CREATIVE ACTIVITIES
AND CURRICULUM
FOR YOUNG CHILDREN

CREATIVE ACTIVITIES
AND CURRICULUM
FOR YOUNG CHILDREN

11e

MARY MAYESKY

CENGAGE
Learning®

Australia • Brazil • Japan • Korea • Mexico • Singapore • Spain • United Kingdom • United States

Creative Activities and Curriculum for Young Children, **Eleventh Edition**
Mary Mayesky

Senior Product Manager: Mark Kerr

Content Developer: Kassi Radomski

Content Coordinator: Joshua Taylor

Product Assistant: Coco Bator

Media Developer: Renee Schaaf

Senior Marketing Manager: Kara Kindstrom

Content Project Manager: Samen Iqbal

Senior Art Director: Jennifer Wahi

Manufacturing Planner: Doug Bertke

Rights Acquisitions Specialist: Tom McDonough

Production Service: Teresa Christie, MPS Limited

Photo Researcher: Krystyna Sperka Borgen

Text Researcher: Christie Barros

Copy Editor: Julie McNamee

Designer: Lisa Buckley

Cover Image: Top image of two girls: Exactostock/
SuperStock; bottom image of boy with dino:
© Sean Justice/Corbis

Compositor: MPS Limited

For product information and technology assistance, contact us at
Cengage Learning Customer & Sales Support, 1-800-354-9706

For permission to use material from this text or product,
submit all requests online at **www.cengage.com/permissions**
Further permissions questions can be e-mailed to
permissionrequest@cengage.com

Library of Congress Control Number: 2013938468

ISBN-13: 978-1-285-42817-8

ISBN-10: 1-285-42817-X

Cengage Learning
200 First Stamford Place, 4th Floor
Stamford, CT 06902
USA

Cengage Learning is a leading provider of customized learning solutions with office locations around the globe, including Singapore, the United Kingdom, Australia, Mexico, Brazil, and Japan. Locate your local office at **www.cengage.com/global**

Cengage Learning products are represented in Canada by Nelson Education, Ltd.

To learn more about Cengage Learning Solutions, visit **www.cengage.com**

Purchase any of our products at your local college store or at our preferred online store **www.cengagebrain.com**

Printed in the United States of America
1 2 3 4 5 6 7 17 16 15 14 13

Dedication

To Casper, my amazing husband. You have been with me through so many editions, shoring me up in ways too numerous to mention. Thank you for *your* creative touch reflected in the many delightful photos in this edition.
I am eternally grateful.

Contents

PART 2 Planning and Implementing Creative Activities   81

PART 4 The Early Childhood Art Program 254

12 Program Basics: Goals, Setting Up, Materials, and Strategies 255

Preface

Nothing is different, yet everything has changed. Those seven words express what this edition represents—change, yet consistency. While this may seem a paradox, it so aptly suits what this edition means to me.

Everything has changed. With new editions, the focus is most often on changes, and this edition has many. A quick leafing through the pages will reveal the birth of many new standards icons throughout the chapters. The placement of these icons is intended as a helpful way to point out the applicable NAEYC and DAP standards in each chapter. In addition, the first thing that greets you when you open this text is a standards correlation chart, which presents the chapter-by-chapter placement of these standards.

Despite this new emphasis on professional early childhood education standards, it is my firm belief that creativity is not prescriptive. It is important to honor each individual's perceptions and approach to ideas. So you, as early childhood teachers, may find other standards applicable in each chapter.

Standards on the national level have certainly changed, and this is reflected in this 11th edition. The No Child Left Behind movement has waned in the United States, as the majority of states have applied and received waivers that allow them to focus on other ways to improve education for children in their respective states. Stepping in to fill the void are the Common Core State Standards, developed not at the federal level but at the state level. These standards are specifically addressed in the chapters on language arts and mathematics. Thus, we now have a new set of standards, built on a more local level.

Another exciting change is the addition of the boxed feature, "Brain Research Says," in applicable chapters. This reflects the importance of neuroscience and its application to early childhood education.

You will also note the addition of TeachSource Videos in each chapter, along with related questions. This new feature allows students to see the application of concepts in an actual classroom setting, and they provide a way of learning beyond reading pages of a book.

Finally, there is a subtle change in this book's title to **Creative Activities and Curriculum for Young Children**. The addition of the words "and curriculum" simply highlights the application of creativity across the curriculum, as well as in the arts. While this has been the case since the second edition, the name change makes this more apparent.

Amid all this change, I said "nothing is different" in that I continue to encourage you to keep children at the center of your practice. I hope the joy of working with young children that brought you to this profession will continue to sustain you through all the ups and downs the world throws your way. Over the years, I have seen many educational trends come and go. Regardless of the latest trends, always rely on your own professional judgment to guide you in your work with young children. Let this knowledge be your "inner teacher" to guide you in your journey.

Nothing is different in that early childhood teachers continue to learn and find developmentally appropriate uses for technology in the classrooms. They continue to use technology for their own professional education, connecting early childhood teachers around the world to the betterment of our profession. Nothing is different as we continue to deal with budget shortfalls because early childhood teachers have long known how to stretch a dollar.

Nothing is different in that I continue to hope for each of my readers that this eleventh edition assists you in your teaching journey in today's challenging world and that you find in these pages concrete, usable ideas to help you in your work with young children.

Nothing is different in that, as in all of the previous editions, this edition is designed for those who are dedicated to helping children reach their full potential. It is written for people who want to know more about creativity, creative children, creative teaching, and creative curriculum and activities. It continues to be my intent to provide readers with sound developmental theory and practical application of these theories, which you can use in actual classroom settings.

Finally, my belief in the absolute necessity of creativity in our world continues unchanged. In a world where the only constant appears to be change, young children need to know how to ask questions and to search for their own answers. They need to know how to look at things in many different ways, and how to create their own sense of beauty and meaning in life.

New Features

Although this book's foundation is creativity, creative activities, and creative curriculum, there are numerous new features. Although I mentioned some of these new features at the beginning of the preface, I have summarized all of them here.

- **NEW! Integrated coverage of NAEYC Standards and DAP Criteria** with icons in the text, a list of standards covered at the beginning of each chapter, and a Standards Correlation Grid on the inside front and back covers helps students make connections between what they learn in the text and professional standards.
- **NEW! Learning Objectives** at the beginning of each chapter correlate with main chapter headings and show students what they need to know to process and understand the information in the chapter. Learning Objectives are also integrated into the end-of-chapter Summary, so by the time students complete the chapter, they should be able to demonstrate how they can use and apply the knowledge and skills learned in the chapter.
- **NEW! TeachSource Videos** on CourseMate feature footage from the classroom to help students relate key chapter content to real-life scenarios. Critical-thinking questions within the text provide opportunities for in-class or online discussion and reflection.
- **NEW! Digital Downloads** of forms, important lists, and more are found in the text and can be downloaded from CourseMate and printed out, so students can review key concepts or use them in the classroom.
- **NEW! Did You Get It?** quizzes allow students to measure their performance against the learning objectives in each chapter. One question for each learning objective is featured in the textbook to encourage students to go to CengageBrain.com, take the full quiz, and check their understanding.
- **NEW! Brain Research Says** boxed feature includes information about recent brain research, such as executive functions of the brain and "prime times" for visual, auditory, language, physical, motor, emotional, and social development.
- **NEW! Integrated coverage of diversity** and multicultural curriculum ideas throughout the book in place of separate chapters.

- **NEW activities** for preschool, kindergarten to grade 3, and grades 4 to 5 in every chapter and more infant and toddler information and activities throughout.
- **NEW content in Think About It and This One's for You!** boxed features throughout.
- **NEW title** more specifically categorizes this book as a curriculum book.

Updated Content

Updated content throughout includes new or updated information on the following:

- **Emergent curriculum** (Chapter 5).
- **Children with special needs**, particularly Asperger's/Autism Spectrum Disorder in Chapter 5, and throughout the book.
- **Preschool play** and the importance of free play and recess (Chapter 7).
- **Teacher talk techniques** for encouraging play with children with disabilities (Chapter 7).
- **Technology**. Although Chapter 8 is still devoted to technology (as in previous editions), even more information is now included throughout the text, such as the joint position statement on technology from NAEYC and the Fred Rogers Center for Early Learning and Children's Media.
- **Music experiences** for infants and children up to age 2 (Chapter 17).
- **Common Core State Standards** in math and language arts and related activities (Chapters 18 and 20).
- **Stages of art development** for infancy to 18 months
- **STEM and STEAM** (Chapter 19).
- **Overweight and obesity in America** (Chapter 21).

Organization

This edition is divided into 5 parts and 22 chapters, which helps to streamline the overall content in the book.

- Part 1, Fostering Creativity and Aesthetics in Young Children: Theoretical Basis, presents a general discussion of various child development theories. Included in Part 1 are chapters on creativity, promoting creativity, the concept of aesthetics, and promoting aesthetic experiences.
- Part 2, Planning and Implementing Creative Activities: Developmentally Appropriate Practice,

presents a general discussion of planning and implementing creative activities. Included in Part 2 are chapters on creativity; creativity for children and teachers; developmentally appropriate activities; creative environments, play development, and creativity; and using technology to promote creativity.

- Part 3, Art and the Development of the Young Child, includes chapters on art and physical-mental growth, art and social-emotional growth, and developmental levels in art.
- Part 4, The Early Childhood Art Program, presents the basics of setting up the art program and includes chapters on two- and three-dimensional activities. Parts 1–4 set an appropriate theoretical stage for application of these theories in specific curriculum areas presented in Part 5.
- Part 5, Creative Activities for Early Childhood, covers creativity in the early childhood curriculum areas.
- Health and safety issues previously covered in Chapter 23 are now addressed throughout the text. Diversity and multicultural curriculum ideas previously found in Chapters 24 and 25 are now also included throughout.
- Streamlined end-of-chapter features now include a Summary organized by learning objectives, a Key Terms list, and Learning Activities.

Creative Activities and Curriculum for Young Children is written for anyone who is interested in teaching children but particularly for busy people who work with children in early childhood settings.

Acknowledgments

The author gratefully acknowledges the contributions of the many people who helped bring this eleventh edition into existence: Casper Holroyd for his continued understanding of my need for purposeful work as well as for the many wonderful photos of children; my daughter, Claire M. Holroyd, who never flagged in her enthusiasm as she listened to my ongoing saga of writing adventures; and my stepdaughter, Jane H. Holding, who kept the business humming along keeping my involvement at a minimum.

Gretchen M. Shaffer, director; and the children, staff, and parents at Highland Children's Center.

Mr. Robert Grant, principal; Dawn Wade, visual art teacher; Betty Ann Holding, 5th grade teacher; and the teachers, staff, children, and parents at Lacy Elementary School, Raleigh, NC.

Gretchen M. Shaffer, director; staff; teachers; and the parents and children at Highland Children's Center.

Dr. Jo Allen, president of Meredith College; Laura Davidson, Dean of Library Information Services; and Gerry Sargent, administrative assistant to the Dean of Library Information Services, Meredith College.

Gary W. Baird, principal; Lisa Coster, teacher; and the parents and children in Mrs. Coster's kindergarten class at Lead Mine Elementary School, Raleigh, NC.

Gregory D. Ford, principal; Amanda Hummel and her staff, and the teachers, parents, and children at Hilburn Drive Academy, Raleigh, NC.

Jacqueline Jordan, principal; and the teachers, parents, and staff at Underwood Gifted and Talented Elementary School, Raleigh, NC.

Sincere thanks to my developmental and project editors for their constant assistance and support during the process of publication.

Special thanks to Jane Barrett, my superb yoga instructor, and dear friend, who twice a week listened and gave me the three hours of respite and release from writing, which helped me survive yet another edition.

A Note of Caution

In all of the activity suggestions in this text, knowledge of the child's developmental level is the most basic guideline for use of any activity. However, in the interest of preventing any undue accidents and spread of infections, a few extra cautions follow.

An important note of caution is necessary regarding the use of egg cartons in any and all activities with young children. Because of the risk of the spread of salmonella, it is important that all egg cartons be washed with warm, soapy water and allowed to dry completely before use. For a similar reason, the same washing and drying procedure is required before using all Styrofoam trays that have held meat, fish, or poultry. Another important note is regarding the use of balloons with children under the age of 3. Use of balloons with this age group is not recommended due to the danger of accidental aspiration. And finally, the use of any small objects that could fit into a child's mouth must be avoided for children under the age of 3.

Instructor Resources

Cengage Learning's Education CourseMate brings course concepts to life with interactive learning, study, and exam preparation tools that support the printed textbook. CourseMate includes the eBook, quizzes, Digital Downloads, TeachSource Videos, flashcards, and more—as well as EngagementTracker, a first-of-its-kind tool that monitors student engagement in the course. The accompanying instructor website, available through login.cengage.com, offers access to password-protected resources such as PowerPoint® lecture slides and the online Instructor's Manual with Test Bank. CourseMate can be bundled with the student text. Contact your Cengage sales representative for information on getting access to CourseMate.

PowerPoint® Lecture Slides

These vibrant Microsoft® PowerPoint lecture slides for each chapter assist you with your lecture by providing concept coverage using images, figures, and tables directly from the textbook!

Online Instructor's Manual with Test Bank

An online Instructor's Manual accompanies this book that contains information to assist the instructor in designing the course, including sample syllabi, discussion questions, teaching and learning activities, field experiences, learning objectives, and additional online resources. For assessment support, the updated test bank includes true/false, multiple-choice, matching, short-answer, and essay questions for each chapter.

Professional Enhancement Booklet

The Professional Enhancement booklet for students, which is part of Cengage Learning's Early Childhood Education Professional Enhancement series, focuses on key topics of interest to future early childhood teachers and caregivers. Topics of interest include the No Child Left Behind Act and its impact on the creative arts; reflective practices; differentiated instruction; special topics in language arts and additional language arts activities; special topics in mathematics, social studies, and nutrition; information on appropriate art centers for different ages of children with examples of guidelines for use; and ideas for storing and maintaining art materials and equipment. Students will keep this informational supplement and use it for years to come in their early childhood practices.

CourseMate

Cengage Learning's Education CourseMate brings course concepts to life with interactive learning, study, and exam preparation tools that support the printed textbook. Access the eBook, Did You Get It? quizzes, Digital Downloads, TeachSource Videos, flashcards, and more in your Education CourseMate. Go to CengageBrain.com to register or purchase access.

- Critical Thinking Forum—in this section, you have the opportunity to respond to "This One's for You" and "Think About It" concepts. Various creative activity scenarios and thought-provoking questions test your understanding of the text's content. You can share your ideas with classmates and interact informally with your instructor online.
- Web Activities—These activities direct you to a website(s) and allow you to conduct further research and apply content related to creative activities for young children.
- Web Links—For each chapter, a summarized list of Web links is provided for your reference.
- Sample Quizzes—Questions are provided online to test your knowledge of the material presented.
- Observation Sheets—These may be printed out and used for further observation of specific concepts in actual classroom settings.
- PowerPoint Presentations—These presentations cover the main points of each chapter and can serve as either an introduction to each chapter or a good tool for reviewing the chapter.

Reviewers

The author and editors at Cengage Learning wish to thank the following reviewers for their time, effort, and thoughtful contributions, which helped to shape the eleventh edition.

Amy Allen
The University of Toledo

Audrey Beard
Albany State University

Cindy Calhoun
Southern Union State Community College

Sharon Carter
Davidson County Community College

Evia Davis
Langston University

Susan Finkel
University of Wisconsin-Oshkosh

Jamie Harmount
Ohio University

Ginger Harris-Pike
Central Carolina Community College

Jennifer Johnson
Vance Granville Community College

Sharon Little
South Piedmont Community College

Leslie Malanoski
Athens Technical College

Mary McGuire-Schwartz
Rhode Island College

Ann McKitrick
San Jacinto College

Vicky Milstead
Angelina College

Bridget Murray
Henderson Community College

Sandra Owen
Cincinnati State Technical and Community College

Amy Pennington
Wisconsin Indianhead Technical College

Sandy Putnam-Franklin
University of Massachusetts Boston

Deborah Ravacon
Montgomery County Community College

Tina Rose Turriglio
College of St. Rose

Dr. Sara Rutledge
Mount Aloysius College

Donna Satterlee
University of Maryland Eastern Shore

Ruslan Slutsky
The University of Toledo

Chareve Stokes
Midlands Technical College

Joseph Todaro
Bronx Community College

Donna Walker
South Suburban College

Lisa White
Athens Technical College

Joanne Yantz
Colorado Mountain College in Dillon

About the Author

Mary Mayesky, Ph.D., is a certified preschool, elementary, and secondary teacher. She is a former professor in the Program in Education at Duke University, former director of the Early Childhood Certification Program, and supervisor of student teachers. She has served as assistant director for programs in the Office of Day Services, Department of Human Resources, State of North Carolina. She is also the former principal of the Mary E. Phillips Magnet School in Raleigh, North Carolina, the first licensed extended day magnet in the Southeast. She has served several terms on the North Carolina Day Care Commission and on the Wake County School Board.

Dr. Mayesky has worked in Head Start, child care, kindergarten, and YWCA early childhood programs and has taught kindergarten through grade 8 in the public schools. She has written extensively for professional journals and for general-circulation magazines in the areas of child development and curriculum design. She is a member of Phi Beta Kappa and was named Woman of the Year in Education by the North Carolina Academy of the YWCA. Her other honors include being named Outstanding Young Educator by the Duke University Research

Council, receiving the American Association of School Administrators Research Award, and being nominated for the Duke University Alumni Distinguished Undergraduate Teaching Award. A collection of personal stories about her educational experiences can be found in her book, *Remembering Mrs. O'Donald: Growing, Learning, and Teaching*. Her most recent published appearance was in *Vogue Pattern Magazine*, modeling a dress she made for a wedding, which was chosen for the magazine's *What We're Sewing* section.

A marathon runner, Dr. Mayesky has completed 19 marathons and received many awards in road races and senior games. She also enjoys studying and teaching yoga, sewing, biking, gardening, and reading on the radio for the blind at the Triangle Radio Reading Service.

Casper Holroyd

Fostering Creativity and Aesthetics in Young Children

Theoretical Basis

Part 1 presents a general discussion of various theories relating to child development. Beginning with the concept of creativity, theories, techniques, basic program components, and their relationship to the growth of creativity in young children are presented.

In essence, Part 1 sets the theoretical stage for application of these theories in later parts.

REFLECTIVE QUESTIONS

After studying this section, you should be able to answer the following questions.

1. How could I change my current teaching strategies to better encourage the development of creativity in young children?
2. How do I encourage the development of a child's aesthetic sense in my classroom environment, lessons, and activities?
3. Are my teaching strategies based on the principles of creative development? How many of them encourage convergent thinking? How many encourage divergent thinking?
4. What thinking styles do my children have? Do I adapt my teaching to fit these individual differences?
5. Using the information about creativity and aesthetics, how will I now question my students about concepts and ideas?
6. As I plan classroom methods and management systems, am I keeping in mind the importance of

cultivating creativity and the aesthetic sense in children?
7. What am I doing to help young children recognize their own uniqueness, creativity, and aesthetic sense?
8. What instructional strategies are best for the development of creativity and the aesthetic sense in young children?
9. What role will creativity have in my planning of curriculum for young children?
10. How will I talk with young children about their art and what they feel is beautiful?
11. How will I share with parents the importance of nurturing a child's creativity and sense of beauty?
12. How have I changed as a result of my learning about creativity and aesthetics?

The Concept of Creativity

Take a few minutes to watch a 4-year-old child in action. At one moment, he is building a tower out of blocks. Suddenly, he spots one of his friends playing with a homemade finger puppet. He wants to make one, too. A bit later, he is playing with a guinea pig, stroking its fur and tickling its chin. Next, he is placing long, wide strokes of color on a piece of paper and getting spots of paint on everything in sight.

What is this? Now he is at the sand table building a sand castle with a high sand tower that keeps falling over. He seems to have discovered something. It is easier to build a tower out of blocks than out of sand, so he is back building with wooden blocks. It looks as though he is back where he started, except that the new block tower does not look anything like the one he started earlier.

Learning Objectives

After studying this chapter, you should be able to:

1-1 Define creativity. Compare and contrast the kinds of creativity.

1-2 List the ways in which children and teachers benefit from an environment in which creativity is encouraged.

1-3 Discuss the ways creativity has been expressed throughout history.

1-4 List several characteristics of creative children, including positive and negative aspects of each characteristic.

1-5 Name five things a teacher can do to help children develop a willingness to express creativity.

naeyc

NAEYC Program Standards

1c Using developmental knowledge to create challenging learning environments.

1b Knowing and understanding the multiple influences on development and learning.

DAP

DAP Criteria

2E1 Teachers arrange meaningful experiences that are intellectually and creatively stimulating, invite exploration and investigation, and engage children's active, sustained involvement.

2F3 Teachers present novel experiences and introduce stimulating ideas, problems, experiences, or hypotheses.

2F5 Teachers provide experiences for children to be genuinely successful and challenged.

PHOTO 1-1 Teachers must realize the importance of creativity for all children.

Watching active young children studying the world around them is exciting. A couple of things become clear almost immediately. First of all, children are full of curiosity. They seem to enjoy investigating and finding out things. Second, they seem quite capable of doing this successfully. They are creative in finding answers to problems that arise from their curiosity. A child can figure out how to reach a needed block that somehow got thrown behind the piano. Another child selects interesting materials to make a finger puppet that is different from all the others. Young children seem to have a natural ability to come up with creative answers, approaches, and ways to use materials.

People who work with young children need to understand creativity and have the skills to help and encourage children to express their creative natures. They must realize the importance of creativity for both children and teachers (see Photo 1-1). They need to be able to identify creativity in children and be able to help them develop a willingness to express this creativity.

1-1 What Is Creativity?

naeyc Perhaps the most important thing to realize about creativity is that everyone possesses a certain amount of it. Although some people are a little more creative and some a little less, no one is totally lacking in creativity.

Preschoolers often ask parents 100 questions in a single day (Hoefferth, 1998). This behavior reflects the enormous power curiosity has on a child's

creativity and motivation to learn in early childhood (Strom & Strom, 2002; Taylor, 2000). Young children tend to be highly open, curious, and creative (see Photo 1-2). Unfortunately, many adults want children to conform. As outside pressures from adults grow, the children's environment closes in on them. They find it less and less rewarding to express interest in things, to be curious, and to be creative in investigating their world. To avoid this, it is important to know ways of encouraging a child's creativity. To begin with, one should understand the meaning of the term **creativity**.

There are many meanings for this word:

- A definition by one writer on the subject, May (1975, p. 39), describes creativity as the "process of bringing something new into being."
- Paul Torrance (1970), a pioneer in the study of the creative process, suggests that creativity is the ability to produce something novel, something with the stamp of uniqueness upon it.
- More recently, creativity has been defined as a combination of abilities, skills, motivations, and attitudes (Honig, 2006).

PHOTO 1-2 A child's sense of wonder and delight is evident when she is allowed to be creative.

Take a moment to assess your own creativity by reading the two lists below. See if you can find yourself in either (or maybe both!) of these lists.

Passive Approach to Life—Do I . . . ?
- ☐ Get bored frequently
- ☐ Have few deep challenges in my life
- ☐ Have mostly temporary enjoyment, with little or no lasting product
- ☐ Have lots of prestructured activities
- ☐ Have little control over events in my life
- ☐ Observe rather than act
- ☐ Have few self-sufficiency interests
- ☐ Kill time
- ☐ Have few distinguished accomplishments
- ☐ Feel mentally "old"
- ☐ Have set opinions and attitudes

Creative Approach to Life—Do I . . . ?
- ☐ Have challenging interests
- ☐ Enjoy self-enriching activities
- ☐ Experience continuous satisfaction and tangible results
- ☐ Have a youthful spirit
- ☐ Aspire to more as I achieve new goals
- ☐ Enjoy the essence of a culture
- ☐ Stay mentally flexible through new insights
- ☐ Pursue creative interests
- ☐ Enjoy selected planned participation in activities
- ☐ Find my own self-enriching activities
- ☐ Experience personal achievement and involvement
- ☐ Feel at home in many conditions
- ☐ Use my time to develop self
- ☐ Get involved in life

© Cengage Learning

FIGURE 1-1 Creativity checklist.

TeachSource Digital Download   Download from CourseMate.

Much like athletic ability, creativity is really a combination of many different abilities, so it is more useful to think of many types of creativities (Ripple, 1999, p. 629). The term *creativity* has many interpretations. One researcher separates the types of creativity as follows:

- **"Capital C" creativity** involves bringing into existence something genuinely new that receives social validation enough to be added to the culture. An example of Capital C creativity is the invention of the lightbulb.
- **"Small c" creativity** involves ideas or products that are new to the person but only to the person.

An example of small c creativity is a child's new use of blending finger-paint colors (Ripple, 1999).

The following definition may help the student understand the concept of creativity better. Creativity is a way of thinking, acting, or making something that is original for the individual and valued by that person or others. A person does not have to be the first one in the world to produce something for it to be considered a creative act. Creativity can be found anywhere—at home or school as easily as in art or science. (See Figure 1-1, Creativity Checklist.) As Paul Torrance, considered "the father of modern creativity," puts it, "Creativity is an infinite phenomenon. A person can be creative in an endless number of ways" (1971).

1-1a The Creative Process

When someone is creating something, the activity usually consists of two parts. The first part has to do with originality—the discovery of an idea, plan, or answer. The second part has to do with working out, proving, and making certain that the idea or answer works or is possible. The first part—discovering—involves using imagination, playing with ideas, and exploring (see Photo 1-3). The second part—process—involves using learned skills, evaluating, and testing.

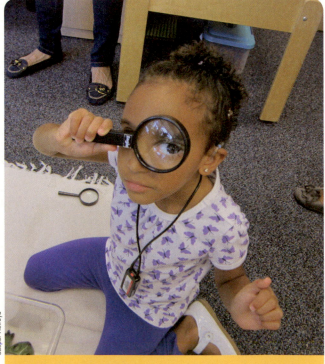

Casper Holroyd

PHOTO 1-3 Creativity involves questioning and exploring.

THIS ONE'S FOR YOU!

This One's for You! Research on Definitions of Creativity

In addition to the definitions of creativity in your text, the following research review provides more information on these definitions.

According to Piirto (2004), *creativity* as a scientific term has its roots in psychology. Other researchers believe that what constitutes creativity has not been defined or featured in a clear and unambiguous way (Ferrari, Cachia, & Punie, 2009). Also, the nature and definitions of creativity vary across cultures (Starko, 2003) and seem to be value- and culture-specific (Craft 2005).

Two researchers reviewed 42 explicit definitions and 120 collations (a familiar grouping of words used to convey a meaning, that is, *creative thinking*) of creativity from 1953 to 2009 (Kampylis & Valtanen, 2010). They state that the noun *creativity* itself is not only relatively new and fashionable but also confusing, even misunderstood. They found that the noun *creativity* first appeared in printed form in 1875. It derives from the Latin *creates* which means, "to make, produce," and is related to the Latin *crescere* (arise, grow).

Their analysis and comparisons of the collected definitions reveal that creativity researchers' and theorists' definitions of creativity generally all have the following key components:

1. Creativity is a key ability of individual(s) (person).
2. Creativity presumes an intentional activity (process).
3. The creative process occurs in a specific context (environment).
4. The creative process entails the generation of products (tangible or intangible). These creative product(s) must be novel (original, unconventional) and appropriate (valuable, useful) to some extent, at least for the creative individual(s) (Kampylis & Valtanen, 2010, p. 198). These key components are commonly summarized and referred to in the literature as the 4Ps of creativity: person, process, press, and product (Richards, 1999).

In working with young children, you will have many opportunities to see young children involved in all of the 4Ps of creativity, as well as in the key components of creativity as described in the preceding research.

Mihaly Csikszentmihalyi, a researcher on the creative process, describes it as one that normally takes five steps (1997, p. 79).

1. Preparation—Becoming curious about interesting ideas or questions.
2. Incubation—Ideas churn around below the threshold of consciousness, subconsciously making connections.
3. Insight—When an understanding is realized. The "aha" moment when the puzzle starts to fall together.
4. Evaluation—Deciding if the insight is valuable and worth pursuing.
5. Elaboration—Translating the insight into its final work. This is the physical realization of the idea or question.

These stages spiral continuously as the individual pursues the problem. Creativity in Csikszentmihalyi's theory is not linear (Csikszentmihaly, 2008). Creativity is about capturing those moments that make life worth living. Creativity's objective is to offer an understanding of what leads to these moments, whether it's the excitement of the artist at the easel or the scientist in the lab, so that knowledge can be used to enrich people's lives.

1-1b Thought Processes and Creativity

naeyc **DAP** Two kinds of thinking produce solutions to problems: **convergent thinking** and **divergent thinking**. Convergent thinking usually results in a single answer or solution to a question or problem. Divergent thinking opens things up and results in many answers to a single problem.

For example, if a child is asked to count the number of fish in an aquarium, there is only one correct answer. This is a question that leads children to convergent thinking. On the other hand, if a child is asked to tell as many things as possible about the aquarium, many correct statements can be made. Questions such as this encourage divergent rather than convergent thinking. Creativity requires both divergent and convergent thinking. Both types of thinking are important to creativity. Consequently, the teacher's challenge is to avoid replacing one with the other. Another way to think about this is that children must learn the "way things are done" (convergent thinking) before truly experiencing the creative process. For example, a child needs to learn how to hold and use a paintbrush (convergent learning) before she can experience the process of painting. An older child

PHOTO 1-4 Creativity occurs across the curriculum.

Casper Holroyd

products. Original products are one of the characteristics of creativity with older children.

Creativity goes beyond possession and use of artistic or musical talent. Creativity is evidenced not only in music, art, and writing but also throughout the curriculum, in science, social studies, and other areas.

Encouraging older children's creativity is vitally important (see Table 1-1). Many times at the middle elementary level, teachers identify their main instructional goals as helping children build cognitive and social skills. But the great engine that drives innovation and invention in society comes from people whose flame of creativity was kept alive in childhood. Research shows that, if not nurtured, creativity takes a nosedive by fourth grade. Young children who were awesome artists in preschool no longer color the sky orange and pink just because they love the glowing colors (Honig, 2006).

must learn the rules (for example, what the parts of a book report are) before she can begin to break or change the rules to be creative (for example, giving a book report as a board game).

In dealing with young children, the focus should be on the process—that is, developing and generating original ideas. This focus on the process encourages the development of creativity across the curriculum instead of being confined to art and music activities (see Photo 1-4).

1-1d Variety and Creativity

A certain kind of creativity allows people to express themselves in a way that makes others listen and appreciate what they hear. Some creative abilities enable people to discover meaning in nature—meaning that others had not understood before (see Table 1-2).

1-1c Creativity and Older Children

With older children, creativity involves greater emphasis on the criterion of high-quality, original products or solutions. The development of creative products emerges later in the child's development. An example of this is seen in fourth- and fifth-grade science fair projects. It becomes very apparent that some projects are more creative than others. For example, a student who created and tested a new chair design may seem to have an idea of a different quality than another student who investigated which commercial cleaning product worked best on stains.

At this level with older children, creativity is perceived as original products or original solutions. Creativity with older children is more than the generation of ideas because it involves the creation of

© 2015 Cengage Learning

▶ ❚❚   **TeachSource** Video

Infants and Toddlers: Creativity

1. Using the information in your text, discuss the pros and cons of this teacher's modeling of clay bird nests to the group of toddlers.

2. Give examples of convergent and divergent questions the teachers used in this activity.

Watch on CourseMate.

Table 1-1 Free yourself—to be creative.

One of the pioneers of research into children's creativity, Paul Torrance (1962), felt that we had to free ourselves to be creative before we can ever really be creative teachers. Here are some of his suggestions:

- Don't be afraid to fall in love with something and to pursue it with intensity.
- Know, understand, take pride in, practice, develop, exploit, and enjoy your greatest strengths.
- Learn to free yourself from the expectations of others and to walk away from the games they impose on you. Free yourself to play your own game.
- Find a great teacher or mentor who will help you.
- Don't waste energy trying to be well rounded.
- Do what you love and can do well.
- Learn the skills of independence.
- Continue to be a student of life; allow yourself to explore new ideas, people, and places.
- Participate in joyful exercise or movement activities on a regular basis—skating, dancing, running, playing on the playground with neighborhood kids.

How many of these apply to you? Are you free to be a creative teacher? Pick one or two of the suggestions that you most want to work on and then go!

TeachSource Digital Download   Download from CourseMate.

Table 1-2 Creativity quotes.

The following are some quotes to inspire you in your creative endeavors as teachers of young children.

- "I am always doing that which I cannot do, in order that I may learn how to do it."–Pablo Picasso
- "The illiterate of the 21st century will not be those who cannot read and write, but those who cannot learn, unlearn, and relearn."–Alvin Toeffler
- "The chief enemy of creativity is 'good' sense."–Pablo Picasso
- "Creativity requires the courage to let go of certainties."–Erich Fromm
- "I'm always thinking about creating. My future starts when I wake up every morning. Every day I find something creative to do with my life."–Miles Davis.
- "It's a miracle that curiosity survives formal education."–Albert Einstein
- "If I had influence with the good fairy who is supposed to preside over the christening of all children, I should ask that her gift to each child in the world would be a sense of wonder so indestructible that it would last throughout life."–Rachel Carson
- "My mother said to me, 'If you become a soldier, you'll be a general; if you become a monk, you'll end up as the Pope.' Instead, I became a painter and wound up Picasso."–Pablo Picasso

Creativity changes at different levels of development. Most people have ideas about what creativity is in adulthood, but what might we look for in a young child? It is crucial that early childhood teachers see creativity as part of the developmental process. For young children, a critical criterion for creative potential is originality (Tegano, Moran, & Sawyers, 1991). Thus, teachers of young children must understand the process that leads to original thinking.

1-1e Originality

Originality can be seen in a kindergarten classroom where children are making collages from pieces of torn tissue paper. Mary's experimenting with the material leads to her discovery of a way to make three-dimensional bumps in the collage. Her discovery of the three-dimensional aspect is a form of originality. Though making three-dimensional collages is certainly not a new idea in a kindergarten classroom, it is

Creative Thinking and Brain Hemispheres: Hard/Soft Thinking

"Hard" and "soft" thinking are terms often associated with creativity, and they reflect the neurological processes associated with different hemispheres of the brain. Research suggests that the right side of the brain is visual and processes information in an intuitive and simultaneous way, looking first at the whole picture and then at the details (**soft thinking**). The other hemisphere—the left brain—is verbal and processes information in an analytical and sequential way, looking first at the pieces and then putting them together to get the whole picture (**hard thinking**) (Heilman, 2005).

The right side of the brain is often associated with characteristics such as intuition, imagination, emotions, feelings, and artistic creativity. The left side is usually associated with planning and organizing, logic, analytical thinking, and deduction. The right side of the brain is sometimes referred to as the "artist," whereas the left side is regarded as the "judge." The following chart presents the differences between hard and soft thinking (Robinson 2010).

Hard Thinking	Soft Thinking
Certain	Doubtful
Close down	Open up
One right answer	Many right answers
Exact	Approximate
Fast	Slow
Black and white	Many shades of gray
Analysis	Hunches
Logic	Intuition
Differences and categories	Similarities and connections
Rational	Dreamlike
Precise	Diffuse
Serious	Playful

It can be argued that creative thinking is a process involving both hard and soft thinking and that it is important to know when each is appropriate. Every person has a "judge" and an "artist," and both are required to be creative (Robinson, 2001). Even those who are very creative and thrive on spontaneity and uncertainty also need to seek order and be analytical to be successful. It is now believed that the most powerful creative thinking occurs when the left and right sides of the brain combine (Robinson, 2010).

an *original* idea for Mary at that particular time. Consider another kindergarten classroom where the children are embellishing full-size outlines of their bodies. Most children are adding hair, faces, and clothes to their outlines, while Luis is making an internal drawing of his skeleton. Luis's drawing of his skeleton is an original idea for him at that particular time.

1-1f Process over Product

DAP naeyc Let's return to Mary and her three-dimensional collage. Teachers of young children need to be grounded in the process over product philosophy. The teacher's observation of the *process* that leads to originality (exploration and experimentation with the materials) is more valuable than any *judgment of the product* (the three-dimensional bump may have been imperfect and collapsed in the end). (See Photo 1-5.) Remember that young children do not always have the skills to make a creative product (an elaborate painting or a workable invention), and so the process that leads to originality is the focus of creative potential.

Casper Holroyd

PHOTO 1-5 The process that leads to originality is the focus of creative potential.

Early childhood classrooms are full of examples of the process of original thinking. We see complex dramas unfold as children act out scenes of their own design, discover clever block-building solutions, and demonstrate unique interpersonal problem solving (Tegano et al., 1991).

Did You Get It?

A gym teacher designs a new game that encourages both cooperative play and aerobic activity. The game quickly spreads in popularity, and other gym teachers within the district incorporate the game into their curricula. What type of creativity has the game's creator demonstrated?

a. "capital C" creativity
b. "small c" creativity
c. combination creativity
d. linear creativity

Take the full quiz on CourseMate.

1-2 Importance of Creativity: Benefits for Teachers and Children

DAP naeyc Creativity is the mainspring of our civilization: from the concept of the wheel, through the steamboat, the telephone, the automobile, the airplane, radio and television, computers, automation, the electronics industry, nuclear power, and space travel. Great inventions, scientific discoveries, the pushing back of frontiers, and all forms of artistic expression—painting, literature, music, drama—have depended on creative thinking of the highest order. Thus, the progress of civilization and humanity's present evolutionary stature are essentially the result of creative thinking and innovation. Our inherent creativity contributes to the very quality of our lives.

The rapid changes of our present age require that problems be tackled creatively. It is difficult to foretell exactly what knowledge will be necessary to solve future problems creatively. What the young are learning now will surely become obsolete. Everyone can and must continue to learn throughout life, but knowledge alone is no guarantee that future problems will be met effectively. Only a strong creative ability will provide the means for coping with the future.

Children want to express themselves openly. They want to bring out new ideas and have new

experiences. They enjoy creativity and benefit from it in many ways, including the following:

● Learning to feel good about themselves
● Learning to seek many answers to a problem
● Developing their potential to think
● Developing their individuality
● Developing new skills
● Experiencing the joy of being different

Teachers also benefit from encouraging creativity, in such ways as the following:

● Being able to provide for more and greater variety in the program
● Learning to recognize children for their unique skills
● Being able to develop closer relationships with children
● Having fewer behavior problems
● Using a minimum of standardized curricula and external evaluation

---

Did You Get It?

A fifth grade teacher assigned her students the task of writing a new ending to a traditional fairy tale. Which benefit of encouraging creativity is she most likely to gain?

a. Being able to develop a closer relationship with her students.
b. Minimizing behavior problems.
c. Learning to recognize children for their unique skills.
d. Being able to provide for more and greater variety in the program.

Take the full quiz on CourseMate.

1-3 Creativity throughout History

The human desire to be creative has been present throughout history in all communities. From the existence of prehistoric cave paintings, we can see that human beings have made their mark using the materials available to them. The desire to represent and share experiences with others—for example, through art, music, and dance—seems to be a basic human characteristic.

Creation stories passed on by religious and cultural groups reflect this same creative desire. A number of these use the imagery of human creativity to express divine creativity. The clay of the potter is used as the raw material of creation—the Creator molds and sculpts the clay to create human beings. For example, the Chinese story of creation describes how Numa, the mother goddess, created people from the river mud to ease her loneliness. Jewish, Christian, and Islamic traditions describe God creating man and woman from the dust of the ground. In Greek mythology, Prometheus uses clay to make little images of the gods (Duffy, 2010).

All of these myths emphasize the desire to create, the pleasure in creating, and the sense of ownership toward the created. This same sense of pleasure and satisfaction derived from the creative process is part of all human experiences, whether it is finding a new solution to a problem, preparing a special meal, or completing a challenging assignment.

Did You Get It?

In the Old Testament, the female Israelites are described as singing and dancing after the parting of the Red Sea. What basic tenet of the human experience does this show us?

a. The female expression of happiness is through song and dance.

b. The human desire to represent and share our happiness has been present throughout history.

c. People across the globe like to sing and dance.

d. The human tendency to express thanks and joy.

Take the full quiz on CourseMate.

1-4 Characteristics of Creative Children

DAP **naeyc** Paul Torrance, a noted expert on creativity in children, has frequently emphasized that the kind of behavior teachers identify as desirable in children does not always coincide with characteristics associated with the creative personality. For example, teachers who think they value uniqueness may find that when a child has spilled her milk because she tried an original method of holding the cup with her teeth, they don't like creative exploration as much as they thought they did!

This lack of conformity can be inconvenient, but teachers should realize that some creative individuals possess character traits that aren't always easy to appreciate. Some of these less attractive qualities include stubbornness, faultfinding tendencies, the appearance of haughtiness and self-satisfaction, and apparent discontent (Torrance, 1962). Yet it is easy to see that stubbornness might be a valuable quality when carrying through a new idea or that finding fault and being discontented could result in questioning and analyzing a situation before coming up with suggestions for improving it.

In all fairness, we must admit that we do not know at present if these less attractive attitudes lie at the root of creativity or are the result of mishandling by teachers, peers, and families as the child matures. On the other hand, Torrance also found that creative children possess many likable qualities, such as determination, curiosity, intuition, a willingness to take risks, a preference for complex ideas, and a sense of humor.

We point out these possible problems of encouraging creativity in children not to discourage teachers from fostering such behavior but to enlighten them so that they will not subtly reject or discourage creative responses out of failure to recognize the positive side of such behavior. Ideally, understanding creativity will result in increased acceptance and valuing of creativity in young children (see Photo 1-6). Acceptance is vitally important because it encourages children to develop their creativity further. Let us now summarize the ways to encourage creativity in all young children.

Casper Holroyd

PHOTO 1-6 Basic to creativity is a warm acceptance of each child's individuality.

PHOTO 1-7 Effective teachers help children feel joy in their creative productions.

1-5 Helping Children Express Creativity

naeyc **DAP** There are at least eight things that can be done for children to help them express natural creative tendencies.

1. **Help children accept change.** A child who becomes overly worried or upset in new situations is unlikely to express creative potential.
2. **Help children realize that some problems have no easy answers.** This may help prevent children from becoming anxious when they cannot find an immediate answer to a question or problem.
3. **Help children recognize that many problems have a number of possible answers.** Encourage them to search for more than one answer. Then they can evaluate all the different answers to see which ones fit the situation best.
4. **Help children learn to judge and accept their own feelings.** Children should not feel guilty for having feelings about things. Create an environment where judgment is deferred and all ideas are respected, where discussion and debate are a means of trying out ideas in a nonthreatening atmosphere.
5. **Reward children for being creative.** Let children know that their creative ideas are valued. In fact, the more creative the ideas or products, the more greatly they should be rewarded. It is also useful to help children realize that good work is sometimes its own reward.
6. **Help children feel joy in their creative productions and in working through problems** (see Photo 1-7). Children should find that doing things and finding answers for themselves is fun. The adult should establish the conditions that allow this to take place.

7. **Help children appreciate themselves for being different.** There is a tendency to reward children for conforming. This discourages creativity. Children should learn to like themselves because they are unique (see Photo 1-8).
8. **Help children develop perseverance—"stick-to-itiveness."** Help children by encouraging them to follow through. Provide chances for them to stick with an activity even if everyone else has moved on to something different.

PHOTO 1-8 A child who meets with unquestioning acceptance of her unique approach to the world feels safe expressing her creativity.

Creativity and the Human Brain

Highly creative thinkers are often stereotyped as dreamers or absent-minded professor types who struggle with deadlines and completing projects. Although these behaviors are often negatively viewed by a society that emphasizes productivity and efficiency, these behaviors may actually be expressions of low levels of neural activity in the brain, which are essential to the creative process.

Studies involving EEG brain scans suggest that low brain arousal seems necessary for the initial (ideation) stage of the creative process, especially for those who are considered highly creative (Haier & Jung, 2008; Martindale & Hasenfus, 1978).

Low levels of arousal in the neurons in the brain during creative ideation (Fink & Neubauer, 2006; Haier & Jung, 2008) allow the scattered, multidimensional thinking necessary for innovative ideas.

In their research, Jausovec (2000) and Martindale and Hasenfus (1978) compared highly creative people to more average ones and found highly creative individuals were more likely to exhibit low cortical energy levels during creative problem solving than their more typical counterparts.

The reverse, high brain arousal is associated with less creative, unoriginal responses (Martindale & Armstrong, 1974).

Another researcher suggests that high neural arousal may cause the brain to zero in too quickly on a common thought and end the idea search before any innovative associations can occur (Gnezda, 2011). Longer idea searches are important because, according to Guilford (1967), a larger quantity of ideas produces more opportunities for unusual association.

So, while it may seem to the casual observer that a creative person in the early stages of the process is idle or not on task, the person may be working hard internally, scanning his or her brain for as many high-quality ideas as possible (Gnezda, 2011).

Low neural arousal levels do not last throughout an entire creative process. Later in the process, when the person is settling on a new combination of thoughts (that is, perceiving the insight of a creative idea), his or her brain will turn up the neural activity level (Martindale & Hasenfus, 1978). The creative person experiences the excitement of inspiration, also called *illumination* (Wallas, 1926) or an "aha" moment.

Considering this research, you may now take a different view of those "daydreamers" and "slow starters" in your work with young children.

THIS ONE'S FOR YOU!

Creative Inventions

Creative approaches to problems and innovative uses for common objects are the basis for the following inventions.

- Ear muffs. Chester Greenwood was born in Farmington, Maine, in 1858. Greenwood was a grammar school dropout. While testing a new pair of ice skates, 13-year-old Chester grew frustrated at trying to protect his ears from the bitter cold. After wrapping his head with a scarf, which was too bulky and itchy, he made two ear-shaped loops from wire and asked his grandmother to sew fur on them. In the beginning, his friends laughed at him. However, when they realized he was able to stay outside skating long after they had gone inside freezing, they stopped laughing. Instead, they began to ask Chester to make ear covers for them, too.

At age 17, he patented an improved model with a steel band, which held them in place. With Greenwood's Champion Ear Protectors, he established Greenwood's Ear Protector Factory. He made a fortune supplying Ear Protectors to U.S. soldiers during World War I. For the next 60 years, Chester's factory made earmuffs, and earmuffs made Chester rich. Farmington, Maine, is now the Ear Muff Capital of the World.

- Band-Aids®. At the turn of the century, Mrs. Earle Dickson, an inexperienced cook, often burned and cut herself. At that time, a bandage consisted of separate gauze and adhesive tape that you would cut to size and apply yourself. Mr. Dickson, a Johnson & Johnson employee, got lots of practice bandaging his wife's hands, but he noticed that the current type of bandage would soon fall off her fingers. Out of concern for his wife's safety, he decided to invent something that would stay in place and protect small wounds better. So, he began to prepare bandages ahead of time so that she could apply them by herself when needed. He combined a piece of surgical tape and a piece of gauze and then covered it with crinoline to keep it sterile. This became the first crude adhesive strip bandage.

Earle's boss, James Johnson, saw his invention and decided to manufacture Band-Aids to the public and made Earle Dickson Vice President of Johnson & Johnson.

Sales of Band-Aids were slow until Johnson & Johnson decided to give Boy Scout troops free Band-Aids as publicity stunts. By 1924, Band-Aids were machine made, sold sterilized in 1939, and made with vinyl tape in 1958. (http://inventors.about.com/od/bstartinventions/a/bandaid.htm)

Summary

1-1 Define creativity. Compare and contrast the kinds of creativity.

Creativity is a way of thinking and acting or making something that is original for the individual child and valued by that person or others. Capital C creativity involves bringing into existence something genuinely new that receives social validation enough to be added to the culture. An example of Capital C creativity is the invention of the lightbulb. Small c creativity involves ideas or products that are new to the person, but only to the person. An example of small c creativity is a child's new way of blending finger paint colors. Young children are naturally creative. This means they behave in ways and do things that are unique and valued by themselves or others. Creativity in preschool children is stimulated when they are allowed to think divergently.

1-2 List three ways in which children and teachers benefit from an environment in which creativity is encouraged.

Children benefit from an environment in which creativity is encouraged by:

- Learning to feel good about themselves
- Learning to seek many answers to a problem
- Developing their potential to think
- Developing their individuality
- Developing new skills
- Experiencing the joy of being different

Teachers benefit from encouraging creativity, in such ways as the following:

- Being able to provide for more and greater variety in the program
- Learning to recognize children for their unique skills
- Being able to develop closer relationships with children
- Having fewer behavior problems
- Using a minimum of standardized curricula and external evaluation

1-3 Discuss the ways creativity has been expressed throughout history.

The human desire to be creative has been present throughout history in all communities. We can see from the existence of prehistoric cave paintings that human beings have made their mark using the materials available to them. The desire to represent and share experiences with others—for example through art, music, and dance—seems to be a basic human characteristic.

1-4 List several characteristics of creative children, including positive and negative aspects of each characteristic.

Some characteristics of creativity that are less attractive are faultfinding, stubbornness, appearance of haughtiness, self-satisfaction, and apparent discontent. Other characteristics are determination, curiosity, intuition, a willingness to take risks, a preference for complex ideas, and a sense of humor.

1-5 Name five things a teacher can do to help children develop a willingness to express creativity.

There are at least eight things that can be done for children to help them express natural creative tendencies:

- Help children accept change.
- Help children realize that some problems have no easy answers.

- Help children recognize that many problems have a number of possible answers.
- Help children learn to judge and accept their own feelings.
- Reward children for being creative.

- Help children feel joy in their creative productions and in working through problems.
- Help children appreciate themselves for being different.
- Help children develop perseverance—"stick-to-itiveness."

Key Terms

capital C creativity   4
convergent thinking   5
creativity   3

divergent thinking   5
hard thinking   8
process over product   8

small c creativity   4
soft thinking   8

Learning Activities

Self-Evaluation

After reading this chapter, take some time to evaluate your own creativity by answering the following questions:

- How do you express creativity in your own life?
- How would you explain the importance of creativity to someone else?
- Is there agreement between yourself and those you live and work with about the importance of creativity?
- How do you encourage creativity in your work with young children?

Changing the Known

Although creative thinking can be hard thinking that does not mean it can't be fun. This activity is designed to prove it. Try it alone or with a few classmates. When the activity is completed, it may be enjoyable to compare lists with those of others.

A. Materials needed: paper, pencil, watch (or clock).

B. Time allowed: 2 minutes.

C. Task: List as many uses as you can (not related to building or construction) for a standard brick. Do not worry if some of them seem silly. The important thing is to think of using something in a new and different way.

It might be fun to try this exercise with a number of different objects: a nail, powder puff, paper clip, key, belt, cup, book, or other objects.

Just Suppose

Creative thinking occurs when one imagines what might be. It is a way of "playing" with the mind. Here is an exercise that allows you to experience this type of creative process. It can be done alone or with a few classmates.

A. Materials needed: paper, pencil.

B. Time allowed: unlimited.

C. Task: From the following 9 possibilities, choose any number of tasks.

1. "Just suppose" there is nothing made of wood in the room. What would change? What would things look like? What dangers might exist? What would you be unable to do?

2. "Just suppose" (try this with other people) you cannot use words, either written or spoken, for an hour. How can you communicate? What is frustrating about it? What is pleasing about it? What would it mean if it continued for days?

3. "Just suppose" you receive a million dollars and must spend it within two minutes. Make a list of ways to spend the money, and compare lists with others in the class.

4. "Just suppose" you were the first person to meet a man from Mars and could ask him only three questions. What would they be? Compare your questions with those of others in the class.

5. "Just suppose" you were with Julius Caesar when he met Cleopatra for the first time. If you could say only one sentence, what would it be?

6. "Just suppose" you could be any person in the world for one hour. Who would it be? What would you do? Compare responses with classmates.

7. What would happen if all people awakened tomorrow morning to find themselves twice as large?

8. IMAGINE! Create seven sentences for which the seven-letter word *imagine* would be the acronym. All sentences should reflect in some way your thoughts about creative thinking, imagination, and ingenuity based on what you have learned by reading this unit.

Example: **I**deas should not be hoarded or hidden.

Many small solutions are necessary to solve big problems.

All people are created creative.

Good ideas drive out bad ideas.

Innovative ideas are resisted by "spectators."

Never mind what others think—use your own judgment.

Enjoy your fantasies—that's what they are for!

Now it's your turn!

9. Pick one or two characteristics associated with creativity that you want to increase in your own life. For example, you might want to become more open to experience or be more persistent. For a month, try to exercise that characteristic whenever you can. Record your efforts and see if you find that the characteristics can be changed.

10. Creativity is not always expressed in school-appropriate ways. For one week, pay careful attention to students causing disturbances in your room. Do you see evidence of creativity in their behavior? Propose and explain ways you could channel that originality in other ways. Get input from your fellow students on your ideas.

11. Name a brand name or specific product and imagine what kind of personality it would have, if it were to become human. For example, consider the washing detergent Kaboom! What kind of personality would it have? Be as descriptive as possible in your answer, including a list of personality traits as well as a physical description.

12. Ask a fellow student to write down the start of what can be a story. Something like, "Standing right next to the fire truck was...." or "I had never seen such a...." After this, ask for an end such as "never again will this happen to me" or "this was the best party I've ever attended!" Now, you write the story that goes in between the beginning and ending sentences, but your challenge is to write a story completely different from what people would assume from the start.

   A variation on this activity is to ask someone to give you a random title and write a story about it. This can also be a good group activity as well.

13. Stretch your creativity by trying these:
    * Draw the taste of chocolate.
    * Imagine clouds had strings. What things would happen? What would you do?
    * Imagine you could instantly change your age. What age would you be, and what would you do?
    * Imagine what would happen if Martin Luther King, Jr., had not been assassinated.
    * Describe how you write with invisible ink.
    * Explain what one plants to grow a seedless watermelon.

14. Divide a large piece of paper into squares, and list one characteristic associated with creativity in each square. Leave the paper on your desk for two weeks. Each time a student does something to demonstrate a listed characteristic, put his or her name in that square. After the first time, just use tally marks. Be sure to mark the characteristic, even if it is displayed in a negative way. At the end of two weeks, see which names are listed most often. Are they the names of students you consider creative?

15. Next week, plan one class activity that you believe is truly unusual or novel, something no student in your class would have experienced before. Observe how your students respond. What does this tell you about your teaching?

16. Give each other some problems or a specific problematic situation. Your job will be to solve the problem with not just one but five different solutions. In the end, you will state which solution you prefer the most and why. All five listed solutions should be rational and logical. When you know you have to give five solutions, you will understand that there may be many different ways of doing things. Ask yourself, "Is there a better way to do this?"

17. **What-ifs**

    Choose a "what if?" from the following list, and then draw a picture or create a photomontage showing how life would be changed by this new condition.

    What if . . .

    it rained sneakers every day?

    animals had people for pets?

    you had a dragon for a next-door neighbor?

    cows could fly?

    people were magnetic?

    Picasso had painted *American Gothic*?

    everyone lived on his or her own island?

    the oceans were made of chocolate pudding?

    every day at 2:00 p.m., gravity went away for 20 minutes?

    works of art came to life?

    nothing could be thrown away?

    all the art in the world was stolen by aliens?

    Write a short story to go along with your picture.

18. **Creative Challenge**

    What if you are trapped inside a box? This box is made of planks of wood all nailed together on the outside very tightly. All you have with you is a bow and one arrow, a piece of cardboard, a crayon, and everything you are currently wearing. You can include whatever is in your pockets, too. (No cell phones!) Now, think of as many ways as possible for getting out of that box with only those items. How are you going to "step out of the box"?

19. **Run-on Sentence**

    Write one sentence consisting of 26 words where each word begins with consecutive letters of the alphabet. Start with the letter R, for example, "Rocky said that until viewing Willy's x-ray...". Try starting with a different letter and see how far you can go with your sentence.

References

Craft, A. (2005). *Creativity in schools: Tensions and dilemmas.* London, New York, NY: Routledge.

Cxikszentmihalyi, M. (1997). *Creativity: Flow and the psychology of discovery and invention.* New York, NY: Harper Perennial Modern Classics.

Csikszentmihalyi, M. (2008). *Theory of creativity - flow: The psychology of optimal experience.* New York, NY: Harper Perennial Modern Classics.

Duffy, B. (2010). *Supporting creativity and imagination in the early years.* 2nd edition. Berkshire, England: Open University Press.

Ferrari, A., Cachia, R., & Punie, Y. (2009). Innovation and creativity in education and training in the EU member states: Fostering creative learning and supporting innovative teaching. *Literature Review on Innovation and Creativity in Education and Teaching in the EU Member States (ICEAC).* Luxembourg: Office for Official Publications of the European Communities.

Fink, A., & Neubauer, A. C. (2006). EEG Alpha oscillations during the performance of verbal creativity tasks: Differential effects of sex and verbal intelligence. *International Journal of Psychophysiology, 62*(1), 46–53.

Gnezda, N. M. (2011). Cognition and emotion in the creative process. *Art Education, 64*(1), 47–52.

Guilford, J. P. (1967). Factor analysis, intellect and creativity. In A. Rotherberg & C. R. Hausman (Eds.) *The creativity question*, pp. 200–208. Durham, NC: Duke University Press.

Haier, R. J., & Jung, R. E. (2008). Brain imaging studies of intelligence and creativity: What is the picture for education? *Roeper Review, 30*(3), 171–180.

Heilman, K. M. (2005). *Creativity and the brain.* New York, NY: Psychology Press.

Hoefferth, S. (1998). *Children at work and play.* Ann Arbor, MI: University of Michigan Institute of Social Research.

Honig, A. S. (2006). Supporting creativity in the classroom. *Scholastic Early Childhood Today, 20*(5), 13–14.

Jausovec, N. (2000). Differences in cognitive processes between gifted, intelligent, creative, and average individuals while solving complex problems: An EEG study. *Intelligence, 28*(3), 229–240.

Kamplysis, P. G., & Valtanen, J. (2010). Redefining creativity: Analyzing definitions, colorations and consequences. *Journal of Creative Behavior, 44*(2), 191–214.

Martindale, C., & Armstrong, J. (1974). The relationship of creativity to cortical activation and its operant control. *The Journal of Genetic Psychology, 124*(2), 311–320.

Martindale, C., & Hasenfus, N. (1978). EEG differences as a function of creativity, stage of the creative process, and effort to be original. *Biological Psychology, 6*(3), 157–167.

May, R. (1975). *The courage to create.* New York, NY: W. W. Norton.

Piirto, J. (2004). *Understanding creativity.* Scottsdale, AR: Great Potential Press.

Richards, R. (1999). Four P's of creativity. In M. A. Runco & S. R. Pritzker (Eds.) *Encyclopedia of creativity*, Vol 1, pp. 733–742. London: Academic Press.

Ripple, R. (1999). Teaching creativity. In M. A. Runco & S. R. Pritzker (Eds.), *Encyclopedia of creativity* (Vol. 2). San Diego, CA: Academic Press.

Robinson, Sir K. (2001). *Out of your minds—Learning to be creative.* Oxford, GB: Capstone.

Robinson, Sir K. (2010). *The element: How finding your passion changes everything.* New York, NY: Penguin.

Starko, A. J. (2003). *Creativity in the classroom: Schools of curious delight.* (3rd ed.). Mahwah, NJ: L. Erlbaum Associates.

Strom, P., & Strom, R. (2002, March). Too busy to play. *Parenting for High Potential,* 18–22.

Taylor, M. (2000). *Imaginary companions and the children who create them.* New York, NY: Oxford University Press.

Tegano, D. W., Moran, J. D., III, & Sawyers, J. K. (1991). *Creativity in early childhood classrooms.* Washington, DC: National Association for the Education of Young Children (NAEYC).

Torrance, E. P. (1962). *Rewarding creative behavior: Experiments in classroom creativity.* Englewood Cliffs, NJ: Prentice Hall.

Torrance, E. P. (1970). *Encouraging creativity in the classroom.* Dubuque, IA: William C. Brown.

Torrance, E. P. (1971). Creativity and infinity. *Journal of Research and Development in Education, 4*(3), 35–41.

Wallas, G. (1926). Stages in the creative process. In A. Rothenberg & C. R. Hausman (Eds.) *The creativity question*, pp. 69–73. Durham, NC: Duke University Press.

 Visit CourseMate for this textbook to access the eBook, Did You Get It? quizzes, Digital Downloads, TeachSource Videos, flashcards, and more. Go to CengageBrain.com to log in, register, or purchase access.

2

Promoting Creativity

Creative thinking is not a station one arrives at but a means of traveling. Creativity is fun. Being creative, feeling creative, and experiencing creativity is fun. Learning is more fun for children in settings where teachers and children recognize and understand the process of creative thinking. Incorporating creative thinking into all areas of the curriculum contributes to a young child's positive attitude toward learning. As one student teacher commented, "I used to think that if children were having too much fun, they couldn't be learning. Now I understand how they are learning in a more effective way." This chapter addresses the relationship of creativity and the classroom environment, providing guidelines for encouraging creative thinking in the early childhood program throughout the day. In subsequent chapters, the same emphasis on creativity is applied to specific curriculum areas.

Learning Objectives

After studying this chapter, you should be able to:

2-1 Describe the relationship between creativity and the curriculum.

2-2 Describe the role of play and exploration in promoting creativity.

2-3 List three points to consider when modifying the curriculum to encourage creative thinking.

2-4 List four beliefs associated with the philosophy of differentiated instruction in the early childhood curriculum.

2-5 Demonstrate four questioning strategies to encourage creative thinking in young children.

naeyc

NAEYC Program Standards

1a Knowing and understanding young children's characteristics and needs.

1c Using developmental knowledge to create healthy, respectful, supportive, and challenging learning environments.

DAP

DAP Criteria

2E1 Teachers arrange meaningful experiences that are intellectually and creatively stimulating.

2F3 To extend the range of children's interest and the scope of their thought, teachers present novel experiences and introduce stimulating ideas, problems, experiences, and hypotheses.

PHOTO 2-1 Creativity is part of each day and is not limited to art activities.

Casper Holroyd

Creativity is an integral part of each day. It is part of circle time, reading time, and lunchtime—it is not limited to art, music, creative movement, or dramatic play (see Photo 2-1). Creativity needs to be a natural part of the curriculum and the learning environment. Children need knowledge and skills to be creative. This unit will help you understand how to attain these goals. Throughout this unit, keep in mind that creative thinking is contagious—from teacher to child, from child to teacher, and also from child to child and teacher to teacher.

2-1 The Relationship between Creativity and the Curriculum

DAP **naeyc** To express their creative potential, young children need knowledge and skills. Both knowledge and skills are necessary before creative potential can have true meaning (Amabile, 1996). Children cannot develop high-level creative thinking skills without the basic knowledge and skills of a particular area, in the same way that a great chef must develop basic culinary skills before creating a gourmet recipe. The curriculum is the teacher's choice of what knowledge and skills are important and also developmentally appropriate for a particular group of children (Bredekamp, 2009).

An example of the need for a knowledge base emerged in the early pilot testing of a measure of creative potential for young children. The researchers were trying to adapt the classic "uses" task for preschool children. In this task, the children are asked to name all the uses they can think of for a common item. The number of original (that is, unusual) answers serves as one measure of creativity (Torrance, 1962; Wallach & Kogan, 1965). The researchers were puzzled when a group of preschool children could think of only a few uses for common objects such as a clothes hanger and a table knife. The researchers realized that the reason for the limited response was that the children had little or no knowledge and skill in the use of clothes hangers and table knives. In fact, most preschool children are not allowed to use these items. Knowledge and skills, then, are a prerequisite for creativity. Later research came up with better results when the children were asked to think of all the ways to use a box and paper, items about which the children had a working knowledge (Moran, Milgram, Sawyers, & Fu, 1985; Rushton & Larkin, 2007). Creativity evolves from a knowledge base—without knowledge, there is no creation. A child must understand in order to invent.

Thus, one important goal for the early childhood teacher is to provide an adequate base of knowledge and skills for children, while at the same time providing an environment that encourages creative thinking in the use of the knowledge and skills (Torrance, 1995). The curriculum is the guide by which teachers determine *what* will be presented to children. Creativity is fostered according to *how* the curriculum is presented to the child (Runco, 2008).

> To live a creative life, we must lose our fear of being wrong.
>
> —Joseph Chilton Pierce

Did You Get It?

A preschool teacher trying to encourage creative thinking handed a group of her three-year-old students a rake and asked them to think of alternate uses for it. How was her activity flawed?

a. Three-year-olds lack the imaginative ability to think of alternate uses for an item.

b. Three-year-olds can only think concretely, not abstractly.

c. Three-year-olds cannot work effectively in groups.

d. Three-year-olds lack knowledge about rakes.

Take the full quiz on CourseMate.

Creativity and Pretend Play

Two researchers studied the relationships among pretend play, creativity, emotional regulation, and executive functioning in children. They assessed pretend play using the Affect in Play Scale (APS), which measures children's cognitive and affective processes, such as organization of a plot or use of emotions.

Sixty-one female participants, in kindergarten through fourth grade, were assessed using the APS to measure pretend play ability, a divergent-thinking task (the Alternate Uses Test), a storytelling task to assess creativity, a measure of executive functioning (the Wisconsin Card Sorting Task),

and parent report on the Emotion Regulation Checklist (ERC).

Using correlational analyses, they found that pretend play was significantly related to creativity as measured by divergent thinking and storytelling. Divergent-thinking ability, in turn, was significantly related to creativity in storytelling. No significant relationships were found with executive functioning.

The results of this study support theories that suggest play, creativity, and emotion regulation are linked (Hoffman & Russ, 2012). This study gives early childhood teachers further evidence that encouraging expressive free play with young children is conducive to creative thinking.

2-2 Promoting Creativity through Play and Exploration

DAP **naeyc** Let's take a look at a preschool classroom where computers are available and observe the process of exploration as it leads into play. At first, the computer is novel, and children engage in randomly punching keys—exploring what the keys can do. This leads to the eventual realization that specific keys have specific uses. This process of exploring the computer to discover what it can do may take several months, depending on the frequency of the child's exposure to the computer. When the child has gained an understanding of what the computer can do, she may move on to another question: "What can I do with the computer?" Equipped with the skills gained through exploration (using a mouse, for example), the child truly begins to play with the computer.

Here again, it is important for the child to have basic knowledge of what a computer can do and the skills to operate it. But young children also need to explore the computer before any more formal experiences take place. Then, after they have acquired knowledge and skills, they can use the computer creatively.

As children explore and play with materials in their environments, they are also in a sense shaping the brain (Catania, 2008). Those who research the human brain contend that experience, particularly in childhood, sculpts the brain (Fischer, Immordino Yang, & Weber,

2007). The brain changes physiologically as a result of experience. New connections are formed every day in active interaction with the environment. Hands-on activities stimulate various regions of the brain, and active participation helps young children form stronger mental association with their existing understandings (Hinton, Miyamoto, & Della-Chiesa, 2008; Rushton & Larkin, 2007). Therefore, the opportunities to learn actively in an environment provided throughout life and particularly in the early years help to create unique individuals. Other researchers put it this way: "Throughout life, we are both shaped by and shaping our environment" (Fischer et al., 2007). Passive observation in the early childhood program is never enough. As the ancient Chinese proverb states, "Tell me and I forget. Show me and I remember. Let me do and I understand." Thus, the role of exploration and play is central to the development of creativity—at all ages.

Did You Get It?

A kindergarten teacher allows his students full access to the classroom art supplies. What type of growth are his actions promoting?
  a. brain growth
  b. personality growth
  c. growth of interpersonal skills
  d. growth of reading skills

Take the full quiz on CourseMate.

2-3 Modifying Curriculum to Encourage Creativity

DAP **naeyc** Curriculum may be viewed as an outline of knowledge and skills to be learned rather than as a recipe for how they must be taught. The term *learn* implies that exploration and play are part of the process; the term *recipe* denotes a careful following of steps in a specific order and amount to come up with one precise product. As we know, young children are not all the same, so differing amounts and various combinations of ingredients are necessary for each child. Each child learns the same knowledge and skills in a unique way (see Photo 2-2); therefore, the recipe is continually modified. Keep in mind that developmental needs serve as a guide to the sequence in which all concepts are introduced.

Creativity and curriculum complement each other. The curriculum is a guide to the knowledge and abilities that are necessary to develop creative thinking skills. The curriculum provides the content around which creativity may develop. How the content is

Casper Holroyd

PHOTO 2-3 The curriculum must allow children to be both physically and mentally active.

Casper Holroyd

PHOTO 2-2 Each child approaches creative activities in her or his own unique way.

presented to the child is the means to creative development. When modifying curriculum to encourage creative thinking, consider the following points:

- The curriculum must be developmentally appropriate for young children. This means it will allow children to be both physically and mentally active, engaging them in active rather than passive activities (see Photo 2-3).
- Be alert to and aware of children's interests. Choose materials and activities that are meaningful to children in your group. Children, like you, are drawn to materials and activities that interest them (see Photo 2-4). Be sure to involve them in choosing materials and activities for the curriculum.
- Provide a variety of materials that encourage children's creative exploration. Allow children ample time not only to physically explore but also to mentally explore—think about—what they are doing (see Photo 2-5).
- In planning curriculum, consider all the types of learning styles and multiple intelligences (ways of learning) of children in your group.

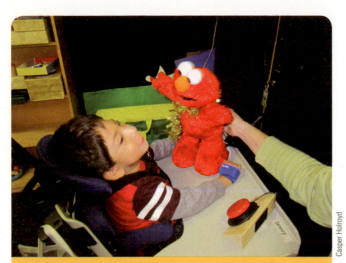

PHOTO 2-4 Children are drawn to materials that interest them.

PHOTO 2-5 Children need lots of time to physically and mentally explore—to think about what they are doing.

(More information about learning styles and multiple intelligences is found in Chapter 5.) Plan activities that meet the different needs of all learners.

● Encourage children's divergent thinking and curiosity. Let them ask questions and search for solutions to their problems.

● Encourage older children's curiosity by giving credit in your grading system for questioning. In this strategy, students are concretely rewarded for curiosity.

● Be sure to provide opportunities for children to interact and communicate with other children and adults in an atmosphere of acceptance.

A note of caution is needed here in our discussion, especially about choosing creative activities for young children. Remember, a teaching activity that produces an enjoyable or creative outcome does not necessarily enhance creativity unless the *students* have the opportunity for creative thinking. There is a difference between creative teaching (the *teacher* is creative) and teaching to *develop children's creativity*. For example, when you examine books of so-called creative activities, you may find adorable illustrations and unusual activities, but the input from students is fairly routine. A color-by-number dragon filled with addition problems may have been an original creation for the illustrator, but completing the addition problems and coloring as directed provide no opportunities for originality on the part of students. A crossword puzzle in the shape of a spiral was an original idea for its creator, but it still requires students only to give accurate (convergent) responses to clues and fill in the correct spaces. In both of these examples, those who created the materials had the opportunity to be creative. The students did not. In other instances, classroom teachers may use enormous personal creativity in developing activities that allow few opportunities for students to be original.

Teaching to enhance creativity has a different focus: the essential creativity is on the part of the students. If the students developed a new form of crossword puzzle, they would have the opportunity to exercise creative thinking. Creativity can also be developed as students devise their own science experiments, discuss a fairy tale from the viewpoint of a character in it, or rewrite *Snow White* as it might be told by the stepmother. When we teach to enhance creativity, we may well be creative as teachers, but we also provide students the knowledge, skills, and surroundings necessary for their own creativity to emerge. The results may not be as flashy as the activities book, but they include real problem finding, problem solving, and communication by students.

It is also important to remember that challenges are not just for our students. We can also challenge ourselves as teachers. One way to do this is to reflect on the ways we are providing challenges in our program. When modifying the curriculum to encourage creative thinking, we need to ask ourselves the following questions:

● Do I take time to observe children in action before stepping in to "teach"?

● Do I provide opportunities for children to use new understandings and skills in many different situations before moving to the next skill?

Casper Holroyd

PHOTO 2-6 With open-ended materials, children are free to be creative.

choose more physical ways—touching, smelling, tasting, and climbing.

● Realize that to some degree, these differences are related to temperament differences in the exploratory drive.

● Recognize that some children are more timid, while others are more comfortable with novelty and physical exploration.

● Understand that even the timid child will be very curious; he may require more encouragement and reinforcement to leave safe and familiar situations.

● Try to redefine "failure." In real life, curiosity often leads to more mess than mastery, but it is how we handle the mess that helps encourage further exploration and thereby creativity.

● Use your attention and approval to reinforce the exploring, curious child.

● When exploration in the classroom is disruptive, contain it by teaching the child when and where to do that particular kind of exploration. For example, "Claire, let's play with water outside" (Perry, 2009).

● Do I provide open-ended activities for children each day (see Photo 2-6)?

● Do I add or modify the materials in learning centers or stations as I perceive children are ready for change?

● Do I feel comfortable being challenged? How can I challenge myself to grow as a learner and teacher?

2-3a Curiosity: A Direct Link to Creativity

Children are curious by nature. From the moment of birth, they are drawn to new things. When children are curious about something new, they want to explore it. Because exploration is a crucial part of the creative process, curiosity is directly linked to creativity.

To ensure that children's curiosity doesn't fade, the following are some tips to encourage curiosity in young children.

● Recognize individual differences in children's styles of curiosity. Some children may want to explore with only their minds, while others may

2-3b Integrated Curriculum and Creativity

DAP **naeyc** The curriculum that encourages creativity the most in young children is an integrated, whole curriculum. In an **integrated curriculum,** the artificial divisions among content areas are reduced. Although many teachers find it convenient to think about what the child will learn as separate categories of information, the integrated curriculum is not designed in that way.

Most often, an integrated curriculum is designed around a unit of study centered on a specific theme or project. The unit of study contains a coordinated series of learning activities planned around a broad topic that involves the whole group. A unit in an integrated curriculum involves all of the content areas (reading, math, art, music, social studies, and so on). Integrated curriculum units provide the topics and framework for planning activities for children. The length of time for the unit may vary, taking weeks or months. The amount of time depends on the topic and the interests of the children.

In an integrated curriculum, children are able to experience learning as a whole. For example, they can explore the idea of neighborhood and community by reading books, hearing stories, drawing and painting a

PHOTO 2-7 Young children explore their world in many ways.

Casper Holroyd

community mural, and planning and preparing foods from their neighborhood and community. In this broad approach to learning, they are able to express themselves creatively in many areas and not just in the area of the arts (see Photo 2-7). Part 5 presents many areas of the curriculum and creative approaches to each of these areas.

Did You Get It?

When teaching addition, a second grade teacher gives the students small items to count and shows them how to write out the problems. Which method of modifying the curriculum to encourage creative thinking is the teacher applying?

   a. Providing opportunities for the children to interact with other children.
   b. Planning activities to meet the needs of all learners.
   c. Encouraging divergent thinking and curiosity.
   d. Allowing children ample time for mental thinking.

Take the full quiz on CourseMate.

2-4 Differentiated Instruction and Creative Early Childhood Curriculum

naeyc Another term associated with effective curriculum for learners is differentiated instruction. Differentiated instruction is a philosophy of teaching and learning based on a set of beliefs that relate to encouraging creativity in your children. The beliefs of differentiated instruction are as follows:

● Children who are the same age are different in their readiness to learn, interests, styles of learning, experiences, and life circumstances.
● These differences in children affect what they need to learn, the pace at which they need to learn it, and the support they need from teachers and others to learn it well.
● Children learn best when they can make a connection between the curriculum and their interests and life experiences.
● Children learn best when learning opportunities are natural.
● Children are more effective learners when classrooms and schools create a sense of community in which children feel significant and respected.
● The central job of teachers and schools is to maximize the capacity of each student. (Tomlinson, 2000)

Differentiated instruction is a refinement of, not a substitute for, high-quality early childhood curriculum and instruction. Differentiated instruction is present in the early childhood classroom when the curriculum and instruction fit each child and children have choices about what to learn and how. Also, children taking part in setting learning goals is further evidence of differentiated instruction. Finally, in the early childhood classroom, with differentiated instruction, the curriculum connects with the experiences and interests of individual children.

Differentiated instruction is not a new phenomenon in early childhood education. The one-room schoolhouses of the past offered teachers the challenge of finding ways to work with students with wide-ranging needs. The contemporary approach to differentiating has been shaped by the growing research on learning—drawing from the best practices in special education, gifted education, and multi-age classrooms; recent research on the brain and multiple intelligences; and developments in authentic assessment.

In summary, the aim of differentiating instruction is to maximize each child's growth by meeting each child where he or she is and helping the child progress from there. In practice, it involves offering several different learning experiences in response to children's varied needs. Chapter 5 provides more specific information about activities for different learning styles and multiple intelligences.

2-4a Creative Early Childhood Curriculum and Learning Styles

DAP naeyc One of the components of differentiated instruction is an understanding of the different ways children learn. Children think and learn in different ways. In any group of children, a variety of different learning characteristics will always be present.

An important factor in understanding learning styles is understanding brain functioning. Both sides of the brain can reason, but by very different ways, and one side of the brain may be dominant. When we talk about a person who is right-brained or left-brained, we are referring to learning preferences based on functional differences between the hemispheres (sides) of the brain.

The left brain is considered analytic in approach. This means that a left-brained (successive processor) person prefers to learn in a step-by-step sequential format, beginning with details leading up to understanding a concept or acquiring a skill.

The right brain is described as holistic or global. This means that a right-brained (simultaneous processor) person prefers to learn beginning with the general concept and then going on to specifics.

Children who are right-brained are those whose right hemisphere of the brain is dominant in their learning process. This is in contrast to the majority of children, whose left hemisphere is dominant in their learning style. Each hemisphere of the brain has distinctly different strengths and behavioral characteristics.

Everyone uses both hemispheres of the brain, but some may use one side more than the other. For instance, you might have a dominant right hemisphere, which simply means that it is your preferred or stronger hemisphere in which you tend to first process most of the information you receive. That does not mean you don't use your left hemisphere. You may use your right hemisphere 60% of the time and your left hemisphere 40%. Similarly, when we talk about children who are right-brained or left-brained, we do not mean they use only one hemisphere but simply that they use one hemisphere to a greater extent than the other.

The right- and left-brain hemispheres have specialized thinking characteristics. They do not approach life in the same way. The left-hemisphere approach to life is part to whole, which means it sequences, puts things in order, and is logical. The right hemisphere learns whole to part, which means it does not sequence or put things in order. Rather, it looks at things in an overall way or holistically. Let's consider specific skills and in which hemisphere those skills are best developed.

2-4b Left Hemisphere

The skills best developed in this side of the brain are handwriting, understanding symbols, language, reading, and phonics. Other general skills best developed here are locating details and facts, talking and reciting, following directions, and listening and auditory association. Children must exercise all of these skills on a day-to-day basis in school. We give children symbols; we stress reading, language, and phonics. We ask for details, insist that directions be followed, and mostly, talk at children. In short, most of our school curriculum is left-brained. We teach to the child who has a dominant left brain.

2-4c Right Hemisphere

The right hemisphere is associated with an entirely different set of skills. The right hemisphere has the ability to recognize and process nonverbal sounds. It also governs the ability to communicate using body language.

Although the motor cortex is in both hemispheres, the ability to make judgments based on the relationship of our bodies to space (needed in sports, creative movement, and dance, for instance) is basically centered in the right hemisphere.

The ability to recognize, draw, and deal with shapes and patterns as well as geometric figures lies in the right hemisphere. This involves the ability to distinguish between different colors and hues and the ability to visualize in color.

Singing and music are right-hemisphere activities. Creative art is also in debt to the right hemisphere. Although many children who are left-brained are quite good in art, the "art" they make is structured; it must come out a certain way. They are most comfortable with models and a predictable outcome. Their pictures, or the things they create, are drawings made for Mother's Day or turkeys drawn for Thanksgiving.

THIS ONE'S FOR YOU!

What Type of Learner Are You?

As discussed in this chapter, both sides of the brain can reason, but by very different ways, and one side of the brain may be dominant. Find out which type of learner you are by checking off which of the following characteristics best describes how you learn. Although you probably will have checks in both lists, you most likely will have a majority of checks in one list, which generally indicates that particular style as your dominant learning style.

Check off the characteristics that are *most* like you in both of the following lists.

Left (Analytic)

Successive Hemisphere Style

1. ☐ Verbal
2. ☐ Responds to word meaning
3. ☐ Sequential
4. ☐ Processes information linearly
5. ☐ Responds to logic
6. ☐ Plans ahead
7. ☐ Recalls people's names
8. ☐ Speaks with few gestures
9. ☐ Punctual
10. ☐ Prefers formal study
11. ☐ Prefers bright lights while studying

Right (Global)

Simultaneous Hemisphere Style

1. ☐ Visual
2. ☐ Responds to tone of voice
3. ☐ Random
4. ☐ Processes information in varied order
5. ☐ Responds to emotion
6. ☐ Impulsive
7. ☐ Recalls people's faces
8. ☐ Gestures when speaking
9. ☐ Less punctual
10. ☐ Prefers sound/music background while studying
11. ☐ Prefers frequent mobility while studying

Children who are left-hemisphere dominant are good at other-directed art.

Children who are right-hemisphere dominant create "mystery" pictures. They show the pictures to you, but they aren't quite sure what you are looking at until they start talking about it. For example, they may show raindrops falling and the sun shining at the same time

After listening to a story, children who are right-brained can retell the story in their own words without any difficulty. However, they are so creative that they usually add their own details and ending. From an adult's perspective, it may seem they are exaggerating or embellishing, but in their terms, they are simply being what they are. They change stories, add details, and alter endings to meet their emotional needs. Feelings and emotions appear to be most dominant in the right hemisphere.

Now, armed with all of this information on children who are right- or left-brained, you need to reflect on your own work with children and ask yourself if your curriculum is directed toward only one type of learner. Are you in tune with the right-brained learners? You may find it helpful to go to the library and take out books with specific curricular ideas for children who are right-brained. At the very least, you need to be aware of yet another way in which each young child is unique. And finally, you may want to find out what kind of learner you are by using the checklist in the This One's for You! box, above.

2-4d Promoting Creativity Through Positive Acceptance

Adults who work with young children are in an especially crucial position to foster each child's creativity. In the day-to-day experiences in early childhood settings, as young children actively explore their world, adults' attitudes clearly transmit their feelings to the child. A child who meets with unquestionable acceptance of her unique approach to the world will feel safe in expressing her creativity, whatever the activity or situation.

The following are guidelines on how to help transmit this positive acceptance to children, which in turn fosters creativity in any situation.

- Openly demonstrate to young children that there is value in their curiosity, exploration, and original behavior.
- Allow children to go at their own pace when they are carrying out an activity that excites and interests them.
- Let children stay with what they are making until they feel it's finished.
- Let children figure out their own ways of doing things if they prefer to do so.
- Keep the atmosphere relaxed.
- Encourage guessing, especially when the answers make good sense.
- Let the creativity activity be the reward and refrain from stock "rewarding" comments such as "good job." Instead, comment on the work, "I notice you are using many diagonal lines."

2-4e Working with Older Children

DAP naeyc In the upper elementary grades, teachers have an even greater challenge to promote creativity because the curriculum often dominates the program. There are often state-level guidelines for what to teach, at what level, and with specific books and materials. Even in this situation, you can encourage creativity in your classroom. Here are some suggestions to help you get started.

To encourage creativity with older children:

- Use tangible rewards (stickers, prizes) as seldom as possible; instead, encourage children's own pride in the work they have done.
- Avoid setting up competitive situations for children.
- Downplay your evaluation of children's work. Instead, lead them to become more proficient at recognizing their own strengths and weaknesses. Encourage children to monitor their own work rather than rely on your surveillance of them.
- Whenever possible, give children choices about what activities they do and about how to do those activities.
- Make intrinsic (internal) motivation a conscious factor in your discussions with children. Encourage them to become aware of their own special interests and to take their focus off the extrinsic (external) rewards.

- To build children's intrinsic (internal) motivation, help them build their self-esteem by focusing on and appreciating their unique talents and strengths.
- As much as possible, encourage children to become active, independent learners rather than to rely on you for constant direction. Encourage them to take confident control of their own-learning process.
- Give children ample opportunities for free play with various materials, and allow them to engage in fantasy whenever possible.
- In any way you can, show children that you value creativity—not only do you allow it, but you also engage in it yourself.
- Whenever you can, show your students that you are an intrinsically motivated adult who enjoys thinking creatively.

It may help to also consider these additional points on working with older students.

Time. Give students extended, unhurried time to explore and do their best work. Stand aside when students are productively engaged and motivated to complete an interesting and creative task.

Space. Provide students with an area to leave unfinished work to be completed later. Create an inviting workspace that has natural light, harmonious colors, and stimulating resources.

Materials. Provide an abundant supply of interesting and useful materials, including writing and art materials that students can use freely to invent, experiment, and demonstrate ideas and products.

Climate. Create a classroom atmosphere where students understand that mistakes are acceptable and it is appropriate to take risks. Allow a reasonable amount of noise, mess, and freedom.

Enrichment. Introduce students to out-of-class experiences so they encounter ideas to use in classroom learning. Help students reflect on their experiences and what they mean to them.

Even when you feel burdened by state standards and high-stakes testing, it's worth the effort to create a classroom environment that is both visually and mentally stimulating. Students need to be certain that a spark of learning—that electricity—is present in their daily lessons. Otherwise, you might as well turn out the lights and send the kids home.

Research on Benefits of the Arts in Education

Numerous studies done over the past years have demonstrated the amazing benefits of having art as part of a well-rounded curriculum. The following research studies reveal the power of art to inspire, motivate, and educate today's students.

In 2006, the Solomon R. Guggenheim Museum study on arts education showed a link between arts education and improved literacy skills. In this study, the Guggenheim sent artists into schools to teach students and help them create their own masterpieces. Children who took part in the program performed better on six different categories of literacy and critical thinking skills than those who did not

In 2009, the Center for Arts Education published a report that suggests arts education may improve graduation rates. Taking a look at the role of arts education in New York public schools, this report found that schools with the lowest access also had the highest dropout rates. Conversely, those with the highest graduation rates also had the greatest access to arts education and resources. Although undoubtedly a number of other factors play into graduation rates, it was reported that many at-risk students cited participation in the arts as their reason for staying. Participation in these activities had a quantifiable impact on levels of truancy, delinquency, and academic performance.

In 2010, a study of Missouri public schools found that greater arts education led to fewer disciplinary infractions and higher attendance, graduation rates, and test scores. Using data submitted by the state's public schools, the Missouri Department of Education and the Missouri Alliance for Arts Education compiled this report. They found that arts education had a significant effect on the academic and social success of their students. Those with greater arts participation were more likely to come to class, avoid being removed, and graduate. They also demonstrated greater proficiency in math and communication.

In 2011, a study called "Reinvesting in Arts Education" found that integrating arts with other subjects could help raise achievement levels. Arts education may not just help raise test scores but also the learning process itself. In this report on the Maryland school system, it was found that skills learned in the visual arts could help improve reading, and the counterparts fostered in playing an instrument could be applied to mathematics. The researchers and school officials believe that arts education can be a valuable education reform tool and that classroom integration of creative opportunities could be key to motivating students and improving standardized scores.

Did You Get It?

On an apple-picking trip, a teacher makes sure to show the students the different varieties of apples. Which tenet of differentiated instruction is the teacher following?

a. Children learn well when the instruction is directed at their level of understanding.
b. Children learn well when the opportunities to learn come naturally.
c. Children learn well in group instruction.
d. Children learn well outside of a classroom environment.

Take the full quiz on CourseMate.

2-5 Creative Questioning Strategies to Encourage Creative Thinking

Just the way a question is phrased or asked sets the stage for creative replies. For example, the request, "Describe (or tell me about) the sky . . ." would certainly elicit different responses than, "What color is the sky?" In the first, more open-ended (divergent) request, children are encouraged to share their personal feelings and experiences about the sky. This might be color or cloud shapes or even how jets, birds, and helicopters can fill it at times. The second question is phrased in such a way that a one-word (convergent) reply would do. Or even worse, it may seem to children that there is one and only one correct answer!

In asking questions, then, a teacher can foster children's creativity. Let us now consider more specific examples of activities that focus on creative questioning. These activities suggest various ways of asking questions and are designed to draw out the creative potential in young children. Activities that deal directly with specific art forms and media are found in later sections of this book.

1. Making things better with your imagination.
One way to help children think more creatively is to get them to "make things better with their imagination." Ask children to change things to make them the way they would like them to be. Here are some examples of questions of this type.

- What would taste better if it were sweeter?
- What would be nicer if it were smaller?
- What would be more fun if it were faster?
- What would be better if it were quieter?
- What would be more exciting if it went backwards?
- What would be happier if it were bigger?

2. Using other senses.
Young children can stretch their creative talents by using their senses in unusual ways. For example, children may be asked to close their eyes and guess what has been placed in their hands. (Use a piece of foam rubber, a small rock, a grape, a piece of sandpaper, and so on.) Another approach is to have children close their eyes and guess what they hear. (Use sounds like shuffling cards, jingling coins, rubbing sandpaper, or ripping paper.)

When doing this exercise, the children should be asked for reasons for their guesses to make the activity more fun and create a better learning experience.

3. Divergent-thinking questions.
Any time you ask children a question requiring a variety of answers, you are encouraging their creative thinking skills. Here are some examples using the concept of water.

- How can you use water?
- What floats in water?
- How does water help us?
- Why is cold water cold? Why is hot water hot?
- What are the different colors that water can be? Why?
- What makes water rain? What makes it stop?
- What always stays underwater?

Divergent-thinking questions using concepts such as sand, ice, smoke, cars, and similar topics are fun for children. They also encourage openness and flexibility of thinking.

4. What-would-happen-if?
The "What-would-happen-if?" technique has been used successfully by many teachers of young children to spark good thinking-and-doing sessions designed to ignite imaginations. Some of the following questions may be used.

- What would happen if all the trees in the world were blue?
- What would happen if everyone looked alike?
- What would happen if all the cars were gone?
- What would happen if everybody wore the same clothes?
- What would happen if every vegetable tasted like chocolate?
- What would happen if there were no more clocks or watches?
- What would happen if you could fly?

5. In how many different ways?
Another type of question that extends a child's creative thinking is one that begins, "In how many different ways . . .?" A few examples are provided here.

- In how many different ways could a spoon be used?
- In how many different ways could a button be used?
- In how many different ways could a string be used?
- In what new ways could we use this? How could it be modified to fit a new use?

All of these questioning strategies are intended to help an adult encourage creativity in young children. Children may also generate these types of questions once they have been modeled for them. Often, the use of these strategies is enough to begin a long-running and positive creative experience for the child as well as the teacher. They are limited only by the user's imagination. More of these types of questioning activities are provided at the end of this chapter.

2-5a Motivating Skills for Teachers

Some children need help in getting started. The fact that the activity is labeled "creative" does not necessarily make the child "ready to go." A child may be feeling restless or tired or may feel like doing something else. All teachers, even those with good ideas, face

▶Ⅱ **TeachSource** Video

© 2015 Cengage Learning

Preschool: Cooking Activities

1. Consider the comments the teacher made to the children as they made their "snack bugs." Discuss how they reflect the information in this chapter on motivating skills for teachers.

2. How would you alter this cooking activity so that it encourages more divergent thinking?

Watch on CourseMate.

child-initiated activities and self-selection of creative materials, and emphasize voluntary participation of the children in the activities presented. Teachers are giving children opportunities for fun if they honestly can answer "yes" to these questions:

● Is the activity exciting?
● Is the activity in a free setting?
● Can the children imagine in it?
● Can the children play at it?
● Is there a game-like quality to it?
● Are judgments avoided?
● Is competition deemphasized?
● Will there be something to laugh about?

Goals. Permit children to set and reach goals. Most of the excitement in achieving a goal is in reaching for it. Children should be given opportunities to plan projects. They should be allowed to get involved in activities that have something at the end for which they can strive. If the completion of an activity is not rewarding to a child, then the value of that activity is questionable.

Variety. Vary the content and style of what the children can do. It is wise to consider not only what will be next, but how it will be done, too. For example, the teacher has the children sit and watch a movie, then they sit and draw, and then they sit and listen to a story. These are three different activities, but in each of them, the children are sitting. The content of the activity has changed but not the style. This can, and does, become boring. Boring is definitely not creative.

Habit is one of the worst enemies of creativity. Teachers who set the standard for valuing creativity by taking a chance on a "crazy" idea may positively influence the expression of creative potential by many children.

Challenge. Challenge children. This means letting them know that what they are about to do is something that will be exciting to try. An example of this is letting the children know that their next activity may be tricky, adventurous, or mysterious. It is the "bet-you-can't-do-this" approach with the odds in favor of the children.

Reinforcement. Reinforce the creative behavior of children. The basic need here is for something to come at the end of the activity that lets the children feel they would like to do it again. It could be seeing the teacher's smile, receiving a compliment, reaching the goal, hanging up the creation, sharing with a friend, or just finishing the activity. The main thing is that the children feel rewarded for and satisfied with their efforts.

this problem. There are several ways to help children become motivated for the creative process.

Physical needs. Make sure children are rested and physically fit. Sleepy, hungry, or sick children cannot care about creativity. Their physical needs must be met before such learning can be appealing.

Interests. Try to find out, and then use, what naturally interests the child. Children want to not only do things they like to do but also be successful at them. Whenever children feel that they will succeed in a task, they are generally much more willing to get involved. Parents may be good resources for determining the child's interests.

Friends. Permit children to work with their friends. This is not possible or advisable all the time, but some teachers avoid ever putting children who are friends together in working situations. They worry that these children will only fool around or disturb others. When this does happen, one should question the task at hand because it is obviously not holding the children's interest.

Activities for fun. Allow the activity to be fun for the child. Notice the use of the word *allow*. Children know how to have their own fun. They do not need anyone to make it for them. Encourage

The children's feelings. Try to make sure children feel good about what they are doing. Some teachers believe that if a child is working intensely or learning, that is enough. This may not be so. The most important thing is not what children are doing but how they *feel about* what they are doing. If children feel bad about themselves or an activity while doing it, this is a warning. The teacher must be continually in touch with how the children are feeling. This is the result of listening, watching, and being with the children in a manner that is open and caring.

2-5b How to Inspire Creativity: Research Perspective

Although many parents, art teachers, and even politicians believe that arts make you smarter, much current research shows these claims to be unfounded. In a study by Ellen Winner and Lois Hetland (2007) of students taking art classes, their analysis showed no evidence that arts training actually *causes scores* to rise. Although they believe that there is a very good reason to teach arts in school, it's not the reason that art supporters commonly fall back on.

In a study of several art classes in Boston-area schools, they found that arts programs teach a specific set of thinking skills rarely addressed elsewhere in the curriculum. Far from being irrelevant in a test-driven education system, arts education is becoming even more important as standardized tests exert a narrowing influence over what schools teach.

These researchers believe that the implications are broad not just for schools but also for society. As schools cut time for the arts, they may be losing their ability to produce not just the artistic creators of the future but innovative leaders as well.

The standardized tests we use in many of our schools today are almost exclusively focused on verbal and quantitative skills, which reward the child who has a knack for language and math and who can absorb and regurgitate information. This type of testing reveals little about a student's intellectual depth, creativity, or desire to learn (Winner & Goldstein, 2011).

As schools increasingly shape their curriculum to produce high test scores, many life skills not measured by tests just do not get taught. In their study, funded by the J. Paul Getty Trust, these researchers spent an academic year in two local Boston-area schools to determine what happens inside arts classes. They videotaped and photographed classes and analyzed what they saw. They also interviewed teachers and their students.

They watched student–teacher interactions repeatedly to identify specific habits and skills and then coded the segments to count the times each were taught.

In their analysis, the researchers found that while students in art classes learn techniques specific to art, such as how to mix paint, they are also taught a remarkable array of mental habits not emphasized elsewhere in school. They identified eight "studio habits of mind" that art classes taught, including the development of artistic craft (Winner & Hetland, 2007).

Such skills included visual–spatial abilities, reflection, self-criticism, and the willingness to experiment and learn from mistakes. All of these skills are important in any number of careers but are widely ignored by today's standardized tests (Hetland, Winner, Veenema, & Sheridan, 2007).

Another of these habits was persistence. Students worked on projects over sustained periods of time and were expected to find meaningful problems and persevere through frustration. Each of the skills and habits they identified has a role in life and learning.

Finally, the researchers, who both have long histories in arts education, were startled to find a systematic emphasis on thinking and perception in the art classes they studied. In contrast to the reputation of the arts as mainly about expressive craft, they found that teachers talked about decisions, choices, and understanding far more than they talked about feelings.

In their summary, Winner and Hetland state their belief that while art teachers rightly resist making their classes like "academic" classes, teachers of academic subjects might well benefit from making their classes more like art classes (2007).

For students living in a rapidly changing world, the arts teach vital modes of seeing, imagining, inventing, and thinking. Those who have learned the lessons of the arts—how to see new patterns, how to learn from mistakes, and how to envision solutions—are the ones most likely to come up with the answers needed most for the future.

Did You Get It?

Which question would best encourage creative thinking?

   a. How many ducks are in the water?
   b. What is your favorite color?
   c. How can we stay warm in the snow?
   d. Why is the sky blue?

Take the full quiz on CourseMate.

Summary

2-1 Describe the relationship between creativity and the curriculum.

Creativity is fun. Incorporating creativity into all areas of the curriculum contributes to a young child's positive attitude toward learning. Teachers who encourage children to work at their own pace and to be self-directed in a relaxed, nonjudgmental atmosphere are fostering creative development.

2-2 Describe the role of play and exploration in promoting creativity.

The process of exploring to discover the characteristics of objects is essential to the development of a child's creativity. As children explore and play with materials, they are acquiring the knowledge and skills necessary to eventually use these materials creatively.

2-3 Demonstrate four questioning strategies to encourage creative thinking in young children.

Four questioning strategies to use with young children include asking them to "make things better with their imagination;" using their senses in unusual ways; asking divergent-thinking questions; using "what-would-happen-if" questions; and extending creative thinking by asking "in how many ways?"

2-4 List three points to consider when modifying the curriculum to encourage creative thinking.

When modifying curriculum to encourage creative thinking, consider the following points:

- The curriculum must be developmentally appropriate for young children. This means it will allow children to be both physically and mentally active, engaging them in active rather than passive activities.
- Be alert and aware of children's interests. Choose materials and activities that are meaningful to children in your group.

- Provide a variety of materials that encourage children's creative exploration.
- In planning curriculum, consider all the types of learning styles and multiple intelligences in your group.
- Encourage children's divergent thinking and curiosity. Let them ask questions and search for solutions to their problems.
- Encourage older children's curiosity by giving credit in your grading system for questioning.
- Be sure to provide opportunities for children to interact and communicate with other children and adults in an atmosphere of acceptance.

2-5 List four beliefs associated with the philosophy of differentiated instruction in the early childhood curriculum.

The beliefs of differentiated instruction are as follows:

- Children who are the same age are different in their readiness to learn, interests, styles of learning, experiences, and life circumstances.
- These differences in children affect what they need to learn, the pace at which they need to learn it, and the support they need from teachers and others to learn it well.
- Children will learn best when they can make a connection between the curriculum and their interests and life experiences.
- Children will learn best when learning opportunities are natural.
- Children are more effective leaners when classrooms and schools create a sense of community in which children feel significant and respected.
- The central job of teachers and schools is to maximize the capacity of each student.

Key Terms

analytic 24	holistically 24	simultaneous processor 24
differentiated instruction 23	integrated curriculum 22	successive processor 24
global 24	left-brained 24	
holistic 24	right-brained 24	

Learning Activities

- Examine today's newspaper. What evidence of creative thought do you see in the stories or advertisements? Look for original ideas that are appropriate to the situation. Are all creative ideas socially appropriate?
- One of the most interesting and effective ways to explore creativity is to undertake a creative project of your own. Identify a problem, and invent something to address it. For example, an invention might be an enormous version

of a dentist's mirror that allows the user to check for leaves in the gutters without climbing a ladder, or a device that signals forgetful teenagers to retrieve their wet laundry. Look around for everyday annoyances or dilemmas that you might solve. What things around you might be improved, simplified, or made more elaborate? Alternatively, you might want to undertake a creative writing project, artistic endeavor, or other creative task.

Whatever you choose, record your thoughts, feelings, and activities. How do you feel about creativity as you contemplate such a project?

- This is a small-group activity designed to help you focus on seeing "creatively." The object is to create something artistic out of lots of curved and straight lines. Each student has a piece of paper and a marker. Each student draws squiggles and swirls all over their paper and then switches papers with a neighbor. Each student then must create something out of the squiggles and swirls drawn by their partner. Or a student may choose to just fill in the areas with different colors of designs. This is a great activity to get you thinking in unique ways and creating something out of nothing.

- With this quote in mind—"A house is a machine for living in" (Le Corbusier)—describe the kind of house you see yourself living in some day. Focus on visual images in your description.
  1. How does it relate to creativity?
  2. List some of your reactions.

- Practice your fluency of thought with this game. At first you may find that you can think of only a few sentences, but if you persist, many more will occur to you. Write five-word sentences from the five given letters GAMES, one word for each letter:
  1. Great Animals Make Everything Sensational.
  2. Giving Anonymously Makes Everyone Secure.

  Now see how many sentences you can produce in exactly 5 minutes, and share them with your classmates.

- "Become" one of the following objects and dramatize its characteristics in class:

bicycle	tire pump
wheelbarrow	hose
rake	beach ball

  Describe how you felt. Would children's dramatizations of these be similar? Different? Explain.

- Tape 10 to 15 minutes of classroom interactions in which you play an instructional role. Analyze your interaction in terms of the kinds of questions you used, the amount of time you waited for children to respond after asking a question, and the way you responded to children's talk.

- Observe a classroom and note the creative experiences available to children. To what extent do the experiences offered seem to contribute to the development of creativity? Describe your impressions and suggestions for improvement for the curriculum in creative expression.

- Observe a teacher and describe the kinds of questions used, the amount of time allowed for children to answer, and the kinds of responses made to children. Do you think the communication you observed is effective in encouraging divergent thinking? Why or why not?

- Practice your own divergent thinking by playing the activity, "In how many different ways?" described in this chapter. Use a variety of objects: a key, a Lego® block, a paper clip, a spatula, a paper cup. Compare your responses to those of several children.

- Also play the "Making things better" game described in this chapter, comparing your responses to those of several children. Whose responses—yours or theirs—best meet the criteria for being creative?

- Observe a preschool child and a fifth-grade student in drawing activities. Do their approaches to art indicate any differences in their apparent levels of creativity? Is one age more creative than the other?

- Observe in several upper-level elementary non-art classes. Notice differences in the ways teachers reward creative behavior, such as when a student asks probing questions, comes up with different ways of doing things, enjoys experimenting, isn't satisfied with easy answers, and questions the teacher. Which teacher responses are most in keeping with the guidelines presented in this chapter?

- With a classmate, examine the same set of student papers or products. Do you agree on which are the most creative or original? Why or why not?

- Compile a creativity portfolio for at least one student. Include evidence of creative activities in at least three areas of the curriculum. You may want to share the information with the student's parents.

- How are creativity killers such as evaluation, reward, competition, and lack of choice operating in your classroom? Investigate whether students are evaluated for creativity in your school district. If they are, examine the assessment procedure. Based on what you learned in this chapter, would you make any recommendations that might improve it?

- From your own peer group of students, select the most creative individuals. Is there general agreement on the selection of these creative persons? What were the criteria on which selections were made? How do these criteria align with those presented in this book?

- **Idea Stimulation.** Choose a specific item for this exercise. It may be something as simple as a shoe or as complicated as a computer. With your fellow classmates, answer as many of the following questions about this item as possible.

  - What would happen if you made it larger? Smaller?
  - What would happen if you took something away and put something else in its place?
  - What could you add to make it better?
  - What would happen if you multiplied it?
  - How could you rearrange it?
  - What would happen if you changed its position?
  - What would happen if you made it stronger?
  - What would happen if you gave it motion? Odor? Light? Sound?
  - What would happen if you put it to other uses?
  - What would happen if you changed the color? Shape? Texture?
  - What would happen if you made it out of a different material?

- **Looking for Shadows.** People usually don't pay much attention to things they see every day. A key to being creative, however, is noticing things that other people often miss. Take shadows. Most people don't bother to look at shadows. But, once you start looking for shadows, you'll discover them everywhere. Looking at shadows is a good way to focus your vision and reacquaint yourself with the world around you.

For this exercise you'll need a flashlight, and a camera.

1. Begin by studying the shadows of things in your room. Shine a strong flashlight on an object. Notice how the position of the light determines the size and shapes of the shadow.

2. Go outside on a sunny day and concentrate on shadows. Watch the shadows of things moving around you. Notice how much detail you can see in shadows. If it's late afternoon, note how the shadows stretch out on the ground. For fun, play with your own shadow for a while.

3. Take a camera and shoot pictures of the shadows you see in your surroundings. Look for both familiar and unfamiliar shadows to record. Select your "best" shadow picture to hang on the class bulletin board.

Activities for Children

Creative Thinking Exercises

- Hand a child a piece of modeling clay, and ask the child to imagine that he or she is the modeling clay.
- Place a child in a different time and place. For example, ask a child to describe how he or she would cook a meal without electricity, silverware, dishes, and so on.
- Ask a child to describe a problem or an event using pictures instead of words.
- Ask a child to solve a problem using the most unusual solutions he or she can come up with.

Water Play Activities for Divergent and Creative Thinking

Water play lends itself to the development of creative thinking in young children. A creative teacher can extend the play of young children by asking thought-provoking, divergent-thinking questions, posing simple problems to solve with water and play objects. Some of these divergent-thinking questions follow.

- Can you make the water in your squeeze bottle shoot out like water from a hose?
- Can you make a water shower for the plants?
- Can you catch one drop of water on something? How many drops of water can you put on a jar lid?
- Can we think of some words to talk about what we do with water or that tell what water can do? (*sprinkle, pour, drip, trickle, drizzle, shower, splash, stir, ripple,* and so on)
- Could we collect some rainwater? How?
- How far can you make the water spray?
- Can you make something look different by putting it in water?
- Can you find some things that float (or sink) in the water?
- Can you make a noise in the water?

Ask children some of the following questions to encourage their creative thinking.

- What are some uses of water?
- What floats in water?
- How does water help us?
- What always stays underwater?
- What are the different colors that water can be?

Follow up children's responses by encouraging them to draw, paint, or model in clay or play dough the ideas about water they experienced during this activity. Generate divergent questions about other topics such as fire, sand, smoke, and ice.

Space Explorers

When children need a "stretch," try one of these for fun.

- Have children pretend they are on a planet in space where they are much heavier than they are on earth. Have them lift their arms as though they weighed twice as much as they do.
- Have children pretend they are on the moon. Have them lift their arms as though they were very light—almost weightless. Also have children "float" across the floor.
- Have children select a familiar activity such as dancing or moving to rhythms and carry out that activity on a strange planet, using slow motion because of increased weight.

Falling Leaves

In this activity, children explore nature's cycles as they recreate the path of a leaf. Use music with a slow, floating quality. ("The Autumn" from *The Four Seasons* by Antonio Vivaldi or "Canon in D" by Pachelbel are two good choices.) You will also need real or construction paper autumn leaves and a photograph or picture of an autumn tree.

- Talk with children about how autumn affects leaves—how they change colors and then fall. Encourage children to move like a leaf as it twists and floats to the ground. Invite a few children to demonstrate some of these motions with their hands—for instance, reaching up high and slowly swaying down using both hands as if they were floating to the floor.
- Create a "woods in fall" atmosphere by bringing in colorful leaves (or cutting them out of paper). Hold each one up, and then let it drop while children brainstorm words to describe its path. Write their words on a large piece of a chart paper.
- Ask children to lift up their hands and copy the path of a floating, tumbling, twirling leaf. You may want to use some of their words from the previously mentioned chart.

Then choose a space for them to recreate the path of a leaf with their bodies. Indicate the path by posting or drawing a picture of a tree at one end of the room and placing a leaf (for the leaf pile) at the other end.

- Group children at the "tree" end of the room. Tell them that in their playing falling leaves they should start with their hands reaching up high into the tree branches to show they are still attached to the tree, and then spin, sway, and float all the way to the designated leaf pile. Suggest that they start on tiptoe and gradually get lower and lower, crouching as they drift and twirl, until they are gently rolling along the floor toward the leaf pile.
- Put on the music and send the leaves on their way, one by one, with a tap for each. When all children have reached the leaf pile, ask them to relax and listen to the music. Repeat the activity, tapping each resting leaf when it's time to walk slowly back to the tree area and attach to the branches to begin again.
- Children also learn by watching each other. Have half the group watch the other half travel the leaf pathway. Add interest by asking the leaves to freeze their positions. Then ask the audience to notice and comment on the leaf shapes and places in their fall. Switch groups and repeat. Encourage children to try out any new movements they observed.

Creative Dramatic Play

One of the best ways children have to express themselves is through creative dramatic play. Here they feel free to express their inner feelings in a creative way. Stimulate this spontaneous kind of drama by providing simple props and encouragement.

- Play the Animal Cracker Game. The child chooses one cracker, looks at it, and then eats it. The child "becomes" that animal for 1 – 2 minutes.
- Read a story, and then let the children act it out.

Circle Creations

- Have children find circle shapes in the room. Then have them draw circles of different sizes on their paper, doing at least five variations.
- Next, have the children find five different ways to make circular shapes with their bodies. Tell them to hold each shape still as if they were having a photo taken. Ask them to try to repeat their five ideas.
- Then, have the children discover with a partner five different ways to make circle shapes together. They might change the level from high to low, face different directions, or use different parts of their bodies.
- Then, have the children do the same thing in a small group.
- When finished, ask the children to describe the ways they formed circles. How did they create circular shapes with a partner or a group? How was making circles with a partner or group different from making circles alone?

Creative Construction

- Gather a collection of recycled materials such as soup cans, oatmeal containers, cereal boxes, scraps of fabric

and paper, glue, and scissors. Challenge the children to create buildings, creatures, designs, and so on from these recycled materials. For children in kindergarten and up, let them choose a theme, such as favorite animals or famous buildings and then use the materials to make creations along this theme.

Creative Games

Have children create with their bodies a "machine" piece by piece. Some players become parts that move and make noise while others operate the machine. Others can guess what it is. Try making a lawnmower with people as wheels, body, and handle and have another player push it. Everyone can join in the sound effects as it cuts the lawn. More good objects to play include: CD or MP3 player, garbage disposal, toaster, pencil sharpener, and water fountain.

Imagination Game

Divide the children into pairs. Have partners stretch out on their stomachs. One child in each pair holds the ankles of the other to form a snake. Then partners slither around the room and connect to each other to make a bigger and bigger snake. If snakes aren't your thing, then children could be caterpillars or earthworms.

Guess What I Am!

Without saying a word, a child acts out the movement of some object. Suggestions for the game include an airplane making a landing, a cement truck dumping its load, or a clock telling the time of day. The child may think up things to do, or the teacher may whisper suggestions.

Scarves

Give each child in the group a colorful lightweight scarf. Encourage the children to dance with their scarf in response to music. Use a recording on an MP3 player, phone, or other device of instrumental music, or turn the radio to a station that plays music. Encourage children to express their thoughts aloud as they dance.

Drawing for Creative Expression

Encourage children to use imagination in expressing their observations, ideas, and feelings through drawing. Have them try some of the following:

- Draw a picture showing how you would improve human beings.
- Design a special machine or device to help the President of the United States.
- Draw a picture that shows how you would weigh an elephant.
- Design a machine that makes peanut butter.
- Draw a picture of a jelly bean factory.
- Design an underground city.
- Design a dog-exercising machine.
- Draw a picture that shows how you would make your school a better place.
- Draw as many animals as you can on one page—some real, some imaginary.

- Draw a map for a brain surgeon. Do the same for a heart surgeon.
- Draw a picture of something that can't be seen.
- Draw a picture of an angry sea or a noisy city. The lines you make should help to express the mood of your picture.
- Complete and then illustrate one of the following statements:
  - "If only I could . . . "
  - "Wouldn't it be strange if . . . "
  - "Can you believe I saw . . . "

Becoming an Object

The teacher names inanimate objects. Children show with their bodies the shapes of the various objects. If the object is moved by an external force, they show with their bodies how the object would move. For instance, they may move like the following:

- An orange being peeled
- A standing lamp being carried across the room
- A wall with a vine growing over it
- A paper clip being inserted onto paper
- An ice cube melting
- A balloon losing its air
- A cloud drifting through the sky, slowly changing shapes
- Smoke coming out of a chimney
- A twisted pin being thrust into paper
- A rubber ball bouncing along the ground
- A boat being tossed by the waves
- An arrow being shot through the air
- A steel bar being hammered into different shapes

Activities for Older Children (Grades 4–5)

Brainstorming Activities

What if?

Divide the class into brainstorming groups of about 8–10 students each. Ask them to come up with the most unique "what if" question and answer they can think of. They are to start with "what if?" and finish with some unusual situation. For example: What if people didn't need to sleep? What if we elected presidents by lottery? After the groups have settled on their particular questions and answers, have the groups share their questions and answers.

Creative Problem Solving

Break the students into groups of three. Name a problem with which everyone is familiar, for example, how to reduce the number of homeless people on the streets. Then assign each group a familiar figure from history, fiction, or current events, and have the group determine how that person would solve the problem. For example, what if Martin Luther King, Jr., were to tackle the homeless problem? What if Spiderman were to try it? The pope? As a starting point, suggest that the students consider what particular expertise the person would bring to the problem and what his or her objectives would be.

Telling Tableaus

Tableaus are "frozen pictures" in which groups of students freeze or pose to act out a scene, a saying, a book title, and so on. Before starting tableaus, discuss the skills necessary to be a good "freezer" (that is, eyes staring blankly, no movement, frozen expression). Have students work in groups, and give each group a caption (or better yet, have the students choose their own). Give students 5–10 minutes (more, if needed) to develop their scene and practice their frozen poses. Don't allow any props.

To begin the performances, have the first group come to the front of the room. Turn off the lights, and have the other students close their eyes as the first group sets up their scene. When the scene is set, turn on the lights, and have the students open their eyes. Then read the caption or have the class guess the title, whichever you feel is appropriate. Continue through the tableau scenes until all groups have had a chance to perform.

Television Drama

Record a part of a television show that will interest your students. Students will be able to tell you which are their favorite shows if you aren't sure. Show students a couple of minutes of the recording, and then turn it off. Discuss the creativity the characters are using. Show more of the program, and stop it at a critical point in the story. Have students work in pairs to brainstorm decisions the characters could make. Then turn the show back on to see what decision the character actually made and what happened as a result of that decision. Have students determine whether the characters came up with creative decisions and then defend their position.

Fairy Tales—Not Just Fancy

Fairy tales are naturally creative and full of fantasy. Use fairy tales for these activities for older children's creative exercises.

Creative fairy tale puppet show. Create a puppet show to retell your favorite fairy tale to the class. Change one thing about the story and see if the class can guess the change.

Fairy tale rating. Read four fairy tales of your choice. Rate them in order of your most to least favorite, and explain why you rated them as you did. Write a short review of your favorite fairy tale explaining why everyone should read it.

Fairy tale journal. Pretend you have been put into a fairy tale, and in journal form, discuss the events and characters you meet. Discuss what you like and dislike about the characters. Include at least eight entries.

Fairy tale logic. Choose a song that you think tells a story similar to one of the fairy tales you've read, and then write a short essay explaining why you chose this song and why it relates to your fairy tale.

Fairy tale music. Compose a song that tells the story of one of the fairy tales. Perform it for a group of students, and have them guess which fairy tale your song represents.

Fairy tale picture book. Create a picture book for your favorite fairy tale. Read it to another class.

Fairy tale day. Plan a fairy tale day for the class, including activities for the entire day. This may include dressing up as your favorite character, eating fairy tale foods, playing games, and reading fairy tales.

Fairy tale rewrite. Rewrite a fairy tale from the perspective of one of the minor characters in the story. Read your story to the class.

Fairy tale game. Create a board game with a fairy tale theme. Include all of the main parts of the story in the game. Let students play the game and give you feedback. Make any changes that would make it more fun to play.

Five Whole Minutes—A Brainstorming Idea

Brainstorm with children a list of different things they think they can do in 5 minutes. Put the list aside. Have children do various things in 5-minute intervals (e.g., read, exercise, color, do math, walk, sit perfectly still, and so on). Discuss their reactions. Talk about time management and how 5 minutes can be used most effectively.

Looking at Things in New Ways

Artists develop their visual abilities by continuous practice and use. They practice by looking at things closely, drawing them, and recording them in their mind's eye. Have your students (and you, too!) try some of these visual exercises to develop visual abilities.

- Draw a picture of something (such as a bicycle or a shoe) showing it from different views on the same page.
- Fill a page full of drawings of bugs, seashells, or something you collect.
- Examine an object for 1 minute. Put the object away. Then draw a picture of what you remember about it. When you've finished, look at the object again and see how much you remembered about it.
- Use a magnifying glass to draw enlarged views of water drops, hair, plant leaves, and other small items.
- Go through a magazine and cut out a picture of something you like or find interesting to look at. Draw a picture of this image—only turn it upside down. This will make you look closely at what you're drawing.
- Draw a family member or friend from memory.
- Sit under a tree and draw the tree from your point of view. Draw other things around your backyard (or school yard) from unusual points of view. Or take pictures instead of drawing in this exercise.

- Take off your shoe and examine it closely. Feel its contours, look inside, and turn it upside down. After you've done this, draw a picture of it. Try this with other common objects around you.

Take a Drawing Break

When you find you have 5–10 minutes to fill, have your students take a "drawing break" by drawing some of the following:

- Your lunch
- The teacher
- A friend
- Your hand holding something
- A small object big
- A car
- A dream or a nightmare
- A leaf
- Yourself

Creative Problem Solving—No Hands Allowed!

The objective of this activity is for students to use creative thinking and problem-solving skills to figure out ways to carry a variety of items without using their hands. In advance, gather together an assortment of large and small objects, such as cardboard boxes and stuffed animals. Set out the items for children to choose for the game.

- Meet as a group and invite children to talk about different ways people carry large and small objects. Ask children to demonstrate how they would hold and carry a box. Then, challenge them to think of other ways they might hold and carry the same box.
- Help children pair off and explain that each pair will work together to carry a cardboard box across the room. The only rule: No hands allowed!
- Give a box to each set of partners and invite them to figure out different ways to lift and hold the box without using their hands.
- After partners have had time to experiment, gather everyone together, along with the boxes, in an area with a lot of floor space. Ask partners to take turns carrying their boxes all the way across the room and back.
- Invite partners to choose an object of a different size from among the assorted items you had set out earlier. Encourage children to work together to find an original way to transport the new item across the room and back. Encourage children to experiment with a variety of objects.
- Now combine sets of partners so that children are working in groups of four. Challenge them to move an object or two, making sure that everyone touches the object without, of course, using their hands.

Experience Journal

Have children explore their environment. Pick a nearby location—a mall, a park, any area—they enjoy exploring. Ask children to visit that location as an artist, writer, scientist, historian, or mathematician. They should observe their surroundings carefully and record their observations. Have children reflect on how their point of view affected their experience.

Historical Research

Have children go to the library and locate a newspaper from the day they were born. Have them examine the headlines, the advertisements, the sports pages, and the classified ads. Encourage children to ask relatives what they remember about that day. Arrange for children to listen to music or watch a movie that was popular during that time. Try to be aware of what children are learning and how they feel as the project progresses. Did history come alive? Have children record their feelings and think about what their experiences were like as an authentic historian.

Animal Artwork

The "scratch art" of a Jack Russell terrier named Tillamook Cheddar was featured on CNN. His owner gave him pieces of carbon paper wrapped around cardboard, which the little dog loved to dig at and scratch designs on. Go to his website, www.tillamookcheddar.com, and decide if you think that his work is art or not. Should a dog have an exhibit in art galleries?

References

Amabile, T. M. (1996). *Creativity in context.* Boulder, CO: Westview Press.

Bredekamp, S. (Ed.). (2009). *Developmentally appropriate practice in early childhood programs serving birth through age 8* (3rd ed.). Washington, DC: National Association for the Education of Young Children.

Catania, A. C. (2008). Brain and behavior: Which way does the shaping go? *Behavioral and Brain Sciences, 31*(5), 516–517.

Fischer, K. W., Immordino-Yang, M. H., & Weber, D. (2007). Toward a grounded synthesis of mind, brain, and education for reading disorders: An introduction to the field and this book. In K. W. Fischer, J. H. Bernstein, & M. H. Immordino-Yang (Eds.), *Mind, brain and education in learning disorders* (pp. 1–20). Cambridge, NY: Cambridge University Press.

Hetland, L., Winner, E., Veenema, S., & Sheridan, K. (2007). *Studio thinking: The real benefits of visual arts education.* New York, NY: Teacher's College Press.

Hinton, C., Miyamoto, K., & Della-Chiesa, B. (2008). Brain research, learning and emotions: Implications for education research, policy and practice. *European Journal of Education, 43*(1), 87–103.

Hoffmann, J., & Russ, S. (2012, May). Pretend play, creativity, and emotion regulation in children. *Psychology of Aesthetics, Creativity and the Arts. 6*(2), 60–68.

Moran, J. D., III, Milgram, R., Sawyers, J. K., & Fu, V. R. (1985). Original thinking in preschool children. *Child Development, 54,* 921–26.

Perry, B. D. (2009). Emotional development: Curiosity—the fuel of development. *Scholastic Early Childhood Today.* Retrieved from http:www2.scholastic.com/browse/article.jsp?id=4043

Runco, M. (2008). Creativity and education. *New Horizons in Education, 56*(1), 18–23.

Rushton, S., & Larkin, E. (2007). Shaping the learning environment: Connecting developmentally appropriate practices to brain research. *Early Childhood Education Journal, 29*(1), 25–33.

Tomlinson, C. A. (2000). Reconcilable differences: Standards-based teaching and differentiation. *Educational Leadership, 57*(8), 7–11.

Torrance, E. P. (1962). *Guiding creative talent.* Englewood Cliffs, NJ: Prentice Hall.

Torrance, E. P. (1995). *Why fly? A philosophy of creativity.* Westport, CT: Ablex Publishing.

Wallach, M., & Kogan, N. (1965). *Modes of thinking in young children: A study of creativity-intelligence distinction.* New York, NY: Holt, Rinehart, & Winston.

Winner, E., & Hetland, L. (2007, Sept. 2). Art for our sake: School art for our sake: School art classes matter more than ever—but not for the reasons you think. *Boston Globe,* http://Boston.com/news/globe/ideas/articles/2007/09/02/art_for_our_sake/

Winner, E., & Goldstein, T. R. (2011). *The impact of arts education: What do we know?* Paris, France: Organization for Economic Cooperation and Development.

 Visit CourseMate for this textbook to access the eBook, Did You Get It? quizzes, Digital Downloads, TeachSource Videos, flashcards, and more. Go to CengageBrain.com to log in, register, or purchase access.

Casper Holroyd

The Concept of Aesthetics

Just as creativity is nurtured in the early childhood classroom, a child's aesthetic sensitivity—the sense of and appreciation for beauty in the world—is cultivated in much the same way. In this chapter, we explore the concept of aesthetics and the ways in which early childhood teachers can create an environment in which the young child's aesthetic sensitivity can blossom and grow.

Learning Objectives

After studying this chapter, you should be able to:

3-1 Define aesthetics.

3-2 List three things a teacher can do to help children develop their aesthetic sensitivity.

3-3 List five benefits of aesthetic sensitivity in children.

3-4 List at least three art elements to discuss with children.

naeyc

NAEYC Program Standards

2a Involving families and communities in their children's development and learning.

4c Teachers use a broad repertoire of developmentally appropriate teaching/learning approaches.

5c Using their own knowledge, appropriate early learning standards, and other resources to design, implement, and evaluate meaningful, challenging curricula for each child.

DAP Criteria

3D2 Teachers plan curriculum experiences to draw on children's own interest and introduce children to things likely to interest them.

1E2 Teachers foster in children an enjoyment of and engagement in learning.

3-1 Aesthetics

The term **aesthetics** refers to an appreciation for beauty and a feeling of wonder. Aesthetic experience begins with and depends on the senses. It is seeing beauty in a sunset, hearing rhythm in a rainfall, and loving the expression on a person's face. Each person has an individual, personal sense of what is or is not pleasing.

The **Aesthetics Movement** in the art world began in early 1800 and lasted the decade. In the art world, the term *aesthetics* was invented or adapted from Greek by the German philosopher Alexander Baumgarten, whose work *Aesthetica* was published in 1750. In this particular work, the word was defined to mean the "science of the beautiful" or the "philosophy of taste." The word was used with its opposite, "Philistine," which in this context meant "one lacking culture" whose interests were bound by material and commonplace things as opposed to the high-minded spiritual and artistic values of the aesthetes. By 1880, the Aesthetic Movement in the arts was a well-established fact and the name itself became a part of everyday speech.

In the center of the movement was a close-knit group of self-appointed "experts" who passed on to their followers standards of color, ornament, and form for all aspects of art. These standards were in direct opposition to the ornate Victorian style. The Aesthetic Movement preferred the simple and sensible over the ornate. One of the most influential figures of the whole movement was Oscar Wilde, who lectured and spread the word of the Aesthetic Movement. The famous painter, Whistler, was another supporter of the Aesthetic Movement.

Aesthetic experiences emphasize doing things for the pure joy of it. Although there can be, there does not have to be any practical purpose or reason for doing something. The goal of aesthetic experiences is a full, rich life for the child. You may take a ride in a car to feel its power and enjoy the scenery rather than to visit someone or run an errand. In the same way, a child plays with blocks to feel their shapes and see them tumble rather than to build something.

Young children benefit from aesthetic experiences. Children are fascinated by beauty. They love nature and enjoy creating, looking at, and talking about art. They express their feelings and ideas through language, song, expressive movement, music, and dance

Casper Holroyd

PHOTO 3-1 Opportunities for aesthetic experiences abound in the early childhood program.

far more openly than adults (see Photo 3-1). They are not yet hampered by the conventional labels used by adults to separate each art expression into pigeonholes. Young children experience the arts as a whole. They are creative, inquisitive, and delighted by art.

On the contemporary arts scene, **multimedia artwork**, such as walk-in sculpture environments; mixes of live dance and films; and art exhibitions with drama, where actors move into the audience to engage it in the drama, are all ways adults are integrating the arts. Like young children, they are learning to experience the arts as a whole.

This exciting art form may be novel for sophisticated adult artists, but it is a familiar approach for young children. For instance, in early childhood programs, it is a common occurrence to find young children singing original songs while they paint or moving their bodies rhythmically while playing with clay. Young children naturally and unself-consciously integrate the arts—weaving together graphic arts, movement, dance, drama, music, and poetry in their expressive activities (see Photo 3-2).

Casper Holroyd

PHOTO 3-2 Children grow in their aesthetic appreciation as they are actively involved in creative learning experiences.

Children sometimes see and say things to please adults; teachers must realize this and the power it implies (Auzmendi et al., 1966). Teachers who prefer that children see beauty as they themselves do are not encouraging a sense of aesthetics in children. They are fostering uniformity and obedience. Only children who choose and evaluate for themselves can truly develop their own aesthetic taste. Just as becoming literate is a basic goal of education, one of the key goals of all creative early childhood programs is to help young children develop the ability to speak freely about their own attitudes, feelings, and ideas about art. Each child has a right to a personal choice of beauty, joy, and wonder.

Children gain an aesthetic sense by doing, that is, sensing, feeling, and responding to things. It can be rolling a ball, smelling a flower, petting an animal, or hearing a story. Aesthetic development takes place in secure settings free of competition and adult judgment.

The capacity for aesthetics is a fundamental human characteristic. Infants sense with their whole bodies. They are open to all feelings; experience is not separated from thinking. A child's aesthetic sense comes long before the ability to create. All of an infant's experiences have an aesthetic component—preferring a soft satin-edged blanket, studying a bright mobile, or choosing a colorful toy. These choices are all statements of personal taste. As infants grow into toddlers, the desire to learn through taste, touch, and smell as well as through sight and sound grows, too. The ability to make aesthetic choices continues to grow through preschool (see Photo 3-3). Preschoolers' ability to perceive, respond, and be sensitive becomes more obvious and more refined. This is obvious in their spontaneous creations using a wide variety of materials.

To develop an aesthetic sense in children, one must help them continuously find beauty and wonder in their world. This is any child's potential. In fact, it is the potential of every human being. To create, invent, be joyful, sing, dance, love, and be amazed are possible for everyone.

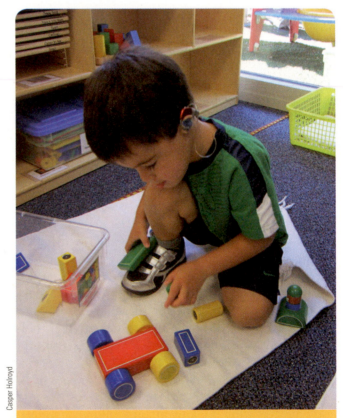

Casper Holroyd

PHOTO 3-3 The capacity to make aesthetic choices continues to grow through preschool.

TeachSource Video

Infants and Toddlers: Cognitive Development and Imaginative Play

1. Using the material from your text, explain how the teacher in this video could expand the children's aesthetic experiences in her questioning about animals.

2. Discuss how this teacher could involve more of the children's senses in this activity.

Watch on CourseMate.

Did You Get It?

A kindergarten teacher discourages her young student from coloring with black crayons, and encourages her to use "pretty" colors such as pink and purple. From a creativity perspective, what is the main flaw in the teacher's approach?

a. She is not helping her student fulfill her potential to find beauty in the world.

b. She is expressing ethnic stereotypes.

c. She is placing gender expectations on her student.

d. She is directing her student instead of allowing her to make choices on her own.

Take the full quiz on CourseMate.

3-2 DAP Developing Children's Aesthetic Sensitivity

Aesthetic learning means joining what one thinks with what one feels. Through art, ideas and feelings are expressed. People draw and sculpt to show their feelings about life. Art is important because it can deepen and enlarge understanding. All children cannot be great artists, but children can develop an aesthetic sense—an appreciation for art.

Teachers can encourage the aesthetic sense in children in a variety of ways. For example, science activities lend themselves very well to beauty and artistic expression. Because children use their senses in learning, science exhibits with things such as rocks, wood, and leaves can be placed in attractive displays for children to touch, smell, and explore with all of their senses. With their senses, they can experience artistic elements such as line, shape, pattern, color, and texture in these natural objects.

Sensory awareness is nourished by teachers who help young children focus on the variations and contrasts in the environment: the feel and look of smooth bark and rippling rough bark, the heaviness of rock and the lightness of pumice stone, the feathery leaf and the leathery leaf, the slippery marble and the sticky tar. Aesthetic appreciation of nature is not confined to the sense of sight. Appreciation of the outdoors may include listening to the song of birds, the smell of newly cut grass, or the soft feeling of moss on a rock. All these are opportunities for expression in the arts, poetry, sound, movement, and many other art forms.

The arts are developed best as a whole. After hearing a story, some children may want to act it out. Some may prefer to paint a picture about it. Others may wish to create a dance about it, and some may want to make the music for the dance. These activities can lead to others. There should be a constant exchange, not only among all the art activities but also among all subject areas. This prevents children from creating a false separation between work and play, art and learning, and thought and feeling.

A teacher can invite, encourage, or stimulate children's aesthetic experiences by:

● Offering possibilities for firsthand, vivid personal perceptions with trips, resources brought into the classroom, and new materials and equipment

● Asking questions to encourage personal, felt responses

Having one's interest and energy *invited* is not the same as being persuaded to move toward a goal predetermined by someone else. For example, holding

Casper Holroyd

PHOTO 3-4 Provide children with many opportunities to look at and talk about art.

- Display fine-art prints on bulletin boards and walls so that children can easily see them. Be sure to change them regularly. If they are up too long, they will quickly fade into the background.
- Include art objects on the science table, where appropriate. Geodes, shards of pottery, and crystals are all good starting points.
- Invite guest art educators into the classroom to show children art objects to look at, touch, and talk about.
- Give children an opportunity to choose their favorites from a selection of fine-art prints.
- Display fine-art prints near the writing and art centers.

3-2a DAP naeyc Suggestions for Aesthetic Experiences with Older Children

Children experience a developmental shift around ages 7 to 8 that allows them to deal with more abstract ideas (more information about this shift is in Chapter 10). At this point, older children not only are able to experience the arts aesthetically but also begin discussing their own opinions, aesthetic tastes, and experiences. Thus, the teacher can engage children in grades 4 to 5 in discussions about what is art and why they consider something to be art or not. The following is an example of a combination 4th- to 5th-grade class involved in this type of aesthetics discussion.

This example demonstrates the type of environment for older children in which questioning is valued. In such an environment, students will feel comfortable raising questions about art and expressing their reactions to it. Teachers of older children need to encourage rather than suppress discussion of aesthetic questions as they emerge. This is done by providing students the time and environment for art-related experiences and inquiry.

In their unit on art and history, prints of the work of Civil War photographer Matthew Brady were displayed and discussed. The fact was brought up by the teacher that Brady frequently repositioned and rearranged bodies of dead soldiers and other objects in composing war scenes to be photographed. The teacher used this fact to encourage the students' responses to her initial question: "Is there anything about Brady's practice that should disturb us?"

up a model of a finished product may stimulate the child's desire to make one like it, or demonstrating how it is produced may invite the child's interest in seeing if she can do it, too (see Photo 3-4). Although these approaches are direct and fast ways to get a group of children to work, by themselves they *do not invite* the individual child to raise his own questions or to draw upon his own experiences and interests.

In the classroom, most invitations to art work are offered in the whole group situation. Yet, the teacher knows that effective aesthetic response is individual and freely given, and not always in line with the group project.

The early childhood environment can be set up in such a way as to encourage this type of aesthetic discussion by implementing the following suggestions.

- In addition to the typical art center, include books about artists in the reading area.
- Include "real" art books in the reading and quiet areas of the room. These do not necessarily have to be children's books; young children will enjoy looking at artwork in any book.

Art, Aesthetics, and Nature in the Life of the Child

The outdoors has something more to offer than just physical benefits. Because the natural world is filled with beautiful sights, sounds, and textures, it is the perfect place for aesthetic experiences for young children.

Preschoolers learn much through their senses. Outside there are many different and wonderful things for them to see (animals, birds, and green plants), to hear (the wind rustling through the leaves, a bird's song), to smell (fragrant flowers and the rain-soaked ground), to touch (a fuzzy caterpillar or the bark of a tree), and even to taste (newly fallen snow or a raindrop on the tongue). Children who spend a lot of time experiencing things through television and computers are using only two senses (hearing and sight), which can seriously affect their perceptual abilities as well as their aesthetic development.

In this overly electronic and technical world, it seems old-fashioned to include nature study in the early childhood curriculum. Yet, sometimes looking back is necessary to move forward for the sake of the child. Looking back to the teachings of Friedrich Froebel, the founder of the kindergarten, can help us see the value of nature study in the early childhood curriculum.

Froebel was a passionate advocate for art and nature studies as well as for their integration. He spent most of his life (1782–1852) in or very near the Thuringian Forest of central Germany, a breathtakingly beautiful area of wooded old mountains, rolling hills, and green valleys. As a young man, he worked as a forester, studied mineralogy, and collected and classified plants—anything that would keep him outdoors.

Nature study was the foundation of Froebel's pedagogy. He saw it as an essential pathway to understanding the interconnectedness of all things. Froebel believed children's intellectual, moral, and spiritual development were all dependent upon their relationships with nature. When referring to nature in his autobiography, he wrote, "Every contact with her elevates, strengthens, and purifies (Froebel, 1889, p. 82).

Froebel preferred to engage children in self-directed dialogue with nature, each other, and supportive adult guides. He believed that through nature, children would not only learn the secrets of the world around them but also learn about themselves and their unity with the world.

Today, our students may be quite familiar with how to search for stream beds on the Internet to write a report for their science class, but they might have never seen the phenomenon firsthand in a way that enables them to describe it using their own words or drawings.

When we look back, we find that even this divide between childhood and nature is not a new concern. In 1883, G. Stanley Hall published results of a study focused on what children did and did not know in a variety of areas, including nature studies. He found, among other things, that 77% of 4- to 8-year-old children in Boston had never seen a crow, 56% had never seen a sparrow, and 63% had never planted a seed (Hall, 1883).

More recently, Louv holds that children need to interact with nature for the sake of their abilities to learn and create. Nature deficit, as explained by Louv (2008), has highlighted the need to reconnect childhood with nature. Art, as a natural language of childhood, is uniquely equipped to make the connection participatory and expressive, permeated with imaginative problem identification and solving.

So, we have a 150-year history full of rich rationale and examples to encourage early childhood teachers to return nature to the curriculum. As we have seen in this chapter, aesthetic development is easily encouraged in a natural setting. Many activities can be taken outdoors for the children's aesthetic benefit. How much more exciting it is to hear a story sitting on the grass on a sunny day! How much more alive science activities can be when they are taking place in a natural setting!

Now when asked why your children are so often outside instead of in the classroom, you can say Froebel made you do it!

The discussion led the students in many directions involving such issues as differences between "real" photographic art and "staged" art and which was art in the truest sense. They also questioned the worth of Brady's work in general, with students evaluating each in their own way. Some saw the work as "political" and of little artistic worth. Others saw it as an artist using his "props" just like any other artist does. One student compared it to a still-life painting the class had seen earlier.

Needless to say, this discussion led to a lot of research into Matthew Brady's life and work. But more importantly, the discussion helped students learn how to reflect upon and present their own opinions of art and to consider the views of others.

THIS ONE'S FOR YOU!

The Real Christina's World

Andrew Wyeth's famous painting, *Christina's World*, shows a crippled woman dragging herself across a field toward a farmhouse. A tour of the house, which was declared a National Historic Landmark, offers a fascinating, in-depth look at the real world of Christina Olson and her family. It also reveals Wyeth's relationship with them.

Wyeth spent 30 years producing about 300 works of art depicting the Olsons and their home. Wyeth met the Olsons in 1939 through his wife, Betsy. Wyeth's father had a summer home nearby. Betsy, whose family also spent summers in the area, was 10 when she met Christina, who was beloved by local children for her cookies and storytelling. After the Olsons died, the house was briefly used as an art gallery.

Wyeth got the inspiration for *Christina's World* after seeing Christina crawling across the field in May when it was lush and green. But when he painted the picture, he used fall colors, adding to the painting's stark and lonely mood.

And though he observed Christina from an upstairs window, heading away from the house as she pulled herself to a garden where she grew flowers, he chose to depict her heading toward the house, up a hill.

Christina was 55 when Wyeth finished the painting, but the figure in the painting is of a young, shapely woman in a pretty dress. Wyeth used his wife and an aunt as models for this painting.

When the work was finished in 1948, the Wyeths hung it in their home and invited the Olsons over for dinner. Not a word about the painting was said during the meal, but afterward, Christina kissed Wyeth's hand in a sign of approval. The painting was then shown at a Manhattan gallery and was purchased by the Museum of Modern Art for $1,800. Wyeth received $1400; the gallery got $400.

Christina's World remains an immensely popular and well-known painting, but experts also consider it a masterpiece of twentieth-century realism in the American Gothic tradition (Harpaz, 2011).

If we could see the miracle of a single flower clearly, our whole life would change.

—Buddha

Did You Get It?

A fourth grade teacher demonstrates how to make a model of the constellations. The teacher's approach might fail to ignite a sense of aesthetics because it

  a. asks them to view the world around them as something that can be copied.
  b. science-based and art-based.
  c. shows them something that naturally occurs instead of something that they create.
  d. does not invite the children.

Take the full quiz on CourseMate.

3-3 DAP naeyc Benefits of Aesthetic Sensitivity

An **aesthetic sense** does not mean, "I see," or "I hear." It means, "I enjoy what I see," or "I like what I hear." It means that the child is using taste or preference. Aesthetic sensitivity is important for children because it improves the quality of learning and encourages the creative process. Aesthetic sensibility in children has many other benefits, too.

- Children are more sensitive to problems because they have more insight into their world. This means they can be more helpful to other children and to adults.
- Children are more likely to be self-learners because they are more sensitive to gaps in their knowledge.
- Life is more exciting for children because they have the capacity to be curious and to be surprised.
- Children are more tolerant because they learn that there are many possible ways of doing things.
- Children are more independent because they are more open to their own thoughts. They are good questioners for the same reason.
- Children can deal better with complexity because they do not expect to find one best answer.

3-3a Aesthetic Experiences

DAP naeyc Aesthetic experiences for young children can take many forms. They can involve an appreciation of the beauty of nature, the rhythm and

THIS ONE'S FOR YOU!

Van Gogh's Yellows

It's hard to imagine some of Vincent van Gogh's signature works without the vibrant strokes of yellow that brightened the sky in *Starry Night* and drenched his sunflowers in color. But the yellow hues in some of his paintings have mysteriously turned to brown, and a team of European scientists has figured out why.

Using X-rays, they found the chemical reaction to blame—one never before seen in paint. Van Gogh's decision to use a lighter shade of yellow paint mixed with white is responsible for the unintended darkening, according to a study published in *Analytical Chemistry*.

In some of Van Gogh's paintings, the yellow has dulled to coffee-brown. The discoloration is serious in about 10 of them, said Koen Janssens, an analytical chemist at Antwerp University in Belgium who co-authored the study.

The problem is the lead-chromate paint he used. It was called chrome yellow, part of a generation of paints that were far brighter than previous yellow ochre shades. Soon after their introduction in the nineteenth century, it became apparent that chrome yellow would degrade under sunlight.

Although conservators took pains to protect Van Gogh's paintings from the sun's ultraviolet rays, the gradual darkening continued. The effect was unpredictable, afflicting the yellow in some works, while sparing others.

What was causing Van Gogh's sunflowers to wither and the golden tone in his daylight scenes to dim? And why did the victims appear to be picked at random?

After trying other tests without success, the researchers hit the paint with a high-intensity X-ray. They found that the colorfast samples were made of chromium in its pure, crystalline form.

The darkened sample contained sulfates, which are associated with white pigment. Those sulfates, Janssens said, probably helped reduce the chromium's oxidation state from chromium-6 to chromium-3, taking on an increasing greenish hue that contributed to the overall darkening (Van der Snickt et al., 2009)

---

imagery of music or poetry, or the qualities of works of art. Far from being a specialized talent, the recognition of aesthetic qualities comes quite naturally to children.

For instance, let us consider **art appreciation**. What adults have come to regard as strictly a "museum-type" experience—seeing and appreciating good artwork— is an enjoyable experience for young children whose fear of the "intellectual" is not yet developed. Art appreciation can occur in the early childhood program through the combined experiences of learning to look at and learning to create visual arts. Introducing young children to art appreciation should be a series of pleasurable experiences with time to look, enjoy, comment, and raise questions. It is a time when children learn to "see" with their minds, as well as their eyes. They begin to feel with the painter, the sculptor, or the architect and to explore their ideas and techniques.

As early childhood teachers, we don't ask ourselves whether language appreciation should be emphasized in our programs. We automatically encourage children to express themselves verbally and reflect on the words used by others. We want children to have fun with language, to appreciate its variety and its shades of meaning. Why should we not do the same for visual imagery—that is, encourage children to go beyond art's functional aspects and find satisfaction in its aesthetic possibilities (Epstein, 2001)?

Early childhood teachers have a responsibility to provide the very best our culture has to offer by introducing young children to a range of fine art by recognized artists, not merely what is easiest or most familiar.

Most children have plenty of exposure to cartoon characters, advertising art, and stereotyped, simplistic posters. These do not foster aesthetic development and are sometimes demeaning to children. Teachers often say, "Children like them," but the fact that children like something—for example, candy and staying up late at night—does not necessarily mean it is good for them. Children might never have seen a Van Gogh sunflower, a mother and child by Mary Cassatt, or a sculpture by Henry Moore. Yet, young children can learn to appreciate such fine art as these, as well as arts and crafts from many cultures, if introduced to them in the early years. From such experiences, children also gradually learn the concepts of design.

Colors speak all languages.

—Joseph Addison

3-3b Multicultural Aesthetic Experiences

naeyc Aesthetic experiences can also be **multicultural aesthetic** experiences. Multiculturalism is so much more than curriculum—it is a worldview. Art is an ideal means of conveying multiculturalism. Multiculturalism honors heritage, community, and tradition. Art objects from different cultures expand beyond their mere physical experience. A Pueblo pot, a Peruvian textile, and a Celtic illumination each represent centuries of culture and civilization. Works of art are valued for their artistic contribution, originality, purpose, collective identity, and universal appeal. In using art reproductions and actual art objects such as pottery in the early childhood program, you are not only providing amazing aesthetic experiences, but you are also bringing the cultures of the world into children's daily lives.

In the past, roll sheets that once listed Billy, Betty, Jack, and Sue are now joined by Jamar, Okezie, Shanta, Esperanza, and Thuy. Every one of the names on the roll sheet brings tradition along with hopes, fears, and dreams. Each student brings the gift of self and of culture. What a thrill to see a big smile grow on the face of a shy student who is new to the United States when the art activity or object is a familiar reminder of family and home! We all want to feel valued and recognized. Pride in cultural heritage helps students learn. Art is a reaffirmation of who we are. Thus, multicultural art objects provide more than aesthetic experiences to young children.

> The work can wait while you show the child the rainbow, but the rainbow won't wait while you do the work.
>
> —Patricia Clifford

Did You Get It?

Thomas, age 5, is concerned when his friend Luke starts to cry. He approaches Luke and tries to comfort him. Which benefit of having developed an aesthetic sense is Thomas demonstrating?

a. independent thinking
b. more sensitivity to problems
c. an appreciation of complexity
d. a willingness to question

Take the full quiz on CourseMate.

3-4 Language for Talking about Art: Art Elements

DAP **naeyc** During group discussions, children should be encouraged to talk about the design qualities of a specific color, the movement of lines, the contrast of sizes and shapes, and the variety of textures. They should be helped to think and feel, as individuals, about a certain art object or piece of music. Their understanding of aesthetics, and their willingness and ability to discuss its concepts, will increase with experience.

As you talk about art with young children, start to introduce the language of art. For example, the teacher may say, "You made a secondary color here," or in another instance, "I see you drew straight lines, zigzag lines, and diagonal lines in your drawing of our school." Talking about art in this way strengthens language development at an age when children are quickly developing a language system and vocabulary (Althouse, Johnson, & Mitchell, 2003).

The **language of art** is an expansion of the language of the early childhood classroom. Each language has its own system of words and rules of grammar. The language of visual art has its own system. The words of the language are the *elements* of art. They are the basic visual symbols in the language of art. Just as there are basic kinds of words in a spoken language such as nouns, verbs, adjectives, and adverbs, there are basic kinds of **art elements**: *line, shape/form, color, space, pattern,* and *texture*. These six elements are the visual building blocks that the artist puts together to create a work of art. No matter what materials are used, the artwork will contain one or more of these visual elements. Sometimes one element will be more important than the others. The following are definitions for each of these elements with examples of using them in discussing art with young children.

- **Line** is a continuous mark on a surface. Lines have a direction: horizontal, vertical, and diagonal. Lines may be straight or curved, fat or thin, or long or short.

  Example: "I notice you made your house with vertical and horizontal lines."

- **Shape and form** are two terms to describe the contours of enclosed spaces in art. *Shape* is used to refer to two-dimensional works such as drawings and paintings that can be measured by height and width. *Form* is used for

1. *Hue* is the color name, such as blue-green. There are primary, secondary, and tertiary colors. The **primary colors** are red, blue, and yellow. The **secondary colors** are orange, violet (purple), and green. The **tertiary colors** are red-violet, red-orange, blue-violet, blue-green, yellow-orange, and yellow-green.

   Example: "You used so many nice primary colors in your collage—red and blue especially."

2. *Value* refers to the relative lightness or darkness of a hue. Tints and shades are made when white (tint) or black (shade) is added to a hue.

   Example: "I see you have made a lovely green tint for the leaves on your tree."

3. *Intensity* is varied by adding a hue's complementary color, the color opposite it on the color wheel, to the hue. For example, red becomes duller, less intense, when its opposite color, green, is added to it.

   Example: "The intensity of your red flowers is great!"

● **Space** refers to the areas above, below, between, within, and around an object. Space is created as an illusion in two-dimensional artwork (see Photo 3-6). A three-dimensional art form—a sculpture, for example—has actual space such as width, height, and depth. Young children learn to create space by several means: overlapping, scale (size), and placement of shapes.

Example: "Scott, I can see in your picture how big your house is in your neighborhood."

PHOTO 3-5 This artwork reflects the art elements of shape/form, color, and balance.

Casper Holroyd

three-dimensional pieces such as sculpture and architecture that can be measured by height, width, and depth (see Photo 3-5). Shapes and forms may be described as *geometric*, *organic*, or *free-form*.

Geometric forms are mathematically precise forms based on the following geometric shapes: square, rectangle, triangle, circle, oval, and diamond. Organic forms are those that are natural. Free-form shapes are images made of straight or curved lines or a combination of both.

Examples:

"Look at that big yellow circle in the center of your drawing!" (geometric)

"Did you see how Mark made an organic-shaped design with his printing tool?" (organic)

"Watch how Eric uses his crayons to make a free-form design for a border." (free-form)

● There are three characteristics of color: **hue**, **value**, and **intensity**.

Casper Holroyd

PHOTO 3-6 Space is created as an illusion in two-dimensional artwork.

- **Texture** refers to the way something feels or looks like it would feel. It can be rough (such as a sandpaper alphabet letter) or soft (such as a chalk drawing); it can be furry (as in a piece of fabric) or slick (as in manipulating finger paint). It can be real, such as a piece of tree bark glued in a collage, or it can be visual, such as the implied bark of a tree trunk drawn with crayons.

Example: "I see you used that piece of velvet to give the puppet's face a soft, smooth texture."

3-4a Some Other Art Terms

The following list includes more art terms to use in the classroom:

- **Foreground, middle, and background.** The areas in a piece of art that appear closer to the viewer, next closest, and farthest away.
- **Contrast.** This is created by putting lighter colors next to darker ones.
- **Light.** The illusion created with lighter colors such as white.
- **Design concepts.** Three design concepts in art are **pattern** (repetition and rhythm), **balance**, and **unity**.

  1. **Pattern** (repetition and rhythm) is created when a particular shape, color, or motif (design) is repeated in a rhythmic way. Patterns provide harmonious or decorative effects in works of art.

     Example: "Tell me how you made that pattern around the edge of your picture."

  2. **Balance** is the principle of design that deals with visual weight in a work of art (see Photo 3-7). Balance may be *symmetrical*, *radial*, or *overall*.

     Example: "Adding flowers on both sides of your house gives your picture balance, Sally."

  3. **Unity** is the feeling of wholeness or oneness in an artwork that is accomplished by using the elements and principles of art (see Photo 3-8). A unified artwork seems harmonious; nothing should be added or removed.

     Example: "Rose, that round grouping of flowers gives your painting a sense of unity, bringing it all together."

Teachers can make children's art experiences meaningful through thoughtful dialogue. For example:

Casper Holroyd

PHOTO 3-7 When a child adds trees to each side of her drawing, she is creating balance.

- Use descriptive rather than judgmental terms when talking about art. Say "I see . . ." or "It makes me think of . . ." rather than "I like it" or "It's pretty." Praise such as "Good work!" sets the teacher above the child artist in a superior judgmental position. It may leave the child artist anxious about whether you will at some later time announce that you do not like the child's efforts. And if you inadvertently pass over one child, does this overlooked child then worry that he or she is not "a good artist"? Respond to the child's efforts not from your head, but from your heart. Rather than pronounce a judgment, try describing your heartfelt response to the art. Use, "In your art, I feel (an emotion)" statements. For example, "I feel happiness, sadness, fear, love, power." You will create a better

Casper Holroyd

PHOTO 3-8 A unified artwork seems harmonious. Nothing needs to be added or removed.

PHOTO 3-9 Children develop their aesthetic senses by doing, sensing, and responding.

connection with the child by saying "I feel an emotion" rather than "I feel THAT YOU are showing (an emotion)." The "that you" makes an assumption. Thus, avoid phrases such as "I feel . . . that, like, as if . . . you are showing . . . ." Using your *own* emotions, no one can argue about what you feel (see Photo 3-9).

- After a small-group art activity, encourage children to look at one another's work and ask them, "Why do you think they look so different from one another even though you all made them out of the same paper and markers?"
- Introduce language to talk about the affect and aesthetics of the artwork. For example, "These colors look sad" or "All these little dots look busy on the page" or "This big, bright circle makes my eye keep coming back to it."
- Ask children to reflect on artistic intentions and feelings. "Why do you think this artist makes little pictures but that artist makes big pictures?" is a question that young children can ponder.

Aesthetic experiences for young children should be chosen according to their interests and level of understanding. For young children ages 2 to 4, use artwork that is colorful and reflects a subject matter familiar to them, such as children, families, and animals. Older children can explore more abstract imagery, although research suggests that young children, while preferring both abstract and realistic art, tend to gravitate more toward abstract art (Danko-McGhee, 2006). Such details as dates and the social–political implications of a piece of art or music have no relevance for young children. Instead,

a painting may appeal to them because of its bold colors as well as familiar subject.

Art appreciation also includes the development of an awareness of the aesthetic qualities of everyday man-made objects (see Photo 3-10). Children are surrounded daily by an endless number of objects such as furniture, clothing, toys, buildings, and machines, along with countless images in films, television, newspapers, books, magazines, advertisements, and exhibits. Examples of good and bad design can be found in all areas of the environment. With guidance and experience, children will become more sensitive to their environment and eventually will develop more selective, even discriminating, taste.

3-4b The Aesthetic Environment: Art Elements in Action

DAP **naeyc** The classroom environment can help young children develop their aesthetic sense. The elements in the early childhood classroom, just like

PHOTO 3-10 Children gain an aesthetic sense by using many kinds of art materials.

those in a painting, all work together to produce a unified, aesthetically pleasing environment for young children. Simply visualize the early childhood room as a canvas, and each part of this canvas (room) is important to the entire composition (program). Next, consider the basic art elements listed below and how they are applicable to an aesthetically appealing early childhood environment.

Color/Hue. Just like in a piece of artwork, the use of color can create very different effects. Lots of blue in a painting gives the viewer a calm, quiet feeling. Bright reds and oranges create the opposite effect. Just as bright colors can dominate a painting, the same applies to color in the classroom. Too many bright colors may detract from art and natural beauty. If you have a choice, it is best to choose soft, light, neutral colors for walls and ceilings. This neural background allows children's artwork to stand out.

Just as color can be used to create unity and balance in a painting, it can also be used to create an aesthetically balanced early childhood classroom. For example, you can use color to coordinate learning centers so that children begin to see them as wholes rather than as parts. For the same reason, avoid having many different kinds of patterns in one place, as they disturb the balance in the room and can be distracting and overstimulating for young children.

Space. The way the artist creates space in a painting either gives the viewer a definite sense of "openness" or "closeness" or maybe a feeling in between the two. In the classroom, the sense of space is created by placement of the furniture and equipment.

Group similar furniture together to enhance the spacious feel of the room. Keep colors of furniture, such as shelving, as natural and neutral as possible. This helps focus children's attention on learning materials on the shelves. When choosing furnishings, select natural wood, which is more aesthetically appealing than metal or plastic. If furniture must be repainted, use one neutral color for everything so that there is greater flexibility in moving it from space to space. Instead of a mismatched collection that breaks up the space in the room, one color of furniture creates a sense of spaciousness because all things "fit together."

Balance. When a child adds flowers to both sides of her house, she is creating balance in her art. In the same way, a teacher can create balance in the early childhood classroom by arranging materials in an orderly, aesthetically pleasing manner. For example,

rotate materials on shelves rather than crowding them together. Crowded shelves are unbalanced as well as unattractive. They are also hard for children to use and maintain. Aesthetically pleasing containers for holding materials are natural wicker baskets and storage tubs. If storage tubs are used, put all of the same kind together on one shelf to maintain a sense of balance. For the same reason, if cardboard boxes are used for storage, cover them with a neutral color paper or paint them.

Composition. Just as this art element refers to the arrangement of the objects and spaces in a piece of art, it can also apply to the various arrangements in the classroom. To create an aesthetically pleasing environment, be conscious of the fact that everything in the room has an aesthetic effect. For this reason, decorate your classroom with care. Mount and display children's artwork rather than simply taping it to the wall. Provide artwork by fine artists from many cultures and avoid garish, stereotyped posters. Make sure that most artwork is displayed at the children's eye level. Be careful to avoid too many visual stimuli when displaying materials in the classroom. Consistently use one pattern or color combination on all display areas throughout the room. Display work by every child, but not every child's work in every display. Allow children to choose what they want displayed. Encourage children to help you create and change displays. They will take pride in seeing their work go on display.

Use shelf tops to display sculpture, plants, and items of natural beauty such as shells, stones, and fish tanks. Avoid storing teachers' materials on the tops of shelves. If there is no other choice, create a teacher "cubby" using a covered box or storage tub.

The information in this section can help you create a "masterpiece" environment for the young children in your care.

Did You Get It?

When setting up her preschool classroom, a teacher chooses to group all the tables together. Which element of an aesthetic environment is she introducing?

a. hue
b. space
c. balance
d. composition

Take the full quiz on CourseMate.

Aesthetic Awareness in Young Children—Theorists' Views

Many theorists study and write about young children and aesthetics. As teachers of young children, it is important to be aware of this area of early childhood education and how it relates to classroom practice. The following summary of some of their ideas provides more ideas about young children's **aesthetic development** and how to enhance it.

Teaching young children ways to appreciate art is not the daunting task that it appears to be. At a very young age, children are quite capable of having an aesthetic experience on their own, whether it is the delight of mixing different-textured foods on the high chair tray or becoming visually engaged with a mobile suspended over the crib (Danko-McGhee, 2006).

When children express preferences for colors, shapes, sounds, tastes, and textures, they are actually making aesthetic choices. Long before young children can speak, their responses to shapes, colors, and other stimuli around them help to form their own special style of interacting with the world (Schirrmacher, 2005).

As young children grow, they continue to exercise their aesthetic senses while observing lines, textures, shapes, colors, and designs found in their environment. This includes images in picture books and artwork found in museums and in the popular media. These aesthetic experiences provide a starting point for understanding that there is a "language of art" (Anderson & Milbrandt, 2005, p. 4). Knowledgeable teachers can facilitate this learning process by pointing out to the child what is to be found in the beauty of an object or work of art.

Developmentally appropriate ways of engaging young children in appreciating works of art include *play, conversations,* and *authenticating the experience* (Danko-McGhee, 2006). *Play* involves finding connections between an artwork and the child by using tangible objects. *Conversations* engage the child in talking about the artwork with a focus on language details. When viewing art, adults can serve as role models for young children by using rich language to describe aesthetic qualities found in nature and in works of art. And finally, *authenticating the experience* guides children into related art activities. During this "appreciating" process, children develop their perceptual discernment. "Looking at, reflecting upon, creating, and experiencing art teaches, guides, and refines perception. True perception requires thought" (Anderson & Milbrandt, 2005, p. 16).

Having an aesthetic experience is the result of being deeply affected by sensory perception and increases our cognitive (mental) abilities. Through sensory perception, we are prompted to reflect and think (Csikszentmihalyi, 1996; Eisner, 2002; Goodman, 1984; Parsons & Blocker, 1993; Siegesmund, 2000; Smith, 2002).

Aesthetic education need not be exclusive to art activities. Eisner (2002, p. 43) suggests: "Aesthetic experience is in no way restricted to what we refer to as the fine arts. . . . Aesthetic experience, therefore, is potentially in any encounter an individual has with the world."

Maxine Greene (2001) suggests that teachers follow the thoughts of Herbert Read and instruct students to experience what it "feels like to live in music, move over and about a painting, travel round and in between the masses of sculpture, dwell in a poem (p. 302)." We should teach our students to pay heed to and use their senses and feelings to understand the qualities of what is perceived in everything. In so doing, we should create more chances for students to find those "a-ha" moments by simply asking questions or calling attention to the elegance of uncomplicated tasks and everyday situations (Flannery, 1977).

Teachers can help their students to slow down, to smell the bread baking in the school kitchen, to listen to morning sounds, to catch and taste a raindrop, and to feel the stippling on the cinder block hall walls. Teachers can extend these lessons by allowing time for students to talk to their peers and write about their feelings and responses to their aesthetic experiences. Students begin to embrace authentic and meaningful learning as they come to realize that they are the agents that create these experiences, and they do not need to have something that an artist delivers to the classroom for passive appreciation (Heid, 2005).

Summary

3-1 Define aesthetics.

The term *aesthetics* refers to an appreciation for beauty and a feeling of wonder. Aesthetic experience begins with and depends on the senses. Each person has an individual, personal sense of what is or is not pleasing. Aesthetic experiences emphasize doing things for the pure joy of it. The goal of aesthetic experiences is a full, rich life for the child.

3-2 List three things a teacher can do to help children develop their aesthetic sensitivity.

- Provide many opportunities to create art.
- Provide many opportunities to look at and talk about art.
- Help children become aware of art in their everyday lives.

3-3 List five benefits of aesthetic sensitivity in children.

Aesthetic sensitivity in children provides the following benefits:

- It improves the quality of learning and encourages the creative process.

- Children are more sensitive to problems because they have more insight into their world.
- Children are more independent because they are more open to their own thoughts.
- Children are better questioners for the same reason.
- Children can deal better with complexity because they do not expect to find one best answer

3-4 List at least three art elements to discuss with children.

Basic art elements to discuss with children are line, shape/form, color, space, pattern, and texture. Some other art terms to discuss are foreground, middle and background, contrast, light, balance, and unity.

Key Terms

aesthetic development 51
aesthetic experience 39
aesthetic learning 41
Aesthetic Movement 39
aesthetics 39
aesthetic sense 44
art appreciation 45
art elements 46

balance 48
color 47
hue 47
pattern 48
intensity 47
language of art 46
line 46
multicultural aesthetics 46

multimedia artwork 39
primary colors 47
secondary colors 47
sensory awareness 41
shape/form 46
tertiary colors 47
unity 48
value 47

Learning Activities

Being Aware

To use your aesthetic sense, you must pay close attention to that which is personally interesting. This means being aware of yourself and your surroundings.

A. Try to think a new thought or make a discovery by paying closer attention to yourself.

B. Begin by going to a place that is quiet and relaxing. Sit down and take a minute to rest. Then say, "Now I am aware of . . ." and finish this statement with what you are in touch with at the moment. Notice whether this is something inside or outside of yourself.

C. Make the statement again and see what happens.
   1. Has your awareness changed?
   2. Are fantasies, thoughts, or images part of your awareness?

D. Make the statement again, but this time think of a person.
   1. Who comes to mind?
   2. What does it mean?

E. Try the same sentence, but change your awareness by thinking of different things such as a flower, a picture, someone from the past, a child, your favorite place, and so on.

F. Notice that when thinking of something outside, you cannot think of something inside at the same time.

G. What does this mean for working with children? Compare your answers with classmates, and find out how they feel about this activity.

Moody Colors

1. For this activity, you will need a 9 × 13-inch piece of drawing paper and colored markers or colored pencils.

Think about how artists such as Vincent van Gogh used color to express moods and emotions. Think about how color can affect your emotions.

2. Fold the paper into eight sections.

3. Think of eight different moods or emotions, and write them lightly on the back of each section of the paper.

4. Then draw each mood on the other side. What colors, shapes, and lines best show your mood? The drawings may be realistic, abstract, or somewhere in between.

5. Now you have eight mini drawings or "thumbnail sketches."

6. Show the drawings to a fellow student or friend without telling them what you wrote on the back. See if your friend can guess what mood or emotion you drew. If you like one a lot, you can make it into a full-size drawing.

Fruit

This is an activity to make new discoveries by paying closer attention to everyday things.

A. Take three different types of fruit. Close your eyes and pick each one up. Feel them with your fingers from top to bottom.
  1. How are they different?
  2. How are they the same?

B. Place the fruits against your face.
  1. Do they feel different?
  2. What about the temperature of the fruit?

C. Smell the fruits, being sure to keep your eyes closed.
  1. How different are the aromas?
  2. Which is your favorite?

D. Open your eyes and look at the fruits.
  1. Hold them up to the light.
  2. See if you can see anything new about each fruit.

E. What have you discovered from this activity? (Notice you did not taste or eat the fruit.)
  1. Could you still receive pleasure from the fruit without eating it?
  2. What does this mean for working with children?

F. Compare your answers with those of classmates, and find out their reactions to this activity.

Museum Explorations

Plan a trip to a local museum for a group of young children. Help the children to focus in the gallery with activities such as the following.

- Search for a particularly interesting picture. For example, in a room filled with paintings, ask children, "Can you find the painting where there is a bear, a house, a mother, and a baby?"
- Ask, "What would it feel like to be in the painting? Where would you like to go? What would you like to do if you were there?"
- Ask children to find two pictures that are the same in some way—the same colors, the same subject, the same feeling.
- Explore your own environment. Pick a nearby location—a mall, a park, or any area you enjoy exploring. Visit that location as an artist, writer, scientist, historian, or mathematician. Look carefully and jot down as many interesting ideas, problems, and questions as you can. Reflect on how your point of view affected your experience.

Activities for Children

Art Talk

Display a print of Van Gogh's famous painting *Starry Night*. Ask young children the following questions about the painting.

- What do you see in the painting?
- What do you notice about the colors and lines?
- Show me the most important thing in the painting. Why do you think it is the most important thing?
- How does this picture make you feel?
- What do you think the artist was feeling when he was painting this picture?
- Another kind of questioning about *Starry Night* might be related to having children imagine they are in the scene.
- If you were in the painting, where would you want to be?
- How would that feel?
- What kind of things do you think you would smell?
- What kind of animals might live there?

These questions could be used for any other painting of your choice.

Art in Nature

The beauty of nature is a continuing source of inspiration for young children. Through nature, many children acquire some of their earliest ideas and concepts of design. A variety of experiences can be planned to help children observe and discover color, line, form, pattern, and texture in natural objects.

- Make a bulletin board arrangement of natural objects and materials.
- Begin a collection of natural objects such as flowers, weeds, twigs, stones, shells, seed pods, moss, and feathers for a touch-and-see display.
- Take a walking trip to observe color, shape, and texture in the immediate environment. Share individual discoveries with others during class discussion.
- A nature walk is a great way to enhance children's appreciation of the natural environment as well as encourage aesthetic awareness. On the walk, ask the children to tell you what they're seeing, hearing, and smelling. Encourage them to touch—to discover the

smoothness of a rock, the roughness of bark, and the fragility of a dried leaf. For young children, these are also basic science experiences.

- A listening walk makes for a wonderful aesthetic experience for young children. As you walk with the children, point out the sounds of birds, passing cars, whistling wind, even your footsteps on the sidewalk. What sounds can the children identify on their own? Which are loud and which are soft? Which are high and which are low? What are their favorite sounds? Bring along a tape recorder so the children can try to identify the sounds at a later time.
- Bring a portable boom box outdoors and let the children experience the joy of dancing in a natural environment.
- Show films, conduct dramatizations, or read stories and poems to develop these concepts.
- Arrange a shelf or corner table for things of beauty that children can admire. Contributions can be made by parents, some of whom may have objects that represent art of their own heritage. Keep changing the collection to create variety and contrast that will encourage young children's interest.
- Give children an opportunity to arrange objects in an aesthetically pleasing manner: flower bouquets; fruit and vegetable centerpieces; and collections of dried plants, leaves, and seed pods placed in a ball of clay or block of Styrofoam.
- Offer equipment such as magnifying glasses, kaleidoscopes, prisms, and safety mirrors to help sharpen children's visual sensitivity.
- In describing the children's artwork to them, use terms that relate to the color, form, texture, patterns, and arrangement of space.
- Be enthusiastic about your own sensory awareness, and share your perceptions with children.

What ideas can you add to this list?

Magical Mixing Colors on Ice

Preschoolers are fascinated by how colors can be mixed together to form new ones. This activity combines color mixing with the concept of melting. The children will enjoy making colorful designs on the magic ice, but because food coloring may stain, be sure to wear old clothes and protect your table with newspaper.

For this activity you will need:

- Eyedropper
- Several cubes of ice
- Shallow dish or pan
- 3 plastic bowls
- Yellow, red, and blue food coloring

1. Pour ½ cup of water in each of the bowls.
2. Put a few drops of each color of food coloring into each bowl until the coloring is the desired intensity.
3. Place the ice cubes in the shallow dish or pan.
4. Discuss primary colors and how these three colors can be used to make all of the other colors.
5. Show the children how to use the eyedropper to pick up some of the red color water and dribble it on the ice cube. Watch how the water reacts to the ice cube.
6. Have the children dribble blue water on the same ice cube. Talk about how the blue water combined with the red water to make purple, and discuss the designs the colored water makes on the ice.
7. When the children are done experimenting with red and blue, give them another ice cube, and let them use yellow and blue to make green. Be sure to also experiment with the red and yellow color to make orange, too.
8. After the children have experimented with all of the color combinations, let them mix all of the different colors on the ice to see what happens. You can also show them how to pick up some of the new colors that they made with the dropper and put them on another piece of ice.
9. As they play with the ice, the ice will begin to melt. Ask them why they think the ice is melting, and explain that ice melts when the air temperature goes below 32 degrees because that is the temperature at which freezing occurs.
10. When you are finished with the activity, have the children help you clean up. Although the children may have very colorful hands, they will be sure to remember the lessons learned about making new colors and the cool effect of colored water on ice.

Primary and Secondary Colors Pantomime

Elementary-age children can work on color recognition and affective response to color through pantomime sentences. Have children perform the following actions and then tell how each of the colors made them feel.

- You are the bright yellow sun shining in the summer sky.
- You are a blue bird flying across the blue sky.
- You are a violet opening your petals.
- You are an orange flame flickering atop a candle.
- You are a green leaf floating gently to the ground.
- You are a yellow jacket buzzing around a flower.
- You are a green bug crawling along the ground.
- You are a red fire engine speeding to the scene of a fire.
- You are an African violet growing in a pot.

Children will enjoy creating and playing their own pantomime sentences that incorporate primary and secondary colors. At the close of the activity, invite the children to tell how the colors in these new sentences made them feel.

Lucy's Science Project—Body Sculptures

Science projects and school science fairs give children hands-on opportunities to examine, test, and operate technical devices. These experiences can be applied to the more fanciful invention in the following activity.

Children working in small groups create Lucy's new invention using their bodies and machine-like sounds after hearing the following scenario. They may adapt a device currently in use, such as a computer, or create a futuristic contraption with a real or fantastic purpose.

Lucy is a second grader in the year 2009. She has been assigned the creation of a new technologic device as her science project. As a group, you are to become Lucy's invention. Your task is to create the device, name it, show how it works, and tell the rest of the class what it does.

Aesthetic Experiences in Autumn

The fall is a great time for children to explore the outdoors, learn about seasonal transitions, and develop their aesthetic skills. Nature-related experiences can foster a child's emerging sense of wonder, and the early years of life are the best time to begin providing direct, ongoing interactions with the natural world. Young children learn best when they are in an environment that is familiar and comfortable. Focus on the foliage, animals, and insects in your own backyard, the playground, or a local park before venturing into heavily wooded areas. Keeping safety concerns in mind, adults should allow children to touch, feel, and smell while they explore the environment.

The young child is naturally sensitive to the wonders and beauty of nature: the colors and rhythm of leaves whirled by autumn winds, the texture of dried seeds and weeds, the form and color in the harvest. A teacher can do a number of things to enlarge children's understanding of their world and to encourage them to learn to look, feel, and think.

- Begin a collection of objects from nature for classroom use. Encourage closer observation of design in nature.
- Take children on walking trips to discover and observe the colors, shapes, and textures in trees, plants, clouds, buildings, and vehicles. Individual observation can be shared with others at group time.
- Have children draw and paint the beauty of nature as they see it, using their own feelings and ideas. Their growing visual awareness is gradually reflected in picture making as they mature in the ability to interpret their environment.
- Children can be encouraged to be more aware of their environment in only a few minutes. Discuss the fact that leaves will change color and then watch together to see when this change happens. Make a game of finding the largest, smallest, and most unusually colored leaf. Focus on an evergreen or pine and talk about the needles and pinecones and the fact that they stay green and don't drop off. Talk about people needing jackets and animals growing winter coats.
- Collect leaves of different sizes and shapes. Show the children that one side is smooth and one side is rough. Have them put a piece of paper over the rough side of a leaf and rub a crayon on its side over the paper. The outline of the leaf will show through. It's fun to change colors. This technique can be used with any object that has texture.
- Fall is the time when apples are harvested. Tell children that there are almost 10,000 varieties of apples grown in the world! Buy one each of several kinds in the grocery store. Have children point out the many ways these apples are alike and different. Have children say each apple's name and taste a piece of each. If you cut two pieces from each one, can the children find the ones that taste the same or different?

Activities for Older Children (Grades 4–5)

Seeing Like an Artist

Have the students discuss the objects in the neighborhood around the school and describe the types of lines they are made of. Have students identify lines similar to those found in paintings by selected artists such as Picasso, Monet, Matisse, and so on.

Birthday Parties for Artists

- Ask the children, "If you were planning a birthday party for a famous artist, what would you want the design, based on the style of that artist, to look like? How would you design a cup, plate, napkin, placemat, treat bag, party hat, and balloon to look as if they belonged together?"
- Divide the class into teams of four. Have each team vote for the artist for whom they would plan a party. Have children review the artists they have learned about. List the names of those artists on the board. Display examples of their work, and provide folders with examples of each artist's work for children's review. Discuss the characteristic styles of these artists and how elements of those styles could be incorporated into the design of the party decorations.
- Have student teams decide what their overall design should look like to reflect the style of their artist. Also have each group decide which art materials would best represent their artist.

- Provide white napkins, balloons, paper plates, cups, treat bags, white paper, colored markers, tempera paint, and watercolors for children to make their party accessories.

Look Closely—Pantomime

Older children can be introduced to art history and gain insight into art criticism through this activity. By studying famous paintings, reproductions, or prints, children sharpen critical observation skills while analyzing artistic process and intent.

As an introduction to critical observation, have children study prints of famous paintings and identify people or objects in each print that can be interpreted through pantomime. Several prints (or similar materials) should be selected for study, and children should be given ample time to view each. Prompt thinking with questions such as, "What was the artist trying to say in this work?" or "What does the artist want you to think or feel when you see this?" or "What do you think is the most important image in this picture?" The class can then generate a list of people or objects in the prints that appear significant to them. After an appropriate list has been developed, call out the subjects, and ask children to pantomime them.

Describing a Work of Art

When looking at artwork with your students, it is important to pay attention to what you see. Artists include certain subject matter and arrange the art elements such as lines and colors to help them convey ideas, feelings, or moods.

You can practice with your students their ability to describe works of art. Practice will help them notice details that may contribute to an artwork's message. Here are some ways to practice describing works of art.

- Pretend you are on the telephone with a good friend. You want your friend to imagine the artwork you have seen. Describe the artwork so that the person you are talking with can create a mental image of it.
- As you plan to tell your friend about the artwork, think about the following questions.
  1. Who made the artwork?
  2. When was the artwork made?
  3. What materials did the artist use?
  4. How did the artist use these materials?
  5. What special techniques did the artist use?

Art Challenges

These art challenges are fun for students to work on at the beginning or end of a class or when students finish an assignment.

- Design a *pattern* for a household item such as curtains, a tablecloth, towels, or wallpaper. Think about household *geometric forms* such as a cylindrical trashcan or an ice cube. How could you change them into *organic* forms?
- Discuss what skills it takes to turn a collection of found objects into artwork.
- Create a three-dimensional scene of a forest. Use natural materials such as grass, leaves, and tree bark to add patterns.
- Gather photos from magazines. Identify the shapes in each one.

Artistic Opinions

Aesthetic experiences for older children involve their opinions of art and their ability to express these opinions and to appreciate those of others. The following "art problems" are designed to capitalize on older children's ability to grasp more complex ideas and should encourage discussion about art and aesthetic appreciation.

A. The Problem of the Pile of Bricks

This problem involves the nature of art and such questions as "What is art?" and "Is it representation?" and "Is it the expression and communication of emotion?" Consider the following possibility, based on an exhibit at the Tate Gallery (London) in 1976. A famous artist, known to be a "minimalist" sculptor, buys 120 bricks and, on the floor of a well-known art museum, arranges them in a rectangular pile, 2 bricks high, 6 across, and 10 lengthwise. He labels it *Pile of Bricks*. Across town, a bricklayer's assistant at a building site takes 120 bricks of the very same kind and arranges them in the very same way, wholly unaware of what has happened in the museum—he is just a tidy bricklayer's assistant. Can the first pile of bricks be a work of art while the second pile is not, even though the two piles

are seemingly identical in all observable respects? Why or why not?

B. The Problem of the Fire in the Louvre

The Louvre is on fire. You can save either the Mona Lisa or the injured guard who had been standing next to it—but not both. What should you do?

C. Is Shakespeare a Real Writer?

Lord Byron criticized Shakespeare as follows: "Shakespeare's name, you may depend on it, stands absurdly too high and will go down . . . He took all his plots from old novels, and threw their stories into dramatic shape, at as little expense of thought, as you or I could do" (Henderson, 1986). Is Shakespeare's use of familiar stories an aesthetic defect? Is Byron a good critic of Shakespeare?

Aesthetic Experiences in Autumn for Older Children

An appreciation of the fall season is probably even more important for middle- and upper-elementary-age students than for younger children because they are further removed from the early years' sense of wonder. In addition to carrying out the activities already covered, you may want to approach this changing season with more complex artistic activities. Here are a few suggestions.

Textures

Provide students with a variety of leaves, long grasses, and other natural objects. You might want them to bring in similar natural objects as well. Have them make rubbings using white crayon or oil pastel and black paper. Suggest that students do a repeated rubbing of the item until the entire paper is covered. Discuss the results as a record of textures that can be viewed as artwork as well as a display for science. Students might want to research the types of grass and leaves they used in this activity.

Fall Textures

Have students make and illustrate vocabulary cards for words that describe fall textures. Have them arrange the items by tactile characteristics (e.g., rough, soft, smooth). Encourage them to use these terms appropriately in storytelling and in other activities.

Mystery Textures

Tell students they will make a mystery texture bag. Provide small paper bags for each student. Have them secretly collect items that have varied textures of fall or any season. These are the mystery items whose identities others will be guessing. Have students work with a partner: Partners exchange bags and try to guess what the mystery objects are by feeling the textures.

Lines, Patterns, Textures

Have students bring in large leaves. Place a magnifying glass over one part of the leaf and observe lines, patterns, and textures. Have students create large drawings of the small section of the leaf seen in the magnifying glass.

Varieties of Colors

Have students look selectively for gradations of the color red in leaves and bring their leaves to class. Have them describe the differences in color using descriptors such as *light, dark, shiny,* or *dull*. Focus on other visual elements in the same way. For example, ask students who are wearing rough textures to stand and point them out. Develop an awareness of terms that describe textures, such as *bumpy, prickly,* and *silky*.

Weather Diaries

Have students keep a weather diary with drawings that portray the weather as it occurs at the same time each day for 5 days. The time might be lunch or recess. At the end of 5 days, have students work in small groups to compare and contrast the different interpretations. The total group can choose drawings that best represent the weather for each day. The drawings might be put into a booklet titled "The Weather Diary of Grade Four." Present the booklet to the school library.

New Colors

Ask students to think about colors they have never seen in fall flowers or leaves. Have them create fall drawings or painting using these colors. Discuss the mood or feeling of these works of art with each student.

Photographers' Vision

Bring in books with fall photographs by Ansel Adams, Paul Weston, Alfred Steiglitz, Margaret Bourke-White, and other well-known photographers. Have students discuss the subject matter portrayed by these photographers. Discuss why each may have chosen his or her subject and how the images were planned. Does it look like the fall where you live? What are the similarities? The differences?

Fall Memory Book

Children in the primary grades can create a "fall memory book" with pressed leaves, pictures, and writings about fall activities and specific events they have enjoyed. Wrap the book in paper and put it away until it's almost spring. When they open it again and look at the leaves and read their writings, they will be able to remember fall and can compare the differences in seasonal colors.

References

Althouse, R., Johnson, M. H., & Mitchell, S. T. (2003). *The colors of learning: Integrating the visual arts into the early childhood curriculum.* New York, NY: Teachers College Press.

Anderson, T., & Milbrandt, M. (2005). *Art for life.* Boston, MA: McGraw-Hill.

Auzmendi, E., Villa, A., & Abedi, J. (1996). Reliability and validity of a newly constructed multiple-choice creativity instrument. *Creativity Research Journal, 9*(1), 89–95.

Baumgarten, A. G. (1750). *Aesthetica.* Frankfurt, Germany: Oder Publishers.

Csikszentmihalyi, M. (1996). *Creativity.* New York, NY: Harper Perennial.

Danko-McGhee, K. (2006). Nurturing aesthetic awareness in young children: Developmentally appropriate art viewing experiences. *Art Education, 12*(9), 21–32.

Eisner, E. W. (2002). *The arts and the creativity of mind.* New Haven, CT: Yale University Press.

Epstein, A. A. (2001). Thinking about art: Encouraging art appreciation in early childhood settings. *Young Children, 56*(3), 38–43.

Flannery, M. (1977). The aesthetic behavior of young children. *Art Education, 30*(1), 18–23.

Froebel, F. (1889). *Autobiography of Friedrich Froebel* (E. Michaelis & H. K. Moore, Trans.). Syracuse, NY: C. W. Bardeen.

Goodman, S. (1984). *Of mind and other matters.* Cambridge, MA: Harvard University Press.

Greene, M. (2001). *Variations on a blue guitar.* New York, NY: Teachers College Press.

Hall, G. S. (1883, Jan. – June). The contents of childen's minds. *The Princeton Review,* 249–273.

Harpaz, B. J. (2011). "In an old Maine farmhouse, the real Christina's world." GO Section, *News & Observer,* p. 11D, August 14, 2011.

Heid, K. (2005). Aesthetic development: A cognitive experience. *Art Education, 58*(5), 48–53.

Henderson, D. E. (1986). *Shakespeare.* New York, NY: Vintage.

Louv, R. (2008). *Last child in the woods.* Chapel, Hill, NC: Algonquin.

Parsons, J. J., & Blocker, H. G. (1993). *Aesthetics and education.* Urbana, IL: University of Illinois Press.

Schirrmacher, R. (2005). *Art and creative development for young children.* Clifton Park, NY: Delmar Cengage Learning.

Siegesmund, J. (2000). *Reasoned perception: Art education at the end of art.* Unpublished dissertation, Stanford University, Palo Alto, CA.

Smith, R. A. (2002). *Aesthetics and criticism in art education: Problems in defining, explaining, and evaluating art.* Chicago, IL: Rand McNally.

Van der Snickt, G., Dik, J., Cotte, M., Janssens, K., Jaroszewicz, J., DeNolf, W., Groenewegen, J., & Van der Loeff, L. Van Gogh's Yellows. (2009). *Analytical Chemistry,* 81(7), p. 2600–2610.

Visit CourseMate for this textbook to access the eBook, Did You Get It? quizzes, Digital Downloads, TeachSource Videos, flashcards, and more. Go to CengageBrain.com to log in, register, or purchase access.

Casper Holroyd

Promoting Aesthetic Experiences

People search their world for what is important to them. They look for what they need. They see what they want. This is as true of preschool children as it is of adults.

Imagine that a group of people is taken into a room and asked to look at a table. Some food, a glass of water, and a small amount of money are on the table. Those who are hungry are most likely to look at the food. Those who are thirsty will probably look at the water. Those who are in debt are apt to look at the money. Those who need furniture will probably take a closer look at the table.

Learning Objectives

After studying this chapter, you should be able to:

4-1 Discuss young children's looking and seeing.

4-2 Describe three types of sensing and feeling.

4-3 Choose materials that have good aesthetic potential.

4-4 List four guidelines to help children work with aesthetic materials.

4-5 List six guidelines to use in talking with children about their artwork.

naeyc

NAEYC Program Standards

1b Knowing and understanding the multiple influences on development and learning.

4b Knowing and understanding effective strategies and tools for early education.

DAP

DAP Criteria

1A Children learn about themselves and their world.

2F3 To extend the range of children's interests and the scope of their thought, teachers present novel experiences and introduce stimulating ideas, problems, experiences, or hypotheses.

2F5 Teachers provide experiences for children to be genuinely successful and to be challenged.

Children also look for things they need and want. A tired child looks for a place to rest. A lonely child looks for a friend. The point here is that only when children are physically well, feel safe, and sense that they belong can they be ready to develop an aesthetic sense.

4-1 Looking and Seeing

Children look in many different ways. Touching, patting, poking, picking, and even tasting are ways of looking for young children. Children look for what they need, but they also see what they find to be stimulating. Something can be stimulating to a child for many different reasons—because it is colorful, exciting, different, interesting, changing, moving, unusual, and so on. The list of stimulating things is seemingly endless. However, there are some basic guidelines for preparing a stimulating activity or object.

- **Can children experience it with more than one sense?** Children enjoy what they can touch, see, and hear more than something they can only see or hear.
- **Can children interact with it?** Children tend to enjoy what they can participate in (see Photo 4-1). For children, the picture of a guinea pig will never

replace a live guinea pig. For the same reason, an interactive computer game can never replace the fun and real-life learning experience of playing a game with friends.

- **Are the children interested in it?** Children relate to what is familiar to them and part of their life. Talking about a food that children have never eaten cannot produce the kind of discussion that comes when they talk about their favorite food.
- **Is the activity well-paced?** Something that moves too quickly or too slowly eventually becomes boring. Watch how many children begin to fidget when the story is too long. Notice how children lose interest in toys that may appeal to adults but are too complex for children to use and enjoy.
- **Does it promise to be rewarding?** Is the activity fun, adventurous, or exciting? Does it have something worthwhile at the end? If not, why should the children stick with it? Searching for a piece of a puzzle or looking for a hidden treasure is only fun if the children believe they can find it.

PHOTO 4-1 Children tend to enjoy what they can actively participate in.

Did You Get It?

According to the basic guidelines for preparing a stimulating activity, why is watching a movie less stimulating than climbing on a climbing frame?

a. The climbing frame can be experienced by more than one or two senses.
b. The climbing frame is outdoors.
c. The movie numbs the child's creativity.
d. The movie stunts the child's brain activity.

Take the full quiz on CourseMate.

4-2 Sensing, Feeling, and Imagining

DAP **naeyc** There are basically three types of sensing and feeling. The first is contact with the world outside of the person—actual sensory contact with things and events. It is seeing, hearing, smelling, tasting, and touching. The second is what people feel within themselves. This includes what they experience under their skin. Itches, tensions, muscular movements, discomfort, and emotions are all a part of this type of sensing. The third type of sensing and feeling goes beyond the present and reality. It is usually called *fantasy* and includes dreams, memories, images, and guesses.

PHOTO 4-2 Sensing and feeling are basic to an aesthetic sense.

4-3 Choosing and Organizing Aesthetic Materials

DAP **naeyc** Every teacher has many ideas about what materials are best for children. Sometimes the desired materials are too expensive or difficult to find. Schools have limited budgets, and even ordinary items can seem impossible to obtain. Three resources with great potential include salvage material, commonly known as "junk"; the hardware store; and things the children bring in.

Before describing the organization of these materials, it is helpful to have some guidelines for choosing materials with good aesthetic potential.

- Choose materials that children can explore with their senses (touch, sight, smell) (see Photo 4-3).
- Choose materials that children can manipulate (twist, bend, cut, color, mark).
- Choose materials that can be used in different ways (thrown, bounced, built with, fastened, shaped).

For a child, each of these types of sensing and feeling is very important (see Photo 4-2). All three can take place during the same activity. Any one type can become more important than the other two, depending on what the child needs or wants at the moment. Most teachers are concerned about the child's sensory contact with the outside world. Children do many things that involve touching, seeing, and hearing; yet, what they feel inside and what they fantasize about are also important. The teacher must give attention to these two processes as well. They are part of **aesthetic sensitivity**. Teachers should ask themselves two questions each day when working with preschool children. Both should be answered "yes," followed by the question, "How?"

The first question has to do with the inside feelings of the children: *Have the children done something today that has helped them feel good about themselves?* The second has to do with the fantasies of the children: *Have the children done something today that has helped them use their imagination either in the past, present, or future?*

Lesson plans, activities, and trips should be planned and evaluated with these two questions in mind. If teachers are sincere about answering yes to the two questions, their teaching will relate to all the ways children sense and feel.

PHOTO 4-3 A child expresses his aesthetic sense with different materials.

THINK ABOUT IT

Youth Art Month (YAM)

Youth Art Month (YAM) is an annual observance each March to emphasize the value of art education for all children and to encourage support for quality school art programs. Established in 1961, YAM provides a forum for acknowledging skills that are not possible in other subjects. Art education develops self-esteem, appreciation of the work of others, self-expression, cooperation with others, and critical thinking skills. All of these skills are vital to the success of our future leaders—our children.

During the month of March, you can hold observances of many kinds, in schools, libraries, stores, and other places. Your celebration can include exhibits of children's artwork, posters, a collection of quotes in support of art and art education from leading citizens and from young students on what art means to them. For more information, go to the National Art Education Association website.

The teacher isn't the only source of aesthetic materials. Children themselves enjoy finding materials because it involves exploration and discovery. Sometimes children's search for materials can be focused on something particular, such as objects for painting or building. The search for aesthetic materials also includes seeking new uses for familiar materials. For example, children might explore ways of modifying paint by mixing sawdust, sand, or confetti with it. A natural follow-up to their experimentation in creating a new substance is to have them brainstorm ways in which the paint can be used. As they find that their discovered materials make their day-to-day work more interesting, they become alert to new possibilities. For both teacher and children, this can mean a constant supply of materials and new aesthetic experiences.

Older children will also enjoy collecting materials, but they can go further into associating materials with the elements of art. For example, the materials can be selected and collected according to their design possibilities. Objects can be classified into art categories, such as those to be used for line, shape, texture, size, and color elements. The number and types of classifications will vary by the age level and interest of the children.

4-3a Aesthetic Use of Materials

DAP **naeyc** The uses of materials collected by the teacher and children are limited only by the collectors' interests and imaginations. Of course, storage space and time to search can sometimes set boundaries on the exploration for aesthetic materials. However, what is most important is that the materials and what is done with them become personal statements of the children and teacher. This is not done by *what* is made but by *how* it is made—whether it is an art project, a building project, or another activity. The process of making and the child's personal involvement in it are the keys here—not the finished product.

Children must have the opportunity not only to find materials but also to try them out (see Photo 4-4). This means much experimenting with the materials to determine what children believe they need. A question such as, "What would you like to say with these things?" might help both children and teacher get started. Assessing children's moods may be helpful, too. Do they seem to feel happy, dreamy, sad, gentle, or aggressive? Such questioning can help children reach their own purpose based on their experience and interests.

Casper Holroyd

PHOTO 4-4 Children enjoy materials that require them to use their imagination.

Another important consideration in the creative process is the number of materials. It is important to remember not to give children too many materials too often. Having too much to choose from can overwhelm a child. The qualities of one material can be lost in the midst of so many others. For example, a teacher might have the children work with a certain color or a single material, such as clay or paper. In this way, the children can learn more about making their own aesthetic choices, as well as mastering specific skills.

Although the process of exploring materials is the primary focus of aesthetic experiences, with older children (grades 4 to 5), the process usually involves the creation of more complex works of art. Children at this level pay greater attention to expressing specific ideas in their work. They are more intentional in their approach to using materials. Because they are not distracted by quantity of materials as younger children are, a variety of interesting materials needs to be available for their aesthetic experiences.

> A man who has no imagination has no wings.
> —Muhammad Ali

© 2015 Cengage Learning

TeachSource Video

Preschool: Appropriate Learning Environment and Room Arrangements

1. What are some additional changes that Miss Sheila can make in her room to increase its aesthetic appeal?

2. After carefully observing Mrs. Sheila's "improved" classroom in the video, what do you consider the most important aesthetic change made in this room and why?

Watch on CourseMate.

4-3b Aesthetics of a Creative Multicultural Classroom

DAP naeyc Classroom environments give children and parents strong messages. The classroom conveys attitudes to the children and parents by what is included in the room and what is left out. Omissions can be just as destructive as stereotypes and inaccurate information. Leaving multicultural education out of the curriculum gives children and families the message that it isn't important. It is our job as early childhood educators to make sure that the classroom includes all kinds of people doing all kinds of things and living out their daily lives in many different ways. This may be through visual images such as pictures or representations in the form of artwork and objects from daily life. Remember that displaying just one or two pictures is tokenism. It gives children the message, "Yes, these people are out there in the world somewhere, but you don't have to take them seriously."

We definitely want children to notice and interact with materials on the shelves and the displays on the tables in the room. What we don't want is children wandering around or flitting from area to area because they can't tell what their options are. The overuse of visual displays creates a form of "visual noise" that distracts children from the materials. Rather than filling every inch of wall space with bulletin boards, pictures, and posters, try using these materials as if you were decorating your own home environment. Use and create visual displays to match, reinforce, and expand the materials and learning that take place in each of the interest centers. For example, display works of art in the art area, posters of buildings and environments in the block area, and pictures of people, families, and family life scenes in the dramatic play area.

4-3c Real-Life Representations

Creating an aesthetically pleasing environment that is also multicultural means avoiding the use of cartoon characters such as dolls in costumes, animal characters dressed in ethnic costumes, and stereotypical pictures of people in their traditional dress. Appropriate display materials include artwork and artifacts from existing cultures such as fabrics, paintings, beadwork, rugs, wall hangings, musical instruments, sculpture, wind chimes, and photos (actual or from magazines). Be sure to include posters with art images from around the world to display in the room. Children become familiar with cultural arts through displayed visual materials. Be sure that your children see images that reflect themselves and their own ethnic identity.

4-3d Finding Multicultural Materials

Acquiring a large selection of multicultural display materials for the classroom can be a time-consuming, difficult, and expensive project. You may find some educational catalogues that carry modern, accurate teaching posters and picture sets. NAEYC is a good source for appropriate posters and other visuals. Nationwide chain stores such as Pier I Imports and World Bazaar are other good sources for inexpensive multicultural materials.

Making your own materials and visual displays is perhaps the most viable way to create a multicultural classroom environment. Photographs from magazines provide pictures of people living out their daily lives in the present. Consider starting a multicultural picture file for your common bonds curriculum units.

When you have gathered enough photographs, you can mount and laminate them. Display the photographs separately or create a collage on poster board. Collages may focus on a specific theme such as boys and girls, babies, grandparents, families, homes, or workers. Create a collage of pictures of people from a specific ethnic group. This type of collage is particularly useful because it shows the diversity and individuality within an ethnic group.

In your search for photos, you will find that not all magazines are useful sources of multicultural pictures. Thumbing through popular women's magazines for appropriate photographs will prove this point, as so many images are far from real life. Be careful, too, of *National Geographic* as it can tend to highlight people in faraway places dressed in traditional costumes at special celebrations, and not in everyday life.

Casper Holroyd

PHOTO 4-5 Children must have the opportunity not only to find new materials but also to try them out.

Did You Get It?

Certain materials have good aesthetic potential. What is the limitation of building blocks in terms of aesthetic potential?

a. Children cannot explore them with more than one sense.

b. They cannot be manipulated.

c. They can be used in only one way.

d. They cannot be used in conjunction with others.

Take the full quiz on CourseMate.

4-4 Guidelines for Using Aesthetic Materials

DAP **naeyc** When children are exploring new materials of any kind, the teacher needs to provide guidance (see Photo 4-5). With aesthetic materials, the guidance needs to be very gentle, supportive, and sensitive. This lets the child know that it is acceptable to take chances and be different. The following are some suggestions on how to give young children guidance when using aesthetic materials.

1. **Ask questions aimed at helping children reach out for and get the "payoff" they are seeking.** A question teachers can ask themselves that will help them ask the right question of children is, "What can I ask the children that would help them better understand what they want?" When the children are working with paints, this question may be something about color. When they are working with paper, it may be something about form, such as "What shape would you like it to be?" Even better, ask how paper feels because just seeing a shape is only one way of sensing paper.

2. **Avoid always doing things the same way.** Teaching children over and over to do something in only one way may dull their aesthetic sense. Repetition tells them to stop thinking. For example, why always start to draw in the middle of a piece of paper? Why not sometimes draw from the edges or bottom? Or why not change the shape of the paper on which children draw, using paper in the shape of a triangle, parallelogram, or circle?

PHOTO 4-6 Be positive when discussing the child's work.

3. **Be positive and creative when using models or examples.** Occasional use of models and examples of other children's work is not uncommon in many classrooms today. Their use need not be a negative experience for children if used positively—as a springboard to unlocking each child's own creative approach to a shared, common theme (or object). Many times, a brief look at one or two other children's examples (which should not then be displayed for "copying" during the activity) can help motivate children to get started on making one of their own. Also, using a model produced by another child of the same age can encourage children to believe they can do it, too. Teacher comments throughout activities and the use of examples can help encourage each child to be creative in his or her approach (see Photo 4-6). Statements like, "Claire, I notice that you are using so many bright primary colors," or "Jawan, you used that paper in a very different way to make your own design," clearly communicate the positive acceptance of different approaches.

4. **Help children select the materials they prefer.** This may mean asking children which materials they plan to use first, which materials they may not use at all, and which materials they may possibly use (see Photo 4-7). Be patient with children and choices. Remember: The simplest choices for teachers become major decision-making opportunities for young children. What color paper, what color crayons or paint, what shape and size of paper, and which way to hold the paper are all options children should have. Children may require more time to work if many decisions must be made, but it's time well spent aesthetically and creatively.

5. **Help children "hunt" for aesthetic qualities.** Help children get in touch with what they feel about differences. For example, ask children to show what they like or think is better. Ask what is brighter, darker, happier, or sadder. Encourage older children to identify and analyze more subtle and complex visual relationships such as how light affects our perception of colors, textures, and forms.

6. **Help children use other senses when only one sense seems necessary.** Children can be asked to hear what they see in a drawing or to draw what they hear in music. Colors can be related to feelings, music, and body movements, as well as to seeing. Older children can be encouraged to explore such ideas as how we perceive space and distance in art. They also need to be encouraged to continue to express in their art what they see, know, feel, and imagine.

7. **Help children experience basic elements of art such as line, rhythm, and contrast in many art forms.** Creative movements (or dance) display a strong relationship to the basic art element of line. For example, when children are moving in a wiggly or a twisting way, they can be given a signal to freeze or hold by striking a gong or stopping the music. The teacher might then appreciatively point out the different lines the body makes while it is held or frozen—the continuous curve from back toe through the body to the reaching, stretched fingers. Children can also make similar observations about each other's interesting body line designs in space. It is natural then to circle back from one's understanding of the body line to reaching, curving, or twisting lines in clay, crayon, or paint.

PHOTO 4-7 Teachers need to encourage children to talk together about their art.

The element of **rhythm** is most frequently associated with music, dance, and poetry, but it can be just as much a quality in art. We find it in repeated shapes, colors, and textures that flow in a directional path, such as in children's nature print designs. We also sense rhythm in their block structures of repeated patterns. We know rhythm unmistakably in the pulse of movement and music. Good examples of rhythm in design can be found in the stylized geometric rhythmic patterns of traditional Native Americans in their weaving, pottery, beadwork, and sand painting, which often tell stories about mountains, rivers, sun, and lightning.

The element of **contrast** provides one of the most exciting characteristics in all the arts. Sensitive teachers frequently help children become more aware of the power of contrast by pointing out how two colors next to each other make the shapes stand out. They comment on the roughly textured bark of a tree in contrast to its smooth leaves. Children appreciate the exaggerated features of "evil creature" puppets in contrast to the more subtle features of the heroes and heroines.

The concept of contrast for older children can be expanded from that presented to younger children. Contrast can involve the introduction of the color wheel. They can see on the color wheel how colors that are opposite one another are called *complementary* colors. These complementary colors provide more contrast than colors next to each other on the color wheel, called *analogous* colors. The idea of warm colors (reds, oranges, and yellows) and cool colors (blues, greens, and purples) is another concept appropriate for older children as they learn about creating contrast in their work. Figure 4-1 features additional suggestions about talking with children about their artwork. (See Chapter 3 for additional information on art elements.)

How teachers use art talk with children and how they encourage them to share art talk determines in large part how well children express themselves with art media. The following suggestions are helpful for teachers in facilitating children's art expression.

- *Use correct art terms.* The teacher may say, "You made a secondary color." "How did you make that tint?" "I see you drew straight lines, zigzag lines, and diagonal lines." "Can you point out some free-form shapes in your collage?" Some elements to comment on: line, shape, form, texture, value, space, and color. Some design principles are: balance, movement, repetition, emphasis, and contrast. (See Chapter 3 for a complete discussion of art terms.)
- *Encourage children to reflect on their art experiences.* Keep art portfolios and ask questions about children's work. "Which picture do you like best?" "Which one did you work on the hardest?" When a child spends several days on a painting, talk to the child about the changes you observe each day.
- *Ask convergent questions.* "What color did you make?" "What geometric shape is this?" "What artist did you say the painting reminded you of?"
- *Ask divergent questions.* "What are some materials you could use in your farm picture?" "What ideas do you have about Monet's painting?"
- *Focus children's attention on the way they use art media.* "I see you are drawing circles with the blue marker." "How did you make the sides so high on your clay cup?" "You are making a shade with the black paint."
- *Label the child's actions.* "You are putting blue paint into red paint. What color did you make?" "You are making a shade with the black paint."
- *Introduce new art concepts with actions.* Model an art process as you present a concept. Do this by speaking as you work: "I want a lighter tint of blue for my sky. I think I'll add more white to my blue paint."
- *Verbalize a problem and help children find a solution.* A child becomes frustrated using a white crayon on white paper, and the teacher asks, "Could we see your drawing better if you use a different color crayon? What other colors could you use to help you see the lines?"
- *Encourage children to discuss and arrive at solutions to art problems.* "We need windows for our cardboard school bus. Is there anything in this box that we could use?" "Could we use this piece of plastic?" "Is there anything else we need?"
- *Encourage children to talk about their artwork.* The teacher says, "Tell me about this part of your picture." A child answers, "I drew pets—a cat, a gerbil, and a dog." The teacher says, "Tell me more about what is around your picture." The child answers, "I made a border of stars."

FIGURE 4-1 Suggestions for talking with children about their art. *(Continues)*

TeachSource Digital Download Download from CourseMate.

© Cengage Learning

- *Share art experiences.* Listen to what children say to each other about their artwork. Encourage children to describe the processes they used to create a product.
- *Encourage children to talk together about their art.* Jaime watched Lin drawing a picture of the gerbils. The teacher said, "Lin, tell Jaime about your picture. How did you make brown paint?"
- *Talk with children about artists from various cultures and countries.* The teacher might show children artworks of several well-known artists, such as Monet, Bearden, and O'Keeffe. In this manner the teacher introduces children to a French impressionist, an African-American artist, and a female American artist.
- *Give children time to think about art.* Pose questions about art processes and wait for children to respond. "How did you paint your picture?" "What did you do first?" "How did you make that color?" Reflection is an important part of art process. All artists reflect on their work.

FIGURE 4-1 Suggestions for talking with children about their art. (*Continued*)

Did You Get It?

An art teacher tells her students to always start drawing in pencil and then to add color later. Which guideline for using aesthetic materials does this contradict?

a. avoiding doing the same thing every time
b. helping children to get the "payoff"
c. being positive and creative when using examples
d. helping students use other senses, even when only one seems necessary

Take the full quiz on CourseMate.

4-5 Talking with Children about Their Art

DAP **naeyc** How teachers use art talk with children and how they encourage them to share art talk determines in large part how well children express themselves with art media. The following suggestions are helpful for teachers in facilitating children's art expression.

- *Use correct art terms.* The teacher may say, "You made a secondary color." "How did you make that line?" "I see you drew straight lines zigzag lines, and diagonal lines." "Can you point out some free-form shapes in your collage?" Some elements to comment on include line, shape, form, texture, value, space, and color. Some design principles are balance, movement, repetition, emphasis, and contrast. (See Chapter 3 for a complete discussion of art terms.)
- *Encourage children to reflect on their art experiences.* Keep art portfolios, and ask questions about children's work. "Which picture do you list best?" "Which one did you work on the hardest?" When a child spends several days on

a painting, talk to the child about the changes you observe each day.
- *Ask convergent questions.* "What color did you make?" "What geometric shape is this?" "What artist did you say the painting reminded you of?"
- *Ask divergent questions.* "What are some materials you could use in your farm picture?" "What ideas do you have about Monet's painting?"
- *Focus children's attention on the way they use art media.* "I see you are drawing circles with the blue marker." "How did you make the sides so high on your clay cup?" "You are making a shade with the black paint."
- *Label the child's actions.* "You are putting blue paint into red paint. What color did you make?"
- *Introduce new art concepts with actions.* Model an art process as you present a concept. Do this by speaking as you work, "I want a lighter tint of blue for my sky. I think I'll add more white to my blue paint."
- *Verbalize a problem, and help children find a solution.* A child becomes frustrated using a white crayon on white paper, and the teacher asks, "Could we see your drawing better if you use a different color crayon? What other colors could you use to help you see the lines?"
- *Encourage children to discuss and arrive at solutions to art problems.* "We need windows for our cardboard school bus. Is there anything in this box that we could use?" "Could we use this piece of plastic?" "Is there anything else we need?"
- *Encourage children to talk about their artwork.* The teacher says, "Tell me about this part of your picture." A child answers, "I drew pets—a cat, a gerbil, and a dog." The teachers says, "Tell me more about what is around your picture." The child answers, "I made a border of stars."

- *Share art experiences.* Listen to what children say to each other about their artwork. Encourage children to describe the processes they used to create a product.
- *Encourage children to talk together about their art* (see Photo 4-7). Jaime watched Lin drawing a picture of the gerbils. The teacher said, "Lin, tell Jaime about your picture. How did you make brown paint?"
- *Talk with children about artists from various cultures and countries.* The teacher might show children the artwork of several well-known artists, such as Monet, Bearden, and O'Keeffe. In this manner, the teacher introduces children to a French impressionist, an African-American artist, and a female American artist.
- *Give children time to think about art.* Post questions about art processes and wait for children to respond. "How did you paint your picture?" "What did you do first?" "How did you make that color?" Reflection is an important part of art process. All artists reflect on their work.

4-5a Kid Culture

A kindergarten teacher noticed that similar superheroes Lavagirl and Sharkboy kept popping up in the children's artwork. And when she saw that multiple drawings about these characters emerged in other classrooms, she decided it was time to take notice. *The Adventures of Sharkboy and Lavagirl* was a popular children's movie. This is an obvious example of how visual culture reaches all ages, including our youngest students.

Looking at children's self-directed artwork is a window into children's visual culture. The term kid culture encompasses a broad range of media, including television, computer games, movies, books, comic books, advertising, entertainment, toys, games, and trading cards. Fashion, industrial design and man-made environments, particularly playgrounds, shopping malls, stadiums, and skate parks, are also a part of this culture. Attracted by powerful imagery and opportunities for play, children recreate their visual world through drawings, paintings, sculpture, and mixed media. In art, children are encouraged to pursue their interests, which are frequently influenced by this visual culture.

Although adults may find some aspects of kid culture to be aesthetically unappealing, it is important to remember that children are independent thinkers who develop their own tastes based on exposure. One has to first become familiar with kid culture to discuss it without bias with children in the classroom.

Encourage children to talk about their ideas with each other and you, their teacher. This is how you learn about current trends in kid culture and their strong impact on students' thinking. If you limit students' artwork to topics of your choosing, children will have no opportunity in school to fully explore that which intrigues them: their worlds, real and imagined. When the teacher steps back, permitting children to take ownership of their artistic and creative learning, the content will reflect topics most compelling to each artist. Within that list of student-originated topics, kid culture will always surface (Marshall & Vashe, 2008).

4-5b Displaying Children's Work

An important part of the teacher's role in developing children's aesthetic sensitivity is showing their work to parents and others. A good rule is that if children feel good about their work, let them show it. The work does not have to be complete. It should be displayed at children's eye level so that they, as well as adults, may enjoy it. Not every child in the group has to have his or her work displayed. Consider some of these suggestions when planning displays of children's art:

1. **Wall displays.** Much of what we want to display ends up on the wall—hung, taped, tacked, stapled, placed on a shelf, or otherwise fastened. Ideally, every last piece is thoughtfully and tastefully placed. Rare as that is, it is something to aspire to in early childhood classrooms. Much of common space wall area and classroom walls should be thought of as gallery space and should be well-spaced and orderly to provide the audience either with necessary information on works of art or documentation that expresses the values of the classroom/program and the children's efforts.
2. **Paint or vinyl surfaces.** Neither paint nor vinyl wall surface is a perfect direct surface for display, although they are by far the most widely used with various kinds of tape. Vinyl tends to handle tape without damage, but often taped materials do not stay up on the wall long. Semi-gloss or eggshell painted surfaces allow for careful taping but sooner or later will require touching up or repainting.
3. **Bulletin boards.** Bulletin boards are useful in administration and teacher areas but are less attractive as display vehicles for children's artwork. If you have bulletin boards, be sure they are at a level for children's viewing.
4. **Map rails.** Map rails are one-inch strips of cork for tacking or stapling and can be purchased with

THIS ONE'S FOR YOU!

Create a Classroom Museum

Provide children (of all ages) a year-round aesthetic experience by incorporating a classroom museum into your program. It's "show and tell" in a more meaningful, aesthetic sense. This project will provide many creative opportunities for children to document their progress in many ways throughout the year. Here are the basics to get you started.

What Is a Classroom Museum? A **classroom museum** is a collection of items and artifacts related to a specific theme. Items and artifacts are brought in by the children for display. Using this approach for show and tell, the theme or topic is motivating, and the exhibit grows gradually and joyfully. Children practice decision-making, problem-solving, and communicating skills as they share/add their special selections. Treasures from home, a family-crafted item, or an occasional purchase—each contribution is worthy. The sharing is educational and enjoyable. Museum topics change each month, with teacher/child interest sparking the choice.

Essentials for Success

- Make a high-quality choice for the first museum of the year.
- Determine a clear purpose, and definite goals for the museum as a curriculum tool appropriate for children's development.
- Invite family participation via an informative, friendly August newsletter, a September Parents' Night, and a special museum notice.
- Plan a simple but attractive museum area in the classroom. A suitable physical setup includes a backdrop for hanging pictures and a display table.
- Highlight the children's artifacts and show-and-tell experience.
- Select a child as a curator to encourage responsibility.
- Guide children's selection for show-and-tell artifacts to help foster respect for all contributions and ensure their survival in the classroom (especially fragile or sentimental items).

A good place to start in the beginning of the program year is with a "Me Museum." This is a good topic to start with because it encourages a feeling of community as teacher and children learn more about each other.

Steps to Setting Up the Me Museum

- **Awareness (with children).** Explore the concept of museum. Discuss possible items for a Me Museum. Plan ways that families can help. Frame a family museum notice. Establish routines for sharing.

- **Contributions (from children).** Me Museum artifacts are always surprises. Descriptions delight. Personal histories in bits and pieces come alive. Students can share stuffed animals, baby journals, family photos, toys, travel souvenirs, books or stories, ballet slippers, and other such objects.

- **Integration (with children).** Growth in vocabulary occurs. Expressive language expands. Thinking and problem-solving skills are nurtured.

- **Outcomes (for children).** Child by child, with each contribution, child-centered showing and sharing creates a caring community in which each child is important and friendships emerge.

To Continue the Museum. To create the next month's museum, brainstorm with the children for some possible topics and themes. What do they want to learn about? What provokes their curiosity? What special interest do they want to share/explore with classmates? With everyone inspired and motivated, many ideas are listed, and voting follows (integrating math skills such as counting, graphing, predicting, and comparing).

First choice becomes the next museum, with second place a strong possibility for a future museum. The teacher also selects topics to coincide with curriculum or timely topics. Topics may vary from year to year. The steps of awareness, contributions, integration, and outcome all facilitate museum planning.

movable clips or hooks to attach paper. These offer flexibility and an economical solution in areas where taping to the wall is likely.

5. **Careful display.** Display children's work in careful and respectful ways. It is often better to highlight one or two paintings rather than a mass of work. Framing with simple construction paper mats can highlight and transform children's work.

6. **Arouse curiosity.** Rearrange and display objects in different ways and places so that the children's curiosity is aroused.

7. **Reflect diversity.** Set up displays to show the different ways children have used a medium, such as painting, collage, clay, and so on. Let the room reflect the children's diversity, their likes, their interests—much the way a well-decorated home

reflects the interests and skills of the people who live in it. Children aren't clones, so we certainly don't expect to see 25 identical works of art with different names on them displayed in the room. How does this reflect children's diversity?

8. **Model art talk.** Take time at the end of the day to show artwork to the children, letting them talk about each other's work. Model for them how to make a positive comment.

Be sure to send all artwork home in a way that shows your respect for the artist and the art. Take care with children's work. Rolling dry paintings to take home shows you respect the work and the artist. Folding a wet painting does just the opposite. (More specific suggestions on displaying children's work are covered in Appendix D.)

4-5c Interpreting Children's Creative Work for Parents

Parents can be guided to see what the child enjoyed about the creative work. All people have their own ideas of what creative talent is, parents being no exception. It is important, however, that they understand and know that what their children enjoy and feel about what they are doing is much more important than the finished product.

Parents should also know why some materials are used by their children and others are not. More importantly, parents should learn to approach their child's making of gifts, art exhibits, and displays as demonstrations of the child's aesthetic sense. With these displays, the child is saying, "This is how it is with me."

Parents want to know their children; children's creative work can help parents know more about their children. Teachers can assist parents by showing these visual examples of the creative process and pointing out that they are valuable for the process alone. Teachers can assist parents of older children to see and appreciate the progression of images that are growing more subtle and complex in their child's art.

Very few children will become professional artists, but given encouragement and experience, they can learn to work with many media, enjoy beauty, and discriminate with aesthetic understanding. A person naturally responds to a lovely sunrise, painting, or piece of music. These aesthetic experiences help us live fully in the moment. Such responses do not need to be taught, but a child might need assistance and exposure to appreciate them fully. Aesthetic enjoyment provides an avenue through which people can find focus and achieve balance and tranquility in an increasingly

fast-paced world. Moreover, children who learn to love beauty in nature and in the arts are likely to want to support and protect these valuable resources.

4-5d Developing Your Sense of Aesthetics

Early childhood teachers need to protect the spirit, imagination, curiosity, and love of life and learning in young children as fiercely as we protect our environment. In a similar manner, early childhood teachers need to develop and protect their own aesthetic senses.

As you read through this book, you will most likely find some activities that catch your attention, appeal to your spirit, and reflect your personality and philosophy. In fact, your personality and philosophy must determine how you use any activity. All of the ideas and activities in this book are to be shaped and modified to suit your own needs with a particular group of children. Any idea will only be successful if you like it and are excited to use it with young children. You must mix a lot of yourself into all of your work with young children. Do not hesitate to mix in your philosophy and personality along with those of the children. Add a good portion of energy (yours and the children's), stir in a large measure of imagination, and you are on your way to a truly creative environment for young children.

DAP naeyc 4-5e The World Wide Web and Older Children's Aesthetic Experiences

In the activity sections of this book, you will find many activities for older children that involve references to virtual art museums. These virtual art museums tend to fall into two broad categories: those that are extensions of brick-and-mortar institutions, such as the Metropolitan Museum website and those that exist only online, such as the Virtual Diego Rivera Web Museum. Some virtual art museums such as the State Hermitage Museum function with corporate support, whereas others, such as the American Museum of Photography, are the work of individuals with a special interest or expertise in art. One goal that all virtual art museums have in common is collecting, preserving, and sharing objects of aesthetic, cultural, or historical value with a viewing public dispersed around the world.

Effective use of these digital resources to support student learning depends on a good research question or task that challenges students to apply what they find online in meaningful ways. Internet-based assignments should encourage students to explore, gather information, think critically, and construct their own understandings of the curriculum topic at hand.

THINK ABOUT IT

Aesthetic Judgment of Six-Year-Old Children

The aim of this study was to investigate the effects of aesthetic education on the development of aesthetic judgment of 6-year-old children. The researchers attempted to determine whether there was a significant difference in the aesthetic judgments of children who did and did not receive aesthetic education. The study also sought to establish if there were significant differences in the aesthetic judgments of children who participated in a program of aesthetic education, measured on completion of an aesthetic program and 4 weeks later. The study also considered the pretest and posttest scores of children according to their gender, their socioeconomic level, and their parents' educational level.

The sample was made up of 77 children—38 female and 39 male—randomly selected from state schools representing lower and higher socioeconomic levels in Ankara, Turkey. Twenty-two children were in the experimental group, 23 in the control group, and 32 in a placebo group.

In this study, an aesthetic education program—composed of 20 activities, offered twice a week for a period of 10 weeks—was designed for the experimental group. Each activity lasted for 1.5 – 2 hours. The program primarily involved activities which ensured that children would perceive visually the objects they recognized in their surroundings. The goal of these activities was to make children notice the difference between looking and seeing. The activities were based on artwork, artists, and their techniques. While preparing these activities, aesthetic values such as line, color, texture, form, mass and volume, composition, and space, as well as aesthetic principles such as balance, rhythm, tone, proportion, coherence, contrast, and repetition were taken into consideration.

The primary method used for incorporating aesthetic principles and aesthetic values into educational activities was art critique. Besides art critique, techniques such as music, painting, drama, and excursion-observation were used. A slide projector, overhead projector, and computer were used frequently during the program. The program focused on the artwork of well-known painters such as Van Gogh, Chagall, and Klimt. The children also visited art galleries as well as painting, sculpture, and printing workshops of fine arts faculties to observe real works of art, perceive them by touching, and talk about them.

The children in the placebo group engaged in educational activities that did not support the development of aesthetic judgment, and the children in the control group did not receive any training. Before implementing the education program, the researchers administered a pretest to the experimental, placebo, and control groups (the Taylor-Helmstadter Pair Comparison Scale of Aesthetic Judgment). At the end of the education program, a posttest was administered to all groups. A retention test was administered to the experimental group 1 month after the posttest to identify the permanence of the aesthetic education.

Although there was not a significant difference between the total pretest and the posttest scores for the experimental group, there was a significant difference in the pretest and the posttest scores of boys compared to girls. This may indicate that boys were more willing than girls to take part in the activities and benefited more by this education program when compared to girls. It also found that the educational and socioeconomic levels of parents did not have any effects on the aesthetic judgments of children (Acer & Omeroolu, 2010).

Several months after the end of the aesthetic education program, interviews were held with the children's teachers. They stated that they had observed an increase in the number of the art-related concepts used by the children. Among the recommendations the researchers made for teachers who wish to encourage aesthetic development in children were the following:

● Encourage dialogue and questions about the process and products of art.

● Encourage the creation of unique works of art by using novel techniques.

● Build an art museum and/or gallery in the classroom

● Compare art in the history of society and today's society.

● Get to know culture, art, and social life in other countries. (Acer & Omeroolu, 2010).

For example, the J. Paul Getty Museum website offers a wealth of art images, thematic exhibitions, video clips, and accompanying text. Depending on your students' grade level, you might ask them to choose works of art from two different time periods that appear on the site to write a comparative analysis. Have students share their comparisons and collectively discuss the larger question of "How has art changed over time?"

Another classroom activity involves students becoming virtual art critics. Students choose an exhibition currently showing on a virtual art museum site for critical review. The Smithsonian American Art Museum,

THIS ONE'S FOR YOU!

The Day the Mona Lisa Was Stolen

On Monday, August 21, 1911, the world's most famous work of art, Leonardo da Vinci's *Mona Lisa*, was stolen from the Louvre museum in Paris. That morning, museum employees noticed that the painting was not hanging in its usual place, but they assumed the painting was taken off the wall by the official museum photographer who was shooting pictures of it up in his studio.

By Tuesday morning, when the painting hadn't been returned and it was not in the photographer's studio, museum officials were notified that the painting was gone.

The police were contacted immediately, and they set up headquarters in the museum curator's office. The entire museum was searched from top to bottom. This took a week because of the size of the Louvre—a 49-acre building that runs along the Seine River for 2,200 feet. The only think a detective found was the heavy frame that once held the *Mona Lisa*. It was discovered in a staircase leading to a cloakroom.

After the news became public, French newspapers made several claims as to the nature of the theft. One newspaper proclaimed that an American collector stole the work and would have an exact copy made that would be returned to the museum, while the collector would then keep the original. Another newspaper said that the entire incident was a hoax to show how easy it was to steal from the Louvre.

Many people were questioned about the theft—from museum employees to people who worked or lived nearby. The police even questioned Pablo Picasso. Picasso had previously bought two stone sculptures from a friend named Pieret. Pieret had actually stolen these pieces from the Louvre months before the *Mona Lisa* was stolen. Picasso thought that perhaps his friend might have also stolen the *Mona Lisa*.

Fearful of the implications and bad publicity, Picasso had the sculptures given to a local newspaper for their return to the museum. Picasso wished to remain anonymous, but someone gave his name to the police. After an interrogation, the police concluded that Picasso knew nothing about the theft of the painting.

The painting was recovered 27 months after it was stolen. An Italian man named Vincenzo Perugia tried to sell the work to the Uffizi Gallery in Florence, Italy for $100,000. Perugia claimed he stole the work out of patriotism. He didn't think such a work by a famous Italian should be kept in France. What Perugia didn't realize was that while the Mona Lisa was probably painted in Italy, Leonardo took it with him to France and sold it to King Francis I for 4,000 gold coins.

How did Perugia steal the *Mona Lisa*? He had spent Sunday night at the Louvre, hiding in an obscure little room. Monday morning, while the museum was closed, he entered the room where the painting was kept and unhooked it from the wall. In a staircase, he cut the painting from its frame. While trying to leave the building, he came to a locked door. He unscrewed the doorknob and put it in his pocket. He then walked out of the Louvre and into the pages of history.

Interestingly enough, 10 months before the painting was stolen, the Louvre decided to have all masterpieces put under glass. Perugia was one of four men assigned to the job. Police questioned Perugia after the theft, but his easygoing, calm demeanor settled any doubts of his involvement (Esterow, 1966).

for example, features more than 30 virtual art exhibitions among the main resources available on its website. The teacher is able to introduce the role of the art critic by providing samples of critical reviews to read and discussing what might be included in students' reviews.

A third virtual art museum activity is to have students use artwork that they study online as springboards for their own artistic compositions. Ask students to select a work from an online exhibit that relates to your current unit of instruction. Have students write a one-page analysis of the work they've chosen, using questions that you provide to guide their analysis. Following the writing activity, have students create their own interpretations of a landscape based on an idea or theme that the artists they studied used in their work.

A great place to find museum sites and special online collections is the Museum of Online Museums (MoOM), which includes listings of links to hundreds of museum websites organized by topic.

Did You Get It?

A teacher asks his student, "Which aspects of geometric composition did you include in your picture?" The teacher is using
a. convergent questioning.
b. divergent questioning.
c. independent questioning.
d. aesthetic questioning.

Take the full quiz on CourseMate.

Summary

4-1 Discuss young children's looking and seeing.

Children look in many different ways. Touching, patting, poking, picking, and even tasting are ways of looking for young children. Children look for what they need, but they also see what they find to be stimulating.

4-2 Describe three types of sensing and feeling.

There are three types of sensing and feeling. The first is contact through the five basic senses; the second is what the person feels inside; and the third is fantasy. The third type of sensing and feeling goes beyond the present and reality. It includes dreams, memories, images, and guesses.

4-3 Choose materials that have good aesthetic potential.

Many materials with aesthetic potential can be found. Anything children can explore, manipulate, and use in different ways has aesthetic potential. What is most important is that these materials (and what is done with them) become personal statements of the children.

4-4 List four guidelines to help children work with aesthetic materials.

The following are some suggestions on how to give young children guidance when using aesthetic materials:

- Ask questions aimed at helping children reach out for and get the "payoff" they are seeking.
- Avoid always doing things the same way.
- Be positive and creative when using models or examples.
- Help children select the materials they prefer.
- Help children "hunt" for aesthetic qualities.
- Help children use other senses when only one sense seems necessary.
- Help children experience basic elements of art such as line, rhythm, and contrast in many art forms.

4-5 List six guidelines to use in talking with children about their artwork.

How well teachers use art talk with children and how they encourage them to share art talk determines how well the children express themselves with art. When talking with children about their art, teachers need to use correct art terms, encourage children to reflect on their art experiences, ask convergent and divergent questions, and help children focus attention on the way they use art media. They also need to label the child's actions, introduce new art concepts with actions, and verbalize a problem and help children find a solution. Encouraging children to talk together about their art and talking with children about artists from various culture and countries are also important

Key Terms

aesthetic sensitivity   60
classroom museum   68
contrast   65

kid culture   67
rhythm   65

Learning Activities

Beautiful Things

Everyone has had some experience with beauty and has a special idea about what is beautiful. It can be a very interesting experience to examine this concept with each of the five senses.

A. Write down the three most beautiful things (living or nonliving) that you have ever experienced with each of your five senses.

B. As you write your list, try as much as possible to relive the sensations.

C. Answer the following questions.
   1. Were most of your things living or nonliving?
   2. How many involved people?
   3. Did any of your answers surprise you?
   4. How often do you encounter beautiful things?
   5. Which sense seems to find the most beauty?
   6. How much does finding beauty in life depend on the viewer?
   7. What does this mean for working with children?

D. Compare your responses with those of fellow students.

Amazing Journey

A. Find a quiet place and relax. Close your eyes and think of something that amazes you or produces wonder in you.

B. Think of yourself as that something. (Take some time to get the feel of being it.)

C. Write a description of yourself as this something. (Use plenty of adjectives.)

D. As a result of this experience:
   1. What emotions do you feel?
   2. How are you like what really amazes you?
   3. How are you unlike it?
   4. Would you like to change in any way?

E. Compare your answers with those of your classmates.

F. Do you think children would enjoy using their imaginations like this?

Cyberspace Aesthetics

A. Visit the Vincent van Gogh Gallery online. Look at several works by this artist. Select the artwork that interests you most. What moods do you think the artist is trying to express in this painting? What features in the artwork made you think that? How was the artist able to convey these moods to the viewer?

B. Some works of art are not as easy to analyze because they are nonobjective—that is, they don't show any people, places, or things. Many modern artists work nonobjectively to express their unique ideas and feelings. Go online and find information about Jackson Pollock. How does Pollock communicate this way? Can you explain how his artwork expresses ideas and feelings?

C. Visit the Andy Warhol Museum website. Examine how art is used to commemorate famous people and important events in different cultures around the world. Then check out the Global Children's Art Gallery website (www.naturalchild.org/gallery/) to see how children have pictured their important events.

Hallway Museum

At the beginning of a school year, when you probably don't have children's artwork to display in the hallway outside your classroom, consider creating a hallway museum. Displaying your collection of art reproductions is perfect for this use. Art reproductions are available at museums, as well as online on websites such as Museum Syndicate.

A. If possible, you can pin the art prints to bulletin board strips that can be screwed into the wall. Or you can use removable glue "dots" to hold up your art reproductions directly on the wall. These "dots" can be removed with no damage to the wall.

B. You can put representational artwork in one section and nonobjective artwork in another. For representational artwork, a good combination to hang up includes portraits, still life works, landscapes, and genre paintings.

C. During the first week of school, ask the children to imagine they are in an art museum, and discuss the rules of behavior. Allow the children time to explore the artwork, and then stand in front of an artwork that they reacted to in some way. They can like or dislike the artwork, but they have to explain why they made their choices.

D. You may even develop a worksheet for students to use as they explore the hallway museum. Students can match the artist with the title, determine if it is a portrait, self-portrait, still life, landscape, seascape, or nonobjective.

E. You may also ask students to choose an artwork to rename, along with reasons for their choices. Older students can compare and contrast more than one artwork.

F. A hallway museum can provide students with an introduction to many artists, styles, genres, and media. Through this process, they will also learn and use art vocabulary, learn about museums, and develop skills for critiquing and accessing art.

Aesthetics in the Animal World

Two famous Russian artists started the Asian Elephant Art & Conservation Project (AEACP) to help improve the welfare of domesticated elephants. The nonprofit organization raises funds through donations and the sale of artwork created by elephants that the AEACP has trained to paint. The work is primarily abstract expressionist, but the elephants are also now being instructed on how to create realistic works.

- Go to the Asian Elephant Art & Conservation Project website, and choose a work that you would like to purchase.
- Tell why you would like to have the artwork.
- Would you like to really own a painting by an elephant?
- Do you think that the elephants are the artists, or are the people who train and help the animals with their paintings the true artists?

Making Cross-Curricular Connections

Here are some suggestions for cross-curricular connections using famous artists' work.

- **Math.** Prompt students to recognize repeated geometric shapes in Grant Wood's *American Gothic* and mosaic patterns in M.C. Escher's *Relativity*. Andy Warhol's *One Hundred Cans* is another good example to use to see geometric shapes.
- **History.** Introduce artists in their historical context. For example, ask older students to consider how Mary Cassatt and Berthe Morisot illustrate the limitations placed on nineteenth-century women in society and as artists, and to note that Jasper Johns' *Three Flags* only has 48 stars because Hawaii and Alaska weren't admitted to the Union until 1959.
- **Science.** Explain how Georges Seurat's method of using small dots to demonstrate how our eyes see color.
- **Literature.** Students connect Michelangelo Caravaggio's realistic style and Henri Matisse's *Icarus* to figures from Greek mythology.
- **Pop culture.** Ask students to reflect on Jasper Johns, who was one of the first artists to think about the design of everyday objects around us. Ask students to recognize how Caravaggio's lifestyle and Warhol's celebration of the celebrity have much in common with our contemporary culture.

Activities for Children

Colors of the Animal Kingdom

Collect a variety of books about animals, and give the children time to browse through them. Then explain that different animals use their colors differently.

- Some animals—such as male birds and fish—are brightly colored to attract a mate.
- Some poisonous animals—such as types of frogs and snakes—have bold colors that warn other animals to stay away.
- Some animals adopt the color and pattern of their habitat so they blend in and go unnoticed by either predators or prey.
- And a few special animals—such as the chameleon—can change colors to blend into any environment. For a great story about a chameleon, read *A Color of His Own* by Leo Lionni. Preschoolers will love having their very own chameleons (simply cut out the shape from clear acetate and mount on a wood stick) that will change color wherever they go.

Aesthetic Thinking Through Art

Help the child to think of new ideas in responding to the following prompts.

A. Say to the child, "If you could invent a new means of transportation, what would it be? Draw or construct how it would look."

B. Ask the child, "If you had a funny-shaped piece of paper, what could you make it into?"

C. Ask, "How do you think the world would look to a giant? Draw a picture (or make a model) of it."

D. Ask, "What could you do with this empty box, this stick, this cardboard (beautiful junk)? How could you place it or arrange it to make something that's your very own idea?"

Sensory Experiences

Seeing

A. **Colors.** Have children look for colors in the room: "How many red things can you see?" Or play a guessing game: "I am thinking of something green in this room. What is it?" Colors sometimes tell us important things. Traffic lights tell us when to go or stop, red flags on a road mean danger, and red lights in a building mean an exit. We must obey these signals. We can make different colors by mixing them. (Allow children to experiment with mixing colors.) Show a prism to see the colors. Blow soap bubbles, and look for the rainbow colors in them.

B. **Shapes.** Show blocks or other objects that are circles, squares, rectangles, and triangles. Have children find things in the room that are these shapes. We can see color and shape at the same time. Find a red square, a blue circle, or an orange pyramid.

Listening

A. **Recording voices.** Children can listen to their own voices, to the voices of others, and to classroom sounds. Take a smartphone or tape recorder on field trips and record sounds in animals' environments. Replay to review the trip and to help children remember the sequence of events. Record sounds in the environment: cars passing; steps in the corridor or on the street; children skipping, hopping, running. Ask questions such as, "Do any of the animals sound alike? Which of the sounds was loudest? How would you describe that sound? Can you draw that sound?"

B. **Street corner.** Listen to sounds. Identify them: a car turning a corner, wind blowing past a sign, the click as a light changes, a dog barking, rain dripping, wheels on wet pavement, animal footsteps, high heels on pavement, sneakers on pavement, and noises from buildings.

C. **Classroom sounds.** Listen to sounds of different toys, clock ticking, blocks falling. Have children cover their eyes and ask, "Where does the sound come from? What is the sound?" Have a volunteer walk (skip, run) across the back, the front, or along the side of the room.

D. **Stethoscope.** Listen to heartbeats of children, adults, and animals. Listen to someone's stomach after a snack. Scratch different objects on a tabletop (floor, rug, pipe), and listen to the sound through the stethoscope.

E. **Rhythms.** Beat out simple and then more complex rhythms with clapping hands. Ask children to repeat them. Then have them lead with their own sound rhythms.

Taste and Smell

Be sure to teach children proper precautions in tasting or smelling strange substances.

A. **Cooking.** Make puddings, candy, or cakes. Smell before, after, and during cooking. Identify what's cooking by smell. Taste brown sugar, white sugar, molasses, corn syrup, and maple syrup. Make lemonade with and without sugar. Squeeze tomatoes, apples, and oranges for juice. Question children about which smells they like and which smells they don't like. Draw a picture about smells.

B. **Snack or lunch.** Talk about differences in taste between hamburgers and bologna, between peanuts and peanut butter, or between potato chips and mashed potatoes. (These discussions may also get into sense of touch as well as smell and taste.) Have children guess what they will have for lunch from smells coming from the kitchen.

Touching (Tactile Awareness)

A. **Rough or smooth?** Discuss tactile sensitivity with children. Make available objects of varying textures, such as silk, burlap, feathers, rope, seashells, mirrors, balls, driftwood, beads, furry slippers, and so on. Have children form small groups, and give each group an object. Have each child in the group show how the object makes him or her feel. For example, a feather may stand in a straight line with arms and legs extended and then move "softly," with arms waving gently from side to side.

B. **A collage made for touching.** A texture collage is a bulletin board that all students can contribute to and use later for future projects. Have children bring in materials of different textures—sandpaper, flannel, velvet, burlap, plastic, bottle caps, pebbles, and paper clips—to glue on the board. After the collage is complete, the children can make "rubbings" using charcoal sticks on newsprint. This board should encourage the use of vocabulary-expanding words such as "coarse," "smooth," and so on.

C. **Creative movement.** Discriminate between various textures through movements. Have children feel a texture such as that of silk and interpret it by moving the way it feels. Use a variety of textures that exhibit characteristics: bumpy, smooth, coarse, prickly.

D. **Outdoor textures.**
   1. Words to use: *rough, smooth, bumpy, soft, hard, sharp, cold, warm, wet, dry, same, different.*
   2. At the beginning of the walk, ask children, "How do things feel?" Say, "Let's feel this building," or "Let's feel the back of this tree."
   3. If a child does not know the meaning of the word *rough*, say to her while she feels the tree, "The tree bark feels rough. Let's see if we can find something else that feels rough."
   4. If the child is familiar with the word *rough* and its meaning, say, "Can you find something that feels different from this rough tree?" (Example: a smooth leaf.) Or, "Can you find something that feels the same as this rough tree?"
   5. As you continue your walk, find new objects to touch, and name their textures. Note: For very young children, begin with two simple words that express opposites, such as *rough* and *smooth, soft* and *hard,* or *wet* and *dry.*

E. **Hidden objects in boxes.** Hide objects inside boxes and then have children feel and describe them without seeing them. Have them match a given object with its mate by hunting for the mate in the box without seeing it. Have children match objects by size and shape, or only by shape, by pulling them out of the boxes. (Some children may be able to do this only if they have felt both objects with the same hand.) Put several objects in the boxes to make the task harder; more similar objects also make the task harder.

F. **Hidden multisensory objects.** A multisensory feely bag game is perfect for the development of aesthetic senses and descriptive vocabulary. Place an interesting object in a bag and invite children to use as many different words as they can to describe it as they feel it. Write their words down in rows like a poem—*big, squishy, soft, round . . .* Pillow!

G. **Sandpaper letter game—early elementary.** Provide children with letters cut from sandpaper. Have them work

in pairs. Blindfold one child and have the other child give a letter to the blindfolded one to feel and guess its identity. Award one point for each correct identification. Then have the partners switch places.

H. **Touch the alphabet—early elementary.** Make a collection of tactile objects for the various letters of the alphabet. Use cotton balls for "c," denim for "d," a brick for "b," and so on. Children will experience the tactile relationship as well as the letter/symbol relationship.

Multicultural Activities

Colors and Feelings Lesson Plan

Topics: "Colors," "Feelings," "Books"

Goal: To help children express the feelings they associate with different colors

Materials: Colored construction paper, felt-tip pens, stapler

Method: Begin by asking all children wearing the color blue to stand up. Tell them to look at their blue clothes. Ask, "What do you think of when you see the color blue?" and "How do you feel when you see the color blue?" Repeat this game with many colors. Include skin colors— tan, brown, black, and peach.

Tell children they can make a color book. Work with children one at a time. Ask them what they are reminded of when they see each color and how it makes them feel. Write down their words on that particular colored sheet of construction paper. Put the sheets of paper together and staple the corner to make a simple flip book.

Variations

- Write down children's responses and add them to a bulletin board about color.
- Teach children the names of colors in another language.

What Is Your Color? Lesson Plan

Topics: "Colors," "Bodies," "I'm Me and I'm Special," "Our Community"

Goal: To help children recognize and name skin color

Materials: Pictures of people from a variety of racial groups

Method: Hold up one picture at a time. Ask such questions as: "Who can tell me about this picture?" "Who is this person?" "What color is this person's skin?" "What color is this person's hair?" "Where do you think this person lives?" Encourage children to use descriptive color words such as *tan, ebony,* and *cream* to expand their color vocabularies. Write down children's answers. Make a bulletin board display by posting pictures along with the children's descriptions.

Variations

Mix up the pictures and lay them face down. Select a child to come up and choose a picture from the pile. Ask the child to show it to the class and describe the person in the picture.

Colorful Bubbles

This activity will enhance children's visual perception and aesthetic skills by observing a variety of subtle color variations. They will also see how light can change these colors. Fine motor skills are also developed in this activity as children use eyedroppers.

Materials: Bubble wrap, clear packaging tape, medicine droppers, food coloring, mixing cups, water, and scissors

Procedure:

1. Cut a piece of bubble wrap to a desired size. Use wrap that has at least 5/16-inch-height bubbles.
2. Using clear packaging tape, place bubble wrap onto the surface of a glass window that is at a level reachable for young children.
3. Cut tiny slits into the tops of bubbles. Let the child decide which bubbles to cut.
4. Have children fill medicine droppers with food coloring and squeeze a bit of the liquid into each bubble, filling about 3/4 of the bubble.
5. Add water in varying amounts to the food coloring to make a variety of shades.
6. The child can decide on the color choices and the arrangement of these colors on the bubble wrap. One color can be used and varying amounts of water can be added to investigate the subtle differences in color depending on the concentration of food coloring.
7. Encourage children to mix colors to make new ones.
8. When the project is complete, secure each bubble with a small piece of clear tape.

My Feelings

1. Distribute large pieces of drawing paper and markers to children.
2. Have children close their eyes and listen. Clearly and slowly say words that evoke emotion: *love, hate, cold, soft, fun, laugh.*
3. With their eyes still closed, children move their marker across their paper to reflect the emotion/emotions they feel as you present each word.
4. Have students talk about how each word made them feel. Older children can write their responses on the back of their drawing.

My Imagination—Kindergarten and Up

Materials: String or yarn, scissors, paper, glue, washable markers or crayons

1. Have children glue a 6- to 8-inch-long piece of string or yarn on a piece of paper.
2. Direct children to pass their paper to the person sitting to their left.
3. Have children take this piece of paper and imagine what the visual represents.
4. Have students use markers or crayons to create something from the original string art.
5. Have children discuss what they saw and why it became what it did.

Famous Artwork Fun

Famous works of art are a great venue for talking about word choice. For instance, when examining Van Gogh's *Starry Night,* have children describe the swirling blue skies and bright orange stars. Write down the adjectives they use in large letters on an index card. Put all of the cards into a bag of adjectives and have each child pick one. The child then draws or paints three things that might be described by that adjective. For example, *prickly* could describe a cactus, a pinecone, and a porcupine. Children will enjoy looking at each other's pictures and guessing which adjective they picked.

Rainbow Reflections

Hang a crystal or prism outside in bright sunlight. If possible, place it in front of a light-colored surface, such as a white wall. On a bright, sunny day, take children outdoors where they'll discover the prism or crystal that you've hung up to catch the sunlight. Talk about the rainbow of colors made by the prism. What colors do they see? Have they ever seen a rainbow in the sky?

A. Take down the prism and let the children hold it. What happens when the sun catches it from behind? From the front? What happens when they walk with it? Ask children to carry it to a shady place. Does the rainbow disappear? Explain how the prism bends the sunlight to create colors.

B. There is another way to make a rainbow in the classroom. All that is needed is a glass of water and a sunny day. (Be sure to use a clear glass—the wider the mouth, the better.) When the glass is placed in sunlight, there should be a rainbow where the shadow would fall due to the simple prism, which can be used in lessons about the color spectrum. Point out to children that a rainbow forms outdoors when drops of water in the air act as prisms.

C. Provide markers or paint and large sheets of white construction paper that children can use to create their own rainbows. If possible, provide prisms of different shapes and sizes that children can use to further their rainbow explorations.

Nature Detectives

This activity uses paint chips found in hardware stores to help children learn about different shades of colors and how to find different colors in nature.

Materials: different colored paint chips, light-colored cardstock or construction paper, glue, bag for collecting items, magnifying glass (optional), and binoculars (optional)

Procedure:

1. Take the children on a field trip to the hardware store. Let them pick out different colors of paint chips. Steer them toward the chips that have several different shades of the same color on the same paint chip. If a trip is not possible, gather the chips yourself.
2. Take a nature walk outside and bring the paint chips. If you prefer, bring along a magnifying glass and binoculars. Talk about what season it currently is and what colors you are going to see in nature right now.

3. Give each child one of the paint chips and have him or her search for nature items that match the color. Talk about the different shades of green found in leaves from different trees or the different shades of brown found in different bark. If it is autumn, talk about how leaves in different stages of turning colors will have a different shade of the same color and how the leaves of different trees turn different colors. If you have any colors that you cannot find in nature, ask the child why he or she thinks those colors are not as common in nature.

4. On your nature hunt, collect small items, such as leaves, sticks, flowers, and acorns that match the paint chips.

5. Inside, spread the collection out on a table and examine them with the magnifying glass. Talk about different characteristics of the treasures such as texture and size.

6. Have the children use the paint chips and the collected items to make a nature collage for the season. Show them how to glue the paint chips and nature items onto the paper. If you have heavier treasures, you may need to use tacky glue. If you have lots of treasures, you can make a collage to go with each paint chip.

7. Let the collages dry and then display them in the room. As the seasons change, you can repeat the activity, or just use the original collage as a jumping off point to talk about how the colors of the season are changing.

Mondrian Can Be Elementary

Piet Mondrian's work is interesting and fun to study for even the youngest student because of his simple shapes and primary colors. To get the children started on this Mondrian exercise, show several examples of reproductions of Mondrian's work. Pointing out shapes he used, and introducing red, yellow, and blue as primary colors. Then encourage students to create their own versions.

Materials: 9 × ½-inch or 9 × 1-inch strips of black paper, construction paper in primary colors, scissors, glue, and 9 × 9-inch white construction paper

Procedure:

1. Have students cut out primary-color construction paper squares and rectangles and glue them onto the white construction paper. Next, use the precut black strips of construction paper to create vertical or horizontal lines on the same page. The black strips can outline the edges of the primary color shapes.

2. To extend the activity, discuss the concepts of vertical, horizontal, and intersecting (crossing) lines, as well as the concepts of length and width. Or make a musical extension by using the tune of "Three Blind Mice" and replacing the words with the following: "Red, yellow, and blue. Red, yellow, and blue. Oh, they are the primary colors, oh yes. We mix them together to get all the rest. Red, yellow, and blue. Red, yellow, and blue."

Fence Designs

For this activity, all you need is access to a chain link fence and colored paper cups. Push the cups into the diamond spaces in the fence. Cups need to be large enough to stick by pressure within the openings without collapsing the cup.

Form the pattern by placing cups in the links. You can make a colored flag, or even present a word or phrase, such as "GO TEAM," "WELCOME," or "USA."

Nature Murals

After a walk in the rain, a dance in the wind, or another outdoor experience, plan a group mural. After coming inside, discuss what was seen, heard, tasted, and felt. Discuss with the children things that can be included in a group mural. Allow each child to decide what she or he will make for the mural. Have children create individual works representing their personal experiences. These pictures and designs can be glued onto one large sheet of paper, creating the mural.

Art Walk

A. Discuss with the children the works of art they have created and the patterns and textures they created in their work. Then invite all of them on a walk around the school looking for patterns and textures.

B. Remind the children that art can be made by people when they draw, paint, or sculpt. People also can make useful things more beautiful, such as when they put patterns on clothing, make patterns with floor or wall tiles, or decorate a bulletin board. Have children bring their sketchbooks to sketch patterns they like or do quick rubbings of interesting patterns they find on the art walk.

C. Remind children that art is also found in nature. Have children look for and sketch examples of art in nature as well as in the design and decorative elements of the school building and playground.

D. After the walk, ask children to draw pictures of both man-made and natural art they found during their walk. Then ask them to write or dictate sentences that tell about their pictures. Display children's work to add to the art in your room.

E. As a follow-up to the art walk, invite local interior designers or landscape designers to visit the class to talk about how they use what they know about art to make rooms or yards more beautiful. Ask the visitor to bring along sketches or other visuals to share with the children. With the visitor's help, plan a simple design activity for children.

Fun with Shadows and Clouds

Capitalize on sunny summer days. Help children make and play with shadows cast by their hands, objects, and moving things. Look at clouds long and often. Find shapes that look like the beginning of a story, then tell the story. Look for another cloud figure that gives you an idea for how to continue the story.

Activities for Older Children (Grades 4–5)

Geometric Composition

A. Encourage students to think of ways they can arrange geometric shapes in a nonobjective artwork. Collect objects that can be traced to draw circles, squares, rectangles, triangles, and so on. Have the students trace the objects on white paper, drawing enough shapes to fill the page.

B. Add straight, zigzag, or wavy lines to the composition of shapes.

C. Finish by coloring the composition with markers.

D. Ask the students to describe the lines and shapes they used. Ask them why they placed them where they did.

Cave Drawings

Before this activity, share with the children cave paintings, for example, *The Red Horse* and *The Bull* from the cave paintings at Lascaux, France. Have students imagine they are cave painters in ancient times. What plants and animals would they include in a cave painting? Encourage them to make several sketches before starting. Next, have them copy the best sketch onto a piece of tan-colored construction paper or a brown grocery bag. Use black crayon to outline objects. Make some lines thick and some lines thin.

Use dark reds, browns, and other earth-colored crayons to finish the drawing. Crumble the paper and straighten it out several times. Then glue the drawing onto black posterboard.

Ask the children to point out the different kinds of lines they used. Have them tell you why they chose certain colors for certain objects. Compare their work to the cave drawings from ancient times.

Color Optics

The following are some color optics phenomena older children will enjoy exploring individually.

- **Afterimage.** This is probably the best-known illustration of how our eyes react to color. Have students stare at a page of solid color for about 30 seconds, then look at a dot on a page of white or gray. They will see color on the blank page—usually the complement or near complement of the color of the paper they had stared at. For example, they will see red if they had stared at a green piece of paper, or blue if they had stared at a yellow piece of paper.

- **Juxtaposition.** Color pigments placed side by side in small repeated strokes are altered by our vision to appear to combine, thus forming a different hue. This new optical effect is more vibrant than if the same pigments were blended together. This technique has been used historically by mosaic and stained glass artists, but most effectively by the nineteenth-century postimpressionists such as Georges Seurat. Use a print of his painting, *A Sunday Afternoon on the Island of Le Grand Jatte,* to

explore this concept. Then challenge students to try their hand at this visual mixing of colors.

- **Color relativity.** The color gray appears much lighter when placed on a black background than it does against a white one. This dark/light effect holds true for many other colors as well. Yellow on a green background will appear to contain more red than it does on a white background.

Using pairs of colored sheets of paper, let students make their own discoveries of color optics by placing two samples of the same color on a variety of different backgrounds. Then have them compare results.

Activities Related to the Concept of Line

Lines are basic to art. Lines can convey different moods. Before drawing and painting experiences, you might want to discuss the variety of lines that we encounter in our daily lives. Ask students to think about telephone lines, clotheslines, lines of people, lines of music, and the line of scrimmage. Then ask some of these questions to get them thinking: "What do we associate with lines on a face? Where do you see long pairs of parallel lines? Where do you see more straight lines, in nature or in man-made objects?" (Ask them to look around.) "Where do you see more curves? Which conveys more movement: a straight line or a curvy one?"

To encourage creative use of lines in their work and to explore line and mood with students, ask questions like the following.

A. **Verticals**
 1. What do you see in our environment that is made up of vertical lines? (skyscrapers, trees, telephone poles, rain, Gothic cathedrals, soldiers standing at attention)
 2. What moods or feelings does a series of verticals convey? (heavenward, of the sky, strong, straight, dignified)
 3. Have you ever leaned against a vertical? (yes—a wall, a tree, a lamppost)
 4. When is your body vertical? (when standing)

B. **Horizontals**
 1. What in the environment is predominantly horizontal? (the horizon, the floor, a bed, a table, a still lake or pond)
 2. What moods do these horizontals convey? (grounded, of the earth, relaxed, at rest, calm, serene, expansive)
 3. When is your body horizontal? (when lying down, asleep)
 4. Can you stand or sit on a horizontal? (yes—a sofa, the floor)

C. **Diagonals**
 1. Where do you see diagonals? (a slide, a plane taking off, a ramp)
 2. What feeling is conveyed by diagonals? (action, movement)
 3. When is your body at a diagonal? (when you are running, walking fast, leaning into the wind)

D. **Wavy Lines**
   1. Where do you see wavy lines in the environment? (a wavy ocean, lake, river, snake, rolling hills)
   2. What feelings do they convey? (undulating movement, relaxed, rhythmic, fluid)

E. **Zigzag Lines**
   1. Where do you see zigzag lines in the environment? (lightning, a jagged tear, the earth after an earthquake, crimped hair)
   2. What moods do they convey? (tense, anxious, frenzied)
   3. When does your body form a zigzag? (while jumping on a pogo stick)

F. **Spirals**
   1. What do you see that is shaped in a spiral? (a spring, a slide, water going down a drain, a tornado, a coiled snake)
   2. What feelings do spirals convey? (spinning, swirling, energy)
   3. When is your body in a spiral? (while twirling on the dance floor or doing a pirouette)

Cyberspace Aesthetics

Have students use the Internet for the following aesthetic experiences.

- Kcho (pronounced KA-cho) is a well-known artist from the island of Cuba. Check out some of his large three-dimensional works, which are displayed around the world, at www.artnews.com. Click on "Back Issues," go to the June 2000 issue, and search for "Kcho" or click on "Making Waves." Alternatively, go to http://www.walkerart.org/education/. Click on "Collections." Type "Kcho" in the "Search" box.
- What did you learn about the artist's background? How would you describe Kcho's work? What subjects and themes do you see in most of Kcho's art? What messages do you think the artist is communicating about his culture? How does he use different materials to express himself?
- Ramona Sakiestewa is a Hopi Indian fabric artist. Learn about the artist and her work at the following site: www.ramonasakiestewa.com.
- Describe the design of Sakiestewa's art. What colors, lines, shapes, and textures can be seen? How do you think the work would be different if you saw it in person? Why do you think she uses this medium? What might she want viewers of her tapestries to know about her?

Is This Art?

Present this problem to your students to get them talking about what they consider to be "art."

One day, your teacher says she wants to draw a picture of you. She takes a sheet of paper and covers the whole thing with chartreuse crayon (you know, that yellow-green color), and then she tacks it up on the board. Under it she writes, "This is a picture of my student." Would you be mad? Is this art? These questions will be interesting ones to answer. They will give you insight into how your students think about art.

Artists Like Us

Exposing children to the work of famous artists can help them find their artist within.

Materials: White drawing paper, markers, colored pencils, crayons, books or prints of art by famous artists such as Picasso, Cézanne, Seurat

1. Present the work of a great master such as Picasso for children to observe and discuss.
2. Invite children to notice specific qualities of the works and techniques used. For example, children might notice the unusual Cubist portraits of Picasso. You might ask, "How are these different from other portraits you have seen or even drawn?"
3. Provide art materials for children to create their own portraits in a particular artist's style.
4. Encourage children to give a title to their works and create a famous-artist-inspired art show or class art book.

Variation: Present the Pointillism style of George Seurat. Show how he preferred not to make brushstrokes but to paint by applying small dots of unmixed colors. Provide cotton swabs as painting tools and watercolors for children to paint their own Pointillism painting.

Water Designs Using an Overhead Projector

This is a wonderful way for children to explore the different aesthetic properties of materials—transparent, opaque, and semitransparent. It also encourages experimentation with a variety of materials.

Materials: Overhead projector, glass tray or glass baking dish filled with water, string, yarn, lace, food coloring, cooking oil, eye/medicine droppers, netting, pipe cleaners, feathers, and any other transparent or semitransparent materials

1. Place the glass tray filled with water on top of the overhead projector.
2. Turn on the projector to project light onto a screen or wall.
3. Invite children to experiment with different materials by placing them into the water tray and watching the image project onto the screen.
4. Encourage children to use drops of color and oil to see and document interesting results.
5. Small pieces of string and yarn can be added along with pipe cleaners twisted into interesting shapes to further manipulate the image and see the aesthetic nature of the art materials.
6. Add other materials for further explorations of transparent properties, semitransparent properties, opaqueness, and color mixing.

Variation: More than one projector can be used. Images can be projected as large as the wall to create interesting environments for children. These environments could change on a daily basis depending on the project theme (underwater, forest, sunsets, storms). Musical selections accompanying these themes can be played while imagery is projected.

Nature Sketches

Have students take a sketchbook home and draw 5 to 10 small patches of different textures they find in nature. Under each patch, have students write down the name of the material from which the sketch was made (a tree, a rock, a piece of a leaf). Have students use their sketches to create a colored and enlarged version of these textures on a suitably sized piece of paper. Display and discuss the drawings.

Patterns in Nature

Discuss regular and irregular patterns seen in plants, animals, and other natural forms in the spring. Some irregular patterns are found in the camouflage of animals. Structural patterns tend to be regular, as seen in shells, leaf veins, and many plants.

Forms of Letters

Have students create letter forms by printing them with objects. Almost all letters of the alphabet can be created from straight lines (edge of tongue depressor or cardboard), circles (bottle caps or spools), and half circles (rubber washers cut in half). Students can also use this printing technique to illustrate an original poem.

Group Objects

Have four or five students work in a group, using the objects from the preceding activity (cardboard, bottle caps, spools, and rubber washers cut in half). Have them share their printing objects to make a picture. Brainstorm creative ways to use the objects they have (repeated circles become

animal shapes, edges of cardboard become repeated blades of grass, and so on). Display these pictorial prints in the classroom.

Georgia O'Keeffe's *The Mountain, New Mexico*

Obtain an art print of this work. It is an excellent example of a landscape and varieties of warm and cool colors. If this print is not available, any other landscape with warm and cool colors will suffice.

A. Briefly review the concept that colors are an important way to express moods and feelings in art. Point out that many color words help people to tell about feelings. Examples include "feeling blue," "green with envy," or "red with rage."

B. Explain that artists often refer to these color qualities as *warm* or *cool*. These terms can mean that a color is used to show warm things (a fire) or cool things (a lake). More often, the artist also remembers that colors help to express feelings.

C. Explain that the warm colors in O'Keeffe's painting show the red earth of mountains in New Mexico, but they also help to express the artist's warm feelings about the land: O'Keeffe thought that the forms and colors of the desert and nearby mountains were beautiful. Guide students to see the delicate shading and rhythmic curves that fill the whole painting. Discuss how the painting makes them feel about the place depicted.

D. As a follow-up activity, have students create a picture of a landscape on a planet no one has seen. Have them use warm or cool colors to express the feelings they want to convey about this place.

References

Acer, D., & Omeroolu, E. (2010). A study on the effect of aesthetic education on the development of aesthetic judgment of six-year-old children. *Early Childhood Education Journal, 35*(3), 335–342

Marshall, J., & Vashe, M. (2008). Mining, bridging, and making: Developing and conveying concepts in art. *Art Education, 61*(1), 6–12.

Mulcahay, C. (2009). Providing rich art and activities for young children. *Young Children, 64*(4), 107–112.

 Visit CourseMate for this textbook to access the eBook, Did You Get It? quizzes, Digital Downloads, TeachSource Videos, flashcards, and more. Go to CengageBrain.com to log in, register, or purchase access.

Planning and Implementing Creative Activities

Developmentally Appropriate Practice

Part 2 provides basic information on planning and implementing creative activities for young children using a developmentally appropriate approach. Included is information on developmental levels, developmentally appropriate practice, emergent curriculum, differentiated instruction, and Bloom's taxonomy.

Guidelines for setting up developmentally appropriate environments as well as practical considerations involved in arranging space, equipment, and activity centers are also found in Part 2. The final chapter in Part 2 presents the concept of play and its importance in the early childhood program.

REFLECTIVE QUESTIONS

After studying this section, you should be able to answer the following questions.

1. What do I know about the attention span and activity levels of the young children in my group? How will I include this information in my lesson planning?

2. What can I do to improve the classroom environment for young children in my care by focusing on developmental levels and individual needs and interests of young children?

3. Am I aware of the importance of developmentally appropriate practice (DAP) and how to implement it in my classroom?

4. Is my classroom reflective of the individual differences present in the group of children using it?

5. In planning lessons, do I include activities that address the learning styles (multiple intelligences) of children in my group?

6. Do I use methods of differentiated instruction in my classroom that are designed to meet the children's individual learning styles?

7. Do I plan lessons that encourage children's higher-level thinking using Bloom's taxonomy of learning?

8. Have I created a positive and safe physical environment for the young children in my care? What strengths and weaknesses are evident in my classroom arrangement and management practices?

9. Have I included all of the media I can that are developmentally appropriate for young children in my classroom? What changes do I need to make to improve my use of media with young children?

10. Does my classroom reflect all of the ethnic and cultural groups appropriate for my group of children?

11. How do I encourage independent learning and exploration in the arrangement of my room? In my lesson planning? In my choice and use of media?

12. Do I enjoy being in and teaching in my classroom the way it is currently arranged? Do the children enjoy being there? How can I rearrange it to make it more enjoyable for both myself and the children?

13. Are my room arrangement, choice of media, interest centers, and presentation of lessons enticing to the children's interests? Do they encourage convergent or divergent thinking?

14. How will the needs of children from varying backgrounds be addressed in planning a creative and safe environment?

15. Am I aware of the national standards in the content areas and the approach my state has taken with regard to the No Child Left Behind Act and Common Core Standards?

16. Am I working to develop my teaching skills to become as accomplished a teacher as I can be?

17. Does the environment I create for young children provide space, time, and opportunities for all types of play?

18. What role does play have in the total development of young children?

19. How can I plan and arrange the classroom environment so young children are encouraged to play in a way that emphasizes problem solving and exploration?

20. Have I included enough dramatic play materials for all the developmental levels and multicultural backgrounds of my children?

Casper Holroyd

Children, Teachers, and Creative Activities

Planning creative activities always begins with the child. Each child is unique, with his or her own way of being and responding to the world. The teacher should be aware of each child's level of development, strengths, abilities, and special personality.

Learning Objectives

After studying this chapter, you should be able to:

5-1 Discuss what factors are involved when considering a child's developmental level.

5-2 Discuss the term *developmentally appropriate practice.*

5-3 Discuss the term *differentiated instruction.*

5-4 Discuss the term *multiple intelligences.*

5-5 Explain Bloom's taxonomy and its place in the early childhood environment.

5-6 Explain how differentiated instruction can be applied in working with children with special needs.

5-7 Discuss attention span and activity patterns as they relate to young children.

5-8 Discuss three aspects of the teacher's attitude that have an impact on children's creativity.

5-9 List the general planning guidelines for creative activities.

5-10 Discuss strategies for success on the national level, including legislation, content standards, early learning standards, and standards for teachers.

naeyc

NAEYC Program Standards

1a Knowing and understanding young children's characteristics and needs.

1b Knowing and understanding the multiple influences on development and learning.

2c Involving families and communities in their children's development and learning.

4b Knowing and understanding effective strategies and tools for early education.

6b Knowing about and upholding ethical standards and other professional guidelines.

DAP

DAP Criteria

2H2 Teachers think carefully about which learning format is best for helping children achieve a desired goal, given the children's ages, development, abilities, temperaments, and so on.

3A2 If state standards or other mandates are in place, teachers become thoroughly familiar with these.

3C1 Teachers are familiar with the understandings and skills that are key for that age group in each domain (physical, social, emotional, cognitive).

6b Teachers know about and uphold ethical standards and other professional guidelines.

Casper Holroyd

PHOTO 5-1 The teachers' role is one of encouraging, questioning, and experimentation.

With this knowledge, teachers can relate their own personalities and unique skills to those of each young child. Thus, an atmosphere is created in which both adult and child remain themselves in order to help and respect each other.

Watching a child at play helps an adult understand this young person. A teacher is able to see how the child uses materials and relates to other children. In many educational experiences, and especially in creative activities, the teacher is a facilitator. To **facilitate** means to help along, to guide, to provide opportunities, and to be sensitive and caring without interfering. The meaning as used here is that the teacher allows the young child to deal directly with the materials, with the teacher acting as an aide rather than a leader or judge. Because the emphasis is on divergent thinking and not on right answers in creative activities, judging is not necessary. Guidance and feedback, however, are helpful. Because creative activities are open ended, there are no simple standards for evaluating them. The teacher's role, then, is one of encouraging, questioning, and experimenting (see Photo 5-1).

"Education costs money, but then so does ignorance."
—Sir Claus Moser

5-1 Consider the Child's Developmental Level

DAP **naeyc** In many early childhood books and journals, we often see the phrase **developmental level**. Generally, when we speak of a child's development, we are referring to four major areas of growth: physical,

social, emotional, and intellectual. These areas serve as a framework on which we organize our knowledge and observations of children. These four areas combined make up the individual child. When the needs of a child are met in each of these areas in any particular activity, we can be fairly well assured that the overall growth of that child is being encouraged.

Another aspect of a child's development refers to **individual differences**. For example, two children may be exactly the same age, but they may be performing at different levels in one or more areas of development. Both children may be within the normal range of development. Therefore, a teacher must not only have knowledge of developmental levels but must also tune in to the different levels of each child's progress in the four major areas.

A child's ability is closely related to his or her level of development. If a teacher understands this, failure and frustration can be avoided when planning creative activities. Answers to the following questions can help adults better understand and work with a young child.

- What is special about the child?
- What are the child's interests?
- What are the child's strengths?
- What abilities and skills are already developed?
- What is the child's home life like?
- How does the child relate to adults?
- How does the child respond to other children?
- What are the motor skills (large- and small-muscle) of the child?
- How does the child express himself or herself?
- How does the child speak?
- How does the child solve problems?
- With what materials does the child enjoy working?
- How does the child learn?

When you have answers to these questions, you are able to plan creative activities that meet the specific needs of young children.

Did You Get It?

A preschool teacher notes that one student has many friends, while another excels at completing jigsaw puzzles. To which aspect of developmental levels is the teacher attuned?
   a. individual differences
   b. intellectual varieties
   c. fluctuating abilities
   d. age-expectation differences

Take the full quiz on CourseMate.

5-2 Developmentally Appropriate Practice

DAP **naeyc** Developmental level and individual differences, discussed earlier, are two of the basic components of **developmentally appropriate practice (DAP)**. This term captures a set of core ideas that are the basis of early childhood education contained in a statement adopted by the National Association for the Education of Young Children (NAEYC) Governing Board in the early 1990s and later published as part of the book *Developmentally Appropriate Practice in Early Childhood Programs* (Bredekamp & Copple, 1997). The third and most recent edition of *Developmentally Appropriate Practice* was published in 2009. Most early childhood professionals express general agreement with the basic principles and guidelines of DAP that NAEYC has articulated in these editions. Because a lot has happened in the early childhood field since the first publication in 1997, each edition reflects the growing complexities and changes affecting the profession of early childhood education. It is not possible to gain a thorough understanding of DAP and how to use it effectively in the classroom with only the information in this chapter. Visit the NAEYC website for a deeper understanding of DAP for infants, toddlers, and children aged 2–8. For our purposes, we will discuss some very basic concepts of DAP.

Developmentally appropriate practice means teaching young children in ways that:

● Meet children where they are, as individuals and as a group, by taking into account their physical, emotional, social, and cognitive development characteristics.

● Help each child reach challenging and achievable goals that contribute to his or her ongoing development—a stretch, but not an impossible leap.

● Recognize that what makes something challenging and achievable will vary depending on the individual learner's development in all areas; her store of experiences, knowledge, and skills; and the context within which the learning opportunity takes place (Copple & Bredekamp, 2009).

A cornerstone of DAP is *intentionality*. Teaching that meets learners where they are and that helps them reach challenging and achievable goals does not happen by chance. In everything good teachers do—from setting up the classroom to assessing children to planning the curriculum—they are intentional (Copple & Bredekamp, 2009).

In classrooms that reflect DAP, teachers are in charge, but the environment is organized so that children can choose among numerous hands-on learning experiences. A balance is sought between child-choice and teacher-directed experiences.

Every DAP classroom is structured; however, this is not as readily apparent as the structure of the teacher-directed classroom. Teachers orchestrate the classroom. The classroom is organized around the elements of time, space, and the conceptual framework of the curriculum. Early childhood teachers organize the schedule, the space of the classroom, and the curriculum with the child's physical, social, emotional, and cognitive needs in mind while seeking a balance of child-choice and teacher-led activities.

A teacher in a DAP classroom plans for children to construct knowledge based on what they already know and what they want to find out. The teacher's perspective is a developmental one in which children are expected to develop over time and move from gross approximations to refinement of skills and concepts. For example, in an early childhood classroom, children would be encouraged to write using whatever letters they know. At first, children may know only the letters of their names. As they learn more about sound/symbol relationships and how to produce letters, they will incorporate these symbols into their writing. In traditional classrooms, children are not encouraged to use the information they presently know but are expected to wait until they know all the letters and all sound/symbol relationships before they write.

Developmentally appropriate early childhood classrooms are those that demonstrate, among other important characteristics, maximum interaction among children as they pursue a variety of independent and small-group tasks. The teacher prepares the environment with challenging and interesting materials and activities, and then steps back to observe, encourage, and deepen children's use of them. In a developmentally appropriate environment, teachers ask thought-provoking questions and make appropriate comments (Barclay & Breheny, 2009).

The NAEYC's position statement on DAP in early childhood education calls for a curriculum of active learning organized around learning centers for 4- to 8-year-old children. These strategies include the following:

THIS ONE'S FOR YOU!

Emotional Development and Activity Settings

One of the principles of DAP is taking into account children's emotional and social characteristics. A study conducted by researchers at the University of Virginia examined sources of variability in preschool children's positive and negative engagement with teachers, peers, and tasks, and how that variability was related to both classroom activity settings (for example, teacher-structured time, outdoor time, transitions) and child factors (age, gender).

Participants were 283 socioeconomically and linguistically diverse children drawn from 84 classrooms, 34-63 months old. Each child's engagement was observed and rated multiple times within a single day. Results suggested that children's engagement varied significantly across the preschool day.

Activity settings that provided children with a greater degree of choice (free choice and outdoor time) were associated with more positive engagement with peers and tasks, while teacher-structured activities were associated with more positive engagement with teachers.

Transitions emerged as a difficult part of the day, associated with less positive engagement with teachers and tasks. Older children were rated higher on peer and task engagement.

These findings suggest that both characteristics of the classroom setting and child factors are associated with children's classroom engagement throughout a day in preschool. Child-choice activities, including free choice and peer engagement were associated with more positive task and peer engagement compared to teacher-structured activities. These findings suggest that different activity settings provide children with different opportunities to engage with teachers, peers, and tasks (Vitiello, Booren, Downer, & Williford, 2012).

Understanding these relations, teachers can plan activities to maximize children's opportunities to learn. Such an understanding is certainly in line with the principles of DAP and its effectiveness in the early childhood classroom.

- Children select many of their own activities from among a variety of learning areas the teacher prepares, including dramatic play, blocks, science, math, games and puzzles, books, recordings, art, and music.
- Children are expected to be physically and mentally active. Children choose from among activities that the teacher has set up or that they spontaneously initiate.
- Children work individually or in small, informal groups most of the time.
- Children are provided concrete learning activities involving materials and people relevant to their own life experiences (Copple & Bredekamp, 2009).

In summary, a developmentally appropriate environment for young children is one that empowers children to be curious, to inquire, to experiment, and to think for themselves.

Developmentally appropriate practice does not mean a set curriculum. An underlying question guides the teacher's design and implementation of the curriculum: What are the significant facts, concrete examples, and basic understandings we can examine in studying this topic? Obviously, what would interest

and motivate 3- to 5-year-old children is different from what would interest and motivate 8- to 10-year-old children. Copple and Bredekamp (2009) describe the curriculum of the DAP classroom as one that uses themes, units, and projects. These are developed around knowledge of child development, subject matter disciplines, and the individual children's needs and backgrounds.

Finally, any description of what is developmentally appropriate is really a dynamic concept. It is meant to address nothing more or less than the best thinking of the field at a particular point in time. The position statement on DAP will likely be revisited at a particular point in time to reflect changes in the knowledge and thinking of the field of early childhood education.

5-2a The Reggio Emilia Approach

DAP naeyc In the same vein as DAP, there is a growing interest in integrating art in the early childhood classroom, partially as a result of the widespread interest in the Reggio Emilia approach to early childhood education. In the preschools of Reggio Emilia, a town in northern Italy, children spend time each day expressing their ideas through art media. Activities stem from the interests and ideas of the children. They have an active part in the planning of the curriculum, and their personal input is shown in their creative art experiences. The result is that children express themselves artistically in a much more mature way than most children their age (Douglas & Jacquinth, 2009).

In the Reggio Emilia approach, the arts are integrated into the school curriculum as problem-solving activities rather than as discrete subjects or disciplines taught for their own sake. Children's art making is emphasized to reinforce concepts, and their art products are considered as aspects of their learning. Visual arts are seen as an additional "language," one in which children's ideas and concepts are expressed in art media (Bruner, 2004).

Perhaps the most innovative activity to evolve from the Reggio Emilia approach is a unique form of documentation. American early childhood teachers are familiar with documentation in the form of note taking, videotaping, language experience, written comments, and checklists. However, in the Reggio Emilia approach, documentation in the child's own words is accompanied by artwork or photographs. Documentation panels display the child's work with great care and attention to both the content and aesthetic aspects of the display. Documentation describes in the child's own words—and sometimes the teacher's as well—the images, ideas, and processes represented by the child's artwork. Documentation may appear on trifolds, bulletin boards, or charts. The words of the children or teachers are in large print so that children, teachers, parents, and visitors can easily read them. This form of documentation makes visible the child's learning, as it often shows the process of the art experience from beginning to end (Douglas & Jacquinth, 2009).

Working with children in Reggio ways must begin with reflective practice—looking at the ways you are working and asking questions of yourself and your colleagues. This entails taking responsibility for your own professional development, which requires constant reflection, collaboration, and questioning (Wien, 2008). Gardner (2004) describes Reggio classrooms as the best preschools in the world, "a shining testament to human possibilities" (p. 17). Is it possible to create such shining examples of early childhood education in the United States? It seems that using the visual arts as a basis for learning across the curriculum might be a good beginning.

5-2b Emergent Curriculum

naeyc A concept closely related to both DAP and the Reggio Emilia approach is **emergent curriculum**. Like the Reggio approach, emergent curriculum is built on the strengths of the child. In contrast to standardized curriculum, emergent curriculum arises from the play of children and the play of teachers. The goal of emergent curriculum is to respond to every child's interest. Its practice is open ended and self-directed. The teacher responds to the child's needs and interests and designs the curriculum to fit them (Jones, 2012). Thus, the curriculum emerges from such sources as:

- Children's and teacher's interests
- Developmental tasks
- Things in the physical environment
- People in the social environment
- Unexpected events
- Values held in school, the community, family, and culture
- Daily living, such as caregiving, routines, and conflict resolution (Jones & Nimmo, 1994)

Emergent curriculum focuses on the process of learning. The children have diverse strengths. Early childhood educators in an emergent curriculum build

Video supplied by the BBC Motion Gallery

▶❚❚   **TeachSource** Video

Learning Through Play

1. Discuss how the type of outdoor learning curriculum depicted in this video relates to the information on DAP and the Reggio Emilia curriculum models as described in this chapter.

2. Using the information in this chapter as the basis for your decision(s), what specific aspects of the curriculum presented in this video could you use in your work with young children?

Watch on CourseMate.

on those strengths and interests as they help children construct genuine knowledge for themselves (Jones, 2012). Thus, curriculum emerges from the teacher's planful interaction with a particular group of children.

PHOTO 5-2 Using differentiated instruction strategies, a teacher learns how to spot what works for each child.

DAP naeyc 5-3 Differentiated Instruction

A concept that is a basic part of DAP is differentiated instruction. The term **differentiated instruction** is often associated with individualized planning and teaching strategies for young children. Quite simply, it means providing different types of learning experiences and environments to suit each child's individual needs.

A beginning teacher will soon discover that no two children learn at the same pace or in the same way. Some need lots of practice; others "get it" immediately. Some take to new materials easily; others are slower to accept them. In early elementary levels, some children can learn from reading, while others get more from listening or from visual aids. Some elementary children have trouble writing clearly, but others express complex ideas in art or music.

When using differentiated instructional strategies, a teacher learns how to spot what works for each child (see Photo 5-2). She checks to be sure that lessons contain activities and content that each child in the group can "connect with" in some way.

5-3a Journey to Differentiated Instruction

Every child who walks through the classroom door brings special gifts to the learning table. Each one has some hidden strength that enables him or her to learn. In preparing to differentiate, you have to find out who your learners are—what abilities, interests, and experiences have shaped them. In addition, you must honor the unique developmental needs of each

child. In a differentiated and developmentally appropriate classroom, the teacher is the one who extends, engages, questions, affirms, and challenges children as they are constructing their own knowledge. The following are five steps to differentiated instruction:

Step 1: Know the children.
What skills and abilities do they have?

What differences from cultural background, life experience, and home life influence their ability to learn?

Step 2: Determine the learning goal (see Photo 5-3).
What do you want the students to understand or be able to do? What learning standards and curriculum goals will you address?

PHOTO 5-3 One of the steps to differentiation is determining the learning goal for children.

Step 3: Identify proof or evidence that they understand what has been taught.

What behavior and comments would tell you that students understand?

What products, performances, constructions, and experiments would express understanding of the concepts, skills, and information taught?

Step 4: Plan the learning experience.

How should the concept be introduced?

What teaching strategies should be used?

What learning activities should be used?

What resources are needed?
How will students be grouped?

Step 5: Reassess and adjust according to new needs and changes.

What is the evidence for knowing that children have understood the concepts and processes involved?

What measures (for example, observation, questioning) will give you the information you need to know if the child is on track or if he or she needs further adjustment?

5-3b Characteristics of a Differentiated Classroom

The most obvious feature of a differentiated classroom is that it is child centered. The following are other indicators that differentiated instruction is present.

- Teachers and students accept and respect one another's similarities and differences.
- The teacher is primarily a coordinator of time, space, and activities rather than a provider of information (see Photo 5-4). The aim is to help students become independent, self-reliant learners.
- Children and teachers work together in setting group and individual goals.
- Children work in a variety of group sizes as well as independently (see Photo 5-5). Flexible grouping is evident.
- Time is used flexibly in the sense that pacing is based on student needs.
- Students have choices about topics they want to study, ways they want to work, and how they want to demonstrate their learning.
- The teacher uses a variety of instructional strategies to help target instruction to student needs.

Casper Holroyd

PHOTO 5-4 One of the steps to differentiation is determining the learning goal for each child.

- Students are assessed in multiple ways, and each student's progress is measured at least in part from where that student begins.
- Assessment is an ongoing diagnostic activity that guides instruction. Learning tasks are planned and adjusted based on assessment data.

Casper Holroyd

PHOTO 5-5 In as little time as possible, explain the activity so that the child knows how to begin and proceed independently.

In differentiated instruction, learning, activities, and materials may be varied by difficulty to challenge children at different readiness levels. They may be varied by topics in response to children's individual interests. Activities and materials may also be varied by students' preferred ways of learning or expressing themselves.

> "Education is what survives when what has been learned has been forgotten."
>
> —B. F. Skinner

5-3c Differentiated Instruction and Process Learning

DAP naeyc Another term associated with differentiated instruction is **process learning**. Process learning conceives of learning in terms of its processes rather than its products. In process learning, the focus is on providing children experiences that promote thinking and problem solving without specifically identified outcomes. The early childhood classroom abounds with opportunities for children to actively engage in learning activities rather than listening unquestioningly as they receive the knowledge of others. In process learning, children not only learn by doing but also reflect on the learning process itself. By doing so, they are able to transfer the information learned in one process or learning situation to another. For example, as the child manipulates blocks, continually building up and breaking down structures, he is learning the process of balance. This process involves size, weight, and object placement. These concepts, in turn, can be applied in the science/discovery center with "sink or float" experiments.

5-3d Explaining Process Learning to Parents/Caregivers

naeyc To a casual observer, a child's process-learning experiences may appear to be simply "playing" or just "messing around." Yet this type of learning is crucial in that it is self-initiated, ongoing, and transferable to other learning situations. Early childhood teachers need to explain the importance of process learning to parents and caregivers to encourage children's continued and active involvement in process learning. What may seem aimless is actually active processing, storing,

and receiving information by a child's exploration. Process learning helps children develop information-processing skills that can be applied across the curriculum. Most importantly, process learning emphasizes information discovered by the *learner*. This type of independent, active learning is key to acquiring knowledge all through life.

> ### Did You Get It?
>
> **During the first month of the school year, a first grade teacher spends time individually with each student, asking about their interests. This practice is likely to contribute to the practice of differentiated instruction by**
>
> **a.** helping the children feel comfortable with the teacher.
>
> **b.** helping the teacher recognize the students' abilities.
>
> **c.** encouraging group interaction.
>
> **d.** showing the students that the teacher is interested in them.
>
> **Take the full quiz on CourseMate.**

5-4 Differentiated Instruction and Multiple Intelligences

DAP naeyc When planning early childhood activities using differentiated instructional strategies, an understanding of multiple intelligences is essential if you are to meet the individual needs of children. According to Howard Gardner's multiple intelligence theory, each of us possesses eight "intelligences," or ways to be smart (Gardner, 1999). Some of us are more adept at using our hands; others are good at making rhymes or singing songs. Each type of intelligence gives us something to offer the world. What makes us unique is the way each intelligence expresses itself in our lives.

By recognizing multiple intelligences, we can help children enhance their individual strengths. Yet understanding multiple intelligences means more than focusing on individual characteristics. Just imagine a grown person who could do nothing but write poetry or solve algebra problems. To do everyday things like drive a car or follow a recipe, a person needs to be smart in more than one way.

An emphasis on the multiple intelligences is also relevant in working with young children with disabilities. Although specific disabilities can affect specific parts of the brain, other parts of the brain may not be affected. "Idiot savants," for example, have an extraordinary skill or ability in a specific area despite limitations in other areas of cognitive or social development. Addressing the education of young children with disabilities through the multiple intelligences may help us discover or "awaken" hidden talents. It is important for all young children to discover their own interests and abilities, and this is no less true for young children with disabilities. An emphasis on the multiple intelligences may help children discover what they are good at and put a focus on ability rather than disability. Each of us is smart in all eight ways. Here's how to recognize these multiple intelligences in ourselves and in children.

5-4a Word Smart (Linguistic Intelligence)

At younger ages, children who are word smart enjoy listening and telling stories. They are effective in expressing themselves and convincing others by using language and their rich vocabulary. These children are often successful learners by listening and hearing because they sort information through their listening and repeating skills. Young children with this dominance often demand story after story around bedtime. When they enter school, they have highly developed verbal skills, enjoy developing rhymes and often puns. In short, they tend to think in words. They like oral and silent reading exercises, playing word games, and enjoying a variety of reading and writing materials at learning centers. They also favor making up poetry and stories, getting into involved discussions, debates, creative writing, and telling complicated jokes.

Older children possess strong vocabularies, and, at times, can get so lost in a book that they almost forget about their dinner. At this age, they may subscribe to their favorite magazines or use a word-processing application to keep a personal diary or secret journal.

Older children who are word smart also have a rich vocabulary and are sensitive to the meaning of words, grammar rules, and the function of oral and written language. Journalists, lawyers, and storytellers often demonstrate this type of intelligence.

5-4b Logic Smart (Logical/Mathematical Intelligence)

Children with high logical/mathematical intelligence are curious about how things work. They like to ask questions and investigate. They use numbers easily and enjoy solving problems. They have the ability to understand logical patterns, categories and relationships, and causes and effects. They enjoy working with manipulatives, strategy games, logic puzzles, experiments, and timelines. They tend to be systematic and analytical, and they always have a logical rationale or argument for what they are doing or thinking. They like to use computers.

Older children often become quite skilled at many areas of mathematics, calculus, and science, perhaps even creating a hypothesis for the development of a new invention. Students at this age also enjoy puzzles and recognize patterns in the world around them. Scientists, accountants, and computer programmers generally have this ability.

5-4c Picture Smart (Visual/Spatial Intelligence)

When Gardner first developed the theory of Multiple Intelligences, he lumped the entire visual world under "spatial" intelligence. Today it is more common to sort the visual world into four domains: two-dimensional (images), three-dimensional (objects), four-dimensional (place), and five-dimensional (experiences).

Visual/spatial intelligence represents not only the knowing that occurs through the shapes, images, patterns, designs, and textures we see with our external eyes, but it also includes the images we are able to conjure inside our heads. People with high visual intelligence are able to visualize three-dimensional objects. They take the information and translate it into images and pictures in their minds. When they need to, they have the ability to retrieve the information through the images and pictures they made earlier.

Young children might build cities out of blocks and create impromptu murals on the kitchen and bedroom walls. They like to paint and make interesting designs and patterns from fabric, colored construction paper, and clay. They also love putting together jigsaw puzzles and working with mazes. They like to spend their free time drawing and building with Legos®. These children tend to enjoy daydreaming.

Older children tend to be good at reading maps and finding their way around new places, daydreaming, and creating accurate drawings; they may find it easier to learn information that is presented in images rather than just by words. Older children who are picture smart have the ability to understand geometry

Getting Started with Multiple Intelligences— Try These Ideas

Here are a few classroom activity suggestions that can get you started with multiple intelligences.

● For musical or bodily/kinesthetic learners who persist in drumming, humming, and tapping during quiet work time, provide thin plastic straws for them to tap on desks. This is much less distracting to others!

● For bodily/kinesthetic students who tear paper, scribble on desks, and gouge textbooks, provide a small piece of clay for them to keep in their desks. Allow them to manipulate while working, listening—anytime.

● For musical students, provide a set of headphones with a music tape to aid concentration.

● Before reading a story to your group, take a moment to imagine how you could turn it into a participatory reading event for your children who are musical or bodily/kinesthetic. For example, before you read a story about a particular animal, instruct students that every time you read the animal's name, they are to make a noise like that animal.

● Assign a different mouth noise to represent each punctuation mark you are teaching. When you put sentences on the board that need punctuation, students will vie for the privilege of reading a sentence with the appropriate noisy punctuation, while you or a student adds the marks to the sentence. (If you can't handle the mouth noises, you might try instruments such as a cymbal or rattle.)

● When practicing vocabulary words, let children who are musical make up a rap or song about the spelling (or meaning) of a word/set of facts. Have your spatial learners draw a "word picture" or "math fact picture." First write the word or math fact in the middle of the paper; then draw a picture around it that will help them remember the word. Have your linguistic learners create a crossword puzzle using vocabulary words. Both linguistic and musical learners would enjoy creating a rhyming poem using vocabulary words or math facts.

and recognize the relationships of objects in space. Children with visual intelligence in schools are successful in geometry. They also are very good in visual arts, sculpture, architecture, and photography.

5-4d Music Smart (Musical Intelligence)

Musical intelligence is that special ability to recognize tonal patterns, rhythm, and beat. In other words, it is the ability to understand and express well numerous musical forms. Such learners are most sensitive to environmental sounds, the human voice, and musical instruments. In short, they possess a strong ear for music. Unlike the average person, they are more obviously affected by rhythms, musical patterns tones, and various sounds. You can easily detect a change in their facial expressions, emotional responses, and/or specific body movements when they listen to music.

Music smart also involves the capacity to understand and express oneself musically (see Photo 5-6). Children with this ability can keep time with music, sing in tune, and tell the difference between types of music. They can appreciate melodies and enjoy listening to music and singing to themselves.

Young children can often be heard banging on pots and/or singing nonsense songs to themselves. Children with a dominant musical intelligence may enjoy humming and easily turning sounds into rhythms; they retain melodies and lyrics well.

Casper Holroyd

PHOTO 5-6 Music smart learners often enjoy keyboard activities.

Older children acquire good memories for lyrics, perhaps emitting the odd wince here and there when their friends sing "Happy Birthday" off key. They are often quite skilled at mimicking language accents, sounds, and the speech patterns of others, as well as recognizing different musical instruments in a composition.

Musical children often play a musical instrument. They participate in the school choir or school band. They like to sing or drum to themselves. They can remember and repeat a melody after listening to it only once. They learn through rhythm and melody. They need music to study or learn, and they learn new things more easily if the ideas are sung, tapped out, or whistled.

5-4e Body Smart (Bodily/Kinesthetic Intelligence)

Bodily/kinesthetic intelligence is related to physical movement and the knowledge of the body and how it functions. It includes the ability to use many parts of the body to express emotion, to play a game, and to interpret and invoke effective body language. Children with this ability enjoy and learn best from activities that use the body and involve movement, such as dance, crafts, mime, sports, acting, and using manipulatives.

People with bodily intelligence use their physical selves to communicate and solve problems. They are good with objects and activities involving their bodies, hands, and fingers.

People with bodily intelligence prefer to learn through their body or feelings. These people are more successful in learning if they can touch, manipulate, and move or feel whatever they are learning.

Young children who demonstrate a strong bodily/kinesthetic intelligence are highly coordinated. They enjoy all sorts of athletics and would rather be a participant than a spectator. Also, this way of understanding the world is most evident in young children who have a hard time sitting still and are well coordinated.

Children with high kinesthetic intelligence learn best with activities such as games, acting, hands-on tasks, and building. These children process information by applying it and through bodily sensation (for example, in a classroom where people from history are acted out or an assignment that allows them to build something such as Lego® towers).

Children with bodily intelligence like being physically active, playing sports, dancing, and acting. They like doing crafts and working on mechanical projects.

Older children who demonstrate this type of intelligence may be good dancers or athletes—or particularly good at mimicking the classroom teacher!

5-4f Person Smart (Interpersonal Intelligence)

Person smart is the ability to understand people and relationships. People with interpersonal intelligence understand and care about people and their feelings and interact effectively with them. They approach people with empathy, recognize differences among people, and value their points of view with sensitivity to their motives, moods, and intentions. These people are sensitive to facial expressions, gestures, and voice. They get along with others, and they are able to maintain good relationships with one or more people among family and friends.

Young children with interpersonal intelligence enjoy playing with other children and often have more than one friend (see Photo 5-7). They care about

Casper Holroyd

PHOTO 5-7 The child with person smart intelligence enjoys playing with other children.

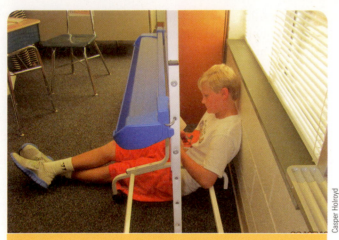

PHOTO 5-8 The child with an intrapersonal intelligence learning style often prefers to work alone.

their friends and like to help solve their problems. They love team activities of all kinds and are very good team members, pulling their own weight and often much more. These children like to teach other children and take part in school organizations and clubs. They have the ability to influence people and are natural leaders.

Older children tend to become natural leaders, picking up on subtle social cues and knowing how to put others at ease. In short, they work well within groups and often end up in leadership roles.

5-4g Self Smart (Intrapersonal Intelligence)

Being self smart is having the ability to think about and understand oneself. People with intrapersonal intelligence are aware of their strengths, weaknesses, moods, and motivations. They effectively use self-discipline to achieve personal goals. They often enjoy working alone, sometimes even shying away from others and going off quietly by themselves (see Photo 5-8). They are often strong willed and self-confident, and they possess definite, well-thought-out opinions on various issues.

These children are self-motivated. They can monitor their thoughts and feelings and control them effectively. Intrapersonal children need their own quiet space most of the time. They prefer to study individually and learn best through observing and listening. They like to play by themselves. They use self-knowledge to make decisions and to set goals. They are sensitive to their own feelings and moods.

Older children may keep journals or logs, express strong emotions and well-developed opinions, and seem blithely unconcerned by other kids' notions of what's "in" and what's "out."

5-4h Nature Smart (Naturalistic Intelligence)

This intelligence involves understanding the natural world of plants and animals, noticing their characteristics, and categorizing them. It generally involves keen observation and the ability to classify other things as well. It may be exercised by exploring nature, making collections of objects, studying them, and grouping them. Children with this type of intelligence may like working on activities related to nature such as fishing, hiking, or camping.

Children with naturalistic intelligence enjoy outdoor activities and have a strong connection to the outside world or to animals (see Photo 5-9). They easily notice patterns and objects from nature. They love collecting flowers, rocks, and leaves. They may enjoy stories, shows, or any subjects that deal with animals or natural happenings. They are interested in the care

PHOTO 5-9 The child with a naturalistic intelligence enjoys outdoor activities.

of animals and zoology. These children also show an interest in endangered species. They easily learn the characteristics, names, and any information about species found in the world.

Older children love to learn the names of trees and flowers and have a good eye for the differences between them. They can spend hours compiling science reports on their favorite animals and exotic plants.

By exploring all of the intelligences, children become well-rounded individuals who are successful in many aspects of life. Early childhood teachers need to recognize these different strengths in children as they emerge. Some children may respond more to words, others to music, and still others to visual stimuli. The point is to plan activities that allow children to express themselves in the way that suits them best. If children have the opportunity to learn in ways that align with their particular intelligence(s) and to improve in those intellectual capacities that are not as strong, they will grow to become intelligent in more ways than one. In summary, the multiple intelligence theory can be a useful way to help children learn and truly understand what they are learning. Although the multiple intelligence theory has powerful implications for teachers, it is not an educational prescription (Nicholson-Nelson, 1998). You must decide how best to use it in your own classroom setting.

Did You Get It?

A kindergarten student who likes to play by himself and insists on completing tasks without the teacher's assistance is most likely displaying _____ intelligence.
- **a.** kinesthetic
- **b.** intrapersonal
- **c.** spatial
- **d.** logical

Take the full quiz on CourseMate.

5-5 Bloom's Taxonomy

DAP **naeyc** Another concept that fits into our discussion of effective teaching strategies is Bloom's taxonomy. Benjamin Bloom and his colleagues developed a classification system that has served educators since 1956. This system is a common structure for categorizing questions and designing instruction. The taxonomy is divided into six levels:

- **Knowledge:** Exhibit recollection of data.
- **Comprehension:** State a problem in one's own words.
- **Application:** Use knowledge in a new way.
- **Analysis:** Distinguish between facts and inferences.
- **Synthesis:** Put parts together to form a whole.
- **Evaluation:** Make judgments about the value of ideas, things.

In the 1950s, Bloom found that 95% of test questions developed to assess student learning required them only to think at the lowest level of learning—the recall of information. Information and/or knowledge alone are not enough. Then and today, knowledge without the ability to know how, when, and where to apply it, is ineffective.

In the early childhood classroom, then, the teacher must help students move up the ladder to higher-level thought. In order to foster children's creativity, higher-level thinking (above the first two levels of knowledge and comprehension) is crucial. As we have learned, the focus of creative activities is not to do things in the "right" way. Rather, the goal is to develop different ways of thinking and learning while being creative, exploring materials, and having fun. As discussed in earlier chapters, creative thinking involves creating something new or original. The aim of creative thinking is to stimulate curiosity and promote divergence. Figure 5-1 presents each level of thinking in Bloom's taxonomy with suggestions on useful verbs, sample question stems, and related potential activities and products for each level.

Did You Get It?

A fifth grade student openly questions a teacher's statements about maintaining one's health, pointing out that some of the facts the teacher quotes have not been proven. Which level of Bloom's Taxonomy is the student displaying?
- **a.** analysis
- **b.** synthesis
- **c.** knowledge
- **d.** comprehension

Take the full quiz on CourseMate.

KNOWLEDGE		
USEFUL VERBS	SAMPLE QUESTION STEMS	POTENTIAL ACTIVITIES/ PRODUCTS
Tell	What happened after . . . ?	Make a list of the main events.
List	How many . . . ?	Make a timeline of events.
Describe	Who was it that . . . ?	Make a facts chart.
Relate	Can you name the . . . ?	List all the . . . in the story.
Locate	Describe what happened at . . .	Make a chart showing . . .
Write	Who spoke to . . . ?	Recite a poem.
Find	Can you tell why . . . ?	
State	Find the meaning of . . .	
Name	What is . . . ?	
	Which is true or false?	
COMPREHENSION		
USEFUL VERBS	SAMPLE QUESTION STEMS	POTENTIAL ACTIVITIES/ PRODUCTS
Explain	Can you write in your own words?	Cut out or draw pictures to show a particular event.
Interpret	Can you write a brief outline?	Illustrate what you think the main idea was.
Outline	What do you think happened next?	Make a cartoon strip showing the sequence of events.
Discuss	What do you think?	Paint a picture of some aspect you like.
Distinguish	What was the main idea?	Make your own book about the story.
Predict	Who was the key character?	
Restate	Can you distinguish between?	
Translate	What are the differences between . . . ?	
Compare	Can you give me an example of . . . ?	
Describe	Can you give me a definition of . . . ?	

FIGURE 5-1 Bloom's taxonomy.   *(Continues)*

APPLICATION		
USEFUL VERBS	SAMPLE QUESTION STEMS	POTENTIAL ACTIVITIES/ PRODUCTS
Solve	Do you know another instance where . . . ?	Make a model to demonstrate how it will work.
Show	Could this have happened in . . . ?	Make a scrapbook about the areas of study.
Use	Can you group by characteristics such as . . . ?	Make a papier-mâché map.
Illustrate	What things would you change if . . . ?	Take a collection of photos to demonstrate a point.
Construct	Can you apply what you learned to some experience of your own?	Make a clay model of . . .
Complete	What questions would you ask of . . . ?	Paint a mural of . . .
Examine	From the information given, can you develop a set of instructions about . . . ?	
Classify	Would this information be useful if you had to . . . ?	
ANALYSIS		
USEFUL VERBS	SAMPLE QUESTION STEMS	POTENTIAL ACTIVITIES/ PRODUCTS
Analyze	Which events could have happened . . . ?	Make a family tree showing relationships.
Distinguish	How was this similar to . . . ?	Put on a play about the topic.
Examine	What was the underlying theme of . . . ?	Design a questionnaire to gather information.
Compare	Can you compare your . . . with that presented in . . . ?	Conduct an investigation to produce information to support a view.
Contrast	What do you see as other possible outcomes . . . ?	Make a jigsaw puzzle.
Investigate	Can you distinguish between . . . ?	Construct a graph to illustrate selected information.
Categorize	What was the turning point in . . . ?	Write a commercial to sell a product.
Identify	What was the problem with . . . ?	
Explain	Can you explain what must have happened where . . . ?	
Separate		
Advertise		

FIGURE 5-1 Bloom's taxonomy. *(Continued)*

SYNTHESIS		
USEFUL VERBS	SAMPLE QUESTION STEMS	POTENTIAL ACTIVITIES/ PRODUCTS
Create	Can you design a . . . to . . . ?	Invent a machine to do a specific task.
Invent	Why not compose a song about . . . ?	Create a new product.
Compose	Can you see a possible solution to . . . ?	Give it a name and plan a marketing campaign.
Predict	If you had access to all resources, how would you deal with . . . ?	Write about your feelings in relation to . . .
Plan	Why don't you devise your own way to deal with . . .	Design a CD, book, or magazine cover for . . .
Construct	What would happen if . . . ?	Write a TV show, play, puppet show, role-play, song, or pantomime about . . .
Design	How many ways can you . . . ?	Devise a way to . . .
Imagine	Can you create new and unusual uses for . . . ?	
Propose	Can you create a new recipe for a tasty dish?	
Devise		
Formulate		
EVALUATION		
USEFUL VERBS	SAMPLE QUESTION STEMS	POTENTIAL ACTIVITIES/ PRODUCTS
Judge	Is there a better solution to . . . ?	Prepare a list of criteria to judge a . . . show.
Select	Judge the value of . . .	Make a booklet about five rules you see as important.
Choose	Can you defend your position about . . . ?	Convince others that . . .
Decide	Do you think . . . is a good or bad thing?	Conduct a debate about an issue of special interest.
Justify	How would you have handled . . . ?	Write a half-yearly report.
Debate	What changes to . . . would you recommend?	Prepare a case to present your view about . . .
Verify	Do you believe?	

FIGURE 5-1 Bloom's taxonomy. *(Continued)*

EVALUATION		
USEFUL VERBS	SAMPLE QUESTION STEMS	POTENTIAL ACTIVITIES/ PRODUCTS
Argue	What do you think about . . . ?	
Recommend		
Assess		
Discuss		
Rate		
Prioritize		
Determine		

FIGURE 5-1 Bloom's taxonomy. *(Continued)*

5-6 Differentiated Instruction and Children with Special Needs

Adapting a classroom to accommodate children with special needs is a process similar to differentiating instruction. In both cases, the teacher provides activities and content, which are appropriate for each student. For this reason, it is essential to know the actual capabilities of each student. The following are some specific ways to adapt (or differentiate) instruction in the early childhood classroom for children with special needs.

- Meet each child at his or her own level of development, foster that stage, and enable the child to move on to the next level. For example, children have individual differences when it comes to motor development. Some children will be able to carry out complex actions such as tying their shoes or doing a complicated drawing, while others may barely be able to draw a line. A child with special needs in the motor area may barely be able to communicate preverbally with pointing, while other children without special needs may have lots of words but differ in the complexity of their thinking. Each needs to be worked with at his or her own level and then helped to advance.
- Tailor the environment to each child's strengths and weaknesses and help all children, special needs or not, build greater competency (see Photo 5-10).
- Interact with children in ways that help them to think and solve problems at their own levels.

Casper Holroyd

PHOTO 5-10 Teachers need to consider the age of the child and attention span when planning activities.

These interactions need to be a part of an ongoing, trusting relationship that children have with you and with each other. Having dynamic relationships is essential while climbing up the developmental ladder (Greenspan, 2001).

- Make sure that the child is gradually using most of his or her senses. For example, if a child has a visual-processing difficulty, begin by offering activities that draw on other senses, including hearing, smell, or touch, as a way to engage him or her. Gradually introduce simple visual-processing experiences. As the child comes to recognize that he or she can succeed, the child will feel more competent and be more inclined to participate in activities he or she finds challenging.

- Increase challenges in manageable, easy steps so children are successful 70% to 75% of the time. Again, keep in mind that it is important to use warm and caring words of encouragement and lively praise as children attempt to meet each new challenge (Greenspan, 2001).

For teachers with little or no previous experience with people with disabilities, having children with disabilities in their classrooms may provide them with the opportunity to learn to value such children for their unique strengths as well as to better understand their disabilities. Teachers and other adults may find that as they become acquainted with children who are disabled, their beliefs about physical or mental limitations are changed. For example, they may find the following:

- Children who are blind do not use alternative sensory channels for information automatically; they must learn to use hearing, smell, and tactile senses as well as movement to replace sight. Adults must help them develop these skills.
- Children with loss of hearing—even if the loss is severe or profound—are not necessarily quiet. They may be constantly babbling, chattering, or using jargon and other forms of unintelligible speech.
- Children with Down syndrome typically appear to be cheerful, compliant, and loving, but they are not always so. They may surprise you with anger and stubborn resistance.
- Children with severe and multiple physical handicaps such as cerebral palsy may have normal or superior cognitive ability masked by their inability to express themselves readily.

5-6a Adapting Instruction for Older Children with Special Needs

DAP **naeyc** Some suggestions for differentiating instruction and adapting a classroom for older children with special needs follow:

- Adapt the number of items that the learner is expected to learn or complete. For example, if typical learners are to know the 50 states, have students with special needs only be responsible

for remembering a certain number at a time. This would be dependent on the student's level of disability.

- Adapt the time allotted and allowed for learning, task completion, or testing. For example, allow the student with a special need additional time to complete timed assignments. If the total project is due by a particular time, have the student complete each portion of the project over various intervals with the required finished project due at a later time.
- Increase the amount of personal assistance you provide with a special-needs learner. For example, allow for peer teaching. Pair the special-needs learner with a more advanced student to provide support.
- Adapt the way instruction is delivered to the learner. For example, provide students with an audiotape and/or videotape of the lesson. Allow for field trips, guest speakers, peer teaching, computer support, or video productions performed by students.
- Adapt the skill level, problem type, or rules about how the learner may approach the work. For example, allow the student to be creative, provided that the task is completed according to the teacher's specifications. The student may draw a picture of the assignment or conduct an interview, depending on the subject. Allow the student to come up with the idea.
- Adapt how the student may respond to instruction. For example, allow students to draw pictures, write an essay, or complete specific computer software programs relating to the lesson.
- Adapt the extent to which a learner is actively involved in the task. Tailor the student's participation in a task to his or her abilities, whether intellectual or physical.
- Adapt the goals or outcome expectations while using the same materials. For example, in a writing assignment, alter the expectations for a student with disabilities who takes longer to write a paragraph.
- Provide different instructions and materials to meet a student's individual goals. For example, instead of requiring the student with special needs to memorize the names of the 50 states, allow her or him to work on a puzzle of the United States.

Working with Young Children Diagnosed with Asperger's Syndrome

Asperger's is classified as one of the autistic spectrum disorders (ASD). It is sometimes mistakenly diagnosed as attention deficit/hyperactivity disorder (ADHD), but early diagnosis is very important in order to redirect brain changes as social skills are developing. The list of ASD symptoms includes notable difficulty with social interaction, sensitivity to stimulation, and intense fixation on particular objects or tasks.

Although Asperger's has only recently become commonly known, it was first described in the 1940s by pediatrician Hans Asperger. An estimated 1.5 million people have Asperger's, and the diagnosis often comes later than other autism spectrum disorders, after age 3 (Eunice Kennedy Shriver National Institute of Child Health and Human Development, 2011).

Teaching a child with Asperger's can seem daunting, especially if you are unfamiliar with the disorder. If you are about to teach a student with Asperger's, understanding the syndrome is your best preparation. Children with Asperger's tend to have normal or above-normal intelligence and high verbal skills, though they may have a hard time expressing their thoughts. As younger children, they may show the ability to focus on one task for a long period of time, but they typically do not understand sarcasm, innuendo, or double meaning and have a hard time reading body language and social clues.

Children with Asperger's may have a very specific and even obsessive interest, such as baseball statistics, trains, or dinosaurs. If a child in your class is interested in a particular subject, incorporating it into your teaching when appropriate can help him focus on the lesson.

Because many children with Asperger's have difficulty with social interaction, they sometimes appear to be misbehaving when they don't mean to be. Some children with Asperger's do not realize that classroom rules apply to them. They may develop their own "rules" and have a high demand to be perfect.

While some students with Asperger's can focus on one subject, you might find they have trouble concentrating in other areas. A visual cue, such as a yellow warning card placed on the desk for distracting behavior or personalized instructions for what to do during down time, can help keep a child focused.

As students grow older and school routines change, different tactics might help. A peer educator to help the student with Asperger's can often help. The peer educator, for example, could meet the student at his locker in the morning. The peer educator could help cue the child about what she needs to get together for classes. Also, sitting the student next to compassionate students or children with similar interests, such as baseball or softball, can improve the atmosphere.

Teaching the other students in your group about ASD can help them handle with maturity and compassion the challenges classmates with Asperger's can present. Although many students may not grasp the concept of the autistic spectrum, they can understand that certain children are more sensitive and need a bit of extra help.

Helping your students understand Asperger's, or at least recognize some of its traits, will help them cope when they experience a child with an Asperger's meltdown. In this instance, another student can often calm down the student just by walking with him. Giving a child time to recompose—by sitting in a special "study desk" or talking to a counselor or teacher in the hall—can help get things back to normal.

Ask what caused the meltdown. For a younger child, it might be the texture of a pencil; an older child may have felt flustered when the room got too chaotic. But often the child may not be able to express what happened without a little digging on your part.

A tiny shift in the environment can make a huge difference for children with Asperger's. If you are not sure just what tiny shift your environment needs, experts recommend talking to the parents, who will most likely know their child better than anyone else.

Before school starts, it is a good idea to meet with parents and children separately. Show the child his cubby or desk, the bathroom, and the cafeteria. Expect that things may be a bit rough in the first few weeks. A positive change in the demeanor of a child with Asperger's typically happens after a few weeks, when they feel more comfortable in their setting.

Keeping the line of communication with parents open can help you work together to provide a positive learning environment. The goal is to help children with Asperger's learn and be able to adapt socially, and early childhood teachers need to consider every way of reaching these special children (Mosteller, 2010).

PHOTO 5-11 Teachers need to consider the age of the child and attention span when planning activities.

5-7 Attention Span, Activity Patterns, and Children's Physical Needs

DAP **naeyc** One must also consider a child's attention span and activity patterns when planning creative activities; it may mean the difference between successful creative learning experiences and creative activities that dissolve into chaos.

5-7a Attention Span

A general rule to remember on the length of a child's interests (**attention span**) is this: The younger the child, the shorter the attention span (see Photo 5-11). It is not unusual for toddlers and 2-year-olds to have a maximum attention span of 2-3 minutes on average. Attention span gradually increases as a child gets older, and a child of 6 can be expected to attend for an average of 15 minutes maximum. A teacher may come to expect a longer attention span than is really possible simply because the child maintains the appearance of attention. More often than not, however, young children make it quite obvious when their attention span is waning—by a yawn, a turned head, fidgeting, excess wiggling, or even by physically leaving—giving clear signs that attention to the task is "turned off."

An early childhood teacher needs to be able to read these obvious signs of lessening (or lost) attention. When they appear, it is time to move on to another topic, suggest a new activity, ask a question, do some "body stretching," or use any other change of pace to get back the child's interest. However, if a teacher has planned developmentally appropriate activities—those that are not too easy and present just enough of a challenge—even very young children will attend longer. Noting which activities keep the children's

interest longer and planning for their frequent inclusion in the program are good ways to work with children's developmental needs and interests. Including activities that appeal to the children's multiple intelligences is also part of planning developmentally appropriate activities for young children.

In direct contrast, many teachers feel compelled to "forge ahead" on their lesson plans despite children's lack of interest or involvement. Although it may be difficult to scrap one's lesson plans in midstream, it is even more difficult to try to "make" children pay attention when the activities just do not match their needs and interests. As many experienced teachers have found, it is far easier to work with children's specific needs and interests, adapting as necessary to meet their changing developmental needs. If, for instance, interest at the art center is waning and children choose to go elsewhere when allowed the option to do so, a teacher needs to reevaluate the activities in that center to see if they are, in fact, a suitable match for the developmental needs of the learners.

Children might be ready to move from tearing and pasting to trying out scissors because their fine motor skills are better developed from previous tearing experiences. Or they may be ready for colored markers as a change of pace from crayons. The point is that by changing activities and equipment to keep them matched to children's present developmental levels,

Casper Holroyd

you are helping those children attend to activities longer *on their own.* Young children will, however, never be bored using the same media over and over again if they have new, interesting, and exciting ideas, thoughts, and feelings to express. With a store of continual, meaningful experiences to think or feel something about, children's stores of ideas, feelings, and imagination will be constantly enriched.

When there is a new thought or feeling pushing to be expressed, children will continually be challenged to find new and different ways to use the same paints, clay, crayons, paper, and markers to give form to their ideas. Think about it: Adult artists use the same materials for decades. What changes is how they use the materials and what they want to communicate (Seefeldt, Galper, & Feeney, 2008).

Another approach to working with short attention spans is to plan around the expected attention span of the children in the group. For example, for a 10-minute circle time, a teacher of a group of 3-year-olds might plan an average of four activities taking about 2-3 minutes each. This could be four different finger plays; two poems, one finger play, and one song; or two Simon Says games and two finger plays. The point is to work with what you know about the group of young children with whom you are working.

Another important point about attention span is its highly individual nature. Some 3-year-olds may attend to a very favorite activity for longer than 3 minutes, while a 6-year-old first grader may not be able to attend to a language arts lesson for 5 minutes! In this case, you need to consider the match between the individual child and the specific activity.

5-7b Activity Patterns

Young children will generally attend better to new activities that are a good match to their present level of development—that is, activities that are neither too difficult nor too easy. It is also important to vary activities so that the new and the old are in an interesting as well as developmentally appropriate pattern for young children. A good **activity pattern** is one that begins with the familiar (or favorite), reviews some other related activities, and then moves on to introduce the new and different. For example, in introducing the letter B, the teacher may begin with a favorite song, "Buttons, the Clown." Then she has the children identify picture cards of foods that begin with B and later introduces the phoneme /b/ and related written words. In a similar activity pattern, a teacher of

4-year-olds begins with a favorite finger play about five little monkeys, has five children role play the monkeys, and then introduces a new book he plans to read about monkeys and their babies, which is part of a new animal unit.

An activity pattern for young children also must take into account their physical characteristics. Children develop large-muscle skills first and enjoy practicing these skills. They also need practice to develop small-motor skills. Therefore, activity patterns should include time for both large- and small-motor tasks. In the previous example, the teacher of 4-year-olds included a large-motor task (jumping like monkeys) with a small-motor task (a finger play). Including both types of activities in one session also helps increase attention span because they are favorite motor activities.

Creative activities for young children must also have a good balance between active and quiet activities (see Photo 5-12). All of one type activity would not be appropriate for the developmental needs of young children. A good rule to remember here follows: The younger the child, the greater the tendency to become overstimulated. Activities for toddlers and 2-year-olds should be limited in number to avoid overstimulation. Activities should be added as children can handle them.

Also, in a single instructional setting (or lesson), young children of all ages need active as well as quiet activities because they have a difficult time sitting quietly for extended periods. In the previous example with first graders, the teacher could provide an appropriate balance of active and quiet activities by having children go to the board and write a *b* on it or even

Casper Holroyd

PHOTO 5-12 Creative activities for young children must have a good balance between active and quiet activities.

Teachers, Parents, and the Economy: A National Survey

The 28th annual *MetLife Survey of the American Teacher: Teachers, Parents, and the Economy* was conducted by Harris Interactive to give voice to those closest to the classroom. The current MetLife survey examines the views of teachers, parents, and students about the teaching profession, parent and community engagement, and effects of the current economy on families and schools. Reports for the entire series are available online.

The survey of teachers was conducted by telephone between October 14 and November 10, 2011, among 1,001 U.S. K–12 public school teachers. The data were weighted where necessary to key demographic variables to bring them into line with their actual proportions in the population. The survey of parents was conducted online between October 18 and October 31, 2011, among 1,086 U.S. adults (aged 21 and older) who are parents or guardians of K–12 public school students. These data were also weighted to bring them into line with their actual proportions in the population.

The student survey was conducted between October 19 and October 27, 2011, among 947 U.S. public school students in grades 3 through 12.

Based on the surveys, the following issues were reported:

● Teachers are less satisfied with their careers; in the past two years, there has been a significant decline in teacher's satisfaction with their profession. In one of the most dramatic findings of the report, teacher satisfaction has decreased by 15 points since the *MetLife Survey of the American Teacher* measured job satisfaction two years ago, now reaching the lowest level of job satisfaction seen in the survey series in more than two decades. This decline in teacher satisfaction is coupled with large increases in the number of teachers who indicate that they are likely to leave teaching for another occupation and in the number who do not feel their jobs are secure.

Several factors distinguish teachers with high job satisfaction from those with lower satisfaction. Teachers with high job satisfaction are more likely to feel their jobs are secure and say they are treated as a professional by the community. They are also more likely to have adequate opportunities for professional development, time to collaborate with other teachers, more preparation and supports to engage parents effectively, and greater involvement of parents and their schools in coming together to improve the learning and success of students.

● The effects of the economic downturn are felt widely and deeply in education. More than three-quarters of teachers have faced budget cuts in their schools in the past year. These budget reductions have been enacted across the full range of school types: urban, suburban, and rural schools, as well as in schools with either low or high concentrations of low-income students, minority students, and English language learner (ELL) students. Two-thirds of teachers report that their schools have had layoffs.

Teachers in schools where layoffs of classroom teachers have occurred are more likely to have witnessed the reduction or elimination of programs and services in their schools. Overall, more than one-third of teachers experienced reductions or eliminations of programs in arts or music, foreign language, or physical education in the past year. Nearly 3 in 10 teachers indicate that there have been reductions or eliminations of health services or social services in their schools.

Beyond reductions in staffing, programs, and services, 6 in 10 teachers report that the average class size in their school has increased. One-third of teachers also indicate that educational technology and materials have not been kept up to date to meet student needs, while 2 in 10 report that school facilities have not been kept in clean or good condition.

● Parent and community engagement has increased in schools but remains a challenge for many schools. Most teachers (91%) and parents (80%) agree that their schools help all parents understand what they can do at home to support a student's success in school, and 83% of students agree that their teachers and parents work together to help them succeed in school.

However, the level of agreement declines for each group from elementary to middle to high school. Secondary school teachers (86% middle school, 88% high school) are less likely than elementary school teachers (93%) to agree that their school helps all parents understand what they can do at home to support a student's success in school.

● Far more students today report that they talk to their parents about school every day (64%) as compared to 40% who said they did so in 1988. The number of students who say their parents visit their school at least once a month has increased nearly threefold since 1988 from 16% to 46% today. (MetLife, 2012)

Child Development Associate Training and Its Impact on Preschool Teachers Beliefs and Practices

Two researchers at Georgia State University conducted a study to investigate the impact of Child Development Associate (CDA) credential training on the beliefs and self-reported practices of preschool teachers. The CDA credential is the entry-level teacher educational qualification for obtaining basic child development knowledge (Bredekamp, 2000). CDA training focuses on teachers' development of specific competencies that are directly tied to early childhood classroom practices. The 120 hours of required early childhood education can be obtained through college coursework, noncollege training, or a combination of the two (Council for Professional Recognition, 1999). Although the CDA credential has been awarded to 200,000 early childhood providers since its inception in 1971 (Council for Professional Recognition, 2007), there are remarkably few studies examining the effectiveness of this credentialing program (Bredekamp, 2000; Peters & Deiner, 1987; Tout, Zaslow & Berry, 2006) on teacher beliefs and self-reported practices.

This study examined the impact of CDA training on the beliefs and practices of early childhood teachers who did not have college degrees or early childhood college coursework. Preschool teachers who were enrolled in CDA classes (N=76) and a comparison group of teachers (N=50) completed two surveys of beliefs and practices.

Seventeen CDA programs in the study were located in urban, suburban, and rural locations across the state of Georgia. Seventy-six teachers enrolled in CDA training completed the study. As required by CDA, all participants were working as child-care providers or teachers in center-based care. To control for the influence of prior college coursework, only teachers who had no early childhood coursework in the past 10 years, and no college degree (associate's or bachelor's) were eligible to participate in the study.

Fifty child-care providers who were not enrolled in CDA training completed the study. Participants had to meet the same education criterion as CDA participants and had to be interested in obtaining or pursuing a CDA credential, early childhood diploma, or associate's degree in the future.

The scale used to measure the child-care providers' beliefs and practices was the Early Childhood Survey of Beliefs and Practices (ECSBP) (Marcon, 1999). The ECSBP focuses on participants' conceptions of early childhood beliefs and self-reported practices on a continuum from a teacher-directed style of teaching to one that is more child-centered (developmentally appropriate).

Repeated Measures Multivariate Analyses of Variance indicated that the CDA training teachers decreased the amount they endorsed beliefs and practices that contrast with DAP over time more than the comparison teachers. They increased their beliefs in DAP after the CDA course. These results suggest that CDA training can be an effective means of increasing the developmental appropriateness of beliefs and self-reported practices of early childhood teachers, which past research suggests will ultimately impact classroom quality (Heisner & Lederberg, 2011).

---

having them walk over to an object beginning with the letter *b*. This way, children's physical inability to sit quietly for extended amounts of time is considered in the lesson. In the example of the teacher of 4-year-olds, we see similar planning for active (jumping) behavior and quiet (listening to a story) behavior. By following the more active activity with a quieter activity, the teacher is working with the physical needs of young children to be active and to rest after exertion.

5-7c Transitions from Group Times

naeyc Transitions from group times to the next activities can be chaotic if group times are uninteresting, too long, or too demanding. If children in a group become wiggly and uncomfortable, you can expect a difficult transition. Even a short, interesting group time can end with a mad exodus if precautions are not taken.

Children don't settle down immediately between activities. They need time to transition between active and more concentrated, quiet play. Getting rid of wiggles on demand is seldom an easy process. Each child has her or his own way and time to achieve quiet. A group of young children without wiggles would be cause for concern. A healthy group of children needs a patient teacher, one who can accept the various ways in which individual children respond to the request for quiet.

THIS ONE'S FOR YOU!

Transitions That Work During the School Day

Transitions can be one of the most challenging parts of any school day. These times of the day find children moving and/or changing from one activity to another. Designing a schedule that minimizes transitions and maximizes the time children spend engaged in developmentally appropriate activities is the first step in decreasing challenging behavior.

Occasionally, children may experience challenges during transitions when they do not understand expectations or if program staff is inconsistent in the structure or the implementation of transitions. The following suggestions are meant to provide guidance to best support children and staff with successful transitions:

- Plan for transitions in your day as you would plan for any group activity. Remember that transitions have a beginning, middle, and end, like other activities. Transition activities can be anything from reading a book, telling a story that actively involves children, or singing songs and saying rhymes that involve hand and/or body movements.

- Prepare materials *ahead* of time and have them easily accessible so that your attention is always on the children instead of trying to find your materials.

- Show respect for children's needs by giving them warnings before transitions. Visual and/or auditory cues help children know when a change is about to occur. Examples of possible cues or signals could be turning the lights off, ringing a bell, singing a special song, or saying something like, "Hands go up!" or "One, two, three all eyes looking at me!" Be sure to give the signal about 5 minutes before the change is to occur and say to the children, "The next time… you hear the bell, the lights go out, or you hear me say "Hands go up!"… it will be time to clean up, go inside, come to group, and so on." Ask the children to give a "thumbs up" so you know they heard the transitional warning.

- For children who are new to your class, take a long time to transition, or have difficulty with transitions, give them individual guidance *prior* to when you give the whole class their warning that a transition is about to happen. Touch, guide, and speak to them about the upcoming transition and help them think about what they will need to do to transition to the next activity. For example, tell the child that it will soon be time to clean up and to think about what he or she wants to pick up when it is cleanup time.

- Try to make certain that enjoyable activities follow less motivating ones. For example, a statement like, "After everyone is finished cleaning up, we will go outside," encourages more cooperation and compliance.

- Give age-appropriate directions, with one direction at a time. Be clear and specific, and be careful not to talk too much.

- Teach children the expectations for the classroom routines. Consider providing visual routine charts and/or picture clues that "show and tell" children what to do with their body as they transition. For example, when lining up to go from outside to inside, children should put both of their feet on a mark on the floor and hands by their side.

- Consider what the children and adults will do during these times. For example, once most of the classroom is cleaned, one teacher can continue to facilitate cleanup, and the other can sit on the carpet reading books with the children.

- Avoid moving "whole" groups of children. Transition children one at a time or in small groups.

- Reduce the number of transitions in your school day. Remember that with transitions, less is more! Consider what transitions can be eliminated or incorporated in other times of the day. For example, you might consider having snack as a center activity and allow children to go to that center as they would go to any center in the classroom.

- Remember that the teacher always sets the tone, so be sure to consistently give advance publicity for the next activity and to use a voice of excitement.

Another suggestion for preventing chaotic transitions from group times is to share the day's schedule with the children at the beginning of the day so they know what will happen. Any special rules may need to be reviewed. Then as each activity begins and ends, reminders will suffice: "Do you remember what we are going to do after our story today?" "When we get ready for our walk, we will need to get our coats. How can we do that without bumping into each other when we leave the circle?" When children help with the plans and participate in setting the limits, they are more apt to understand, remember, and be willing to help enforce the rules. Do not forget to give positive reinforcement when things go well, not just reminders when someone fails to remember. However, positive reinforcement should not become so automatic or

Younger Children in the Classroom Likely Overdiagnosed with ADHD

The youngest children in the classroom are significantly more likely to be diagnosed with attention deficit/hyperactivity disorder (ADHD)—and prescribed medication—than their peers in the same grade, according to a study in the Canadian Medical Association Journal (Morrow et al., 2012).

ADHD, which is often treated with prescription medication, is the most commonly diagnosed behavioral disorder in children. This study has shown a link between the relative age of children and diagnosis of ADHD and prescription of medication. Younger children in the same grade as children who may be almost a year older may appear to be immature compared with their older peers. This apparent lag in maturity has been called the "relative-age effect" and influences both academic and athletic performance.

Researchers from the University of British Columbia were interested to see whether this relative age effect was present in Canada and looked at a large cohort of 937,943 children in British Columbia, a province where the cutoff for entry into kindergarten or grade 1 is December 31. The research included children who were between 6 and 12 years old at any point during the 11-year study.

Researchers found that children were 39% more likely to be diagnosed and 48% more likely to be treated with medication for ADHD if born in December compared to January. Due to the Dec. 31 cutoff birth date for entry into school in British Columbia, children born in December would typically be almost a year younger than their classmates born in January.

"The relative age of children is influencing whether they are diagnosed and treated for ADHD," said lead author, Richard Morrow, University of British Columbia. "Our study suggests younger, less mature children are inappropriately being labeled and treated. It is important not to expose children to potential harms from unnecessary diagnosis and use of medications" (2012).

There are significant health and social ramifications of inappropriate diagnoses of ADHD. Medication to treat ADHD can have negative health effects in children such as sleep disruption, increased risk of cardiovascular events, and slower growth rates. Younger children who have been labeled ADHD may also be treated differently by teachers and parents, which could lead to negative self-perception and social issues.

Boys who were born in December were 30% more likely to receive a diagnosis of ADHD than boys born in January. Girls born in December were 70% more likely to receive a diagnosis of ADHD than girls born in January. Similarly boys were 41% more likely and girls 77% more likely to be given a prescription for medication to treat ADHD if they were born in December than if they were born in June. (Morrow et al., 2012)

---

mechanical that children begin to doubt its sincerity. Some genuine response—a smile, pat, or word—is always more effective than a stock phrase.

5-7d Transitions to Free-Choice Times

A key strategy for avoiding mad dashes at the beginning of free-choice times is the assurance that children will have ample time for their favorite activities. If free-choice time is too short or few activities are interesting, some children will run to grab their chosen activity. Others will flit about aimlessly and not bother to start anything because they know they will have to stop soon. It is important to have enough interesting things to do and to use a system that allows children to select a second activity if the first is not satisfactory. Children who are bored or frustrated during free-choice time are rarely cooperative when it is time to clean up. A free-choice time that is too long, however, will give you tired children who are no longer constructively busy and are ready to misbehave. It takes flexibility and a good eye for the quality of work and play to know the right amount of time for free play.

5-7e Transitions to Group Times: Back Together

Moving into a group time is often facilitated by a little advance publicity. It builds interest to have something in a bag and as the children ask about it, say, "I'll show you at group time." Children will look forward to group times in which they have a chance to show their block building, artwork, or the book they have drawn and stapled. The morning planning time can give advance notice of exciting things to come, and reminders can keep interest alive throughout the day.

From the first arrival at group time, there should be a teacher or classroom assistant in place to be with the children. Trying to control behavior at a distance is always hazardous and never more so than during a transition.

Sometimes teachers let children look at books until all are ready for story time or music. When the last things are put away at cleanup time, the teacher walks over to the rug and says, "Time to collect the books." Some children have just arrived and have opened the cover of their favorite storybook. Some children are in the middle of reading their favorite book. Some children may resist, and some might cooperate, but they will all be left with the feeling that the teacher does not value books except as a tool to keep them quiet.

You might try this different approach. When all the children are seated and looking at books, sit down with them. You may share books with some of the children or just wait for a reasonable period of time. Then you may give a warning that it will soon be time to put the books away. As children finish, collect their books and allow others to finish while you begin the discussion or possibly a finger play to occupy those who are through. When most books have been collected, then you may have your group activity. This process respects children and their interest in books.

> "Be careful what you say to children. When their bones are brittle and their hair silver, they will quote you in their hearts."
>
> —Rheta Grimsley Johnson

Did You Get It?

Which activity is most likely to hold a three-year-old's interest for a long period of time?
- **a.** watching a video
- **b.** playing a challenging game of "Simon Says"
- **c.** playing on a swing set
- **d.** drawing pictures with crayons

Take the full quiz on CourseMate.

5-8 Consider the Teacher/Caregiver: Attitude

DAP **naeyc** Attitude is basic to facilitating creative activities with young children. Some teacher attitudes and ideas that help facilitate creative behavior in young children include the following:

- **Tolerate small mistakes.** When children do not have to worry about being perfect, they have more energy to be creative.
- **Avoid telling the child the best way to do things.** To tell a child the best way implies, first, that the teacher knows it; second, that the child does not know it; and third, that the child has to ask the teacher to know the next time.

Be concerned about what children are doing—not about the final product. In creative activities, young children are in a process—playing, drawing, painting, and building. Although they are interested in mastering tasks and producing things of which they are proud, they are not like adults. The final product may not be as important as experimenting or as using their minds and senses while doing it. That is why young children often build a complex structure with blocks and then take great joy in knocking it over. They want to see what happens!

Older children enjoy the process of creating as well as younger children. However, older children will show more concern for the product, which is natural at this developmental level. Encouraging an open, "what-if?" approach to creative activities will help the older child concentrate on the process as well as the product.

5-8a Speaking with Children

DAP **naeyc** The way a teacher speaks to and with a young child can mean the difference between the child's positive feelings of self and those not-so-positive feelings. Cherish their uniqueness. The following suggestions may be helpful as you work with young children and help them grow.

- Before speaking to children, get their attention. Putting your hand on a child's shoulder or speaking the child's name helps. As much as possible, stoop to the child's eye level.
- The younger the child, the simpler your statement should be.
- Act as if you expect your words to be heeded. Young children are influenced by the confidence in the adult's tone and action.

- Give children time to respond—their reaction time is slower than yours. Try not to answer your own questions!
- Tell children what they *can* do rather than what they *cannot* do. Use positive rather than negative suggestions or statements.
- Give only as much help as is needed, and give simple directions. Use manual guidance to aid verbal suggestions with young children.
- Use encouraging rather than discouraging statements: "You can do it," not "Is it too hard?"
- Use specific rather than general statements: "You need to put on your socks and now your shoes," not, "Put on your clothes."
- Use pleasant requests rather than scolding: "You will need to pick up your materials now," not, "Get those things picked up."
- Use substitute suggestions rather than negative comments: "Use that pencil from the drawer over there," not, "Don't use that."
- Give a choice between two things when possible. You might say, "Will you wash your face, or shall I help you?" This means the child will be washed in any case. Never give a choice where there is none, such as, "Do you want to wash?" when washing is necessary. Try not to say, "Would you like to?" if you do not intend to abide by the child's choice.
- Remember to show disapproval in what the child does when necessary, but never disapproval of the child. You can say, "You are a good climber, but you will need to climb on the jungle gym. This roof is not solid enough."
- Working with a child—trying to tell or show the child how to do it alone—is better for learning than doing it for the child.
- Keep your promises to children. For example, if you say you will let someone have a turn later, be sure to offer that turn as soon as you can, even though the child may have found another activity. Let the child decide whether to leave the present activity to take a turn.
- Encourage children to use language (to replace physical force, crying, whining, and so on) to communicate their problems, needs, and wishes.

Children learn through example. Many things, such as manners, are "caught," not always necessarily "taught."

Resist the temptation to always have quiet and order. Silence may not be the spirit of joy. Cleanliness may not be the companion of discovery. Timing and flexibility are all important in these matters.

Get involved. The teacher who is painting, drawing, and working beside the children or accompanying them on a field trip or a walk is a companion and friend. To children, the activity must be worth doing if the teacher is doing it, too. This helps motivation and is a legitimate entry into the children's world. Besides, it's fun! Be careful, however, not to cause children to copy what you are doing. Be sure to "slip away" before this happens.

Did You Get It?

A five-year-old pours too much glue on her paper, drenching the page. In order to foster creativity, the teacher should comment,

a. "That's okay, here's another paper."

b. "It's okay, but next time, tilt the glue bottle the same way I do to avoid spilling it."

c. "What do you think you should do next?"

d. "Who can help clean up the glue?"

Take the full quiz on CourseMate.

5-9 Strategies for Success: General Planning Guidelines

DAP **naeyc** Teachers plan creative activities with children's needs and interests in mind. In addition to assessing whether the planned activity is developmentally appropriate for a particular group of children, there are some general planning guidelines to follow that will help ensure the success of these activities.

5-9a Preparation

Often, teachers attempt a creative activity that they have not experienced before. They may have read about it in a book, heard about it from a friend, or seen it at a workshop. They try it because they feel it should work and the children should gain something from it. Often it does succeed, but sometimes it does not. The unfortunate part is that when it does not, the teacher may not know whether it was because of the activity itself or the way it was prepared for and offered. For any activity, especially for a first-time experience, the following suggestions may be helpful.

Try the activity before presenting it to the children Do this physically, if possible, or else mentally. Sometimes things sound better than they really are. The children should experiment, not be experimented on.

Make sure all necessary equipment is available. Too few scissors, paints without brushes, and paper without paste can cause a great deal of frustration. Creativity and frustration don't mix well.

Think through the activity. Review in your mind (and on paper) the best way to present the activity, step by step. Consider what might be the best time of the day for the activity. Think about how you will distribute the materials. Think through the activity and write down the necessary steps in sequential order.

Modify the activity, if necessary, to meet the developmental needs of the children. Few activities are right for all cultures, all situations, or every type of child. Be sure to include appropriate materials for children with special needs. All teachers must be sensitive to this.

Briefly explain the activity so that the children know how to begin and proceed. For this part, rules are not necessary but understanding is.

After the children have started, circulate among them. Offer suggestions where helpful, and answer questions as needed. Try to let the children answer their own questions as well as solve their own problems. The teacher's role remains that of facilitator.

5-9b Presentation of Creative Activities

The success of any creative activity is influenced by how it is presented, which in turn is affected by how prepared the teacher is for guiding the children in the activity. In planning for each activity, the teacher should do the following.

> Identify goals for the activity.
> Identify possible learning from the activity.
> List the materials necessary for the activity.
> Determine how to set up the activity.
> Decide how to stimulate the children and how to keep their interest alive.
> Anticipate questions the children might ask.
> Plan ways to evaluate the activity.
> Consider follow-up activities.
> Consider cleanup time and requirements.

A broad range of creative activities should be included each week. This gives children a variety of choices to suit their many interests. Not only should each curriculum area be highlighted, but certain types of behavior should also be considered. Dramatic play, creative movement, singing, outdoor activities, and small-group projects should all take place within each week.

Do not move too fast when presenting new ideas or activities for young children. As we learned earlier, when using methods of differentiated instruction, time is flexible and is based on the needs of the child. Children need time to explore and create with new materials. For the very young child, even more time may be needed. Activities should be repeated so that the children learn new ways of approaching the material and expand their understanding through repetition. Purposely leave out specific art activities in the classroom for several days so that if a child does not want to try it the first day or the second day, she has another chance.

Proper sequencing should be given close attention. Activities should build upon each other. For example, some children may want to taste, feel, and smell an apple before they draw or paint one. Once a child is involved in a creative activity, a few words of encouragement may be all that is needed to keep the child interested. It is useful to watch for children who are having problems. A little help may be needed to solve a small problem. Children need enough time to finish an activity. Be sure children are not stopped just when they are beginning to have fun.

5-9c Completing a Creative Activity

At the end of each day, the teacher evaluates the day's activities. Ideas for the next day can be revised or created based on what then appears best. What were the successes of the day? How interested were the children in what they were doing? What did their conversation and play indicate? What does the teacher feel like doing? The key words are *question*, *think*, *feel*, and *decide*. A person who works with young children must always be open to new information and feedback.

> ### Did You Get It?
>
> A preschool teacher allots six sessions each week to playing with clay and often leaves the clay out where the students can approach and touch it. From a creativity viewpoint, the value of the teacher's approach is that it
>
> **a.** gives a focus to the classroom.
> **b.** minimizes fighting over materials.
> **c.** strengthens the students' manipulative abilities.
> **d.** expands the students' understanding of the clay.
>
> **Take the full quiz on CourseMate.**

5-10 Strategies for Success— The National Level

DAP naeyc All of the information in this chapter so far has centered on the developmental approach to teaching young children. This is, and will continue to be, the most basic and direct approach to working with young children in creative activities and in all other areas. However, anyone who teaches young children in the United States today needs to be aware of the three-pronged national focus on (1) legislation in education, (2) content standards, and (3) standards for teachers. What follows is a brief description of each of these three areas.

5-10a Legislation and Education

In 2001, Congress authorized the No Child Left Behind (NCLB) Act. This particular act has been highly publicized for its dramatic emphasis on improving U.S. schools to create more equitable educational opportunities for all children. NCLB is intended to provide all children with a fair, equal, and significant opportunity to obtain a high-quality education. One of the most significant provisions of NCLB is the requirement that states set standards and conduct annual assessments to gauge school districts' progress in improving students' academic achievement. Schools were given report cards based on student performance, and many schools were labeled as "failing" if subgroups of students did not reach proficiency. Critics of the program claimed that the high stakes led teachers to "teach to the test." Most recently, the Department of Education has allowed waivers for some states, which the majority of states have applied for. In lieu of the NCLB, states that requested a waiver were able to opt out and develop their own standards and forms of student testing.

The idea of launching a common set of national standards called the Common Core Standards, began in 2009 as an initiative of the National Governors Association and the Council of Chief State School Officers. This initiative did not come from the federal government. The U.S. Department of Education's Race to the Top grant competition spurred many states to reform curriculum and embrace the Common Core Standards.

The Common Core Standards establish a clear and consistent map for what students should learn from kindergarten through high school to better prepare them for college and career.

Governing English language arts and math, the standards are meant to be more rigorous, with a goal of producing high school graduates who are critical thinkers, effective communicators, and problem solvers. More information on English and math Common Core Standards can be found in Chapter 18 and Chapter 20.

5-10b Content Standards

State departments of education are required to develop challenging academic content standards and academic assessments, both under the NCLB and the Common Core Standards.

These content standards are important for preschool teachers as well as K–5 teachers. Although most national standards are written for grades K–12, they are often written in broad language, making them applicable in some cases to prekindergarten. Some national standards written for the primary grades begin with pre-K. Also, most states have developed or are developing their own content standards, and these often include pre-K content standards. Head Start has developed its own set of standards, the Head Start Child Outcomes Framework (2009). These serve as a framework of building blocks that are important for school success.

As a result of the development of content standards, many early childhood teachers have been increasingly integrating the subject matter standards into their programs for several years and have been involved in the standards movement in many states. Most teachers recognize that we must have expectations and standards for our early childhood programs. But they also know the nature of learning at this age, and they carefully define how content standards are most appropriately and effectively incorporated into preschool and kindergarten programs. Because a program uses playful ways to build children's success does not mean the curriculum is not rigorous or content based. It means that it is just right for what's best for 3-, 4-, and 5-year-old children.

With regard to the emphasis on assessment that is part of both the NCLB and Common Core Standards, observation of young children is at the heart of early childhood practice. As we have seen earlier, the early childhood curriculum grows out of an understanding of the young child. Knowing as much as possible about each child's uniqueness, strengths, and needs, educators can create an effective environment to support development and learning for all ages.

As early childhood professionals, we must create our own definition of assessment rather than yielding to others' definitions. Owning the word, we can keep its meaning from narrowing to the domain of standardized tests or high-stakes evaluation. Owning the word in our developmental sense, we can keep the conversation focused on the *uses* of assessment—not assessment as an end in itself but as a means of helping young children and families reach valuable goals.

5-10c Early Childhood Learning Standards

Content standards are no longer the domain of elementary education. Early learning standards for preschool children are all around us. Early childhood standards have been implemented across the United States in mathematics, science, social studies, social/emotional development, physical development and health, and the creative arts.

Just what are early learning standards for preschool children? The Early Childhood Education Assessment Consortium of the Council of Chief State School Officers (CCSSO) defines early learning standards as those that "describe expectations for the learning and development of young children across the domains of health and physical well-being; approaches to learning; language development and symbol systems; and general knowledge about the world around them" (http://www.ccsso.org).

Most of the learning standards developed are for the preschool years, ages 3–5. However, some states have also developed (or are developing) standards or expectations for infants and toddlers.

All of these state early learning standards have many features in common and are based on generally accepted knowledge of child development. The differences lie in the formatting or the inclusion of specific content or developmental areas. On the federal level, Head Start developed a Child Outcomes Framework in 2000. This framework is now an important part of the evaluation of the effectiveness of Head Start programs across the country. Standards for children younger than kindergarten age differ from those for older children because the primary tasks of young children are to acquire and refine foundational skills—skills that will help them successfully learn content in the later grades. The National Association for the Education of Young Children (NAEYC) and the National Association of Early Childhood Specialists in State Departments of Education (NAECS/SDE) in a joint policy statement suggest that early learning standards can be a valuable part of a comprehensive, high-quality system of services for young children (NAEYC, 2009).

However, throughout the field of education there is cause for concern about how these standards are used. In the same joint NAEYC and NAECS/SDE position statement, the authors warn that there are educational and developmental risks for vulnerable young children if standards are not well developed and implemented (NAEYC, 2009).

However, there are some definite benefits to standards if they are used in the proper way.

- Standards reinforce the fact that there is an incredible potential for learning and growth in the infant, toddler, and preschool years and that there is value and importance in providing high-quality early childhood programs for children's long-term success in school and in life.
- Standards help establish expectations for children at different ages and create a commonality for communication about children's accomplishments and capabilities.
- Standards provide a framework for accountability—a way for early educators to show parents, the community at large, and themselves just what children are learning in early childhood programs (NAEYC, 2009).

Just as with all other national standards, there are some definite drawbacks to early learning standards:

- They can lead to teaching only to the standards in a cookie-cutter style curriculum.
- They bring a pressure of accountability with the risk of a push down in curriculum and inappropriate expectations for younger children.
- They can result in testing and other inappropriate assessment methods being used with young children.
- Direct instruction is often assumed to be the only way to guarantee that standards are addressed. Children's learning in self-directed, exploratory ways is not trusted.

Many experienced early childhood teachers very likely could add to this list of arguments against early learning standards. Yet it is crucial for early childhood educators to take an active interest in these early learning standards to ensure that the best interests of young children are served in their use. As in all issues related to young children, educators need to be constantly vigilant that the developmental needs of our youngest citizens are acknowledged and respected in all standards and curriculum issues.

The third and final focus in our discussion directs the issue of standards for the teacher.

5-10d Standards for Teachers—INTASC Standards

Interstate New Teacher Assessment and Support Consortium (INTASC) standards are model standards for licensing new teachers. Drafted by representatives of the teaching profession, along with personnel from 17 state education agencies, these standards represent a common core of teaching knowledge and skills that will help all students acquire twenty-first-century knowledge and skills. An important attribute of these standards is that they are performance based—that is, they describe key indicators, or what teachers should know and be able to do, rather than listing courses that teachers should take in order to be awarded a license.

Did You Get It?

The NCLB and the Common Core standards emphasize assessment. A preschool teacher can use assessment in a way that promotes creativity by

a. focusing on observation as a means of helping students to develop.
b. testing students in a group format.
c. evaluating students while they are playing.
d. developing his or her own assessment methods.

Take the full quiz on CourseMate.

Summary

5-1 Discuss what factors are involved when considering a child's developmental level.

When we speak of a child's development, we are referring to four major areas of growth: physical, social, emotional, and intellectual. These areas serve as a framework on which we organize our knowledge and observations of children. These four areas combined make up the individual child.

5-2 Discuss the term developmentally appropriate practice.

The teacher's plans need to take into consideration: (1) children's needs and interests, (2) their developmental levels, and (3) available materials and resources. These are the basic concepts in developmentally appropriate practice (DAP).

5-3 Discuss the terms differentiated instruction and process learning.

Differentiated instruction involves providing different types of learning experiences and environments to meet children's individual needs. Process learning is another term associated with differentiated instruction. It conceives of learning in terms of its processes rather than its products. In process learning, the focus is on providing children experiences that promote thinking and problem solving without specifically identified outcomes.

5-4 Discuss the term multiple intelligences.

Gardner's multiple intelligence theory provides further insight on how to meet children's needs by knowing how each child is "smart." According to his theory, each of us possesses eight "intelligences": word smart, logic smart, picture smart, music smart, body smart, person smart, self smart, and nature smart. By recognizing multiple intelligences, we can help children enhance their individual strengths.

5-5 Explain Bloom's taxonomy and its place in the early childhood environment.

Bloom's taxonomy gives us a tool to encourage children's higher-level thinking. It is divided into six levels: knowledge, comprehension, application, analysis, synthesis, and evaluation. In the early childhood classroom, the teacher helps students move up the ladder to higher-level thinking (above the first two levels of knowledge and comprehension).

5-6 Explain how differentiated instruction can be applied in working with children with special needs.

Adapting a classroom to accommodate children with special needs is a process similar to differentiating instruction. In both cases, the teacher provides activities and content, which are appropriate for each student. For this reason, it is essential to know the actual capabilities of each student. The following are some specific ways to adapt (or differentiate) instruction in the early childhood classroom for children with special needs.

- Meet each child at his or her own level of development, foster that stage, and enable the child to move on to the next level.
- Tailor the environment to each child's strengths and weaknesses, and help all children, special needs or not, to build greater competency.
- Interact with children in ways that help them think and solve problems at their own levels.
- Make sure that the child is gradually using most of his or her senses.
- Increase challenges in manageable, easy steps so children are successful 70% to 75% of the time.

5-7 Discuss attention span and activity patterns as they relate to young children.

A teacher should have reasonable expectations of how long young children can be attentive in certain activities. A general rule to remember on the length of a child's interests (attention span) is this: The younger the child, the shorter the attention span. Attention span gradually increases as a child gets older, and a child of 6 can be expected to attend for an average of 15 minutes maximum. It is also important to vary activities so that the new and the old are in an interesting as well as developmentally appropriate pattern for young children. A good activity pattern is one that begins with the familiar (or favorite), reviews some other related activities, and then moves on to introduce the new and different. The teacher should also know how to supervise these activities so that there is a good balance between active and quiet ones.

5-8 Discuss three aspects of the teacher's attitude that have an impact on children's creativity.

A teacher's attitude is basic to facilitating creative activities with young children. Some teacher attitudes and ideas that help facilitate creative behavior in young children include the following:

- Tolerate small mistakes.
- Avoid telling the child the best way to do things.
- Resist the temptation to always have quiet and order.
- Get involved working beside the children.

5-9 List the general planning guidelines for creative activities.

To ensure the success of creative activities, careful planning is essential. The following are guidelines for preparation:

- Try the activity before presenting it to the children.
- Make sure all necessary equipment is available.
- Think through the activity.
- Modify the activity, if necessary, to meet the developmental needs of the children.
- Briefly explain the activity so that the children know how to begin and proceed.

- After the children have started, circulate among them.
- Once the creative activity is finished, its success should be evaluated in terms of individual and program goals.

5-10 Discuss strategies for success on the national level, including legislation, content standards, early childhood learning standards, and standards for teachers.

The No Child Left Behind legislation of 2001 has most recently been revised to allow states to request waivers from many of the adequate yearly progress (AYP) requirements for all schools. Due to the NCLB, state departments of education have developed academic content standards to measure students' academic progress. Across the United States, early learning standards are now available for preschool children. Most of these standards are for the preschool years, while some states have also developed standards or expectations for infants and toddlers. The Interstate New Teacher Assessment and Support Consortium (INTASC) standards are model standards for licensing new teachers. These standards represent a common core of teaching knowledge and skills that will help all students acquire twenty-first century knowledge and skills. These standards are performance based—that is, they describe key indicators, or what teachers should know and be able to do, rather than listing courses that teachers should take in order to be awarded a license.

Key Terms

activity pattern 103	developmental level 84	individual differences 84
Asperger's Syndrome 101	differentiated instruction 88	key indicators 113
attention span 102	emergent curriculum 87	national standards 111
Bloom's taxonomy 95	facilitate 84	No Child Left Behind (NCLB) Act 111
Common Core Standards 111	Gardner's multiple intelligence	process learning 90
developmentally appropriate	theory 90	Reggio Emilia approach 86
practice (DAP) 85		

Learning Activities

A. Check the list of attitudes found in this unit that facilitate creative behavior in young children.
   1. Choose one example of each from your personal life in which you demonstrate the attitude.
   2. Decide whether this is an attitude you already possess or one that you need to work on in order to improve.
   3. Explain how you might go about modifying those attitudes in need of improvement.

B. There are strategies that teachers use to create a good climate for creative activities. There are other factors that may cause a child's creativity to be hindered by a teacher.
   1. Make a list of five dos and don'ts for creative activities in the early childhood setting.

   2. If possible, compare and discuss your list with those of your classmates.
   3. Observe a teacher who is supervising a creative activity in an early childhood classroom. What does he or she do to facilitate children's expression of creativity?

C. Using the information in this chapter on planning and presentation of creative activities, plan a creative activity for (a) 3-year-olds and third graders or (b) 4-year-olds and fourth graders. In your activity plan, consider the following:

- Developmental needs of the children
- Attention span
- Physical ability

- Activity level
- Appropriate materials
- Appropriate motivation

D. Use the observation sheet on MindTap to assess your own multiple intelligences. Were you surprised by anything you learned about yourself? Can you apply this learning to your teaching? How?

E. Use the observation sheet on MindTap to help you reflect on your personal teaching style. Which intelligences are the strongest in you? Which are the weakest? Are you neglecting types of activities because of your own weaknesses?

F. Find the National Standards for Arts Education on the Kennedy Center's ArtsEdge website. Find curricula, lessons, and activities linked to these national standards that you can use with children in your group.

G. Hands-On Multiple Intelligences Activities

Hands-on experience is the easiest way to explain multiple intelligences. Here's an exercise to try with your fellow students to learn more about Gardner's eight areas of intelligence.
1. Give each person an apple.
2. Ask participants to experience their apples using Gardner's eight intelligences.

Examples:

Linguistic intelligence: Have participants describe how the apple looks.

Bodily kinesthetic/intrapersonal intelligence: How does the apple feel? Touch the apple.

Logical/mathematical intelligence: What shape is the apple? Sort apples by color and size. Share the apples.

Interpersonal intelligence: Compare the apple to your neighbor's apple.

Kinesthetic Intelligence: Taste the apple.

Transition Ideas

Transitioning from one activity to another can be a taxing experience. Students often become engrossed in what they are doing and don't want to move on to the next activity. They may become confused when they are asked to end one activity and start another. Using specific activities for transitions can help avoid chaos and headaches. Here are some suggestions for transition activities to try with your group of children.

Clapping

Clapping can serve as a means of indicating a transition from one activity to another. When the time comes that you want children to switch activities, loudly clap out a pattern. Upon hearing the clap, the children are to stop what they are doing and repeat the clap, giving you their undivided attention. You will probably have to clap your pattern a few times before you have everyone's attention. However, with each series of claps, you will gain more and more of the children's attention and eventually have all of their attention. Once you see all eyes on you, tell children what you expect them to do.

Magic Wand

Young children are often fascinated by magic and all things associated with it. Use this to your advantage when it comes to transition times with toddlers. Decorate a wooden dowel or empty paper towel roll to look like a magic wand using either paint or markers, sequins, faux stones, and ribbons. When it's time to transition, pull out your wand, wave it in the air, and recite a silly rhyme, such as, "Rise and shine, it's cleanup time.!" You'll grab the children's attention and be able to tell them what you want them to do next.

References

Barclay, K., & Breheny, C. (2012). Hey, Look Me Over! Assess, Evaluate & Conference with Confidence. Published online August 28, 2012. Taylor & Francis Online, http://taylorandfrancis.com.

Bredekamp, S. (2000). CDA at 25: Reflections on the past and projections for the future. *Young Children*, September, 15–19.

Bruner, J. (2004). *The rights and potentials of children and adults*. Crossing Borders International Conference. Reggio Emilia, Italy.

Copple, C., & Bredekamp, S. (Eds.). (2009). *Developmentally appropriate practice in early childhood programs serving children from birth through age 8* (3rd ed.). Washington, DC: NAEYC.

Council for Professional Recognition (1999). *Preparing professionals as child development associates: A guide for designing the delivery of CDA training*. Washington, DC: Council for Professional Recognition.

Council for Professional Recognition (2007). *History and Mission of the Council for Professional Recognition & CDA*. http://www.cdacouncil.org Accessed September 5, 2012.

Douglas, K., & Jaquinth, D. (2009). *Engaging Learners through art making: Choice-based Art Education in the Classroom*. New York, NY: Teachers College Press.

Education Policy Research Unit. (2009). *NCLB school evaluation system is a flawed reform tool*. News release. Arizona State University: Author.

Eunice Kennedy Shriver National Institute of Child Health and Human Development. (2011). Autism Spectrum Disorders (ASDS). http://www.nichd.nih.gov/health/topics/asd.cfm. Accessed September 5, 2012.

Gardner, H. (1999). *Intelligence reframed: Multiple intelligences for the 21st century*. New York, NY: Basic Books.

Gardner, H. (2004). The hundred languages of successful educational reform. *Children in Europe*, 6, 16–17.

Greenspan, S. I. (2001, September). Creating an inclusive classroom. *Scholastic Early Childhood Today,* 33–34.

Jones, E. (2012). The emergence of emergent curriculum. *Young Children* 67(2), 66–68.

Jones, E. (1977). "Introduction: Curriculum Planning in Early Childhood Education." In *Curriculum is what happens: Planning is the key*, ed. L. L. Dittman, 4. Washington, DC: NAEYC.

Jones, E., & Nimmo, J. (1994). *Emergent curriculum.* Washington, DC: NAEYC.

Marcon, R. A. (1999). Differential impact of preschool models on development and early learning of inner-city children: A three-cohort study. *Developmental Psychology,* 35(2), 358–375.

MetLife Survey of the American Teacher: Teachers, Parents, and the Economy (March 2012). Available at https://www.metlife.com/teachersurvey.

Morrow, R. L., Garland, E. J., Wright, J. M., Maclure, S. T., & Dormuth, C. R. (April 17, 2012). Influence of relative age on diagnosis and treatment of attention-deficit/hyperactivity disorder in children. *Canadian Medical Association Journal (CMAJ),* 184: 755–762.

Mosteller, R. (Sept./Oct., 2010). When a student has Asperger's: Integrating a child with Asperger's means expecting the unexpected. *Instructor,* 46-49.

NAEYC and the National Association of Early Childhood Specialists in State Departments of Education (NAECS/SDE). (2009). *Early learning standards: Creating the conditions for success.* Available at http://www.naeyc.org/positionstatements

Nicholson-Nelson, W. (1998). *Developing student's multiple intelligences. New York, NY: Scholastic.*

Peters, D. L., & Deiner, P. L. (1987). The reality of early childhood: Head start and the Child Development Associate (CDA). *TECSE,* 7, 48–58.

Seefeldt, C., Galper, A., & Feeney, S. (2008). *Continuing Issues in Early Childhood Education.* Upper Saddle River, NJ: Prentice Hall.

Tout, K., Zaslow, M., & Berry, D. (2006). Quality and qualifications. In M. Zaslow & I. Martinez-Beck (Eds.). *Critical issues in early childhood professional development* (pp. 77–110). Baltimore, MD: Brooks.

Vitiello, V. E., Booren, L. M., Downer, J. T., & Williford, A. P. (2012). Variation in children's classroom engagement throughout a day in preschool: Relations to classroom and child factors. *Early Childhood Research Quarterly,* 27(1): 210–220.

Wien, C. A. (2008). (Ed.). *Emergent curriculum in the primary classroom: Interpreting the Reggio Emilia approach in schools.* New York, NY: Teachers College Press.

Visit CourseMate for this textbook to access the eBook, Did You Get It? quizzes, Digital Downloads, TeachSource Videos, flashcards, and more. Go to CengageBrain.com to log in, register, or purchase access.

Casper Holroyd

Creative Environments

The setting in which a creative activity takes place is very important. Young children are very aware of negative moods and environment. A dark room or crowded space can have much more effect on them than a rainy day. The arrangement of space and the type of equipment provided have a dramatic impact on a child's creative experiences. The impact is even greater on children with special needs.

Learning Objectives

After studying this chapter, you should be able to:

6-1 Describe an appropriate physical environment for creative activities for young children.

6-2 List five safety factors to be considered in the early childhood environment.

6-3 Discuss the main considerations involved in the arrangement of space and equipment in the early childhood classroom.

6-4 Describe the condition and organization of materials in interest centers that encourage children's creativity and developing skills.

6-5 Discuss the decisions involved in setting up activity centers.

6-6 List six factors that are important when selecting equipment to be used in creative activities for young children.

6-7 Describe multicultural learning centers.

naeyc

NAEYC Program Standards

1c Using developmental knowledge to create healthy, respectful, supportive, and challenging learning environments.

2a Knowing about and understanding diverse family and community characteristics.

DAP

DAP Criteria

1E3 Teachers ensure that the environment is organized and the schedule follows an orderly routine that provides a stable structure within which development and learning can take place.

2E3 Teachers organize the daily and weekly schedule to provide children with extended blocks of time in which to engage in sustained play.

2C6 9,10

6-1 DAP naeyc General Guidelines for Appropriate Physical Environments

The aesthetics of the early childhood environment were discussed earlier in Chapters 3 and 4. Here we will consider some basic guidelines for a physically appropriate early childhood environment. This is as important as the aesthetics of a room, because a positive physical environment is one of the keys to the success of the creative activities that take place within it. The following points are some things to consider when evaluating the physical space in early childhood programs.

- Proper heat, light, and ventilation are important. Remember that children live closer to the floor (see Photo 6-1) than do adults and that warm air rises and is replaced by cooler air. It may be helpful to install a thermostat or thermometer at their level so you can be aware of the temperatures they are experiencing. However, it must also be remembered that children of all ages are more active than adults and that they may not feel cool at temperatures that may be uncomfortable for you.
- Consider the source of natural light in the room. Children are likely to be more comfortable if they do not face directly into strong sunlight when they work. For children with visual difficulties or limited vision, make sure the room has plenty of light.
- Chairs should be light enough for the children to handle and move without too much noise. Because the chairs are used at tables for creative activities, the kind without arms should be used. For children in wheelchairs, provide small stools for the child's feet when placing the child at a table.
- There should be some tables that accommodate from four to six children for group activities. Rectangular tables are better for art activities involving large sheets of paper. Some small tables designed to be used singly or in combinations are quite versatile. Tables with washable surfaces such as Formica are best.
- Shelves should be low and open and not too deep so that children have a chance to see, touch, and choose materials independently. Shelves that are sturdy but easy to move are more flexible in room arrangement and help create interest centers.

Did You Get It?

Although the weather is hot, a group of 4-year-olds does not seem to mind playing outside. What most likely explains their heat tolerance?
  a. their closeness to the ground
  b. their high level of creativity
  c. their low level of sensory awareness
  d. their memories of the mother's womb

Take the full quiz on CourseMate.

PHOTO 6-1 Provide sufficient floor space for young children to allow them to stretch out if they wish.

Casper Holroyd

DAP naeyc 6-2 Safety Factors

Special consideration should be given to safety in the physical environment. Some important safety checks follow.

- Be sure that all low window areas are safe.
- Beware of and remove toxic, lead-based paints and poisonous plants, particularly berry-producing plants.
- All art materials *must* be certified nontoxic. Resist the urge to keep or use any unlabeled materials. More specific information on safe art materials is found in Chapter 12.
- With all materials, ask yourself: Will the item be likely to cause splinters, pierce the skin, or cause abrasions? Will the attractive glitter stick under fingernails? Are the fumes from a spray

irritating? Will a 2-year-old child's tongue-test transfer color from the object to the mouth?

● Avoid using scented felt-tip markers, which teach children bad habits about eating and sniffing art materials. A good rule of thumb: If the label on a marker reads "nontoxic" or *does not* read "permanent ink," the ink is probably water based. Not only are water-based varieties safe to use, they are easier to remove from walls and clothes!

● Try out new materials yourself before creative activities to become aware of any potential safety problems. Most young children can learn to be careful workers when they understand hazards. A teacher, when discussing how to use scissors, might ask, "How can you hide the point in your fist so that you will not hurt yourself and others when you are putting them away?" Two- and three-year-old children will usually need to have adults set rules—for example, "Clay is for modeling, not for eating." Children 4 years of age and older can cooperatively decide on rules and regulations for safe

handling of tools, materials, and equipment. However, older children may still need verbal reminders or simple signs.

● For children with visual impairments, keep the arrangement of furniture stationary until the child is familiar with the room. Be sure to warn the child when changes are made in the arrangement of the room and/or equipment.

● Regularly check to see that fire exits, fire alarms, smoke detectors, and fire extinguishers are in working order and are placed appropriately in the classroom.

● Familiarize yourself and the children with fire exits and fire drills.

Did You Get It?

The best way of presenting scissor safety to a classroom of 5-year-olds is to say,

    a. "Remember to cut only paper, and nothing else."
    b. "Never run with scissors."
    c. "Watch me to learn the safe way to use scissors."
    d. "Let's make a list of safety rules."

Take the full quiz on CourseMate.

DAP naeyc 6-3 Main Considerations in the Arrangement of Space and Equipment

Teachers must consider many things when arranging space in an early childhood program, including the following factors.

6-3a Children's Age and Developmental Levels

The age and developmental levels of the children using a room dictate how that room should be arranged. A group of 2- and 3-year-old children, for example, would do quite nicely in a simple, small, enclosed space. At this age, children may be overwhelmed by too large a space or too much equipment in it. Yet as their large-motor skills are developing rapidly, the space should be big enough for active, large-motor activities. Here is where balance is very important. Also, because coordination is not well developed yet in 2- and 3-year-olds, the space should be as uncluttered as possible.

▶❚❚ **TeachSource** Video

© 2015 Cengage Learning

Preschool: Appropriate Learning Environment and Room Arrangement

1. Evaluate the equipment observed in this video with regard to the selection criteria in your text. Does this equipment fit the criteria? Why or why not?

2. What additional equipment would you suggest and why? What equipment would you remove? Give a rationale for your choice(s).

Watch on CourseMate.

In contrast, a 5-year-old child has better coordination because of a more centralized center of gravity and doesn't fall as frequently as a 2- or 3-year-old child. More equipment in a room will not present a space or safety problem for the 5-year-old. However, the space needs to be large enough to allow children of this age to run, jump, climb, and pretend. In organizing space for young children, then, there should be enough open space for the children to move around safely and comfortably at their level of physical coordination and to work together cooperatively and freely. Adequate room also needs to be available and easily accessible for children in wheelchairs and with walkers. Approximately 40–60 square feet per preschool child is recommended. Middle- and upper-level elementary students can and need to work in a much larger area than younger children. A larger working space allows for their larger physical size and provides room for various student groupings that naturally arise out of project work, which is an appropriate instructional method for this age group.

6-3b Supervision

Another consideration in arranging for young children is the supervision of that space. Open play spaces should not be so large that it becomes difficult to supervise the children properly. A common technique is to divide the space up into interest centers or activity areas with limited numbers allowed at each center. (Interest or activity centers are discussed later in this chapter.) When breaking up the space in such a way as to facilitate supervision, using low, movable barriers, such as child-level bulletin boards, bookshelves, or room dividers, provides a clear view of the area and permits a more flexible use of the space itself.

In supervising a group that includes children with special needs, the teacher needs to be aware of the specific limitations of these children and to check throughout the day that their needs are being met. For example, in working with children in wheelchairs, the teacher should ensure that they are not in the same position for long periods (more than 20–30 minutes). The teacher should also be aware of when to move children who use wheelchairs to the proximity of ongoing activities.

6-3c Flexibility

Space should be kept as open and flexible as possible so it can be adjusted as children grow, develop, and

Casper Holroyd

PHOTO 6-2 Choose materials that are simple in design and versatile.

change in their needs. Your early childhood program certainly should not look the same on the last day of the year as it did on the first day of the year! The early childhood environment must reflect the young children in it—changing and developing along with them (see Photo 6-2). In response to children's growing ability to deal with more concepts, the room should now incorporate additional equipment, supplies, and interest centers. Conversely, materials, equipment, and even whole centers need to be removed to storage when children have outgrown them. This same idea holds true for older children in middle- and upper-elementary grades. The classroom that never changes is boring and a less-than-stimulating learning environment for these children. In a flexible environment, space can easily be rearranged to fit these new centers without major renovations.

This same flexibility holds true when working with children with special needs. For example, at the beginning of the school year, children who are visually impaired need to be in a room where there is assigned seating. This will aid in helping them learn their classmates' voices and names. The reason for assigned seating needs to be clearly explained to the class so they can understand the importance of the seating arrangement. Another helpful suggestion is to make sure children understand that they should identify themselves before speaking.

6-3d Traffic Flow

Even when increasing activity options in a room, space should be as free as possible to allow the traffic

PHOTO 6-3 Space should be as free as possible to allow easy movement between activities.

PHOTO 6-4 Older children need more room for special projects.

to flow between activities (see Photo 6-3). For example, the **traffic flow** should not interfere with activities that require concentration. A language arts center is more likely to be used by children if it is away from the noise of people coming and going. The block corner, too, will be used more often if it is planned for a space that is free from interruption and traffic.

Older children will enjoy an arts center that is situated in an area where they can concentrate and work without a lot of interruptions (that is, away from the door or other heavy-traffic areas). (See Photo 6-4.)

Involve children in arranging the space. Sometimes children as young as 4, as well as older children, may help determine where particular centers should be located and the reasons for such decisions. For example, a kindergarten teacher, introducing the woodworking bench, held a discussion with the children about where it should be placed. They wisely considered safety and noise factors in making their decision. Older children can actually help move desks, tables, and other equipment to carry out their own space reorganization plan. You may even tape arrows to the floor to teach the children traffic patterns for moving about the room.

6-3e Personal Space

In the early childhood years, children are growing physically and intellectually and developing their sense of self. For this reason, it is very important to plan space in such a way that each child has a place of her or his own (see Photo 6-5). Having a place of one's own to keep personal belongings, extra clothes, artwork, and notes to take home helps encourage a child's developing sense of self. A snapshot of the

PHOTO 6-5 Each child needs a personal space in the early childhood program.

child used to label the **personal space** is a good way, too, of assisting the growth of a sense of self. A snapshot removes all doubt that the place is private property even before a child has learned to recognize his or her name. Each child needs to be able to count on having a place belonging only to him or her.

It is only by firmly establishing an understanding of ownership that a young child learns about sharing. Having a cubby of one's own helps the child learn about possession and care of self, which are both basic to a growing sense of independence.

If there is not enough space for individual cubbies, labeled dishpans, clear plastic shoeboxes, large round ice cream containers, or even plastic milk crates can be used. Making personal space important recognizes each child's personal needs. This says to the child, "You are important."

In developing a positive self-concept, young children also need privacy. Besides respecting a child's private cubby, the space should be arranged so that there are quiet places to be alone. Especially as children grow intellectually, they need space and time to reflect and think. Quiet places to be alone encourage this reflection where children can enjoy their own thoughts and mental perceptions of the world. Older children have no less need for privacy and personal space. The classroom needs to have a designated space where a student's need to be alone is respected.

Children with attention deficit disorders (ADD) have a more intense need for concentration in a designated personal space. They tend to be most successful when they have their own materials and space in which to work. Even a cardboard box on a table can function as a study carrel for children with ADD.

6-3f Planning for and Displaying Children's Artwork

The way you plan for and display children's artwork tells children a lot about how much you value their work. Here are some suggestions on how to manage children's artwork in a way that shows children you value their work.

- Plan your artwork exhibits so they reflect children's ideas and experiences. Ask children to help select the items to be displayed. They may want to (or have you) write down why this particular work is meaningful to them. For instance, they like the medium, color, or subject.
- Enliven students' artwork by providing interesting backgrounds. Use gift-wrapping, colored paper, maps, sheet music, foreign newspapers, and wallpaper samples to encourage children's creativity.
- Make interesting groupings of children's artwork. Feature a specific theme, stress a particular color, or highlight a special medium.
- Display artwork outside as well as inside the classroom. Use the hallway and stairwell walls and other flat surfaces, such as doors, for your gallery. A sheet of butcher paper or bulletin board paper can be attached to a wall to define a display area and unify the works of art.
- Exhibit artwork in various stages. Include photos of the work in progress for documentation so others can enjoy the process, too.
- Place artwork at children's eye level. Label the displays with large, easy-to-read letters, and make up simple but catchy titles. Older children can make up these titles as well as cut out or write them out for the display.
- Handle work respectfully. Let the children know that you appreciate and value their skills and creativity. Frame or mount their work attractively. (Use backgrounds with contrasting colors and interesting textures, such as burlap or corrugated cardboard.) Encourage the young artists to sign their own names. Be sure not to write on their work without permission. Take dictation on a separate strip of paper. Older children may want to write a short statement to accompany their work.
- Mobiles and kites are best displayed from the ceiling. Make certain that all materials are well attached and that the items hung from the ceiling are secure so they do not fall or set off sensor alarms. As with all displays, it is important to know your school's policies about the types of adhesives allowed. Hot glue has a tendency to peel paint, low-temperature glue guns may not work on some surfaces, and double-sided tape can leave a residue. Humidity and the wall's surface both affect what will and will not work. Reusable tacky putty sticks to most surfaces and leaves few marks.
- Showcase work in exciting ways. Instead of stapling work to bulletin boards, hang pictures with clothespins from clotheslines. You can also use tree branches to display mobiles. Create a free-standing kiosk with four display sides from a cardboard refrigerator carton. A cardboard, folding, pattern-cutting board can be used to display art on both sides.

● Two-dimensional works of art can be mounted on larger contrasting or neutral-toned paper. The top and sides are usually of equal width with the bottom larger, unless the work is square, in which case all four sides are equal in width. When matting art, a 2- to 3-inch mat is standard, with the bottom being an inch wider than the top and sides. The mat acts as a resting place, so when arranging mounted or matted art, the works should not overlap.

● Arrange special areas for fragile or three-dimensional work. Supply stable shelves or low tables to display wire and clay sculptures or woodwork. Use cardboard "shadow boxes" for added emphasis and protection. Arranging sturdy boxes of varying heights and covering them with complementary cloths allow sculptures to be equally viewed. If sculptures are of varying sizes, the largest should always be placed toward the back and the small works in front. Arranging works in odd numbers creates interest as well.

● Provide individual display space. Have each child choose his or her own small area of a bulletin board that has been divided into sections. Let him or her select and change dated samples to document growth.

● Organize a space where parents can collect artwork. Designate the top compartment of the child's cubby as the "art shelf" or create an art "mailbox" from a large, partitioned, cardboard beverage carton turned on its side. Use cardboard mailing tubes to send home rolled-up artwork to prevent folding, creases, and tears.

6-4 Activity/Interest Centers that Encourage Children's Creativity

DAP **naeyc** One approach to fostering creative activities and use of materials is to provide as part of the environment **activity centers** or **interest centers** and to identify activities and materials for each, based on the group of children in the class.

An activity or interest center is a defined space where materials are organized in such a way that children learn without the teacher's constant presence and direction (see Photo 6-6). It is a place where children interact with materials and other children to develop certain skills and knowledge. Activities in each activity center are planned by the teacher according to the developmental needs of the children (Kostelnik & Grady, 2009).

Learning centers are places where children learn through direct interaction with other children and their environment. In centers, children learn through doing in an environment carefully prepared for their personal and active exploration.

An early childhood program organized around activity centers encourages creativity by giving children many opportunities to play, experiment, and discover as they engage in activities that help them with problem solving, learning basic skills, and understanding new concepts. In activity centers, young children can manipulate objects, engage in conversation and role playing, and learn at their own levels and paces. Materials in the interest centers also allow the children to experience various cultural and ethnic groups represented in their world.

Figure 6-1 presents the basic interest centers found in most early childhood programs. Figure 6-2 shows

Casper Holroyd

PHOTO 6-6 Art materials need to be organized to provide easy access for children.

ART AREA: This is a place for painting, collage making, cutting, pasting, and chalking. It should be located near water and light and away from large-motor areas.

HOUSEKEEPING/DRAMATIC PLAY CENTER. This is a place for acting out familiar home scenes with pots, pans, and dishes and to "try out" social roles, real-life dialogues, and grown-up jobs. It includes props that are specific to a wide variety of ethnic and cultural groups represented in the class.

BLOCK-BUILDING AREA. Here children can create with both large and small blocks, Tinker Toys®, logs, Legos®, etc.

MANIPULATIVE AREA. Activity in this center enhances motor skills, eye–hand coordination, and mental, language, and social skills through the use of play materials such as puzzles, pegboards, and games.

SCIENCE/DISCOVERY CENTER. Here children can learn about nature and science. They can display what they find at home or on nature walks. It is a place to discover, explore, and ask questions.

MUSIC CENTER. This center provides a place for children to listen to CDs or iPods, to sing, to express themselves creatively in dance, and to play musical instruments. Music from many cultures and ethnic groups is included.

LANGUAGE ARTS CENTER. In this center, children can be alone with their thoughts as they explore the world of books. Books in languages other than English for bilingual and ELL/ELS students as well as books representing a multicultural approach are included.

SAND AND WATER PLAY AREA. This is a place children learn through sensory experiences with sand and water.

THE SOCIAL STUDIES CENTER; PEOPLE AND PLACES. This is a special area where children can study about families, different cultures, ethnic groups, community awareness, specific occupations, and lifestyles.

WOODWORKING CENTER. This center provides children the opportunity to develop their large and small muscles by sanding, gluing, fastening, drilling, and sawing wood.

OUTDOOR PLAY AREA. This center provides a natural learning environment where activities from indoor learning areas can be extended.

FIGURE 6-1 Basic interest centers in early childhood programs.

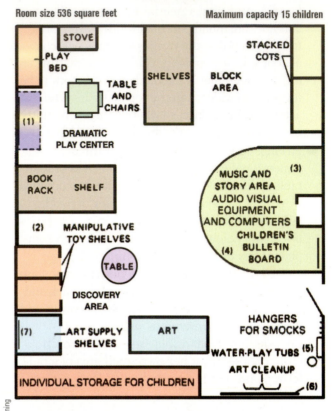

ROOM PLAN

Room size 536 square feet   Maximum capacity 15 children

© Cengage Learning

1. A second bed or folding mat   4. Rug
2. Child-size rocking chairs   5. Wastebasket and paper towels
3. Adult rocking chair   6. Adult bulletin board above tubs
7. Windows

FIGURE 6-2 Sample classroom arrangement using interest centers.

TeachSource Digital Download   Download from CourseMate.

how interest centers can be arranged in a classroom. Again, this arrangement is a suggestion, to be adjusted to the needs of the children.

Did You Get It?

A group of girls and boys play together in a preschool classroom at the doll activity center. Which aspect of the center most likely contributes to the children's creativity?

  a. the variety of dolls and doll clothing available

  b. the absence of the teacher at the center

  c. the gender heterogeneity of the children at the center

  d. the availability of multicultural dolls at the center

Take the full quiz on CourseMate.

THIS ONE'S FOR YOU!

The Organic Classroom

An organic classroom—one that focuses on reducing, reusing, and recycling—reflects the world's growing need for global awareness of better environmental practices. The following are some practical and easy-to-implement strategies to help your classroom be an organic one. These activities can teach children to become environmentally responsible now and in the future.

- Stock the writing table with individual dry-erase boards and markers or chalkboards and colored chalk.

- Cover a table with a large piece of butcher paper for joint activities such as stamping and drawing. This reduces paper usage while fostering cooperation.

- Teach (and remind) children to replace the caps on markers, glue sticks, and other costly consumables that will dry out if not stored properly.

- Make a Paper Rule. If a paper scrap is worn, ripped, and withered, it gets recycled. Otherwise, the paper goes in a scraps box. Students become aware of the potential uses for paper scraps, and the scraps box becomes an immediate destination for collage activities. Neatly trimmed scraps are more likely to be selected than torn ones.

- Trade materials with other teachers in your school. By recycling, you can freshen up your classroom and offer children new experiences without purchasing new items.

- Offer natural materials (for example, seeds, shells, twigs) in the art center in place of expensive craft materials. Use natural items in collages, to frame a picture, or with stamp pads for prints.

- Keep a stack of old cloth towels, some cut into washcloth sizes. Have your students use these instead of paper, especially for large spills and very messy hands. Keep a laundry bag in the classroom and take the towels home to wash them.

- Give families the option of receiving classroom newsletters and other communications online instead of sending home paper copies.

- Host a school-wide clothing-, book-, or toy-swap during open houses and parent–teacher conferences. Invite families to bring their unwanted materials to trade for items brought by others.

- Create a lending library where families can borrow books and educational materials for a few weeks at a time.

- Ask families to lend or donate real items, such as a computer keyboard or cloth placemats, needed to create a variety of themed settings (for example, office or restaurant) in the dramatic play center.

6-5 Decisions Involved in Setting up Activity Centers

naeyc Before setting up activity centers, you have to make a number of decisions about which centers to use, when to use them, and where they can best be placed in the classroom. Some of the questions to be addressed include the following.

- Will centers be offered all day, every day; part of the day; or only some days of the week? The ideal choice is to offer activity centers for a large block or blocks of time every day at approximately the same time. This lets children plan ahead, make choices, and get involved in activities. It allows teachers initially to structure learning centers throughout the room and gradually add, remove, or modify centers during the year.

- What room features offer potential settings for centers? You can make creative use of walls, floor, chalkboards, tables, and nooks and crannies.

- Should there be limits on the number of children using any specific center? If so, how will this be determined, and how will children know what the limits are? Activity centers need to be planned so children can work individually or in small groups of various numbers. The size of a small group of children at any center is determined by the amount of materials available, the purpose of the center, physical space considerations, and the need to avoid overstimulating confusion. Signs with stick figures and numbers can indicate the number of children who can use a specific center. For some children with ADD who may wander from center to center, make a photo display of the centers so the child can select from the photos to make an individual schedule of what she plans to do.

- What kinds of centers will provide a workable balance in terms of content? This will depend on the characteristics of the children and staff.

● How free should movement in and out of the centers be? Ideally, children should move at their own paces, guided by the teacher. This allows for more individualization within the program.

● How will children know what to do in each center? Some centers will require more direction than others. You may want to use pictures or symbols for routine directions (hands with a faucet of running water to remind children to wash; aprons on pegs to facilitate art and cooking cleanup without having to mention it). Be sure your centers have the appropriate equipment for children with special needs. For example, children with physical disabilities may need to use art materials in different ways, such as lying on the floor over a bolster pillow to draw. For children who are auditorily impaired, be sure to provide in your centers many activities that use senses other than hearing. For the child who uses a wheelchair, which places him at a different height than the other children, it

may be possible to use a beanbag chair for floor-time activities. For a child who does not have the strength to stand for long periods, a table-top easel will let the child sit in a chair while painting.

● As we learned in the previous chapter, young children have many ways of learning. You can incorporate what you've learned about these multiple intelligences by including appropriate materials and equipment in your activity centers that appeal to multiple intelligences. Figure 6-3 presents a list of suggested materials and activities for preschool and kindergarten children. Figure 6-4 has the same information for grades 1 through 5. You don't need to include all of these items in each center, but it is important to have a variety of materials for the multiple intelligences of children in your group.

● For elementary students, is there a place for storing ongoing projects? Milk crates or storage containers can be used for this purpose.

WORD SMART
Books
Maps
Magazines
Pipe cleaner letters
Chalkboard
Dry-erase board
Rice/sand/shaving cream/
    finger paints
Texture letters
Construction paper
Laminator
Pencils/pens/markers
Overhead projector
Letter puzzles

LOGIC SMART
Manipulatives
Counters
Abacus
Legos®/blocks
Geo boards
String art
Cuisenaire rods
Blocks
Play money
Puzzles
Marbles/beans

Geometric shapes
Straws/string/clay
Pattern blocks

PICTURE SMART
Legos®/blocks
Colored pencils/markers/
    crayons/paint
Puppet theater
Tongue depressors
Glitter
Manipulatives
Clay
Posters
Puzzles
Sand/water

MUSIC SMART
iPod
Musical instruments
Headphones
Cassette/record/CD player
Keyboard
Music books
Video camera
Kitchen utensils for making sound
    effects
Recordings of nature sounds

Toy microphones
Posters of composers
Tape recorders/blank tapes

BODY SMART
Audiocassette tapes
CDs and CD player
Beanbags
Large-motor equipment
Dress-up clothes and other props
    for dramatic play
Manipulatives

SELF SMART
Books
Puzzles
Art supplies
Cassettes/cassette players
Computer
Microscope
Reference materials
Writing materials
Clay
Musical instruments
Tape recorder

PERSON SMART
Art supplies
Sports equipment

FIGURE 6-3 Materials for multiple intelligences—preschool to kindergarten. *(Continues)*

Musical instruments
Puppet theatre
Books
Video recorders
Seeds/gardening tools
Computer
Cooking supplies

NATURE SMART
Terrarium
Microscope
Ant farm
Seeds
Soil
Bird feeders
Bird guides
Gardening tools
Magnifying glass

FIGURE 6-3 Materials for multiple intelligences—preschool to kindergarten (*Continued*).

TeachSource Digital Download Download from CourseMate.

WORD SMART
Reference books
Glue
Encyclopedias
Scissors
Computer
Desktop publishing software
Bulletin board
Thesaurus
Dictionary
Letter stencils
Sentence strips
Variety of paper
Newspapers
Notebooks
Magazines
Bookmaking materials
Student-made books
Writing utensils
Books on tape

LOGIC SMART
Pattern blocks
Protractors
Unifix cubes
Balance scales
Tape measures
Puzzles
Rulers
Strategy games
Construction sets
Objects to serve as counters
Dice
Cuisenaire rods
Collections for sorting/classifying
Science equipment

PICTURE SMART
Markers
Art prints
Crayons
Video equipment
Collage materials
Videotapes
Pastels
Charts
Graphic software
Colored pencils
Computer
Stencils
Puzzles
Rubber stamps
Graphs
Drafting supplies
Posters
Architectural supplies
Paints
Clay
Variety of drawing paper
Lego® sets

MUSIC SMART
iPod
Tape recorder
Recording equipment
Headphones
Musical software
Tapes/CDs
Keyboard with headphone
Homemade instruments
Books on musicians and music
Instruments

SELF SMART
Private, quiet place
Personal collections
Journals
Bulletin board/small chalkboard
Writing materials
Posters/pictures of individuals strong in this intelligence
Stories, books, and articles dealing with character development
Self-checking materials
Independent projects

BODY SMART
Costumes
Puzzles
Miscellaneous props
Sand
Hats and scarves
Craft supplies
Construction sets
Tools
Stacking blocks
Building materials
Puppets
Sports books and magazines
Tactile learning materials
Scissors

PERSON SMART
Large table for students to sit around
Group games and puzzles
Autobiography and biography books
Conflict resolution materials and posters
Tutoring activities
Group projects
Board games
Comfortable chairs/rugs
Writing paper

FIGURE 6-4 Materials for multiple intelligences—grades 1 to 5.

TeachSource Digital Download Download from CourseMate.

THINK ABOUT IT

Activity Settings and Daily Routines in Preschool Classrooms of Low-Income Children

Children from low-income families attend a variety of early learning programs prior to kindergarten. Some programs are specifically designed to provide prekindergarten readiness development opportunities. Others are primarily concerned with meeting the child-care needs of working parents. Many programs focus on both of these goals. As a result, early learning settings may vary greatly with respect to the services provided, the structure and size of the program, and the setting itself (home-based or center-based). Past research has shown that participation in early learning programs can help to alleviate socioeconomic disparities in school achievement by increasing children's academic and social readiness for formal schooling (Howes et al., 2008)

The purpose of this study was to examine activity settings and daily classroom routines experienced by 3- and 4-year-old low-income children in public center-based preschool programs, private center-based programs, and family child-care homes. This study involved a variety of early childhood education programs serving low-income children in Los Angeles County, California, representing a range of diverse learning settings available to low-income children. The study analyzed 125 classroom settings over a 2-year period.

Two daily routine profiles were identified using a time-sampling coding procedure: (1) a High Free-Choice pattern in which children spent a majority of their day engaged in child-directed, free-choice activity settings combined with relatively low amounts of teacher-directed activity, and (2) a Structured-Balanced pattern in which children spent relatively equal proportions of their day engaged in child-directed, free-choice activity settings and teacher-directed small- and whole-group activities.

For each early learning program, highly trained research staff conducted observations to measure global quality of the interactions and academic experiences provided.

All programs, whether publicly or privately funded centers or family child-care homes, were observed using the same set of tools. These observational tools were selected to measure a wide variety of instructional practices and features of the child-care environment for the purpose of providing rich but quantitative documentation of children's daily experiences.

Children in Structured-Balanced classrooms had more opportunities to engage in language, literacy, and math activities, whereas children in High Free-Choice classrooms had more opportunities for gross motor and fantasy play. Children in Structured-Balanced classrooms experienced significantly more scaffolded interactions with their teachers than children in classrooms that fit the High Free-Choice routine profile.

Children in Structured-Balanced classrooms had higher vocabulary scores than children in High Free-Choice classrooms. Yet, there was no significant effect of daily routine profile on math reasoning despite the fact that children in Structured-Balanced classrooms engage in more math-related activities than children in High Free-Choice classrooms. Children's social–emotional behaviors also did not differ as a function of daily routine profile, which suggests that neither routine is more likely to support or suppress children's development in the social–emotional domain.

The researchers found that the Structured-Balanced profile was most common for all program types. This finding challenges the commonly held belief that family child-care programs are always less structured than center-based programs. Among the three program types sampled, public programs had the highest proportion of classrooms that fit the Structured-Balanced profile; however, private center-based programs were equally likely to have either activity profile (Fuligni et al., 2012).

6-5a Condition and Organization of Materials in Activity Centers

Activity centers with materials that are in good condition, arranged and placed far apart on open shelves, tell a child that materials are valued and important enough to be well cared for. What kind of message does a child get from crowded, open shelves with a mixture of materials and broken or missing pieces? What kind of message does he or she get from torn books?

Young children work best in a predictable environment where materials are organized and can be found repeatedly in the same place. Organizing materials can help children develop self-help skills and self-control, as well as help them learn to respect materials and use them well. For example, cutouts of tools or other equipment help children learn to identify materials and return them to the proper place. Organizing open storage shelves by labeling them clearly with pictures and words makes it possible for children to find materials they want to work with. When shelves are clearly labeled with few objects on them at a time, putting things back in place becomes an easier task for young children.

Labeling, too, can be done in the block area by cutting out the shapes of the blocks in colored Con-Tact® paper and pasting them on the back and shelves. Clear labeling of shelves helps even very young children become independent in the use and maintenance of their environment.

For children who are visually impaired, cut out tactile shapes and attach them to shelves to assist them in finding and replacing blocks in the manipulative area. One of the challenges for the visually impaired student is maneuvering the materials. Work trays are one way for keeping track of art materials and managing and keeping materials accessible. Nonskid rubberized shelf liner is handy for keeping items from slipping away and preventing spills. A cafeteria tray with rubber shelf liner attached to the bottom provides a controllable boundary for the student's materials. For Braille readers, labels may be helpful. Ask the students what they prefer.

6-5b Color Coding in Activity Centers

A tried-and-true method for helping children function independently and successfully with activity centers is the systematic use of colors and symbols. Children can quickly learn a color-coding system even if they do not yet know how to read. Colors and symbols can be used to identify activity centers, to manage children's movement in and out of centers, and to let children independently find and replace assigned materials.

Special symbol and color codes help children identify and locate each center. The symbol identifies what is learned in the center. The color code helps children easily locate the center in the classroom. For example, the art center's symbol might be a paintbrush, and its color code might be red. A card would be hung at the entrance to each center with its corresponding symbol and color code.

To manage traffic in and out of the centers, the card at the center's entrance would also indicate the number of children allowed in the center at one time. It could be a number of stick people or the actual numeral, depending on the children's knowledge of written numbers. That corresponding number of color-coded clothespins would be attached to the bottom of the card. For example, the art center might allow 10 children and thus have 10 red clothespins. The clothespins are children's "tickets" to the centers. Children must pin on the clothespin when they enter the center, wear it while using the center, and replace it on the card when they leave. When no clothespins

are on the card, the center is full, and children must choose another activity until a clothespin is available.

6-6 Selecting Equipment for Creative Activities

DAP naeyc The kinds of equipment available to young children can either promote or discourage creative expression. If equipment is to encourage creative activities, it should have certain characteristics.

- **Simple in design.** Too much detail destroys children's freedom to express themselves. Crayons, blocks, clay, sand, paints, and even empty cardboard boxes are examples of simple but useful equipment for young children.

- **Versatile.** Equipment should be usable by both girls and boys at their developmental level for many kinds of activities.

- **Stimulating.** Equipment should be the kind that allows children to do things that motivate them. If adults must supervise children every minute they are using the equipment, this may hinder creativity. Long explanations on how to use the equipment should not be necessary.

- **Large and easy to use.** Because of the growth of muscles during this time, very small equipment can cause young children to become anxious. Big trucks and wagons are just right. Large, hollow blocks are better than small, solid ones.

- **Durable.** Breakable equipment is soon broken by 2- to 5-year-old children. Equipment made of hard wood such as maple is less likely to splinter than equipment made of soft wood such as pine. Rubber-wheeled riding toys are preferred to those with wooden wheels. For older children as well, durability of equipment is important. For example, a higher-quality brayer will last far

Hints for a Smoother Daily Program

If you, like most teachers, are always looking for ways to improve the daily operation of your program, you may want to think about using some of the following general hints.

- Store small books easily and neatly in plastic napkin holders. These can be found at discount stores and even at garage sales.

- When odd parts of toys and games turn up around the room during the day, forget trying to return them to their proper place each time they are found. Instead, make a special container just for toy and game parts. A zipper-type plastic bag works well for this purpose. Not only will this save time during the day, but you will also always know where to look if a part is missing.

- To preserve posters, pictures, and other items you want to last from year to year, cover them with clear Con-Tact® paper. The items will be easier for children to handle, and dirt and finger marks can be wiped off easily.

- Spray new puzzles and game boards with clear varnish (outdoors and away from the children, of course). You'll find they last much longer.

- Empty food boxes used in the housekeeping corner and for other learning games will be sturdier if you stuff them with newspaper and then tape them shut. Be sure to brush all crumbs out first.

- When sanitizing furniture and fixtures with bleach and water, put the mixture into an empty spray bottle that has been thoroughly washed and dried. The spray bottle is easy to use, and it will protect your hands from the harsh bleach.

- Instead of using tape to hang paper shapes on a wall with a hard finish, try sticking them on with dabs of toothpaste. The toothpaste can be washed off the wall when you change decorations.

- When a child paints a picture that you want to display on a wall, attach the paper to the tabletop with masking tape. The tape keeps the paper from sliding during painting, and when the child has finished, you can unpeel the ends of the tape from the table and use them to retape the painting to the wall.

longer through vigorous printing use by this age group.

- **In proper working order.** Nothing impedes creativity more than things that don't work. Do a daily quick checkup on equipment to see that it's in good working order. Older students can help with this inventory and write down a to-do list of specific repairs needed. Even better, select materials that are the best quality you can afford. It's cheaper in the long run.

- **Available in proper amounts.** Too many toys or too much equipment can decrease the effectiveness of those materials. Too many blocks can overwhelm children, and they may never start to build. Equally frustrating is too few blocks to complete a creation. Work for a balance in amount of equipment.

- **Designed to encourage children to play together.** Many pieces of equipment are designed for one child to use alone. However, children need to work together and find out what others are thinking and doing. Therefore, equipment designed to get children together should also be provided.

- **Safe.** Safety is a key consideration in selecting equipment for young children. Among the safety factors to consider are whether the equipment is developmentally appropriate (for instance, you would not select for 18-month-olds toys that are small enough to be swallowed easily), whether nontoxic and nonflammable materials were used in the manufacture of the equipment, whether the materials have any sharp edges or rough areas that could cause injury, and whether the physical environment allows for the safe use of the equipment. (Appendix F provides more complete information on appropriate toys and equipment for early childhood programs.)

6-6a Other Considerations

In selecting equipment and materials for creative activities, keep these additional considerations in mind.

- Do not choose a material or piece of equipment because it looks "cute" to you. Instead, select each item with some developmental purpose in mind (see Photo 6-7). For example, ask yourself,

PHOTO 6-7 Select each piece of equipment with a developmental purpose in mind.

Casper Holroyd

and you may need more blocks, more cars and trucks, and so forth. Also consider the age of the children in the group. Because 2- and 3-year-old children spend much of their time in egocentric (solitary) play or parallel play (playing next to but not with another child), there must be enough blocks, people, animals, cars, and dishes to allow several children to engage in similar play at the same time. Yet another strategy is to have duplicate or very similar copies of favorite items on hand.

"What contribution will the item make to the growth of small- or large-motor skills of the children? How will it help a child's intellectual growth? Self-esteem? Will it encourage the growth of social skills?"

- Resist the temptation to buy inexpensive merchandise as a matter of course. Select equipment that is sturdy and durably constructed because it will get hard use. In the long run, a high-quality, durable item will last longer and be more cost effective over time than one that is less expensive but poorly constructed.

- Consider each new item of equipment in light of what you already have. Work toward a balanced environment, one with many sources of creative expression: working alone, in pairs, or in small or large groups. In addition to equipment for large- and small-motor skills, select items that appeal to the sensorimotor explorations of young children. Equipment should be stimulating to see, interesting to touch, and satisfying to maneuver. This applies to equipment for older children as well.

- Purchase all major equipment in child size rather than doll or toy size. It is also important to have real-life and adult-sized equipment where appropriate. Real hammers and screwdrivers in a smaller adult size (not toy tools) work best in construction projects.

- Consider the total number of children and how many at a given time are to use the equipment. Ten 2- or 3-year-old children need a basic supply of equipment. Add several more children,

> ## Did You Get It?
> A preschool teacher has noticed that few children approach the classroom's well-stocked block center. What change would most likely encourage interest in the center?
> **a.** removing half of the blocks
> **b.** adding more-colorful blocks
> **c.** adding interesting blocks that require some adult explanation
> **d.** posting signs above the block center
>
> **Take the full quiz on CourseMate.**

6-7 Interest Centers and Multicultural Learning

DAP **naeyc** Multicultural education includes teaching children about their own culture—their ethnic heritage. It also means exposing children to other cultures and helping them be comfortable with and respect all the ways people are different from each other. It is teaching children how to relate to one another and how to play fair.

Begin introducing **multicultural curriculum** by adding materials that reflect the culture of your children and the local community. Later, add a variety of materials and objects to represent diversity in the world and the many ways people live out their daily lives. You can also teach through the **multicultural interest center** by adding materials to each area that support the unit theme. Here are some ideas on how to incorporate multicultural materials into some specific learning centers.

6-7a Art Area

In a multicultural classroom, the art materials must include colors, patterns, and textures from other cultures. Try adding origami paper for folding, rice paper for painting, and red clay for modeling. Collage materials could also be available such as magazines with picture of people from different cultures, a file of precut pictures, or fabric scraps of imported cloth. In addition, the art area should be stocked with skin-colored crayons, markers, paint, paper, collage materials, and play dough. Consider setting out hand mirrors so that children can look at themselves or other people. Include visual displays illustrating the artwork, color schemes, and visual patterns of other cultures.

In our global society, we need to help children understand that there are many ways of doing things and many ways of seeing the world. Looking at art from different cultures helps children do this. Providing open-ended experiences based on well-known artwork gives children rich exposure to art as well as cultural experiences.

6-7b Block Area

Blocks adapt well to a multicultural environment because they are the most versatile piece of equipment in the early childhood classroom. If you add multicultural accessories and props to a full set of hardwood unit blocks, you will guide and expand children's play. Such props can include a variety of transportation toys such as trains, buses, double-decker buses, planes, jets, cars, horses and carts, ferries, barges, canoes, and sleds. Multiethnic, nonsexist wooden play figures as well as small dolls and paper dolls from other countries increase the variety of people. Try adding palm leaves, coconut branches, corn husks, pine branches, bark, pine needles, stones, and straw for creating roofs, houses, and fences.(Be sure that children are not allergic to any of these materials.) Display pictures of buildings from different parts of the world such as a pagoda, tree house, adobe, thatched hut, log home, sod home, tent, earth-sheltered home, apartment building, trailer, and hotel. Rubber, plastic, wooden, cloth, and carved-bone animals representing the jungle, tropical forest, desert, and forest will also enhance children's play.

6-7c Music Area

Build up a broad selection of both vocal and instrumental music. Ask parents to make a CD or MP3 of the music their family and children enjoy at home. Use music from different cultures as background music during free play and rest time. Teach children songs with simple words and melodies from other cultures and teach them songs that encourage differences, acceptance, and cooperation. Add instruments such as maracas, Tibetan bells, gongs, gourds, metal and bongo drums, woven jute rattles, wooden flutes, brass bells, conch shells, castanets, wooden xylophones, and guitars to the set of traditional rhythm instruments. Many cultures use drums and drumming as their main instrument. Though expensive, a good drum provides a wonderful sound that can serve as the basic background instrument for many music activities.

6-7d Dramatic Play

The dramatic play area, like other centers, must allow children to explore a variety of lifestyles, including family systems, economic class, and culture. In this area, children try on the roles of people of different ages, skills, and occupations. Rather than teaching a particular culture, the dramatic play props should emphasize the many ways of going about our daily lives such as kinds of food to eat, types of eating utensils, and ways of dressing. Begin with items children have in their homes and expand from there.

6-7e Manipulative Area (Table Toys)

This area can be enhanced with multiethnic, nonsexist puzzles available through many common toy catalogues. Sets of graduated items from other cultures such as wooden dolls or animals make fun sequencing games. Make your own activities such as sorting foreign coins, shells, bottle caps, ethnic fabric squares, and other raw materials. Make lotto, classification, and matching games such as "Which One Is Different?" "Match Ups," and "Mothers and Babies." Because of stereotyped packaging, make it a practice to take toys out of their original container and display them in plastic dish tubs or on trays.

6-7f Science Center

Multicultural activities might include a collection of rocks and shells from different parts of the world. Terrariums and miniature indoor gardens model different types of soil, ground covering, and vegetation. The display might include a small cactus garden in sand, a planting of ferns in soil heavy with peat and sphagnum moss on the top, a bonsai display with smooth pebbles, a fish tank with plants that grow under the water, a Norfolk Island pine tree with bark chips, a dwarf citrus tree in sandy loam, a palm tree, bamboo shoots in water and marbles, or a tropical flowering ornamental such as a hibiscus or azalea. Include pictures and photographs of gardens from around the world. Grow herbs that are used in cooking ethnic foods in a sunny window. Cilantro, lemon grass, oregano, basil, mint, sage, sweet grass, and parsley are good choices. Add smells and scents from other cultures to the smelling jar kit. Create collections of different kinds of grains, beans, and soils. Examples of grains include wheat berries, rye berries, oats, millet, corn, couscous, barley, white and brown rice, red rice, and wild rice. A complete assortment of dried beans would include black-eyed peas, baby limas, black beans, pinto, kidney, great northern, soybeans, and lentils. Some teachers may choose not to use food as a teaching tool. This decision is based on personal values, and each teacher must make her or his own choice.

6-7g Sensory Table

You can also integrate a multicultural approach to your sand and water table areas. Try to include textures and smells that represent not only the children in the class but other cultural groups as well. Many of the grains and dried beans listed under the science area can be purchased in large quantities to use in the sensory area as children use them to learn about comparing and measuring amounts and the characteristics of the various grains. Other dry materials for the table include whole nuts in the shell, bark, dry leaves, coffee beans, soil, raw wool, raw silk, and flax. (Be sure to be aware of any allergies children may have to any of these materials.) When exploring liquids with children, try adding a scent to the water. Small bottles of essential oils in various floral, wood, citrus, and herbal scents can be purchased at health food stores or international gift shops.

The sensory table can also be used for dramatic play. The addition of small people figures, transportation toys, twigs, rocks, and miniature plastic plants to a base of sand, soil, or water allows children to create environments that are unfamiliar as well as recreate environments that are common in their everyday lives. For example, children in the coastal areas of North Carolina and South Carolina could play "beach" with wet sand, shells, and small people figures. Likewise, for children in an urban setting, a high-rise construction site could be created with a layer of dirt, a crane, trucks, small building blocks, and play figures.

6-7h Language Arts Center

Display books that emphasize diversity, ethnicity, different lifestyles, and cooperation. Include alphabet and counting books from other cultures. A CD player and story CDs add to the interest area. Look for stories that include ethnic background music and narration by a person from that culture. You and the children can supplement your current library with homemade books. For example, take pictures of children and create your own books. Have children make books about themselves and their families.

In addition to planning for centers that reflect a multicultural curriculum, it is important to plan activities in these centers to reflect this curriculum. Rather than watering down elementary school activities and social studies lessons, try adapting proven early childhood activities. Avoid using worksheets, coloring pages, and craft projects. Go through your own activity files and curriculum books, as well as the activities in this book. Think about how they might be modified to teach multicultural concepts.

For example, use the curriculum to help all students learn about each other's families. Using the common bonds topic of "family," you might have children interview their relatives and tell the story about how and when their family first came to the United States. Students, unless they are of Native American descent, will discover that their ancestors were all once immigrants. You might also give all parents and even other relatives of your students an opportunity to visit your classroom and tell about their family traditions. Regardless of where children are from, they have much to offer each other in sharing family and cultural backgrounds. A positive incidental effect of this activity is that you will avoid unintentionally making a new student feel singled out or on display.

Did You Get It?

A fifth-grade teacher decides to introduce her students to Chinese landscape painting. What creativity fostering teaching objective is she likely to have in mind?

a. showing her students a different way in which they can paint

b. helping her students understand alternate ways of viewing the world

c. teaching her students how to value nature

d. explaining the difference between pencil drawings and paintings

Take the full quiz on CourseMate.

Summary

6-1 Describe an appropriate physical environment for creative activities for young children.

To ensure the proper environment for creative expression in young children, careful attention must be given to safety, amount and organization of space, light, sound, and furniture. Planning the environment in the early childhood program involves knowledge of children's needs, as well as attention to traffic flow in the room, children's developing skills, and safety. Arrangement of personal space for each child also needs to be planned.

6-2 List five safety factors to be considered in the early childhood environment.

Safety involves having the appropriate space, supervision, and developmentally appropriate equipment, materials, and activities. It is also important that equipment be stored properly so that children can reach it easily, thereby developing their self-help skills.

6-3 Discuss the main considerations involved in the arrangement of space and equipment in the early childhood center.

A balance between teacher planning and children's self-direction is necessary. Interest or activity centers help children make their own choices. The placement and organization of the various activity centers have an impact on how creative materials within them are used by children, how safe the environment is, and how children's self-help skills are encouraged

6-4 Describe the condition and organization of materials in interest centers that encourage children's creativity and developing skills.

Interest centers that encourage children's creativity and developing skills are organized in such a way that children learn without the teacher's constant presence and direction. An early childhood program organized around activity centers encourages creativity by giving children many opportunities to play, experiment, and discover as they engage in activities that help them with problem solving, learning basic skills, and understanding new concepts. In activity centers, young children can manipulate objects, engage in conversation and role playing, and learn at their own developmental level and pace.

6-5 Discuss the decisions involved in setting up activity centers.

Decisions must be made about when the centers will be offered; what room features offer potential settings; limits on the number of children in a center; what kinds of centers will be available; movement in and out of centers; and how children will know what to do in the centers.

6-6 List six factors that are important when selecting equipment to be used in creative activities for young children.

Because creative activities are so important in promoting children's development, careful attention must be directed toward the selection and care of creative materials and equipment. The best equipment is simple in design, versatile, easy to use, large, durable, working properly, available in needed amounts, designed for group play, and, above all, safe.

6-7 Describe multicultural learning centers.

Multicultural learning centers include materials that reflect the culture of the children in the group and the local community. They also include a variety of materials and objects to represent diversity in the world and the many ways people live out their daily lives.

Key Terms

activity centers   123

interest centers   123

multicultural centers   131

multicultural curriculum   131

personal space   122

traffic flow   121

Learning Activities

A. Choose one activity center from the list provided in this chapter. Design your own unique version of this activity center. Describe it in detail. List the items and activities it would include.

B. Draw an ideal room plan for creative activities. Imagine you have all the money, materials, and space necessary. Be creative. After drawing it, list what you feel is important in it, starting with the most important feature. Share this list with classmates and discuss it.

C. Using small blocks or any other similar object, show how you would arrange space in a room to ensure smooth traffic flow and noninterference among interest centers in the room.

D. Go through a school supply catalog. Find examples of furniture, shelving, and play objects that you would include in planning your ideal room in the activity preceding. Explain your choices in a developmental context.

E. Obtain a toy and equipment catalog or go to a toy store. Make a list of materials that would be useful for children's play. Imagine that you have $1,250 to spend on some additional equipment for your classroom. Make a list of items you would purchase. Assume you may not go over the $1,250 limit.

F. Explain the statement: "Form follows function" in terms of structure in the classroom. With your ideas and observations in mind, design an ideal classroom for you, a creative teacher.

Classroom Activities

A. **Natural objects and random "calling on."** To make calling on students truly random, gather enough flat, smooth rocks such as river rocks so that you have one for each child. Paint the children's names on them. Put them in a basket and use them for calling on children. At year's end, children take them home as a tangible reminder of their time in your classroom.

B. **Foamy cleanup.** To help students really get into keeping their desks squeaky clean, try using shaving cream as an incentive. Spray each desk with a generous amount of shaving cream on the desktop. Then, let the children use their fingers to practice letters, numbers, their names, and so on before you wipe it away. Children will love it and it really does get the desks squeaky clean.

C. **Bulletin board idea.** Try using felt and fabric for your bulletin board backgrounds. Fabric doesn't fade as much as bulletin board paper, and staple holes are barely noticeable. You can fold up the fabric to use again next year. Or you can change fabric backing in the middle of the year to perk up your room.

D. **Sticky words.** To prevent word cards from landing on the floor, make them "sticky words." In a well-ventilated area, spray a light coat of spray adhesive (the kind used to mount photos, available in craft stores) on construction paper, following directions on the can to make a nonpermanent bond. Word cards can easily be repositioned on this sticky paper but won't get knocked out of place if the desk gets bumped accidentally.

Also, the cards stand out on the colored construction paper background, helping children with ADHD better focus on them. Store sheets of sticky paper in pairs with sticky sides together and then just peel them apart to use. When the paper starts losing its stick, simply respray with adhesive.

E. **"Don't interrupt" reminder.** If you don't want students interrupting small group or individual student conference time on a daily basis in your classroom, try this idea. To help students remember not to interrupt, wear a headband with decorative animal ears or antennae. Or if you prefer, you can wear any type of hat that you choose. This headwear serves as a visual reminder that you are busy listening to the person or group in front of you.

F. **Help is on the way!** When you are busy with a small group or an individual child, students are not expected to sit alone at their desks for an extended time pondering an assignment they do not understand. Have three students who finish their work quickly and accurately be "student helpers." Have the helpers wear plastic visors or any special headwear. This way they are readily visible as the designated helpers. The visors also allow you to tell at a glance if the people talking and out of their seats are helpers or if they are students who are not following class rules.

G. **Reading with cell phones?** Students are often asked to read material silently at various times during the day. Yet some students don't comprehend what they read when they read silently. To allow for student learning differences, try using "cell phones" in your classroom. This doesn't mean that children bring cell phones from home and call their friends and families for reading help! Instead, make "cell phones" from PVC elbows. Two 90-degree PVC elbows connected to one another are just the right size for a "cell phone" for students to read into. They can read quietly into the mouthpiece of the "cell phone" and are able to hear their voices amplified in their ears. The classroom is a soft hum of students reading at their own pace and comprehending what they are reading. This is also an excellent tool for students to use to read their own writing.

References

Fuligni, A. S., Howes, C., Huang, Y., Hong, S. S., & Lara-Cinisomo, S. (2012). Activity settings and daily routines in preschool classrooms: Diverse experiences in early learning settings for low-income children. *Early Childhood Research Quarterly, 27*(2), 198–209.

Howes, C., Burchinal, M., Pianta, R., Bryant, D., Early, D. M., & Clifford, R. M. (2008). Ready to learn? Children's pre-academic achievement in pre-kindergarten programs. *Early Childhood Research Quarterly, 23*(1), 27–50.

Kostelnik, M. J., & Grady, M. L. (2009). *Getting It Right from the Start: The Principal's Guide to Early Childhood Education.* Los Angeles, CA: SAGE/Corwin Press.

Visit CourseMate for this textbook to access the eBook, Did You Get It? quizzes, Digital Downloads, TeachSource Videos, flashcards, and more. Go to CengageBrain.com to log in, register, or purchase access.

Casper Holroyd

Play, Development, and Creativity

Some children are busily involved in activities in an early childhood program. One group of children is removing the wheels from the wooden trucks in the room. Now they are having races by pushing the wheel-less trucks along the floor. One child notes the scraping sound being made, while another discovers that the trucks without wheels make marks on the floor.

Learning Objectives

After studying this chapter, you should be able to:

7-1 Discuss the concept and qualities of play.

7-2 Discuss the play theories of Parten, Smilansky, Piaget, and Vgotsky.

7-3 Discuss the importance of play to human growth and development.

7-4 Describe developmentally appropriate childhood games.

7-5 Discuss ways the environment can be adapted to encourage social play experiences for children with special needs.

7-6 Discuss some reasons children engage in violent play and how to deal with this type of play.

naeyc
NAEYC Program Standards

1b Knowing and understanding the multiple influences on development and learning.

2a Knowing about and understanding diverse family and community characteristics

4c Using a broad repertoire of developmentally appropriate teaching/learning approaches.

DAP
DAP Criteria

2E4 Teachers provide experiences, materials, and interactions to enable children to engage in play that allows them to stretch their boundaries to the fullest.

2F1 To develop initiative, teachers encourage children to choose and play their own learning activities.

2I3 Recognizing the self-regulatory, linguistic, cognitive and social benefits that high-quality play affords, teachers do not reduce play opportunities that children critically need.

One child is preparing a tea party for three friends. The child has baked an imaginary cake and has just finished putting on icing. Now the table is being set and the chairs arranged. Another group of children is carefully observing several small furry animals on the other side of the room.

Are these children working? Are they playing? Is there a difference between work and play for a young child? Must children be involved in games to be playing? Must toys be involved? Is play natural, or can children be taught to play?

The answers to these questions are important. They help define the meaning of the word *play*. The answers lead to an understanding of how children benefit from creative play. They give direction for the purchase and placement of creative materials that guide children's play. They help adults plan activities that help children grow through creative play.

Casper Holroyd

PHOTO 7-1 Play is essential in the lives of young children.

7-1 The Concept of Play

For adults, play is what they do when they have finished their work. It is a form of relaxation. For young children, play is what they do all day. Playing is living, and living is playing.

Young children do not differentiate between play, learning, and work. Children are by nature playful. They enjoy playing and will do so whenever they can. Challenges intrigue them. Why do children love to play? Because play is intrinsically motivated—that is, no one else tells them what to do or how to do it. An activity ceases to be play, and children's interest dwindles, if adults structure or even interfere inappropriately with play.

For older children, learning may be work. When they complete their work, then they can play. For young children, mental development results from their play. Growth of their ability to deal with the problems of life—social development—results from play. Growth of their imaginations results from play. Muscles develop in play, as well.

Play is an activity. It does not necessarily result in a product. It may involve one child or groups of children. It may be built around toys and tools or may involve nothing more than the child's imagination. A play period may last a few minutes or go on for days.

Play is the mechanism by which children learn—how they experience their world, practice new skills, and internalize new ideas—and is therefore the essential "work of children" (see Photo 7-1) (Paley, 2004).

Through this continuous and expanding process, early skills give rise to new ones, and new experiences are integrated with previous ones. Through play, children learn about the world and engage in activities that encourage their cognitive, emotional, and social development (Elkind, 2007). For example, when a child bangs on a drum, she learns she can create a sound. Through play, she learns the important concept of cause and effect (Guyton, 2011).

7-1a Qualities of Play

Although we often refer to things as "child's play" when referring to something purely simple in nature, definite qualities are associated with child's play. The following are some of the qualities that distinguish play for young children from other activities:

- Play is a process. The outcome is not as important as the process itself.
- Play is child-initiated. The activity is done for no other reason than the child wants to do it.
- In play, everything and anything can happen; a sheet over a table becomes a castle, and the little girl inside is the princess.
- Play becomes the arena for testing rules, both logical and illogical. Rules freely appear and disappear in children's play; they may be simple or complex, and they are created from children's previous knowledge. An example of rules in play is the "rule" of roles. For example, when young

children play in the housekeeping center, you will often hear one of the children assigning roles to each of the other children ("You be the mommy").

● Play is very much an activity of the mind. Children may become deeply engrossed in their play and find it difficult to stop when asked. Play involves the mind in an active process as a child investigates, explores, and inquires (Hurwitz, 2003).

In the early childhood classroom, play and the curriculum should be deeply connected. A high-quality curriculum for young children should rely heavily on play. Learning to identify different types of play may give you further understanding of their importance. Types of play include the following.

● Practice play—play that children do repeatedly, solely for pleasure, such as playing in sand and pouring it through their fingers.
● Constructive play—play where children construct or create something, such as block building.
● Rough-and-tumble play—play that involves laughing and pretending; as the name implies, it can get a little rough. (This is not aggressive play and, when done in a safe area, is an acceptable form of play.)

● Dramatic play—play that gives children the opportunity to take on the role of another person, an animal, or even an object.
● Games with rules—play governed by a set of rules, such as a game of Duck, Duck, Goose.

Understanding these categories helps teachers plan appropriate play activities to meet the developmental needs of the whole child (Hurwitz, 2003).

Did You Get It?

Two preschool children scatter pillows on the floor and then jump from pillow to pillow, pretending that crocodiles will eat them if they touch the floor. From a playing perspective, their game

a. meets the qualities associated with child's play.

b. is considered low quality play, as it does not include manipulatives.

c. shows imagination, but it violates the rules of play.

d. reveals their deep-seated phobias, and their teacher should continue to observe them for signs of further disturbances.

Take the full quiz on CourseMate.

▶❚❚ TeachSource Video

© 2015 Cengage Learning

2-5 Years: Play in Early Childhood

1. Which scene(s) in the video would you describe as organized play? Explain your reason(s) for this/these choices.

2. What information concerning the importance of play covered in your text is not included in this video? Why is this important to consider?

Watch on CourseMate.

7-2 Play: Theories of Parten, Smilansky, Piaget, and Vgotsky

DAP **naeyc** Early childhood researchers have developed a number of theories of play over the years. Mildred Parten, one of the early researchers, developed the notion of the sequence of play (Parten, 1932). According to Parten, there is a general sequential order of play activities that may be observed in young children. These types of play activities may be classified according to stages.

The earliest stage of play is onlooker behavior in which the child plays passively by watching or conversing with other children engaged in play activities. Also in early toddlerhood, a child at first generally plays alone (see Photo 7-2). This stage is termed solitary play. Using all of their senses, children explore long before they use any objects in their play. They touch, smell, see, and listen. Manipulating and handling materials are important parts of play experiences. In these early play experiences, children are more involved with the manipulation of materials than they are with the uses of them. Gradually, as the toddler's social realm expands,

PHOTO 7-2 In early toddlerhood, a child first generally plays alone.

Casper Holroyd

he or she will engage in **parallel play**. Parallel play occurs when a child plays side by side with other children with some interaction but without direct involvement.

As the number of relationships outside the home increases, the child's ability to play with other children develops further. At this point, the child may engage in **associative play**. This type of play may take the form of the child's merely being present in a group. For example, a child who participates in finger plays during circle time or group time is engaging in associative play. Common activities occur between children. They may exchange toys and/or follow one another. Although all the children in the group are doing similar activities, specific roles are not defined, and there is no organized goal (such as building something or pretending to have a tea party). Eventually, as they grow more comfortable with their social ties, young children will begin to talk about, plan, and carry out play activities with other children. This type of play, marked by mutual involvement in a play activity, is called **cooperative play**. Children cooperate with others to construct something or act out coordinated roles.

Sara Smilansky (1968), another researcher of play, investigated how dramatic play helps children develop socially. Generally, preschoolers' play becomes

more social as they get older. Smilansky (1968) found that by engaging in socio-dramatic play (dramatic play that involves more than one player), their social skills were enhanced. She also found that participation in socio-dramatic play requires a high level of social ability, including cooperation, negotiation, sharing, problem solving, self-regulation, and appreciation of another's play efforts. The amount and complexity of fantasy play have been found to be predictors of social skills, popularity, and positive social activity (Smilansky & Shefalya, 1990).

In addition to these theories on play, there are different kinds of play, different stages of play, and different purposes underlying play. The play of preschool children is different from the play of toddlers, which is different from the play of school-age children.

Generally, children under the age of 3 engage in exploratory play. Their objective is to explore the world through physical actions, to experiment with their movements, and discover what they can do. They poke, dump, taste, stroke, and pull whatever they encounter in order to learn about their world. From 3 to 7 years of age, however, children's actions become more "play" than exploration, and efforts to know and understand become more important than sensory experiences. Play can also be either **free** (or **spontaneous**) play or **organized play**. In either type, children may work alone or in a group. Each type may involve materials and equipment, or it may not. Basically, free play, as its name suggests, is flexible. It is unplanned by adults. It is a self-selected, open exercise. Organized play is also open and flexible. However, some structure is provided in terms of materials and equipment.

Teachers can promote organized play by providing representational toys and dress-up clothes. Representational toys strongly resemble real objects, such as dolls, toy vehicles, dishes, cooking utensils, stoves, telephones, and doctor kits. Dress-up clothes can include handbags, lunch boxes, briefcases, hats of various kinds, and jewelry. These representational toys prompt children to pretend to engage in the activities of others, that is, to do the things they see adults do. This is often called "dramatic" play, as children act out the roles of grownups in their lives. (More specific information about dramatic play is provided in Chapter 15.) They pretend to feed the baby, drive to work, cook dinner, talk on the telephone, and so forth. Props relevant to children's culture and community can enrich their efforts to construct and express their understanding of significant events and people in their lives (see Photo 7-3).

Casper Holroyd

PHOTO 7-3 Playing with toy "friends" is a common sight in early childhood.

Jean Piaget (1962) defined play as assimilation, or the child's efforts to make environmental stimuli match his or her own concepts. His theory holds that play, in and of itself, does not necessarily result in the formation of new cognitive structures. Piaget claimed that play was just for pleasure, and while it allowed children to practice things they had previously learned, it did not necessarily result in the learning of new things. In other words, play reflects what the child has already learned but does not necessarily teach the child anything new.

Piaget describes **imaginative play** as one of the purest forms of symbolic thought available to the young child. According to Piaget, play permits the child to fit the reality of the world into his or her own interest and knowledge of the world. In this sense, imaginative play contributes strongly to the child's intellectual development. Some researchers even maintain that symbolic play is a necessary part of a child's development of language (Oliver & Klugman, 2007; Porter, 2009).

In contrast, Lev Vygotsky (1978) states that play actually facilitates cognitive development. Children not only practice what they already know, they also learn new things. Play does not so much *reflect* thought (as Piaget suggests) as it does *create* thought (Vygotsky, 1978).

Play, according to Vygotsky, offers the child opportunities to acquire information that sets the foundation for additional learning. For example, through playing with blocks, a child learns the idea of equivalents (that things can be equal) by discovering that two small blocks equal one larger one; or through

playing with water or sand, the child acquires knowledge of volume, which eventually leads to developing the concept of reversibility. In Vygotsky's view, make-believe reaches its highest level of development in the preschool and kindergarten years.

Observations of children at play are full of examples to support both Piagetian and Vygotskian theories of play. A child who puts on a raincoat and a firefighter's hat and rushes to rescue his teddy bear from the pretend flames in his play house is practicing what he has previously learned about firefighters. This supports Piaget's theory. On the other hand, a child in the block center who announces to his teacher, "Look! When I put these two square blocks together, I get a rectangle!" has constructed new knowledge through her play. This supports Vygotsky's theory. Whether children are practicing what they have learned in other settings or are constructing new knowledge, it is clear that play has a valuable role in the early childhood classroom.

Children gain an understanding of their environment as they investigate stones, grass, flowers, earth, water, and anything else. Through these experiences, they eventually begin to make their own generalizations: Adding water to earth makes mud. A puddle of water disappears in sand. The inner part of a milkweed pod blows away in the wind. Wet socks can be dried out in the sun.

As children play, they develop spatial concepts; as they climb in, over, and around the big box in the yard, they clarify concepts of "in," "over," and "around." They hear someone call the box "gigantic," and *gigantic* becomes a new word that attaches to a specific meaning. In the sandbox, words such as *deep, deeper,* and *deepest* begin to have meaning through play experiences.

The theories of play are summarized in Figure 7-1. Whatever the theory, imaginative play comes naturally to young children, gives them great pleasure, and is crucial to the development of their thinking and learning. When they use their imaginations, children think about people, places, and things that aren't right there in front of them (see Photo 7-4). In this way they are involved in *abstract* or *symbolic* thinking.

Symbolic thinking lays the groundwork for later learning in reading, writing, and math. For example, to understand what they are reading, children have to be able to see a picture of what each word stands for in their minds. Similarly, to solve math problems, such as adding three apples and four oranges, children have to picture them in their minds.

Parten	Play is a measure of child's increasing social maturity.	Developmental stages of play: onlooker, solitary, parallel, associative, and cooperative
Piaget	Play is assimilation—child makes world adapt to him.	3 stages of play: sensorimotor, symbolic, and games with rules
Smilansky	Play aids child's social development.	6 criteria of dramatic play: imitative role play, make-believe, verbal make-believe, persistence in role play, interaction, and verbal communication
Vygotsky	Play directly supports the development of child's cognitive powers.	Symbolic play promotes abstract thinking.

© Cengage Learning

FIGURE 7-1 Summary of the theories of play.

Casper Holroyd

PHOTO 7-4 Children often invite teachers to enter their imaginative play.

Did You Get It?

Connor, age 4, is enthralled with superheroes, and he regularly engages in imaginary superhero play with his classmates. A few years later, at age 10, he is a popular class leader who is elected to student council. Whose theory would fit with Connor's trajectory?

a. Piaget's
b. Urie Bronfenbenner's
c. Lev Vygotsky's
d. Smilansky's

Take the full quiz on CourseMate.

7-3 DAP naeyc Importance of Play to Human Growth and Development

Children learn best in an environment that allows them to explore, discover, and play. Play is an important part of a developmentally appropriate child care program. It is also closely tied to the child's physical, mental, emotional, and social growth.

7-3a Physical Growth

Play contributes to muscle development in many ways. Throwing a ball or lifting objects helps children's large muscles develop. Placing an object on top of another and grasping tools also add to a child's small muscle development and hand–eye coordination. Play that requires children to look for objects, feel textures, smell various odors, hear sounds, and taste substances helps them develop their senses.

Children spend hours perfecting such abilities in play and increasing the level of difficulty to make the task ever more challenging. Anyone who has lived or worked with infants will recall the tireless way they pursue the acquisition of basic skills. Babies will repeatedly enjoy peek-a-boo long after the adult is ready to stop the game. Toddlers' falling and getting up time and time again is another example of this persistence. (For more specific examples of play for infants and toddlers, see Figure 7-2.) In older children, this repetitious physical activity is also a major characteristic of play. It is evident on playgrounds, where we see children swinging, climbing, or playing ball with fervor.

As a child gains control of his body, self-concept is enhanced. When a child runs, she feels exhilarated. When a child uses the last bit of strength to accomplish

When infants and toddlers are not sleeping, they are engaged in play and exploration, two important avenues to building understanding of their world. The following are ages and characteristics of play at each age.

Birth to 4 Months

Babies explore their new world with their eyes and ears. Some ways to play with a baby of this age are to:

- Provide bright, moving objects for babies to practice focusing on.
- Move your face and objects close to and away from babies. This helps the baby judge the relationship between objects and between themselves and objects.
- Provide babies different views by holding them in various places, such as in your lap or on your shoulder.
- Let the baby see herself in a mirror.
- Talk to babies in playful ways. Smile and repeat soft sounds. Stop between sounds and watch for them to smile or move in response to your voice. If you get a playful response, repeat the sounds.
- Sing to the baby. Make up songs for the baby. Dance with the baby on your shoulder.
- Play with the baby's hands and feet, gently patting and rubbing.

Four to 8 Months

At this stage, infants can now also use their hands and mouths to explore their world. Some ways to play at this age are:

- Choose toys that move or make sounds in response to the baby's actions. Best choices are toys that turn, honk, rattle, pop up, or play music when the baby pushes, punches, hits, or pokes them.
- Check all toys for safety. Be sure toys are small enough for baby's hands to hold, but not small enough to fit entirely in the mouth.
- Buy washable toys and toys made of tough, durable material. Check all toys for sharp edges or points and for small parts that could fall off.
- Watch but don't interrupt when the baby is exploring new objects. Keep other children (especially older children) from interrupting play.
- Entertain the baby with playing This Little Piggy Went to Market.
- Sing songs to the baby when diapering, changing clothes, etc.

8 to 12 Months

By this age, babies are now fully active in exploring their world. Almost all babies crawl and creep, many walk around the room holding onto furniture, and some are already walking on their own. Babies at this age are able to drop, throw, pull, and squeeze objects. Some suggestions for play at this age are:

- Provide toys that challenge the baby's skills of pulling, pushing, poking, and punching.
- Provide objects to put in and dump out of containers. Some suggestions are plastic bowls, plastic storage boxes, baskets, and shoe boxes. Be sure that items to put in are small enough to fit in the containers, but too big to fit in the child's mouth. Some good items to put in containers are plastic lids, yarn balls, blocks, and rings from stack-a-ring toys.
- Read to the baby.
- Play pat-a-cake, peek-a-boo, and copy cat with the baby.
- Play So Big with the baby. Stretch the baby's arms gently over her head, asking, "How big is baby? Soooo big!" After a while, baby will hold her arms up by herself to respond to this question.
- Babies of this age enjoy the sensory feeling of moving through space in such activities as riding piggyback, swinging in a child seat, riding in a wagon or a stroller, and dancing in an adult's arms. They also enjoy bouncing on an adult's knee to the accompaniment of a song or verse.

FIGURE 7-2 Infant and toddler play.

(*Continues*)

12 to 18 Months

Children at this stage are great experimenters, trying out things to see what happens. The first pretend play occurs in this group when infants begin to act as if they are doing daily activities. They pretend to sleep, eat, or wash.

Some suggestions for play are:

- Provide safe places (indoors and outdoors) for walking, moving, and climbing.
- Provide opportunities for going in and out, through, and under objects such as tunnels, cabinets, tables, and so forth.
- Provide lifelike toys for daily activities such as cleaning, eating, bathing, and riding.
- Read to the toddler, talking about the book as you go.
- Participate with the child in pretend activities. Let the child "pour" you a glass of milk, and say, "Mmmm, it's delicious." Allow the child to comb your hair or pretend to wash your face. Then, extend the play to a doll and continue the actions and language.
- Encourage language development by talking about play as it happens. "The baby is asleep." Or "I'm going to have such neat hair after you comb it."
- Collect simple pictures of familiar items for the child to practice naming (Sluss, 2005).

FIGURE 7-2 Infant and toddler play. (*Continued*)

TeachSource Digital Download   Download from CourseMate.

a goal, he gains a better sense of self. As the child discovers her own strength, she develops feelings of competency and worth. A young child is quite physical in play, playing with his whole being. As the child plays, she decides what to do and how to do it, does her own planning, and implements those plans in her own ways.

When children have a chance to be physically active, they continually gain strength. As they become more adept, they become more adventurous and learn to take reasonable risks to test their strength. When children set their own challenges, they are less likely to have accidents. Without predetermined goals, they can pace themselves and discover what they can and cannot do.

A youngster in the middle childhood years (5–8 years of age) develops physically in his or her play. At the beginning of this period of growth, the child is almost continuously active, whether standing or sitting. Toward the end of this period, however, movements of the 8-year-old child have become fluid and graceful. He has developed poise. In fact, he is continually on the go—jumping, running, chasing, or wrestling. There is an increase of speed and smoothness in fine-motor movements. The child approaches objects rapidly and smoothly, and releases them with sure abandon. Organized games with rules to follow are beginning to be popular with this age group.

During the later childhood years (in grades 4 to 5), the need for vigorous play is still important for children. A glance at children of this age group reveals one factor that stands out above all others: Children of this age vary widely. The children in the group may be about the same age, even in the same grade, but the similarities end there. They vary widely in their sizes, interests, activities, and abilities, and these differences, in turn, influence every aspect of their development. The child, other children, parents, and teachers should realize that these differences are quite normal.

This age group has good muscular control, has a general increase in strength, is particularly sturdy, is keenly interested in sports, and acquires the skills for games readily. Watching these children at play, one often wonders if they ever get tired. They have a lot of stamina. Arms grow longer, and hands and feet grow bigger. Some children at this stage are clumsy and awkward as a result of the uneven growth of the different body parts.

Children who are 8 to 12 years old select increasingly demanding physical play, which gives them a greater opportunity to develop muscle control and coordination. At this age, boundless amounts of energy and enthusiasm are hallmarks of their play. Children in this group enjoy running, tumbling, climbing on jungle gyms, and swinging. As they grow in motor skills and confidence, they begin more advanced forms of play such as roller skating, skipping rope, skateboarding, and throwing and catching. Children's increased physical abilities and improved coordination also allow participation in team sports and other organized activities in which one's physical ability affects the outcome of the game.

Teacher–Child Interactions During Preschool Free Play

The purpose of this study was to test a model of adult-child play interactions in preschool classrooms, based on the work of Vygotsky (1978). The model predicts that adults will tailor the play support they provide to the immediate needs of individual children, which will lead to subsequent independent play.

Classroom interactions between 8 preschool teachers and 32 students were videotaped, transcribed, and analyzed over a 6-month period. Interviews were conducted with the 8 adult participants to confirm and elucidate findings from observed classroom behaviors.

Participants were eight early childhood education professionals—two head teachers, four assistant teachers, and two student assistants—who taught in two full-day preschool classrooms in a university child development center serving a culturally and socioeconomically diverse population in a small New England community. The two head teachers held master's degrees in early childhood education and had 25 and 10 years of teaching experience, respectively, in community-based child care. One of the assistant teachers held a master's degree in early childhood education and had 4 years of experience in a private preschool. The other three assistant teachers held bachelor's degrees in fields unrelated to education and had between 2 and 4 years of experience in Head Start or child care. The two student assistants had less than a year of classroom experience and were completing introductory coursework in psychology and early childhood education.

The two preschool classrooms in which participants taught were part of a high-quality child development center located on a moderate-sized state university campus. The center was funded by the state, with some support from the university, and served primarily children and families from the local community. The population was made up of 32 children ages 3 and 4 of diverse backgrounds. The philosophy of the program and observed daily activities reflected a traditional, play-based, Piagetian-influenced orientation. The daily schedule of both classrooms blended long periods of self-guided play in clearly defined learning centers with group experiences, outdoor time, snacks and lunch, and naptime.

Adult participants were each video recorded during four or five 30-minute observations over a 20-week period as they interacted naturally with children during free-play periods in the classroom. This yielded 19 hours of recorded teacher–child play interaction for analysis.

Free play was defined as a time when children were able to make independent choices regarding their activities. So, play was broadly defined in this study as any activity that was self-guided and intrinsically motivated. Recordings were made during regularly scheduled free-play periods in each classroom. Teachers were not asked to rearrange daily activities or alter their interactions with children in any way during these sessions. Adults were informed on the mornings when recordings would be made but not of the precise times when they would occur.

Child play behaviors were sorted into three basic categories related to the amount of needed adult guidance: much need, some need, and no need. Level of guidance was categorized into four distinct levels: direct, indirect, observation, and no interaction. Good-fit interactions were defined as one of the following: need for much support, followed by direct adult guidance; need for some support, followed by indirect guidance; and no need for support, followed by either observation or no interaction.

Results of the study indicated that the head teachers and assistant teachers performed a higher frequency and rate of good-fit interaction than did student assistants. Yet, any adult subject, regardless of professional role, achieved a relatively high rate of success in promoting autonomous play when good-fit interactions were implemented. Percentage of good-fit interactions leading to autonomous play ranged from 61% to 78% across all adults in the study. Good-fit interactions more frequently led to autonomous subsequent play than poor-fit interaction.

In summary, the purpose of this study was to test a model of teacher–child play interactions based on the work of Vygotsky. This model predicts that adults will often respond to children's play behaviors with good-fit interactions and that these will lead to more independent subsequent play. Overall, the findings of the study confirm this model. Thus, this study contributes to a growing body of research suggesting that the quality of teacher–child interactions can be a critical component for supporting children's development in early educational programs (Trawick-Smith, & Dziurgot, 2011).

7-3b Outdoor Play/Recess

Children have two classrooms—one indoors and one outdoors (see Photo 7-5). The outdoor play environment should be an extension of the indoor classroom. The outdoor play area should be a learning environment as carefully planned as the indoor activity centers. Outdoor play should encourage motor and social skills as well as help children refine existing cognitive structures and construct new ones. Used in this way, the outdoor play environment provides a basis for observational assessments in all areas of development.

However, with the passage of federal and state standards and testing requirements, many schools started to lessen or even eliminate time children spent outdoors or at recess. The arguments against recess involved both academic time and safety issues. Some administrators believed their schools' test scores would improve if children spent more time on schoolwork. Some feared lawsuits from playground injuries. What are children learning outdoors that they could not learn inside? There is considerable research (Jarrett, 2002; Staempfli, 2009) to suggest that outdoor play/recess has many benefits for children, such as the following:

- Children are less fidgety and more on task when they have recess, and children with ADHD are among those who benefit most.
- Research on memory and attention shows that recall is improved when learning is spaced out rather than concentrated. Recess provides breaks during which the brain can "regroup" (Jarrett & Waite-Stupiansky, 2009).
- On the playground, children exercise leadership, teach games to one another, take turns, and learn to resolve conflicts.
- In a free-choice situation, children learn negotiation skills in order to keep the play going.
- Recess before rather than after lunch leads to healthier eating.
- Children who are active during the day are more active after school. Children who are sedentary during the day tend to remain sedentary after school.
- Teachers rated children's behavior as better in classes where children had at least 15 minutes of recess (Barros, Silver, & Stein, 2009).

See End of Chapter Activities for group games to use outdoors and at recess.

PHOTO 7-5 Children have two classrooms—one indoors and one outdoors.

Casper Holroyd

Did You Get It?

Nikita, age 10, is a verbally advanced child who can read for two hours at a sitting. She dislikes sports and runs rather slowly. Nikita's physical development is

a. abnormal for her age, as the typical 10-year-old should be active for at least three hours daily.

b. within normal range, as 10-year-olds display a wide variety of levels of physical activity.

c. of concern, as she is at the low end of the average range.

d. typical of girls, who are far less active than boys.

Take the full quiz on CourseMate.

7-4 Developmentally Appropriate Childhood Games

DAP **naeyc** Do you remember how it felt when you were eliminated from musical chairs? It probably didn't feel good being a "loser." Children know that to avoid being labeled a "loser," they must do whatever it takes to win. And what teacher hasn't seen this lead to children pushing, poking, and shoving while playing this game?

Games, like any other early childhood activity, are opportunities to promote children's development in one or more of the cognitive, social, emotional, and physical areas. When we select games, we need to be sure they are developmentally appropriate, just as we do when planning an activity for the rest of the curriculum (Pica, 2009).

In planning games for young children, ask yourself, "What will the children learn from the game—self-confidence, problem solving, cooperation, trust, and improved motor skills? Or rejection, competition, failure, and humiliation?" (Staley & Portman, 2000, p. 67).

Neil Williams created the Physical Education Hall of Shame, a list of children's games he considers inappropriate for physical education programs. In this list he includes Dodge Ball, Musical Chairs, and Red Rover (find the full list at www.auburn.edu/~brocksj/4360hastietext/hallofshame1994.pdf). These games are developmentally inappropriate because they tend (1) not to foster children's development; (2) to embarrass children in front of their classmates; (3) to focus on eliminating children; and thus, (4) to afford players limited participation time in the activity; and (5) to carry a high risk of injury or harm (Williams, 1994).

NAEYC's most current position statement on developmentally appropriate practice states that play allow children "to stretch their boundaries to the fullest in their imagination, language, interaction, and self-regulation" and offer opportunities for children "to practice their newly acquired skills" (Copple & Bredecamp, 2009, p. 18). It's really quite easy to modify a game so that it fits these guidelines. Here are some ways to do that.

7-4a Modify Musical Chairs

Instead of playing this the traditional way, modify it so it is a cooperative game. In this game, when the music stops, the goal is for children to find ways to share the remaining chairs. This way there is no one "loser." Compared to the traditional version, in this modification, children practice problem solving and prosocial behaviors.

7-4b Modify Simon Says

Simon Says can also be modified so it is a more cooperative game for young children. Start by dividing the class into two groups instead of one large group. Have the children arranged in either two circles or two lines. When a child moves without Simon's permission, he leaves his original circle or line to join the other group, and he continues playing. Full participation allows children to acquire the listening, direction-following, and movement skills that are the objectives of Simon Says (Pica, 2009).

7-4c Modify Duck, Duck, Goose

Another example of changing a game to make it more cooperative is Duck, Duck, Goose. This game usually involves physical activity for only one or two players and a good deal of waiting for the rest of the children. Also, some players are repeatedly chosen to be the goose. To modify this, have the children stand in a circle and walk in place as the game is played. This way all players engage in more physical activity. Also, make it a rule that the child who is "it" can't choose someone who has already been the goose. This way, more children will have a chance to chase. When the game is modified this way, all the children benefit from a low to moderate level of physical activity as well as practice in walking in place, chasing, and fleeing (Pica, 2009).

7-4d Older Children's Play and Cognitive Development

DAP **naeyc** Older children learn many concepts through play. They learn about such things as rules of the game and strategies in play. They begin to learn about their own skill levels in various activities and to develop preferences for specific sports and activities.

Children's increasing cognitive abilities allow them to participate in more advanced forms of organized games and team activities where rules guide actual behaviors. Although younger children often play together (actually, they may only be playing near each other), they also often play alone. Children between the ages of 8 and 12 might also play alone either by choice or by necessity. However, their increasing cognitive abilities (especially in those 10–12 years of age) allow them to play with others in situations requiring consistent or complex rules. The cognitive abilities of 10- to 12-year-olds also allow for more advanced forms of play such as word games, riddles, and other literacy-related play.

Today's technology allows older children many new forms of play. Children can play a wide array of computer games either alone or with another child. Software, such as for chess, requires that children think and participate in active decision making, while other software requires writing and complex thinking. As technological advances become even more commonplace in our society, children will have even greater access to problem-solving programs, CDs, applications (or "apps"), and simulation programs. Many 8- to 12-year-old children who have benefited from computer use in schools are sufficiently computer literate to play with the latest technologically advanced computer and video games.

THINK ABOUT IT

The Importance of Recess and Free Play

The purpose of this study was to determine the contribution of unstructured recess on children's school-day physical activity levels and to examine if recess and school-day physical activity levels varied by gender and grade level. One-hundred sixty third- to fifth-grade students from two elementary schools (50% girls) wore pedometers during four recess periods.

Data were collected during four school days within a one-week period. Each day, upon arriving at school, students fastened their pedometer to their waistband and obtained a data recording sheet for that day. Before leaving for recess students were prompted by a teacher or researcher to record their step count. After recess, students were again prompted to record their step count. The pre-recess step count was subtracted from the post-recess step count to calculate the number of steps recorded during recess. At the conclusion of the school day, students recorded their final step count and placed their pedometer into a collection container.

Playground areas at both schools were very similar. Both had large open areas including grassy fields, play structures, blacktopped basketball courts, hop scotch areas, fun hoops, and several trees for shade. A variety of playground balls (kickballs, basketballs) and jump ropes were available for the students to use during recess.

Results of the study indicated that youth accumulated 17% to 44% of their school-day physical activity during a 15-minute unstructured recess. This is fairly significant given that recess time only accounts for about 4% of the total time in school (one 15-minute recess out of a 410-minute school day). Regardless of physical activity level (least active vs. most active), approximately one-third of students' school-day physical activity was accumulated during recess.

Recess was most influential with fourth-grade girls, as it contributed approximately 44% of their school-day physical activity. Yet, in terms of gender, there were no differences in activity level during recess between boys versus girls. On average, boys in third and fourth grades were more active during recess than girls.

With respect to grade level, recess made the greatest relative contribution to school-day physical activity for fourth-grade students, accounting for approximately 40% to 44%. This is because the fourth graders had a greater recess step count but lower school-day step count, on average, compared with third and fifth graders.

Recess periods evaluated in this study were unstructured, consisting of free play for the children. The researchers suggest that due to the fact that physical activity choices are varied and personal in nature, a recess environment that offers both structured physically activity opportunities and free-play opportunities is advocated. They also recommend that teachers and administrators provide adequate equipment for children during recess to improve physical activity levels (Erwin et al., 2012).

7-4e Emotional Growth

One of the keys to the quality of children's emotional health is how they feel about themselves. Creative play activities help a child develop a positive self-concept. In play activities, there are no right or wrong answers. Children are not faced with the threat of failure. They learn to see themselves as capable performers. Even when things do not go well, there is little pressure built into play. Thus, young children learn to view themselves as successful and worthwhile human beings through creative play. This is an important first step in developing a positive self-concept.

Children also learn to express and understand their emotions in creative play experiences. They may be observed almost any place in the early childhood setting expressing their feelings about doctors by administering shots with relish or their jealousy of a new baby by reprimanding a doll, but creative play is not necessarily limited to the expression of negative feelings. The same doll that only a moment ago was being reprimanded may next be lulled and crooned to sleep in the rocking chair.

Another emotional value of creative play is that it offers the child an opportunity to achieve mastery of her environment. The child has control of the situation, using what props she chooses and in the manner she prefers. The child is in command. She establishes the conditions of the experience by using imagination and exercises her powers of choice and decision as the play progresses.

Play is a safe and acceptable way to test out the expression of feelings. Through play, children can re-create experiences that have been important to them and elaborate on experiences that have special meaning. The child can relieve anxiety or stress through play activities and feel perfectly safe in doing so. For example, Susan gets pleasure out of hammering on a piece of wood. She feels strong as she swings the hammer and sees the deep indentations she is making in the wood. Woodworking, thus, is providing a medium through which she can release tension or aggression in an acceptable way.

Children in the middle- and upper-elementary grades grow emotionally when engaged in play with their peers. Playing together, children learn to accept each other's styles and personalities and learn how it feels to be accepted as part of the group. After the child gains acceptance among his peers, he begins to have self-respect and feels confident and adequate in attempting new problems and activities.

PHOTO 7-6 Children establish relationships as they play together in the early childhood program.

Casper Holroyd

7-4f Social Growth

Play is a characteristic behavior of children at all times and places. Nonetheless, it varies with social class and culture. Smilansky (1968) initiated a new line of play research studies with her finding that socio-dramatic play was more common among children of advantage than it was among those with less advantage.

At the early childhood level, however, there is likely much more similarity in children's play than difference across both culture and social class (Cote & Bornstein, 2009). This is true because young children are less socialized and more apt to create their own play than to adopt socially transmitted play activities. For the young, and to a degree all ages, play has personal meaning and value not dealt with in traditional theory and research.

Although there has been a great deal of research on play since these theories were offered (Center on Education Policy, 2008; Jarrett, 2002; Oliver & Klugman, 2007), we really have no new theories of play, according to David Elkind (2003), noted child developmentalist. Elkind asserts that all the research on play simply represents one side of the issue—the adult side. Adults, in his opinion, look at children's play as, in one way or another, facilitating healthy development. Although he does not deny the developmental value or meaning of children's play, Elkind maintains that play has a personal, experiential value of equal, if not greater, importance (2003).

As teachers of young children, we need to resist the pressure to transform play into work—into academic instruction. We encourage true play by making certain that we offer materials that leave room for the imagination—blocks, paint, paper to be cut and pasted—and that children have sufficient time to innovate with these materials.

Children learn social skills as they relate to others during play (see Photo 7-6). As a child becomes proficient in his social relationships, he learns to deal with more than one person at a time. As a group participant, he discovers that not everyone behaves in the same way and that some forms of behavior are not acceptable. When Yuki takes a block from Manuel's building, Manuel pushes her away. Next time, she does not try that. In one situation, Yuki learns that crying will get her what she wants, while in another, it does not work at all. Children establish social relationships as they sit side by side playing with clay, dough, and other manipulative materials. A child discovers that she can make some decisions about what she will or will not do. If a child does not wish to push a wagon, he can play somewhere else. The child cannot, however, always be the one to tell others what to do. Sometimes the child takes the role of leader and sometimes she finds the role of follower satisfying (see Photo 7-7).

When children play together, they learn to *be* together. The development of common interests and goals takes place among children during creative play. They must learn to "give a little" as well as "take a little" when involved in creative play activities. Whether two small children are arguing over the possession of a toy or a group of children are playing together on a jungle gym, play helps children grow socially.

PHOTO 7-7 Young children learn social skills as they relate to others during play.

of games. This developmental task is actually enhanced when facilities, equipment, and play space are made available for children of this age group. Too often, the importance of vigorous play for children of this age group is overlooked because they seem so "grown up."

Did You Get It?

The game "Duck, Duck, Goose" is not considered a developmentally appropriate game because

   a. its rules are too simplistic.
   b. it focuses on eliminating children.
   c. even a young child will consider the game too "babyish."
   d. it lacks the main elements of fun.

Take the full quiz on CourseMate.

Children ages 10 to 12, in particular, develop the social skills necessary to participate in complex, cooperative forms of play. Their enhanced social skills allow them to see others' perspectives and allow them to realize the benefits of playing socially and cooperatively with other children. At this age, play that requires social skills might consist of games, team sports, and organized activities.

Children, especially 10- to 12-year-old children, shift allegiance from parents and teachers to peers. They are beginning to seek freedom and independence, which results in their playing away from home and often away from direct adult supervision. Children might visit ball fields, playgrounds, and recreation centers where others play or where special equipment is available to them.

At school, teachers can assist older children through play activities at recess, noon, or during class time to become more proficient in skills for ordinary games. Yet, the acquisition of physical skills needed in ordinary games involves more than physical maturation. It is a matter closely tied to social adjustment.

A child who is socially comfortable with other children will try and try until he or she can participate without ridicule from others. The teacher needs to help children feel socially comfortable in the area

7-5 Adapting Environments to Encourage Social Development for Children with Special Needs

DAP **naeyc** Play for children with special needs may not look like what is normally viewed as play. Put a ball in front of a 2-year old who is typically developing, and the child will probably try to throw, hit, or kick it. A child who has a disability may or may not react to a ball placed in front of him. That is why it is essential that knowledgeable adults facilitate play for children with special needs. The adult must know how to intervene in a way that supports play.

Teachers need to work with other adults and experts to develop specific plans to create environments that facilitate play for children with special needs. In making these plans, the following points should be considered.

● Remember that children with special needs are children first.
● Use children-first language when you discuss the child. Never refer to the child by the name of the disability.
● Make appropriate adaptations for the child. Recognize that you do not know everything you need to know about how to include this child in play. Each child is unique, and each disability is unique. Ask questions about how to adapt the classroom and materials to encourage the child's play.
● Children with special needs may not always initiate play. They may not engage in play on

their own. Teachers must intervene to encourage play and to use strategies that will encourage self-generated play.

● The nature of a child's special condition will affect the play. For example, a child who has cerebral palsy and is in a wheelchair may need specialized assistance in motor areas but may be willing to challenge anyone in a game of checkers.

● A child who has visual impairments may need special assistance to participate in board games but be able to move around the room with minimal assistance.

Play for children with special needs must be individualized to reflect the child's assets. Their play may not look like typical child play. Each child will have a unique way of playing. Teachers must know the child well enough to understand that child's unique play (Sluss, 2005).

Teachers should arrange the physical environment and daily schedule to facilitate opportunities for children to interact and continue to model appropriate behaviors for these children. Research indicates that selection of toy materials and their arrangement in the room is significantly related to increased frequency of positive social behaviors and decreased frequency of negative behaviors in special-needs children (Morrier, McGee, & Daily, 2009).

One way to arrange the physical environment to promote social interaction is to use specific toys. When social toys (for example, blocks, balls, miniature cars) rather than isolate toys (for example, crayons, modeling dough, puzzles) are used during playtimes, children engage in more interactions and less solitary play (Sluss, 2005). Balls encourage interaction between two children when they roll or toss them to each other. Wagons and toys that require two children encourage cooperation. Water play and house play are also designed to stimulate social play.

Limiting the space available to children during playtime and placing children with special needs in close proximity to peers during group time and play sessions increase social interactions (Harper & McClusky, 2003). Increasing the proximity of children and limiting the space available to children can be accomplished by creating play centers and by assigning seats during group times, ensuring that children with special needs always have peers who are typically developing on both sides of them (Harper & McClusky, 2003). These strategies can be designed around children's Individual Educational Plan (IEP) goals and can be

made part of the general curricular and daily activities. When children play together, the play is greater than the sum of its parts. It may seem only to be water play, encouraging physical (gross and fine motor development), social (interactions with other children), and cognitive development (sensory stimulation, language development). But, it is more; it is enjoyable. Children are playing and having fun, which is the essence of play for all children (Sluss, 2005).

7-5a Play and Children with Special Needs

DAP **naeyc** Children with disabilities and delays often lack the skills they need to enter into and maintain play with others (Stanton-Chapman, Denning, & Jamison, 2008). Adults may need to scaffold or support the child by providing hints or assistance to help them enter into and benefit from interactions with their typically developing peers (Stanton-Chapman, Kaiser, & Wolery, 2006).

During free play or center time, early childhood teachers typically assume the role of a manager who helps children get ready to play (for example, providing materials for play, giving suggestions for use of materials). Although this level of support may be appropriate for many children, children from at-risk environments or children with disabilities may need the teacher to assume a more active role for quality play to take place. To enhance their play, early childhood teachers need to enter children's play and provide support to make it a quality experience for the children involved, although not so much support that play is stifled.

7-5b Teacher Talk

Teacher talk is a key form of adult support that early childhood teachers can use to enhance the play of children with disabilities and promote peer interactions. Teacher talk refers to specific help that teachers provide to children to encourage richer play experiences. It is most effective when it is implemented in ongoing classroom routines. Teacher talk can take several different formats (Sharpe, 2008).

● *Recasting*: A teacher changes a child's word into a more appropriate word (for example, child says, "cutter" and teacher says, "scissors").
● *Repeating*: A teacher restates what a child has said (for example, child says, "My dolly is sick" and the teacher says, "Your dolly is sick").

Multicultural Play

Teaching children about all kinds of cultures is no more complicated than playing a game. The following are some games from around the world you may enjoy using with children:

Chile: Corre, Corre la Guaraca

This game's name translates to "Run, Run, la Guaraca." Chilean children typically speak Spanish, but Guaraca is actually a nonsense word.

This is a game for five or more children, ages 5 and up. You will need a handkerchief for this game.

Players sit in a circle while a runner jogs around the outer rim with a handkerchief. The seated children are not allowed to watch and have to cover their eyes. They sing, *"Corre, corre, la Guaraca,* who looks back will be bopped on his head." Trying not to be felt, the runner drops the handkerchief on a child's back and runs. If he makes it around the circle before the player realizes that it's on her back, the seated player is out. If the seated player catches on, she must tag the runner. If she succeeds, the runner is out. If she fails to tag him, they play again, but this time player 2 is the runner.

Greece: Statues

American children may not be familiar with the classic *Discus Thrower*, but Greek children have access to some amazing marble statues that date to ancient times. After a trip to the museum, it's only natural that they would incorporate some of these awe-inspiring characters into an imaginative game.

This game is appropriate for four or more children, ages 4 and up. Choose one player to be "It" and have her stand, eyes covered, in the center of a large, open playing area. She starts to count, at least to 10, but she can go higher. The point is that there's no set ending number; only "It" knows when she'll stop and open her eyes. While "It" is counting, the others scatter around, never sure when she'll yell "Agalmata!" (That's "statue" in Greek. Tell the children to yell it to be authentic, or to just say "statue" if that's easier.) On this cue, players freeze, taking on poses that mimic famous statues. They can pull from any statue they've ever seen a photo of—a javelin thrower, *The Thinker*, even the Statue of Liberty. Children are allowed to use found items, such as sticks, a ball, or a Frisbee, to add a touch of realism. "It" tags any statues that are moving—they're out—then tries to make the steady ones laugh or move. The last player remaining composed is the winner and becomes the new "It." This game is great for practicing balance, too.

Sumatra: Semut, Orang, Gajah

This large Indonesian island is home to the Sumatran elephant, which has made its way into this children's game, similar to the American, "Rock, Paper, and Scissors." Children play *Semut, Orang, Gajah* to determine the first player in a game or simply for fun.

This game involves two players, ages 3 and up. Players pump their fist up and down to the count of three. On four, they straighten their arm and give one of three signs: Pinky out is "ant" (*semut*), pointer finger out is "man" (*orang*), and thumb out is "elephant" (*gajah*). The elephant beats man because it is stronger; man defeats the ant because he can step on it and squash it. And the ant? It can crawl into the elephant's ear, bite him, and drive him crazy, so the ant beats the elephant! If players make the same signs, they go again. Two out of three wins.

Israel: Go-Go-In

During midsummer, when fresh apricots are in season, Israeli children play games with the small, smooth pits known as go-gos, which are plentiful and perfect for tossing. They tote customized boxes and challenge their friends to toss pits for points.

For this game, you will need two or more children, ages 5 and up. If you can't locate apricot pits, you can use acorns or small stones. You will need 100 (or fewer) or at least 20 per player. You will also need a shoebox for each player.

With a grown-up's help, players must first prepare their boxes by cutting six holes of varying sizes along the lid's top. The smallest hole should be just slightly bigger than the go-go, with the others incrementally larger. Each hole is given a point value, usually 1 (for the largest opening), 2, 5, 10, 50, and 100 (for the most challenging hole).

The game begins like this: Standing about five feet away (or closer if that's too difficult), a player tries to throw one of his pits into another player's box. If he makes it, the point value of the hole determines how many go-gos that player must give him. If he misses the box entirely, he loses his one go-go. So the children don't have to lug around buckets of pits or stones (on the chance someone gets one in the toughest hole, he'd have to pay up 100!), feel free to lower the point values on the smaller holes. Children can also personalize their shoebox by decorating if it desired

● *Expanding*: A teacher extends or adds to what the child has just said (for example, child says, "I painted," and the teacher says, "You painted in red and blue").

● *Questioning*: The teacher begins a back-and-forth interaction with a child (for example, teacher says, "What did you build?" child answers, "A house"; teacher replies, "Who lives in your house?").

● *Prompting*: A teacher provides a specific cue to a child (for example, teacher says, "I think Marc is talking to you").

Teacher talk is one technique that early childhood teachers can use to support and encourage play opportunities for children with disabilities.

7-5c Adaptation

Toys for children who have disabilities may need to be adapted. Toys can be adapted with low-tech or high-tech changes. High-tech adaptations are generally requested by an IEP and used by someone trained in assistive technology (see Photo 7-8).

Yet low-tech adaptations are just as useful and can be done by adults in the classroom. Some examples are adding large knobs to puzzles, adding Velcro© to blocks, or adding grips to crayons and markers. Simple items such as muffin pans and Nerf© balls can be turned into a game. The muffin pan and soft balls is an activity generally recommended as the infant's first puzzle, but it is equally effective with children who have motor delays. Putting marbles in a hollow ball

PHOTO 7-8 Play is possible with technology, too!

Casper Holroyd

allows children with visual impairments to feel and hear the movement of the marbles inside the ball.

7-5d Accessibility

Some toys in the room should be accessible to all children. All preschoolers should be able to access blocks, dolls, books, or balls without a teacher's assistance. But be careful in that some children may become overstimulated by too many available materials. If this is creating a problem, rotate toys on a regular basis. A survey of the room can determine the level of accessibility of the toys and play materials. Consider the needs of the individual children. Materials for art should be accessible to children in wheelchairs. If a child has visual impairments, signs with large pictures or signs in Braille can be used depending on the child's degree of impairment. Being sure that the placement of the shelves and materials is stable will also help children navigate the classroom (Sluss, 2005).

Did You Get It?

A teacher hands a 3-year-old child with Down Syndrome a doll, and the child simply stares at it. What can you infer from this situation?

a. The child needs the teacher to help her engage with the toy.

b. Children with Down Syndrome cannot be expected to engage in play.

c. Special needs children play well with other children but cannot play independently.

d. If special needs children are not taught to play with toys in the first year of life, they will be unable to learn to play later on.

Take the full quiz on CourseMate.

7-6 Violent Play

DAP naeyc Play, as we have discussed in this chapter, is viewed as an essential part of the early childhood program. In our world today, however, violent play can often be a problem because of the frequency of war and superhero play in the early childhood years. Some teachers question the importance of play when it is often focused on fighting. Some teachers resort to planning other activities that are easier to manage. Another solution some teachers use is to reduce playtime. This may seem to reduce problems in the short term, but it deprives children of the wide-ranging developmental benefits play provides. Before we consider how to deal with the problem of war and superhero play, it is important to consider some of the reasons for this type of play.

7-6a Some Reasons for Violent Play

Children are exposed to far more violence today than their teachers have experienced in their lives. Yet teachers must help today's children face and deal with this exposure to violence. Let us consider what impact the presence of violence has in a child's life.

Violence in everyday life. Many young children are exposed to some form of violence in their everyday lives. They may see violence in their homes and communities as well as in entertainment and news on the television screen. It's hardly surprising that children are bringing it into their play.

If you watch children's violent play, you will see that they often focus on the most graphic, confusing, scary, or aggressive aspects of violence. It is this context they are struggling to work out and understand in their play. Usually, the children who seem most obsessed with war play have been exposed to the most violence and have the greatest need to work it out (Porter, 2009).

Feelings. Most young children look for ways to feel powerful and strong. Play can be a safe way to achieve a sense of power. From a child's point of view, play with violence is very seductive, especially when connected to the power and invincibility portrayed in entertainment. Children who use war play to help themselves feel powerful and safe are children who feel the most powerless and vulnerable (Porter, 2009).

Media, toys, and violence. Many of the action figures so popular today are highly structured toys. Just by the way they look and work, they give children powerful messages about the content and direction of play. In contrast, open-ended toys such as blocks and stuffed animals can be used in many ways that the child controls.

Many of the action and war games toys are linked to violent movies, TV shows, and video games. These toys have strong appeal because they promise dramatic power and excitement. Often, these toys cause children to replicate violent stories they see on the screen. Many young children get stuck imitating media-linked violence instead of developing creative and imaginative play.

Working with children's violent play. There are no simple or perfect solutions to children's violent play. However, here are some ways to approach the problem.

- Wherever possible, reduce the amount of violence children see. Most of young children's exposure to violence occurs in the home, so family involvement is crucial. Teachers can help families learn more about how to protect children from violence through parent workshops and family newsletters. Teachers can also help parents learn to deal with the violence that still gets in. In addition, teachers can provide parents with information on how to choose open-ended toys and toys with nonviolent themes.

- Promote imaginative and creative play. Be aware of the difference between imitative play and creative or imaginative play. Imitative play occurs when children engage in the same play with violence day after day and bring in few new or creative ideas of their own. Piaget called this kind of behavior *imitation*, not play (Porter, 2009). In imitative play, children are less likely to work out their needs than in imaginative play.

- Take time to observe children's play and learn what children are working on and how. Use this information to help children move beyond their imitative play that focuses on violent actions. Help children learn new ways to work out the violent content of their play. For example, children can work out their feelings by pounding nails into wood, rolling and pounding out clay, and knocking down stacks of blocks.

- Encourage children to deal with issues of violence by expressing their feelings in painting, drawing, or telling stories. Older children can write down their thoughts in stories or poetry.

- Talk with children about violent play. As children struggle to feel safe and make sense of violence, they need to know adults are there to help them in the process (Porter, 2009). Talk with children to learn what confuses and scares them. When a child raises an issue about something that frightens her or him, it helps to ask an open-ended question. For example, simply ask, "What have you heard about that?" That way you can respond more exactly to what is troubling the child.

- It is important to keep in mind that children do not always understand violence as adults do. They may have misconceptions. Try to correct these misconceptions. ("The planes that go over our school do not carry bombs.") Help children sort out fantasy from reality. ("People in real life can't change back and forth like the Power Rangers do.")

● Encourage children to engage in creative play so they can transform violence into positive behavior. Provide them with props, time, and a positive environment in which to act out violent ideas in more positive ways. Guide them in their approach so they might learn firsthand how to treat each other in peaceful ways. Praise them for their efforts ("I'm glad that in real life you could solve your problem with Scott by. . ."). These real-life experiences can help defuse some of the harmful lessons children learn about violence.

Given the state of our world, young children now more than ever need to find ways to work out the violence they see. For many, play helps them do this. We

have a crucial role in helping meet young children's needs through play.

Did You Get It?

A teacher encourages her 6-year-old student to draw a picture depicting violence. What positive learning objective might the teacher have?

a. helping her student to deal with issues of violence through artistic expression

b. helping her student recognize that violence is an inalienable part of life

c. helping her student connect to her classmates who regularly express violence

d. helping her student avoid violent media by making violence a part of her classroom life

Take the full quiz on CourseMate.

Summary

7-1 Discuss the concept and qualities of play

For young children, play is what they do all day. Playing is living, and living is playing. Young children do not differentiate among play, learning, and work. Children are by nature playful. They enjoy playing and will do so whenever they can.

There are definite qualities associated with child's play. Some of these qualities that distinguish play for young children from other activities are the following:

- It is a process. The outcome is not as important as the process itself.
- Play is child-initiated. The activity is done for no other reason than the child wants to do it.
- In play, everything and anything can happen; a sheet over a table becomes a castle, and the little girl inside is the princess.
- Play becomes the arena for testing rules, both logical and illogical. Rules freely appear and disappear in children's play; they may be simple or complex, and they are created from children's previous knowledge.
- Play is very much an activity of the mind. Children may become deeply engrossed in their play and find it difficult to stop when asked.

7-2 Discuss the play theories of Parten and Smilansky. Piaget and Vgotsky.

Parten theorized that there is a general sequential order of play activities that may be observed in young children.

These types of play activities may be classified according to stages.

In Parten's theory, onlooker play is when the child plays passively by watching or conversing with other children engaged in play activities. Solitary play is when a child plays alone. Parallel play occurs when a child plays side by side with other children with some interaction but without direct involvement. Associative play takes place when a child plays in a group. Smilansky found that dramatic play enhanced children's social skills. Cooperative play marked by mutual involvement in a play activity. Piaget and Vgotsky.

Piaget defined play as assimilation—the child's efforts to make environmental stimuli match his or her own concepts. He described imaginative play as one of the purest forms of symbolic thought available to the young child. Vygotsky states that play actually facilitates cognitive development. Play does not so much reflect thought as it does create thought. Play usually develops in a natural sequence that evolves from a child's level of socialization.

7-3 Discuss the importance of play to human growth and development.

Creative play has specific purposes in the early childhood program: to promote physical, mental, social, and emotional growth. Play contributes to muscle development and hand–eye coordination. Play also helps children develop their senses. When children have a chance to be physically active, they continually gain strength. Play helps children develop important mental concepts. Children learn to sort, classify, and probe for answers in play. Creative play helps a child achieve mastery of his or her environment.

7-4 Describe developmentally appropriate childhood games.

Developmentally appropriate games allow children to learn self-confidence, problem solving, cooperation, trust and improved motor skills.

7-5 Discuss ways the environment can be adapted to encourage social play experiences for children with special needs.

Toys can be adapted with low-tech or high-tech changes. All preschoolers should be able to access blocks, dolls, books, or balls without a teacher's assistance. Be aware that too many available materials may overstimulate some children. Consider the needs of the individual child with special needs. For preschool children who have difficulty interacting with peers, teachers must plan, develop, implement, and monitor interventions to promote social interactions during play.

7-6 Discuss some reasons children engage in violent play and how to deal with this type of play.

Young children today are exposed to violence in their homes, communities, and in entertainment and news on the television. Children engage in violent play to feel powerful and strong. Play can be a safe way to achieve a sense of power. Also, many of the action figures popular with children give powerful messages about the content and direction of play in contrast to more open-ended toys such as blocks and stuffed animals.

Wherever possible, reduce the amount of violence children see; promote imaginative and creative play; help children work out their feelings in nonviolent ways; encourage children to deal with issues of violence by expressing their feelings in paintings, drawing, or telling stories; talk with children about violent play; and encourage children to engage in creative play so they can transform violence into positive behavior.

Key Terms

associative play 139	onlooker behavior 138	spontaneous play 139
cooperative play 139	organized play 139	teacher talk 150
free play 139	parallel play 139	
imaginative play 140	solitary play 138	

Learning Activities

A. Observe children of various ages at play. Without letting them know you are watching, observe one or more children from each age group at play for periods of at least 10 minutes for each group. How are the play activities similar? How are they different? Observe children in these two groups: (1) kindergarten through grade 3 and (2) grades 4 to 5. How are their play activities similar? How are they different? What were the most prevalent forms of play observed in each group? Were you surprised by what you saw? Why or why not?

B. Select one play activity and discuss how it contributes to a child's growth in each of four areas of development discussed in this chapter (physical, mental, social, emotional). Choose an activity for each of the age groups discussed in this chapter. Compare and contrast the activities for each age group.

C. Observe the dramatic play of a group of 3-year-olds and a group of 5-year-olds. In what ways is their play different? How is it similar? Observe dramatic play for a group of children in each of these age groups: (1) kindergarten through grade 3 and (2) grades 4 to 5. In what ways is their dramatic play different from each other? How is it similar? Did you observe anything that surprised you? Share your observations with your fellow students.

D. Try the animal cracker game. This is a game that children enjoy and that helps them develop a better understanding of the creative possibilities of games.
   1. Obtain a box of animal crackers. Stand before a full-length mirror and, without looking, take one of the crackers from the box. Look at it and then eat the cracker. With that action, you "become" the selected animal for 2 minutes. Observe your behavior as that animal. Do this a number of times.
   2. Answer the following questions about this activity.
      a. How did you feel about doing this?
      b. How is creativity different from silliness?
      c. How do games help people develop creativity or become more creative?

E. Select an activity that children engage in for the sheer joy of doing it. List the learning involved.

F. Record the conversations of two children playing together. Is there evidence from the discussion that one child is dominating the play? If so, on what did you base your conclusions? Compare your findings with others in class.

G. Visit a local playground. Describe the equipment available. Which pieces were most popular? Why do you believe this was so? What aspects of the arrangement and equipment are conducive to children's play? Explain.

Activities for Children

Toddler Play

- Gather up some plush animals and arrange them in a circle around the child. Ask her to make each animal's special sound, and then call on each animal as if in a classroom: "Cow, you're next. Cow says . . . ."
- Toddlers love to explore, especially when there's treasure at the end! Using a ball of brightly colored yarn, mark a trail through the room and place a small treat at the end. Help the toddler follow the trail as it runs around the room and ends with his fun surprise. If the toddler gathers up the string as he goes, the path will be easier to follow.
- Box Fun. Toddlers love big boxes to play in—but don't expect complex play with them. A toddler may not be ready to rocket to the moon in the TV box, but she'll relish the cozy space, the flaps to open and close, or maybe the chance to hide away with a blanket and take a nap.
- Fun Footwork. Unroll large sheets of paper on a washable surface, and put a few colors of tempera paint out on paper plates. Let the toddler step in the paint with bare feet, and then hold his hands while she "paints" her foot prints all over the paper.
- Cardboard boxes offer toddlers the opportunity for a great deal of beneficial play. Take sturdy cardboard boxes of different sizes and tape them together with packing or duct tape to form long "trains." Make segments of varying heights by propping some boxes on sturdy pillows or padding. Then place the trains in a padded area or surround them with pillows. Encourage the toddlers to climb on top of the train at one end and crawl the length of the train. Moving up and down onto the different levels promotes motor planning, eye–hand coordination, and balance. You can also have them crawl through open boxes taped together in "tunnels," which will increase their body awareness.
- Stuff an empty tissue box with scarves or large pieces of nylon or similar fabric. Toddlers enjoy pulling the fabric out. Turn on some music and let the children dance with their scarves.
- Add materials to a water or sand table. A large plastic tub or box can be a portable sand table. Put in foam packing "peanuts," cotton balls, shredded paper, or even dirt. Hide some small plastic toys in the box. Give the child some scoops, funnels, or cups with which to dig for fun and to develop eye–hand coordination.

Expanding Play Experiences

One way to encourage and expand children's play is by changing the materials they normally use in activity centers. Add some of the following materials to your interest centers to expand children's play experiences.

Dramatic Play Center

- Add open-ended materials such as sheets and scarves or a large cardboard box. Ask children, "What can you do with this?"

- Have a box of unusual items (tools, beach ball, funny glasses, hats) that children can choose from when they want to add a new element to their play.
- After reading a favorite story, provide props to go with it and have children retell the story in their own way.

Block Center

- Add rope and small balls. Ask the children, "What can you do with these?"
- Add aluminum foil and flashlights to inspire new types of building.
- Have pictures of unusual buildings in the center to inspire children's building.

Shadow Play

A. In a group, perhaps outdoors on a bright day, encourage children to make silly movements and observe their own shadows. Introduce a quick "copycat" (follow-the-leader) game: "Everybody jump! Everybody hop! Now, everybody dance!"

B. On the playground, play a shadow touch game. Have the children in the group make one connecting shadow by having their shadows touch each other's. Then play shadow tag.

Imagination Exercises

Children enjoy "being" animals or other pretend things. These activities are good for large-muscle development as well as for creative play. In these activities, encourage children to move slowly and quietly. After they interpret the object or animal in their own way, suggest that they hold the positions while continuing to breathe slowly.

A. *Tree.* Together, close your eyes and think about different trees you've seen. Then stand up and raise your arms to look like a tree. Breathe slowly in and out and try to hold the pose for about 30 seconds.

B. *Mountain.* Sit on the floor, legs crossed or in any position that's comfortable. Slowly raise your arms to create a mountain peak. As you hold this position, have children pretend they, too, are huge, quiet mountains. You, or someone in the group, can describe the peaceful scenes you might see below.

C. *Cat.* Find a comfortable way to curl up like a cat and pretend to be sleeping in a warm, comfy place, such as near a fireplace or in a sunny place. Then wake up and stretch.

D. *Turtle.* Pretend you are a turtle by rounding your back like a shell and tucking your head, arms, and legs under the shell. Hold this pose for a bit, and then very slowly stretch out your neck, arms, and legs (Church, 1993).

The following are some creative play activities that require the use of large muscles and that promote large (gross) motor skills.

Guess What I Am

Without saying a word, a child tries to act out the movements of some object. This may be an airplane making a landing, a rooster strutting around the barnyard, a cement truck dumping its load, or a clock telling the time of day. The child may think up things to do, or the teacher may whisper suggestions.

Water Play

A water table or a large tub is filled with water and used for creative water play. Children pour, mix, and stir the water. Soap may be added so they can create suds, too. They may also enjoy using water and a large paintbrush to "paint" a fence or the school building. A variety of objects can be put together to make a boat that floats. (Aluminum foil works well for this.) Creative cleanup can be developed by children as they find how water, tools, and materials can help them clean up messes.

Playing With a Hose

A child enjoys playing with a hose connected to an outlet with the water on strong. Children learn about what happens when they put their thumbs over the nozzle. They discover the push effect as water leaves the hose. They make rain by sprinkling water into the air. They create a rainbow. They hear different sounds as the water strikes different materials.

For a realistic gas pump hose to use outdoors with riding toys, fit an old piece of garden hose with a pistol grip nozzle. These nozzles are available at hardware stores.

Challenges

Look around the room to find ways to encourage children's creative play. Try some of these.

- *In the Housekeeping Corner.* How many ways can you use a scarf, pillowcase, or paper bag? What can you invent to help you carry your baby doll or your groceries? What do you need to change your house into a pet store?
- *In the Block Center.* What can you build that can be a place to park all the cars and trucks? How many ways can you build a road that is as long as the classroom? How many ways can you build a bridge, castle, apartment house, or tower?
- *In the Science Center.* How many different objects can you use to invent bubble blowers? How can you use sponges to pick up things? How many ways can you use paper to make wind?
- *At the Sand and Water Table.* What can you invent that will keep the sand (or water) from leaking out of the colander? How many different materials can you use to invent a boat that floats? What can you invent that will move sand from one container to another?
- *In the Outdoors.* How many ways can you make a shadow? What can you invent to dig with in the sand? How many ways can you balance a beach ball between you and a friend?
- *In the Art Center.* How many ways can you change a piece of paper without using a tool? What can you invent with newspaper, paperclips, and rubber bands? How can you draw with more than one crayon at a time?

Play in the Great Outdoors

- Set up an obstacle course with old tires, large appliance boxes, and tree stumps. Moving through it will teach important concepts such as over, under, through, and around.
- Bring the parachute or an old sheet outside and play parachute games (shaking it, circling with it, making waves with it, or bouncing foam balls on it).
- Chasing bubbles gives children a chance to run!
- Bring a portable boom box outdoors and let the children experience the joy of dancing in a natural environment.

Group Games

Kick the Can

Kick the Can is a little like tag. Players draw a large circle on the ground and put a can or other object in the middle. The player who is "It" guards the can. Other players try to run in and kick it out of the circle. When someone kicks the can, the It player must go to get it back. Meanwhile, the other players run to hide. When It gets back to the circle, he or she yells "Freeze!" and the others must stop. It calls out the names of the players he or she can see, and they are prisoners. Then It must find the other players. But if someone who's hidden can run and kick the can, the prisoners are free. If there are no prisoners, one of the hiding players can run into the circle and shout, "Home free!" Then everyone runs back to the circle, and the last player to get there is It for the next round.

Ghost in the Graveyard

This tag game is also called Midnight Ghost. It can be played with any number of children. One person is chosen as the ghost. While everyone else stays at a home base, the ghost runs away and hides. The groups chants, "one o'clock, two o'clock, three o'clock…" up to 12 o'clock, then shouts "Midnight! I hope I don't see the ghost tonight!" Then all the children run around. When someone sees the ghost, he or she yells, "Ghost in the graveyard!" and tries to run away. If the ghost catches you, you become a ghost, too. In the next round, all the ghosts hide and the others count again. The last person caught is the ghost for the next round.

Mother, May I?

Line up the children facing you, about 10 feet away. Give commands to one child at a time, such as, "Claire, take one hop forward." If Claire responds, "Mother, may I?" you can say either "Yes, you may" or "No, you may not." If your reply is "yes," make sure that Claire says "Thank you" before she goes. Anyone who forgets her manners or makes a move without permission is sent back to the starting line. Keep playing until one child reaches Mother. Give each child a chance to be Mother. This game helps teach children respect. To avoid frustration over misunderstood consequences ("I didn't know I had to say thank you"), make the rules of the game perfectly clear before you get started.

The Hot or Cold Game

Choose one child to be the Finder. Send him out of the room while the rest of the players hide an object, like a red ball, somewhere in the room. Ask the Finder to come back and look for the ball, while the other players call out hints: "You're getting hotter" or "you're getting colder." Play until the object is found, then give everyone a turn as the Finder. This game puts the emphasis on encouraging other players, not competing against them, so children learn to help each other out in a fun setting.

I Spy

Take turns spotting nearby objects and describing them: "I spy with my little eye something that is green . . . ." The other players try to guess what the object is: "A tree!" "Jorge's shirt!" Whoever guesses right gets to be the net "spy." This game teaches patience and how to listen politely while other players have their turn.

Australian Skippyroo Kangaroo

This is a popular game played in many Australian preschools and kindergartens to help teach children their classmates' names as well as good listening skills. Children sit in a circle and an adult asks one child to go into the middle—she is the first Skippyroo, the kangaroo. Skippyroo crouches forward on the floor with her eyes closed while the kids in the circle chant: "Skippyroo, kangaroo, dozing in the midday sun, comes a hunter, run, run, run." At this point, an adult points to a child sitting in the circle, who then touches Skippyroo's shoulder and says, "Guess who's caught you just for fun?" and waits. Skippyroo tries to name the owner of the voice and if she guesses correctly, swaps places. The game begins again and continues until all the children have had a chance to be Skippyroo.

Activities for Older Children (Grades 4–5)

Marble Games

Children have been playing marble games since ancient Roman times, more than 2,000 years ago. Early marbles made of clay have been found in Egyptian tombs and in Native American burial grounds. Around 120 years ago, machines were invented to make marbles. In most marble games, players shoot their marbles. They aim for another player's marbles or for a target, such as a hole in the ground.

Ring Taw. In this marble game, players make a circle about 3 feet wide on the ground. Each player puts several marbles in the circle.

A larger circle is drawn around the first one. Players choose a starting point on the outside of the circle. They use a taw, or shooting marble, to try to hit another player's marble out of the inside of the ring.

If the shooter hits a target marble and it goes out of the ring, the person gets one point. If his shooter stays in the ring, he may shoot from the place his taw stopped.

As long as he continues to knock a target marble out of the ring, his turn continues. His turn stops if his taw does not hit a target marble or if his taw leaves the ring. The winner is the player with the most points. For more ideas for marble games, visit www.landofmarbles.com.

New Games

Invent new class games. Divide the class evenly into cooperative learning groups. Have each group brainstorm ideas for a new game to play at recess or in gym class. Groups should determine the basic rules of play and any penalties. Allow one group per day to teach its new game to the rest of the class. Use anonymous feedback cards as a way for each member of the class to offer compliments or suggestions for improvement to each group's game. Offer each group time to assess its game and make changes. Record final game rules in a class game book.

How Other Kids Play

Have students meet Lornah Kipligat, a world-class athlete who started a girls' running camp in her native Kenya.

What's It Like to Be a Kid in Kenya?

Explore photo albums from students in South Africa, Kenya, Ghana, and Uganda.

Pictograms

Have the students try their hands at Chinese pictograms with Sagwa interactive games.

References

Barros, R. M., Silver, E. J., & Stein, R. E. K. (2009). School recess and group classroom behavior. *Pediatrics, 123*(2), 431–438.

Center on Education Policy. (2008). *Instructional time in elementary schools: A closer look at changes for specific subjects.* Retrieved from www.cep-dc.org/

Church, E. G. (1993, February). Moving small, moving quiet. *Scholastic Pre-K Today,* 42–45.

Copple, C., & Bredekamp, S. (2009). *Developmentally appropriate practice in early childhood programs serving children from birth through age 8* (3rd ed.). Washington, DC: NAEYC.

Cote, L. R., & Bornstein, M. H. (2009). Child and mother play in three U.S. cultural groups: Comparisons and associations. *Journal of Family Psychology, 123*(3), 355–365.

Elkind, D. (2003, May). Thanks for the memory: The lasting value of true play. *Young Children, 58,* 46–50.

Elkind, D. (2007). *The power of play: Learning what comes naturally.* Reading, MA: Da Capo Press.

Elkonin, D. B. (2005). Chapter 1: The subject of our research: The developed form of play. *Journal of Russian and East European Psychology, 45*(1), 22–48.

Erwin, H., Abel, M., Beighle, A., Nolan, M. P, Worley, J., & Riggs, R. (2012). The contribution of recess to children's school-day physical activity. *Journal of Physical Activity and Health, 9*(3), 442–448.

Guyton, G. (2011). Using toys to support infant-toddler learning and development. *Young Children, 14*(3), 50–56.

Harper, L., & McCluskey, K. (2003). Teacher-child and child-child interactions in inclusive preschool settings: Do Adults inhibit peer interactions? *Phi Delta Kappan, 18*(2), 163–184.

Hurwitz, S. C. (2003). To be successful—Let them play! Childhood Education, Winter 2002/2003, 100–101.

Jarrett, O. W. (2002). *Recess in elementary school: What does the research say?* ERIC Digest, ED466331 2002-07-00. Retrieved from www.ericdigests.org /2003-2/recess.html

Jarret, O. W., & Waite-Stupiansky, S. (2009). Recess—It's indispensable. *Young Children, 64*(5), 66–69.

Leong, D. J., & Bodrova, E. (2012). Assessing and scaffolding make-believe play. *Young Children, 67*(1), 28–34.

Levin, E. D. (2003). *Teaching young children in violent times: Building a peaceable classroom* (2nd ed.). Cambridge, MA: Educators for Social Responsibility.

Morrier, J. J., McGee, G. G., & Daily, T. (2009). Effects of toy selection and arrangement on the social behaviors of an inclusive group of preschool-aged children with and without autism. *Early Childhood Services: An Interdisciplinary Journal of Effectiveness, 13*(2), 157–168.

Oliver, S. J., & Klugman, E. (2007). Building a play research agenda: What do we know about play? What new questions do we need to ask? *Exchange: The Early Childhood Leaders' Magazine, 14*(4), 14–17.

Paley, V. (2004). *A child's work.* Chicago, IL: University of Chicago Press.

Parten, M. (1932). Social participation among preschool children. *Journal of Abnormal and Social Psychology, 27,* 243–269.

Piaget, J. (1962). *Play, dreams, and imitation in childhood.* New York, NY: W. W. Norton.

Pica, R. (2009). Learning by leaps and bounds. What makes a game developmentally appropriate? *Young Children, 64*(2), 66–69.

Porter, C. L. (2009). Predicting preschoolers' social-cognitive play behavior: Attachment, peers, temperament and physiological regulation. *Psychological Reports, 15*(6), 132–138.

Sandlund, M., McDonough, S., & Hager-Ross, C. (2009). Interactive computer play in rehabilitation of children with sensorimotor disorders: A systemic review. *Developmental Medicine and Child Neurology, 15*(3), 173–182.

Sharpe, T. (2008). How can teacher talk support learning? *Linguistics and Education, 19*(2), 132–148.

Sluss, D. J. (2005). *Supporting play: Birth through age 8.* Clifton Park, NY: Thomson-Delmar Learning.

Smilansky, S. (1968). *The effects of socio-dramatic play on disadvantaged preschool children.* New York, NY: Wiley.

Smilansky, S., & Shefatya, L. (1990). *Facilitating play: A medium for promoting cognitive, socio-emotional and academic development in young children.* Gaithersburg, MD: Psychosocial & Educational Publications.

Staempfli, M. B. (2009). Reintroducing adventure into children's outdoor play environments. *Environment and Behavior, 141*(2), 268–273.

Staley, L., & Portman, P. A. (2000). Red Rover, Red Rover, It's time to move over! *Young Children, 55*(1), 67–72.

Stanton-Chapman, T. L., & Hadden, D. S. (2011). Encouraging peer interactions in preschool classrooms: The role of the teacher. *Young Exceptional Children, 14*(1), 17–27.

Stanton-Chapman, T. L., Denning, C. B., & Jamison, K. R. (2008). Building requests and turn-taking skills in young children with disabilities. *Psychology in the Schools, 45*(7), 644–664.

Stanton-Chapman, T. L., Kaiser, A. P., & Wolery, M. (2006). Building social communication skills in Head Start children using storybooks: The effects of prompting on social interactions. *Journal of Early Intervention, 28*(3), 197–212.

Trawick-Smith, J., & Dziurgot, T. (2011). "Good-fit" teacher-child play interactions and the subsequent autonomous play of preschool children. *Early Childhood Research Quarterly, 26*(2), 110–123.

Vygotsky, L. (1978). *Mind in society: The development of higher psychological processes.* Cambridge, MA: Harvard University Press.

Williams, N. F. (1994). The Physical Education Hall of Shame, part 2. *Journal of Physical Education, Recreation & Dance, 65*(2), 17–20.

8

Using Technology to Promote Creativity

Today's preschoolers can answer the Sesame Street song's question, "Can you tell me how to get to Sesame Street?" in many ways. The way to Sesame Street can be found via TV, DVR, computer, a tablet such as an iPad, netbook, smartphone, or Microsoft's Kinect Sesame Street TV. And it's a good bet that there will be more ways in the near future.

Learning Objectives

After studying this chapter, you should be able to:

8-1 Summarize the position of the National Association for the Education of Young Children with regard to technology for children from birth through age 8.

8-2 List the pros and cons concerning the use of technology with young children.

8-3 Discuss several examples of technology used in the early childhood program.

8-4 Discuss the value of computers in early childhood programs.

8-5 List at least five characteristics to consider in choosing developmentally appropriate computer software.

8-6 List the four basic types of children's websites.

naeyc

NAEYC Program Standards

1c Using developmental knowledge to create healthy, respectful, supportive, and challenging learning environments.

4c Using a broad repertoire of developmentally appropriate teaching/learning approaches.

DAP

DAP Criteria

2H2 Teachers think carefully about which learning format is best for helping children achieve a desired goal.

2J1 Teachers incorporate a wide variety of experiences, materials and equipment, and teaching strategies to accommodate the range of children's individual differences.

PHOTO 8-1 Computers are a part of many children's preschool experience.

Casper Holroyd

Technology, especially computers, is a part of many children's preschool experiences (see Photo 8-1). You can generally find at least one computer available for children's use during learning center or free-choice time. Technology—computers, tablets, netbooks, digital cameras, videos, video games, interactive CDs, DVDs—is definitely here to stay in the early childhood program.

With the growing use of technology in the early childhood program, teachers more than ever need to know the best ways to use technology with young children. This chapter provides a basic framework of information about using technology in developmentally appropriate ways in the early childhood program.

8-1 NAEYC Technology Position Statement and Developmentally Appropriate Practice

DAP **naeyc** Before beginning any discussion of technology in the early childhood program, it is important to consider developmental appropriateness of technology and young children.

As we have seen in Chapter 5, developmentally appropriate practice (DAP) is an underlying premise of all educational experiences for young children. Although the theories of DAP have been widely adopted in many aspects of the early childhood curriculum, developmental appropriateness is still largely absent from the methods in which the computer is used with young children. To ensure that computer technology enhances the learning experiences of young children, standards of DAP must be applied to using technology just as they are to other materials and methods in the classroom. Technology does not drive purposeful learning; teachers' intentional instructional planning does. The National Association for the Education of Young Children's (NAEYC) 2012 position statement, "Technology and Interactive Media as Tools in Early Childhood Programs Serving Children from Birth Through Age 8" (NAEYC, 2012) reflects the ever-changing digital age and provides guidance for early childhood educators about the use of technology and interactive media in ways that can optimize opportunities for young children's cognitive, social, emotional, physical, and linguistic development. NAEYC defines technology as a broad range of digital devices such as computers, tablets, multi-touch screens, interactive whiteboards, mobile devices, cameras, DVD and music players, audio recorders, electronic toys, games, e-book readers, and older analog devices still being used such as tape recorders, VCRs, VHS tapes, record and cassette players, light tables, projectors, and microscopes (NAEYC, 2012).

The main recommendations of the NAEYC position statement are found in Figure 8-1. When thinking of computer integration across the classroom curriculum, it is helpful to think of software as a manipulative. That is how most children see the computer—as something to manipulate or control. Any teacher who has spent a few moments with high-quality early childhood software can see that the computer is not unlike other early childhood materials such as books, play dough, and blocks. With the right kind of software, computers are open ended and discovery oriented, with three-dimensional screen manipulatives that are controlled with various devices. The child simply points the mouse, clicks, and drags the objects on the screen to the desired location (see Photo 8-2). Sometimes the graphics are static, as in a picture book, and sometimes they are animated (birds fly, people walk). Therefore, computer graphics constitute manipulatives, as do blocks and puzzles.

1. Select, use, integrate, and evaluate technology and interactive media tools in intentional and developmentally appropriate ways, giving careful attention to the appropriateness and the quality of the content, the child's experience, and the opportunities for co-engagement.

2. Provide a balance of activities in programs for young children, recognizing that technology and interactive media can be valuable tools when used intentionally with children to extend and support active, hands-on, creative, and authentic engagement with those around them and their world.

3. Prohibit the passive use of television, videos, DVDs, and other non-interactive technologies and media in early childhood programs for children younger than 2, and discourage passive and non-interactive uses with children ages 2 through 5.

4. Limit any use of technology and interactive media in programs for children younger than 2 to those that appropriately support responsive interactions between caregivers and children and that strengthen adult–child relationships.

5. Carefully consider the screen time recommendations from public health organizations for children from birth through age 5 when determining appropriate limits on technology and media use in early childhood settings. Screen time estimates should include time spent in front of a screen at the early childhood program, and with input from parents and families, at home and elsewhere.

6. Provide leadership in ensuring equitable access to technology and interactive media experiences for the children in their care and for parents and families. (NAEYC, 2012)

FIGURE 8-1 Recommendations on the use of technology: NAEYC and the Fred Rogers Center.

Source: From "Technology and Interactive Media as Tools in Early Childhood Programs Serving Children from Birth through Age 8," a joint position statement issued by the National Association for the Education of Young Children and the Fred Rogers Center for Early Learning and Children's Media at Saint Vincent College, adopted January 2012.

PHOTO 8-2 Learning to point, click, and move objects on a screen are basic computer skills for early elementary students.

Casper Holroyd

Like other manipulatives, computers can be used in many ways. They can be used wisely in a way that enhances development or in less appropriate ways that interfere with that development. No one would argue against crayons as a necessary staple in the early childhood program. But this does not mean we support having 2-year-olds use crayons to color shapes on a ditto page or trace letters of the alphabet on a workbook page. Similarly, computers are advocated as an appropriate tool for use with young children, but only if they are used in a manner that supports curiosity and exploration, not as an expensive worksheet.

In working with children under the age of 5, it is important to think of the computer much like a dessert instead of the main meal. Children in this age group learn best through active, physical exploration of their environments. An occasional use of the computer is appropriate with children under 5 years of age. But sitting down and working on a computer for long periods of time each day is not appropriate to the developmental needs of these children. For younger children, the American Academy of Pediatrics revised its 1999 statement that said no TV and no screens for children less than 2 years old, to more recently advising caution with parents using screens for babies under 2 (American Academy of Pediatrics, 2010).

8-2 Deciding to Use Technology: Pros and Cons

DAP naeyc The time children spend in front of computers is time they don't have for physical activity and a host of other important activities. In making decisions regarding the use of technology in teaching and learning, teachers should carefully examine what is gained and lost when making decisions about the amount of time students spend interacting with computers and other media. For instance, when students type information, they are losing time formerly used to write—an activity that develops important handwriting and small-motor skills.

When we make the decision to have students use a computer, for example, we must think about both the gains made from using the computer (such as quick access to information) and the losses (learning to use the library, handwriting, face-to-face social skills, hands-on experiences, and understanding that simply finding mountains of information does not equate to thoughtful, accurate learning). If the computer is selected for a given activity, we need to be aware of what we are losing in the process and then make a decision about whether to provide additional time to develop the knowledge and skills that are lost when we use the technology.

> "It took 19 years for the color TV to reach 10 million users. The VCR took 12 years. CD players, 7 years. The iPad, 9 months."
>
> –A tweet made during 2011's International Society for Technology in Education Annual Conference key note speech.

8-3 Technology that Develops Creativity

DAP naeyc Technology provides variety, interest, involvement, and reinforcement. One of the most important advantages it provides is a chance for children to develop their creativity. This occurs when they design, manipulate, and express themselves using the technology examples that follow.

8-3a Video Recordings

It is possible for children to plan and produce video recordings of class activities. They can record dramatic presentations, dancing, field trips, and other activities in and around the school.

Today, fairly inexpensive video recording equipment is available to schools. It is lightweight, portable, and easy to use. Video can do all the things that movies and slides do, is less expensive, and can be reused. Mistakes can be erased or deleted. Children see the results of their work right away. Video can be used with dramatic play activities: A play can be recorded, and a children's art show can be recorded. Some children enjoy telling stories or retelling favorite events. Playtime games can be created and taped. Many portable units can be taken on field trips. Video recordings made on field trips can be used to spark creative storytelling and the creation of new games.

Movies can be obtained from a library or rental company. These movies can be used to introduce engaging activities. Creative dramatics, for example, can begin with a movie that introduces a story and several characters. At a particular point, the movie can be turned off, and children take the parts of the characters in acting out their own ending to the story. DVDs or videos might also be used to inspire children's ideas for painting and drawing.

8-3b Photography

Young children enjoy taking pictures. Taking photographs is yet another creative way for children to experience their world. Photography is an outlet for self-expression that has potential for all ages. This is due in large part to the low cost and simplicity of many cameras, which allow even the novice to take well-focused pictures. Children can share the special world of their school with others through pictures and words.

It is important, especially with younger children, to keep responsibilities simple. Explain that taking pictures is a fun activity and children can take pictures of whatever they would like to remember about their experiences at school. For example, a class of second graders came up with these ideas: happy places, happy people, special places, and special people. With older children, you may be a bit more abstract. A class of fourth graders could be asked to take pictures of friendship in as many images and ways they can find. An interesting approach to photography with upper-elementary-grade children is to focus on common themes generated by the teacher or the children. Some of these might be pictures of special people or places or pictures of people or places that make you happy or even unhappy. Children can journey around the school to document the images in their mind's eye. Don't provide too specific guidelines for what they photograph. Let the child be the leader.

Plan to spend some time explaining and demonstrating how to take a picture, frame the picture, activate the flash, and so forth. Leave the cameras in the art center, and let children practice with them. After they have practiced taking pictures for a while, they will be ready to really use the cameras.

When children are taking photos for the first time, a teacher or another adult needs to be on hand to help with the mechanics of looking through the viewfinder, pressing the buttons, and answering questions as they arise.

When children are out taking pictures, be sure they have notebooks and pencils with them to record where each picture was taken and its significance. So they do not forget what they have photographed,

children need to write a note about each picture right after they take it. The notes can become stories later. Be certain that the students understand that their personal impressions are what you want them to describe.

Today's digital cameras make it possible to instantly see the picture you've *just* taken (and erase it if you don't like it). These cameras have incredible educational possibilities, from making labels for the classroom to showing parents their children's creations during parent–teacher conferences.

The power of a digital camera is measured in megapixels—the more a camera has, the sharper the picture. A classroom camera should have at least 5 megapixels and strong rechargeable batteries. A digital camera with a fast shutter speed and the ability to take several photographs in a row (sports setting) works well. It is easy to snap a series of back-and-forth expressions between a child and a teacher, or a series of movements, such as a child learning to tie his shoe for the first time—without having to wait for the camera to process the first image.

A digital camera is a great tool for teachers. You can take pictures of children's artwork throughout the year to create a portfolio of each child's work. You can take pictures of each child, print them, and post the photos on each child's cubby or personal space area.

Digital cameras can be used to photograph and document children's progress. Many times when children are working with materials, especially creating with blocks or art materials, the final product misses the thinking and process that goes into the completed work. Documenting with photographs helps to show the progress and also gives the child opportunities to revisit her or his work.

It is a good idea to download and organize your photos and video clips onto the computer soon after taking them. It is helpful to have a computer nearby to help get into the habit of downloading photos quickly and regularly. Easy access to a computer can allow you to share photos or video clips on the same day they are recorded.

Label each downloaded image with the day it was taken and a short description. Teachers can use the photographs to record child growth over time when conferencing with families and use concrete images to support thoughts, anecdotes, and observations.

Back up your photos on an external hard drive on a regular basis. This preserves the photos in case of a computer failure. Saving video clips and older

THINK ABOUT IT

The Effect of Fast-Paced Cartoons on Young Children's Executive Functions

The typical child began watching TV at 4 years of age in 1970 and consumed 3-4 hours/day. In contract, the typical child today begins watching at 4 months and is engaged with media for up to 8 hours/day (Vandewater et al., 2007; Zimmerman et al., 2007).

This has led some to distinguish between today's generation of children, the "digital natives," and their parents, who will remain "digital immigrants."

This study focused on rapid paced children's programming (for example, *SpongeBob SquarePants*) and its effect on preschool children's executive function. Executive function includes the ability to control one's attention, stay focused on specific instructions, and wait for a reward (delayed gratification) (Lillard & Peterson, 2011).

Sixty 4-year-olds were randomly assigned to watch a fast-paced cartoon *(SpongeBob SquarePants)*, watch an educational cartoon (PBS' *Caillou),* or draw with crayons or markers for 9 minutes.

They were then given four tasks tapping their executive function, including delay of gratification and Tower of Hanoi tasks (stacking disks in order of size). Parents completed surveys regarding TV viewing and children's attention.

Children who watched the fast-paced TV cartoon performed significantly worse on the executive function tasks than the children in the other two groups, when controlling for child attention, age, and TV experience. Children who watched 9 minutes of a fast-paced cartoon had impairment in their executive function (for example, self-regulation, working memory) compared to children who were assigned a drawing task and those who watched educational TV.

The researchers concluded that connecting fast-paced TV viewing to deficits in executive function, regardless of whether they are transient, has profound implications for children's cognitive and social development that need to be considered and studied further. Parents, too, should be aware that fast-paced TV shows could at least temporarily impair young children's executive function. Teachers need to consider planning transitions between intense periods and activities that require the child's focus (Lillard & Peterson, 2011).

---

photo files to a hard drive and then deleting them from the computer can ensure enough memory on the hard drive to avoid slowing down the computer (Luckenbill, 2012).

Some other ways to use a digital camera follow:

- Experiment with time-lapse photography. Take a picture of the children in front of the same tree each month to see the seasons change.
- Preserve memories. The next time a child cleans up, snap a picture.
- Decorate bulletin boards with photos of active, happy children.
- Allow the children to become the photographers. Take pictures in the classroom, on the playground, and on walking trips. Children can view their finished photos from the camera or with a teacher on the computer, identifying what they thought was important. Inexpensive, throwaway digital cameras are available that are well suited for children's use. You will be amazed and delighted as you see the world through children's eyes.

8-3c Editing Digital Images

Basic editing can be done on the camera or with any number of photo-editing software programs. A number of software programs and Web-based photo services are available to support your photo editing and layout design. These tools make it easy to import and export photos, edit, add special effects, and organize photos into albums. Three of these sources are briefly described here.

- Picasa2—Free download from Google with one-click editing and effects.
- Shutterfly—This free software download is a great way to store and edit digital photos. Use one click to edit tools to enhance lighting, crop, and even create collages of 4 to 100 photos.

● Snapfish—This online photo service from HP facilitates camera or computer uploads—even email photos from a mobile phone. Install PhotoShow for more features.

All of these photo tools let you email photos to share with colleagues or parents to highlight special events.

8-3d iPods and MP3 Players

The iPod is a portable digital music player that can also be used to store photos or even movies. The first iPods contained hard disks; later versions were RAM-based with more reliable performance. iPod content can only be managed by a computer running iTunes, which makes it possible to browse, store, and purchase digital content. Today, a variety of digital music players are available for children, including the Playskool Made for Me MP3 Music Player, or Peapod Toys' SweetPea3.

8-3e CDs and CD Players

If digital music is not easily accessible to your classroom, using CDs and CD players is another possibility. CDs can be used in computers, providing sound effects and narration on early childhood computer software. Playing recorded music on a CD is an excellent source of musical experiences for young children.

8-3f Interactive Whiteboards in Elementary Classrooms

Interactive whiteboards (IWBs), also called Smart Boards, are large screen-like boards that are placed in front of a class and connected to a computer and data projector. Any computer image can be projected onto this sturdy surface. Teachers and students can write directly on the board to make notes and highlight all sorts of amazing images.

Whiteboards were initially developed for and used in the business world, but they are now more widely used in higher education, and they're becoming more common in K-12 schools (see Photo 8-3) (Lacina, 2009). Almost across the board, teachers report that their students are highly engaged in activities with IWBs (Curwood, 2009).

IWBs appeal to children's multiple intelligences, providing opportunities for visual/spatial and bodily/kinesthetic learners than can be hard to accommodate in the print-based classroom. They also allow you to reach your students through a variety of media (see Photo 8-4). For example, if you are studying Kenya,

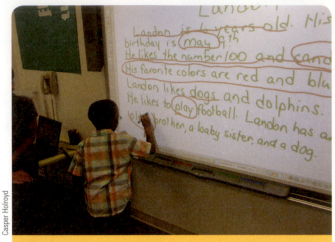

PHOTO 8-3 A whiteboard is becoming a standard piece of classroom equipment.

your students might use Google Earth to project the country on the whiteboard, zooming in and out to see the terrain, and clicking on photos that show details, daily life, flora, and fauna. Then, when students dive into the reading, they have a variety of background knowledge and increased motivation.

IWBs allow users to annotate computer screen information and highlight key visual points. This technology allows presenters to make their notes directly on the whiteboard itself using either a finger or an electronic stylus. They can also use a remote device to operate the whiteboard like a mouse operates a computer.

Some teachers prefer standing at the front of the room using the IWB. Other teachers like to circulate throughout the room while teaching, using a wireless

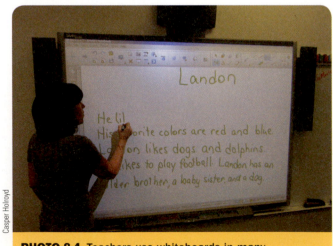

PHOTO 8-4 Teachers use whiteboards in many curriculum areas.

pad that allows them to control their computer and whiteboard while moving about. Whatever is on a computer screen can be shown on a whiteboard for an entire class to see.

IWB manufacturers are now packaging teaching suggestions that include lessons, activities, and clip art. Whiteboard vendor websites often have places where teachers can share and download images and lesson templates. See activities at the end of this chapter for suggestions on uses for an IWB in the classroom.

8-3g Technology and Multiple Intelligences

Technology can help meet the needs of various learning styles. The multiple intelligences, as discussed in Chapter 5, can be enhanced with the use of technology. The list in Figure 8-2 covers the types of technology and software suitable for each of the multiple intelligences. When integrating technology into the early childhood program, teachers need

to make sure to keep in mind the needs of all learners and use various methods and techniques suitable for each.

Did You Get It?

A second grade teacher uses a whiteboard, or smartboard, to teach a lesson about varieties of birds. In addition to writing facts about birds, she shows her students pictures and video clips. Her methods meet the standards of Developmentally Appropriate Practice because she

a. integrates media into her classroom, as recommended by educational experts.

b. is appealing to different intelligences by using both verbal and visual cues.

c. uses a whiteboard, which the children prefer to a traditional blackboard.

d. is teaching about birds, thereby meeting standards for a multicultural curriculum.

Take the full quiz on CourseMate.

Following Howard Gardner's theory of multiple intelligences, teachers can encourage development by providing enrichment opportunities in each of the areas of the intellect. The following are suggestions on how to integrate technology with each of the multiple intelligences.

Linguistic Intelligence (Word Smart)

Use of word-processing programs can help teach language, writing, editing, and rewriting skills. Also, the Internet is invaluable for learning. Through email, children can improve their language skills. Other technologies children may benefit from follow.

- Desktop publishing programs
- Programs that allow children to create stories, poems, and essays
- Multimedia authoring
- Videodiscs to create presentations
- Tape recorders

Logical/Mathematical (Logic Smart)

Computer programs can teach logic and critical thinking skills. These are also in game formats that can motivate children's thinking. For example, drill-and-practice math programs, while building mathematical conceptualization and functions skills, also offer engaging games that maintain young learners' interest. Database programs help explore and organize data and information.

Other technologies children may benefit from are listed here.

- Problem-solving software
- Computer-aided design programs
- Strategy game software
- Graphing calculators
- Multimedia authoring programs
- Spreadsheet programs

FIGURE 8-2 Technology and multiple intelligences.

(*Continues*)

© Cengage Learning

Visual/Spatial (Picture Smart)

Graphics programs help develop creativity and visual skills. Also, browsing the Internet and organizing files and folders will develop some spatial understanding. Other technologies children may benefit from follow.

- Drawing programs
- Image-composing programs
- Paint programs (Photopaint, Microsoft Paint)
- Reading programs with visual clues
- Web-page programs
- Three-dimensional software
- Software games
- Spreadsheet programs that allow children to see charts, maps, or diagrams
- Multimedia authoring programs

Musical Intelligence (Music Smart)

Some computer programs help write or play music. Other technologies that children may benefit from include these:

- Music-composing software
- Videodisc player
- Programs integrating stories with songs and instruments
- Reading programs that relate letter/sound with music
- Programs that allow children to create their own music
- CD-ROMs about music and instruments
- Tape recorders
- Word processors to write about a movie or song

Bodily/Kinesthetic (Body Smart)

Using computers will help develop eye–hand coordination. Working with a computer will allow children to become actively involved in their learning. Other kinesthetic technologies children may benefit from are listed here.

- Software games that allow contact with the keyboard, mouse, joystick, and other devices
- Programs that allow children to move objects around the screen
- Word-processing programs
- Animation programs

Interpersonal (Person Smart)

Students can work in groups of two to four on computers. Working in groups will strengthen children's communication and cooperation skills. Technologies children may benefit from include these:

- Computer games that require two or more people
- Programs that allow children to create group presentations (PowerPoint)
- Telecommunication programs
- Email
- Distance education
- Helping others with any programs

Intrapersonal (Self Smart)

The computer can help children build individual skills. It allows for differences in children's learning styles and abilities. Children may work at their own pace with computers. Other technologies children may benefit from follow.

- Any programs that allow children to work independently
- Games involving only one person
- Brainstorming or problem-solving software
- Instructional games
- Word processors for journaling and recording feelings
- Developing multimedia portfolio
- Video editing

FIGURE 8-2 Technology and multiple intelligences (*Continued*).

8-4 Value of Computers in Early Childhood Programs

DAP **naeyc** Computers, as we have seen, have found their way into the preschool setting, taking their place beside the finger paints, play dough, books, and other media found within the early learning environment. Computer programs have been developed for young children that allow them to produce colorful graphics, music, and animations.

Children of the twenty-first century will use computers as integral parts of their daily lives (see Photo 8-5). Yet children who are plugged into computers to do drill and practice engage in convergent thinking. In fact, these programs are just another version of convergent ditto sheet-like work. It is important to realize that using computers with young children is a process of exploration and discovery for both you and the children. How you use computers the first year in your classroom will probably be very different from how you use them 5 years later.

Based on recent research, some general conclusions about the value of computers with preschool and other children in early childhood programs may be made.

● *Computers can be used effectively with young children.* Researchers have consistently observed high levels of spoken communication and cooperation as young children interact at the computer. Compared with more traditional activities, such as puzzle assembly or block building, the computer elicits both more social interaction and different types of interaction. Children in comprehensive, technology-enhanced programs make progress in all developmental areas, including social, fine

PHOTO 8-6 Working with a computer can instigate new instances and forms of collaborative work.

motor, gross motor, communication, cognition, and self-help skills (Ching, 2009; Lee, 2009).

● *Computers can be interactive.* The term **interactive** here means that the computer used with young children provides a vehicle for two types of interaction: child-to-computer and child-to-child. Child-to-computer interaction depends to a great extent on the software. Some software requires children to choose one response, which is then corrected. Other programs have been developed that allow children to use information on the screen to make more than one response.

Child-to-child interaction at the computer depends on the arrangement of the environment. When children work near each other by the computer, they discuss what they are doing and assist each other as they work. Some software is also designed for, or lends itself better to, participation by more than one child.

The teacher and the software together also make a difference. By placing two child seats in front of the computer and one at the side for adults, the teacher is encouraging cooperation between children as well as interaction with an adult. Such an arrangement encourages children to work cooperatively and to converse as they work on the computer.

Computer work can instigate new instances and forms of collaborative work—such as helping or teaching, discussing and building on each other's ideas, cooperating, and praising (see Photo 8-6). It can also increase social interaction between children with disabilities and their

PHOTO 8-5 Children of the twenty-first century will use computers as integral parts of their daily lives.

typically developing peers (Clements & Sarama, 2003a; Robinson et al., 2009).

● *Placement of computers can encourage children's learning.* The ideal placement of the computer center is in a visible location. The monitors are situated so that they can be seen from throughout the classroom (Lee, 2009). Children are interested in what's happening in the computer center, although they may be working in another center. All of this stimulates peer mentoring, social interaction, language development, and cooperative play. In addition, a highly visible computer center enables you to supervise this area without leaving your current location. You need to move to the computer center only when it is necessary to assist children, or you can ask another child who is not busy if he or she is willing to help. This helps encourage children's independent learning as well as peer teaching. Strive for a 10:1 ratio (or better) of children to computers to encourage computer use, cooperation, and equal access by girls and boys.

● *Age and computer use.* Age doesn't appear to be a limiting factor in computer use. Even 2-year-old children can work proficiently on the computer using age-appropriate software that requires only simple key presses or pointing with a mouse. One researcher watched children as young as 3 use Google to look up sites and an 8-year-old check his mom's email to download a game (Buckleitner, 2010). Preschoolers can easily start the computer, load disks, type on the keyboard, and understand pictorial cues.

During the preschool years, children should have many opportunities to explore open-ended, developmentally appropriate software programs in a playful, supportive environment. These experiences will help them develop the basic skills needed to use technology equipment, such as opening and closing programs, saving and printing documents, and navigating the screen using a mouse. This will help children become confident in their ability to use a computer and will provide the foundational skills needed to use more advanced applications for purposeful work as they grow older.

As children enter the primary years, they can begin to use familiar technology tools as a part of their academic program. At the same time, adults should model the use of technology in support of the curriculum and learning experiences children are engaged in. For example, adults can model the use of technology for communication by using email and word-processing programs with children to communicate with families and others important to the classroom community. Adults can model the appropriate use of technology in many other ways, such as documenting events in the classroom using digital still or video cameras and creating multimedia electronic portfolios that document children's learning (Ching, 2009). This way, children can see firsthand the purposeful use of technology and benefit from exposure to more advanced applications that they will eventually use independently.

● *Children prefer action.* Just as in other aspects of their play, children like action with computers, and they do not necessarily choose to follow the rules of games. They watch what happens when they press new keys, and they purposely may try to squash all the keys at one time. One of the strengths young children bring to computer use is their fearless experimentation!

A good environment for young children includes many experiences that involve the senses, adult–child and child–child conversation, and a host of other age-appropriate activities. Computers can supplement, but do not substitute for, experiences in which children can discover with all their senses. Technology is a tool, and as such it should be used because it is the best tool for the job (Parette et al., 2009).

Only after a sound, basic program has been developed should teachers consider buying a computer. First should come blocks, sand and water tables, art materials, books, and all other proven elements of a good program for young children.

Did You Get It?

A kindergarten teacher brings her children into the school's computer lab, then sets up each child in a chair in front of his or her own computer. She is failing to take advantage of the full potential of school computer use because she

    a. does not have a full complement of computers in her classroom.

    b. has the children work individually rather than in pairs.

    c. expects the children to sit instead of roaming around during computer use.

    d. does not allow the students free access to the computer room.

Take the full quiz on CourseMate.

8-5 Choosing Developmentally Appropriate Software for Young Children

DAP **naeyc** Teachers basically have two options to assist them in selecting developmentally appropriate software. First, they can use a software rating scale to evaluate software themselves. Many evaluation forms, such as the **Haugland/Shade Software Developmental Scale** (Haugland & Wright, 1997), can help teachers understand the key component of quality software.

Second, several individuals and organizations have designed systems that teachers can use to evaluate software. The advantage of using an existing software evaluation system is that previewing software is unnecessary because it has already been extensively field tested by teachers, parents, and children. Table 8-1 presents a list of online sources of educational software reviews.

Research shows that different types of software have different effects (Clements & Samara, 2003b). Open-ended programs foster collaboration. Drill-and-practice programs encourage turn taking but also may encourage a competitive spirit. Violent programs can lead to aggressiveness (Clements & Samara, 2003b). The following 11 criteria distinguish software that is developmentally appropriate:

1. *Age appropriateness.* The concepts taught and their method of presentation reflect realistic expectations for young children.
2. *Child control.* Children are active participants, initiating and deciding the sequence of events, rather than reactors, responding to predetermined activities. The software needs to facilitate active rather than passive involvement (Lee, 2009). The pace is set by the child, not the program.
3. *Clear instructions.* Because the majority of preschool children are nonreaders, spoken directions are essential (Bergen & Wang, 2008). If printed instructions are used, they are accompanied by spoken directions. Directions are simple and precise. Graphics accompany choices to make options clear to the children.
4. *Expanding complexity.* Entry level is low; children can easily learn to manipulate the software successfully. The learning sequence is clear; one concept follows the next (NAEYC, 1996). The software expands as children explore, teaching the skills they are ready to learn. Through the expanding complexity of the software, children build on their knowledge.
5. *Independent exploration.* After initial exposure, children can manipulate the software without adult supervision.
6. *Process orientation.* The process of using the software is so engaging for children that the product becomes secondary. Children learn through discovery rather than being drilled in specific skills. Motivation to learn is intrinsic, not the result of praise, smiling-face stickers, or prizes.
7. *Real-world representation.* The software is a simple and reliable model of some aspect of the real world, exposing children to concrete representation of objects and their functions.
8. *Technical features.* The software has high technical quality that helps the young child pay attention. It is colorful and includes uncluttered, realistic, animated graphics. Realistic sound effects or

Table 8-1 Educational software reviews on the Internet.

Site	Information available
California Learning Resource Clearinghouse (CLRN)	Provides information needed for the selection of supplemental electronic learning resources aligned to the State Board of Education academic content standards.
Children's Technology Review	A monthly PDF newsletter that summarizes products and trends in children's interactive media.
Educational Media Reviews Online (EMRO)	Online database of video, DVD, audio CD, and CD-ROM reviews on materials from major educational and documentary distributors. Reviews are written by librarians and teaching faculty in institutions across the United States and Canada.
Superkids Educational Software Review	Provides reviews and ratings of software and practical and fun tools for online and offline use.
Tech & Learning	Provides resources and strategies for integrating digital technology into the K-12 classroom.
Learning Village	Reviews and recommends educational software.

© Cengage Learning

What Would Maria Montessori Say About the iPad?

Among Montessori groups, the use of technology-based materials such as the iPad is debated. Many feel that Montessori would appreciate the deep, intuitive connection the iPad fosters between content and user, taking working with knowledge to another level (Buckleitner, 2010).

Plenty of evidence suggests that Montessori herself was a bit of a geek. She wrote about the promise of Roentgen Rays (later renamed X-rays) in 1912 and accurately predicted wonderful things from the "Marconi Telegraph" (a.k.a. the radio) (Buckleitner, 2010).

She was also a consummate game maker, constantly fiddling with innovative materials such as sand paper to perfect a new self-teaching gadget. Because she always put a child's interests ahead of any formal curriculum, it's a safe bet she would have encouraged a child's use of technology.

Here are some further reasons Montessori would be "pro-iPad":

● Montessori was a scientist who was future-centric. She understood that she was living in a changing time and that children needed to be exposed to modern materials. She was in the business of preparing children for their future, to live to their full human potential, so she would have wanted them to embrace and feel empowered by every element of the environment, including technology.

● She would be discriminating about the types of apps she loaded on her iPads. She would look for noncommercial apps that promoted active learning, were self-correcting, were multileveling, and empowered children. A word Montessori used frequently was "didactic" as in "didactic materials," or working toward one right answer; a feature found in many of the better designed apps.

● In designing apps, she would compensate for the iPad's sensory limitations of just sight and sound, using apps in concert with real, concrete experiences. She would use the iPad to supplement traditional experiences rather than to replace them. After the trip to the apple orchard, she would give each child their own apple, to hold, smell, and taste. Only then would she read a story about the apples, or let them "pick" abstract apples on a multitouch screen.

● Because Montessori frowned on the notion of shaping a child's behavior with external prizes and punishments, she would recommend apps where the process, in itself, is rewarding. Montessori would probably insist that every children's app should have a "no candy lane" mode, that perhaps costs a few lire/euros more (Buckleitner, 2010).

Source: From "What Would Maria Montessori Say about the iPad?" by Warren Buckleitner in Children's Technology Review, November 2010, Vol. 18, No. 11, Issue 128, Pages 5-6, www.childrenstech.com. Reprinted by permission.

music correspond to objects on the screen. The software loads from the disks and runs fast enough to maintain the child's interest.

9. *Trial and error.* The software provides children many chances to test alternative responses. Through resolving errors or solving problems, children build structures and knowledge.

10. *Visible transformations.* Children have an impact on the software, changing objects and situations through their responses (NAEYC, 1996).

11. *For bilingual students,* translation of both languages, preferably in real time, is an important feature. A program that allows the student to toggle between languages provides instant translations of each page.

In this list, it is important to note that software may have a developmental approach to learning without having all of the criteria. Some software has more developmental criteria than other software. You need to choose software that includes as many of these criteria as possible.

Did You Get It?

A computer game presents a picture of a house with many doors. Preschool students click on the doors to find interesting games in various rooms of the house. A group of children becomes so involved in the game that they don't notice they are learning new skills. This game meets the standards of Developmentally Appropriate Practice because it has

   a. process orientation.
   b. clear instructions.
   c. expanding complexity.
   d. trial and error.

Take the full quiz on CourseMate.

8-6 Basic Types of Children's Websites

naeyc **DAP** There are four basic types of children's websites: information sites, communication sites, interaction sites, and publication sites.

8-6a Information Sites

Enhanced with sound and videos, information sites are rich reference resources that teachers and parents can use to model or assist children in answering questions, making new discoveries, and building knowledge. For example, a virtual trip to the zoo gives children opportunities to see pictures, hear animal sounds, and view movies of animals exploring their natural habitats. The National Zoo from the Smithsonian Institute is such a website. A virtual tour of a dinosaur museum is another possibility. Another example is taking an online tour of Italy to learn more about the children's electronic pen pals from Rome.

8-6b Communication Sites

At communication sites, children interact with teachers, friends, relatives, or classrooms across the street, in another city, or even across the globe. Using simple email addresses, children and classroom groups write letters, compose stories, create poems, or work on a class project. For example, "The Way We Are" is an e-pals project in which students learn about other people and cultures and then produce a PowerPoint show about what they learned.

Also through email, children can ask "experts" questions in various disciplines. One example is Ask Dr. Math. This provides classrooms not only with the answers to questions but also with the opportunity to explore a variety of math-related occupations. Another communication option is to join the Twitter community. Twitter allows users to send and read messages that are limited to 140 characters. The content of these short messages, or "tweets," offers a mixture of day-to-day chats as well as useful information. See Twitter4Teachers for a list of teachers by grade level and subject area. The best way to regularly use Twitter is to reflect on what's happening in your classroom and to raise issues or share resources that might interest other teachers.

8-6c Interaction Sites

Interaction sites are similar to software programs, using sound, animation, sound effects, and high-quality, realistic graphics. An example of an interaction site is Lego Universe, a Massively Multiplayer Online Game (MMOG) designed for children and adults. This is the first MMOG game involving Lego bricks in a virtual, public, shared space. Players can communicate with one another through various layers of chat and build anything they can dream up. As they build, children (and adults) can chat or team up to participate in Lego-based

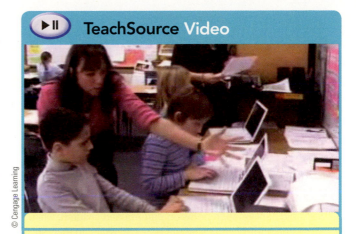

© Cengage Learning

▶❚❚ **TeachSource** Video

Teaching Technology Skills: An Elementary School Lesson on PowerPoint

1. Using the information in this chapter, what other type(s) of technology could Miss Defusco use to teach this same lesson?

2. Were these two teachers using technology in a developmentally appropriate manner with their writing projects? Explain your answer using the information provided in this chapter.

Watch on CourseMate.

adventures. Another example of an interaction site is Club Penguin. After registering (which requires a valid email address), children are asked to choose one of several penguin worlds to join. At any time, children can use a map to jump in or out of a game, or visit their own igloo, which serves as a home base. This Web experience is very easy to get into and play with no risk or downloads other than Adobe Flash Player, which is becoming standard on nearly every browser. As a language experience, the program gets children busily typing with others, and a variety of games require logical thinking and strategy.

Also at Club Penguin, students can learn responsible skills, such as don't give your address, last name, password, physical description, current location, or other identifying information. Teachers can use these sites to teach students about digital citizenship within a controlled environment so they know how to conduct themselves in the uncontrolled real world.

8-6d Publication Sites

The Internet can be used as a resource for actually publishing children's work on publication sites. Even 3-year-olds can understand that when their work is displayed on the Internet, everyone in the world can see it.

THIS ONE'S FOR YOU!

Technology for Children with Special Needs

When the iPad debuted, there was a lot of talk about whether people beyond the iPhone and Mac faithful would use such a thing. But it became very clear to a particular group of people—advocates for those with autism spectrum disorders—that the device could be a new tool for communication and education in that community, which is something perhaps even Apple didn't foresee. Some autism-related apps aid conversation between parents and children, while others help with learning words or social skills. In fact, so many autism-related apps are now available for the iPad and other iOS devices that there's an app called Autism Apps, which provides a comprehensive list of the available apps.

The popularity of the iPad for use with autism-spectrum disorders revolves around accessibility, the idea that websites, apps, hardware, and other technology should be designed in ways that do not shut out those with disabilities, from blindness to hearing loss to other physical limitations. Kel Smith, founder of a technology accessibility company, has been studying technology shifts like this one for his book, *Digital Outcasts: Moving Technology Forward without Leaving People Behind.*

Smith started his book on the premise that there are entire populations of people who are being left behind by technology. Then he realized in the process of writing and research that they're the ones driving the innovation and moving it forward. They're forming their own solutions at a very grass-roots level (Gallaga, 2012).

Smith's company Anikto (the Greek word for "open") has for years been advocating more accessible Web design, hardware, and software. In recent years, he has found that the somewhat broad concept is becoming readily adopted as companies realize they're leaving money on the table by not making their websites or tech products accessible.

The idea that designers should think about accessibility because it's in their own best interests in addition to being altruistic makes a lot of sense. Also, the cost for individuals and nonprofits to create their own Web design tools and apps has also fallen, making it easier than ever for technology for the disabled to be distributed and for online communities to get the word out about them.

Another big shift is that, for years, accessibility was largely focused on how the Web is viewed on computers, that is, how the online world interacts with computers, mouse devices, and text-to-speech assistive devices. But now, many people's Web browsing is moving to mobile devices such as smartphones, which have much smaller screens. Technology that relies on gestures and movement, such as Microsoft's Xbox 360, is also becoming more common. These new interfaces can be a double-edged sword. They provide a whole new array of possibilities and a whole new array of problems for special populations.

Improvements in accessibility are likely to benefit not just those with special needs. The aging population of baby boomers is going to widen the definition of what constitutes a disability. That will increase the need for products that are mindful of people with limited motor skills or hand–eye coordination, those who have problems reading text that's too small, or anyone who is hard of hearing (Gallaga, 2012).

Imagine their pride! Motivation for learning is sparked as they create new pictures and stories. A number of websites post children's work, such as KidPub. Photos can be shared on an Internet website such as Flickr, which hosts free images and videos for an online community. One of the advantages of using a publication site is that students' work is exposed to a wider audience than typically occurs with a school-based website. For examples of art programs that post student work on Flickr, see the photo streams of Darien Public Schools' art department in Connecticut and Fortismere Secondary School's art and photography department in North London.

8-6e A Note of Caution!

Although the potential of the Internet is tremendous, some precautions must be addressed. Anyone can place anything on the Internet, some of which may be harmful to young children. A screening device is essential, such as Kid Desk: Internet Safe, Net Nanny, or Cyber Patrol. Another helpful screening device is a PG Key. The PG Key resembles a USB flash drive and plugs directly into the USB port of a child's computer. It allows adults to control when the child uses the computer. When it is unplugged, the computer can't be used. In addition, it locks in Safe Search, which allows the freedom to search the Web but prevents most of the unwanted and dangerous content from showing up.

Also, it is probably best for children to use a pen name when on the Internet—the name of their dog, cat, or favorite stuffed animal.

8-6f Blogs

A blog is basically an online journal. The key to the blog's popularity is how simple it is to construct and maintain. The blogger simply types in his or her thoughts and clicks "post." The blog handles the rest automatically, with the new posting appearing at the top of the blog Web page, followed by previous postings in reverse chronological order.

A blog, which requires no special software, no knowledge of HTML, and virtually no time, can substitute for a traditional website if your aim is to have a simple medium for communication.

8-6g Types of Blogs

Some of the most common types of blogs being used in schools today are classroom news blogs, mirror blogs, showcase blogs, and literature response blogs. Blogs often incorporate more than one of these primary functions, and, given the creative minds of effective teachers and the rapidly changing nature of literacy on the Internet, many more types will probably emerge in the future.

Classroom news blogs. Many classroom blogs are used to share news and information with parents and students. Often this is the first type of blog a teacher will use. Teachers update classroom news blogs on a regular basis, posting homework assignments, providing updates on curriculum for parents, and sharing any other information that could benefit the home–school connection. Parents do not necessarily have to be your target audience. You may want to establish a dialogue with students in the upper grades. With a blog, you can create a message and invite students who visit the blog to add their comments. Or the target audience could be your fellow teachers.

Mirror blogs. Mirror blogs allow bloggers to reflect on their thinking—hence the "mirror" title. A teacher may post a response about a workshop recently attended, sharing insights learned. While reading a new professional book on literacy, a blogger might post quotes or compelling new ideas found in the book to a mirror blog. Many teachers not only post their own reflective thinking but also include student reflections. Student comments of this type might include thoughts about lessons or content learned.

For example, you can write every morning before students come in or every afternoon when they leave. In a mirror blog, you can reflect on the completed class day, analyzing skills met and standards addressed in preparation for the next day's lessons. Blogging becomes something like an electronic log or journal of the class's successes and identified needs for reteaching. If the blog is made public, then parents, students, and even colleagues can follow the progression to improve their support for classroom learning.

Showcase blogs. Many teachers use blogs to post student art projects, podcasts (audio clips), and writing in showcase blogs. Of particular interest are the ways in which second language learners can use these spaces to write and respond in their second language in more authentic ways and for more authentic audiences. *Have Fun with English! 2* is an Edublogs award winner where students from Portugal practice their English. The blog is a combination of student and teacher writing, artwork, and even audio messages from students. Many of the blog posts are student podcasts describing their day with the written text just underneath.

Literature response blogs. Literature response journals are common in elementary classrooms. A literature response blog simply moves this idea online, where the teacher may sometimes post a prompt and invite student responses to a text. Using blogs to bridge a familiar in-school activity with this out-of-school tool provides students with a different medium for literature response.

Many resources are available online to help you set up and organize a blog, such as Free Blogs for Teachers.

8-6h Wikis

Although blogs may be the easiest websites to maintain, they're not great for large, collaborative class projects that sort a lot of information onto separate Web pages. For that, it may be easier to have children contribute to a wiki. A wiki is a website that allows readers to add and edit content. The popular Wikipedia, an online encyclopedia, is one example. ("Wiki-wiki" means "hurry quick" in Hawaiian.)

It's a great way to make a large website without knowing HTML or Web design. The wiki format allows students to easily link to each other's work using the same collaborative method and internal linking that you see on Wikipedia.

You can easily set up a wiki on any topic children are studying with a free account. Another wiki service is *Wikispaces*, one of the first wiki services that educators embraced. As a result, there are literally thousands of Wikispaces that you can look to for samples of what's possible.

Perhaps your instructor has a wiki as a useful way to eliminate handouts. Or you as a teacher may use a wiki to enable parents to follow along with what

THIS ONE'S FOR YOU!

Technology for the Youngest Learners

Some preschool children come to school with little or no experience with technology. Here are some suggestions to help the youngest learners become familiar with the technology tools in your classroom:

- *Set up a play computer.* Setting up a play computer in the drama center can be a good way for students to role-play proper computer care. Begin with reviewing how they should avoid touching the screen and use gentle mouse clicks. Students can also practice "typing" on a pretend keyboard.

- *Go part by part.* Start off slowly, introducing a single computer to students and naming some of the parts, such as mouse, keyboard, monitor, and screen.

- *Be attentive to ergonomics.* The computer screen should be positioned so that children can view it without craning

their necks. Seating should allow their feet to touch the floor. If the chair is too tall, try providing students with a small box to rest their feet on. When using the mouse, their hands should be level with their forearms.

- *Start with their names.* To help acclimate students to the keyboard, provide them with their names on a card and let them type their names repeatedly. It's a great way to get them using the Enter key.

- *Hand washing.* Be sure to have some wet wipes on hand to wipe down keyboards after use. Keep in mind that a child could have an allergic reaction to peanut butter residue on a dirty keyboard.

With a little thought on your part and some guidance and enthusiasm, you can help children embrace ever-changing technologies.

---

is happening in your class. At the upper-elementary levels, it may be a useful tool for students who missed class to download work that needs to be made up. A wiki in the best sense helps students (and teachers) to work together and build upon each other's work, allowing everyone to get involved.

8-6i Personal Learning Network

A **personal learning network** refers to a collection of people and resources you can consult to learn something or to get answers to your questions. Building learning connections is not a new practice for teachers. From the time we enter the classroom, we gather useful curriculum resources and periodically call on colleagues for advice, read educational journals, and attend professional conferences in order to improve our understanding of pedagogy and the subjects we teach. With the aid of some online tools, you can expand your existing learning network to include people and resources from all over the world.

A good way to get started building your personal learning network is to set up a social bookmarking account. Social bookmarking is a variation of the popular practice of saving and organizing links to Web pages (sometimes called "favorites") that you want to remember and return to at a later date. In a social bookmarking system, links are usually shared with selected

people through groups or networks. Because your links are stored online rather than on your computer, they are available through any computer connected to the Internet.

Social bookmarking sites encourage users to organize their collections of bookmarks with tags, which are keywords associated with the content of a linked page. Other features available through some social bookmarking services include subscription feeds that inform you when new bookmarks have been added to your network or group, plus the ability to highlight and annotate bookmarked pages.

Two social bookmarking services that are popular among teachers are Delicious and Diigo, which offer educator accounts with features intended to serve the needs of K-12 teachers.

Did You Get It?

A website allows children to play virtual games with other users of the site, even though they don't know the other users in real life. This type of website is a(n)

 a. interaction site.
 b. communication site.
 c. information site.
 d. publishing site.

Take the full quiz on CourseMate.

Summary

8-1 Summarize the position of NAEYC with regard to technology for children from birth through age 8.

Technology and interactive media are to be used in ways that optimize opportunities for young children's cognitive, social, emotional, physical, and linguistic development.

8-2 List the pros and cons concerning the use of technology with young children.

When making the decision to have students use a computer, a teacher must think about both the gains made from using the computer (such as quick access to information) and the losses (learning to use the library, handwriting, face-to-face social skills, hands-on experiences, and understanding that simply finding mountains of information does not equate to thoughtful, accurate learning). Teachers need to be aware of what is lost in the process and then make a decision about whether to provide additional time to develop the knowledge and skills that are lost when using the technology.

8-3 Discuss several examples of technology used in the early childhood program.

Examples of technology appropriate for use in early childhood programs are video recordings, photography,

iPods and MP3 players, CDs and CD players, and interactive whiteboards (IWBs).

8-4 Discuss the values of computers in early childhood programs.

Computers can be used effectively with young children; computers can be interactive; placement of computers can encourage children's learning; computers can be easy for children to use; and computers appeal to children's preference for action.

8-5 List at least five characteristics to consider in choosing developmentally appropriate computer software.

Characteristics to consider when choosing software are age appropriateness, child control, clear instructions, expanding complexity, independent exploration, process orientation, real-world representation, technical features, trial and error, visible transformation, and language translations.

8-6 List the four basic types of children's websites.

The four basic types of children's websites are information sites, communication sites, interaction sites, and publication sites.

Key Terms

blog   174
classroom blog   175
communication sites   173
digital camera   164
Haugland Software Development
    Scale   171

information sites   173
interaction sites   173
interactive   169
literature response blog   175
mirror blog   175

personal learning network   176
publication sites   173
showcase blog   175
wiki   175

Learning Activities

Taking Creative Photos

Obtain an inexpensive camera or use your smartphone to shoot a series of photos trying to make each picture creative.

A. Photograph the following:
   1. a beautiful sunset
   2. an ugly, broken-down house
   3. a beautiful building
   4. interesting-looking people
   5. a flower in bloom
   6. an animal
   7. a brightly colored bird
B. Use the pictures to tell a creative story about some experience.

Digital Camera Activities

Make-a-Face Gallery

Take pictures of each child in your group with a digital camera. Turn off the flash, and zoom in close on each child's face, capturing every detail. Print each picture on an 8½ × 11"-inch sheet of paper and make a "face gallery" bulletin board. If you don't have a color printer, don't worry—the pictures look great in black and white.

Bringing Home to School

Offer parents a classroom camera (or a disposable camera) to take home for the weekend. Provide a "shot list" of ideas that includes their children's bedroom, pets, favorite toys, and family members. Any 2.1-megapixel or digital camera works well. Use the photos to make a poster or bulletin board featuring that child. If you don't have a digital camera, use a disposable camera. Some manufacturers produce disposable digital cameras ideally suited to this activity.

Additional Activities

Record interesting sounds. Invite the children to identify the sounds. Try any or all of the following.

1. a computer keyboard
2. a door closing
3. a car starting
4. a jet plane taking off
5. voices
6. music
7. popcorn popping

Activities for Using an Interactive Whiteboard

Hints for Using the Whiteboard

- **Mount on the wall**—An IWB can be an invaluable resource, but you don't want it to clutter floor space. Mount the board on a wall and hang the projector from the ceiling so you don't have to continually realign.
- **Prepare seating**—Give students a place to sit. For young students and to avoid jostling the board or its tray, place carpet squares in front of it as a boundary reminder. A line of masking tape on the floor works as well.
- **Store markers**—Store markers somewhere else. It's too easy for them to be mistaken for one of the computerized markers, and ink is a difficult substance to try to remove.
- **Post instructions**—In the event that substitute teachers or other adults will be using this equipment, it's not a bad idea to permanently post a note beside it that reads, "This is a Smart Board. Please do not use regular markers on it."
- **See the bigger picture**—Scan the pages of a social studies or science book onto the whiteboard so the whole class can experience the book at once. The pictures and diagrams will be big enough for the whole class to see. You are also able to write on the pages and point things out.
- **Play all sorts of games**—The touch-and-drag feature of the whiteboard puts sorting activities in the students' hands. Have the students touch the item on the whiteboard and drag it to its appropriate location in the sort. You can do category sorts (herbivores and carnivores) and word sorts (parts of speech, number of syllables, initial sounds). You can also do "mystery sorts" where you can begin sorting without giving away the rule.

Encourage volunteers to figure out the sorting rule, and then let them create their own mystery sorts.

- **Spin a better story web**—This is a second-grade activity that is related to the *Magic Tree House* books by Mary Pope Osborne. Use the whiteboard to create a story web spanning several of these books. By using different colors, shapes, and fonts, you can create a much more intricate yet easier-to-read web than would have been possible with traditional chart paper or overhead transparency. When you want the students to have a hard copy, just print copies, and they can add their own ideas or take them home to share.
- **Keep things fair**—Use your IWB to introduce all kinds of concepts, from fact families to vocabulary. The children usually want a turn. To make your choice equitable, draw "fair sticks" (which are virtual popsicle sticks programmed with students' names) to see who gets to go to the board.
- **Build a word cloud**—Wordle is a fantastic online tool with many possibilities on an IWB. Students enter a piece of text and the program builds a "word cloud" based on the most frequently used words within the text. Entering the text of a favorite storybook or a chapter of a novel can reveal key vocabulary. Or you can challenge kids to create a word cloud based on the vocabulary from your latest unit of study.
- **Teach media literacy**—All IWB software allows you to draw over websites, documents, and applications. Teachers use this capability to teach children critical thinking and responsible Internet use. You can pull up a website and highlight information that suggests it's a legitimate source as well as any clues or indications that it may not be the best place for valid information.
- **Play with Magnetic Poetry**—Pull up the Magnetic Poetry® website, and have students experiment with all four Magnetic Poetry Kids' Kits on a stylish digital fridge. Drag and drop adjectives, verbs, and nouns to learn about parts of speech, proper sentence construction, and poetic forms.
- **Design a digital robot**—Students will enjoy exploring all the tools on Sodaplay, an interactive website at which users build animated models and machines. One favorite Sodaplay application is Moovl, which lets children easily make their words and images shimmy and shake.
- **Create customized flashcards**—FlashcardDB earns raves from teachers for its ease of use, broad application, and great possibilities on the whiteboard. You can easily create a custom set of flashcards in minutes as well as access other educators' cards and teaching tools. The Study mode allows children to "flip" the cards and quiz themselves in a flash.

Activities for Children

Photo Activities

Picture Puzzles

Glue an enlarged photograph of each child to construction paper. Then use a paper cutter to cut each photo into three horizontal strips. Spread your new puzzle pieces out on the table or floor, and have the children create brand

new faces by combining different features. As students play, invite them to say or write the personality traits their "people" might exhibit if they were real. For example, "She has Meg's love of sports and Drew's great math abilities." For easy storage, hole-punch the strips and put them in a binder, allowing children to mix and match during free time.

Picture Walks (Kindergarten and up)

Children take pictures while walking through the school neighborhood, around the school building, or while on a field trip. During circle time, have children talk about and describe their pictures.

Matching Game

Have children take pictures of objects and other children in their class. Put the pictures in random piles, and have the children work in small groups to locate the objects/ people that are in the photos in the room. This can be fun and challenging when the photos show only a part of the object and the child has to figure out what object has been photographed. For example, a child may have taken a photograph of the table leg, the end of a pencil, or a classmate's red sneaker. Children can search the room to find the match to their picture.

Classroom Newsletter

Create a classroom newsletter so that the children have opportunities to share their pictures. Each child should have multiple opportunities to have his or her photos included in the classroom newsletter. Let the children choose which photos to include. The newsletter can have photos of special events and class trips but also everyday events that the children have photographed. The newsletter creates a natural opportunity for children to talk about school experiences through photographs.

Photo Storytelling

Photographs can be used to create stories, illustrate ideas in stories that the children have developed, or retell events. Through photos, children can create stories that reflect their everyday experiences. Take pictures of the events of one entire class day, and write a group story about a day in the life of your classroom, accompanied by the children's photographs. As the children become more experienced using cameras, have them take pictures of activities in the classroom and "write" their own story about a typical day in their classroom. Having the children "write" means either having the children dictate their story to you or having them make approximations using scribbles or some forms of writing.

Alphabet Bodies

Give students practice in teamwork, problem solving, and communication by having them build different letters with their bodies. Then capture the results on film. First, ask children how they might build a particular letter. How many children will need to work together? How will their bodies need to be positioned? Encourage children to use listening and language skills to complete each letter-making task. Then snap away! Stand on a sturdy chair to get a better angle. Post the photographs or paste them into a scrapbook to familiarize children with the alphabet. Or make a super-simple game of Concentration by duplicating the photos to use as cards.

Music and Friends

This is a terrific getting-to-know-you activity. Play a round of musical chairs that will help students learn one another's names and interests. Place a photo of each child on the front of a chair back. (There's no need to have one less chair in this noncompetitive version of the game.) Invite children to stand in a circle around the chair and start the music. When the music stops, children sit down on the nearest chair. Ask each child to identify whose photo is on his or her chair. Older students may also share something special about that classmate. Later on, challenge children by using photos of arms and legs instead of faces.

Me Puppets

Have children cut their faces or bodies from large, close-up photographs, then mount them on heavy paper and laminate them. Attach a craft stick or glove to the back of the puppet using tape or strong glue. Children might like to change their puppet's appearance by adding cloth or paper and marker costumes. Children can use the me-puppets to tell stories and practice storytelling skills. Invite children to act out favorite stories or create new ones—starring themselves, of course. Try using the puppets during large-group time as a fun, alternative way for students to express themselves.

Twisting

Put a photographic twist on the classic game of Twister™. Make the game board by cutting out large, blown-up photos of each child and gluing them to sturdy cardboard circles. Laminate and attach the circles to a Twister board or to the floor with strong tape. Small groups can take turns playing by having one "caller" announce a name and a right or left hand/foot direction. For example, "Place your right hand on Casper." Older children can give more complex directions, such as "Place your foot on a friend who has brown hair," or "Place your hand on a friend who can play the violin."

Changing Faces

Children can "change" their faces again and again by simply laying transparency paper over their photographs. Using markers, children can add a moustache, change hair color, add a hat, or make any other change—silly or serious—that they want. Have children think and write about how they perceive themselves in these changes. Wipe off the marker as many times as desired to make new changes.

Technology Choreography Movement Activity

In this activity, children learn about technology and interpret their understandings through creative movement.

A. Prepare a tape recording (no more than three minutes) of the sounds of various machines, such as an electric can opener, microwave, coffee maker, or mixer. It is not necessary to have many sounds. Rather, juxtapose the sounds of different lengths and repeat them during the three-minute recording.

B. Play the tape. After the students identify the source of the sounds, discuss the ways in which technology (in the kitchen, garage, or other places) helps us do our work. Assign children to work in pairs or independently to prepare a choreographed interpretation of the sounds on the tape. Ask children to think about the function of the technology as they select movements.

C. Play the tape three or four times for rehearsal and preparation. Encourage students to select appropriate movement, depending on the function and "feeling" of the technology. The interpretation may take the form of finger movements, a hand jive, dance, or creative movement. Perform the choreography and critique the movements as to their connection with the function of technology.

Internet Activities—Grade 3 and Up

Your students can monitor leopards in South Africa, volcanoes in Italy, or insects in Iowa without ever leaving your classroom, thanks to webcams—permanent cameras that transmit pictures over the Internet. Here's where to find some of the best kid-friendly cams:

- **JellyCam**—Your students will be fascinated by the fantastic creatures in the Oregon Coast Aquarium's moon jelly exhibit. http://www.aquarium.org
- **Monterey Bay Aquarium**—Seven different cams offer a look at marine life in the aquarium's exhibits. See penguins, otters, sharks, and more! http://www.montereybayaquarium.org
- **Volcano Watch**—It's a known fact that kids love volcanoes. Here, satellite images let them monitor the world's most active ones. http://www.ssec.wisc.edu/data/volcano.html

Google Earth

If you're looking for a stellar example of how technology can bring abstract concepts to life, look no further than Google Earth. Google Earth turns your Windows computer into a dynamic superglobe, combining the ability to search and zoom down with enough resolution to view your own backyard. The program is an extension of Google Maps and uses satellite images taken over the past 3 years, combining them with local points of interest plus facts from Google.

You can zoom to a specific address or fly along a route. You can also view annotations left by other Google Earth users. Younger children can get a sense of how their neighborhood fits into their town, their county, their state, and their continent. Other educational applications are numerous, both for mapping and geography, as well as other more indirect uses, including science, history, and math.

Google Earth is free for personal use, although upgrade versions are also available.

Try the following activities with Google Earth:

- Search for your community by using your ZIP code or another search method.
- List human-made structures as you view your community.
- Locate your school. Record its elevation and its latitude and longitude reading.
- Zoom in on and identify some of the smallest features you can view near your school. List what you see.
- Locate and list two or more other interesting features that you see in or near your community.

More Internet Explorations for Children

- Teach your students how to be safe on the Internet by visiting SafetyClicks. They can play games to become Internet savvy, visit other sites, watch a cartoon, and get tips on how to use the Web.
- Invite students to find the basics of surfing the net on the Albion website. Click on "Netiquette." After exploring this site, ask children to define the terms *netiquette, online behavior,* and *cyberspace.*
- Find a directory of games, where children will find games and artwork by other students and lots of other fun activities.
- Become a wolf for a day at WolfQuest. WolfQuest is a 3D wildlife video game by the Minnesota Zoo and game developer Eduweb. WolfQuest is the first video game funded by the National Science Foundation. You'll also learn how a real wolf thinks and what the wolf eats. You'll need to register, and then download and install the file on your computer. Once you do, you can form your own pack with kids from all over the world.
- Make your own game. The best way to play a good game is to make one yourself. Try Cartoon Network's Ben Ten Alien Force Game Creator where you can drag and drop walls, ramps, and barriers into place. Then you can sprinkle your game with enemies or gems to collect. Your finished game can be saved and shared with others. There are 210 other games at Cartoon Network.

References

American Academy of Pediatrics, Council on Communications and Media. (2010). Policy statement on media education. *Pediatrics, 126,* 1–7.

Bergen, D., & Wang, A. (2008). The effects on children's creativity of super-realistic technologically-enhanced toys. *International Journal of Psychology, 43*(3), 16–24.

Buckleitner, W. (Nov. 2010). What would Maria Montessori say about the iPad? *Children's Technology Review, 18*(1), Issue 128.

Ching, G. S. (2009). Implications of an experimental information technology curriculum for elementary students. *Computers and Education, 53*(2), 419–428.

Clements, D. H., & Samara, J. (2003a). Young children and technology: What does the research say? *Young Children, 58*(6), 34–40.

Clements, D. H., & Samara, J. (2003b). Strip mining for gold: Research and policy in educational technology—a response to "Fools Gold." *Educational Technology Review, 11*(1).

Cogill, J. (2003). The use of interactive whiteboards in the primary school: Effects on pedagogy. *Research Bursary Reports* (Coventry, Becta).

Curwood, J. S. (2009). Education 2.0: Case for interactive whiteboards. *Instructor, 118*(6), 29–32.

Gallaga, O. L. (May 21, 2012). Gadgets help the challenged adapt. *Austin American Statesman.* In *News and Observer Connect* section, Section D, p. 1.

Haugland, S., & Wright, J. (1997). *Young children and technology: A world of discovery.* New York, NY: Allyn & Bacon.

Lacina, J. (2009). Interactive whiteboards: Creating higher-level, technological thinkers? *Childhood Education, 85*(4), 270–272.

Lee, Y. (2009). Pre–K children's interaction with educational software programs: An observation of capabilities and levels of engagement. *Journal of Educational Multimedia and Hypermedia, 18*(3), 289–309.

Lillard, A. S., & Peterson, J. (2011). The immediate impact of different types of TV on young children's executive function. http://pediatrics.aapublications.org/.

Long, C. (2006). Getting wiki with it. *NEA Today, 25*(2), 16–17.

Luckenbill, J. (2012). Getting the picture: Using the digital camera as a tool to support reflective practice and responsive care. *Young Children,* 67(2), 28–36.

NAEYC, (2012). Technology and interactive media as tools in early childhood programs serving children from birth through age 8. Retrieved from http://www.naeyc.org /content/technology-and-young-children

NAEYC. (1996). NAEYC position statement: Technology and young children: Ages three-eight. *Young Children, 10,* 11–16.

Parette, H. P., Blum, C., Boeckmann, N. M., & Watts, E. H. (2009). Teaching word recognition to young children who are at risk using Microsoft PowerPoint coupled with direct instruction. *Early Childhood Education Journal, 36*(5), 393–401.

Robinson, L., Schneider, C., Daytner, G., Johnson, J., & Hutinger, P. (2009). *Early childhood technology integrated instructional system (EC-TIIS): Phase 3. Final report. Macomb, IL:* Center for Best Practices in Early Childhood Education, Western Illinois University.

Smith, H., Higgins, S., Wall, K., & Miller, J. (2005). Interactive whiteboards: Boom or bandwagon? A critical review of the literature. *Journal of Computer Assisted Learning, 21*(9), 91–101.

Straub, E. T. (2009). Understanding technology adoption: Theory and future directions for informal learning. *Review of Educational Research, 79*(2), 625–649.

Thompson, S., & Williams, K. (2008). Using photography to tell a story. *Social Studies and the Young Learner, 20*(3), 18–21.

Vandewater, E. A., Rideout, V. J., Wartella, E. A., Huang, X., Lee, J. H., & Shim, M. S. (2007). Digital childhood: Electronic media and technology use among infants, toddlers and preschoolers. *Pediatrics.* Retrieved from http://www.pediatrics.org/cgi/content/fall/119/5/e1006.

Zimmerman, F. J., Christakis, D. A., & Meltzoff, A. N. (2007). Television and DVD/video viewing in children younger than 2 years. *Pediatric & Adolescent Medicine, 161*(5), 473–479.

Visit CourseMate for this textbook to access the eBook, Did You Get It? quizzes, Digital Downloads, TeachSource Videos, flashcards, and more. Go to CengageBrain.com to log in, register, or purchase access.

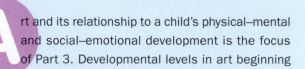

PART 3

Art and the Development of the Young Child

Art and its relationship to a child's physical–mental and social–emotional development is the focus of Part 3. Developmental levels in art beginning with the scribble stage up t[...] presented in Part 3.

REFLECTIVE QUESTIONS

After studying this section, you should be able to answer the following questions.

1. Are the young children in my group able to fully develop their physical and mental potential in the room and the activities I have planned?

2. Do I have sufficient and appropriate art materials for both large- and small-motor activities? What can I add to improve my program? What can I remove? Have I made appropriate changes for children with special needs?

3. How am I encouraging the development of self-concept in young children in my classroom management and teaching practices?

4. What are the strengths and weaknesses of my art program as it relates to the development of self-concept? What can I do to improve it so that it is more conducive to the development of a positive self-concept for young children?

5. Does my classroom reflect the range of individual differences in social–emotional and physical–mental development present in the group? How can it be improved?

6. At what levels in the development of art-related skills are the children in my group? Have I planned activities and lessons to fit these levels?

7. Are my teaching practices based on knowledge of social–emotional, physical–mental, and art development levels? Is this knowledge reflected in my choice of materials, supplies, and interest centers?

8. Am I aware of each child's individual schema? Can I recognize them? How do I speak with children about their art?

9. How can I assist parents in their understanding of children's development in art? Of a child's physical–mental development? Of a child's social–emotional growth?

10. Do I encourage young children to verbalize their feelings? Do I encourage this process by modeling consideration of their thoughts and actions?

11. What can I do to improve my current teaching practices in the art program?

12. Am I satisfied that the social–emotional, physical–mental, and developmental levels of art are being appropriately addressed in my teaching strategies? What can I change to better meet the individual needs of young children in all of these areas of development?

© Cengage Learning

Art and Physical—Mental Growth

This chapter presents the ways in which art relates to physical and mental growth. Physical, mental, social, and emotional growth all occur together in a child, but physical and mental growth are discussed separately here for the sake of clarity.

Learning Objectives

After studying this chapter, you should be able to:

9-1 Discuss the relationship between art and physical (motor) development.

9-2 Discuss the relationship between art and mental development.

9-3 List and describe the basic elements of the human brain.

9-4 Discuss the critical periods of the brain for visual and auditory, language, physical and motor, and emotional social development.

9-5 Explain the relationship between art and vocabulary development and how art can be a part of the total early childhood program.

NAEYC Program Standards

1a Knowing and understanding young children's characteristics and needs.

1b Knowing and understanding the multiple influences on development and learning.

DAP Criteria

3A1 Teachers consider what children should know, understand, and be able to do across the domains of physical, social, emotional, and cognitive development.

3C1 Teachers are familiar with the understandings and skills key for that age group in each domain (physical, social, emotional, and cognitive).

9-1 Art and Physical (Motor) Development

naeyc DAP The term **motor development** means "physical growth." Both terms refer to growth in the ability of children to use their bodies.

In an early childhood program, dancing, drawing, painting, pasting, and other activities that exercise muscles aid a child's motor development (see Photo 9-1). Exercising muscles in creative activities aids both small- and large-muscle development. Before we consider each of these types of motor development, let us look at the overall pattern of growth and development.

9-1a Pattern of Development

The process of human development follows a general pattern that includes growth in three basic directions (Figure 9-1). The first of these is called *large- to small-muscle* or **gross-motor development** to **fine-motor development**. Large- (gross) to small- (fine) motor development means that large muscles develop in the

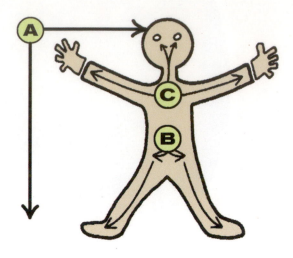

THE BODY DEVELOPS FROM

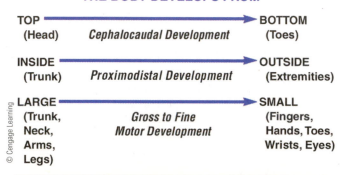

© Cengage Learning

FIGURE 9-1 The pattern of development.

neck, trunk, arms, and legs before the small muscles in the fingers, hands, wrists, and eyes develop. This is why young children can walk long before they are able to write or even scribble.

The second direction of growth, from head to toe (or top to bottom), is called **cephalocaudal development**. This growth pattern explains why a baby is able to hold up his head long before he is able to walk—the muscles develop from the head down.

The third pattern of development is from inside to outside (or from center to outside) and is called **proxomodistal development**. This explains the ability of a baby to roll over before he is able to push himself up with his arms. Because the inner muscles of the trunk develop first, rolling over comes before pulling or sitting up. Understanding these basic principles of development, especially large- to small-motor development, is important in planning appropriate art activities for young children. Let us now consider large- and small-motor development.

Casper Holroyd

PHOTO 9-1 Large motor skills are developed in dancing, too!

9-1b Large-Muscle Development

A child's proportions are constantly changing as he or she grows because different parts of the body grow at different rates. Physical disproportions are common from birth to approximately age six as the upper body is generally longer and not in proportion to the lower body. As a consequence of these body proportions in which the legs and body are not developed in proportion to the upper body region, toddlers and preschoolers have a high center of gravity and are prone to falls.

By age 6, however, body proportions are more similar to those of an adult. When the child has matured to adult-like proportions, his or her center of gravity is more centrally located so that he or she achieves a greater sense of physical balance and is able to be more purposeful in movements (see Photo 9-2).

Because large muscles in the arms, legs, neck, and trunk develop first, by the time children reach preschool age, they are able to use large muscles quite well. They can walk, run, sit, and stand at will. They can use their arms and hands quite easily in large movements such as clapping and climbing. Younger children enjoy large-motor play activities. Most 3-year-olds and many 4-year-olds are actively using their large muscles in running, wiggling, and jumping. They are not yet as developed in small-motor skills (such as cutting, tying, or lacing) as 5-year-olds.

The early childhood art program gives the child a chance to exercise large-motor skills in many ways other than just in active games. Painting with a brush on a large piece of paper is as good a practice

PHOTO 9-3 Small muscles in the hands and fingers are exercised in play dough activities.

for large-muscle development as dancing. Whether by using broad arm movements made in brush strokes or moving to a musical beat, it is only by first developing these large muscles that a child can begin to develop small-motor skills.

Creative activities in the early childhood program provide many opportunities for exercising large-muscle skills. Activities that exercise large muscles include group murals, tracing body shapes, easel painting, clay pounding, and crayon rubbings. (See the end of this chapter for suggested activities.)

9-1c Small-Muscle Development

Small muscles in fingers, hands, and wrists are used in art activities such as painting, cutting, pasting, and clay modeling (see Photo 9-3). These small-motor art activities and any other activity that involves the use of small muscles help exercise and develop a child's fine-motor control.

Small-muscle skills are different for a child at different ages. For example, many 3-year-olds do not have good small-muscle development, so the muscles in their fingers and hands are not quite developed enough to enable them to use scissors easily (see Photo 9-4).

Practice in crushing and tearing paper, and later practice in using blunt scissors, all help small muscles develop. The better the small-muscle development, the easier it will be to cut with scissors. Small muscles can grow stronger only by practice and exercise. A teacher encourages a child to exercise these small muscles in small-motor artwork, such as tearing, pasting, working with clay, making and playing with puppets, and finger painting.

PHOTO 9-2 Outdoor play is excellent for large-motor skill development.

PHOTO 9-4 Cutting with scissors is a challenge for preschool children.

Small muscles are often better developed in 4- and 5-year-olds. However, small-motor activities are still necessary for continued small-muscle development. Drawing with pencils, crushing paper into shapes, modeling figures with clay, and making mobiles are examples of more advanced small-motor activities.

Working with small muscles in small-motor art activities helps make learning to write much easier for the child. The control over hand and finger movements used for finger painting and clay modeling is the same control the child needs to be able to write. Early childhood art activities give the child a chance to practice and develop the small-motor skills needed in schoolwork to come.

Four stages of fine-motor development set the stage for early writing success: whole arm, whole hand, pincher, and pincer coordination (Carvell, 2006). Fine-motor development begins with strengthening and refining the muscles of the whole arm. As young children participate in large arm movements, such as painting a refrigerator box with paint rollers and water or tossing a beach ball into a laundry basket, they use their entire arm. This full arm movement is a precursor to muscle development of the hand.

Pouring water from one container to another and squeezing water from a turkey baster develop the muscles of the whole hand. Strengthening the hand muscles leads to the ability to coordinate the finer movements of the fingers. Children develop the pincher movements by pressing the thumb and index finger together. Clipping clothespins on a plastic cup, stringing beads, and tearing paper are activities that support this development.

Pincer control is the final stage of fine-motor development. With other skills in place, children are now prepared to properly grasp markers, pencils, and other writing utensils as they engage in authentic writing activities. This coordination allows the thumb, index, and middle fingers to act as a tripod, supporting the writing utensil and enabling small, highly coordinated finger movements (Huffman & Fortenberry, 2011).

9-1d Large- and Small-Motor Activities

The early childhood art program should have a good mixture of both small- and large-motor tools and activities (see Photo 9-5). A child needs to develop both large and small muscles, and artwork provides this chance.

The teacher must respect each child's need to develop both large and small muscles at any age. This means a teacher needs the right equipment and, more importantly, the right attitude for the level of each child (see Photo 9-6). The right attitude is one that lets the child know it is all right to try many large- and small-motor activities at any age. In this type of art program, not all 4-year-olds are expected to cut well, to button a shirt successfully, or to be able to do

PHOTO 9-5 Art activities involve small- and large-motor skills.

PHOTO 9-6 Tricycle play is a fun exercise for large muscles.

Casper Holroyd

either at all. Five-year-olds, as well as younger children, may enjoy pounding clay for no other purpose than the fun of pounding. Older children should also be allowed this same freedom of expression with both large- and small-muscle activities. Although they may appear more physically developed, middle- and upper-elementary children still enjoy "messing around" with clay and even finger paint.

Art activities provide both fine- and gross-motor experiences. As children create—thrusting sticks into plastic foam, forming small shapes with a marker, using a paintbrush at an easel—they move back and forth between large, sweeping motions and small, discrete movements. These movements help children develop control and coordination of both fine and gross muscles. Both types of development are important for the child's growth, not only for forming letters and numbers later in school but also for overall physical movement. Offering children a variety of different materials, such as crayons, easel paint, scissors, recycled materials, and clay, helps them develop the various muscles in their arms and fingers.

9-1e Hand–Eye Coordination

In the early childhood program, as children exercise their small and large muscles, they also improve their **hand–eye coordination**. Hand–eye coordination refers to the ability to use hand(s) and eyes at the same time. Painting is a good example of an activity in which hand–eye coordination comes into play. When children paint, they use their eyes to choose the colors, their hands to hold and use the brush, and their eyes to follow the brush strokes.

Hand–eye coordination is also used in clay modeling, making a mobile, pasting, and finger painting. In all of these art activities, the child is receiving practice in coordinating (using together) the hands and eyes.

9-1f Art Activities and Reading Readiness

Hand–eye coordination is important for future schoolwork. Many reading experts believe that good hand–eye coordination helps a child learn to read. They believe that the ability to use hands and eyes together in activities such as painting or playing ball helps a child learn the motor skills needed in reading. Holding a book in two hands and using the eyes to read from left to right require simple hand–eye coordination.

Reading experts believe that the growth pattern of large to small muscles affects reading ability. In other words, a child must have a chance to develop large muscles before being able to use small muscles—such as the eyes in the left-to-right movements of reading. The side-to-side or lateral movements developed in such activities as painting and printing are helpful in developing left-to-right tracking in reading. Thus, art activities are important for future reading because they exercise and develop hand–eye coordination and left-to-right tracking.

Explorations with art materials also offer opportunities to sharpen perceptions of form. Children note relationships between artistic two- and three-dimensional forms and the environment. Statements like "My clay is round like a pie," "I drew a square like that book," or "Look at the funny shape of my puppet's head; it's not like my head" indicate that children are learning about form while being involved in creative activities. **Visual acuity**—the ability to see and recognize shape and form—is implicit in all art activities. It is also an ability that needs to be developed for beginning reading.

9-1g Motor Control

All that we have discussed thus far about muscle growth and hand–eye coordination falls under the general category of motor control. As children grow, they progressively gain control over their bodies.

Children growing in small- and large-muscle skills and in hand–eye coordination are growing in total motor control. (Figure 9-2 contains suggested activities in art and other curriculum areas to enhance overall motor control for children ages 2 through 10.) The child's work in various activities demonstrates this growing motor control. An observant teacher can assess an individual child's motor skills in one activity

CHARACTERISTICS	SKILLS AND SUGGESTED ACTIVITIES
The Two-Year-Old Very active, short attention span	Provide pushing and pulling toys. Encourage play with pounding bench, punching bags, and soft clay. Provide opportunities both indoors and outdoors for active free play that involves climbing, running, sliding, and tumbling.
Interest in physical manipulation; ability to stack several items; pull apart, fill, and empty containers	Provide stacking cups or blocks for stacking and unstacking. Provide pop-apart toys, such as beads, for taking apart. (Large enough not to swallow.) Provide opportunities for filling and emptying containers with sand, water, rice, beans, rocks, etc.
Increased development of fine-motor skills	Provide crayons, chalk, paint, and paper for scribbling and painting. Be sure all materials are lead-free and nontoxic. Allow the child to "paint" the sidewalk, building, wheel toys, etc., with clear water and a brush large enough to handle. Provide opportunities to play with play dough, finger paint, paper for tearing, etc.
Increased development in language skills	Encourage the child to talk with you. Use pronouns such as "I," "me," "you," "they,"and "we." Encourage the child to use these words. Talk with the child about pictures. Ask her to point to objects or name them. Always give the correct name for objects. Give directions to follow: "Close the door," "Pick up the doll." Be sure to make this a fun game. Teach the child the names of unusual objects such as fire extinguisher, thermometer, screwdriver, and trivet.
Likes to imitate	Encourage finger plays. Recite nursery rhymes. Encourage the child to repeat them. Play I Am a Mirror. Stand or sit facing the child and have him copy everything you do.
Shows interest in dramatic play	Provide dolls, dress-up clothes, carriage, doll bed, toy telephones for pretend conversations.
The Three-Year-Old Increased development of large-motor skills	Provide opportunities for vigorous free play indoors and outdoors. Provide opportunities for climbing, jumping, riding wheel toys. Play Follow-the-Leader, requiring vigorous body movements.
Greater control over small muscles	Provide opportunities for free play with blocks in various sizes and shapes. Provide a variety of manipulative toys and activities such as pegboard and peg sets, Tinker Toys, puzzles with three to eight pieces. Encourage children to dress and undress themselves, serve food, set the table, water the plants.
Greater motor coordination	Provide art activities. Encourage free expression with paint, crayons, chalk, colored pens, collage materials, clay, play dough. Be sure all materials are lead-free and nontoxic.
Increased development of language skills and vocabulary	Provide opportunities each day for reading stories to children in a group or individually. Encourage children to tell stories. Tape-record their stories. Encourage children to talk about anything of interest.

© Cengage Learning

FIGURE 9-2 Motor skills and characteristics of children ages 2 through 10 years, with suggested activities to encourage physical development.

(Continues)

CHARACTERISTICS	SKILLS AND SUGGESTED ACTIVITIES
Beginning to understand number concepts. Usually can grasp concepts of 1, 2, and 3. Can count several numbers in a series but may leave some out.	Count objects of interest, e.g., cookies, cups, napkins, dolls. When possible, move them as you count. Allow children to count them. Display numbers in the room. Use calendars, charts, scales, and rulers.
Enjoys music and is beginning to be able to carry a tune, express rhythm	Provide music activities each day. Sing songs, create rhythms. Offer opportunities for children to move their bodies to music. Encourage children to make up songs. Record them and play them back for the children to dance to or to sing along with.
Curious about why and how things happen	Provide new experiences that arouse questions. Answer the questions simply and honestly. Use reference books with the child to find answers. Conduct simple science activities: What will the magnet pick up? Freeze water, make ice cream, plant seeds, make a terrarium, fly a kite on a windy day.
The Four-Year-Old Good balance and body coordination; increased development of small- and large-motor skills	Provide opportunities each day for vigorous free play. Provide opportunities for the child to walk on a curved line, a straight line, a balance beam. Encourage walking with a beanbag on the head. Games: "See how fast you can hop," "See how far you can hop on one foot," "See how high you can jump." Provide opportunities to throw balls (medium-sized, soft), beanbags, yarn balls.
Small-motor skills are developing most rapidly now. Drawings and art express world around them.	Provide opportunity for variety of artwork. Encourage children to tell a story or talk about their finished projects. Encourage children to mix primary colors to produce secondary colors. Name the colors with them.
Increasing hand–eye coordination	Encourage children to unzip, unsnap, and unbutton clothes. Dressing self is too difficult at this point. Encourage children to tear and cut. Encourage children to lace their shoes.
Ability to group items according to similar characteristics	Play lotto games. Group buttons by color or size. Provide a mixture of seeds. Sort by kind. At cleanup time, sort blocks according to shape. Play rhyming word games.
Increased understanding of concepts related to numbers, size and weight, colors, textures, distance and position, and time	In conversation, use words related to these concepts. Play "follow direction" games. Say, "Put the pencil beside the big block," or "Crawl under the table." Provide swatches of fabric and other materials that vary in texture. Talk about differences. Blindfold the children or have them cover their eyes and ask them to match duplicate textures.

FIGURE 9-2 Motor skills and characteristics of children ages 2 through 10 years, with suggested activities to encourage physical development. (*Continued*)

TeachSource Digital Download   Download from CourseMate.

CHARACTERISTICS	SKILLS AND SUGGESTED ACTIVITIES
Awareness of the world around them	Build a simple bird feeder and provide feed for birds. Record the kinds of birds observed. Arrange field trips to various community locations of interest (park, fire station, police station).
Has a vivid imagination; enjoys dramatic play	Provide variety of dress-up clothes. Encourage dramatic play through props such as cash register and empty food containers, tea set, and child-sized furniture.
The Five- and Six-Year-Old Good sense of balance and body coordination	Encourage body movement with records, stories, rhythms. Encourage skipping to music or rhymes. Teach them simple folk dances.
A tremendous drive for physical activity	Provide free play that encourages running, jumping, balancing, and climbing. Play tug-of-war. Encourage tumbling on a mat.
Development and coordination of small muscles in hands and fingers	Encourage opportunities to paint, draw, cut, paste, mold clay. Provide small peg games and other manipulative toys. Teach sewing with large blunt needle and thread into egg cartons or punched cards. Provide simple carpentry experiences.
Increased hand–eye coordination	Allow children to copy designs of shapes, letters, and numbers. Show a child how his name is made with letters. Encourage catching small balls.
Ability to distinguish right from left. Can discriminate between weights, colors, sizes, textures, and shapes	Play games that emphasize right from left. Games can require responses to directions such as "Put your right hand on your nose" or "Put your left foot on the green circle." Play sorting games. Sort rocks by weight; blocks by weight or shape; marbles or seeds by colors. Match fabric swatches.
Increased understanding of number concepts	Count anything of interest—cookies, napkins, cups, leaves, acorns, trees, children, teachers, boys, chairs, etc. Identify numbers visible on a calendar, clock, measuring containers, or other devices.
Enjoys jokes, nonsense rhymes, riddles	Read humorous stories, riddles, and nonsense rhymes.
Enjoys creative, dramatic activities	Move body to dramatize opening of a flower, falling snow, leaves, rain, wiggly worms, snakes, blowing wind. Dramatize stories as they are read. Good stories to use are: *Caps for Sale, Three Billy Goats Gruff, Three Bears.*
The Seven- to 10-Year-Old Good sense of balance and body coordination. More directed in their drive for physical activity. Good development and coordination of small muscles in hands and fingers	Encourage movements that challenge the child such as horizontal and vertical jumps. Introduce more complex motor skills such as relay races obstacle courses, etc. Encourage free play that allows running, jumping, balancing, throwing, and catching. Introduce basic sports such as baseball, basketball, and soccer. Provide many challenging and diverse art activities that allow for fine-motor exercise. Encourage three-dimensional projects such as woodworking, papier mâché, costume-making, etc.

FIGURE 9-2 Motor skills and characteristics of children ages 2 through 10 years, with suggested activities to encourage physical development. (*Continued*)

CHARACTERISTICS	SKILLS AND SUGGESTED ACTIVITIES
Improved hand–eye coordination	Continue to encourage tossing, throwing, and catching skills. Use activities that incorporate several skills such as dodge ball.
Learns to apply and refine perceptual skills developed earlier	Challenge children in art activities to see and express shape, form, color, and line in a variety of media. Provide activities that allow them to learn to identify and analyze relationships such as how light affects perception of colors, textures, and form.
Growing facility with use of numbers; can think more flexibly. Has an increasingly sophisticated sense of humor	Introduce the use of calculators for math problems. Challenge them with basic probability and estimation activities/problems. Allow them to work in small groups for problem solving. Provide joke books, humorous books, nonsense riddle and rhyme books. Encourage them to write their own humorous pieces.
Enjoys dramatic activities, but self-consciousness is becoming an issue	Encourage children to express themselves in short performances such as sketches, vignettes, "freeze-frame" scenes, and pantomime. Provide opportunities for them to see dramatic activities of other students (middle-school play, dance rehearsal, etc.). Provide books, music, and artwork of great artists for children to experience. (Gallaghue & Ozmun, 2005)

FIGURE 9-2 Motor skills and characteristics of children ages 2 through 10 years, with suggested activities to encourage physical development. (*Continued*)

TeachSource Digital Download   Download from CourseMate.

and make judgments about his or her likely skill or ability in another area. For instance, when considering art activities, a teacher recognizes that early scribbling is the beginning of motor control. Initially, children hold the crayon and scribble with very little motor control. As they grow in motor control, they can control the direction of their scribbles, then control lines to make basic forms, and finally draw pictures.

Therefore, a teacher can assess children's general motor control by knowing their artwork. For example, the teacher who knows that a certain 5-year-old cannot yet cut with scissors knows how to reply to parents who ask if this child is ready for piano lessons. Observing each child's motor control in artwork helps the teacher know each child's motor control in other areas as well.

Did You Get It?

A preschool teacher gives his students beads to string on yarn. Which type of skills are his students developing?

a. pincher development
b. proxomodistal development
c. gross-motor control
d. pincer control

Take the full quiz on CourseMate.

9-2 Art and Mental Development

naeyc DAP Art activities involve children mentally as well as physically. They involve both the physical ability to use art tools and the thinking processes involved in the creation itself. Let's now consider how art and thinking skills are related in art activities.

Creating art is a complex mental process. It involves mental skills such as problem solving, predicting, design, and cause and effect. For example, think about a child who wants to draw a person. First, the child needs to remember what she or he knows about how people look, then identify the important features, and represent them on paper through shapes and lines. That is no small achievement for a 3- or 4-year-old! Working with art materials, the child learns new concepts such as how colors can change and how paper can be used in many ways. These and similar experiences help the child develop more flexible thinking, an important mental skill that is discussed later in this chapter.

Just as art reflects children's thinking, it also enhances it. Consider an older child who wants to draw an ant and a mosquito. The child learns about the similarities and differences between the two insects by observing; then, through drawing, the child clarifies and reinforces what she or he has learned.

Art helps children gain a great deal of knowledge in more direct ways as well. As children experiment and investigate, they learn about the physical nature of tools and materials. What will the brush do if I hit it on the paper this way—or that way? How can I make the foil plate stick to the wood? How much glue is okay to use on the tissue paper? When you offer a wide variety of materials for children to investigate freely, you broaden their opportunities for learning.

9-2a Concept of Change

Change is an important concept for children to understand, and it is one that develops slowly. Piaget (1955), in his writings about the growth of intelligence in young children, emphasizes the fact that mental growth is aided by a child's active exploration of the environment. The child, according to Piaget, gradually comes to understand how things can change as he or she experiences different materials in various situations in the environment. For example, by using color, mixing colors, and making colors lighter or darker, the child learns that things can change. Clay can change from hard to soft. Plaster can change from liquid to solid. (See Figure 9-3 for a more detailed explanation of Piaget's stages of mental development.)

Sensorimotor Stage: Birth to two years
Uses all senses to explore the world. Nonverbal communication.

Gains object permanence—objects exist even when not seen. Example: Remove a toy from a very young child and object won't be missed because child can't see it. Once child achieves object permanence, she remembers the toy and will cry to get it back or search for it.

Moves from reflex action to directed actions toward a goal. Example: Child sees object and tries to get it by crying and crawling.

Preoperational Stage: two to seven years
Child begins to carry out mental actions (operations) that require forming and using images and symbols. Example: Uses symbols for objects and people. Likes fantasy and imaginative play, makes mental images and likes to pretend.

Rapid language growth. By age four, a 2,000-word vocabulary is average.

Has trouble reversing actions (making transformations) or understanding how objects can change shape but still be the same object. Example: Child doesn't think a tall glass of milk poured into a short fat glass is the same amount of milk.

Has inflexible thinking; does not think about something from more than one perspective. Example: Child focuses on the shape of glass of milk, thinking the taller glass has more milk even when the same milk is poured into a short fat glass.

Understanding other points of view is difficult because child is egocentric (centering on his or her own experiences). Example: Child thinks everyone thinks, feels, and sees as he does.

Concrete Operations: seven to 11 years
Develops basic concepts of objects, numbers, time, space, and causality.

Develops reversibility (two-way thinking). Example: Amount of milk is the same when poured from tall glass into short fat glass.

Can classify by different categories. Example: Child understands how a group can be a subset of another, such as animals and plants are both living things.

Uses concrete objects to learn and draw conclusions. Manipulation of objects aids the child's understanding.

Basic logic develops, but is tied to physical reality. Abstract thinking and hypothetical problem solving is not yet possible.

Formal Operations: 11 to 15 years
Child can think abstractly and hypothetically.

Can generate diverse possible solutions for problems.

Can evaluate alternatives based on many criteria.

Can form and test hypotheses, using scientific method.

(Piaget, 1950, 1952, and 1955).

FIGURE 9-3 Summary—Piaget's Stages of Mental/Cognitive Development.

TeachSource Video

2–5 Years: Piaget's Preoperational Stage

1. What other conservation tasks using different materials could you do with young children in addition to the ones shown in this video?

2. How can you relate the preoperational child's irreversibility to the information in your text concerning executive functions of the brain?

Watch on CourseMate.

"Learning by doing" in art helps children grow mentally because they grow more flexible in their thinking. They learn to think of things in the context of change, realizing that not all things are permanent. The ability to think this way is called **flexible thinking** (see Figure 9-4).

Art activities with a variety of materials encourage flexibility of thought. In making a collage, the characteristics of different items are compared, and relationships are discovered between new and familiar items. Flexibility of thought is encouraged as children associate particular tools with certain processes and learn which tools work best with various materials. For example, a thin brush will make a thin line with paint, and a thick one creates a broader stroke. A sharp needle is needed to sew through felt, but a blunt one works well for open-weave fabrics.

Being able to think flexibly helps children become mentally prepared for later school experiences. Math, spelling, and science all require thinking that can deal with change. In science, for example, a cooking lesson involves changes that ingredients go through in the process of becoming a cake. In math activities, a child learns how numbers can change by adding and subtracting. In spelling, children learn how words change with plurals, suffixes, and prefixes. Flexibility in thought processes is, therefore, basic to most of a child's subsequent learning experiences.

9-2b Art and Sensorimotor Development

As children grow physically, they also grow mentally. This is because young children learn by doing. Piaget, in his work with young children, describes a child's learning by doing as *sensorimotor development*.

The word **sensorimotor** derives from the two words *sensory*, referring the five body senses, and *motor*,

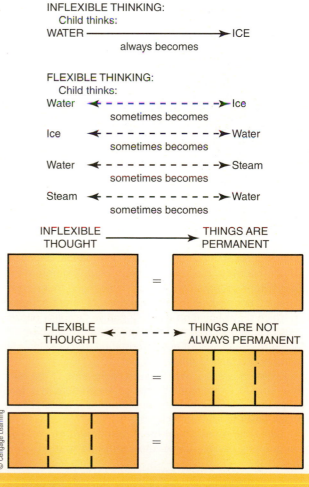

FIGURE 9-4 Flexible and inflexible thinking.

Executive Functions:
Building Blocks of Cognitive Development

Executive function skills are crucial building blocks for early cognitive development. These skills can be described as the ability to focus, hold, and work with information in mind, filter distractions, and switch gears. Acquiring these early building blocks is one of the most important and challenging tasks of the early childhood years. Young children will need to rely on their emerging executive function skills to help them as they learn to read and write, remember steps in solving math problems, and take part in class discussions and group projects (Center on the Developing Child at Harvard University, 2011). In the research on executive functions, three dimensions are most often highlighted: working memory, inhibitory control, and cognitive/mental flexibility. These functions, which are not entirely distinct, work together to produce competent executive functioning.

Working memory is the ability to hold and use information in our heads over short periods of time. It enables children to remember and connect information from one step to another ("Go to the rug and sit down.") An example for an adult would be the ability to return to a place in a book after being interrupted by a phone call.

Inhibitory control is the skill to master and filter one's thoughts and impulses in order to resist temptations, distractions, and habits, and to pause and think before acting. It is the skill you are using as you read this section when you would rather be doing something else. Children use this skill to wait until they are called on when they know an answer, to ignore distractions, and to stay on task at school (Center on the Developing Child at Harvard University, 2011).

Cognitive or mental flexibility is the ability to easily switch gears and adjust to changed demands, priorities, or perspectives. It allows a person to apply different rules in different settings. With children, we teach them to use "inside" and "outside" voices and the different situations in which they should be used. Cognitive flexibility allows us to catch mistakes and fix them, to revise ways of doing things in light of new information, to consider a new perspective, and to think creatively.

Children use this skill to learn exceptions to the rules of grammar, to approach a science experiment in different ways until it works, or to try out different ways to get the block tower to stay upright.

Scientific research on the development of executive functioning reveals some important information on the effects the environment can have on the development of these skills. Chaotic and unpredictable environments can lead to poor self-regulatory behaviors and impulse control (Evans & Wachs, 2010). A number of other studies have shown that exposure to highly stressful early environments is associated with deficits in the development of a child's working memory, attention, and inhibitory control skills (Lengua, Honoroda, & Bush, 2007; Maughan & Ciccheti, 2002; and O'Connor et al., 2000).

Damaging fear and toxic stress are likely mechanisms that explain these effects, in part, because they affect the chemistry of brain circuits involved in the development of these capabilities (Center on the Developing Child at Harvard University, 2005, 2008; Pollak, Cicchetti, & Klorman, 1998; Sanchez et al., 2001). Under such conditions, the brain goes into high "fight or flight" mode, when it's necessary to calm down, plan, and execute a well-thought-out response. In children (and adults) acute stress can lead to a temporary "blip" in executive functioning (Arnsten, 1998). Thus, chronic fear and anxiety associated with living in highly threatening, chaotic, or stressful environments can make it very difficult for young children to engage their executive abilities—even in situations (for example, school) where they may, in fact, be safe (Liston, McEwen, & Casey, 2006; Liston et al., 2009).

Mounting research is revealing that children from lower (versus higher) socioeconomic backgrounds show poorer performance on tests of working memory, cognitive flexibility, and inhibition (Kishiyama et al., 2009; Li-Grining, 2007; and Noble, McCandliss, & Farah, 2007). One reason that social class may be related to the development of executive function skills is that young children with greater access to resources experience environments that are more likely to contain features that protect and foster the development of these skills (for example, responsive caregiving, order and predictability, and freedom from sustained threats). This underscores the importance of efforts to improve children's early environments and experiences as a strategy for increasing the likelihood of positive developmental outcomes in executive functioning skills (Center on the Developing Child at Harvard, 2011). It also underscores the importance of early childhood teachers providing safe, predictable environments for all young children.

referring to the physical act of doing. Sensorimotor learning involves the body and its senses (sensory) as they are used in doing (motor).

For Piaget (1955), the foundation of all mental development takes place in physical knowledge—the knowledge that comes from objects. Children construct physical knowledge by acting on objects—feeling, tasting, smelling, seeing, and hearing them. They cause objects to move by throwing, banging, blowing, pushing, and pulling them. They observe changes that take place in objects when they are mixed together, heated, cooled, or changed in some other way. As physical knowledge develops, children become better able to establish relationships (comparing, classifying, ordering) between and among the objects they act upon.

9-2c Sensorimotor Learning in Art

An example of sensorimotor learning in art is modeling with clay. In using clay (the motor activity), children use their senses (sensory), such as touch and smell, to learn about clay and how to use it. A teacher can *tell* the children how clay feels and how to use it, but children truly learn about clay by physically *using* it themselves. A child needs this sensorimotor exploration with clay and many other art materials.

In the art program, children learn many things in this sensorimotor way—learning by doing. Many ideas and concepts are learned from different art activities. Just as children exercise different muscles in art activities, they also learn new concepts in many kinds of art activities. Exploring and creating with art materials encourages children to use their senses to become more aware of the environment.

Did You Get It?

While drawing with crayons, a 5-year-old realizes that colors that blend well are suited for backgrounds and that colors that create sharper lines are useful for drawing foreground figures. What skill is this child developing?

   a. sensorimotor awareness
   b. sensory integration
   c. preoperational thought
   d. flexibility of thought

Take the full quiz on CourseMate.

9-3 Brain Development: Basic Elements

naeyc **DAP** Much like the overall pattern of physical growth, the brain grows in sequential fashion, from top to bottom, or from the least complex part (brain stem) to the more complex area (cortex).

The basic elements of the human brain include the following:

- The *brain stem* is at the base of the skull and controls most basic life activities, including blood pressure and body temperature.
- The *midbrain* is at the top of the brain stem and controls motor activity, appetite, and sleep.
- The *cerebellum* is behind the brain stem and coordinates movement and balance.
- The *limbic system* is in the central part of the brain and controls emotions, attachment, and memory.
- The *cortex* is the top layer of the brain and is about the depth of two dimes placed on top of each other. The cortex is the "executive branch" of the brain that regulates decision making and controls thinking, reasoning, and language.

The cerebral cortex contains 80% of the neurons in the brain. Because it is the least developed part of the brain at birth and keeps developing until adolescence and even beyond, the cortex is more sensitive to experiences than other parts of the brain.

Neurons are the functioning core of the brain. Each cell body is about one-hundredth the size of the period at the end of this sentence. A neuron has branches of *dendrites* emerging from the cell body. These dendrites pick up chemical signals across a *synapse,* and the impulse travels the length of the axon. Each axon branch has a sac containing neurotransmitters at its tip. The electrical impulse causes the release of the neurotransmitters, which, in turn, stimulates or inhibits neighboring dendrites, like an on-off switch. These connections are miracles of the human body. But to understand their power, you have to multiply this miracle by trillions. A single cell can connect with as many as 1,5000 other cells (Zero to Three, 2012). This incredibly complex network of connections is referred to the brain's "circuitry" or "wiring." Experiences shape the way circuits are made in the brain.

A remarkable increase in synapses occurs during the first year of life. The brain develops a functional architecture through the development of these synapses or connections. For example, if a parent repeatedly calls a child a certain name, then connections will form that allow the child to recognize that name over time as referring to her, and she will learn to respond. From birth, the brain rapidly is creating these connections that form our habits, thoughts, consciousness, memories, and mind.

By the time a child is 3 years old, her brain has formed about 1,000 trillion connections—about twice as many as adults have. A baby's brain is superdense and will stay that way throughout the first decade of life. Beginning at about age 11, a child's brain gets rid of extra connections in a process called "pruning," gradually making order out of a thick tangle of "wires" (Center on the Developing Child at Harvard, 2005).

The remaining wiring is more powerful and efficient. As the synapses in a child's brain are strengthened through repeated experiences, connections and pathways are formed that structure the way a child learns. If a pathway is not used, it's eliminated. Things done a single time are somewhat less likely to have an effect on brain development. Conversely, when a connection is used repeatedly in the early years, it becomes permanent. For example, when adults repeat words and phrases as they talk to babies, babies learn to understand speech and strengthen the language connections in the brain (Zero to Three, 2012).

Did You Get It?

A teacher shows her 2-year-old students how a toy operates day after day. What is the benefit of repeating information to a small child?

   a. It helps the teacher relate to the child.
   b. It helps brain connections to become permanent.
   c. It helps the child relate to the teacher.
   d. Routine makes a child feel comfortable in the classroom.

Take the full quiz on CourseMate.

9-4 Critical Periods of Brain Development

DAP **naeyc** Brain development proceeds in waves, with different parts of the brain becoming active at different times. The brain's ability to respond to experience presents exciting opportunities for a child's development. Learning continues throughout life. However, "prime times" or "windows of opportunity"

exist when the brain is able to absorb new information more easily than at other times. While this is true especially in the first three years of life, it continues throughout early childhood and adolescence. For example, young children learn the grammar and meaning of their native language with only simple exposure.

Although later language learning is possible, it usually is slower and more difficult. Providing children with the best opportunity for learning and growth during the periods when their minds are most ready to absorb new information is important, as detailed in the following.

1. Visual and Auditory Development—The prime time for visual and auditory development, or a child's capacity for learning to see and hear, is from birth to between 4 and 5 years of age (Center on the Developing Child at Harvard, 2005). The development of these sensory capacities is very important for allowing children, especially babies, to perceive and interact with the world around them. During the first few months, especially, babies need to see shapes, colors, objects at varying distances, and movement for the brain to learn how to see. Babies also need exposure to a variety of sounds so their brain can learn to process that information and allow for responsiveness by hearing something.

2. Language Development—The prime time for language development and learning to talk is from birth to 10 years of age (Center on the Developing Child at Harvard, 2005). Children are learning language during this entire period. However, the prime time for language learning is the first few years of life. Language skills depend critically on verbal input (or sign language, for babies with hearing impairments) in the first few years or certain skills, particularly grammar and pronunciation, may be permanently impacted (Zero to Three, 2012). Many experts believe that the critical period for language learning begins to close around 5 years of age and ends around puberty. They believe that this is why individuals who learn a new language after puberty almost always speak it with a foreign accent.

   Children need to hear you constantly talk, sing, and read to them during these early years. Responding to their babbling and language efforts is also important during this critical period. Children vary in their language development

Opportunities to Affect Students' Brains

Brain research has uncovered some powerful connections for educators to make in the classroom. Here are some of these:

● The human brain can and does grow new neurons. We now know that new neurons are highly correlated with memory, mood, and learning. Of interest to educators is that this process can be regulated by our everyday behaviors. Specifically, it can be enhanced by exercise, lower levels of stress, and good nutrition. Schools can and should influence these variables (Kempermann, Wiskott, & Goge, 2004).

● The ability of the brain to rewire and remap itself by means of neuroplasticity is profound. The *Journal of Neuroplasticity* explores these and related issues. Schools can influence this process through skill-building, reading, meditation, the arts, career and technical education, and thinking skills that build student success. Neuroscientists Michael Kilgard and Michael Merzenich verified that when the correct skill-building protocol is used, educators can make positive and significant changes in our brains in a short time (2006).

● Good nutrition is about far more than avoiding obesity. The journals *Nutritional Neuroscience* and the *European Journal of Clinical Nutrition* explore the effects on our brain of what we eat. The effects on cognition, memory, attention, stress, and even intelligence are now emerging. Schools and teachers that pay attention to nutrition and cognition (not just obesity) will probably support better student achievement (Jensen, 2008).

● The study of the value of exercise to the brain has shown that physical activity and exercise is strongly correlated with increased brain mass, better cognition, mood regulation, new cell production, and increased reading ability (Jensen, 2008). The reason for this is that the cerebellum is part of the brain that processes movement as well as cognition. The connection between the two is powerful and demonstrates how domains of growth are deeply connected. In older children, research has shown a connection between physical fitness and the brain. Children between the ages of 9 and 10 years old tend to have a bigger hippocampus and better memory than their peers who are less fit (Chaddock et al., 2010). The hippocampus is the center brain area and part of the foundation for learning and memory.

● Brain development is "activity-dependent," meaning that the electrical activity in every circuit—sensory, motor, emotional, cognitive—shapes the way that circuit gets put together. Like computer circuits, neural circuits process information through the flow of electricity. Unlike computer circuits, however, the circuits in our brains are not fixed structures. Every experience—whether it is seeing one's first rainbow, riding a bicycle, reading a book, sharing a joke—excites certain neural circuits and leaves other intact. Those that are consistently turned on over time will be strengthened, while those that are rarely excited may be dropped away. Or, as neuroscientists sometimes say, "Cells that fire together, wire together." The elimination of unused neural circuits, also referred to as "pruning," may sound harsh, but it is generally a good thing. It streamlines children's neural processing, making the remaining circuits work more quickly and efficiently. Without synaptic pruning, children wouldn't be able to walk, talk, or even see properly (Zero to Three, 2012).

during these first years, so teachers should allow for some variation in children's abilities at different ages.

3. Physical and Motor Development—The prime time for physical and motor development in children is from birth to 12 years of age (Center on the Developing Child at Harvard, 2005). Children become physically ready for different aspects of motor development at different times. A child needs several years to develop the coordination skills to play catch with a ball easily, and even then refinement of such skills continues into a child's early adolescence. Teachers should monitor a child's motor development but be patient because children vary in their rates of development.

4. Emotional and Social Development—The prime time for emotional and social development in children is birth to 12 years of age. Differing aspects of emotional and social development, which incorporate higher capacities, such as awareness of others, empathy, and trust, are

THIS ONE'S FOR YOU

Your Amazing Brain

"The brain," wrote Emily Dickinson, "is wider than the Sky." And the more you learn about your brain, no doubt will you will agree. The following are some interesting facts about your brain and its power:

● Our brain contains 100 billion neurons (nerve cells), our gray matter. Each neuron has an axon—a little arm—that transmits information in the form of electrical impulses to the dendrites—receivers—or nearby neurons. Dendrites branch twig-like from each neuron. Between axon and dendrite, the synapse is the point of connection. Axons commune with dendrites across the synaptic gap. A single neuron can make between 1,000 and 10,000 connections. At this moment, your neurons are making, it could be, a million billion connections.

● Failure to learn new things kills neurons. People who vegetate before the TV are killing their neurons. People who never do anything new or meet anyone new are killing their neurons. People who never read or learn a new game or build a model airplane or cook up a new recipe or learn a new language are killing their neurons. To keep your neurons, learn something new every day. Begin now. Doing so requires no particular genius.

● Genius is nothing you can be born with. No one is born with it—not Mozart, not Picasso, not Tolstoy. In any field, world-class achievement demands thousands of hours of practice. Dozens of cognition studies have produced the same result: geniuses practice more. Neural pathways require repeated stimulation to gain a "genius" level of mastery. The neurons must be stimulated and restimulated, over and over again. Essential to this learning process, to this process of achieving supreme mastery, is the hippocampus.

● The hippocampus is at the core of what is known as declarative memory—memory of facts and events that can be recalled later for conscious reflection. Memories of what you did this morning, of which candidate you voted for, of whether you were supposed to pick up milk on your way home, all depend on the hippocampus. The sea horse-shaped structure is located above the eye, about an inch behind the forehead. It is part of the limbic system, the chief purveyor of emotion. We remember what is emotional. Fear, essential for survival, is provided to us by our almond-shaped amygdalae, also part of the limbic system. Fearful events fire up the amygdalae, and the amygdala sends its projections all over the brain, but especially to the hippocampus. The amygdala can "smell a rat." It receives sensations directly from the nose and sets off alarms with no intervening cognition. We remember what we fear. And we remember what we like, what we want, what we love, and what triggers our reward system. We attend to what is meaningful, what is emotionally resonant, whether positive or negative. We remember what we pay attention to.

● Stress shrinks the brain. Not normal stress or necessary stress, but chronic stress—chronic anxiety or clinical depression. The view that chronic stress destroys dendrites, neural pathways, and even entire neurons, especially in the hippocampus, is gaining acceptance as studies go forward (Center on the Developing Child at Harvard, 2011).

Stress revs up the adrenal gland to pump glucocorticoids such as cortisol. Cortisol sparks the production of epinephrine (adrenaline), which tenses muscles, narrows blood vessels, and prepares you to run for your life. When the emergency ends and cortisol subsides, then all is well. But in chronic stress, the emergency never ends. Cortisol bathes the hippocampus continuously, killing its neurons (Long, 2010). So, the best thing you can do for your brain is to quit worrying needlessly and stop stressing out over every little thing.

important at different times. For example, the real prime time for emotional attachment to be developed is from birth to 18 months, when a young child is forming attachments with critical caregivers. Such development provides the foundations for other aspects of emotional development that occur as children grow.

Emotional intelligence is critical to success in life. The part of the brain that regulates emotion, the amygdala, is shaped early on by experience and forms the brain's emotional wiring. Early nurturing is important to learning empathy, happiness, hopefulness, and resiliency (Center on the Developing Child at Harvard, 2005).

Social development, which involves both self-awareness and a child's ability to interact with others, also occurs in stages. For example, sharing toys is something that a 2-year-old's brain is not fully developed well to do, so this social ability is more common and positive with toddlers who are 3 or older. Early childhood teachers' efforts to nurture and guide children will assist in laying healthy foundations for social and emotional development.

9-5 Art, Vocabulary Development, and the Total Program

In the art program, children also have opportunities to naturally expand their vocabularies. An expanding vocabulary about creative materials and processes is a natural partner to the activity itself. Children working with art materials will naturally use descriptive terms for the media and the resulting creations. The teacher's use of particular words to compare size, weight, color, texture, and shape influences children's descriptions of their artwork. Previous knowledge is combined with new information as oral language develops. "Gushy, mushy, wet paint," chanted 3-year-old Laura as she pushed the finger paint around on the tabletop. "Gushy, mushy, red paint," responded one of her tablemates.

As children grow and develop through art, they begin to use words such as *thick, thin, hard, soft, straight, curved, dark, light, smooth,* and *sticky.* Vocabulary that indicates direction is also quickly assimilated into the children's arena of understanding when they work with art materials. Five-year-old children show how much they have learned with statements like these: "I wrote my name at the top," "I put a board under the clay," and "I drew smoke coming out of the chimney."

The teacher introduces words like *soft* and *smooth* to describe the feel of velvet material. Scraps of burlap are called *rough, bumpy,* or *scratchy.* Even the word *texture* is one that can be used with young children. As they feel the different kinds of cloth, the different "feels" can easily be called "textures." Children then put together in their minds the feel of the velvet with the words *soft, smooth,* and *texture.* This is sensorimotor learning—learning through sensing as well as by association.

Learning to notice the different way things feel teaches a child about concepts that are opposite, which is important in subjects such as math and science. The difference between hard and soft is similar to the difference between adding and subtracting in math; both ideas are opposites. A child learns in art that soft is not the same as hard. In math, a child learns that adding is different from or the opposite of subtracting. Mastering opposite concepts used in doing artwork thus helps the child learn the mental concepts needed later in other school subjects. (See Chapters 3 and 4 for more information on art concepts and vocabulary to use with young children.)

The early childhood art program helps a young child grow in social, emotional, physical, and mental ways. It gives children a chance to be themselves and grow at their own individual paces. Art should not be the only part of the early childhood program where this growth can occur. Freedom for growing at the child's own pace should be part of the whole early childhood program. The exploring, creating, and relaxing parts of artwork should be part of all the other early childhood activities. (Activities in these other curriculum areas are included in subsequent chapters.)

Art helps a child grow through creative thinking and feeling, not only about art but also about all other things. The confidence and good feelings about themselves and their work that children develop in art apply to other things in and out of school. Seen in this way, art cannot be thought of as a separate part of the program. It is and always must be an approach to learning inseparable from all the rest.

Summary

9-1 Discuss the relationship between art and physical (motor) development.

In an early childhood program, drawing, painting, pasting, and other activities that exercise muscles aid a child's overall motor development. Exercising muscles in creative activities aids both small- and large-muscle development. The process of human development follows these general patterns: gross-motor development to fine-motor development, cephalocaudal development, and proxomodistal development. According to Piaget, young children learn mentally as they do things physically. Their mental development, in his theory, falls in these stages: sensorimotor, preoperational, concrete, and formal operations. In the art program, children learn many important concepts that are used later in other learning experiences. Art activities involve children in sensorimotor learning through the use of the body, senses, and mind. Involving all the senses in art activities helps provide a complete learning experience for young children.

9-2 Describe the relationship between art and mental development.

Artwork also helps in developing their mental abilities: learning to think flexibly; being able to see fine differences; being able to hear, listen, and follow directions; and learning new words. Finally, art helps children develop a creative mental attitude that will help them succeed in all school subjects. The creative aspects of art cannot and should not be separate from the total early childhood program.

9-3 List and describe the basic elements of the human brain.

The basic elements of the human brain include the following:

- The brain stem is at the base of the skull and controls most basic life activities, including blood pressure and body temperature.
- The midbrain is at the top of the brain stem and controls motor activity, appetite, and sleep.
- The cerebellum is behind the brain stem and coordinates movement and balance.
- The limbic system is in the central part of the brain and it controls emotions, attachment, and memory.
- The cortex is the top layer of the brain and is about the depth of two dimes placed on top of each other. The cortex is the "executive branch" of the brain

that regulates decision making and controls thinking, reasoning, and language.

9-4 Discuss the critical periods of the brain for visual and auditory, language, physical and motor, and emotional social development.

1. Visual and Auditory Development—The prime time for visual and auditory development, or a child's capacity for learning to see and hear, is from birth to between 4 and 5 years of age (Center on the Developing Child at Harvard, 2005). The development of these sensory capacities is very important for allowing children, especially babies, to perceive and interact with the world around them.

2. Language Development—The prime time for language development and learning to talk is from birth to 10 years of age (Center on the Developing Child at Harvard, 2005). Children are learning language during this entire period. However, the prime time for language learning is the first few years of life.

3. Physical and Motor Development—The prime time for physical and motor development in children is from birth to 12 years of age (Center on the Developing Child at Harvard, 2005). Children become physically ready for different aspects of motor development at different times.

4. Emotional and Social Development—The prime time for emotional and social development in children is birth to 12 years of age. Differing aspects of emotional and social development, which incorporate higher capacities, such as awareness of others, empathy, and trust, are important at different times.

9-5 Explain the relationship between art and vocabulary development and how art can be a part of the total early childhood program.

The early childhood art program helps a young child grow in social, emotional, physical, and mental ways. It gives children a chance to be themselves and grow at their own individual paces. In the art program, children have opportunities to naturally expand their vocabularies. An expanding vocabulary about creative materials and processes is a natural partner to the activity itself. Art should not be the only part of the early childhood program where this growth can occur. Freedom for growing at the child's own pace should be part of the whole early childhood program.

Key Terms

cephalocaudal development   184
executive functions   195
fine-motor development   184
flexible thinking   192

gross-motor development   184
hand–eye coordination   187
motor development   184

proxomodistal development   184
sensorimotor   192
visual acuity   187

Learning Activities

A. Observe children in a preschool program. Include observations in the art center, the block center, and the housekeeping/dramatic play center. Describe the small- and large-motor development of children as demonstrated by their play in each of these areas.

B. Using the information in Figure 9-2, create your own activities for each of the age groups presented in this chart.

C. Listen to a group of children painting. Record or take notes on their conversations. Compare your observations to the information in this chapter on vocabulary and art. Discuss your findings with your classmates.

D. Visit an early childhood classroom. Survey and describe the equipment and materials in the room for suitability for the following:

- Small- and large-motor activities
- Hand–eye coordination activities
- Reading readiness activities
- Motor coordination activities

E. Using your observations from the previous item in this list, describe the strengths and weaknesses of the supplies and equipment in the classroom you visited. What would you suggest as ways to improve it?

F. Play a game using Piaget's theory of mental development in which you say an age and students have to identify the stage in which the age belongs and act out a characteristic of thinking for that stage.

Activities for Children

The following activities are designed to help children exercise both small- and large-muscle skills and develop hand–eye coordination. Try the activities yourself, with your classmates, and with children.

Small-Motor Activities

Pincer Activities

Get that Cork! For this activity you will need corks in a variety of sizes, a bowl of water, and tweezers.

Put the corks in the bowl of water. Children use the tweezers to try to capture the floating corks.

Clip It Fun

For this activity, you will need a variety of small barrettes, hair clips, and elastic bands; dolls with hair, brushes, and combs; and a tray for these materials.

Children use the hair fasteners or elastic bands to divide the dolls' hair into small sections. Clips that fasten in different ways and small elastic bands support a range of motor skill levels.

Dropping Buttons

For this activity, you will need buttons and four plastic containers with lids.

Cut a slit in each lid and label each container with a color. Children sort the buttons by color and drop them into the appropriate containers.

Tongs

For this activity, you will need spring-handle metal tongs, sorting trays (ice cube trays, egg cartons, divided dishes, or small containers), and items to sort (counting bears, acorns, buttons, pom-poms).

Show the children how to use their thumb, middle and index fingers to manipulate the tongs. Children use the

tongs to pick up the items and sort them into separate compartments or containers.

Whole Hand Activities

Squeezing Sponges

You will need a small sponge, divided food dish, and water.

Fill one side of the dish with water. Children transfer the water from side to side by dipping and squeezing the sponge.

Matching Lids

Gather together two baskets and a collection of plastic containers with matching lids (spice jars, margarine tubs, yogurt cups, shampoo containers, hand cream jars, etc.). Sort the containers and lids into separate baskets. Children match and attach the lids to the correct containers.

Cornmeal Sifting

For this activity, you will need a crank-style sifter, 1-cup plastic measuring cup, large bowl, and cornmeal.

Place the empty sifter in the bowl. Children use two hands to pour the cornmeal into the sifter, and then turn the crank handle to sift the cornmeal into the bowl.

Whole Arm Activities

Down Under Art

You will need a large sheet of drawing paper, tape, and crayons or markers.

Tape the paper to the underside of a table. Children lie on their backs under the table, extend the arm with crayon or marker in hand, and draw on the paper.

Rings and Ribbons

Gather together a set of plastic bracelets and 12 inches of colored ribbon for each bracelet.

Attach a ribbon to each bracelet using a simple slipknot. Play music. Children wear or hold their bracelet, using their bracelet arm to make big circles, wave the ribbons high and low, and do any other creative movements they desire.

Stirring Situation

You will need a large pot, long wooden spoon, and dry beans, pebbles, or pasta.

Put the dry ingredients and the spoon in the bowl, and place them in the dramatic play area. Children pretend to "stir the soup" using a large circular arm motion.

Additional Small-Motor Activities

A. Decorate a Shirt

Have children color a picture on a white or light-colored shirt using wax crayons. Press newspaper over the picture and on the ironing board. The picture will stay indefinitely.

B. Watercolors and Salt

Children love to paint with watercolors, but sometimes the colors seem too subtle and quiet. Once a picture is done (using enough water to make it a moist picture), bring out table salt and sprinkle a little over the picture while it is still wet. The salt causes the paint to separate and gives the painting a completely new look. This is a good activity to carry out when talking about change in objects: The teacher can discuss with the children what they see as changing in the painting.

C. Printing with Feet and Hands

Equipment: Finger paint and finger paint paper.

Procedure: Children step in finger paint and print their right feet and left feet and then their hands. This work could be saved and used in social studies for a book "all about me."

D. Shaving Cream Art

An easy-to-do favorite is to take shaving cream and put a few squirts of it in an empty water table. With food coloring, dye the shaving cream the color the children choose. Watching the shaving cream turn color is half the fun; the other half is to finger paint with the colored shaving cream and save the design on paper. To save the design, put a clean sheet of white paper over the design drawn by the child, rub the paper, and lift. Hang to dry.

Shaving cream is also great to use when there are a few minutes until cleanup time and the children are restless. Squeeze a dab of shaving cream on a table in front of each child. Show how it grows and changes and how designs, mountains, and squeezy-feely shapes can be made from the cream. When the time allotted is over, each child can clean up with a sponge. The children and the table will shine and smell good.

E. Creative "Found" Sculpture

On a neighborhood walk, on a field trip, or from a child's weekend trip with his or her family, collect an assortment of wood scraps such as driftwood, weathered boards, seashells, stones, twigs, dried flowers, pine cones, and leaves. Use either a flat stone or piece of wood for the base

of the sculpture. The rest is up to the child's imagination; animals, designs, birds, and the like can be created. Have children simply assemble their creations and glue them together in place on the base. Markers can be used to draw in faces, make decorations, or add necessary details.

Hand–Eye Coordination Activities

A. Water Pouring

Set up a pan filled with water. Provide different-sized plastic containers, squeeze bottles, funnels, and strainers. Children enjoy pouring water from one container to another.

B. Block Bowling

Set up a long unit block on the floor. The children sit in a circle around it. Each child has a chance to knock it down by rolling a ball at it.

C. Music and Painting

Play music while the children paint.

D. Ball Rolling

Play catch with the children who are able, or roll the ball to the children who cannot catch yet. Notice which ones can catch and return the ball. Compare this ability with their motor control in art.

E. Painting with Water (Outside Activity)

Fill a bucket with water and let the children "paint" the building or sidewalk with water. Children should use large paintbrushes (1 to 2 inches wide) and buckets of water small enough to be carried around.

F. Weed Brushes

On a nice day, take the children on a walk collecting Queen Anne's lace, wild oats, goldenrod, and interesting grasses. The next day, let each child dip these items into different colors of tempera paint and use them as paintbrushes, using either one or several different colors. If the children do not want to paint with their "weed" brushes, they can simply dip their weeds in colors, leave them to dry, and take them home in a plastic bag. These dried, colored weeds make a pretty arrangement.

G. Repeated Natural Forms Collage

Another nature collage can be made using seeds, pods, and other things scattered on the ground and left by the wind.

- Children may classify the objects as large, small, round, straight, rough, smooth, hard, and soft.
- A Styrofoam egg carton is a good receptacle for small objects. (Be sure to wash it out with hot, soapy water before using it.)
- The objects may be arranged into a pattern of repeating forms, using contrasting shapes, textures, and colors. A group display tells the story of nature's materials.

H. Natural Designs

After collecting a variety of natural objects from their outdoor walks, some children may want to arrange them in bouquets. Provide children a variety of containers such as tin cans, old vases, or paper cups. They will also need sand, marbles, pebbles, clay, play dough, or salt clay to make a base to hold their natural bouquets. Children place objects randomly in the base until they are satisfied with their arrangement. The more objects available, the more interesting the arrangements will be. They are nice decorations for the housekeeping center, as well as a centerpiece for snack time.

I. Nature Walk Photographs

Take photographs during an outdoor walk. A digital camera, a regular camera, or even a disposable camera all work equally well for this activity. Try to take pictures that show a sequence of events. Back in the classroom, display the photographs in sequence. Have children think of captions for the pictures, then the story of the event, following the sequence shown in the pictures. Children who are not yet writing can dictate their captions and story to the teacher. They can also dictate their stories on a tape recorder to enjoy at a later time.

J. Favorite Collections Display

During your outdoor walks, encourage children to collect items that appeal to them. They may enjoy collecting items such as leaves, acorns, small pinecones, twigs, interesting rocks, and so on. These items can be displayed in box lids, on pieces of cardboard, or on paper plates. If children prefer, these items can be glued onto a base for a more permanent arrangement.

Activities for Checking Motor Control

A. Artwork Samples

Collect examples of artwork from children aged 2–6. Categorize the examples by the degree of children's motor control as evidenced in the artwork.

B. Obstacle Course

Make an obstacle course of chairs, tables, or blocks to climb under, over, or around. Notice how easy or difficult it is for children aged 3, 4, and 5.

C. Action Songs

Sing an action song such as, "If You're Happy and You Know It," using different directions: "Clap your hands," "Clap your hands and tap your head," "Clap your hands and shake your head." Notice which children can perform the combined actions and which can do the single actions. Note their ages.

D. Rope Games

Put a long rope on the floor in a zigzag pattern and have children walk on it. Note how many of the children can do this and how well they can do it. Put the rope in a straight line and have children pretend it is a tightrope. Have them "walk the tightrope" with a real or pretend umbrella in their hands for balance. Note the balancing ability of each child.

Two children take turns holding the rope very high at first and then gradually lower and lower. The rest of the children go under the rope without touching it.

Place the rope straight out on the floor. The children walk across it, hop on one foot across it, hop on two feet across

it, crawl across it, jump across it, and cross it any other way they can think of. Note each child's physical control.

Large-Motor Activities

A. Blanket Statues/Shapes (suitable for kindergarten and up)

Have children make shapes using their bodies. Have them experiment with as many shapes and forms as they choose. Then involve them in making "blanket statues." A child stays frozen in one position, and a blanket is placed over the child to create a statue. Two children can create partner statues: One child rests on hands and knees, and a second child rests on her or his back. Or two children stand three or four feet apart, facing one another, with their arms raised and reaching across, fingertips touching in an arch. These are just suggestions. Let children's creativity direct their movement. This activity is a good opportunity to take photographs that can later be displayed. Older children may want to write captions for their photographs, creating their own documentary of the activity.

B. Can You Guess What I Am?

Collect about 15 to 20 different animal pictures. Place these in a box on a chair over to one side. From a group of children (a small group of four or five works best) seated on the floor, and the teacher chooses one child to pick out a picture from the box. The child then "acts out" the animal in the picture for the others to guess. Whoever guesses the animal is the next to pick out a picture to act out. As a variation, use transportation pictures such as a train, truck, jet, car, boat, and bus.

C. Body Creations

Invite children to create different shapes by using their bodies. For example, three children might stretch out on the floor, joining their bodies in a way that creates a triangle. Four children might position their bodies to create a square, four others can create a rectangle, and so on. Ask others in the group if they know the names of the shapes their classmates are creating. Introduce terms such as *square, triangle,* and *rectangle.* Continue the activity until all children have had an opportunity to participate. Photograph the activity and post the photos where visitors can see them.

Activities for the Senses

The following activities are designed to exercise the senses. Try the activities yourself, with your classmates, and with children.

Seeing Activities

A. Exploring With a Magnifying Glass

Provide children magnifying glasses and a tray full of different objects—stamps, coins, rocks, and leaves. Encourage young children to talk about what they are seeing. They might also want to draw or paint what they've seen.

With older children, talk about the qualities of color, line, shape, and other visual elements they see magnified in the objects. Provide opportunities for them to sketch what they see. Challenge them to draw a pattern or design using what they've seen through the magnifying glass.

Use the magnifying glass outside on a nature walk. Encourage children to talk about what they see. Provide them opportunities to express their reactions to "nature under glass" in two- and three-dimensional activities.

B. Paper Towel Telescopes

Collect paper towel rolls for telescopes. Children use the paper towel roll to see their world in a sharper focus. Looking through a tube such as this helps children focus on a single area.

Encourage children to talk about what they see. Maybe later they will want to draw or paint about what they have seen. Older children can be challenged to see if they can see specific elements of design through their telescope.

C. Examining Objects in Different Colors

Have children look at the things around them through transparent plastic or colored cellophane. They can see how the brown table looks through "yellow" or how the blue sky looks through "red." When children seem to understand how the color of different objects changes when seen through another color and have been satisfied using just a single color, they may look through two colors at once (superimpose red over blue) and see still another change.

D. See-Through Colors

Looking through color strips will help children learn how colors combine to make new colors—specifically, how the combination of two primary colors creates a secondary color. The children can relate the colors to familiar objects.

Materials: Scissors; red, yellow, and blue cellophane papers. (You can find colored cellophane paper in the wrapping paper section of a variety store. It is most readily available at Easter time when it is used to cover baskets.)

Preparation: Cut the red, blue, and yellow cellophane into strips about 4 inches long and 2 inches wide.

Procedure: Gather four children together. Give each child a color strip. Have them first look through their individual color strips by holding them up to the light. Each child names something that is the color of the strip—for example, blue is the color of water or the sky. Each child should have a turn.

Put children with different color strips into pairs. Each child in the pair looks through the two strips to see what new colors are made. The teacher then gives each pair another strip, making sure that each pair has a set of red, blue, and yellow. Allow children to explore and

exchange color strips. When interest begins to wane, call the children together. Let each pair name the colors produced, and name something that is that color.

Variations: Allow children to cut up pieces of cellophane to make their own color combinations. They might tape the pieces together to make stained glass designs.

Encourage the expression of emotional and impressionistic responses of the children caused by colors. For example, "Yellow is the color of sunshine, and it makes me feel happy." "Blue is the color of the ocean, and I like the waves in the ocean."

E. Room Noises
1. Have children close their eyes and name the different sounds they hear in the room.
2. Make up noises and sounds (birds singing; blocks dropping; sawing wood; bells, drums, and other instruments; tearing paper; water splashing). Have children guess what they are.
3. A child closes both eyes while another child speaks. The first child tries to guess who is speaking.

F. Rattlesnake

You will need a small plastic bottle with beans inside. The group closes their eyes and the "leader" walks around shaking the bottle. The group then points to the direction from which they hear the sound and identifies the level of sound (that is, "high" or "low"). This can be played with one child as well.

G. Sound Cans

Place four different substances—a small block, a piece of clay, a piece of cotton, a small amount of sand—in four identical cans. When all the lids are on, shuffle the cans. The child guesses what is in each can by the noise made as the can is shaken.

H. Parrot Talk

Use a paper bag puppet of a parrot, or just use your hands and fingers to look like the mouth of a parrot talking. Discuss with the child how parrots like to repeat everything they hear. Let the child speak first while you are the parrot and repeat everything the child says. Then you speak first and the child repeats. Begin with a single word and build up to a full sentence. Nonsensical words may also be used.

Variation: Talk with the child about echoes and how they repeat the sounds two or three times. After you have echoed something the child has said or a noise the child has made, by tapping for instance, let the child be your echo.

Activities for Older Children (Grades 4–5)

A. Link Art to Dance and Physical Movement

Older children have well-developed large and small muscles as well as good overall motor coordination. Challenge them to use these skills in creative ways. Choose several artists' works that have a good deal of movement in the composition. Some suggestions are Vincent van Gogh's *Starry Night,* Jackson Pollock's

Water Birds, Jacob Lawrence's *Strike,* or Edgar Degas's *Ballet Scene.* Review with children the elements of line and movement in art while viewing one of the prints. Have them discuss the ways the artist used lines in the painting to show movement.

Tell students that they will take turns modeling and drawing different movements. Then have volunteers pantomime individually or in small groups various kinds of movements such as those in dance, in a sport, or in a type of exercise. Have students observing the movements draw lines that represent or reflect the movements they are seeing.

Continue the activity until students have filled their sheet of drawing paper with colorful lines. Then have students exchange roles.

B. Understanding Composition by Posing a Picture

One of the most effective ways to help students understand the overall composition or structure of a work of art is to have them pose as a painting or sculpture. This requires some advance preparation on the part of the teacher. Scour your attic, basement, closets, and the local resale shop for old items of clothing and props that resemble those depicted in the artwork you have chosen to pose. Be creative. For example, in posing *Washington Crossing the Delaware* by Emanuel Leutze, you might borrow oars from a boat store. Diego Rivera's *The Flower Carrier,* Jan Van Eyck's *Arnolfini Marriage,* George Caleb Bingham's *Wood Boatmen on a River,* Pieter de Hooch's *Interior with People,* and Vincent van Gogh's *The Bedroom of Van Gogh at Arles* are all good choices for posing.

Assign clothing, props, and their position to your students and have them really study that part of the painting to notice facial expressions, body positions, and relationships to other figures, the background, and so forth. If you have a large group, split it in half or thirds and have an audience comment on the accuracy of each group's pose. Everyone gets to participate, and students remember the artwork better by recalling their own part in it. Posing is not only great fun but also of value in increasing understanding. For example, ask students which poses were easier to hold in order to point out how some paintings create a feeling of motion or imbalance, while others give the impression of equilibrium or stability.

C. Recreating a Still Life

An activity similar to posing can be done with still-life painting. This involves having children re-create with real objects one of the paintings they have been studying.

Bring in as many items as possible that are found in selected works of art. These artworks might include William J. McCloskey's *Wrapped Oranges,* Albert Dummouchel's *Still Life,* Margaret Burroughs's *Still Life,* Laura Wheeler Waring's *Still Life,* and Gustave Caillebotte's *Fruit Displayed on a Stand.*

Ask each child to identify an object and place it in its proper position so that the finished arrangement approximates the original as closely as possible. This exercise enables students to comprehend some of the basic concerns of the still-life painter: the use of light, the concepts of balance and harmony, the question of focus, and the problem of rendering three-dimensional objects on a two-dimensional surface.

D. Shadowplay

Students often have difficulty determining the source of light in a painting. A simple way to demonstrate how shadows help us determine where light is coming from is to shine a flashlight on a ball from a variety of angles (behind the ball, to the left of the ball, above the ball, below the ball). Place the flashlight in the position before turning it on, and ask the students if they can guess where the shadow will fall. (This exercise works best if the area around the ball is fairly plain and darkened somewhat so that the shadows can be seen clearly. Also the flashlight beam should be smaller than the ball.) One teacher did this activity near Groundhog's Day and substituted a toy stuffed animal for the ball.

E. Matching Colors Under Different Lights

To demonstrate to students that light influences the way we see color, bring in various paint chips or cloth swatches. Be sure to have multiples of the same color available. Have students view identical color samples under different light sources (fluorescent, incandescent, and natural). They will soon discover that it is almost impossible to match colors under different lighting conditions. The most accurate light for viewing colors is daylight.

F. More Telescopes

Visual perceptiveness is an important skill that comes into use not only when looking at a painting but also when reading a book, examining a map, or even doing a math problem. To hone this ability, encourage students to look carefully for details in a painting. One way to accomplish this is to use "telescopes." These are simply 4- × 6-inch index cards that students roll up into tubes and look through. The teacher can ask students to find certain things in a painting and will be able to tell by the angle of the telescopes if the child is looking in the correct place. This is a technique artists have used themselves: Frederic Church handed out a rolled up piece of cardboard to everyone who came to see his painting *Heart of the Andes* when it was exhibited in 1864.

G. Magnification—Once Again

The use of a magnifying glass can heighten the enjoyment for older children when looking at certain paintings, especially those that are extremely detailed. Allow students to use the magnifying glass one at a time and give them specific instructions as to what they should find. Explain to them that artists use very thin brushes in order to paint the tiniest details. The sixteenth-century Flemish master Pieter Brueghel the Elder supposedly used only a few cat's hairs as a brush for his miniscule figures. Thus, a magnifying glass enables us to appreciate the artist's creation more thoroughly. It also intrigues students to see even more than the eye alone can see.

H. Creative Color Thinking

Have children gather in small groups. Ask a recorder in each group to write down, in columns, the names of the basic colors on the color wheel. Have the students identify adjectives that are often used to describe varieties of each color, such as "sky" blue, "fire engine" red, and "grass" green. While the students work, set up columns on the board so students can compile the unique adjectives and place tally marks by those identified by more than one group. Discuss the connotations of the adjectives for yellow, red, and orange in relation to ideas or experiences of warmth. Discuss the connotations of the words listed for blue, green, and violet in relation to experiences of coolness.

I. Online Learning: Enlighten Me

Check out the website Enlighten Me. Play the Peetnik Mystery using a phone book, a Who's Who, and a map to help Penn Peetnik and her friends solve a mystery. In this activity, students make "phone calls" and find locations, which helps them practice mapping skills, research, and real-life problem solving to find clues that lead to a solution. Also on this site, children can make a book, write a book review, or print Super Thinker posters. Super Thinkers also has games, stories, and many more activities.

J. Textures

Provide students with a variety of leaves, long grasses, and other natural objects. You might want them to bring in similar natural objects as well. Have them make rubbings using white crayon or oil pastel and black paper. Suggest that students do a repeated rubbing of the item until the entire paper is covered. Discuss the results as a record of textures that can be viewed as artwork as well as a display for science. Students might want to research the types of grass and leaves they used in this activity.

K. Texture Words

Have students make and illustrate vocabulary cards for words that describe textures in nature. Have them arrange the items by tactile sense (for example, rough, soft, smooth). Encourage them to use these terms appropriately in storytelling and in other activities.

L. Mystery Textures

Tell students they will make a mystery texture bag. Provide small paper bags for each student. Have them secretly collect items that have varied textures associated with fall or any of the other seasons. These are the mystery items that others will be guessing. Working in pairs, students exchange bags and try to guess what the mystery objects are by feeling the textures.

M. Lines, Patterns, Textures

Have students bring in a large leaf. Have them place a magnifying glass over one part of the leaf and observe its lines, patterns, and textures. Have students create a large drawing of the small section of the leaf seen in the viewfinder.

N. Varieties of Colors

Have students look selectively for varieties of color in leaves and bring them to class. Have them describe differences using terms such as *light, dark, shiny,* or *dull*. Focus on other visual elements in the same way. For example, ask students who are wearing rough textures to stand and point them out. Develop an awareness of terms to describe textures such as *bumpy, prickly,* and *silky*.

O. Weather Diaries

Have students keep a weather diary with drawings that portray the weather as it occurs at the same time each day for five days. The time might be lunch or recess. At the end of five days, have students work in small groups to compare and contrast the different interpretations. The total group can choose drawings that best represent the weather for each day. The drawings might be put into a booklet titled "The Weather Diary of Grade Four." Present the booklet to the school library.

References

Arnsten, A. (1998). The biology of being frazzled. *Science*, 280 (5370), 1711–1712.

Carvell, N. R. (2006). *Language enrichment activities program (LEAP)*, vol. 1. Dallas, TX: Southern Methodist University.

Center on the Developing Child at Harvard University. (2011). Building the brain's "Air Traffic Control" system: How early experiences shape the development of executive function. Working Paper No. 11. http://www.developingchild.harvard.edu.

Center on the Developing Child at Harvard University. (2008). Mental health problems in early childhood can impair learning and behavior for life. Working Paper No. 6. http://www.developingchild.net.

Center on the Developing Child at Harvard University. (2005). Excessive stress disrupts the architecture of the developing brain. Working Paper No. 3. http://www.developingchild.net.

Chaddock, L., Erickson, K. I., Prakash, R. S., Kim, J. S., Voss, M. W., VanPatter, M., Pontifex, M. B., Raine, L. B., Konkel, A., Hillman, C. H., Cohen, N. J., & Kramer, A. F. (2010). A neuroimaging investigation of the association between aerobic fitness, hippocampal volume, and memory performance in preadolescent children. *Brain Research*, *1358*(28), 172–183.

Evans, G. W., & Wachs, T. D. (Eds.) (2010). *Chaos and its influence on children's development: An ecological perspective*. Washington, DC: American Psychological Association.

Gallaghue, D., & Ozmun, J. (2005). *Understanding motor development: Infants, children, adolescents, adults* (6th ed.). New York, NY: McGraw Hill.

Huffman, J. M., & Fortenberry, C. (2011). Developing fine motor skills. *Young Children*, *14*(3), 100–103.

Jensen, E. P. (2008). A fresh look at brain-based education. *Phi Delta Kappan*. Retrieved from http://www.pdkintl.org.

Kempermann, G., Wiskott, L., & Goge, F. (2004). Functional significance of adult neurogenesis. *Current Opinion in Neurobiology*, April, 2004, 186–191.

Kilgard, M., & Merzenich, M. (2006). Cortical map reorganization enabled by nucleus basalis activity. *Science, 279*, 1714–1718.

Kishiyama, M. M., Boyce, W. T., Jiminez, A. M., Perry, L. M., & Knight, R. T. (2009). Socioeconomic disparities affect prefrontal function in children. *Journal of Cognitive Neuroscience, 21*(6), 1106–1115.

Lengua, L. J., Honorado, E., & Bush, N. R. (2007). Contextual risk and parenting as predictors of effortful control and social competence in preschool. *Journal of Applied Developmental Psychology. 28*(1), 40–55.

Li-Grining, C. P. (2007). Effortful control among low-income preschoolers in three cities: Stability, change, and individual differences. *Developmental Psychology, 43*(1), 208–221.

Liston, C., McEwen, B. S., & Casey, B. J. (2009). Psychosocial stress disrupts prefrontal processing and attentional control. *Proceedings of the National Academy of Sciences, 106*(3), 912–917.

Liston, C., Miller, M. M., Goldwater, D. S., Radley, J. J., Rocher, A. B., Hof, P. R., Morrison, J. H., & McEwen, B. (2006). Stress-induced alterations in prefrontal cortical dendritic morphology predict selective impairments in perceptual attention set-shifting. *The Journal of Neuroscience, 26*(30), 7870–7874.

Long, P. (2010). My brain on my mind. *American Scholar, 79*(1), 20–37.

Maughan, A., & Ciccheti, D. (2002). Impact of child maltreatment and interadult violence on children's emotion regulation abilities and social–emotional adjustment. *Child Development, 73*(5), 1525–1542.

Noble, K. G., McCandliss, B. D., & Farah, M. J. (2007). Socioeconomic gradients predict individual differences in neurocognitive abilities. *Developmental Science, 10*(4), 464–480.

O'Connor, T. G., Rutter, M., Beckett, C., Keaveney, L., & Kreppner, J. M. (2000). The effects of global severe privation on cognitive competence, extension and longitudinal follow-up. *Child Development, 71*(2), 376–390.

Partridge, K. (2009). *The reference shelf: The brain.* New York, NY: H. W. Wilson.

Piaget, J. (1950). *The psychology of intelligence.* New York, NY: Harcourt Brace.

Piaget, J. (1952). *The child's conception of number.* New York, NY: Humanities Press.

Piaget, J. (1955). *The child's conception of reality.* London, England: Routledge & Kegan.

Pollak, S. D., Cicchetti, D., & Klorman, R. (1998). Stress, memory, and emotion: Developmental considerations from the study of child maltreatment. *Development and Psychopathology, 10*(4), 811–828.

Sanchez, M. M., Ladd, C. O., & Plotsky, P. M. (2001). Early adverse experience as a developmental risk factor for later psychopathology: Evidence from rodent and primate models. *Development and Psychopatology, 3*(3), 419–449.

Thompson, P. M. (2006). Growth patterns in the developing brain detected by using continuum mechanical tensor maps. *Nature, 204*, 190–193.

Zero to Three (2012). General Brain Development. Retrieved from http://www.zerotothree.org/site/PageServer?pagename=ter_key_brainFAQ.

 Visit CourseMate for this textbook to access the eBook, Did You Get It? quizzes, Digital Downloads, TeachSource Videos, flashcards, and more. Go to CengageBrain.com to log in, register, or purchase access.

Casper Holroyd

Art and Social–Emotional Growth

The term **social–emotional growth** refers to two kinds of growth. Emotional growth is the growth of a child's feelings, and social growth is the child's growth as a member of a group.

Learning to be a member of a group involves many social skills. Young children, for example, must learn to relate to other children and adults outside the family. Often, a child's first experience of sharing an adult's attention with other children occurs in the early childhood setting. Of the social skills involved in learning to work

Learning Objectives

After studying this chapter, you should be able to:

10-1 Define the terms *self-acceptance*, *self-concept*, and *unconditional positive acceptance*.

10-2 List the points included in planning the art program to encourage a child's self-concept and self-acceptance.

10-3 Discuss how the art program helps a child in child-to-child relationships.

10-4 Discuss how the art program aids child-to-teacher relationships.

10-5 Discuss how the art program helps in child-to-group relationships.

naeyc

NAEYC Program Standards

1a Knowing and understanding young children's characteristics and needs.

1b Knowing and understanding the multiple influences on development and learning.

2a Knowing about and understanding diverse family and community characteristics.

DAP

DAP Criteria

1A Children learn about themselves and their world and also how to develop positive constructive relationships with other people.

1B Relationships are an important context through which children develop and learn.

3C1 Teachers are familiar with the understandings and skills key for that age group in each domain (physical, social, emotional, and cognitive).

in a group, children have to learn how to share materials, how to take turns, how to listen to others, and how and when to work on their own—to mention just a few!

This chapter covers both the social and emotional growth of the child as they occur in the early childhood art program. Although social–emotional growth occurs at the same time as physical–mental growth, the two are covered in separate chapters within this text for the sake of clarity. The developmental concepts learned and applied in this and the following two chapters are applicable to all other creative activities and materials.

This chapter is divided into four main sections: (1) self-concept and self-acceptance, (2) child-to-child relationships, (3) child-to-teacher relationships, and (4) child-to-group relationships.

10-1 Self-Concept, Self-Acceptance, and Unconditional Positive Acceptance

DAP **naeyc** Self-concept can be defined as the child's growing awareness of his or her own characteristics (physical appearance as well as skills and abilities) and how these are similar to or different from those of others.

All children like to feel good about themselves (see Photo 10-1). This good feeling about oneself is called *self-acceptance* or *self-esteem*. Children who feel good

PHOTO 10-1 All children like to feel good about themselves.

Casper Holroyd

about themselves and believe they can do things well have a good sense of self-acceptance.

This feeling of self-acceptance was one of the main concepts espoused by noted psychologist **Carl Rogers.** He felt that every human being has a single "force of life," which he calls the **actualizing tendency,** or **self-actualization**. It can be defined as the built-in motivation present in every human being to develop his or her potential to the fullest extent possible. Rogers believes that all creatures strive to make the very best of their existence. Among the things that humans instinctively value is **positive self-concept** (that is, self-esteem, self-worth, a positive self-image). Children achieve this positive self-image by experiencing the positive regard others show them over their years of growing up. Without this self-regard, children feel less positive and often helpless, and they may fail to become all they can be (Rogers, 1995).

Children who have a positive self-concept accept their strengths and limitations. The early childhood program provides an environment that nurtures the development of a positive sense of self and a good self-concept in each child. And according to Rogers, such an environment is **psychosocially safe** for young children (Thorne, 2003).

Children learn to accept themselves from birth all the way throughout life. According to Rogers, children grow in **self-acceptance** when they receive **unconditional positive acceptance** from the people in their lives. They learn about themselves by the way they are treated by others. The way parents hold their baby makes the baby feel accepted. A baby who is held closely and with tenderness learns to feel loved and good. The only way babies understand this is by physical touch because they do not yet understand words.

As babies grow into young children, they continue learning to accept themselves. When toddlers are encouraged and praised for messy but serious attempts to feed themselves, they learn to accept themselves and feel good about what they do. If children are accepted positively and unconditionally as they are, they learn to accept themselves.

Another psychologist whose work centered on the importance of a psychologically safe environment for children was **Erik Erikson** (Erikson, 1950). He developed a set of **stages of psychosocial development** that he felt characterized human social development. See Figure 10-1 for more information on these stages and their application in the early childhood years. Basically, his ideas centered on the influence of culture on a child's social–emotional development.

Stage 1: Trust vs. Mistrust
Birth and first year
Most fundamental stage
Trust based on dependability and quality of caregivers
Successful completion: Child feels safe and secure in the world
Unsuccessful completion: Failure to develop trust, fear, belief world is inconsistent and unpredictable

Stage 2: Autonomy vs. Shame and Doubt
Early preschool childhood/preschool years
Child develops greater sense of personal control
Child learning to control body functions leads to feeling of control and sense of independence
Child gains control over food choices, toy preferences, clothing selection
Successful completion: Child feels secure and confident
Unsuccessful completion: Sense of inadequacy and self-doubt

Stage 3: Initiative vs. Guilt
Preschool years
Child asserts power and control over the world through directing play and other social interactions
Successful completion: Child feels capable and able to lead others
Unsuccessful completion: Sense of guilt, self-doubt, and lack of initiative

Stage 4: Industry vs. Inferiority
Ages 5–11 (approximately)
Through social interaction, child begins to develop a sense of pride in accomplishments and abilities
Successful completion: Children who are encouraged and commended by parents and teachers develop feelings of competence and belief in their skills
Unsuccessful completion: Child doubts ability to be successful

FIGURE 10-1 Erikson's Stages of Psychosocial Development (1950)—Early Childhood Years.

In the early childhood program, children must continue to learn to accept and feel good about themselves (see Photo 10-2). The art program can be of special help in this area. When children feel they can do things well in art, they grow in both self-confidence and self-acceptance.

In the art program, young children learn more about themselves and their capabilities and affirm their sense of self. For example, a child at the easel used many bright colors and was proud of his accomplishment. "I'm Harry and I like to paint pretty colors. Write my name at the top," he calls out to his teacher. This 3-year-old child's growing concept of self is evident as he views what he has painted. The good feelings about oneself, which can be fostered through art, are essential for positive development of self-concept.

A good self-concept is equally as important to middle- and upper-elementary students. They, too, need the same encouragement and emotionally safe environment in which to express themselves creatively. Just because they are physically bigger and appear surer of themselves doesn't mean a teacher can overlook the development of their self-concept in creative activities.

At the primary level and above, state and national standards often overpower teachers with lists of objectives, goals, and mandated learning experiences.

PHOTO 10-2 The early childhood program is a place where children can relax and be themselves.

Casper Holroyd

Often in this situation with older children, teachers may impose art activities on children from a prescribed curriculum without consideration for the child's interest or concern for his or her personal experiences. This approach takes less time than it takes to listen to children, to get to know them, and to adapt the curriculum by putting the child at the center. It is far easier for adults to dictate to children.

In this adult-directed model, children learn primarily to follow directions. They are directed through one activity after another, activities that often are related to the seasons of the year or holidays. Then, children are evaluated primarily by how well they are able to follow directions.

The importance of changing such an adult focus is clearly explained by the renowned art educator, Viktor Lowenfeld:

> Because every process involves the whole child, and not only a single segment, art education may well become the catalyst for a child-centered education in which the individual and his creative potentialities are placed above subject matter, in which the child's inner equilibrium may be considered as important as scientific achievements. (1957, p. 11)

This approach is one that obviously builds the child's self-acceptance. An early childhood teacher needs to plan the art program in such a way that it gives each child a chance to grow in self-acceptance. To do so, the program should be child centered, which means that it is planned for the age and developmental levels of the children in it.

Naturally, if the program is child centered, it is, in turn, developmentally appropriate—meeting the specific individual needs of each child. The art program is planned around the developmental needs of the child. In this way, the teacher has clear guidelines for selections of appropriate materials and activities for the level of each child in the program. (Developmental levels in art and related activities for these levels are covered in Chapter 11.)

10-2 Planning the Art Program: Encouraging Self-Acceptance and Self-Concept

DAP **naeyc** A climate of psychological safety is essential to the growth of a child's self-acceptance and self-concept. This safe, accepting environment doesn't just happen. It is carefully planned with the following points included in the planning:

- **Accept children at their present developmental level.** If the adult accepts the child in a positive way, the child feels this acceptance. This does not mean that the child should not be challenged. Art activities can be planned that are a slight challenge for the child's present level, but they must not be so hard that they frustrate the child. By feeling successful in art activities, children learn to feel more sure about themselves and their skills.

  Self-confidence is built on a circular relationship between the child and teacher. When the teacher shows confidence in a child, it helps that child develop greater self-confidence (see Photo 10-3).

  When 4-year-old Rathnam was sweeping broad, free strokes of blue, red, and white paint across his paper, the colors inadvertently mixed at various places. Suddenly he stopped, his brush

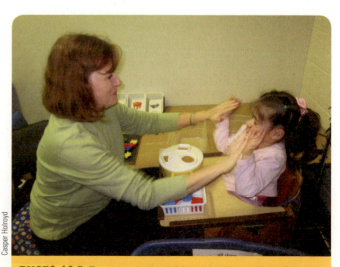

PHOTO 10-3 Teachers help children develop self-confidence when they celebrate a job well done with the child.

Casper Holroyd

Did You Get It?

A fifth-grade art teacher criticizes her student's sculpture, telling him it is too messy and difficult to interpret. This teacher is harming her student's

  a. self-concept.

  b. unconditional positive acceptance.

  c. stage of psychosocial development.

  d. artistic skills.

Take the full quiz on CourseMate.

in midair, as he squinted hard at his painting. "Look, it's pink up here! And look at this," he said, pointing to a hazy lavender area.

"Yes," said his teacher, catching the excitement of the moment. "And you made them—you made those special colors."

Without hesitation Rathnam responded, "Oh, that's red and white, mixed."

"So now you can make pink whenever you want," summarized the teacher.

"Yeah," whispered Rathnam with a touch of pride and awe. "I'll mix red and white."

In this way the teacher made clear her confidence that Rathnam could repeat purposefully a technique for changing color that he had discovered accidentally. Rathnam's response highlighted a moment of self-confidence in his ability to control this responsive art medium.

● **Provide an environment that is comfortable for the age level of the group.** Plan the room so that it is a place where children can feel at home. It should have tables and chairs that are the right size for young children. A room for older children needs the same care in planning. This age group needs chairs and tables of the appropriate size and strength. There is often a widening difference in physical size in grades 4 to 5, so a mixture of sizes is often necessary if equipment is to be appropriate for this age group. For example, small desks and chairs often aren't the right size for fifth-grade children who have had a growth spurt. It's hard for children to feel good about themselves when they are too big for the chairs! If necessary, there should be a covering on the floor and work areas so that children can work freely without worrying about spills. It is hard for children to feel good about themselves and their work when they are always being told they are "too messy." If sponges and towels are within reach, children can clean up their own messes. A little responsibility like this is fun for them, as well as a good way to help them develop independence and confidence. By being in charge of keeping their own areas clean, children learn to feel good about how they can take care of themselves. This strengthens their self-acceptance and personal pride.

● **Provide an environment that is appropriate for children with special needs.** Adapt the environment so that children with special needs can successfully function in the program.

● **Provide materials and activities that are age appropriate.** By giving children tools they are able to work with at their age and skill level, the teacher helps them have more success in art projects. Success helps them grow with pride and confidence and know that they can do things well. Success breeds success.

● **Provide creative materials and activities that the children can work on and complete by themselves.** Activities that children can finish themselves help them feel more self-assured and confident about their art ability. To do this, teachers need to be good observers to know exactly what materials and activities are developmentally appropriate for each child. This match between children's developmental levels and appropriate activities and materials is an ever-changing one, as children continue to grow and develop in the early years. The creative process offers opportunities for children to gain a spirit of independence and a sense of personal autonomy when the choice of medium, process, or kind of expression is their own.

Did You Get It?

An art teacher arranges her classroom for fourth graders with both large and small desks and chairs. Her likely objective is to

a. allow the students to produce different art styles that require different heights.

b. allow students from younger classes to join, increasing the students' understanding of others.

c. prevent students in the front of the classroom from blocking students seated in back.

d. provide the students with a comfortable environment.

Take the full quiz on CourseMate.

10-3 Child-to-Child Relationships

DAP naeyc Only after a child has developed self-acceptance is it possible for him or her to accept other children. In the early childhood art program, there are many chances for a child to be with other children of the same age (see Photo 10-4). Children who have had positive creative experiences are the ones who can honestly accept their own abilities and those of other children.

PHOTO 10-4 The early childhood program offers many chances for a child to be with other children.

The art program is a good place for child-to-child relationships, where children can work, talk, and be together. If art activities are developmentally appropriate for children, they provide a relaxed time for exploring, trying new tools, and using familiar ones. They also allow children many chances to interact with each other.

The freedom of art itself encourages children to talk about their own work or the work of other children. Working with colors, paint, paper, paste, and other materials provides children an endless supply of things to talk about.

10-3a Sharing Ideas and Opinions

Art activities also provide endless opportunities for a child to learn how other children feel about things. For example, a 3-year-old boy may hear for the first time how another child his own age feels about his painting. At home, this child may hear mostly adult comments; in the early childhood setting, he can experience the ideas and feelings of an age-mate. An action as simple as putting easels side by side encourages this type of social learning. In the same way, fourth- and fifth graders will learn a lot about each

other's ideas and opinions as they work together planning and creating a mural for a class project.

Although this sharing can be new and exciting for a child, it can also be hard for some children to accept at first. Children may have good feelings about themselves and their work in art; likewise, they can learn to accept ideas about their work from others.

The chance to share ideas and talk about one's own work or the work of others is the beginning of a new type of relationship. It is a sharing relationship. The child begins to see that other children have different ideas and feelings. This type of sharing encourages the child to understand that people can have different feelings and ideas and still be friends. A child can learn that everyone does not have to agree all the time and can share ideas and opinions.

By the time children are in the fourth grade, they are capable of developing rather strong friendships. It is good to encourage these friendships because the social development of children is furthered as they gain feelings of inner security in having a friend. By the time children are in the fourth or fifth grade, they are being prepared socially for peer group interaction. It is this association with a peer group that is the focus of social development of this age group. Within a peer group, the needs of the child are met in the following ways:

- The child finds models for behavior and achievement among peer group members and their activities (see Photo 10-5).
- The peer group makes it possible to get the attention that the child discovers he or she needs and wants.

PHOTO 10-5 Learning to function as a member of a group is an important social skill.

- The child learns to view himself or herself in different ways as he or she identifies with the group.
- The group furnishes a support system in asking or doing certain things.
- The child is growing toward maturity with the help of the peer group as the child learns to rely less on his or her parents.

10-3b Social Competence

Social competence, the ability to get along with others, is another important factor in child-to-child relationships. During the past two decades, a large body of research has accumulated, which indicates that unless children achieve minimal social competence by about the age of 6 years, they have a high probability of being at risk throughout life. These risks are many: poor mental health, dropping out of school, low achievement, and other school difficulties (McClellan & Katz, 2003).

The single best childhood predictor of adult adaptation is *not* IQ, *not* school grades, and *not* classroom behavior, but rather the adequacy with which the child gets along with other children. Children who are generally disliked, who are aggressive and disruptive, who are unable to sustain close relationships with other children, and who cannot establish a place for themselves in the peer culture are seriously "at risk" (Hartup, 2002, p. 347).

Working together in the early childhood program, children learn how to get along with each other. Sharing materials and ideas, children learn the give and take of being in a group—the skills of social competence.

10-3c Expression of Feelings

The creative art process allows children to visually translate personal feelings as well as ideas (Dewey, 1958; Lowenfeld & Brittain, 1987). Art thus becomes an emotional catharsis. The use of color and the size or placement of representations frequently reflect healthy emotions that are difficult to express in words.

It is not unusual for a teacher to notice that children vigorously pounding clay or energetically hammering nails seem to be relieving tension or frustration. Children who are afraid of the dark may paint some brown or black or purple renditions to express this feeling. Bright colors or symbols of smiling faces may express happy experiences. Art as a vent for

Casper Holroyd

PHOTO 10-6 The early childhood program provides many opportunities for child-to-child as well as adult-to-child relationships.

feeling is universally acknowledged for artists of all ages (Lowenfeld & Brittain, 1987).

Expressing strong feelings through art rather than through destructive acts may provide catharsis for emotions. Teachers who accept the reality of children's feelings can understand children better and help them cope with distressing feelings (see Photo 10-6). In the same way, teachers who accept children's expressions of their desires and delights can share, and thus intensify, children's joy.

10-3d Cooperation and Sharing

Working together with other children in creative activities gives a child the chance to learn about being with others. Being with others teaches a child the value of sharing and cooperation.

Working with limited amounts of crayons, paint, and paper means that a child has to share. The child soon learns that sharing is a part of being in a group. One can of red paint for two young painters is a real-life lesson in sharing. Likewise, sharing woodworking tools in the creation of three-dimensional structures teaches fourth and fifth graders how to deal with limited equipment in a cooperative way.

Cooperation among children is also part of the art program. A child learns the meaning of cooperation while helping another child glue seeds on a paper, clean a brush, or button a painting shirt. This is truly learning by doing. This is actively learning social competence.

Mirror Neurons and Emotions

Each child's brain is unique, and varying levels of individuality exist. Different levels of neurochemicals can create different emotions. Too much of one chemical or too little (for example, dopamine, a neurotransmitter that creates a feeling of well-being) will impact the child's mood and therefore his or her ability to want to learn or simply respond (Rushton, 2011).

The human brain has nerve cells called **mirror neurons** that allow us, without thinking, to mimic the feelings and movements of people around us. The child's mirror neurons reflect their external world. Research (Iacoboni et al., 2005) suggests that a positive, enthusiastic teacher sends signals to the child's mirror neurons, which, in turn, can impact how the child receives the learning objectives being delivered. How we present not only ourselves but also the phenomenal journey of learning is critical to the child's emotional development (Rushton, 2011).

Mirror neuron networks throughout the brain confirm the importance of the teacher's moment-by-moment actions as the child's neurological synapses "mirror" the teacher's actions and reactions. Some researchers (Hurley & Chater, 2005; Winerman, 2005) speculate that these same mirror neurons affect the mood of the individual observing the instructor. At a subliminal level, children observe the teacher's expression and disposition and internalize how the teacher is feeling. Neuroscientists believe that an ability to empathize with another human being is due, in part, to the activation of the mirror neuron networks being activated by what we observe (Rushton, Juola-Rushton, & Larkin, 2010).

It is vital then that early childhood teachers model various dispositions such as caring, cooperation, and authenticity so that our children may become positive contributors to society (Carr, Fauske, & Ruston, 2008). The subtle changes in our disposition, attitudes, and body language can impact what a child feels, thinks, and believes. This, in turn, sets in motion any number of chemical reactions that can either help or hinder learning.

Learning first requires that children are attentive to what is being taught. Mixed signals can confuse a child. If a teacher's body language indicates she is not interested in the topic or that she is nervous because she is not sure about the lesson, the message being interpreted by the child at a neurological (and unconscious) level is apt to be one of confusion, anxiety, and distraction (Rushton et al., 2010).

As early childhood teachers, we can use the information provided in this research to encourage children's positive social–emotional development by our own positive emotions and attitude as we interact with young children.

Did You Get It?

Two preschoolers work together at an art station, sharing markers and pencils and commenting on each other's drawings. These children are developing

   a. unconditional positive regard.
   b. social competence.
   c. essential artistic skills.
   d. psychomotor skills.

Take the full quiz on CourseMate.

10-4 Child-to-Teacher Relationships

DAP **naeyc** The teacher in the early childhood program is a very important person in the child's eye. Children look up to their teachers and tend to take them very seriously. A child learns new ways to be with an adult in the early childhood program. The teacher is an adult, but not the child's parent; therefore, a new type of relationship opens up (see Photo 10-7). Of course, it is different in several ways from the adult–child relationship at home.

PHOTO 10-7 Children in the early childhood program learn to be with an adult other than a parent.

The school setting is unlike the home situation. Children learn how to be and act in a place other than the home. They learn how it is to be in a larger group than the family and how to share an adult's attention with other children.

The children learn about art as well as about themselves from the teacher. The teacher helps them feel that it is safe to be themselves and to express ideas in their own ways. The sensitive teacher lets the child know that the fun of participating in and expressing oneself in art or other creative activities is more important than the finished product. The teacher encourages older children to explore the many ways to express their ideas in the growing complexity of their work, which is characteristic of this age group. A teacher opens up many new art skills and feelings for the child and is thus a very important person in the eyes of the child.

The teacher may be the first real adult friend for the child. It is, therefore, important for a good child–teacher relationship to develop during the art program. A positive feeling between teacher and child affects all of the child's school days to come.

10-4a Building Rapport

Building a warm and friendly feeling, a **rapport,** between teacher and child is not always easy; it does not happen quickly. The best learning and teaching take place, however, when the child and teacher have this feeling for each other (see Photo 10-8).

Casper Holroyd

PHOTO 10-8 The best learning and teaching take place when the child and the teacher have a good rapport.

THINK ABOUT IT

Teacher–Child Interactions and Teacher–Child Relationships: First to Third Grade

The quality of children's relationships with teachers in early elementary grades has implications for their academic and behavioral outcomes in later grades (Hamre & Pianta, 2006). The current longitudinal study uses data from the National Institute of Child Health and Human Development Study of Early Child Care and Youth Development (NICHD SECCYD) to examine associations between children's temperament at preschool age (approximately 4-1/2 years old), teacher–child interactions and relationships in first grade, and teacher–child interactions and relationships in third grade. Prior research indicates that characteristics and behaviors of both children and teachers impact teacher–child relationship quality (Baker, 2006; Ewing & Taylor, 2009).

The present study targets children's gender and temperament (the child's biologically based style of responding to people, events, and situations) as predictors

of teacher–child relationship quality. More specifically, it examined the connections between child shyness, effortful control, and gender and teacher–child relationship quality from first to third grade (Rudasill, 2011).

Children and their first- and third-grade teachers from the NICHD SECCYD study were participants in the study. For this study, 1,364 mother–child pairs were randomly selected. Data for the study were collected in Phase I when children were preschool aged (approximately 4-1/2 years) through first grade, and at Phase II, when study children were from second through sixth grades. Teachers became involved in the study if they had study children in their classes.

Data from the first time point were obtained from mothers during a laboratory visit. Data from first- and third-grade time points were obtained via observations of classrooms and from surveys distributed to teachers in the spring of each school year. Data were analyzed with path analyses using structural equation modeling.

Results show that children lower in shyness, lower in effortful control, and boys were likely to have more conflict in their relationships with first-grade teachers. Similarly, children with lower effortful control and boys were more likely to be rated by third-grade teachers as having conflictual relationships. Teacher–child conflict in first grade predicted conflict in third grade, and teacher-initiated interactions in third grade were positively related to conflict in third grade (Rudasill, 2011).

Shyer children initiated fewer interactions with teachers in first grade. Children lower in effortful control initiated more interactions with teachers in first- and third grade and received more teacher-initiated interactions in first grade. Boys were more likely than girls to receive teacher-initiated interactions in third grade. Child-initiated interactions in first grade were negatively associated with teacher-initiated interactions in third grade. Shyer children initiated fewer interactions with teachers in first grade and third grade. Boys were more likely than girls to initiate interactions with teachers and receive interactions from teachers in third grade (Rudasill, 2011).

Results from the path analysis indicated that children with lower shyness, higher effortful control, and girls, were more likely to have close relationships with first-grade teachers. Similarly, children with higher effortful control and girls were more likely to be rated by third-grade teachers as having close teacher–child relationships. Teacher–child closeness in first grade predicted closeness in third grade. Child-initiated interactions in third grade were positively related to closeness in third grade (Rudasill, 2011).

Children's gender and early temperament ratings predicted the frequency of interactions they initiated with their third-grade teachers. Children with lower levels of both effortful control and shyness were more likely to initiate interactions with third-grade teachers in the teacher–child conflict and closeness models. Boys were more likely to initiate interactions with third-grade teachers in the closeness model.

Findings from this longitudinal study point to two overlapping mechanisms that may help explain the quality of children's relationships with teachers. The first is that certain child characteristics seem to directly contribute to the nature of teacher–child relationships. For example, girls in this study had closer relationships with teachers in both first and third grades. The second is that early teacher–child relationship quality and teacher and child behavior establish patterns for later relationship quality and behavior. This is evidenced by the study's finding of reciprocity between child and teacher behavior both within and across grades, as well as the consistency with which first- and third-grade teachers rated relationships with children as conflictual and close (Rudasill, 2011).

Results of this study have definite implications for early childhood educators concerning the importance of teacher–child relationships. It is important that we as early childhood educators be aware of the importance of high quality teacher–child relationships for children's positive academic and social outcomes. It is also important to keep in mind how important the role early teacher–child relationships have in predicting future teacher–child relationships. Teachers need to be aware of the fact that certain characteristics, such as low effortful control, may place children at risk for poor teacher–child relationships. Teachers need to encourage and facilitate child-initiated interactions in their classrooms, as these may promote teacher–child closeness among children who are more likely to have less closeness in their relationships with teachers.

The following are some ways in which the child–teacher relationship may be enhanced.

- Welcome each child into the room. Make the child feel wanted and special.
- When speaking to children, look into their eyes.
- When speaking to children, use their names.
- Understand that children like to feel proud of themselves.
- Talk with and listen to every child as much as possible.
- Use a normal speaking voice.

10-4b Acceptance

In addition to accepting children at their individual developmental levels when planning the arts program, teachers have countless opportunities to model an accepting attitude for children. When Mirelis derisively called 3-year-old Sharon's crayon picture a "scribble scrabble mess," the teacher matter-of-factly commented, "Sharon is hard at work trying out many different crayons. That's exactly how everybody begins—with big, colorful lines." Sharon smiled contentedly; Mirelis said, "Oh," and went off thinking her own thoughts but perhaps somewhat responsive to the teacher's casual yet positive acceptance of the legitimacy of scribbling in that classroom.

From such small incidents, which collectively reveal an attitude, Mirelis may realize she is accepted as a person who warrants an explanation, while Sharon may feel the teacher accepts her as she is. When children feel accepted by people who are important to them, they are better able to develop a sense of trust in those people.

When the teacher accepts and respects each child's physical and artistic abilities, the children then accept each other. By accepting each other, they learn about ideas, opinions, and feelings different from their own. These new ideas make the art program richer and more exciting for children.

10-4c Provide an Environment That Respects Individuality

As discussed earlier in Chapter 5, each individual child possesses eight "intelligences" or different learning styles. For instance, some children learn best by listening and hearing (word smart/linguistic intelligence) while others learn best by manipulating objects in their environment (body smart/kinesthetic intelligence). For this reason, teachers need to appreciate how differently children respond to new art activities just as to any other new experiences (see Photo 10-9). Some children eagerly plunge into new activities, attracted perhaps to new materials or the newness of the venture, while other children temporarily hold back. Still others retreat to the safety of the familiar and are reluctant to take risks with new materials or processes.

Sensitive teachers, trying to provide a climate in which children can take risks in their own ways, will accommodate the differences they observe in children. Three-year-old Mary refused her teacher's invitation to try finger painting. She apparently had the same conflicting feelings she had expressed when clay was introduced. She wanted to play with messy materials but was anxious about getting carried away in her play and becoming too dirty. Her response to the invitation was to run away and play with the little cars across the room.

Eventually, she drove her car toward the finger painting area while accompanying herself with a steady, persistent engine sound of rhum-rhum-rhum. She barely glanced at the children who were finger painting and then turned and raced back to the block area. Once again, Mary approached and stopped her engine sounds. She looked at the painters with sidelong glances, pretending to examine the wheels on her car at the same time. The teacher, noting Mary's interest and reluctance, decided to give her more time. His only comment that day was, "When you decide you want to finger paint, you can pick the color you want." After a few days, Mary announced, "I want blue." The teacher had read Mary's nonverbal behavior correctly; her individual pattern of response had been respected.

A similar approach works with older children as well. For instance, some children may be reluctant to work with a new art technique such as printing using a brayer for the first time. A sensitive teacher accepts this and allows alternative activities for all students.

▶❙❙ TeachSource Video

Preschool: Emotional Development

1. Which aspects of the child-to-teacher relationship as described in your text are demonstrated by the teacher in this video? Give specific examples in your answer.

2. Using the information in this chapter and in Chapters 1 and 2, evaluate the activities this teacher used to assist the children in expressing angry feelings. What other additional activities would you use?

Watch on CourseMate.

PHOTO 10-9 Create an environment that respects individuality.

Casper Holroyd

© 2015 Cengage Learning

THIS ONE'S FOR YOU!

Helping Young Boys in Today's Early Childhood Classrooms

Research shows that boys, particularly African American and Latino boys, are more often labeled as having behavior problems and are often isolated, referred for evaluations, prescribed medication, and even suspended and expelled while still in preschool (Ferguson, 2000; Smith, 2002; U.S. Department of Education, 2003; Gilliam, 2005; Barbarin & Crawford, 2006; Mead, 2006). To counteract these trends, teachers are encouraged to use instructional approaches that motivate and engage African American boys and support positive emotional development in African American boys (Barbarin, 2010).

Boys typically enter early childhood classrooms less developmentally mature than girls in terms of literacy and social–emotional skills (Gropper et al., 2011). Therefore, it is essential for early childhood settings to provide opportunities for all forms of play to help children acquire such skills naturally. Play not only provides a physical outlet for boys and helps to decrease instances of acting out (Baptiste, 1995), but it also allows boys to express themselves through dramatic play and to learn how to negotiate social–emotional challenges (Miller & Almon, 2009).

Depriving boys in particular of dramatic play time limits their literacy development. As children mature, their dramatic play becomes more complex and, with skillful guidance from their teachers, can include assigned roles, written parts, and organized plays that display a rich use of language and literacy skills.

Research bears out the positive effect that dramatic play has on comprehension and metalinguistic awareness, which are precursors to reading and writing (Roskos & Christie, 2000; Marcon, 2002). Opportunities for this type of play are essential for boys who need lots of practice to build vocabulary and social skills.

Because young boys have a great need for physical activity, a highly structured, teacher-directed learning environment that emphasizes seat work and worksheets is counter-productive. This approach especially does not meet boys' physical, cognitive, and social–emotional development needs. The early childhood development concept of teaching the whole child is the most compatible and successful approach for young boys in an early childhood environment.

Another helpful approach when working with young boys in early childhood settings is the use of note taking (Cohen et al., 2008). This technique allows teachers to observe and record children's behavior as a way of coming to know each child as an individual. It allows the teacher to stand back and watch children while refraining from judgment about what is happening. The information gathered can provide insights about an individual child that enable the teacher to adapt curriculum and materials to better meet that child's needs. This is particularly important for boys, who may run into difficulty when their socially or emotionally immature behaviors are dismissed as "acting out" or "being off task." Teachers who use this observation and recording strategy could view these instances as opportunities to look deeper into what boys' behavior may suggest about their social–emotional needs and to build relationships with individual children.

Did You Get It?

Mr. Delta, a preschool teacher, is always careful to call each of his students by name when speaking to him or her. Mr. Delta is working on developing

  a. psychosocial stages.
  b. rapport.
  c. independence
  d. unconditional positive regard.

Take the full quiz on CourseMate.

10-5 Child-to-Group Relationships

DAP naeyc When taking part in creative activities, a child learns to be in a group. Being in a group at school is not the same as being in a family. In school, the child is a student as well as a member of the group.

As a member of a group, the child learns many things. In art, a child learns how to follow—for example, learning to use a paintbrush by following directions. When making a mural with a group of children, a 5-year-old learns to follow and work with group ideas in planning the project. Learning to follow rules about cleanup is another way a child learns to follow in a group.

A child learns how to lead in a group, too. For example, a 6-year-old boy who is in charge of his group's paint learns to be a leader with responsibility. Children who can go ahead with ideas on their own are learning the qualities of a leader, too. Thus, in art projects, children have many chances to learn to sometimes be leaders and sometimes be followers.

Being a member of a group is a social learning experience. A group of children engaged in a creative project is a little social group for the child. In such a group, children learn how to share and cooperate. They learn that being in a social group has advantages, such as being with other children their own age, working, sharing ideas, and having fun with them. Children also learn that it is sometimes a disadvantage having to work with the group's rules and that it is not always easy to take turns or to play with others each day in school.

A child learns to respect the rights and ideas of others by being a member of a social group. Learning to respect others is also a part of the child's life outside the school. The things children learn about being members of a group in school help them as members of social groups outside the school.

Because young children are naturally egocentric, they face the difficult, yet necessary, task of moderating their self-interest to cope with group living. Young children must learn the self-discipline inherent in cooperating, in taking turns, and in adapting when necessary to group interests and needs. Skill in resolving interpersonal conflicts gradually develops. Creative art activities that take place in an open and flexible atmosphere provide a valuable setting for these social learnings.

How fortunate that creative experiences that give children so much pleasure should also be so effective in helping them to learn about themselves, other people, and how better to negotiate the real conditions of group living.

10-5a Learning about Diversity

By age 3, children have an awareness of differences in language, skin color, or customs. By age 4, children become aware of differences associated with handicaps. This awareness depends somewhat on how obvious the difference is. Even in the early childhood years, however, children are developing attitudes toward other racial groups.

With an understanding of the developmental sequence through which children become aware of differences, adults can better teach children about diversity. For preschoolers, the initial focus should be on increasing knowledge about similarities and differences among children. This knowledge can be revealed through awareness of different foods, family

structures, celebrations, and cultural traditions. All adults need to model support and understanding of cultural diversity.

A preschooler's primary means of learning is through play. Play across cultures often involves the use of toys. Toys and other things that children play with reflect culture and provide insight into the norms and values of a society—hence, the importance of Show and Tell. Because toys and playthings have an important influence on the play of young children, adults need to make sure that the toys available are appropriate and reflect cultural diversity. Adults should evaluate toys and make sure that they are varied and span different developmental areas. Toys also should be examined to be sure that they are accessible and do not reflect a cultural bias (Gonzalez-Mena, 2009).

Young children are naturally curious about differences. One way they make sense of the world is to sort it into different categories. At the same time they divide objects or actions or people into groups, they are also trying to separate right from wrong and good from bad. Their intent is not to judge but merely to organize a complex and challenging environment.

However, this mode of thinking can sometimes lead young children to label anything that differs from them as negative or undesirable. Our response as early childhood educators is to support their fascination with differences while helping them understand that diversity is normal and not inherently good or bad. By addressing and valuing the differences among ourselves and the children and family in our programs, we can encourage the acceptance of diversity among the children who turn to us as an example (Epstein, 2009).

Did You Get It?

A kindergarten teacher asks four of his students to plan and paint a mural together. From a developmental perspective, his actions are

   a. conducive to his students learning social skills.

   b. inadvisable, because the students are likely to argue.

   c. bound to be good for students who are leaders, but harmful to followers.

   d. not Developmentally Appropriate Practice.

Take the full quiz on CourseMate.

Summary

10-1 Define the terms *self-acceptance, self-concept, and unconditional positive acceptance.*

Self-concept can be defined as the child's growing awareness of his or her own characteristics (physical appearance as well as skills and abilities) and how these are similar to or different from those of others.

Self-concept is the good feeling a person has about himself or herself.

Unconditional positive acceptance is the positive feelings the child gains as he learns to accept himself and is accepted by others.

10-2 List the points included in planning the art program to encourage a child's self-concept and self-acceptance.

The following points need to be included in planning: Accept children at their present developmental level; provide an environment that is comfortable for the age level of the group; provide an environment that is appropriate for children with special needs; provide materials and activities that are age appropriate; and provide creative materials and activities that the children can work on and complete by themselves.

10-3 Discuss how the art program helps a child in child-to-child relationships.

In the art program, children who have positive creative experiences are able to honestly accept their own abilities and those of other children. The art program is a good place for child-to-child relationships, where children can work, talk, and be together.

10-4 Discuss how the art program helps in the child-to-teacher relationship.

A child learns new ways to be with an adult in the early childhood art program. The teacher is an adult but not the child's parent; therefore, a new types of relationship opens up for the child.

10-5 Discuss how the art program helps in child-to-group relationship.

When taking part in creative activities, a child learns to be in a group. In art, the child learns how to follow and follow rules. A child learns to lead in a group as well. Being a member of a group is an early social learning for the child.

Key Terms

actualizing tendency 209	mirror neurons 215	self-actualization 209
Carl Rogers 209	positive self-concept 209	social competence 214
Erik Erikson's stages of psychosocial development 209	psychosocially safe environment 209	social–emotional growth 208
	rapport 216	unconditional positive acceptance 209

Learning Activities

A. Your first peer group may have been made up of children in your neighborhood or classmates in school. Can you remember their names? What did they look like? How did they behave toward you? How did you feel about your involvement with this group?

B. During these early years, who were the popular, amiable, rejected, or isolated children with whom you came into contact? How would you rate yourself?

C. What happened to this group? What caused it to break apart? Can you remember how you felt about this change?

D. You have a time machine. Would you go back to your childhood to give the child you were a message? Or would you go forward to the future and give your own child a message? What would those messages be? Share them with your classmates.

E. Think of a teacher who made a positive difference in your life. Try to recall an interaction with this teacher. What did your teacher say and do? How did you respond? Take a moment to reflect on the ways this teacher made a difference to you. Now think about a child you currently teach. Fast-forward about 10 years and imagine that this child (now a teenager) is telling a friend about you, her preschool teacher, and about being in your classroom. What do you hope this teenager will say about you?

F. Think about your childhood years. Can you remember being afraid, worried, anxious? Write down several of your unpleasant memories, including the situation that created this feeling. Now think about your work with children. Have you created similar situations for children? Share your memories and thoughts with your classmates.

G. Psychological safety requires that every child in your room feel accepted, important, and valued. Examine the images of children and adults found in your room. Consider those in textbooks, posters, calendars, and any other available materials. Think about the mixture of genders and races portrayed. Will it support psychological safety for all your students?

H. Make a slot in the top of a lidded shoebox. Decorate the box and write the words "Private Letters" on it. Then encourage students to write letters or cards (or draw pictures) to you. Be sure to answer each letter individually. Some students may use the letter box as an opportunity to write more personal notes describing their feelings, thoughts, or problems. Remember to respect the confidentiality of all letters.

I. Share your feelings with your students. If you provide a space on the board for students to write their names when they're having a hard day, remember to include your own name from time to time.

J. Allow students the chance to be heard. Set up "One Minute and Be Heard" sessions. Children need to realize that you will listen to them, but it is important that you set boundaries, too.

Activities for Children

Toddlers

Emotions in the Mirror

Help toddlers identify feelings and build vocabulary and classification skills. Sit with the toddler in front of a mirror. Hold up a picture of a child looking surprised. Tell him this is a "surprised face" and have him practice copying this face in the mirror. Ask him when he might feel surprised. Repeat this activity using different pictures showing emotions such as happy, silly, angry, and sad.

Matching

Create a set of 8–10 cards showing four or five emotions, making 2 of each emotion. Help the toddler match the emotions. For more advanced toddlers, turn the cards over and play a game of memory with the cards. Or create a pattern of sad and happy faces using face stickers. Give the toddler his own stickers and have him copy your pattern.

Sorting

Sit with the toddler on a rug and spread out 8–10 circles with faces drawn on them. Help the child sort the faces into two piles: sad and happy. Talk with the toddler about what being happy feels like, and ask him what makes him feel happy. If the toddler can't come up with any ideas, suggest situations such as playing with friends or eating an ice cream cone, and ask the toddler whether he feels happy or sad when doing the activity. Talk about sad feelings the same way.

Observation Skills

Start by discussing good feelings. Ask the toddler to practice smiling and laughing, reinforcing that doing so expresses being happy. Play music and dance around or even do some jumping jacks! Talk to the toddler about how the exercise makes him feel. Jumping and dancing can make you feel excited and energized. If the toddler is quite verbal, encourage him to share how exercise makes him feel. You could also say, "Your cheeks are pink, and you are smiling. Do you feel happy?"

Group Effort Activity

To encourage and develop children's self-esteem, cooperation, and group effort, try this activity. You will need a table, crayons, markers, paper, and tape. Cover the top of the table with paper, attaching it with tape. In the middle of the paper write the title of the picture—for example, "Our Group Art." Allow children to draw pictures on the paper during group or free choice time. When the picture is finished (to everyone's liking), take it off the table, and tape it to the wall or put it on a bulletin board. As a variation, use different shapes or colors of paper. Use a round table or a rectangular table, or an animal or tree shape. Or try to have a special theme for the group artwork: nature, families, animals.

Random Moments of Good Manners

Keep a digital camera on hand to encourage children's polite behavior. Look for opportunities to "catch" children using their manners. Snap pictures of these moments and jot down the occasion and manners that were used on sticky notes. Later, print the pictures and display them on a bulletin board with a brief caption describing the situation.

Mirror Activities

Use a large, full-length or small, hand-held mirror to encourage self-awareness with toddlers, preschoolers, and children in grades kindergarten through grade three and grades four through five.

- With toddlers—Bring children to the mirror, one at a time. Encourage them to look at themselves in the mirror. Have them point to various parts of their body as you name the part: "Show me your nose." "Where is your tummy?" "Point to your mouth."

- With kindergarten through third-grade students—Ask them as they look at themselves such questions as, "Why do people look in mirrors?" "Why do people look at themselves?" "What do you like about you that you see in the mirror?" Then have two children look in the mirror together. Have each child tell the other what is special about him or her.

- With fourth and fifth graders—Have them look in the mirror. What features do they see that remind them of their parents, siblings, a famous person, or other relatives? What is special about what they see? What lines and shapes do they see in their image? Have two children look into the mirror. Have them compare the lines and shapes they see in each other's face. Ask them to tell each other what is special about their images. Does either one look like a famous person?

Activities for Self-Awareness, Self-Acceptance, and Cooperation

What's Your Name?

Invite students to research the meaning of their names using a baby name book or website. Have students write the original meaning on a piece of construction paper. Then challenge them to think of a more personal meaning. For example, "The original meaning of Hannah is 'grace.' But to me, Hannah means strong runner, good friend, and cupcake lover." Encourage students to use descriptive words in writing their own meanings. Or the teacher can write them down for the student. Display students' work on the bulletin board.

Making a Web of Friends Game

Materials: Ball of thick white yarn

Gather a group of 10 children or more. Ask the children if they think people can spin webs like spiders. After the discussion, tell them that you will try to spin a web as a group. Everyone sits in a large circle. Show the children the ball of yarn. Explain that you will begin spinning the web by holding the end of the yarn ball tightly in your lap and picking a friend to toss the remaining ball to, saying something like, "I pick Claire to help spin our web." When she catches it, share something you like about her. Remind her to hold the yarn string tight in her lap as she picks the next friend to toss the yarn ball to.

Continue until the ball is completely used. The number of times a child is picked doesn't matter after everyone has had at least one turn. It's fun to see how huge your life-size web has become. Variation: See if the group can stand up together without getting tangled in the web!

Put Your Feelings in a Letter

Materials: large construction paper, any color; markers, chalk or paint, large letter stencils (for youngest children)

Start by talking with students about how art can be a way to portray your feelings. You can link this lesson to Leonardo Da Vinci or Claude Monet because of how their art changed with their feelings. Trace or sketch the first letter of the students' names (or have them do it). Have the students fill their letters in with colors and /or pictures that portray a happy feeling, a sad feeling, and so on. Have the students share their letters with the class and explain their feelings.

Skin Color Matching Activity

Set out a variety of nylon knee-high stockings in various shades such as tan, black, white, yellow, red. Encourage the children to try them on their hands and arms or legs and feet. Ask questions to help children increase their awareness of skin color. For example, "Can you find a stocking that is like the color of your skin?" or "What color is that stocking on your arm?" Ask the children to try another color stocking. Then ask if it is lighter or darker than their own skin color. Be sure to tell the children that no one's skin is really white, pink, yellow, or red. Emphasize that skin color differences are interesting and desirable.

Body Shapes

Objectives: To encourage children's positive feelings about themselves and their bodies and to encourage cooperation among children.

Equipment: Large pieces of brown paper, crayons, and paints.

Procedure: Have a child lie down on a piece of paper. Have another child use a crayon to trace the first child's body outline on the paper. Then have the first child paint or color in his or her body shape outlined on the paper.

Encourage children's self-awareness by having them notice what they are wearing and the colors before they paint their outline.

Patty-Cake (for 3-Year-Olds)

Objectives: To learn to use body parts and to learn other children's names.

Procedure: Teacher begins by singing and clapping: "Patty-cake, patty-cake, baker's man. Bake me a cake as fast as you can. Roll it and pat it, mark it with a (use a child's initial). Put it in the oven for (use a child's name) and me."

1. Use all the children's names in the song. (Or each child can have a turn to sing the song and name another child in the group.)
2. Repeat it often so that children learn each other's names.

Hands On

Cover one wall with brown kraft (wrapping) paper. With bright paint (one color for each letter), write the title, "Hands On!" at the top of the paper. Children then place handprints randomly on the board by first pressing hands on a paint-coated sponge and then pressing directly on the paper. Label each print with the child's name and date.

Pattern Prints

Prepare the bulletin board by measuring off horizontal lines on backing paper to create one horizontal stripe/space for each child. At the left end of the stripes, list children's names. Then, offer children a variety of materials for printing (rubber stamps, printing letters, etc.) and an inked pad or sponge soaked in tempera paint. Allow children to create any pattern or design they would like to make.

Names

Cover a large bulletin board with a bright, solid background. Divide paper evenly into a grid design, thus providing each child with a 12-inch-square space on the board. With a marker, print each child's name in large letters at the top of the space, leaving at least 11 inches of paper exposed under each name. First, use the board as a basis for a matching game—children must match name cards to their name printed on the board. Then invite children to decorate their name with markers, crayons, or paints. As the year progresses, children can copy their names in a variety of other materials (older preschoolers may enjoy using yarn, sparkles, etc.).

Line Up

To help children recognize their own body shape, notice other people's body shapes, and represent their physical characteristics, try this activity. You will need a large sheet of butcher paper, masking tape, felt-tip markers, and crayons.

Tape up the butcher paper on a wall or fence. Have the entire class line up next to one another with their backs to the paper. Draw around their bodies with a felt-tip pen. Each child can stand away from the wall as soon as you finish tracing their body. They'll enjoy looking at their outline as well as watching you trace the rest of the class. When finished, encourage the children to look at the mural. Can they recognize each other's outline? How do they know? Distribute crayons or markers and encourage the children to draw their face, color in their skin and hair, and color in their clothes. Display the mural in the hallway or classroom.

Variation: As a group, decide how each person's body should be colored in.

I Like

You will need a tape recorder. Individually ask children to name something they like or are interested in. Record these statements and create a pause on the tape. After the short pause, ask each child to say his or her name and record it. During group meeting time, play the tape for the children, asking them to identify the child after each statement of interest. The children can check their guesses when they hear the name of the child recorded on the tape.

As a follow-up to this activity, play the tape in the art center. Some children may want to express what they heard on the tape with paint, markers, clay, or another medium. Another possible use for the tape is in the book corner. Have earphones on the tape player so children can listen quietly to their own and their friends' voices and comments. Some children might want to dictate a story about something they heard on the tape.

This Makes Me Feel Happy

A. Bring an object to a small group and say, "I would like to share something with you that makes me happy." Explain why the object makes you happy. For example, "Here is a necklace that someone I like very much gave to me. When I wear it, it reminds me of that person, and I get a good feeling." Then, "I would like to give you a chance to share something with us and tell us how it makes you happy."

B. Ask children to obtain something to bring back to the group. Give each child an opportunity to share her or his object with the group. This can take place over several days as children bring sentimental objects from home. (See Chapter 7 for ideas on making a class museum to display these special objects.)

Me-Mobiles (Older 4-Year-Olds)

You will need: (1) a selection of magazines (school and department store catalogs, nature, sports, as well as any popular family magazines); (2) scissors; (3) paste; (4) construction paper; (5) wire hangers; (6) yarn (or string); and (7) name tags large enough to fit in the central triangle of the hanger.

Tie the child's name tag to the central portion of the hanger and allow at least three strings to dangle from the bar of the hanger. Have children look through magazines and cut (or tear) out three or more pictures that reflect a favorite thing or activity. Have children paste the pictures on the construction paper and then tie or staple the mounted pictures to the strings attached to the hanger. Encourage children to talk about their selections. Hangers can be hung on a "clothesline" in the classroom or in any other appropriate place.

Fill Your Talent Plate!

In this activity, you are giving children the opportunity to discover that people all around them possess many talents. This activity also helps develop language and fine-motor skills.

For this activity, you will need magazines, newspapers, photographs, scissors, glue, and paper plates.

Prior to carrying out the activity, discuss with children the meaning of the word *talent,* and emphasize that everyone has special talents. Talk about personal talents of people the children know that will help them connect the meaning of the word with their own experiences.

Direct children to find pictures that show people doing things they are good at. Show children how to cut the pictures out and glue them on a paper talent plate. After children are finished with their talent plate, they might show it to a peer or help a partner.

Faces Charades

Start by singing songs such as "If You're Happy and You Know It" and play Simon Says to introduce the idea that facial and body expressions can convey meaning. Focus on changes in mouths, eyes, and eyebrows.

Preparation: With a small group of children in front of a wall mirror (or small, unbreakable hand mirrors) suggest that they make faces with these or other expressions: You mean *yes,* you mean *no,* you are very tired, you are very excited, you are angry, you are happy, and so on. When they are able to read each other's expressions, children are ready for Faces Charades!

Procedure: Write one word or idea on an index card. Draw a picture to illustrate the feeling, or use pictures cut from magazines.

Mix up the cards. Have children choose a leader to pick the first card. The leader makes a face according to the directions on the card. The other children try to figure out what feeling the leader is expressing. The player who guesses correctly gets to pick the next card.

Variations: Cards could be of animals, favorite story characters, or any other topic that appeals to children and can be acted out.

With toddlers, you might begin with two or three very different feelings. They could tear pictures from recycled magazines to help distinguish facial expressions.

Multicultural Activities

Everyone Is Different

Topics: "I'm Me and I'm Special," "Alike and Different," "Our Five Senses," "Bodies," "Our Community"

Goal: To help children discover that all people have physical characteristics that make them unique

Materials: White paper or 3- × 5-inch cards, black ink pad, pen, magnifying glass

Method: Encourage children to make prints of their thumbs by pressing their thumb on the ink pad and then on the paper. Label each print with the child's name. At group time, show children the prints. Talk about how everyone has patterns of lines on the skin of their fingers, how each person has a different pattern, and how each person's fingerprints are different from everyone else's. No two are alike. Set out the prints and a magnifying glass on the table so children can examine the similarities and differences in the fingerprints.

Variations

Make two sets of prints for each child. Mix them up and see if children can match them.

Hair

Topics: "I'm Me and I'm Special," "Boys and Girls," "Alike and Different," "Clothes We Wear," "Bodies"

Goal: To help children notice hair as a distinguishing physical characteristic and discover that some people express their culture through hairstyle

Materials: Pictures of a variety of people with different hairstyles, a hand mirror, empty hair care containers, scarves, turbans, rubber bands, hair clips, old hair dryers, old curling irons, old crimping irons

Method: Show pictures of different hairstyles to children. Ask them to touch their hair. Talk about how hair has texture and curl; how some people have fine hair and some people have coarse hair. Some people have straight hair, and some people have curly hair.
Pass around the mirror so that children can look at their hair. Talk about how different people differ in the color and length of their hair. Set out hair care materials in the dramatic play area for children to use during free-choice play.

Variations

- Write down children's descriptions of their hair. Let each child draw a self-portrait to accompany the description.
- Have children make collages using pictures from a variety of magazines showing all kinds of hair and hair styles.

Photography and Self-Concept

Taking pictures of themselves and their classmates in different contexts wearing different clothing can help children understand that people remain fundamentally the same, even though they may look different from day to day. Have the children take pictures of each other on different days when they are wearing different clothing and when they are dressing up in the dramatic play area. Have them identify who is in the picture. Talk about how children and other people can look different, depending on what they are wearing. Have the children take photos of their classmates wearing different hats and talk about how they look. Have the children identify pictures of themselves and then discuss what is the same and what is different about each picture. Use points of confusion when children cannot identify themselves in a picture as a teaching moment to talk about how appearances can be different, but the person inside is the same.

Half of Me

Materials: Pieces of lightweight cardboard, old magazines and catalogs, markers, crayons, or paint and paintbrushes, blunt-tip scissors, glue

Procedure:

1. Have children go through magazines and catalogs to find a picture of something they like. Have them cut the picture out and glue it to a piece of cardboard. Then have them cut the picture in half. An adult or older child can help the younger ones with the cutting.
2. Put the halves in a box or bag.
3. Pass around the box or bag of half pictures and ask each child to take out one of the pieces. Continue passing the box or bag until all the pieces have been taken.
4. Ask a child to hold up one of his or her half pictures. Ask the other children to look through their pieces to see who has the other half. Invite those children to come together to fit the pieces together. Children can leave the completed piece on a table.
5. Ask which child selected this picture. Then ask this child to talk about why this was a picture he or she liked. Continue the activity until all the children have had a chance to talk about their chosen pictures.

Let's Draw!

Topics: "I'm Me and I'm Special," "Friends," "Alike and Different," "Our Five Senses"

Goal: To help children notice facial features and the uniqueness of each person

Materials: Drawing paper, felt-tip pens, crayons

Method: Have children find a partner and ask them to sit across from each other at a table. Encourage children to draw a picture of their partner's face. Ask them to look at their partner. Then ask: "What color is his skin? What color are her eyes? Does he have freckles? What color is her hair? How long is his hair? Is her hair straight or curly?" The drawing probably won't look like the partner.

That's all right because it's the looking at the features of another person that is important. Have children exchange their drawings when they are finished.

Variations

- Have children describe themselves to each other before they begin drawing.
- Have children share their drawings with the class at group time.
- Play a guessing game during group time. Have children look at each drawing and guess who it is.

Photo Masks

Topics: "I'm Me and I'm Special," "Boys and Girls," "Friends," "Changes," "Alike and Different," "Feelings"

Goal: To help children explore diversity by taking on another person's identity through role playing

Materials: Close-up photographs of people's faces (choose people in your school that exemplify a variety of differences), rubber cement, poster board, hole punch, scissors, string

Method: Have the photos enlarged to 8 × 10 inches. Cut out the photo around the hair and face. Mount the photo on poster board using rubber cement. Cut out the eyes so the child can look through them. Punch a hole on both sides above the ear. Tie a 12-inch piece of string through each hole. Introduce the masks at group time. Set them out on a "discovery table" with a mirror or in the dramatic play area. Observe the children and notice their conversations as they try on different masks.

Variation: Record the children's voices or write down what they say as they take on other people's identities.

Face Puzzles

Topics: "I'm Me and I'm Special," "Bodies," "Alike and Different," "Friends"

Goal: To help children discover that each person's face is unique because of the color and shape of its features, but that all faces are similar because the features are in the same place on each person

Materials: Camera (digital or instant), rubber cement, poster board or foam core, mat knife or Exacto knife, pencil, ruler

Method: Take a close-up photo of each child's face. Have the photos enlarged to 8 × 10 inches. Glue the photo to the foam core or poster board and let dry. Using a ruler, mark off the photo in fourths vertically and horizontally. With a pencil, lightly draw lines for cutting out the pieces. This results in sixteen 2-inch squares. Cut out the pieces with the Exacto knife, and put the child's name or initials on the back of each piece. During group time, give the pieces to each child in a plastic bag. Encourage them to try to put together their face puzzle. As they work on their own puzzle, talk about where the eyes, nose, and mouth are located on a person's face. When the children have completed their puzzles, ask them to hold up the piece that shows their mouth. Talk about how each person's mouth is different. Continue with the other facial features.

Variations: Combine three or four puzzles and see if children can unscramble them and make the correct faces. Or, set the puzzle pieces out in a tub and let children freely explore putting the pieces together to create different faces.

Activities for Older Children (Grades 4–5)

A. Older children can use cameras and take each other's pictures. They may take photos on a field trip or during a special project, or at whatever time they want. A "documentary" of their experience can be created by arranging the photos in a special order and then writing an explanatory text to go with the photos. Or have older children take pictures of each other according to a specific idea or theme, such as lines/shapes in faces, dark-haired/light-haired friends, and so on.

B. Older children can sketch the body outline of another student by projecting a light onto a blank wall that has a large sheet of paper taped on it. Students can trace each other's "standing shadow" with a large dark marker. They may want to decorate the outline or fill it in with words and phrases describing that person. The point is to do another person's outline to learn more about that person. Asking questions about favorite foods, clothes, TV or movie stars, cars, and so on is a good way to learn information to fill in the outline.

C. With older children, make a mural after a field trip. Have them work as a group to decide which part of the field trip they want to feature as the topic of their mural. Encourage them to include as many art techniques as possible in their mural (for example, collage, finger paint, tempera painting, printing, three-dimensional add-ons).

D. Give older children a chance to learn more about each other in "Talk Time." A talk time break gives them an opportunity to visit with their friends. As we know, the development of strong friendships and a peer group are characteristic of this age group. They can talk about what they did last night, their new item of clothing, what they are going to play at recess, a book they have been reading—anything they feel is important to share with their classmates. This type of experience also provides an opportunity for developing social interaction and for finding out that their friends have special interests and mutual concerns. Teachers who use this technique find that when children know they are going to have a time to visit freely, they refrain from visiting at inappropriate times. Teachers can join in the conversations, thus using this break as an information-gathering time.

E. **Family Name Crossword.** Have students write their names in large block letters in the center of a piece of paper. Then challenge them to fill in the names of their family members and pets by building off the letters in their own name, crossword-style. If students are stumped, allow them to use additional words describing what family means to them, such as *love* or *happiness*. Display the crosswords on a bulletin board for families to enjoy during an open house night. As an extra challenge, you might create a jumbo crossword that includes the names of everyone in your class.

F. **Jump-Rope Names.** Get the kinesthetic learners in your classroom off their feet and onto the playground with this active jump-rope name game. Distribute jump ropes to groups of three students and challenge them to come up with a skipping rhyme for each group member's name. Students might simply spell out their names, jumping at leach letter, or they might develop more elaborate routines. After 15 to 20 minutes of practice, have the groups perform their routines for the entire class.

G. **Celebration of Life.** Set aside a day to celebrate life. The purpose of this day is to help each child feel good about herself or himself and to recognize how precious the gift of life is. Provide each student with several blank business cards. Have them fill in their own name, address, and phone number. Then ask them to draw pictures of or list their special talents, their place in the family, or their favorite things. During group time, have them share and explain their cards.

H. **Personal Trophies.** Challenge students to make a trophy for a family member that honors something that person does well. Students might use clay, gold tempera paint, and paintbrushes.

Look at reproductions of Greek sculpture and a variety of commercial trophies featuring athletic forms. Explore different ways of modeling figures. Try working flat from clay slabs, like gingerbread men. Flattened clay balls make good bases for clay figures. Let the clay figures dry and then paint them with gold tempera paint.

I. **Personal Memories.** Motivate your students to create art and writings based on their personal memories. Share with them the following websites.

- Two contemporary artists who make art based on their personal memories are Carmen Lomas Garza and Faith Ringgold. Both have strong online presences with their personal websites. Lomas Garza, a self-described Chicana narrative artist, creates images about everyday events in the lives of Mexican Americans based on her own childhood memories and experiences in South Texas. Her website includes an artist's statement, images of her artwork, a biography, and much more (http://carmenlomasgaza.com).

- Ringgold is an African American artist well known for her illustrated children's books, such as *Tar Beach*. Her website offers many features, including a biography, a test about prejudice, a story to read and illustrate, frequently asked questions, and a link to send a message to the artist (http://faithringgold.com).

- Older students may want to explore Mexican painter Frida Kahlo. She is another artist who painted from personal experience. There are a variety of websites about this artist.

- Encourage your students to write autobiographies including artwork, photographs, and any other images they choose to include.

J. **What Is a Friend?** This activity helps build children's awareness of characteristics a friend ought to possess. Divide students into teams of three or four. Each team must decide on a list of characteristics they all agree are important in a friend. Have them list these characteristics on a piece of paper.

Have each team work together to rank the characteristics in order of importance. The characteristic they have agreed is most important should be listed as number 1, the second-most important as number 2, and so on. When they are finished, have the students look over the paper and decide which characteristic(s) can best be applied to themselves.

Finally, explain to students that sometimes when people work in a group, positions or ideas have to be compromised so that the group can come to an agreement. Ask students to think about whether that happened to them, and whether they would have come up with the same answers if they had done the activity on their own. Remind students that if they choose not to, they need not share their list with anyone.

K. **Friendship Recipes.** As a group, discuss the characteristics of a good friend. Ask older students to list at least five important friendship attributes, such as humor, availability, kindness, loyalty, and common interests. Write the descriptions that come up on a chart to refer to again and to add to as the class thinks of new descriptions. Using these friend characteristics, have students write their own "recipes" for how to make a friend. You may compile these into a class-made book titled *Friendship Recipes*. Older students might work in teams to develop a mutually agreed-upon recipe. The team's final recipe can be written on an index card in recipe format. Use a cookbook as a guide.

L. **Caring Ropes.** For this activity, use a 20-inch leather strip or rug-yarn length for each student. Ask students to keep track of their caring deeds toward others. Each time they perform a deed, invite them to tie a knot in the rope. Keep the ropes in an accessible place, such as a desk.

M. Georgia O'Keeffe's *The Mountain, New Mexico*— Exploring Feelings. Obtain an art print of this work. It is an excellent example of a landscape featuring varieties of warm and cool colors. If this print is not available, any other landscape with warm and cool colors will suffice.

Briefly review the concept that colors are an important way to express moods and feelings in art. Point out that many color words help people tell about feelings. Examples include feeling blue, being green with envy, or being red or purple with rage.

Explain that artists often refer to these color qualities as "warm" or "cool." These terms can mean that a color is used to show warm things (a fire) or cool things (a lake).

The artist also remembers that colors help to express feelings.

Explain that the warm colors in this painting show the red earth of mountains in New Mexico, but they also help to express the artist's warm feelings about the land. Georgia O'Keeffe thought that forms and colors of the desert and nearby mountains were beautiful. Guide students to see the delicate shading and rhythmic curves that fill the whole painting. Discuss how the painting makes them feel about the place depicted.

As a follow-up activity, have students create a picture of a landscape on a planet no one has seen. Have them use warm or cool colors to show and express the feelings of the creatures that inhabit this planet.

References

Baker, J. A. (2006). Contributions of teacher–child relationships to positive school adjustments during elementary school. *Journal of School Psychology, 44*, 211–229.

Baptiste, N. (1995). Adults need to play, too. *Early Childhood Education Journal*, 33–36.

Barbarin, O. A. (2010). Halting African American boys' progression from pre-K to prison: What families, schools, and communities can do! *American Journal of Orthopsyciatry, 80*(1), 81–88.

Barbarin, O., & Crawford, G. M. (2006). Acknowledging and reducing stigmatization of African American boys. *Young Children, 61*(6), 79–86.

Carr, C. J., Fauske, J., & Rushton, S. (2008). *Teaching and leading from the inside out: A model for reflection, exploration, and action*. Thousand Oaks, CA: Corwin Press.

Cohen, D., Stern, V., Balaban, N., & Gropper, N. (2008). *Observing and recording the behavior of young children*. New York, NY: Teachers College Press.

Cornett, C. E. (2003). *The arts as meaning makers*. Upper Saddle River, NJ: Merrill/Prentice Hall.

Dewey, J. (1958). *The philosophy of education*. New York, NY: Corwin.

Epstein, A. S. (2009). *Me, You, Us: Social–emotional learning in preschool*. Ypsilanti, MI: HighScope Educational Research Foundation.

Erikson, E. (1950). *Childhood and society*. New York, NY: W. W. Norton.

Ewing, A. R., & Taylor, A. R. (2009). The role of child gender and ethnicity in teacher-child relationship quality and children's behavioral adjustment in preschool. *Early Childhood Research Quarterly, 24*, 92–105.

Ferguson, A. (2000). *Bad boys: Public school in the making of black masculinity*. Ann Arbor: University of Michigan Press.

Gersch, I. (2009). A positive future for educational psychology—If the profession gets it right. *Educational Psychology in Practice, 25*(1), 9–19.

Gilliam, W. S. (2005). *Prekindergarteners left behind: Expulsion rates in state prekindergarten systems*. Policy Brief, series no. 3. New York, NY: Foundation for Child Development.

Gonzalez-Mena, J. (2009). *50 Strategies for communicating and working with diverse families* (2nd ed.). Upper Saddle River, NJ: Pearson.

Gropper, N., Hinitz, B. F., Sprung, B., & Froschi, M. (2011). Helping young boys be successful learners in today's early childhood classrooms. *Young Children, 66*(1), 34–41.

Hamre, B. K., & Pianta, R. C. (2006). Early teacher–child relationships and the trajectory of children's school outcomes. *Child Development, 72*, 625–638.

Harmel, K. (1999). *UF researcher: Teachers' nonverbal clues affect student's performance*. Retrieved at http://www .sciencedaily.com/releases/1999/01/990122130911.htm

Hartup, W. W. (2002). *Having friends, making friends, and keeping friends: Relationships as educational contexts*. Urbana, IL: ERIC Clearinghouse on Elementary and Early Childhood Education, ED345–854.

Hurley, S., & Chater, N. (Eds.) (2005). *Perspectives on imitation: Mechanisms of imitation in animals*. Cambridge, MA: MIT Press.

Iacoboni, M., Molnar-Szakacs, I., Gallese, V., Buccino, G., Mazziotta, J. C., & Rizzolatti, G. (2005). Grasping the intentions of others with one's own mirror neuron system. *PLoS Biology, 3*(3), e.79.

Lowenfeld, V. (1957). *Creative and mental growth* (3rd ed.). New York, NY: Macmillan.

Lowenfeld, V., & Brittain, W. L. (1987). *Creative and mental growth* (8th ed.). New York, NY: Macmillan.

Marcon, R. A. (2002). Moving up the grades: Relationship between preschool model and later school success. *Early Childhood Research & Practice, 4*(1).

McClellan, D., & Katz, L. G. (2003). *Young children's social development: A checklist*. Urbana, IL: ERIC Document EDO PS–93–6.

Mead, S. (2006). *The evidence suggests otherwise: The truth about boys and girls.* Washington, DC: Education Sector.

Miller, E., & Almon, J. (2009). *Crisis in the kindergarten: Why children need to play in school.* College Park, MD: Alliance for Childhood.

Rogers, C. (1995). *On becoming a person: A therapist's view of psychotherapy.* Boston, MA: Houghton Mifflin Harcourt.

Roskos, K., & Christie, J. E. (2000). (Eds.) *Play and literacy in early childhood: Research from multiple perspectives.* Mahwah, NJ: Erlbaum.

Rudasill, K. M. (2011). Child temperament, teacher–child interactions, and teacher–child relationships: A longitudinal investigation from first to third grade. *Early Childhood Research Quarterly, 26,* 147–156.

Rushton, S. (2011). Neuroscience, early childhood education and play: We are doing it right! *Early Childhood Education Journal, 39,* 89–94.

Rushton, S., Juola-Rushton, A., & Larkin, E. (2010). Neuroscience, play, and early childhood education: Connections, implications, and assessment. *Early Childhood Education Journal, 37,* 351–361.

Smith, R. A. (2002). Black boys: The litmus test for No. Child Left Behind. *iEducation Week, 22*(9), 40, 43.

Thorne, B. (2003). *Carl Rogers.* Thousand Oaks, CA: Sage.

U.S. Department of Education, Office of Special Education Programs. (2003). *25th annual report to Congress.* Washington, DC: Author.

Winerman L. (2005). The mind's mirror: A new type of neuron—called a mirror neuron—could help explain how we learn through mimicry and why we empathize with others. *Monitor Psychology, 36*(9), 48–52.

 Visit CourseMate for this textbook to access the eBook, Did You Get It? quizzes, Digital Downloads, TeachSource Videos, flashcards, and more. Go to CengageBrain.com to log in, register, or purchase access.

Casper Holroyd

Developmental Levels and Art

As children grow older, they change in height and weight and gain new skills. They also develop different abilities in art. The artwork of a 3-year-old is different from that of a 4- or 5-year-old. It is different in the way it looks, as well as in the way it is made.

For many years, people have been trying to explain why all children the world over draw the way they do. There are many theories of children's art, each of which offers an explanation for why children produce art and suggests strategies for teachers. Basic to all of these theories are two facts. The first is that all children go through definite stages in their development of art. The second is that the pace of each child's development in art varies with the child.

Learning Objectives

After studying this chapter, you should be able to:

11-1 Define the concept of developmental levels/stages of art and their importance in early childhood education.

11-2 Describe the scribble stage, including appropriate materials for use in this stage.

11-3 Explain the basic forms (preschematic) stage, including appropriate materials for use in this stage.

11-4 Discuss the pictorial (schematic) stage, including appropriate materials for use in this stage.

11-5 Discuss the gang stage, including appropriate materials for use in this stage.

naeyc

NAEYC Program Standard

1b Knowing and understanding the multiple influences on development and learning.

3b Knowing about and using observation, documentation, and other appropriate assessment tools and approaches.

DAP Criteria

2B2 Teachers continually gather information about children in a variety of ways and monitor each child's learning and development to make plans to help children's progress.

4A Assessment of young children's progress and achievements is ongoing, strategic, and purposeful.

11-1 Developmental Levels/Stages of Art

Just as young children experience various stages of physical development, they also develop art abilities in a gradual process, going through specific stages. These stages are called developmental levels. A developmental level is a guide to what a child can do in art at different ages, but it is not a strict guideline. Some children may be ahead of or behind the developmental level for their age. Developmental levels tell the teacher what came before and what is to come in the artwork of the young child.

There is no exact pattern for each age level. Not all 3-year-olds behave alike, nor are they completely different from 4-year-olds. But there is a gradual growth process that almost every child goes through. There is also considerable overlap between stages. Stages of art development as presented in this chapter should be viewed as fluid and dynamic—not as static and rigid. Sometimes children will not fit neatly into each stage at approximately the "correct" age. Two stages may be represented in one work, and a child may regress before advancing to the next stage. An understanding of developmental levels helps an adult accept each child at the child's present level, whatever it is.

From 1830, when Ebenezer Cooke first drew attention to the successive stages of development found in children's drawings, to Rhoda Kellogg's *Analyzing Children's Art* (1970), and Viktor Lowenfeld's *Creative and Mental Growth of the Child* (1987), teachers have based their objectives for art activities on the idea that children's art is developmental. (See Figure 11-1 for a summary of several art theories.) While each art theory varies (for example, in the number of proposed stages), they all propose a similar pattern of development—one of progressing from scribbling to more realistic representations. Ability in art develops as the child grows and matures. Each stage is a part of the natural and normal aspects of child growth and development. These stages are sequential, with each stage characterized by increasing progress. Even though stages in art have been identified and accepted, the age at which children progress through these stages is highly individual. As children's bodies and minds mature, so does their art ability. Children learn to paint, model, and build as they learn to walk—slowly, developing in their own way. They learn each new step in the process, as they are ready for it. As a general guide, art development progresses from experimentation and exploration (the scribble stage in drawing), to the devising of basic forms, to the forming of symbolic figures and their naming.

Herbert Read, *Education Through Art* (1966)

Scribble: 2–4 years
Line: 4 years
Descriptive Symbolism: 5–6 years
Descriptive Realism: 7–8 years
Visual Realism: 9–10 years
Repression: 11–14 years
Artistic Revival: 14 years

Rhoda Kellogg, *Analyzing Children's Art* (1970)

Scribble Stage—20 basic scribbles: 2-year-olds
Combine Stage (Diagrams)—Basic shapes: 3-year-olds
Aggregate Stage—Two or more diagrams: 4-year-olds
Pictorial Stage—Representational art: 5-year-olds

Victor Lowenfeld and Benjamin Brittain, *Creative and Mental Growth* (1987)

Scribbling Stage—First Stage of Self-expression: 2–4 years
Preschematic Stage—First Representational Attempts: 4–7 years
Schematic Stage—Achievement of a Form Concept: 7–9 years
Gang Stage—Dawning Realism: 9–11 years
Stage of Reasoning—Pseudonaturalistic: 11–13 years

© Cengage Learning

FIGURE 11-1 Summary: Theories of art development.

Older children continue to develop and refine their abilities in art as they create more complex works of art and give greater attention to their expressive intentions. The following discussion of the development of children's drawing is intended to serve as a general guide to the overall process of development in art. The basic developmental levels, or stages, apply to all art media. For the sake of clarity, children's drawing will be the primary focus of the discussion.

11-1a Infants (Birth to 18 Months)

Long before the child picks up a crayon and begins to scribble, many earlier stages in art development occur with children of this age group. Here are some of these basic steps in art development with infants:

● Child responds to visual elements present in the environment such as light, color, and patterns.

- Child participates in and enjoys a variety of tactile/sensory experiences such as water and texture.
- Child explores the shapes of objects.

To encourage the infant at this early stage of art development, adults need to do the following:

- Provide pictures, mobiles, and other types of displays in the environment.
- Display pictures and art at the child's level.
- Involve the child in water play, texture books and toys, and so on.
- For older infants, provide finger paint, large crayons, and other appropriate art materials.

11-1b Children's Drawing

Three developmental levels in drawing are of concern to the early childhood teacher: the **scribble stage**, the **basic forms stage**, and the **pictorial** (or first drawings) **stage**. The realism stage, generally covering children ages 9 years old and older, is of concern to teachers in the upper-elementary levels.

Did You Get It?

A 16-month-old is presented with finger paints by her caregivers at her daycare center. From a developmental perspective, this is

- **a.** developmentally appropriate.
- **b.** above the child's level of ability.
- **c.** inadvisable, as it is dangerous to the child's development.
- **d.** appropriate only for gifted 16-month-olds.

Take the full quiz on CourseMate.

11-2 The Scribble Stage

naeyc DAP Most children begin scribbling at about 1½–2 years of age. Children can be given a crayon or marker as soon as they no longer put everything in their mouth. They will scribble with anything at hand and on anything nearby. Their first marks are usually an aimless group of lines. Yet these first scribbles are related to later drawing and painting. They are related to art just as a baby's first babbling sounds are related to speech.

The crayon may be held upside down, sideways, with the fist, between clenched fingers, or with either hand. Children may be pleased with their scribbling and get real enjoyment from it. They enjoy the pure physical motions, the kinesthetic pleasure, involved in scribbling. It is the act of doing—not the final product—that is important to the child. When a child gets her or his hands on materials, the child begins to manipulate and explore randomly. This exploration delights the child and therefore leads to further manipulation and discovery.

If you watch a baby draw or a toddler scribbling, you know it is a sensorimotor activity. As a child draws or paints, every part of the child's body moves, all working to move the crayon or brush across the paper. After the child begins the movement, it's difficult to stop! As a consequence, whatever surface the child is working on often becomes covered with paint and crayon.

From the moment the child discovers what it looks like and feels like to put these lines down on paper, he has found something he will never lose—he has found art. This wonderful thing happens to every child when he is about 2 years old (Kellogg & O'Dell, 1967).

11-2a Early Scribble Stage: Disordered or Random Scribbling

During the early scribble stage, the young child does not have control over hand movements or the marks on a page. Thus this stage is called **disordered or random scribbling.** The marks are random and go in many directions. The direction of the marks depends on whether the child is drawing on the floor or on a low table. The way the crayon is held also affects how the scribbles look. But the child is not able to make the crayon go in any one way on purpose. The child has neither the desire nor the ability to control the marks. (See Figure 11-2 for some examples of random scribbles.)

Because it is the sensory experience of making marks that is important at this stage, the child doesn't even realize that she or he is producing these scribbles. The early scribbler doesn't make the connection between herself or himself and the scribbles. In fact, these children receive as much satisfaction from just handling the materials—dumping the crayons out of the box, putting them back in again, rolling them across the table or in their hands—as they do from scribbling!

Art is such a sensory experience at this age that children may use crayons in both hands as they draw, singing along in rhythm to the movements they are making. They may not even notice the crayon they're working with isn't leaving marks on the paper.

Because it is the process that is important to children when they're toddlers, there's no need to label

Children's drawings reflect growth in thinking (cognition) and in physical control (gross and fine motor) over materials and tools.

Note: All ages listed here are approximate. All children develop at highly individual rates.

Ages   **Characteristics of Stage**

1–2 years *Random Scribbling*. Exploration of tools and materials, showing increasing fine and gross motor control. Single and multiple dots and lines (horizontal, vertical, wavy, and diagonal) produce some twenty basic scribbles that eventually include loops, spirals, and circles. Some examples:

2–7 years *Shape Making*. Scribbles begin to be used intentionally to make basic shapes or diagrams. Children combine shapes and use overlapping. Eventually, shapes form aggregates (three or more diagrams together). Some examples:

3–5 years *Symbol Making*. Lopsided geometric shapes are made. Mandalas and suns are drawn and eventually become human figures. At first, arms and legs stretch out from the head. Eventually the torso emerges and human figures appear more and more complete. Some examples:

FIGURE 11-2 Example of development in children's drawings.

Source: All above examples based on Kellogg (1970) and Lowenfeld and Brittain (1987).

their scribbles with their names or ask for stories or titles to accompany the scribbles. For young children in the early scribble stage, it is appropriate for adults to comment on the process. Focusing on the process, you might say, "You covered the entire paper," "Your whole arm moved as you worked," or "You moved your crayon all around and around." These are the kinds of comments appropriate in the scribble stage. They are specific, and they are geared to the developmental level of the child. Be sure to save samples of scribbles from time to time, using portfolios to keep a visual record of the child's progress (see Photo 11-1). (Portfolios are discussed in detail later in this chapter.)

A further insight into this stage of art development is provided by Rhoda Kellogg, who points out that

PHOTO 11-1 Example of random scribbling.

"visual interest is an essential component of scribbling" (1970, p. 7). She divides children's scribbles into 20 basic varieties that have no specific developmental order. (See Figure 11-3 for a summary of these basic scribbles.)

11-2b Later Scribble Stage: Controlled Scribbling

At some point, children find a connection between their motions and the marks on the page. This may be about six months after the child has started to

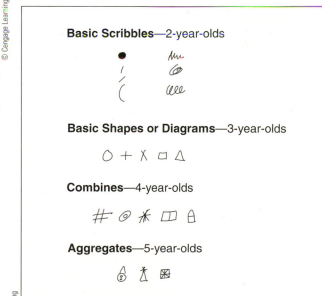

Basic Scribbles—2-year-olds

Basic Shapes or Diagrams—3-year-olds

Combines—4-year-olds

Aggregates—5-year-olds

Example of Mandala

FIGURE 11-3 Examples of Rhoda Kellogg's stages of development in preschool.

Source: All above examples based on Kellogg (1970).

Casper Holroyd

© Cengage Learning

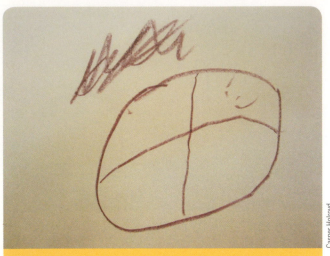

PHOTO 11-2 Example of controlled scribbling and early mandala.

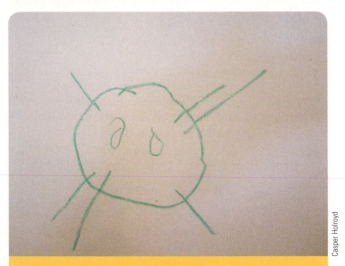

PHOTO 11-3 Example of a more developed mandala.

scribble, but the time will vary with each child. This very important step is called **controlled scribbling**. The child has now found it possible to control the marks (see Photo 11-2). Many times, an adult cannot see any real difference in these drawings. They still look like scribbles—but they are different in a very important way.

The controlled scribbler knows that she is making the marks being made on the paper. She wants to see what will happen when she tries making different kinds of marks and squiggles. Using repeated motions, the child can make distinctive diagonal, horizontal, and vertical lines as well as big and small circle shapes (see Photo 11-3). Unlike the random stage where the child is not totally aware of the marks she is making,

now she intensely watches her scribbles. The child's gradual gaining of control over scribbling motion is a vital experience for the child. She or he now is able to make the marks go in the direction desired. Most children scribble at this later stage with a great deal of enthusiasm because coordination between seeing and doing is an important achievement.

Because children enjoy this newfound power, they now may scribble in lines, zigzags, or circles. When they repeat motions, they are gaining control over certain movements. They can become very involved in this type of scribbling.

Controlled scribbling is described in Kellogg's developmental theory as placement patterns of these 20 basic scribbles. Each child has one or more favorites that he or she uses repeatedly. The difference with these placement patterns, however, is that unlike uncontrolled scribbles, they "require both seeing and the eye's guidance of the hand" (Kellogg, 1970, p. 23). At this point, the child's eyes have definitely begun to guide his or her hands, and the child places the scribbles repeatedly in patterns that are visually pleasing to him or her (see Photo 11-4).

In this later scribbling stage, repeated movements among the scribbles begin to appear. At a basic level, the child is beginning to organize his or her environment. One universal form seen most often in this stage

PHOTO 11-4 As the child develops muscle control and hand–eye coordination, she is able to make basic forms at will.

is the mandala—a variety of circular patterns. During this stage, children also make sweeping, wavy, bold, and rippling lines.

11-2c The Scribble Stage and Two-Dimensional Media

The term two-dimensional media refers to any art form that is flat. Art in two dimensions has only two sides, front and back. Examples of two-dimensional art processes are painting, drawing, printing, and scribbling.

Children just beginning to scribble need tools that are safe and easy to hold and use. For a child between the ages of 1½ and 3, large, nontoxic crayons are good tools for two-dimensional artwork. Pencils are dangerous for the young child and are also too difficult to hold and use. A good-quality, kindergarten-type crayon is the best tool. Crayon quality is determined by how much wax can be scratched off the paper—the more wax, the poorer the quality. The child will have to press so hard to get a good color that his fingers (and the resulting drawings) will become cramped. The smaller the child, the better (and bigger) the crayons should be. The crayon should be large and unwrapped so it can be used on both the sides and ends. Good-quality crayons are strong enough to hold up to rough first scribbles. They also make bright, clear colors, which are pleasant for the child to use.

Because motion is the chief enjoyment in this stage, the child needs large blank paper (at least 18" × 24"). This size allows enough room for wide arm movements and large scribbles in many directions. The paper should always be large enough to give the child a big open space for undirected, random scribbles. Paper can be in a variety of shapes, such as rectangular, triangular, circular, and oval.

If possible, a child in the scribble stage should use large white paper. Crayon scribbles show up better on white paper, so the child can see more easily the results of the scribbling. The classified section of the newspaper is also appropriate paper for beginning artists. The small print of the advertisements makes a neutral, nonintrusive background for scribbling, and this section of the paper provides a generous supply of material for young scribblers, which encourages the frequency of their scribbling.

The child needs only a few crayons at a time. Because motor control is the main focus in the early period of the scribbling stage, too many different crayons may distract the child in the scribbling process. A box of 32 crayons, for example, would become an

object of exploration itself and hence a distraction from the act of scribbling. This type of interruption breaks up arm movement as well as total physical involvement. New crayons may be added when a new drawing is started. The tools should mark clearly and easily.

▶❚❚ **TeachSource** Video

© 2015 Cengage Learning

Preschool: Family Interactions, School, and Community

1. In the early part of this video, name the developmental stage the child using crayons is in and the reason for your choice.

2. Based on your observation of the children as they make their "Me Books," what developmental level(s) do the children represent? Give specific examples in your answer.

Painting is another good two-dimensional art activity for children in the scribble stage because it offers children the most fluidity. Paintbrushes for 2- and 3-year-olds need to have 12-inch handles and ¾-inch to 1-inch bristles. Paint for 2- and 3-year-old children should be mixed with a dry soap so it is thick enough to control. The paper for painting may need to be heavier than newsprint because children will repeatedly paint the paper until it disintegrates. For these first painting activities, beginners should paint while seated at a flat table rather than while standing at an easel. It is difficult for young painters to control drips on an easel. Also, these beginning artists are likely to become distracted if they are standing at an easel and wander off. A good deal of monitoring is required with toddlers because they are tempted to taste the materials and carry them about the room.

For toddlers, the major value lies in simple experimentation with colors and textures.

11-2d Observation of the Scribble Stage

The student observer of young children (1½–3 years) should keep in mind the following points while observing scribbling. A copy of the observation sheet (Figure 11-4) may be used to record your observations.

Age. Note the age of the child. Keep in mind the average range for the scribble stage (1½–3 years). See how the child fits in the range. There may be an overlap between stages.

Motor control. Note how the child holds the crayon: with two fingers, clenched fingers, or a fist. If the child uses a two-finger grip, this is the start of good motor control. The other methods of holding the crayon show less motor control. See if the child can hold the crayon without dropping it during the entire drawing. This also shows good motor control. Note any other things that might show the child's degree of motor control.

Arm movements. In scribbling, a child may use one type of arm movement or a variety. Note if movements are wide, long, short, jabbing, or of other kinds. The type of arm movement used affects the basic forms the child will make in the future. For example, if circular scribbles are being made, later these scribbles become circles.

Types of scribbles. Note the kind of scribbles the child is making. They may be controlled or uncontrolled, circular, lines, or others mentioned earlier.

Use of paper. There are many ways of using paper for scribbling. Some are moving across the paper from left to right, moving across the paper from right to left, scribbling on only one part of the page, and moving the paper to make marks in the other direction. See if the child seems to know how to use the paper. Older scribblers often have more control over the paper.

Try the following activities, observing and noting what happens.

- Provide the child with some soft, colored chalk. See if this new tool causes any differences in the way the child scribbles.
- Change to a smaller paper. See if there are any differences in the child's arm movement, type of scribbles made, and use of paper.

CHILD	AGE	MOTOR CONTROL	ARM MOVEMENT	TYPES OF SCRIBBLES	USE OF PAPER	EARLY PERIOD	LATER PERIOD

COMMENTS:

FIGURE 11-4 Scribble stage observation form.

© Cengage Learning

● Place two extra colored crayons in the child's view. See if the child uses them. Then see if scribbles look different when the child uses many colors. Compare an all-one-color drawing with a many-color drawing.

11-3 The Basic Forms/Preschematic Stage

naeyc **DAP** Basic rectangle, square, and circle forms develop from scribbles as the child finds and recognizes simple shapes in the scribbles (see Photo 11-5). More importantly, they develop as the child finds the muscle control and hand–eye coordination (use of hand(s) and eyes at the same time) to repeat the shape.

In Kellogg's theory, basic forms are called **emergent diagram shapes.** These "diagrams are made with single lines forming crosses and outlines of circles, triangles, and other shapes" (Kellogg, 1970, p. 39).

PHOTO 11-5 Notice how this child combined basic forms in this example.

At this stage, the child's drawings look more organized. This is because the child is able to make basic forms by controlling the lines. A child in the age range of 3–4 years is usually in the basic forms stage. This stage is also referred to as the **preschematic stage.** This means that in this stage, basic forms are drawn in and of themselves and not to represent a particular object. For example, the child draws a rectangular form over and over in a variety of sizes. At this point, this rectangle is not the child's schema or idea of a house. It is simply a controlled drawing of a basic form.

During this stage, children hold their tools more like adults do and have a growing control over the materials. Children can now control their scribbles, making loops, circular shapes, and lines that are distinguishable and can be repeated at will. Children at this age value their scribbles. By age 3 or 4, children will not draw if their marker is dry. Children now ask to have their names put on their work so it can be taken home or displayed in the room.

It is important to note, again, that there may be an overlap between developmental levels in art. For example, one 3-year-old child may be drawing basic forms and an occasional scribble. Another 3-year-old child may still be totally in the scribble stage. Developmental levels are meant merely as guidelines, not as set limits on age and ability levels.

11-3a Early Basic Forms Stage: Circle and Oval

Generally, the first basic form drawn is the oval or circle. This marks the **early basic forms stage.** It develops as children recognize the simple circle in their scribbles and are able to repeat it. Both the oval and the circle develop from circular scribbles. Following the discovery of the oval or circle, the child will begin to elaborate on it by adding dots and perhaps lines.

Another early basic form in this stage is the curved line or arc. This is made with the same swinging movement of an arm used in the early scribble stage. Now, however, it is in one direction only. This kind of line gradually becomes less curved, and the horizontal and vertical lines come from it. Making an intentional arc-shaped line reflects more developed motor control.

In Kellogg's full-fledged diagram stage, children begin to draw six different diagrams: the rectangle, the oval, the triangle, the Greek cross, the diagonal cross, and the odd shape.

Casper Holroyd

Marker Maintenance

Markers are wonderful for young artists. But busy artists frequently lose caps from these tools, often resulting in dried-out markers. Replacing dried-out markers can be expensive, so here are a few hints on marker maintenance to help preserve markers as long as possible:

● Solve the lost cap/dry-out problem by setting the caps with open ends up in a margarine or whipped topping container filled with plaster of Paris. Make sure the plaster does not cover the holes in the caps. When the plaster dries, the markers can be put into the caps and will stand upright until ready for use again.

● Give new life to old, dry felt-tip markers by storing them tips down with the caps on. When the markers become dried out, remove the caps and put in a few drops of water. This usually helps "revive" them.

● Recycle dried-out markers by having children dip them in paint and use them for drawing.

● Make your own pastel markers by adding dry tempera paint (or food color) to bottles of white shoe polish that come with sponge applicator tops.

● Purchase empty plastic roller-top bottles from a school supply store. Fill them with watery tempera paint and use them as a different type of marker.

11-3b Later Basic Forms: Rectangle and Square

As muscle control of 3- to 4-year-olds continues to improve, more basic forms are made in their drawings. The rectangle and square forms are made when the child can purposefully draw separate lines of any length desired. The child joins the separate lines to form the rectangle or square. This indicates the later basic forms stage. The circle, oval, square, and rectangle are all-basic forms made by the child's control of lines.

11-3c The Basic Forms Stage and Two-Dimensional Media

Children in the basic forms stage have enough motor control and hand–eye coordination to use different tools. In addition to crayons, the child may now begin to work with tempera paint. Tempera paint is the best kind for children because it flows easily from the brush onto the page. Liquid tempera in 16-ounce squeeze bottles is a convenient way to provide paint for beginning painters. Powdered tempera is also appropriate because it can be mixed with water to the desired consistency (very thick for beginners). Be sure to mix dry tempera well out of children's reach because it contains silica, which is not safe for children to breathe.

Large lead pencils are good for children in the later period of this stage; there is less danger of injury with these older children. A variety of papers can be supplied, from newsprint to construction paper. These children should be allowed plenty of time with the basic tools of drawing, painting, modeling, cutting, and pasting and should not be rushed into other media. The basic developmental goal for this age is the control of the media and tasks of drawing, painting, or modeling. (A complete list of appropriate materials is included in Chapter 12.)

Felt-tip pens or colored markers are excellent tools for this stage. They provide clear, quick, easily made, and nice-looking marks. In the basic forms stage, when the child really enjoys seeing the marks come out as desired, these pens are best. They require little pressure to make bold marks. Felt-tip pens should be nontoxic and water soluble so that most spots can be washed out of the child's clothes. (See "Think About It . . . Marker Maintenance" for suggestions on prolonging the life of colored markers.)

The largest paper size is not as necessary in this stage as in the scribble stage. Because the child now has better motor control, it is easier to keep marks on a smaller space. Room for wide, uncontrolled movements is not as necessary. Make available paper of many sizes and shapes, different colors and textures of paper, and a variety of colored pencils and markers. Children in this stage like to make basic forms in many colors and ways as an exercise of their skill.

Student observers should realize that children of this age like to repeat forms and should not try to force them to "make something else" to fill up the paper. It is important that children practice making their own basic forms. The forms may look simple, but each drawing is a great motor achievement for them. The children may rightly be quite proud of their basic form drawings.

11-3d Observation of the Basic Forms Stage

The student observer of young children in the basic forms stage should keep in mind the following points when observing children. The points may then be recorded on a copy of the observation form, Figure 11-5. If students are observing children in both the scribbling and basic forms stages, observations of each stage may be compared to help highlight the differences in these two stages.

Age. Note the age of the child. Look back at Figure 11-2 and Figure 11-3 on p. 233 for the average age range for the basic forms stage. See how the child fits in the range. See if there is an overlap between stages.

Motor control. See how the child holds the crayon. Note if it is held very tightly or if the child can draw with sureness and ease. Also note if the child draws with a lot of arm movement or uses just the hand to draw. The child who uses more hand movement and less arm movement is showing improved motor control. In the basic forms stage, children generally use fewer unnecessary arm movements.

Types of basic forms. Write down the number and type of basic forms mentioned earlier that the child can draw. See if the shapes are well drawn or rough and unclear. Rough, less clear forms are made in the early stage. A child in the later basic forms stage draws clear, easy-to-recognize shapes.

In drawings with a variety of forms, see if one form is clearer than another. Clearer forms are the ones that the child first began to draw. The less clear forms are in the practice stage and eventually become clearer.

Use of paper. Use the same checkpoints for the use of paper that were used in the scribble stage section. In addition, see if the child fills the page with one or many basic forms. If the same shape is made over and over, it means the child is practicing a new basic form. Practice like this occurs at an early point in the stage.

CHILD	AGE	MOTOR CONTROL	ARM MOVEMENT	TYPES OF SCRIBBLES	USE OF PAPER	EARLY PERIOD	LATER PERIOD

COMMENTS:

© Cengage Learning

FIGURE 11-5 Basic forms stage observation form.

11-4 The Pictorial/Schematic Stage

naeyc **DAP** With the two earlier stages mastered, children now have the ability to draw the variety of marks that make up their first pictures. This occurs at the next developmental level in art—the **pictorial stage**. Many 4-year-olds and most 5-year-olds are generally at this level. The *schematic stage* refers to the child's ability to use his or her own special variety of marks, or *schema*. More details on schema follow later in this section.

In Kellogg's theory, children move on from the diagrams stage and enter the pictorial stage when they begin putting diagrams together to form combines or aggregates, which are basically two diagrams put together, or three or more diagrams put together. After children can put these shapes into combinations and aggregates, they are able to make drawings that begin to be a picture of someone or something in particular. In this way, these shapes allow for a natural transition from children's abstract to pictorial work.

Pictures or first drawings are different from scribbling in that they are not made for pure motor enjoyment. Instead, they are made by the child for a purpose. The basic forms perfected in the preceding stage suggest images to the child that stand for ideas in the child's own mind. A new way of drawing begins. From the basic forms the child is able to draw, only particular ones are chosen. Miscellaneous scribbling is left out. In this way, children draw their first symbols. A **symbol** is a visual representation of something important to the child; it may be a human figure, animal, tree, or similar figure. Art in which symbols are used in such a way is called **representational art**. This means there has been a change from kinesthetic, or sheerly physical, activity to representational attempts. The child realizes that there is a relationship between the objects drawn and the outside world and

that drawing and painting can be used to record ideas or express feelings.

The ability to draw symbols in representational art comes directly from the basic forms stage. The basic forms gradually lose more and more of their connection to body motion only. They are now put together to make symbols, which stand for real objects in the child's mind. In scribbling, the child was mainly involved in a physical activity, trying out the materials to see what she could do with them. Now the child is expressing in the scribble something of importance to her. The drawing may seem to be a scribble, but it is now a "man" or a "dog"—a definite symbol representing something in the child's life.

The human form is often the child's first symbol. A human figure is usually drawn with a circle for a head and two lines for legs or body. These are often called "tadpole" figures because of their large heads on a tiny body with extended arms. Other common symbols include trees, houses, flowers, and animals. The child can tell you what each symbol stands for in the drawing.

Further attempts to make symbols grow directly from the basic forms the child can make. Flowers and trees are combinations of spiral scribbles or circles with attached straight lines for stems or trunks. Houses, windows, doors, flags, and similar objects are simply made up of rectangles and straight lines.

It is a common adult practice to label these first drawings "children's art" because they contain recognizable objects. If children's drawings appear to be mere scribbles to an adult, they are not considered children's art because they don't look like "something." Yet being able to identify objects in a child's work does not make it children's art. Art is self-expression and has value in any form and at any stage.

Because art is now representational, children need tools that can be easily controlled and thus facilitate their ability to produce the desired symbols. Thinner crayons and paintbrushes and less fluid paints can now be made available so children can express their ideas and feelings with greater realism. Children over age 5 will want to be able to select representational colors, so a variety of colors of paint, crayons, and markers are necessary.

Naming and owning the art produced are also important to children in this stage. These children may ask you to record the names of their paintings or drawings as well as write stories to go with their drawings. These children recognize other children's work at this point. They will want to take their work home, as well as contribute some to display in the classroom.

Art Training, Attention, and Cognition

Researchers are finding evidence that when children find an art form that sustains their interest, the subsequent strengthening of their brains' attention networks can improve cognition more broadly (Posner & Patoine, 2009). The following specialized neural networks are involved in the aspects of attention:

- The *alerting* network, which enables the brain to achieve and maintain an alert state
- The *orienting* network, which keeps the brain attuned to external events in our environment
- The *executive attention* network, which helps us control our emotions and choose among conflicting thoughts in order to focus on goals over long periods of time

Recent research offers a possibility that focused training in any of the arts strengthens the brain's attention system, which in turn can improve cognition generally (Hyde et al., 2009).

The brain has a system of neural pathways dedicated to attention. We know that training these networks

improved general measures of intelligence. And we can be fairly sure that focusing our attention on learning and performing an art—if we practice frequently and are truly engaged—activate these same attention networks (Posner & Patoine, 2009).

The idea that training in the arts improves cognition is generally consistent with a basic function of the brain called *activity-dependent plasticity*. This function refers to the ability of the brain to change in response to what you do. Put another way, behavior shapes and sculpts the brain networks. What you do in your day-to-day life is reflected in the wiring patterns of your brain and the efficiency of your brain networks (Posner & Rothbart, 2007).

Being aware of the importance of the arts to the developing human brain gives us even more reason to be sure to provide young children every opportunity to explore their creativity in the early childhood art program. Painting, drawing, and sculpting can all help shape and sculpt children's brains and improve their attention and cognition.

11-4a Portfolios for Developmental Assessment

The pictorial stage is an excellent point at which to begin keeping a portfolio of the child's work, if you haven't started yet. Samples of the child's early, initial representational artwork will be a record of the development of the child's first symbols. As representational development proceeds, this may be forgotten without the portfolio sample. For example, when Claire first made a scribble that she called "doggy," her teacher noted it on the sample and kept it in Claire's folder. Over the year, a collection of these various samples gave quite a graphic story of Claire's progress in art.

Keeping portfolios does not mean, however, collecting and keeping all of the child's work. Items in a child's portfolio should reflect how the child is progressing in art. Each piece in the portfolio needs to be selected with this question in mind: "What does this piece tell me about this learner?" For example, selected samples of scribbles from the early and later scribble stages tell a great deal visually about how a child is progressing. In contrast, keeping all of the child's scribble work samples in the file would make it difficult to clearly see the child's development.

Digital cameras are very useful in keeping portfolios of children's artwork. See Chapter 8 for details on digital portfolios, and see Figure 11-6 for a checklist of what to include in a child's portfolio.

The most obvious advantage of a portfolio/file is the fact that it is visible evidence of the child's development in art. From the earliest selections in the portfolio to the most recent, one can see the child's progress in art.

A portfolio/file can greatly aid the teacher during parent–teacher conferences. It is a collection of work samples that indicate how a child is developing in this area. It reduces the subjectivity of discussions by helping both teacher and parent focus objectively on the portfolio. Parents may see the obvious growth and learning evidenced in the child's artwork. Another excellent advantage of the portfolio is that it encourages growth of the child's aesthetic sense of choice. By involving the child in selection of pieces for the portfolio, the child learns about the process of selection. Of course, learning to be selective is a very complex skill and will take time for the child to develop. But like any other skill, given the time,

A child's portfolio should contain pieces of work that are evidence of a child's development and progress. The following are suggested items to include in a child's portfolio.

_____ Work samples—These are examples of a child's work, such as drawings, photos of block buildings, finger paintings, etc. Collect a variety of samples for each type of art activity.

_____ Observations—These are written observations about a child. For example, notes on how the child handled the paintbrush, used scissors for the first time, or made basic forms with a crayon.

_____ Anecdotal records—These are factual, nonjudgmental observations of observed activities. These provide essential information about a child's progress and activities in the classroom and information on what occurs in the classroom's everyday environment.

_____ Interviews—These are notes on questions that teachers ask children so as to gain understanding about the child and the child's development in art and other areas of the curriculum.

_____ Developmental checklists—These are lists of developmental characteristics and traits arranged in a logical order. As teachers observe children, they can use these checklists to note the presence or absence of behaviors. These lists give both teachers and parents a good idea of where the child is developmentally.

FIGURE 11-6 Checklist: What to include in a child's portfolio.

TeachSource Digital Download Download from CourseMate.

© Cengage Learning

opportunity, and guidance to make selections of one's own work for the portfolio (or file), the child will develop his or her own personal preferences. Be sure to date, label, and write a short comment on each piece added to the portfolio. The label should describe the media/materials used, and comments should be on some significant aspect of the piece, for example, "First time Jorge named an object in a drawing. This one he called 'Daddy.'"

For all of these reasons, then, using a portfolio in the early childhood art program has definite merits. Alongside these merits are some pitfalls one needs to keep in mind. Most important, if you plan to use portfolios for developmental assessment, stick to it for the whole year. Beginning a portfolio with good intentions

and then only sporadically filling it with work reduces its importance as the year goes on—this type of portfolio is best left out of the program entirely. To be of use in developmental assessment, the portfolio needs to be as complete as possible, reflecting the process of artistic development as a whole. Many teachers find it helpful to include in their monthly planning a week set aside for portfolio selection. This way, they are sure to have it on their list of priorities. Of course, there should always be time for spontaneous inclusions whenever they occur.

11-4b Early Pictorial (First Drawings) Stage

In the **early pictorial (first drawings) stage**, a child works on making and perfecting one or many symbols (see Photo 11-6). The child practices these symbols, covering sheets of paper with many examples of the same subject. For example, a child may draw windows and doors over and over in each drawing. Also at an early point in this stage, a child's picture may be a collection of unrelated figures and objects. This type of picture is a sampling of the child's many tries at making different symbols. At this point, pictures are done very quickly.

During this early pictorial stage, the child is searching for new ideas. Symbols change constantly. A picture of a man drawn one day differs from the one drawn the day before. In this stage, often a great variety of forms represent the same object. Early first drawings are very flexible in appearance. Children are assigning meaning to the shapes they make. These shapes will stand for whatever the child wishes, regardless of whether they are accurate reproductions.

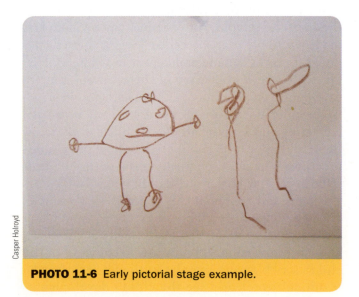

Casper Holroyd

PHOTO 11-6 Early pictorial stage example.

11-4c Later Pictorial (First Drawings) Stage: Use of Schema

In the **later pictorial (first drawings) stage**, through practice, a child draws symbols easily and more exactly. Many 4-year-olds and most 5-year-olds generally perfect to their own liking and take pride in producing a series of many symbols. A child at this point often likes to see these symbols set clearly and neatly on the page. They are now drawn one at a time with few or no other marks on the page. They are clear and well drawn (see Photo 11-7). If children can draw the letters of their name on the page as well, they may feel this is all that belongs in the picture.

For a while, children are content to make these finished yet isolated examples of their drawing skill, but it is not long before more complex drawings are made. Children 4–5 years of age are generally able to use their symbols in drawings to tell a story or describe an event. The naming of these symbols is an important step in that the artwork becomes a clear form of visual communication. It may not look any different, but the child now calls the circle a "sun" because it represents a specific object to the child.

By 5½–6 years of age, children generally are ready to make a picture of many things in their experience or imagination. Their drawings are made up of combinations of symbols they are familiar with and that have meaning to them. Children create new symbols as they have new experiences and ideas. However, children at this point can't be expected to make pictures of the unfamiliar or of things they have not personally experienced. Another common error made by well-intentioned teachers is a misunderstanding of

this stage by expecting all children 5 years old and older to be able to use symbols in their art. This is not a valid expectation because the age at which children begin to use symbols is as highly individual as the age at which they learn to walk. Children use symbols when they are ready—and no sooner. Creative expression is the goal at this and all ages; a child's art does not have to include specific symbols, such as a house, tree, or animals, unless the child chooses to include them.

Children need to repeat art processes over a period of time in order to become competent with and feel secure about using materials to express ideas and feelings. At 4 and 5 years old, children who have had many opportunities to paint will frequently move easily from manipulative scribbling to expressive symbolic or representational art.

In the later pictorial stage, each child has a special way of drawing the human form, houses, and other symbols. This individual way of drawing is called a **schema**. A schema, or individual pattern, often can be seen in drawings by the age of 6. A schema comes after much practice with drawing symbols. As the child becomes more skilled in drawing, his or her drawing begins to show the child's direct experiences coming from his or her mind onto the paper. Once the child has a schema, symbols become special marks. A schema is special for each child, just as a signature is unique for each adult. One child may tell another, "That's Chad's drawing; I recognize his trees," or "I know it's Zarina's painting because she paints her skies that way." These children have developed a schema that is clearly their own, easily recognizable by others.

Importance of schemas. The schema drawn by a child represents something important to the child, something that is part of the child's environment and experience. A schema is much more than an individual way of drawing, it is a mental structure that the child uses to organize and process his or her knowledge of the world. These schemas about the child's world, other people, food, and nature are created based on the child's experiences. Thus, a child's schema is highly individual and reflects things of emotional importance.

Children draw a schema in a picture not according to actual size but in a size that shows the emotional importance of the object to them. For example, people and things important to a child might be drawn large and with many details. If a tree is drawn, the limbs may

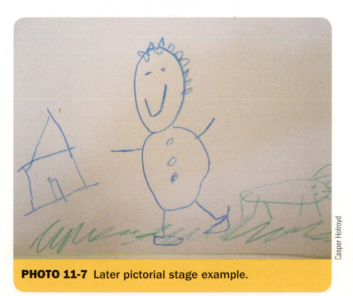

PHOTO 11-7 Later pictorial stage example.

Casper Holroyd

THIS ONE'S FOR YOU!

Art DOs with Young Children

Knowing the stages of art development in young children is just a starting point. It is crucial that you know how to talk with young artists about their work. Here are some dos to keep in mind when you are working with young artists.

● DO accept a child's work as he or she creates it. Avoid correcting or adding to a child's work. Understand that when children draw huge hands, construct unreal proportions, or leave out items that you might consider essential, they are concentrating on what is important to them at the moment. Accept their work as they create it. Observing what is emphasized or omitted will give you an important insight into a child's development.

● DO understand that children's coordination and muscle development will grow as a result of creating their own artwork. Avoid using coloring books. Don't be fooled into believing that filling in pictures in a coloring book will improve a child's coordination.

● DO offer art materials every day in the week. Children need an ongoing experience with materials so that new growth and discoveries can be made.

● DO remember that children need continuity. They will not be bored if you offer them opportunities to paint, draw, build, paste, and model every day. Personal growth takes place through repeated experiences with open-ended materials.

● DO avoid offering coloring books or precut patterns to the children. These are just another way of saying, "You are not capable; you do not have the ability."

● DO offer children open-ended materials (paint, clay, crayons, wood, blocks) so that they may make discoveries for themselves.

● DO be mindful of the words you use with young children when discussing their art work. Try to avoid asking a child, "What is that?" It's not even appropriate to try to guess. Casually saying that a painting or drawing is "great" or "terrific" does not make a child aware of his or her individuality. Avoid making models for the children, even when they protest that they "can't do it." They cannot possibly duplicate what an adult has created. Your model is a way of saying, "I know you are not able to do a good job."

● DO tell children why you like their work. Comment on the red line near the blue circles or mention the two blue dots. Commenting on what you see helps children become more consciously aware of their work. Help children think about what they want to paint, draw, build, or model; for example, ask, "How does a cow eat?" or "How many legs does the animal have?"

● DO see each child's work as individual and avoid comparing children's work or showing preferences. Be sure to pay attention when children are commenting about each other's work. For example, hearing something like "Oh, that's just scribble scrabble" can be responded to by saying, "That's Dustin's design" or "That's Shania's idea."

● DO help the children feel confident about their work and take pride in it. Stress the individuality of each creation. Respect the many different ideas children have even though they are using the same materials.

● DO be sure to talk with parents about their child's art as often as possible, in an everyday, nontechnical way. Also be sure to express to parents the value of their child's art at *all* stages. Parents don't always know the importance of a scribbled drawing to the child's development, or the great stride controlled scribbles represent in the child's overall art development.

---

be made larger because the tree is used for climbing. If it is an apple tree, the apples may be drawn very large.

Children express other responses to their environment in their drawings. A painting showing a child walking on wet grass may show the feet and toes large in size. This may show how the child felt after a walk in the early morning.

11-4d Importance of First Drawings

At about the same time children develop their own schemas, they begin to name their drawings. Naming a drawing is an important step for children. It is a sign that their thinking has changed; they are connecting their drawings with the world around them. This is the beginning of a new form of communication—communication with the environment through art.

Soon a 5-year-old may think: "My daddy is a big man; he has a head and two big legs." She then draws a head and two big legs and names her drawing "Daddy." Through drawing, the child is making a clear relationship between her father and her drawing. The symbol of a man now becomes "Daddy." Of course, a child will not verbally name all objects every time a picture is made.

In their use of schemas, children express their own personalities. They express not only what is important to them during the process of creating but also how aware they have become in thinking, feeling, and seeing. From early drawings to the most complex, they give expression to their life experiences.

11-4e Observation of the Pictorial (First Drawings) Stage

Keep in mind the following points when observing children in the pictorial stage. You may want to use a copy of the observation form (see Figure 11-7) to record your observations.

Age. Write down the age of the child. Check to see what the average age range is for the pictorial stage. See how the child fits in this range. There may be an overlap between stages. For example, you may see figures as well as simple, basic forms in one drawing.

Combination of basic forms. See how the child puts basic forms together to make figures. Very simple combinations mean the child is at an early point in the stage. An example would be a flower made up of a single circle and one-line stem. On the other hand, a flower of many circles with oval petals and a stem of many leaves is a more complex combination of basic forms and would show that the child is at a later point in the stage.

Size of figures. A child in both the early and later periods of this stage may use size to show importance. The large figure represents something important to the child. Note, for example, children may draw themselves or other figures such as their mother in a very large size. Extra-large heads on a small body are found mainly in the early period of this stage.

Notice the relative size of certain things in the picture. For a child who likes animals, a dog may be far larger than the human form. Here, too, size indicates that the object is important to the child.

Number of figures. Mark down the number of figures in each drawing. A drawing with few figures or a single figure means that the child is at an early point in the stage. The child making this type of drawing is working on developing a symbol.

At a later point, the child can draw many types of symbols and figures in one drawing. Also, drawings at a later point look as if they tell a story with the figures.

Details. Note the type and number of details a child uses in a drawing. They indicate at what point the child is in the stage.

Figures with only a few details are made in the early pictorial stage. For example, a circular head, round body, and stick arms and legs make up an early human form. A picture of a man with details such as full arms, hands, and fingers is a sign that the child is at a later point in the pictorial stage.

CHILD	AGE	COMBINATION OF BASIC FORMS	SIZE OF FIGURES	NUMBER OF FIGURES	DETAILS	USE OF FIGURES	NAMING DRAWINGS	EARLY PERIOD	LATER PERIOD

COMMENTS:

FIGURE 11-7 Pictorial (first drawings) stage observation form.

See if certain objects are drawn in greater detail than others. A child's experience with certain objects can cause this increase in detail. As an example, tree limbs may be unusually large in the drawings of children who love to climb trees. Special sensory experiences can also cause increase in detail. For example, a child may draw large raindrops in a drawing after a walk in the rain.

Use of figures. Note how the child uses figures. See if the paper is filled with many unrelated figures that simply fill space and look like practice forms. Lack of connection between figures can mean the child is at an early point in the stage; the child is practicing a symbol and is not yet ready to tell a story with it.

If there seems to be a connection between figures, the child is at a later point. This type of drawing is a narrative drawing, that is, one that tells a story. It is a visual form of communication for the child.

Naming drawings. Be sure to listen to the child who wants to talk about a drawing. Note if the child names certain objects or figures, or refers to the entire drawing, but never force the child to tell you "what it is." Naming must come only through the child's own idea. It is an important step in the child's ability to communicate. Naming is only worthwhile if the child sees meaning in the work and takes the initiative in naming it.

Casper Holroyd

PHOTO 11-8 Children in the gang stage are no longer content with symbolizing their environment.

Children of this age are no longer content with symbolizing their environment (see Photo 11-8). Their searching minds tells them that there is something they must know about the structure of things in order for them to be "right" in their visual statement. This is the first time that children become aware of a lack of ability to show objects the way they appear in the surrounding environment.

At this point, the child becomes more aware of how things look in her drawings. She looks at her own drawing with a critical eye and raises questions. "What is wrong with the arms? They are too short and don't seem to bend right." "Why doesn't the figure really look like it's running?" "The people are too big for the house. What can I do about it?" This awareness is often expressed with more detail in the child's schema. Drawings are still far from naturalistic. Children at this age discover space in their drawings, and it is often depicted with overlapping objects in the drawings. Children of this age also begin to draw the horizon line to separate land from sky.

Because children of this age are becoming more social minded, they are beginning to compare their work with other children's. Their growing self-awareness is to the point of being extremely self-critical, often becoming critical of their own work, wanting their images to be very realistic. Children at this point often become frustrated if realism can't be achieved. The "I-can't-draw" syndrome typically starts to emerge at this stage.

Because of their awareness of lack of ability, drawing often appears less spontaneous than in previous stages (less vital and lively).

Did You Get It?

A child draws a picture of her family. The picture is composed of four figures, and each figure is comprised of a circle atop a rectangle, with stick arms and legs protruding at the sides and bottoms. Her drawing falls into the category of

  a. kinesthetic art.
  b. representational art.
  c. simple art.
  d. abstract art.

Take the full quiz on CourseMate.

11-5 The Gang Stage

naeyc DAP Children ages 9–12 fall into the **gang stage** of art development, according to Viktor Lowenfeld (1987). The title of this stage reflects the fact that children of this age are more independent of adults and more anxious to conform to their peers.

Teachers of children in this stage need to encourage the child's self-accepting attitude. The teacher must be ready with specific and direct answers to the child's questions about his work. Vague answers will not satisfy a child at this stage, but will turn the child off and eventually smother his or her desire for or interest in this valuable process of personal expression. Discuss proportions of the figure. Have a child pose, walk, jump, or move his or her arms. Take the class outside to see and to sketch a tree, a house, or animals—to broaden concepts of structure, form, color, relationships, texture, movement, and action. Have children bring natural and man-made objects into the classroom for study. Show good examples of art that will assist the child in his or her feeling for picture organization, balance, and unity (see Photo 11-9). Use the bulletin boards and other visual aids as tools for clarifying ideas and building design concepts.

While the continuous use of the crayon in the same way is satisfying in the earlier stages, it can eventually become a boring tool for the child at this stage. Encourage the child to explore new possibilities with the crayon. Introduce new techniques. Provide opportunities for the child to experiment so that he or she may discover the various effects that can be achieved with crayons when combined with different materials

PHOTO 11-10 Art experiences for children in grades 1–5 need to focus on prior creative experiences and build on these.

and used with other tools. (See Chapter 13 for these activities.)

Help children realize that they can still express themselves by exploring new uses for familiar media. For example, printing using brayers (rollers) and wood blocks is one way to encourage exploration at this stage. Group projects such as murals are also appropriate at this age because they allow children to "pool" their talents. In such a project, each child can contribute at his or her own level.

11-5a Other Stages of Art Development—Grades 1–5

Art experiences for children in grades 1 through 5 should focus on prior creative experiences and build on these (see Photo 11-10). The stages of artistic growth outlined here focus on skills portraying space, proportions, and movement or action. Each stage is typical of many children at a particular grade level; however, it is not unusual to find a range of developmental levels within a class or within the work of single students during a year. Similar variations can be expected in students' ability to respond thoughtfully to artwork. At each stage of development, some students will have greater interest and skill in responding to art than in creating art (or the reverse).

Stage 1 (usually Grades K–2). Children begin to create visual symbols to represent figures such as people, houses, and trees. The figures often seem to "float" in

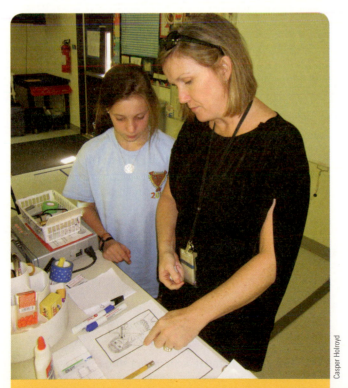

PHOTO 11-9 Teachers can help older children in the gang stage plan their art projects.

space. Proportions are related to the importance of a feature in the child's experience. Movement is often suggested by scribble-like lines. Three-dimensional artwork reflects the level of prior instruction and practice in using media and the physical coordination students have developed.

Stage 2 (usually Grades 1–3). In picture-making, lines or borders are often used to represent the ground below and sky above. Figures may be placed along a line or at the lower edge of the paper. Proportions are shown through relative size—a house is larger than a person. Action is implied by the general position of lines and shapes, rather than subtle shifts in direction. Children who receive instruction will show general improvement in using three-dimensional media and applying design concepts as they work.

Stage 3 (usually Grades 3–6). Students try out new ways to portray space in the pictures they draw and paint. These explorations often reflect remembered functional or logical relationships more than visual recall or observation. General proportions improve, as well as the use of diagonals to suggest action. Many students develop a strong affinity for three-dimensional work and are willing to try out new media and techniques that require several steps.

Stage 4 (usually Grades 4–6). In picture-making, students search for ways to portray recalled or observed space. Some students begin to use perspective to imply near and distant objects. Movement is suggested through more subtle angles and curves. Individual styles and preferences for two- or three-dimensional work become more evident, along with increased skill in applying design concepts to create expressive work.

Did You Get It?

To reengage her students in the artistic process, an art teacher offers her students printing wood blocks and stencils to use in addition to the printing tools they already have. She is probably working with students at the _____ stage.

  a. gang
  b. pictorial
  c. representational
  d. early-scribble

Take the full quiz on CourseMate.

Summary

11-1 Define the concept of developmental levels/stages of art and their importance in early childhood education.

Just as young children experience various stages of physical development, they also develop art abilities in a gradual process, going through specific stages. These stages are called developmental levels. A developmental level is a guide to what a child can do in art at different ages, but it is not a strict guideline. Some children may be ahead of or behind the developmental level for their age. Developmental levels tell the teacher what came before and what is to come in the artwork of the young child.

11-2 Describe the scribble stage, including appropriate materials for use in this stage.

The scribble stage occurs in children of about 1½–3 years of age. It covers the time from the child's first marks to more controlled scribbles. At this stage, the child enjoys the pure motion involved in scribbling.

  Wide, good-quality crayons are the best tools for the scribble stage. Large paper should be given to the child to allow room for wide arm movements. Age, motor control, use of paper, and type of scribbles should be noted in scribble stage observations.

11-3 Explain the basic forms (preschematic) stage, including appropriate materials for use in this stage.

The basic forms stage covers approximately ages 3 to 4 years. The child develops more muscle control and hand–eye coordination through scribbling. Basic forms come when children can see simple forms in their scribbles and are able to repeat them. The oval or circle is usually the first basic form, followed by the rectangle or square. Children now enjoy seeing forms emerge as a result of their own will. A wider variety of art materials can be used with children in the basic forms stage. In addition to crayons, the child may now begin to work with tempera paint, felt-tip pens, and colored markers. Large lead pencils are good for children in the later period of this stage.

11-4 Discuss the pictorial (schematic) stage, including appropriate materials for use in this stage.

The pictorial stage generally occurs from ages 4 to 6. Basic forms made in the prior stage are put together to make up symbols. The human form, birds, flowers, and animals are examples of some symbols. Naming drawings is an important part of first drawings. Children can now communicate outside themselves and with their world. A child's artwork is very individual and expresses the child's own personality.

In the pictorial stage, children make the most varied and complex drawings. Points to note in observing this stage are the age of the child and figures and details in the drawings. Thinner crayons and paintbrushes and less fluid paints are appropriate for this stage. A variety of colors of paint, crayons, and markers are necessary so children can express their ideas and feelings with greater realism.

11-5 Discuss the gang stage, including appropriate materials for use in this stage.

This term, developed by Viktor Lowenfeld (1987), refers to the fact that peer groups assume more importance to the child than ever before. Children aged 9–12 fall into the gang stage. The child becomes more aware of how things look in his drawings. Children at this age discover space in their drawings, which is often depicted with overlapping objects. Children of this age also begin to draw the horizon line to separate land from sky. Encourage children in this stage to explore new possibilities and techniques for crayons. Allow the child to experiment with different materials and new tools.

Key Terms

basic forms stage 232
controlled scribbling 234
developmental levels 231
disordered or random scribbling 232
early basic forms stage 237
early pictorial (first drawings) stage 242
emergent diagram shapes 237

gang stage 246
later basic forms stage 238
later pictorial (first drawings) stage 243
mandala 235
pictorial stage 240
portfolio 241

preschematic stage 237
representational art 240
schema 243
scribble stage 232
symbol 240
two-dimensional media 235

Learning Activities

Selecting Appropriate Materials for Art Experiences

A. Visit a preschool classroom. Examine the tools that are available for children to work with—paintbrushes, scissors, and crayons, to mention a few. Inventory these in terms of how many are available, the condition of the various tools, and their suitability in terms of design and quality for young children.

B. Using toy and equipment catalogs that can be cut up, compile a catalog that pictures appropriate early childhood art materials in terms of the many uses covered in this chapter. Select and annotate each entry in each category in terms of age level, appropriateness, appearance, versatility, durability, and safety.

C. Consider the following quote:

When my daughter was about seven years old, she asked me one day what I did at work. I told her I worked at the college—that my job was to teach people how to draw. She stared back at me, incredulous, and said, "You mean they forget?" (Howard Ikemoto)

How would you answer this child? Why do you think we "forget" how to draw? What can you as a teacher do to help children continue drawing?

Scribble Stage Experiences for the Student

A. Exercise 1. Goal: To experience some of the lack of motor control of a young child in the scribble stage.
  1. Use the hand opposite your writing hand to "draw" a crayon picture.

2. Discuss the following with your classmates:
  - The clumsy feeling of the crayon in your hand
  - Your lack of control over your finger and hand movements
  - Your inability to draw exactly what you desired
  - Your difficulty in controlling the crayon, the paper, and your hand movements all at once

3. Try painting on your knees at an easel. Discuss how it felt and how it may have affected your painting. After this experience, what would you change about your approach to easels and painting for young children?

B. Exercise 2. Goal: To experience the pure motor pleasure of scribbling.
  1. Close both of your eyes and do a crayon scribbling.
  2. To experience feelings similar to the young child's, consider and discuss the following with your classmates:

  - Your difficulty in overcoming your adult need for seeing as well as doing
  - How it feels to move your hand and fingers for movement's sake alone
  - What forms you see in your scribbles
  - Your feelings about how your drawing looks

Recognizing and Evaluating the Three Art Stages

Obtain samples of drawings from children 1½ to 5 years of age. Separate the samples into three groups, one for each stage. Give reasons for the stage selected for each sample, especially for the samples that are not clearly defined.

A. Note and explain the differences in scribble stage examples:
   1. Early or later scribbling period
   2. Type of scribbles (circular, jagged, etc.)
   3. Control of crayon

B. Note and explain the differences in basic forms examples:
   1. Type of basic forms used
   2. How clear and exact the forms are
   3. Child's control of the crayon
   4. Early or later basic forms period

C. Note and explain the differences in pictorial examples:
   1. Early or later period
   2. What basic forms are combined into symbols
   3. Observable symbols

D. Using the same drawings, see if you can determine why some people believe children draw what they feel, know, and see.

E. Make a list of children's books that feature outstanding illustrations that could be used to introduce children to the concept of the artist as well as to different techniques and a wide variety of art materials.

F. Work with a small group of children (or even one child) to try to motivate art with a firsthand experience, such as touching a tree, petting a kitten, or observing a moth. Then ask the children to draw a picture. Identify how this experience influenced the drawings.

G. Obtain samples of drawings from children in grades 1 through 5. Separate them by grade level. Using the stages presented in this chapter, discuss how each sample fits (or doesn't fit) the general characteristics of that grade level/stage.

H. Collect samples of drawings from one grade level only (grades 1 through 5). Sort them according to how they represent the grade level stage. For example, sort them out by grouping the samples most near the characteristics of the grade level stage down through those with the least characteristics of the grade level stage. Discuss the ranges of abilities represented in these samples. Share your ideas about how you would work with each of the children whose samples you have in your collection.

I. Observe a child who is making his or her first representational symbols. Keep a verbatim record of his or her comments for several different 15-minute periods. What relationship is there between the child's verbal and graphic expression?

J. From a collection of paintings by 5-year-olds, list the objects that are painted with a visually established color–object relationship. List those objects that are painted with no visually established color–object relationship. What might cause some of these color choices?

K. Collect drawings of a human figure done by a second-grade class. Find how many different symbols are used for nose, mouth, body, arms, and so forth. What percentage of these children is using geometric shapes for their expression? Compare with drawings done by third graders to see if the percentages change.

L. Keep a list of the different reasons for exaggerations, omissions, or neglect of parts as shown in drawings. Illustrate each from examples of children's work.

M. Plan an art lesson that includes drawing people. Carry it out with kindergarten, second-grade, and fourth-grade children. Use the same art materials and paper size for all classes. Compare the finished products and note the differences in developmental levels.

Activities for Children

A. Display prints of famous artwork. Examples: Mondrian's *Composition with Red, Blue, and Yellow,* Pollock's *Detail of One (#31, 1950),* and Van Gogh's *Cypress Trees.* See if these examples affect the children's choice of colors, type of figures made, and amount of detail in their pictures.

B. Play music during part of the art period. Compare the drawings made with music to those done without music.

Some Variations on Easel Painting

- Use a number of shades of one color.
- Use colored paper—colored newsprint comes in pastel shades, or the backs of faded construction paper can be used.
- Use the same color of paint with same color paper.
- Use black and white paints.
- Use various sizes of brushes, or both flat and floppy ones, with the same colors of paint.
- Paint objects the children have made in carpentry, or paint dried clay objects.
- Paint large refrigerator-type boxes.
- Work on a long piece of paper to produce murals.
- Paint the fence with water and large brushes.
- Draw firmly on paper with crayons, and paint over it to produce "crayon resist" art.
- Use all pastel colors. Start with white and mix in color a bit at a time.
- Set up a table with many colors of paint, and encourage children to select the colors they prefer.

Cracked Paint and Crayon Drawings

Have children draw with crayons an image or design on a piece of paper. Crumple up the picture, but don't tear it. Have them smooth out the drawings and brush over them with watery tempera paint. The paint will go into all the little cracks in the paper. After it dries, have children brush a coat of thinned white glue onto the drawing. This gives it a shiny effect.

Painting with Soft Objects

Have children dip a cotton ball in a shallow dish of wet paint and then smear it or squish it on paper or another surface. Also have them try dipping a cotton ball into dry powdered paint and rubbing it across dry paper. This creates an interesting soft effect.

Cornmeal Paintings

Mix a variety of colors of dry tempera paint with cornmeal and place the mixture in shakers. The children take a craft stick and dip it into a bowl of glue, then drop the glue onto a piece of heavy poster board or construction paper, creating lines, circles, and different designs. The child then shakes color on the glue with the shakers. When finished, spray with hairspray (in a well-ventilated area) to preserve the painting.

Surprising Designs

Young children love discovering the final product of crepe paper art. Cut several different shapes and sizes of crepe paper in a variety of colors. The children lay the crepe paper on heavy white poster board or construction paper and paint vinegar over the paper with a paintbrush. Set aside to dry. When the picture is dry, brush the paper away, and a beautiful design will be underneath.

Cotton Swab Painting

Have children dip cotton swabs into paint and use them as brushes.

Button Printing

Glue buttons onto small wooden dowels for children to use in printing. Vary the sizes, shapes, and designs of buttons.

Sponge Painting

Cut sponges into different shapes. Have children dip each shape in paint and then dab, press, or rub it on paper.

Paper Towel Painting

Have children wad a paper towel into a ball, dip it in paint, and dab, press, or rub it on paper.

Crayon Surfaces

Try a variety of surfaces for crayon drawings. Children may enjoy drawing with crayons on these surfaces for variety:

fabric	sticks and stones
egg cartons	spools and clothespins
paper towel rolls	cardboard
sandpaper	Styrofoam trays
wood scraps	

Finger Painting with Ice Cubes

For this variation of finger painting, use regular finger paint and glossy paper, but do not wet the paper as you normally would to prepare for finger painting. Give each child an ice cube with which to spread and dilute the paint while making designs on the paper.

Printing

A. Toy Prints

Have children dip the wheels of an old toy car, truck, or other toy in paint and then make tracks on paper.

B. Plastic Alphabet Letters and Numbers

Have children dip plastic alphabet letters and numbers in paint and print them on paper.

C. Paper Cup Printing

Have children dip the rim of a paper cup into paint and then press the rim on a piece of paper to make a design.

D. Comb Printing

Have children dip the teeth of a comb into paint and print with it by drawing it along a sheet of paper.

E. Printing with Clay

Have children pound clay into small, flat cakes about an inch thick. Then they may want to carve a design on the flat surface with a pencil or popsicle stick. If desired, the design is either brushed with paint or dipped in paint and pressed onto paper to print the design.

Fabric Painting

Wrap small pieces of burlap, nylon netting, or other textured fabrics (2½" to 3" square) over a sponge that has been attached to a clothespin or secured to a dowel with a piece of string or elastic. Have children dip the fabric into paint and press onto a surface.

Pinecone Printing

Roll whole or pieces of pinecones in paint. Children can dip the large ones with flat bottoms into paint and print images and designs.

Combination Painting

Thicken tempera paint with liquid starch. Divide the paint into individual portions. Have children use this paint in their paintings. While the paint is still wet, children can sprinkle the painting with any of the following for attractive combination paintings: salt, coffee grounds, eggshells, glitter, tiny Styrofoam balls, seeds, sequins, or tiny beads. The media dry in the paint for interesting effects.

Ideas to Encourage Drawing

Try some of the following ideas to encourage children in kindergarten to grade 3 to use their imagination in expressing their observations through drawing.

- Draw a picture of something that can't be seen.
- Draw as many animals as you can on one page.
- Draw a map for a brain surgeon or for a heart surgeon.
- Design a special machine or device to help the President.
- Draw a picture showing how you would improve human beings.
- Draw a picture of an angry sea or a noisy city.
- Draw a picture that shows how you would make your school a better place.
- Draw a picture that shows how you would weigh an elephant.

- Design an underground city or an underwater city.
- Design a dog-exercising machine.

Drawing for Break Time

When you have several minutes to pass, encourage children to draw some of the following.

- Their shoe
- Their lunch
- The teacher

- A friend
- Their hand holding something
- A small object big
- A car
- A dream
- A nightmare
- A leaf
- Themselves

Activities for Older Children (Grades 4–5)

Scribble Art

Have each child make a scribble line on a piece of paper. The child then passes the paper to another child on the left. The child receiving the scribble is challenged to turn the scribble into an image or a design. Challenge the children to be as creative as they can be in transforming the scribbles.

Variation on a Scribble

Give each student a 6- to 8-inch-long piece of string or yarn, glue, and a piece of paper. Students glue the string or yarn into a scribble-type shape. Students pass their paper to the person sitting to their left.

Students take this piece of paper and imagine what the string brings to mind. Students use markers or crayons to create something original from the string. Have students discuss what they saw and why it became what it did.

Direction Drawing

The purpose of this activity is to help children see how, following just one set of directions, everyone will come up with his or her own unique works of abstract art. There are two basic steps in this activity: (1) teacher calls out directions for the children, and (2) children draw what they hear.

Here are some ideas on directions to call out for this activity. Of course, you can make up your own.

- Draw five circles—any size—anywhere on your paper.
- Draw four straight lines from one edge of your paper to the other.
- Draw two more straight lines from one edge of your paper to the other, but this time, make the lines cross over the lines you have already drawn.
- Draw two curved lines beginning at the edge of the paper and ending up somewhere in the middle of the paper.
- Fill in three of the five circles.
- Fill in four areas of your paper however you would like.

When the drawings are complete, have students sign their work. Display the work in the classroom. Discuss how the drawings look the same. Discuss how they are different.

Come up with more directions, and try the activity again. You will be amazed at the unique qualities of all of the drawings.

Line Shape and Space: Maps from the Air

Discuss students' experiences in seeing actual or televised views of the Earth from high in the sky. Have students describe any differences between extremely high views (many weather reports have satellite views) and views closer to the ground (hot air balloon or low-flying aircraft).

You may want to explain that some artists are fascinated with map-like views of the Earth. They have created original artwork to suggest the special arrangements of lines and shapes that people cannot see from the ground. Good examples of artwork to use for this are Clause Herbert Breeze's *Canadian Atlas: Position of London,* Judith Wittlin's *Cincinnati,* or *Late Evening Traffic* by Yvonne Jacquette.

If you can't obtain artwork prints, have a city map available to show the grid-like structures common to many cities and rural areas where the land is flat. From the air and on maps, you can see graceful curves made by freeways. Point out the differences between an actual map and the paintings. (A map is more complex and has labels.)

Discuss the similarities and differences between the simple map and a painting. Guide students to see how the organic lines and shapes—those with complex, irregular curves—are related to natural forms such as the rivers, borders of an island, and surrounding land. Have students identify geometric lines and shapes that suggest the human-made environment (grid lines, long lines that might be highways) in the maps.

Bring in old maps that can be cut apart and used for artwork. Have students work in small groups to identify sections of the maps where interesting organic or geometric lines and shapes occur. Ask students to offer explanations for these designs in relation to concepts from this lesson. Then have students change the map into an abstract design by adding crayon or oil pastels or by cutting along lines and creating new shapes. Compare and contrast the results.

Skeletons

Artists learn to see and sketch things in two ways. One way is to look for geometric shapes. The other is to look for lines that show the skeleton or hidden structure of an object. Bare trees in winter are perfect to study as skeletons for shape and drawing activities.

Take a few trips outside with sketchbooks and observe the barren trees for shapes and designs. Remind children to look at them as if they were skeletons. This shape is hidden when the leaves are on the tree. Help students find geometric shapes in these skeletons. Use words such as *circle, oval,* and *ellipse* to describe shapes of trees. Encourage children to sketch what they see. Discuss any geometric shapes they see in terms of how the shapes all combine into one design—the tree itself.

Light Sources

Set up an environment with a light source and several geometric forms. Have students develop some experiments that will allow them to move the light source or the forms a measured distance from each other. Have them observe and draw the changes in the length and the shapes of the shadows cast when they move the light source or the objects.

Awareness in Nature

Ask students to look for examples of unusual shapes and colors in the environment (sunsets, changing colors and shapes of clouds, puddles of water with reflections). Have students use the wet-into-wet technique (painting on a wet piece of paper) to create paintings of the sky with soft, fuzzy clouds of different shapes. Note possibilities for pictures of stormy skies, sunsets, and so on.

Integrated Art Activity: Science/Independent Research

Have students look through science books for illustrations of linear structures (snowflakes, bones, blood circulation, plants, geological formations, and the like). Have them select a small section of one of the illustrations and draw a similar structure on a large sheet of paper. After they have completed the drawing, have them use dark colors of crayons or oil pastels to increase the width of lines, making an abstract design. Shapes between the lines might be colored as well. Display the work and discuss relationships between the "artistic structure" and the structure shown in the scientific illustration.

Integrated Art Activity: Language Arts/Aesthetic Awareness

Explore the connotations of phrases such as "the blues," "I'm feeling blue," "green with envy," and the like. Ask students to give additional examples of the use of color-related words to describe moods or feelings. Write the phrases on the chalkboard, in two columns, so students can compare and contrast phrases for warm colors and cool colors. Have the students select one of these phrases and create an artwork that uses the phrases as a title and is dominated by variations on the color in the title.

Integrated Art Activity: Language Arts/Art Criticism

Ask students to speculate on reasons why many artists like to create paintings that portray flowers in vases. There are many reasons. Flowers in general are symbols of a cycle of life. Cut flowers are often symbolically related to the concept of enjoying moments of beauty. The colors, lines, textures, and other qualities provide a challenge for artists to interpret. The paintings are also enjoyed by many people, especially in homes where the image of a vase of flowers can add a feeling of warmth or happiness. You might want to display prints of flower paintings, such as Van Gogh's *Sunflowers* or any of Georgia O'Keeffe's flower paintings during this discussion. Provide students an opportunity to create their own flower paintings.

Aesthetic Awareness

Have students cut out some black-and-white photographs from old magazines or newspapers. Provide them with viewfinders. (See the telescope activity in Chapter 10.) Have them place the viewfinder over the photograph and look for the darkest area of the photograph. Show them how to trace around the edges of the hole of the viewfinder to mark the place on the photograph, then cut out and save the piece. Have them continue to identify and cut out four or five other pieces that differ from each other in value. Have students arrange the pieces in a light to dark sequence. Ask pairs of students to check each other's arrangements.

References

Harris, M. E. (2009). Implementing portfolio assessment. *Young Children, 64*(3), 82–85.

Read, H. (1966). *Education through art*. New York, NY: Pantheon Books.

Hyde, K. L, Lerch, J., Norton, A., Foregeard, M., Winner, E., Evans, A. C., & Schlaug, G. (2009). Musical training shapes structural brain development. *Journal of Neuroscience, 29*(2), 3019–3025.

Kellogg, R. (1970). *Analyzing children's art*. Palo Alto, CA: National Press Books.

Kellogg, R., & O'Dell, S. (1967). *The psychology of children's art*. New York, NY: CRM, Inc.

Lowenfeld, V. (1975). *Creative and mental growth of the child* (6th ed.). New York, NY: Macmillan.

Lowenfeld, V., & Brittain, W. (1987). *Creative and mental growth of the child* (8th ed.). New York, NY: Macmillan.

Posner, M. I., & Patione, B. (2009). How arts training improves attention and cognition. The Dana Foundation. Retrieved from http://www.dana.org/news/cerebrum/detail.aspx?id-2320.

Posner, M. I., & Rothbart, M. K. (2007). Research on attention networks as a model for the integration of psychological science. *Annual Review of Psychology, 58*(2), 1–23.

 Visit CourseMate for this textbook to access the eBook, Did You Get It? quizzes, Digital Downloads, TeachSource Videos, flashcards, and more. Go to CengageBrain.com to log in, register, or purchase access.

PART 4

The Early Childhood Art Program

Part 4 covers early childhood program basics such as goals, setting up, materials, and strategies. Also included are chapters on two- and three-dimensional artwork. In these chapters, you will find information on materials, setting up by age group and specific two- and three-dimensional activities.

REFLECTIVE QUESTIONS

After studying this section, you should be able to answer the following questions.

1. How do my classroom art activities reflect the emphasis of process over product?

2. When I set up art activities for young children, what activities and materials do I plan to use for each different age and developmental level present in the group?

3. How do I avoid falling into a routine when planning, setting up, and using art activities with young children?

4. Am I keeping the early childhood program basic goals in mind as I plan lessons and activities?

5. Am I planning developmentally appropriate two- and three-dimensional art activities for all of the children in my group?

6. How are children using the two- and three-dimensional materials I have provided for them? Do they appear motivated and involved in exploring them?

7. How can I improve the appeal as well as range of two- and three-dimensional activities I currently use with young children?

8. What skills do the young children in my group already possess with regard to two- and three-dimensional media? Have I planned lessons and activities to match these skills?

9. What instructional strategies are best for young children's learning and enjoyment with two- and three-dimensional media?

10. How will I modify my lessons and activities as children become more proficient in their use of art materials?

11. Have I considered children with special needs in my lesson planning?

Program Basics: Goals, Setting Up, Materials, and Strategies

Art experiences are an essential part of the early childhood curriculum. Yet creative experiences do not just happen. They are the result of careful planning. This chapter covers three major areas of concern in planning for children's creative art experiences: (1) program goals, (2) setting up for art activities, and (3) using basic art materials and equipment.

Learning Objectives

After studying this chapter, you should be able to:

12-1 Discuss goals for the early childhood art program.

12-2 Describe the basic setup for the early childhood art program.

12-3 Discuss how to plan art activities for toddlers.

12-4 Discuss how to plan art activities for young preschoolers.

12-5 Discuss how to plan art activities for older preschoolers and kindergarteners.

12-6 Explain how to adapt art activities for children with special needs.

12-7 List some basic materials and equipment and their use in the early childhood art program.

NAEYC Program Standards 1c   Using developmental knowledge to create healthy, supportive, and challenging learning environments.

DAP

DAP Criteria

2H2   Teachers think carefully about which learning format is best for helping children achieve a desired goal considering children's ages, development, abilities, temperaments, and so on.

3C2   Teachers carefully shape and adapt the experiences they provide children to enable each child to reach the goals outlined in the curriculum.

12-1 Basic Goals of the Early Childhood Art Program

naeyc **DAP** The early childhood art program provides the time and place for children to express thoughts, ideas, feelings, actions, and abilities in a variety of media and activities. In the art program, children are free to actively participate in exploring art ideas and materials, discovering all the wonderful possibilities they provide. This exploration and discovery, as we learned in Chapter 5, is provided by a developmentally appropriate curriculum for young children. In addition, all the principles of DAP are applicable to the early childhood art program as well as to all other parts of the curriculum.

Just as in the early childhood profession in general, there are national standards in the arts. National standards in the arts (dance, music, theater, and visual arts), first developed in 1994 by experts in arts education, are currently under revision. The current and soon to be revised standards are designed to describe what a child with a complete, sequential education in the arts from K–12 should know and be able to do at various grade levels in each artistic discipline. They are divided into three main groups: K–4, 5–8, and 9–12. Most states have standards based on the national standards in place for arts education, and other states are in the process of developing them. Most state standards are for dance, music, theater, and visual art and for grades K–12, but this varies from state to state and district to district. For more information on these standards, visit the National Art Education Association website.

12-1a Process, Not Product

Art programs provide young children many opportunities to work with a variety of materials and techniques to express themselves creatively.

The first and main goal in all art experiences is **process over product**. In the process, the child expresses experiences and feelings. The expression of one's *self* is what is important here, not what the finished product looks like. Lowenfeld and Brittain express the importance of a child's creating through art in this way:

> "Art is not the same for a child as it is for an adult. For a child, art is primarily a means of expression. No two children are alike, and in fact, each child differs even from his earlier self as he constantly grows, perceives, understands, and interprets his environment. A child is a dynamic being; art becomes for him a language of thought". (p. 7, 1987)

Another reason that it is better to emphasize the process of art in early childhood programs is that young children are not yet skillful users of materials. Much of their creative effort is expended in the manipulative experience of trying materials out and becoming acquainted with them. Also, young children are more interested in *doing* than in *producing* and rarely, if ever, have a planned product in mind when they take up their paintbrushes or select collage materials. This sort of advance planning belongs to children on the verge of kindergarten age. Older children in middle- and upper-elementary levels will be more purposeful in their creative activities. However, this does not change the fact that the main objective of their artistic endeavors is self-expression.

Children take paints, bits of cloth, clay, wood, and stone and put them together into products that express their own ideas. In the art program, emphasis must be on continued satisfying experiences with many kinds of materials and a continued involvement in the process of making. Creative activities provide opportunities for self-expression by allowing children to construct something that is uniquely their own.

12-1b Needs of the Children

A second major objective of the art program is to meet the needs of children. This means that the program must be designed for their age, ability, and interest levels (see Photo 12-1). Thus, a program for 3-year-olds

Casper Holroyd

PHOTO 12-1 The early childhood art program must be designed for a child's age, ability, and interest level.

is set up to have the right materials and activities for a group with a limited interest span and limited motor control. It has materials and activities that interest them and that they can use without a lot of adult help. Two-year-olds are at the point of learning how to tear and paste and do not require scissors, whereas 3- and 4-year-olds are generally able to use scissors independently. The same applies to art activities for 4-, 5-, and 6-year-old children. In a mixed age group, the program must be set up with a variety of materials and activities available to all children in the group. For middle- and upper-elementary students who are beginning to create more complex works of art, there needs to be an increased supply of materials and equipment for creative expression. The teacher's job at this level is to maximize students' use of these resources as they continue to develop their imaginations in art experiences.

Another way a teacher meets the individual needs of children is to provide art materials appropriate to the multiple intelligences of the children in the group. (See Chapter 5 for more information about multiple intelligences.)

12-1c Originality and Independence

The third important objective of the early childhood art program is to give each child the chance to think originally and to learn to work independently. In creating art, a child can use and explore all kinds of materials. This encourages original, divergent thought. Also, giving children materials that they can control at their physical level encourages independent work. Materials that appeal to a child's multiple intelligences encourage exploration. For example, providing a child who is logic smart blocks and clay encourages this child to create models and structures, which are a natural expression of his or her logical/mathematical skills. These two attributes—originality and ability to work on their own—are basic to children's creativity.

With older children, you can expect and plan for a higher degree of independence in use of materials. With ready access to a variety of materials, if allowed, children are able to be self-directed and choose the materials they need to express ideas. At this level, instead of relying on the teacher to pass out supplies and lead a lesson, self-directed, independent children are able to gather their own materials for creative work.

Most important of all, in order to encourage a child's originality and independence, be sure that you avoid using "creative fakes" with young children. These are the "cute" ideas that masquerade as creative

activities. Examples of these are ditto sheets, craft kit projects, worksheets, or any activity that results in identical products from each child. Another important routine to avoid is showing children an example or model of a previously made article before starting an activity. This practice limits and may even stifle a child's creativity. Viewing such a sample, the child may think, "This is what my teacher likes. I need to make something just like it."

12-1d Creative Thinking

The fourth goal in the early childhood art program is for children to be creative thinkers. Creative children work freely and flexibly. They attack each problem without fear of failure. Children in an art program that is right for their developmental level are able to work creatively, freely, and flexibly. They can handle the material in the setting, which helps them feel confident about their abilities. If children do not feel secure, safe, and comfortable with themselves, the teacher, and the other children, they will not be able to take the risk or meet the challenge involved in producing art.

As we have learned, all children have multiple intelligences or ways of learning. These individual learning styles will influence how each child will work in art activities. See Figure 12-1 for a summary of these learning styles and appropriate art activities for each style.

12-1e Individualized Progress

Finally, the fifth goal of the art program is to allow children to grow at their own pace. Activities may be planned to stimulate children, but true growth comes only at their own pace. Just as children learn to walk on their own, they learn to paint by painting in their own way.

In the art program, young children are given time to grow, explore, and experiment with materials at their own pace. Barely out of the sensorimotor stage of development, 2- and 3-year-olds are respected for being 2 or 3. These young children are expected to explore materials; to enjoy feeling, tasting, and playing with crayons; to scribble and mess around; to find out how paint feels on their hands and faces; and to experiment with soft clay. Children are not hurried or pressured into representing their ideas or feelings through art; similarly, they are not expected to be interested in a product, much less to produce one.

Children who have had the opportunity and time to explore and experiment with materials as toddlers are ready at 3, 4, and 5 to find out how they can gain control over the materials and use them to express themselves. In turn, preschoolers who have had the time and freedom to develop their art ability will enjoy using these skills to express themselves visually in a wide variety of media.

A STUDENT WHO IS . . .	WILL ENJOY ART PROJECTS THAT . . .	AND WILL ENJOY HELPING OUT IN THE CLASSROOM BY . . .
Person Smart *The Socializer* • interactive • communicative • group-oriented • extroverted	• are group projects • require giving/receiving feedback • require group leaders	• distributing and collecting materials • mediating
Self Smart *The Individual* • individualistic • solitary • self-reflective • introverted	• are individual projects • focus on feelings, dreams, or self are goal-oriented	• arranging items in storage spaces • assisting teacher before or after class
Body Smart *The Mover* • physically active • hands-on • talkative	• involve physical motion such as dancing or acting • involve touching various objects, materials, and textures	• running errands • role-playing safety rules • distributing and collecting materials
Word Smart *The Word Player* • oriented toward language, words, reading, and writing	• involve spoken or written words • involve storytelling	• reading instructions aloud • labeling storage spaces • creating "rules" posters
Logic Smart *The Questioner* • inquisitive • experimental • oriented toward numbers, patterns, and relationships	• involve patterns, relationships, or symbols • require problem solving	• arranging or classifying materials for distribution • helping solve problems
Picture Smart *The Visualizer* • imaginative • creative • oriented toward colors, pictures	• involve colors and designs • involve painting, drawing, or sculpture • require active imagination	• creating displays of artworks • designing charts and posters
Music Smart *The Music Lover* • oriented toward music, rhythmic sounds, and environmental sounds	• involve rhythmic patterns, singing, humming, responding to music, keeping time, or listening for sounds	• thinking of cleanup songs • thinking of safety songs • creating displays about music or musicians

FIGURE 12-1 Learning styles and art activities (Gardner, 1993, 1999).   *(Continues)*

(Gardner, 1993, 1999)

A STUDENT WHO IS . . .	WILL ENJOY ART PROJECTS THAT . . .	AND WILL ENJOY HELPING OUT IN THE CLASSROOM BY . . .
Nature Smart *The Outdoors Lover* • interested in the outdoors • oriented toward animals, insects, and nature in general	• involve collecting objects of nature • involve observing and recording weather • involve identifying plants and insects • involve tree rubbings • involve creating his or her own animal or insect	• working in the garden • caring for classroom pets and aquarium • arranging collections of natural objects
Acquiring English	• require limited word usage • involve terminology from their first language • involve simple name/word games	• creating labels and posters in their first language • creating images or icons for bulletin boards • sharing elements of their culture with other students

FIGURE 12-1 Learning styles and art activities (Gardner, 1993, 1999) (*Continued*).

TeachSource Digital Download   Download from CourseMate.

Did You Get It?

Process over product is best demonstrated by a scenario in which

a. children play with clay but don't bring home a completed sculpture.

b. elementary school students compete in an art contest.

c. a kindergarten teacher encourages her students to produce pictures to be sent to a magazine for publication.

d. students' artwork is displayed during parents' night at a school.

Take the full quiz on CourseMate.

12-2 Basic Set Up for Art Activities

Whether setting up an art center or an entire room for art experiences, there are certain basic guidelines for arranging the environment. The age of the group will always be the major consideration in planning, as each age group has varying abilities and interests requiring different arrangements. Specific requirements for different age groups are covered in Chapter 6. At this point, our discussion covers basic guidelines that cross age levels. The following are considerations that are basic to setting up art activities.

12-2a General Considerations

The art area should be arranged for ease in cleaning up and dispensing materials. One type of arrangement that works well is to separate wet from dry materials. For example, clay and paint centers can be placed near the room's water source.

To work creatively with art materials, children need to be free from constraints and worry related to keeping themselves and their work spaces clean. Children will need smocks to protect clothing, supplies for covering work surfaces, and tools for cleaning. Men's shirts with the arms cut off make good smocks, or children can wear an old set of clothes for art activities. These "art clothes" will be like an art journal: the various spots and splashes on them are reminders of past art projects! Some teachers ask parents to provide old adult-sized t-shirts as they are easier to put on than button-down shirts, especially for younger children. Children will also need to know where to place work in progress for safekeeping and where wet items can be left to dry. Providing these arrangements is part of the teacher's responsibility as a guide and facilitator.

Sharp materials such as scissors must be placed out of reach of children who have not yet mastered handling them independently and safely. Usually such materials are dispensed from a teacher-height counter placed in a location convenient to children's work tables. Easels are placed out of the way of traffic so that children can work without being jostled. Next to the easels are places for children to hang paint smocks and a rack to drape paintings to dry. The rack where children's paintings are hung is situated so that the children do not have to carry their wet paintings through areas where other children are working to hang them.

Drying racks are convenient to have in early childhood classrooms. However, the commercial type can be expensive. An inexpensive substitute can be assembled in the same manner as a bookshelf. Cardboard is placed on top of four brick or block supports (one in each corner). Several layers are built so paintings can be left on the shelves for drying. Two other methods for drying paintings are (1) hanging paintings on a clothesline suspended above the head of the tallest adult and (2) using a portable, folding clothes-drying rack. However, paintings can drip in both of these methods. Windowsills can also be used, especially for drying three-dimensional artwork.

Masonite boards cut in 10-inch squares are convenient for transporting wet or unfinished clay work and assemblages to a place where they can dry. Children can work directly on the boards when they start their modeling and construction. These boards can frequently be obtained from scrap piles at a lumberyard or can be purchased inexpensively. Foam core board or heavy corrugated cardboard can also be used. To enlarge table surfaces for drying artwork, cover the tabletop with large pieces of cardboard. You can find these at warehouse-type stores where they are used to hold large lots of merchandise on pallets. They are generally discarded every day and are available for the asking.

A place for children to wash after using wet materials must also be nearby. If you don't have the convenience of a sink in your room, a plastic kitchen tub half filled with water and placed on a low stand next to the paper towels and wastebasket works well. Include a bucket of small sponges near the art area. They are easy for children to use and can be rinsed and used again.

12-2b Set Up for Daily Art Activities

Set up art materials so that children have daily art experiences. The teacher should make sure every day that there are designated places, equipment, and materials for art experiences. For example, every day the teacher should prepare easels with paper and paints for

Casper Holroyd

PHOTO 12-2 Have enough supplies so children know where to get them and can work independently.

children's use. This way, activity proceeds smoothly in the easel area, and the teacher is free to manage the rest of the classroom.

Have a supply of paper, crayons, pencils, and clay available in a set place every day for children's use. Tearing, cutting, and pasting supplies should be ready and easily available, too. (Specific suggestions about supplies and their care are provided later in this chapter.) As part of this preparation, the teacher guides the children in learning the necessary use and care of all equipment as it is set up.

Being prepared in all these ways ensures that children will have the supplies they need, will know where to get them, and will know how to use them—which encourages them to pursue independent, creative activities on a daily basis (see Photo 12-2).

12-2c Set Up for Weekly Art Activities

To enhance children's creative experiences, the teacher plans for and sets up weekly art activities in addition to the children's daily experiences. For example, a teacher might plan a unit on printing (see Chapter 13 for more information about printing), using each week to introduce a specific technique of printing. This, of course, would be in addition to and not in place of children's regular art experiences. The teacher plans in advance to set up a table or other area with printing supplies and equipment. Scurrying around for "things to print with" at the last minute can be avoided in this planned weekly approach.

Work of the previous week is evaluated before new plans are prepared. Even though plans have been carefully thought through, a teacher must be prepared to make changes resulting from unexpected events. For example, a sudden snowstorm extends the amount of time the children will play outdoors. Or one morning the road outside the building is being repaired, and huge machines appear on the street. The wise teacher recognizes this event as a good learning experience and arranges time for children to observe the workers.

In weekly plans, teachers plan for a balance between the familiar and the new as they make decisions about how materials and equipment are to be used. Teachers need not be concerned that children may lose interest if the same activities are offered week after week. If children have freedom to use materials in their own ways, they do not tire of working with the same ones. After children have gained success in using a material, they enjoy repeating the experience.

Because some activities require more supervision than others, a teacher needs to consider how many activities will be available for a given period. The number of activities chosen that requires close supervision depends on the number of adults assigned to the room. After making careful observations and deciding upon the activities for the week, the teacher must think through what would be the best use of his or her time—for example, whether to give special attention to the block area or to the art area. If a new material or technique is being introduced, it generally requires teacher supervision. In this case, the teacher usually sits with a small group and participates in the activity with them. Unless there are several teachers in a room, it is unlikely there would be more than one group activity requiring close supervision.

In weekly and monthly planning, consideration must be given to the time of the year and to the developmental levels of the children. At the beginning of a school year, too many choices and too much open space may be upsetting to children because they are not yet familiar with the room or the school. At a time when a teacher's goal is to help children feel comfortable in the school, too many new and exciting materials can be overwhelming and distracting. The same is true for older children at the beginning of a new school year. Children will feel more comfortable as the year begins by using media and equipment they have become familiar with the previous school year. Therefore, materials offered at the beginning of the year should be those that are familiar to most children. For example, even a very shy child can feel secure at a table with crayons and paper. As children begin to know each other, feel more comfortable in the room, and become aware of the daily routines, additional materials can be introduced and activities can be expanded.

Set up the art area so that it facilitates children's creative experiences. While specific materials and their use are discussed individually later in this chapter, some general ideas apply to the use of materials by young children. Children work better in a predictable, organized environment where art materials can always be found in the same place. For example, art materials on open storage shelves at child level make it possible for children to find the materials they want to use easily and independently. Also, when materials such as paper or paste are spaced far apart on shelves, putting things back in place becomes an easier task for young children. Using placemats or trays on child-size tables helps organize space into individual work areas.

Art activities in the early childhood program work best on child-level tables and easels. Although some children may occasionally enjoy working on the floor, it is important to have a table set up for regular art activities. It is a good idea to have a limit on the number of children for each art activity/area to ensure the proper space for children as well as sufficient materials for each child. In addition to the general considerations discussed earlier, there are some age-specific, considerations when setting up art activities.

Did You Get It?

During the first week of kindergarten, a teacher limits classroom art supplies to paper, scissors, and glue. From a developmental perspective, her purpose is to

a. encourage the students to think more creatively.

b. allow students to gradually develop their creativity.

c. prevent messes.

d. provide the students with a comfortable environment.

Take the full quiz on CourseMate.

12-3 Planning Art Activities for Toddlers

naeyc DAP Very young children benefit from a program divided into well-defined areas in which they have freedom to move, explore, and make decisions about activities and materials. However, when planning for this age range, special considerations must be kept in mind. Toddler-appropriate art activities and those for young 2-year olds toddlers must involve sturdy materials that do not include tiny pieces that might be swallowed.

Teacher Tips

The way a teacher sets up her or his own materials, supplies, and space can make or break the child's and teacher's successful experiences in art. The following are some suggestions for arranging supplies for art experiences as well as for displaying children's artwork:

● Scissors holders can be made from gallon milk or bleach containers. Simply punch holes in the container and place scissors in holes with the points to the inside. Egg cartons turned upside down with slits in each mound also make excellent scissors holders.

● Paint containers can range from muffin tins and Styrofoam egg cartons to plastic soft drink cartons with yogurt containers in them. These work well outdoors as well as indoors because they are large and not easily tipped over. Place one brush in each container; this prevents colors from getting mixed and makes cleanup easier.

● A great tool for organizing craft supplies is a large metal popcorn tin (the ones that are popular around the holidays). Fill the tin with paper towel tubes. Use the tin for sorting pipe cleaners and paper strips, placing different colors in each tube. You will save time finding the right colors and when checking which colors are running low.

● Keep pencils from falling on the floor with Velcro. Attach a 1-inch strip of Velcro (the rough side) to the corner of each desk. Then attach a strip of the soft side of the Velcro to a pencil, just under the eraser. In addition to keeping the pencils handy, it keeps them from being sharpened down too much. This helps make pencil stumps a thing of the past.

● When markers have dried out, pour ½ inch of nail polish remover into a paper cup and let the marker tips soak in the solution for 30 seconds. Let them dry for 5 minutes before using. The acetone in the remover restores moisture without diluting the color and draws ink down to the tip of the markers.

● Mr. Clean Magic Erasers are the best for cleaning dry erase boards. They even can remove permanent marker stains from dry erase boards.

● Store posters in cardboard tubes from paper towels or toilet paper. Slip the cardboard core over the outside of a rolled-up poster. Label or color-code the tubes to keep them categorized for easy access. You can flatten the hardboard tubes for easy storage in small resealable plastic bags until needed.

● Crayon pieces may be melted down in muffin trays in a warm oven. When cooled, these are nice for rubbings or drawings.

● Airtight coffee cans and plastic food containers keep clay moist and always ready for use.

● For clay sharing, mold clay in the shape of a cake. Place the "cake" on a small table and use a plastic knife to slice it. Each child can work with a "slice" of clay.

● Individual watercolor sets can be made by pouring leftover tempera paint into egg carton cups. Set them aside to dry and harden. Use the paints with water and brushes just as you would ordinary paint sets.

Some more ideas for different types of paint containers.

● Cupcake or muffin tins are excellent for painting with several colors at a time.

● Styrofoam egg cartons work well when children are painting with cotton swabs. Cut cartons in thirds to make four-part containers, and pour small amounts of paint into each egg cup.

● Store liquid tempera in recycled glue or dishwashing liquid bottles. Paint can be squirted quickly and neatly into paint cups from these bottles.

● Sponges can be good paint holders, too. Cut a hole the exact size of the paint jar or cup in the center of the sponge, then fit the jar/cup in the hole. Besides keeping paint containers upright, the sponges also catch drips.

● Cotton-ball painting is more fun (and neater) when you clip spring-type clothespins to the cotton balls. Children use the clothespins like handles. The same clothespins can be used when printing with small sponge pieces.

Put only a few materials out at a time so that young children are not overwhelmed with too many choices. Materials should be rotated often, and children should learn to work on the floor or table area nearby and not carry materials across the room.

Art materials, such as crayons, play dough, colored markers, chalk, and paint, as well as materials such as sand and water, should be frequently available to children of this age. These materials are presented under the supervision of an adult so that appropriate use is encouraged. Also, because children of this age have difficulty sharing, duplicates of materials will help cut down on competition for the same items.

Traffic patterns and the children's distractibility must also be considered when art or any other interest areas are arranged in the room. Arrange activities requiring running water, such as play dough and painting, conveniently close to sinks. Walking babies and younger toddlers are prone to falling, grabbing, and running; therefore, they need clear, open spaces. They are also easily distracted by other activities, making task completion or cleanup difficult unless areas are visually divided. The need for occasional solitude and quiet is especially important at this age. Toddlers can easily become overstimulated if exposed to too many activities at once. In view of all these considerations, dividing and organizing a room becomes an art in itself. Several arrangements should be tried to determine which one best fits the children's needs.

Did You Get It?

A preschool director who arranges the toddler classroom by leaving six square feet of the floor empty and placing art tables in a corner is meeting the requirements of developmentally appropriate practice (DAP) by

a. confining art to a small corner.
b. ensuring that all the children will work together on art projects.
c. giving the room a clear appearance.
d. preventing problems of falling and grabbing.

Take the full quiz on CourseMate.

12-4 Planning Art Activities for Young Preschoolers

naeyc **DAP** Art activities for 2- to 4-year-old young preschoolers must address the fact that most children of this age have a limited span of interest and attention. Many activities, even the most interesting, hold their interest for less than 10 minutes. However, it should be remembered that each child is different, and interest spans may be shorter or longer depending on the individual child.

The point is that the teacher must, first of all, plan activities that appeal to the interests of the young preschooler. Simple, basic art activities are most interesting to children in this age group. Second, the teacher must be prepared to accept the fact that the activity may hold the child's interest for only a short time. It helps to remember that a period of time that seems short to an adult may be quite long to the young preschool child. Finally, alternative and extra activities

should always be available for those children who may not be interested in the first activity planned or who finish the activity faster than the teacher had anticipated.

Because 2- and 3-year-old children require considerable supervision, many teachers prefer to introduce or arrange only one supervised art activity each day. Sometimes they will divide the whole class into small groups for simultaneous participation. Unless there are several adults, this can be a difficult undertaking. In such a setup, a one-to-one interaction between teacher and child—which is so necessary in the early years—will be limited. In addition, whole-group participation in art can frequently lead to conformity of response rather than individuality of expression.

In one popular method for organizing supervised art activity, teachers have children take turns coming to an area where materials for art are arranged. The space will usually accommodate four to six children and provides opportunities for peer interaction as well as for interaction with the teacher. This arrangement allows for freedom of choice and gives children a chance to grow toward autonomous decision making about the kind of art they will do.

With the young preschool group, it is usually best to use only the basic materials at first. This helps keep the art program from being too confusing for the child. Using only a few crayons or paints or pasting one or two kinds of things at first is a good idea. It encourages children to experiment with each new tool and medium. They learn to use the basic tools and materials first. When they have acquired the basic skills, more colors and variety can be added.

Why and when to provide a variety of materials for early childhood art deserves thoughtful consideration. After children have had opportunities to explore the basic expressive materials, varieties of the basics can be introduced, providing children do not become overwhelmed. However, 2- and 3-year-old children and some less secure older children may still need consistency because sameness and simplicity provide a sense of security. Observant teachers will notice when a child begins to lose interest in using art materials or when a child keeps repeating the same colors of crayon or paint daily. Then it may be time to offer that child the stimulation that accompanies a change of medium or novel material. Let us now consider specific activities for the interest, ability, and skill levels of young preschool children.

© 2015 Cengage Learning

TeachSource Video

Preschool: Family Interactions, School, and Community

1. Discuss the art materials and equipment used in the "Me Book" activity in this video with regard to the ease of use and appropriateness for the young children using them.

2. What would you change in this activity and why?

3. Note and comment on the children's artwork displayed on the walls using the information in this chapter on children's art displays.

Watch on CourseMate.

12-4a Collage

Making a collage is a good activity for young preschoolers because it can be completed quickly and is within their interest span. It also encourages the use of small muscles as children tear and paste. Young preschoolers also benefit mentally as they learn to choose items and to arrange them in a collage. As they paste together a collage, they learn about the feel, shape, and color of many things and develop the ability to use things in unusual ways. (For more information about the techniques of collage, see Chapter 13.)

At times, it may seem as if young preschoolers focus more on the paste than on the items being pasted, but that is part of the fun. The teacher must be sure that the objects available are suitable for the child who is using them. For example, it is important to keep tiny, inedible objects away from children who still put things in their mouths.

With young preschoolers who are new to this activity, begin with just one thing to paste. A good idea is for them to make a tear-and-paste collage. To do this, provide the children with pieces of newspaper, colored tissue, or any colored scrap paper that tears

easily. Show them, if necessary, how to tear large and small pieces. Then have them paste these torn bits of paper on colored construction paper in any way they choose. This is a good activity for young preschoolers who do not want or are not yet able to use scissors. Some scissors should be available for children who want to try cutting the pieces to paste on the collage (see Photo 12-3). However, children should not be forced to practice cutting.

As children master the basic technique of pasting, more objects can be added to the collage. Some good things to add are large buttons, bits of cloth and paper (use different colors, textures, and shapes), and bottle caps. Care must be taken to ensure that the materials are not sharp, not painted with lead paint, and not small enough to swallow.

For a change of pace, different materials may be used for the backing of the collage. Children may use pieces of cardboard to paste things on, or shoebox lids, or even pieces of burlap. Teacher and children should use their imaginations to come up with ideas for new and different collage materials.

Painting. Young preschool children also get much satisfaction from working with paint and experimenting with color and form. Painting at an easel is not as easy for young preschoolers as painting on a table (see Photo 12-4). It is difficult for this young artist to control drips at an easel. Also, while standing at an easel, the young child may be easily distracted and wander away. Often, young children of this age paint one color on top of the other and enjoy the

Casper Holroyd

PHOTO 12-3 Blunt-tipped scissors should be available for young preschool aged children interested in cutting pieces of paper for a collage.

PHOTO 12-4 For preschool-aged children, painting at a table is easier than painting at an easel.

effect. But most of all, they enjoy the movement involved in painting. Finger paint is an especially good medium for this age group, as it can be manipulated over and over again (see Photo 12-5). In this way, the process is stressed, not the product. This is very important for children, who at this age are learning the basic ways to use paint. This age group enjoys the feel (and sometimes the taste) of the paint. They may even use their upper arms and elbows to help them in their designs.

PHOTO 12-5 Finger painting is a good medium for preschoolers.

To save on the cost of finger paint paper and to try something new, have children finger paint on a Formica table top, an enamel-top table, a sheet of smooth Formica, or even linoleum. When this is done, a print can be made from the child's finger painting by laying a piece of newsprint paper on the finger painting and gently rubbing it with one hand. The painting is transferred in this way from the tabletop to the paper. More finger paint activities are suggested later in this chapter. There may be some preschool children who do not like the feel of finger paint. These children should never be forced to use finger paint. Instead, another art activity should be arranged that the child will enjoy. (For more information about painting, see Chapter 13.)

Printing. Printing with objects is an art activity that is appropriate for the age, ability, and interest level of young preschool children. In a basic printing activity, the child learns that an object dipped in or brushed with paint makes its own mark, or print, on paper. Children use small muscles in the hand and wrist as they hold the object, dip it in paint, and print with it on paper. They learn that each object has its own unique quality because each thing makes its own imprint.

For the young preschool child, stick prints are a good place to start. In this type of printing, children dip small pieces of wood of various sizes and shapes into thick tempera paint and press them onto a piece of paper. Twigs, wooden spools, wood clothespins, and bottle caps are objects suitable for 3-year-olds to use in printing.

After stick printing is mastered, printing with other objects is an appropriate activity for children in this age group. A good way for young preschoolers to begin printing is to "walk" the inked object (for example, a wooden spool, a pinecone, a potato masher) across the paper in even "steps." When it gets to the other side, they walk it back again. By making three or four lines—or walks—the child has made a pattern.

After one color is used, the object can be wiped clean, and another color can be used. Three-year-olds like to try many colors with the same printing object. They may even print over their first prints in a different color. More printing activities for young preschool children are found in Chapter 13 and at the end of this chapter.

Crayons. Crayons are the most basic, most familiar, and easiest tool for young preschoolers to use. Supply your classroom with thick ones. Large, thick crayons are easier to hold, and they don't break as easily as thinner crayons. Crayons can be used to make attractive colored marks on paper.

You can test the quality of your crayons by coloring a small area, putting pressure on the crayon. If you can scratch the wax off the paper with your fingernails, the crayons are not of a good quality. There is too much wax in the crayon, and it is not well intermixed with the pigment. In good crayons, pigment and wax are equally combined, and the wax cannot be scraped off the paper. Crayons of good quality can easily be combined to form new colors by putting different layers of colors one on the other. Color an area with blue and put a layer of yellow over it. If the resulting color is not a vivid green, your crayons are of poor quality.

If thick crayons are not available in your community, buy the thin ones, but remember that they break easily. The easiest way to avoid tears and frustrations resulting from broken crayons is to break all new crayons and put them on a tray after you have peeled off the paper. The child, without hesitancy and fear that the crayon may break, can put as much pressure on it as he or she wants, and there is no competition between those who keep their crayons in "newer" condition and those who don't.

By using only pieces of crayons, the child may be encouraged to experiment with different crayon techniques, employing the broad side as well as the pointed end. Don't worry about buying a box with many colors of crayons. The more "ready-made" colors you present the child, the less will she use her imagination and creative urge to produce new colors by mixing. In general, boxes with few colors are sufficient to produce the rest by mixing, if the need for more colors arises. This need, however, depends on the age, development, and personality of the child.

Buy regular newsprint (unprinted newspaper) for crayon work. An 18- × 24-inch sheet of paper is just right. The child should have plenty of paper and should not be restricted in its use.

While most young preschoolers have crayons, they often use them only for drawing on paper. There are, however, several other ways to use crayons that the teacher might try to vary the program for young preschoolers.

- *Crayons and a variety of materials.* Crayons can be used to draw on many surfaces. Cardboard in any form (including corrugated cardboard, paper gift boxes, and food trays) provides a good surface for crayon drawings, as does Styrofoam. Crayon on sandpaper also creates an interesting effect.
- *Crayon rubbings.* Crayon rubbing is a technique that young preschool children can easily master. To make a crayon rubbing, the child puts a piece

of paper over a textured surface and rubs the sides of a peeled crayon over the paper. The crayon picks up the texture on the paper, forming a design. Have children experiment with bumpy paper, food trays, bark, leaves, the sidewalk, bricks, and corrugated cardboard. This is a good activity for developing both small and large muscles.
- *Crayon resist.* Another way to use crayon is in crayon-resist drawings. To make a resist drawing, the child first draws a picture on paper with crayons, pressing hard. She or he then paints over and around the crayon drawing with thin paint (tempera paint diluted with water). A dark-colored paint works best. The dark color fills in all the areas that the crayon has not covered. In the areas covered with crayon, the crayon "resists," or is not covered by, the paint. Crayon resist gives the feeling of a night picture. It is a thrilling experience for the child to see the changes that come when the paint crosses the paper.

See Chapter 13 for additional activities and techniques using crayons.

12-5 Planning Art Activities for Older Preschoolers and Kindergarteners

naeyc DAP   Just as in the case of the younger preschool child, there are preferred and suitable materials and art activities for older preschoolers and kindergarteners (ages 4–6). Although there may be considerable overlap, children in this age group generally differ significantly from younger preschool children.

Preschoolers and kindergartners who are 4–6 years old share some general traits. Small-muscle development in the fingers, hands, and wrists is much improved. Whereas younger preschool children may have great difficulty buttoning their clothing or using scissors, most in this older group do not. Many are able to use crayons, colored markers, and even pencils and pens. Because these children are very interested in life beyond home and school, art activities making use of outside environments (for example, television characters) can be stimulating. Youngsters of this age paint and draw with more purpose. Designs and pictures are within their abilities. These will probably be somewhat simple but nonetheless fun and exciting for the children to do.

If various materials are available to children 5 years of age and older, they can discover alternative ways of accomplishing similar tasks. For example, if glue does not hold, children may try tape or a stapler. If other fibers are available in addition to yarn, children will experiment and discover possibilities for knotting, stitching, or weaving with each. Children, finding some materials more satisfying than others, are more apt to use them to express ideas. With variety, older children come to understand that color, line, form, and texture can be expressed through different materials.

The first cooperative or group art projects will usually take place in kindergarten. In most cases, children discuss the joint effort but work individually. Then the teacher helps arrange the individual contributions into a whole. (See Chapter 13 for a discussion of the group mural as an example of this group approach.)

Art activities for children in grades 1–5 should allow them to express their creative potential. Children in this age group will continue to use all of the basic materials and equipment discussed thus far but in more varied and challenging ways (see Photo 12-6). New equipment such as brayers for printing and pastels for painting may be introduced at this point.

PHOTO 12-6 Children in grades 1–5 will use basic materials in new, more challenging ways.

Did You Get It?

A kindergarten teacher helps her students plan a mural. The students discuss the plan, and then each paints a different portion of the mural. From a developmental perspective, this activity is

  a. appropriate to the students' developmental level.

  b. inappropriate, because five-year-olds are not yet ready to work together.

  c. acceptable, but far from ideal, as the work is distributed rather than worked on cooperatively.

  d. not developmentally appropriate practice.

Take the full quiz on CourseMate.

12-6 Adapting Art Activities for Children with Special Needs

Many early childhood programs today include in their classrooms children with special needs. Although this book is not intended as a resource for teaching special education, this section is intended to provide some very basic information on how to adapt the art program for children with special needs.

12-6a Developmental Delays and Physical Impairments

It takes many repetitions for the child with developmental delays to fully learn a new skill. For this reason, some children will appear to have mastered the task one day but then be unable to perform the same task on another day. This type of inconsistency is common for children with developmental delays (Gould & Sullivan, 1999).

Open-ended art activities are most appropriate for children with developmental delays. Some effective techniques to use are demonstration, task breakdown, and hand-over-hand assistance as needed. It also helps to demonstrate the activity by doing it first while the child watches. Another approach is to break down an activity into a series of small steps. It is most important to help the child complete one step before going on to the next. In addition, you may find that some children will need you to physically guide their hands. This would involve placing a crayon in the child's hand and then gently moving the child's hand and crayon across a sheet of paper.

Some children with developmental delays may have weak hand muscles and a poor grasp. For these children, short, stubby art instruments are frequently easier to grasp than commercially available crayons, markers, and brushes. You can adapt materials by breaking chalk and preschool crayons into small, short pieces.

Some other suggestions for working with these special needs children follow:

- Place masking tape or colored tape or draw colored lines with a permanent marker about 1 inch from the end of the paintbrush end to show the child where to place fingers on the brush.
- Use large pieces of paper for art activities to allow for large arm movements characteristic of children with developmental delays.
- In art activities, place the paper on a horizontal surface such as a table or the floor, or tape it to a large easel, door, or wall. Be sure to place a large sheet of plastic, such as a shower curtain or plastic tablecloth, underneath the paper to protect the surface.
- Stabilize the paper with tape, clips, clothespins, or other fasteners to prevent excess slippage. At the same time, encourage the child to use his or her nondominant hand to hold the paper down.
- Children with cerebral palsy will benefit greatly from consistent physical and/or verbal cues to use the less functional hand as a stabilizer while painting with the other.
- Place paper inside a sturdy shirt-size box that will provide walls to contain extraneous movements of the paintbrush or other tool.
- Use thickened paint to provide more resistance and feedback. Paint can be thickened with cornstarch, salt, sugar, flour, sawdust, or sand.
- Students who are mentally challenged may have difficulty grasping complex ideas in art and other subjects. Even so, they often respond to art in a direct and insightful manner. They are often able to portray their ideas or feelings more successfully through art than through words. Simplify and separate into specific steps any more difficult activities. Encourage independent thinking about the ideas to be expressed.

Students who have impaired mobility due to physical impairments may need to use alternate tools and materials for some activities. Rehabilitation specialists may help you solve unique problems. A number of special tools are available for students with physical impairments (such as a mouthpiece that holds a pencil or brush).

In working with children with physical impairments that affect the upper body, arms, hands, or fingers, you will need to make some modifications similar to those mentioned earlier for art activities such as stabilizing paper, using the nondominant hand to hold the paper down, and so forth.

12-6b Visual Impairments

The term *visual impairment* is a general term that includes all levels of vision loss from partially sighted to complete blindness. The child with visual impairments learns about the objects and people around him or her through the senses of touch, smell, taste, and hearing. A child with a visual impairment is unable to observe and imitate others as they explore the environment. Because of this, the child will need to learn how to investigate the world around him or her. You can help by offering verbal descriptions about what the room looks like, where furniture and playthings are located, and what other people in the room are doing. Students with visual impairments can participate in discussions about artwork, especially with regard to themes portrayed in art that are related to the student's own experience. In art activities, provide materials to create tactile, kinesthetic artwork—clay, textured paper, cloth, small boxes, or wood blocks that student can arrange.

Although some children with visual problems prefer dimmed lighting, most need bright, even lighting. To help reduce glare, use a table with a dull finish on it. If you don't have this type of table, tape light-colored construction paper on top of the table. Place the table in an area of the room where the lighting is optimal to reduce glare and shadows. Another way to reduce glare from reflection of light is to use pastel paper instead of white paper for art activities. (Ponder & Kissinger, 2009).

Some other suggestions for working with children with visual impairment follow:

- Use high-contrast materials, such as dark or bright colors on light paper. Red, yellow, and orange are the easiest colors for a child with low vision to see, especially on a dark blue background.
- Place a piece of mesh or screening under the paper the child is coloring with a crayon so that the child can feel the raised finished product.

Arts and Crafts—Two Different Processes

Many people think of "arts" and "crafts" as if they are the same thing. The process of making art and the process of making crafts are related but different activities.

Painting with tempera colors and making a birdhouse are two quite different activities. While one is an open-ended of unstructured activity (painting), the other is a structured, goal-oriented one (making a bird house). Thus, painting is an art activity, and making a birdhouse is a craft activity. The early childhood art program can provide both types of activities and allows the child to explore and learn from both.

The main differences between arts and crafts are listed here:

Craft Activities	Art Activities
Product oriented	Process oriented
Engage cognitive skills and problem solving	Engage imagination and feelings
Require specific materials and instruction	Use basic supplies and open-ended instruction
Involve assembly of three-dimensional materials	Involves two- and three-dimensional materials

Craft activities often are looked down on by many art teachers as less creative than pure art activities. However, definite thinking skills are developed in craft activities. Craft activities help children develop problem-solving skills from experimenting with a wide range of materials. Also, decision making is constant and continuous in assembling and decorating projects. Visual thinking skills and three-dimensional information processing are exercised in the process of assembling materials.

Your goal as a teacher of young children should be to help children experience the joy of creativity and the satisfaction of mastery. Both concepts relate to the process of art. But while adults focus on the process of art, school-age children are often concerned with the product. Too often they want their project to look good and be worthy of admiration. So, it's important to keep both the process and product in mind when you plan an art activity. You can do this by providing a variety of art materials that are stimulating, age appropriate, and easy to be successful with and by providing just the right amount of instruction and inspiration.

- Show the child how to hold a crayon or marker and what to do with it if he or she has never held a crayon or marker before.
- Hang paper at eye level, either at the easel or taped to the wall. Placing the paper on a vertical surface allows the child's head and eyes to remain in a neutral position while he or she is working.
- Use markers or crayons instead of paint. When using paint, the child has to constantly change visual orientation as he or she looks from the paper to the paint and back to the paper. Markers and crayons reduce the amount of visual shifting.
- Add materials to paint such as thickeners and fragrances so the child will experience the smell as well as the paint itself. Try sand, salt, flour, cornstarch, sawdust, lemon juice, vanilla extract, and ground cinnamon.
- Allow extra time to complete projects, encourage frequent breaks, and suggest a low-key,

relaxing activity to follow (see Photo 12-7). Doing art activities can be extremely fatiguing for a child with visual impairments (Gould & Sullivan, 1999).

12-6c Attention Deficit/Hyperactivity Disorder and Behavioral Issues

Students with attention deficit/hyperactivity disorder (ADHD) can be a challenge for any teacher. Children with ADHD display the behaviors associated with short attention span as well as those associated with hyperactivity. Children with attention deficit disorder (ADD) display signs of short attention span but not hyperactivity.

Some techniques to use with these children follow:

- Plan freeform art activities such as painting, finger painting, and drawing to hold children's interest for extended periods. These activities allow them to enjoy expressing themselves in a nonverbal, nonthreatening manner.

Casper Holroyd

PHOTO 12-7 Children with special needs often benefit from relaxing projects after completing an art project.

- To transition children out of one art activity and into another, use a timer or provide another type of cue that marks the end of an activity. For example, an end-of-playtime song before the cleanup song gives children a few minutes to get used to the idea that cleanup time will follow shortly.
- Give children clear expectations before they begin an activity. For example, you might state that they will have 15 minutes to work on the activity and that you will give an advance warning when that time is almost up.
- Allow active children to either stand at the art center table or kneel on a chair. These positions are sometimes easier to maintain than sitting in a chair. If a particular child prefers to sit, however, make sure that the chair is the appropriate height, and the child's feet are flat on the floor.
- Allow children to lie on the floor while working on an art project. This position allows most of the body to come into contact with a hard surface, providing the type of pressure touch that can be calming to the child who is active or agitated. (Lee, 2008).
- Provide children with as many choices as possible to reduce noncompliant behavior. Offer choices that are acceptable to you, but give children the sense that they are in control. For example, ask the child whether he or she would like to use a fat paintbrush or a skinny one, the blue paper or the white.
- Provide an adequate work area with well-defined boundaries. If possible, move the easel next to the art table and allow the child with

ADHD to work there alone. Another possibility is to place the child's paper onto a cookie sheet at the table. This provides a clear, separate area for the child to concentrate on during the activity.
- Make use of the children's excess energy by allowing them to do classroom errands. Such errands can include walking notes from the teacher down to the office, putting chairs up on desks at the end of the day, helping the teacher put supplies away, or hanging up visuals.
- Establish quiet zones, create time for one-on-one interactions, listen to children's needs, and solve problems together. (Lougy 2007).

Let us now consider some specific art activities and the required materials and strategies for each. More in-depth information and activities for grades 1 through 5 are found in Chapters 13 and 14.

Did You Get It?

A four-year-old boy with special needs has difficulty focusing on painting. He repeatedly walks away from his easel and disturbs the other students working on their own paintings. What would be an appropriate intervention to use to help the boy perform the activity?

  a. instructing him to bring his easel into the closet and paint alone to avoid distraction

  b. placing his paper on the floor and allowing him to lie down while he paints

  c. telling him that he will not be allowed to participate in art activities until he learns to focus on his own work

  d. directing him to a simpler, less challenging art activity

Take the full quiz on CourseMate.

12-7 Basic Equipment, Materials, and Use

The following section contains lists of basic art materials needed in the early childhood art program and related strategies for their use. Basic recipes for making finger paint, paste, and other related materials are found at the end of Chapter 13. In choosing from the lists, the teacher must keep in mind the motor control, coordination, and overall developmental level of children in the group.

12-7a Drawing Materials and Use

The following are basic drawing materials and use:

- Sturdy sheets of paper (manila or newsprint, 8" × 12" or 12" × 18"). Spread the paper on a table or on the floor, or pin it to a wall or easel. Paper of different shapes and colors may be used for variety.
- A basket of jumbo crayons about 3/4 inch in width. These are a good size for the muscle control of small fingers. Unwrap the crayons so they can be used on both the sides and the ends.
- Watercolor markers in many colors and tip widths. (Be sure they are not permanent markers.) Colored markers come in beautiful, clear colors. Compared with paint, they have the additional advantage of staying bright and unsullied until children use them up.
- Make sure that crayons have the AP or CP label to ensure that they do not contain lead. Most schools set out crayons or pens jumbled together in a basket. However, you might try assembling them in separate boxes so that each user has an individual, complete set. This cuts down on arguments and means that all colors are available to each child as he or she requires them. Another alternative is to store crayons in wide-mouth containers according to color—all red crayons in one container, all blue in another.
- Crayons are an ideal medium for children: They are bold, colorful, clean, and inexpensive. They consist of an oily or waxy binder mixed with color pigments. They are of various types, some soft, some semi-hard, some for general use with young children (kindergarten or "fat" crayons). Crayons work well on most papers.

12-7b Chalking Materials and Use

The following are basic chalking materials and uses:

- A blackboard and eraser, and/or a stack of wet or dry (or both) paper.
- A container full of colored and white dustless chalk.
- Chalk is inexpensive and comes in a variety of colors. Its most typical use is with chalkboards, but young children do not seem to use it very effectively there. They do better if they can mark on the sidewalk with it—perhaps because the rougher texture of the cement more easily pulls the color off the stick, and because children

seem more able to tell what they are doing as they squat down and draw. It is, of course, necessary to explain to them that they may "write" with chalk only on special places.

- Some young artists apply chalk in separate strokes, letting the color blending take place in the viewer's eye. Others are not reluctant to blend the colors and do so successfully, although the colors may get muddied. Of course, there is no need to caution children against this; they should be encouraged to explore by rubbing with fingers, a cotton swab, or other suitable implement. Most children will select and use chalks easily.
- Chalk drawing is best done on a paper with a slightly coarse, abrasive surface. This texture helps the paper trap and hold the chalk particles. Many papers have this quality, including inexpensive manila paper.
- Chalks are brittle and easily broken. They are also impermanent, smearing very easily. Completed works should be sprayed with a "fixative" (ordinary hairspray works well); this should be done with proper ventilation.
- Chalk strokes can be strengthened by wetting the chalk or paper. Various liquids have also been used with chalks for interesting results. Chalk sticks can be dipped in buttermilk, starch, and sugar water. Liquid tends to seal the chalk, so teachers must occasionally rub a piece of old sandpaper on the end of the chalk in order to break this seal and allow the color to come off again.
- Fat, soft chalk of different colors mixes with ease and provides a great beginning for small-motor, free expression. Chalk discourages tight, inhibited work and makes free expression easy. Covering each piece of chalk with a piece of aluminum foil, leaving about half an inch of the chalk exposed, prevents smearing. It also prevents the transferring of colors from one piece of chalk to another while they are stored.
- If a slippery surface is desired, liquid starch may be applied to the paper before the dry chalk. There is less friction with starch, and the paper is less likely to tear.
- Soaking pieces of large chalk in sugar water (one part sugar and two parts water) for about 15 minutes and then using the chalk on dry paper is another method of application. Sugar gives the chalk a shiny look when dry.

12-7c Brush Painting Materials

The following is basic information on **brush painting**:

- Two easels (at least) with two blunt-tipped nails sticking out near each upper corner to attach the paper. (Paper can also be held on the board with spring-type clothespins.) Easels must be at the right height so that a child can paint without stretching or stooping. Children can also paint seated at a table covered with newspapers or an old shower curtain.
- Sheets of paper (18" × 24" plain newsprint), white or in assorted colors.
- Three or four jars of tempera paint. These may be mixed with powdered detergent for proper consistency.
- Paint containers. These must have flat bottoms so they will not tip over easily. Quart milk cartons (cut down) are good because they can be thrown away after using. Also, plastic fruit juice cans with lids work well when unused paint must be stored.
- Large, long-handled brushes in each jar. Those with 12-inch handles and ¾-inch bristle length are easy for young children to use. Soft, floppy, camelhair brushes allow the child to swoop about the paper most freely. When wet, the brush should have a pointed end: stiff, flat brushes make it harder to produce free movements. See Figure 13-2 in Chapter 13 for more information about paintbrushes.
- Smocks. An old shirt with the sleeves cut to the child's arm length makes a practical smock. Oilcloth or plastic aprons are also good. Extra art smocks can be made easily from either large plastic trash bags or newspaper. Cut openings for the child's head and arms at the end of a plastic trash bag.
- A place to dry finished paintings.

12-7d Mixing Paint

Although **mixing paint** in large quantities saves teachers time, the children enjoy making it so much and this is such a good learning experience for them that mixing a fresh batch each day with one or two children helping stir is generally preferred. A surprising amount of tempera is needed in relation to the quantity of water to make rich, bright, creamy paint; thus it is best to put the tempera into the container first and then add water bit by bit. Instead of water, some

teachers prefer using liquid starch because it thickens the paint mixture. However, this does increase the expense. It is also helpful to add a dash of liquid detergent, as this makes cleaning up easier. Another avenue to easier cleanup is to cut a poster board that has been laminated on both sides to fit the easel. Tape the laminated poster board over the easel so that as the students paint on the easel and get ready for the next child, the student can easily wipe off the paint with a damp cloth, rag, or paper towel. It helps the student learn how to clean up, keeps the center clean, and develops eye–hand coordination in a fun way.

At the easel, it may help children to see that if they wipe the brush on the side of the jar, the paint does not drip or run. An adult can show children that keeping each brush in its own paint jar keeps the color clear.

Keep several pieces of paper clipped to the easel at once. Many teachers prefer to write the child's name on the back of the paper to avoid the problem of having him or her paint over it. A developmental portfolio kept at school for each child, containing dated paintings, delights parents at conference time, enabling them to see how their child's skills have developed during the year. You can use a digital camera to take photos of selected pieces of each child's artwork for a video presentation of her or his painting experiences throughout the year.

Easel painting. With easel painting, teachers like to start with only the three primary colors (red, blue, and yellow) in the beginning of the year and then add other colors in the second month or so. Each container of blue tempera paint should be labeled with a strip of blue paper on which is clearly printed the word BLUE. (Label other containers in the same way.) Brushes should be thoroughly washed and kept in good condition. Teach children how to wipe up and wash the art area after its use.

At the end of each day, wash all paintbrushes thoroughly in running water, and dry them with bristles up before putting them away. Wash easels and vinyl aprons with a wet cloth and soap if necessary. Wash and put away containers. Cover leftover paint with a tight lid or aluminum foil. Hang up aprons and smocks.

12-7e Finger Painting Materials and Use

The following is basic information on **finger painting materials** and use:

- Paper that has a shiny surface. This can be butcher paper, shelf paper, special finger paint paper, freezer wrap, or glossy gift wrap.

Art Stimulates the Brain

Every culture on the planet has art forms. Why is that? Neuroscientists continue to find clues as to how the mental and physical activities required for the arts are so fundamental to brain function (Perso et al., 2011).

Visual arts excite the internal visual processing system to recall reality or create fantasy with the same ease (Sousa, 2006). In those cultures without reading or writing, the arts are the media through which that culture's history, mores, and values are transmitted to the younger generations and perpetuated.

Many of the things that young children do as play—singing, drawing, dancing—are natural forms of art. These activities engage all the senses and wire the brain for successful learning (Sousa, 2006). When children enter school, these art activities need to be continued and enhanced. Brain areas are developed as the child learns songs and rhymes and creates drawings and finger plays.

The arts are not just expressive and affective, they are deeply cognitive (Gullatt, 2008). They develop essential thinking tools: pattern recognition and development, mental representations of what is observed or imagined, and careful observation of the world to name a few.

Research studies have examined both stand-alone arts programs as well as those that integrate concepts and skills from the arts in other curriculum areas. One intriguing revelation of these studies is that the most powerful effects are found in programs that integrate the arts with subjects in the core curriculum (Bodilly, Augustine, & Zakaras, 2008). Researchers suggest that arts integration causes both students and teachers to rethink how they view the arts and generates conditions that are ideal for learning (Perso et al., 2011).

Studies consistently show the following in schools where arts are integrated in the core curriculum:

- Students have a greater emotional investment in their classes.
- Students work more diligently and learn from each other.
- Art and music teachers become the center of multi-class projects.
- Learning in all subjects becomes attainable through the arts.
- Curriculum becomes more authentic, hands-on, and project-based (Perso et al., 2011).

- A water supply to make the paper damp. A damp sponge or rag works best. Water may also be sprinkled directly onto the paper.
- Finger paint. This can be special finger paint or dry tempera paint mixed with liquid starch or liquid detergent to make a thick mixture.
- Racks to dry the finished work.
- A smock for each painter.
- A nearby sink with running water for washing hands and cleaning up, or a bucket of soapy water, sponges, and paper towels.
- For finger painting, tables should be covered with linoleum, Formica, or plastic, and children should wear smocks. Plenty of paper towels and clean rags should be provided. Smooth-surfaced paper is dipped in a pan of water and spread flat on a table.
- The quickest, simplest way to make finger paint is to combine liquid starch with dry tempera. This may be done by pouring a generous dollop

of starch onto the paper and then sprinkling it with dry tempera. Alternatively, some teachers like to stir the dry pigment into an entire container of starch base. No matter how the paint is originally prepared, you need to be ready to add more ingredients as children work. While mixing, strive for rich, brilliant color and sufficient paint to fill the paper completely if the child wishes. Children must be allowed to experiment with the paint as they wish, using their fingers, the palms of their hands, their wrists, and their arms.

Prepared finger paints may be used, or the children may help mix a recipe from Chapter 13. If the recipe is used, the mixture may be separated into three or four parts and coloring added—either food color or the powdered tempera used for easel painting. Children like to add their own color; they may use salt shakers containing powdered paint and mix in the color with their fingers. Adding soap flakes (not detergents)

Art Displays

There are so many more ways to display children's artwork than just on the bulletin board. Here are some ideas to help get you started on new ways to display the work of young artists:

- Involve the children in selecting work for display.

- Add children's commentary, narrative, or description to the display. Be sure to write the narrative or description on a separate Post-it note or paper rather than on the children's artwork.

- Personalize displays. On a large bulletin board, mark sections off for each artist. Take children's photos and invite them to draw self-portraits to hang in their own gallery. Encourage children to discuss and select the rest of the artwork they wish to display in their section of the bulletin board. See Chapter 8 for suggestions on using a digital camera for presenting children's artwork.

- Make interactive displays. Have children make and display a group collage of materials that encourage viewers to touch it when they see it. Make peephole covers for pictures. Tape the peephole cover on one side of the picture. Encourage children to guess what's under the peephole, then lift it up to see if they guessed correctly.

- Suspend wire sculptures from clear fishing line.

- Make floor display cubes out of cardboard boxes with taped-on, clear cellophane tops for peek-a-boo viewing.

- Make an elastic "clothesline" for displaying artwork. Stretch a length of ¼-inch elastic along the wall chosen for display. Staple it in place. Use miniature clothespins to hang the children's artwork. The elastic stretches slightly, and the clothespins are always in place as instant hang-ups for new artwork.

- For an interesting display method, place a huge sheet of clear, shatterproof Plexiglas over children's artwork on the classroom floor. Encourage children to take a closer look at their artwork on their tummies.

- Consider dividing your display into categories by media—watercolors, easel paintings, tabletop paintings, mixed media (collage, sand painting)—or by type, such as paintings, sculptures, or construction projects.

- Be certain to display at least one example of *every* child's work.

- Create display panels with borrowed tri-fold screens or buy wooden lattice panels from your local garden-, hardware-, or lumber store. Secure them on wooden stands and use to display art work. Place heavier sculptures on tables or in safe places on the floor under one of these panels.

- Paint a large cardboard box to use as a three-dimensional kiosk to hang pictures on. Use shoeboxes to display children's clay work.

- Show off young children's creative work at their eye level on classroom walls or bulletin boards. Keep bulletin boards low so children can help attach materials to them. Toddlers can safely touch displays if you slide drawings down behind clear Plexiglas frames.

- To keep artwork accessible, use press-on cork tiles to create low bulletin boards for toddlers. Use different levels of paper or cloth-covered boxes as pedestals to display clay sculptures. Display delicate clay miniatures in the partitions of a beverage six-pack carrier placed on its side.

---

to the paint mixture increases variety. Finger painting can also be done with interesting materials such as cold cream and shaving cream. Be sure to check the list of ingredients on the label for any ingredients children may be allergic to.

Finger painting variations. Another method of finger painting is to cover a table with white oilcloth and let the children work on the oilcloth. The mixture can later be washed off with a hose or faucet. This activity is good for all ages.

For a change, use waxed paper instead of regular finger painting paper. Its transparent quality will lend an interesting effect. A combination of any liquid dishwashing detergent and dark-colored tempera paint (one part paint, one part soap) can be applied to waxed paper. Cover the surface evenly so the painter can make a simple design with his or her fingers.

Finger painting without paper is another variation. Children finger paint directly onto plastic trays or a table top. When each child finishes, place a piece of paper on top of the finger painting and rub across the back of the paper. Lift the paper from the tray or table top, and you will have a print of the finger painting. The trays are easily rinsed off in the sink.

12-7f Pasting Materials and Use

The following is basic information on pasting materials and use:

- Small jars of paste. (Or give each child a square of waxed paper with a spoonful of paste on it. This prevents waste.) A wooden tongue depressor is a good tool for spreading the paste, or paste can be spread with the fingers. Glue sticks can also be used.
- Sheets of plain or colored manila or construction paper in many sizes.
- Collage materials. Some of these can be paper shapes in different colors, scraps of cloth, feathers, yarn, tinfoil, string, beans, sawdust, bottle caps, buttons, Styrofoam packing pieces, rock salt, bits of bark, and any other things that look interesting.
- Blunt scissors, for both left- and right-handed children.
- Pasting should be done away from climbing toys, building blocks, and similar large-motor activities. All the materials for pasting should be on a shelf at child level. Collage and pasting materials should be placed on a separate table and be sorted into shallow containers, such as baskets or clear plastic boxes, so that children can readily see the kinds of things that are available and consider how they will look when arranged together. Some children will enjoy tearing and pasting, while others will prefer cutting and pasting. Of course, children should learn the safety rules for using scissors early in the year. The teacher must also be sure that all young children have only blunt scissors.
- Keep paste in small plastic containers or jars. To help children learn to keep lids on jars, mark the bottom and top of each jar with a number or a colored X. Show children how to match up the jar with its lid by matching colored Xs or numbers. In this way, children learn to keep the lids on the jars and to recognize numbers and colors as well. Show children how to rinse out paste brushes and where to return all pasting material. Set up a place to put finished work to dry.
- Using common recycled household disposables will make cleanup easier. Aluminum pie tins and frozen food trays are both excellent for holding paint, paste, or glue for table activities.

At the end of the activity, you may want to recycle the aluminum. Another way to make cleanup easier after pasting is to fold over the top edges of a large paper bag, then tape the bag to one end of your work table. When children have finished their projects, scraps can easily be swept off the table into the bag, which can then be tossed into the trash.

12-7g Scrap Art Materials and Use

The following is basic information on scrap art materials and use:

- Paste, glue, glue stick, tape, and stapler.
- Colored tissue paper.
- Colored sticky tape, gummed circles, stars, and designs.
- Tempera paint, chalk, crayons, and colored markers.
- Odds and ends of scrap material—egg cartons, Styrofoam pieces, plastic containers and lids, pinecones, feathers, and buttons. For scrap art activities, all materials need to be in good order. This is because this type of activity requires a large supply of materials. A special place is needed for all supplies that is within the child's reach and at eye level.
- Scraps of cloth may be kept in one box with scrap pieces glued on the outside to show the child at a glance what is in the box. Clear plastic shoe boxes are excellent for scrap art storage, as children can easily see the contents. Buttons may be kept in a muffin tin, feathers in a plastic bag, and old bits of jewelry for puppets in a plastic shoe box. The point is to keep each material in a specific place so that it is ready for planned or spontaneous projects.
- Organizing material in this simple, easy-to-find way helps children learn to work on their own. Having glue, glue sticks, scissors, paper, and all other materials on shelves at the child's height also encourages independent work. Cleanup time is much easier, too, when the children can see "what goes where" and can reach the places where materials are supposed to go.

12-7h Potter's Clay and Play Dough Materials and Use

The following is basic information on potter's clay and play dough materials and use:

- Potter's clay or play dough (mixed from the recipes at the end of Chapter 14 and kept in an airtight container).

● Clay or play dough table (select a table that is easy to clean, such as one with a Formica top, or spread large pieces of plastic for protection).

● Tools for clay work (toy rolling pins, cookie cutters, spoons, and blunt plastic knives).

● Working with clay and play dough requires a place away from all active centers such as building blocks, wheel toys, and climbing toys. The tables should be covered with Formica or oilcloth to make cleaning easier. Young children also enjoy working with clay on individual vinyl placemats, Masonite boards, burlap squares, or brown paper grocery bags. Newspaper does not work well because when it gets wet, bits of paper may mix with the clay.

● For clay projects that are meant to be hardened and possibly painted later, set up a good place for drying. Because these objects may take a few days to dry, this place must also be away from frequently used areas.

● Before starting any three-dimensional projects that require several stages such as molding, drying, and then painting, the teacher must be aware of children's interest spans. Some of these projects take longer than other art activities, and some children may lose interest and not finish the project. The teacher must also consider the time needed for preparing the material, making the objects, drying them, and painting them. Then it must be decided if the children's interest is strong enough to last through the time needed for the whole project. It is an unpleasant experience for both teacher and children when a project is too rushed. This takes the joy out of the activity for all involved.

Potter's clay. Potter's clay may be purchased in moist form at any art supply store. This is much easier to deal with than starting with dry powder. The clay is available in two colors—gray and terra cotta. (Terra cotta looks pretty, but stains clothing and is harder to clean up.) Clay requires careful storage in a watertight, airtight container to retain its malleable qualities. When children are through for the day, form it into large balls, press a thumb into them, and then fill the holes with water and replace the clay in the container. If oilcloth table covers are used with potter's clay, they can simply be hung up to dry, shaken well, and put away until next time.

Making play dough. Children should participate in making dough whenever possible. If allowed to help make the dough, children learn about measuring, blending, and cause and effect. They also have the chance to work together and practice cooperation.

The doughs that require no cooking are best mixed two batches at a time in separate deep dishpans. Using deep pans keeps the flour within bounds, and making two batches at a time relieves congestion and provides better participation opportunities. Tempera powder is the most effective coloring agent because it makes such intense shades of dough; adding it to the flour before pouring in the liquid works best. Dough can be kept in the refrigerator and reused several times. Removing it at the beginning of the day allows it to come to room temperature before being offered to the children—otherwise it can be discouragingly stiff and unappealing. The addition of flour or cornstarch on the second day is usually necessary to reduce stickiness.

Dough variations. All the dough recipes at the end of Chapter 14 have been carefully tested and are suitable for various purposes. In preschool centers where process, not product, is emphasized, the dough and clay are generally used again and again rather than the objects made by the children being allowed to dry and then sent home. For special occasions, however, it is nice to allow the pieces to harden and then to paint or color them. Two recipes included in Chapter 14 serve this purpose particularly well: ornamental clay and baker's dough. For dough to be truly satisfying, children need an abundance of it rather than meager little handfuls, and they should be encouraged to use it in a manipulative, expressive way rather than in a product-oriented way.

Cleanup. For clay cleanup, sponge off tables, mats, and boards. Burlap squares can be stacked and shaken when dry, and grocery bags can be thrown away. Clay-caked hands and tools should never be washed in the sink because clay can clog the drain. Instead, have children wipe off their tools and hands with paper towels, then wash them in a basin filled with soapy water. When the clay particles settle, you can let the soapy water down the drain and throw the sediment in the trashcan. Children may rinse their hands in the sink, and the tools may be left to dry on paper towels.

The cooked cornstarch recipes are the only ones that are particularly difficult to clean up because they leave a hard, dry film on the pan during cooking. However, an hour or two of soaking in cold water converts this to a jellylike material that is easily scrubbed off with a plastic pot-scrubbing pad. If pans are soaked during nap time, children will be quite interested in the qualities of this gelatinous material when they get up. You might even have one or two of them work on scrubbing the pot clean!

12-7i Woodworking Materials and Use

The following is basic information on woodworking materials and use:

- A bin of soft lumber pieces (leftover scraps of lumber)
- Supply of nails with large heads
- Wooden spools, corks, and twigs
- Wooden buttons, string, and ribbons to be nailed to wood or tied to heads of nails already hammered into the wood
- Bottle caps
- Small-hand tools (hammer and nails are best to start with; saws, screwdrivers, a vise, and a drill may be added later)
- Workbench
- Sandpaper
- A vise or C-clamp placed near the corner of the workbench, flush with the table top
- Safety goggles

For older children:

- Screws and screwdrivers—standard and Phillips
- Pencils, rulers, and tape measures
- Files, planes, levels
- Crowbars

Carpentry needs to be done in a special area away from other activities. Provide children plenty of good wood and satisfactory tools. A sturdy workbench of the right height is helpful.

The most basic woodworking tools are hammers and saws. Hammers should be good, solid ones—not tack hammers. Supply crosscut saws that can cut with or across the grain of the wood; these should be as short as possible. A well-made vise in which to place wood securely while sawing is invaluable. Preferably there should be two of these, one at each end of the table. (Inexpensive C-clamps can also be used for this purpose, or a board can be nailed to the table while the child saws it, but this leaves the troublesome chore of removing the nails afterward.)

Very young children enjoy sawing up the large pieces of Styrofoam that come as packing for electronic equipment. Hammering into such material or into plasterboard

is also quick and easy and does not require more force than 2- and 3-year-old children can muster. Older children need plentiful amounts of soft wood to work with.

Cabinet shops are a good source for scrap lumber. Only smooth lumber should be used. Pieces of various lengths and sizes add interest. The greater the variety of wood, the greater the challenge for building. An old tree stump is great fun for children to pound countless nails into.

Woodworking needs careful adult supervision because children can easily hurt themselves or each other with a hammer and saw. General guidelines for adult supervision include the following:

- Stay very close to the woodworking activity. Be within reach of each child.
- There should be no more than three or four children for one adult to supervise. Only one child at a time should use a saw.
- Show children how to saw away from their own fingers and from other children. Show them how to avoid hitting their fingers with the hammer.
- Hand out nails a few at a time.
- Never turn your back on the activity for even a few seconds.
- Make a wall-mounted tool board to store frequently used tools. Less-used tools can be stored in a cupboard. The outline of each tool can be marked on the board so children can figure out where to hang each tool. (More woodworking information is found in Chapter 14.)

Some variations for woodworking follow:

- Remember to vary the tools the children use as their skill (and self-control) increases.
- Purchase a variety of nails by the pound, not by the little box, from a hardware store. Children love an assortment of these. They can be set out in small foil pie plates to keep them from getting mixed up. These pie plates can be nailed to a long board to prevent spilling.
- Offer various kinds of trims to go with woodworking, such as wire; thick, colorful yarn; and wooden spools (with nails long enough to go through the spool).
- Have children wear safety glasses.
- Offer round things for wheels, such as bottle caps or buttons.
- Provide dowels of various sizes that will fit the holes made by the different sizes of bits.
- Younger children may use a rubber mallet with golf tees to pound into Styrofoam.

12-7j Safety

For all the activities in this chapter and in any art activities for young children, be sure that you are not using any unsafe art supplies. Potentially unsafe art supplies include the following:

- Powdered clay. It is easily inhaled and contains silica, which is harmful to the lungs. Instead, use wet clay, which cannot be inhaled.
  Paints that require solvents such as turpentine to clean brushes. Use only water-based paints.
- Cold-water or commercial dyes that contain chemical additives. Use only natural vegetable dyes made from beets, onion skins, and so on.
  Permanent markers, which may contain toxic solvents. Use only water-based markers.
  Instant papier-mâché, which may contain dust, lead, or asbestos. Use only black-and-white newspaper and library paste or liquid starch.
- Epoxy, instant glues, rubber cement, or other solvent-based glues. Use only water-based white glue.
  Aerosol spray paints, which may contain toxic solvents; spraying makes them even more hazardous.

The teacher should always do the following:

- Read labels.
- Check for age appropriateness. The Art and Creative Materials Institute labels art materials AP (approved product) and CP (certified product) when they are safe for young children, even if ingested. These labels are round. A product bearing the square "Health Label" is safe only for children older than 12 years.
  The best way to avoid exposure to hazardous chemicals is to *read the label* and follow the directions. Most hazardous consumer products are required to provide identification of hazardous chemicals on their labels. Label warnings should be taken seriously. They exist because chemicals contained in these products can be hazardous when inhaled, ingested, or absorbed through the skin. Read labels carefully and look for the following:

  DANGER—extremely flammable, corrosive and/or highly toxic
  POISON—highly toxic
  WARNING or CAUTION—less toxic

  Other key phrases to look for include HARMFUL IF SWALLOWED, AVOID SKIN

CONTACT, and FLAMMABLE, all of which indicate acute, or short-term, hazards. Older products (for example, an old bottle of rubber cement) or "professional" products (for example, some paints and photographic solutions) may not carry a warning label. Keep children away from unlabeled products.

- Check for ventilation requirements. In most cases, one open window or door is not sufficient ventilation. You can stay safe by opening windows and turning on a fan, or, weather permitting, take your art projects outside.
- A list of materials safe for young children is available from the Art and Creative Materials Institute's website. Always use products that are appropriate for the individual user. Children in grade 6 and lower and adults who may not be able to read and understand safety labeling should use only nontoxic materials.
- Do not eat or drink while using art materials. Wash up after use. Clean yourself and your supplies.
- Never use products for skin painting or food preparations unless indicated that the product is meant to be used in this way.
- Do not transfer art materials to other containers. You will lose the valuable safety information that is on the product package. Also, ingestion of these products can be avoided by keeping materials in their original containers.
- Imported art materials should be looked upon with extreme caution. Other countries have not developed the rigid safety codes adopted by the United States. Do not accept or use old art materials that may have been left in the school or donated by some well-meaning adult. If the materials do not bear the current safety codes, toss them out!
- If a marker stains the clothes or hands and does not clean up with simple soap and water, it is not appropriate or safe for young children to use.
- Use plastic containers for washing brushes; glass is dangerous in the hands of young children.
- Paper cutters should not be used by elementary children (or younger!). The paper cutter should be kept out of students' reach and left in a locked position always with the blade turned to the wall or out of reach.
- Know your students. Be aware of students' allergies. Children with allergies to wheat, for example, may be irritated by wheat paste used

in papier mâché. Other art materials that may cause allergic reactions include chalk or other dusty substances, water-based clay, and any material that contains petroleum products. (Qualley 2008).

- Be aware of students' habits. Some students put everything in their mouths. (This can be the case at any age.) Others act out or behave aggressively. Use your knowledge of individual students' tendencies to help you plan art activities that will be safe for all students.
- A good rule of thumb about markers is that if the label on a marker says "nontoxic" or does not say "permanent ink," the ink is probably water-based. Not only are water-based varieties safer to use, they are easier to remove from the wall!

Did You Get It?

A preschool teacher's assistant randomly places crayons and markers in baskets and then sets one basket on each table where students are coloring. From a developmental perspective, what is the drawback of this system?

a. The children are likely to argue over colors of crayons.
b. The children will not learn proper organization methods.
c. This system does not teach children how to categorize colors.
d. This system gives too much power to the assistant instead of the teacher.

Take the full quiz on CourseMate.

Summary

12-1 Discuss the basic goals for the early childhood art program.

The first and main goal is the emphasis on process over product. The expression of one's self is what is important here, not what the finished product looks like.

A second major objective of the art program is to meet the needs of chidren. This means that the program must be designed for their age, ability, and interests. The third objective is to give each child the chance to think originally and to learn to work independently. The fourth goal is for children to be creative thinkers. The fifth goal is to allow children to grow at their own pace.

12-2 Describe the basic setup for art activities in the early childhood art program.

The early childhood art program is a part of the early childhood curriculum in which children have the chance to work with many kinds of materials and techniques.In setting up for art activities, the basic considerations are physical environment and space, ease of cleanup, and setting up for daily and weekly art activities, including these additional issues:

- The age of the group will always be the major consideration in planning as each age group has varying abilities and interests requiring different arrangements of space in the environment.
- The art area should be arranged for ease in cleaning up and dispensing materials. One type of arrangement that works well is to separate wet from dry materials.
- To work creatively with art materials, children need to be free from constraints and worry related to keeping themselves and their work spaces clean.
- The teacher should make sure every day that there are designated places, equipment, and materials for art experiences.

- To enhance children's creative experiences, the teacher needs to plan for and set up weekly art activities in addition to the children's daily activities.

12-3 Discuss how to plan art activities for toddlers.

Toddlers are very active and want to explore everything. For this reason, they need materials that are sturdy—practically indestructible—and do not include tiny pieces that might be swallowed. Only a few materials should be put out at a time so toddlers are not overwhelmed by too many choices. Art materials, such as crayons, play dough, chalk, and paint, need to be frequently available to toddlers. These materials should be presented under the supervision of an adult to encourage their appropriate use. In setting up art (and all other) centers for toddlers, a teacher should arrange lots of space and clear traffic patterns because toddlers are prone to falling, grabbing, and running.

12-4 Discuss how to plan art activities for young preschoolers.

Young preschool children, 2–4 years of age, have a limited interest span. Even the most interesting activities hold their interest for only approximately 10 to 15 minutes. Thus, the teacher must plan several activities and alternative activities for this age group. Some appropriate art activities for children of this age are easel and finger painting, printing, collage, coloring with crayons, using play dough, making simple puppets, and sculpting.

12-5 Discuss how to plan art activities for older preschoolers and kindergarteners.

Older preschool children and kindergartners (4–6 years of age) have begun to develop better small-muscle control in the fingers, hands, and wrists. For this reason, they enjoy cutting with scissors, using smaller paintbrushes, and trying out a wide variety of colored markers. All of these activities are also appropriate for middle- and upper-elementary level students.

12-6 Explain how to adapt art activities for children with special needs.

It takes many repetitions for the child with developmental delays to fully learn a new skill. For this reason, some children will appear to have mastered the task one day but then be unable to perform the same task on another day. Open-ended art activities are most appropriate for children with developmental delays. Some effective techniques to use are demonstration, task breakdown, and hand-over-hand assistance as needed. It also helps to demonstrate the activity by doing it first while the child watches. Another approach is to break down an activity into a series of small steps. It is most important to help the child complete one step before going on to the next.

Students who have impaired mobility may need to use alternate tools and materials for some activities. Rehabilitation specialists may help you solve unique problems. A number of special tools are available for students with physical impairments (such as a mouthpiece that holds a pencil or brush).

For children with visual impairments, you can help by offering verbal descriptions about what the room looks like, where furniture and playthings are located, and what other people in the room are doing. Students with visual impairments can participate in discussions about artwork, especially with regard to themes portrayed in art that are related to the student's own experience. In art activities, provide materials to create tactile, kinesthetic artwork—clay, textured paper, cloth, small boxes, or wood blocks that student can arrange.

12-7 List some basic materials and equipment and their use in the early childhood art program.

Basic art materials needed in the early childhood art program include drawing materials, chalking materials, brush materials, mixing paint, finger paint, pasting materials, scrap art, potter's clay, play dough, and woodworking materials. There are also unsafe materials that should not be used in an early childhood classroom.

Key Terms

brush painting 272
chalking materials and use 271
crayons 265
drawing materials and use 271
finger painting materials and use 272

mixing paint 272
pasting materials and use 275
printing 265
process over product 256
potter's clay and play dough
   materials and use 275

scrap art materials and use 275
toddler-appropriate art activities 261
woodworking materials and use 277

Learning Activities

A. It is hard to truly appreciate the individual merits of the dough recipes unless they are actually available for inspection and experimentation. As a class project, have volunteers make them up and bring them to class to try out.

B. Suppose a bad fairy has waved her wand and ruled that you can select only three basic types of creative, self-expressive activities to use for a whole year in your preschool. Which three would you select and why? Answer the same question for a group of older children, grades 1 through 5.

C. Suppose that same bad fairy has waved her wand again, and now you are allowed to purchase only paint and glue (no paper even!) for your creative activities. How limiting is this? What self-expressive activities would you actually be able to offer under these circumstances? How might you go about acquiring the necessary free materials to make them possible? Be specific.

D. Visit one or possibly several early childhood programs and observe the arts activities. Keep in mind these points in observing:
   1. Are the equipment and activities right for the age, ability, and interest levels of the children?
   2. Is the area well planned for each activity?
   3. Are the children free to make what they want with the material?

E. Set up a classroom, real or imagined, for one or more of the following activities:

- Finger painting
- Collage
- Making puppets

Consider the following in setting up the activity:

- Location of water source
- Preparation of area
- Preparation of materials
- Preparation of children
- Teacher preparation
- Activity itself
- Cleanup
- Drying and storage space for work in progress or finished works

F. Draw up a plan of a room set up for art activities for 3-, 4-, and 5-year-old children.
   1. Include the following areas:

brush and finger painting	crayon and chalk work
clay	woodworking
puppetry	scrap art
papier-mâché work	

2. Show on the plan where the following areas would be found:

storage space   water source(s)

child-level shelves   light source(s)

drying areas

G. Ask children what they think is the hardest part about cleaning up. Record their answers. See if there is one thing that is mentioned more than others. Check on the problem to see if it is caused by room setup, supply setup, water source, or something else.

H. Go on an odds-and-ends hunt.
1. See how many different kinds of things can be found for use in art projects. Things to look for include spools, Styrofoam, feathers, buttons, and foil.
2. Sort the material and store it in the best way possible. Label each container so that children will know what is inside.

I. Choose a grade level from grades 1 through 5. Draw up a room plan for art activities for this grade level.

Include the same areas and requested information as in question F.

J. In the year 105, paper was invented by Ts'ai Lun, an official of the Chinese Imperial Court at the Han Dynasty in China. Lun's paper was made from bamboo and mulberry fibers, fishnets, and rags.

What did people use before paper? Can you name 10 uses of paper? Of what other material can paper be made? Do you know what paper is made of now? Does your school recycle its paper?

K. Try these cleanup secrets after an art activity.

For grades K–2: Have the children form a line and march around the room to fun music. When you see a piece of trash, the child in front picks it up and then goes to the end of the line. The next child in line has a turn. Children will love this.

Grades 3–5. Wander around the room and make a note of three pieces of trash. Give children one minute to clean. Reward the finders of your "secret scraps" with a small something from your "goodie box."

L. Compare a list of the various art materials used in several kindergarten classes. Rank these in order of value for the child. Are there any materials used that cannot be justified as being of value for development? Explain your answers.

References

Bodilly, S. J., Augustine, C. H., & Zakaras, L. (2008). Revitalizing arts education through community-wide coordination. Rand Corporation. Retrieved from http://www.rand.org/pubs/monographs/MG702.html.

Gardner, H. E. (1993). *Multiple intelligences.* New York, NY: Basic Books.

Gardner, H. E. (1999). *Intelligence reframed. Multiple intelligences for the 21st century.* New York, NY: Basic Books.

Gould, P., & Sullivan, J. (1999). *The inclusive early childhood classroom: Easy ways to adapt learning centers for all children.* Beltsville, MD: Gryphon House.

Gullatt, D. E. (2008). Enhancing student learning through arts integration: Implications for the profession. *High School Journal, 91*(4), 12–25.

Lee, I. M., Balestrino, M. D., Phelps, R. A., Kurs-Lasky, M., Chaves-Genecco, D., Paradise, J. L., & Feldman, H. M. (2008). Early histories of school-aged children with attention-deficit-hyperactivity disorder. *Child Development, 79*(6), 1853–1868.

Lougy, R. A. (2007). *Teaching young children with ADHD: Successful strategies and practical interventions for Pre-K–3.* Thousand Oaks, CA: Corwin.

Lowenfeld, V., & Brittain, W. L. (1987). *Creative and mental growth of the child* (8th ed.). New York, NY: Macmillan.

Perso, T., Nutton, G., Fraser, J., Silburn, S. D., & Tait, A. (2011). The "arts" in education: A review of arts in schools and arts-based teaching models that improve school engagement, academic, social, and cultural learning. Centre for Child Development and Education, Menzies School of Health Research.

Ponder, C., & Kissinger, L. (2009). Shaken and stirred: A pilot project in arts and special education. *Teaching Artist Journal, 7*(1), 40–46.

Qualley, C. A. (2008). *Safety in the artroom.* Worcester, MA: Davis Publications.

Sousa, D. A. (2006). How the arts develop the young brain. *School Administratori, 63*(11), 8–14.

 Visit CourseMate for this textbook to access the eBook, Did You Get It? quizzes, Digital Downloads, TeachSource Videos, flashcards, and more. Go to CengageBrain.com to log in, register, or purchase access.

 Casper Holroyd

Two-Dimensional Activities

Using as a framework the basic information about developmental levels, creativity, aesthetics, the principles of art and design, and planning and implementing creative activities presented thus far, let us now take a closer look at the general processes of drawing/picture making, printmaking, and collage. Note that specific ages are not listed for many of the activities in sections of this chapter because many of the activities are designed to be springboards for art experiences and are not limited to certain age groups. Use your knowledge of the developmental levels of the children in your group as a guide to choosing and using activities in this and all chapters of the book. You will, however, find the

Learning Objectives

After completing this chapter, you should be able to:

13-1 Discuss the various ways to motivate children in their use of the various two-dimensional media in this chapter.

13-2 Describe the tools, materials, and techniques involved in the activity of painting in the early childhood program.

13-3 Describe the tools, materials, and techniques involved in printmaking in the early childhood program.

13-4 Define collage, and describe the tools, materials, and techniques involved in collage in the early childhood program.

naeyc
NAEYC Program Standards

1c Using developmental knowledge to create healthy, respectful, supportive, and challenging learning environments.

DAP
DAP Criteria

2E1 Teachers arrange firsthand, meaningful experiences that are intellectually and creatively stimulating . . . by providing a rich variety of materials, challenges, and ideas that are worthy of the child's attention.

3D2 Teachers plan curriculum experiences to draw on children's own interests and introduce children to things likely to interest them.

developmental information provided in the previous sections helpful in determining which activities to initiate with children. Children's reactions to the suggested activities will determine the appropriateness of the choice. Their interest, enthusiasm, and ability to do the activity should be your guide to each activity's appropriateness.

13-1 Motivating Children

naeyc **DAP** To young children, the act of drawing and painting comes naturally. It is a means by which they communicate visually their ideas and feelings about themselves and their world. They may work in paint, crayon, or chalk; each material has its own distinct characteristics for the child to explore.

Sensitive teachers understand and appreciate the charm and freshness of children's early drawings and paintings. They **motivate children** by helping them recall their experiences and record these in art media. Because teachers respect the individuality of each learner, they inspire and encourage each child to express personal reactions about the world as she or he understands it. In this way, children discover and build their own unique style of expression. Each child's picture is different from the others in the class, just as her or his appearance and personality are different.

At this point, it is important to note that the terms **picture making/drawing** in this chapter refer to any and all forms of purposeful visual expressions, beginning with controlled scribbling. A common error associated with picture making or drawing is to equate it with artwork that contains recognizable objects or figures. Children's pictures and drawings (artwork) may take any form, just as long as the child is expressing herself or himself visually in a nonrandom way (see Photo 13-1).

When properly motivated, the child eagerly examines materials and looks forward to proceeding with the activity. Most young children are eager to express themselves in their drawings. However, some children may need more encouragement than others to take the first step. Sometimes a few motivating ideas from the teacher can liven up a child who seems to be less motivated than usual.

Reading a familiar story or singing a song can stimulate art. For example, the artwork in children's books by artists such as Leo Lionni and Eric Carle are excellent choices to motivate a child's creativity in art activities. The colorful collage work in their children's books provides perfect examples of this medium and is sure to encourage children to create their own special collages. Such stimulation is most successful when children are

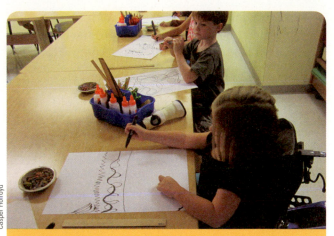

PHOTO 13-1 Children's pictures and drawings may take any form.

Casper Holroyd

able to associate themselves with the story, poem, or song. They might be asked to think about the character they liked the best, a new ending for the story, or the part that surprised them or pleased them the most and then to draw or paint what they thought.

There are many ways of motivating that awaken the child to the world of color, shape, size, texture, action, and mood. Some of the following ideas may help stimulate children's spontaneity and experimentation:

- Take a walking trip using careful observation.
- Use a digital camera to take pictures on a walking trip. Take pictures of things seen, events, products, and work being done. Then discuss these images, reflecting on them and their significance. Discuss the colors, lines, and other design principles reflected in the images.
- On the trip, gather a collection of objects for a "touch-and-see" display.
- Put up an interesting bulletin board or case display of your children's and your artwork.
- Dramatize stories, animals, birds, and so on.
- Encourage children to try using materials in different ways if children do not discover them on their own. For example, you might say, "I wonder if the back and side of the crayon will make the same kinds of marks as the pointed end?"
- Exhibit sincere pleasure when a discovery is announced, and share it with others in the group.
- Encourage children to bring materials from home to incorporate into their art.
- Share the works of several artists that represent the same or similar theme. This will help children understand that they can draw in many different ways.

- Display the work of each child at some time during the year, and call attention to the fact that everyone sees things differently (nonrealistic use of color included).
- Offer found materials that can be used as accessories or tools for artwork. Children will find a variety of ways to create with them. For example, they will use buttons for stringing, glued designs, wheels on toys, or eyes for a puppet or as objects for printmaking.
- Add new materials that match the group's interest at particular times. Children who live in snowy areas may need lots of white paint. Temperate spring seasons will stimulate use of pastel colors. Gold and silver papers will spark experimentation with holiday decorations. Furry fabrics may intensify interest in animals and pets.
- Make papers available in many kinds, shapes, and colors. The variety will lead to more responses and experimentation with techniques.

Children's growing awareness is gradually reflected in their pictures as the ability to interpret their environment increases. As the process continues, the teacher and children can evaluate their progress and consider how pictures might be varied, different media used, and any other changes children might suggest.

Did You Get It?

How does a preschool teacher displaying the work of each of her students at different times during the school year relate to the children's development of creativity?

a. She motivates them to engage in art.
b. She stunts their creative initiative.
c. She embarrasses them by highlighting their differences in ability, causing them to stop creating art.
d. She neither contributes to nor detracts from their creative initiative.

Take the full quiz on CourseMate.

13-2 Development of Painting Skills

A child's development of painting skills occurs in a specific sequence (see Figure 13-1). At the beginning of this developmental sequence, infants can distinguish bright and dark and have some color perception, especially clear, bright colors such as red. Early experiences with paint involve squeezing and manipulating thick paint and the trickling effect of thin paint. These explorations are crucial, as during this period children are developing mastery of paint and an understanding of the technique that can be used to control it. Once these skills have been acquired, children can use paint for their own purposes. Later, children explore paint's ability to cover surfaces, to overlap, to mix, and to layer.

As their technical skills develop, children are able to place blocks of color alongside each other to create a patchwork effect. Paint is also used in a linear fashion to draw. The ability to handle paint and to draw accurately gradually come together and children are then able to use paint to create unique, personal images. An interest in mixing paint is present from an early stage, and children need opportunities to practice these skills. As their mixing skills improve, children should have the chance to mix their own colors in response to what they see (Duffy, 2010).

"A picture is not thought out and settled beforehand. While it is being done it changes as one's thoughts change. And when it is finished, it still goes on changing, according to the state of mind of whoever is looking at it. A picture lives a life like a living creature, undergoing the changes imposed upon us by our life from day to day. This is natural enough, as the picture lives only through the man who is looking at it."

—Pablo Picasso

13-2a Painting with a Brush

naeyc **DAP** **Painting with a brush** encourages the spontaneous use of color (see Photo 13-2). Finger painting, covered in Chapter 12, is another form of painting that is enjoyable for children.

Materials. Basic materials for painting with brushes include the following:

- Watercolor paint sets. These are actually dehydrated tempera colors in concentrated cakes. They provide easy and convenient paint for individual use or group activity in the classroom.

Birth to 1 year
- Explore texture using all their senses. For example, the texture of food
- Are aware of color and light, especially clear, bright colors such as red

1–2 years
- Explore the textural qualities of paint using feet, hands, mouth
- Use hands, feet, and fingers to manipulate paint on surfaces
- Are aware of color in their environment
- Use paint to make purposeful marks

2–3 years
- Use paint to make separate marks
- Ask the name of the color of objects and know the names of some colors
- Are able to sort and match color hues

3–4 years
- Know the names of primary colors
- Are interested in mixing their own colors
- Enjoy exploring a range of brushes and surfaces
- Use paint to produce separate and overlapping blocks of color
- Are able to sort and match color shades

4–5 years
- Are able to name secondary colors
- Are able to mix their own colors, know that adding white lightens a color and that black darkens it
- Choose the appropriate brushes and paper for task. For example, know that thin brush will produce fine line
- Use paint to produce representational forms and patterns
- Describe their intentions, and comment on outcomes in their painting
- Are starting to match colors used in painting to colors seen, when representing realism

At 6 years
- Include fine detail in their paintings
- Are able to mix a wide range of colors with exactness
- Place small areas of color accurately
- Place colors side by side with precision

(Duffy, 2010)

FIGURE 13-1 The development of painting from birth to age six.

Source: Duffy, B. (2010). Supporting creativity and imagination in the early years. 2nd edition. New York: McGraw-Hill Education. Reproduced with the kind permission of Open University Press. All rights reserved.

TeachSource Digital Download   Download from CourseMate.

PHOTO 13-2 Painting with a brush is a popular preschool art activity.

Casper Holroyd

Flat-tip and Round-tip Brushes—Basic Information

The best brushes are made of natural hairs from animals such as hogs.

Basic Flat Brush Sizes

Length	Width of Bristles	Ages Appropriate
8"	1"	Toddler and up
12"	½"	4 years and up
6"	½"	4 years and up
12"	¾"	3–4 years
6"	¾"	3–4 years
12"	¼"	5 years and up
8"	¼"	5 years and up

Basic Round Brush Sizes (With Pointed Tips)

8"	¾"	6 years and up
8"	½"	6 years and up

FIGURE 13-2 Flat-tip and round-tip brushes—basic information.

© Cengage Learning.

These watercolor sets should never be too dry and hard. Try to make an indentation with your fingernail. If the watercolor is too hard, it is not the type to buy for young children. Some watercolors come in oval button shapes. Children will enjoy using these more than the square ones because they do not have to manipulate their brush to get into the corners and because ovals are more suited to brush movements. Also, small sets are preferred to larger ones. Smaller sets encourage children to mix their own colors. Many paint sets include a plastic paintbrush. Discard this, and be sure to use paint brushes with natural fiber bristles.

● When buying brushes, be sure to buy those that are labeled "all media" or "for use with oils, acrylics, and watercolors." Brushes that target watercolor alone will be too soft for young children's use. Don't buy wall-painters' brushes or those where all fibers are the same length and end in a flat tip. Brushes with plastic bristles are appropriate only if the brush tapers

to a point like a natural bristled brush. (See Figure 13-2 for suggested brush sizes for children of various ages.) Students should have the opportunity to experiment with a variety of brush sizes when painting. Thick lines can be created by gently pressing down on the brush. Thin lines can be created by lightly touching the surface of the paper with the tip of the brush. Use a wide brush for covering large areas with paint.

● To use paints in cakes: Place a few drops of water on the surface of each cake of color to moisten the paint. Never grind the brush into the cake or onto the paper. The child holds the brush as he would a pencil but farther back on the handle. Dip the brush in water and brush the surface of the moistened cake to obtain smooth, creamy paint.

● To use powder paint (tempera): Fill a can ¼ full of dry paint. Add water slowly, stirring constantly until the paint has the consistency of thin cream. A small amount of liquid starch or liquid detergent may be added to the mixture as a binder. Use enough paint to make good, rich colors. For best results, prepare paint when needed; large amounts kept over a period of time have a tendency to sour. Containers for use with powder paint include milk cartons, juice cans, yogurt containers, coffee cans, plastic cups, and cut-down plastic bottles. A set of paints can be carried easily if containers are placed in tomato baskets, soft-drink carriers, boxes, or trays.

- Individual pieces of paper, at least 12- × 18 inches: roll paper, manila paper, newspaper, wallpaper, newsprint, freezer paper.
- Water containers for painting and rinsing brushes: coffee cans, milk cartons, juice cans, and cut-down plastic bottles. Half-gallon plastic containers with handles (the kind used for milk) are light and can be filled to carry water during the painting lesson.
- Paper towels or scrap paper for blotting brushes while painting.
- Newspapers to protect painting area. Painting may be done on paper-covered tables or desks, or on paper pinned to a bulletin board or fastened to a chalkboard. Painting can also be done on the floor if it is protected with newspaper.
- A bucket of child-sized moist sponges for cleanup.

13-2b Care and Storage of Materials

- Lay paintings horizontally to dry before stacking. An unused floor space along the wall is suitable for this purpose (see Chapter 12).
- Wipe paint sets clean with paper toweling. They can be stored in a cardboard carton.
- Students should always thoroughly rinse their brush tips between colors of paint. Next, they should gently blot the brush on a paper towel to test for missed paint. If paint appears on the towel, it should be rinsed and tested again. Sometimes paint gets deep inside the bristles and needs more rinsing.
- Rinse brushes under gently flowing water. Do not use hot water.
- Place a small amount of soap in the palm of the hands.
- Gently rub the bristles of the brush in soapy palms. This will remove stubborn paint from deep inside the bristles.
- Rinse the brush under gently running water to remove all of the soap.
- Blot, gently reshape the bristles into a point, and store brushes to dry upright in a container.
- Clean brushes after each use. Neglect will cause the brush to lose its shape. Never rest a brush vertically on its bristles.

Processes. Painting with brushes may require some demonstration of the following techniques:

- How to prepare paint trays for use. A drop or two of water is placed in each paint color to moisten it.
- How to use a variety of brush strokes. Encourage children to paint directly, using full, free strokes.

Use the point, side, and flat surface of the brush. Try wide lines, thin lines, zigzag lines, and dots and dabs.
- How to mix colors on the paper as they paint. Try dipping one side of the brush in one color, and the other side in a second color to blend paint in one stroke.
- How to create textures. Paint with bits of sponge, crushed paper or cloth, cardboard, string, sticks, or an old toothbrush. A stiff brush with most of the paint removed creates interesting textural effects.
- How to handle excess paint or water on a brush.
- How to clean paint trays.
- How to rinse and dry brushes.

13-2c More Painting Hints

- Thicken easel paint with liquid starch to cut down on drips.
- To help paint stick better to slick surfaces such as foil, waxed paper, Styrofoam, or plastic, mix dry tempera with liquid soap.
- To keep paints smelling fresh and sweet, add a few drops of mint extract, oil of wintergreen, or cloves.
- For an added sensory experience, try adding lemon flavoring to yellow paint, mint to green, vanilla to white, and peppermint to red paint. You might want to caution children—especially younger ones—not to taste the paint.
- Keep dated examples of each child's work in the child's portfolio to reflect his or her growth and development in creative expression. Children will enjoy seeing their progress in control and expression over the year.
- Use a digital camera to create a digital portfolio of children's artwork. One day every month, put a reminder on your calendar to carry a fully charged digital camera throughout the day. Snap the highlights of the day but especially zoom in on children's artwork. At the end of the day, empty the camera into a dated folder to keep on your hard drive. After about four months, select about 10 pictures from each folder and print them, grouped by month. This is a fun way for parents and children to see how much they've developed over the course of the year and their progress in art. See Chapter 11 for more suggestions about using portfolios with children's artwork.

More ideas on painting activities for children as well as recipes for making various types of paints are found at the end of this chapter.

13-2d Crayons

Most young children are introduced to using crayons before starting school. (See Chapter 12 for additional information about crayons.)

Materials. Crayon drawings may be done on a wide assortment of surfaces, such as newsprint, wrapping paper, newspaper, construction paper, corrugated board, cloth, and wood. This is an ideal medium for all children because it is bold, colorful, clean, and inexpensive. Crayons work well on most papers. They can be applied thinly to produce semitransparent layers of subtle color, and these layers can be coated with black crayon and scratched through for crayon etchings.

Processes. Encouraging children to experiment with crayons and to explore the use of different parts of the crayon leads to the discovery of new methods that satisfy their need for expression. The wax crayon has great versatility.

The best way to get bright, rich color from the crayon and onto the paper is by pressing hard. A cushion sheet placed underneath the drawing will assist children in creating bright colors easily.

- Make thin lines with the point of the crayon, and make heavy lines with the blunt end or side of the crayon.
- Vary the pressure to create subtle tints or solid, brilliant colors.
- Make rough texture by using broken lines, dots, jabs, dashes, and other strokes with the point.
- Create a smooth texture by using the flat side or by drawing lines close together in the same direction with the point.
- Twist, turn, swing the crayon in arcs, and move it in various ways to achieve different effects.
- Repeat motions to create rhythm.
- Notch the side of a crayon. This creates negative lines when the crayon is used on its side, resulting in interesting designs with each stroke.
- Use crayons to make designs and patterns on finger-paint paper. Then finger paint over the crayon design.
- For older children, combine the use of crayons and textiles. Children make their design with wax crayons directly onto a piece of cloth. Place the cloth between two pieces of paper and press with a warm iron. This will tend to set the design somewhat permanently in the fabric. Variations in the weave and texture of the cloth will affect the design.

See the end of this chapter for crayon batik and crayon chip activities.

Avoid using coloring books or photocopied papers. Children who are frequently given such patterns to color are, in fact, being told that they and their art are inadequate. A pattern of a dog for children to color says to them—more clearly than words could—"This is what your drawing should look like; this is the *right* way to make a dog." Instead of coloring book pages, provide children a variety of art supplies, media, large blocks of time, and the freedom to work at their developmental level.

The crayon offers new areas of creative interpretation when used in combination with other materials (see Photo 13-3):

- Use crayon and white chalk on colored construction paper.
- Make a crayon rubbing by placing shapes or textures under paper and rubbing over the surface.
- Make a crayon resist by first drawing in brilliant color, and then covering the drawing with watercolor paint.
- Paint a colorful background, allow it to dry, and then draw directly over the painted surface with chalk or crayon.
- Use white crayon underneath a color to make a brighter color.

Casper Holroyd

PHOTO 13-3 Crayon and water color drawing.

● Use Cray-Pas (oil pastel crayons) on colored
const. construction paper. Apply the oil pastels thickly
to get rich colors.

More crayon activities are found at the end of
this chapter.

13-2e Pasting

Paste serves a useful purpose, and its properties also
make it a valuable medium for creative expression.
Many teachers have given up using paste in favor of
glue sticks. These are easier to use and infinitely less
messy than "old-fashioned" white paste. However, the
stickiness, texture, odor, and changes that take place
as old-fashioned white paste is used provide children with opportunities for many discoveries. When
a young child picks up paste in his hands, the child
will almost automatically spread it over his fingers and
squeeze it or roll it to feel its stickiness. Before long,
the child spreads the paste over his hands, sometimes
even rubbing it into the palms. As paste dries, a child
feels a different sensation. When the child begins to
wash his hands, the paste is transformed from hard to
sticky to slimy, a phenomenon of great interest to a
child. Paste is a medium that can stimulate a child to
repeated explorations of the properties of matter.

Given sufficient paste and a piece of paper, a child
almost invariably smears the paste on the paper as
though it were finger paint. She moves her hand across
the page with sweeping motions. In some places on
the paper, the child smooths the paste until it is slick
and shiny. In other places, the child forms lumps of
paste and then enjoys pressing down on the lumps to
smooth them out. The paste-smeared paper becomes
an artistic creation for the child.

Having explored paste in this manner, a child
reaches for small pieces of paper and pastes piece upon
piece, using large quantities of paste in the process.
The child is excited by what can be accomplished
with the medium. When the child attempts to lift the
mound of paper that has been created, very often the
paper tears. The child discovers that paste is heavy.

Adults should avoid instructing children on the
uses of paste and allow them to make their own discoveries. Eventually a child will begin to create a
collage, arranging random shapes of varied colors on
large paper. At first, the child may pay no attention
to design; later she will learn to carefully arrange the
pieces to achieve a pleasing balance (see Photos 13-4a
and 13-4b). By adult standards, it may appear that the
amount of paste children use is exorbitant, but their

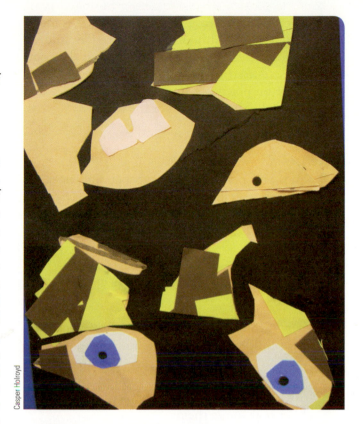

Casper Holroyd

Casper Holroyd

PHOTO 13-4 When cutting and pasting, a child may start
out not paying attention to design, but will later learn to
carefully arrange the pieces.

explorations are limited if they cannot have as much paste as they need. Although most paste for children is nontoxic, a teacher should be certain that the commercial paste used in the classroom is safe because children often put paste in their mouths. Paste can also be made by the child and/or the teacher.

13-2f Torn Paper and Pasting

Materials

Kinds of paper: construction paper, wallpaper, gift wrap, metallic paper, tissue paper, newspaper, illustrated magazine pages

For mounting: newsprint, construction paper, cardboard, wallpaper, newspaper (classified ad pages), cardboard box lids

Paste, glue sticks, scissors, brushes

Process

Demonstrate cutting and tearing paper shapes. Have children cut and tear paper shapes (see Photo 13-5).

Show a variety of papers different in color, and texture and encourage children's suggestions about how to use them.

Demonstrate pasting the torn pieces to the background.

PHOTO 13-5 Teachers can demonstrate cutting and tearing paper shapes, and then children can do it.

Casper Holroyd

- Point out how torn paper creates a textured edge, while cut edges appear smooth.
- Point out how, in tearing paper, greater control of the paper is achieved by tearing slowly with fingers close together.
- Encourage children to choose light and dark colors for interesting contrast and different sizes or shapes and a variety of papers for textural effects.
- Overlap or group paper shapes to produce new shapes and new combinations of colors and textures.
- Change the texture of cut paper by wrinkling, crumpling, slitting, and folding out.

Older children are eager to use scissors in collage and other pasting activities. There are some general safety points to remember when scissors are used with children:

- Children should always cut away from their bodies.
- Children should never point scissors at anyone.
- Children should never walk with scissors or spin them on the table.
- There are scissors specially made to spring open for students who are physically challenged.
- Many scissors on the market today can be used with the right or left hand. If these are not available, keep a supply of "lefty" scissors for students who need them.

Older children who have mastered scissoring skills will enjoy cut paper activities. Some suggestions for working with cut paper follow.

- Encourage children to think about the shape of an object and its edges before cutting.
- Plan the composition. Cut the big, important shapes first, then cut details, patterns, and textures, and glue last.
- Use a variety of shapes. Repeat shapes and change their size for variety. Repeat colors by changing their intensity or value for variety.
- Create textured areas by folding, fringing, pleating, curling, and weaving the paper.
- Overlap shapes to give depth and distance to a cut paper composition. Create distance in cut paper by working from the background forward.
- Glue small shapes, details, patterns, and textures to larger shapes before gluing them to the background.

- Glue around the outside edge of the shapes, not over the entire back of the shape.
- Create identical shapes by folding the paper once and remembering that the fold is the middle of the shape.
- Use positive and negative shapes in the composition. The positive shape is the cut shape. The remaining paper is the negative shape.
- Use the lightest colors first when creating with tissue paper. Cut and arrange all the big, important shapes before gluing. Change the arrangement of the shapes until a pleasing composition is found.

Suggested projects

- Paper collage: Use papers of various textures, colors, sizes, and shapes to create a design or picture. See the section on collage later in this chapter.
- Mosaics: These are made with small pieces of torn or cut colored paper. Making a mosaic can be a very exciting project for older children because it combines the elements of drawing, cutting, pasting, and putting a puzzle together. It may also be used as a group project. Begin by cutting colored paper into small square pieces (1/2"). When enough pieces have been cut, the group can try a mosaic picture. It's best to start with a simple picture, such as an animal, a tree, or a flower. After children have decided what they want to create, they select the colors that suit the idea they have in mind. Then they apply the bits of paper with glue, starting with the central figure or object and working toward the edges. Mosaics are attractive when they are pasted onto a background of colored paper or cardboard. More complex mosaics can be made by combining a variety of materials, such as gravel, pebbles, seeds, pods, and various types of grains. When using these materials, a stronger glue—like craft glue—is required.
- All-over design: Cut or tear related shapes of different sizes and colors to form a design.
- Cut-paper mural: Select a topic. Each child may cut shapes and combine them in a group mural.
- Three-dimensional picture: Paper pieces on some parts of the picture may be curled, fringed, or fastened only at the edges to allow them to protrude from the background.
- Pasting can involve anything and everything that can be stuck to paper, wood, cardboard, or together: tissues, scraps, corks, feathers, popcorn, Styrofoam pieces, yarn, paste, colored paste, and white paste. It's even possible to paste with glue on brushes or with glue on figures.
- Montage: The word montage literally means "putting together." Montage is an art form in which a number of smaller items have been put together. For example, a photomontage is made by cutting and joining a number of pictures into a large design. Children might make a family photomontage. After gathering some photos of important events in their family's life, they can cut or tear the photos into different sizes and glue them onto construction paper. Before gluing, encourage children to try different arrangements. Discuss such art elements as contrasting lines, colors, patterns, value (of colors), shapes, and size as children work at arranging their montages. When the child is satisfied with her or his design, gluing can proceed.

After the glue is dry, children may use markers to outline some areas or embellish the montage. Have them think about and create details surrounding the event, not just the event itself. When the montage is complete, encourage the children to tell stories about the pictures they have chosen.

13-2g Murals

A storytelling picture or panel intended for a large wall space is called a mural, another form of picture making. A suitable topic for a mural may come from children's personal experiences at home, at school, or at play, or it may relate to other school subjects. In the classroom, mural making is a versatile art activity; it may involve a large group or just a few children, depending on the size of the mural. Mural-making projects are excellent for "person smart" children who enjoy activities involving other children. Of course, murals are a natural fit for children who have the picture smart (visual) learning style.

With young children, mural making should involve simple, informal, spontaneous expression with a minimum of planning. Tedious planning destroys much of the intuitive quality and reduces interest. In contrast, older children will enjoy planning a group mural almost as much as making it. Have older children think about the composition of the mural—what they could include in it. Some design elements to consider when making a mural with older children follow.

○ Varied sizes and shapes
○ Varied breakup of foreground and background space
○ Overlapping shapes
○ Shapes extending out of the picture
○ Quiet areas to balance busy ones
○ Large objects or figures at the bottom and smaller ones at the top to create the illusion of distance

Materials

○ Kraft paper, roll paper, newspapers, wall paper, and colored construction paper
○ Crayons, brushes, and paint
● Scissors, water and container, and collage materials

Processes

○ Watercolor paint allows for spontaneous bold design and brilliant color, ideal for murals.
○ Cut or torn paper is a flexible medium suitable for murals, permitting many changes and parts as the mural progresses. Other techniques for manipulating paper are folding, curling, pleating, twisting, fringing, and overlapping. Place background paper on a bulletin board, and then plan, pin, and move parts before attaching. Various papers such as tissue, wallpaper, illustrated magazine pages, and metallic paper add interest. Topics for group murals are limited only by the imagination of the children. Providing children a variety of experiences both in and out of the classroom will stimulate them to express their ideas visually in a mural. Sometimes an ordinary group discussion will nudge children to become interested in creating a mural.

Did You Get It?

Is it developmentally appropriate for a daycare teacher to give her two-year-old students brushes and thick paint for them to use?

a. No, because children at that age should be exposed to brushes.
b. No, because it is frustrating for young children to work with messy substances.
c. Yes, because they cannot yet handle crayons.
d. Yes, because it helps them to gain mastery over the paint.

Take the full quiz on CourseMate.

13-3 Printmaking

naeyc DAP Long before they enter the classroom, most children have already discovered their footprints or handprints, made as they walk or play in snow or wet sand. In a basic **printmaking activity**, the child learns that an object dipped in or brushed with paint makes its own mark or relief print on paper (see Photo 13-6). This process can be repeated over and over again to create a design. Children use small muscles in the hand, wrist, and fingers as they hold the object, dip it in paint, and print with it on paper. They learn that each object has its own unique quality—that each thing makes its own print. Techniques range from a simple fingertip printing to carving a Styrofoam plate and printing with it. The emphasis should be on the free manipulation of objects and experimentation with color, design, and techniques.

The teacher may begin by encouraging children to search for objects from the home or classroom. Household items, kitchen utensils, hardware, discarded materials, and many objects of nature are useful in relief printing. Gradually, the child learns to look and discover textures, colors, and patterns that exist all around.

In their first attempts to organize shapes into a design, young children usually work in a random fashion. These early experiments help them develop a better understanding of the printmaking process and of the possibilities for a variety of designs.

Casper Holroyd

PHOTO 13-6 A basic printmaking activity is dipping an object in paint, then dipping it on the paper, and repeating over and over again.

The History of Printing

As you plan printing activities for children, you might be interested to know that there is a very long history to this medium. The history of printing started around 3000 BC with the duplication of images. The use of round cylinder seals for rolling an image onto clay tablets goes back to the early Mesopotamian civilization before 3000 BC where they are the most common works of art to survive and feature complex and beautiful images (British Library, 2012).

Cylinder seals were typically about 1 inch in length, engraved with written characters of figurative scenes, or both. They were used as an administrative tool, a form of signature, as well as jewelry and as magical amulets (Porada, 1993).

In both China and Egypt, the use of small stamps for seals preceded the use of larger blocks. In Europe and India, the printing of cloth preceded the printing of paper or papyrus. This probably was also the case in China.

The earliest woodblock printed fragments are from China. They consist of printed flowers in three colors on silk. They are generally assigned to the Han Dynasty before the year 220 (Vainker, 1990). The oldest woodblock printed book is the *Diamond Sutra*. It carries a date of "the 13th day of the fourth moon of the ninth year of the Xiantong era" (that is, May 11, 868) (British Library, 2012).

In Europe, block printing was long practiced by Christians as a method for printing on cloth, where it was common in 1300. Images printed on cloth for religious purposes could be quite large and elaborate. When paper became more readily available around 1400, the medium transferred very quickly to small woodcut religious images and playing cards printed on paper. These prints were produced in very large numbers from about 1425 onward (Hind, 1967).

Block printing, then, is an ancient medium. Yet it still holds the interest of young children today. Try a few of the suggested block print activities at the end of this chapter to continue in this long tradition.

13-3a Helping Children Get Started in Printmaking

The following suggestions are some ways to introduce printmaking activities:

- Paint hands and feet, and then "print" them on paper.
- Point out and discuss examples of repeated design in clothing, wrapping paper, and wallpaper in which objects appear again and again, up and down and across the whole material.
- Have children print repeat designs using found objects, such as a sponge, rubber eraser, stick, and bottle cap, or natural materials, such as leaves, twigs, stones, and bark.
- Soap is an easy material for even the younger child to handle. First, the teacher levels the surface of the soap block by shaving with a straight knife blade. Younger children might use the unleveled block, although it is always better to cut below the surface of the brand name. Using a knife or a spoon, gouge the desired design in the block of soap. The parts cut away will not print. Ink the soap with tempera paint using a paintbrush or roll paint on with a brayer. Older children are able to carve the soap themselves with a plastic knife. Challenge older pupils to experiment with arrangements and pressures to create greater variety in their prints.

The creative teacher demonstrates any necessary processes of using materials and tools without dictating what the final product will look like. He or she provides stimulation and guidance in the use of children's original ideas and encourages children to experiment with various objects and techniques.

Gradually, through their printmaking experiences, children discover for themselves the following:

- The amount of paint needed to obtain clean edges.
- The object must be painted each time it is printed. Print by pressing slowly and firmly.
- The amount of pressure needed to get a print.
- How the shape and texture of an object determine the shape and texture of the print.
- How to repeat a print over and over to create a design.

THIS ONE'S FOR YOU!

WD-40: The Teacher's Friend

In 1953, a fledgling company called Rocket Chemical Company and its staff of three set out to create a line of rust-prevention solvents and degreasers for use in the aerospace industry in a small lab in San Diego. It took them 40 attempts to get the water displacing formula (whose basic ingredient is fish oil) worked out. WD-40, which stands for Water Displacement perfected on the 40th try, is still in use today.

The most interesting piece of WD-40s history is the uses for the product, now numbering in the thousands. These uses include everything from silencing squeaky hinges and removing road tar from cars to protecting tools from rust. But they get even crazier than that. Some of the more interesting stories include the bus driver in Asia who used WD-40 to remove a python snake, which had coiled itself around the undercarriage of his bus, or when police officers used WD-40 to remove a burglar trapped in an air conditioning unit. The following list contains additional, more common uses for WD-40.

You will find many appropriate places in the early childhood program for this product.

WD-40 does the following:

- Removes gum and crayon from walls, plastic tables, compressed wood furniture, and chalkboards
- Lubricates small rolling toys
- Lubricates sticky drawers
- Removes tape marks from the wall where posters have been hung
- Lubricates moving parts on playground equipment
- Removes Kool-Aid stains from carpet and fabric
- Removes grape juice and tomato stains from cloth
- Removes marker stains from the floor
- Keeps scissors working smoothly
- Rids rocking chairs and swings of squeaky noises
- Makes umbrella stems easier to open and close
- Removes all traces of duct tape

13-3b Printmaking Materials

Materials for printmaking may include the following.

- Paint. Any of the following are suitable: tempera paint (see Photo 13-7) in sets of eight colors, powder paint in a thin mixture, food coloring, and water-soluble printing ink.
- Stamp pad. Discarded pieces of felt or cotton cloth inside a jar lid, cut-down milk carton, frozen food tin, or similar waterproof container can be saturated with color to create a stamp pad. Another way to make a stamp pad is to fold a paper towel or similar absorbent paper in several layers. Then place it in a shallow dish such as a small foil plate and saturate it with paint.
- Paper. Absorbent papers suitable for printing include newsprint, manila paper, wallpaper, tissue, construction paper, classified pages of the newspaper, plain wrapping paper, or paper towels. Avoid using paper with a slick finish because it does not absorb paint and ink well.
- Cloth. Absorbent pieces of discarded cloth can also be used to print on, such as pillowcases, sheets, men's handkerchiefs, old shirts, and napkins.
- Other items. Also have newspaper for covering tables, brushes for applying paint when not using a stamp pad, and cans for water.

Casper Holroyd

PHOTO 13-7 Marker and tempera paint picture of a "happy monster."

13-3c Printmaking Techniques

The following are some common printmaking techniques suitable for young children.

Found object printing. With a few familiar objects, such as forks, spools, sticks, buttons, bottle tops, some paper, paint, and a brush, children can learn to print their own designs. Objects found in nature, such as leaves, weeds, seeds, and stones, can also be used.

Fingerprints. Children press one of their fingers onto a stamp pad or a tray filled with thickened tempera and then onto a piece of newsprint. Encourage children to experiment using different fingers, singly or in combinations. Afterward, they can add details with markers and crayons.

Texture prints. Children prepare a printing block that consists entirely of a variety of textures. This might include natural materials such as pebbles, seeds, or other items that are glued to a stiff cardboard backing. Or children can cut and punch in cardboard to create different textures. Children then paint the block with a wide brush and then press the block onto a piece of paper.

Another texture print that involves only simple materials is a sandpaper print. The child colors on a sheet of sandpaper using wax crayons. The design is developed directly on the sandpaper and then placed face down on the paper. The teacher goes over the back of the sandpaper with a warm iron and the melted wax will transfer into a textured print onto the paper.

Monoprinting. To create a monoprint, apply paint to paper. Carefully place a sheet of paper over the painting and rub smoothly from the center out to the edge. If desired, children can draw in crayon on the top sheet of paper, pressing the lines into the paint on the bottom sheet. Pull the print gradually, starting from one corner.

Styrofoam prints. Children draw a picture or design using permanent markers on a flat piece of Styrofoam. These markers will dissolve the foam. They then use a brush or sponge to apply a thin layer of tempera to the surface of the tray. They place a piece of construction paper over the tempera and rub. Another way to print with Styrofoam is to make a pattern, picture, or design by squeezing glue onto the Styrofoam. After the glue has dried, tempera paint is applied to the entire surface. Place a piece of construction paper over the paint and rub. Because this is a two-step process, it is more appropriate for children in the middle- and upper-elementary grade levels.

Pieces of Styrofoam can also be used as printing plates after cutting them into shapes and pasting them on a background. The same applies to heavy cardboard.

Printing for older children. Older children, as we have seen in Chapter 12, continue to refine their creative skills throughout the elementary grades. In printing experiences, children in the middle- and upper-elementary levels are usually able to use a brayer (an ink roller) with a printing plate. Brayers in various sizes can be purchased at art supply stores.

The brayer is rolled in a shallow pan filled with a small amount of water-soluble ink or tempera paint. A metal or plastic tray or small cookie sheet works well for this. The child rolls the brayer over the ink to spread an even coat on the brayer. Then the ink-coated brayer is rubbed over the printing plate (for example, a cut out design on Styrofoam) until the whole surface is covered with ink. It works best to roll the brayer in one direction, and then in another at right angles.

The child then places paper on top of the inked plate and presses it down gently with the palm of the hand. She rubs the back of the paper with her fingertips or the back of a spoon, being sure to cover all areas, including the edges. Finally, the child pulls the paper away from the block. This is called "pulling the print." Now the print is ready to dry.

Some hints for working with older children and printing with brayers follow:

- Set up three printing centers in a classroom. You may want to use a different color of ink at each center. Keep centers neat and well stocked with paper and ink.
- As students are ready to print, direct them to a center to roll the ink on their blocks with the brayer. Then have them take their inked blocks and papers to their desks and do the actual printing there. This will prevent long lines at the centers.
- For cleanup, drop a folded piece of newspaper in the pan filled with ink. Roll the brayer on the newspaper. This will remove a great deal of the ink from both the pan and the brayer. Unfold the newspaper and refold it with the dirty side inside. Crumple and throw away the newspaper. After most of the ink is out of the pan, it is easy to rinse both it and the brayer at the sink.

Paper stencils. The 4- to 5-year-old child can begin to use paper to make stencils in a most creative manner. Each child is given four or five pieces of drawing paper about 4 inches square. With scissors, the child cuts holes of various sizes and shapes in the center of each piece. It is a good idea to cut more than one hole per piece. When the holes have been cut, each child is given a tissue, small piece of cotton, or piece of cloth. This is rubbed on a piece of colored chalk to pick up enough dust to stencil. Then the child selects a shape and places it on the paper on which the design is to go. The child rubs the tissue across the hole, making strokes from the stencil paper toward the center of the opening. This is continued around the edge of the opening until the paper under the stencil has a clear print. The same shape can be continued across the paper, or other shapes and colors may be added according to the child's preference.

A child can choose the shapes and combinations desired. The same technique can be used with wax crayons and felt-tip markers instead of chalk. The crayons and markers are applied directly on the stencil. Unbleached muslin or cotton material can be used to print on as well.

The spatter technique. Simple spatter or spray printing is both fascinating and fun for children. It also has the advantage of allowing for a wide variety of patterns and shapes. Children can work individually or with partners on this project.

Have several children bring in old toothbrushes. Besides toothbrushes, only a small amount of watercolor paint and paper are needed. "Spray" the paint with a toothbrush. This is done by dipping the brush in paint and gently pulling a straight-edged object (ruler, emery board, or tongue depressor) across the ends of the bristles. This causes the bristles to snap forward, throwing small particles of paint onto the paper.

Children create designs by placing small, flat objects on the paper. When the bristles snap the small particles of paint forward, the object prevents the spray from striking the paper directly under the object. This leaves the shapes free of paint spray while the rest of the paper is covered with small flecks of paint.

This technique has endless possibilities. Not only can a variety of shapes be used, but colors can also be superimposed on one another. Natural forms such as twigs, leaves, and grass are excellent for this activity. Several forms can be combined, leading to interesting arrangements with unlimited variety. A field trip is a good way to find new print forms and shapes, thus encouraging children to find and learn about beauty in their own environment. Another strength of this project is that it avoids stereotyped designs and ready-cut patterns. The children create beauty for themselves.

13-3d Suggestions for Printmaking Experiments

With color

- Alternate thin watercolor with thick, opaque tempera paint.
- Use a light color to print on dark paper, or vice versa.
- Use thin tempera paint on colored paper or cloth so that the color of the background shows through.
- Combine two sizes of objects of the same shape.
- Combine objects of different sizes and shapes.
- Use one object in various positions.
- Try overlapping and grouping objects.

With texture

- Vary the amount of paint used in printing.
- Use objects that create different textures, such as sponges, corrugated paper, wadded paper or cloth, stones, vegetables, and sandpaper.

With background paper

- Use a variety of shapes and sizes of paper.
- Paint background paper and allow it to dry before printing.
- Paste pieces of tissue or colored construction paper onto background paper, allow to dry, and then print.
- Print a stippled design on the background with a sponge, allow to dry, and then print with a solid object.

With pattern

- Print a shape in straight rows or zigzag. Repeat design to create an all-over pattern.
- Use a different shape for each row, and add a second color in alternate rows.
- Print in a border design with a single shape or group of shapes.

More ideas for printmaking are found at the end of this chapter.

> **Did You Get It?**
>
> **Printmaking is an activity that teaches young children many skills, including**
>   **a.** how to form letters.
>   **b.** how to recognize patterns.
>   **c.** how to copy forms by drawing freehand.
>   **d.** how to blend colors.
>
> **Take the full quiz on CourseMate.**

13-4 Collage

naeyc DAP A collage is a picture made by applying various materials to a flat surface. The word *collage* comes from the French word *coller*, meaning "to paste or stick." As an art expression, collage was developed in France during the early part of the twentieth century by the artists Pablo Picasso and Georges Braque, and in Germany by Kurt Schwitters. Collage was further developed in Germany at the Bauhaus, an experimental school of art. A collage is the product of selecting, organizing, and arranging materials of contrasting color and texture and attaching them to a flat surface.

One way children become aware of things around them is by touching. Through manipulation of everyday objects, they grow in sensitivity to shapes and textures and discover ways to use them in creating new forms and images. With added experience, the tactile sense becomes an instrument of knowledge and a tool of expression. Unlike the imitation of texture in drawing and painting, the textural materials in collage are real.

Children may be interested to know that when the painter Henri Matisse became ill and was too infirm to paint standing in front of an easel, he changed his working process and medium. Because he was confined to his bed or a wheelchair, he began to make large collages with shapes he cut out of papers that had been painted by his studio assistants. When children begin their collage experiences, they may become very interested in knowing about how Matisse overcame his disability and continued to produce art (Thompson, 2005).

13-4a Helping Children Get Started in Collage Activities

The following suggestions are designed to help motivate children in their initial collage activities:

- Arouse children's awareness of texture by passing around various materials for them to touch and examine. Discuss the qualities of various textures by asking: "How do these materials feel? Are they smooth? Hard? Soft? Fuzzy? Sharp? How can we use these materials?"
- Arrange a "touch-and-see" display.
- Discuss sources of collage materials and encourage children to collect them.
- Demonstrate making a collage: Select and arrange materials on a background and demonstrate methods of fastening using paste, thread, and staples.
- Assess qualities of materials in relation to ideas to be expressed (for example, gold paper

is bright and "shiny like the sun," and cotton is soft and white "like snow").

Materials

- Background: manila paper, construction paper, cardboard, and shirt board
- Collage materials: paper and cloth scraps, magazine pages, yarn, string, ribbon, lace, and any other items the children and teacher collect
- Natural materials: leaves, twigs, bark, seed pods, dried weeds, feathers, beans, ferns, sands, small stones, and shells
- Scissors, brushes, paste, glue sticks, stapler, and staples

Sort and keep materials of a similar nature in boxes to facilitate selection.

Processes

- When working with beginners, limit the number of collage materials. This lessens the confusion in selection.
- Encourage children to use materials in their own way. Instead of giving exact directions, suggest ways of selecting materials for variety of shape, size, color, and texture.
- Demonstrate how materials may be cut, torn, or left in their original shapes.
- As children arrange and rearrange the shapes on the background, they may form a representational picture or compose an abstract design.
- Throughout the work period, emphasize thoughtful use of space by overlapping and grouping shapes, and trying different combinations of colors and textural surfaces.
- Create three-dimensional effects by crumpling flat pieces of material and attaching them to the background in two or three places. Other techniques include overlapping, bending, folding, rolling, curling, and twisting paper.
- Include buttons, braids, fabric pieces, tissue, or yarn for added interest and accent.
- Use glue or staples to fasten heavy materials and plastics.
- Display the collage in a shadow box, using a box lid as a frame. It can also be mounted in an old picture frame or on a sheet of colored construction paper.
- Create a nature collage using all natural materials.
- Make a paper or cloth collage, exploring a variety of one kind of material. Do the same with leaves, buttons, or one kind of material children enjoy.

THINK ABOUT IT

A New Form of Finger Painting

While many people might think of finger painting as child's play, Japanese artist, Seikou Yamaoka, shows us that this art form can truly be used to create something of artistic beauty. Yamaoka uses only his finger tip to create digital masterpieces on his iPhone using the $2.99 app, Art Studio. One of his recent works is a portrait of a geisha, which he created on his iPhone4S. Yamaoka first sketched the portrait in black and white and then added stunning swipes of vivid color to bring the piece to life.

The entire iPhone finger painting took him about 4 hours to complete. This artist has created many stunning finger paintings while commuting on the train. His goal is to create images that look more akin to watercolor than digital art. A collection of his work can be seen on Yamaoka's official Facebook page. Technology has given rise to a whole crop of new artists like Yamaoka who are lucky enough to experience a synergy between their artistic and technological skills (Huffington Post, 2012).

Source: (Huffington Post, July 30, 2012, Used by permission.)

© 2015 Cengage Learning

▶❚❚ TeachSource Video

Preschool: Family Interactions: School and Community

1. What specific two-dimensional activities are represented in the "Me Book" activity? Are they developmentally appropriate for the ages of the children in the group? Why or why not?

2. Using the information presented in this chapter, what additional two-dimensional activities would you include in this "Me Book" project? What additional materials would be required for these activities? Give your rationale for including them in the lesson.

Watch on CourseMate.

● Keep a collection of old magazines on hand. Have students tear or cut out sections of pages with large areas of interesting colors, textures, or patterns that might be used for collages. Have them create collages with these. Allow them to trade magazine pages with one another.

● Collages can often send the viewer a very strong message. Have students make a collage mural about littering. Discuss how litter pollutes the school grounds and the environment. Talk about the types of items that comprise litter. Have students cut pictures from magazines of things that could litter the playground or cause environmental pollution. Students can also draw objects for the mural. Give the mural a title that reinforces the message of the artwork.

After students have completed collage activities, have them write about their artwork. More collage activities are found at the end of this chapter.

Did You Get It?

A teacher can increase the sensitivity of young children to texture and shapes through the creative activity of
a. printmaking.
b. collage.
c. museum visits.
d. freehand drawing.

Take the full quiz on CourseMate.

Because older children enjoy creating more complex works in their art experiences, collage is an excellent medium for this age group. Here are some collage ideas for this age group:

Summary

13-1 Discuss the various ways to motivate children in their use of the various two-dimensional media in this chapter.

Help motivate children by having them recall their experiences and record these in art media. Reading a familiar story or singing a song can stimulate art experiences. Motivation can involve reading children's books with noteworthy art, such as that of Eric Carle and Leo Lionni, to inspire children in their own creations. Other ways to motivate children include taking walking trips, taking pictures on the walk, putting up interesting bulletin boards, dramatizing stories, encouraging children to try using materials in different ways, showing sincere pleasure when a discovery is announced, encouraging children to bring materials from home to use in their art, and offering found materials that can be used in art work.

13-2 Describe the tools, materials, and techniques involved in the activity of painting in the early childhood program.

Basic tools for painting include brushes of the appropriate size for the developmental level of the child, watercolor paint sets, tempera paint, individual pieces of paper, water containers for painting and rinsing brushes, paper towels or scrap paper for blotting brushes while painting, newspapers to protect the painting area, smocks for the children, and a bucket of child-sized moist sponges for cleanup.

Painting with brushes may require some demonstration of how to prepare paint trays for use, how to use a variety of brush strokes, how to mix colors on the paper as they paint, how to create textures, how to handle excess paint or water on a brush, how to clean paint tray trays, and how to rinse and dry brushes.

13-3 Describe the tools, materials, and techniques involved in printmaking in the early childhood program.

In printing activities, the child learns that an object dipped in or brushed with paint makes its own mark or relief print on paper. This process can be repeated over and over to create a design. Techniques range from a simple fingertip printing to carving a Styrofoam plate and printing with it. Emphasis should be on the free manipulation of objects and experimentation with color, design, and techniques. Printmaking materials include paint, stamp pads, paper, cloth, and found objects for printing. Some techniques for printmaking are found object printing, fingerprints, texture prints, monoprinting, and Styrofoam prints. Older children include paper stencils spatter printing, and printing with a brayer.

13-4 Define the term collage, and describe the tools, materials, and techniques involved in collage activities in the early childhood program.

A *collage* is a picture made by applying various materials to a flat surface. The word *collage* comes from the French word *coller,* meaning "to paste or stick."

Collage activities involve selecting, organizing, and arranging materials and then attaching them to a surface. Materials for collage include background paper and assorted materials such as paper, cloth scraps, magazine pages, yarn, string, ribbon, lace, found and natural materials, as well as any other the children and teacher collect. Other materials include scissors, brushes, paste, glue sticks, stapler, and staples. When working with beginners, it is important to limit the number of collage materials. Encourage children to use collage materials in their own way. Encourage the thoughtful use of space by overlapping and grouping shapes and trying different combinations of colors and textural surfaces. Three-dimensional effects can be created by crumpling paper, as well as bending, folding, rolling, curling, and twisting paper.

Key Terms

brayer 295	motivate children 283	printmaking activity 292
collage 297	mural 291	spatter/spray painting 296
crayons 288	picture making/drawing 283	stencils 295
montage 291	pasting 289	tempera 286
monoprint 295	painting with a brush 284	

Learning Activities

A. Think creatively and develop a list of "unlikely" two-dimensional art materials. Concentrate on using recycled materials such as newspaper, magazines, cardboard, and so on.

B. Observe a preschool child painting at an easel. Describe how the child handled the brush, the application of paint, and amount of time spent painting. Then observe a first-grade child painting at an easel and describe these same

things. What does your observation tell you about easel painting at various developmental levels? What would you change in either situation to enhance the painting experience for each child?

C. Make a collage, painting, or drawing that expresses one of the following:

- How you would improve human beings
- A special machine or device to help the President

- How you would weigh an elephant
- A machine that exercises a dog
- Something that can't be seen
- An underground city

After you have finished your work, see if your fellow students can guess which topic you chose. Then try the same activity with children. Compare their work with yours and that of your fellow students. Discuss the similarities and differences in each group.

D. Choose one of the children's books in the following lists by Eric Carle or Leo Lionni:

- Books by Leo Lionni: *Alexander and the Wind-up Mouse* (1970), *Frederick* (1973), *Swimmy* (1973), *The Biggest House in the World* (1973), *Fish is Fish* (1974), *The Alphabet Tree* (1990), *Little Blue and Little Yellow* (1995), *Inch by Inch* (1995), *Matthew's Dream* (1995), *It's Mine!* (1996), *A Color of His Own* (1997), *Tico and the Golden Wings* (2000), *Let's Play* (2003), *Pezzettino* (2006)

- Books by Eric Carle: *The Mixed-up Chameleon* (1988), *Do You Want To Be My Friend?* (1988), *The Very Busy Spider* (1989), *Polar Bear, Polar Bear, What Do You Hear?* (1997), *The Very Hungry Caterpillar* (1994), *The Grouchy Ladybug* (1996), *The Very Quiet Cricket* (1997), *From Head to Toe* (1999), *The Very Lonely Firefly* (1999), *Brown Bear, Brown Bear, What Do You See?* (1996), *Papa, Please Get the Moon for Me* (1999), *Eric Carle's Very Little Library* (2003),

Panda Bear, Panda Bear, What Do You See? (2006), *Baby Bear, Baby Bear, What Do You See?* (2009), *Eric Carle's 123* (2009)

Plan a collage lesson for young children with one of these books that features collage work in your lesson introduction. Discuss the results of your lesson and the role this book played in the effectiveness of your lesson as it is reflected in the children's work.

E. Explain how you would use Garner's multiple intelligences to choose specific art activities for young children. Use at least two intelligences in your answer, giving specific examples.

F. As teachers of young children, we encourage children to be keen observers of the world around them and to reflect these observations in their artwork. This activity is designed to give you the chance to practice drawing from observation and recollection by one or more of the following activities.

- Take an object apart and then draw it.
- Examine an object for 1 minute. Put the object away. Then draw a picture of what you remember about it.
- Show someone how to do something in a sequence of drawn pictures.
- Draw yourself looking in a mirror.
- Draw an object from three different views.
- Draw a map showing your route from home to school. Include local landmarks in your map.

Activities for Children

Painting

Dip and Dye. This technique comes from the old Japanese technique of folding and dipping paper in dye. Put diluted food coloring or strong tempera paint in small bowls. Children fold paper towels or any other absorbent paper in half, quarters, thirds, and so on. They then dip the corners of the folded paper towel into the bowl of dye and allow time for the color to be absorbed. After the child has dyed the four corners of the folded paper, he or she blots the paper between several layers of paper towels or newspapers to remove the excess color and force it evenly through the layers of paper. The paper is then dipped in another color that is darker than the first. Dipping occurs on a corner or side that was not dipped before, or the paper may be redipped on the tip, a corner, or an edge that was dipped before. If paper is redipped, it should be removed before the dye completely covers the first color. After the packet is blotted between papers again, it is carefully unfolded and placed on newspapers to dry. Children will want to make several sheets of this decorative paper because no two ever come out of the dye baths looking exactly alike. Two and three dips in the dye baths create merged and blended tones, while a pleasing repetition of colored shapes results from the way in which the paper was folded before it was dipped in the dye.

The brightly patterned paper may be pressed with an iron and used for gift wraps, stationery trims, program covers, greeting cards, or for covering cartons, boxes, cans, books, and notebooks.

Bubble Wrap Painting. Lay a piece of bubble wrap on a table so that the bubbles are facing up. Have the child cover the bubbles with tempera paint. Then place a piece of construction paper on top of the bubbles. Press down on the paper so that all of the bubbles are able to make a print. Lift up the construction paper and see the design. See what happens when some of the bubbles pop when pressing down on the construction paper. How do the popped bubbles print differently than the ones with air still in them? If you use more than one color of paint, how do the paints blend?

Spoon Painting. You will need liquid tempera colors, cups, spoons, construction paper, and water bowls. Cover tables with newspapers. Provide children with cups of paint and spoons. Explain that they will be painting without using brushes and without the spoons touching their papers. Demonstrate spooning the paint onto the paper and tipping the paper in different directions to make the paint move. Show students how to place the spoon into the water bowl before reusing it. Students will get streams of color on the paper.

Rainbow Painting. Use white crayons to draw simple pictures or designs on white paper. Then make a rainbow of lines over the picture, using different colors of watercolor paints. Watch as the drawings magically appear through the rainbow.

Variety Painting. For a change, try using household implements to paint or print with. Try a comb, an old toothbrush, string, an old wheel toy, sponges, a wadded bit of paper towel, alphabet letter magnets, and other safe items from the kitchen drawer. Try different motions, such as pulling the object across the paint or quick dabbing onto the paper.

Finger Painting with Ice Cubes. For this variation of finger painting, use regular finger paint and glossy paper, but do not wet the paper as you normally would to prepare for finger painting. Give each child an ice cube with which to spread and dilute the paint while making designs on the paper.

String Painting. You will need two pieces of white drawing paper for each child, tempera paint in bowls, and 12-inch lengths of string (at least three per child). Provide several lengths of string for each bowl of tempera paint. Hold one end, and then dip the string into the paint. Lay the string on the paper to create a design. Redip and repeat, or use a new string and a new color. For a variety, try dropping the string onto the paper. For a print design, lightly press a second sheet of paper on top of the string design.

Pulled String Painting. You will need yarn or string, bowls of tempera paint, construction paper or drawing paper, and a damp rag or sponge. Dip the string or yarn into a bowl of tempera paint. Do not squeeze paint out of the string. Lay the string on a sheet of paper in any design, leaving the tail end of the string off the edge of the paper. Place another piece of paper over this. Lay a hand gently over the paper and string. Pull the string from the paper, keeping the hand pressing gently on the top of the paper. Remove the top paper and see the string design! For a variation, try a folded sheet of paper and place the string inside. Try several colors, one at a time, adding each color after the first is done. Try a rope dipped in paint, and place it between very large sheets of paper. Many hands can help this time!

Smash Painting. You will need white construction or drawing paper (let the children cut or tear it into interesting shapes), plastic cling-type wrap cut a bit larger than the pieces of paper, plastic eye droppers, tempera paint in three colors (white, dark blue, and light blue), and markers.

Children pick up one color of paint with an eyedropper and drip it onto the paper. Repeat with the next two colors. Then children place the plastic wrap on top of their paper and rub, causing the paints underneath to blend and swirl. Talk about the colors being created. When the child is pleased with the blended colors, remove the plastic wrap and enjoy the design. After the paintings are dry, children can add details and designs with markers and crayons.

Splotch Paintings. Mix some paint in a small cup of water. Make sure it is dark enough to show up on the paper you are using. The child "spills" some paint onto her or his

paper. Watch as the puddle of paint forms an organic or free-form shape. Children can tilt the paper in different directions to spread the spill if they like. Allow the organic shape to dry. The child can use her or his imagination to turn the shape into a picture or a design.

Flashy Painting. You will need black or very dark construction paper, glitter, white glue, and newspapers. Cover the work area with newspapers. The child spreads the glue on the paper in shapes and designs. Sprinkle glitter on the paper. Slide the excess glitter off the picture and back into the glitter container. Repeat the glue and glitter process with different colors of glitter. Let the glue dry.

Homemade Paints. The following are paint recipes that are fun and different.

Watercolors

1 tablespoon white vinegar
1½ tablespoon baking soda
1 tablespoon cornstarch
½ teaspoon glycerin
food coloring

Mix vinegar and baking soda in small bowl and allow foaming. After foaming stops, add cornstarch and glycerin. Stir well (up to a couple of minutes). Portion the mixture into a paint palette, muffin tin, or similar container, and add food coloring. Make the colors dark; drying and use will lighten them. Allow watercolors to dry in a warm place for several hours or overnight. Makes one set of watercolors.

Shiny Paint

white glue
tempera paint (liquid)
dish detergent

Pour glue into small cups. Mix your choice of liquid tempera paint into each. Use to paint on wood, paper, or cardboard as you would any paint. Paint will dry shiny as if glazed. Variations: Paint pinecones, driftwood, rocks, or glass. Try painting with sponge brushes for a very smooth finish. To help paint adhere to shiny, smooth surfaces, add a few drops of dish detergent.

Salt Paint

⅛ cup liquid starch
⅛ cup water
1 tablespoon tempera paint

Mix together and apply to paper with a brush. Keep stirring the mixture. Paint will crystallize as it dries to a salt-like texture.

Puffy Paint

flour
salt
water
tempera paint

Mix equal parts of flour, salt, and water in a bowl. Add a small amount of tempera paint to the mixture and pour into a small plastic squeeze bottle. Repeat the procedure, making as many colors as you wish. Squeeze onto heavy paper or cardboard to make designs. Mixture will harden into puffy shapes.

Sand Paint

tempera paint (powder)
sand

Mix dry tempera paint with sand. Let children spread glue on picture and sprinkle on sand.

Cornstarch Paint

1 tablespoon cold water
2 tablespoons cornstarch
1 cup boiling water
food coloring

Combine cold water and cornstarch. Stir until smooth. Add boiling water and stir again until smooth. Add food coloring until paint is desired color. Let cool. Store this paint in a covered container. If it dries, add wate to thin it.

Cold Cream Paint

six-sectioned muffin tin
1 teaspoon cornstarch
½ teaspoon cold cream
½ teaspoon water
food coloring

Mix all but the food coloring for each section of the muffin cup. Decide what food coloring color to add to each cup and mix.

Painting—It's Great Outdoors!

Break away from traditional thinking about painting inside at a table or an easel. Many exciting painting adventures await you and the children in the great outdoors. Here are a few ideas to get you started.

Water Painting. Preschoolers enjoy painting the side of a building or the sidewalk with large paintbrushes and buckets of water. The broad strokes enhance gross motor development and hand–eye coordination. This activity can also lead to a rudimentary discussion of evaporation.

Weed Painting/Printing. Go outside and collect a variety of weeds to use as paintbrushes. Queen Anne's lace is one that works especially well. Children dip the weed into a small, shallow container of paint. Then they can either print with the weed or use it as an interesting paintbrush.

Root Painting. Help children dig up dead plants and save the roots (with the stems attached). Or ask families to gather roots that children can use. Be sure that you have nontoxic roots that are bushy, with stems sturdy enough to serve as root brush handles. Mix a variety of tempera paint to a medium consistency and pour it in juice cans, paint cups, or ready-to-use frosting containers. Gather paper—any kind will do—and put it in a bag or basket to take outside.

Set up easels on a grassy area, or cover a picnic table with newspapers. Put out the paper and paint. Give children lots of time to experiment and create designs and pictures with their root brushes.

Mud Finger Painting. Fill a dishpan with dirt (high clay content works best, but any "clean" soil will do). Fill another dishpan with water. Provide several large, washable trays and several plastic scoops for the soil and the water. Set up a table, preferably near a faucet with a hose. Place the trays, dishpans, and scoops on the table with smocks nearby. Children put on smocks and scoop soil and water onto their trays. Let children enjoy experimenting with this new "mud finger paint" they create by mixing water and soil together.

Outdoor Weaving. Gather long scarves, pieces of ribbon, cording, and rope in many colors, and rolls of crepe paper in as many colors as possible. Locate a nearby chain link fence. Children weave the ribbons, crepe paper, and other materials in and out of the links on the fence to create a colorful woven design on the fence. (This is not painting, but it's a fun outdoor activity!)

Sun Prints. Collect a variety of items with interesting shapes: spools, forks, cookie cutters, seashells, stray puzzle pieces. Gather several sheets of bright construction paper. Be sure not to use construction paper guaranteed not to fade. Dark blue, purple, and green construction paper work well. Attach the construction paper to one side of a large flat sheet of cardboard. Children choose shapes from the collection and place them anywhere and in any way they like on the paper. Leave everything in the sun. In a day or two, go outside and remove the objects. When the objects are removed, the sun will have bleached the paper, leaving dark silhouettes in an interesting design.

Printing

Line Printing. You will need 2-inch-wide strips of various lengths of manila tag paper, one sheet of 9- × 18-inch white drawing paper per child, paperclips, staplers, and three plates of tempera paint per group (for example, warm/cold colors). Children fold, curve, pleat, and so on, their strips of manila tag paper and either paperclip or staple the form. They then dip each strip form into different colors of tempera paint and print onto their drawing paper to demonstrate the element of line.

Bubble Prints. You will need 1 cup of water, food coloring, ¼ cup liquid detergent, ¼ cup liquid starch, straws, printing paper, and a 6- to 8-inch bowl. In the bowl, mix the water, drops of food coloring, liquid detergent, and liquid starch. Let children blow bubbles in the bowl using a straw. (Poke a hole in the top of the straw to prevent children accidentally sipping with the straws.) Blow until the bubbles form a structure above the rim of the bowl. Make a print by laying a sheet of white paper across the bowl rim and allowing the bubbles to pop against the paper. Talk about the lines, shapes, and patterns the bubbles make on the paper.

Pipe Cleaner Printing. Pipe cleaners can be bent into almost any shape desired and will carry paint well. These shapes glued to a heavy cardboard backing make a printing plate that is simple enough for young children but also suitable for more controlled expression by older children. Paint the pipe cleaners using thick tempera paint and press the inked plate to the paper. Or ink the block with a brayer, first having put a cardboard or pipe cleaner down either edge of the cardboard backing to keep the background clean. Press the block face down to a paint-soaked pad of paper toweling, lift by the edges, and print.

Berry Nice Prints. You will need plastic berry baskets, construction paper, tempera paint, a container large enough to dip the berry basket in, and paper. Talk about the lines children see in the plastic berry basket. Discuss how the lines cross and how they make squares. Talk about which kinds of prints the children think the baskets will make on paper.

Dip the berry basket in paint. Press the basket onto the paper. Repeat, overlapping the shapes. Continue until the pattern or design is completed. For variety, make contrasting designs by printing with white paint on black paper. Print with different colors of primary colors and watch the colors mix.

Circle Challenge. You will need paper cups of various sizes, Lifesavers candy, small round plates, and any other circular shapes to print, tempera paint, a shallow container for paint, brushes, and paper.

Talk about circles. Have children identify as many circles as they can in the room. Discuss which things in a circle shape the children can think of to use in printmaking. Challenge children to bring from home as many of these items as they can.

Begin by printing with one circular printing object. Print this on the page, making a pattern or a random design. Use another circular object and print with it on the page. Try printing one line with one size circle. Do another with a different-sized circle. Alternate large and small circular shapes in one line. Print zigzag, horizontal, and vertical lines with circle shapes.

For variety, repeat the activity with another shape—square, rectangle, even triangles!

Pinecone Prints. You will need pinecones, a thin mixture of tempera paint, a container for the paint, and paper. Talk with children about pinecones, their shapes, how they feel, and how they smell.

Give each child a piece of paper. Dip a pinecone in tempera paint. Press the pinecone onto the paper. Use all sides of the pinecone to make prints.

Plunge Into It! You will need new plungers of various sizes, large sheets of butcher paper, various colors of tempera paint, and foam trays or plates.

Cover the art area with newspaper. Tape the newspaper to the floor. Lay out butcher paper, and tape it to the floor as well. Prepare paints in trays. Set plungers in paint trays.

Have children dip the plunger in paint and press the plunger onto the butcher paper to make a print. Continue printing to create a design or pattern. Add other round objects to print such as paper cups or towel rolls. Use two plungers at a time, each with a different color of paint. Use the paper as a giant class mural. Use the print as wrapping paper or book covers.

Tin Can Prints. Don't overlook the lowly tin can as a printing object. It can be the basis of a very versatile printing surface. Be sure the edges of the can are smooth before using it for printing. The end of the can dipped in paint makes a circular shape that can be combined in an over-all pattern, preferably using different sizes of cans.

Use the side surface of the tin can as a base for a printing plate. First, cut both ends from the can so that it will be easier to handle in the printing process. Then glue shapes cut from felt, cork, or even heavy paper and lines made from string or heavy cord around the outside of the can.

Paint the raised surfaces using thick tempera paint. Or roll the can over an inked plate so that the raised areas pick up the color. Then the can is rolled across the printing paper to make a design. The prints may be placed in rows to completely fill the page, or the can may be rolled in different directions.

Bottle Top Prints. Have the children collect bottle tops ranging from soft drink bottles to larger jars. Paint these with thick color to make circular prints. Try the textures of the edge of the bottle tops. Glue felt or cork to the top to make new designs. Combine these with the tin can prints described previously, thus mixing solid shapes and linear prints.

Toothpick Prints. Children create the print by pasting toothpicks to a piece of heavy cardboard in a design and then using this as a printing block.

Roller Prints. Almost any type of roller can be used to make a direct print. Collect large wooden dowels, round curtain rods, or even a rolling pin to make roller prints. Paint a design on the roller using lines and solid areas in a variety of colors. Quickly roll this across the paper and note the print made. It will fade out quickly as the paint dries on the roller. Paint the same design again and start at a different part of the paper to make the print. Continue until the child is finished with the design.

Using a wooden roller or a heavy cardboard cylinder, build up a relief surface by gluing on shapes of felt, corrugated cardboard, or cork. Or use knives and nails to cut and gouge a design in the surface of the wooden dowel. Spread some printing ink or thick tempera paint on a nonporous surface and roll the prepared roller through it and onto the paper.

Yarn Prints. You will need yarn, glue, scissors, cardboard or oak tag, paper, tempera paint, and crayons. Talk about how designs can be repeated to make patterns. Discuss how lines can be zigzag, horizontal, vertical, and so on.

Use crayons to draw a pattern, design, or picture on the cardboard. Outline parts or all of the picture with white glue.

Apply yarn to the glue. Let the yarn and glue dry thoroughly. Brush tempera paint over the picture. Place another piece of paper over the picture. Press lightly with the palm of the hand. Peel off the paper to see the string print.

Crayons, Markers, and Chalk

Sugar and Chalk Pictures

If thick pieces of colored chalk are soaked for a few minutes in a sugar-and-water solution, they provide young children with a drawing medium that is closely related to paint in both appearance and approach. One part of sugar should be dissolved in three parts of water and placed in pie pans for soaking the chalk. This technique will delight children with its rich, velvety, intense tones and its direct and instant application on the paper. They will find that they can draw an object easily, and quickly fill in all the areas. It dries quickly on the paper, and the colors do not tend to run into each other and smear. If the chalk pieces become dry while the children are using them, they may be dipped in the sugar-and-water solution and be reactivated. The finished pictures do not rub off as regular chalk drawings do.

Chalk Blend Backgrounds. Rub and blend light pastel colors of chalk on a plain sheet of heavy paper. Dip a small comb in black tempera paint and use the comb with paint to make interesting repeat patterns on the paper. Spray the entire picture with hairspray to prevent smearing. Be sure to spray in a well-ventilated area.

Using Chalk in Picture Making. Don't overlook the creative possibilities of chalk as a medium for young children's drawing and picture making. Here are some creative ways to use chalk:

- Texture: Place thin paper, such as tissue paper or tracing paper, over a surface with a unique texture, for example, sandpaper, bricks, or corrugated cardboard. Then rub over the paper with the side of the chalk so that the texture of the object appears. Numerous textures can be used for many interesting effects.
- Chalk on wet paper: Using colored chalk on wet paper (construction paper or toweling), glide the chalk over the damp surface to give a flowing motion to the drawing. This process provides bold and colorful pictures.
- Starch and chalk: Pour a small amount of liquid starch on a sheet of paper. Dip the colored chalk in the starch and create a unique art experience.
- Wet chalk: Soak chalk in water for several minutes before using it on a dry surface. The wet chalk can be used on windows, paper, ceramic surfaces, and numerous other slick areas. This chalk medium reacts much like a finger-painting activity and provides a leaded glass appearance.

Line Stories. Create a story using different types of lines. For example, a line is a dot that went for a walk in the snow. Each set of subsequent lines can be different things (for example, thin parallel lines are sled tracks, thin curvy lines are bike tracks, spiral lines could be a snake, and so on).

Scribbles. Discuss scribbling, how it looks, and how much fun it is to do. Explain that this activity begins with scribbling.

The child makes a large scribble on the paper. Outline parts of the scribble with a marker. Fill the outlines with crayon. Leave some areas uncolored.

Some variations: Make rules for filling the scribbles (for example, "You can't put the same colors next to each other." "You can only use primary colors." "Use only complementary colors."). Challenge children to make scribbles using straight lines and angles. Have a group of children make a scribble picture mural. Scribble using crayon, and then paint the spaces using tempera paint.

Be Like Picasso

When he was a boy, Picasso would bet his friends that he could draw anything using just one line. He always won his bets. In the book *Picasso's One-Liners* (1997), you can find a delightful assortment of his one-line drawings accompanied by his one-line quotes. Now try to be like Picasso in this activity!

1. Give students a stack of copy paper and a black fine-tip marker. Students take turns suggesting objects for the class to draw (animals work especially well), using just one line.
2. Each student gets a turn to name a subject.
3. Then everyone draws that subject using just one line, not lifting the marker until they are finished.

Students close their markers and lay them down to signal when done. When everyone is finished, students hold their drawings up for everyone to admire.

Encourage students to avoid simply drawing an outline of the object, and to let their pen explore the insides of shapes, adding texture, pattern, and detail that would not appear with just an outline. There are no such things as mistakes in this activity.

Drawings may end unexpectedly when the pen reaches a "dead end," but this is part of the fun.

Disappearing Line Drawings. You will need hard soap (the type from hotels works well), black construction paper, crayons, water, and a sink or large tub of water.

Talk with the children about lines in drawings and how they can be straight, curvy, horizontal, vertical, zigzag, and so on. This project is messy, so you may want rubber gloves and a newspaper-covered drying area.

Give each child a piece of black paper. Do a line drawing with the soap. The drawing should have lots of outlined areas in which to color. Note that the soap will not work for areas the children want white; for these areas, the children must use white crayon. Color in the drawing. Light colors work best. Rinse the drawing until the soap lines disappear. Allow to dry. Variation: Draw a design using only shapes. Repeat the process.

Crayon-Rubbing Pictures. You will need crayons, textured surfaces (for example, sandpaper, pieces of screen, cardboard), and newsprint or another thin-type paper.

Discuss the pieces of textured surfaces with the children. Use descriptive words such as *coarse, bumpy,* and *crisscross.*

Make an outline drawing with a pencil on thin paper. Hold the drawing against a surface that has a definite texture. Rub the crayon over all areas of the drawing, filling the area with an interesting texture pattern. The texture will transfer to the paper by the crayon. Place the paper against another texture and transfer this texture to another part of the drawing. Textures may be repeated or overlapped. Continue until all areas are filled with texture rubbings.

Crayon Batik. You will need crayons, paper, water, a container for water, a thin solution of tempera paint, brushes, and paper towels.

Discuss the fact that the term *batik* refers to a design with wrinkles. Talk about which kind of picture or design the children would like to make in this activity.

The child makes a drawing or design with crayons on paper. Soak the paper in water. Crumple the paper into a ball. Uncrumple the paper. Flatten it out. Blot off excess water with paper towels. Flow diluted tempera paint over the surface with a wet brush. Let the batik dry thoroughly. Variations: Draw with light-colored crayons and cover the drawing with dark tempera paint. Draw with dark-colored crayons and cover the drawing with light tempera paint. After the batik has dried, add more design elements or details with markers.

Tie-Dye

Materials

- Large pans of water
- Marbles, rocks, pebbles, wooden spools, cubes, and any other objects (one for each color of dye used)
- Rubber bands to tie the cloth
- String
- Pieces of old sheets, undershirts, or cloth squares to use as a scarf
- Liquid dye (cold-water dyes are easiest to work with)

The art of tying knots in fabric and dipping it in dye is more than 3,000 years old, so this "new" way of decorating material is actually one of the oldest. Young children enjoy the surprise achieved in creating the blurry-edged patterns resulting from a process that is actually an updated version of an ancient process called *bandhnu* in India. The designs created are determined by the manner in which the material is folded or tied. The color doesn't penetrate the tied portions.

Fill a large pot one-third full of water. Add the liquid dye and stir. The brightness of the color will depend on how much dye you add.

Circles—large and small, regular and irregular—can be tied in several ways. Tiny ones are made by pinching up bits of the fabric and winding a thread or narrow rubber band around them. Slightly larger circles can be tied over beads or marbles. A grouping of a number of small circles makes a fun arrangement, too. Large circles are created by picking up bigger loops of the material. Concentric circles are made by tying in a series or marbles or golf balls. Where the cloth is tied between the marbles, there is a very definite edge to the ring. By tying in cubes, pebbles, beans, spools, clothespins, and little sticks, an infinite variety of rings may be made. Fabric may be pleated and the pleats tied together, leaving gaps between the strings. This will produce an all-over cobweb effect.

The fabric should be dipped in water and squeezed before the child begins to tie knots. Strong white string is best for tying. Thread may be used for fine circles and narrow tape for wide bands. For very young children, rubber bands work best.

Show children how to tie-dye by placing the objects inside the cloth and fastening them with a rubber band. (Adults may need to tighten the rubber bands.) Dip the cloth in the dye. Leave it in the dye bath until the desired color is reached. Remember, colors will be lighter when the fabric dries. Remove the rubber bands, and the design is revealed. When the item is removed from the dye, it should be squeezed out and rinsed thoroughly in cool water.

You will probably find it best to schedule your tie-dying for a pleasant day so you can do the work outdoors, stringing up clotheslines for finished pieces to dry on.

Torn-Paper Collage. Tape a large sheet of construction paper onto an easel or wall. Explain to the children that you will pass around some construction paper and that everyone will be invited to tear up a piece. Children may tear their paper into very small pieces or big pieces—whatever they choose. Show them how to tear the paper and assist those who may need help. Invite children to glue their torn paper onto the large sheet of construction paper. When finished, engage children in a discussion about the torn-paper collage. Discuss how some may have layered paper; ask them to notice designs or shapes that were created or to find images that may be recognizable to them.

Next, invite children to create their own torn-paper collages. Suggest they choose a sheet of construction paper for their use and one or two colors for tearing. Older children may be able to work with several colors of construction paper.

Display all of the collages so that children can observe each other's work. Encourage them to talk about the things they observe.

Keep materials in a basket or tray in the art area so children can continue to experiment with torn-paper collage. Encourage collaborative work by inviting children to work in pairs or groups of four to make torn-paper collages together.

Matisse Cutouts. "A pair of scissors," said Matisse, "is a marvelous instrument." Your students will think so, too, as they follow the steps below to create their own paper collages.

As a group, brainstorm favorite activities. Swimming? Football? Soccer? Once children have chosen a subject, invite them to create a Matisse-like cutout. Ask children what shapes or symbols represent their favorite activities. (For example, for football, children might mention the distinctive shape of the ball or the lines of the goalposts.)

The children cut their shapes out of colored construction paper. Encourage them to use their imaginations.

Next, have them create the backgrounds for their collages, using two to four colored rectangles of paper. For example, a soccer background might include green for the field, gray for the bleachers, and blue for the sky. Then they glue their rectangles to the white paper.

Last, have the students arrange the cutout shapes on the backgrounds. They may want to add additional shapes to indicate action or energy, such as bursts or squiggles. After the collages dry, show them off on a hallway bulletin board.

Multicultural Two-Dimensional Lesson Plans

Light and Dark

Objective: To help children explore the concepts of light and dark; to help children notice the variations of skin color in terms of light and dark.

Materials: A set of pictures of people with different skin colors, easel, easel paper, paint brushes, four shades of the same color paint (preferably brown)

Description: During group time, show the children the pictures of people with different skin color. Have the children look at their skin. Ask such questions as: "Is your skin light or dark?" "Does it ever get darker than it is now?" "Does it ever get lighter?" Also ask the children if they know how to make a color darker or how to make a color lighter. Show them the four containers of paint. Talk about how each container holds a different shade of the color brown. Ask, "Which one is the lightest? and "Which one is the darkest?" Tell the children that they can experiment with the light and dark shades of paint at the easel during free choice time.

Variations: Use paint swatches instead of a picture set.

Older children can experiment with mixing shades of paint for use at the easel. Have them choose a color and slowly add white paint to create lighter shades. This gives children the experience of beginning with dark and changing it to light.

Finger-Paint Mixing

Objective: To help children explore shades of skin color by combining colors as they finger paint.

Materials: Liquid starch, black, brown, red, yellow, and white powder tempera paint, finger-paint paper, smocks, small plastic bowls, teaspoons

Description: Put a small amount of each color of powder tempera paint into bowls and set them out on a table. Ask the children to put on a smock to protect their clothes. Show the children the five colors of paint. Ask them, "What do you think will happen if you mix the colors together?" Then ask the children to look at their skin color. Encourage them to mix the colors so that the finger paint matches the color of their skin. Give each child a piece of finger-paint paper, and pour approximately 3 tablespoons of liquid starch directly onto the paper. Tell the children they can spoon the powder tempera onto their paper and mix the colors and starch together with their hands. Compare the color of the finger paint with each child's skin color and ask them questions to help them figure out how to make the finger paint the same color as their skin.

Variations: After the painting has dried, encourage the children to draw a face on their artwork.

Color Collage

Objective: To help children associate positive images and feelings with the color black.

Materials: Gray construction paper, magazines, scissors, glue

Description: Set out magazines and scissors on a table. Ask the children to think of things that they like that are black in color. Talk about how there are many wonderful things in our world that are black. Give each child a piece of gray construction paper. Talk about how the color gray comes from mixing black with white. Encourage the children to go through the magazines and cut out pictures of their favorite black things. Allow the children to glue their pictures to the paper any way they choose.

Variations: Repeat the activity focusing on the color brown. Use tan construction paper instead of gray.

Go on a "color walk" to look for all of the beautiful black and brown things in the world.

Have a "Black Day" at school where everyone wears black and brings a favorite black object to school. Do the same for the color brown.

Set up a discovery table with black objects. Encourage the children to put the objects next to their skin. Do the same with the color brown.

Make and use black and brown play dough.

References

British Library (2012). *Diamond Sutra* (868). Accessed October 16, 2012, from http://www.bl.uk/onlinegallery /hightours/diamsutra/index.html.

Duffy, B. (2010). *Supporting creativity and imagination in the early years.* 2nd edition. New York, NY: McGraw-Hill Education.

Hind, A. M. (1967). *An Introduction to a history of woodcut.* Mineola, NY: Dover Publications.

Huffington Post. (2012). Seikou Yamaok, iPhone finger painting artist, creates digital watercolors. Accessed July 30, 2012, from http://www.huffingtonpost.com /news/seikou-yamaoka.

Porada, E. (1993). Why cylinder seals? Engraved cylindrical seal stones of the ancient Near East,

fourth to first millennium, B.C. *The Art Bulletin, 75*(4), 563–582.

Thompson, S. C. (2005). *Children as illustrators: Making meaning through art and language.* Washington, DC: NAEYC.

Vainker, S. (1990). In Anne Farrer (Ed.) "Caves of the thousand Buddhas." British Museum publication, ISBN 0-7141-1447-2.

 Visit CourseMate for this textbook to access the eBook, Did You Get It? quizzes, Digital Downloads, TeachSource Videos, flashcards, and more. Go to CengageBrain.com to log in, register, or purchase access.

14

Three-Dimensional Activities

The term **three-dimensional art** refers to any art form that has at least three sides. Three-dimensional art is "in the round," which means that one can look at it from many sides. Modeling with clay, working with play dough, making creations with paper boxes, and creating other sculpture forms are examples of three-dimensional art activities (see Photo 14-1).

Learning Objectives

After studying this chapter, you should be able to:

14-1 Describe the development of three-dimensional awareness and the developmental levels involved in working with three-dimensional media.

14-2 Explain modeling and describe its benefits for children.

14-3 Discuss some guidelines to follow for successful modeling activities.

14-4 Explain the value of clay in the early childhood program.

14-5 Describe the strategies for working with clay.

14-6 Define assemblage, and give specific examples of assemblage activities for children.

14-7 Explain how to adapt assemblage activities for children with special needs.

14-8 Discuss how cardboard may be used for three-dimensional activities.

14-9 Describe the benefits of woodworking experiences for young children.

NAEYC Program Standards
1a Knowing and understanding young children's characteristics and needs.
1c Using developmental knowledge to create healthy, respectful, supportive, and challenging learning environments.

DAP

DAP Criteria
3C1 Teachers are familiar with the understandings and skills key for that age group in each domain (physical, social, emotional, and cognitive).
3C3 In determining the sequence and pace of learning experiences, teachers consider the developmental paths that children typically follow and the typical sequences in which skills and concepts develop.
3D2 Teachers plan curriculum experiences to draw on children's own interests and introduce children to things likely to interest them.

PHOTO 14-1 Three-dimensional objects can be created with many different materials.

Three-dimensional art projects give tactile stimulation and provide an emotional outlet through touch because of the versatility of the materials. Work in three-dimensional media also provides children the opportunity for growth in all developmental areas. Children grow physically as they use their hands, fingers, and arms creating three-dimensional objects. Their hand–eye coordination also develops as they work with clay and other three-dimensional materials in such activities as assemblage and woodworking. Growth in language occurs naturally as children work with three-dimensional media, expanding their vocabularies as they learn new words to describe these materials and the process of using them. Self-confidence and self-concept are enhanced as children grow in their control over the forms created with three-dimensional materials.

14-1 Developmental Levels and Three-Dimensional Media

naeyc **DAP** We experience the world through three dimensions: height, width, and depth. Babies have an awareness of this from very young ages. For example, babies are aware of size consistencies; they know objects remain the same size as they move toward us even though they look as if they are becoming larger (Granrud, 2006). This ability is often overlooked, and we often limit children's access to representing in three dimensions, giving

preference to two-dimensional artwork. Yet, construction and malleable materials give children the opportunity to represent the world in three-dimensional forms.

Research in children's block play shows how access to these materials enables children to develop their representations of the world in ways that two-dimensional materials cannot match (Kersh, Casey, & Young, 2008). Although blocks do not have the fluidity of paint or the preciseness of drawing with a pencil, they can be used just as creatively as these or other art materials. Blocks can be moved and rearranged an infinite number of times to produce the most satisfying design, whereas paint, for example, once applied to paper becomes a permanent feature of the artwork.

Three-dimensional models, whether of clay, wood, blocks, or any other material, can have a top, bottom, sides, front, and back, as well as an inside and outside. If they are large enough, they can be walked around and entered. Children often use a wide range of objects in their three-dimensional representations and often not necessarily materials specifically designed for the purpose. For example, many adults who live with young children have experienced chairs and tables being turned into spaceships and boats, and cans from the cupboard being used to create towers. Although these three-dimensional representations do not occur in convenient times, they are evidence of a creative approach to the use of materials and growing confidence in three-dimensional representations (Duffy, 2010). Figure 14-1 presents the stages in the development of three-dimensional awareness and representation.

Just as in drawing, there are basic stages of development in working with three-dimensional material, much the same as there are for two-dimensional media. Although the names of stages in two-dimensional art do not apply (a child does not "scribble" with clay), the same processes of growth and basic ideas for each stage apply.

14-1a Random manipulation

At first, clay is squeezed through the fingers in a very uncontrolled way. This random manipulation is comparable to the early scribble stage. The child at this point is exploring the media. The child is interested in the qualities of the material: what it feels like and what it can do. With both clay and crayons, the child in this age range has little control over hand movements. The feel of the clay in his or her hand while squeezing—the sheer physical pleasure alone—is what the child enjoys about the clay.

Just as children make early scribbles in many directions, they also make early clay forms in many ways. A

Birth–1 year

- Experiences the world in three dimensions
- Handles, feels, and manipulates three-dimensional objects and materials using hands, fingers, and mouth.
- Uses eyes to explore form
- Enjoys manipulating food
- Experiences three-dimensional construction as mobiles

1–2 years

- Heaps objects and demolishes structures
- Mixes and stirs flour and water
- Manipulates dough and clay
- Tears and crunches paper

2–3 years

- Constructs using ready-made forms, for example, blocks, bricks, boxes
- Uses construction materials, such as blocks, horizontally, for example, will line up blocks to create a road
- Stacks, rolls, and lines up objects
- Uses hands to roll, pinch, coil dough and clay

3–4 years

- Builds using raw materials such as clay and wood
- Uses hands and tools to manipulate materials and creates forms
- Adds features to surfaces using fingers and tools
- Uses construction materials vertically, for example, will balance blocks to create towers.

4–5 years

- Uses fingers and tools to create forms that represent ideas
- Engages in complex block play, for example, uses blocks to create a structure than can be entered
- Is interested in decorating the surface of malleable materials such as clay
- Can record constructions through drawings

At 6 years

- Is aware of a variety of natural and manufactured forms
- Expresses his/her own ideas in a variety of media
- Can produce plans for three-dimensional structures and follow them.

(Duffy, 2010)

FIGURE 14-1 Development of three-dimensional awareness and representation.

Source: Duffy, B. (2010). Supporting creativity and imagination in the early years. 2nd edition. New York: McGraw-Hill Education. Reproduced with the kind permission of Open University Press. All rights reserved.

child of this age beats and pounds clay for no special purpose. The child will explore by pushing, tearing, pounding, smoothing, and so on. The child does not try to make anything definite with the clay. What is made depends on whether the child pounds, flattens, or squeezes the clay. Although a child may occasionally identify a mound of clay as a house or a ball of clay as a car, he or she is usually more interested at

this point in the manipulation of the material and discovering what he or she can do with it than in the object created.

14-1b Patting, Rolling, and Making Shapes

As children's muscle control develops, they begin to pat and roll the clay with purpose. This matches the

▶Ⅱ **TeachSource Video**

Infants and Toddlers: Creative Development

1. Observe the toddlers' use of the play dough in this video and describe the developmental level(s) in three-dimensional media observed. Give specific examples in your reply.

2. Which of the guidelines for successful modeling in this chapter are represented in this video? What additional guidelines would you include to further encourage children's modeling in this video activity?

Watch on CourseMate.

controlled scribbling stage. In both scribbling and clay work, children enjoy seeing the effects of their movements. They find that they can use their hand movements to make the clay go in desired ways. At this point, a child may roll the clay into thin lengths or ropes (sometimes called "snakes"), pound it, or shape it into balls. Often, children will make whole families of coils or balls, sometimes covering their entire work surface. Lines drawn with crayon and rope lines or "snakes" made of clay are proof of the child's growing motor control.

14-1c Circles and Rectangles

An older preschool child able to draw basic forms can also make clay into similar forms. Rolling clay to make balls is an example of a basic form (circle) in clay. Boxes made of clay are examples of basic forms (rectangles) in a three-dimensional material. In drawing and in working with clay, the circle is one of the first basic forms made. In both two- and three-dimensional media, the child is able to make this form by controlling the material. The rectangular form usually comes after the circle. Just as in

scribbling, the rectangle is made with clay when the child can shape it into whatever length desired.

14-1d Forming Clay Figures

Many children aged 4 to 5 can put together basic clay forms to make up figures. This is equivalent to the pictorial stage in two-dimensional media. Most children in this age range like to make specific things with clay. They combine basic forms to build objects that are like figures in drawing by making simple things out of basic forms. The child working with clay puts together a round clay ball (circle) for a head and a clay stick-type line or lump for a body. This is similar to the stick figure made in early first drawings.

Later, in working with clay, children 5 years and older may put these forms together in more complex ways. After they have mastered basic shapes, they may make a person with legs, arms, fingers, and feet (see Photo 14-2). This parallels the later pictorial stage, when a child draws with more details. Children at this stage do not make the same forms over and over again for practice as in the stage before. This is because a child of 4 or 5 has the motor control and hand–eye coordination to easily make any form desired. Clay is now used to make a definite object, a symbol for something important to the child. These forms are made in the child's own special way, just as in drawing.

PHOTO 14-2 In using clay, some children may make each part separately, and then put them together in a whole figure.

14-1e Development of Schema

This special way, or schema, of working with clay is the same for two- and three-dimensional media. It comes from much practice in making symbols and is the child's own special way of making these symbols. In developing their personal schemas, just as in drawing, children may make things that are more important to them (symbols) larger than things that are less important. They may also use more details for an important clay figure. At this stage, these details may be made by putting other pieces on the clay, such as buttons for eyes, straws for legs, and cotton for hair. Children at this point also like to create designs by sticking objects into the clay such

as dried flowers, seeds, wooden sticks, feathers, beads, pipe cleaners, and wire. Creating textures by pressing various fabric and found objects into clay is another appropriate way of extending children's natural desire to design and explore with three-dimensional materials.

Children start to name their clay objects at about the same time they start to name their drawings. This is just as important with clay as with drawing. In both cases, it means children are expressing their ideas in art. They can now tell other people just what these ideas are by naming their work. Figure 14-2 summarizes and compares the developmental stages of two- and three-dimensional art.

NON-REPRESENTATIONAL USE OF 3-DIMENSIONAL MEDIA		
Use of 3-Dimensional Media	**Relationship to 2-dimensional media**	**Characteristics**
Early experiences	*Early scribble stage*	Holds material passively. Turns it aimlessly. No deliberate manipulation. Attaches material to other objects
Early modeling	*Later scribble stage*	Material handled kinesthetically. More active handling. Material fingered, pounded, stretched, pulled apart and joined together, hammered on table, folded, patted, squeezed, poked, pinched
Purposeful Modeling	*Early basic forms*	Discovers rolling motion. Makes 1st recognizable shape, Makes rolled dough shapes. Material still handled kinesthetically
REPRESENTATIONAL USE OF 3-DIMENSIONAL MEDIA		
Use of 3-Dimensional Media	**Relationship to 2-dimensional media**	**Characteristics**
Transitional Stage	*Later Basic Forms*	Awareness of possibility to make things with material. Relates actions to objects created (ball bounces). Creates objects for no particular reason. Objects not representative of idea or concept. Needs to verbalize missing parts

FIGURE 14-2 3-Dimensional Media: Pattern of Development   (*Continues*)

© 2015 Cengage Learning

REPRESENTATIONAL USE OF 3-DIMENSIONAL MEDIA		
Use of 3-Dimensional Media	**Relationship to 2-dimensional media**	**Characteristics**
Early to later representational stage	*Early and later pictorial stage*	Child sets out to make specific object Tadpole men 3 forms of human figure: upright standing column, ball/slab dough with facial features, separate parts (face and body) Makes ball or flattened ball with facial features. Standing column develops into figure with body details. Makes ball/slab dough with facial features, separate parts (face and body) Makes ball or flattened ball with facial features. Standing column develops into figure with body details. No need to verbalize parts.

FIGURE 14-2 3-Dimensional Media: Pattern of Development

TeachSource Digital Download   Download from CourseMate.

Did You Get It?

At Angela's first birthday party, she picks up her piece of birthday cake and squeezes it, allowing the icing to ooze through the spaces between her fingers. At what stage of development in three-dimensional art is Angela?

   a. random manipulation
   b. patting and rolling
   c. shape forming
   d. development of schema

Take the full quiz on CourseMate.

14-2 Modeling

naeyc **DAP** Modeling—manipulating and shaping flexible material—has many benefits for young children (see Photo 14-3). It helps them develop tactile perception, which is the understanding and appreciation of the sense of touch. Modeling also helps develop the child's adaptability to change as he or she interacts with an ever-flexible material. In modeling three-dimensional objects, the child's concepts of form and proportion are strengthened as the child learns to make objects with his or her hands. Older children develop an appreciation for sculpture and

pottery as they appear in our environment when they create their own original sculpture and simple pottery.

Three-dimensional art is often an underexplored area of the arts in many early childhood programs. And yet, the overarching ideas of sculpture (one of the most basic of three-dimensional arts) are form, space, and material—qualities that are seen in hundreds of everyday contexts. Clay and play dough are excellent materials for developing and enhancing children's individual learning styles. Modeling with

PHOTO 14-3 Manipulating or shaping flexible material, or modeling, has many benefits for young children.

these substances has appeal for the body-smart learner because it involves tactile experiences such as squeezing, shaping, and physical manipulation. The child with an interpersonal learning style finds working with clay alongside other children a very natural learning environment. The child with a visual learning style will find clay an ideal material for making models and other similar projects involving measurement. Clay also makes a great base for a natural objects display piece for the child with a nature-smart learning style.

14-2a Materials

The soft, plastic quality of natural clay has a strong appeal for children of any age (Photo 14-4). Salt clay may be substituted for modeling; it is quite a suitable modeling material for young children. To prepare salt clay, mix together 2/3 cup of salt, 1/2 cup of flour, and 1/3 cup of water. Add a small amount of dry powder paint or food coloring, if desired, while the mixture is moist. When the clay is left white, the dried piece has a crystalline sheen or "snow" effect caused by the salt. Finished objects dry to a durable hardness.

Paper pulp (papier-mâché), another modeling material, is easy to work with, does not crack or break readily, and is inexpensive. It can be made in either of two forms: as a pulp or in strips applied to a base. It can be molded into various three-dimensional shapes when it is wet and painted when it is dry. This medium is not appropriate for very young children because it is created in a two-step process that involves a sustained interest span. (See chapter end for papier-mâché paste recipes.)

PHOTO 14-4 The soft, plastic quality of natural clay has a strong appeal for children of any age.

To prepare paper pulp:

1. Shred pieces of soft paper, such as newsprint, paper towels, newspaper, or facial tissue, into small bits or thin strips.
2. Soak several hours in water.
3. Drain, squeeze out the extra water, and mix the pulp with prepared wheat paste to the consistency of soft clay.
4. Let the mixture stand for an hour before beginning to work with it.

You can make a mold out of nonhardening clay and cover it with petroleum jelly. Then cover your mold with one or two layers of the paper pulp and let dry for 24 hours. Do a few more layers and let dry again. Cut the whole thing in half. Take the molding clay out. Tape the papier-mâché forms back together. Put three, four, or even five layers of paste-soaked newspaper strips over the tape. Make sure it covers the split well. Let dry and then paint. The second type of papier-mâché involves the use of paper strips. To prepare paper strips:

1. Tear newspaper or newsprint into long, thin strips about 1/2-inch wide.
2. Dip the strips into a wheat paste or starch and white glue mixture, and then put down a layer of wet strips over the shape to be covered.
3. Continue putting strips on the form until there are five or six layers. This thickness is strong enough to support most papier-mâché projects.

Good forms that can be used as foundations for papier-mâché include the following: rolled newspapers secured with string or tape, blown-up balloons, plastic bottles, paper sacks stuffed with newspapers and tied with string, and wire or wooden armatures used as skeletal forms.

Did You Get It?

Modeling has many benefits for young children, including

a. developing their multicultural awareness.
b. teaching them about art history.
c. developing their ability to copy a preexisting form.
d. developing their adaptability to change.

Take the full quiz on CourseMate.

14-3 Guidelines for Successful Modeling

naeyc **DAP** The following suggestions encourage children's modeling activities:

● Make it clear to children that in working with modeling materials, the emphasis is on process

THINK ABOUT IT

Assemblage: Recycling, Recreating

The idea of transforming ready-made objects into works of art was popularized in the early twentieth century by French artist Marcel Duchamp, who sought to show that mass-produced objects held aesthetic qualities. The found object movement *(object trouve)* featured new works of art created by transforming material objects and endowing them with novel, different meanings.

Duchamp perfected the concept when he made a series of *ready-mades,* completely unaltered everyday objects selected by Duchamp and designated as art. The most famous example is *Fountain* (1917), a standard urinal purchased from a hardware store and displayed on a pedestal resting on its side. In its strictest sense, the art term *ready-made* is applied exclusively to works produced by marcel Duchamp, who borrowed the term from the clothing industry while living in New York, and especially to works dating from 1913 to 1921 (MOMA, 2012).

In the past decade, there has been a demonstrated growth of exhibitions and other venues related to found object/assemblage art. This resurgence in popularity, coupled with the fact that assemblage addresses the national visual arts standards content standard 4—understanding the visual arts in relation to history and cultures—makes working with reclaimed objects a particularly useful practice for young children (Eckhoff & Spearman, 2009).

Using reclaimed objects in artwork involves the creation of new and innovative artwork from what were once considered non-art items or objects of waste. Introducing reclaimed materials into the early childhood art program provides children with unique opportunities to connect ordinary, discarded objects with unique, personal artistic creations. The transformation of objects used in assemblage pieces asks viewers to reconsider the notion of "valuable" as they are challenged to look at everyday objects with a new perspective (Taylor, 2006).

If using found materials in assemblage is to be an enriching experience for young children, early childhood teachers need to do more than provide a variety of these materials for children. Children need time to develop understandings of reclaimed materials. Children need to look, feel, compare, describe, contrast, and exchange observations with one another. During this process of active exploration, the teacher acts as a facilitator or guide. Taylor (2006) offers a series of questions that can act as a sufficient guide for teachers to engage in discussions with children about the objects they explore and contemplate for inclusion in an assemblage. For example:

- What story does it tell you?
- Does it remind you of an event, a specific time in history or in your life, a place, or a state of mind?
- How can you bring that story to life? (Taylor, 2006, p.9)

You might supplement these questions with additional ones that look at the material object and its cultural identity. For example:

- Where do you think this object came from?
- Why do you think that someone labeled this object as "waste?"
- How can you transform this object to tell the story that you thought of before? (Eckhoff & Spearman, 2009)

These challenging questions encourage children to think deeply about materials and how they can transform them with their imaginations.

---

rather than product. Modeling with clay interests and absorbs children, who will enjoy working with it because of the feelings it generates in them, the pleasure of discovery they experience, being able to put their mark on it, and its change-friendly properties. Very rarely should clay be used with young children to make something permanent. Rather, clay is played with at a table with others and made back into a ball and stored away after children are finished.

- Introduce new tools for modeling to add variety to clay activities. Provide sticks, tongue depressors, a garlic press, Popsicle sticks, nails, combs, and paper clips. Of course, any tools small enough to put in the mouth should not be used with any young children, especially toddlers. All preschoolers need to be supervised in their use of modeling tools.
- Encourage children's efforts at all levels and all stages of growth. Some children find satisfaction in manipulating a modeling material without making anything. Others, in the symbolic stage, give names to objects such as balls, pancakes, and coils. All efforts in modeling should be encouraged.
- Avoid blocking children's thinking by diverting them from one method of working with

modeling materials to another. One child may pull, pinch, or squeeze the material into a desired shape with head, arms, and legs extended. Another may make each part separately, then put them together into the whole figure. Some children may combine the two ways of working. No one method is better than another.

- When children are ready for other techniques, demonstrate how to do the following:
  - Moisten both parts when joining pieces of clay together, then pinch and work them together so they will not separate when the object has dried.
  - Avoid delicate parts that break off.
  - Smooth the material to prevent cracking.
  - Create texture using fingernails or carving tools.
  - Depict action by bending the head or twisting the body.
  - If a child has difficulty with attaching smaller pieces of clay to a larger piece, demonstrate how to "pull" a smaller piece of clay out of the larger mass. Just be sure your suggestion helps the child accomplish his or her own goal for the clay.

Wrap unfinished clay work in plastic bags or aluminum foil, or place it in a covered can with the child's name attached. A small lump of modeling material can be used as a magnet to pick up crumbs at cleanup time.

14-3a Encouraging Older Children's Modeling Activities

Children who are in the middle- and upper-elementary grades enjoy more exploration and challenge with modeling activities. This is a good age to introduce the work of potters. Having a potter visit your class to demonstrate how pottery or clay sculptures are made can motivate children's work in clay. As an alternative, a teacher or parent can arrange a field trip to a potter's studio so that children can see a potter's wheel, kiln, and other special tools and ways of working with clay.

Bring in beautiful earthenware serving pieces to show children these "common" dishes, bowls, and cups are made from clay. Explain that for thousands of years, people have used clay to make utensils for eating. For members of the earliest cultures, clay was important for more than its artistic potential. Objects used in everyday life, such as vessels used as containers for a variety of materials from water to grain, were made from this substance taken from the earth. Bits and pieces of such vessels, called *shards*, help archeologists determine the age as well as the social, artistic,

and religious aspects of particular cultures. Many of the clay pieces and other ceramic works now in museums had a functional importance long before museum curators gathered them as works of art for display.

Children of this age can also begin to learn about and appreciate the work of sculptors. Art prints of the sculpture work of Henry Moore are a good place to begin discussing the qualities of form, subject, and theme in sculpture. Obtain samples of sculpture pieces from a museum gift shop or from local art stores. Encourage children to view these pieces from all sides. Have them identify basic geometric forms they see in sculpture examples. Encourage children to create sculpture pieces of their own. Suggestions for more activities involving clay and play dough are provided at the end of this chapter.

Did You Get It?

One first-grader manipulates a clump of clay into the shape of a dog, and another forms the separate shapes of a body, head, and legs, then attaches them together to form a dog. Their teacher should approach their different methods by

  a. recognizing that the former student is far more sophisticated in his abilities.

  b. recognizing that no method is superior to other methods.

  c. recognizing that the latter student is far more sophisticated in his abilities.

  d. modeling the correct way to form an elephant.

Take the full quiz on CourseMate.

14-4 The Value of Clay

naeyc DAP Too little attention is given to the use of clay in the early childhood program. Many ideas can be carried out better in clay than in paint. If a child has not developed enough confidence to express himself or herself freely in painting, he or she can do so with greater ease in modeling. In modeling with clay, the child can change his or her artistic concept at will because clay is pliable. If a painting does not turn out as anticipated, it cannot be changed, and the child may become discouraged. A clay object, on the other hand, can be altered multiple times.

At all ages, work with clay gives the child many chances for creative experiences. Most children like the damp feel of clay. They like to pound it, roll it, poke holes in it, and pull it apart. Just as in drawing, it is the fun of working with the clay that counts. The end product is not as important as using it; a child becomes really involved in the process. Children should not be restricted in the size of their modeling. If they do not have enough clay, their modeling may be so small that they have difficulty in handling it. Have at least a five-pound bag of clay available for children's use.

Potter's clay is a very good three-dimensional material for young children. Playing with clay is an exciting manipulative experience. It is pliable and thus provides a very different experience than working with paint. Preschoolers and children in all grade levels enjoy working with potter's clay. It is easy to use because it is soft and elastic. It is best bought in moist form because the dry powder is difficult to prepare, and the silica dust is unhealthy for children to inhale. Plasticene, a plastic-type clay, is more expensive and is much harder for the young child to use because it is not as soft and elastic as real clay. To make it easier for young children to use, warm and soften cold or hard Plasticene by rolling it between your hands.

To make the play dough and clay area satisfying for toddlers in their first experiences with modeling clay, use a small, low table. Although many different props can be used (utensils, cookie cutters, play dishes), most of the activity with this medium comes from the use of hands and fingers (Photo 14-5). Squeezing, patting, pulling apart, and rolling all help develop small muscles and make the experience relaxing and successful for toddlers. Many young children like to watch and vocalize to their friends while they use dough. If the housekeeping area is nearby, toddlers

PHOTO 14-6 Children who are hesitant to touch clay might be willing to start by gently patting it with a teacher or a friend nearby.

may even initiate simple imaginative games around themes of cooking, eating, and family celebrations.

Play dough can be made from water, flour, and salt; the colors can be varied each time. (Recipes for various doughs for three-dimensional activities can be found at the end of this chapter.) Toddlers enjoy helping mix the dough, which can be refrigerated when not in use.

Children who perceive clay as "messy" or "slimy" may not want to work with it. Never force the issue! Be patient and give these children lots of time and plenty of opportunities to see the fun others have with clay. Some teachers find that involving timid children first in a "cleaner" aspect of clay work, such as mixing up play dough, helps involve them on a gradual basis. Hesitant children might feel more comfortable sitting near you as you pat the dough and describe how it feels. Acknowledge these simple participations. As children feel more comfortable, they may eventually try patting clay gently with you or a friend (see Photo 14-6).

PHOTO 14-5 Adding interesting items to use with play dough fosters children's creativity.

Did You Get It?

One advantage of providing clay instead of paint when working with young children is that

a. children can feel more confident about freely expressing themselves with clay.

b. clay is a cleaner material than paint.

c. clay is more developmentally appropriate for children younger than five.

d. clay places fewer societal expectations on its users than paint does.

Take the full quiz on CourseMate.

14-5 Strategies for Working with Clay

naeyc DAP Working with clay requires planning and forethought. A lack of planning can result in a teacher's constantly having to remind the children about the right use of clay. Proper setup will make this unnecessary. Some tips for clay setup follow.

- The tables used for working with clay should be placed away from wheel and climbing toys. They should be covered with linoleum or Formica to make cleaning easier. If the tables in the room are Formica-topped, additional covering is not usually needed.
- The number of children at a table at one time should be limited, allowing each child enough room to spread out and use as much arm and hand movement as he or she needs.
- Each child should be given a lump of clay at least the size of a large apple or a small grapefruit. The clay may be worked with in any way the child wants. Two basic guidelines are helpful: The clay may not be thrown on the floor, and no child may interfere with another child's work.
- The teacher may sit at the table and play with clay, too; this adds to the social feeling of the modeling experience. But the teacher should avoid making objects for the child to copy. This discourages the child's creative use of the clay.
- When children are finished modeling, clay needs to be stored until its next use. It is best to form it into balls, each about the size of an apple. A hole filled with water in each ball helps keep the clay just right for use the next time. Keep the clay in a container with a wet cloth or sponge on top of the clay. The container should be covered with a tight-fitting lid. (Margarine tubs with plastic lids work well.) Clay becomes moldy if it is too wet and hard to handle if it becomes very dry. If clay should dry out, it can be restored to a proper consistency by placing the dried-out clay in a cloth bag and pounding it with a hammer until it is broken into small pieces. After the clay soaks in water, it can be kneaded until it is the proper consistency again. If clay does become moldy, there is no need to throw it away. Simply scrape off the moldy area and drain off any water collected in the bottom of the container.

Did You Get It?

A preschool teacher sits with her students, playing with a clump of clay while they work with their clay. From a developmental perspective, her actions are

a. helpful, as they contribute to the social feeling of the clay experience.
b. disadvantageous, as they cause the children to feel inhibited.
c. inadvisable, as they don't contribute to the creative process.
d. recommended, as children will not know how to play with clay without the teacher's demonstration.

Take the full quiz on CourseMate.

14-6 Assemblage

naeyc DAP As an art form, assemblage refers to placing a number of three-dimensional objects, natural or manmade, in juxtaposition to create a unified composition. Materials are combined in a new context to express an abstract, poetic, or representational theme. Assemblage makes use of three-dimensional space, resembling a still-life arrangement as objects are first selected, then grouped and regrouped. Assemblage art can also involve the creation of new and innovative artworks from what were once considered objects of waste. Through their use in assemblage pieces, reclaimed objects are endowed with a new meaning.

There are many ways to make an assemblage. One way is to put things together. Small boxes, a paper cup, a cardboard roll, and an egg carton can be glued together. Another way to make an assemblage is to build up a form, using materials you can shape yourselves. For older children, cardboard is a good material for shaping an assemblage with building up a form. Cardboard can be found anywhere, and it is easy to work with. Children just need scissors and glue to cut and stick the cardboard shapes together. They can bend, twist, fold, cut, or glue shapes to make a sculpture.

14-6a Encouraging Assemblage Activities

Try some of the following suggestions to introduce children to assemblage:

- Encourage children to bring objects from their environment and containers for assemblages.
- Display and discuss collected items.

THINK ABOUT IT

Research on Young Children and Three-Dimensional Media

Researchers at the University of Massachusetts Boston have conducted several extensive studies of children's three-dimensional modeling of clay figures (Golomb, 2007, 2004; Golomb & McCormick, 1995). They also studied children's approach to two- and three-dimensional tasks that had a specific theme, while the material and conditions were varied. In one study, the two-dimensional media consisted of drawing on paper and representing themes with felt cutouts; the same themes were also made with three-dimensional items on a Plexiglas board (Gallo, Golomb, & Barroso, 2003). The results from these studies highlight the role of the medium and the significance of experience with the art form.

One of the most striking findings of these studies concerns **dimensionality**. Instead of flattening the human and animal figures as they are in children's drawings, the great majority of the children while modeling paid some attention to the different sides of the figure, at times working on all six sides: front, back, long sides, top, and bottom. This finding applied to the youngest children (4-year-olds) as well as the oldest (13-year-olds).

A progression similar to that of the developmental stages in two-dimensional art can be seen in the modeling of animal figures: First global shapes, then tadpole-like figures, followed by a fully differentiated figure composed of head, body, four legs, and a tail. The majority of the modeled animals are upright standing figures, which is significantly higher than is the case for the human figures (83% vs. 57%). The children's strategy was to turn figures upside down to attach the front and hind legs, sideways to model the tail, and frontally to attach the head and differentiate the orientation of the head from the sides of the body (Golomb, 2007).

Also noteworthy was the use of different models on diverse tasks. For example, the children used a very specific, easily recognizable model for the human figure (upright with torso and limbs) and an upright standing three-dimensional model for an animal. Other differences between children's representation in two- and three-dimensional media were also found in the representation of facial features. In drawing, facial features are rarely omitted in children's drawings, but in modeling there was a high incidence of faceless human and animal figures. In contrast to the facial omission, the body was represented in most three-dimensional models of the youngest children.

With age and practice, they report a growing interest in size differences and in attempts to enliven the figure by action and gesture and by the addition of such details as clothing and accessories in the case of the human, spots on the turtle, and a collar on the dog. In general, they found differentiation of form was mostly age related, with older children being more skillful and able to model better-balanced sculpture. However, they found that age per se does not guarantee skill. Although technical skill improved with age, many sculptures continued to be modeled crudely at the higher age levels. Often, the technique of the older children was not better than that of the youngest.

In summary, their research supports the idea that when children become representational in the three-dimensional medium of clay, approximately during their fourth or fifth year, they exhibit some basic three-dimensional understanding. From the very beginning of their work with clay, children develop representational concepts that are three-dimensional in nature, and they refine them with continued practice. They found much evidence that the young artist struggles with problems older children must also confront: how to create a satisfying representation in a medium (clay) that requires balance, uprightness, and the modeling of multiple sides, all of which require great skill and practice. Once again, we must acknowledge the great challenges young children face in their creative development. We too must acknowledge the important role early childhood teachers play in supporting this development.

- Explore ways of arranging the various objects, emphasizing the variety of shapes, sizes, colors, textures, and methods of fastening the objects.
- Explore ways of making items for an assemblage. Some materials for an assemblage follow:

- Containers: Wooden boxes, cardboard boxes, cigar boxes, matchboxes, suitcases, egg cartons and crates, packing cartons. These may be painted or decorated if children desire.
- Mounting boards: Pasteboard, corrugated cardboard, wood, crates, picture frames.

- Objects: Wooden forms or scrap lumber, driftwood, screening, corks, cardboard boxes, spools, discarded toys, household items, articles of nature (such as seeds, weeds, stones, twigs), and any other interesting items.
- Adhesives: Paste, glue, staples, tape.
- Tools: Scissors, stapler, hammer, nails, pliers.
- Encourage children to collect objects that are meaningful to them. Almost any area of interest or everyday experience is a possible theme for assemblage.
- Show children how to select objects for an assemblage according to an idea, topic, size of container, or variation in line, form, color, and texture. Demonstrate how to use multiple items for repetition of shapes.
- Encourage children to alter or transform three-dimensional forms so that they lose their original identity and take on a new meaning. They can be bent, twisted, stretched, crumpled, or painted.
- Extend possibilities for assemblage by cutting out pictures or illustrations and pasting them over cardboard, wood, or other substantial material.
- Glue, staple, or even nail objects together or onto a mounting board.
- Encourage children to arrange and rearrange objects until the desired effect is achieved. Distribute paste and other fastening materials after the arrangement has met with the child's satisfaction.

Did You Get It?

A fourth-grade teacher who has her students design a miniature neighborhood of the future inside a shoebox is involving her students in which three-dimensional activity?

a. containment
b. assemblage
c. adapting nature to art
d. multicultural awareness

Take the full quiz on CourseMate.

14-7 Assemblage Adaptations for Children with Special Needs

naeyc **DAP** Many of the assemblage activities in this chapter and in the collage activities in Chapter 13 involve a child's working with glue and paste. This type of activity may be challenging for certain children with special needs. The following are some suggestions for modifying the gluing and pasting processes for those children who find this type of activity challenging.

14-7a Developmental Delays

If the multistep process of gluing is too complicated for the child, make a collage or assemblage without glue by using contact paper or another type of sticky base. Turn the paper sticky side up and tape it into a cookie sheet or shirt box. The child only needs to place selected items onto the sticky surface to complete the activity. No glue or tape is needed.

The following are some additional suggestions for working with children who have special needs:

- Try not to overwhelm the child with too many choices. Offer only one or two materials at a time.
- Help the child organize his or her space by providing containers for each type of collage/assemblage material.
- Provide the child with a large collage/assemblage base to compensate for less mature hand–eye coordination.
- Provide a glue stick instead of white glue for children who have difficulty controlling the amount of glue needed.

14-7b Physical Impairments

For children with arm, hand, and finger control limitations, some of the following ideas may be useful.

- Stabilize the base of the collage/assemblage by taping it to the work surface to prevent slipping. A piece of nonskid shelving material or a placemat can also be used to stabilize the base of the assemblage.
- Use a 6-inch-long, 1- to 2-inch-wide dowel piece with a sponge attached to spread glue. It may be easier for a child with a weak or poor grasp to hold onto this dowel. Another alternative is to provide a wide paintbrush for applying glue.
- Place glue in an aluminum pie plate that has been taped to the work surface. The pie plate is easier for a child with limited motor control to reach and use.
- Make certain all necessary materials are placed within the child's reaching distance.
- Minimize fatigue by reducing the number of steps of the collage/assemblage process.

14-7c Attention Deficit/Hyperactivity Disorder

Children with attention deficit/hyperactivity disorder (ADHD) frequently exhibit poor organizational skills. The following are some suggestions to assist a child with ADHD in collage/assemblage activities:

- Have an adult available to sit with the child and guide him or her through the activity, providing ample praise and frequent feedback at each step of the process.
- Do not place all the project materials out on the table. Too many materials will distract and confuse children who are impulsive and easily distracted. Set out only the particular material needed for the next step of the activity. When that step is completed, set out the material for the next step, and so on.
- Place each collage material in a separate container, and place the child's collage/assemblage base in a shirt box or on a cookie sheet to help define his or her workspace.

14-7d Visual Impairments

Both children who are blind and children with low vision enjoy assemblages and collages. These children are able to use their heightened sense of touch to guide them through the process and then feel their finished product at the end. Here are some suggestions for facilitating their work with collage/assemblage:

- Add yellow food coloring or yellow tempera paint to the glue so it is more easily visible on the collage surface. Use a contrasting dark blue paper for the collage base.
- Add sand, sawdust, or other textures to the glue to enhance tactile feedback.
- Use a small squeeze bottle or a commercial glue stick for ease of use instead of the dip-and-spread method.
- Place glue in an aluminum pie plate to provide a larger target for dipping the gluing utensil. Place colored tape around the edge of the pie plate to emphasize its boundaries.
- Mark the edges of the collage paper with a bright color paint, marker, or tape to help indicate the boundaries.
- Line a shallow baking pan with a piece of non-skid shelving material, and place the collage materials in the pan.
- Guide the child's arm and show him or her where each material is located. Be sure to also say what you are doing and describe the position of each item. For example, you might say, "I am moving your hand to the right side of the pan, almost to the edge, to find the buttons".

Did You Get It?

How can a teacher enhance a visually impaired four-year-old's collage experience?
- **a.** give her only a few materials at a time to avoid overstimulation
- **b.** minimize fatigue by reducing the number of steps needed to complete the collage
- **c.** add sand to the glue
- **d.** give her crayons to draw with instead

Take the full quiz on CourseMate.

14-8 Cardboard Construction

naeyc DAP Cardboard, an indispensable material for construction projects, stimulates and challenges the imagination of children on all levels. It is readily available in various forms. Such commonplace objects as milk and egg cartons, apple-crate dividers, towel tubes, and assorted sizes of boxes offer unlimited possibilities for creative art projects.

14-8a Encouraging Cardboard Construction Activities

Gather together an assortment of cardboard materials. Some suggestions follow.

- Assorted cardboard boxes, cartons, corrugated cardboard, paper cups, and paper plates of all sizes
- Recycled materials: paper bags, yarn, string, buttons, feathers, cloth, tissue paper, scraps of construction paper, and wrapping paper
- Paste, glue, tape, crayons, colored markers, paint, brushes, scissors, stapler, and staples

Most topics of interest to young children can be adapted to cardboard construction projects. Creations are as endless as the imaginations of young children. Some possibilities for creative construction projects include using boxes for making various buildings, houses, cities, and even neighborhoods. Young children also enjoy making such things as imaginary animals, people, and favorite characters from a story out of various cardboard rolls and containers. Some children have even made costumes out of boxes large enough to fit over the child's body. Cars, trucks, and trains are some other favorite construction projects with young children. Cardboard construction provides a wealth of possibilities for creative expression in arts and crafts projects as well.

Some suggestions for facilitating cardboard construction follow.

Have the cardboard construction materials out and available for children to explore on their own. Encourage children to stack materials or combine them in different ways. Encourage children to explore the possibilities for creating they may discover while playing with the materials.

Discuss with children and demonstrate (if needed) ways of fastening boxes together, covering them with paint or paper, and adding other parts or features.

Encourage children to select as many objects as they need for their construction.

Cover boxes with waxed surfaces with a layer of newspaper and wheat paste that is allowed to dry before painting. Tempera paint mixed with liquid starch adheres well to box surfaces.

Create textured surfaces by using corrugated cardboard, shredded packing tissue, or crinkled newspaper.

Allow the shapes and sizes of cardboard objects to suggest ideas for a project. An oatmeal box can become the body of an elephant; a milk carton will transform into a tall building.

Use a variety of materials to complete a design, such as pieces of ribbon, buttons, sequins, spools, and so on.

Older children are able to appreciate lessons combining three-dimensional assemblage projects with architectural ideas. For example, after drawing their plans for a building or structure, students might like to use boxes, cardboard, or cut-and-fold paper techniques to make three-dimensional models of their buildings. Students who are particularly excited by such projects may wish to create realistic settings for their structures as well, using sand, pebbles, dried moss, and the like to create their own miniature scene.

More assemblage activities are found at the end of this chapter.

Did You Get It?

The creative value of using cereal boxes and other cardboard containers in art activities is that it
   a. teaches children the importance of recycling.
   b. provides the teacher with useful storage containers.
   c. helps children with their drawing and painting.
   d. stimulates children's imaginations.

Take the full quiz on CourseMate.

14-9 Woodworking

naeyc **DAP** Woodworking involves a range of activities from hammering nails to sanding, gluing, and painting wood. As with other three-dimensional activities, woodworking can be an excellent medium for fostering a child's creativity if the process, and not the product, is emphasized.

14-9a Planning for the Woodworking Experience

Planning for the woodworking area and related experiences is the key to success. Thought must be given to time allotment, location of the woodworking area, limits, number of children working at one time, and the role of the teacher. The following criteria need to be considered:

● Enough time should be allotted for children to explore materials without feeling rushed. If the woodworking area is a popular one, the teacher may find it necessary to set up time allotments to give all children a chance to participate.

● The workbench should be situated so that several children can move around and work without bumping into one another. It should be located out of major traffic patterns to avoid interruptions and accidents, and away from quiet areas so the noise will not disturb others. Weather permitting, and with adequate supervision, woodworking can be done outdoors.

● A specific limit should be set in advance regarding the number of children working at one time. Usually, one teacher can comfortably supervise three or four children. No more children than the set limit should be allowed in the woodworking area at one time. Teachers can enforce this number by requiring all children who are woodworking to wear an apron and safety goggles and then supplying only that number of aprons and goggles in the center.

- Tools and materials should be geared to the ability level of the children using them.
- The teacher needs to familiarize himself or herself with the use of woodworking tools and materials in order to give effective guidance and set reasonable limits. To create enthusiasm for woodworking, it is important that the teacher be excited about its possibilities. The carpentry area must be constantly supervised to avoid accidents.

14-9b Guidance for Woodworking Activities

In guiding children in woodworking activities, the teacher must first help them become familiar with the tools. In introducing the saw, for example, show the children how to hold the saw at a 45-degree angle and gently move it back and forth rhythmically. Children do not have to use a great deal of force or power for sawing; the saw will do the work on its own. Demonstrate how to fasten the wood in a vise and hold the wood with the left hand while sawing with the right hand, or vice versa for left-handers.

The rules of saw safety must be emphasized, including where to keep the hands, how to carry the saw, and where to lay it down.

In introducing the hammer, show children how to set a nail by gently tapping it into the wood. It can be driven using more vigorous strokes while holding the hammer near the end of the handle. Make a series of holes in various pieces of wood, showing how to set nails into these premade holes. Avoid too many detailed instructions or providing models or patterns. These things limit the children's initiative, independence, and creativity.

To prevent children from becoming frustrated, show them how to make handling wood easier by laying it flat and securing it with a vise. Allow children to try out their own ideas, but guide them in choosing the proper tools to use for carrying out those ideas.

14-9c Selecting Tools for Woodworking Experiences

When buying tools and equipment for woodworking, choose adult-type tools of good quality that withstand hard use. Tools should also be able to be resharpened, be reconditioned, and have broken parts replaced.

- Saws. Three types of saws are generally sold for woodworking purposes: the rip saw, the crosscut saw, and the coping saw. The rip saw has coarse teeth for cutting wood in the direction of the grain. The crosscut saw is designed to cut across the grain, while the coping saw is designed for use on thin wood and for cutting curves. Of the three saws available, the crosscut saw is the easiest for young children to manage. An 8- or 10-point saw (teeth per inch) is the most satisfactory size for children's use.
- Hammers. A 10- to 13-ounce claw hammer, with a broad head, is the most satisfactory for use by young children.
- Plane. A plane may be provided for children's use. If it is available, the blade should be adjusted to make small cuts, and children should be cautioned to use it only on surfaces free from nails, screws, or knots.
- Workbench. The workbench used must be strong, sturdy, and stable. An old door or heavy wooden packing box is ideal for a homemade workbench. Or a pair of sawhorses connected with a heavy board can be easily set up. All workbenches should be about 16 to 18 inches high, just under a child's waist height, for the most convenient work.

Optional tools
- Pliers for holding nails as children are setting them
- Scissors for cutting sandpaper and string
- Screwdriver
- Rasp for smoothing a rough or splintered edge against the grain and for rounding corners on wood
- 1-foot ruler, yardstick
- Pencil
- C-clamp

14-9d Storage and Care of Tools

A special wall-mounted tool board is essential for storing frequently used tools, while infrequently used tools can be stored in a cupboard. Paint the outline of each tool on the board so children can see where to put them away.

Saws should be professionally sharpened and oiled once or twice a year and wrapped in newspaper for long-term storage. Tools should be kept free from dust and rust; lightweight machine oil or WD-40 will remove any rust that forms.

14-9e Choosing and Using Woodworking Materials

Woods. The wood provided for young children in the woodworking area should be unfinished, smooth, and porous enough for children to pound or saw. Pine, balsa, poplar, and basswood are good, soft woods for children's use. Children work best with small pieces of wood of varying sizes, shapes, and thicknesses. Lumberyard scraps of doweling, molding, and mill ends offer endless possibilities when provided along with basic wood pieces.

Store wood in a container that allows visibility and accessibility to the child. Plastic vegetable bins work well for this.

Nails. Nails are supplied in pennyweights (dwt), which refers to the length of the nail. Common nail sizes are 2 dwt or 10; 4 dwt or 1 1/20; 6 dwt or 20; 8 dwt or 2 1/20; and 10 dwt or 30. At first, most children have trouble pounding nails without bending them, so 1 1/20 nails with large heads are best. Store nails in small jars according to size to allow children to select them easily.

Glue. Glue can be used by children who have not mastered the skill of pounding nails well enough to fasten wood pieces together. A quick-drying, all-purpose glue can be used for this purpose. Glue can also be used to make wood sculptures, attach accessories, and strengthen joints.

Screws. Screws may be provided in the woodworking area but are often difficult for young children to handle. They can be made more manageable by making a guide hole with a nail first. Older children can work more easily with screws and a screwdriver than

young children. Provide both standard and Phillips-head screwdrivers with a variety of screw sizes.

14-9f Additional Materials

- Sandpaper in four weights: coarse, medium, fine, extra fine (mount sandpaper on wooden blocks and use in a back-and-forth motion)
- Brushes of medium and narrow widths
- Tempera paint for painting completed creations
- Accessories such as string, rubber bands, small pieces of rubber, scraps of leather, pieces of cloth and carpeting, bottle caps, pieces of Styrofoam, and metal gadgets (for example, cup hooks, staples, and paper clips)

Did You Get It?

What is the best educational approach to woodworking?
   a. It is a dangerous activity best left to professionals.
   b. It should not be used in schools because most parents would not approve of it.
   c. It is useful if the children can then use the finished product.
   d. It teaches creativity only if the process, not the product, is emphasized.

Take the full quiz on CourseMate.

Summary

14-1 Describe the developmental levels and three-dimensional media.

Just as children have different drawing abilities at each age, they work with clay in different ways at each age. When young children first learn to use a three-dimensional material such as clay, they go through much the same process as a child using crayons in the scribble stage. In work with both crayons and clay, children at this age have little control over their hands or the material. They enjoy the feel of the clay but do not have good control in working with it.

Older preschool children who can draw basic forms such as circles or rectangles can also make clay into similar forms. Balls and boxes are examples of basic forms in clay. Children's muscle (motor) control helps them make these forms. Children in this age group can also put together basic forms in clay to make up figures. This is similar to making figures in the pictorial stage of two-dimensional media.

Children name their clay objects at about the same time that they name their drawings. Naming is an important form of communication in both two- and three-dimensional media.

14-2 Explain modeling and describe its benefits for children.

Modeling refers to the manipulation and shaping of flexible materials. Modeling activities help children develop their sense of touch, their adaptation to change, their concepts of form and proportion, and, especially in older children, their sense of aesthetics.

14-3 Discuss some guidelines to follow for successful modeling activities.

Make it clear to children that in working with clay, the emphasis is on process rather than product. Introduce new tools for modeling to add variety to clay activities. Encourage children's efforts at all levels and all stages of growth. Avoid blocking children's thinking by diverting them from one method of working with clay to another. Demonstrate new techniques when children are ready for them.

14-4 Explain the value of clay in the early childhood program.

In modeling with clay, the child can change his or her artistic concept at will because clay is pliable. A clay object can be altered multiple times. Work with clay gives the child many chances for creative experiences. Playing with clay is an exciting manipulative experience. It is pliable and thus provides a very different experience than working with paint.

14-5 Describe the strategies for working with clay.

Tables used for working with clay should be placed away from wheel and climbing toys. They should be covered with linoleum or Formica to make cleaning easier. The number of children at a table at one time should be limited, allowing enough room to spread out and use as much arm and hand movement as he or she needs. Each child should be given a lump of clay at least the size of a large apple. The teacher may sit at the table and play with the clay, too. When children are finished modeling, clay needs to be stored until its next use.

14-6 Define assemblage and give specific examples of assemblage activities for children.

Assemblage is a creative activity that involves placing a number of three-dimensional objects together to create a unified composition. Stabiles and mobiles are also examples of three-dimensional artwork. Everyday materials found in the school or home environment are media for this type of activity.

14-7 Explain how to adapt assemblage activities for children with special needs.

If the multistep process of gluing is too complicated for a child with developmental delays, make a collage or assemblage without glue by using contact paper or another type of sticky base. For children with arm, hand, and finger control limitations, stabilize the base of the assemblage by taping it to the work surface to prevent slipping. For children with ADHD, have an adult available to sit with the child and guide him or her through the activity. Also, do not place all the project materials out on the table. For children with visual impairment, add sand, sawdust, or other textures to the glue to enhance tactile feedback. Place glue in an aluminum pie plate to provide a larger target for dipping the gluing utensil. Mark the edges of the collage paper with a bright color paint, marker, or tape to help indicate the boundaries. Guide the child's arm and show him or her where each material is located.

14-8 Discuss how cardboard may be used for three-dimensional activities.

Cardboard is an indispensable material for construction projects. It stimulates and challenges the imagination of children on all levels. Most topics of interest to young children can be adapted to cardboard construction projects. Creations are as endless as the imaginations of young children. Some possibilities for creative construction projects include using boxes for making various buildings, houses, cities, and even neighborhoods. Young children also enjoy making such things as imaginary animals, people, and favorite characters from a story out of various cardboard rolls and containers. Cars, trucks, and trains are some other favorite construction projects.

14-9 Describe the benefits of woodworking experiences for young children.

Woodworking, another three-dimensional activity, involves a range of activities from hammering nails to sanding, gluing, and painting. Woodworking experiences for young children contribute to their total development. These experiences must be planned so that appropriate, good-quality tools are provided for the children's use. Close supervision is required in woodworking.

Key Terms

assemblage 318	modeling 313	random manipulation 309
dimensionality 319	paper pulp (papier-mâché) 314	three-dimensional art 308

Learning Activities

Exercise 1

Goal: To experience how a child aged 1½–3 years works with clay.

A. Use the hand opposite the writing hand.

B. Use a piece of real clay about the size of a large apple.

C. Squeeze the clay in one hand only.

D. Keep these points in mind:

1. How it feels to lack good muscle (motor) control
2. How hard it is to make an exact object
3. How the clay feels in the hand

Exercise 2

Goal: To feel the differences in clay.

A. Prepare large balls of real clay, Plasticene (oil-based) clay, and play dough.

B. Use the hand opposite the writing hand to squeeze and feel each of the three clay balls. (This should help you experience both the child's lack of muscle control and different materials.)

C. Consider the following points while working with each of the three balls of clay.
1. Which is the easiest to squeeze?
2. Which feels the best?
3. Which is the most fun to use?
4. Is the type most fun to use also the easiest to use?

D. Try the previous activity with children aged 1½–3 years. Ask them the same questions. Compare answers.

Exercise 3

Goal: To help you understand how children feel when they are given a model to copy.

A. Collect several small glass or porcelain figures. These could be decorative birds, glass dolls, or any other finished figure from a variety store or other source.

B. Using clay, create a copy of one of the figures, including its intricacies.

C. Examine and discuss your finished object.
1. How did it feel to copy such a difficult model?
2. Was it a pleasant or frustrating experience?
3. Did this copying exercise make you feel happy about working with clay? Did it make you like to copy?
4. How do you think children feel about trying to copy models the teacher sets up?
5. Why is it undesirable for a teacher to have children copy a model?

Exercise 4

Obtain some pictures of modern sculpture. (Henry Moore's are good examples.)

A. Show the pictures to the children before they work with clay.

B. See if there are any effects on their work in relation to the following:
1. Kinds of objects made
2. New shapes made
3. More or less clay work done
4. Change in the way objects are made
5. Change in the way child works with clay

Exercise 5

Read an exciting story to children before they work with clay. For example, try Maurice Sendak's *Where the Wild Things Are* or Dr. Seuss's *And To Think That I Saw It on Mulberry Street.*

A. Do not tell the children what to make.

B. See if their work with clay shows any influence from the story regarding the following:
1. Type of figures made
2. Size of figures made
3. Details of figures made

Exercise 6

To add variety to play dough activities, try one of these variations:

A. Work a drop of food flavoring and a drop of food coloring into your play dough recipe. Match scents with colors, such as mint flavoring with green and lemon flavoring with yellow.

B. Use a tasty mixture of peanut butter and powdered milk as play dough for another three-dimensional taste treat. Be sure to be aware of any children with peanut allergies.

C. Make your play dough recipe slippery by adding a little vegetable oil.

Activities for Children

Using Recycled Materials in Three-Dimensional Activities

Recycled materials are perfect for three-dimensional art activities. They are free, readily available, and full of artistic possibilities. Here are some possibilities to start you thinking about (and using) recycled materials for three-dimensional art activities.

Paper Bags

• Collect large paper bags with attached paper or plastic handles (at least one for each child); additional paper shopping bags to use as masks; a variety of materials such as juice cans, egg cartons, plastic-foam pieces, empty boxes, fabric scraps, and straws; and scissors, glue, tape, crayons, and paint. Cut off the bottoms of the bags that have attached handles. Children can wear the bags as costumes by stepping into them and using the paper or plastic handles as shoulder straps. Arrange the collage and scrap materials on a table nearby so children can decorate their costumes with them.

• **Make a class mascot.** Provide children with two large paper shopping bags, colored yarn, and scrap materials that can be easily crumpled, including clean rags, newspaper, and pieces of cotton fabric. Invite children to choose pieces of scrap materials, crumple them, and stuff them into the paper bags. To make the mascot's head, have children stuff the first bag halfway full, and then tape it closed. Children use markers, paint, or decorative materials to make a face. Invite them to decide together on special characteristics, such as what color yarn to glue on for hair. Encourage them to work together to make a mascot that represents the whole class.

Boxes

- **Moving things.** Collect several medium-size appliance boxes that will hold one or two children. Invite children to use the boxes to make a vehicle. Provide them with smocks, paintbrushes, and tempera paint and invite them to paint their vehicle. If they want to make a train, attach the boxes to one another with twine, and place the train in your dramatic-play or outdoor area.
- **Measuring.** Invite children to use the boxes for measuring, asking them to find out things like how many shoeboxes tall they are. Record their answers. Now, ask them to lie down on the floor and measure the length of their bodies using the smallest boxes. Encourage them to estimate how many boxes long they will be. Afterward, compare their estimation with the actual answer. How many boxes long or wide is the classroom?

Paper Tubes

- **Tube puppets.** Invite children to make tube puppets to use in dramatic play. Provide children with sturdy paper tubes similar to the length and weight of tubes used to hold foil or cellophane wrap. Set out a variety of materials, including googly eyes, glue, yarn, felt, markers, scissors, oak tag paper, and small paper plates. Children might base their puppets on favorite storybook characters.
- **Tube bird binoculars.** Tape together two toilet tissue rolls. Let children decorate these with crayons, markers, and any other exciting "extras." Punch a hole on the outside of each of the tubes and string a ribbon or piece of yarn to make a strap for the binoculars. Go outside and start bird watching!
- **Music makers.** Use small paper tubes to make shakers for children to use during music and group-singing time. Invite children to decorate and individualize their shakers. Provide tempera paint, glue sticks, and collage materials. Enclose both ends with cardboard pieces secured with masking tape.
- **Counting the days.** Collect small paper tubes (from paper tissue rolls) to use for this counting activity. Get a large spool of twine and invite a child to string on a paper tube each day of school. Each child can take a turn decorating the tube and writing the number for each day on it. Invite the class to predict how long their "tube necklace" will be. Record their prediction and then compare on the last day of school.

Egg Cartons

- **Use your imagination.** Provide children with cardboard and Styrofoam egg cartons and a variety of construction materials, including tape, glue, string, paper, scissors, feathers, buttons, markers, and paint. Invite them to use the materials to create their own works of art.
- **Sand experimenting.** Invite children to investigate the different ways they can use the cartons to manipulate sand. Give them a spray bottle filled with water so that they can moisten sand in the carton. Can they use the egg cartons as a mold to create interesting shapes?

- **Floating experiments.** Give children cardboard and Styrofoam egg cartons and invite them to make boats to use at the water table. Have them predict which type of egg carton will work best in water. Record their responses. Now have them conduct their experiment. Does the size of the carton affect how it floats? Can they cut up the cartons to make smaller boats? Will the cartons sink if they are filled with water?

Three-Dimensional Textured Artwork

Impasto painting allows young children to explore a thick-textured material while creating expressive artwork. Provide children with toilet paper. Have the children tear the paper into pieces. Mix glue and the paper in a bowl until it becomes a gooey mixture. Children dip their fingers into the bowl and finger paint the mixture on heavy black paper. Let dry for two days. When the pictures are dry, children use different colors of paints and brushes to paint the picture. This makes a beautiful three-dimensional painting.

Clay-Coil Pots

For this activity, you will need potter's clay, a large plastic garbage bag, and tape. Split the garbage bag at the seams and tape it to the top of your work area.

Give each child a grapefruit-sized ball of potter's clay. Show children how to make snakes by rolling out pieces of clay into coils. Make several coils or one very long coil. Roll a small ball of clay and flatten it into a round shape for the bottom of the pot. Moisten the edges of the round bottom piece with water. Wrap the coils around the round bottom piece. Continue wrapping the coil around and around, putting coil upon coil. Moisten the pieces together as you coil. Let the pot dry before painting or decorating. Children can also make free-form coil sculptures.

Matching Toy Prints

Assemble a few small toys, such as cars, figures of animals, blocks, plastic shapes, and so on. On a flat piece of play dough or clay, make prints from these items. (You may do this with or without the children watching.) Then have the children match the toys to the prints. Alternatively, you can make prints out of obvious objects such as a coin, key, or small action figure. Then have the children figure out what made the print.

You can also flatten out a large piece of play dough or clay and let the children drive cars on it to make tracks or "streets." They can use other pieces of play dough to make houses, trees, and other objects around the street.

Crepe Paper Clay

For this activity you will need crepe paper, 1 cup of flour, 1 cup of salt, a large container, and water. Place crepe paper in a large container and add enough water to cover the paper. Soak for about 1 hour until most of the water absorbs into the paper. Pour off excess water. Save this colored water for dye in other projects. Add small amounts of flour and salt until the mixture is clay-like. Mold and form shapes by hand with crepe paper clay. Let the forms dry before painting.

Pipe Cleaner Sculpture

For this activity, you will need a flat sheet of Styrofoam, pipe cleaners of various lengths and widths, beads in various sizes, hole sizes and colors, and any other objects with a hole in them (such as straws, pasta, and so on).

Lay out the materials on the table or work area. Show children how the pipe cleaners can be stuck into the Styrofoam. They can slide beads, straws, pasta, and other interesting items onto the pipe cleaners.

Brown Bag Surprise

For this activity, you will need lunch-size brown paper bags and items such as paper tubes, sections of egg cartons, foil, cellophane, fabric, gift wrap, feathers, sequins, yarn, bubble wrap, paper plates, Styrofoam cups, stickers, glue sticks, child safety scissors, markers, and crayons.

Place different items into individual brown bags for each child. Vary the items in each child's bag to encourage different types of experiences.

Give each child a surprise bag full of art materials. Children use the materials to create their own special art project, creating whatever they want. One child might decide to create a flat collage while another opts to make a three-dimensional assemblage. When children have finished creating their artwork, ask them to write about it. They can write about how they made their work or what materials they used, or they can make up a story to accompany the work. Encourage them to use invented spelling and to be creative. Assist those who need it with their writing.

Invite children to share their work with the group. Encourage them to describe how they made their artwork. Find an area in the classroom to display children's artwork and writing.

Foil Sculpture

For this activity, you will need aluminum foil, masking tape, paintbrushes, liquid detergent, and tempera paint.

Crumple the foil into individual forms, shapes, or creations that when assembled will create a piece of sculpture. Join these forms together, if desired, with tape. Color can be added to the surface by painting with a drop or two of liquid detergent mixed in the tempera paint.

Line Sculpture

Give each student a single piece of wire about a yard long and ask them to bend this "line" into an object. Students will enjoy creating these simple line sculptures. This activity can serve as a stepping-off point for an investigation of Alexander Calder and his wire innovations.

Nature Jewelry

Make nature bracelets by attaching a ring of masking tape backwards (sticky side out) around children's wrists. As you embark on a nature hike, have children collect natural objects to stick to their bracelets. Then ask them to classify the objects as living or nonliving.

Natural Object Sculpture

For this activity, you will need natural materials (seeds, twigs, pinecones, seed pods, stones, driftwood, and so on), quick-drying glue, clear quick-drying spray, paint, construction paper, and felt.

Collect a number of natural objects of various sizes and colors. Arrange several of these items to create a small piece of sculpture. When satisfied with the creation, glue it together. Paint or colored paper can be added to enhance the design. Spray with clear spray to preserve the finish. (Spray with optimum ventilation, preferably outdoors.) Glue a piece of felt to the bottom to prevent scratching.

Wire Sculpture

Use lengths of 18-gauge wire to twist and form three-dimensional sculptural forms. First, have children create sketches of their ideas. Then, they bend and twist the wire together to hold a form. Use a piece of play dough or clay for the base. Display the finished works alongside their sketches.

Spool Sculpture

For this activity, you will need spools (a variety of sizes), assorted fabric pieces, glue, and anything that will serve to stimulate children's imaginations as decorations.

Each of the spool sculptures is made differently according to the imagination of the artist. Basically, the procedure involves "dressing" the spool, which serves as a body. Materials are added for clothing and are glued onto the spool. If desired, a child may use the spool purely as a base; it does not have to be a figure to dress. Details can be made with drawing materials, and bits and pieces of yarn, ribbon, and other similar materials can be glued on for interest.

Box Sculptures

For this activity, you will need boxes of different sizes and shapes, paste, tempera paint, brushes, construction paper, and scraps of fabric and trim.

Have children bring in an assortment of boxes. Be sure to include cereal boxes because they make great bases for box sculptures.

Use one box as a base. Glue smaller boxes on to make a sculpture design. Glue on cut-construction-paper details. Add fabric and trim scraps for more design details. Children may want to make a city of box sculpture buildings. They may choose to paint the sculpture. Boxes can become robots, imaginary animals, and anything else children can imagine.

Variation: For toddlers and young preschoolers, another use for cardboard boxes in various sizes is to build a train. Collect several cardboard boxes large enough for a child to sit inside. Put out a variety of supplies—markers, stickers, construction paper, glue—and tell each child to turn his or her box into a train car. After they've decorated the outside of their boxes in whatever way they can think of, help them arrange the cars one behind the other. Then, hop aboard for an imaginary train ride! Be prepared to hang onto these boxes; the children will want to get together and ride the track again and again.

Milk Carton Construction Fun

For this activity, you will need milk, juice, or cream cartons (different sizes—all cleaned and dry!); white acrylic paint; gesso or white latex house paint; pencils; paintbrushes; tempera paint; and containers for water.

Discuss homes and neighborhoods with the children. Talk about the different styles of places to live: houses, apartments, condos, and so on. Talk about shapes and sizes and such details as windows, doors, roofs, and stairways.

Have children cover the carton with white acrylic, gesso, or latex house paint. Let the paint dry thoroughly. Draw windows, doors, and so forth on the carton. Paint the carton (using tempera paint) to look like a house.

Children may want to make several houses for a neighborhood. They may even create a town/village from a favorite story.

Imaginary Animals

For this activity, you will need a collection of boxes of various sizes and shapes, paste, masking tape, stapler and staples, scraps of colored paper, fabric, trim, buttons, and yarn.

Talk about animals and their shapes, sizes, and colors. Give children a collection of boxes of various sizes and shapes.

Have children stack the boxes and rearrange them until they are satisfied with their arrangement. Shapes and sizes of boxes may suggest certain animals, such as an oatmeal box for an elephant or a long, narrow box for a giraffe's neck. Smaller boxes or towel rolls can be used for legs or a head. Fasten boxes together with glue, masking tape, or a stapler. Glue on details using scraps of colored paper, fabric, trim, buttons, or yarn.

Textured surfaces can be created by using corrugated paper or egg cartons for bodies of animals. Wood shavings, bark, or wrinkled-paper scraps can be glued to the boxes to create interesting textures. Exaggerated features help to create dramatic effects, such as large buttons for eyes, frayed string or rope for a mane or tail, or pieces of cloth for ears.

Egg Carton Buggy Things

For this activity, you will need egg cartons cut into single cups, pipe cleaners cut into small pieces, buttons, scraps of fabric and trim, crayons, and markers.

Discuss bugs, real and imaginary, with children. Talk about colors, shapes, "feelers," legs, and textures. Talk about other creatures, real or imaginary.

Give each child one egg cup. Have them attach pieces of pipe cleaners for legs, buttons for eyes, and pipe cleaners for feelers. Details may be added with crayons or markers. Pieces of fabric or trim can be glued on for even more details.

String a thread through the top of the egg cup to hang the creations, or make a family of creatures. Tell stories about the creatures' adventures in the bug world. Make houses for the buggy creatures out of milk cartons or other recycled boxes. Decorate the houses with markers or crayons.

Egg Carton Gardens

For this activity, you will need tops from Styrofoam egg cartons, scissors, pipe cleaners, toothpicks, construction paper, crayons, markers, glue, glue brushes, glitter (optional), and twigs.

Give each child a top from a Styrofoam egg carton. Talk about flower gardens, real or imagined. ("Which kind of flowers can you see in your mind?" "Which kinds of flowers do you see in a garden?" "Think of colors and shapes.")

Children cut or tear the construction paper into flower shapes, or any shapes they want. Children decorate the flower and/or shapes with crayons and/or markers. Glitter can be applied to the shapes that have been brushed with glue. Insert a toothpick or pipe cleaner into the flower. Poke the flower into the Styrofoam egg carton top. Add twigs to fill the egg carton top as desired.

For variations: Make an egg carton zoo. Fill the egg carton top with paper animals. Create an egg carton top filled with paper "people." Classmates, family members, and characters from a favorite storybook all make fun additions! Older children might enjoy creating a scene from a favorite story in the egg carton top.

Construction Paper Characters

For this activity, you will need construction paper, tape, scissors, crayons, markers, tempera paint, brushes, yarn, buttons, pieces of trim, and fabric scraps.

Talk about the people who are important in the child's life. Talk about those people's sizes, shapes, and other characteristics. Think about these things when making the construction paper creations.

Form the body by rolling the paper into a tube and taping it on the ends. The tube is both the body and the head of the person. Feet cut from construction paper can be taped on the bottom of the tube. Glue on features made of pieces of construction paper. Glue on yarn or pieces of construction paper for hair. Add fabric or trim scraps for clothing details. Features can be drawn on with crayons, markers, or paint.

For variation: Make a family of construction paper characters. Older children may want to make favorite characters from storybooks. Famous characters from history make good subjects for older children.

Construction Paper Buildings

For this activity, you will need construction paper, crayons, markers, tape, stapler and staples, and markers.

Discuss types of buildings with children, such as houses, barns, silos, and apartment buildings. Talk about the shapes, colors, and details on these buildings.

Give each child a supply of colored construction paper. Have them roll paper and tape the ends for round shaped buildings. Fold paper for roofs. Tape four pieces of paper to make square or rectangular buildings. Add such details as windows and doors with crayons, markers, or paint.

For variation: Have children add cut-paper windows and doors, chimneys, and balconies. Children might make several buildings to create a city, small town, or farm. Store windows can have merchandise painted on, cut out and pasted on, or made and set behind cellophane windowpanes.

Rock Sculptures

For this activity, you will need rocks of various sizes, glue, markers, paint, and scraps of fabric and trim.

Go outside and collect the rocks for this activity. Talk with children about the rocks—their colors, shapes, sizes, lines, textures, and other details. Ask them to think about what they would like to make with the rocks.

Use one rock for a base. Glue on a rock for a head or simply for another part of the sculpture. Glue on other details with bits of trim and fabric. Draw on details with markers or paint.

Variations: Make a family of rock people. Make a zoo filled with rock animals. Make abstract sculptures out of rocks. Glue small pebbles to paper boxes for unusual gifts.

Pebble Painting

Gather enough pebbles so that you have three different-sized pebbles that are cleaned for each student. You will also need three primary colors of tempera paint, three spoons per student, white paper cut into a shape of a pebble, and boxes no deeper than 4 inches.

Start by reading *Sylvester and the Magic Pebble* by William Steig. After finishing the story, introduce the pebble painting activity to the children.

1. Students first choose three different-sized pebbles.
2. Students tape the paper to the box.
3. Students dip two pebbles into the two colors they choose.
4. Placing the pebbles on the paper, students start to shake or tilt the box, creating a design.
5. After pebble painting with the two colors is completed, students then use all three primary colors and pebbles to paint their second painting.

When they are finished, have a designated drying place for all pebble paintings.

Styrofoam Sculpture/Stabile Construction

For this activity, you will need Styrofoam of various sizes and shapes (sheets, broken parts of packaging materials, "peanuts"), white glue, pieces of cardboard (optional), toothpicks, scraps of fabric, trim, ribbon, markers, tempera paint, and brushes.

Talk with children about the collection of Styrofoam. Discuss the size and shape of the pieces. Ask children to think about what they would like to create with these pieces.

Use a piece of cardboard or sheet of Styrofoam as a base. Glue pieces of Styrofoam onto the base. Use toothpicks to add small pieces to the design. Have children continue gluing on pieces until they are satisfied with their design.

Children can use markers to draw details on the sculpture and paint it with tempera paint. They can also glue on pieces of fabric, trim, and ribbon for interesting effects.

Variation: Suggest children make a list of things that they have in their homes that could be recycled and used for art projects. Send the list to families along with a note requesting that they collect some of the items to donate to the classroom art area.

Cornstarch

Believe it or not, a fascinating modeling medium is plain old cornstarch. Mix 2 cups warm water and 3 cups cornstarch to make a fascinating substance for children's three-dimensional play.

Put ingredients in a bowl and mix with your hands. This mixture will solidify when left alone, but turns to liquid from the heat of your hands. Magic!

Involve the children in making the cornstarch recipe. Have them feel the dry cornstarch. Encourage their reactions to it, using their senses of sight, smell, touch, and even taste. Add a little water, and let the children mix it and feel it again. It is lumpy. After this lumpy stage, you can add a little more water until it's uniformly moist. Wet cornstarch forms an unstable material, which is fun because of its unexpected behavior—it breaks, but it also melts. It doesn't behave like glue, or like milk, or like wood; it's a liquid and it's a solid, too. If you rest your fingers lightly on the surface of the cornstarch mix, it will let your fingers drift down to the bottom of the container. If you try to punch your way to the bottom, it will resist.

Cornstarch works well in a baby bathtub set on a table, with a limit of two or three children using the entire recipe. If you leave it in its tub overnight, by morning it will be dry. Add some water, and it becomes that wonderful "stuff" again. Be sure to invite children to watch this event.

This is a clean sort of play. The white, powdery mess on the floor can be picked up easily with a dustpan and brush or a vacuum cleaner.

Children will enjoy this cornstarch mixture again and again because it feels good and behaves in such an interesting way.

Dioramas/Scenery Boxes

A diorama is a three-dimensional scene inside a box. This activity can be used with students in kindergarten through grade 5. The materials required for this activity include a shoe box for each student, scissors, construction paper, glue, thread, black marker, and tape. Optional materials include tin foil, small boxes, markers, pencils, crayons, paint, or tissue paper.

1. Ask the students to bring in a shoe box for this activity.
2. A few days in advance, ask the students to think of a scene they would like to create in the shoe box. Tell them they may bring in their own objects to include in the scene.
3. On the day of the project, place all the materials on a table where everyone can reach them.
4. Ask two to three students to come to the table at a time and choose a few of the materials.
5. The student makes the background and the bottom of their scene first. Construction paper, paint, or other materials may be used for a background.
6. Students need to decide what they will put in the box and what materials they will make their items out of (maybe a box for a bed in a bedroom or a kitchen cabinet, and so on.).
7. While the items are being constructed, the teacher walks around the room with the thread and gives each student the needed amount. (The thread will be used to hang objects in the box, for example, fish in the ocean, birds in the sky, and so on.)
8. All objects should be glued in the box so they will not fall off. When the items and the background are complete, the students should create some sort of texture or pattern on the objects.
9. Children may choose to hang some of the items or all of them. If the items are not hung in the box, the students use paper folded back and forth to make the objects pop out. Items may also be glued anywhere in the box.
10. After they are finished, students may want to explain their scene to fellow students.

Soft Sculptures

Materials: scissors, glue, socks and stockings, yarn, crumpled newspaper, tissue paper, pillow stuffing, nylon stockings, felt pieces

Collect mismatched socks and stockings, the larger the better.

Children stuff a sock with newspaper, tissue paper balls, pillow stuffing, or nylon stockings. Tie the sock closed with a piece of yarn. Older preschoolers can use a plastic needle and yarn to sew felt or fabric scraps onto their soft sock sculpture. Younger children can glue on designs cut out of pieces of felt.

Sewing on Burlap

For this activity, you will need large plastic needles, 12- × 12-inch pieces of burlap (taped around the edges with masking tape), jumbo crayons, and various kinds of yarn (precut).

1. Show the children how to go in and out of the fabric with the needle.
2. Have children practice making stitches on a 4-inch square of burlap with a needle and some yarn before they start this project.
3. Let the children brainstorm some shapes they could sew, such as shapes in the room, from nature, and so on. Each child decides on a shape to sew and then draws it on the burlap with a crayon.
4. Help the students thread their needles.
5. Students use the running stitch (going in and out of the fabric) to follow the outlines they have drawn.

Activities for Older Children (Grades 4–5)

Masking Tape Masks

For this activity, you will need box lids, plastic bowls, gallon milk jugs (cut in half), discarded CDs, wooden spools, carry-out containers, plastic cups, foil, discarded computer parts, masking tape, tempera paint, and assorted embellishment materials.

Introduce masks by examining photographs, authentic wooden masks, papier-mâché masks, and ceramic masks. Have students brainstorm ideas for their own masks and sketch the ideas on paper.

Have students create a base using a box lid, plastic bowl, or milk jug, and then select objects to tape on top of their base. Foil is an excellent material to use when you don't have the shapes you need.

Completely cover the objects and base of the mask with two layers of masking tape. Use small pieces on awkward spaces and shapes. Make sure the tape is lying flat and is smooth. Cover the mask with gesso and let dry.

Have students select a base paint color, and then paint their masks. When the base paint is dry, students add facial details and designs with different colors of tempera.

Optional: Add embellishments using a hot glue gun (teacher use only).

Display the masks and discuss how they were made. Can students think of a function or purpose for their masks? Can they think of other sculptures that they could make using masking tape?

Basic Mobiles

Materials: Thread, supports (heavy stove pipe wire, strips of wood, or dowels), wire cutters, glue, and materials for making objects to be suspended (paper, wire, plastics, cardboard, straws, plaster, clay, and so on)

1. Decide the number of units to be used in the mobile and their method of construction. These objects can be made from paper, wire, papier-mâché, wood, or a combination of

any of these materials. Remember that an effective mobile should contain objects that have some kind of relationship to each other.

2. Attach a thread to each object.

3. Cut a support (a piece or wire or small wood dowel) and suspend an object from each end, making sure that it hangs evenly and that the separation is great enough to prevent objects from touching.

4. Place a spot of glue on the very ends of the wire or dowel to help hold the thread of each object when tied in place. The threads supporting the objects should be comparatively short but of different lengths.

5. Tie another thread to the wire or dowel supporting the mobile by the thread. Slide the thread back and forth on the wire or dowel until it finds a point of balance. Secure it with a spot of glue.

6. The thread holding the section just completed should be tied to the end of another wire or dowel and held in place with glue. Suspend an object from the other end of the wire or dowel.

7. Any number of sections can be added as long as balance is maintained.

8. Note: A wire stretched in a seldom-used corner of the room will enable the children to hang their mobiles while working on them. There is no limit to the ways a mobile can be constructed after the principles of movement and balance are understood.

Creating Soft Wire Sculptures

A. Have students use three pipe cleaners to create a simple "skeleton" of a person.

B. Other pipe cleaners can be wrapped around the skeleton figure to suggest the form of muscles. Encourage children to help one another.

C. After students bend their sculptures into different poses, each pose is drawn on paper. The poses can be planned to create an action picture of a group of people. The poses might be planned and drawn to show a favorite sport, game, dance, or other activity such as a family watching television or enjoying a picnic. Drawings of all the skeleton figures should be made first. Then the students can draw in the details—clothes, faces, and the like.

D. Encourage students to draw the skeleton figures so they are about the same size as the wire sculpture. If the skeleton lines are carefully observed in each pose, their final drawings should be easy to complete and have interesting poses.

Memory Boxes—Assemblage

Students in middle- and upper-elementary grades are often involved in collecting things that express their interests. Talk about what collecting means to them. How are the things we save and collect reflections of parts of ourselves? Introduce the idea of a memory box for presenting their personal memorabilia. Have students bring in a shoebox or any other small box.

- First, have students prepare their memory boxes. They can paint the inside and outside of their boxes. A dark color, such as black or brown, works best because the objects of the assemblage will stand out more and the composition will be more unified.

- After the boxes have dried, preferably overnight, students will be able to compose their assemblages. Have them look through their memorabilia collections and select objects they want to use. To avoid having students glue their objects in place before they have experimented with various compositions, do not pass out glue until everyone has had a chance to explore different combinations. Students should be advised to select objects with contrasting qualities in order to create interest and variety—objects with varying sizes, colors, shapes, and textures.

- Remind students that composition is the organization of parts into a unified whole. They should carefully consider the placement of each part of their assemblage to make a composition that is pleasing to them. Remind them that they should place objects so that they can be seen as the box stands upright or hangs on a wall; they should not compose the box to be viewed from above.

- Have students use white glue to attach all the parts of their assemblage. When the glue has dried overnight, set up a display of all the memory boxes.

- Students might be interested in shadow boxes. You may be able to find boxes with interior divisions, such as boxes used to package Christmas tree ornaments or various kinds of fruit, and use these interior divisions to create a shadow box display. A memory box with interior cardboard divisions (tiny interior shelves) can also be created by cutting and attaching strips of carefully measured cardboard to the inside of a box. In this way, memorabilia items need not be glued down but only set on the cardboard "shelves."

Multicultural Awareness

Discuss examples of papier-mâché sculpture that students may have seen such as piñatas (Mexico) or large modeled heads or floats used in parades, puppets, and masks (Europe, the Americas, Asia). Ask students to explain why papier-mâché is used as a medium for those art forms instead of other materials. (In many cultures, paper is inexpensive or is saved and recycled. The paste for papier-mâché can also be made easily from a variety of inexpensive "sticky" materials, such as flour and water.)

This is a good way to introduce and motivate students for a class papier-mâché project.

Community Awareness

Have students research the buildings on the block or area nearest to their homes. Have them focus on the materials that have been used and varied textures or patterns they see. Suggest they draw the materials, patterns, or textures on unlined index cards and place labels on the back of each card, naming the material. If they are unable to name the material, an adult may assist or the drawing can serve as a reference for library research. When the drawings are completed, have the class sort and display them in groups in relation to the type

Trophy Sculptures

For this activity, you will need Styrofoam or wood blocks, pipe cleaners, glue, paper, markers, and small pieces of decorations. This activity gives children the opportunity to create an original trophy and present it to someone they want to congratulate.

Have children think of someone they want to congratulate for a noteworthy accomplishment by awarding that individual a personalized trophy. Have students use pipe cleaners to form the trophy person or object. Use small pieces of decoration to make the figure more fun. When satisfied with their figures, students glue them to the pieces of Styrofoam or wood blocks. Students can attach labels to the front of the blocks bearing the awardees' names and messages of congratulations. Be sure to have children sign their work.

A trophy can be made from just about anything. Interesting things can be glued on a paper plate for one kind of a trophy. Some things to glue for a trophy are natural objects from outside or even magazine pictures and words.

Positive and Negative Space—Hand Sculpture

Discuss with children the concept of positive and negative space. The space an object takes up is positive space. The "air" around it is negative space. When we create a painting, objects are positive space and are surrounded by negative space.

Have children trace their hands on a piece of cardboard. The cutout hand is the positive space, and the cut piece of paper is the negative space. Use the cutout cardboard hand as the base for the sculpture. Have the children try to figure out how to get the negative space to stand up (bend in half, bend bottom pieces to make a stand, use the cut out hand to support it).

Cut out other hands from construction paper—use different "poses": thumbs-up, peace sign, fist, and so on. Add these to the base. Stress the idea of three-dimensional sculpting.

Early American Weaving

Older children can experience the Native American and Colonial American art of weaving with this activity that uses a modern twist on a traditional craft. The simple instructions in this activity are for a woven belt or sash.

For this activity, you will need five small beverage straws, four-ply yarn (solid color), four-ply yarn (variegated), thin wire, and masking tape.

To set up your loom:

1. Cut solid yarn into lengths three times the desired length of the finished product. You will need five of these, one for threading each straw.
2. Cut approximately 10 yards of variegated yarn and roll into a ball. Bend thin wire to form a "needle."
3. For each of the beverage straws, thread the wire needle with a length of solid yarn, pull the wire through the straw, and tape one end tightly to the straw.

4. After all straws have been threaded and taped, begin weaving.

Weaving the belt:

1. Hold all five straws, with the taped ends up, in one hand.
2. Using the end of the ball of variegated yarn, begin weaving with an "under/over" pattern from the bottom of the straws (where you are holding them) to the top (taped edge). When you have woven to the top of the straws, carefully push the weaving down a few inches. *Do not push all of the weaving off the straws.*
3. Continue until you have reached a desired length, and tie off the ends.

Recipes for Papier-Mâché

Papier-Mâché Paste

3 cups water   ½ cup flour
A drop of two of wintergreen

Mix the water and flour together in a large saucepan. Heat the mixture over a medium heat, stirring constantly. Add a few drops of wintergreen.

Caution: Wintergreen is toxic. It smells like yummy gum, but don't be tempted to taste it. You use wintergreen to retard molding. After a while, the paste will thicken. When it does, remove from the stove and let it cool.

If you are going to use your paste right away, leave it out. Make sure your project is well ventilated while drying.

Wheat Paste Method

Wheat paste or wallpaper paste
Warm water

You can get wheat paste at most hardware stores or art supply stores. Mix wheat paste and water until it is thick and creamy. Store in a container with a tight lid. Use it within 2 to 3 days.

Glue Paste

Dilute white glue (Like Elmer's) 5 parts to one part.

Recipes for Dough and Other Plastic Materials

1. *Cooked Dough*
   ½ cup flour   2 cups boiling water
   ½ cup cornstarch   ½ cup salt
   (blend with cold water)

   Method: Add salt to boiling water. Combine flour with cornstarch and water. Pour hot mixture into cold. Put over hot water and cook until glossy. Cool overnight. Knead in flour until right consistency, adding color with flour.

2. *Cooked Dough*
   4 tablespoons   ½ cup boiling water
   cornstarch   ½ cup salt

   Method: Mix cornstarch and salt. Add color if desired. Pour on boiling water, stir until soft and smooth. Place over fire until it forms a soft ball. In using, if it sticks to fingers, dust hands with cornstarch.

3. *Sawdust and Wheat Flour Paste*

   4 parts sawdust   1 part wheat flour

   Method: Make paste of wheat flour and water. Add sawdust. Presents interesting sensory appeal.

4. *Uncooked Play Dough*

   3 cups flour   1 cup water

   ¼ cup salt   1 tablespoon oil
   coloring

   Method: Mix flour with salt; add water with coloring and oil gradually. Add more water if too stiff; add more flour if too sticky. Let children help with the mixing and measuring. Keep dough stored in plastic bags or a covered container.

5. *Salt Dough*

   1 cup salt   ¾ cup cold water

   ½ cup cornstarch

   Method: Combine all ingredients in a double boiler placed over medium heat. Stir the mixture constantly; in about 2 to 3 minutes, it should become so thick that it follows the spoon mixing it. When the consistency is similar to bread dough, place on wax paper or aluminum foil to cool. When dough is cool enough to handle, knead for several minutes. It is then ready to use. To store for up to several days, wrap in wax paper or place in plastic bags.

6. *Fragrant Play Dough*

   2½ cups flour   1 tablespoon alum powder

   ½ cup salt   3 tablespoons oil

   2 cups boiling water dash or two food coloring

   1 package unsweetened Kool-Aid

   Method: Combine flour, alum powder, and salt. Stir in oil and boiling water. Add food coloring and Kool-Aid.

7. *Ornamental Clay* (suitable for dried objects)

   1 cup cornstarch   1¼ cups water

   2 cups baking soda

   Method: Cook ingredients together until thickened, either in double boiler or over direct heat—stir constantly. When it is cool enough, turn it out and let children knead dough and make it into whatever they wish. If used for ornaments, make hole for hanging ornament while dough is still moist.

8. *Baker's Dough* (suitable for dried objects)

   4 cups flour   1 to 1¼ cups water
   1 cup salt

   Method: Mix ingredients to make the dough easy to handle. Knead and shape as desired. Bake at 350°F for 50 to 60 minutes. Material will brown slightly, but baking at lower temperatures is not as successful.

Soapy Sculpture Dough

Add this soap dough mixture to your modeling materials. It is white and very pliable and easy for children to manipulate. To make the soapy mixture, pour a box of soap flakes into a large container. Add water slowly until the mixture is the consistency of paste. Invite the children to mix it with you. Then have the children form grapefruit-sized balls with a lump of the mixture. Provide enough of these balls so each child has his or her own modeling "soap." You may want to supply toothpicks, pipe cleaners, buttons, and sequins for children to decorate their soap dough creations.

References

Duffy, B. (2010). *Supporting Creativity and Imagination in the Early Years.* 2nd edition. New York, NY: McGraw-Hill Education.

Eckhoff, A., & Spearman, M. (2009). Rethink, reimagine, reinvent. *Art Education, 62*(2), 10–16.

Gallo, F., Golomb, C., & Barroso, A. (2003). Compositional strategies in drawing: The effects of two and three-dimensional media. *Visual Arts Research, 28*(1), 2–23.

Golomb, C. (2004). Sculpture: Representational development in a three-dimensional medium. In E. Eisner & M. Day (Eds.), *Handbook of research and policy in art education* (pp. 329–358). Mahwah, NJ: Erlbaum.

Golomb, C. (2007). Representational concepts in two- and three-dimensional media: A developmental perspective. *Psychology of Aesthetics, Creativity, and the Arts, 1*(1), 32–39.

Golomb, C., & McCormick, M. (1995). Sculpture: The development of three-dimensional representation in clay. *Visual Arts Research, 21*(2), 35–50.

Granrud, C. E. (2006). Size consistency in infants: 4-month olds' responses to physical vs. retinal size. *Journal of Experimental Psychology, Human Perception Performance 32*(6), 1398–1401.

Kersh, J., Casey, B. M., & Young, J. M. (2008). Research on spatial skills and block building in girls and boys: The relationship to mathematical learning. In *Contemporary Perspectives on Mathematics in Early Childhood Education,* by Saracho, O. N. & Spodek, B. Charlotte, NC: Information Age Publications.

MOMA. (2012). Art Terms. Accessed October 22, 2012, at http://www.moma.org/collection/theme.php?theme_id=10.

Taylor, T. (2006). *The altered object.* New York, NY: Lark Books.

 Visit CourseMate for this textbook to access the eBook, Did You Get It? quizzes, Digital Downloads, TeachSource Videos, flashcards, and more. Go to CengageBrain.com to log in, register, or purchase access.

PART
5

Creative Activities for Early Childhood

Infusing a creative approach into every area of early childhood curriculum is the focus of Part 5. Building and expanding on the theory presented in Part 2, the chapters in Part 5 cover several areas of the early childhood curriculum in which a creative approach is appropriate. These curricular areas include dramatic play and puppetry, movement, music, language arts, science, math, food experiences, and social studies.

All of the activities presented in Part 5 are based in developmental theory yet are simple to reproduce and expand upon. All are presented in the hope that they will be adapted to children's individual needs, abilities, and interest levels. Information on adapting activities for children with special needs is included where appropriate throughout Part 5. Activities in Part 5 are designed to be springboards to many learning experiences limited only by the child's and teacher's imagination and creativity.

Unlike simple manipulation of media, such as pounding clay and finger painting covered in Part 3, the activities offered in this section generally require more skill on the part of the children and more instruction (at least initially) by the teacher. They tend to have a more definite focus and direction. In using these activities, considerable latitude must be allowed for individual ideas to be expressed. These are valuable activities that provide opportunities for purposefulness and challenges to skills that children will enjoy. They also increase the variety of experiences available to young children in full-day centers.

In all chapters in Part 5, the teacher should always consider the developmental level of a child or a group of children before initiating any activity. Activities are included for children from preschool through grade 5. Appropriate age and/or grade levels are indicated on these activities.

Finally, while guidance of a child's activities is appropriate, each child should be given the freedom to adapt these activities and the processes used to his or her own creative needs. In other words, the approach should not be "What is it?" but "Tell me about what you've made." Most important, emphasis in all activities should be on the process and not the end product.

Rather than displaying a model or sample product at the beginning of an activity, have the children talk about their own ideas and plans for the activity. The beginning, middle, and end of every activity is the child—unique and singular in his or her own way.

REFLECTIVE QUESTIONS

After studying this section, you should be able to answer the following questions.

1. Do I use puppets as an instructional tool for encouraging creativity and dramatic play?

2. Have I included enough materials for puppet making for all the developmental levels, special needs, and multicultural backgrounds of my children?

3. Have I provided opportunities for young children to express themselves creatively in movement and music activities?

4. How will I modify my language arts activities so that they are appropriate for the multicultural children in my group?

5. At what levels of listening skills are the young children in my group? Do my lessons and activities meet these individual levels?

6. Have I presented language arts experiences that are appropriate to the children's current level of emerging literacy?

7. How can I be sure my classroom centers and activities are conducive to the young child's active science exploration?

8. Am I aware of the different levels of mathematic thinking present in my group of children?

9. Are my teaching practices reflective of antibiased curricular principles?

10. Have I planned developmentally appropriate food and nutrition experiences for young children? Do these practices help establish lifelong positive habits?

11. In what ways can I improve the science experiences for young children in my program?

12. In considering my language arts curriculum, what are the areas I most need to improve? What positive steps can I take to implement these improvements?

13. In what ways are children verbalizing their mathematical thinking? Do I encourage this process by providing materials and activities that foster mathematical thinking?

14. As I evaluate my classroom's physical arrangement, how can I adjust it to better represent the curriculum areas of most importance to the young children who use it?

15. Does my current math and science curriculum provide an appropriate match to the developmental levels of the children in my group?

16. What are some specific ways I can be more creative (in my instructional strategies) in curricular areas outside the arts curriculum?

17. How can I integrate art and creative activities into my entire curriculum?

18. In what way can I improve the range of language arts experiences so that the language arts are related to other curriculum areas?

19. Do my teaching and classroom practices emphasize respect for individual differences in language development? Individual differences in math and science understanding? Individual cultural differences?

20. Can I verbalize the rationale for each area of my curriculum and how it helps develop the creativity of young children?

Dramatic Play and Puppetry

"I am being *magic*!" crows Miguel, dressed in a "superman" cape and a painter's cap. "I can fly anywhere I want!" As he flaps his arms and swoops around the room, he is joined by Claudia dressed in a dancer's tutu. "Wait for me. I can fly, too!" she says. The two children glide around the room for a minute or two, until they notice Jaime sitting by himself in the block corner. Moving in his direction, Miguel invites him to join them in flight. "Jaime, I can make magic, so you can fly, too." Jaime joins Miguel and Claudia for a short time, until he spots an opening at the computer where he "lands" for another activity. Claudia soon decides to land as well, deciding to be a doctor and make a house call to check on a sick baby in the home center. Miguel continues to "be magic" for a few more moments before he too "lands" and becomes the concerned daddy of the sick baby.

Learning Objectives

After studying this chapter, you should be able to:

15-1 Discuss the importance of dramatic play to a young child's development.

15-2 Discuss what children learn in dramatic play.

15-3 Discuss ways to adapt dramatic activities for children with special needs.

15-4 Discuss the difference between dramatic play and creative dramatics.

15-5 Discuss appropriate ways to use puppets in the early childhood program.

naeyc

NAEYC Program Standards

1a Knowing and understanding young children's characteristics and needs.

1c Using developmental knowledge to create healthy, respectful, supportive, and challenging learning environments.

DAP

DAP Criteria

2E3 Teachers organize the daily and weekly schedule to provide children with extended blocks of time in which to engage in sustained play, investigation, exploration, and interaction (with adults and peers).

2E4 Teachers provide experiences, materials, and interactions to enable children to engage in play that allows them to stretch their boundaries to the fullest in their imagination, language, interactions, and self-regulation.

These children are happily engaged in dramatic play, a natural and essential part of a child's development. It is spontaneous and child directed. It is fluid, changing momentarily as children's imaginations move them to explore "being" things and "trying on" many roles.

15-1 Importance of Dramatic Play

naeyc **DAP** In the preceding scene, it is obvious that **dramatic play** is an excellent means for children to develop their creativity and imaginations. Dramatic play allows them to exercise their special, instinctive ways of dealing with reality. They need no written lines to memorize or structured behavior patterns to imitate in order to fantasize their world. What they do need is an interesting environment and freedom to experiment and be themselves.

Dramatic play provides children one of the best ways to express themselves. They are free to express their inner feelings in a safe, creative way. Often, teachers find out how children feel about themselves and others by listening to them as they carry out dramatic play. The pretending involved in such dramatic experiences, whether planned or totally spontaneous, is a necessary part of development. In the dramatic play center, children can act out feelings that often cannot be expressed directly. For example, the child who is afraid of the doctor can express this fear by giving shots to dolls or stuffed animals in the center. In like manner, a child can act out with a friend a visit to the dentist. Thus, children can learn to deal with their anxieties as well as act out their fantasies through creative dramatic play. Through the imitation and make-believe of dramatic play, children sort out what they understand and gain a measure of mastery and control over events they have witnessed or taken part in—making breakfast, going to work, taking care of the baby, and going to the doctor (see Photo 15-1). Dramatic play helps children enter and begin to make sense of the world of adults.

15-1a The Beginnings of Dramatic Play

The beginning of dramatic play is visible in the actions of children as young as 1 year, who put a comb to their hair, for example, and pull it along the side of their face, imitating the activity that has been performed on them with the same "prop." Given the right prop, the baby will imitate the behavior associated with that prop. For example, if offered a cup, the baby drinks; a hat, the baby puts it on his head; or a pillow,

© Cengage Learning

PHOTO 15-1 In the dramatic play center, children are free and safe to try on many social roles.

the baby puts his head on it. Adults often describe this as "pretend" play, but it is more accurately prepretend play because it involves only actions that are known to the child.

Actual dramatic play begins when a child uses a prop for something other than the activity for which he or she has seen it used by an adult. Thus, a hairbrush becomes a sailing boat, a wooden block becomes a hairbrush, and a stick becomes a bridge. This usually happens when the child is about 2 years old; that is the age when children seem to be capable of making an "as if" transformation of an object, a necessary prerequisite to pretend play involving objects, others, and themselves.

15-1b Development of Dramatic Play

As children grow and develop, so does their dramatic play. From simple imitative movement, children move on to more complex dramatic play. It is important for teachers of young children to be very good observers and listeners, to see what children play with, to watch what they do with the materials, and to listen to what they say about the props and materials provided to them. It is equally important that the teacher becomes part of the play of the child but—and this is essential—at the child's present developmental level. We all remember the relative who insisted that the Fisher Price garage

PHOTO 15-2 Creative dramatic play often begins with one child, and others soon join.

Casper Holroyd

15-2 Young Children's Learning in Dramatic Play

naeyc **DAP** Dramatic play occurs daily in the lives of young children. It is one of the ways that children naturally learn. They constantly imitate the people, animals, and machines in their world. They enjoy recreating the exciting experiences of their lives. Dramatic play is their way of understanding and dealing with the world.

Dramatic play is also an important medium for language development, as it encourages fluency in language. A child who is reluctant to speak in other situations is almost compelled to speak in order to be included in dramatic play. As play becomes elaborate, a child's language becomes more complex. When children talk with each other in a nondirective setting, such as the dramatic play center, it is possible for the flow and quality of language to develop. If others are to understand his or her role, a child needs to explain what he or she is doing so that friends will respond in appropriate ways. If the child is to understand what they are doing, he or she must listen.

When children become involved in complex make-believe, they need to listen and respond to each other. A child speaks convincingly to others when she wants them to change the nature of the play. If they still do not understand, she may try to find other ways to persuade them. When she needs to elaborate on her ideas, the child is likely to use a longer sequence of words and move from two words to more complex syntax.

As children play together, they learn new words from each other. At their make-believe restaurant, Maria prepared tacos and Justin ordered fruitcake from the menu. Justin liked the sound of the new word, *tacos*. He pretended he was eating one, even though he did not know what a taco was.

As children play, they repeat words and phrases they have learned and enjoy saying them. They name objects, talk about what they are doing, and plan as they go along. They begin to recognize the importance of planning and take time to formulate more detailed plans for their dramatizations.

15-2a Dramatic Play in the Dramatic Play Center

One of the best places for children to express themselves in creative, dramatic play is the dramatic play center (see Photo 15-3). Here, in a child-sized version of the world, children are free and safe to express how they feel about themselves and others. While they carry out dramatic play in this center, they can

could only be a garage, not a part of the fortress wall, and the legendary behavior of the adult who gives the young child a gift of an electric train or racing car set and proceeds to insist that it be played with in terms of adult reality. In adult play, there is no flying of cars one over the other to win and no make-believe drivers, only Grand Prix racers. No wonder the adult ends up playing by himself, while the child returns to playing with the racing car box. This way, the child is allowed to pretend without adult guidance and limitations.

Many times creative dramatics begins with one child, and others soon join in (see Photo 15-2). Playing store with a storekeeper and a number of customers is a form of creative dramatic play. Speaking on a toy telephone to a friend is another form. Puppet shows in which children use finger puppets and make up a story as they go along is still another form.

Did You Get It?

A one-year-old child picks up a hairbrush and makes brushing motions in her hair. This action is considered prepretend play because

a. the child is familiar with the action.

b. it is an action used in real life.

c. it demonstrates a lack of creativity.

d. it is an instinctive response.

Take the full quiz on CourseMate.

Casper Holroyd

PHOTO 15-3 One of the best ways for children to express themselves is through creative dramatic play.

pretend to be many different kinds of people, "trying on," so to speak, many social roles.

The dramatic play center provides endless opportunities for the teacher, as a facilitator of learning, to broaden children's horizons. The center can be decorated and rearranged to represent an area that pertains to specific content. Possibilities include creating a home, hospital, post office, grocery store, and more. The change of seasons as well as certain holidays can be easily incorporated in this center. For example, during fall, a child's rake, sweaters, and pumpkins might be included in the center. During the winter months, mittens or a child's shovel may be additions to the center. For spring, the teacher may add plastic or silk flowers and a variety of hats. Supplies in the dramatic play center should reflect the activities in the classroom and extend the skills being taught elsewhere in the room as well as introduce new skills. Be sure to include clothing, dishes, and dolls that are familiar and represent each of the ethnic and cultural groups in your classroom. (See Figure 15-1 for the benefits of dramatic play and recommended materials to encourage early childhood dramatic play.)

Activities in the dramatic play center afford the child experiences in the following social interactions:

- clarifying adult roles
- trying out social skills
- getting along with others
- sharing responsibilities
- making group decisions
- controlling impulsive behavior

- recognizing cause and effect
- developing positive attitudes about oneself and others
- enjoying the fantasy of the grownup world
- using oral language spontaneously
- practicing the use of symbols, which are subskills in reading
- learning social ease and confidence in one's own strengths

Materials*

full-length mirror
child sized stove
child sized refrigerator
sink
closet or rack of clothes
cooking/eating utensils
table and chairs
tea set
telephone
stethoscope
props for cleaning (broom, mop, dustpan, pail, sponge, rags, duster)
play dough
doll bed, doll carriage, baby highchair

rocking chair
empty cans
empty multicultural food boxes
mirror/hand mirror
carriage
multicultural dolls and doll clothes
iron/ironing board
puppets
a variety of hats, dresses, shirts, ties, belts, scarves, shoes, pocketbooks, and jewelry
an old suitcase (for "trips")
doctor's satchel, bandages, cotton balls, play syringe, pill bottles, a play thermometer, play money

an old briefcase
dress-up gloves, rubber gloves, baseball gloves, garden gloves
open-ended materials such as large sheets, scarves, and cardboard boxes.
a "challenge box" of unusual items (tools, large beach ball, and funny glasses) to add new elements to their play. Challenge children: "What can you do with this?"
props from favorite stories to encourage retelling experiences.

*Add objects as needed for special emphasis.

FIGURE 15-1 Benefits of and materials for dramatic play.

© Cengage Learning

Dramatic Play Kits:
Post Office and Mail Carrier: Index card file, stamp pads, stampers, crayons, pencils, stickers, envelopes, hats, badges, mail bag, supply of "resident" or other third-class mail
Firefighter: Hats, raincoats, badge, boots, short lengths of garden hose
Grocery Store: adding machine, play money, paper pads, pencils or crayons, paper bags, empty food cartons, wax fruit, cans with smooth edges
Plumber: wrenches, sections of plastic pipes, toolkit, hats, and shirts
Painter: paint cans full of water, brushes of different sizes, drop cloth, painter's hat
Mechanic: tire pump, tool kit, boxes to become "cars," shirt, hat
Entertainer: CD player, musical instruments, costumes

FIGURE 15-2 Dramatic play kits.

© Cengage Learning

Teachers of young children further encourage children's dramatic play by providing kits containing "props" for them to use. Dramatic play kits are created by assembling a variety of everyday items into groups that have a common use or theme. Children select the props and use them in groups or alone to play roles or create dramatic play experiences. Just letting the children know about the use of these kits is often enough to get them started. Materials for these dramatic kits can be kept together in shoeboxes or other containers. Some common types of dramatic play kits are found in Figure 15-2.

Imagination can also be used to transform regular classroom items into "new materials." Chairs can become trains, cars, boats, or houses. A table covered with a blanket or bedspread becomes a cave or special hiding place. Large cardboard cartons that children can decorate become houses, forts, and fire stations.

It is important to emphasize a gender-neutral approach in teaching, especially in the dramatic play area. For example, boys' dramatic play must be encouraged in an early childhood program as much as girls' dramatic play. A good tactic to encourage boys' participation is to change the themes of the dramatic play corner to topics that interest some boys. Include open-ended materials in the dramatic play areas such as blocks, flashlights, a rope, and small balls. An observant teacher, sensitive to both sexes' dramatic play and developing sex-role concepts, even gives cues that encourage all children to play in all centers.

Remember also to provide outdoor materials and equipment for pretending and role play. With more space and fewer boundaries, outdoor dramatic play is often robust and highly mobile. Children will make use of anything available—wagons, tricycles, and other wheeled toys for cars, buses, trains, and boats; large packing boxes, boards, sheets, ropes, and tires for houses, stores, forts, and caves; and sand and sand utensils for cooking, eating, and building. They may also enjoy the addition of some "indoor" materials (hats, scarves, baby dolls, dishes, chalk) to their outdoor dramatic play (see Photo 15-4).

15-2b Teacher's Role

Entering into the child's dramatic play is an important point of consideration here. The teacher should not be the leader or the organizer of the dramatic play and must try not to form premature conclusions or make

Casper Holroyd

PHOTO 15-4 An outdoor area can also have dramatic play activity opportunities.

Puppets and ESL Activities

In addition to the information in this chapter on the ways to use puppets in the early childhood program, using puppets with children who are learning English as a second language (ESL) is yet another excellent use. Using puppets is like having two fluent English speakers in class, and two fluent English speakers are better than just one!

Puppets introduce another proficient English speaker into the classroom for the teacher to speak to. This is important, as one natural language learning strategy adopted by children is that of observing and then imitating conversations conducted by the people around them. The puppet allows this dialogue modeling to take place in the classroom. For example, imagine that the teacher wants to demonstrate how to ask for a colored pencil in English. She places a red pencil and a blue pencil to the right of the puppet (out of reach of her left hand to necessitate the pencil being passed to her by the puppet), then turns to the student and has the following dialogue:

> Teacher: "Enrico, may I have a pencil please?"
> Puppet: "Yes, what color?"
> Teacher: "Red, please."
> Puppet (handing over pencil): "Here you are."
> Teacher: "Thank you."

The pencils are then placed on the far left of the teacher and the roles are reversed. Enrico asks for the pencil and the teacher passes it to him. After modeling the dialogue again, the teacher may then invite a child to come to the front and take one of the roles, while the teacher speaks for the puppet.

Some children feel hesitant to speak in English because they are unsure of the pronunciation of certain words or of exactly how to express themselves. In such cases, puppets can act as a psychological support for the child. When a child speaks through the puppet, it is not the child who is perceived as making errors but the puppet, and children find this liberating. Thus, puppets can encourage students to experiment more with the language and "have a go" when they may have otherwise remained silent.

Have your own puppet as a special friend. Introduce yourself to the puppet in front of the class. Next, have the children introduce themselves to their puppets from the privacy of their own seats. No one will be listening to them as everyone is talking to their own puppets at the same time. This is a good fluency activity with no need for teacher correction. Later, when the children are comfortable using puppets, ask a child to tell about himself in front of the class. The puppet speaks for the child, which should ease the discomfort level.

ESL children will also enjoy singing along to a favorite song with their puppets. Choose a song that is familiar and one that the children can make their puppets dance and do the actions to as the class sings. For example, with "The Wheels on the Bus," the puppets and children can make all of the motions mentioned in the song.

---

assumptions for the child. The teacher observes and asks questions about what the child says and helps to draw out information from the child, maintaining the conversation on the theme provided by the child, but at a pace that allows the child to feel comfortable and pleased with the conversation. The teacher also encourages children's play by providing props that extend the play but do not change the theme. In doing so, teachers provide for further dramatic play and thereby create a more effective basis from which thought processes and imagination can develop. Teachers help children with their thinking by making statements about their work—*not* evaluative statements, such as, "I like your cake," or assumptive ones, such as, "What a naughty cat, eating up all the meat!"—but statements of the obvious on which the child can expand, such as, "It's a bright yellow color!"

When observing the dramatic play of children of various ages in the dramatic play center, the perceptive teacher can detect definite developmental and age differences. Younger children 2 to 4 years old generally are involved in dramatic play for a much briefer period of time than children 5 years of age and older. Before the child is 2 years old, for example, he may say, "Nice baby," when he hugs a doll and then move on. After the age of 2, the child's dramatic play may begin to combine several ideas, in contrast to the single idea dramatization of the younger child. The older child may hold a doll and pretend to feed the "baby" a cookie. He may decide to put the baby to bed, covering the doll with a blanket because it is time for "baby to take a nap." This process of imitating what has been observed is called **modeling behavior**.

Instances of such modeling behavior in the dramatic play center and elsewhere are even more prevalent in older children. For example, a 5-year-old child will feed the baby, discussing why milk is good for him or her, telling the baby it is nap time, and instructing the baby that children must "be good" and listen to their parents. This dramatization is in marked contrast to that of the 2-year-old.

Early childhood teachers also need to be aware that children involved in dramatic play also use materials from various parts of the room to support their play. For example, a child who needs some pretend money to put in a purse may decide to make some in the art area, or even go to the manipulative area to gather beads, chips, or small Lego® blocks to use as money.

Whether they are searching for materials or on their way to another related location, it is perfectly natural and appropriate for children involved in dramatic play to move about the entire space as part of their play. Confining role players to one area or part of the room frustrates rather than supports their intentions. When their use of space and materials conflicts with other children's use of space and materials, the opportunity for group problem solving arises.

15-2c Multicultural and Multiple Intelligences and Dramatic Play

Dramatic play is a natural avenue for participation by children from diverse language and multicultural backgrounds. Children who are bilingual can participate easily in dramatic activities that call for nonverbal communication. The dramatic play area can also be a place where children learn the words for their play props. For example, name tags can be made for objects in the dramatic play center in both English and children's native languages.

Dramatic play also appeals to children's various learning styles or multiple intelligences. The body-smart learner gets obvious enjoyment from the active, physical movement involved in dramatic play. The child who is word smart enjoys the ongoing dialogue that is so naturally a part of the dramatic play experience. The child with a person-smart learning style thrives in dramatic activities involving constant interaction with other children. The child with a picture-smart learning style enjoys creating the visual scenes that provide the background for dramatic play scenarios.

Did You Get It?

Two preschoolers are playing in a castle in a dramatic play center. One of the children announces, "I am a nobleman!" The other child is not familiar with that term, but nevertheless responds, "I am a nobleman, too!" From a developmental perspective, how can we interpret this interaction?

a. A child is experiencing negative peer pressure.

b. A child is unusually gifted verbally.

c. The first child is stunting the imagination of the second child.

d. The second child's language skills are broadening.

Take the full quiz on CourseMate.

15-3 Adapting Dramatic Play for Children with Special Needs

naeyc DAP The following suggestions are designed to help teachers include children with special needs in dramatic play.

- Because the child should feel free to experiment and take risks, be careful not to make too many rules for his or her play. Enforce only those rules that are really needed for the child to play safely.

- Let the child take the lead. This may involve some patient waiting for the child to choose something to do.

- To encourage children to play together, define the space where children can play and keep it small. For example, position housekeeping toys around a small area rug and remind children that they need to stay on the rug while they are playing.

- Children with attention deficits, autism, and developmental delays tend to flit from center to center. Children cannot fully benefit from the learning experiences in a center if they are there only a moment or two. Be firm and require that children initially spend at least 5 minutes in a center of their choice. Then gradually build on the amount of time the child can focus on dramatic play. If 5 minutes is impossible for the child, start with the amount of time the child can currently tolerate.

- To help children put away dramatic play props and toys, label shelves with pictures as well as words.

- Try to let the child play with other children as much as possible. The more often you interact with children, the less often children interact with their peers (Gould & Sullivan, 2004).

15-3a Developmental Delays

Adults may be tempted to intervene too much in the play of children with developmental delays. Children need an opportunity to play at their level of ability and to independently initiate play activities. If you need to intervene when the child is playing in a group, be as unobtrusive as possible. For example, you could simply sit down as part of the children's play and become a character or prop so that you could subtly make suggestions.

Other suggestions for working with children with developmental delays follow.

- Offer dramatic play materials that are familiar and part of the child's daily life experiences.
- Encourage verbalization during play by asking questions and encouraging communication with other children.
- Some children with developmental delays fatigue very easily. Make sure that the child has supportive seating.
- The child who is not yet proficient at dramatic play may be able to carry out some kind of support role in the play, such as being the patient at a doctor's office. You can make this happen by having the appropriate props nearby or by verbally suggesting the role.
- Bring out a few props at a time to avoid unnecessarily distracting the child.
- Provide some dress-up clothes that are simple to get on and off and do not have tiny buttons or snaps. Large clothes are easier to get on and off.

15-3b Attention Deficit/Hyperactivity Disorder and Behavioral Issues

Two traits—high activity levels and distractibility—may prevent children from participating in dramatic activities. These children are more able to focus on dramatic play that they have chosen and that is of personal interest. Novelty is very important. Adding a single novel toy to a play setting may be enough to refocus the child's attention. For example, if the child is playing in the dramatic play center and seems to be losing interest, add a doctor's kit with stethoscope and play syringe and cue the child to return to the play with a question such as, "Is the baby sick?"

Additional suggestions for working with these children in dramatic activities follow.

- Help children learn how to work out conflicts when playing with other children. In order to circumvent a child's acting out aggressively, offer the child help in verbalizing what is bothering him or her (Deiner, 2009).
- Make sure that there are clear behavioral consequences for inappropriate behavior. Carefully consider whether the rules you make are really necessary.
- Exciting activities that are new or offer a lot of sensory input should be preceded and followed by calming activities. Involvement in dramatic play could be followed by quiet time sitting on a beanbag chair with a favorite toy.
- If the child attempts to leave the center after a few moments of play, ask the child to stay and do one more thing. However, children should be allowed to leave play situations that are not productive.
- Hyperactivity in and of itself does not get in the way of learning. If the child is focused on the play activity while actively moving about, there is no need to intervene. This is different from the child who cannot focus on the play or the other children and is darting aimlessly around the classroom. That child needs adult intervention to settle down to play.
- Reduce distractions in the dramatic play center by hanging sheets or lengths of fabric from the ceiling to section off the center from the rest of the room. Dramatic play could also take place in a large box or under a table that has been draped with a sheet.
- Set a timer to help the child stay in a play center. The timer provides an auditory cue for when the child can move to another center and gives the child a sense that his or her involvement in the center has a definite beginning and end.

15-3c Visual Impairments

Children with vision impairment may have not had the opportunity to learn how to play by observing others. The child may also have had limited experience with exploring and manipulating objects. It is important that children with residual (limited vision) be encouraged to use their vision. Children who are blind should be encouraged to explore the sensory properties of objects.

- Help the child explore the dramatic play area and to discuss what the objects are and what they are used for. Ask the other children in the center to explain the ongoing play to the child who is visually impaired (Deiner, 2009).

- Intervene if the child is always assigned subordinate roles in play such as that of the baby or patient. Suggest another role.
- Encourage the child who is blind to develop social skills that will help interaction with other children. The child should learn to turn his or her face toward people when they are talking and to keep his or her head in midline (Gould & Sullivan, 2004).

Did You Get It?

A teacher insists that her students spend at least five minutes at the play center of their choosing before moving on to another play center. From a developmental perspective, her actions are

a. inappropriate, because they eliminate free choice.

b. appropriate for students with attention disorders or autism.

c. inappropriate, because they stunt the children's imagination.

d. appropriate for all types of students.

Take the full quiz on CourseMate.

15-4 Creative Dramatics versus Dramatic Play in the Elementary Grades

naeyc DAP *Dramatic play* is the free play of very young children in which they explore their universe, imitating the actions and traits of those around them. It is an accepted part of the preschool and kindergarten curricula. While adults rely on reason and knowledge, children use play and imagination to explore and understand their world. It makes sense, then, for teachers to use these two resources—play and imagination—as learning tools. Dramatic play is the child's earliest expression in dramatic form, but it is not the same as **creative dramatics**.

Dramatic play is fragmented, existing only for the moment. It may last for a few minutes or go on for some time. It even may be played repeatedly, but it is a repetition for the pure joy of doing. It has no clear beginning, no end, and no development in the dramatic sense (see Photo 15-5).

PHOTO 15-5 Dramatic play has no clear beginning or end, and it may last for only a brief time.

The term *creative drama* is generally used to describe the improvised drama of children age 6 and older (see Photo 15-6). Creative dramatics builds on the free creative play of the preschool years. It is an extension of the natural activities of early childhood. The make-believe play of home, yard, and sidewalks can have new dimensions as it is incorporated into new learning experiences in the elementary classroom.

Creative drama goes beyond dramatic play in scope and intent and may make use of a story with a

PHOTO 15-6 Creative drama is the term generally used to describe drama activities for older children.

Puppet Play and Autistic Children's Communicative Skills

In this study, preschool autistic children in Mashhad, Iran, comprised the statistical population. A pretest and post-test (The Early Social Communication Scales—ESCS) was administered to both the intervention and control groups of preschool children (100 in each group).

The children in the intervention group participated in a puppet program on a daily basis. This program was designed to encourage children's eye contact, social interaction, initiating requests, pointing to objects, and giving objects. The control group participated in a traditional preschool program. After one month, children in both the intervention and control group were given the ESCS as a posttest.

Findings indicated that in terms of the ESCS, there was a statistically significant difference between the control and the puppet group with the puppet group scoring statistically significantly higher. The puppet group also scored higher on eye-contact subscales, initiating requests, and responding to social interaction. On the subscales of pointing to objects and giving objects, there were no statistically significant differences in the two groups. Qualitative findings from parental reports also indicated that the puppet intervention was effective. Thus, the researchers concluded that puppet play therapy was effective for achievement of communication skills of autistic children in this study (Moshen et al., 2011).

beginning, a middle, and an end. It may, on the other hand, explore, develop, and express ideas and feelings through dramatic enactment. Creative drama is, however, always improvised. This makes it different from performing a play. Actors in a play read or memorize lines written by somebody else. In creative dramatics, actors create their own words to convey meaning. Dialogue is created by the players, whether the content is taken from a well-known story or is an original plot. Lines are not written down or memorized. With each playing, the story becomes more detailed and better organized, but it remains extemporaneous and is at no time designed for an audience. Participants are guided by a leader rather than a director; the leader's goal is the optimal growth and development of the players.

15-4a Guidelines for Creative Dramatics with Elementary Students

The following are some specific steps you may find helpful in setting up creative dramatic experiences for elementary children.

Provide a structure. While pretending is very natural for children, improvising a short drama can be an abstract process. Children will need structure to guide their actions and dialogue during the initial stages. The teacher can provide this structure by modeling and demonstrating the basic story, as well as possible actions, dialogue, and characterizations. In story reenactments, be sure everyone gets a turn. But try to avoid repeating the play over and over again in the

same setting, as children will probably become bored. Instead, repeat it once a day over the course of a week to maintain children's interest. It is best to keep early dramas short and simple, using only two to four characters. Older students and those with experience in creative dramatics will need less structure.

Encourage open-endedness. Creative dramatics is spontaneous and changeable. Although it works best when teachers provide a beginning structure, this structure should be flexible and open ended. As students become more comfortable with creative dramatics, they will begin to use ideas and experiences from their own lives to create unique variations on the original themes. Using a prepared script would prevent this kind of creativity and individualization. It is a good rule not to use written dialogue.

Promote a safe environment. Creativity is enhanced when the teacher creates a fun, safe environment. Closing the classroom door during the initial learning stages of creative dramatics can help to develop a sense of safety and community. A teacher who is willing to take creative risks by modeling and participating in creative dramatics encourages the children's participation. Positive, specific feedback that acknowledges actors and their efforts will put students at ease to continue acting creatively. Finally, a teacher should never force students to participate in creative dramatics; rather, he or she should always ask for volunteers.

Provide feedback. Students like to receive feedback, both formal and informal. Informal feedback

Dramatic Play and Cognition Control

In this study, dramatic play activities were a large part of the Tools of the Mind curriculum, designed to improve preschooler's executive functions (EFs) (Diamond et al., 2010). EFs, which are also called cognitive controls, are critical for success in school and life. EFS include such skills as self-control and maintaining attention to tasks.

The Tools curriculum is based on Vygotsky's insights into EF and its development (Vygotsky, 1978). The core of this curriculum is 40 EF-promoting activities, including telling oneself out loud what one should do (self-regulatory private speech – 18 activities), dramatic play (18 activities) and activities to facilitate memory and attention (19). These activities in the Tool curriculum had been refined through 12 years of research in preschools and kindergartens (Diamond et al., 2010).

Tool teachers spent 80% of each day promoting EF skills. The study population consisted of 147 preschoolers (62 in the regular preschool curriculum and 85 in the Tools curriculum) in their second year of preschool (average age: 5.1 years in both groups). All children came from the same low-income, urban neighborhood and were randomly assigned to the regular or Tools curriculum. The regular curriculum developed by the school district (dBL) was based on literacy and included thematic units. Both dBL and Tools covered the same academic content, but dBL did not address EF development. After 1 year, educators in one school were so convinced that the Tools children were doing substantially better that they replaced the regular curriculum with the Tools curriculum for all preschool children in that school.

The researchers conducted multiple regression analyses with age, gender, curriculum, and years in curriculum as independent variables. The EFs of the children in the Tools group were significantly improved in the study population of 4–5 year olds in regular public schools with regular teachers. Being in the Tools curriculum resulted in superior scores on objective neurocognitive EF measures in comparison to closely matched peers in the non-Tools curriculum.

In their summary, the researchers state that although dramatic play is often thought frivolous, it may be essential. Tool uses dramatic play to help improve EF as they state, "If throughout the school day, EFs are supported and progressively challenged, benefits generalize and transfer to new activities. Daily EF 'exercise' appears to enhance EF development as much as physical exercise builds bodies" (Diamond et al., 2010). Thus, based on this study, dramatic play provides young children yet another positive benefit in the early childhood program.

---

is best when a teacher responds in a way that is appropriate to the dramatic experience (for example, laughing at the comedic parts). After a drama is over, the teacher can give more formal feedback by processing the experience with students and recognizing those things that were done well.

Take your time. Allow students to slowly become comfortable with creative dramatics. Remember, creative dramatics is meant to be an enjoyable learning experience. Make having fun your number one priority.

The following are some examples of creative dramatics experiences:

- In a third-grade classroom, students using creative dramatics "become" metal containers, expanding with heat and contracting with cold. These expanding and contracting movements are put into a drama and are eventually accompanied by a dance.

- In a first-grade classroom, children become clouds releasing raindrops, shimmery rays of sunshine, and seeds that grow roots, sprout, and squeeze their faces through the dirt.

- A fourth-grade teacher introduces a dramatic activity having individuals or small groups of students repeat the same line while portraying different qualities or characters. She says in a very mysterious way, "Are you going to wear the red hat to the fair?" She says in a very angry way, "Are you going to wear the red hat to the fair?" She asks the students, "How might a mouse ask the same question? How might a clown ask the same question?" After five minutes, students are thinking creatively and are ready to move into a dramatic activity.

- In a third-grade classroom, students are performing "The Three Billy Goats Gruff" with a twist. The teacher tells the actors before they begin that they can only use dog language. That is, they will have to act out the whole drama using only barks and pants. This forces children to convey meaning and develop characterization using only their faces and bodies while watching and reacting to other actors.

In all of these examples, teachers are using creative dramatics to reinforce concepts in the curriculum. In the process, these teachers are creating an active learning experience that is fun, allowing the students to work together to achieve a common goal and allowing everyone to be successful.

This is the essence of creative dramatics. Creative dramatics is a form of imaginative play that helps elementary students learn in an active, enjoyable way.

Casper Holroyd

PHOTO 15-7 Puppets fascinate and involve children in a way few other art forms can.

Did You Get It?

A young child pushes a toy vacuum cleaner along a carpet, pretending to clean it. This activity is best described as

  a. creative drama.
  b. dramatic play.
  c. imaginative repurposing.
  d. effective modeling.

Take the full quiz on CourseMate.

15-5 Puppets in the Early Childhood Classroom

Puppets are very important in the lives of young children. Even the youngest of children in the early childhood program is familiar with the puppets on *Sesame Street*. Puppets can be used for almost any of the dramatic experiences that have been described here. They offer the child two ways to express creativity: (1) the creative experience of making the puppet, and (2) the imaginative experience of making the puppet come to life.

Puppets fascinate and involve children in a way that few other art forms can because they allow children to enter the world of fantasy and drama so easily (see Photo 15-7). In this magic world, children are free to create whatever is needed right then in their lives.

15-5a Using Puppets

naeyc DAP The use of puppets usually begins in the nursery or preschool, where they are invaluable when readily available for dramatic play. Teachers can teach finger plays with simple finger puppets; hand puppets can act out familiar nursery rhymes. Music time is enhanced by a puppet leading the singing and other

puppets joining in. The shy child who is reluctant to sing often will participate through a puppet. Puppets are also excellent for concept teaching and can help clarify abstract concepts and demonstrate concrete concepts. For instance, in the preschool the concepts of "above," "below," "behind," "in front of," and so on can be clearly shown with the puppet.

Puppets allow you to say "silly" things to your class. For example, in a science class about how the position of the sun appears to change in the day and makes the puppet's shadow shorter, one teacher used the puppet to tell children someone must have washed it to make it shrink! The children told the puppet that the shadow couldn't have shrunk, and they explained in words understandable to other children what had happened. The children talked to the puppet as if it were a person separate from the teacher.

Puppets allow children freedom to talk when they are not sure about things. Also, children sometimes are aware that the teacher "knows the answer," and thus may not respond to a question or prompt. However, a puppet probably doesn't know an answer, so children's responses and explanations are more readily forthcoming and fuller.

Some of the larger puppets have hands like gloves so the teacher can make the puppet manipulate equipment and other resources. This is particularly helpful in sorting activities, as the puppet is able to join in just like another child. If, for example, children are sorting rocks on the basis of their characteristics, the teacher can make the puppet move rocks from one group to another to promote further discussion. The puppet's actions can encourage children to justify their choice of groupings if the puppet disagrees with their classification. As they explain their ideas, children can consider the validity of their claims or recognize possible flaws in their reasoning.

Another argument for using puppets in the classroom is that they can be used by the teacher to mirror desirable behaviors. The puppet can model the way claims can be justified and reasons given for a point of view. There is no right or wrong way to use a puppet, but teachers have found it valuable to give the puppet a distinct character. If the character is consistently maintained by the teacher, children can be allowed to "take over" animating the puppet: They already know what the puppet is like—they don't have to invent a new character.

Puppets are wonderful tools for demonstrating social skills with young children. You can use them to enact a scenario that represents a frequent troublesome behavior in the classroom or an issue that one or more children are experiencing in their lives. Puppets help the children see the situation from a new perspective. For instance, if children in your group are having trouble sharing toys, you might act out a similar situation during circle time using puppets.

Puppets are used most successfully when teachers have introduced them slowly to the class and have developed a strong sense of identity for the puppet. Care needs to be taken to maintain the puppet's character, even when it is not being used. Give the puppet a seat to sit in and watch the children at work; assign a child to look after the puppet each day. It is crucial that puppets talk to children; puppets that listen to children and "whisper" to the teacher aren't as effective with young children. Puppets can effectively be used to introduce a lesson or to "talk" to small groups when children are discussing their ideas. Teachers have noticed that their classes become more animated when puppets join in the lesson. Children want to talk to the puppet and hear what the puppet has to say.

Puppetry, as a form of dramatic play, is a sure means of stimulating creative storytelling in younger children. Some teachers record spontaneous puppet skits, and by writing them down, show children how they have created a story. In a room with a climate of flexibility and freedom, children are bound to come up with countless ideas for using their puppets (see Photo 15-8). Some suggestions are presented here:

- Put together a puppet center—puppet materials, props, and theater—for children to use during the day (see Photo 15-9).
- Consider having a specific puppet for each center area. This puppet could remind the class that it is music time, for instance, and be used

PHOTO 15-8 Children can come up with many different ways to use puppets.

to give directions and explain new concepts. If the puppet has trouble in an area, the children could teach it and straighten out its confusion. Through such dramatic experiences, self-confidence and skills are strengthened.
- Felt boards and puppets work well together. A puppet with hands can effectively help the adult or

PHOTO 15-9 Puppet centers can be used by children throughout the day.

child put pieces on or take them off the felt board. One teacher who was teaching toddlers the parts of the face used a rather "stupid" puppet that kept making mistakes by putting the parts in the wrong place. The children had a lot of fun correcting it.

- In music experiences, teachers find that puppets help young children develop a feeling for rhythm and music interpretation by moving the puppets to the beat. They also encourage reluctant children to sing because the puppet does the singing for the child. Puppets with moving mouths are most effective but not necessary.
- Social studies is a natural area for puppets; it presents countless opportunities to dramatize holiday ideas, represent particular ethnic customs, or portray the roles of various community helpers.
- Use puppets to help children voice feelings, such as fear; other activities can include using high- and low-pitched voices and making squeaking, growling, and chirping animal sounds.
- Provide opportunities for enactments of published or original stories.
- Encourage children to present original work. Young children may have difficulty manipulating puppets and saying words at the same time. Record the story in advance so that the children can then focus on the puppets' actions.

These suggestions are simply intended to be idea starters. The use of puppets in the classroom is limited only by imagination—yours and the children's.

15-b Kinds of Puppets

Some of the most common and easiest puppets to make are stick puppets, hand puppets, finger puppets, people puppets, wooden spoon puppets, mitten and sock puppets, paper plate puppets, play dough puppets, Styrofoam ball puppets, ping-pong ball puppets, and cylinder puppets.

Stick puppets. The simplest of all puppets, stick puppets are controlled by a single stick (any slim, rigid support) that goes up inside the puppet or is attached to the back of it.

Stick puppets are fun and easy to make. The teacher can use sticks from the lumberyard, large twigs, pencils, or wooden popsicle or craft sticks. With this type of puppet, the child puts a bag or piece of cloth over the stick and stuffs the bag or cloth with wads of newspaper or cotton. The child then ties the

▶❚❚ **TeachSource** Video

© 2015 Cengage Learning

Preschool: Emotional Development

1. Evaluate this teacher's use of a puppet with this group of preschool children with regard to the information presented in this chapter. Is her use of a puppet in this lesson consistent with the uses for puppets as discussed in this chapter? What specific aspect of her use is most consistent? Least consistent?

2. What other type(s) of puppet(s) could this teacher use for this same lesson? Give specific examples in your answer.

3. Why do you suppose the puppet in the video has no facial features? How would having facial features on this puppet change the lesson?

Watch on CourseMate.

top of the bag to the stick, making a head. A rubber band may be used instead of string to form a head.

The child can then paint the head or make a face with crayons, markers, or colored paper and paste. Scrap yarn, wood shavings, and buttons are also good materials for the puppet's face. Scrap pieces of fabric can be used to "dress" the puppet; wallpaper samples provide inexpensive material for puppets' clothes.

With the stick, the puppet is moved around the stage or turned from side to side. It has the advantage of being a good first puppet for preschoolers because a stick can be attached to any little doll, toy animal, or cutout figure, and the puppet is easy to operate.

Bag puppets. The common paper bag in any size makes a good bag puppet for young preschoolers. The bags are stuffed with wads of newspaper and tied, stapled, or glued shut. A body is made with a second bag stapled to the first, leaving room for the child's hand to slip in and work the puppet.

A face can be made with paint, crayons, or colored paper and paste. Odds and ends are fun to use for the face, too. Buttons make eyes; crumpled tissue, a nose; and yarn, hair. The search for the right odds and ends to make the puppet is as much fun as using the finished puppet later.

Hand puppets. Frequently called "glove" or "mitten puppets," these are the most popular for young children. These can be made in child or adult sizes by tracing around your hand or the child's hand in a mitten shape, or around your fingers or the child's fingers for a glove shape. There are many types of hand puppets, but most can be classified into two general groups: (1) those with moving mouths and (2) those with moving hands.

The first (with moving mouths) is any sort of hand covering—a handkerchief, sock, mitten, or paper bag—inside of which one's fingers open and shut, forming the mouth of the puppet. The second kind has a head and two hands and is operated by putting one or two fingers in the head and one in each hand. This kind of puppet can freely pick up objects and make hand motions, thus putting more realism into a performance.

Finger puppets. The three general types of finger puppets are the following (see Figure 15-3):

- Finger-leg. Finger puppet in which two fingers (usually the index and middle fingers) serve as the puppet's legs.
- Finger-cap. Finger puppet that slips over an individual finger.
- Finger-face. Puppet made by drawing a face on a finger with a felt pen. Usually, one can perform with quite a few puppets of this type at one time. They are great for finger plays!

Some advantages of finger puppets include the following.

- They are easy to manipulate, even by a toddler.
- They encourage small muscle action.
- They are inexpensive to make.
- One child alone can put on a performance with an "entire cast."
- They maintain interest because they are always easy and quick to make.
- They can be made in spare moments, as materials are small and mobile.

Wooden spoon puppets. You will need wooden spoons, yarn, string, material scraps, glue, and construction paper. Draw a face on the wooden spoon. Glue

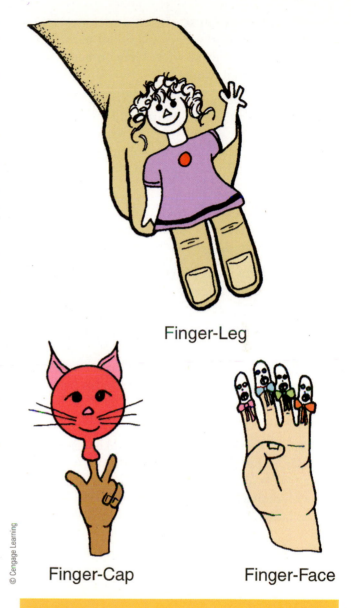

Finger-Leg

Finger-Cap   Finger-Face

© Cengage Learning

FIGURE 15-3 There are many kinds of finger puppets. Three examples are shown here.

on yarn or string for hair and scraps of material for clothing.

Two-faced (paper plate) puppets. Draw a face on the back of each paper plate. Add features with various types of materials. Insert a stick between the paper plates and glue it into place. Staple edges together.

Play dough puppets. Place a small amount of play dough onto a finger. Mold play dough into a face shape covering the finger. Add beads, toothpicks, and other small objects for facial features and added emphasis.

Styrofoam ball puppets. Insert a stick into a Styrofoam ball. Cover the Styrofoam ball with fabric. Tie the fabric around the stick. Glue on buttons and felt scraps for facial features.

Ping-pong ball puppets. Cut an X-shaped hole out of a ball. Place a piece of lightweight fabric on your finger. Cover the area of the ball with sturdy glue. Force the ball at the X onto the fabric on your finger. While the glue is drying, draw or paste a face onto the puppet.

Sock puppet. Pull the sock over your hand. Glue or paint facial features onto the toe of the sock or decorate as desired.

Finger puppets from gloves. Recycle stray gloves and use them for finger puppets. Recycle old rubber gloves, too, by drawing features on rubber glove fingers with marking pens. Glue pom-poms on each finger for the "head" and glue on bits of cloth or felt for facial or character details.

Old mitten puppets. A child can slip his hand into an old mitten and make the puppet "talk" by moving his thumb up and down against the four fingers.

Cardboard cylinder puppet. To make a cardboard cylinder puppet, place a cardboard cylinder from paper towels or toilet tissue over the fingers. Decorate with desired features. The cylinder could be used for the body, and a Styrofoam ball or ping-pong ball could be placed on the top for the head. Decorate as desired.

People puppets. Also called humanettes, these are half-person and half-puppet. The easiest people puppet for children is a large paper sack put over the head. Holes are cut out for the eyes, and facial features and decorations are added with paint or paper and paste. The bags can be turned up slightly above the shoulder or cut away on the sides for armholes. People puppets make a natural transition from puppetry to creative drama. Also, shy children generally feel more protected behind this kind of puppet than all the other types. Be sure not to force a child to use this type of puppet if the child does not like his or her head covered!

More ideas for puppets are found at the end of this chapter.

Did You Get It?

Christian, a 4-year-old, is shy and reluctant to speak to the teacher because he is afraid of giving the wrong answers. Which creative activity is most likely to encourage him to answer the teacher's question?
- **a.** puppet play
- **b.** pretend play
- **c.** creative drama
- **d.** collage making

Take the full quiz on CourseMate.

Summary

15-1 Discuss the importance of dramatic play to a young child's development.

Dramatic play is an excellent means for developing creativity and imagination in young children when it is related to the child's personal sense of reality without imposed adult standards. It provides children one of the best ways to express themselves in a safe, creative way. Through dramatic play, children sort out what they understand and gain a measure of mastery and control over events they have witnessed or taken part in. Dramatic play helps children enter and begin to make sense of the world of adults.

15-2 Discuss what children learn in dramatic play.

Dramatic play is an important medium for language development and learning to listen and respond to other children, and it is a natural source for many other types of learning.

15-3 Discuss ways to adapt dramatic activities for children with special needs.

Be careful not to make too many rules for the child's play. Let the child take the lead. Encourage children to play together; define the space where children can play and keep it small. Children with attention deficits, autism, and developmental delays need to be assisted in choosing centers and spending at least 5 minutes in a center of their choice. Help the child with visual impairments explore the dramatic play area to discuss what the objects are and what they are used for. Encourage the child who is blind to develop social skills that will help interaction with other children.

15-4 Discuss the difference between dramatic play and creative dramatics.

Dramatic play is the free play of very young children in which they explore their universe, imitating the actions and traits of those around them. Creative drama is generally used to describe the improvised drama of children age 6 and older.

Dramatic play can be adapted so it is appropriate for children with special needs. Dramatic play kits are easy to make and help develop opportunities for creative play. The use of puppets provides opportunities for creative movement, dramatics, and language development. Creative dramatics refers to informal drama that is created by the participants. It goes beyond dramatic play in scope and intent. The term creative dramatics is generally used to describe the improvised drama of children age 6 and older.

15-5 Discuss appropriate ways to use puppets in the early childhood program.

Teachers can teach finger plays with puppets. Music time is enhanced by the use of puppets. Puppets are also excellent for concept teaching and can help clarify abstract concepts and demonstrate concrete concepts. Puppets allow children the freedom to talk when they are not sure about things. Puppets can help to mirror desirable behaviors. Puppets are wonderful tools for demonstrating social skills with young children. Puppets can also encourage creative storytelling in younger children.

Other uses of puppets in the early childhood program include helping shy children express themselves, having children introduce themselves, and teaching new concepts in various areas.

Key Terms

bag puppet   350
cardboard cylinder puppet   352
creative dramatics   345

dramatic play   338
finger puppets   351
humanettes   352

modeling behavior   342
people puppet   352

Learning Activities

A. Create two dramatic play kits not listed or suggested in this chapter. Think divergently! Compare your kit with those of your classmates.

B. Make up a play kit of "props" children might use in one of the following activities.
   - Playing mail carrier
   - Playing dentist
   - Playing airline pilot
   - Playing waitress/waiter

C. Make one of the types of puppets discussed in this chapter. Demonstrate its use to your classmates before you use it with children. Describe how you plan to use the puppet with children in the future.

D. If you had $200 to spend for drama equipment in setting up a new room in your first year of teaching, what would you buy and why? Itemize each purchase, and give at least three uses for each item. You may use a school supply catalog for assistance in your purchasing.

   Do this for a preschool class, a class in the kindergarten to grade 3 group, and in a class in the grade 4 to 5 range. Discuss the differences in each level and how they affected your purchases.

E. Observe in two early childhood rooms. What roles did you observe children playing in dramatic activities? How do you think these roles are related to children's real-life experiences? Explain.

   Consult the teacher in each of the two rooms you observed to learn how information obtained through

observing children's dramatic play is utilized (if at all) in guiding children or in making future plans. Give examples.

   In each of the rooms you observed, what limits were placed on children during dramatic play? How do you think these limits would change in an outdoor dramatic activity?

F. Make plans for bringing in new pieces of equipment and new props to help extend children's dramatic roles in each of the situations you observed. Bring them in, and then observe how children use these materials.

G. Visit an early childhood program. Interview the director, a head teacher, and a parent. Ask each how important they feel dramatic play is to their child(ren). Ask each to share their opinions about the last (or most currently produced) school program involving the child(ren). Compare the answers you received. Discuss the similarities and differences you found in these interviews.

H. Invite some children and adults to participate in creative dramatics together. See if you notice any differences in the ways they approach the activities. Adults should all have a chance to participate! You might also try this activity with students of different ages. What do you observe in their approaches?

I. As you observe at an early childhood center, make a record of the roles taken by boys and those taken by girls as they engage in dramatic play. Discuss in class.

J. Draw a plan of what you consider to be a good dramatic play center in a classroom for young children. Draw a second plan of the same area, showing how you might rearrange it and describe what you would hope to accomplish through these changes.

K. Try your hand at planning a drama in which you would take a role. Practice on something short, like a fable or Mother Goose piece. Consider the following:

1. Examine the story for problems and themes. What is this really about? What is the conflict? Who has the problem? For example, *Jack and the Beanstalk* is about how goods are not equally distributed and how people are never satisfied with what they have.
2. List groups or individuals that might be affected by the problem. For example, the giant's family who now has no income; Jack's mother, wife, and friends, who see a changed Jack; neighbors who don't like having a thief around.
3. Under what circumstances might these individuals come together (for example, some kind of meeting)?

For example, a counseling session for Jack's materialistic addictions.

4. Choose a role and plan a short introduction speech about who you are and why you are there (counselor).
5. Plan the roles that the children can become. For example, children can choose to be any of the characters affected by Jack's greed.

L. Using the information in this chapter on drama, jot down ways you might use drama in an elementary classroom.

M. From this chapter and class discussion, write a "letter to parents" in which you describe what creative dramatics is and why you plan to incorporate it into your classroom. Try to make your letter both brief and informative.

Activities for Children

Puppets for toddlers. Put a puppet on your hand or finger, and a small group of toddlers will gather in front of you. The magic of puppets helps toddlers increase their attention span. Children who would normally not last long in a group activity will be fascinated enough to sit down and stay awhile. Choose puppets children can interact with—shake their paw, tickle their ears, and give a kiss. And don't forget to have a puppet sing-a-long! You can make small finger puppets for the children to use on their fingers, too. Ideas for finger puppets are found later in this section.

Puppets for times of the day. Use a special puppet to begin your morning meeting. Children like seeing the puppet every day, and this routine can also help them make transitions to and from the group. You can also use the puppet to welcome children, lead the hello song, or discuss the events of the day. It can also be used to share a recent experience that may be similar to one a child in the group has had. A puppet can also talk about feelings regarding a classroom situation that needs discussion. A large puppet that has an expressive face and moveable arms would be good in this situation.

Puppets for group time. Here are some ideas for using puppets at group time:

- Use a puppet for teaching alphabet letters (for example, a lamb puppet for the letter L). If focusing on a particular color, the puppet might wear the chosen color in a paper hat and a scarf.
- Make simple stick or finger puppets representing characters from a favorite book. Do this, too, for story-songs such as "This Old Man" or "I Know an Old Lady." Children can use the puppets to play the different roles in the story or song.
- Use a puppet to introduce a story. When the story is finished, the puppet can discuss it with the children.
- Designate a special puppet, such as a Riddle Puppet, for asking children "What am I thinking?" or to play an "I Spy" game. Children will know a riddle is coming whenever you bring out this puppet.

Puppets and Math

- Have a puppet that is always backward . . . he adds instead of subtracts . . . he multiplies instead of divides . . . he even counts backward. Have the children point out his errors and correct them.
- Have a puppet that goes crazy every time he hears a certain number. Choose your work problems so that the number is in the correct answers. Whoever gets the problem right first gets the puppet for the next problem.
- Have a puppet that always has a secret number, concept, or word. He will only give the children hints. When they figure it out, he will be approached by another puppet that will tell him a new secret.

Puppets for transition times. Use a puppet to announce cleanup or any other change in activity. The transition puppet might have a bell it rings or a drum it plays. Set aside a special puppet just for this role so that the children do not confuse it with others in the room. The puppet can also excuse children from group time with a song, riddle, or direction. "Anybody who is wearing BLUE can go wash their hands." Later in the year, children will enjoy taking turns using this puppet and providing the directions.

Puppets as peacemakers. A puppet can be an impartial negotiator. Try a puppet when an argument arises or a problem occurs in the classroom. Children can take their case to the puppet. Children are often more willing to listen and cooperate when they problem solve with an "impartial" puppet friend. You can even use homemade sock puppets set aside solely for this purpose to help children express their feelings.

Puppets as school-to-home connections. Puppets, like dolls and stuffed animals, are wonderful for creating a home–school connection. Children can take the puppet—along with the puppet's overnight bag and journal—home for the weekend to visit with the family. Don't forget to pack the disposable camera so that children can record its adventures. This take-home puppet should be large enough that children can dress it up and play with it.

Puppets as classroom friends. Introduce a new classroom family member to the class—a puppet! Children will delight in telling the puppet all about the rules and even give it a tour of the room after group time. This is especially effective with shy children. You may see them chatting away to the puppet in a way you have never seen or heard them before. A full-body puppet that looks like a stuffed animal is good for this activity because children will want to carry it around to the different centers in the room and sit next to it at snack time.

Rubber Household Glove Puppet

These gloves provide a smooth surface for adhering small picture images such as drawings, photos, greeting cards, or magazine pictures. Cut out images and laminate with clear contact paper or plastic laminate for permanency, if desired. Put a piece of double-stick tape on the back of each image, and secure the images to the tips of the glove.

Garden Glove Puppet

Garden gloves come in an interesting variety of designs and colors while making a sturdy glove for all-around use. Sew or glue small pieces of Velcro to the tops of the glove. Make characters from pom-poms, and glue corresponding pieces of Velcro to the backs of the pom-poms for attaching to the glove. Felt scenery such as a clock, moon, or trees can be attached to the palm area of glove by means of Velcro or a button.

Puppet Theater Ideas

Tabletop. Drape a blanket over a table. Children can crouch behind it and use the surface as a stage. Props can go beneath.

Appliance Box. Cut off the back of a large appliance box (often available free at appliance stores). Cut a hole in the front. Let children decorate with paints and markers.

Door Frame. Hang a simple curtain on a tension rod halfway up your classroom doorframe. Performers stand in the hall; the audience sits in the room.

A Quiet Puppet

Cut the bottom and top off a cereal box. Put any puppet on your hand and stick it up through the box. When children need to quiet down, bring down your hand to hide the puppet in the box, as if the puppet is frightened by the noise. When children are quiet, stick the puppet back up. Let children use the puppet in the same way.

Paper Cup Finger Puppet

Give each child a paper cup. Explain how this cup will be their puppet's head. They can paint or use felt-tip markers to draw on the features. Yarn hair can be attached with glue. Paper ears or noses can be added. Cut two paper circles in the side of the cup to place fingers in the cup to work the puppet.

Body/Box Puppet

Make a box puppet in which the child becomes the puppet. Each child will need a lightweight cardboard box

(12" × 24" or 24" × 30"). Often, the first body puppets may all be ponies and horses. If the children really love these puppets, you may later want to vary the construction and produce birds, airplanes, fish, or the like.

For each puppet, remove the bottom of the cardboard box. Center a hole in the top of the box. The child's torso should comfortably fit into this space. In the middle of each side, an inch or two down from the top, cut a rectangular hole for handles. The child holds the puppet body up by the two handles. Staple a horse/pony head to the front of each body and horse tails (yarn or rope or crepe paper) to the end of each box. Have the children paint their body puppets, adding spots, saddles, blankets, manes, and faces. Once dry, the horse and pony puppets can be put into action!

Shadow Puppets

In this activity, children experiment with the effects that various light and puppet position have on shadows they make with their arms and hands. Children work in pairs to trace their shadows and create puppets with them.

Dim the lights and use flashlights to cast light on an open wall or chalkboard. Let children play, making hand puppets with their arms and hands on the open area.

Working with a partner, children trace each other's shadow puppets onto oak tag or poster board with markers.

Children (or adults) cut each traced hand shadow from the paper. Details are added to the hand shadow with crayons and markers.

Attach a craft or popsicle stick to the back of each shadow puppet with glue. Let the glue dry before using the puppet.

Pop-Up Puppets

For this activity, you will need poster board, crayons, glue, paintbrushes, scissors, markers, tempera paint, a small box, and craft (or popsicle) sticks.

Cut off the sides of the box to make a puppet theater. Paint the box. On the poster board, draw and color people and animals. Cut them out and glue each one to the top of a craft or popsicle stick.

An adult cuts slits into the bottom of the puppet theater so the puppet characters can pop up through the floor.

Balloon Puppets

For this activity, you will need balloons, markers, paste, pieces of yarn and trim, and masking tape. (Never use balloons with children under 3 years of age.)

Blow up the balloons, one for each child. (If children are able, let them blow up the balloons. Some children will need assistance.) Tie the ends of the balloons.

Talk about how to handle the balloons so they will not break. Have extras on hand in case they do break.

Tape the balloons to the table. Use markers to make faces on the balloons. Glue yarn on top for hair. Add other pieces of fabric for clothing. Untape the balloons when children are finished decorating them and enjoy.

Use balloons of different shapes to create fanciful animals. Make a balloon body with other balloons taped to the head.

Box Puppets

For this activity, you will need small boxes (from pudding or gelatin), construction paper, paste, scissors, scrap pieces of fabric and trim, masking tape, markers, and crayons.

Give each child two small boxes. Tape the two boxes together, keeping the openings on both free. Cover the boxes with construction paper. The top box is the eye and top of the mouth. The bottom box is the bottom part of the mouth. Add bits of colored paper for eyes, a mouth, and other details. Add ears on the side of the boxes if desired. When all adhesives are dry, use and enjoy the puppet. To use the puppet, place four fingers in the top box and the thumb in the bottom box to work the mouth.

Variations: Use large boxes for big puppets. Be sure, however, that the boxes are small enough for little hands. Have fun making big tongues on the bottom box that will wag when the puppet talks. Add yarn hair that will be floppy and fun when the puppet moves.

Envelope Puppets

For this activity, you will need white envelopes, markers, scissors, and crayons.

Give each child a white envelope. Seal the envelope. Holding the envelope lengthwise, draw a face on the top of the envelope. Add facial details with markers and crayons. Cut off the short bottom edge of the envelope. Slip the puppet on the hand and use as a puppet.

Flower Puppets

Use individual flowers as puppets to talk to children about nature. Flowers can be purchased at any variety store. Hold the flower in your hand and let it "talk" to the children.

Pom-Pom Puppets

For this activity, you will need pom-poms of varying sizes and colors, popsicle or craft sticks, paste, a hole punch, construction paper, scraps of fabric, yarn, and trim. Talk about the pom-poms. Discuss what kind of puppets could be made with them. Talk about colors, details, features, and so on.

Glue a large pom-pom to the stick. Glue on pieces of construction paper for features and details. Use smaller pom-poms for other details. Use a hole punch on colored construction paper. Glue on the colored circles from the hole punch, if desired. Add fabric strips to the stick for clothing. Glue on yarn for hair.

Variations: Make a group of pom-pom puppets for a group sing-along. Let children choose the songs. Make animals for the song "Farmer in the Dell," and use them as you sing the song. Use cotton balls instead of pom-poms, but be aware that cotton balls are less stable decorations.

Stuffed Animal Puppets

Put those plush toys to work! They can be ready-made puppets for telling stories explaining directions, introducing a new activity, and so on.

One way of turning a stuffed animal into a hand puppet is to split the back seam and remove the body stuffing. You now have an instant hand puppet. Put your hand into the toy's cavity, and you're ready to perform.

The best thing about using a stuffed animal, however, is that you don't have to remove the stuffing. A stuffed animal is already a puppet. Simply articulate your animal by making it walk or use its paws, "playing" with it just the way you did when you were a kid.

Stuffed Animal Stick Puppets

For this activity, you will need popsicle sticks, twigs, pencils, small stuffed animals, and yarn or rubber bands.

Collect small stuffed animals. Attach a small stuffed animal to a stick or a pencil with a piece of string or rubber band. Dress the puppet with scraps of fabric and trim. Use this puppet like a stick puppet.

Variations: Attach small dolls to sticks to make puppets. Act out a fairy tale or a favorite story with the stuffed-animal stick puppets. Dress the stuffed animals with fabric, ribbon, and trim scraps.

Duster Puppets

Use feather or other small dusters with handles. Children use their imaginations to add eyes, nose, mouth, hats, and even clothes by gluing on these details. Children make the duster puppet move by using the handle on the duster.

Lint Brush Puppets

Recycle old two-sided lint brushes for puppets. These brushes have two sides. One side can be a smiling face, and the other a frowning face. Glue on large pom-poms for hair, wiggly eyes, and the other features from pieces of felt. You can even give the puppet a tie or bow with a fabric scrap.

Lonely Glove Finger Puppets

After cold weather is gone, what do you do with lonely, single gloves? Like socks, they always lose their mates. Make a finger puppet by cutting off the fingers from the glove. Use fabric glue to attach to the glove fingers small pom-poms for tails and feet, felt shapes for beaks. Add googly eyes, feathers for birds' wings and chenille stems (pipe cleaners) for claws. Slip the glove finger puppet on the finger and the fun begins!

Portable Puppet Stage

A portable puppet stage provides a special place for the children to tell stories and pretend with their puppets. While stages can be constructed, cardboard three-sided display units that you decorate make excellent stages and are easy to obtain from most craft or teacher-supply stores. One unit can be used in the story corner, or children can create individual stages to use on their own.

To use the display unit as a puppet stage, cut out a good-sized opening from the middle panel for the puppet to be seen through. Decorate to suit a particular story. For example:

- Sponge paint a wild-animal or farm-animal scene.
- Stamp the child's hand print and add the child's name for use with a variety of stories.
- Paint on a flower garden.
- Use markers to make a zoo scene.
- Use crayons to create a circus.
- Glue on collage items.

Set the three-sided unit on a table top when a puppet tale will be told, and fold for easy storage.

Finger Puppet Playhouse

Make a playhouse that will accommodate many finger puppets. You will need a large cereal box, paint, a craft knife (for the teacher's use), and markers. Paint a wide, tall cereal box. Cut out windows and a door for the puppets to use. Cut a large hole in the back of the box for children to put their hands through. Use markers to outline where the windows and door are on the back of the box as well, so the storyteller can tell the story and move the finger puppets more easily. A town can be created with several boxes and puppets for the houses. Children can use the playhouse and finger puppets for neighborhood conversations and storytelling from one house to another. Provide several houses in the story corner and rotate the puppets to develop children's imaginations.

Multicultural Puppet Lesson Plan

Topics: "I'm Me and I'm Special," "Boys and Girls," "Friends," "Alike and Different," "Colors," "Feelings," "Folk Tales," "Books," "Bodies"

Goal: To give children an opportunity to make a three-dimensional object that represents themselves and to gain skills in verbal self-expression

Materials: Collection of tan, beige, cream, brown, peach, and other skin-colored socks; felt scraps; and assorted fabric trim, yarn, buttons, glue, mirrors

Method: Explain to children, "I brought some materials so that you can make a sock puppet that looks just like you." Let children select the color of sock they want to use for their puppet. Encourage them to choose one that is like their skin color. Set out the mirror and materials on a table. Children may want to look in the mirror when deciding how to make their puppet's facial features and hair. Talk about the similarities and differences between the puppets. For example, you might say, "Each puppet is different because it looks like the person who is making it."

Variations

- Set up or make a puppet stage and encourage children to act out a story or classroom situation.
- Have children use their puppets to sing along during a favorite song.
- Have children use their puppets to act out a favorite finger play or poem.

Activities for Older Children (Grades 4–5)

Paper Puppet Portraits

A portrait on paper can be used as a hand puppet. The portraits can be of a biographical or historical subject or self-portraits drawn by the children. You will need paper, crayons, markers, scissors, glue stick, tape, and Popsicle sticks.

Children draw a face on typing or drawing paper. Glue the drawing to the popsicle stick and tape it, too, for extra strength. Then let the children tell the story of their lives (or of the historical subject) using the puppet portrait.

Aesthetic Awareness

Have students relate terms for movement in dance to terms that describe actual or implied motion in the visual arts. Examples include *glide, dart, slide, pivot, hop, sway,* and *twirl.* Have students create pantomimes or dances based on motions in nature such as a bird flying, a fish swimming, and a leaf falling. Have students invent vocal or instrumental sounds that seem to fit these motions, then orchestrate the sounds in different ways.

Creative Drama Exercises

The following are some exercises to get elementary children started on creative dramatics. Refer to the guidelines presented in this chapter to help you use these activities.

- Walk like the following: an elephant, a feather, a grasshopper, cooked spaghetti, uncooked spaghetti, a very quiet mouse, a very careful chicken.
- Blow a bubble, catch it in the air, and then set it down very carefully on the table.
- Walk into the kitchen, take a jar of pickles out of the refrigerator, open the jar, and eat one. It is very sour.
- Brush your teeth in the morning.
- Prepare and eat ice cream with spinach on top.
- Come into a room, look around, and hide in the closet.
- You are walking through a room when your foot gets stuck on some glue. You sit down to think and other parts of you get stuck, too.
- You are a mouse looking at some cheese on a mouse trap. Can you take it off?
- Lift something heavy, light, smelly, gooey, small, big, wiggly, or shaky.
- Tell a story without using any voice.
- Using only your face, be angry, surprised, sleepy, hurt, afraid, funny, or silly. Be someone who just heard a very loud noise.

Narrative Pantomime

Explain that in narrative pantomime, someone tells a story while others use their faces and bodies to show the story. Have everyone find a personal space in the center of the room. Be sure there is room around each child so they do not bump into one another.

Give each child a card with an animal name on it. (Arrange duplicates, but do not tell students.) Say, "When I say 'Start!' everyone is to show her or his animal in a variety of ways (for example, shape, moves, size). Stay in your personal spot. At the 'Freeze!' signal, everyone should stop. Start!"

After the activity, discuss with children their concentration, their unusual ideas, their focus, and so on. Then repeat the exercise in slow motion.

Creating Costumes for Creative Dramatics

For fun and affordable costumes, use Fabric Fun® Pastel Dye Sticks. Create costumes for drama activities, flags, personal banners, ethnic costumes, quilt blocks, and much more. Students of all ages will enjoy transforming their clothing into works of art with these brilliant colors. Simply draw or stencil a design directly onto the fabric with the dye sticks, cover the design with a piece of paper or a paper towel, and then the teacher presses it with an iron to make the drawing permanent. Fabric Fun® is available in sets of 7 and 15.

References

Deiner, P. (2009). *Inclusive early childhood education: Development, resources, and practice.* Clifton Park, NY: Delmar Cengage Learning.

Diamond, A., Barnett, W., Thomas, J., & Munro, S. (2010). Preschool program improves cognitive control. *Science, 31*(8), 1387–1390.

Gould, P., & Sullivan, J. (2004). *The inclusive early childhood classroom: Easy ways to adapt learning centers for all children* (2nd ed.). Beltsville, MD: Gryphon House.

Moshen, A., Ali, A. G., Abbas, B., & Mohsen, S. Y. (2011). The effect of puppet play therapy intervention on communicative skills of autistic children. *The Quarterly Journal of Fundamentals of Mental Health, 13*(1), 442–57.

Vygotsky, L. S. (1978). *Mind in society: The development of higher psychological processes.* Cambridge, MA: Harvard Press.

Visit CourseMate for this textbook to access the eBook, Did You Get It? quizzes, Digital Downloads, TeachSource Videos, flashcards, and more. Go to CengageBrain.com to log in, register, or purchase access.

Creative Movement

Movement is a powerful communicator that can fascinate or repel and delight or disgust us. And yet, unlike the use of words, movement is not a communication form often considered to be part of the basics in most schools, even in early childhood programs. Perhaps it is so basic we simply take for granted that we all know how to use it effectively. But we don't. Creative movements are frequently the part of the curriculum that teachers are most unprepared to integrate in their classrooms.

In the United States, body image is very important; beautiful body images bombard us daily in the media. We have become very sensitive about our bodies. It is not surprising that teachers are sometimes uncomfortable using creative movement, especially if they're not sure exactly what that means.

Learning Objectives

After studying this chapter, you should be able to:

16-1 Discuss the importance of creative movement activities for young children.

16-2 List the benefits of creative movement activities.

16-3 Discuss guidelines for planning creative movement activities to meet young children's needs.

16-4 Discuss some general ways to adapt creative movement for children with special needs.

naeyc

NAEYC Program Standards

1a Knowing and understanding young children's characteristics and needs.

1c Using developmental knowledge to create healthy, respectful, supportive, and challenging learning environments.

DAP

DAP Criteria

2C Teachers carry out the curriculum through their teaching in ways that are geared to young children in general.

2F Teachers have the skills to adapt curriculum, activities, and materials to ensure full participation of all children.

Rather than focusing on the lack of use of creative movement in many early childhood settings, we can simply acknowledge the ways movement is important in our lives and move on to strategies for using kinesthetic ways of knowing in creative ways, which is the focus of this chapter. Most important is to start with some foundational truths: We all love to move. It feels good to walk, run, wiggle, and shake. We also remember what we *do* more easily than what we are told or what we only read about.

It is the same for young children—they learn by doing. They are immensely active and energetic. Movement activities are natural avenues for this energy. Reaching, jumping, balancing, and hopping are experiences that teach children how to understand and negotiate the world.

Physical movement is the young child's first means of nonverbal communication. Closing his or her eyes, crying, shaking—a nonverbal infant very clearly communicates a need for attention! Physical movements provide one of the most important avenues through which children form impressions about themselves and their environment.

Anyone entering a preschool classroom cannot help but be aware of children's constant activity and movement. In fact, movement is valuable at any age to combat lethargy and spark an interest in our environment. We know children's physical and motor development influences, and is influenced by, all other aspects of development: cognitive, language, social, and emotional. Even so, early childhood teachers too often believe that children's motor skills will develop on their own. Therefore, they do not consciously plan for motor skill development as they do for other areas. This chapter addresses the importance of motor skill development and provides some guidelines for adults working with young children.

Movement activities concern the whole child and not just physical fitness and recreation. Through creative movement activities, a child is able to express his or her creative self in a very natural way.

16-1 The Importance of Creative Movement Activities for Young Children

naeyc DAP To a child, physical movement and exercise are pleasurable and fulfilling activities because the young child is busy acquiring all sorts of large- and small motor skills during the early years of life. The child's main learning strategy is through physical

Casper Holroyd

PHOTO 16-1 Creative movement reflects the mood or inner state of a child.

manipulation of his or her world. Creative movement activities, more than any other type of activity, offer children rich opportunities for the development of their total selves.

Creative movement reflects the mood or inner state of a child (see Photo 16-1). In creative movement, children are free to express their own personalities in their own style. They do not have an example to follow or an adult to imitate. Creative movement can occur in any situation where children feel free and want to move their bodies. It can be done to poetry, music, rhythm, or even silence. By feeling a pulse, beat, idea, or emotion, children's bodies become instruments of expression. They are musical notes running along a keyboard or wheat waving in the wind. They are anything they want to be. Their movement is an expression of that being.

There is usually no planning or forethought on the part of children in creative movement (see Photo 16-2). They forget about themselves and let the music's rhythm or an idea carry their bodies away. There is no pattern of movements to be practiced or perfected. Young children are free to move about in any mood the music or rhythm suggests to them.

PHOTO 16-2 Movement is a natural part of young children's lives.

Did You Get It?

After two months of practice, a group of children performs a choreographed dance for an audience of parents. Why isn't this considered creative movement?

a. The dance is not a personal expression of mood.

b. An audience is observing it.

c. The children are dancing in a group.

d. The dance is accompanied by music.

Take the full quiz on CourseMate.

16-2 Benefits of Creative Movement

naeyc DAP Creative movement is a joyful experience for children. And in this joyful experience, children are benefiting in sensory awareness, social development, body awareness, concentration, and personal development.

16-2a Sensory Awareness

Children perceive the world though their senses. All senses are engaged when children explore different aspects of movement. The kinesthetic sense increases as children literally feel the shapes and actions their bodies are making. Visually, children respond to the images they see as well as the images they create. The auditory sense is stimulated as children respond to sounds (and music) they make or hear. Tactile experiences such as running with bare feet, performing specific floor movements, or swirling a scarf heighten children's awareness of their sense of touch. Such full sensory awareness

experiences lead to a greater understanding of themselves and their surroundings. It strengthens children's imaginative powers and increases their ability to experience life with greater meaning.

16-2b Social Development

Creative movement encourages children to interact with their environment and with each other as they share space and explore movement together. Movement activities encourage children to realize their own uniqueness, as well as recognize and appreciate the uniqueness of others. As children move creatively, they express their personal feelings and preferences (see Photo 16-3). In movement activities, children learn to cooperate within a social structure and appreciate the different responses of other children.

16-2c Body Awareness

Creative movement activities help children gain a better mental picture of their own bodies. Controlling their own bodies is the first type of control children have over themselves. It is the first step toward developing internal control and self-discipline. Body awareness is an essential part of becoming aware of our feelings because they exist in our minds and bodies. When we feel angry or excited, we feel it in our whole self. Body awareness is also important in the development of spatial orientation. Children who do not perceive the space of their own bodies may frequently misjudge distances or bump into things. Movement activities also help with the development of motor

PHOTO 16-3 Creative movement gives children a chance to express their personal feelings.

skills. Creative movement activities focus on body awareness, motor fitness, rhythmic skill, strength, flexibility, coordination, endurance, and physical vitality.

16-2d Concentration

Children grow in self-control as they learn to concentrate and focus. Children must learn what it feels like to concentrate. When children learn what focusing feels like, it can be a frame of reference for other activities where concentration is more difficult to achieve. Concentration is essential for learning in the classroom.

16-2e Personal Development

As children engage in creative movement activities, they are developing such personal traits as respect, self-esteem, and purpose. Experiences in creative movement help children respect the working space of others as they learn about "personal space" and "shared space." Children also learn to recognize, appreciate, and respect differences in the people with whom they come into contact. Children learn and respect the fact that all bodies come in various sizes and shapes. They also learn to respect these differences in their peers.

Self-esteem is the greatest benefit from incorporating creative movement into your curriculum. As children learn more and develop new skills, their self-esteem increases. A child's self-esteem is also enhanced through participation in creative movement activities where her or his contributions are acknowledged and valued.

Creative movement can teach children to become more aware of themselves, sensitive to others, and actively conscious of the world they share. They can find meaning and exhilaration in activities that nourish rather than harm them. Creative movement provides an opportunity for all children, regardless of age, special needs, or developmental stage, to interact with each other, release energy, and have fun.

Other curricular activities can emerge from a creative movement experience. For example, reading time can involve looking at books related to dance and children making connections to their own movement experiences. Creative movement activities can also lead to children expressing emotions from their movement experience in drawings, paintings, and music activities. Children can be encouraged to explore new and creative uses of familiar objects such as dress-up clothes, balls, hoops, or free-flowing fabrics in their creative movement experiences. Creative movement also may encourage children to use familiar objects in new, creative, and imaginative ways that in turn facilitate their abstract thinking of the physical world.

Did You Get It?

The creative movement of swaying like a flower in the wind is most beneficial to
  a. social development.
  b. the development of concentration.
  c. personal development.
  d. the development of sensory awareness.

Take the full quiz on CourseMate.

16-3 Guidelines for Planning Creative Movement Activities to Meet Young Children's Needs

naeyc **DAP** All movement activities best serve young children's needs when they address their current developmental levels. The following guidelines provide a framework to help teachers of young children be more effective in this important aspect of their work. (Appendix A presents a general measure of the average ages at which young children acquire physical skills.)

When planning creative movement activities for children, teachers need to keep in mind the characteristics of each age group (see Photo 16-4). Refer to Chapters 9 through 11 for characteristics of preschool children. Figure 16-1 summarizes the growth and development characteristics of children from kindergarten to grade 5.

PHOTO 16-4 When planning creative movement activities, teachers need to keep in mind the characteristics of each age group.

Casper Holroyd

CHARACTERISTICS	NEEDS	TYPES OF EXPERIENCE
Kindergarten, Grades 1 and 2		
1. Spurt of growth of muscle mass	1. Vigorous exercise requiring use of large muscles	1. Running, chasing, fleeing type games; hanging, climbing, exercises
2. Gross movement skills becoming more refined	2. Exploration and variations of gross motor skills; chance to refine skills	2. Self-testing activities of all types; dance activities, movement tasks
3. Manipulative skills still unrefined but improving; will catch balls with body and arms more so than hands	3. Opportunities to manipulate large or medium-size objects; throw small balls	3. Ball-handling activities; work with beanbags, wands, hoops, progressing from large to smaller objects
4. Imaginative, imitative, curious	4. Opportunities for expression of ideas and use of body	4. Creative dance, story plays, creative stunt and floor work; exploration with all basic skills and small equipment
5. Very active, great deal of energy	5. Ample opportunities for vigorous play	5. Running, games, stunts, large apparatus-like swings, jungle gym, slides
6. Short attention span	6. Activities that take short explanations and can be finished quickly	6. Simple games, simple class organization so activities can be changed quickly
7. Individualistic or egocentric	7. Experiences to learn to share or become interested in others	7. Much small group work, exploration of movement activities
Grades 3 and 4		
1. Gross-motor patterns more refined and graceful	1. Use of skill for specific purposes	1. Introduce specific sport skills; expressive style skill utilized in dance; traditional dance steps
2. Hand–eye coordination improved; growth in manipulative skills	2. Opportunities to handle smaller objects; more importance placed on accuracy; throw at moving targets	2. Ball-handling activities, use of bats, paddles, target games
3. Sees need to practice skills for improvement of skill and to gain social status	3. Guided practice sessions, self-testing problem situations	3. Drills, skill drill games, self-testing practice situations; task setting
4. Increased attention span	4. Activities with continuity; more complex rules and understandings	4. Organized games with more complex rules and strategy
5. More socially mature, interested in welfare of group	5. Make a contribution to large or small group, remain with one group for a longer period of time, help make and accept decisions with a group	5. Team activities, dance compositions with small groups
6. Greater sex differences in skills; some antagonism toward opposite sex (Gr. 4)	6. Ability grouping	6. Combative type stunts, folk dance; after-school activities, clubs

FIGURE 16-1 Summary chart of growth and development characteristics of children from kindergarten to grade 5.   (*Continues*)

CHARACTERISTICS	NEEDS	TYPES OF EXPERIENCE
Grade 5		
1. Coordination highly developed, keen interest in proficiency in skills	1. Need to learn more difficult skills; more coaching on refinement of skills; use of skills in games, routines and compositions	1. Lead-up games to sports in season; instruction and practice in sport skills; more advanced dance step patterns and folk dances; track and field; apparatus routines, intramurals
2. Greater sex differences in skills and interests; most prefer to play and compete with own sex	2. Separation of sexes in classes or within classes for some activities	2. Co-educational dance; swimming, gymnastics, recreational games; sexes separate in team sports and fitness activities; intramurals for each sex
3. Good skills and physique important to social acceptance	3. Instruction and practice sessions in skills, understanding of fitness elements	3. Fitness tests; developmental exercises; work with apparatus
4. Group spirit is high, allegiance to group is strong	4. Need to belong to a group with some stability; make rules, decisions, and abide by group decisions; longer term of membership on a squad or team	4. Team games, tournaments, group dance compositions, sport squads with student leaders, track and field meets
5. Social consciousness of need for rules and abiding by rules; can assume greater responsibility	5. Participate in setting rules, opportunities for squad captains or leaders	5. Student officials; plan and conduct tournaments in class and after school; students plan own strategy, line-ups, etc.
6. Flexibility decreases	6. To maintain flexibility within structural limitations	6. Stunts, tumbling, developmental exercises

FIGURE 16-1 Summary chart of growth and development characteristics of children from kindergarten to grade 5. (*Continued*)

TeachSource Digital Download   Download from CourseMate.

As with any age group, preschoolers need to practice skills in order to learn them. Children of this age need many opportunities for practice. Several different activities should incorporate use of a particular skill, thus allowing for extended overall practice time and preventing children from getting bored. For example, teachers may want to prepare two or three movement activities, or include several variations of an activity.

16-3a Preschool Creative Movement

Movement activities will be more successful when the children understand how to work cooperatively in a given space. Beginning individual movement activities generally start with children working in their own spaces, interacting only occasionally. Even after children are functioning well in the entire space, using it wisely and creatively and showing respect for one another, movement in self-space is always useful for warm-up activities. Warm-up activities are designed to free the children and stimulate their involvement in creative movement activities.

Before the movement activities begin, everyone finds his or her own space. Young children may enjoy using imaginative labels such as "your own igloos, space ships, tepees, nests," usually something that specifically ties in with the rest of the lesson. Getting every part of the body moving is always a good way to begin. Children start by moving just one part and add others as side-coached by the teacher until everything is in motion (fingers, then hands, and so on). This simple activity can be done with different sequencing (beginning with toes, for example), or sitting or lying down rather than standing, or expending different amounts of energy, or changing the tempo.

TeachSource Video

© 2015 Cengage Learning

2–5 Years: Observation

1. Using the basic guidelines for using music to introduce creative movement presented in this chapter, which of these guidelines are evident in this video? Give specific examples in your answer.

2. What specific additional guidelines would you add to enhance the children's creative movement experience?

3. How would you adapt this music/movement activity in the video for use in an early childhood classroom?

Watch on CourseMate.

The use of space is one way in which the teacher helps the children control their behaviors during movement activities. In addition, she will want to develop some kind of signal with which she can get their attention, begin and end activities, and generally serve as a means for instant communication with the children. Some teachers use the light switch for such control, flicking it on and off to get total group attention. One advantage of the light control is that it is quiet and does not break into creative movements as much as some other kinds of signals. A disadvantage is that it eliminates the use of the room light for purposes other than drama—sensory effect and heightens certain dramatic situations.

Holding up an arm or showing a "quiet" sign of some kind is also unobtrusive but may not work when children are very deeply involved in their activity. A simple and easy-to-remember signal with a rhythm instrument works well for most teachers and children. A couple of beats on a drum or a few shakes of a tambourine gets attention.

16-3b Creative Movement in the Elementary Classroom

Most elementary teachers find it harder than kindergarten and preschool teachers to incorporate creative movement activities into their curriculum. The use of movement in the elementary classroom can be challenging. By their very nature, creative movements are unstructured. Too often, this type of activity can become chaotic and uncontrollable. The following suggestions may help you manage creative movement activities in the elementary classroom.

Define expectations. Let students know that you expect them to work and behave with the discipline of a dancer. Movement time is a time to focus and work with the body. Be clear that you expect the students to use and remember the "space bubble," that is, one's personal space.

Prepare the room. Because a gym or large space may not be available, the movement activity may have to take place in the regular classroom. Establish a routine for preparing the space. For example, put all the desks to the sides of the room and back in place at the end of the activity. Have the children rehearse and memorize the procedure. Although this may take some extra effort, this is time well spent in the smooth beginnings and endings of movement activities.

Cues. The more auditory and visual cues you can provide for students, the better. Try to use a variety of visual cues and sounds. For example, you can use handclaps, a tambourine, a drum, an electronic keyboard, or any other number of percussive instruments. The command "Freeze!" is very effective in stopping a student immediately.

Spatial arrangements. Use different patterns in class. Have students arrange themselves in various patterns such as lines, circles, dispersed patterns, groups, sitting, or standing.

Working with partners. Either pick partners for students or let them choose their own. Younger children may have more difficulty picking their own partners. Tell students that they are expected to work productively with their partners. If students are not working well together, change their partners. Review all of the rules of an activity before the students start working with their partners.

Time limits. To help keep students on task, set time limits. It is especially important to give time limits when students are working with partners or in a group.

Commenting on students' work. When you speak about a student's work, use movement vocabulary. For example, "I see Mario in a low twisted shape" or "I see Clancy in a high curved shape that reminds me of the wind." Be generous with praise and use thoughtful corrections.

Remember that creative movement is a language and a physical skill that requires practice. Be patient. With time and instruction, students will become adept at using movement to communicate ideas and concepts (Griffiths, 2009).

16-3c Outdoor Creative Movement Activities

More and more, early childhood professionals recognize the potential of the outdoors as a classroom extension and time outdoors as an opportunity to promote children's development. They maintain that outdoor space should be used not only for the enhancement of physical skills but also for the development of children's social, emotional, creative, and cognitive abilities (Isenberg & Jalongo, 2000; Essa, 2010; Gordon & Browne, 2010).

The teacher's role in supporting outdoor play is *play leader*—someone who interacts with children by asking leading questions and providing guidance for certain skills, such as cooperating and taking turns. The play leader's role is critical because static playgrounds, with traditional swings and slides and their typical uses, do not always stimulate children's physical, cognitive, or creative development.

Play equipment associated with activities performed in one prescribed way limits children's natural, imaginative play. A child is unlikely to look at the jungle gym and decide to pretend to be clothes hanging on the line to dry; but a play leader can suggest such a creative movement activity. The children benefit from adult assistance in discovering more creative movement possibilities.

If a teacher brings a portable CD or MP3 player outdoors, the children can play Statues, creatively moving on the equipment until the music is paused and then "freezing" until the music begins again. Look for unusual ways children can use the playground space and static playground equipment. Use the open areas of the playground for large group creative movement activities that are inconvenient or impossible to do indoors. Suggest games such as Follow the Leader, which is more challenging, fun, and appealing when there is a lot of space to explore and obstacles such as trees and jungle gyms that have an impact on the course taken. If the playground has a low balance beam (four inches off the ground), suggest creative ways the children can travel on it—tightrope walkers, gymnasts, butterflies, inchworms, cats stalking their prey, or elephants. Have the children think up their own creative movements as well.

Adults who enrich children's outdoor experiences offer new opportunities for children to express themselves creatively, stretch their imaginations, and be continuously challenged. Teachers who interact with children on the playground can make the outdoors an extension of the indoors and encourage creative movement learning in both environments (Pica, 2011).

16-3d Transitions and Creative Movement Activities

Using creative movements during transitions is an excellent group management technique. Whenever young children move from activity to activity in transitional times, they often lose their focus and may even get a bit confused and disruptive. The following strategies may help children move more easily from one activity to another.

- Have children pretend they and their classmates are cars in a train, with you as the engine. Assign one child to be the caboose—to turn off the lights and close the door.
- Turn your jump rope into a dragon, worm, caterpillar, or other animal by attaching a head at one end of the rope and a tail at the other end. Have children make the body and legs by holding onto the rope with one hand and walking down the hall and out to the playground.
- Have children imagine they are tired puppies, yawning, stretching, and rolling on the floor. Direct them to lie very still. (Suggested for the beginning of rest time.)
- Construct a "feel" box or bag or a "look" box or bag. Place an item in the bag or box that will suggest the next activity or topic for each child to feel or look at.
- To help children quiet down between activities, clap a rhythm for them to copy. Start by clapping loudly, and then gradually clap more softly until your hands are resting in your lap.
- Have children pretend to be a bowl of gelatin and shake all over.
- Have children pretend to lock their lips and put the key in a pocket.
- Show children how to put on "magic" ears for listening.

- Have children pretend to walk on tiptoe in boots, Indian moccasins, or elf shoes.
- Have children do two things at once. Examples: tap heads and rub stomachs, clap hands and stand on one foot, snap their fingers and nod heads, and so on.
- Have children march in place as they count by 2, 5, or 10, recite the ABCs, say the multiplication tables, and so on.
- When children transition to their chairs, have them pretend to swim like a fish, prance like a horse, hop like bunny, move like a turtle, walk like an elephant, and the like.
- With older children, have children choose a partner. Have one student slowly print a current spelling word on his or her partner's back. The partner guesses which word was printed. Have them take turns doing this.

16-3e Guidelines for Using Music and Poetry to Stimulate Creative Movement Activities

Let us now consider how music and poetry can encourage children's creative movement in the classroom.

Music. Listening to music is a natural way to introduce creative movement (see Photo 16-5). Distinctive types of music or rhythm should be chosen for initial

PHOTO 16-5 Listening to music is a natural way to introduce creative movement.

© Cengage Learning

movement experiences. Many resources are available that can give teachers ideas on this topic.

In order to provide the music or rhythm for creative movement, only a few items may be necessary. A tape or CD player with some tapes or CDs, mp3 players and electronic music files on computers, sticks, and bells may be more than enough.

Some basic guidelines for using music for creative movement follow.

- Make it clear that anything the children want to do is all right, as long as it does not harm themselves or others.
- Ensure that children understand that they do not have to do anything anyone else does. They can do anything the music or an idea "tells" them to do.
- Allow a child to "copy" someone for a start, if the child wants to.
- Encourage children to respect each other as different and able to move in different ways.
- Encourage children to experience freedom of movement, the relationship of movement to space, and the relationship of movement to others.
- Show children how to move in their personal space. This space can be explained by having the children think of an imaginary circle or bubble around themselves.

The teacher may begin the experience by playing a CD or tape. Music that has a strong and easily recognized beat or rhythm is best. Children should not be told what to listen for. Let them listen first and then ask them to think about what the music is "telling" them.

While children are listening, the teacher may turn the music down a bit lower. The teacher might talk with each child about what the music is saying. Some children may already be moving to the music by this time, and the teacher may join in. Children may go anywhere in the room and do anything that the music "tells" them to do. For this exercise, clapping, stomping, and even shouting are all possible and helpful. When appropriate, a quieter piece of music may be played to allow children to rest and to give them a sense of contrast.

As children become involved in movement explorations, try to redirect, challenge, and stimulate their discoveries by suggestions such as, "Do what you are doing now in a slower way," "Try moving in a different direction or at a different level," or "Try the same thing you were doing but make it smoother or lighter."

Some creative movement activities with music can also be done with a partner. Some possibilities follow.

- Have children face a partner and do a "mirror dance" with their hands and arms. Challenge partners to do a mirror dance with their feet and legs and then with different facial expressions.
- Have children hold hands with a partner and skip, slide, leap, and gallop until they hear a signal. Then they should find a new partner and continue to move to the music.
- Direct children to move the same way their partner moves until they hear the signal, and then move in a different way.
- Pair children with partners. Ask: "What interesting body shapes can you and your partner make together? Can the two of you create an interesting design in the space you share? Practice until you and your partner can make three different designs to music."

This general approach can be adapted to movement with dolls and puppets; movement of specific parts of the body, such as hands, feet, or toes; and movement in different kinds of space or groups. The imaginations of the children and the teacher are the only limits.

Older children may begin to be a bit self-conscious and need other suggestions to encourage their creative movements. They often enjoy working in small groups for this reason. A small-group activity involving mirror movements, copying, and shadowing is appropriate for older children. For example, working together in groups of three or more, children perform movements matching the leader of the group. The leader leads the group in a sequence of movements that the rest of the group copies as closely as possible. A second member takes over as leader, moving in a different sequence. Then, the third member leads the group in yet another sequence of movements. In this type of activity, the group's size helps students overcome the fear of the "whole class looking at me." It is also easier for children of this age to participate in a group when they know everyone else will be participating along with them in the activity. See the end of this chapter for more creative movement activities for older children.

Poetry and prose. For creative movement, poetry has rhythm as well as the power of language. It is not necessary to use rhyming verses at all times. In the beginning, poems that rhyme may help to start a feeling of pulse and rhythm. Poems should be chosen that fit the young child's level of appreciation. By adult standards, they may be quite simple. They are often short, vivid, lively descriptions of animals or motion, but children should not be limited to these, as there are many books and collections available with a wider variety. The local library is the best resource for this. The American Library Association website is another good source for poetry books.

A suggested beginning may be to ask children to listen to a poem. After they have heard it, they may pick out their favorite characters in it. Discuss who these characters are and what they do. Read the poem a second time; suggest that children act out their characters as they listen to the poem. Anything goes—children may hop like bunnies, fly like planes, or do whatever they feel. (More suggestions are at the end of this chapter.) Encourage each child to move in his or her own way, and encourage as many variations as you see! As readings continue, more complex poems may be selected, containing a series of movements or simple plots. The same general idea can also be carried through with prose.

As children become more comfortable in acting out poetry read aloud, they may become more sensitive to the less obvious actions or emotions described by the poetry. When stories or poems that have several characters and more complex interaction are read, the entire selection should first be read for listening only. Then it can be discussed to get some idea of children's understanding and appreciation. If the children are interested, several readings may be necessary.

Older children are able to sustain their interest for a longer period of time and enjoy the procedure of listening, picking out roles, and acting out what is read. They may also enjoy adding costumes and props to their creative movements.

16-3f Art and Creative Movement

Much of art is movement. Drawing, painting, and working with three-dimensional materials all involve movement. Lines and shapes are everywhere in art.

Creative movements can be planned so that they connect visual art with movement. The following are some suggestions to get you started.

Dance and art. Children can dance a painting or paint the dances they create. The kinesthetic pleasure of dance can motivate children to want to move, and this need to express themselves can extend to scribbles, drawing, painting, and modeling.

An example of how to help children connect dance with art is to show artwork with physical motion in it.

Effects of Exercise on Brain Health and Cognition across the Lifespan

A group of researchers at the University of Illinois at Urbana-Champaign reviewed findings from 111 recent research studies on the effects of exercise and strength training on the brains of humans ranging in age from young children to elderly adults in nonpathological populations. They focused on the relationship between physical activity and cognition and brain health.

Their review suggests that aerobic exercise is important for getting a head start during childhood on cognition abilities that are important throughout life. For example, physical inactivity is associated with poorer academic performance on standard neuropsychological tests, while exercise programs appear to improve memory, attention, and decision making (Voss et al., 2011). These effects extend to young adults and elderly adults, with solid evidence for aerobic training benefitting executive functions, including multitasking, planning, and increasing the volume of brain structures important for memory.

Exercise appears to change brain structure, prompting the growth of new nerve cells and blood vessels. It also increases the production of neurochemicals, such as BDNF and IGF-1, which promote growth, differentiation, survival, and repair of brain cells (Colcombe et al., 2006).

Research indicates that childhood physical inactivity, and subsequent reduced aerobic fitness, is associated with poorer academic achievement (Castelli, Buck, & Erwin, 2007; Chomitz et al., 2009) and lower performance on standard neuropsychological tests (Buck, Hillman, & Castelli, 2008; Sibley & Etnier, 2003). The majority of scientific literature supports a general benefit of aerobic fitness on childhood cognitive performance (Voss et al., 2011). One study found that 3 months of aerobic exercise training improved executive function abilities in 7- to 11-year-old overweight children (DHHS, 2008).

In summary, the researchers found that cross-sectional and longitudinal studies support a positive association between aerobic fitness and enhanced performance in both the classroom and laboratory (Sibley & Etnier, 2003; Troiano et al., 2008). Furthermore, neuroimaging evidence supports a beneficial association between childhood aerobic fitness and improved brain function and structure. Thus, while all exercise might not provide the "easy fix" to enhance brain and cognition across the lifespan, ample evidence supports exercise as one of the most effective means available to improve mental and physical health (Voss et al., 2011).

(Degas's dancers are a natural choice.) Discuss how motion is shown in the work and why a particular step is "frozen" by the artist in the painting. Then let the children do the painting as a dance with movements and dance the painting as they think it would look before and after the artist "froze" the motions.

Creative movement and sound collages. Sounds of the body, city, nature, animals, machines, and children's names can all suggest movement. Brainstorm a category with students, and then stretch it for movement possibilities. Encourage children to think of the shape, size, rhythm, energy, and vocal quality of the words. Break into small groups and ask each group to make a collage of sounds and movements. Groups can then plan a freeze-move-freeze dance and perform it. This activity could be followed by a visual art collage around the same topics danced.

Dance a painting (older students). Display a print and ask students to brainstorm all the shapes, movements, and emotions they can see in it. Direct attention to the foreground, middle ground, and background of the painting in subjects such as landscapes, seascapes, and still life. Divide children into small groups. Have each group decide a way to dance the painting, using a beginning-middle-end structure. The goal is not to merely pantomime but to think divergently: What movements came before this moment in the art? During this moment? After this moment? What is just outside the subject matter (for example, other people, movements)? After students prepare, they can take turns presenting. Background or mood music can be added.

Magic wand. Display an art print featuring a scene from history with several figures in it. Have children assume the figures' positions. Tell them that when you touch them with a magic wand, they should move in ways the figure might move. Remind children about bending and walking, using curved and straight lines, and positive and negative space. You can also add emotions: "Move as if you are in a hurry."

Artists that move. Set up a station with art books or assign students to locate art that includes movement (for example, paintings by Matisse and Degas). Discuss how artists show movements through line, shape of body, and use of space.

Sculpture or architecture dances. Display pieces of sculpture or pictures of buildings or furniture. Ask about space, curves, and movements and how each sculpture might move if it came to life. Ask students to show the size, energy, and flow of these pieces with their bodies.

Did You Get It?

The developmentally appropriate purpose of a fourth-grade teacher who has her students move all the desks and chairs to the back of the classroom before starting creative movement activities is to
   a. give the students a physical warm-up.
   b. prevent the activity from turning into chaos.
   c. comply with Board of Education requirements.
   d. mark the beginning of the activity.

Take the full quiz on CourseMate.

16-4 Adapting Creative Movement Activities for Children with Special Needs

naeyc **DAP** When involving children with special needs in movement activities, adapt the prompts and challenges to reflect their social, cognitive, and physical abilities. For example, if a child uses a wheelchair, be certain the space allows for free movement. Include prompts for the parts of the body the child can move. Even if a child is not verbally expressive, it's important to include him in the discussion by making eye contact and affirming his accomplishments.

Creative movement activities can benefit children with special needs because they can participate at their own level of ability. For example, children who are physically challenged can move parts of their body to music or keep a beat by blinking their eyes. Props such as feathers, instruments, or scarves do not have to be held with the hands but can be placed or

attached to an appropriate area of the child's body or equipment. All children with special needs can feel a sense of belonging to a group and a sense of joy at being able to learn on a fundamental movement level. The necessary modifications are often simple; it is basically a matter of focusing on what the children can do as opposed to what they cannot. Large-motor activities are important for children with special needs because they help children gain in strength, endurance, and coordination. This section uses the term *gross-motor movements* in place of creative movements.

During gross movement experiences, it is important not to do too much for children with special needs. They need the chance to figure out how to get their bodies to do what they want them to do, to problem solve, and to make choices. Whenever possible, gross-motor movement should take place outside or in a large indoor area where there is ample space and children can move freely.

16-4a General Suggestions

- Follow large-muscle activities with quiet activities to help children to calm and focus on other learning experiences.
- Be animated and energetic during movement activities. Children will be more motivated and focused.
- Integrate gross-motor activities into the daily schedule as part of the curriculum, during transitions, and at cleanup time (See Photo 16-6).
- Modify your expectations for how long a child can do a gross-motor activity. If the child has muscle weakness or attention problems, she might lack the endurance to sustain activity. Children with special needs do not need to participate in gross-motor activities in the same way or as long as typically developing children. Partial participation is a valid form of involvement for some children (Petersen, 2008). Build strength and endurance from the child's current level of skill.
- Encourage parents to send children to school in sneakers so that they can participate fully in gross-motor activities.

16-4b Developmental Delays

Many children with special needs have low muscle tone and poor strength. Because of this, movement is difficult, so the child often doesn't move. This results in increased muscle weakness. It is important that the child is encouraged to have an active lifestyle in

THINK ABOUT IT

Day-Care Centers and Children's Physical Activity

Three-quarters of U.S. preschool children are in child care, and many are not achieving the required levels of physical activity. Daily physical activity is essential for motor and socioemotional development as well as the prevention of obesity. Little is known about the barriers to physical activity in child care.

This research study's objective was to identify potential barriers to children's physical activity in child-care centers. The research group consisted of 9 focus groups with 49 child-care providers (55% African American) from 34 centers (inner-city, suburban, Head Start, Montessori) in Cincinnati, Ohio. Three coders independently analyzed verbatim transcripts for themes.

The results of this study identified three main barriers to children's physical activity in child care: (1) injury concerns; (2) financial; and (3) a focus on "academics." Stricter licensing codes intended to reduce children's injuries on playgrounds caused playgrounds to be less physically challenging and interesting. In addition, some parents were concerned about potential injuries, which required staff to restrict playground play for their children.

Small operating margins of most child-care centers limited their ability to install abundant playground equipment. Child-care operators felt pressure from state mandates and parents to focus on academics at the expense of gross-motor play. Because children spend long hours in care and many lack a safe place to play near their homes, these barriers may limit the children's only opportunity to engage in physical activity.

The researchers concluded that societal priorities for young children—safety and school readiness—may be hindering children's physical development. In designing environments that optimally promote children's health and development, child advocates should think holistically about potential unintended consequences of policies (Copeland et al., 2012).

school and at home. The suggestions that follow are especially helpful to the teacher of young children.

- Use exercise videos or tapes with a child who is developmentally delayed. In these videos, the same movement and exercises are repeated, which gives the child an opportunity to practice and enables him to feel confident in his ability to keep up with the class.
- Encourage the child to participate in gross-motor activities for gradually longer periods.
- Always demonstrate the activity first.
- Allow children to watch a role model engage in the activity before attempting it themselves.
- Familiarize yourself with gross-motor developmental sequences. If the child's gross-motor skills are at the 2- or 3-year level, she may be reluctant or unable to participate in gross-motor activities that have been designed for typically developing 4-year-old children.

16-4c Physical Impairments

Space in the room may be a problem if you have a child in the group who is physically impaired. The

PHOTO 16-6 Integrate gross-motor activities into the daily schedule.

child might bring lots of equipment to school, such as a prone stander, a chair of some sort, and a wheelchair. Some children might have walkers or crutches. This child will also need space to maneuver between furniture. Keep the following recommendations in mind.

- During movement activities in the classroom, it is fine to assist the child, but slow movements are best. Quick movements might increase muscle tightness.
- Avoid always giving the child physical assistance to move, and encourage the child to do what he or she can to move independently.
- The child with physical impairments who is walking may be able to do whatever the other children are doing but for a shorter time or shorter distance.
- Occasionally, the child with physical disabilities can play the role of "time keeper" or "music director" by turning the music on and off during a musical activity, but this should not be the child's only role. It is important that the child also be part of the movement activity.

16-4d Attention Deficit/Hyperactivity Disorder and Behavioral Issues

Movement activities can be calming for children with hyperactivity and behavioral difficulties, but they can sometimes be overstimulating and disorganizing. Large-motor activities need to be structured with clear rules and expectations. Observe if the child is becoming overstimulated and redirect the child to an activity where he or she can become calm and regroup (Kaufmann & Ellis, 2007). You will find the following practices helpful as you deal with children with behavioral issues.

- Teach children how to manage their behavior in gross-motor activities. Children need to be taught that there is no pushing, that indoor voices should be used, and that equipment must be shared on occasion. Instruction in these skills will have to be given frequently until the child has mastered them and can remember them even in the excitement of the activity.
- Notice and give praise when the child is following the rules during gross-motor play (Kaufmann & Ellis, 2007).
- Some children who have AD/HD are highly sensitive to being touched and may perceive an innocent bump from another child as being a push. To avoid this, make sure that each child has enough space in movement activities. Define

the child's personal space during movement activities with hula hoops or rug squares.
- Make sure to maintain eye contact when giving instructions.
- Structure gross-motor activities to eliminate waiting.
- Keep activities short. A child may be able to participate for a few moments and then need to move on to some other kind of activity.
- If you aren't offering a choice, give clear directions rather than posing a question. Don't say, "Do you want to walk on the balance beam?" if you mean, "Walk on the balance beam" (Warren & Coaten, 2008).

16-4e Visual Impairments

Studies have shown that children with visual impairments tend to have poor levels of physical fitness (Petersen, 2008). These children will need lots of encouragement to move independently. When giving directions to the child who is visually impaired, be very clear and avoid vague words such as *this*, *that*, and *over there* (Warren & Coaten, 2008). Be careful not to encourage anxieties by being overprotective of the child with visual impairments. Describe the movement experience or play equipment before involving the child. Let the child explore the equipment with his or her hands before attempting to use it.

When giving directions to the child with visual impairments, use the child's name to get the child's attention and give him or her additional time to process directions and respond (Warren & Coaten, 2008). Tell the child what will be happening next, especially before physically assisting him or her through a movement experience. Instead of just naming objects, describe them for the child (Kaufmann & Ellis, 2007).

Did You Get It?

During a creative dance activity in a preschool classroom, a wheelchair-bound student watches and moves his upper body along with the rhythm of the music. For meeting the needs of physically challenged students, this activity

a. is a failure because it precludes the child's involvement.

b. is appropriate for this student.

c. meets the needs of most special needs children, but does not meet the needs of this student.

d. is developmentally inappropriate for the student.

Take the full quiz on CourseMate.

Summary

16-1 Discuss the importance of creative movement activities for young children.

Young children learn by doing, and movement activities are a natural avenue for children's learning. Movement activities contribute to the total development—physical, mental, social, and emotional—of young children. Movement activity is as vital for children as art and other subjects because in movement activities, young children acquire skills, knowledge, and attitudes that help them discover and understand their bodies and their physical abilities and limitations.

16-2 List the benefits of creative movement activities.

Creative movement reflects the mood or inner state of an individual. Creative movement is a joyful experience for children. The benefits are sensory awareness, social development, body awareness, concentration, and personal development.

16-3 Discuss guidelines for planning creative movement activities to meet young children's needs.

In planning creative movement activities for young children, the developmental level of each child is the starting point.

The information provided in developmental skill charts (such as Appendix A) for young children can be used to get some idea of what to expect of children physically at different ages. The most important thing to remember is that the individual child is the measure, not any chart of developmental skills.

16-4 Discuss some general ways to adapt creative movement for children with special needs.

Some general suggestions include the following:

- Follow large-muscle activities with quiet activities to help children calm and focus on other learning experiences.
- Be animated and energetic during movement activities.
- Integrate gross-motor activities into the daily schedule as part of the curriculum, during transition, and at cleanup time.
- Modify your expectations as needed for how long a child can do a gross-motor activity.

Key Terms

creative movement   360
creative movement activities   360

Learning Activities

A. Observe a group of children involved in movement activities of any kind. Record evidence of each of the following situations.
   1. A child discovers a new way to move.
   2. A child uses small and/or large muscles in the activity.
   3. A child discovers what other children are like as a result of the activity.

B. At the end of a long lesson (with children or your own classmates), try this movement activity to help you understand the importance of movement activity at all ages.

   Toss around a small, soft ball for a few minutes, using these rules: You must be sitting in your seat, you cannot "whip" the ball at someone, and you may not throw it to someone who chooses not to play. The object is to see how many times you can catch the ball consecutively. This requires cooperation and encouragement. Everyone is given the chance to play, even if they aren't the world's best catchers. Encouraging one another leads to a higher count. See how high you can go with this one!

   In the classroom, you can change the rule to correspond to your current lessons. For example, every student who catches the ball must name an adverb in language arts class, solve a problem in math, explain a date in history, or define a term in science. The purpose of movement is

to wake up and revitalize students for their next learning experience.

C. Think about an everyday movement (for example, washing the dishes or combing your hair). Take a minute and explore it. Go beyond "pretending" to do dishes or whatever movement you choose. Instead, explore the movement potential itself, by moving using different body parts than would normally be used. Try doing the movement fast, and then very slowly. Feel the essence of the movement.

D. Transformations. Brainstorm with your fellow students the word *transformation,* its definition and implications. Think of types of transformation. Things that go through a *fast* state of transformation (for example, cells, atoms, and so on), a *slow* state of transformation (for example, human beings, plants, and so on), and a *very slow* state of transformation (for example, rocks, creation of the mountains, a sea becoming a desert).

Create body movements using the following transformation concepts as a warm-up:

- A huge rock shrinking smaller and smaller through erosion
- An egg hatching into a baby bird, and then developing into an adult flying bird

- A tiny seed growing into a tall sunflower
- A cell dividing into two cells, demonstrating cellular division (using two students)

Try adding sound and/or music for extra effect and to enhance the mood. What kinds of sounds would be fitting to show erosion of a rock as opposed to a lively bird hatching segment?

After experiencing this activity with your fellow students, how would you adapt this activity to use with young children?

Activities for Children

Suggested Creative Movement Interpretations

Movement explorations and creative movement experiences can be used to interpret nearly every experience, creature, or phenomenon. Have children act out one of the following movement interpretations. (This list can be expanded with endless possibilities.) Join in the fun!

1. Life cycle of butterfly
   a. Caterpillar crawling
   b. Caterpillar eating grass
   c. Caterpillar hanging very still from branch or twig
   d. Chrysalis hanging very still
   e. Butterfly emerging from chrysalis
   f. Butterfly drying its wings
   g. Butterfly flying
2. Piece of cellophane, lightweight plastic, or plastic wrap
   a. The teacher holds the item in his or her hands without children seeing it. Children are encouraged to guess what the item might be, interpreting their guesses through movement.
   b. The teacher opens his or her hands, the children watch the plastic move, and then interpret what they see through movement.
   c. The piece of plastic is used for movement exploration.
3. Shaving cream
   a. Spurting from aerosol can
   b. Foaming up
   c. Spreading on face
   d. Being used for shaving
4. Airplane sequence
   a. Starting motor
   b. Taking off
   c. Flying
   d. Arriving
   e. Landing safely
5. Popcorn
   a. Butter melting
   b. Popping
   c. Everyone ending in a ball shape on the floor, all "popped"
6. Water
   a. Dripping
   b. Flooding
   c. Flowing in a fountain
   d. Freezing
   e. Melting
   f. Spilling
   g. Spurting from a sprinkler
7. Laundry
   a. Inside washing machine
   b. Inside dryer
   c. Being pinned to clothesline
   d. Drying in a breeze
8. Fishing
   a. Casting out
   b. Reeling in
   c. Pretending to be a fish
   d. Fly fishing
   e. Pretending to be a hooked line
   f. Frying and eating fish

Shape and Movement Game

Cut out various shapes from construction paper. Have children scatter around the room. When you hold up a triangle, they can only move their heads. When you hold up a circle, they move only legs. For a square, they move only shoulders. For a rectangle, they move only hips. For an oval, they move their entire bodies. Change shapes rapidly. Encourage children to be creative in their movements. Playing music during this activity makes it even more fun.

Show Me Movements

Children should be scattered around the room with adequate space between them. Call out challenges like the following.

1. Show me how small (tall, wide, tall, thin, and so on) you can be.
2. Point to the farthest wall; touch it and return to your own place.
3. Point to the nearest wall; touch it and return to your own place.
4. Standing in your own place, make your feet move fast.
5. Make them move slowly.
6. Show me how slowly you can walk.
7. Show me how fast you can walk.
8. Be a tree (wall, ball, river, and so on).

Guide children toward looking at objects in the room and noticing where they are located. Have children close their eyes and point to objects in the room that you call out (for example, the door, chalkboard, window, wastebasket, floor, ceiling, playhouse area, wagons, or teacher's desk).

Shadow Movement Activities

On a sunny day, go outside for a "shadow hunt." Encourage children to look for shadows made by your school building, playground equipment, bushes, and their own bodies. Talk about how large shadows, such as those from trees, make the cool, shady areas people enjoy on hot days.

Inside, play a shadow game. Start by playing a cassette, MP3 music file, or CD. As the music plays, have children dance or move in any way they choose, trying to avoid stepping on one another's shadows or letting shadows "step on" them.

Encourage children to watch the patterns their shadows make as they move. After a short time, stop the music and say, "Freeze!" Children then stop moving and hold their positions until the music starts again. After you do this a few times, have a child operate the player. Let children take turns being in charge of the music.

For younger children, place a ball on the pavement of your outdoor play space on a sunny day. Invite children to take turns jumping on and off the shadow of the ball.

After older children try their own creative movements, have them move in specific ways as they try to avoid one another's shadows. For example, ask children to move like mice approaching a piece of cheese, like monkeys jumping from tree to tree, or like lively kittens running after a ball of yarn.

Variation: Change the game to number freeze. Call out a set of numbers. Tell children that they need to freeze when they hear the number seven. Continue the game by encouraging children to freeze as you call out other specified numbers.

Running Movements

Before starting this activity, go outdoors and make a mental note of landmarks such as trees, the end of a sidewalk, a large bush—anything that can serve as a marker for a running path. Make sure that there are no sharp edges or items children might run into.

Take your group outside and gather them together a short distance from one of the markers you spotted earlier. Explain that you are going to make a running path together. Say, "Let's mark our path with these streamers. Come help me tie these markers on."

Together, walk around and tie a different color streamer onto each of the markers you've chosen. Then step back and say, "Hey! Let's all run over to that tree with the blue streamer. Come on and run with me!"

Let your enthusiasm and delight fill the mood of the activity as you encourage children to participate. Catch your breath and call out, "Come on, let's run to the yellow streamer!"

Later, hand out streamers for children to carry as they run. Partners can share ends, and you can call out various ways to move—like a duck, like a robin, like a bear—as they run around the play space.

The fun in this activity is laughing and being silly together. In no way is this a race or a contest to see who can go the farthest or fastest.

Line Challenges

Use a tape or chalk to make a line on the floor and encourage children to see how many things they can do: jump over the line, walk on the line, hop along the line, stand on the end of the line, stretch out on the line, slide on the line, tiptoe across the line, roll over the line, lie beside the line, run around the line, or skip round and round the line. Then have children make up their own challenges.

Jet Planes

Encourage children to use creative movements in becoming a jet plane. Pretend you are a jet plane. Use your body to show the jet: on the ground, in the air, climbing up into the clouds, nose diving, coming in for a landing, and on the ground again. Take off again. This time, your jet is a stunt plane. It can write in the sky. It can make loops and turn upside down. Now make a number 2. Make a 3. Now make a 5. Can you make an S? How about a P? Make the shape of a funny animal. How about a wiggly worm?

Classical Music and Movement

Selected sections of the music of Saint-Saëns' *Carnival of the Animals* are excellent for encouraging the acting out of various animal movements. These movements can include crawling, walking on all fours, jumping, and flying. Tell children the title of the music and play it for them to enjoy. Encourage them to move their bodies the way they think the animal in the music would be moving.

Another piece of music that is good for creative movements is Tchaikovsky's "Dance of the Little Swans" from *Swan Lake*. It's a natural for some fun tip-toeing!

For marching experiences, use Herbert's "March of the Toys" from *Babes in Toyland* or Grieg's "Norwegian Rustic March" from *Lyric Suite*.

For running movements, try Bizet's "The Ball" from *Children's Games*. Bizet's *Children's Games* also has a section titled "Leap Frog," which is great for creative jumping movements. In the same composition, Bizet's "Cradle Song" encourages swaying and rocking movements. "The Swan" by Saint-Saëns from *Carnival of the Animals* is also good for swaying and rocking movements.

Prokofiev's "Waltz on Ice" from *Children's Suite,* Tchaikovsky's "Waltz" from *The Sleeping Beauty,* and Khachaturian's "Waltz" from *Masquerade Suite* are all excellent pieces of music for waltzing and smooth gliding creative movements.

Rope Skills

Lay out various lengths of rope in a straight line on the floor as if they were tightropes. Challenge children to try some of these skills. Can you do this while moving backward? Walk the "tightrope" with eyes shut. Jump from side to side across the rope without touching the rope. Hop from side to side without touching the rope. Lay your rope in the pattern of a circle. Get inside the circle, taking up as much space as possible, without hanging over the edges. Make up a design on your own. See if you can walk it. Can your friend? Can you walk your friend's design?

Unwinding

Children pretend they are windup toys, such as dolls, dogs, monkeys, rabbits, or clowns. The teacher winds up the toys and the children begin moving at a brisk pace, getting slower and slower until they are completely "run down" and stop or collapse to the floor. The teacher or a child rewinds the toys and the sequence is repeated.

Collapsing

The teacher explains that "collapsing" means relaxing a body part or the whole body, allowing gravity to pull it down to earth. Children stand and stretch tall, and then slowly collapse (relax) one part at a time—first the fingertips, then the wrists, elbows, arms, head, and shoulders, and so on—until they are left collapsed on the floor.

Imagination and Creative Movement

Combine full-body stretching and children's creativity in these fun movement activities.

- Invite children to imagine that their foot is a paintbrush and that they need to cover the ground with a beautiful painting.
- Suggest they pretend to be zookeepers giving a giraffe a bath. Make sure they reach all the way up to wash behind his ears!
- Ask them to make believe that they are leaves on a tree. Suggest that the leaves break away from the tree and float down to the ground.
- Invite children to use their bodies to make shapes. Can they make a square? A circle? A triangle?

Creative Movement Games

Suggest a game of "Jack-in-the-box" to children. Say, "Wind yourself down and shut the door—then pop up on the count of four. Make your own music while winding yourself down." Continue the movement experience by asking children to stretch slowly like a rubber band and then snap back quickly. Say, "Quickly twist yourself into a knot; then slowly stretch your elbow to the ceiling and untie the knot."

Creative Movement—Machines

Collect pictures of machines that children are familiar with such as a computer, hand mixer, hair dryer, blender, and so on. Choose one of the pictures and ask the children to think about how this machine moves. Invite the children to move their bodies and create the sounds of that particular machine. Show a picture of another machine, and invite children to create movements and sounds for that machine.

Musical variation: Use rhythm sticks or a drum and play slow rhythmic beats. Invite one child to be in charge of the pictures. Explain to the children that when their classmate holds up a picture they will move like that particular machine. Children not comfortable with moving can play instruments or take turns holding up the pictures.

Magnet Movements

Pretend to have a large magnet. Ask children to imagine that this magnet can pull them toward it or push them away. Say, "The magnet is pulling you to the ceiling, higher, higher, higher. Never take your eyes away from the magnet. Now the magnet is pulling you quickly to the floor. Watch to see what the magnet does next and act it out." This movement activity is most successful when the teacher acts out the effects of the magnet along with the children.

Poison Ivy Movement Activity

Discuss what poison ivy is. Ask children if any of them have had a rash from poison ivy. Talk about how it feels. This discussion leads naturally to this activity.

Designate a small area in which children can move freely. Have them move around in this space without touching anyone with any part of their bodies. If they do touch someone, they will get "poison ivy" and must move to the side and swing their arms up and down, side to side, or hop on one leg as it "heals." Call out instructions for the children to change direction, pace, and type of movement.

Falling Rain Dance

For this activity, you will need long pieces of materials, such as colorful scarves, and recorded instrumental music.

Play instrumental music that changes tempo often, fast to slow and back again. Tell children they're going to pretend to be raindrops falling to the ground. Dance together, moving your bodies to the music—move slowly when the music is slow, faster as the tempo picks up. When the music stops, all dancers fall down into puddles.

Next, give children scarves. Encourage them to have fun holding the scarves and moving to the music. Try tying the scarves to children's clothing or wrists. Then continue your rain dance with added drama.

Remember to dance with the children and share your enthusiasm. Choose a variety of types of music. Don't tell children how to move, just set a mood and allow them to move as they feel like moving.

When working with younger children, be sure to have a well-defined area for their movement. This will help to keep them safe and prevent their getting "carried away with the music" and bumping into other children.

For older children, play a wide variety of music with varying tempos. Talk with them about how the different types of music make them feel. Then give children the opportunity to demonstrate these feelings by moving independently or in small groups.

For another variation, divide the children into two groups. Provide rhythm band instruments for one group and scarves for the other. Go outdoors and invite the children with instruments to play improvised music while the children with scarves dance to their tunes.

More Outdoor Activities

On a rainy day, draw children's attention to the weather. Look through the window together. Ask questions such as, "What is happening outside today?" "What is making the puddles?" Then put on your rain gear, grab umbrellas, and go for a short rainy day walk. Help children notice the rain and the wind. Together, look at rain fall onto leaves, the grass, and into puddles.

Go outdoors on a sunny day and ask children if they can move like raindrops. Can they drip-drop into puddles? Can they drop onto leaves? How would a raindrop move in the wind?

Recite this poem as they move.

> All the rain is falling down,
> Falling, falling to the ground,
> The wind goes swish right through the air,
> And blows the rain 'round everywhere.   (Church, 1998)

All of these activities can also be done indoors. Just be sure you have a clear area so children can move freely about.

Jiggly Jello

In an open area, gather players into a close group. Tell them they have been changed into a bowl of Jello (any flavor you like). Pretend you are shaking the bowl. Begin by slowly waving your hands as if you were conducting an orchestra. Jiggle quickly and vibrate the Jello more. Children are encouraged to act exactly like the Jello would. Stop shaking the Jello. Usually Jello will shake for a while until it slows down to a stop.

Jumping Jello

This is a variation of a follow-the-leader game. Divide the group into two "bowls" of Jello, for example, strawberry and lime. Two leaders are selected to shake up each bowl of Jello. The two groups of flavors stand mixed together in one close group. Leaders stand in front of the group and begin jiggling their flavors simultaneously as players follow their respective leader. In this game, leaders can make their Jello hop on one foot, twist, turn, shimmy, or shake a leg.

Creative Animal Dance

Introduce the activity by either reading a book that shows a variety of animals or showing children pictures of different types of animals. Ask the children to describe how the different types of animals move. Does an elephant move quickly or slowly? What about a fish or a butterfly? If they have pets at home, invite them to demonstrate how their pet moves. Play some instrumental music and invite children to move like some of the animals in the books or photographs. The next day, divide children into small groups and ask each group to make up a dance using a specific animal movement. Work with each group and assist them as they think about how the animal moves. Then invite them to choose a musical selection for their dance. Allow time for everyone to perform their animal dances for their friends. Extend the children's creative thinking and movement activities with a game of animal pantomimes. They can act out different animal movements and let their friends try to guess what they are. They can also use animal movements during transition times as they move from one area to the next.

Music and Movement—Balloons, Inside and Outside

For this activity, you will need a balloon that has been blown up and a 3-foot piece of string or ribbon for each child.

Gather everyone together in a large room where children can move about freely and safely. Offer each child a blown-up balloon and let him or her play with it. Observe children's play and make comments to challenge and expand their movements. You might say, "Look at Jim! He taps his balloon to keep it in the air. Let's use our bodies to hit our balloons, too." Model new movements and make fun suggestions to extend children's movement explorations.

Before going outdoors, offer to tie the other end of their string or ribbon to their wrists.

Move outdoors and take time to note the effect of the wind on the movements of the balloons. Give children time to run and move with their balloons. Try to do some of the same movements you did inside, and encourage children to compare their movements and the movements of their balloons with and without the wind.

Note: Young children are often frightened by the sound of a balloon bursting. If possible, use extra-thick balloons and blow them up only part of the way. If a balloon bursts, react in a calm and comforting manner. Always keep extras on hand.

Balloons let loose can be harmful to our environment because they often land in streams, rivers, and oceans where fish and wildlife swallow them and choke. Be careful that the balloons you use come back into your setting.

For younger children: Take a kite outdoors on a windy day. Give children turns flying the kite. Discuss the movements of the kite as children watch it dip and dive through the air.

For older children: Have children work in pairs or in small groups to keep a balloon in the air on a calm day. See if children in the group can use movements different from their classmates to keep the balloon in motion.

Making Friends with Movement and Music

This is a good activity early in the school year to help children get to know one another. Divide children into pairs so that each has a partner. Explain that you will turn on music and each pair will dance together at the same time. Tell the children that when you stop the music, they will "freeze," holding a position. Practice freezing before you begin. Invite them to "dance and freeze" with the same partner for a few rounds. Next, call out "change partners," and suggest children choose another dance partner. Do this several times so that everyone gets to dance with a few different friends.

Extension: Find a variety of pictures in books and magazines that show people or animals moving. Create a list of words with children that describe the different movements such as running, hopping, pedaling, lifting, bending, or dancing. Then, set out art materials, ask them to draw pictures that illustrate one of the movements listed, and include the "movement word" below the picture.

Yes, Let's

This is a silly, fun game. The group stands in the space waiting for someone to call out, "Let's all pretend to try on hats" (or any other similar suggestion). The group then responds with great enthusiasm "Yes, let's!" The group then pretends to try on hats until someone calls out a new request, such as "Let's all hop like a bunny!" The group then responds again, "Yes, let's!" They hop up and down until a new suggestion is made and accepted. This is a good, short, energizer and a good game for transition times.

Van Gogh, Lines, and Movement

Use an art print of Van Gogh's *Starry Night*. Have the children look at the painting and name the kinds of lines they see in it. Then have the children move their bodies to show each kind of line they see. Have the children look around the room and see how many different kinds of lines they find. Ask them to "paint their ideas" using their bodies and motion rather than using a brush and paint.

For younger children: Children walk around doing whatever they want to with their arms and bodies. When the teacher says "Stop!" the children "freeze" and hold that position until the teacher says "Go!" Encourage children's movements of all kinds.

Activities for Older Children (Grades 4–5)

Movement, Line, and Shape

Artists use lines and shapes to send "wordless" messages or feelings to people. Show students prints of several artists' work that exemplify such use of lines and shapes. Good examples for this would be works of Mondrian (for squares and rectangles), Georgia O'Keeffe (for curvy, round shapes), and Salvador Dali (for clear lines of various shapes). Using the work of one or more of these (or other artists), have students pick out some shapes and convert themselves into the geometric figures used by the artists.

To make body sculptures, the teacher divides the class into small groups and asks them to pick a geometric shape in the artist's work and to make that shape with their bodies. Give them some rehearsal time. Children use their bodies to create the shape they see in the artist's work. Six children, for example, would be used to form a rectangle. They might do so by lying on the floor and connecting limbs so that four form the top and bottom and two form the sides. Larger versions of the shapes can be created by using more children to form each body sculpture. The groups show their body shape sculpture to the rest of the class and viewers identify the shape they see.

To build on this activity, divide the class into two groups. Each group is asked to prepare a body sculpture in which several shapes are linked. One, for example, might have a triangle, a circle, and a square linked by connecting body parts. The other group has to identify the shapes present in the sculpture.

A further challenge would be to invite the children to invent new shapes and demonstrate them for the larger group. Together, have them come up with creative titles for their original inventions.

Clay and Blobs

For this activity, you will need plasticene or clay; large sheets, blankets, or bedspreads; and a variety of recorded music (marches, jazz, lullabies, circus, electronic, carnival, or sound effect records that includes lightning, train wheels, bells, and so on).

1. Have the children explain what a *blob* is (a shapeless mass, something that can change shape).
2. Give each child a blob of clay to make a "happy blob" (no faces allowed!). Share blobs and search out what the children's blobs have in common. Repeat the process by making "Sad," "Frightened," "Funny," or other blobs.
3. Then hold up the sheets, blankets, and bedspreads, and explain that these will become the "skins" that will be used to transform them into life-sized blobs.

4. Collaborate in terms of three or four members each, and have students arrange themselves under a single "skin" as they work together in response to a specific type of blob. For example:
   - Popcorn blob
   - Blob made from Jello, glass, wood, sponge, or mud
   - Blob that is cold, freezing, warm, or very hot
   - Blob that lives under water, in the sky, or on the moon
   - Blob that is brave, frightened, silly, or pompous
5. Play some music or sound effects to enhance the mood concept as the teams improvise. For example, a popcorn blob could pop to some lively ragtime, while a cloud blob could float to some soft blues music.
6. Variations: Challenge each blob team to work out and present a specific thematic skit for the rest of the group to guess. For example: War and Peace, Rock Concert, Sinking Ship, Growing, Enchanted Forest, Approaching a Beast from Another Planet, Electronic Brain Going Haywire, Floating Cloud on a Sunny Day, or Stormy Day.

Classical Music and Creative Activities

Play Stravinsky's ballet *Firebird*. Discuss the story of King Kastchei, the Firebird, the Prince, and the Princess. The children might enjoy making masks for the hideous ogres found in the "Infernal Dance of King Kastchei." Students could act out the parts in the story as well as narrate what happens in the ballet. Other students can be chosen to be either "low," "medium," or "high" creeping demons according to the dynamics of the music. When the theme isn't playing, the monsters can "freeze" until the theme comes back again. Children can make a class project of the performance with costumes and masks.

Creative Movements

Children use their bodies for the following activities:

- Explore a range of movements involving body parts (that is, bend, stretch, twist, turn, push, pull, swing, sway).
- With a partner, facing each other, one moves and the other mirrors the movements. Move a body part. Keep that part moving as you transfer the movement to another part.
- Working with a partner, do the same movement your partner does. Now do the same movement with another body part.
- Create a dance with your partner using two different movements suggested by each person.
- Begin a movement in one body part and gradually transfer the movement to adjoining body parts. Try moving in different ways.

- Create a dance in which the movement flows from one dancer to another.
- Explore moving different body parts in unison.
- Move body parts in opposition.
- Combine a movement. Create a dance combining unison (or opposition) movements of different body parts.
- Put a piece of elastic around two body parts. Initiate a movement with one and have the attached part move with it. Initiate another movement and have the attached part resist the movement. Combine two or three movements initiated by the attached body parts moving in sequence or in resistance to the movement.
- Working with a partner, attach a piece of yarn loosely to a body part (not around the neck) and to the same body part of your partner. One begins the movement with the attached body part following the movement. Try moving in different ways.
- Create a dance with each person initiating a movement in turn, which is followed by the attached body part of the partner.

Emotions

Compose a word list and ask students to move across a space, either one at a time or all together, while expressing a specific word when called out. Word list examples include glad, ecstatic, carefree, puzzled, scared, cheerful, goofy, sad, edgy, and terrified.

Inanimate Forms

Have students move across a space expressing one of the following ideas:

- Floating bubble
- Mechanical bulldozer
- Piece of uncooked spaghetti
- Piece of cooked spaghetti
- Tiny mouse
- Two-ton elephant

Have students suggest other ideas to express in creative movements.

In How Many Ways?

Write the following question on a sheet of chart paper: How many ways can we move our bodies?

Show the children the question. Ask the group if they can think of 20 different ways they can move their bodies. Write the numbers 1 through 20 on the paper and then write down the different ways children suggest they can move their bodies.

Use a camera to record some of the different ways the children move their bodies during this activity. Be sure to photograph each child in the class.

Ask the children to stand up. Ask them how many ways can they move their bodies while standing? Have they reached 20 yet? If so, can they think of more ways they can move their bodies?

How many ways can they move their heads? How about their mouths and eyes? Who can raise his eyebrows, turn his tongue, or move his nostrils?

Extension: Use the photographs to create a class book. Glue each photograph onto a sheet of paper. Have the children write information describing their photograph. Invite the class to create a title and cover for their book. Bind the pages, read the book together, and then place it in the library area for everyone to enjoy.

Can You Guess?

Divide the class into small groups of four to six. Give each group the name of an object or thing written on a piece of paper. Each group must then, within a set time limit (usually 7 to 10 minutes is a good length of time), make a machine out of their bodies that makes their object or thing. Be sure to make it clear that the group is to become the machine that *makes* the object, *not* just become the object itself. In presenting their machine, children may make sounds but may not talk in words. Bring the groups back together and have them present their machine. When they are finished, the other groups may guess what their machine was making. Suggestions for things to make include rainbows, dreams, community, friends, monsters, solar system, a school, or other things appropriate for your group.

Linking Literacy and Movement

Can you dance your ABCs? Students work in groups to create the shapes of the letters of the alphabet with their bodies. Students can be very creative, using all different parts of their bodies to get the letters just right. This is a great activity for English-language learners to "feel" the shapes of the letters and to better recognize them when reading and writing. This activity educates the whole child—mind, body, and soul.

Scrabble and Movement

Students spell out words using letters they hop, skip, and jump to collect. Divide the class into groups of two or three. Each group should receive a set of index cards that reflects the same distribution of letters as a Scrabble set (nine As, two Bs, twelve Es, and so on). Divide a large open space in half, and send all the groups to one half and have them spread out their cards face up. (Cards should not overlap.)

Bring students back to the empty half of the playing area. On your signal, and one group member at a time, students hop, skip, or jump (you provide the directions) to their cards, pick one up, and bring it back to the group. When a group has enough cards to spell a word, they bring their word to you to verify and record it. Students take turns collecting letters and spelling words until you call time. Words of four letters or less get one point, and words with more than four letters get two points. Total the points per group and for the entire class. Celebrate success!

Movement and Math

Give students a chance to move while they add and subtract. Have partners take turns kicking large foam dice as far as they can. It doesn't matter where the dice land because they can't hurt anyone. When the partners have their two numbers, they make as many number statements as possible. For example, if they kick a three and a six, students can calculate $3 + 6$ and $6 + 3$. Have students try this activity with multiplication as well (6×3 and $\times 3\ 6$). Your students will get a real kick out of doing math!

Planet Hoop

Invite students to take an amazing journey to space in their very own "spaceships." First give each student a plastic hoop. Have them stand inside their hoop, holding it at waist level to make spaceships. Have them crouch with their hoops at the "launching pad" (the ground) and jump up to "blast off" at your signal. Count backward from 5 to 0, and then yell, "Blast off!" Give suggestions on how students might move (hop, skip, walk, gallop) as they "fly" their spaceships around the room to the tune of Gustov Holst's "The Planets." Fade the music out when it is time to "land" on a planet. Direct students to land by placing their hoop on the floor and sitting inside it.

When they are seated, conduct a read-aloud to share facts about the planet each student is visiting. Volunteers might take turns reading orally. Then have students blast off again! After visiting several planets, have students travel back to Earth. This might be a good time to discuss how Earth is different from other planets.

References

Buck, S. M., Hillman, C. H., & Castelli, D. M. (2008). The relation of aerobic fitness to stroop task performance in preadolescent children. *Medicine and Science in Sports and Exercise, 40,* 166–172.

Castelli, D. M., Buck, S. M., & Erwin, H. E. (2007). Physical fitness and academic achievement in third- and fifth-grade students. *Journal of Sport and Exercise Psychology, 18,* 1–8.

Chomitz, V. R., Slining, M. M., McGowan, R. J., Mitchell, S. E., Dawson, G. F., & Hacker, K. A. (2009). Is there a relationship between physical fitness and academic achievement? Positive results from public school children in the Northeast U.S. *Journal of School Health, 79,* 30–37.

Colcombe, S., Erickson, K., Scalf, P., Kim, J., Prakash, R., Mcauley, E., Elavsky, S., Marquez, D., Hu, L., & Kramer, A. (2006). Aerobic exercise training increases brain volume in aging humans. *Journal of Gerontology: Series A: Biological & Medical Sciences, 61,* 1166–1180.

Copeland, K. A., Sherman, S. N., Kendeigh, A., Kalkwarf, H. J., & Saelens, B. E. (2012). Societal values and policies may curtail preschool children's physical activity in child care centers. *Pediatrics, 129*(2), 265–74.

DHHS. (2008). Physical activity guidelines advisory committee report. Washington, DC: US Department of Health & Human Services, edited by Services DoHaH2008.

Essa, E. (2010). *Introduction to early childhood education.* Belmont, CA: Wadsworth.

Gordon, A., & Browne, K. W. (2010). *Beginnings and beyond.* Belmont, CA: Wadsworth.

Griffiths, F. (2009). *Supporting children's communications and creativity through music, dance, drama and art: Creative conversations in the early years.* London, England: David Fulton.

Isenberg, J. P., & Jalogo, M. R. (2000). *Creative expression and play in the early childhood curriculum.* Upper Saddle, NJ: Prentice-Hall.

Kaufmann, K., & Ellis, B. (2007). Preparing pre-service generalist teachers to use creative movement in K–6. *Journal of Dance Education, 7*(1), 7–13.

Petersen, D. (2008). Space, time, weight and flow: Suggestions for enhancing assessment of creative movement. *Physical Education and Sport Pedagogy, 13*(2), 191–198.

Pica, R. (2011). Taking movement education outdoors. *Young Children, 66*(4), 58–60.

Sibley, B., & Etnier, J. (2003). The relationship between physical activity and cognition in children: A meta-analysis. *Pediatric Exercise Science, 15,* 243–256.

Troiano, R. P., Berrigan, D., Dodd, K. W., Masse, L. C., Tilert, T., & McDowell, M. (2008). Physical activity in the U.S. measured by accelerometer. *Medicine & Science in Sports and Exercise, 40,* 181–188.

Voss, M. W., Nagamatsu, L. S., Liu-Ambrose, T., & Kramer, A. F. (2011). Exercise, brain and cognition across the lifespan. *Journal of Applied Physiology.* Retrieved from http://jap.physiology.org/content/early/2011/04/25/japplphysiol.00210.2011.full.pdf+html.

Warren, B., & Coaten, R. (2008). *Dance: Developing self-image and self-expression through movement: Using the creative arts in therapy and healthcare: A practical introduction* (3rd ed.). London, England: Routledge/Taylor & Francis Group.

Visit CourseMate for this textbook to access the eBook, Did You Get It? quizzes, Digital Downloads, TeachSource Videos, flashcards, and more. Go to CengageBrain.com to log in, register, or purchase access.

Creative Music

Lisa sang to herself in a sing-song way while drawing with crayons: "One purple, two purple, three purple, four purple." Next to her, William was humming the jingle for a fast-food restaurant advertisement and keeping rhythm with his coloring strokes. Out on the playground, Drew chanted, "I-am-going-to-be-a-lawn-mo-wer," and as he slid down the slide, he made a sound like a lawn mower. Picking up his cue, Inez and Christy slid down after him, each on her stomach and making motor-growling sounds.

Learning Objectives

After studying this chapter, you should be able to:

17-1 Discuss the importance of music for young children.

17-2 Outline some basic goals for music activities for young children.

17-3 List guidelines for planning music activities for young children.

17-4 Explain how to vary the rhythm of the music program.

NAEYC Program Standards

5a Understanding content knowledge and resources in academic disciplines.

5b Knowing and using the central concepts, inquiry tools, and structures of content areas of academic disciplines.

DAP Criteria

2D Teachers plan for learning experiences that effectively implement a comprehensive curriculum so that children attain key goals across the disciplines, including music.

3D Teachers consider what children should know, understand, and be able to do across the curriculum, including music.

Musical experiences like these are a common occurrence in a young child's life. Children love the sound of their own voices, and chanting is the way they experiment with sound and rhythm. Chants are half-speaking, half-singing sounds that often accompany young children's play. Making up original chants and songs and moving rhythmically to musical beats are quite natural to a young child, for whom music is a favorite avenue for creative expression.

17-1 Importance of Music for Young Children

Music is one of our greatest inheritances as human beings. So global is the human experience of music that it has often been called the universal language of humankind. Music is all around us, which is a testimony to its great importance for adults. Music is equally important for children from infancy on (see Photo 17-1). Children sing to communicate thoughts and feelings. They sing as they play. They grow silent and intent when they hear unusual sounds. They become quiet and relaxed when they hear soothing sounds. They move their bodies in concert with the sounds they hear. Music is central to the human experience of children, just as it is to adults. For this reason, music should be an important part of the early childhood curriculum.

Every child begins life immersed in the most basic element of music—rhythm. The steady beat of the mother's heart introduces the baby to patterned sound. Into the safe, suspended world of the womb also come outer-world voices with unique rhythms and timbre. The unborn child responds, physically, to these external sounds, showing an innate desire to listen and learn.

PHOTO 17-2 It is appropriate to expose children to a variety of music, including music they play themselves.

So, even before birth, children hear sounds in their brains. The child's world, too, is filled with music. Infants' windup musical teddy bears, crib mobiles, and go-to-sleep lullabies are just a few examples of early introductions to music. Young children respond quite naturally to music with rhythmic movement, and they also create their own musical patterns in original chants and songs as well as in unaccompanied rhythmic movements such as swinging, tapping, and even rocking in a chair. Activities that make up the natural beginnings of musical learning right in the home can be extended by the early childhood teacher to classroom music activities.

We know a foreign language is best learned when the brain is still growing rapidly, and this is also true for the language of music. So the obvious conclusion is that early years need to be musically rich. Young children are more open to types of music—from classical to country—and it is what they hear the most that becomes what they like and value. The teaching implication is to take advantage of this openness to musical diversity by providing experiences with a wide range of styles, types, periods, and cultural music experiences.

In an early childhood program, music of all kinds is appropriate (see Photo 17-2). For example, the sounds of a slow Duke Ellington tune and a fast, rhythmic portion of Stravinsky's "Rite of Spring" are equally appropriate for young children. Background music in the early childhood classroom can be as soft and soothing as Schubert's "Cradle Song" or a Brahms lullaby. For a change of pace to a livelier mood, classics such as "Tambourine" by Gretry or Bach's "Badinerie" can be used. Good music of all types has a place in all early childhood programs.

PHOTO 17-1 Music is important for children from infancy on.

Musical Experiences Improve Brain Functions

Music seems to be related to very primal parts of the brain (Hudson, 2011). Our bodies cannot help but react physiologically to musical input (Thaut & Kenyon, 2003; Hasan & Thaut, 2004). This implies that even the youngest children have the potential to inherently respond to music (Geist, Geist, & Kuznik, 2012).

Recent music neuroscience research indicates that steady beat does affect attention behaviors in humans. We typically process steady beat in the premotor cortex of the brain, an area also related to attention (Bengtsson et al., 2008). Zentner and Eerola (2010) found that 120 infants, ages 5–24 months, were more engaged with rhythm-only stimuli (for example, a steady drum beat) than with speech-only stimuli. The results of this study indicate that children have the potential to be more engaged when listening to steady beats than when listening to verbal-only instructions. Therefore, it is conceivable that listening to a steady beat pattern during certain teaching activities (such as mathematics) in the early childhood classroom could promote better attention and increased engagement in young children (Geist et al., 2012).

In other research, a longitudinal study (Hyde et al., 2009) with 32 nonmusician children over 9 months was conducted to determine 1) whether functional differences between musician and nonmusician children reflect specific predispositions for music or result from musical training, and 2) whether musical training improves nonmusical brain functions such as reading and linguistic pitch processing. Event-related brain potentials were recorded while 8-year-old children performed tasks designed to test the hypothesis that musical training improves pitch processing not only in music but also in speech. Following the first testing sessions, nonmusician children were randomly assigned to music or to painting training for 6 months and were tested again after training using the same tests. After musical (but not painting) training, children showed enhanced reading and pitch discrimination abilities in speech. Remarkably, 6 months of musical training seemed to significantly improve behavior and to influence the development of neural processes as reflected in specific pattern of brain waves. These results reveal positive transfer from music to speech and highlight the influence of musical training. Finally, they demonstrate brain plasticity in showing that relatively short periods of training have strong consequences on the functional organization of the children's brain. (Hyde et al., 2009).

You do not have to be able to play an instrument or be able to read music in order to plan appropriate music experiences for young children. It often helps to view teaching music as an *experience* to be offered, rather than a subject to be taught. It also helps to think of music experiences as ways to explore, test, and investigate ideas by connecting music to topics studied. In this way, the focus is on student participation and the process, not perfect singing or competence in playing an instrument.

As with other areas of the curriculum, **developmentally appropriate music activities** can be planned only if the teacher understands the developmental levels of the children involved. Although individual rates of development vary widely, the sequence of development follows a particular pattern. Figure 17-1 shows some important behavioral characteristics for each stage of development, along with their effect on a child's experiences with music. This material is based on the theories of Piaget (Wadsworth, 1979)

and Erickson (1963). Figure 17-1 may be used as a guide for choosing from the musical activities for children listed at the end of this chapter.

Did You Get It?

A father plays classical, country, pop, and folk music for his six-month-old son. Developmentally speaking, this father's activities are

a. recommended because they will help the child learn the language of music.

b. useless because a baby cannot distinguish between styles of music.

c. questionable because they might further musical development, but not enough information is known about the topic.

d. inadvisable because playing different styles will confuse the child.

Take the full quiz on CourseMate.

AGE	BEHAVIORAL CHARACTERISTICS	MUSIC EXPERIENCES
Newborn to 1 month	Responds to stimuli by moving entire body.	Quiet singing and rocking soothe the baby. Scary sounds avoided. Sound stimuli important.
1 to 4 months	Changes from hearing to listening. Turns head toward stimulus. Follows moving objects with eyes.	Same as for newborn.
4 to 8 months	Involved in purposeful activity. Reproduces interesting events. Develops hand–eye coordination.	Hits suspended bells again and again to reproduce the sound.
8 to 12 months	Anticipates events, shows intention. Knows that objects have functions. Imitates actions.	Hits drum or xylophone with stick. Claps hands to music. Hits instrument to produce a sound. Understands purpose of instrument.
12 to 18 months	Invents new actions. Uses trial and error to solve problems.	Experiments by hitting instrument in different ways with different objects.
18 to 24 months	Creates new actions through prior thought. Imitates actions after person leaves.	Continues music activity after adult stops. Listens to radio, dances to it.
2 years	Steps in place. Pats. Runs. Increases language. Has limited attention span. Attends to spoken words a few at a time. Develops independence, is very curious. Tendency to tire easily.	Enjoys action songs and moving to music. Can learn short, simple songs. Enjoys activities with short, simple directions. Many opportunities to experiment with instruments and sound. Opportunity for frequent rest breaks in strenuous rhythmic experiences. Avoid prolonged activities.
3 years	Jumps, runs, and walks to music. Has self-control. Attentive, has longer attention span. Uses more words. Compares two objects. Participates in planning. Initiative emerges.	Special music for special movements. Can wait for a turn. Longer songs or small-group experiences can be planned. Experiments with sound comparisons. Suggests words for songs or additional activities. Can recognize several melodies and may have several favorites. Choices important along with an opportunity to try out own ideas.
4 years	Has better motor control. Interested in rules. Plans ahead with adults. Likes to imagine.	May begin skipping. Rule songs and games appropriate. Can make suggestions for music activities. Adds words to songs. Creates songs on instruments. Makes dramatic movements. Likes to experiment with the piano. Likes to play music over and over. Can identify simple melodies.

FIGURE 17-1 Developmental characteristics and music experiences.   *(Continues)*

© Cengage Learning

AGE	BEHAVIORAL CHARACTERISTICS	MUSIC EXPERIENCES
5 to 6 years	Has good motor control. Likes to have rules. Vision not yet fully developed; eye movements slow; likely to have trouble seeing small print or making fine linear distinctions when music staff is not enlarged. Heart in stage of rapid growth. Begins to read written symbols.	Able to sit longer. Enjoys songs and dances with rules. Can follow specific rhythm patterns. May pick out tunes on the piano. Likes musical movies but may become restless. Strenuous activity periods should be brief. May be able to read words to songs.
7 to 8 years	Concerned with rules. Cooperation and competition. Logical thought processes emerge. Can compare more than two objects after first object removed (seriation). Thoroughly enjoys group play, but groups tend to be small. Boys and girls play together.	Can read words to songs, Rule dances and songs especially valued. Better able to tell reality from fantasy. Can compare three or more sounds or pitches. Likes duets and doing anything musical with a friend. May want to take piano or dancing lessons. Likes group activities including singing games, playing informal instruments, phrase games.
9 to 11 years	Has more developed language arts skills. Understands rules and strategies of games. Peer group assumes greater importance. Logical thought processes are present. Has more flexible thought. Enjoys play with peer group. Boys and girls prefer same-sex play. Begins to see others' opinions and ideas as unique.	Can create original lyrics. Enjoys dances with varied steps and patterns. Begins to enjoy small-group singing experiences, such as duets, trios, chorale. Can compare sounds, pitch, rhythms in music. Can understand elements of music such as tone, basic notations, styles, and forms of music. Introduce harmony and part singing for small groups. Provide duet singing experiences, all-boy, all-girl singing groups. Enjoys multicultural music and dance.

FIGURE 17-1 Developmental characteristics and music experiences. *(Continued)*

17-2 Goals for Young Children's Music Experiences

naeyc DAP Music is a common and enjoyable occurrence in a young child's life (see Photo 17-3). One of the main goals of musical activities for young children is to maintain this natural appreciation of musical experiences. Focusing and then building on this natural enjoyment of music will help you produce the most successful and joyous music program for young children. As in all early childhood activities, it is the process—not the finished product—that teaches and enriches a young child.

Other goals of the early childhood music program include the following.

- Numerous opportunities to sing a wide variety of songs
- Frequent exposure to various forms of music with wide ranges of rhythms, tempos, and moods
- Opportunities to hear and learn about music from different cultures and ethnic groups
- Frequent opportunities to express feelings and emotions in song, rhythm, and movement
- Opportunities to expand listening skills
- Developing an increased enjoyment of music
- Frequent opportunities for group participation

PHOTO 17-3 Music is an enjoyable experience in a child's life.

© Cengage Learning

Opportunities to explore their own creativity in music

Experience in playing simple instruments, moving to rhythms, and expressing emotions in motion during musical activities

Learning to identify some basic musical concepts and terms, such as loud and soft, fast and slow, and high and low

For older children, these goals also include the following:

Opportunities to sing in parts, in rounds, and in harmony

Learning about a variety of major musical works such as operas, ballets, symphonies, concerts, and chamber music

Listening experiences with instruments and tonal qualities of strings, woodwinds, brass, and percussion

Recognizing basic meter and rhythmic notation by sound

Did You Get It?

A preschool teacher hands out instruments to her students and asks them to create a song together because one of the goals of early childhood music programs is to

a. compose songs.

b. learn to play an instrument.

c. create dissonant sounds.

d. give opportunities for group work.

Take the full quiz on CourseMate.

17-3 Guidelines for Planning Music Activities

naeyc **DAP** The two keys to success in all your musical endeavors are **flexibility** and **acceptance**. You should be able to accept more than one kind of response to a music activity and adapt the activity accordingly. If, for example, the child in a planned clapping activity chooses to pat the rug or his leg, accept the response and imitate it as you continue the activity. In fact, the child may interpret your imitation of his response as a form of praise, thus making the enjoyment of what he is doing even greater. Or if the child is more interested in just listening to music than in dancing to it, accept that, too. Try to catch the child for your dancing activity at another time, when he is in a dancing mood. In other words, take your cues from the children and build enjoyment and learning on what they already find enjoyable. Build, don't tear down, the joyful world that music naturally creates for young children.

With these guidelines in mind and with an understanding of the developmental needs of children at different ages, a teacher may plan appropriate musical activities for young children. Let us now consider some examples of specific musical experiences appropriate for young children.

17-3a Musical Experiences

Infants and very young toddlers experience music by hearing it, by feeling it, and by experimenting with pitch and timbre as they vocalize. Adults can provide infants and toddlers music experiences daily while giving children caring, physical contact. Singing to children during changing and feeding times is a basic way to provide music experiences for very young children. Following is some more specific information on this age group and appropriate musical experiences.

Infants – 18 months. A child in this age range can be expected to exhibit the following musical aptitudes:

● Child becomes calm when sung to, or spoken to with a soothing voice.

● Child shows interest in and responds to music.

● Child enjoys producing music and other sound with rattles, bells, music boxes, and so on.

● Child delights in new ability to produce sounds (smacks lips, squeals on purpose, and so on).

Musical learning activities for infants are as follows:

- Provide the child many musical experiences in a variety of ways—singing, musical toys, and so on.
- Encourage the child's interest and participation in musical activities such as listening to favorite songs and making simple movements such as clapping or touching the head or belly.
- Encourage the child to make his or her own music and sounds such as banging spoons on a tray, chapping, giggling, mimicking sounds, and so on.
- Expose the child to a variety of types of music (lullabies, classical, children's songs, and so on) from a variety of cultures/languages/backgrounds.

PHOTO 17-4 Toddlers enjoy experimenting with a variety of sound-making instruments.

Casper Holroyd

Toddlers (18 months – 3 years). Children in this age group can be expected to exhibit these general musical aptitudes:

- Clapping, bouncing, and beginning to dance to music
- Using instruments to produce rhythm and musical sounds
- Experimenting with a variety of sound-making objects (See Photo 17-4).
- Participating in musical activities such as singing, dancing, finger plays, and so on
- Knowing and asking for favorite songs
- Participating in group singing activities for short periods of time

The following are some age-appropriate musical activities for toddlers:

- Provide musical experiences in a variety of ways (singing, musical instruments, recorded music, and so on).
- Plan for and encourage the child's participation in musical activities, including through repetition.
- Expose the child to a variety of types of music from a variety of cultures, languages, and backgrounds.
- Provide the child simple instruments and toys that make sounds.

Preschool – 3 years and up. When children enter the preschool program, music continues to be an important part of their lives. In the classroom, preschoolers need to hear all kinds of music. Adults need to talk about this music and how it expresses feelings. Rocking, patting, touching, and moving with children to the beat, rhythm patterns, and melodic direction of the music are all appropriate musical experiences for preschool children.

▶❚❚ **TeachSource** Video

© 2015 Cengage Learning

Learning Math Through Music and Movement Activities in Early Childhood

1. What specific elements of music are covered in this video?
2. What other instruments other than the tambourines could the children make to practice rhythm?
3. In the alligator game led by the male teacher, Chad, what other visuals would you use in this lesson to better interest the little girl in this activity?

Watch on CourseMate.

THINK ABOUT IT

Music Education Can Help Children Improve Reading Skills

Children exposed to a multiyear program of music involving increasingly complex rhythmic, tonal, and practical skills display superior cognition performance in reading skills compared with their nonmusically trained peers, according to a study published in the journal, *Psychology of Music.* Authors Joseph M. Piro and Camilo Ortiz from Long Island University report that data from this study will help clarify the role of music study on cognition and shed light on music's potential to enhance school performance in language and literacy (2009).

The study involved two U.S. elementary schools, one that routinely trained children in music and one that did not. They aimed to investigate the hypothesis that children who received keyboard instruction as part of a music curriculum increasing in difficulty over successive years would demonstrate significantly better performance on measures of vocabulary and verbal sequencing than students who did not receive keyboard instruction.

Using a quasi-experimental design, the investigators selected second-grade children from two schools located in the same geographic area with similar demographic characteristics. Children in the intervention school (n=46) studied piano formally for a period of 3 consecutive years as part of a comprehensive intervention program. Children attending the control school (n=57) received no formal musical training on any musical instrument. Also, they had never taken music lessons as part of the general school curriculum or in private study. All students were pre-tested for their reading skills at the start and close of the standard 10-month school year.

Results analyzed at the end of the year showed that the music-learning group had significantly better vocabulary and verbal sequencing scores than the nonmusical control group. The researchers suggest that the study of how music may also assist cognitive development will help education practitioners to go beyond the sometimes hazy and ill-defined "music makes you smarter" claims and provide careful and credible instructional approaches that use the rich and complex conceptual structure of music and its transfer to other cognitive areas (Piro & Ortiz, 2009).

Source: http://www.sagepub.com/repository/binaries/press/2009/music_instruction_reading_skills.pdf.

If you don't know how to begin incorporating music into your program, simply start at the opening of the day. Sing in your classroom as the children are arriving. In the mornings, to warm up your voice and the children's voices, hum a little bit. Show children all the possibilities of song. Sing high, then low. Sing softly, then loudly. Change the words of a familiar song such as "Twinkle, Twinkle, Little Star." Change the melody. Play with your song, just as you would take a ball and dribble, roll, or twirl it. There's certainly more than one way to play with a ball. The same is true for a song.

Sing when you are doing routine tasks. Remember that making up the words is fine. Children will pick up on the joyful atmosphere you are creating and also begin spontaneous singing as they move around the classroom. Use familiar tunes as "frames" for songs describing movements. Many children know the tune to "Row, Row, Row Your Boat," "Mulberry Bush," and "Twinkle, Twinkle, Little Star," and can easily sing along with you—especially if you have lots of repetition in the words. Children will often make up verses themselves, spurring literacy learning. In such an environment, teaching songs and singing are a natural part of the early childhood program.

Playing music during periods of the day is another opportunity for a musical experience. Adults can further encourage the musical development of infants and toddlers by exposing them to a wide variety of vocal, instrumental, and environmental sounds. Simple things such as talking about the sounds children hear on their walks outside—if they are loud sounds or soft, if they are near or far away—are basic beginning music experiences for very young children.

Listen to the sounds of young children playing in the dramatic play area, on the playground, in the sandbox, and in the building block area. You will often hear young children in these everyday situations singing, humming, or chanting familiar songs. Songs and singing are a common occurrence in the everyday life of a young child.

17-3b Introducing Music Elements

Although musical terms alone do not create music, early childhood teachers need to understand and teach basic elements so that there is a common language to

Rhythm: Movement of sounds through time. In songs, the words usually match the rhythm.

Beat and **Accent:** Have to do with the rhythmic pulse, like the steady beat of a clock ticking. The accent is where the strongest emphasis is placed as in *one* two three, *one* two three.

Tempo: The speed, how fast or slow the music is.

Syncopation: Uneven rhythms as in jazz, yet the beat remains steady.

Melody (tune): A series (more than one) of musical tones falling into a recognizable pattern. When we sing words, they become melodies.

Pitch: The high or low tones in the sound pattern.

Timbre (Pronounced "tambur"): Tone color or unique qualities of sound (e.g., voices or sounds made by plucking, beating, rattling, or blowing various instruments).

Dynamics: Volume or relative loudness or softness of the sound; gives emotional intensity.

Texture: Layering of instruments and/or voices to create a thin or full feeling. Melodies, rhythms, and timbres can be combined to create different textures. Music made by an orchestra is an example of a full texture.

Harmony: The blending of sounds, e.g., chords; two or more pitches simultaneously.

Form: Structure, shape, or distinct pattern or a piece of music or a song. Related to *style* or *genre*.

Ostinato: Simple, rhythmic or melodic content repeated over and over to accompany a song.

FIGURE 17-2 Summary: Basic elements of music.

© Cengage Learning

discuss music and concepts to use when exploring music creation. In other words, to integrate music into the curriculum, teachers and students need some basic understanding of the tools of music. This is similar to the basic art concepts introduced while children are working with two- and three-dimensional media. **Spiral teaching** can be used in this instance. In spiral teaching of music elements, the teacher presents the basic facts about music without worrying about the details. For example, the teacher calls it "marching music" instead of duple time, or "swinging music" instead of ¾ time. Then, as learning progresses, more and more details are introduced while at the same time they are related back to the basics. For example, the teacher now adds the word "tempo" so the song now has a "slow tempo" rather than just being "slow." The caution is for teachers not to kill the joy and spirit of music through overanalysis of music elements. Figure 17-2 contains a summary of the **basic elements of music.** Specific suggestions on working with the basic elements of music are available in the Activities for Children section at the end of this chapter.

17-3c Teaching Songs

The way in which you teach songs and singing to young children reflects the same natural and enjoyable place music holds in a young child's life. Always consider the developmental level of the children and keep songs for younger children simple—easy lyrics, limited melody (not too high or too low), and a catchy beat.

The method you choose to present a song to children will depend on the mood and the nature of the song itself. Following are the basic ways to present a song to young children:

- **Phrase-wise method.** Introduce the song with a brief story, discussion, or question. Sing one phrase and ask children to repeat it, then sing two phrases, and so on.
- **Whole-song method.** Present the whole song in a variety of ways: rhythmic moving, dancing, playing instruments, or dramatizing to make repetition interesting and meaningful.
- **Modeling.** The teacher or another student who knows the song models it (sings it) for the rest of the group. They join in as the song is repeated.
- **Combination of phrase-wise and whole-song method.** The teacher sings and presents the whole song but asks the children to respond to the easiest part of it with voices, hands, or an instrument.

The following suggestions are intended to help you present songs and singing experiences in the early childhood program in a way that maintains the young child's natural musical interest.

- Choose songs that have a natural appeal for young children. Popular topics include the children themselves, family members, animals, seasons, toys, and holidays. Be sure to include songs for all ethnic and cultural groups represented in the class, as well as in the larger community group. Be aware that not all children will participate in singing activities. This may be due to cultural reasons—not a lot of singing in the home, for instance—or for personal reasons, such as shyness. Pay attention to the songs you choose. Select one in the right key (in other words, not too low and not too high) so children can sing it. Sometimes, it's not the song but the arrangement that is difficult. Be aware that some songs are not designed for the average singer (as anyone who has tried to belt out a rendition of "The Star-Spangled Banner" can tell you).

● Be aware that learning a song is really quite a complicated process for young children. It involves listening, understanding and remembering words, having correct pronunciation, and remembering and singing a tune. That is quite a number of skills to be coordinated in a short period of time. Many young children find this difficult. Choose songs with a clear, strong melody. If the melody is easy to follow, it will be easier to remember.

Try out all songs yourself first.

After you've chosen a song, learn it yourself—and learn it well. Nothing is less inspiring to eager songsters than a teacher who has to check notes while teaching a song.

Based on the length of a song, you may want to teach it in sections, by verses, or even in short phrases. Often, a song's wording may be a bit tricky, and you may want to practice key words a bit more. Whatever method you choose, remember to be light on practice and heavy on praise. Don't make learning a song work; instead, give children lots of verbal encouragement during singing activities.

Visual aids can help add to the pleasure of singing and song activities. Pictures of key characters in the song or a series of pictures of key song events add interest to song activities. For example, a flannel board with farm animals for "Farmer in the Dell" helps add interest to this old favorite song. Use puppets to accompany you when teaching a song to children. If you're shy, this will help, as children can't help but focus on the puppet and not you!

Keep on hand a list of songs you have taught the children. They really enjoy singing old favorites, and

Casper Holroyd

PHOTO 17-5 Encourage all attempts at singing—each child will perform at his or her own level.

it's easy to forget which songs they know. You may want to post the list with some associated picture words so that children can choose their favorites.

● Encourage all attempts at singing (see Photo 17-5). Just as with other developmental skills, each child will perform at his or her own unique level. Thus, there is never any reason to compare children's singing or encourage children to compete with one another. If you ever had the experience of hearing a group of children attempting to out-shout one another in a choral performance, you will know firsthand the results of encouraging competition between young children in singing.

● Add movements, gestures, and props when appropriate for the song and for the children. A too-heavy emphasis on gimmicks to teach a song is unnecessary if you have chosen a song that interests children and is of an appropriate level of difficulty for them to learn. Added devices need to be thought of as "spices" and used as such: A few appropriately placed hand gestures in a song are like a dash of cinnamon in the applesauce. An entire routine of cute gestures and too many props adds too much "spice" to the recipe. Let preserving the integrity of both the song and the children be your guides in the use of all "extras" in teaching songs to young children.

● Include the new song in other areas of the curriculum by playing the song softly during center time or rest periods.

● Introduce new books related to the song's topic in the language arts area.

THIS ONE'S FOR YOU!

Start the Music!

The National Association for Music Education (NAfME), Texaco Foundation, National Association for the Education of Young Children (NAEYC), and the U.S. Department of Education developed Start the Music in 2000. This is a series of projects and events designed to help bring age-appropriate music education to every child in the United States. These organizations solicited the expertise of early childhood music educators, music therapists, education association administrators, early childhood educators, and healthcare providers to identify best practices for early childhood music education and to develop strategies to implement those practices.

Developmentally and individually appropriate musical experiences are guided by these beliefs (MENC, 1995):

● All children have music potential.
  ● They bring their own unique interests and abilities to the music learning environment.
  ● They can develop critical thinking skills through musical ideas.
  ● They come to early childhood music experiences from diverse backgrounds.
  ● They should experience exemplary musical sounds, activities, and materials.
● Young children should not be expected to meet performance goals.

● Their play is the work.
● They learn best in pleasant physical and social environments.
● They need diverse learning environments.
● They need effective adult models.

Start the Music recognizes the role adults play in assisting young children in their musical development. Families, caregivers, and teachers can all help children grow musically (Neely, Kenney, & Wolf, 2000, p. 1) by doing the following:

● Immersing children in musical conversations while singing, speaking rhythmically, moving expressively, and playing musical instruments. By doing these things, we stimulate children's initial awareness of the beauty and the structure of musical sound.

● Encouraging children's musical responses by smiling, nodding, and responding with expressive sounds and movements. In doing so, we show children that music making is valuable and important.

● Finding ways to encourage and motivate children's playful exploration, interpretation, and understanding of musical sound.

● Start the Music recognizes that all children are individuals and that music experiences should be a part of every child's world.

● Include art activities related to the song's topic throughout the week's activities.
● Record children singing the song. Have the recording available in the listening center for children to enjoy (with earphones or without). Play the recording during your next musical activity session. You may want to record the next version—with rhythm instruments, with a "solo" performance by one of the children, or with any other new variation you and the children prefer.
● Refer to Appendix E and make rhythm instruments like the circle embroidery hoop, egg shaker, and small plastic bottle rattles as an activity in the arts and crafts center. Have children use these as a rhythmic accompaniment to the song.
● Use the instructions provided in Appendix E to make "flutes" out of paper towel or tissue paper rolls. Have children decorate them with crayons,

colored markers, and stickers, and use their "flutes" to hum along to the song.

17-3d Breathing for Singing

Explain to children that breathing for singing is different from regular breathing and that they need to breathe more deeply for singing. Try this exercise to help them breathe more deeply. Have the children stand or sit "tall" with one hand on their abdomens below their waists and the other on their chests. Have them inhale to the count of three and then exhale to the count of five. Only the bottom hand should move as they inhale and exhale. Explain that the exhale lets the "old" air out and the inhale lets the "new" air in. As they inhale "new" air, they will feel their abdomens grow bigger and their chests stay still. When this happens, they know they are breathing deeply. Explain as they sing songs, they need to breathe deeply.

17-4 Varying the Rhythm of the Program

Just as variety is the spice of life, variety provides the same spark for the early childhood music program. Although young children enjoy the stability that routine provides, it is important to vary these routines to prevent lessening their, and your own, interest in music. Consider how many people can't remember the words to our national anthem, even though they've heard it innumerable times: It has become so routine that people don't really hear it anymore. The same thing can happen in your early childhood music program if you have too rigid a routine.

Varying the rhythm of the music program helps hold children's interest and makes the experience enjoyable. Variety can be provided in your choice of music, your method of presentation, and your lesson planning. In choosing music for young children, your own interests as well as the children's can improve variety in musical selections. Children's music need not be exclusively from music resource books. In an early childhood classroom, music selections can include classical, jazz, rap, rock, reggae, pop, and Native American, to name only a few. Young children are very interested in what's new and different and enjoy hearing popular music. In fact, most preschool children can name their favorite pop singers and their latest hits. Although music experiences should expose young children to a wide variety of musical styles, a music program including popular songs gives young children a familiar sound and a friendly starting point. Developmentally, it is appropriate to begin with the familiar, using it as a base for the introduction of new concepts to the child.

Variety in choice of music can also be provided by the families of the children. A teacher may find a rich source of musical variety by asking families to share the names of their favorite music or to share tapes, records, or CDs with the class for special activities. In preparing for special ethnic and cultural celebrations, for example, you might find families willing to share favorite holiday music with your group. Some parents may be willing to sing for the group or bring in special instruments for children to see and hear. The key is to go beyond your likes and the dictates of curriculum guides into the children's lives, their parents' lives, and the community at large, where a variety of music awaits you and your group.

17-4a Variety in Presentation

We've already discussed several basic methods of presenting a song. In addition to these basics, you need to consider other ways to add variety to your presentation of songs and musical experiences for young children.

● Vary the time of day you have musical activities. Switch from afternoons to mornings and vice versa. Also, don't neglect the spontaneous inclusion of a song during the day. Mixing up a recipe together is an excellent time to vary your program by singing as you work with the children. Singing a song on a nature walk is another. Swinging and singing on the playground is fun. And who can refrain from a song ("The Wheels on the Bus" is an obvious example) on a bus trip? In essence, plan for the unexpected occasion to sing and have a mental repertoire of songs to sing with the children. Singing can make an ordinary event joyous, so start making a list of favorites for this very reason.

● Vary your presentation by having the children choose the songs they want to sing and how they want to present them. Be sure to have available puppets, pictures, rhythm instruments, and audiovisual or other necessary equipment for their creative choices.

● Play games with music. Musical chairs is only one of these games. Games can focus on voice recognition. For example, a child is challenged to guess who is humming the song or who sang the last verse. A "name that tune" game is also a way to vary the presentation of songs. Play, sing, or hum a few bars of a song for the children to guess. Charades, or acting out a song, is an appropriate musical game for older children.

17-4b Variety in Lesson Planning

The key to variety in lesson planning is cross-curricular planning. More specifically, music need not be planned for only one area of the curriculum. Music should cross all curricular areas by specifically planning for it to do just that. Here are some suggestions for this specific planning.

- When making lesson plans for the week, include music in at least two other curricular areas. For example, plan to play music during art activities, and note which selections you will use on which day. Be sure to make a note to have the tape/CD ready and the tape/CD player set up for the days required. Then, plan to read a book at group time that relates to the new song(s) introduced that week. Plan to locate the book early.
- Use music as your cue to adding new materials and props to the dramatic play center. For example, engineer hats, trains, and railroad signs are natural additions when you've planned to teach "I've Been Working on the Railroad" to children. Putting the book *The Little Engine That Could* (Piper, 2002) in the language arts center is another example of a music-inspired topic used in another curricular area.
- Review past lesson plans to assist you in your future planning. We are creatures of habit and often tend to get in a rut when making lesson plans. Review past plans to see what kinds of music you have been introducing, the method of presentation, and curricular coverage. If a pattern is obvious, then you need a change! Make a conscious effort to find new types of music or methods of presentation, or plan a new schedule of times/days for music. If you are bored with the lessons and the planning of music lessons, the children will reflect your lack of engagement in their half-hearted participation.
- Use a variety of sources for music experiences for young children.

17-4c Rhythm Activities

Rhythm is present from life's earliest moments, when a baby hears its mother's heartbeat. Infants continue to enjoy rhythms in many everyday situations, such as the soothing ticking beat of a windup swing or the soft sounds and smooth rhythms of a lullaby. One of a child's earliest musical experiences is clapping and

moving to rhythmic music. Using rhythm instruments to follow the beat and feel the rhythm follows as one of the most accessible and enjoyable early childhood musical experiences. While learning a new song can be difficult for many young children, rhythm instrument activities are quite easy! With most of them, the child is simply copying one motion at a time. There is nothing to remember. Using rhythm instruments involves the body in keeping a beat and feeling rhythm, so children are fully participating musically. They're really creating the music themselves. And children love playing these instruments. Young children, who love movement and motion in general, are naturally drawn to the use of rhythm instruments. Listening first to the music for its rhythmic pattern and then matching the beat with rhythm instruments is the most familiar method of introducing rhythm instruments. Having young children listen to the music and clap out the beat with their hands or tap it out with their feet is another appropriate, traditional rhythm activity.

Rhythm instrument activities encourage technical exploration as well as expand movement repertoire and vocabulary. When you verbalize each movement as you do it with the children ("Now we're twirling the shakers" or "Can you click the tops of your sticks together?"), you are encouraging their exploration and learning. These activities also help children develop an awareness of rhythm, phrasing, tempo, dynamics, and other elements of music in a natural way that is suited to their developmental level and their active style of learning.

A teacher can also help a child's development of rhythm by focusing on the natural movements of the child. For example, teachers can follow a child's natural walking or running tempo by accompanying the child's steps on the drum. This can quickly become a game as the child, realizing that his steps dictate the beat of the drum, walks faster and slower.

Following children's galloping and skipping with the drum can also illustrate through sound the asymmetrical nature of those rhythms. The drum can emphasize the accent when running children leap over an object, or it can mark groups of beats (meter). Teachers can also mark the beat as children jump over a series of sticks laid out in parallel formation or pass a ball from hand to hand. Teachers provide a more fulfilling movement experience by fitting the external music source, such as a drumbeat, to the child's movement. Some teachers feel that percussion instruments such as drums are merely

Music Activities for Special Needs Children

A child with autism may not react well to being touched by another. When playing musical games, make adaptations to the movement so that the game can be played with individual movement. A child with disabilities may feel more comfortable and perform better in music activities if she is partnered with a "music friend" who can help during music activities. Ask the child which peer she would like as a music friend. Be sure that the child chosen is willing. Explain ways the friend could be helpful. For example, the music friend could repeat or clarify the directions of an activity.

If a child with a disability responds to music in a way that is disruptive to the class, it may be that the child has difficulty processing sensory input. Consult with the child's parents to determine how this is handled in the home. Be sure to read the child's IEP so that strategies you use are consistent with those being implemented in other aspects of the child's life.

A child with a developmental delay may be slow to acquire a new skill. Be sure to provide multiple opportunities for the child to practice the new skill. Keep in mind that he or she may not have the ability to retain the skill, and expect that you may have to teach the child that skill again.

---

noisemakers. Drums, however, can be used for musical conversations as children ask each other questions using patterns, as they drum out the rhythm of their names, as they count/drum out the syllables in their names, or as they simply explore the sound of a drum. The drum can be available for children's exploratory free play, for a guided experience with an adult at circle time, or for small-group interaction in a play center.

17-4d Strategies for Using Rhythm Instruments

Whenever rhythm instruments are added, they should have a specific purpose. Instruments are not used just to make "noise" but rather to enhance an activity. Instruments should be in good condition. Be sure children know the proper use of rhythm instruments before beginning any activities. Allow children to explore instruments freely before attempting a structured activity. Direct them to handle instruments with care, playing them to make a musical sound, rather than just noise. Demonstrate a "noisy sound" and then a "musical sound," guiding children to compare and contrast the two. Invite children to take turns exploring the instruments one at a time.

Set up rules for using rhythm instruments, but keep the rules clear and very simple. For example, "Keep the instrument away from your face" is a good, simple rule. Be sure to maintain order at the beginning and throughout all of the activity. Have children keep their hands in their laps while you pass out and collect instruments. Try using simple signals for starting and stopping that don't require your shouting over the music. Holding up rhythm sticks in a crossed formation is a good visual "stop" signal. Holding the rhythm sticks straight up can be a visual "start" signal. Have children practice picking up and playing, then stopping and putting down instruments on your signals. Using rhythm instruments, children learn to listen for a pattern of sounds in the music. In beginning rhythm activities, it's a good idea to choose music with a clear, easy-to-hear beat or rhythm. Marches and many types of ethnic music are excellent choices for this strong beat.

Some children may have difficulty hearing rhythms and/or reproducing them. This can be handled in the same way you would handle a reluctant singer. Specifically, never force the child to copy your pattern to use a rhythm instrument or practice this activity. Your emphasis should be on the child's natural enjoyment of music (see Photo 17-6). Whether the child can reproduce a rhythm is not essential to his or her enjoyment of music. As many an adult can attest, not being able to sing on key or reproduce rhythms does not affect one's enjoyment of music.

Rhythm instruments may be made by the children as well as by the teacher. Refer to Appendix E for using recycled materials such as toweling rolls, pebbles, and spools to make rhythm instruments as yet another creative outlet for young children.

Organize with Music: Songs for Interest Centers

To add a new, interesting feature to your room, try a song for each area in your room to help direct children to an area as well as to provide new ideas for play. First, list the songs you (and the children) are familiar with, and then sort them according to the classroom area. For example, have children lay "miles of track" in the block areas to the tune of "I've Been Working on the Railroad." Then have them build boats with blocks to the tune "Row, Row, Row Your Boat."

Next door in the dramatic play area, as the children are "cooking" cakes, they can be encouraged to sing the "Happy Birthday Song." "The Wheels on the Bus" can be acted out with chairs arranged in rows, with a cap for the driver, and even a cardboard steering wheel.

"If You're Ready and You Know It" (a handy version of "If You're Happy and You Know It") can signal time to assemble on the rug for group time. Or start singing a familiar song like "I'm a Little Teapot" at the beginning of cleanup time and see if, after two verses, cleanup time is finished.

Your language arts center probably holds a number of nursery rhymes and storybooks already set to music. Why not use "Jack and Jill" one week, and then "Hot Cross Buns" another? These nursery rhyme books will become very popular as children try to match words and pictures to the songs you sing.

Art projects are easy to organize in the art corner to songs such as "Frosty the Snowman," which can inspire painting with cotton balls for fun. "Old MacDonald" is a great springboard for animal pictures, murals, designs, and so on

"Jingle Bells" can be a year-round favorite. Sing it complete with bells, triangles, drums, and xylophones. "The Ants Go Marching" is another good tune for active participation as children enjoy marching in time to the music.

Keep a song in your heart in your classroom. Use singing to help organize space and activities. Singing will draw you together at circle time, as well as help foster group cooperation. Try it for variety and fun!

PHOTO 17-6 With children of all ages, emphasis needs to be on the child's natural enjoyment of music.

Casper Holroyd

17-4e Music Experiences for Older Children

With children in the middle- and upper-elementary grades, teachers are able to offer a wider array of musical experiences. Children of this age need to have broad experience with a variety of forms and styles of music. They need to have an abundance of listening experiences with the world's finest music, including the classics, multicultural, folk, and composed music. By the end of fifth grade, students should have been exposed to the main periods of music history and be acquainted with composers and repertoire from each period. For these older children's listening experiences, the following are the periods of musical history and composers associated with each period:

- Baroque—Bach, Handel, Corelli
- Classic—Haydn, Mozart, Beethoven
- Romantic—Weber, Schubert, Schumann, Mendelssohn, Chopin, Wagner, Liszt, Brahms, J. Strauss, Tchaikovsky, Moussorgsky, Saint-Saëns, MacDowell, Grieg
- Post-Romantic and Impressionist—R. Strauss, Sibelius, Dukas, Debussy, Ravel, Respighi
- Modern   Stravinsky, Bartók, Kodály, Prokofiev, Hindemith, Villa-Lobos, Copland, Thomson, Menotti, Bernstein

- Light Classic—Gershwin, Rodgers and Hammerstein, Gilbert and Sullivan, Irving Berlin
- Jazz and Popular—Miles Davis, Marsalis, Basie, the Beatles, Elvis
- Ethnic and Folk—Frere Jacques, Danny Boy, Clementine, Home on the Range, Bicycle Built for Two

The varied treatment that composers have given musical elements has resulted in different styles of music. The labels that are given these styles are also applicable to art and literature. For example, music experiences in the Impressionist music of Debussy can be associated with Impressionist paintings of Mary Cassatt. Art and music can both be enjoyed from the Impressionist style and time in history. The same is true for music of all periods.

Singing is an important classroom activity for children in the middle- and upper-elementary grades. Opportunities to sing in parts (harmony) or in rounds (like "Row, Row, Row Your Boat") are enjoyable musical experiences for children of this age. They are becoming more familiar with vocal ranges, female (soprano, mezzo-soprano, and alto) and male (tenor, baritone, and bass). They are able to sing simple melodies while reading a musical score. They are learning more about musical notation as well. For example, they can begin to recognize and understand what a whole note, half-note, and rest notations mean.

Did You Get It?

A teacher playing early folk songs for her students when teaching a unit on American history is

a. inadvisable, as it distracts the students from the real subject.

b. recommended, as it fulfills the need for cross-curricular lesson planning.

c. neither positive nor negative, as it does not enhance or detract from the students' learning.

d. unlikely to teach the students anything new.

Take the full quiz on CourseMate.

Summary

17-1 Discuss the importance of music for young children.

Children sing to communicate thoughts and feelings. They sing as they play. They grow silent and intent when they hear unusual sounds. They become quiet and relaxed when they hear soothing sounds. They move their bodies in concert with the sounds they hear.

Music is central to the human experience of children, just as it is to adults. For this reason, music should be an important part of the early childhood curriculum.

Every child begins life immersed in the most basic element of music—rhythm. The steady beat of the mother's heart introduces the baby to patterned sound. The unborn child responds, physically, to these external sounds, showing an innate desire to listen and learn.

Young children respond quite naturally to music with rhythmic movement, and they also create their own musical patterns in original chants and songs as well as in unaccompanied rhythmic movements such as swinging, tapping, and even rocking in a chair. Activities that make up the natural beginnings of musical learning right in the home can be extended by the early childhood teacher to classroom music activities.

17-2 Outline some basic goals for music activities for young children.

The most basic goal for music activities for young children is to maintain the children's natural appreciation of musical experiences. Another goal is to focus on the process and not the product in all music activities. Other goals include giving children many opportunities to sing a wide variety of songs; to enjoy frequent exposure to various forms of music; to hear and learn about music from different cultures and ethnic groups; to express feelings in music and song; to expand listening skills; to develop an increased enjoyment of music; and to learn to identify basic musical concepts.

17-3 List guidelines for planning music activities for young children.

Appropriate musical experiences for young children must take into account the child's developmental level and need for self-expression. Careful planning is essential in providing successful learning experiences for children. Young children can be introduced to the elements of music by spiraling instruction, beginning with basic information and gradually adding information on these elements. For example, the teacher calls it "marching" music instead of duple time. The term "duple time" will be introduced at a later time after the initial learning of "marching" music is fully understood.

You do not have to be able to play an instrument or have a perfect singing voice in order to share music experiences with children. It is helpful to think of it as offering children a musical experience rather than a subject to be taught. In planning musical experiences, the teacher must consider many things. First, the teacher must plan for the developmental level of the group. Next, it is important to include activities from each area of music—singing, rhythm, instruments, movement, listening, and musical concepts such as loud and soft. It is equally important to be flexible and happy when presenting musical activities to children. You must enjoy yourself as much as the children.

17-4 Explain how to vary the rhythm of the music program.
The music program may be varied by the choice of music, variety in presentation, and variety in lesson planning.

Children's music should reflect your interests and the children's interests. The families of the children can also provide variety in choice of music. Variety in presentation includes varying the time of day you have musical activities, varying the presentation, and playing games with music. The key to variety in lesson planning is cross-curricular planning. Music should cross all curricular areas.

Key Terms

acceptance in teaching music   386
basic elements of music   389
developmentally appropriate music
    activities   383
combination of phrase-wise and whole-song
    method   389

flexibility in teaching music   386
music elements: rhythm, beat, accent,
    tempo, syncopation, melody, pitch,
    timbre, dynamics, texture, harmony,
    form, ostinato   389
phrase-wise method   389

spiral teaching   389
rhythm instruments   393
varying the rhythm of the music
    program   392
whole-song method   389

Learning Activities

A. Form a group of three or four children from your program, neighborhood, or local school. Spend at least 15 minutes with them singing songs they know and new ones you teach them. Following this session, write an anecdotal record for each child commenting on (a) participation in singing, (b) attitude, and (c) knowledge of songs. Compare and contrast the children and comment on the likenesses and differences you found in each anecdotal record.

B. From your own childhood, recall several popular singing games and action songs that you have not found in this chapter. Record each song along with clear directions on how to play the game or move to the song. Share the activities with your classmates.

C. To comprehend how much music is a part of your life, at the beginning of the week, start a weekday music diary. At the end of each day, draw or write about a musical activity you had that day (dancing, listening to music, singing, playing a musical instrument, watching a music video, and so on). On Friday, share with your classmates what you experienced musically in the week.

D. Choose one of your own favorite songs (popular, rock, country and so on,). Teach it to your fellow classmates, using one of the methods discussed. Discuss your experience, including the following points: How well did your "class" learn by the method you chose? Did you feel comfortable using this method? Discuss how you would feel teaching a song you didn't especially like. Would it make any difference in your effectiveness?

E. Using a box of animal crackers and one of the suggested rhythm instruments (preferably a drum) or a hand-clapping accompaniment by your classmates, try the following creative/interpretive movement to rhythm activity.
  1. Take out one animal cracker and note what animal it is.
  2. "Become" that animal, acting it out by walking, hopping, sliding, and so on.

3. Have one (or several) of your classmates pick up your rhythm and beat or clap, accompanying your movement.
4. See who can guess what animal you are. Whoever guesses correctly gets the next opportunity to "become" an animal.

F. Using a concept song such as "Round the Mulberry Bush" (describing a daily routine), make up several verses and accompanying motions. Share your song and actions with your classmates for comments and improvements. Record your song to use later with a group of young children. Examples of other concept songs include "Old MacDonald Had a Farm," "If You're Happy and You Know It," and "The Wheels on the Bus."

G. Make a drum (tin coffee can with plastic lid, empty oatmeal carton with lid) for the following rhythm activity.
  1. Beat a rhythm on the drum for walking, running, skipping, and hopping movements.
  2. Beat out a pattern of rhythm and have your peers repeat it by clapping hands (or by using their own handmade drums).
  3. Imitate a pattern clapped (or made on a drum) by one of your peers in the class.
  4. Sing a song (your own creation, if you like) to accompany a rhythm you make on your drum.

H. Obtain a music supply catalog. Choose $150 worth of teaching materials. Explain why you chose each item, for what age group, and how you plan to use it.

I. Make a set of simple rhythm instruments as suggested in Appendix E. Use these instruments in a demonstration lesson on rhythm for your classmates.

J. Choose one of the composers from a particular period of music mentioned in this chapter. Obtain a CD, tape, or music file of one of the pieces referred to in this chapter. Make a lesson plan for grade 3, grade 4, or grade 5 using this piece of music. Relate the music to art and language arts activities of the same period. Share your plan with your fellow students.

K. Think of a familiar song. Take a few minutes to brainstorm all you could teach with just that one song. Write a lesson plan that uses the song in at least two curricular areas.

L. Try using your singing voice when giving directions throughout the day with the children in your class or with your classmates. There is something calming and quieting about the use of the voice. You may find children listening to directions more carefully and maybe even communicating with one another by singing, following your model. You will also be protecting your own voice with this practice.

M. Make a "Thinking about Music" bulletin board. Label it "What Can Music Give Us?" Divide the board into four squares. In three of them, put a picture of a person

the students know something about. Each of the three people should be from different cultures and time periods and have different needs (for example, Daniel Boone, Martin Luther King, Jr., and King Tut). Using the three profiles, ask the students what music can offer different people. Write these things under each person's image. In the fourth square, draw a blank person, labeled, "Me." Students then write things that they feel music offers them in that square.

N. Make a bulletin board illustrating the four ways a voice may be used: talking, whispering, singing, and calling. Using a sheet of paper fitting the bulletin board, divide the paper in four equal boxes with a marker. In each box, list one of the ways the voice can be used. For example, in one box, list *talking,* in another *whispering.* Then list *singing* and *calling* in the other two. Add pictures or photos of a child doing each of these things. Encourage your students to bring in pictures of themselves showing them using these four voices.

Activities for Children Using Music Elements

Rhythm

Rainstorm. Sit in a circle with eyes closed. A leader begins by rubbing his palms together. The person to the right picks it up until the whole group is participating. Then the leader switches to hand claps and that moves around the circle. Next is thigh slaps, and then foot stomps, with periodical "claps" of lightning. Reverse the order to show the storm dying out.

Rhythms Circle. Stand in a circle with one person as IT. IT creates any rhythmic phrase desired, and the phrase is passed around the circle to the right until the phrase returns to IT. The person to IT's right then becomes IT. The rhythmic phrase may be clapped, sung, or done in any way that IT chooses.

Follow the Leader Rhythms. Use rhythm instruments, homemade or purchased (sticks, tambourines, drums, cymbals). One child is the leader and plays different rhythms. Everyone echoes the rhythm on their instruments.

Ostinato

Repeat a Beat. Make a sound and repeat it a number of times: tap the floor, click your fingers, slap your leg, or repeat a syllable (dum dum dum). Tell children to listen carefully and to count how many times they hear the sound. Then they repeat the sound exactly. Let the children take turns making a sound while others count and repeat the patterns.

Texture

Voices Thick and Thin. Use poems or stories and assign different numbers of children to participate in solo and choral readings or parts. Ask the children how it sounds when more people are reading compared to fewer. This

should produce "thicker"- and "thinner"-sounding stories. Repeat the activity using singing voices. Relate to using individual versus multiple instruments by playing recordings of the same song or music done by an orchestra and an individual instrument.

Timbre

Guess Who? In a group, tell children to close their eyes and someone will be tapped on the shoulder. Whoever is tapped says a word, like "hello." The others guess who spoke. Each time a correct response is given, ask "How did you know who spoke?" The answer will be related to the uniqueness of the person's voice. Repeat the activity. In a follow-up session, play the game again but have the children sing "hello." Stress how each person's speaking voice is unique and so is each person's singing voice.

Pitch

Teach your students that shorter instruments such as a piccolo produce a higher pitch, or frequency, because the air vibrates more quickly in a small space. Longer instruments (such as a tuba) produce a lower pitch because the air vibrates more slowly in a large space. Let them observe the phenomenon by tapping on color-coded bottles filled with different amounts of water.

Dynamics

Dialing Dynamics. Dynamics has to do with volume. Make a volume dial out of cardboard or use an old clock. Label "soft" to "loud" on the dial with the musical symbols *pp* (very soft), *p* (soft), *f* (loud), *ff* (very loud), and *mfz* (loudest). Have children sing a familiar song or talk as someone turns the dial or volume button. The children should sing or speak according to what the dial reads. For example, if the dial says "pp," children sing or talk very, very softly. Variation: Teach hand signals to show dynamics, such as a hand up high for loud, and a hand down much lower to show a softer sound.

Science, Music, Loud and Soft

To reinforce the musical idea of loud and soft sounds, try the following simple science experiment. Explain to the children that vibrations in the air produce sounds. Loud sounds have very big vibrations. Soft sounds have very small vibrations. Demonstrate this by stretching a balloon over a plastic or glass jar, fastening it tightly with a rubber band. Sprinkle the top with salt. Use a pair of cymbals or your voice to show that loud sounds make the salt jump around more than soft sounds. Ask them, "What is going on here?"

Musical Activities for Children

My Special Music

The object of this activity is to have children listen and dance to a variety of music that reflects the various classroom cultures.

Materials: CD player or cassette recorder, collection of multicultural music, collection of multicultural children's instruments and rhythm instruments, favorite personal music selection, chart paper

In advance, send a note home asking families to send a favorite musical selection that reflects their culture or selection that their child enjoys at home. Remind families that the music must be appropriate for the classroom.

Start by sharing a musical selection that reflects your culture or is special to you. Explain why you like the music. Tell children the name of the music, where it is from, and the names of the musicians. Invite the children to clap or dance to the music.

Then tell the children that they will each have a day to share their special music with the class. Begin each day with one child's music. Write the child's name and a short description about the featured music on a sheet of chart paper to review during morning meeting time.

Provide opportunities for the class to listen to and dance to the music during the day. Provide rhythm instruments to play along. What do they notice about the music? Is it fast or slow? Have they ever heard this type of music before? Does it remind them of other music they have heard in the classroom or at home?

Is there a special dance that is done with the music? Invite children or other family members to teach the dances. Children can also create their own dances to accompany the music.

Keep the music in the listening area so that children can have additional opportunities to listen.

Musical Listening Activities

The following activities help young children sharpen their musical listening skills. They are most successful when used as fun "musical challenges" for young children and not as rote exercises. Space them throughout your daily and weekly activity planning, not just in the music portion of your curriculum. The auditory and listening skills they develop are used in all curriculum areas.

A. *Listening for specific sounds and being able to tell what they are* (auditory discrimination).

1. Have a child play a musical instrument such as a bell, tambourine, drum, triangle, or wood block. Another child closes his or her eyes and identifies the object played.
2. A variation of the same game is to have two sounds played with both being identified. The number can gradually be increased to see how many can be identified at once.
3. A child can go to the piano or some other instrument and hit a high or low note. Children can show with their hands, arms, or body whether the note is high or low.
4. Identifying the sound of a bell, drum, or some other musical instrument from a specific position in the room. Children close their eyes and identify where the sound came from. They might also identify the instrument and tell whether the tone was loud or soft.
5. Children identify instruments by comparing two different tones, such as large and small horns, large and small bells, and wood blocks and play blocks.

B. *Listening for sounds of nature.* The children close their eyes and listen for the rain, leaves rustling, the wind, birds, hail, snow, and so on.

C. *Listening for school sounds.* Children listen for children walking, people laughing, bells ringing, and so on.

D. *Listening for outdoor sounds.* Children listen for whistles, trucks, cars, train, airplane, and so on. Encourage children to use descriptive words for the sounds, such as, "It is like a *bang*" (*buzz, knock, crash*).

Musical Imaginations

Ask children to think of a small animal and a large animal. Divide the class into two groups. Have one group be the small animals and the other be the large animals. When you play music with high notes, have the small animals move and dance. When you play low notes, have the large animal group move and dance.

Sharing Prerecorded Music

Try using the Suzuki method when introducing children to a musical classic such as "Peter and the Wolf." Before actually introducing the classic, play the piece as background music for several weeks, during center time, for example. Then, when you tell the story of Peter and the Wolf, children already will have learned to distinguish the various melodies in the piece and will be able to anticipate what comes next. Follow up with another few weeks of just listening to the piece. Using the Suzuki method, children will never forget the music they learned.

Instrument Identification Game

Set up the music center with two chairs and tables separated by a divider. On one side of the divider, place several rhythm instruments on the table. On the other side, place pictures of the instruments. As the child on one side plays an instrument, the child on the other side holds up the picture of the identified instrument.

Listening Book

Play a piece of music with no singing. Let children draw pictures and dictate a story to go with the music. Repeat the activity several times, and keep adding to the listening book.

"The Blue Danube" Waltz

Swinging and rocking are favorite movements of young children, and Strauss waltzes possess a compelling feeling of movement that even adults find hard to resist. Children enjoy swinging not only their own bodies to Strauss waltzes, but they also enjoy swinging with a doll or favorite stuffed animal or puppet. Very young children may not be able to swing their arms in parallel motion because of the developmental inability to cross the midline of the body. Thus, the teacher may need to model symmetrical arm movements. By 3 years of age, some children will be able to swing arms in parallel action.

Animals/Insects

Use the following classical musical selections for creative movements in acting out animals or insects. You may want to introduce the piece by giving its name and briefly discussing how this animal or insect would move.

- Griffes—"The White Peacock"
- Liadov—"Dance of the Mosquito"
- Rimsky-Korsakoff—"Flight of the Bumblebee"
- Saint-Saëns—"The Swan" from *Carnival of the Animals*
- Bizet—"Leap Frog" from *Children's Games*
- Debussy—"Golliwog's Cakewalk" from *The Children's Corner Suite*

Edgar Degas – School of Ballet

Edgar Degas (1834–1917) was an Impressionist painter. Degas is famous for his paintings and pastel drawings of dancers, depicting a busy dance school. Point out in this painting how Degas used contrast—the white costumes contrast with the room's dark walls and warm yellow light. Ask the children to think of ways that music can show contrasts (fast/slow; soft/loud; short sounds/long sounds). Have each child choose two contrasting colors, such as blue and orange, green and pink, yellow and purple, or black and white. Invite them to paint a picture using only the two colors they choose.

Starry Night by Vincent van Gogh

This painting seems to quiver with motion. Discuss with children what the artist might be trying to portray (simple answers: a windy night, comets). Help them compare the painting's visual elements to elements in music, such as higher and lower start to pitches and darker and lighter colors to different tone colors. Invite children to paint or draw their own version of a night sky. Volunteers may then "play" their picture using simple instruments such as a kazoo, recorder, and so on.

Water Lilies by Claude Monet

Claude Monet (1840–1926) painted most of his water lily paintings in the last decade of his life. Painted on enormous canvases in the Impressionist style, they are some of his most moody, abstract works. Ask children to recall moods in music you have used with them. Then ask for their ideas on the mood of *Water Lilies*. Is the mood happy? Sad? Angry? Calm? Encourage them to explain why they think so.

Then invite them to draw a picture of themselves, portraying a particular mood. Help them to brainstorm a list of possible moods, such as happy, sad, angry, calm, excited, peaceful, and silly. Discuss what colors might be best to show different moods. For example, children might use bright colors to show "happy" and cool blues to show "calm."

Activities for Older Children (Grades 4–5)

Sing a Picture

Display a landscape, seascape, or cityscape, and ask students to brainstorm all the sounds associated with different parts of the picture. Encourage them to think creatively about what "might be." Come to an agreement on a sound for five or six parts of the picture and then discuss the pitch, dynamics (areas that are louder or softer), and how many times the sound should be repeated. Point to each area and have students make the sounds, holding them or repeating them, as decided. Next, try harmonizing sounds or doing the sounds of the picture in round form.

Variation: Use prints with several people in them, and break students into groups to find songs or create songs their

characters would sing. Come back together and have each group present the songs of their characters.

Finding Musical Elements in Art

Have students find musical elements in a piece of art. For example, students can compare folk art and folk music. They might also find rhythm in art, texture, tempo, style aspects, and dynamics (areas that are louder or softer).

Bilingual Music

- Ask students of various cultural backgrounds to bring in CDs of their music heritage. Spend a few minutes each day listening to salsa music, steel drums, Irish dances and so forth. Ask students: "Why do you think different cultures make different kinds of music? Can music be characterized in any way?" Connect this to your study of various countries of the world and/or to current events.

- Ask students to think of a song that's meaningful to them and write a paragraph explaining why. When appropriate, have students bring in their music selection and play it for the rest of the class.

Music History

Have students research the different musical styles that were popular when their parents and grandparents were growing up. Assign groups of students to a particular era and have them create a CD with representative music from their assigned era.

Technology and Music

The way we listen to music has reflected the rise of technology. Discuss with students how they listen to music today (online, cable television, satellite radio, CDs or MP3s, and iPods). Compare these with AM radio, tapes, vinyl records, and even wax cylinders! What did people do for music before any of those inventions came to be?

Illustrate a Song

Have each child choose a favorite song to illustrate, or the whole class can do the same song to find all the ways one song could be interpreted. Students might create a group mural of a song, or songs can be cut apart, line by line, with children working on illustrating their part. By assembling all the art, the entire song is then depicted (for example, "Home on the Range" will work nicely).

Musical Mural

While teachers frequently provide background music during art activities, rarely do children have the chance to demonstrate their musical imaginations in a complete and satisfying way. Rather than treating the music as "wallpaper music" (that is, present but not really a point of focus), this mural activity invites children to give shape to their thoughts and feelings associated with a piece of music. Whether they have visions of sugarplums or rap jive movements dancing in their heads, the teacher's task is to guide children in developing their imagery into a story told through a mural.

Begin with a musical selection that is programmatic and concrete, such as "Peter and the Wolf." After discussing major episodes, assign children to particular scenes of the story to illustrate on panels of the mural. Let children flesh out details of the story through visual elements (colors, shape, perspective, and line). Draw their attention to musical aspects that help tell the story (volume, speed, instrumentation).

Next, children can progress to more abstract listening exercises connected to various content areas. The class, for example, could be divided into groups with each group painting a picture based on *Pinocchio, Pocahontas, Sleeping Beauty,* or *The Nutcracker Suite* (language arts), or using other pieces of music such as "La Mer" (science), or "The

Blue Danube" (science), or "The Moldau" (social studies). Children can create the mural prior to learning the title and/or story of the music.

This exercise encourages active listening. Ask children what story they hear in the music. Do they all hear similar stories? How does the story they have envisioned match the actual title of the piece? What do they think the composer had in mind? These are only some of the questions that can be used to help children compare/contrast while integrating concepts from several content areas.

Art History/Aesthetic Awareness

Gather several musical selections from composers of the Impressionist era listed in this chapter. Choose one or two to play for your class. Explain that the music is from a period called "Impressionism" and that this was a movement in art as well. Obtain and display art prints of Impressionist painters such as Monet and Cassatt. Briefly discuss Impressionism in art: Impressionism developed in France during the 1860s. The artists who worked in this style wished to portray the qualities of light and color at a particular time of day. They usually took their paints outdoors so they could see and study colors. The unusually light and bright colors in Impressionist paintings shocked many critics of the 1860s. Impressionist painters rarely used black or gray. For shadows, they preferred deep violets, blues, and the like. They also preferred to use patches or dot-like areas of color rather than strong outlines. They wanted the eye to "blend" colors, and they developed a technique whereby they placed small dots of color next to each other, allowing the eye of the viewer to "blend" them together.

Students may want to paint in a manner similar to that of the Impressionists to experiment with this technique. Of course, painting outdoors is the best way to experience this style!

Handel's Water Music

George Frideric Handel, a German composer, wrote *Water Music* specifically for a party that King George I of England was giving. Handel's music was performed on boats floating up and down the Thames River. The King liked the music so much that the musicians played it over and over. Let the students enjoy listening to this music.

Then, divide the class into small groups. First, have them decide upon a favorite piece of music. Ask them to plan how they would present it for a party. As they plan, encourage them to use props and sets for their presentation. Then have each group perform the chosen song for their classmates.

"Octopus's Garden"

This song was made popular by the Beatles. Have students listen to the song, paying attention to how the melody moves, where there are repeated pitches and movement up and down. Have them discuss what the words express. Then let them sing the song and sway with the beat as they sing. Point out the meter, so they may understand the idea of two beats per measure.

Then invite the student to create movements that represent an underwater garden. Encourage them to use many levels (lying on the floor, kneeling, standing, and so on). Have them vary the texture as well, moving above, with a partner, and as an entire class. Suggestions include swaying underwater plants (moving their upper bodies side to side), and propulsion of fish and sea turtles (with arms as fins) as well as octopi (with pulsing arms or fingers).

Musical Collage

Ask students to think of one of their favorite songs. Have students create collages using light and dark images cut from magazines and newspapers. Ask them to arrange the collage visually in the same order as their song: Light (loud) images are placed where the song's loud, and dark (soft)

images are placed where the sound is soft. Have students share their finished artwork with the class, describing the song their piece represents.

Songs for Different Journeys

Ask the students to think of a different journey from history, from stories their families have told, or from their own experiences. Have students create artwork that depicts these journeys. Encourage them to use multiple colors. Use tempera paint, markers, or watercolors on paper or cardboard. After they have finished, ask students to name a song that expresses the feelings of the artwork. Then ask them what songs, if any, the people shown in the art might have sung while traveling.

References

Bengtsson, S. L., Ullen, H. H., Ehrsson, T., Hashimoto, T., Kito, T., Naito, E., Forssberg, H., & Sadato, N. (2008). Listening to rhythms activates motor and premotor cortices. *Cortex, 45*(1), 62–71.

Erickson, F. (1963). *Childhood and society.* New York, NY: W. W. Norton.

Geist, K. Geist, E. A., & Kuznik, K. (2012). The patterns of music: Young children learn mathematics through beat, rhythm, and melody. *Young Children, 67*(1), 74–80.

Hasan, M. A., & Thaut, M. H. (2004). Statistical analysis for finger tapping with a periodic external stimulus. *Perceptual and Motor Skills, 99*(2), 643–61.

Hudson, N. J. (2011). Musical beauty and information compression: Complex to the ear but simple to the mind. *BMS Research Notes, 4*(9).

Hyde, K. L., Lerch, J., Norton, A., Forgeard, M., Winner, E., Evans, A. C., & Schlaug, G. (2009). Musical training shapes structural brain development. *The Journal of Neuroscience, 29*(10), 3019–25.

MENC (National Association for Music Education). (1995). *Pre-kindergarten music standards.* Reston, VA: MENC.

Neely, L., Kenney, S., & Wolf, J. (2000). *Start the music strategies.* Reston, VA: MENC.

Piper, W. (2002). *The little engine that could.* Uhrichsville, OH: Barbour.

Piro, J. M., & Ortiz, C. (2009). Music education can help children improve reading skills. *Science Daily.* Retrieved from http://www.sciencedaily.com/releases/2009/03/090316075843.htm.

Thaut, M. H., & Kenyon G. P. (2003). Rapid motor adaptations during syncopated rhythmic sensorimotor synchronization. *Human Movement Science, 223*(3), 321–38.

Wadsworth, B. (1979). *Piaget's theory of cognitive development.* (2nd ed.). New York, NY: Longman.

Zentner, M., & Eerola, T. (2010). Rhythmic engagement with music in infancy. *Proceedings of the National Academy of Sciences, 107*(13), 5768–73.

Visit CourseMate for this textbook to access the eBook, Did You Get It? quizzes, Digital Downloads, TeachSource Videos, flashcards, and more. Go to CengageBrain.com to log in, register, or purchase access.

Creative Language Experiences

The following scene demonstrates the power of a young child's language, both verbal and nonverbal. It also demonstrates very clearly the fact that adults often assume they know exactly what young children are saying and respond to them on this basis. Yet, communicating can be a more complicated process than this, as the scene should emphasize.

Learning Objectives

After studying this chapter, you should be able to:

18-1 List and explain the four distinct skills in the development of language.

18-2 Discuss strategies for enhancing language development.

18-3 Define the terms *deficit approach* and *transformational approach* with regard to supporting Dual Language Learners (DLL) and English Second Language (ESL) learners.

18-4 Discuss the antibias curriculum (ABC).

18-5 Define *emerging literacy* and *emergent reading*.

18-6 List some guidelines to follow when reading to infants, toddlers, and preschool children.

18-7 Discuss the importance of poetry for young children's language development.

18-8 List the guidelines for story reading groups.

18-9 Define the Common Core Standards, and explain their importance in the early childhood language arts program.

naeyc

NAEYC Program Standards

1a Knowing and understanding young children's characteristics and needs.

3d Knowing about assessment partnerships with families and with professional colleagues.

5a Understanding content knowledge and resources in academic disciplines.

5b Knowing and using the central concepts, inquiry tools, and structures of content areas or academic disciplines.

DAP

DAP Criteria

1E4 Children hear and see their home language and culture reflected in the daily interaction and activities of the classroom.

3A1 Teachers consider what children should know, understand, and be able to do across disciplines, including language and literacy.

On a warm, sunny, fall afternoon, the store was filled with shoppers, many browsing the racks of women's sale-priced clothes. Among them were a grandmother and her daughter, who pushed a pretty toddler along in a stroller. The child wore a large patch over her right eye. Soon she filled the air with pleading cries, "Off, off!"

Her mother simply responded, "The doctor said you have to wear the patch, honey. We can't take it off."

When the child continued to cry "Off, off!" in a plaintive voice, the grandmother took a more direct approach, saying, "Now, I'll have no more of that. You can't take the patch off."

The little girl looked at her grandmother and then resumed her cries, "Off, off!" But this time, when she received no response from her cries, she tugged on the arm of her coat, saying, "Off, off!" She wanted her coat off, not her eye patch!

18-1 Development of Language: Four Distinct Skills

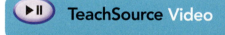 Two points can be made from this scene: (1) We can never underestimate the ability of a young child to get her message across, and (2) we should never overestimate our understanding of a young child's message. In this chapter, we will explore these points and many other facets of language development.

Language is part of a child's total development. As with physical growth, there is a definite developmental pattern to a child's use of language. Four distinct skills are involved in the development of language: speaking, listening (in the sense of comprehending or understanding speech), writing, and reading. Each of these, in turn, has its own pattern of development.

Ability in one language skill is not always directly related to competence in another. For example, many young children—like their adult counterparts—are far better speakers than listeners! In the early childhood program, language experiences must take into consideration the developmental levels of children in each of these four distinct parts of language development. Emphasis in preschool programs, however, is not on teaching writing and reading. Developing skills that are related to reading and writing helps prepare a child for more formal instruction in these skills in later years. Although this chapter focuses on the development of language skills in the early years, activities and resources are provided for older children where appropriate. Reading and writing skills will be handled as emerging literacy

skills in this chapter. The term *reading readiness* is often used in reference to these skills as well. However, the author prefers the term *emerging literacy* because it encompasses a broader range of prereading skills development.

18-1a Development of Speech

Speech is a form of language in which words or sounds are used to convey meanings. The ability to speak is not necessarily related to the ability to understand. For example, infants make many sounds as they practice vocalizing that probably do not mean nearly what eager adults like to read into them. Three-year-old children, as another example, can sing along, not missing a single word of popular songs on the radio, without really knowing what the words mean. Many children can sing the alphabet song and not know what letters really mean.

In the development of speech, there are differences among children in the age at which they begin to learn to speak and the rate with which they achieve competence. The overall developmental sequence with which speech is acquired, however, generally follows the basic sequence presented in Figure 18-1.

▶❚❚ **TeachSource Video**

© 2015 Cengage Learning

Language Development: Oral- and Literacy-Related Activities in an Early Childhood Setting

1. Give specific examples of children's emerging literacy skills that you observed in this video.

2. Using the guidelines to follow when reading to young children found in this chapter, evaluate Marantha's reading to her class.

3. Are the children in this class using controlled verbal communication? Give specific examples to support your answer.

Watch on CourseMate.

AGE	TYPICAL LANGUAGE SKILLS
0–6 months	<ul><li>Cries in different ways to say, "I'm hurt, wet, hungry, or lonely."</li><li>Makes noises to voice displeasure or satisfaction.</li><li>Babbles.</li><li>Recognizes and looks for familiar voices and sounds.</li></ul>
6–12 months	<ul><li>Waves bye-bye.</li><li>Responds to name.</li><li>Understands names of some familiar objects.</li><li>Shows interest in picture books.</li><li>Pays attention to conversation.</li><li>Says first word (maybe).</li></ul>
12–18 months	<ul><li>Identifies family members and familiar objects.</li><li>Points to a few body parts such as nose, ears.</li><li>Follows simple, one-step instructions.</li><li>Says two or more words.</li><li>Imitates familiar noises such as cars, planes, birds.</li><li>Repeats a few words.</li><li>Looks at person talking.</li><li>Says "Hi" or "Bye" if reminded.</li><li>Uses expressions like "Uh-oh."</li><li>Asks for something by pointing or using one word.</li><li>Identifies an object in a picture book.</li></ul>
18 months to 2 years	<ul><li>Says about 50 words but can understand many more.</li><li>Echoes single words that are spoken by someone else.</li><li>Talks to self and jabbers expressively.</li><li>Says names of toys and familiar objects.</li><li>Uses two to three word sentences such as "Daddy bye-bye," "All gone."</li><li>Hums or tries to sing simple songs.</li><li>Listens to short rhymes or finger plays.</li><li>Points to eyes, ears, or nose when asked.</li><li>Uses the words "Bye," "Hi," "Please," and "Thank you" if prompted.</li></ul>
2–3 years	<ul><li>Identifies up to 10 pictures in a book when objects are named.</li><li>Uses simple phrases and sentences.</li><li>Responds when called by name.</li><li>Responds to simple directions.</li><li>Starts to say plural and past tense words.</li><li>Enjoys simple stories, rhymes, and songs.</li><li>Uses two- to three-word sentences.</li><li>Enjoys looking at books.</li><li>Points to eyes, ears, or nose when asked.</li><li>Repeats words spoken by someone else.</li><li>Vocabulary expands up to 500 words.</li></ul>

FIGURE 18-1 Children's development of language ability.

Source: From Oesterreich, L. (2004) Understanding Children, "Language Development." Iowa State University Extension. http://www.extension
.iastate.edu/Publications/PM1529F.pdf

(*Continues*)

AGE	TYPICAL LANGUAGE SKILLS
3–4 years	• Talks so 75 to 80% of speech is understandable. • Says own first and last name. • Understands location words such as over, under, on, and in. • Understands now, soon, and later. • Asks who, what, where, and why questions. • Talks in complete sentences of 3 to 5 words: "Mommy is drinking juice." "There's a big dog." • Stumbles over words sometimes—usually not a sign of stuttering. • Enjoys repeating words and sounds over and over. • Listens attentively to short stories and books. • Likes familiar stories told without any changes in words. • Enjoys listening to stories and repeating simple rhymes. • Enjoys telling simple stories from pictures or books. • Likes to sing and can carry a simple tune. • Recognizes common everyday sounds. • Identifies common colors such as red, blue, yellow, green.
4–5 years	• Recognizes some letters if taught and may be able to print own name. • Recognizes familiar words in simple books or signs (STOP sign, fast-food signs). • Speaks in fairly complex sentences—"The baby ate the cookie before I could put it on the table." • Enjoys singing simple songs, rhymes, and nonsense words. • Adapts language to listener's level of understanding. To baby sister: "Daddy go bye-bye." To mother: "Daddy went to the store." • Learns name, address, and phone number if taught. • Asks and answers who, what, why, where, and what if questions. • Names six to eight colors and three shapes. • Follows two unrelated directions. "Put your milk on the table, and get your coat on." • Likes to talk and carries on elaborate conversations. • Likes to shock others by using "forbidden" words.
5–6 years	• Speaks with correct grammar and word form. • Expresses self in pretend play. • Writes first name, some letters, and numbers. • Reads simple words.

FIGURE 18.1 Children's development of language ability. (*Continued*)

Similar to the pattern of physical development (see Chapter 9), acquisition of speech develops from general to specific.

At first, the child's speech consists of sounds that are vague and difficult to understand. Yet even in these early stages of life (from birth to 36 months), very young children can communicate quite effectively with a minimum of vocabulary. See Appendix B for a summary of the basic characteristics of these early levels of speech development and some related activities for language development at each level.

Gradually the development of speech progresses to clear and distinct words that carry specific messages, which we call *controlled verbal communication*. Generally, by the age of 3 years, children are rapidly building their vocabularies. They continue to increase the

THINK ABOUT IT

Using "50-Cent" Words with Young Children

The young child's vocabulary is highly sensitive to early adult input, which is critical to preventing later reading comprehension difficulties (Dickinson et al., 2003). Also, vocabulary is causally related—that is, it helps reading comprehension (Dickinson et al., 2003)—and it is highly correlated with the rate of learning new words (Hart & Risley, 1995). Thus, a meager beginning vocabulary slows the rate of vocabulary learning, which compromises reading comprehension (Collins, 2012).

Two widely examined contexts for early language development are conversations and storybook reading (Dickinson & Tabors, 2001). Pan and colleagues (2005) found that exposure to unfamiliar words in mothers' talk with children is related to children's vocabulary growth. Research on teachers' talk at mealtimes shows a positive relationship between conversations and preschoolers' vocabulary development (Cote, 2001).

Although numerous studies have examined vocabulary acquisition, most focus on common words—that is, high-frequency vocabulary (Collins, 2012). A few studies examine children's acquisition of sophisticated, or low-frequency, vocabulary. Dickinson and Porche (2011) find that preschool teachers' use of complex vocabulary during play contributes to children's reading comprehension in fourth grade. Research shows that among preschoolers in families with low incomes, there is a positive relationship between the amount of exposure to sophisticated words and supportive explanations during conversations with parents and children's later vocabulary (Weitzman & Snow, 2011).

In storybook reading contexts, Beck and McKeown (2007) find that kindergartners and first graders from families with low incomes learn sophisticated words from robust instruction during read-alouds. Preschoolers who hear rich explanations of sophisticated words learn significantly more words than children who do not (Collins, 2010). These studies provide compelling evidence for the benefits of teaching sophisticated vocabulary, the 50-cent words so to speak, to children in preschool through first grade (Collins, 2012).

---

number of words in their speaking vocabulary for the next few years.

18-1b Development of Rules of Speech

As children learn to speak, they begin to put words together in patterns and gradually learn the grammatical rules of their language. They follow a sequence of language development from sounds without meaning to single words to two-word sentences to more complex structures. Jenny moves from saying, "Juice," to saying, "My juice," to saying, "Give Jenny apple juice." Children usually use nouns before pronouns, and *I* and *me* are often the first pronouns used.

Children usually learn the names of objects first and gradually make finer discriminations. They notice likenesses and differences. For Elise, all four-legged animals are dogs. Later she identifies dog, cat, cow, and horse, and further refines her classification to little dog and big dog.

Concepts of time and space are difficult for young children to comprehend. William cannot tell the difference between tomorrow and next week. He knows only that it is not now. After much practice and experience, children begin to recognize shades of meanings and become more precise and facile with language. Philip talks about his warm blue coat, and Alice knows that hers is bright blue because she has heard her mother describe it that way.

Children draw generalizations about how words come together to form sentences. Then they overgeneralize, not realizing that there are exceptions to rules. If "I cooked the egg" is a correct grammatical construction, then "I tooked the ball" seems equally correct to Estefan. Instead of saying, "I forgot the picture," Sam is likely to tell his father that he "forgotted" the picture. When Ella says, "I runned down the hill," she demonstrates an advanced stage of language development, using a grammar rule she discovered for herself. Children learn rules about past tense as they become familiar with the language. In a similar manner, they learn the rules about plurals. If the plural of *house* is *houses*, should not the plural of *goose* be *gooses*?

A child hears sounds all around. Adults, other children, radio, and television all provide aural stimulation. As children learn to speak, adults need to accept the language they produce. Whatever the nature of the sounds they make, they should be encouraged to talk and not be restrained by criticism or corrections. If the adults around them speak well, children usually begin to use words correctly, too. A child who has many verbal interactions with adults is likely to develop greater verbal proficiency and confidence in the use of words than one who has not had such experiences.

18-1c Development of Listening

Just exactly how a child learns to listen to and understand language has been studied by many researchers and language experts. Some argue that language and thought grow somewhat independently, at least in the early stages of language development. This view does make sense when you consider the fact that young children are often able to learn words and phrases that have no meaning for them. (Remember how 3-year-olds can sing popular songs yet do not understand the words.)

Listening is not a passive receiving of information. Good listening involves receiving and processing incoming information. Listening is more than simply hearing because good listeners filter out much of what they hear in order to concentrate on a message.

Children are not the only ones who should listen, and teachers are not the only ones who should speak. Rather, children and teachers need to be good listeners, and children should listen to one another as carefully as they do to adults. Good listeners are *active*. They get involved with what they hear, both intellectually and emotionally. Active listeners give complete attention to what they hear. They are active in that they process the information, make pertinent comments, and ask relevant questions.

Young children may act as if they understand concepts at a level that they cannot yet express in words. Because young children think in simple, basic ways, they have difficulty comprehending adult language that is abstract or too complex. Abstraction is beyond the thinking capabilities of the young child in preschool and early elementary years. The teacher or child-care worker who is not aware of these language limitations of young children can easily lose their attention. For example, a visiting firefighter who described the fire hose as "a supplementary antiincendiary device" obviously was unaware of the language level of the audience and more accustomed to addressing adults! In the same manner, a teacher who directs a child pulling another's hair to "be nice" is too general and abstract in her directions. A more appropriate, direct, and less abstract request for a young child would be, "Caleb, don't pull Jane's hair."

Physical conditions affecting the listener (deafness, hunger, fatigue, illness, and physical environment) can impair the listening process or influence the quality of listening. The environmental climate or atmosphere in the early childhood program should motivate listening. The atmosphere needs to be one in which children are free to express their ideas; they should feel that their contributions will be accepted and respected.

18-1d Literacy

> "When we teach a child to draw, we teach him how to see. When we teach a child to play a musical instrument, we teach her how to listen. When we teach a child how to dance, we teach him how to move through life with grace. When we teach a child to read or write, we teach her how to think."
> —Jane Alexander, chair for the National Endowment for the Arts

All the information discussed to this point falls under the general term *literacy*. Literacy in its most general sense is a mastery of language—speaking, listening, writing, and reading. Literacy learning, as discussed earlier, begins in infancy and continues through life. In helping children develop literacy, we must respect the language the child brings to school and use it as a base for language and literacy activities. To develop literacy, we build on what the child already knows about oral language, reading, and writing. Children's literacy grows when we encourage them to see themselves as people who can enjoy exploring oral and written language.

Did You Get It?

A teacher says to her first-grade students on the playground, "All of you have the agility needed to ascend the climbing structure." She then explains the meaning of "agile," "ascend" and "structure." Her actions are

a. recommended, as she is helping her students develop vocabulary.

b. unnecessary, because first-graders cannot develop higher-level vocabulary.

c. not recommended, because she is hurting the feelings of students who are not verbally gifted.

d. potentially harmful to her students.

Take the full quiz on CourseMate.

18-2 Enhancing Language Development: Strategies

naeyc DAP A true mastery of language requires social interaction. A classroom in which children are given many opportunities to interact with others is one in which language development is fostered. A teacher can create an environment that fosters language development of young children by creating a child-centered classroom where young children are given many opportunities to pursue their own interests and are trusted to know what it is they want and need to learn (see Photo 18-1).

18-2a Language Experiences during Self-Initiated Play

When children move freely to activities of their choice in self-initiated play in a child-centered environment, more language is used with greater richness of speech than when children are in teacher-centered classrooms where formal instruction dominates the program. When children discover they can satisfy needs by speaking, they gain confidence in their abilities to speak and begin to value language.

Interaction is an important part of communication (see Photo 18-2). Children speak and listen as they play with clay, play dough, paint, pegs, blocks, sand, and water. If they feel comfortable when they talk, they are more likely to experiment with language. In a housekeeping area, children talk to each other as they reenact familiar roles. Midday snack arrangements provide natural settings for conversations. Such

PHOTO 18-2 A true mastery of language requires social interaction.

activities as playing with blocks, pounding and rolling clay, and experimenting with magnets all offer children rich opportunities to speak, listen, and exchange ideas with others.

18-2b Language Experiences in Small-Group Activities

In small groups, children are more likely to talk to each other and to the teacher and have less anxiety than when they are expected to respond in large groups. Sharing time in an early childhood program is best when it involves a small group of three to five children. In a large group, it is necessary to limit each child's conversation so that several children have an opportunity to speak, and this limitation tends to discourage children from talking. A group of three to five is a more natural situation for young children.

Formal discussion periods are neither as interesting nor as meaningful as informal conversations in a small group. A child who takes a treasured item out of her or his pocket to share with two or three friends is probably enjoying a very personal experience. But when Show and Tell time is made into a daily ritual in which many children are expected to participate, the personal excitement may disappear for the speaker. The telling supersedes the sharing, and the personal reactions of peers are not part of the experience. When incorporated into a program at an appropriate time, Show and Tell can be valued by all as a sharing experience. When it is a teacher-centered language lesson, its value is likely to be lost. Early childhood classrooms should reflect these

PHOTO 18-1 Pretend reading is an important step in a child's developing literacy.

and many other opportunities for young children's developing language skills. In these more intimate settings, the teacher can focus on encouraging rich conversation between herself and the children, fostering the use of "rich words" to broaden the children's vocabularies. See the Think About It box on page 407 for research on the relationship between the growth of children's vocabulary and the use of "rich" or "50-cent" words with preschool children.

Did You Get It?

From a language development perspective, what is the disadvantage of a kindergarten teacher taking half of her students to a side of the room and then initiating a discussion with those students about the upcoming holidays?

a. Students who do not celebrate holidays for religious reasons will feel left out.

b. Young children cannot carry on a guided discussion.

c. She is initiating the conversation, thus stunting the students' creativity.

d. The large group size will discourage the students from speaking.

Take the full quiz on CourseMate.

18-3 Supporting Dual Language Learners and English Second Language Development: Deficit versus Transformational Approach

naeyc **DAP** Pre-K–12 students who are Dual Language Learners (DLLs) represent a fast-growing segment of the total student population in the United States. During the 2007–2008 school year, more than 5 million (11%) of the almost 50 million total student enrollment were learning English (NCELA, 2010).

There is great linguistic diversity among the DLLs themselves in US public schools. According to the Migration Policy Institute's analysis of the US Census Bureau's 2009 American Community Survey, 150 languages are spoken among students nationwide who are English language learners, with Spanish the home language of the majority of them (Batalova & McHugh, 2010). One study projects that students who speak a language other than English at home or who are acquiring proficiency in English will comprise 40% of K–12 students by the 2030s (Thomas & Collier, 2002). These

demographics suggest that teachers need to acquire new knowledge and skills and adjust their instructional strategies to better serve this ever-expanding student population.

Based on this information, the early childhood teacher plays a critical role in the lives of linguistically and culturally diverse young children. It is important to remember that children will not learn literacy skills in a language they do not yet speak. This is why it is so important to support the continuous development of the child's primary language while providing meaningful experiences with English.

There is a danger in working with non-English-speaking children of taking a deficit perspective. This type of perspective sees the child as lacking skills, a deficit caused by not speaking English. A **deficit perspective** is one that often distorts teachers' vision when interacting with children from marginalized communities: children of color, children who speak a language other than English, children whose families are poor or working class (Garcia, Jensen, & Scribner, 2009). A deficit perspective attributes many children's school failure to perceived deficits within the children, their families, and their cultures (Alvarado, 2008). For example, parents are often cited for not reading to their children, not valuing education, not using enough discipline (or disciplining their children too strictly), not speaking English at home, and/or for family "dysfunctions" that interfere with children's learning (Garcia, Jensen, & Scribner, 2009).

In direct contrast to the deficit perspective is the **transformational perspective**, which is based on the assumption that communities possess "funds of knowledge," reservoirs of knowledge and skills shared by community members (Gonzalez-Mena, 2009). On one level, this means that what families know about music or literacy can contribute to learning activities or be topics of study. At a deeper level, it means we must view families as knowledgeable and skillful as well as understand and respect teaching and learning relationships in homes and communities (Gonzalez-Mena, 2009).

These funds of knowledge are often invisible to those who are unfamiliar with lives that are different from their own. Traditional nods to multiculturalism, such as a piñata or Kwanzaa *kinara*, miss the point. Understanding others means paying close attention to ways of learning in families and communities, listening and questioning actively, and interacting in meaningful experiences (Gonzalez-Mena, 2009).

What does all of this mean for teachers? NAEYC answers this question by urging early childhood educators to accept the legitimacy of children's home language, respect and value the home culture, and promote and encourage the active involvement and support of all families (NAEYC, 1996). Similar position statements by other organizations, such as the National Council of Teachers of English (NCTE) and the International Reading Association (IRA) note that such an approach not only provides multiple pathways to learning but also has the potential to broaden the world views of children and teachers.

18-3a Implementing a Transformational Perspective

All of these ideas about a transformational perspective look good on paper, but putting them into practice is yet another issue. To help you get started in developing more of a transformational perspective in your work with bilingual students, consider some of the suggestions that follow.

- *Validate children's home language.* Learn and use as many words as possible in the child's home language. Encourage other children to use these words as well.
- *Build respect and positive connections with children and families.* Ask them about their background (country of birth, length of US residency, languages spoken at home), culture (food, customs, values), and children's education experiences (prior schooling, proficiency in home language and English). Use the knowledge to support children and meet their communication needs.
- *Understand that children learning English as a second language tend to acquire receptive (understanding) language skills faster than expressive (communication) skills due to their observing and listening.* Encourage and model verbal communication and word usage. During choice time, show children pictures of the play areas and ask, "Would you like to play in the kitchen?" or "Would you like to play with blocks in the block area?"
- *Determine the level of each child's communication skills in English and the home language through ongoing, careful observation.* Take notes about the child's use of verbal and nonverbal communication: Under what conditions is the child most likely to communicate? In which language is the child most successful at communicating?

How does the child use words or gestures and for what purpose? Use knowledge of a child's communicating skill set to provide opportunities to practice and expand those skills in English and/ or the home language.

- *Be aware that DLLs may have the skills to communicate effectively in their home language but lack the proficiency to do so in the second language.* Be mindful that children learning a new language may go through a "silent period" when they tend not to speak much (Chen & Shire, 2011). Encourage them to communicate in their home language (especially if there is a bilingual adult or child in the classroom for support), and help them recognize that their communication skills in their home language can be transferred to the second language.
- *Use familiar, culturally relevant literature.* Use children's rhymes from the children's language to teach rhyming and letter sounds. This encourages the bilingual child's participation in oral recitations.
- *Help children share personal stories.* Write down the children's dictated stories and help them act them out. Most children want to share stories from their lives.
- *Create activities around songs from home.* Let the children share their favorite songs with classmates. They can learn each other's songs and how the songs connect to their individual worlds. You can create song books and play the songs at the listening center. Songs can be posted on charts with the children's drawings and photos.
- *Use environmental print.* With a bag from a fast-food restaurant, a movie advertisement, and a photo of a local store sign for example, in Spanish, teachers can show children that they know and can read many words. They can then use those words to make connections to other words (Gonzalez-Mena, 2009).
- *Use the universal language of the arts.* Bilingual children can participate easily in dance, art, and drama activities that call for nonverbal communication; the arts are universal languages used to communicate when words cannot or when words are inadequate for ideas and feelings.
- *Use folk literature.* Folk literature is a universal literary form, so it is one place to begin to integrate multicultural art. Many plot lines, like that

of "Cinderella," have been found in hundreds of cultures and written in dozens of languages. Include stories from students' language and cultural heritages. Encourage students to share cultural stories from home, and use these for drama, dance, art, and music activities.

● *Use name tags.* Name tags or hats can be made for characters during drama (for example, tags with *stepsister, mother, father, and prince* in both English and the child's native language).

● *Make a word box.* Give every child a small recipe box with empty index cards at the start of the year. Keep this "word box" nearby so that new words can be collected and used or referred to for children's writing activities. Make sure that each word is accompanied by a small, simple sketch representing that word.

● *Create a print-rich classroom.* Look around your classroom. How many words do you see? A print-rich classroom has meaningful words taped, glued, or written on objects and equipment in each learning center. These words can be written in both English and in the child's native language. To make labels, use any word processor with a large, clear font. Type out a list (in both languages), print it on regular paper, and tape the printed words on objects. Digital cameras are great for adding pictures to these labels.

The early childhood setting becomes a home away from home, the first contact with nonfamily members, the first contact with culturally different people, and the first experience with nonnative speakers. A teacher's attitude and knowledge base are crucial in making the early childhood program accepting and appreciative of diversity (DeBruin-Parecki, 2007).

18-3b Guidelines for Establishing the Classroom Climate for DLL/ESL Learners

The possibilities are endless for teachers of young children who, as role models, are in a unique position to establish the tone or "classroom climate" through decision making, collaboration, interactions, and activities. It is possible to offer the best teaching we can to all young children who are experiencing English as an unfamiliar language. We can help these young children by following some general guidelines.

● Accept individual differences with regard to language-learning time frames. It's a myth that young children can learn a language quickly

and easily. Avoid pressures to "rush" and "push out" children to join the mainstream classroom. Young children need time to acquire, explore, and experience second-language learning.

● Accept children's attempts to communicate because trial and error are a part of the second-language learning process. Negotiating meaning and collaborating in conversations are important. Children should be given opportunities to practice both native and newly established language skills. Adults should not dominate conversations; rather, children should be listened to. Plan and incorporate opportunities for conversation within dramatic play, story time, puppetry, peer interactions, social experiences, field trips, cooking, and other enriching activities.

● Maintain an additive philosophy by recognizing that children need to acquire new language skills instead of replacing existing linguistic skills. Afford young children an opportunity to retain their native language and culture. Allow young learners ample social opportunities to practice emerging linguistic skills.

● Provide a stimulating, active, diverse linguistic environment with many opportunities for language use in meaningful social interactions. Avoid rigid or didactic grammatical approaches with young children. Children enjoy informal play experiences, dramatizations, puppetry, telephone conversations, participation in children's literature, and social interactions with peers.

● Incorporate culturally responsive experiences for all children. Valuing each child's home culture and incorporating meaningful, active participation will help children develop interpersonal skills and contribute to eventual academic and social success. See Figure 18-2 for more suggestions.

Did You Get It?

His new preschool teacher discourages Vladimir, a recent immigrant from Russia, from using Russian words, insisting that he learn the English words for classroom items and activities. His teacher is approaching his language acquisition from a _____ perspective.

a. transformational
b. deficit
c. immigrant-experience
d. molding

Take the full quiz on CourseMate.

Here are some more strategies you can use to differentiate instruction for English as a Second Language Learners or Dual Language Learners.

- Start with what children know. Learn key words and sentences in the child's primary language. These words will help children feel connected to the adult, and give the message that the adult is interested in the children's language.

- Start slowly. Allow time for children to adjust to the new surroundings before approaching them with questions and directions. Use children's names during the activities without actually directing the speech to them.

- Use on-the-spot labeling in meaningful contexts. Identify "teachable moments" to talk about object(s) a child is using or about his/her actions at that particular moment, e.g., "You picked the book" or "Yes, it is blue."

- Double the message. Use words along with plenty of gestures, body language, and actions.

- Use repetition. Say the same thing many times. Emphasize the word you want them to learn, "Look at the hand. See how Mario traced his hand. Do you want to trace your hand?"

- Talk about the here and now. Remember, children (and adults) use context to understand the message. "It is cold outside. We put our jackets on to go outside."

- Expand and extend. Once children begin to use new words, add to what they say. "Yes, cookie. Is this a chocolate cookie? May I eat it?"

- Keep it short. Once the adult gets along well with the child, talk to that child for short periods in the second language. The child may not understand at first, but by hearing the second language in a variety of situations, the child will eventually begin to notice, play with, and grasp intonation patterns and sounds.

- Fine-tune your language. Simplify your messages and use short sentences. "I like your shirt." "Is it new?" "Did you get it yesterday?"

- Accept the use of any combination of a child's home language and English. Do not criticize or directly correct a child for code-switching (mixing languages).

- Recognize children's attempts to use English. Provide positive feedback when children try to use English to communicate.

- Focus on what the children are saying. Focus on the child's message rather on how well the child is using the second language. Allow children to talk or not to talk in accordance with their own paces or abilities.

- Focus on one language at a time. Avoid immediate translations. Constant translations may cause children to tune out the second language.

- Be a good language role model. Although it is common for children learning a second language to "mix" two languages in the same sentence, as a language role model, use one language at a time. Talk in ways you want children to talk.

- Use English songs and finger plays to teach simple vocabulary. Songs such as "Head, Shoulder, Knees and Toes" and "The Wheels on the Bus" teach parts of the body, directional movements, and simple nouns.

- Up the ante. Use your judgment and knowledge of the child to decide when to insist the child use verbal communication instead of gestures.

© Cengage Learning

FIGURE 18-2 Additional suggestions for teaching second-language learners.

18-4 The Antibias Curriculum (ABC)

naeyc DAP Creative teachers promote an inclusive environment, which addresses both the daily life realities of cultural diversity and the potentially biased attitudes and behaviors that are part of this reality. The early childhood teacher creating an inclusive environment plans the curriculum to address the cultural differences represented by the children in the group and in the society in general. This inclusive curriculum reflects sensitivity to all cultural groups in all areas of the curriculum. Related inherently to the inclusive environment is the concept of an antibias curriculum (ABC). This concept, developed by the NAEYC's ABC Task Force and Louise Derman-Sparks (Derman-Sparks & ABC Task Force, 1989), is an excellent starting point for planning an inclusive, antibiased curriculum. The Task Force's booklet contains excellent suggestions on ABC planning, working with parents, and suggested books and materials, which are all essential in preparing an inclusive environment for young children of all cultural groups.

The language arts curriculum is an excellent starting point for the ABC because there are hundreds of good-quality books for children representing a multitude of ethnic groups. Teachers of young children need to select literature that reflects the perspectives, experiences, and values of all ethnic and cultural groups. Choosing and using multicultural books with young children is discussed later in this chapter.

18-4a Multicultural Book Center

DAP An essential part of the ABC is the inclusion of multicultural books. When planning your book center, be sure to fill it with children's books about diverse cultures. By including many bilingual children's books, you will be helping second-language learners feel more at home in your classroom. Reading bilingual books—books that contain words in languages other than English—gives children a very good opportunity to be exposed to multiple languages. Teachers who have bilingual and multilingual books in their classrooms are sending the message that they acknowledge the importance of those languages and cultures. These teachers, by exposing their students to different alphabets and words, are also raising awareness of diversity for the English speakers in their group.

You may find that using a children's book in a child's native language can help acquaint a beginning English language learner with the topic at hand. Also, a book in the child's native language might serve well to soothe feelings of frustration and exhaustion common among second-language learners.

18-4b naeyc DAP Picture Books and Multicultural Learning

Good children's literature features real or imagined African Americans, Asians, Hispanics, Native Americans, Caucasians, Middle Easterners, and a whole rainbow of other children and adults. Children can come to know these multicultural characters intimately by identifying with them as you read stories about how children from different cultures play, work, and live; how they eat, dress, and go to school; and how they feel, act, and even "act out." Introducing children to picture book characters in the stories and activities

you provide is an especially effective way for children to get to know children from other cultures. The experience can be almost as real as having a new child from a different culture in the class.

Even if the book characters are children from a different culture, young children have no difficulty choosing them as models. Children enjoy the characters in their storybooks, and if the story appeals to them, they want to hear it over and over. They come to love the characters in the stories they love. Such stories subtly let them know that multicultural children are accepted in our society because they appear in storybooks.

Although you may have different cultures represented in your group, children are exposed to even more cultural groups by adding multicultural picture books to your book corner. Be sure to read a multicultural book on a regular basis as a natural part of your daily activities. Remember, high-quality multicultural books are *first and foremost* children's literature. Let children enjoy the story first. Then you might discuss the cultural aspects of the story. If you make the reading of a multicultural story book a multicultural lesson every time you read one, children will sense that it is a "kind" of book because of the way you handle its reading. Instead, try talking about all the things that children share in common with the characters in the story. With the vast majority of multicultural books available today, this shouldn't be hard.

18-4c naeyc Parents, Language Arts, and the Multicultural Classroom

Creative language arts involve more than teaching information directly to children. It involves the child and his or her individual culture. Here are some suggestions to bring families into classrooms where they are valued as experts who have something to teach teachers about their children.

- Talk with families to learn how their children communicate important needs and wants (for example, "milk," "hungry," "hurts," "diaper/potty"). Sometimes these needs, wants, and feelings may be expressed in the child's home language. Providers and teachers can be encouraged to learn this vocabulary themselves so they will recognize the words more easily when children use them (August & Shanahan, 2008).
- Help parents compile booklets with rhymes and stories the parents learned as children that they can share in learning areas.

- Encourage parents to bring from home literacy materials, such as tapes and music CDs, videos in their home languages, calendars, and newspapers, plus paper, envelopes, and stamps that they and their children can use to write letters in the writing center (August & Shanahan, 2008).

- Involve children and family members in creating shoe box biographies—shoe boxes filled with artifacts that prompt stories about their lives—and picture books about home activities.

- Teachers and caregivers need to look for ways to incorporate aspects of children's cultures into daily routines because children become more interested in the learning process when activities look familiar to them.

- Offer written information in languages other than English as an important way to reach out to culturally diverse families.

- Teachers should always ask families how to pronounce a child's name and not assume they know. Nor should they create an "American" name for a child because they can't pronounce the child's given name.

- Be sensitive to the cultural shifts that immigrant students or other students with minority family and community cultures must make as they move between school and home. This transition may be most difficult at the beginning of the school week, after students have been immersed in their home culture over the weekend. Teachers need to be sensitive to transitional challenges and collaborate with families to develop mechanisms to ease the stress caused by them.

- Help parents gain the skills to negotiate the education system and knowledge of the norms of behavior that govern schools (Hirschler, 2005). Without this information, many minority parents, especially new immigrants, may not feel competent to negotiate the system on behalf of their child or feel knowledgeable enough to support their child's efforts. Teachers can help by talking with parents directly rather than using more formal written communications, such as letters or notes. This is particularly valuable to families from cultures in which personal connections and conversational language are the preferred ways of gathering information (Cruzado-Guerrero & Kenreich, 2008).

Did You Get It?

How does a preschool teacher who asks her students' parents to send in Jamaican music because they emigrated from Jamaica fulfilling the requirements of an antibias curriculum?

a. She exposes the students to a range of music, honing their music appreciation.

b. She values the family as experts who can contribute to the classroom.

c. She stimulates the students' language development.

d. She promotes creative play.

Take the full quiz on CourseMate.

18-5 Emerging Literacy and Emergent Reading

naeyc DAP If *reading* is defined as "the interpretation of symbols," it could be said that a child begins reading the day he or she is born. Literacy emerges as a baby gets excited when he sees his bottle. The baby stops crying when Mother enters the room and smiles. The baby gurgles with pleasure when members of the family stop to play with him. He is responding to what he "reads" into the actions of others. These experiences are all examples of emerging literacy, which precedes understanding the printed word.

Not all children should be expected to learn to read in the same way, at the same rate, or at the same age. Children begin by reading pictures, taking great delight in recognizing objects with which they are familiar. As adults read to children, thereby exposing them to words in the books they read, children begin to understand that printed words say something.

Pretend reading of favorite books is an activity familiar to many parents and teachers of young children. During pretend reading—also called *emergent reading,* children practice reading-like behaviors that build their confidence in themselves as readers.

Adults interested in emergent or pretend reading have long assumed that children imitate adult reading—that is, they pick up reading-like behaviors and story language after adults read aloud to them. We can see the beginnings of independent emergent reading when children participate in adult read-alouds by "reading along" with an adult reader—mumbling, echoing phrases, and completing sentences and phrases when the adult reader pauses.

During emergent reading, children combine several information sources: the pictures and print in the book;

THINK ABOUT IT

Digital Storytelling

Storytelling is one of the oldest forms of communication, which creates connections and stretches our imaginations. The need to share and interpret stories in the classroom is still important, but we just have more ways of telling it using technology. Varying your lesson presentation between traditional storytelling and online sources can be engaging for students living in a world filled with technology. Capture the attention of your students by integrating some of these great online resources.

- **Dallas Art Museum**—Arturo's Art Stories from the Dallas Museum is most appropriate for elementary students. It uses animation, audio, and user interaction to explore the meaning behind artwork. These stories could easily be used as an introduction to a unit or as an independent student activity.

- **Screen Actors Guild**—Another site useful for younger students is Story Line Online presented by members of the Screen Actors Guild. Listed among other children's classic stories, *When Picasso Met Mootisse*, written by Nina Laden, is read aloud by an actor and is a change of pace from a traditional read-aloud story during class.

- **Memorial Art Gallery**—Students in fourth grade through high school will enjoy the variety of world

cultures represented in Picturing the Story from the Memorial Art Gallery at the University of Rochester. This informative site offers several interactive features, including a "looking tour" of a work of art while listening to a professional storyteller or watching the description told in sign language.

- **Delaware Museum**—The Art of Storytelling, sponsored by the Delaware Art Museum, is an engaging website appropriate for all levels. The first of three categories on the site lets you experience a story about a piece of fine art by listening or reading content created by website visitors. In the second category, choose an inspirational work of art and write or record an audio story about it. The third category contains a collage builder that uses images from the collection to create a new composition producing new meanings or stories.

Technology has never been more relevant and integrated into the lives of students as it is today. Online content can help you reach these techie kids and achieve some of your instructional goals. There's more than one way to tell a story, and these online resources will help.

---

input from adult listeners, as well as their own memory for having heard and discussed the book previously; their personal experiences; and their background knowledge about the world, language, and how stories sound. In emergent literacy programs, children enjoy and participate actively in reading experiences long before they are readers in the conventional sense of the word.

Both participation in read-aloud sessions and emergent reading give children opportunities to learn about the language and the meaning of reading in a natural setting. By giving children opportunities to interact with books through read-alouds and emergent readings, teachers help children grow as competent and confident readers (Dunst, Trivette, & Hamby, 2007).

Conventional reading involves total development—emotional, social, physical, and intellectual readiness. A child who has not yet acquired large-muscle control will not be able to develop more refined skills, such as matching shapes and recognizing patterns needed for reading. Some children are

not interested or physically ready to read until they are 6, 7, or even 8 years of age. When children are forced to engage in reading activities before they are physically, intellectually, or emotionally ready, reading can become a burden. Vision, hearing, diet, and physical coordination are all factors to be considered. Eye-muscle development is necessary and cannot be rushed. Speaking skills are needed for success in reading. And motivation is a primary factor for success.

18-5a Read-Alouds and Emergent Reading

Children who participate in read-aloud sessions and do their own emergent reading of favorite books grow as readers because they are engaged in authentic, natural literacy, not in instruction-focused tasks that break up reading into separate "skills." Practice in the natural activity of emergent reading is a good preparation for later, conventional reading.

18-5b Prewriting Skills

Another skill that is part of a child's emerging literacy is writing. In the preschool and early childhood period, a child is developing the physical skills needed to write later on in school. It is not the goal to have young children "practice" letters and words in the early childhood language arts program. Instead, the goal is to provide young children with opportunities to practice the hand–eye coordination and small-muscle skills needed to be able to write.

For preschoolers, writing is a part of the total language experience, preceded by many fine-motor-control activities. Writing begins when children first become interested in making their own marks, and it continues to be a part of their everyday experiences. When children show an interest in writing, large pieces of paper are made available along with crayons, felt-tip pens, and pencils.

For preschoolers, reading and writing are closely related. Writing can be part of the language experience of children when children dictate stories for the teacher to write down.

Use children's artwork in conjunction with reading and writing. Besides making the obvious use of illustrations for stories, early readers can give titles to their work. Asking children if they would like to give their work a title reflects the teacher's valuing their work (see Photo 18-3). Some children may want to give their work a title; others may not. Young children can also use photographs to tell stories that the teacher writes down. Preschool children might bring their baby pictures to school and then be photographed by the teacher. Mount both pictures side by side and then have children dictate descriptions of what they could do as babies and what they can do now that they are "big." Children can share the displayed individual books. A language experience approach such as this encourages literacy. Using cartoon boards and cartoon balloons enhances writing and reading motivation. Children can dictate or write captions in the balloons, stating what different characters in the strips are saying.

18-5c The Language Arts Center

All of the previously mentioned forms of emerging literacy and early reading quite naturally take place in the early childhood language arts center. When planning your language arts center, keep in mind that it is essential to create a place where children can explore the world of books. A language arts center is an important part of every early childhood classroom as well as

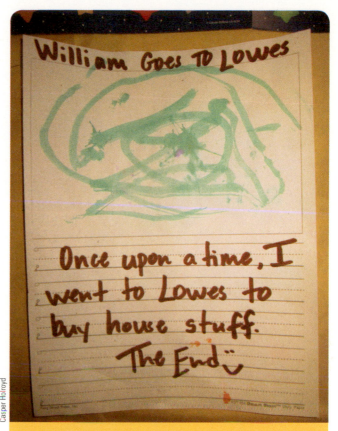

Casper Holroyd

PHOTO 18-3 Some children will want a title and the "story" to go with their artwork.

elementary classroom. As you use books during circle time, children will realize the magic of books—that they have good make-believe stories or are full of facts and have pretty pictures. Children will then want to explore those books on their own, so they need to have a well-organized place where they can go and read.

Think about the physical space first and be sure you find a place that is away from the more active goings-on in the room, a place where the child can quietly explore books (see Photo 18-4). Gather together a table, some chairs or soft cushions, and shelves for books, tapes, CDs, and magazines. Nearby, create a listening center with recorded books. In the listening center, children can examine books and learn how they work by following text while listening to a recording. When covering some units, you might want to create an unusual seating place. For example, you might make an airplane out of a large box as you talk and read about types of transportation.

Take time to decorate nearby bulletin boards or tops of shelves with book jackets, pictures, flowers, and special collections related to the books you have in the book center. If you choose to display the letters of

Casper Holroyd

PHOTO 18-4 Provide a quiet language arts center where kids can go to read.

the alphabet, be sure you do so in a developmentally appropriate manner. These guidelines are helpful.

- Place letters where children can see them. Alphabet displays too far above children's heads are of little use. Letters need to be at eye level where children can examine them.

- Place letters where children can refer to them as they work and play. When they are writing, children are far more likely to make use of letter guides that are close at hand. Teachers can apply alphabet strips to tabletops or laminate letter-writing guides that children can take off a shelf and bring with them to wherever they are writing.

- Place letters where children can handle them. Children notice the shapes of letters when they do alphabet puzzles or use letter-shaped cookie cutters in damp sand or dough. Magnetic letters and alphabet blocks allow children to explore letter/sound connections, arrange and rearrange letters to form words, and become more aware of the sequences of sounds within words.

Set up a writing center offering a variety of writing tools (pencils, crayons, markers, magnetic letters), paper (different shapes, sizes, and colors), and other

kinds of writing surfaces (chalk boards and magnetic boards). Encourage writing by providing an alphabet chart and posting a list of children's names. Include book-making materials (hole punch, stapler, shoelaces, or thick yarn) and ready-made blank books for children to fill. Provide individual mailboxes for children (and for yourself) so children can send and receive messages.

Offer a variety of books and magazines. Include books related to topics you and the children are exploring. Rotate books frequently as children build skills and discover new interests.

Display books on low shelves, with the covers facing out. Place certain kinds of books on the shelves so that they are readily available at all times—Mother Goose books; poetry books; a children's simple encyclopedia (there are some two-and three-volume sets); "sense" books where children can touch, scratch, and smell as they look; and some of the classic stories with which children are already familiar, such as *Goldilocks and the Three Bears*, *The Three Little Pigs*, and *The Cat in the Hat*. Books reflecting ethnic diversity should always be available for children's use. Books portraying ethnic diversity of children in the group as well as those not represented in the group need to be on the shelves.

As concepts—the alphabet, numbers, animals, families, and transportation—are introduced, provide a special bookshelf or display area where children can find books on those subjects and expand their knowledge about each concept.

You can begin to introduce the organization of a real library by color-coding the different types of books with a colored dot fastened to the bottom edge of each book. Then, use paper strips on the shelves so that children can replace the books where they belong just by matching the strip on the shelf with the mark on the book.

Help children determine what rules should be followed as they read in the language arts center; these should relate to behavior, care of books, and removal of books from the area.

Did You Get It?

Although she does not yet know how to read, five-year-old Jordan likes to leaf through books and look at the pictures. Jordan can best be described as a(n) _____ reader.

   a. emergent
   b. conventional
   c. budding
   d. dramatic play

Take the full quiz on CourseMate.

18-6 Reading with Infants, Toddlers, and Preschool Children

naeyc **DAP** The way teachers use stories is as important as the stories themselves. Infants and toddlers come to a story experience with few if any preconceived notions about what that experience *should* be like. This gives the teacher plenty of room to be creative and imaginative.

18-6a Reading with Infants and Toddlers

Within that flexibility, there are some factors to keep in mind when reading stories with infants and toddlers in order to make the story experiences we share with them as enjoyable and productive as possible.

- Allow freedom and choice. Participation in story sharing should not be compulsory for very young children. Children should be invited to join in, and if they are interested in participating, they will let you know. Try to share stories with children throughout the day, not only during a fixed period in the schedule. Initiate stories when the situation seems right, and make time when children do the initiating.

- Adjust expectations to fit children's abilities and preferences. Your understanding of child development should, in principle, inform when you share stories and which stories you select. For example, a hungry child will not usually be interested in a story, even if that story is one of her favorites. A toddler busy pushing his doll in the stroller will probably not want to stop for a story, either. And even if it seems like the optimal time for sharing a story, when distractions seem minimal, toddlers often will wander away if they are not ready for the type of story being shared or if something else captures their attention.

- Keep story groups small and intimate. Because one of the key benefits of sharing stories with infants and toddlers is fostering close relationships among the story participants, it is best to share stories with no more than three children at a time, so everyone can nestle close. Keeping groups small also allows each child to be an active participant. One or even a very few children can join in a story's refrain without being too noisy or disruptive for the other children in the room. Small groups also make it easier to maintain children's interest through eye contact and gentle touches. Larger groups are likely to

PHOTO 18-5 Show pleasure and enthusiasm when reading to toddlers.

Casper Holroyd

require the adult to spend more time keeping order than sharing the story, which takes away from the enjoyment.

- Show pleasure and enthusiasm. Your attitude as you share stories is critical if you want these experiences to be successful for infants and toddlers (see Photo 18-5). Very young children are influenced greatly by our behavior, and they are keen observers of what we do and say. If we are enthusiastic, interested, and clearly enjoying the story, children will be more likely to feel these things, too. Pleasure is contagious—and so is boredom.

- Be expressive. Being expressive when sharing a story helps young listeners engage with what they are hearing. Being expressive might mean using a soft voice for a gentle bedtime story, or making your voice loud and growling like a tiger when telling a story about zoo animals. This also entails changing your tone of voice or accent for different characters. Another part of being expressive is using gestures, facial expressions, and body language in ways that support the story. If young children are accustomed to hearing expressive language, they will use it themselves when they begin to tell their own stories.

- Use props. Story sharing can be enriched with the careful use of props or other supplementary resources. However, props are not necessary for every story and can sometimes be distracting. For example, a teacher might introduce a large puppet to tell the story of the Little Red Hen; but if the children are more interested in the puppet than the story, then the prop might not be adding to the story experience itself.

● Follow children's cues. Children give many different cues or signs about how they like the stories we share with them. For the youngest children, those cues are likely to be conveyed through sounds and body language, such as gestures, wriggling, and facial expressions. As infants become toddlers, they can respond more explicitly by saying things such as "Again," "More," and "No," or even by getting up and simply walking away. Whenever possible, repeat a story that children express interest in hearing again. Depending on the length of the story and children's interest level, some story sessions could be quite long, while others will be much shorter. The desire for repetition, which is valuable for building vocabulary and developing language skills, shows that children are engaged (Birckmayer, Kennedy, & Stonehouse, 2009).

Casper Holroyd

PHOTO 18-6 Read favorite books repeatedly to encourage reading.

18-6b Reading with Preschool Children

By becoming aware of the benefits of linking emergent reading to read-aloud sessions and by arranging classroom space and time to promote these activities, teachers can maximize the benefits of reading aloud and emergent reading in early childhood classrooms in the following ways.

● Invite children to participate actively in read-aloud sessions. Ask questions that require children to predict what will happen next and to link the story to their own experiences. As books become more familiar to children, pause before familiar or repeated patterns and allow children to complete the reading. Give children opportunities to choose their favorite books to be read to the group.

● Provide frequent opportunities for young children to engage in book handling and emergent reading. Although for many years many classrooms have featured daily book browsing time, there are still too many classrooms in which children look at books only as a transitional or optional activity with books available to children who have finished other "required" activities or who choose to look at books during "free-choice" times. As a result, children who have had less experience with books or who work slowly have little occasion for self-directed interaction with books. Teachers

should instead establish daily "serious reading time" when all children are expected to be involved with books in whatever manner is most comfortable for them—browsing through books, looking at pictures, or emergently or conventionally reading.

● Read favorite books repeatedly to encourage emergent reading (see Photo 18-6). Follow through by making these books available for children to look at on their own or with other children and adults. Children are more likely to choose books and engage in emergent reading with books that are familiar to them. Set up the classroom so that familiar books are available and visible to children during independent time and free time. Arrange for reading aloud to be done in or near the language arts center so that children see the connection between hearing books read and reading them on their own and that books read by the teacher can be easily put in the language arts center. Schedule time for children to independently read or look at books soon after the teacher has read to them, again highlighting the connection between the adult read-aloud and children's independent involvement with books.

● During read-aloud and independent-involvement times, teachers have opportunities to observe children's emerging literacy in real-life situations. Become more aware of how children respond during read-aloud sessions (a tape recorder might be useful). Which of the children asked and answered questions? Which ones participated in reading by chiming in on familiar parts or by making predictions? How do children's questions and comments change over several readings of the same book? What kinds of questions and comments came from you, the teacher?

● By listening to children's emergent readings (live or taped), teachers can see how much book content and book language children incorporate. Do children use the distinctive language of books? Do they use literary formulae such as "once upon a time"? What sources of information do children use when they "read"? Do they use the pictures, the print, memory of the text and discussion, and their personal experiences?

● Educate parents about the ability of their child to "pretend read" books and to participate in reading through "completion reading." Some parents worry that "pretend reading" will result in bad habits that will prevent children from learning to "really read." Reassure all of these parents that their children's reading-like behaviors, even though they may not involve attention to print, are a source of future reading success. Parents also need to understand that allowing children to participate in read-aloud sessions through joint reading and discussion can enrich the literacy experience for parents and children.

18-6c Children's Books

When reading books to very young preschool children, toddlers, or children in the early elementary grades, it is important choose these books with care. They must be right for the developmental level of the child (see Photo 18-7). The pictures should be easily seen and the story easily understood by young listeners.

"ABC" or alphabet books for young children also must be chosen carefully. Very young children need simple, uncluttered alphabet books. Words should represent familiar, concrete objects, with a beginning *apple* rather than *atom*.

First alphabet books typically pair initial sounds with words, and these associations should depict regular sounds. Pages that proclaim "*K* is for *knife*" or "*G* is for *gnu*" bewilder rather than educate. These key words should also have unambiguous names: "*B* is for *bow-wow*," in a book filled with objects rather than sounds will confuse the child who identified the animal as a dog.

Casper Holroyd

PHOTO 18-7 When reading books to young children, make sure they are the right developmental level of the child.

In addition, illustrations must be obvious and straightforward. Complications in naming lead to misunderstandings. One preschooler, upset because she had read an alphabet book incorrectly, sadly pointed out this problem: "I said '*R* for *rope*' but the book meant '*S* for *snake*.'" There are three additional features characteristic of good ABC books:

● Well-written ABC books focus on a central idea or concept, and the alphabet sequence merely provides a story format. You should look for ABC books that follow a limited subject such as endangered species rather than a broad subject such as wild animals.

● The best ABC books provide thoughtful features such as bilevel text and addenda, with bilevel text appearing on the page in two font sizes for two reading skill levels. Younger listeners enjoy the illustrations and sometimes notice the letters of the alphabet or the larger print. Beginning readers may explore the accompanying text, which appears in smaller print size.

● Good-quality ABC publications invite the response or involvement of the children in the read-aloud experience, and they also provide teachers with a rich source of ideas for extended activities in the early childhood setting. ABC books can be starting points for group projects or individual activities.

Children interacting with their first texts are not reading in the traditional sense of relying solely on the printed word. Instead, as emergent readers, they depend on illustrations to create meaning.

Consequently, in initial alphabet books, only one or two objects should appear on the page, acknowledging the young child's perceptual and spatial skills. There's plenty of time later on to hunt for hidden pictures, sort out numerous nouns, or locate obscure objects after letter–sound correspondence has been mastered.

Did You Get It?

A teacher who is reading aloud and frequently stops to ask the students to consider what actions the book's characters will take next is probably reading to
- **a.** preschoolers.
- **b.** toddlers.
- **c.** first- and second-graders.
- **d.** third- and fourth-graders.

Take the full quiz on CourseMate.

18-7 Poetry and Language Development

naeyc DAP Poetry is part of the magic that motivates children to love reading. The educational benefits of including poetry in the early childhood program are many. Exposure to poetry raises children's level of general language development and vocabulary development and whets their appetite for reading, too!

Some other benefits of including poetry on a regular basis in the early childhood program include the following.

- Poetry's often playful approach to language helps children think about language forms as well as meaning. The predictable rhythms of Mother Goose rhymes naturally segment speech sounds and expose and highlight phonetic similarities and differences in a way that normal speech does not.
- Children take pride in learning to recite short poems. Thus, poetry can be used to stimulate the development of memory, which will aid in future learning. Knowing poems enhances feelings of competence, which is important for young children. Young children who continually hear poetry read effectively, and those who have the opportunity to join informally in reciting it will soon have quite a repertoire of memorized poetry without any effort. It is quite appropriate to expect 3- and 4-year-old children to happily chant finger plays, Mother Goose rhymes, and short poems such as those found at the end of this chapter.

- Finger plays, or poems recited and accompanied by appropriate body movements, help develop coordination and muscle tone. Asking children to invent their own movements helps them develop problem-solving abilities. Some of these poems also help in learning to name body parts ("Hokey Pokey," for example).
- Acting out poetry can be a fun and beneficial drama and speech activity for children of all ages. By allowing children to organize and act out poems using props and costumes, the teacher encourages the development of creativity and positive self-concept as well as of language.
- Children can be encouraged to illustrate favorite poems to display in the classroom or to take home, thus stimulating artistic expression and development while aiding language development. Using colored chalks, paint, markers, and crayons, many young artists will illustrate the mood of the poem more movingly than we ever could have imagined!

Let poetry fill your and the children's days. Why not recite a verse while lining up to go to lunch? Memorize short poems to recite when waiting for stragglers to take their seats. Start the day with a poem; end the day with one as well. Create the job of poetry selector for the job chart. Poetry can rhyme or not, speak to deep emotions, or lift us with light language and witty wordplay.

Check out the Reading is Fundamental website for more tips on using poetry to build literary skills. You will find many ideas for incorporating poetry into the curriculum.

18-7a Selecting Appropriate Poems

Using poetry in the classroom will, of course, be much more valuable and enjoyable if the poem selection is made carefully with the children's interests and needs in mind. Not all children have the same needs. And by no means are all children at the same developmental level. Choose poetry that meets all developmental levels in the group.

Another important criterion for selecting poetry to present in any classroom is that the teacher should like it, too. It is not possible for a teacher to read a poem well or generate much enthusiasm for it if he or she does not enjoy it.

- When selecting poems, think about what the children are likely to find appealing. From approximately 3 to 6 years of age, young children like things that seem relevant to them. For

What to Look for in Children's Books

Children today live in an exciting media-driven time of television, video games, and computers, yet no medium can stir a child's imagination like the pages of a good book. There is an enormous selection of children's books available today. The following are some general guidelines on what to look for in choosing children's books from preschool through grade 5.

Baby Books. There are four basic kinds of baby books.

- Board books feature sturdy cardboard pages that can be wiped clean.
- Touch-and-feel books have cloth, feathers, fur, and familiar "feely" things attached to them for little ones to discover.
- Cloth books are made of safe, washable material.
- Bath books are constructed of soft, durable plastic and can take a lot of abuse.

What to look for:

- Simple text and art
- Repetition and bouncy rhymes
- Bright and familiar photos or artwork (there should be a connection between baby's surroundings and the book's pictures)
- A sturdy book that can handle many spills
- Rounded corners for safety
- Right size and shape for little hands
- A book you will enjoy as well; baby will recognize your enjoyment

Preschool. Preschool books are on a higher level than baby books but on a slightly lower level than picture books. In addition to hardcover and paperback, preschool books come in a variety of novelty formats. Among them are the following.

- Lift-the-flap books have sturdy pages and flaps to lift that reveal hidden words or pictures.
- Pop-up books have paper-engineered pages that make pictures three-dimensional.
- Pull-tab books have tabs to pull to change the pictures.

Some books combine all of these features. These kinds of books are designed to be played with as much as to be read—yet another way to show that books are fun. What to look for in preschool books:

- A book that clearly covers the concept you are trying to teach
- A book that helps develop children's sense of humor
- Easy and fun story line
- Clear and easy-to-read text
- Colorful, high-quality illustrations that children can connect to their own lives and situations

Picture Books. Picture books are one of the most popular forms of children's books and are appropriate for a wide range of ages and reading levels. Picture books have varying amounts of art and text. Some are even wordless! Some story lines are simple, while others are quite complex. Subjects can be beautiful, funny, moving, scary, or just plain silly. What is important is that you find a picture book the children in your group will relate to and enjoy.

What to look for:

- Art or photography children respond to
- Story lines that elicit questions and discussions
- Stories that develop children's sense of humor
- Stories that help with children's issues—such as sibling rivalry or going to school
- Stories you enjoyed as a child and would like to share with children
- Titles recommended by reviewers and award committees

Early Readers. These books are designed to supplement a child's reading program at school. As with picture books, early readers cover a wide variety of subjects. They are illustrated, though the emphasis is more on text than on illustrations. Early readers are targeted toward specific reading levels or by grade. As every child is different, you may want to judge on your own which reading level is appropriate.

What to look for:

- A reading level that will challenge but will not intimidate children
- Clear text (the print size varies with reading levels)
- A topic that will stimulate further interest in reading
- Favorite artists children have enjoyed at an earlier level of reading
- Nonfiction subjects children enjoy, such as sports, history, fantasy, or adventure
- New subjects to introduce to children, such as fantasy and folklore

Fiction. When we enter the world of fiction, we leave behind colorful pictures and favorite characters, and subject matter becomes more complicated. The early readers are the stepping-stones to these more advanced works.

What to look for:

- Books with a reading level that will challenge and stimulate
- Books with a subject that interests the young reader; many children want to pick out their own books at this age
- Some of the more popular and enduring titles that are available in different editions (the trim size of the books may vary, and the cover art may vary as well, but almost without exception the text remains the same)
- Some classic tales in abridged formats

Computer Assisted Instruction (CAI) and the Development of Early Literacy Skills in Young Children

Numerous research studies have shown an important link between the development of phonological awareness and advancements in reading (Macaruso & Rodman, 2011). Phonological awareness, the ability to analyze the sound structure of language, is a key component in acquiring phonic word-attack skills. The ability to segment words into syllables and smaller units of sound and to blend these units back into words provides a foundation for mastering phonics, the letter-sound mapping used to identify words in print.

Two studies examined the efficacy of using computer-assisted instruction (CAI) to supplement a phonics-based reading curriculum for preschoolers and kindergarteners in three elementary schools in an urban community north of Boston, Massachusetts. Students in 14 preschool classes participated. The 14 classes consisted of both morning and afternoon classes of seven teachers. For each teacher, one class was randomly assigned to be a treatment class, and the other class was designated a control class. Students who turned 5 years old by the end of the school year were eligible for the study. There were 50 students in the treatment classes and 48 in the control classes. Students came from diverse sociocultural backgrounds: Caucasian (32% treatment, 40% control), Hispanic (37% treatment, 40% control), Asian/Mid-Eastern (26% treatment, 13% control), and African American (5% treatment, 7% control). A greater percentage of treatment students than control students qualified for free or reduced lunch (63% treatment, 20% control).

All students participated in 200 minutes (20 ten-minute sessions) of computer-assisted programs. All treatment and control classes were engaged in a Language and Emergent Literacy Skills program developed by the preschool staff in the school system. The CAI was designed for independent student use, requiring minimal teacher involvement during a session. Teachers were instructed to have students use the CAI programs.

For preschoolers, the treatment group made significantly greater gains than controls in phonological awareness. For the kindergarten children, treatment students with low pretest scores made significantly greater gains than controls, particularly in word reading. Overall, preschoolers and low-performing kindergartners benefited from intensive practice provided by CAI programs.

The researchers found that CAI use allowed low performers in the treatment group to show even greater gains than low performers in the control group. The CAI programs provided treatment students with opportunities to engage in systematic and structured exercises that specifically address individual needs. Overall, they concluded that well-structured CAI programs can deliver the kind of intensive practice that young children benefit from in acquiring early literacy skills (Macaruso & Rodman, 2011).

(Macaruso & Rodman 2011).

something to be relevant to children, it must somehow relate to the world as they know it, if not directly to them. By selecting poetry about familiar objects, events, and feelings, the teacher takes a major step toward making poetry interesting and enjoyable for young children. Older children enjoy poetry that challenges their imagination and thinking skills.

● Focus on popular topics. There are certain subjects that almost all young children enjoy. For this reason, these subjects are traditionally dealt with in most early childhood programs—self-awareness, the senses, the family, feelings, transportation, seasons, holidays, animals,

plants, water, earth, sky, and so on. By selecting poems that deal with these subjects as they are being emphasized in class, you can capitalize on the interest generated by other classroom activities: science, social studies, music, and so on. Many children's poetry books classify poems according to these categories, making it easy to find appropriate poems.

The American Library Association website is an excellent resource for high-quality children's books for young children of all ages. You can also locate current and past Caldecott and Newberry award-winning books at the American Library Association (ALA) website. Simply enter the titles "Newberry" and/or

"Caldecott" in the search bar to access this page. See the "This One's for You!" box on page 423 for guidelines on what to look for in choosing books for children.

Encourage frequent use of the language arts center. This means that you need to change the displays and what books are available so that children will want to explore continually to see what is new. It's hard to be interested in a shabby collection of books casually tossed on a table in the corner of the room!

Involve the children in decorating the language arts center. They can help you change the display or make pictures for use on the library corner bulletin board. Then the book center will be a place where they feel they belong.

Did You Get It?

A nursery school teacher recites the first lines of poems, then expects her students to recite the remaining lines. From a developmental perspective, she

a. expects too much from her students.

b. is enriching her students' language development.

c. is squelching her students' natural creativity.

d. is engaging in an inappropriate activity.

Take the full quiz on CourseMate.

18-8 Guidelines for Story Reading Groups

Reading to young children has a few very general requirements. For instance, it is best to work with children's short attention spans by choosing books that are not too long. Young children's visual discrimination also requires books that have pictures large enough for them to see. (Remember, the small muscles of the eyes are the last to develop to maturity.) A book with a story that is simple, yet interesting in its wording, is also good for young children.

Children in the middle- to upper-elementary levels still enjoy illustrated books, but the story is becoming equally as important to them. These children begin to enjoy fiction in which the subject matter becomes more complex. The variety of subjects available for use with older children reflects their expanding interests and personalities. Types of books of special interest to this age group are science fiction, fantasy, mystery, and tragedy as well as books on relationships, humorous tales, horror stories, and sports. Consider

the following suggestions to help you read stories to young children more effectively.

- Select a suitable spot that is quiet, away from distracting noises and activities. In the language arts center, have books displayed at children's eye level. Have books already read out for children to look at and "re-read" themselves.

- There is no law saying that reading aloud is always a large-group activity. In fact, it is often very difficult to read to a large group of young children because interest and attention span differences multiply as the group increases in size. Ideally, a small group of six to eight children is a more manageable and comfortable size for reading effectively. With toddlers, a group of two to three children is best.

- See that everyone is seated comfortably. Avoid crowding. Be sure that you as storyteller can see all the children's faces and that they can see yours. Rugs on the floor in a semicircle facing the teacher make a good seating arrangement. Sitting in chairs is uncomfortable for young children and causes a distraction if a child falls out of one.

- If using a book, be sure to hold it so that all can see it. Do not hold the book in your lap. The best plan is to hold it out to one side up beside your cheek. This means that you must be able to read the story out of the side of your eye without turning the book toward you.

- Be sure you like the story you read; otherwise, you will put little enthusiasm into the telling of it.

- Know your story well! If you do not, you will focus too much of your attention on the book. You must be free to notice the reactions of the children. Also, knowing the story well means that you will be able to tell it with appropriate enthusiasm, expression, and emphasis. Sounds are better made than read. For example, crow for *cock-a-doodle-do* and bark for *bow-wow* instead of just reading the words.

- Read the story unhurriedly with an interesting, well-modulated voice. Read naturally—do not "talk down" to the children or have a special "storytelling" voice.

- Do not comment so much throughout the story as you read it or point out so many things in the pictures that you break the thread of the story and spoil its effect.

● Encourage comments and questions but not to such a degree that it interrupts the flow of the story.

Practice reading a book to a group of children. Then go back to these guidelines to check to see if you used them effectively with children. It takes a good deal of practice to achieve mastery of the skill of story reading. If you make the experience a fun learning experience for yourself with the children, you are halfway there!

Reading to toddlers is an activity they truly enjoy. Here are a few guidelines for reading to this age group.

● While you read to toddlers, follow the lines with your fingers. This helps toddlers who are learning that pages are read from top to bottom and from left to right and that pictures and printed words are related to each other.

● Give toddlers a choice of books. Books at this age are good for memory development. As toddlers remember story lines, they begin to choose what they want to hear over and over again. Listening to preferred choices again and again increases a toddler's sense of self and security. Give toddlers several choices of books, and you'll learn just which ones they love.

● Choose interactive books. Some toddlers may have difficulty sitting still. Try to find books that encourage their participation by pushing moveable parts, uncovering a hidden character, making a figure pop up, or patting the bunny.

● Use books that toddlers can carry. Toddlers like to possess books. Look for ones with handles or large plastic rings that toddlers can clutch and carry around as precious possessions.

● Show your pleasure. As you settle down to read, let children know you enjoy books and reading together. After all, toddlers are great copycats. If you are involved in a simple story, toddlers will get swept into the tale. As you encourage them to help turn pages, toddlers become truly involved with books for pleasure, for learning, and for life.

18-8a Storytelling

In today's modern world, storytelling has become a lost art. Despite a strong connection between storytelling and literacy, many teachers do not engage in storytelling to children. They may offer regular picture-book readings but neglect storytelling. Yet, the ancient art of storytelling is a vital way to inspire children's imaginations as well as language and listening skills. Storytelling is *not reading from a book to children*. In storytelling, the teacher weaves the story using his or her voice and expressions to compel the child's attention and interest.

Storytelling events that actively engage listeners in the making of the story create a shared experience that bonds the teller and the listeners. This personal interaction and active participation are very different from the story viewing that young children frequently experience in today's high-tech world (Isbell, 2003). Stories presented in a form such as television, videos, or movies cannot personally involve children or invite them into the story.

Storytelling isn't limited to just one kind of story. When you develop your storytelling curriculum, be sure to include a good variety of these story types:

● Fables—Short tales that have a moral and communicate a truth about life. The main characters in fables are often animals that act and think like humans.

● Fairy tales—Stories that often feature fairies, elves, genies, pixies, leprechauns, and other make-believe characters.

● Legends—Stories that revolve around incidents that are believed to have taken place in a particular culture's history.

● Folk tales—Stories that come to us from many parts of the world. These stories reflect a particular country or people's flavor and preserve cultural traditions.

● Poetry—Rhyming poetry, in particular Mother Goose rhymes, is a source of excellent storytelling for young children.

18-8b Tips for Storytelling

Discover the right story to tell.
● Look for stories that are age appropriate.
● Find stories that you love.
● Check picture books written for different age levels.
● Collect stories from family, friends, and community.
● Create your own stories.

Learn the story.
● Read it several times.
● Break it into a beginning, middle, and end.

Speak naturally.
- Use your normal speaking voice.
- Use sound effects, such as unusual voice and story sounds, sparingly.

Use simple, natural gestures. Add gestures when they add to the story, but don't overuse them.

Polish the story. Tell it, retell it, and retell it.

Once you have a story ready to tell to your satisfaction, the next step is to share it with the children.

- Make eye contact with your listeners.
- Introduce the story.
- Tell the story looking directly into your listeners' eyes.
- Encourage your listeners to interact with you.
- Enjoy and work with your audience's enthusiasm.

A puppet is a natural prop to use when storytelling. Even a shy child will relate to a puppet. Puppets are also multisensory vehicles for storytelling. They create an art and language experience that children can understand. When you find a special puppet, give it a personality and a home, and you'll be amazed how children interact with it. Use it in your story and throughout your curriculum.

Some stories include sound effects or repeated phrases that children can play with or repeat during the story. Listening to stories draws attention to the sounds of language and helps children develop sensitivity to the way language works. Children, as listeners and participants, experience the joy of the repetitive phrase, "The sky is falling" or the musical quality of the chant, "fee-fi-fo-fum." Developing auditory discrimination connects the sounds of words, phrases, and passages, influencing phonemic awareness in a meaningful way (Isbell, 2003). When children begin to "read" a familiar story, these sound phrases are often the first words of the story they identify and repeat.

Drawing children into the telling helps them understand how the story works, what phrases are repeated, and the sequence of action. Active participation in literacy experiences can enhance the development of comprehension, oral language, and the sense of story structure (Birckmayer et al., 2009). By providing immediate feedback to the storyteller and sharing observations, the children create the experience together.

Did You Get It?

From a developmental perspective, a mother who moves her fingers along the lines while reading books to her toddler is
- **a.** exposing her child to the fundamentals of reading.
- **b.** detracting from the reading experience.
- **c.** wasting her time, because it does not teach her child anything.
- **d.** teaching her child letter recognition, which is appropriate at this age.

Take the full quiz on CourseMate.

18-9 Common Core Standards—English Language Arts

The **Common Core State Standards** is a state-led effort coordinated by the National Governors Association Center for Best Practices (NGA Center) and the Council of Chief State School Officers (CCSSO). The standards were developed in collaboration with teachers, school administrators, and experts to provide a clear and consistent framework to prepare our children for college and the workforce. These standards define the knowledge and skills students should have within their K–12 education careers so that they will graduate high school able to succeed in entry-level, credit-bearing academic college courses and in workforce training programs.

The mantra of common core advocates is "fewer and deeper." There may be fewer items on the learning checklist, but students will be expected to dig deeper and become higher-order thinkers. For example, in language arts, children will dive into nonfiction texts in addition to stories, and they will hone reading through other subjects such as history, science, and social studies. They will be expected to infer, analyze, and cite evidence to back up ideas they glean from reading. There will be more research projects, more writing, and more speaking to develop students' communication skills (NGA Center, 2010).

What's new for students under the Common Core in language arts? The following is a short summary of what is new:

- In elementary school, half of reading should be nonfiction and informational texts. Nonfiction will grow to a 70% share by 12th grade.

Key Ideas and Details

1. Read closely to determine what the text says explicitly and to make logical inferences from it; cite specific textual evidence when writing or speaking to support conclusions drawn from the text.
2. Determine central ideas or themes of a text and analyze their development; summarize the key supporting details and ideas.
3. Analyze how and why individuals, events, and ideas develop and interact over the course of a text.

Craft and Structure

4. Interpret words and phrases as they are used in a text, including determining technical, connotative, and figurative meanings, and analyze how specific word choices shape meaning or tone.
5. Analyze the structure of texts, including how specific sentences, paragraphs, and larger portions of the text (e.g., a section, chapter, scene, or stanza) relate to each other and the whole.
6. Assess how point of view or purpose shapes the content and style of a text.

Integration of Knowledge and Ideas

7. Integrate and evaluate content presented in diverse media and formats, including visually and quantitatively, as well as in words.
8. Delineate and evaluate the argument and specific claims in a text, including the validity of the reasoning as well as the relevance and sufficiency of the evidence.
9. Analyze how two or more texts address similar themes or topics in order to build knowledge or to compare the approaches the authors take.

Range of Reading and Level of Text Complexity

10. Read and comprehend complex literary and informational texts independently and proficiently.

The ELA Writing Standards, likewise, are divided by grade level into four broad categories:
Text Types and Purposes
Production and Distribution of Writing
Research to Build Present Knowledge
Range of Writing

FIGURE 18-3 Common Core State Standards: Ten anchor standards in reading.

- Literacy is developed in other disciplines—history, science, and social studies, through reading and analyzing documents such as the Declaration of Independence and the Gettysburg Address.
- Students should be able to dig into texts with the ability to answer questions, analyze information, cite evidence, and defend a claim.
- Students must be able to collaborate respectfully with others on shared projects, to be partners in problem solving, and to know how to communicate in both formal and informal settings.
- Students should master several types of writing—argument, explanation, and narrative. (NGA Center, 2010)

The 10 ELA Reading Standards describe what it means to be literate. The standards are organized by grade level: K–5, 6–8, 9-11, 11–College, and Career Ready. The CCSS take the 10 anchor standards in reading and spiral them up a staircase of sophistication over time. Figure 18-3 presents the 10 anchor

Did You Get It?

A fifth-grade teacher who assigns his students a story to read, then asks them to write what they have learned from the story using quotes from the text as evidence is trying to teach his students

a. emergent reading skills.
b. dramatic thought.
c. creative intelligence.
d. higher-order thinking.

Take the full quiz on CourseMate.

standards in language arts. The Common Core Standards hinge on students encountering appropriately complex texts at each grade level in order to develop the mature language skills and the conceptual knowledge they need for success in school and life (CCSS, 2010). It is important to note that the standards do not tell teachers how to teach, but they are designed to help figure out the knowledge and skills their students should have so that they can build the best lessons and environments for their classrooms (NGA Center, 2010). You will find activities at the end of this chapter addressing specific common core language arts standards.

Summary

18-1 List and explain the four distinct skills in the development of language.

Language is a part of the child's total development. Similar to physical growth, there is a definite pattern of development related to a child's growth of language involving four distinct skills: speaking, listening, writing, and reading. Each of these four skills can develop at different rates in each individual child. This is why one child can be better at speaking than a peer who listens better than she or he speaks. A teacher of young children needs to understand each child's developmental level in each of these language skills in planning appropriate language arts experiences.

18-2 Discuss strategies for enhancing language development.

A classroom in which children are given many opportunities to interact with others is one in which language development is fostered. Creating a child-centered classroom where young children are given many opportunities to pursue their own interests and trusted to know what it is they want and need to learn is another way to enhance language development. Teachers can also enhance language development during self-initiated play and in small-group language experience activities.

18-3 Define the terms *deficit* and *transformative* approaches with regard to supporting DLL and ESL learners.

A deficit perspective is one that often distorts teachers' vision when interacting with children from marginalized communities: children of color, children who speak a language other than English, and children whose families are poor or working class. A deficit perspective attributes many children's school failure to perceived deficits within the children, their families, and their cultures. For example, parents are often cited for not reading to their children, not valuing education, not using enough discipline (or disciplining their children too strictly), not speaking English at home, and/or for family "dysfunctions" that interfere with children's learning.

In direct contrast to the deficit perspective is the transformational perspective, which is based on the assumption that communities possess "funds of knowledge," reservoirs of knowledge and skills shared by community members. On one level, this means that what families know about music or literacy can contribute to learning activities or be topics of study. At a deeper level, it means we must view families as knowledgeable and skillful as well as understand and respect teaching and learning relationships in homes and communities.

18-4 Discuss the antibias curriculum (ABC).

This inclusive curriculum reflects sensitivity to all cultural groups in all areas of the curriculum. This concept, developed by the NAEYC's ABC Task Force and Louise Derman-Sparks (Derman-Sparks & ABC Task Force, 1989), is an excellent starting point for planning an inclusive, antibias curriculum. The Task Force's booklet contains excellent suggestions on ABC planning, working with parents, and suggested books and materials, which are all essential in preparing an inclusive environment for young children of all cultural groups.

18-5 Define *emerging literacy* and *emergent reading*.

Readiness for reading is termed *emerging literacy*. This term refers to the time immediately before a child learns to read printed symbols as well as to the continuous development of prereading skills that begins at birth. Pretend reading of favorite books is an activity familiar to many parents and teachers of young children. During pretend reading—also called *emergent reading,* children practice reading-like behaviors that build their confidence in themselves as readers.

18-6 List some guidelines to follow when reading to infants, toddlers, and preschool children.

With infants and toddlers: allow freedom and choice; adjust expectations to fit children's abilities and preferences; keep story groups small and intimate; show pleasure and enthusiasm; be expressive; use props; and follow the children's cues. With preschool children: invite children to participate actively in read-aloud sessions; provide frequent opportunities for young children to engage in book handling and emergent reading; read favorite books repeatedly to encourage emergent reading; during read-aloud and independent-involvement times, observe children's emerging literacy; and educate parents about the ability of their child to "pretend read."

18-7 Discuss the importance of poetry for young children's language development.

Exposure to poetry raises children's level of general language development and vocabulary development and whets their appetite for reading. Poetry's often playful approach to language helps children think about language forms as well as meaning. Children take pride in learning to recite short poems. Finger plays, or poems recited and accompanied by appropriate body movements, help develop coordination and muscle tone.

18-8 Discuss guidelines for story reading groups.

The following are some basic guidelines for story reading groups: Select a spot that is quiet, away from distracting noises and activities. A small group of six to eight children is ideal. See that everyone is comfortably seated and not crowded. Hold the book so that all can see it. Be sure you like the story you are reading to the children. Know your story well. Read the story unhurriedly with an interesting, well-modulated voice. Do not comment so much throughout the story that you break the thread of the story. Encourage comments and questions but not so much that it interrupts the flow of the story.

18-9 Define the Common Core Standards and explain their importance in the early childhood language arts program.

The Common Core State Standards is a state-led effort coordinated by the National Governors Association Center for Best Practices (NGA Center) and the Council of Chief State School Officers (CCSSO). The standards were developed in collaboration with teachers, school administrators, and experts to provide a clear and consistent framework to prepare our children for college and the workforce. The 10 ELA Reading Standards describe what it means to be literate. The standards are organized by grade level: K–5, 6–8, 9–11, 11–College, and Career Ready. The CCSS take the 10 anchor standards in reading and spiral them up a staircase of sophistication over time.

The Common Core Standards hinge on students encountering appropriately complex texts at each grade level in order to develop the mature language skills and the conceptual knowledge they need for success in school and life.

Key Terms

antibias curriculum (ABC)   413
Common Core State Standards   427
deficit perspective   410

inclusive environment   413
literacy   408

pretend reading   415
transformational perspective   410

Learning Activities

A. Observe an early childhood program and describe the language development of the children. Record at least three statements from the children to share with your classmates. Discuss your findings in class.

B. Visit a library and ask a librarian to recommend two good books for each of the following age levels: 2-year-olds, 3- and 4-year-olds, and 5-year-olds. Compare the books on the following points:
   1. Number of pages
   2. Average number of sentences per page; average number of words per sentence
   3. Theme of the book
   4. Number of illustrations and size

   Discuss how the books were similar and different for each age group. If possible, bring your books into class. Share your ideas about them with your classmates.

   Make a second visit to the library and ask a librarian to recommend two good books for each of these levels: kindergarten to grade 3 and grades 4 to 5. Compare these books on the same points.

C. Give examples from your own experience with young children of the various language skills discussed in this chapter. For example, do you know any children who are better talkers than listeners? Better listeners than talkers?

D. Study the language development of a child 3–6 years of age and compare it to the information presented in Figure 18-1. What similarities do you find? What differences

do you find? You may wish to make comparisons with another child of approximately the same age.

E. Based on the information given in this chapter about selecting appropriate books, begin a story file with at least five excellent books for children 3–6 years of age. Make a card for each book. On the card, include the title of the book, author, illustrator, publisher, copyright date, age level the story is appropriate for, and a brief summary of the story.

F. Go to a drugstore or variety store and look over the inexpensive books for children offered there. Select and purchase a desirable and undesirable one and bring them to class. Be ready to explain their weak and strong points.

G. Observe groups of children at play to collect examples of their language. Group examples according to the ages of the children. What similarities and differences do you observe?

H. Observe in a classroom where young children have free-choice activities. Select three activities and, for five minutes during each activity, record children's language as they play. During which activity was there the most talking? Why do you think this was so? How would you change the activities to encourage more talking? Explain.

I. Using a digital camera, snap a few photos of an early childhood classroom, school, students, and staff. Print out the photos and place them at a center where students can arrange them to tell a story. Have the students share their stories in writing or with their class.

Poems for Young Children

Animals

My Rabbits

My two white rabbits chase each other
With humping, bumping backs.
They go hopping, hopping
And their long ears
Go flopping, flopping
And they make faces
With their noses up and down.
Today I went inside their fence
To play rabbit with them
And in one corner under a loose bush
I saw something shivering in the leaves.
And I pushed
And I looked
And I found
There in a hole in the ground,
Three baby rabbits hidden away
And they made faces
With their noses up and down.

If You Find a Little Feather

If you find a little feather,
A little white feather,
A soft and tickly feather
   It's for you.
A feather is a letter
From a bird
And it says,
"Think of me,"
"Do not forget me."
"Remember me always."
"Remember me at least until the little feather is lost."
So—if you find a little feather,
A little white feather,
A soft and tickly feather,
It's for you.
Pick it up, and put it in your pocket.

There Once Was a Puffin

Oh, there once was a puffin
Just the shape of a muffin
And he lived on an island
In the
    Bright
      Blue
         Sea!
He ate little fishes,
That were most delicious,
And he had them for supper
And he
    Had
      Them
         For tea.
But this poor little puffin,
He couldn't play nothin',
For he hadn't anybody

To
   Play
      With
         At all.
So he sat on his island,
And he cried for a while, and
He felt very lonely,
And he felt
    Very small.
Then along came the fishes,
And they said, "If you wishes,
You can have us for playmates,
Instead
    Of
       For tea."
So they now play together
In all sorts of weather
And the puffin eats pancakes
Like you
    And
       Like me.

Caterpillar

A fuzzy, wuzzy caterpillar
On a summer day
Wriggled and wriggled and wriggled,
On his way.
He lifted up his head
To get a better view.
He wanted some nice green
Leaves to chew.
He wriggled and he wriggled
From his toes to his head
And he crawled about until
He found a comfy bed.
He curled up tight
In a warm little wrap
And settled himself
For a nice long nap.
He slept and he slept
And he slept until
One day he awoke
And broke from his shell.
He stretched and stretched
And he found he had wings!
He turned into a butterfly
Such a pretty-colored thing.
Oh, how happily
He flew away,
And he flew and he flew
In the sun all day.

Mice

I think mice
Are rather nice.
Their tails are long,
Their faces small.
They haven't any

Chins at all.
Their teeth are white,
They run about
The house at night.
They nibble things
They shouldn't touch
And no one seems
To like them much.
But I think mice
Are nice.

If I Were a Fish

I like to play in water
And if I were a fish,
I'd have water all around me
In a big glass dish.
My tail would make it splatter
'Til it splashed the sky,
And the mother fish would only say,
"No, don't get dry!"

Tiny Tim

I had a little turtle.
His name was Tiny Tim;
I put him in the bathtub
   To see if he could swim.
He drank up all the water;
He ate up all the soap;
And woke up in the morning
   With bubbles in his throat.

Seeds and Plants

Mister Carrot

Nice Mister Carrot
Makes curly hair,
His head grows underneath the ground—
And early in the morning
I find him in his bed
And give his feet a great big pull
And out comes his head!

The Apple

Within its polished universe,
The apple holds a star,
A secret constellation
To scatter near and far.
Let a knife discover
Where the five points hide.
Split the shining ruby
And find the star inside.

Seed

In the heart of a seed,
Buried deep so deep,
A dear little plant lay fast asleep.
"Wake," said the sunshine
"And creep to light."
"Wake," said the voice of raindrops bright.
The little plant heard
And rose to see
What the wonderful world
Outside might be.

Dandelions

Oh dandelions as yellow as gold,
What do you do all day?
I wait and wait in the tall green grass
Till the children come out to play.
Oh dandelion as yellow as gold,
What do you do all night?
I wait and wait in the tall green grass
Till my yellow hair turns white.
And what do the little children do
When they come out to play?
They pick me up in their hands
And blow my white hair away.

Birthdays

Five Years Old

Please, everybody look at me.
Today I'm five years old, you see.
After this, I won't be four,
Not ever, ever, anymore;
I won't be three, or two, or one,
For that was when I'd first begun.
Now I'll be five awhile, and then
I'll soon be something else again!

The Birthday Child

Everything's been different
All the day long.
Lovely things have happened,
Nothing has gone wrong.
Nobody has scolded me,
Everyone has smiled.
Isn't it delicious
To be a birthday child.

When I Was One

When I was one,
I had just begun.
When I was two,
I was nearly new.
When I was three,
I was hardly me.
When I was four,
I was not much more.
When I was five,
I was just alive.
But now I am six,
I'm as clever as clever
So I think I'll be six now
For ever and ever.

Action Poems

A Swing Song

Up, down
Up and down,
Which is the way to London Town?
Where? Where?
Up in the air,
Close your eyes, and now you are
   There.

Swinging

Hold on tightly, up we go
Swinging high and swinging low.

See-Saw

See-saw Margery Daw,
Jack shall have a new master.
He shall have but a penny a day,
Because he won't work any faster.

The Ball

Bounce the ball and catch the ball
One, and two!
Bounce the ball and catch the ball,
And I throw it back to you.
Bounce the ball and catch the ball,
One, two, three!
Bounce the ball and catch the ball,
And toss it back to me.

Blocks

Blocks will build a tower tall,
Blocks will make a long, long wall,
Blocks will build a house or plane,
A truck, a tunnel, or a train.
Get the blocks, so we can see
What they'll build for you and me.

Soap Bubbles

Fill the pipe!
Gently blow;
Now you'll see
The bubbles grow!
Strong at first,
Then they burst,
Then they go to
Nothing, oh!

All Excited

I wondered and I wondered
When I could go to school.
They said I wasn't old enough
According to the rule.
I waited and I waited
I was patient as could be.
And now—I'm all excited
It's time for school for me!

The Train

My train runs on a track
Chug-a-chug, chug-a-chug
Slow at first, then faster,
Chug-a-chug, chug-a-chug,
Chug-a-chug-chug!
Round and round the wheels go
Just listen to the whistle blow,
Toot-toot-toot!
Chug-a-chug, chug-a-chug,
Toot-toot-toot!!

Toys

See the toys on my shelf?
I can count them by myself.
One, two, three, four, five.
Here's an airplane, zoom, zoom,
And a drum, boom, boom,
A ball that bounces up and down.
A top that spins round and round.
A telephone, so I can say,
"Come and play with me today."

Raggedy Ann

Raggedy Ann is my best friend
She's so relaxed, just see her bend.
First at the waist, then at the knee
Her arms are swinging, oh so free.
Her head rolls around like a rubber ball,
She hasn't any bones at all.
Raggedy Ann is stuffed with rags,
That's why her body wigs and wags.

The Cupboard

I know a little cupboard
With a teeny tiny key.
And there's a jar of lollipops
For me, me, me.
It has a little shelf, my dears,
As dark as dark can be,
And there's a dish of Banbury Cakes
For me, me, me.
I have a small fat grandmomma
With a very slippery knee,
And she's the keeper of the cupboard
With the key, key, key.
And when I'm very good, my dears,
As good as good can be,
There's Banbury Cakes, and lollipops
For me, me, me.

If I Were

If I were an owl,
At night I'd prowl.
If I were a bear,
At night I'd growl.
If I were a sheep,
At night I'd bleat.
But since I'm a child,
At night I sleep.

Personal Topics

New Shoes

I have new shoes in the fall time.
And new shoes in the spring.
Whenever I wear my new shoes
I always have to sing.

Shoe Lacing

Across and across the shoe we go,
Across and across, begin at the toe.
Criss and cross us over and then,
Through the hole, and across again!

Loose Tooth

I had a little tooth that wiggled
It wiggled quite a lot;

I never could be sure if it
Was coming out or not.
I pushed it with my tongue
To see if it would drop;
But there it stayed and wiggled
Until I thought I'd pop.
My auntie tied it with a string
And slammed the kitchen door!
And now I haven't got a tooth
That wiggles anymore.

But Then

A tooth fell out
And left a space
So big my tongue
Can touch my face.
And every time
I smile, I show
A space where something
Used to grow.
I miss my tooth,
As you can guess.
But then, I have to
Brush one less!

Washing

With soap and water,
I rub my hands;
With the bubbly suds,
I scrub my hands,
Rubbity, scrubbity scrub!
Rub my hands
And scrub my hands,
Til no more dirt is seen!
Rub and scrub;
Rub and scrub
And then my hands are clean!

Naughty Soap Song

Just when I'm ready to start
    On my ears,
That is the time that my
    Soap disappears,
It jumps from my fingers, and
    Slithers and slides
Down to the end of the tub
Where it hides,
And acts in a most disobedient
    Way,
And that's why my soap's
    Growing thinner each day.

Activities for Children

Language Activities

Name Games

Playing with children's names can build sensitivity to the sounds of language and the use of words.

- The patterns and rhymes found in children's names can be explored. Begin by clapping the rhythm of children's names: Ste–pha–nie, Rich–ard, Al–li–son. Children can use rhythm sticks, drums, or triangles to follow the beat of their names and find ways to jump, step, hop, or slide to the rhythm of their names. These activities will attune children to the sound of words.

- Children's names can also be used to further understanding of the connection between the spoken and written words. Children's names are spoken and then written over cubbies, on paintings and artwork, and on other personal objects. Use lists of children's names whenever possible so the similarities and differences between names can be observed. You might list all of the children who have a birthday during each month or those voting to name the guinea pig Christina and those voting to name it Andrea. Other lists might name each child who has brown, black, or blonde hair.

Hello in Different Languages

This can be a fun, warm-up, get-to-know-you activity with a cross-cultural theme. Ask your students to come up with the word "hello" in as many different languages as possible. Before they make suggestions, ask the group to guess how many collective languages the group will be able to come up with. After the activity, check to see if the final number of "hellos in different languages" was close to the group's guess.

Variation: Have a list of "hello" in lots of different languages from which you can read out. This is especially useful for groups who don't know many different languages as well as to learn, have fun, and illustrate the range of different languages.

Variation: Choose one of your classroom rules such as "Be Respectful" and research how to say it in another language—ideally a language that you know is spoken in a student's home. If you have an interactive whiteboard, pull up an online translator, such as http://babelfish.yahoo.com. Practice pronouncing the rule in the other language and discuss where that language is spoken. If you like, ask families to share the translation in a language that is important to them

Outdoor Language Experiences

Outdoor play materials can be used for language experiences. These can promote awareness of the printed word in young children. Tricycle paths can have traffic signs (commercial or teacher-made). The workbench can have rebus (picture) charts to describe something to build. Animal cages and insect containers can have rebus instructions for care. In addition, seed packages can be used to label plants in the garden, graphs of plant growth can be created, and collections of nature objects can be gathered and labeled. Charts of pictures of safety rules can be on display.

Recycled Materials for Language Experiences

- Mail-order catalogs. These are a comfortable hand size for young children and have more pictures and fewer words than regular magazines. Use them to find categories of colors, objects, beginning sounds, and so on. Be sure to screen them first for any inappropriate pictures.
- Purse story. Fill old pocketbooks with assorted items such as tickets, keys, lists, make-up, combs, and so on. Have children examine the contents of the purse and tell about the owner. List their ideas. Draw pictures of how the owner of the purse might look. Tape stories about the owner.
- Original picture books. Photograph events throughout the year and have the children use these pictures to tell stories. Place photos and children's stories in a self-sticking photo album to become a permanent part of the book corner.
- For older children, use catalogs for language arts activities. Discuss words used to describe materials. For example, find synonyms for *soft usable;* explain what *preshrunk wash and wear,* or *telescoping* mean; rewrite descriptions of items to give them another meaning.

Ball Stories

This is a game that focuses on language skills as well as large- and small-motor skills. Have children sit in a circle. (It may be helpful to tape masking tape on the floor to establish boundaries.) Use a medium-sized, soft, ball (spongy Nerf balls available in most discount stores work well). Begin with a story-starter line such as, "Once upon a time there lived a frog," and then toss the ball to a child in the circle. He or she says the next line to the story and tosses the ball to another child, who adds a line. The activity goes on until each child has had a chance to catch the ball and add a line to the story. The likely silliness of the story enhances the experience by adding laughter and humor to your language arts program.

Because children have different levels of development in social skills and speech and language skills, do not expect each child to add a line to the story. Some may simply attempt to catch the ball and then toss it to another child. Some may want to add a word, a phrase, a partial sentence, or an idea. Others will be willing to add many lines to the story, depending on their language skills and their level of creativity.

Feely Bag Stories

Put a few toys, small stuffed animals, and dolls into a bag. Feel around inside the bag and pull out a toy. You might start the story by saying, "Once upon a time there was a . . . (little bear). He was happily walking along until, OOPS! He bumped into a . . ." At this point in the story, pass the bag to one of the children and ask him or her to pull out another toy and continue the story. After everyone has had a chance to pull out a toy and add to the story, use your toy to create a "happily ever after" ending.

Activities for Multiple Intelligences

As we have learned earlier, all children have different learning styles or multiple intelligences. When working with young children in the language arts, try using some of the following activities to reach these various learning styles.

Body-Smart Activities

- Have children make letters with clay or paint, in sand or flour, or on the computer.
- Have children use hand movements and body formations to show letters.
- Trace letters on the child's palm, and help the child trace sandpaper letters.
- Use jump rope chants with letters for exercise breaks.
- Lead children in a game of Simon Says with commands such as "Simon says write a *B* in the air."
- Write each vocabulary word on a piece of paper, and crumple the first one up around a small object like an eraser. Then crumple each paper over the first piece, one by one until you have a large paper ball. Have children toss the ball back and forth, but before a child throws the ball to a classmate, he or she removes one layer and reads the word.

Music-Smart Activities

- Use simple poems and rhythmic, repetitive stories.
- Use lyrics to simple songs to practice letters and reading.
- Sing the sounds.
- Use alphabet songs.
- Use tongue twisters to practice and isolate specific words.

Picture-Smart Activities

- Have children make pictures out of letters or groups of letters.
- Use different colors on bulletin boards to represent specific sounds.
- Have children draw "word pictures" to show the meaning of words. For example, *tall* would be written with tall letters, and *rain* would be written with drops of water around it.
- Have students draw a picture to represent the word and write the word inside the picture.
- Have children practice writing sight words over and over again in a rainbow of different colors. Have them write a sight word in one color, whispering the letters as they write. Next, have them trace over the top of each letter in four other colors. Make sure children write the entire word with the same color.

Number-Smart Activities

- Have children write sight words, numbered from 1 to 25, on a poster board. When children ask how to spell a word on the list, refer them to the appropriate number on the poster.
- Make dice for classroom use with letters instead of dots on them.
- Use a flannel board with cloth letters or a metal board with magnetic letters. Show students how new words are formed by changing one letter (*fine, dine, line*).
- Locate letters numerically in the alphabet by creating a poster that shows letters ordered that way (A1, B2, and so on).

Word-Smart Activities

- Provide language experiences by writing down stories as children tell them to you.
- Use word flash cards.
- Teach prereading skills—holding books, turning pages, and reading from left to right.
- Use tracing activities.
- Have students learn word families—words that are phonetically alike or sound similar.
- Use echo reading. Students repeat what is read.
- Write words you want the students to practice on slips of paper and put them into an empty water bottle. Fill the rest of the bottle with popcorn kernels, brightly colored buttons, or other small objects. Then screw on the lid, and shake it up. The students have to find the "hidden" words, read them, and cross them off the word list.

People-Smart Activities

- Make reading a social event in the classroom.
- Have students take turns reading letters, words, sentences, and so on.
- Have student partners read (or look at) a book together.
- Have students teach younger children the alphabet and sight words.
- Have reading parties at which children read individually and in small groups and listen to guest readers who are visiting the class.
- Arm children with clipboards and have them seek out words in newspapers, on the classroom wall, and in the hallway at school. This is an activity that can be done alone, in groups, in pairs, in centers, and at their desks. In word hunts, children make connections between their work with words and their actual reading and writing. The goal is not to memorize a list but to gain the tools to become a more confident contextual reader.

Self-Smart Activities

- Provide a quiet, cozy reading corner.
- Give students opportunities to read silently.
- Provide books that have a high-interest value.
- Keep special "Book Favorites" lists on a bulletin board where students can write their "All-Time Favorites."
- Have children practice reading aloud to a stuffed animal.
- Have children listen to a tape-recorded story and follow along in the book.

Word Charades

Write the sight words you are studying on index cards. Each child picks two index cards and looks up each word's meaning in the dictionary. Children take turns acting out, drawing, or expressing the meaning of their words in another creative way. The rest of the class tries to guess the meaning of the word. The first player to guess correctly wins that index card. The player who has the most cards at the end of the game gets to write the words on the chalk/ whiteboard, while the others write the words in their journals.

Mysterious Words

Discuss names with children. Ask specific questions and invite children to stand and find partners: "Who has ___ letters in his or her name?" "If your name begins with a ___, stand up." "Whose name has two vowels?" Play this game until children become familiar with the similarities between their name and their friends' names.

Then pass out 9- × 12-inch white construction paper and white crayons. Invite children to write their names on the white paper with the white crayon as many times as they like. Assure children that their magic name will appear when they complete the last step.

Pass out watercolors and paintbrushes. Have the children paint over the entire sheet of paper. Their names appear like magic!

After this activity, children most likely will want to make another mystery painting. They might make a card for someone special by writing a secret message and telling the person how to reveal that message.

Listening Exercises

Noisy Story

The noisy story develops vocabulary and skill in sequencing of story events. It also permits pupils of varying levels to participate. Prepare a set of cards, each card having a noisy word on it: PEEP, BANG, BUZZ, ROAR. Give each child a card, considering individual reading levels. Select a leader to begin the noisy story, using the noisy word on his or her card. The other children take turns adding to the story, using the words on their cards. The leader might start the story by saying, "Bill fed the baby chick, and it went *peep*." The next child might add, "The baby chick was scared when the balloon went *bang*." The story would be completed when all the children have had a turn. Other groups of words could be used: action words, animal words, people words, toy words, and so on. The game could also expand to include writing the story, illustrating the story, acting the story out, and many other creative activities.

Are You Listening?

Fill eight margarine tubs (with plastic lids) with different materials: for example, two with flour, two with buttons, two with nails, and two with pins. Have children find the two that sound alike by shaking them.

Whose Voice Is It?

Form a circle of several children. Blindfold one child or have the child cover his or her eyes. Have this child stand in the middle. Direct children to regroup so that each will be in a different place in the circle. Then have each child make a simple statement such as, "I like to play games." The child in the center then points to one child and identifies this child or asks questions (up to three) that must be answered in a sentence. If the child who is IT guesses correctly or fails to after three times, IT returns to the circle, and another child becomes IT.

Story Stick

Every culture throughout history has told stories to teach, explain, preserve history, and entertain. Making up a story as a group allows each child the opportunity to share his or her own unique ideas in a creative activity. In this activity, each person will have a chance to add a part to the story. Before beginning, remind the students that the story has a beginning, middle, and an ending. It also must include who, what, when, where, and why.

You may work with the entire class or with a smaller group of students. Have students form a circle and select a stick that will be used as a cue for passing the story from person to person. The story stick is handed to the next student when it is his or her turn to tell the next part of the story.

Let the children decide who will begin the story. That person can then take the story stick and hold it while saying, "Once upon a time…." You may want to have each student add one sentence to the story at a time.

After the story is finished, ask the children to choose one word that describes the story. Ask the children why they chose to add the part they did. And then ask them what title they would give the story.

Miscellaneous Activities

Story Plot Reporters

Discuss with children the relationship between a story's events and its plot. Then invite students to take the role of news reporters who are covering the events that make up the plot of their favorite story. First, work with children to help them condense their story into six to eight main events that include the first and last events of the story. Write their dictated versions of each event on note cards, or ask them to draw a picture of each event. Have them put their cards in order. Then, using their sequenced cards as prompts, have children present their story-plot reports. You might provide a toy microphone (or paper towel tube) for them to use in their presentation.

Comics-Style Sequence Frames

After reading aloud a story, help children determine the main events and their sequence in the story. Next, hand out six 4-inch squares of white paper to each child. Instruct children to illustrate a different main event on each square, being sure to include the first and last events of the story. Then have children sequence and glue their drawings to a 12- × 18-inch sheet of construction paper so that their story resembles a comic strip. If desired, help them write a caption for each story frame. Finally, invite children to use their sequence frames to retell the story to friends and family members.

Activities for Older Children (Grades 4–5)

The following are some suggested activities to liven up the elementary language arts program. Use your knowledge of each child's reading level to choose those activities that are most appropriate.

Book Reports

The following are some fun ways for older children to give book reports (sometimes a dreaded assignment).

- Allow students to choose a friend who has read the same book and have a debate about it.
- Give students the option of illustrating a mural explaining the sequences of the book.
- Have children simulate an interview about the book. They can ask a friend to be their interviewer or interviewee.
- Have students act out or pantomime scenes from the book.
- Encourage students to create a timeline featuring the events that occurred in the story.
- Have students develop a brochure advertising the book.
- Have students make stick puppets that depict characters in the book and display them as though they were giving the report.
- Encourage students to give their report in riddle form; have the class guess what book is the subject of the riddle.
- Allow students to make up comic strips depicting story content.
- Give students the option of creating PowerPoint presentations that relate to the story. Students then present their report using the computer and the PowerPoint slides.
- Allow students to write the report as a newspaper article or as an commercial for television.
- If the story content lends itself to a real-life situation, encourage students to report on the book as a happening in the present environment.
- Allow students to generate some simple sketches on the board as they are giving their report.

Packing Your Suitcase

This activity combines research and writing. Have students imagine that they are going to take a trip to a country of their choice or that they are going to visit relatives in their home country. Have them make a list of clothes that they will need to pack. Then make a second list of the clothes and accessories that they might like to buy there to bring back to friends in the United States. For example, a Russian student might need to pack a warm parka, and a Guatemalan student might want to bring back an embroidered blouse for a friend. Ask students to find out how shoe and clothing sizes are determined in their target country and figure out the sizes of clothing they would need to buy.

Reversibles

Explain what reversible words are with examples (*understand, stand under*). Point out that while such turnabout words differ in meaning as they are reversed, the degree of difference is not the same in each case. Players are to write or tell sentences for six pairs of reversibles, trying to use them amusingly and effectively to show their differences. Here are some reversibles to begin the activity: *understudy, study under; overcome, come over; indoors, doors in; outgoing, going out; overdone, done over; overturn, turn over; withhold, hold with; instill, still in.* This can be modified to include illustrations of the reversibles, a spelling lesson, or working as partners to develop lists.

Invisible Milk Ink Writing

Milk makes a perfect invisible ink to use on cardboard or heavyweight papers such as cardstock or construction paper. Apply milk with a small paintbrush or cotton swab and then let it dry completely. To make the message appear, rub any type of dark powdery substance over the message and the powder will stick to the milk residue. Charcoal, chalk, or graphite from a pencil lead will all work. Try making hidden messages by letting one student write the message in milk and passing it to another student to "decode."

Vocabulary Book

For each subject area, have students keep a vocabulary book of words they are struggling to learn. Then encourage students to use these vocabulary words across disciplines. For students who have difficulty with the writing process and definitions, have them draw a picture to help them remember a word's definition.

Poetry and Movement Activities

Theme dance. Any theme from a poem or book can be danced by first brainstorming all the ways to express the theme with body parts, movements, energy, and use of space and time. For example, the theme that courage comes out of fear can be danced in a frozen shape, movements, and frozen shape three-part dance planned and performed by small groups, who will each present a very different interpretation.

Key topic dance. Make a list of important words or topics in a poem or book. Brainstorm all the movements, shapes, levels, energy, and so on that could be used to convey the topic. Give small groups the choice of a topic or word to plan a dance or a series of creative movements to show it.

Character dance. Any character in a story or book can be explored through movement by considering all the ways a character might move. For example, how would Wilbur in *Charlotte's Web* move if he were happy? Hungry? Afraid? Tired? How is Wilbur's movement different from Charlotte's or Templeton's? How does body shape show something about a character?

Line by line. Read a poem to students first. Give each student or group a line from a poem. Then have them explore all the movement possibilities of the line (for example, the rhythm of the words, the emotions expressed, the images). Encourage more than pantomiming. The poetry can then be danced line by line as a narrator reads, or groups can each plan to perform just one line.

Solutions

On separate paper strips, write these and other problems: lost my door key, scared to give my book report, came to school late, tore my jeans. Post one of the problems on a bulletin board. Working in small groups, children discuss how to respond to and/or solve the problem. Then the groups present and defend their responses. Guide them in considering other responses and solutions.

Reading Pictures

Have students clip magazine photos that show feelings. Show one of the pictures to a group and have them brainstorm the feelings shown in the photo. Then they write what occurred just before the photo was snapped, the dialogue when the photo was taken, and a caption for the picture. For further activities, select photos and ask the students to remark on something happening in the picture. Photos of animals from *National Geographic* work well. Have students describe the weather and location. Next, ask them to tell what happened after the picture was taken, what will happen one day later, one week later.

Pantomime in Language Arts

Prior to the pantomime activity, design a homophone word list with the children. (Homophones are words that sound alike but are spelled differently and have different meanings.) Upon completing the list, children form a circle. The teacher calls out a word and the children pantomime a meaning for that word. Then the homophone is called and the children show that meaning. Try using the following words in this exercise: *ant/aunt; bear/bare; board/bored; buy/bye; clothes/close; eight/ate; flour/flower; grate/great; hear/here; knight/night; lends/lens; marry/merry; prints/prince; ring/wring; shoe/shoo; tow/toe; we/wee; yolk/yoke.*

Activities for Multiple Intelligences

Learning sight words is an important reading skill. Planning sight word activities that are appropriate for children's multiple intelligences or learning styles can make learning sight words fun and challenging. Here are some ideas.

Body-Smart Activities

Sand letters. Fill several shallow tubs with sand. Students can work in groups, taking turns spelling each word in the sand. When their teammates verify that a word is spelled correctly, they erase it.

Playground ball catch. Using a Sharpie marking pen, write sight words all over each of several playground balls. Have students form groups of four and stand in a close circle. One student tosses a ball to another. The student who catches the ball reads the word closest to his or her right thumb. Younger students can read any word on the ball.

Sit up/sit down. Tell students that you are going to be reading them a short story and that any time they hear one of the sight words, they should stand up. After all students are standing up, signal them to sit down. Do the same activity with the story projected on a screen as you read so that students can see the special word being read.

Body letters. Choose several students at a time to come and spell out one of the sight words by forming their bodies into the shapes of its letters as best they can. Their classmates can guess the word.

Music-Smart Activities

Singing songs. During singing time, take time to point out the sight words in song lyrics. You might also have students sing and spell the words in a familiar song.

Consonant-vowel spelling. Have students spell each word out loud to a partner. Tell them to say consonant letters out loud and to whisper the vowels. This helps students become more aware of individual letters and memorize a rhythm as they are spelling. It can lead to a discussion of the patterns of vowels and consonants as they recognize that many words start with a vowel, others have a vowel in between, and still others end with a vowel.

Teachers can have students do the following "music-smart" activities in developing language skills.

- Make up a rap or song about the spelling (or meaning) of a word/set of facts.
- Use maracas, a tambourine, or a drum to beat out the rhythm while spelling words.
- Make up a cheer with motions and words to advertise your word.
- Make up a hand-clapping rhyme or jump rope rhyme about your word.
- Use maracas, a tambourine, or other music-maker to "shake-write" the word in the air.
- Dance to music and write the word in the air with a scarf, light stick, or wand.

Person-Smart Activities

Group spelling. Ask several volunteers to come to the front of the classroom. Pronounce a sight word and have members of the group spell the word, one letter per student. After students understand the game, divide the class into groups of two or three and tell them to whisper the spelling of the word you say. Remind them that they are whispering so that other groups have to rely on their own knowledge to spell the words.

Buddy spell. Ask students to choose partners. Give each pair one set of alphabet tiles or cubes (or index cards with one letter on each card). One student says a word, and the other arranges the letters in the correct order. After the word is correctly spelled, the students change places and continue until they've spelled all the words.

Picture-Smart Activities

Word pictures. Have students write a sight word in large letters in the middle of a sheet of paper and then decorate the page with pictures and drawings.

Word search. Write a short story that includes sight words, and make a copy for each student. Have the students highlight or underline all of the sight words they can find.

Configuration clues. Have students write one word at a time on a sheet of paper. After each word is written, have them draw a box around it so they can see how the word looks (for example, tall letters, short letters). Older students can draw individual boxes around each letter.

Have students implement these additional strategies in learning new words.

- Draw a "word picture." First, write the word in the middle of the paper. Then draw a picture around it that will help you remember the word. Make sure that the picture surrounds the information you are trying to learn.
- Create a word search using the words you are trying to learn.
- Write your word in the middle of the paper. Use crayons or markers to draw around the shape of the word. Keep tracing around the shape using different colors. Finally, use black marker (or fluorescent, or whatever will stand out) to trace over the word while you spell/say it.

Self-Smart Activities

Study time. Give students a list of sight words to tape to their desk. Each day, give them a couple of minutes to study them.

Journal writing. Have students choose two words each day to copy into their personal journals. Ask them to write a sentence or illustrate a sentence that includes the word. Then relate the sentence to something they enjoy doing in their personal time.

Word-Smart Activities

Introducing words. On word strips, write sight words, one to a strip. Introduce students to a few words each week. Explain to students that they will be learning words that are used a lot. After introducing words, hang the strips in a wall pocket so students can see them throughout the day. Any time one of the words appears in a book or someone says it out loud, have students walk to the pocket chart and point to the word.

Student writing. Have students underline the sight words each time they use them in their writing assignments. Older students can keep a Special Word Dictionary where they write these words.

Paper-plate spelling. Write one letter on each of a number of paper plates and give each student several plates. Have students stand if they have a letter that appears in a word you say. If several students stand up at the same time, acknowledge all of them as you reinforce how the word is spelled.

Logic-Smart Activities

Counting letters. To help students who need a mathematical connection to memorize sight words, have them write each word, count its letters, and write the number of letters next to it. For example, students would write *the* and place a "3" next to it. An extension of this is to have students count the consonants and vowels. Students would write *the* and next to it write "C2, V1."

Categorizing words. Give groups of students each a set of index cards with one of the sight words written on each card. Ask them to work as a group to categorize words that might go together. After they are done, have each group explain its categories. For example, students may feel that all the three-letter words or all the words with o in them go together. For many students, categorizing similar words will help them memorize word families. This activity helps to build and strengthen sight word vocabulary as well as to increase students' awareness of phonetic similarities.

Common Core State Standards—Sample Activities

Although many of the preceding activities can be applied to the Common Core State Standards, the following activities are specific examples tied into these standards.

Reading: Craft and Structure

Students interpret words and phrases that are used in a text, including determining technical meanings and analyzing how specific word choice shape meaning or tone.

Tic-Tac-Toe with Antonyms and Synonyms (Primary)

Materials: Blank tic-tac-toe sheets, drawn on scrap paper, pencils, thesaurus or dictionary

Knowing antonyms from synonyms is an important part of the primary grades writing curriculum. It is also a great vocabulary booster. This is a game designed to help develop this skill.

Review with the children that synonyms are words with similar meanings and antonyms are words with opposite meanings. Example: On a hot day, you can get too warm unless you find a way to stay cool. In this example, ask the children to identify a pair of synonyms (hot, warm) and a single antonym (cool).

Then, it's time to play. Start by choosing a word that has many shades of meaning, such as good, nice, cold, bad, or happy. Write the selected word at the top of the tic-tac-toe sheet.

The "x" player chooses a space and marks a small "x." She writes a synonym for the selected word in the same space. Then the "o" player chooses a playing space and marks a small "o." She writes an antonym for the selected word in her space. Play continues until someone gets three in a row. If a player gets stuck, he can consult the dictionary or thesaurus for help.

Reading: Craft and Structure

Students interpret words and phrases as they are used, including figurative meanings.

Clay Indians Vocabulary Fun (Primary)

Materials: sheets of paper, pencils, modeling clay

Idioms such as "that problem was a piece of cake" and "it's clean as a whistle" can be found everywhere from the books children read to everyday conversation. That is why it is important for students to understand the figure of speech that they are using. This activity is a fun way to reinforce this figure of speech.

In this activity, the children use modeling clay to represent the literal meaning of an idiom, which can then be compared to how we use the phrase when we talk or write. To begin, have the children brainstorm all the idioms they know. Then, have them think creatively about how to represent their favorite ones using clay. In the process, they will learn that practicing English grammar can be fun.

Work together with the children to write down as many idioms as they can think of. You can go online if you need help getting started.

Have each student pick the idiom he wants to make into a clay creation. Keep in mind that the idioms that will work best are those that involve people or things. Some examples include the following: Hold your horses. Don't let the cat out of the bag. All in the same boat. Bite your tongue. When pigs fly. You are what you eat.

Have the children think about how they will design their clay creations. Some students may want to sketch it before starting. The children create their idioms using modeling clay. Encourage them to focus on their phrases as they work.

After this activity, discuss how these phrases are used in everyday life. This activity is especially appropriate for kinesthetic learners who learn best by doing hands-on activities.

Reading: Craft and Structure

Students interpret words and phrases as they are used in a text.

Gotcha! Early Reading Game

Materials: Variety of books

Fluency, the ability to read at a constant, relatively fast speed, is an important skill for early readers to learn. This activity focuses on this skill as well as reading comprehension.

Have the children gather with you in a reading group. Tell them you are going to play a reading game together called "Gotcha." In this game, the children call out "Gotcha" when you read the wrong word.

Then begin reading from the book as quickly as you can, with the children following along in their books. Randomly say a different word instead of one in the story. The first time, say an obvious wrong word. For example, you might say, "Ill huff and I'll puff and blow your bicycle down." Do not stress the wrong word.

When the child raises her hand and says, "Gotcha," congratulate her. Then explain that it's her turn to read, and that she should eventually read the wrong word on purpose so that you can try to catch her.

Repeat this game several times, switching roles each time someone says "Gotcha." Be sure to emphasize that the goal is to have fun, not just to catch another child's mistakes.

Reading: Key Ideas and Details (Summaries)

Students determine central ideas or themes of a text and analyze their development and summary

What Is a Summary?

Explain that a summary consists of the main points of a piece of reading. Share a summary of a book you've read as a class. Review the summary sentence by sentence, asking students why they think each point was included and whether anything is missing. Read aloud summaries of other favorite books, challenging students to identify the titles.

Cutting Down

In order to summarize, children need to distinguish major points from less relevant ones. Help students understand what's important by writing the text of a picture book on chart paper. Tell students that you are going to cross out as many words as possible in order for the story to still make sense. Model your thinking as you cross out phrases. Ask students to help you decide what to cross out and what to leave. When finished, read the remaining words.

Three-Fact Biographies

Materials: Strips of paper, envelopes

Label envelopes with the names of people you are studying in class. In each envelope, put strips with different facts about the person. Some should be important, while others less so. For example, an Abraham Lincoln envelope might include facts such as "16th President of the United States," "helped to end slavery," along with "had a dog named Fido." Challenge children to select the facts they think are the most important for each person. Ask them to explain their thinking to a partner.

Summary of a Story

As you read a favorite picture book, tell students that you'd like them to pay attention to the major events of the story. If they hear one, they may raise their hands. If they share an appropriate event, ask them to stand at the front of the room. After reading, invite the standing children to say their events in order. As a class, discuss whether or not they provide an accurate summary.

Bookmark Summary

Invite children to create bookmarks for whatever they are reading. On one side, have students illustrate a scene from their books. On the other, have them write the numbers 1–5. As children read, encourage them to note major events or facts on their bookmarks. Students can use their bookmarks to write a summary of what they've read.

Reading Literature

With prompting and support, students retell familiar stories, including key details.

Filling in Sequentially

Write each of these words on its own large index card: *First, Then, Next, After that,* and *Finally.* Place each card in a separate row on a pocket chart. After sharing a story with students, write the first event on a card and place it next to *First.* Write the last event on another card and place it next to *Finally.* Then challenge children to fill in what's missing. To begin, read aloud the first and last events, using the words *First* and *Finally* in front of the corresponding sentences. Then point to *Then* and have children decide together what happened after the first event. Write their responses on a card and add it to the chart. Continue, recording events to go with *Next* and *After that.* If desired, use different words, such as *Before, After, So, Second,* and so on.

Writing: Production and Distribution of Writing

Use a combination of drawing, dictating, and writing to narrate a single event or several loosely linked events, tell about the events in the order in which they occurred, and provide a reaction to what happened.

Picture This!

Materials: A story the children are currently working on, blank piece of paper, crayons, or colored pencils

Primary students often have a difficult time adding detail and description to their stories. Comparing the process of writing to drawing a picture can help children understand the importance of using detail and description in their stories. This activity is designed to help students "picture" how to improve their stories. It is appropriate for a small reading group setting.

Use a black crayon to draw a large rectangle frame leaving about 2 inches around the rectangle. In this space around the frame, write the following question words, spreading them out so that they look like artsy decorations on the frame: Who? What? How? Where? When? What color? How big?

Choose one of the student's stories to read aloud. As you read, have the child illustrate his story in the blank space in the center of the frame. Tell the child he can only draw what he hears you read in the story.

When you're finished, discuss the drawing with the child. What's missing in the picture? What details could have been added that would make the story more interesting? If the child needs ideas, refer to the question words you wrote earlier in the frame. As the child adds details to his drawing, have him use words to describe the details to you. Then have him go back to his story and write in these extra details.

Finally, turn the completed drawing over, face down, and read the child's improved story out loud to him again. Ask him to picture the story in his head as you read it aloud. Ask, "Can you picture it?" Then turn over the picture and ask him to decide if the picture in his head matches the picture on the paper. If he finds they match well, he can be sure that he has added enough details to the story.

Writing: Production and Distribution of Writing

Students produce clear and coherent writing in which the development, organization, and style are appropriate to task, purpose, and audience.

Writing Together

This writing activity takes a regular task—writing a story—and transforms it into a collaborative writing experience that's sure to have interesting results.

The first child starts writing a story, not letting anyone know what she is writing about. Encourage the child to be as creative as possible—the crazier the better.

When the child has written about a paragraph, have her fold the paper down so that only the last line can be seen. The child then passes the paper to the next person who reads the visible line and continues the story. When this child is finished, he folds the paper over again so that only the last line of her paragraph is visible to the next person. Repeat until everyone has participated. Then unfold the paper and read aloud the funny story.

Writing: Production

Students develop and strengthen writing as needed by planning, reviewing, editing, rewriting, or trying a new approach.

Sentence Scramble Game

Materials: Strips of construction paper in two colors, pencils, two large bowls or containers

Primary students have learned to construct simple sentences, but they are still exploring ways to make their writing more interesting and effective. By turning simple sentences into compound sentences, students are strengthening their writing and communication skills. This hands-on activity gives children practice creating compound sentences, while teaching analytical skills that will help them become better writers.

Pick a topic such as sports, pets, family members, or any other topic of interest to the students.

Have each student write 10 simple sentences on one color strip of construction paper. Next, each student writes 10 connecting words or conjunctions on another color strip of construction paper. Use words such as *and, because, or, but, so,* and *yet.* Words can be repeated more than once. Place the connecting word strips in the other bowl. Ask each child to choose two sentence strips and one connecting word to make a compound sentence. Then, have each child read his sentence out loud. Discuss the compound sentences created by the students. Which sentence was the funniest? Which one made the most sense?

Writing: Production and Distribution

Students produce clear and coherent writing in which the development, organization, and style are appropriate to task, purpose, and audience.

Describe It to Me

How do you describe a zipper? It may seem easy enough, but how easy would it be to explain it to an alien? Explaining everyday items in detail helps develop skills vital to good writing: clarity, timing, details, explanation, and organization. This is a great activity for primary students whose writing style is just beginning to bloom and who are starting to write more and more detailed stories and sentences in school.

Begin by framing the context of the story about aliens who have landed in your neighborhood. You might say, "Friendly, harmless, extremely curious aliens have landed in your neighborhood. You have been charged with the job of writing a manual explaining simple, everyday tasks and items to them so they'll know how to live, eat, sleep, and play on Earth."

Each child chooses an activity to describe: getting ready for bed, how to make a sandwich, and how to use a zipper are all good tasks to use for this activity.

Children write and then read to the class their chosen explanations. Ask the children these questions: Would these explanations be clear to the aliens? How could they be improved upon?

References

Alvarado, C. (Ed.) (2008). *In our own way: How anti-bias work shapes our lives.* Washington, DC: NAEYC.

August, D., & Shanahan, T. (Eds.) (2008). *Developing reading and writing in second-language learners: Lessons from the Report of the National Literacy Panel on Language-Minority children and youth.* New York, NY: Routledge.

Batalova, J., & McHugh, M. (2010). *Top languages spoken by English language learners nationally and by state.* Washington, DC: Migration Policy Institute. Retrieved from http://www.migrationinformation.org/ellinfo/FactSheet_ELL3.pdf.

Beck, I. L., & McKeown, M. G. (2007). Increasing young low-income children's oral vocabulary repertoires through rich and focused instruction. *The Elementary School Journal, 107*(3), 251–71.

Birckmayer, J., Kennedy, A., & Stonehouse, A. (2009). Using stories effectively with infants and toddlers. *Young Children, 64*(1), 42–47.

Chen, J. J., & Shire, S. H. (2011). Strategic teaching: Fostering communication skills in diverse learners. *Young Children, 66*(2), 20–27.

Collins, M. F. (2012). Sagacious, sophisticated, and sedulous: The importance of discussing 50-cent words with preschoolers. *Young Children, 67*(5), 66–71.

Collins, M. F. (2010). ELL preschoolers' English vocabulary acquisition from storybook reading. *Early Childhood Research Quarterly, 25*(1), 84–97.

Common Core State Standards, http://www.corestandards.org/.

Cote, L. R. (2001). Language opportunities during mealtimes in preschool classrooms. In Dickinson, D. K., & Tabors,

P. O. (Eds.) *Beginning literacy with language: Young children learning at home and school*, pp. 205–21. Baltimore, MD: Paul H. Brooks.

Cruzado-Guerrero, J., & Kenreich, T. W. (2008). Making global connections with family book bags. *Social Studies and the Young Learner, 20*(4), P1–P4.

Debruin-Parecki, A. (2007). *Let's read together: Improving literacy outcomes with the adult-child interactive reading inventory.* Baltimore, MD: Brookes Publishing.

Derman-Sparks, L., & ABC Task Force. (1989). *Anti-bias curriculum: Tools for empowering young children.* Washington, DC: NAEYC.

Dickinson, D., McCabe, A., & Clark-Chiarelli, N. (2004). Preschool-based prevention of reading disability: Reality versus possibilities. In Stone, C. A., Silliman, E. R., Herebn, B. J., & Apel, K. (Eds.) *Handbook of Language and Literacy*, pp. 209–277. New York: Guildford Press.

Dickinson, D. K., McCabe, A., Anastasopoulos, L., Peisner-Feinberg, E. S., & Poe, M. D. (2003). The comprehensive language approach to early literacy: The interrelationships among vocabulary, phonological sensitivity, and print knowledge among preschool-aged children. *Journal of Educational Psychology, 95*(3), 465–81.

Dickinson, D. K., & Porche, M. V. (2011). Relation between language experiences in preschool classrooms and children's kindergarten and fourth-grade language and reading abilities. *Child Development, 82*(3), 870–86.

Dickinson, D. K., & Tabors, P. O. (Eds.) (2001). *Beginning literacy with language: Young children learning at home and school.* Baltimore, MD: Brookes.

Dunst, C., Trivette, C., & Hamby, D. (2007). Predictors of and intervention associated with later literacy learning. *CELLreviews, 1*(3).

Garcia, E. E., Jensen, B. T., & Scribner, K. P. (2009). The demographic imperative. *Educational Leadership, 66*(7), 8–13.

Gonzalez-Mena, J. (2009). *Diversity in early care and education.* 5th ed. Washington, DC: NAEYC.

Hart, B., & Risley, T. R. (1995). *Meaningful differences in everyday experience of young American children.* Baltimore, MD: Brookes.

Hirschler, J. A. (2005). *How teachers support English language learners in the classroom.* (Head Start Bulletin 48). Washington, DC: U.S. Department of Health and Human Services.

Isbell, R. T. (2003). Telling and retelling stories: Learning language and literacy. In *Spotlight on young children and language.* Washington, DC: NAEYC.

Macaruse, P., & Rodman, A. (2011). Efficacy of computer-assisted instruction for the development of early literacy skills in young children. *Reading Psychology, 32,* 172–196.

NAEYC (1996). Position statement: Responding to linguistic and cultural diversity: Recommendation for effective early childhood education. *Young Children, 51*(2), 4–12.

NCELA (National Clearinghouse for English-Language Acquisition and Language Instruction). Instruction Educational Programs (2010). *The growing numbers of English learner students: 1997–98–2007/08.* Washington, DC: U.S. Department of Education, Office of English Language Acquisition, Language Enhancement, Academic Achievement for Limited English Proficient students.

National Governors Association Center for Best Practices (NGA Center), Council of Chief State School Officers. (2010). Common Core State Standards. Washington, DC: National Governors Association Center for Best Practices, Council of Chief State School Officers, Washington D.C. Retrieved from http://www.corestandards.org.

Pan, B. A., Rowe, M. L., Singer, J. D., & Snow, C. E. (2005). Maternal correlates of growth in toddler vocabulary production in low-income families. *Child Development, 76*(4), 763–82.

Thomas, W. P., & Collier, V. P. (2002). *A national study of school effectiveness for language minority students' long-term academic achievement.* Washington, DC: Office of Educational Research and Improvement.

Weitzman, Z. O., & Snow, C. E. (2011). Lexical input as related to children's vocabulary acquisition: Effects of sophisticated exposure and support for meaning. *Developmental Psychology, 37*(2), 265–79.

Visit CourseMate for this textbook to access the eBook, Did You Get It? quizzes, Digital Downloads, TeachSource Videos, flashcards, and more. Go to CengageBrain.com to log in, register, or purchase access.

19

Creative Science

When considering creative activities, it is not possible to skip the area of science because true science is a highly creative activity. Consider the following scenario:

Twenty young children in a classroom have each just been given a small box wrapped in brightly colored gift paper with a big ribbon. There are some objects inside each box, and each child is trying to find out what is in her or his box without taking off the ribbon and paper. Some children are shaking their gift boxes. Some are holding them up to their ears and listening very carefully. Others are squeezing them. A few are poking the boxes. They are clearly interested in discovering the contents of what they hold in their hands.

Learning Objectives

After studying this chapter, you should be able to:

19-1 State why science is important to the development of young children.

19-2 Name and describe three general types of science activities.

19-3 Discuss inquiry-based learning and ways to promote it in the early childhood classroom.

19-4 Explain the purpose of the National Science Education Standards.

19-5 Discuss the aesthetics of science in the early childhood program.

19-6 Discuss the discovery center and its importance in the early childhood program.

19-7 Discuss environmental education and its place in the early childhood program.

NAEYC Program Standards

1a Knowing and understanding young children's characteristics and needs.

5a Understanding content knowledge and resources in academic disciplines

5b Knowing and using the central concept, inquiry tools, and structures of content areas or academic disciplines.

DAP

DAP Criteria

2F3 To extend the range of children's interests and the scope of their thought, teachers present novel experiences and introduce stimulating ideas, problems, experiences, or hypotheses.

3A1 Teachers consider what children should know, understand, and be able to do across disciplines…, including science.

Is this a game? It may seem so, but it actually is a way in which children make creative discoveries. In many ways, this is also the way that scientists make creative discoveries. The little gift box is somewhat like the world in which the children live. Children study their own little "world" by shaking the box, smelling it, squeezing it, and looking at it. Each child makes some discoveries but cannot find out everything because the box cannot be unwrapped. Children may be able to make some good guesses after studying the boxes, however. Some things are open to children's discovery; some things are not. Scientists are faced with the same problems. They, too, study the world. They, too, can observe some things and only guess about others.

19-1 Science and the Young Child

For young children, science is about trying to understand the world. Young children are natural scientists who observe the people, animals, and objects in their environment, conduct experiments, and report on their discoveries. Science in early childhood is much broader than what you might at first consider it to be. Try to avoid thinking about science only in terms of activities devoted to "doing" science, such as growing plants or taking a nature walk. Rather, view science as an ongoing part of the total curriculum, woven into daily activities and routines. Science education occurs naturally when Kenzie wonders why a cork floats and a penny sinks, when Mark questions why ice melts, when Kamal observes he can hear his heart beating as he runs, and when Madison wonders why the water she paints on the sidewalk disappears.

There are two things that both the child and the scientist do. They *investigate* (carefully study the world around them) to *discover knowledge* (find answers to questions or problems about that world). Science consists of two phases, or parts, that cannot be separated: investigation and knowledge.

19-1a Importance of Science

naeyc DAP Science is important to young children in a number of ways. First, when children are actively involved in investigating their world, they are learning by doing—the most effective way for young children to learn. In dealing with young children, it has been found that the process of investigating is much more important than the knowledge that comes from

investigating. Young children need a lot of action, not a lot of facts. This does not mean that understanding the world is put aside completely for young children. It just means that *learning how to find answers* is more important than the answers themselves. However, investigation and knowledge are a team. They cannot be completely separated from one another.

Second, science activities help young children develop skills in using their senses. Use of these skills is not limited to science. These skills can be used every day throughout a person's lifetime. Educators use the term *transfer of learning* to describe knowledge and skills that are gained in one area and used in many other areas. Science skills are particularly important because they are so highly transferable. Skills in seeing, feeling, and tasting are not limited to science even though they do represent the basic skills that are taught.

Third, science allows children yet another chance to exercise their creative abilities (see Photo 19-1). Science allows young children a chance to play with ideas and materials in an open environment where there is freedom to explore without fear of being "wrong."

Casper Holroyd

PHOTO 19-1 Young children are naturally curious and enjoy discovery involved in science activities.

19-2 Types of Science Activities

naeyc **DAP**   There are three types of science experiences for young children: formal, informal, and incidental.

19-2a Formal Science

Formal science experiences are planned by the teacher to develop particular skills (see Photo 19-2). A formal science experience that develops young children's fine-motor skills might involve pouring and measuring with tools in the sand and water area. The teacher would plan to include a specific item such as a funnel hung low over the water table or funnels attached to each end of a length of plastic tubing that would serve a specific purpose—the development of fine-motor skills. Although other learning might occur because of these implements' inclusion, they serve a specific developmental purpose.

19-2b Informal Science

Unlike formal science, **informal science** calls for little or no teacher involvement (see Photo 19-3). Children work on their own, at their own rate, and only when they feel like it. They select the kinds of activities that interest them. They spend as much or as little time working at a given activity as they desire. It is when this sort of openness is available to children that creative potential begins to develop.

PHOTO 19-2 The child is observing the effects of light as part of his teacher's planned, formal science activity.

Most informal science activities occur in the discovery (science) center. The discovery center is an area in the early childhood classroom where children can participate in a variety of informal science activities that stimulate curiosity, exploration, and problem solving. In the discovery center, young

PHOTO 19-3 Playing with sand and other materials fosters many informal science experiences.

children develop many skills and concepts in their active exploration of such things as sand, water, magnets, and a multitude of other real-life objects. A more specific discussion of the discovery center follows later in this chapter.

19-2c Incidental Science

Incidental science cannot be planned. It sometimes does not take place once a week or even once a month. Just what is incidental science? A city or town may be struck by a violent windstorm. Limbs of trees are knocked down; whole trees are uprooted. Great sheets of rain fall, and streets become flooded. Children are frightened by the great noise and wild lightning as the storm passes. Finally the storm is over.

Is this the time for an incidental science experience? Of course it is! This is the time for children who are interested to learn many things. They can study the roots of trees; they may have the chance to observe growth rings. They are able to examine tree bark. They can observe what happens to water as it drains from a flooded street. Some might want to talk about their feelings as the lightning flashed and the thunder crashed. Some may want to create a painting about the experience.

A teacher cannot plan such an experience. A good teacher can, however, take advantage of such an opportunity by letting children explore and seek answers to questions. A teacher can encourage children to be more inquisitive and creative.

Did You Get It?

A group of young children take magnifying glasses from a box, and then run around the schoolyard looking at insects and plants through the magnifying glasses. In which type of learning are they engaged?

a. scientific method
b. creative learning
c. informal science
d. formal science

Take the full quiz on CourseMate.

19-3 Inquiry-Based Learning

naeyc DAP **Inquiry-based learning** is a term often used when discussing science experiences for young children. Inquiry refers to investigating to gather information, which is part of human behavior from birth. For children, it is a way of learning about the world driven by interest, wonder, and curiosity. For teachers, it is a way of learning about children's interests, abilities, and theories in order to plan appropriate activities.

Because inquiry is such a basic human learning strategy, it makes sense for teachers to use an inquiry-based approach in their science activities with young children.

Inquiry-based learning is an approach to learning that involves a process of exploring the natural or material world that leads to asking questions and making discoveries in the search for new understandings. There are several ways to promote inquiry-based learning in the early childhood classroom:

- Ask questions that invite constructive input and validate prior knowledge. For example, instead of "Has anyone ever seen a rock before?" ask, "What do you know about rocks?" Ask open-ended questions. For example, "Tell me about what you're wondering." "What do you think might happen if…?" "What do you notice?"

- Encourage children to wait a few seconds before giving an answer to allow time for thinking. Tell the children you are going to ask a question, but you would like them all to close their eyes and think about it for a few seconds before answering.

- Repeat or paraphrase what the children say without praising or criticizing. This encourages children to think for themselves instead of seeking teacher validation. "Scott thinks that sand comes from rocks, and Claire says it is dirt from the ocean. What do you think? Where does sand come from?"

In science activities, encourage children to look closely, notice details, pose questions, and reflect on what they learned. Children's wonderings and reflections are essential to the learning process. Also, talking about their experiences with others allows children to articulate what they have seen or done in a way that makes sense. By listening to what others have experienced, children can understand multiple perspectives. Listening to others' insights and opinions and learning that these are of value is a key skill taught in an inquiry-based classroom (see Photo 19-4).

© Cengage Learning

PHOTO 19-4 In an inquiry-based classroom, children need to ask questions, but they also need to learn to listen to other's insights and opinions.

▶❚❚ **TeachSource** Video

© 2015 Cengage Learning

School Age: Cooking Activities

1. What type of science activity is being presented by this teacher? Give a specific reason for your choice. How could you present this activity in one of the other types of science activities?

2. Is this teacher using inquiry-based learning techniques? Use specific examples from the video in your reply.

3. How could this activity be enhanced so that it involves aesthetics and science?

Watch on CourseMate.

Did You Get It?

A preschool teacher is careful to always use an inquiry-based method of teaching because she wants her students to learn social skills. Inquiry-based learning can promote social skills because children learn to

   a. obey the teacher.
   b. listen to others' opinions.
   c. listen instead of asking questions.
   d. share their materials.

Take the full quiz on CourseMate.

19-4 National Science Education Standards

The National Research Council (NRC) defined performance standards for children at each grade level, from kindergarten through high school back in 1996. These standards present an outline of what students in kindergarten through grade 12 need to know, understand, and be able to do to be "scientifically literate" at each grade level. They promote a dynamic understanding of scientific principles that is always open to review and revision.

Since the introduction of these standards, a joint effort between the NRC, the National Science Teachers Association (NSTA), and the American Association for the Advancement of Science (AAAS) is underway to create the **Next Generation Science Standards (NGSS)**, the foundation for all students to have a solid K–12 science education. The NGSS will be K–12 science standards created through a collaborative, state-led process. The new standards being drafted are based on the **Framework for K-12 Science Education**, which identifies the key scientific ideas and practices all students should learn by the end of high school. Many states have begun work to implement the framework. The vision laid out in the framework identifies what students should know and be able to do to be a functional citizen, which includes being scientifically literate and an effective member of the U.S. workforce.

19-4a STEM/STEAM

Science, Technology, Engineering, and Math (STEM) curriculum areas have become a major focus in education because of the concern that the United States is falling behind in scientific innovation. The pressure is on educators to start early and provide learning experiences in these areas for young children. STEM is a buzzword even referring to preschool (Ashbrook, 2010; Moomaw & Davis, 2010).

STEM has quickly taken hold in education policy circles, but some experts in the arts community and beyond suggest it may be missing another initial to make the combination still more powerful. The idea? Move from STEM to STEAM, with an A for the arts.

Some experts perceive a special connection between the arts and the STEM fields. A 2008 study led by Robert Root-Bernstein of Michigan State University found that Nobel Laureates in the sciences were 22 times more likely than scientists in general to be involved in the performing arts (2008). Others note that Albert Einstein was an accomplished violinist. And then there's the Renaissance figure viewed by some as the personification of STEAM: Leonardo da Vinci, the Italian painter and sculptor who also made a name for himself as a scientist, engineer, and inventor.

Because the arts are a natural part of early childhood education, adding this element may help more teachers find ways to work STEM concepts into the curriculum. STEM is more about facilitating inquiry-based thinking and discovery than about teaching facts and giving answers.

Did You Get It?

While teaching three-year-olds about mixing colors, the teacher has them experiment with mixing different colors and seeing what happens when they add more water to the paint. The teacher's actions reflect the _____ policy.
  a. STEM
  b. STEAM
  c. creative arts
  d. color teaching

Take the full quiz on CourseMate.

19-5 Aesthetics and Science

As we have learned earlier in this text, having aesthetic awareness means being sensitive to beauty in nature and art. Such sensitivity is fostered not by talking about beauty but by experiencing it in a variety of forms—the sight of snow on evergreen boughs, the smell of the earth after a spring rain, the sound of a bird singing overhead, and the feel of a kitten's

fur or the moss on the side of a tree. It is easy to forget how amazing a pebble or a pinecone can be to a young child.

For the young child, the world of nature is an especially appropriate avenue for developing aesthetic sensitivity. An early snowfall in winter may provide a child with his or her first remembered experience of snow. Seeing a rainbow in the sky may be something a 3-year-old has never experienced before. Watching a butterfly move from flower to flower may provide a visual feast that a child has not yet come to take for granted. Beauty is not just in what can be seen. It is present also in what can be touched, felt, and listened to. Because the world of nature is so full of sights, sounds, and textures, it can serve as an incredibly rich and readily available resource for the development of aesthetic sensibilities in young children.

19-5a Science and Art Materials/Activities

Children working with art materials make scientific observations noting, for example, that water makes tempera paint thinner and that crayons become soft if they are left near the heat. Evelyn looks at her wet, drippy painting and says, "I wonder if I can blow it dry with my wind." Drew finds that his clay figure left on the windowsill overnight has "gotten all hardened up" because it is no longer wet.

Experimentation with art materials may lead to many other discoveries about cause and effect. Children notice that colors change as they are mixed and that the sponges used for printing absorb liquid. In contrast, other materials such as plastics are found to be nonabsorbent. In using many materials, children observe differences between liquids and solids and see that other items such as wax crayons and oil paints resist water. In mixing paint from powder, children learn that some materials dissolve in water. The operations of simple machines can be understood through using tools such as scissors and hammers. The potential for developing science concepts is in the art materials and in the processes—ready to be discovered and applied. These experiences are consistent with the national science standard that states that children should understand the properties of materials.

19-5b Animals Link Science and Art

Young children's natural love of animals is a good place to begin when planning art activities that encourage science experiences. Children are intrigued

Casper Holroyd

PHOTO 19-5 This science activity combines drawing, language arts, and scientific observation.

by animals. Studying animals is consistent with the national science standard calling for the study of animals and their environments (see Photo 19-5). Yet, animals provide more than a science experience for children because they stimulate children's artistic exploration as well. Young children, after touching, seeing, hearing, or smelling animals, will be stimulated to use art media for animal representations. Children with an emotional attachment to household or school pets will be additionally motivated to create visual images. Teachers create opportunities for guided learning about animals by providing art media and materials for children to use, by engaging children in discussions about animals, and by reading stories, showing pictures, and singing songs about animals.

Sometimes after a trip to a zoo or farm, children will be stimulated to visually express their ideas about animals. After the class trip to the zoo, 4-year-old Aiden painted an elephant immediately upon returning to school. "Look! Elephants are so funny because they have a tail on both ends," he announced. The teacher accepted his work but, realizing his confusion, clarified the differences between a trunk and a tail. This example shows how art can serve as a vehicle for direct learning by helping children express their understandings. At the same time, the art responses give the teacher clues for further planning. The following are some activities that expand further on the concept of animals/pets and art activities.

- Encourage older children to draw, paint, or model representations of their pets doing something characteristic of that animal.

- Suggest to children that they find pictures for collages showing animals that live in different places, move in various ways, or have different body coverings.
- Provide opportunities for children to make their drawings, paintings, or cutout animals into booklets, murals, jigsaw puzzles, or puppets.
- Offer a variety of boxes, trays, and found objects that children can use to make zoo cages or farm environments for toy animals or models they create.
- Provide scraps of furry fabrics, yarns, and spotted and striped papers in different shapes for children to paste on a background and then add appendages for real or imaginary animals.
- Make a variety of boxes, cardboard tubes, and other found objects available so children can create real or imaginary creatures.
- Provide Styrofoam trays on which children can draw simple animal forms. Pierce the outline at regular intervals for younger children to stitch. Older children can pierce through the trays themselves.
- Transfer children's animal drawings onto felt or burlap. Cut out two duplicate shapes, stitch together, and fill with beans, seeds, or shredded nylon hose for use as toys to toss.

At the end of this chapter, you will find many ideas that may be used as the basis for planning both formal and informal science activities. These, of course, are meant to be starting points. Teachers will think of many more activities that suit their particular groups' interests and abilities.

Did You Get It?

A four-year-old notices that when she rubs her hand over her drawing, the lines she drew with pastels meld and soften. She is learning

   a. scientific inquiry.
   b. the aesthetic principle.
   c. cause and effect.
   d. operation of simple machines.

Take the full quiz on CourseMate.

19-6 The Discovery/Science Center

naeyc DAP The discovery center can be open ended (for example, present students with a box of magnets and electrical supplies with the instructions to see how the items interact), or they can work toward a specific outcome (for example, ask students to find out which items sink or float). The discovery center should have things for the children to "do." It is not a center where children just look at objects. Most teachers use a sand and water table in the discovery center. Here various materials—sand, water, sawdust, mud—can be made available for children to explore, measure, and pour. Sand and water activities are usually informal science and open ended; that is, children can freely explore and manipulate materials with no definite or specified purpose to the activity.

Another type of activity that usually is done in a discovery center is cooking. Recipes that children can prepare individually with a minimum of teacher supervision work well in the discovery center. There are many simple recipes that do not require cooking (see Chapter 21 for examples of such recipes). If heating equipment is used, an adult must always be present to supervise and assist.

The discovery center can house plants and animals for the children to observe. In addition to caring for them, children can also record information about them, such as the amount of food given to the guinea pig each day, the amount of water used for the plant, or the amount the plant has grown (see Photo 19-6).

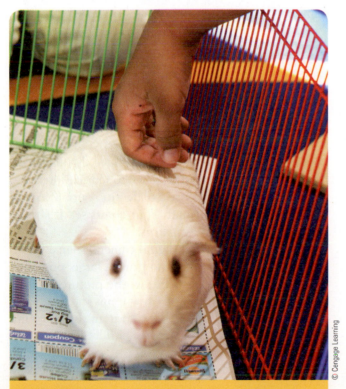

PHOTO 19-6 A discovery center can keep animals for children to observe and to keep track of the amount of food they eat.

© Cengage Learning

"Please touch!" is the implied invitation of an interesting, ever-changing discovery center. Many teachers begin the school year with noble intentions of welcoming nature finds and other objects of scientific interest that children bring from home. Perhaps they initiate the project attractively with a bird's nest propped in a small tree branch, some special rocks, and a recently shed snake skin. If the goal of a changing display is forgotten, the old things will lose their meaning. Because there is little appeal in a dusty nest or a tattered snake skin, it is better to retire the too-familiar objects.

19-6a Discovery Centers—Setup

Try to locate the discovery center in an area that both invites children's participation yet controls distractions. Varying the location to fit the requirements of the activity builds interest. Science is very popular on the days when it takes place under a blanket-covered table! Careful planning of space, materials, and time for science will allow children to work as safely, independently, and successfully as possible.

In preschool and kindergarten classrooms, and in elementary classrooms organized with learning centers, many science activities can be set up for independent use. Printed activity directions can be prepared to guide reading students. Recorded guides for nonreaders can also be made to reduce the amount of direct supervision needed for small-group learning activities.

19-6b Discovery Centers—Younger Preschool Children

Although the activities in this text are intended for children 3 years of age and older, many can be adapted for younger preschool children. Two-year-olds can enjoy simple sensory explorations such as feeling air as they move it with paper fans, spinning pinwheels, or swinging streamers on a breezy day. They can feel rock textures and weights, touch ice and then the water it melts into, and watch and then move like a goldfish. They can taste raw fruits and vegetables that have grown from plants, listen to loud and soft sounds, or gaze through transparent color paddles to see their surroundings in a new light.

Three-year-olds might be expected to engage in similar activities, taking in greater detail. They will be able to direct deeper attention to such things as exploring new dimensions with a magnifying glass. This group can enjoy some of the classifying experiences on a beginning level: sorting rocks from objects that are not rocks; things that float from those that do not float; and objects that are attracted by a magnet from objects that are not attracted.

In formal science activities, younger children need easily distinguished materials and clearly defined steps. For instance, the seeds in a planting experience should be large and easy to see. A fine, dark lettuce seed is hard to distinguish from a bit of dirt, and a child may not be sure of what he or she has actually done after planting it. A large, pale bean or pumpkin seed that is obviously different from the soil would be a better choice.

Very young children can be easily sidetracked in their reasoning by what they observe. To keep the objective of science experience evident to them, avoid using materials with irrelevant, distracting details. For instance, if size comparisons are to be made with measuring cups, use cups of the same color and shape to help children focus on size. Younger children will still be exploring materials with their mouths as well as with their fingers. Nonfood materials must not be small enough to swallow. Foods such as peanuts and popcorn should not be given to children too young to chew them well. As a matter of course, adults should closely supervise any activity for very young children.

Thoughtful questioning, careful listening to children's replies, and comments from the teacher guide formal science activities in the discovery center. Open-ended questions such as "What happens when you . . .?" help children focus their thinking. A question such as "Why do you suppose . . .?" allows children to share their reasoning. Many of us use the pattern of stating the answers we hear from children in the form of a question. We may say, "So the cup of snow melted into a smaller amount of water, right? Isn't that what you found?" This style of questioning reduces children's need to discover answers for themselves, or tells them that the main discovery is to find out what the teacher wants them to say.

19-6c Discovery Walks

An easy way to keep the science discovery area new and exciting is to plan nature discovery walks as a regular part of your curriculum. The desire to collect things is strong in young children. A discovery walk can be a springboard to some memorable science experiences.

Give children shopping bags and take them on a mini field trip to a nearby playground or sidewalk. Ask them to collect anything interesting to add to their bag (keeping safety in mind, of course). You'll be amazed at what your young collectors find, including flattened bottle caps, blades of grass, and even an occasional penny.

Sorting and representing. Ask children to unload their collections into a plastic tray or pan. Start sorting, comparing, classifying, and ordering. Have a

© Cengage Learning 2015

PHOTO 19-7 A magnifying glass is an excellent tool to help children examine their discoveries.

sheet of paper and markers on hand so that they can trace and label their collections.

A closer look. A magnifying glass is great for helping children examine their discoveries (see Photo 19-7). Children can sort their collections by lines, textures, colors, or any other art element. You might add magnetic strips to the backs of rocks and place them in categories (big/little, smooth/rough, shiny/dull, and so on) on a magnetic board.

Displaying objects in the discovery center. When a child brings a collection of objects from home, provide a special place for this temporary display. For objects collected by the class, you can organize and store the displays in clear plastic boxes. This way, the displays can be easily rotated among children.

When you have popular items in your discovery center such as prisms or magnets, have duplicates on hand or use a sign-up system. Two to four children can sit on the floor and explore a collection out on a small carpet square or a bathmat. Four chairs set at a table invite four science investigators.

If you have access to a digital camera, snap a photo of each child's collection and print a large, one-page photo of each collection. Below the picture, write a short "I spy" description of a few items in the collection. For example, write, "I spy an item that is round and has lines on it." This invites children's investigation and close observation.

You can also use interesting collections as table centerpieces for special occasions. If you have access to a video camera, you can make a video about the children's collecting and investigating process and share it with parents.

THIS ONE'S FOR YOU!

Making Sense of Data: A Twenty-First-Century Science Skill

Knowing how to read, interpret, and see trends in graphs is a critical twenty-first-century skill. All learners use this skill throughout their lives because it helps judge whether a claim is supported by evidence. A major aspect of doing science (in and out of the classroom) is asking questions about how the world works and then designing investigations to collect and analyze data that will provide solutions to those questions (McNeill & Krajcik, 2011; NRC, 1996, 2000). But after your students collect data, how can you help them make sense of it?

Young students are capable of asking a, "How many different types of birds come to our bird feeder?" question, designing and carrying out investigations, and then analyzing data to use as evidence to support claims that respond to their questions (NRC 1996, 2000). *Data organization and analysis* is the process of making observations, taking measurements, and sorting out the information in ways that facilitate sense-making, allowing possible patterns to become apparent (Krajcik, 2011).

The ability to analyze data is an essential aspect of scientific literacy and will be critical for young children as they grow in a world that is filled with information. To make sense of data, scientists transform it into various representations. By creating tables, graphs, diagrams, or other visualizations, children can transform data into different forms that will allow them, just as it allows scientists, to see patterns and trends.

Let's go back to the bird feeder scenario. This could be an area where children can practice making sense of data. The children might make a record of the type and number of birds that visit the feeder. A simple list of information might be difficult for children to see a pattern. Children can create a table to more clearly see the pattern of type of bird and how frequently each type visits the feeder. The transformation from list to table helps learners see trends in data—for example, sparrows are the most common bird. After students have constructed their tables, they can write summaries describing what their tables mean. Such summaries are another way to transform data—from numbers to words.

Children could also create graphs of data to make visual representations. Transforming data into graphs will help students see trends in quantitative data. To continue with our bird example, rather than a count of the type of birds, students could create a bar graph. A bar graph of the number versus types of birds is much easier for students to "read" because it more effectively illustrates patterns. In elementary classrooms, students can transform their data into pie charts, bar graphs, and line graphs (NCTM, 2000).

Another way to support students in learning this data-analyzing skill is to have them come up with statements that describe what the graph means. Have them look for a pattern or a trend in the shape of the graph. After students have written their own interpretation, members of the group can compare the statements. If your students are too young to write, you can have them say what they see.

Providing opportunities for students to ask questions about scientific phenomena they encounter in their world is a critical aspect of students learning science. Creating such learning activities will support all students in developing critical scientific practices and developing twenty-first-century capabilities that they will use throughout their lives (Krajcik, 2011).

19-6d Nature-Related Materials in Different Learning Centers

To the language-experience center, you can add books and pictures about nature. You can also add stuffed animals, animal puppets, and a variety of plant and animal flannel-board characters (see Photo 19-8). Choose pictures and other representations of animals that are as realistic as possible versus those that have a cartoonlike appearance.

To add nature-related materials to the manipulative center, you might choose simple puzzles with nature themes (animals, plants, and so on) and shells or pebbles of different colors and sizes. You might also add pinecones, small pieces of bark, dry wood, and other objects found in or near the yard. Similar items could be introduced into the block center as well.

Casper Holroyd

PHOTO 19-8 Stuffed animals are just one type of item that can be added to a nature-related learning center.

Materials from the outdoors also make wonderful additions to the art center. Dried leaves or small pieces of bark can be used for rubbings; seeds, shells, dry grasses, and feathers can be used for collages; evergreen sprigs can be used as paintbrushes.

To the music or listening center, you might add audiotapes of bird songs, ocean sounds, rainforest noises, and other sounds from nature. The dramatic play area can also be enriched with materials from the outdoors. Such materials include camping equipment, garden tools, and a picnic basket filled with a variety of picnic items.

Did You Get It?

A teacher gives each of her three-year-olds three identically sized ice cubes so they can compare how long each cube takes to melt in different assigned places in the classroom. Why should she be careful to give each child three identically sized ice cubes?

a. to minimize jealousy among the students

b. to avoid them from becoming sidetracked by irrelevant details

c. to ease the job of giving out the ice cubes and managing the experiment

d. to ensure their satisfaction with the experiment

Take the full quiz on CourseMate.

19-7 Environmental Education

> "We do not inherit the earth from our ancestors, we borrow it from our children."
> —Native American proverb

Ecologists have varied estimates on how much time is left before we will have wasted natural resources and polluted the Earth to the point where we can no longer survive. Some fear the damage is already irreversible. Others believe that there is still time—provided a profound change in attitude and behavior occurs. For adults, this change means finding new values. For children, it means growing up with an understanding of the environment and a desire to conserve and protect those things essential for continued life on this planet.

If children are to grow up in a world fit for human survival, the environment must be protected. Children should learn about nature from their earliest years. Nature is not the only part of a child's environment,

however. Home, school, and neighborhood are all parts of the child's environment. In fact, everything that contributes to children's experiences—good or bad—is part of their environment. Can a child learn creativity by learning about the environment? Can a child learn to improve the environment? Can young children learn about ecology? The answer to these questions is "yes." Most of all, learning about these things can and must begin when a child is young.

Their environment is one of the most important influences in the lives of children. They need an environment full of love. They need an environment that provides for their other basic needs: water, food, clean air. Children need an environment that provides for their safety, that helps them grow intellectually, and that they can understand and control. In other words, children need to learn about their environment because their lives depend on that environment. This learning can be done in a very creative way. Activities that help children understand their environment can also help them become more creative thinkers. (Bredekamp 2009).

19-7a Types of Environments

For the purposes of this chapter, the term environment refers to two things: man-made and natural things that children meet in their surroundings. Streets, houses, and schools are examples of man-made things in the environment. Trees, grass, and birds are parts of nature. Streetlights, cars, and buildings are man-made. Animals, clouds, and snow are natural things. Noise, light, and smells may be man-made or a part of nature.

Children have many environments in which they live. Home is one. It may be a pleasant part of a child's life or an unpleasant one. School is another environment that influences a child's life, and it, too, may be an enjoyable experience or an unpleasant one. The neighborhood environment may be friendly and safe, or it may be hostile and dangerous. Many people are also part of a child's environment: parents and neighbors, grocers and police officers, and teachers and doctors. The people who make up the communities in which children live may make children feel very good about their lives, or they may make the children feel unhappy.

In these environments, there are also natural things and natural happenings: grass, trees, and flowers; rain, wind, and earthquakes; cats, rats, and beetles. All these things are part of a child's environment. They all affect one another. Nature influences people; people influence nature.

Eight-Year-Olds Publish Study

Biology Letters published a report conducted and written by a group of 8- to 10-year olds from an English elementary school investigating the way bumblebees see colors and patterns. The scientific organization—which is more than three centuries old and includes some of the world's most eminent scientists—said the children reported findings that were a genuine advance in the field of insect color and pattern vision (Hui, 2010).

Working with a neuroscientist from University College London, the children carefully documented their methodology and discussed the data they collected. The group trained bees to go to targets of different colors by giving them a sugar reward, and they reported that the insects are able to learn and remember cues based on color and pattern. The study successfully went through peer review, and the scientists who commented on the students' report in the journal said although the experiments were modest and lacked statistical analyses, they were cleverly and correctly designed. The studies held their own compared to those conducted by highly trained specialists.

Beau Lotto, the scientist who coordinated the study, said she hoped the project could inspire people to approach science in a way that's creative and fun (Hui, 2010).

19-7b Ecology

Ecology is the study of all elements of an environment, both living and nonliving, and the interrelation of these elements. The term comes from two Greek words: *ecos*, meaning the "place to live" or "home," and *ology*, meaning "study of."

If we stop to consider our work with young children, we have probably touched on the subject of ecology frequently. For example, we notice the changes in the weather and discuss how these affect plants, birds, animals, and ourselves. When we plant seeds, hatch eggs, or care for a pet, we notice those things that are necessary for life and growth—nourishment, light, heat, nurturing. We like to examine and observe many organisms, but if we remove an insect from its home, we take care to restore it unharmed to its place after our observation is finished. Consequently, children learn that all life is precious, and no creature is more or less worthwhile than another.

Those of us in early childhood education are also old hands at recycling materials and using up discards. Bits of paper left over from cutting shapes find their way into the collage box instead of the wastebasket. Empty boxes evolve into constructions, large and small. The blank sides of printed sheets of paper are used for drawing. Old newspapers are used for many art projects. We all think twice before throwing anything away, and with a little encouragement, children and their parents soon catch the saving habit.

By our example, we can teach other ways of living a more ecologically sound lifestyle. For example, using durable dishes for food service rather than disposable dishes is an ecologically sound practice. When food and beverages for snacks and meals come in bottles or cans, these containers should be cleaned and the cans flattened and deposited at a recycling center. The use of personal cloth towels instead of paper towels is another good ecological practice. To encourage parents to recycle, you might consider establishing a collection site at your school, perhaps making it a cooperative project run by the parents.

To truly grasp the concept of ecology, young children need opportunities to observe the total process rather than just a portion of it or only the finished product. Help children understand the total process when you explain the need for conservation. Describing how the paper-making process begins with the cutting down of a tree in the forest and ends with the paper products that we use every day helps children understand why it is important that they use only one paper towel to dry their hands.

Incorporating the subject of ecology into the early childhood curriculum is endorsed in the National Science Education Standards. It is particularly relevant to the standard that states that children should develop an understanding of "types of resources" and "changes in environments" (NRC, 1996, p. 138).

These early experiences in ecology will provide students an eventual understanding and appreciation for their part in protecting the environment.

19-7c Ecology and Art

Art, music, dance, movement, and storytelling all provide opportunities for children to express their interests and discoveries developed through environmental education. Setting up easels outdoors may inspire children to paint trees or their feelings about trees. Modeling clay outdoors may encourage children to create their own versions of natural objects in their outdoor play space. Use types of clouds to inspire soft sculptures: stratus, cumulus, and so on. (See Chapter 14 and the appendices for play dough and other modeling material recipes.) In movement activities, children may reflect the wiggle of caterpillars they observed on the playground. In music, the sounds of birds and crickets can be reflected with rhythm instruments or their own voices. They may dance the story of birds, flowers, and animals awakening to the springtime sun. Children's books are also excellent for further expanding a child's understanding and appreciation of the earth. Children's science books are an excellent way to address the national science standard that states, "It is important for students to learn how to access information from books" (NRC, 1996, p. 45).

The preceding are all general ideas on how to incorporate environmental education and ecology into your early childhood program. The following are some more specific activities related to environmental education and ecology for children of all ages:

- When someone in the classroom breaks a toy or piece of equipment, use the opportunity to talk with children about the consequences—that no one can play with the toy or use the equipment until it is repaired and that if it cannot be repaired, no one can ever use it again. Have children discuss ways of preventing this problem.
- Help children (and by your own example) use materials—paint, paper, crayons, and the like—conservatively by saving scraps, storing unused paint, completing a picture before starting another, and keeping pencils and crayons off the floor.
- Encourage children to help care for and clean classroom furniture. Provide cleanup materials for washing off tables and chairs and cleaning up spills.
- Before looking at books, discuss with the children the importance of caring for them. Suggestions might include washing hands, turning pages at the corner, and putting them in a special place away from pets and younger brothers and sisters. Remind them of their disappointment over a missing page in a story.
- Snack time offers an opportunity for children to learn to conserve. The same applies to older children at lunch time. Persuade them to take only what they will eat, to eat all they take, and to refuse what they do not want. Each child should frequently have the opportunity to clean up after snack. Before going on a class picnic, remind children to pick up their trash in the park and discuss with them why this is important.
- During the year, encourage appreciation for the jobs of the school custodian, the garbage collector, and others whose work is essential to maintaining a clean and pleasant environment. Invite these helpers to talk with children about what they do and how the children can help make their job easier.
- Avoid frightening children with threats about results of things they cannot control. (Example: What will happen when there is no clean air left?) Concentrate instead on the things they can do, such as keeping their own yards and school grounds neat, putting their own waste in proper receptacles, having a litter bag in the car, avoiding open burning, keeping pets clean, and so on.

19-7d Environmental Activities in School

A child first learns about caring for the environment by caring for his or her most immediate environment, that is, home, school, playgrounds, and parks. In the early childhood years, the teacher can use everyday experiences to point out to children the importance of caring for the environment.

Getting started. Getting young children outdoors to touch and experience nature is the starting point for learning about ecology and the environment. Unfortunately, a visit to many early childhood classrooms reveals the obvious: indoor time and space are given far more priority than outdoor. Many early childhood programs allot only a short daily period of outdoor time for children's energy release and motor development. In the elementary grades, with state-mandated curriculums, it becomes even more difficult to find time to go outdoors to study and still accommodate all the mandated subjects and time requirements.

PHOTO 19-9 It's important to work outdoor learning experiences into the day.

Increased time for outdoor learning experience can be worked into the daily routine without difficulty, however, at least in good weather (see Photo 19-9). Music, movement, and art acquire new dimensions outside; there is often plenty of space for construction with large blocks, boxes, tires, and boards; and snack and lunch times become picnics. Best of all, the outdoors provides a natural setting, complete with props, for dramatic play. Middle- and upper-elementary-age students enjoy reading and working on projects outdoors. Small reading groups, project work, and other academic activities can often be done just as effectively in the outdoors. Just think how much you, as a student, enjoy reading outside on a sunny, pleasant day!

Even if the outdoor space is a concrete-covered square, children experience more of nature than they would inside. They know the warmth of the sun, the power of the wind, and the coolness of shade; they find plants that spring up in cracks and insects that crawl or fly; and they experience weather in its many forms.

Obviously, the more natural an environment is, the better. Slightly unkempt spaces are more interesting to investigate than blacktop or grassy lawns. In many areas, the edges of property lines where the mower does not reach hold the greatest promise for exploration.

As stated in the national standards on earth and science (Content Standard D), it is important that "all students develop an understanding of the properties of the earth" (NRC, 1996, p. 130). Young children are naturally interested in everything they see around them—soil, rocks, streams, rain, snow, clouds, and rainbows. During the first years of school, they should be encouraged to observe closely the objects and materials in their environment, note their properties, distinguish one from another, and develop their own explanations of how things become the way they are.

Teacher's role. To be involved with nature, all you need are curiosity, joy of exploration, and a desire to discover firsthand the wonders of nature. Young children are naturals at this. Adults take a little longer. The teacher's most important role is sharing enthusiasm, curiosity, and wonder. Adults can best do this by using their legs—stopping and getting down to see what has caught a child's attention (see Photo 19-10). Just the focusing of attention, perhaps with an expression of wonderment— "Look how pretty!" or "Great, you found something amazing!"—can encourage exploration and child–adult conversation. When we share our own ideas and feelings with a child, it encourages that child to explore his or her own feelings and perceptions. In middle- and upper-elementary grades, as children become more familiar with their world, the teacher guides them to observe changes, including cycle changes such as cycles of the moon, predictable trends such as growth and decay, and less consistent change, such as weather.

PHOTO 19-10 Teachers can share in young children's natural curiosity and wonder by getting down to look at what has caught their attention.

THIS ONE'S FOR YOU!

Where the Wild Things Are

In an attempt to give the public a peek into the secret lives of wild animals, Smithsonian Institution researchers have collected all of their motion-triggered camera shots from the field in one place, the Smithsonian Wild website. Before consolidation, these candid photos of vampire bats, jaguars, and everything in between were lodged on various computers, neglected and at risk of being lost.

All over the world, researchers have set up "camera traps," often along forest trails or in trees, which take a photo when the camera's sensor recognizes movement or body heat. Researchers often employ camera traps instead of walking forest trails and carefully watching and recording every sign of an animal's presence. But these line-transect surveys often fail to catch shy, small, or rare species, like the snow leopard, which the cameras have successfully captured.

You can check the website to see what work has been done on any particular species in any area of the world. The pictures are just like collecting a specimen. The Smithsonian plans to enlarge the current cache of 200,000 images with contributions from individuals and researchers associated with institutions and schools (Schipani, 2011).

Source: Schipani, V. (2011). Works in progress: Where the wild things are. Reprinted from The American Scholar, Volume 80, No. 3, Summer 2011, p. 14. Copyright © 2011 by the author.

Pets in the classroom. The best way for young children to learn about animals is to have them in the classroom. Through observing and caring for pets in the classroom, children can do the following.

- Grow in understanding the needs of animals for food and water, as well as safe, clean housing and attention.
- Grow in appreciation for the beauty, variety, and functional physical characteristics of animals (for example, the protective shell on a turtle, the webbed feet on a duckling, and the sharp teeth and claws on a hamster).
- Grow in compassion for and humane treatment of animals.
- Obtain inspiration for many language experiences and creative activities.
- Good classroom pets are guinea pigs, rabbits, parakeets, white mice, hamsters, turtles, salamanders, gerbils, and goldfish. Good short-time (an hour or so) classroom pet visitors are chicks, ducklings, puppies, a setting hen, kittens, and turkey poults. Of course, before purchasing or adopting any pet, be sensitive to the needs of children with allergies.

Children can help plan for the pet by building the cage or preparing the terrarium or aquarium. The necessary food and water pans can be obtained, a food supply can be stored up, bedding can be prepared, and the handling of the pet can be discussed. Arrangements must be made for pet care during all holidays and vacation periods. A trip to a pet shop would be an excellent experience.

Children should help with the care of the pet after it is obtained, but in the final analysis, the teacher is responsible for seeing that the pet is treated well. Children should learn that pets are not toys, that they have feelings, and that when provoked, some of them defend themselves by biting. Children should not be allowed to handle pets excessively or without supervision. It is cruel to let them wrap pets up in blankets and take them for walks in a doll buggy or to allow any other activity foreign to the pet's nature—and children should be helped to understand why. Neglected or mishandled pets give a negative message about responsibility and respect for life.

Besides learning how to care for pets, children can participate in the following activities:

- They can discuss the way pets feel, how they look, the sounds they make, the way they move, the purpose of various parts of the body, the need for food, their homes, their reproduction habits, and other attributes.
- They can create experience charts about an animal's care and characteristics.
- They can tell original stories based on the pet and tape these stories.
- They can draw, paint, or model the pet out of clay.
- They can dramatize the pet's movements.
- They can take a trip to a pet shop or zoo.
- They can show pictures of animals, telling which are tame and which are wild; which fly, hop, or swim; and which live in water or on land.
- They can tell animal stories, recite animal poems, and sing animal songs.

- Older children can write journal entries about their daily observations of the classroom pet.
- They can write stories with the pet as the main character.

Outdoor science. Many activities work well inside the school. Others are more suited to the area outside the school building. All of the following activity suggestions are consistent with National Science Education Standards. They apply most specifically to Content Standard D in Earth Science. This standard is focused on the child's developing an understanding of: properties of earth materials, objects in the sky, and changes in earth and sky.

Beginning activities. Children can learn many different things about nature by being outdoors. However, many young children come to school with limited direct experiences with natural environments. Thus, they may have little understanding and great fear about what may happen to them in their encounters with nature. They may fear the darkness of a wooded area. They may think that all bugs and insects bite or sting. In their minds, an earthworm may be a poisonous snake. Such children need a gradual exposure to the world of nature. They need to become familiar with the trees and bushes in the schoolyard before they feel comfortable hiking in the woods. They need to observe and care for classroom animals before they are asked to welcome a caterpillar crawling across their hand or feel the woolly head of a lamb while on a field trip to a farm.

Young children also need to realize that nature is all around them and that wildlife can be found anywhere. Some children seem to think that wildlife is somewhere very separate and far away from where they live. When asked where he might look to find wildlife, one little boy responded, "Africa." For such children, one of the most meaningful lessons would focus on becoming aware of and comfortable with wildlife in their immediate environment.

Ideas on how to begin with simple experiences include the following.

- Have students watch a bean seed sprout in the classroom and then attempt to plant and tend a vegetable garden.
- Allow children to play with snow in the texture table before making and crawling through tunnels of snow in the schoolyard.
- Have children watch birds and squirrels from a "window on nature" before suggesting that they let a goat eat from their hands.

- Have children walk barefoot in puddles, and then observe their footprints made on the sidewalk.

Bird feeders. Children can design and build bird feeders with the assistance of their parents or another adult. Professionally built bird feeders can also be used outside the classroom.

Children can try to discover what food attracts various kinds of birds. Where is the best place to put a bird feeder? When is the best time of year to watch for birds? What time of day is best for bird watching at a feeder?

Older children enjoy learning the names of the birds they see at the feeders. A book with colored illustrations of local birds can be a research source for this activity. Children can keep records of which birds frequent certain feeders more than others and speculate as to why this is the case. They can make graphs representing use of each feeder.

Cloud and sky watching. On a mild, partly sunny, or cloudy day, children can learn much about their environment. They can lie on the ground and look up at the sky. They may see distinct clouds of many shapes or clouds that join together. The sun may disappear. It may get cool very suddenly. Birds may fly past.

Children may have many different feelings as they lie still and watch the sky. Questions may arise. How do clouds seem to move? What do they look like? Are there many colors in the clouds? What do clouds look like just before a storm? The teacher might have children make up a story about clouds or suggest they paint a picture about their cloud watching.

The sounds of nature. Walking in the woods or along a busy street can be made exciting by listening to the sounds. In the area next to a school, there are many sounds, too. When most of the children are indoors, one or two supervised children may want to go outside and simply listen. They can take a cassette tape recorder along and record sounds, too. Play the tape and encourage children to move like the sounds make them feel.

How many different sounds can they hear? Can they hear sounds made by birds? By animals? What do the leaves in the trees sound like? How do trees without leaves sound? What other sounds can be heard? How do noises made by cars differ from noises made by trucks? How does a person feel if there is too much noise?

What happens to rain water? After a rainstorm, children can try to follow the paths taken by the water. Does all of the water flow into a sewer? Does some of it go into the ground? What happens in paved areas compared to grassy areas? What happens in dirt areas compared to grassy areas?

Older children can learn about the effects of erosion in their own parks and playgrounds. This can easily be done after a heavy rainstorm on the playground or in a nearby park. Making mud pies and mud finger painting are great follow-up activities to these observations.

Animal hiding places. There may be a small hole in the ground or a sand hill in a crack on the playground. Thick grass or bushes serve as hiding places for animals. Under a large rock or near the foundation of the school, there may be places for living things to hide.

Children seek answers to many questions about animals. Why do animals need hiding places? Can a child create a place where an animal will choose to hide? How many natural hiding places can be found? Can children create hiding places for themselves? How do they feel when they are in their hiding places? Can they move like an animal looking for a hiding place? Can they move like that animal as it goes into its hiding place?

If creativity is to be a part of activities such as these, decisions must be left to children. Help from the teacher should not take the form of orders about what to do and what not to do. Advice is good; orders or carefully worded cookbook directions are not.

Plants in the environment. Probably the best way to observe the magnificent color and variety to be found in plants is to visit the places where they can be seen firsthand. The school grounds are the closest source. Children can hunt with you for the tallest tree, the one with the roughest bark, and the ones with needles, pinecones, or smooth leaves. They can hunt for plants that are growing in cracks in the sidewalk, for plants that have been eaten by insects, and for seeds, berries, and roots that are exposed.

Going beyond the schoolyard, trips can be made to the grocery store, supermarket, or farmers' market to examine firsthand the potatoes, carrots, onions, eggplants, peas, cabbages, beets, and other foods. Vegetables are beautiful and occur in many colors, shapes, and sizes. One of each kind brought back to the classroom would provide a wonderful opportunity for children to make comparisons among them.

The same kind of observations can be made with fruits, or with flowers at a greenhouse, shrubs at a nursery, or plants in an arboretum, small neighborhood garden, or truck farm. Plants can be looked at, cooked, taken apart, tasted, felt, counted, smelled, and weighed. They could be compared for color, texture, juiciness, shape, kind of leaf, aroma, size, and outside covering.

They could be classified by the preceding characteristics as nuts, seeds, fruits, roots, leaves, stems, or vegetables, usually eaten raw or usually eaten cooked.

If trips are not possible, each child could be asked to bring one fruit, vegetable, or other plant to school, or the teacher could supply the necessary items from the school budget. Some other suggestions follow.

- Have seed catalogs available in the book center for children to browse through.
- Have children plant seeds in pots, or better yet, if a small garden plot is available, have children use it for planting and nurturing a "crop." Seed dealers can advise you on types that germinate quickly and what care they need. Press a stick such as a tongue depressor down into the soil by the seed when it sprouts. Have children mark the height of the sprout each week as it grows. The date and name of the plant can be put on the stick. If the seeds in some pots don't grow, dig them up to see what happened to them.
- Help children build a model greenhouse in the block center, using planks, large blocks, and packing boxes. They can put their plants in the greenhouse, as well as small trowels, watering cans, a bag of potting soil, and experience charts.
- Have children start plants from seeds, cuttings, bulbs, roots, and tubers. Sweet potatoes, placed in glasses so that half the potato is under water, will produce roots and a luxuriant vine. (Try to find potatoes that aren't bruised.) Bulbs of all kinds can be started. Geraniums and philodendron will produce roots from cuttings placed in water and can then be potted. Pussy willow twigs will grow roots in water.
- Show children how to make top gardens by cutting off about an inch from the top of root vegetables, such as carrots. When children place the cut end in water, new, leafy growth will shoot up.
- Have children break or cut apart seeds of various kinds to study the small plant inside. Then have a plant tasting party. Examples: Seeds—sunflowers; roots—carrots; stems—celery; leaves—lettuce; flowers—cauliflower.
- Help children sprout seeds so that their growth can be studied. A satisfactory way to do this is to cut up blotting paper or paper towels. Place a couple of layers in the bottom of a saucer, moistening the paper thoroughly. Drop six to ten radish seeds on the blotter. Smear a little Vaseline around the edge of the saucer and cover with a piece of window glass. Tiny white root hairs will develop.

● To see roots, stems, and leaves form, have children make a plastic bag greenhouse. They can place folded paper towels inside a plastic, self-locking bag, then staple a line across about 2 inches from the bottom. Children can fill the bags to just below the line of staples with water, and then drop in seeds. Seal the bags and display them on a bulletin board for children to observe their growth and development. Children will be able to see the roots, stems, and leaves form.

Water play experiences. No matter in what quantity or container water is available—in a pool or basin, in a puddle or cup—there are ways to take advantage of its learning potential! A wading pool or large basin lends itself to pouring, sprinkling, and mixing with water, while a cup or a puddle is ideal for floating tiny objects like foil boats or cork stoppers and for dissolving small quantities of sugar or drink mix. Whatever facilities can be provided, water provides a marvelous science experience for young children (see Photo 19-11).

Organizing the play space for water play is a matter of selecting and arranging suitable containers and appropriate equipment. A laundry tub or plastic wading pool can be placed outside with a bench or table nearby to hold objects. If water play is to take place inside, the floor covering must be water repellent, and a shelf can be used for equipment storage; a plastic tablecloth can be a weatherproof carpet and a small card table can substitute for the shelf. Plastic aprons are ideal for clothing protection, but garbage bags with neck and armholes cut serve well, too.

Objects that lead the child to science experiences might include the following:

● Sponges, corks, and light pieces of wood
● Funnels, strainers, colanders, plastic tubing, and siphons
● Spray containers, sprinkling cans, squeeze bottles, and rubber balls
● Plastic pitchers, margarine tubs, plastic cups, and yogurt containers
● Paintbrushes, paint rollers, and washcloths
● Spoons, dippers, plastic syringes, and plastic medicine droppers

Occasionally, bubble bath, cornstarch, food coloring, or other mixables can be added to vary the appearance and physical properties of the water.

Safety tips. Always have an adult with the children in any water play situation. Never leave a child unattended. Use only unbreakable materials for water play activities: never use glass, ceramic, porcelain, pottery, china, or other breakable materials. Always gather materials ahead of time so you do not have to leave children unsupervised.

Develop water play rules with children. Discuss and generate a list of rules that are appropriate to your situation and revise them as needed. For example, you will need one set of rules when children are playing at the water table and another set for the outdoor pool.

Appropriate rules are presented here.

● No splashing is allowed.
● Keep the water in the containers.
● Mop up spills immediately.

Specific activities for water play are included at the end of this chapter.

PHOTO 19-11 Playing at the water table, children learn many science projects.

© Cengage Learning

Two Approaches to Teaching Science to Young Children

In this study, researchers examined two common but different instructional approaches to teaching young children science concepts, vocabulary, and scientific problem-solving skills. One of the approaches was responsive teaching (RT), which involves a child-initiated and child-directed perspective in which teachers provide materials and opportunities for exploration and experimentation but without explicitly and systematically teaching specific concepts. Teachers who use this approach follow a child's lead and facilitate children's exploration by using strategies such as modeling, imitating, describing what children are doing and saying, and providing materials in an environment that challenges children's thinking (Hong & Diamond, 2012).

The second teaching strategy was one that included more explicit instruction (Responsive Teaching + Explicit Instruction: RT+EI). This approach includes guiding and supporting children's learning using explicit as well as implicit strategies that best fit each child's level of understanding and skills. Specific strategies in this approach include explicitly introducing concepts and vocabulary words to which children may not be familiar, directly asking open-ended and challenging questions, and conducting experiments, along with responsive teaching approaches.

Researchers hypothesized that children whose teacher provides both explicit and implicit (responsive) instruction (RT+EI) will outperform children receiving only responsive instruction (RT) on all three issues (that is, concepts and vocabulary, content-general, and content-specific problem-solving) (Hong & Diamond, 2012).

Participants included 104 children (51 boys and 53 girls) aged 4 to 5 years attending early childhood programs in a mid-sized Midwestern community. Children were randomly assigned to small group instruction with one to three classmates, and the small groups were then randomly assigned to an instructional condition: Responsive Teaching (RT), Responsive Teaching and Explicit Instruction (RT+EI), and Control.

Four 15-minute intervention sessions focused on objects' floating and sinking were implemented with the two intervention groups, and four book-reading sessions were provided for the control group. The full cycle of each intervention took approximately 2 to 2 1/2 weeks. Each session was videotaped. Assessments of science

concepts and vocabulary and scientific problem-solving skills related to sinking and floating were completed about 1 week before and after the four intervention sessions.

In the RT intervention, the lessons were taught by choosing and providing materials that would promote an understanding of sinking and floating. In contrast, Responsive Teaching and Explicit Instruction (RT+EI) used both implicit and explicit strategies to teach science vocabulary, concepts, and problem-solving skills by providing a brief lesson (10 minutes) at the beginning of each session.

Results revealed significant effects of instructional approaches on children's learning of science concepts. Children in both intervention groups significantly outperformed those in the control group on measures of science concepts and science vocabulary. There was a significant difference in performance between children in the two intervention groups. These findings suggest that the combination of implicit and explicit teaching strategies may be more effective in teaching new concepts and vocabulary than implicit teaching strategies.

In addition, there was a significant difference in children's performance on content-specific scientific problem-solving skills (that is, making floating and sinking experiments) that were taught as part of the EI intervention. Children in the RT+EI group received significantly higher scores than did children in the control group on these tasks. The performance of children in the RT group was not significantly different from the performance of children in either the RT+EI group or the control group.

This study provides evidence that preschool-aged children can learn science concepts, vocabulary, and age-appropriate scientific problem-solving skills when appropriate guidance and instruction are provided. Both responsive teaching and explicit instruction are useful approaches to teaching young children science concepts, vocabulary, and scientific problem-solving skills at a basic level. However, incorporating explicit strategies into teaching was found to be more effective in promoting children's understanding of science concepts related to objects' floating and sinking (Hong & Diamond, 2012).

Source: Hong, S-Y & Diamond, K. E. (2012). Two approaches to teaching young children science concepts, vocabulary, and scientific problem-solving skills. Early Childhood Research Quarterly 27(3), 295–305.

Summary

19-1 State why science is important to the development of young children.

Science activities help children acquire knowledge about the world around them through investigation of that world. Learning about science is important for all children because it gives them an opportunity to learn by doing. Science activities help young children develop skills in using their senses. These skills can be used every day throughout a person's lifetime. Science also allows children another chance to exercise their creative abilities.

19-2 Name and describe three general kinds of science.

Formal science activities are planned by the teacher to develop particular skills, such as fine-motor skills or awareness of the five senses. Informal science, on the other hand, calls for little or no teacher involvement. Children work on their own and select the kind of activities that interest them. Informal science activities are less structured than formal science activities. Creativity is, therefore, better served by informal than by formal science. Incidental science activities cannot be planned because they are based on events that occur randomly. An effective early childhood teacher makes use of these events to enhance and extend students' learning.

19-3 Discuss inquiry-based learning and ways to promote it in the early childhood classroom.

Inquiry-based learning refers to investigating to gather information. It is an approach to learning that involves a process of exploring the natural or material world that leads to asking questions and making discoveries in the search for new understandings. It may be promoted by asking questions that invite constructive input and validate prior knowledge; encouraging children to wait a few seconds before giving an answer to allow time for thinking; and repeating or paraphrasing what the children say without praising or criticizing them.

19-4 Explain the purpose of the National Science Education Standards.

The National Research Council (NRC) defined performance standards for children at each grade level, from kindergarten through high school back in 1996. These standards present an outline of what students in K–12 need to know, understand, and be able to do to be "scientifically literate" at each grade level. They promote a dynamic understanding of scientific principles that is always open to review and revision.

19-5 Discuss the aesthetics of science in the early childhood program.

For the young child, the world of nature is an especially appropriate avenue for developing aesthetic sensitivity. Children working with art materials make scientific observations, noting, for example, that water makes tempera paint thinner and that crayons become soft if they are left near the heat. Young children's natural love of animals is a good place to begin when planning art activities that encourage science experiences. Children are intrigued by animals. Studying animals is consistent with the national science standard calling for the study of animals and their environments. Because the world of nature is so full of sights, sounds, and textures, it can serve as an incredibly rich and readily available resource for the development of aesthetic sensibilities in young children.

19-6 Discuss the discovery center and its importance in the early childhood program.

The discovery center is where children can actively experience science with natural materials. It is an interesting, ever-changing place for children to observe and interact with natural objects. Discovery walks are an easy to keep the science discovery area new and exciting.

19-7 Discuss environmental education and its place in the early childhood program.

Children should learn about nature from their earliest years. Their environment is one of the most important influences in the lives of children. Children should begin to understand that all forces in the environment affect one another. Animals influence other animals. Plants affect animals. The climate has an effect on the environment. People can make the environment pleasant or unpleasant.

Key Terms

ecology 455
environment 454
formal science 446
Next Generation Science
   Standards 448

Framework for K-12 Science
   Education 448
incidental science 447
informal science 446
inquiry-based learning 447

Science, Technology, Engineering, and
   Math (STEM) 448
Science, Technology, Engineering, Arts,
   and Math (STEAM) 449

Learning Activities

Science Activities

1. Take a field trip. Walk within one square block of your home or school. Identify all of the plant life in this area. How many trees, plants, shrubs, and weeds can you observe?

2. Create a file of resources in the community that could be used to foster children's concepts of their environment and the world around them.

3. Observe in a classroom where there is a living pet or pets. Record children's conversations as they interact

with the pet. Discuss how much they have learned about the animal from direct observation. What did their questions/conversations tell you about their experiences with the pet? Be specific in your answers.

4. Using a pail of water, create a puddle on a playground in order to observe children's reactions as they approach it. Describe the ways in which they play.

5. Plan a science table where children can be involved in making discoveries. List the objects you might include, and describe the types of involvement each object might stimulate. Discuss your list with others in your class.

6. Visit a playground. List natural phenomena that seem to be of interest to children. As you observe children at play, describe behavior that indicates they do take an interest in these phenomena. Compare what interested you at the playground to what interested the children. Discuss the differences between your interests and those of the children.

Making Observations

The ability to make many accurate observations is an important skill for both children and adults. The following activity is designed to test your ability to make observations using all of your senses (seeing, hearing, smelling, tasting, and touching).

Materials: A package of peppermint Life Savers, ruler, book of matches, small nail, sheet of sandpaper, glass of water, and waxed paper.

A. How many observations can you make about the package of peppermint Life Savers? Can you make as many as 40 observations? Try doing this with one or two partners, if possible. Do it for each of the items listed in letter A.

B. List all your observations and write down the sense or senses that you used to make each observation (seeing, hearing, and so on).

Finding Objects for Making Observations

A. Find 10 objects that can be used for making observations. Each object should provide opportunities for an observer to use all five senses. An ice cube is one such object.

B. After finding the 10 objects, try the following.
   1. Decide what other materials would be helpful in making observations of this object (for example, a ruler or magnifying glass). Make a list of these materials.
   2. Collect all materials needed for observing each item, and place them in small packages or boxes.
   3. Choose a partner. Make observations of three of your partner's objects using materials provided by your partner. Then let your partner do the same with your objects and materials.

Finding Materials

A. Visit rummage sales, farm auctions, store sales, and secondhand stores. Look for materials that could be used by children in science activities.

B. Make a list of things that can be bought, how much they cost, and where they can be purchased. Compare your list with the lists of several other students.

C. Prepare a master list of materials for science activities.

Activities for Children

Art and Science Activities

Science is a natural springboard for art activities. Try some of the following activities to get children actively exploring the connection.

Art and Reality. Students can examine how a single object is shown realistically in many different ways by artists. For example, show five different pieces of art that feature an animal. Ask how each gives different information and feels different.

Invisible Animals. Have students examine water under a microscope or with hand lenses and sketch living organisms that reside there. Emphasize close looking to capture specifics. Sketches can be enlarged into full paintings.

Three-Dimensional Habitats. Have students use boxes to create dioramas of an animal's habitat (land or water). They might add clay sculptures, tempera paint, and found objects to their construction.

Scientific Drawings. Examine the drawings of Beatrix Potter and Robert McCloskey, both of whom studied animals and plants carefully to render their images. Students can then choose to do a careful scientific drawing, focusing on important details. Use photos or actual plants for close looking.

Color Science. Provide small groups of students a prism to investigate color. Children can paint or use crayons to record observations and discover colors.

Growing Things. Use pantyhose feet to make living "heads." Fill hose with a teaspoon of grass seed and then a mixture of soil and sawdust. Tie snugly with a string. Paint on face with fabric paint. Put head in a shallow dish and pour water over it. Place in a sunny area and watch the grass "hair" grow.

Step into Painting. Have students think like scientists and tell or write their observations as they look at a piece of art (for example, a landscape). Encourage students to focus on the painting's content and how it might have been made.

Spider Web Analysis. Slide a piece of black construction paper behind a spider web and bring it forward so that the web clings to the paper. Dust with flour or dusting powder. Spray with fixative or non-aerosol hair spray. Discuss the patterns of lines created by the web. Look closely to compare and contrast.

Water Play Activities

In all of the following activities, be sure that an adult is always present when children are playing with water.

Rainbow in a Bowl

This activity shows children that light is made up of color. Place a clear bowl of water away from direct sunlight. Put one drop of clear nail polish in the water. Have children look at the water and nail polish from different angles to see a rainbow of colors. Then ask them to share other times they have seen rainbows, such as in water from a sprinkler on a sunny day.

Miscellaneous Water Play Ideas

- Straws are great for blowing bubbles during water play. To prevent children from sucking up the soapy water by mistake, poke holes near the tops of the straws first.
- Make soap bubbles last longer by adding a few tablespoons of sugar to the soapy water.
- Add variety to the water play area by adding these items and activities:
  - Fill the water table with ice cubes and provide shakers of salt and lengths of string.
  - Punch a row of holes from the bottom to the top of a two-liter plastic soda bottle.
  - Put salt in the water, and then let children try to float and sink objects.
  - Substitute snow for water.
  - Put a large chunk of ice in the water table. Provide safety goggles, rubber mallets, and rock salt.
  - Provide lengths of plastic pipe, whole and also in sections cut in half lengthwise, to use as canals and ramps for rolling marbles, small toy cars, or blocks. Have children use the piping dry, then wet, and compare results.
  - Punch holes in the bottom of milk cartons to make sieves. Use a variety of sizes of cartons, and vary the size of the holes.
  - Add foam or rubber alphabet letters and small fishnets to the water play center. Have students name the letter they catch or catch the letters that make up their name.
  - Encourage children to experiment with varying the amounts of water and air inside zippered sandwich storage bags in floating experiments.
  - Give children heavy aluminum foil to shape into boats.
  - Challenge children to create a boat from found objects, and then move it from one end of the water to the other without using their hands.
  - Challenge children to make a bridge over a portion of the water using scrap materials.

Funny Fish

In this activity, students learn about life under the sea by making a three-dimensional clay artwork of a sea creature.

Materials: Self-hardening clay, mats to place under clay, simple clay tools such as craft sticks and pencils, small strips of paper on which to write student names, shallow bowls of water, paper towels.

Procedure:

1. Ask students to share what they have learned or know about sea life. Ask them to consider which sea creatures would be a good choice to make out of clay. Ask them to share characteristics of fish such as scales, gills, fins, and so on.

2. Give each student a mat and about a ¼ lb. piece of clay. Have students shape the clay into a ball and gently flatten it to about the thickness of a hamburger patty.

3. Demonstrate how to shape the clay into the desired shape, taking care to keep the clay thick enough to holds its shape. Give students extra pieces of clay as needed to add fins and other details. Show students how they can use craft sticks and pencils to add textured details.

4. Have students roll a thick, oblong piece of clay to serve as a support so that the sculpture can stand up on its own. Have students write their names on strips of paper and place them with their pieces so that you can write them on the clay later. Let the pieces harden.

Shadow Hunting

On a sunny day, gather children in a circle outside. Bring a small object such as a book or a doll with you to demonstrate a shadow. Talk about shadows. Does everyone know what a shadow is? Has everyone seen his own shadow? What other kinds of shadows have children seen? As children are sitting in the circle, can they see their shadows and those of their neighbors? What do the shadows look like?

Next, take a shadow walk with children around the school neighborhood. Look for all sorts of shadows—birds, trees, houses, clotheslines, cars, signs, people, animals, and so on. Do the shadows of things look the same as the actual objects? How are they alike? How are they different?

If possible, take a morning and an afternoon walk and observe the same shadows. Do the shadows look different at different times of the day? On your hunt, walk on both sides of the street. Art there places where there are no shadows?

During the walk, have children stand in the shade. Can they see their shadows? (Explain that shade is a shadow.) Look for shadows of moving cars, people, and animals. Do the shadows change as these things move?

After you've finished the shadow walk, have some more shadow fun outdoors. Put on some music and invite children to dance. What happens to their shadows? As your children move, can they make their shadows longer? Shorter? What happens when they move their arms and legs in different directions?

As the children are moving, encourage them to step on each other's shadows. Occasionally, say, "Freeze!" as you stop the music. As the children stand frozen, have them look at their shadows. Do any shadows look the same?

Build a Bird Feeder

Treat a bird to lunch. Cut windows and doors into an empty milk carton or plastic soda bottle. Have children decorate this container in such a way that birds will want to visit. They might paste on colored pictures of big juicy worms, or glue on twigs, leaves, seeds, and other outdoor things with nontoxic glue. (Keep decorations to a minimum so as not to frighten the birds.) Fill the feeder with bird seed and hang it up near windows where children are able to observe the birds enjoying their food.

Pinecones can be used for another type of bird feeder. Help children spread sugarless peanut butter on pinecones and roll them in wild birdseed. Birds love peanut butter, and it provides protein and oil for healthy feathers and bodies. Children can fasten the pinecones to the branches of a tree using floral wire.

Young children are keen observers of nature and will enjoy the variety of birds their feeders attract. See how many birds and what kinds of birds use the feeder. Encourage children to make pictures or paintings of birds that come to the feeder.

More bird-feeding ideas follow.

- Under supervision, even young children can manage to thread peanuts in shells onto a string with a large, dull-tipped rug needle. Hang up these "necklaces" for the birds. Be aware of children who may be allergic to peanuts when using this activity.
- Children can make "bird pudding" from stale bits of bread, raisins, bird seed, and bacon bits, moistened with water and put out for the birds. Put the pudding out as is, or put it into half a coconut shell. A small hole drilled into the coconut shell will enable you to hang it up where it can swing freely as birds land to feed.

Dandelions

In spring, dandelions are everywhere, and children not only notice them but touch them, note their color, count them, and pick them.

Dandelions seed early, rapidly, and in great quantity. They grow fast and recover from damage quickly and powerfully! So children may pick them, dig them up, and tear them apart. Respect for nature is an important aspect of learning about the environment, but exceptions to rules exist in every field of study. Weeds are exceptions because of their hands-on study value for young children.

Ask children if they ever noticed that dandelions let out a milky juice when picked? Or that the stem is hollow? Rub the flower on paper to obtain a yellow pigment, or create a "duplicate" dandelion by rubbing flower, stem, leaves, and soil on the paper. How fast do the dandelions in a lawn grow after being cut? Have children try watching and measuring. How deep do the roots of a dandelion go? Why not dig up some dandelions and determine which is the longest?

Early French explorers named this weed *dent-de-lion,* mispronounced by the English as "dandelion." The original means "tooth of the lion" and refers to the leaves. Can children see and feel "teeth" on the leaves? If you cut several leaves from the plant and superimpose one upon another, you will recognize the diversity of shapes.

Insect Cage

Cut openings in small plastic or cardboard cartons. Cover the opening with fine netting, taping it into place. Fine netting can also be taped over the top of any plastic container to provide a temporary home for insects. The children can observe insect life more easily if the insect cages are made from clear plastic containers.

A clean, empty, half-gallon milk carton also makes a good insect-viewer. Simply cut rectangular holes on two sides of the milk carton. Slip a nylon stocking over the carton and fasten at the top with a rubber band. Insects can be held inside for temporary viewing.

Be sure to release the insect back into its natural habitat after children view it.

Examining Windowsill Dust

Give pairs of students two index cards and have them mount them on a piece of tagboard, date them, and smear them with petroleum jelly. Partners then place one of the cards on the windowsill inside the classroom, and then attach the other with masking tape to the windowsill outside. Each day for a week, have students check their dust-collecting cards, look at them under a microscope, and record their observations. Afterward, discuss what the many particles they see may be, how they got carried through the air, and so on. They may want to illustrate some of the many interesting things they saw under the microscope.

Tornado in a Glass

For this science activity, you will need sugar, water, food coloring, a 12-ounce cup, and a spoon.

Add 3 tablespoons of sugar to 8 ounces of water. Slowly stir in a circular pattern. Wait 10 seconds, and then drop a single drop of food coloring in the center. The dye will form a tornado in the sugar solution, as the rotating force of the water pushes it to the bottom. It will not diffuse into the sugar solution on the sides.

This teaches the principle of diffusion, or spreading out of liquids.

Observing Worms

Make an earthworm observatory with a large glass jar (a large peanut butter jar is good), worms, garden soil, and black construction paper.

Place a layer of small rocks or sand in the bottom of the jar so water will drain. Place two inches of moist soil and sand in the jar. Have children pick up worms and place them in the jar. Cover them with more soil. Keep the soil moist. Seal, using a lid with holes punched in it.

Wrap black construction paper around the jar. After 24 hours, remove the paper. The children should be able to see the worms tunneling through the soil.

Encourage children to talk about what interests them about worms.

Sky Gazer

Save the cardboard tubes from paper towel rolls. Punch two holes at one end of each tube, and loop an 18-inch piece of yarn through them (make one for each child). Have children hang their telescope around their neck. Go outside on a nice, warm day and have children lie down on the grass.

Direct them to use their telescope to look up into the sky. What do they see? Have children look some more. What else do they see?

Bugs are Fun!

For this activity, you will need magnifying glasses, play dough or self-hardening clay, chart paper, and art materials, including construction paper, tissue paper, markers, glue, scissors, yarn, and pipe cleaners.

In advance, read many books about insects. Have pictures for children to look at in your learning centers. Discuss the fact that scientists who study insects are called entomologists. Explain to the children that all insects go by the "3 + 3 rule"; three parts of the body (head, thorax, and abdomen) and three pairs of legs. Show the children this rule using a picture or specimen.

Explain to the children that they will be entomologists for the morning. They are going on an insect hunt together. Ask where they think they would find insects. Where would they hide if they were insects? Tell them that they will observe insects in their natural habitats. Stress to the children that they should not harm the insects; they are scientists observing them in the field. Ask them to watch the way the insects move. What colors are they? How big are they? Look for the 3 + 3 rule.

Take children outdoors to search for insects. Give each child a magnifying glass, which will help narrow their field of vision and focus their attention on a small area. Encourage children to share what they find with one other. Be sure to repeatedly use the scientific names for the body parts in order to build vocabulary. Ask them to specifically look for the head, thorax, and abdomen.

Once back inside, have a group discussion about the insects. Make a chart with a list of insects the children found and the information they collected. Did the 3 + 3 rule help them identify insects?

Invite the children to create an insect of their choice. Have a variety of art materials available so children can choose which medium they would like to use. Encourage them to try to show the 3 + 3 rule in the insect they create. If they want, children can label the parts of their insect or dictate the labels to you.

Remember, some children may be afraid of bugs. Be respectful and let them observe with you or a friend. Also,

young children may become so absorbed in creating their own bug that they make more legs or body parts than is accurate. This is completely acceptable. Talk with the child about the various body parts and legs, and reinforce the vocabulary you are teaching.

Rock Hounds

Young children love rocks! Encourage these "rock hounds" with the following activities.

- Go on a collecting walk with the children. Give each child a paper bag and encourage everyone to look for rocks and pebbles of different sizes, shapes, and colors. Gather children in a circle outside and look over the rock collection together. Have them work in small groups to study and experiment with the rocks.
- Divide children into groups outdoors. Give each group a mound of rocks and pebbles. Encourage children to use magnifying glasses to make close observations. Ask, "How are the rocks the same or different?"
- Invite children to sort the rocks in any way they choose—by size, texture, shape, color, and so forth—onto paper plates. When they are finished sorting, ask them to describe the rocks on each plate.
- Make a chart describing the different ways children classified the rocks. Then invite them to count the rocks on each plate. Together, discuss which plate has the most and the least amount.
- Ask children to arrange the pebbles from smallest to largest in an egg carton. Give out sheets of white paper and pencils; let children trace the smallest and largest pebbles, and then compare their differences.
- Let children use a pan balance to compare the weights of various rocks. Have them predict which rocks will be the heaviest or the lightest. Then have them test their predictions.
- After studying and experimenting with the rocks, help children create a rock museum. Display the rocks in your discovery center with signs describing the biggest, smallest, roughest, smoothest, heaviest, lightest, and so on.
- Older children may use reference books to try to identify the different rocks in their collections.
- Have a "rock 'n' roll" party! Take children to a grassy area outside. Ask them to curl their bodies in a ball as if they were rocks randomly strewn on the ground. Then, invite them to roll their bodies as if they were rocks rolling down a hill.

Activities for Older Children (Grades 4–5)

Aesthetic Awareness—Light

On a sunny day, direct a beam of light through a prism onto a white piece of paper. Have students take turns describing the colors. With white paper and crayons, have them record the colors using yellow and green to achieve a yellow-green, red and purple to achieve a red-purple, and so on. Guide them to see that these colors are similar to a color wheel.

Aesthetic Awareness—Van Gogh's *Irises*

Obtain an art print of this work by Van Gogh. Discuss with children the repetition of the triangular shapes of the iris leaves and the shapes of flowers. Ask if the shapes are exactly alike (they aren't). Discuss how Van Gogh changed the shapes a little each time. These variations help us see differences in each plant. They also add more interest to a work of art. Have students identify comparable variations in the colors of the flowers and leaves. Some children may enjoy creating their own summer flowers using these subtle variations to add interest to their work.

Optical Illusions—A Different Way of Seeing

Ask students to find library books that have optical illusions. These books are usually in the science or art section of a library. Have students look for examples of optical illusions based on positive and negative shapes or "hidden figures." Have students select one of their favorite examples and try to create an original artwork based on the illusion.

Solar System—Science Activities for Multiple Intelligences

The following activities are designed to give children the chance to use their multiple intelligences to learn concepts involved in a study of the solar system. After students have a foundation of knowledge about the solar system from classroom readings and discussions, the following activities can enrich and strengthen their learning.

Solar system model. Have students build a three-dimensional scale model of the solar system (picture/logic smart).

Role-play activity. Have students choose a group of classmates with whom to participate in a role-playing activity. One student is the sun, and each of the other students is a planet. Have students write a script, with the "planets" each saying something about themselves. Students should perform their skit for the class, with all members of the solar system standing in the correct order holding signs to identify themselves (word/picture/person smart).

Solar system tableau. Have students write a several-scene tableau that includes facts and information about the solar system. Choose a group of students to practice and perform the tableau (word/body/picture/person smart).

Solar system song. Have students create a song to teach younger students the order of the planets. The song should have a recurring rhythm and a chorus. Have students perform it for their class and a class of younger students (music/word smart).

Solar system report. Have students write a two-to three-page report about the solar system. They can include three different references and one picture (word/picture smart).

Imaginary journal. Have students write an imaginary journal for a 10-day mission into space. Tell them: "You have been selected as the first student to go into space. Decide where within the solar system your mission goes, and keep a daily log explaining what you are seeing and learning. You'll need to research space missions and spacecraft before writing." Students can find facts about space travel at the Smithsonian National Air and Space Museum website. Direct students to use their last entry to evaluate the entire mission. How successful was it? What would they do differently? How did it make them feel? (word/person smart)

Solar system math. Have students make a chart or graph to show the distance of each planet from the sun. Have them translate the actual distance into a smaller scale and draw the solar system to this scale (logic/picture smart).

Famous astronauts play. Have students research famous astronauts who have played a major role in the exploration of space. They might write a short skit that tells interesting facts and information about these astronauts and their missions and then perform it for the class (word/person/body smart).

Weather Unit Activities for Multiple Intelligences

Verbal/linguistic. Have students read a book about weather and write a short summary of what they learned.

Logical/mathematical. Have students draw a diagram of the water cycle. Alternatively, have them create a monthly weather calendar and a graph showing weather patterns during the month. They might also analyze collected weather data.

Visual/spatial. Have students create a collage of pictures showing different types of weather. They can display data in graphs and charts.

Bodily/kinesthetic. Have students create a weather dance to perform for the "weather spirits." These students might also build weather instruments.

Musical. Have students research and build different types of percussion instruments. They might create a rhythm and teach it to others, or they might write a song using weather words and concepts.

Interpersonal. Have students work together in groups to build instruments, collect data, or perform songs about weather.

Intrapersonal. Have students keep a journal of weather-related activities. They might list their favorite things to do on a day when a particular kind of weather predominates.

Interviewing Inventors

Combine learning to use the library and making oral book reports with learning about inventions that have changed our lives. Before doing this activity, children should select one of the following inventors and read about that person and his or her invention.

Marie Curie—chemical processes, Geiger counter

Alexander Graham Bell—the telephone

Alice Chatham—the astronaut's helmet

Henry Ford—the automobile

The Wright Brothers—the airplane

Thomas Alva Edison—the electric lightbulb, phonograph

Jonas Salk—polio vaccine

Rose O'Neill—the Kewpie doll

Rear Admiral Grace Murray Hopper—computer program compiler

When children know the inventor and the invention well enough to discuss them with classmates, pair up the students. One child assumes the role of the inventor, and the other child assumes the role of the interviewer. Together, they develop and rehearse questions and responses for a radio or television talk show. These are then performed for the class. If the children are interested in switching roles, replay the activity, giving both students an opportunity to become the inventor that they studied.

During the next phase, children imagine that they are inventors. They are to develop a fictitious individual. They then create an autobiography for the inventor they imagine themselves to be and think of an invention for which they are famous. What have they invented? What does it do? After children have had enough time to develop the character and to become familiar with the invention, use the interview format previously described.

Combine the two exercises by having students perform a television news show in which Bell, Ford, and other real inventors are interviewed. Between the interview segments, have children perform commercials for the new devices their imaginary inventors have developed.

Creative Expression: Using Lines

For this activity, you will need: 12- × 18-inch white construction paper, colored markers, sketch paper, pencils, pencils, crayons, paint.

Ask the students how different weather makes them feel. The purpose of this activity is to have them draw a weather scene that reflects a definite feeling. Have them think about different kinds of weather where they live. What mood does it create?

Students then select the type of weather condition they would like to draw, making a rough sketch to plan the scene. Encourage them to experiment with different types of lines. Then decide which lines best express the mood they want to create. Students then draw their weather scene, being sure to use the appropriate lines to create a calm or active feeling.

Letters from the Garbage Heap

To liven up lessons on recycling and decomposition, give small groups of students each a bag with clothespins, a diaper, an aluminum can, a cigarette butt, a rubber eraser, a banana peel, some wood, a plastic jug, a cotton sock, and an apple core. (Photographs or cut-out magazine pictures of the items also work well.) On a clothesline marked in increments with 2–4 weeks, 1–5 months, 1 year, 10 years, 25 years, 100 years, 500 years, and 1,000 years, ask each group to hang its trash, indicating how long they think each item will take to decompose. When groups have finished, reveal the actual times: apple, 2–4 weeks; banana and sock, 1–5 months; cigarette butt, 2–5 years; wood, 10 years; diaper, 25 years; plastic, 25–30 years; eraser, 50–80 years; can, 200–400 years. (A glass bottle takes 1,000 years to decompose!) After talking about how crowded a dump will get if we fill it with so many items that take years to decay, have students write down ways they can recycle to reduce waste.

Artists' Flowers

Have art prints of flowers from at least two artists. Two good prints for this activity would be Van Gogh's *Sunflowers* and Georgia O'Keeffe's *Poppy*. Other floral works by these artists are also good. Of course, you may find many other artists whose paintings of flowers are appropriate for this activity.

The purpose of this activity is to see how two artists express their flowers in two contrasting ways. Each artist has his or her own vision of representing them in art. Be sure to use art terms such as color, line, and shape when discussing these works.

Explain that the artist Georgia O'Keeffe created many paintings of flowers. She once said that she made the flowers large so people would really see the beauty of the colors, shapes, and edges. Explain that the poppy, like other flowers in O'Keeffe's paintings, seems to glow with life and energy. It is a close-up view of a flower in full bloom. Encourage students to make other observations about the painting.

Then lead them in a discussion of Van Gogh's *Sunflowers*, especially their texture. Guide them to describe the mood qualities in Van Gogh's painting. For example, the flowers are on the ground, no longer growing. Many of the seeds are gone, the stems are withered, and the petals look shriveled and dry. Encourage other observations. Contrast and compare the two works, using the scientific analogy of a life cycle.

Emphasize the concept that artists in many times and places have created artworks about the same subject, such as flowers. Each artist creates his or her own picture in a special way—in a different, original style. Ask students to express opinions about which of these artworks they like to see, and discuss reasons for their preferences. Stress that students may like more than one kind of art and that everyone may not like the same work.

Animals

Language Arts Experiences

- Have students write a story in which the main character is an endangered animal who is trying to teach his or her family why the species is endangered.
- Arrange for students to debate in small groups the issue of wild animals being captured and put in a zoo. Are zoos actually a form of cruelty to animals?
- Have students write a short speech (2–4 minutes) about an animal topic that they feel strongly about. Topics might include how to take care of pets, endangered animals, or the similarities between animals and humans.
- Have students write a story in which they become an endangered animal lost in a large city. They might write about how they feel being lost and endangered and what they would do in this situation.
- Have students choose an animal to observe for 15 minutes. The allotted time might be broken down into smaller segments if the animal is hard to observe. Encourage them to write their observations and what they learned about the animal.

Art Experiences

- Have students make a clay model of an endangered carnivore and write a short paragraph telling key facts about the animal.

- Have students work with a partner in designing an advertisement that could be published in a newspaper to promote the preservation of an endangered animal.
- Have students build a three-dimensional habitat model for an animal of their choice.

Movement Experiences

- Have students pretend they are different animals, and then role-play how each animal might react to meeting the other.
- Have students perform a skit in which all of the characters are animals—some endangered and some not. The animals discuss the problems that arise from being endangered.
- Encourage students to invent a game called The Animal Game. They can make up the rules for the game, describe how it is played, and then play it!

Music Experiences

- Have students work in small groups to make up an animal song and record it on a tape recorder.
- Have students write a poem or story about an animal and add animal sounds as they read it to other students.

How Does Water Disappear?

This is an initial experience with evaporation. You will need a sponge, chalkboard, water, and a heavy piece of cardboard.

1. Moisten the sponge.
2. Make a wide, damp streak on the blackboard.
3. Observe for several minutes. What happened?
4. Make two streaks about 1 yard apart.
5. Use the cardboard to fan one of the streaks.
6. Compare the time it took for each to disappear.

Students should learn from this activity that water is absorbed into the air by a process called *evaporation*. Increasing the amount of air moving over the water (fanning) increases the rate of evaporation. The amount of moisture the air already contains (humidity) will be a factor. Hint: If the sponge is just moist, the results will be faster than if it is soaking wet.

An alternate activity is to put a small amount of water (1/2 inch) in two small jars. Seal the lid of one and leave the other open. Observe for 24 hours. Discuss the differences in water remaining in each jar.

Science: A Different View of Things

Discuss the importance of imagination and observation in science. Imagining that people might walk on the moon was the first and most important step in discovering how it might be done.

Have students collect unusual rocks, shells, dried seed pods, and other small objects. Glue several objects to the bottom of a clear plastic box. Challenge students to draw the objects inside the box from each of the points they can see when looking straight through one side of the box. Provide square paper for the drawings.

Have students create drawings from unusual or imagined vantage points, such as being in a hot air balloon, flying in an airplane, being inside of a mine or a cave, looking at things under water, or looking out the window of a rocket while it is being launched or is nearing a planet.

Insects

Contrast the way an artist and a scientist might study insects. Point out that scientists and artists are both very keen observers of nature. The artist is more likely to study insects to discover the beauty or the special lines, shapes, textures, and colors. The scientist may look for the same features but is more likely to want to explain their purpose—protection, reproduction, or food gathering. Encourage students to draw their own versions of insects, using either the artistic or scientific perspective.

Aesthetic Awareness

Discuss texture as a property that we experience by sight as well as touch. Stress that scientists who want to describe and classify living and nonliving things carefully observe and often measure subtle differences in textures (as well as other properties) of objects. Provide magnifying glasses and a variety of textured materials for students to observe, touch, and describe: fine white sand, salt, sugar, flour, baby powder, or varieties of rocks or paper.

Science Outdoors

Take students outside to study the branching structures of trees. Guide them to see relationships between the branching structures in a leaf, among twigs that support leaves, larger branches, and the trunk. Have them identify other natural forms in which linear qualities are evident such as hair and fur, or shells with radial or spiraling edges. Have them draw representations of their observations.

Making Crystals

Making crystals is an amazing and fun science activity. To begin, carefully add 1 cup of very hot water to a mason jar for each child. Then have students help measure and add up to 2 cups of sugar to their water jars, ½ cup at a time, until no more dissolves. By doing this, students will be creating a saturated solution.

Have each student tie a string to a craft stick (or pencil) and a rust-proof paper clip, and then suspend his or her clip just above the bottom of the jar. Cover jars with paper towels to keep dust out. As water evaporates, sugar crystals will form.

In a week or two, remove and dry the strings of crystals. Challenge students to find the edges, angles, and faces of the crystals.

Set up a crystal observation station with salt and sugar on sheets of black paper, a magnifying glass, and a flashlight. Students may notice some of the following characteristics of crystals:

- Crystals have geometric shapes, such as cubes (salt), rectangles (sugar), diamonds, or pyramids.

- Crystals have sharp, straight edges that meet to form angles.
- Crystals are solids.
- Crystal shapes range from simple to very complex.
- Crystals break smoothly and cleanly at their weakest point.
- Crystals' smooth sides are called *faces*.

Jumping Pepper and Lazy Salt

Scatter a teaspoon of coarse salt onto a table and mix it with a teaspoon of ground pepper. To separate the two spices, rub an inflated balloon with a wool cloth and hold it about an inch or so above the mixture. The pepper jumps up to the balloon and sticks to it.

Explanation: The balloon becomes negatively charged when it is rubbed with a wool cloth. As a result, the balloon attracts both the pepper and salt. The pepper "jumps" to the balloon because it is lighter than salt. After most of the pepper has been removed, recharge the balloon and move them closer to the salt.

How fast does it fall?

Students will determine whether the weight of an object affects how fast it falls.

Materials: two pennies, two quarters, two sheets of notebook paper (one flat, one crushed into a ball), other heavy and light objects in the classroom (a baseball and a softball, a small and a large marble, small and large erasers, a short and a long pencil, and so on).

Procedure:

1. Hold two coins, one in each hand, at the same height and simultaneously drop them. Do three trials. Did they reach the ground at the same time?
2. Simultaneously drop two coins of different sizes from the same height. Do three trials. Did they reach the ground at the same time?
3. Simultaneously drop the flat sheet of paper and a coin from the same height. Do three trials. Did they reach the ground at the same time?
4. Simultaneously drop the sheet of paper that was crushed into a ball and a coin from the same height. Do three trials. Did they reach the ground at the same time?
5. Do the same with the crushed sheet and the flat sheet of paper. Do three trials. Did they reach the ground at the same time?
6. Make a chart from your data-collecting record sheet and examine the results.

Weather Science

People often say, "This is a cold April" or "It seems wetter than normal." Challenge students to see if it is true or not. Contact the local weather bureau for last year's daily figures. Have students collect daily data and make comparisons between this year and last in temperature and moisture. Include more years if you want to look at trends. Make tables and graphs so children can see patterns.

Paper Bridges

Make a flimsy bridge by placing a sheet of writing paper over two small plastic drinking cups four inches apart. Place a third plastic cup on top of the paper between the two cups. The bridge collapses. Now, fold the paper into an accordion shape (each fold about ½" wide) and place it on top of the two cps. Place the third cup on top of the folded paper. It supports the weight of the cup.

Explanation: Flat surfaces cannot hold as much weight as vertical surfaces. The weight of vertical surfaces is easily distributed over several sloping paper walls and supported in the high-stability folds. A great example of this is the strength that is found in corrugated iron and corrugated cardboard.

Inventions

Inventors design new products because there is a strong need for them. Students can practice being inventors with these activities.

A. **Robots.** Have students design a robot that performs a needed service, such as one that fights fires or helps people with physical disabilities. Robot design challenges stimulate children to imagine all sorts of incredible inventions. Using a team-based approach builds collaborative skills. Students can create their models using construction paper or recycled household items.

B. **Home sweet home inventions.** Challenge students to design a home that uses alternate energy sources. Challenge students to design homes that withstand catastrophic weather events such as floods, hurricanes, and tornados.

C. **Futuristic thinking.** Have students create a story about how robots will be used in the future. This exercise combines science and technology with social studies and language skills to engender a look into the future. Encourage students to illustrate their stories.

References

Ashbrook, P. (2010). Preschool STEM. NSTA Blog (National Science Teachers Association). Available at http://nstacommunities.org/blog/2010/03/01/preschool-stem.

Bredekamp, S., & Copple, C. E. (2009). *Developmentally appropriate practice in early childhood programs serving children from birth through age 8* (2nd ed.). Washington, DC: National Association for the Education of Young Children.

Hong, S-Y., & Diamond, K. E. (2012). Two approaches to teaching young children science concepts, vocabulary, and scientific problem-solving skills. *Early Childhood Research Quarterly, 27*(3), 295–305.

Hui, W. (2010). "Biology Letters" Science Journal Publishes Study by 8-year old Children on Bumblebee Color & Pattern Vision. *Huffington Post, Huff Post Green.* Retrieved from www.huffingtonpost.com/2010/12/22/biology-letters-science-j_n_800134.html.

Krajcik, J. (2011). Helping young learners make sense of data: A 21st century capability. *Science and Children, 48*(5), 8–9.

McNeill, K. L., & Krajcik, J. S. (2011). *Supporting grade 5-8 students in constructing explanations in science: The claim, evidence and reasoning framework for talk and writing.* New York, NY: Pearson Allyn & Bacon.

Moomaw, S., & Davis, J. A. (2010). STEM comes to preschool. *Young Children, 65*(5), 12–14, 16–18.

NCTM (National Council of Teachers of Mathematics) (2000). *Principles and standards for school mathematics.* Reston, VA: NCTM.

NRC. (2000). *Inquiry and the national science education standards: A guide for teaching and learning.* Washington, DC: National Academies Press.

NRC (National Research Council). (1996). *National science education standards.* Washington, DC: National Academies Press.

Root-Bernstein, R. (2008). Arts foster scientific success: Avocations of Nobel, National Academy, Royal Society, and Sigma Xi members. *Journal of Psychology of Science and Technology, 1*(2), 51–63.

Schipani, V. (2011, Summer). Works in progress: Where the wild things are. *The American Scholar*, p. 14.

 Visit CourseMate for this textbook to access the eBook, Did You Get It? quizzes, Digital Downloads, TeachSource Videos, flashcards, and more. Go to CengageBrain.com to log in, register, or purchase access.

20

Creative Mathematics

Early childhood teachers face the challenging responsibility of opening young children's eyes to the world of mathematics. We can provide creative, stimulating, hands-on experiences that can initiate long-term positive feelings about mathematics, or we can provide a boring stream of workbook pages and dittos. In such a situation, where children are required to sit down, quiet down, and write it down, excitement about math may never have a chance to emerge. Math in the early childhood setting is not a sit-at-your-desk-with paper-and-pencil activity. It is a part of a young child's active life.

Learning Objectives

After studying this chapter, you should be able to:

20-1 Discuss the developmental pattern of learning mathematical concepts.

20-2 Explain the purpose of national mathematics standards in the early childhood program.

20-3 Discuss how mathematics learning occurs in learning centers in the early childhood classroom.

20-4 Define rote counting and rational counting.

20-5 Discuss classification and sorting.

20-6 Discuss comparing.

20-7 Discuss ordering.

20-8 Describe how to present shape and form concepts to young children.

20-9 Describe mathematical concepts appropriate for children in grades 3–5.

naeyc

NAEYC Program Standards

1a Knowing and understanding young children's characteristics and needs.

5a Understanding content knowledge and resources in academic disciplines.

5b Knowing and using the central concepts, inquiry tools, and structures of content areas or academic disciplines.

DAP

DAP Criteria

3A1 Teachers consider what children should know, understand, and be able to do across disciplines, including mathematics.

3c2 Teachers carefully shape and adapt the experiences they provide children to enable each child to reach the goals outlined in the curriculum.

All young children need opportunities to explore their world and experience mathematics through their play. Early mathematical experiences include such basic events as placing crackers in a toddler's hands while saying, "Here are two crackers—one, two," or allowing a 3-year-old to choose how she wants her sandwich cut—into triangles, rectangles, or small squares. As a child arranges stuffed animals by size, a teacher might ask, "Which animal is the smallest?" or "Which is the largest?" Such questions reveal mathematical ideas involved in simple activities and lay the foundation for children's understanding of more complex mathematical concepts as they grow older.

When children recognize a stop sign from the back, focusing on the octagonal shape rather than the red background and the word "STOP," adults have an opportunity to talk about different shapes in the environment. Teachers in any setting can help children look for mathematical connections and relationships, encourage their questions, and promote mathematical discussion about topics that interest them. The most powerful mathematics learning for a child is seldom acquired sitting down in a group lesson.

In this chapter, the emphasis is on this active exploration of mathematical concepts as a natural part of the early childhood program.

20-1 Developmental Pattern of Learning Mathematical Concepts

naeyc **DAP** It is possible to look at the child's construction of mathematical concepts the same way we look at literacy development—as emergent. The idea that literacy learning begins the day that children are born is widely accepted in the early childhood field. Mathematical learning can be viewed in a similar way. Children begin to build the foundation for future mathematical concepts during the first few months of life. In fact, from the moment they are born, children begin to construct ideas about mathematics through everyday routines, experiences, and, most importantly, caring interactions with trusted adults. A key aspect of these interactions involves language—how we talk with infants, toddlers, and young children.

Long before children formally use numbers, they are aware of them through daily experiences. For example, children become aware of sequences in events before they can talk about what is first, second, or third. At the age of 2 or 3, they know that one block on top of another is two blocks, and they know that if they add more, they will have three, even though they

may not know the words *two* and *three*. When they lift objects, they experience lightness or heaviness. Cuddling up in their mother's lap, they feel themselves small and her big. They know all this by the reality of their experience—through living and doing. Thus, children are able to tell differences in sizes of people, animals, and toys before they have any idea about measurement. They recognize, too, the difference between one and many and between few and lots before they acquire real number concepts. They develop a sense of time long before they can tell time by a clock. Their ideas about time grow out of hearing statements like the following: "It's time for lunch." "It's time to go to bed." "We're going for a walk today." "We went to the park yesterday." In such instances, parents reinforce mathematical concepts every day in life's normal routines. Thus, when the child enters an early childhood program, he or she has already experienced many basic mathematical learnings.

This pattern of early use of numbers is similar to the general-to-specific pattern of physical growth (see Chapter 9). In these early stages of mathematical thinking, the child has a general understanding of numbers that will gradually move toward a more specific understanding as the developmental process continues. Thus, a general understanding of time ("It's time for lunch.") develops in a gradual process to a more specific understanding of time ("Twelve o'clock is lunch time."). Children gradually associate 12 o'clock with lunchtime. They learn with their senses, with their whole bodies. Their understandings become parts of themselves. Only after this has happened can they name these experiences. By the time they learn the words *big*, *small*, *light*, *heavy*, or the names of numbers, they will know by their own senses what these words mean. (Geist, 2009).

20-1a Parents as Partners in Mathematical Learning

Because young children begin to learn mathematics from the day they are born, parents are obviously an early childhood teacher's partner in mathematical learning. Early childhood teachers can explain to parents how infants and toddlers begin to notice relationships as they interact with their parents or primary caregivers through songs, rocking, and other verbal and nonverbal communication. They can help parents understand that as a baby crawls through a tunnel or in and out of a cardboard box, he is using his whole body to explore and learn. Placing infants in different positions to encourage the child to pay attention to where things and spaces are in relation to one another is another mathematical learning early childhood teachers can point out to parents. In the same way, early childhood teachers can explain to parents that physical activities introduce spatial relation and set the stage for later understandings of geometry and numbers.

Teachers need to encourage parents to allow their children freedom to explore how their bodies fit in space and to see things from different perspectives, such as "inside" and "outside," and "high" and "low." The teacher may suggest activities to parents to reinforce these concepts, such as providing an expanding tunnel or making one by taping together several cardboard boxes. Also, parents may encourage children to climb on a stack of pillows for the same reasons. Encourage parents to talk about what the child is doing so they can begin to learn the words that describe mathematical concepts: "You were *on* the pillow, and then you climbed *off*. You climbed *up* on the box, and then you jumped *off*."

Parents can also use sequential words to describe events or tasks in order to help children develop mathematical concepts. For example, when the parent explains the day's schedule, the use of sequential words helps children connect events with the order of time: "*First*, we will go outside. *After* we go outside, we will go to the playground. *Next*, we will have lunch. *Later*, we will come home for a nap." Parents are, and will continue to be, the most important math teachers our students will ever have. Here are a few additional suggestions to help parents help you.

- Provide parent workshops. Have them try some of the exploratory, hands-on lessons they might see in their children's classroom. Explain how the concepts fit into the curriculum and why a student-centered, investigative approach is so valuable.
- Offer family mathematics challenges. Group activities can be fun, simple ways to tackle math together. A math scavenger hunt—in which families identify the math they encounter and do over a weekend—is one example.
- Foster positive attitudes. Help parents understand that mathematics is the doorway to many professional careers and that every child can be successful in math.
- Encourage parents to be positive about their own view of math, even if they must acknowledge that it can be challenging.

Did You Get It?

A teacher of two-year-olds likes to hold her students on her lap, saying that it helps her students develop math skills because cuddling

a. helps them to understand that one plus one equals two.

b. sparks creativity, which helps develop mathematical ability.

c. helps them recognize the difference between people of different sizes.

d. is directly correlated with mathematical ability.

Take the full quiz on CourseMate.

20-2 National Council of Teachers of Mathematics (NCTM) Standards

Recognizing the importance of these early experiences in mathematics, the National Council of Teachers of Mathematics (NCTM) has developed a set of Principles and Standards for Children Pre-K–12 (2000). These standards propose mathematical content and processes students should know and be able to use as they progress through school. There are 10 standards—5 content standards and 5 process standards—that apply across the pre-K–12 grade span. (See Figure 20-1 for a summary of these standards.) Within each standard, a number of focus areas are to be emphasized at each grade level.

20-2a Common Core State Standards for Mathematics (CCSSM)

The **Common Core State Standards for Mathematics (CCSSM)** build on the NCTM standards, but they also introduce significant changes to how mathematics is to be taught. The Eight Standards for Mathematics Practice (see Figure 20-2) describe varieties of expertise that mathematics educators at all levels should seek to develop in their students (CCSSM, 2010). Each standard has broad *clusters* of goals for each grade level, which are further grouped under broad mathematical concepts called *domains* (CCSSM, 2010).

The K–5 standards provide students with a solid foundation in whole numbers, addition, subtraction, multiplication, division, fractions, and decimals. This helps young students build the foundation to successfully apply more demanding math concepts and procedures, and move into applications. These standards build on the best state standards to provide detailed

Content

Five standards describe the mathematical content that students should learn.

- number and operation
- patterns, functions, and algebra
- geometry and spatial sense
- measurement
- data analysis, statistics, and probability

Process

Five standards describe the mathematical processes through which students should acquire and use their mathematical knowledge.

- problem solving
- reasoning and proof
- communication
- connections
- representation

Societal Needs for Mathematics

- Mathematical literacy. The underpinnings of everyday life are increasingly mathematical and technologic. Our students will live in a world where intelligent decisions often require quantitative understandings.
- Cultural literacy. Mathematics is a great cultural and intellectual achievement of human kind, and our citizens should develop an appreciation and understanding of that achievement.
- Mathematics for the workplace. Just as the level of mathematics needed for intelligent citizenship has increased dramatically, so too has the level of mathematical thinking and problem solving needed in the workplace increased.
- Mathematicians, scientists, engineers, and other users of mathematics. Equity and excellence both must be the object of school mathematics programs. If schools enfranchise more students while maintaining high standards, there will be a larger number available to pursue these careers.

FIGURE 20-1 Overview of the National Council of Teachers of Mathematics National Standards for grades pre-K–12.

These Standards define what students should understand and be able to do in their study of mathematics. The Standards set grade-specific standards but do not define the intervention methods or materials necessary to support students who are well below or well above grade-level expectations. Standards define what students should understand and be able to do.

1. Make sense of problems and persevere in solving them.
2. Reason abstractly and quantitatively.
3. Construct viable arguments and critique the reasoning of others.
4. Model with mathematics
5. Use appropriate tools strategically
6. Attend to precision
7. Look for and make use of structure
8. Look for and express regularity in repeated reasoning

(CCSSM, 2010)

FIGURE 20-2 Common Core State Standards for Mathematical Practice.

guidance to teachers on how to navigate their way through topics such as fractions, negative numbers, and geometry, and do so by maintaining a continuous progression from grade to grade (CCSSM, 2010). Suggested activities addressing the Common Core Math standards are at the end of this chapter. Let us now take a look at mathematics in action in the early childhood program.

Did You Get It?

In planning her math activities, a kindergarten teacher uses clusters of goals for kindergarten students, as recommended by the
   a. National Council of Teachers of Mathematics.
   b. State Board of Creativity and Mathematics.
   c. Federal Guidelines for Kindergarten Teachers of Mathematics.
   d. Common Core Standards for Mathematics.

Take the full quiz on CourseMate.

20-3 Mathematics Learning in the Early Childhood Classroom

naeyc DAP Everything we know about young children tells us that early math experiences must be hands-on, filled with play and exploration. Young children's understanding of mathematical ideas takes place in an action-based learning environment. Mathematics learning can occur throughout the early childhood curriculum. The following information provides examples of how this can be achieved.

20-3a Mathematics in the Movement Center

As we observe in the movement center, we see children climbing over, ducking under, crawling through, and walking around several pieces of climbing equipment. Anthony approaches a ladder bridge suspended between two climbing frames and hesitates. He ducks under it, just clearing the ladder. He looks back to see what he did and repeats this action several times. "What would happen if you didn't duck?" asks the teacher. Anthony silently stands beside the ladder and indicates with his hand where he would hit his head (an example of measuring vertical distance by eye and comparing lengths).

At the trampoline, Christina counts as Justin jumps. "After 10 times, it's my turn," she tells Justin (an example of using a cardinal number to obtain

access to classroom equipment). The rest of the children begin to count Justin's jumps. "I can jump highest because I am the tallest," comments Juliette (an example of explaining measurement between object and event).

The children in line begin to measure themselves against each other (comparing height). When the teacher asks who jumped the highest today, the children all agree that it was Amanda. "Is she the tallest?" the teacher asks.

"Well, tomorrow I'm going to jump the highest because it's my birthday," says Justin.

"Amanda jumps in the middle of the trampoline," observes Juliette (showing she is thinking about location). "I'm going to try that tomorrow."

These specific learning experiences in the movement center fall under the three mathematics content standards of number and operation, measurement, and spatial sense. In the preceding scenes, we see how moving their own bodies through space helps children learn these specific mathematical concepts.

Playtime will allow children many chances to explore, extend, and refine their spatial discoveries. The children playing on the trampoline are learning to share power, space, things, and ideas as well as to use counting for access and comparing their jumping skills by measuring in a nonthreatening way.

20-3b Mathematics in the Language Arts Center

naeyc DAP Very few teachers need convincing of the benefits of using children's books in the early childhood math program. Children love being read to, and books provide rich sources for learning math (see Photo 20-1). Teaching math through children's books motivates children to learn math in exciting new ways. Learning math through the use of children's books encourages students to think and to reason mathematically while building students' appreciation for both math and literature.

Evaluating Children's Books for Math Learning. When evaluating which books to incorporate in a math activity, first judge the book as a worthy piece of literature. It must have an engaging story line, beautiful language, and a sense of wonder about the world (Eisenhauer & Feikes, 2009). Appropriate picture books present math concepts accurately with visual and verbal appeal. The illustrations and text must engage the reader. The reader or listener

PHOTO 20-1 Pretend reading is an important step in a child's developing literacy.

© Cengage Learning 2015

must be able to find real-world connections in the way concepts are presented. Concepts must also be presented in a way that truly engages the specific audience of young children.

Ask yourself these questions when considering a book for a math lesson.

1. *Would I read this book to the children even if I weren't choosing it for a math lesson?* Books should be used in the classroom because they are enjoyable, not because they teach a lesson. For a book to promote interest in reading as well as be appropriate for math, it must be memorable, use natural language, have captivating images, and stand up to multiple readings.

2. *Does the book stimulate curiosity and a sense of wonder? Are children inspired to do their own investigations?* In the reading of these books, concepts that a teacher may be required to teach, such as proportion, measurement, weight, and shapes, become topics that children want to investigate on their own.

3. *Is the book meaningful to children? Can they make personal connections?* Children should be able to identify with the characters in the book as having similar life experiences, doing activities children normally do.

4. *Are the math connections natural?* When math connections are embedded in a story, the reader

not only enjoys the book but also is intrigued by the math concepts. Mathematical ways of thinking are emphasized; they are not facts presented in an authoritarian tone. As such, children have opportunities to question and pursue solutions (Charlesworth, 2011).

An Example of Using a Children's Book for Math Learning. You will find that children's books can be used to launch many interesting math learning activities. Eric Carle's *The Very Hungry Caterpillar*, which describes the life cycle of a caterpillar through the use of vibrant, collage-like designs, is an excellent example of children's literature that can provide math experiences for a young audience.

Teaching comparisons. Size comparison is the most obvious prenumber concept that can be drawn from this book. The caterpillar changes from a tiny egg laid on a leaf to a small, hungry caterpillar to a big, brown cocoon, and finally to a large, beautiful butterfly. After reading the book to the class, the teacher might discuss with the children the size relationships depicted. Later, children can compare cutouts of phases of the caterpillar's life cycle and arrange them from largest to smallest.

Teaching ordering. The prenumber skill of ordering can be related to both the days of the week and the caterpillar's life cycle. Ask children to tell the order of the days of the week or stages of the life cycle told in the book. Ordering the days of the week in this way can promote an interest in the calendar for daily record keeping of days gone by. The life cycle can be used in a game-like situation in which children order the pictures of the cycle. This sequencing can be made self-correcting by writing the numerals 1 through 4 on the back of the pictures.

Teaching one-to-one correspondence. The fact that the caterpillar ate through a variety of foods one by one can be used to emphasize one-to-one correspondence. A learning center follow-up might require children to match pom-pom caterpillars to plastic fruits to see if there is an equal match or if there are more caterpillars than fruit.

Teaching rational counting. Children can also be asked to rationally count the number of pieces of food the caterpillar ate in the story by counting the number of fruits and then the number of other foods eaten. They might also count the number of days of the week and the life cycle changes. A later concrete learning activity would be to have children count out pieces of fruit or other similar foods eaten by the caterpillar to eat in their own particular snack time. Learning center games could involve the counting of food cutouts found in plastic containers.

Teaching cardinal numbers. The teacher might use a story to emphasize the prenumber skill of recognizing cardinal numbers. As children look at the book, the teacher might ask: "How many things did the caterpillar eat on Saturday? How many on Monday?" Later, children can work with a learning center activity that involves counting holes made by the hungry caterpillar in card stock leaves to determine how many bites the caterpillar took. A self-correcting feature can be included by simply writing the answer on the backs of the leaves.

20-3c Mathematics in the Art Center

naeyc DAP Much incidental learning related to mathematics occurs during art activities. When materials are used for a particular process, children need to remember quantities and their order of use. Children can frequently be heard explaining a process to classmates by saying, "First you tear the strips, then you add the paste, and then you stick them on the balloon." As art projects are planned, children learn to consider the number of items needed and often the shapes that will be required. This experience relates directly to problem solving and measurement—two of the content standards in the national mathematics standards for children.

We hear, "My truck will have four wheels," and "I need a triangle shape of wood for the roof on my house." Children learn to decide "how many" as they draw and paint: how many eyes on the face, fingers on the hand, and buttons on the coat.

Differences and equivalences in number and size frequently concern children. Six-year-old Jonathan calls out, "I want 10 feathers on my peacock, and I have only 9." Bernardo, sitting next to him, responds, "I have more than you; I have 12 feathers."

Children also learn about one-to-one correspondence as materials are chosen and distributed to classmates. Four children need four scissors; five paste cups need five lumps of paste; three needles need three lengths of yarn—all direct, hands-on experiences with the standard of number and operation.

The following scenario further demonstrates how art activities can be used to provide children

practice in areas related to national mathematics standards. Two children are making headbands using shape stamps to make designs on paper strips that will fit around their heads. "This is a skinny square," says Casper, referring to his rectangle stamp. Claire laughs and looks through the shape set. She picks up an oval shape, "This is a skinny circle!" The children laugh some more as they assign names to the other shapes. (Comparing shapes provides experience with the geometry and spatial sense standard.)

Soon they are finished, and Casper holds the strip while Claire measures and cuts the correct length (measurement standard). On the first try, the strip is too short, and they come to the teacher with the problem. "How could you make it longer?" she asks.

Claire thinks they can add some paper to one end of the strip (an example of extending length to make an object longer). Eventually the children make the headbands fit. When two different children approach the center later, Casper says, "You should cut the paper first to be sure it fits." One child takes this advice, but the other ignores him and begins to make designs on the paper strips.

The children in the preceding scenario had a prolonged opportunity to explore and talk about the characteristics of shapes. This was a fun, hands-on learning experience involving the mathematical concepts of shape, measurement, and problem solving.

20-3d Mathematics at the Water Table

naeyc DAP Some of the greatest opportunities for integrating math in children's play occur at the water table. Constant "watery" sounds are heard as children fill containers with water and pour the water back and forth. "This won't hold all the water," Grace comments (an example of measuring volume).

Elbert picks up a bottle and says, "This one is taller. It will hold the most." Grace disagrees. "This one might hold a lot because it's very fat all the way up." (She is comparing size and capacity of containers.) She suggests that they count how many cups each holds and begins to count, but Elbert just continues to pour water from one container to another. (He is comparing capacity by direct measure.) "This one holds six cups!" says Grace (an example of measurement). "How much does yours hold?" Elbert then begins to fill his bottle with water, using the cup and a

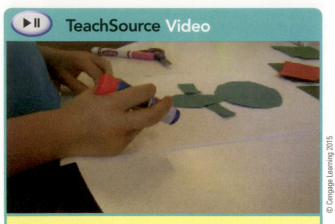

© Cengage Learning 2015

TeachSource Video

Exploring Math Concepts Through Creative Activities: Integrated Curriculum in Early Childhood

1. What basic mathematical concepts are covered in this video?

2. When the child answers, "three" for number of sides on the diamond, how else could the teacher handle this child's number error?

3. What additional center(s) could be included in this shape lesson? Include in your answer the specific center, number concept, and activities you would use.

Watch on CourseMate.

funnel. Grace counts the cups and explains, "It's four and a little bit more—not the whole thing" (a real-life use of measurement—fractions).

In the preceding scene, play reveals a progression of mathematical thought. In this situation, the children's processing of their own experiences shows the way they grow in measurement thinking. They were not concerned with a particular goal or end as much as with the means to achieve it. They did not have a clear plan in mind, and their goals and ends were self-imposed and changed as the activity proceeded.

In addition to these spontaneous mathematical experiences, you can also plan activities at the water table to build children's mathematical concepts. For example, a teacher may construct a math puzzle with three empty plastic glasses. Pour water up to the brim on the first glass. Then fill the second glass halfway, and leave the third empty. Ask children to identify which glass is empty, which is full, and which one is

half-full. Children generally understand the meaning of *full* and can identify the full glass of water. Most children will also understand the concepts of *empty* and *more*, but many children have trouble with *half* and *less*.

This experience at the water table may be continued in the manipulatives area by providing measuring cups of beads, buttons, or other materials for children to further explore the concepts of *full*, *empty*, *fewer*, and *less*. Through repeated interactions and dialogue, children learn some of the vocabulary and concepts that underlie mathematics, such as equations, fractions, and the notion of zero. At the water table, these math concepts are experienced and learned by repeated activity rather than by sitting at a desk trying to do math worksheets.

20-3e Mathematics in the Dramatic Play Center

naeyc DAP Two children are rocking their dolls and sharing a book about a hospital adventure. Suddenly, Corazon stops and says, "My doll is so sick. I have to call the doctor." She looks at a list posted near the telephone and dials (reading and using numbers). "His number is 919-555-1234" (ordering a sequence of single numbers). "Hello, doctor? My baby is so sick. What should I do? Goodbye. My doctor says I have to give my baby eleven pills."

"Oh, well," says Meg. "My baby was so sicker the other day before today" (time sequence). "He had eleventy-seven pills" (using numbers from the teens to the over-twenty digits). The children continue to rock their babies and share the book.

These children are using play to translate their understanding of adult activities into their own actions. Corazon understood how adults use numbers to make telephone calls. Play activity also involves intelligence. Corazon used her understanding of the pattern of telephone numbers—three digits followed by seven digits—to make her call. Her comment to Meg that her baby needed "eleven pills" showed her developing number sense; to Corazon, teen numbers indicate a larger quantity of an item than single digits. Meg's comeback indicated that she, too, is developing a sense of numbers because she knew that numbers ending with *-ty* are larger than numbers ending with *teen*. Meg's verbal description of yesterday was understood by her friend and will be replaced later with the appropriate terms after more

Goals

Activities in this center afford the child experiences in

- creating real and imaginary structures.
- differentiating between sizes and shapes.
- classifying according to size and shape.
- selecting according to space.
- conceptualizing about space, size, and shape.
- defining geometric shapes.
- developing perceptive insight, hand–eye coordination, imagination, and directionality.

Materials

Set of solid wooden unit blocks (approximately 200)

Small wheel toys

Puppets (to use with puppet stage or theater)

Dolls (from housekeeping center)

Dress-up clothes, especially hats

Set of hollow blocks (varying in size)

Miscellaneous construction sets: Tinkertoys, Lego® blocks, Lincoln Logs, Bristle-blocks, Connectos, etc.

Rubber animals (zoo, farm)

Small plastic/rubber people (family, farmer, firefighter, etc.)

Planks, tiles

Old steering wheel

Packing crates, boxes, and ropes

Traffic signs

Books related to building

Pulleys and ropes

Large quantities of "junk" construction materials, egg cartons, milk cartons, rods, spools, small rectangular boxes, etc.

Measuring tapes and unusual things to measure

Pan balance for exploring weight

Playing cards or cards with dots, numerals, or both

FIGURE 20-3 Suggested Goals and Activities for a Block Center.

TeachSource Digital Download   Download from CourseMate.

© Cengage Learning

experiences over time. This scenario can also be related directly to the national standards in math. Two of the standards—"communication" in a mathematical sense and "connections" between mathematics and everyday life—were obvious in the children's play experience.

20-3f Mathematics in the Block Center

naeyc DAP The block center is a perfect place for math experiences. Blocks are especially good for learning math because they are real-life examples of geometric shapes and solids. The block center is usually set up in preschool rooms, but it is just as important in the early elementary classroom. Figure 20-3 lists some suggested goals and block materials to make this center as complete a learning place as possible.

To encourage rich and varied mathematical experiences in the block center, you need to carefully plan the appropriate equipment in this center. For example, the younger the children, the larger their first blocks should be. Smaller blocks can come later, when children feel the need to supplement larger blocks. If you give too many small blocks to children early in the year and insist that they reshelve them neatly, children may come to dislike blocks, defeating your purposes in having them at all. Aside from this, block building is a tremendously satisfying activity that nourishes minds, imaginations, and the development of mathematical concepts. If your block area is popular, and children must wait for turns, make a waiting list—printed neatly for children to read—and set a timer. When you use a timer, children discover that turns are coming around in a fair way. You may also want to post stick-figure pictures indicating how many children can be in the area at one time.

A child building with blocks has many experiences related to math, such as classification (grouping by the same size, for example) and order (putting blocks in order of largest to smallest). Many other basic math ideas are also learned through block building, such as length, area, volume, number, and shape (see Photo 20-2). Both small- and large-motor skills are also developed as children play with blocks.

Cleanup in the block center is another good chance to practice math skills. The following suggestions can help you make this cleanup a true learning experience.

- Ask children to pick up all of the blocks that are curved.
- Ask children to pick up blocks of three different lengths.
- Ask children to pick up blocks according to size.
- Ask children to pick up blocks similar to a specific block that the cleanup director names.
- Ask children to pick up blocks different from a specific block that the cleanup director names.
- Ask children to put away all of a particular shape or size block, and ask how many of that block were used.
- Ask children to stack all of the blocks that go in the lower-left section of the blocks shelf, then stack the lower middle shelf, and so on.
- Ask children to put away blocks in groups of twos, threes, fours, and so on.
- Ask children to put away one dozen long unit blocks.
- Ask children to put away blocks according to size, beginning with the biggest or longest and ending with the smallest or shortest.
- Select certain children to put away certain shapes, for example, rectangles and cylinders.
- Select certain children to collect blocks according to weight.
- Have children put away a certain unit of blocks and all of the blocks that are a fraction of that unit block.
- Use an assembly line to put away blocks. This encourages cooperation.
- Ask children to pick up a number of blocks that are greater or lesser than the number of blocks the cleanup director is holding (Hirsch, 2000; Sarama & Clements, 2009). See Figure 20-4 for more information on all of the learning opportunities possible in the block center.

© Cengage Learning 2015

PHOTO 20-2 While playing with blocks, young children learn many basic math concepts.

Did You Get It?

A teacher reads his preschoolers a book about flowers. The book shows what flowers are growing each month of the year. Which math skill are the children likely to learn from this book?

a. flowers and where they grow.

b. how to care for flowers.

c. counting the pages as the teacher turns them

d. understanding ordering from the progression of months

Take the full quiz on CourseMate.

The block center abounds with learning opportunities for young children. Listed below are a few of them. In the block center, children learn:

Science and math

- Discover that one long block is equal to two short blocks (proportion, fractions).
- Match block shapes to shelf labels (spatial sense).
- Make patterns (triangle, triangle, square, square, and so on).
- Arrange blocks in order of size (sequencing).
- State the number of blocks (counting).
- Stand net to a block tower (comparing, measuring).
- Build ramps and pathways, then race cars and marbles (measuring, spatial reasoning).

Language and literacy

- Learn vocabulary – shapes (arch, cylinder); comparisons (taller, heavier); building terms (enclosure, bridge) – in English and their home languages.
- Talk about structures before, during, and after their creation.
- Make books about structures using photos and text dictated to a teacher.

Social and emotional skills

- Rebuild after a block tower falls (self-confidence, perseverance).
- Put away blocks when finished building (self-regulation, sense of community).
- Offer dress-up items to a friend so they can both be construction workers (cooperation, self-regulation).
- Share ideas with a friend whose building keeps toppling (friendship).
- Construct roads and buildings with a small group (cooperation, sense of community).

FIGURE 20-4 Learning opportunities in the block center.

TeachSource Digital Download   Download from CourseMate.

20-4 Numbers: Rote and Rational Counting

naeyc **DAP** In our preceding discussion, many references were made to various mathematical concepts young children develop through everyday experiences in early childhood learning centers. The following information provides a brief description of these basic mathematical concepts and suggests some related activities for development of these specific concepts.

Children learn numbers by rote. A child often has no comprehension of what these abstract terms mean, but as a result of relevant experiences, he or she begins to attach meaning to numbers. Children talk about monetary values in their play, usually without any comprehension of what a dime or a quarter is. While playing store, Irene glibly sold the apple for a dollar and later sold the coat and hat for 10 cents.

Before the child is 3 years old, he or she often can count to 10 in proper order. Such counting (called **rote counting**), however, may have little specific meaning for the child. The words may be only sounds to him or her—sounds repeated in a particular sequence, like a familiar song. This rote counting is similar to the stage in the development of speech (see Chapter 18) when a child can repeat words without really understanding their meaning.

Quite different from and much more difficult than rote counting is understanding the numerals as they apply to a sequence of objects: that each numeral represents the position of an object in the sequence (button 1, button 2, button 3, and so on). Equally or more difficult to understand is the idea that the last number counted in a sequence of objects represents all the objects in the sequence, the total number of objects counted. This is called **rational counting**. For example, in counting six buttons, the child must grasp the idea that six, the last number counted, tells him how many buttons he has—that he has six buttons in all. Rational counting, a higher-level number understanding, develops slowly for most children. However, carefully structured activities that take one idea and present it to children one step at a time help them grow from a general to a more specific understanding of numbers.

Young children frequently hear counting—as steps are being climbed, objects are being stacked, foods are being distributed, finger plays are being played, familiar nursery rhymes and songs are being enjoyed, and during many other activities. This repetition helps the child memorize the sequence and sounds of numbers, even before the meanings of these numbers are understood. Songs, finger plays, and nursery rhymes using the fingers as counting objects should be common practice in early childhood programs to help young children practice the sounds and sequence of numbers.

True counting ability (rational counting) is not possible until the child understands one-to-one correspondence. In other words, to rote count (to say the number sequence) is one thing, but to count items correctly—one number per item—is more difficult. Very often when a young child is given a series of things to count, the child counts two numbers for one item or two items while saying only one number. Thus, as rote counting develops, teachers should also encourage the skills of **one-to-one correspondence**. Having children touch each object as they count is one way to encourage their grasp of one-to-one correspondence. Repeating this exercise in various experiences throughout the day reinforces the concept of one-to-one correspondence.

Young children should be asked to count only with number names that are meaningful to them, that is, **cardinal numbers** (the numbers one, two, three, and so on). Young children just learning numbers often have difficulty in understanding the relationship between counting and numbers. For example, Beatrix may count, "One, two books." Later, when asked to bring two books to the table, she may count, "one, two" and bring only the second book. **Ordinal number** refers to the place of an object in a series of numbers. The second book in the preceding example is an ordinal number. (The cardinal number is two.)

Did You Get It?

A six-year-old child counts his pennies, pointing to one at a time as he says the numbers. When he has finished counting them, he proudly proclaims, "I have six pennies!" This child has learned
  a. pre-operational counting.
  b. numeral counting.
  c. operational counting.
  d. rational counting.

Take the full quiz on CourseMate.

20-5 Classification and Sorting

naeyc **DAP** Classification and sorting activities are the beginnings that help children perceive a variety of relationships among things in their world. **Classification**, putting together things that are alike or that belong together, is one of the processes necessary for developing the concept of numbers. In order to classify, children must be able to observe an object for likenesses and differences, as well as for attributes associated with purpose, position, location, or some other factor. Children progress through the following stages as they develop the skill of classifying:

● Sorting into graphic collections without a plan in mind. Children may put all of the blocks with a letter on them together and then, ending with a blue letter, continue by putting all blue blocks with the group. When the grouping is complete, they won't be able to tell you why the blocks belong together, only that they do.
● Grouping with no apparent plan. When asked why all the things go together, children respond with some reason but one not immediately clear to the adult: "Well, all these are like Kimiko's."
● Sorting on the basis of some criterion. Children proceed to being able to sort a group of objects on the basis of one criterion. All of the green things or all of the round things go together, but not all of the green and round objects go together in a group.
● Creating groupings on the basis of two or more properties, putting all of the green and round objects together in a group.
● Sorting objects or events according to function, use, or on the basis of a negative concept, such as all of the things that are not used in the kitchen.

Before children can classify and sort, they need to understand concepts such as "belongingness," "put together," "alike," and "belong together." These concepts are acquired over time as children have varied hands-on experiences in the early childhood program.

Your role as teacher is to help children gain these ideas through many experiences with a wide variety of materials selected specifically for classifying and sorting activities. Activity suggestions for classifying and sorting are found at the end of this chapter.

Materials for children's classifying and sorting may be kept together on a shelf in the manipulative toy or

Mathematics, Music, and Math Difficulty

Everyday learning experiences, such as listening to music, are especially important in supporting developing mathematics concepts in children from infancy to 5 years old (Linder, Powers-Costello, & Stegelin, 2011). Music is made up of rhythmic patterns and can be structured to make the patterning simple or complex, depending on the activity. Zentner and Eerole (2010) suggest that infants and toddlers have an innate capacity to not only see patterns but also hear them in music. Reinforcing these capabilities by teaching patterns through music at an early age may benefit children's cognitive abilities (Bell et al., 2009; Meltzoff et al., 2009).

Teaching patterns to very young children is also a key to the concept of emergent mathematics, which parallels the idea of emergent literacy. As with literacy, emergent mathematics suggest the following:

- Mathematical learning begins very early in life.
- Mathematics is related to many other developmental milestones.
- Mathematics develops from real-life situations in which the child is an active participant (Geist, Geist, & Kuznik, 2012).

Neuropsychological case studies have provided support for the involvement of key brain regions in tasks involving number processing and calculations in adults (bilateral posterior superior parietal lobe, bilateral horizontal segment of the intraparietal sulcus, and left angular gyrus) (van Eimeren et al., 2010). Children appear to engage a similar network of brain regions in simple number processing (Ansari & Dhital, 2006). However, children also use the inferior frontal cortex to a greater extent than adults (Cantlon et al., 2008).

---

game area of your room. Boxes or sorting trays (common plastic dishpans and muffin tins work well) are kept with the materials. Sorting trays can be constructed by either attaching a series of metal jar lids to a board or piece of cardboard; mounting a number of clear plastic cups on a board; dividing a board or tray into sections with colored pieces of tape; or by mounting small, clear plastic boxes on a board. Egg cartons, plastic sewing boxes, tool boxes (such as those for storing nuts and bolts), and fishing tackle boxes are also useful for sorting trays and stimulate children to use materials mathematically.

Did You Get It?

Children progress through developmental steps as they learn the skill of classification. A child who groups together toy cars, buses, bicycles, and trains because they are all modes of transportation has reached the _____ level.

  a. second
  b. first
  c. last
  d. third

Take the full quiz on CourseMate.

20-6 Comparing

naeyc **DAP** The skill of **comparing** seems to come easily and naturally, especially when it is a personal comparison: "My shoes are newer than yours." "I've got the biggest." "My sister is little." "You've got more." When children build with blocks, they may be asked to make additional comparisons: "Which tower is the tallest?" "Pick up the heaviest blocks first." "Build something as tall as this." Have children identify parts of their buildings using the vocabulary of comparison.

When different size and shape containers are used in sand and water play, children can make comparisons based on volume. In the early childhood program, these are informal and related to children's actual experiences. "How many blue cups of water will it take to fill this bucket?" "How many are red?" "Which is the heaviest?" "This doesn't hold as much."

Stories and poems, often the folk tales children are already familiar with, offer other opportunities for informal comparisons. *The Three Billy Goats Gruff, Goldilocks and the Three Bears,* and others offer comparisons on the basis of differing attributes.

Throughout the preschool years, ask children to observe and note differences in the objects of their environment, to name them, and to discuss them with one another.

20-7 Ordering (Seriation)

Another mathematical idea that is a vital part of a complete number concept formation is the idea of **ordering (seriation)**. Ordering the environment into series begins when children are very young and continues throughout adult life. The child begins by perceiving opposite ends of a series:

big——————little
heavy—————light
cold————hot
long————short

The intervention of an adult, suitable materials, and appropriate language lead to refinement of these early basic concepts. The comparison of the height of two children is the beginning of ordering, as is the comparison of two sets of things as *more* or *less*. Ordering sticks, blocks, or nesting cups in a sequence that leads gradually from the smallest to the biggest helps children see ordered size relations (see Photo 20-3).

When children line up to go outdoors, they meet another idea of order: Juan stands in front of Ne'Andrea, and Yvonne stands in back of Drew. They may use their understanding of sequence when they say, "I want to be first," or "Jimmy is last."

After listening to the story of *Goldilocks and the Three Bears*, their observations may become more refined as they discuss the story. The story contains big–little and one-to-one relationships in addition to its many other enjoyable qualities.

The idea of ordering in size also appears naturally in other classroom areas. The teacher can make ordering a part of natural discussions in relation to the children's play and activities: sets of cans, bottles, and books can also be used for practicing ordering of size. With younger children, only two objects are compared at first; this will

© Cengage Learning 2015

PHOTO 20-3 Nesting blocks teach about size, shapes, seriation, and ordering.

be extended to three or more objects for older children. Children enjoy ordering and do so spontaneously.

Many table toys provide ordering experiences, as do ordinary objects such as measuring spoons and cups. Your role is to provide materials and sufficient time. When children find the existing materials too easy, you can awaken their interest by encouraging them to use the toys differently, by asking them questions, and by providing additional materials. Ordering activities can include length (sticks), height (bottles), total size (bowls and shoes), weight (stones), color (from light to dark), and other endless possibilities. Suggestions for ordering activities are found at the end of this chapter.

20-8 Shape and Form

naeyc **DAP** Young children need many experiences with shapes and making comparisons between shapes before they focus on naming shapes. Usually, it is

THINK ABOUT IT

Numerical Matching Abilities in Young Children Using a Touchscreen Computer

This study presents the first evidence that preschool children perform more accurately in a numerical matching task when given multisensory rather than single sense (unisensory) information about numbers using a touchscreen computer. Participants were 24 children: 14 girls and 10 boys, mean age 3.94 years; eight 3-year-olds, eight 4-year olds, and eight 5-year-olds (Jordan & Baker, 2011).

Children learned to play a numerical matching game on a touchscreen computer, which asked them to match a sample number with a numerically equivalent choice. To begin a trial, children were required to press a picture of a puppy located in the lower-right corner of the screen; this ensured that children were attending as each trial was initiated.

For trials that contained an auditory sample, the sample tones were played sequentially from the speaker; for trials that contained visual sample elements, these elements appeared sequentially in the center of the screen. Immediately after the last sample element, two choice stimuli appeared. If the child correctly chose the numerical match, a green border flashed around the match, a positive sound occurred (clapping and people cheering), and the child was given a sticker in their cup. In contrast, if the child touched the incorrect choice, the screen turned black, a negative sound was emitted (single, brief tone), and no sticker was provided. Each session contained 30 trials, with approximately one-third of trials visual, one-third of trials auditory, and one-third of trials audiovisual.

Children performed significantly better when provided with multisensory samples. Also there was no speed-accuracy trade-off between single sense and multisensory trial types. Thus, the researchers suggested that multisensory numerical stimuli enabled the preschool children to more precisely match representations of number. They concluded that this is an important finding for our knowledge of the development of numerical processing in typically developing children (Jordan & Baker, 2011). Based on this study's results, activities using more than one sense in teaching number concepts would seem an appropriate approach in the early childhood mathematics curriculum.

---

enough to introduce one new shape at a time. As the new shape is understood, other shapes may be added, thus building new learning on previous learning (see Photo 20-4).

PHOTO 20-4 Children need many experiences with shapes.

In teaching young children about shape and form, it is important to include more shapes than the common geometric shapes of a circle, triangle, rectangle, and square. Because shapes aid in, or are sources of, identification, limiting instruction to the "basic shapes" excludes from the learning environment important aspects of recognition of shapes in general. Yet familiar shapes must be taught before uncommon ones. Most of these unfamiliar shapes depend on previous shape identification and recognition. From the basis of understanding simple shapes, the child is able to build more complex structures.

Shapes of various kinds can be found throughout the child's environment. Words defining shapes should be used often. For example, everyday language should include such statements as "That is a square box," rather than "That is square"; "The clock is round," rather than "This is round"; "Put the book on the square table," rather than "Put it over there." With these phrases, the object and its characteristic shape are made clear to the child. Later on, characteristics such as color, size, texture, and number may be added.

When unfamiliar shapes are introduced, a review of already familiar ones should precede the new introduction. Then children's thinking can be stimulated with such questions as "How is this new shape the same as . . . ?" or "How is this new shape not the same as (or different from) . . . ?" Such comparisons reinforce and review shapes already learned.

Did You Get It?

A teacher decides to introduce shapes to her four-year-old students by teaching recognition of hexagons and oval shapes. Developmentally speaking, her technique is

a. correct, as beginning with complex shapes will challenge the children and aid in their learning.

b. correct, as children understand those shapes more readily than they understand squares and circles.

c. incorrect, as children can understand uncommon shapes on the basis of their understanding of simple shapes.

d. incorrect, as children cannot understand uncommon shapes before they reach grade school age.

Take the full quiz on CourseMate.

20-9 Mathematics: Grades 3–5

Mathematics is a subject most students in grades 3 through 5 like. Students in grades 3 through 5 see mathematics as practical, are challenged with many new ideas, and believe that what they are learning is important. However, sometime between grades 4 and 8, students' interest in mathematics begins to wane. Although they continue to view mathematics as important, students are less likely to characterize it as interesting or to consider themselves good at math by grade 8 (Charlesworth, 2011). It is crucial that mathematics education in the upper-elementary and early middle grades be challenging, relevant, and engaging for students.

The curriculum materials and instructional approaches a teacher uses help students connect mathematical ideas and provide a basis for making them meaningful. Because the amount of content in grades 3 through 5 expands greatly from that of the earlier grades, students need help in building connections and managing the many new concepts and procedures they are encountering. Students in grades 3 through 5 must also understand and bear responsibility for their learning. In math, this means learning how to

examine, ask questions, and consider different strategies—all with the goal of making sense of mathematical ideas and fitting them to other, related areas.

While the 10 standards of the National Council of Mathematics Teachers apply to all grade levels, the instructional emphases for grades 3 through 5 build on those outlined for grades pre-K–2 and extend well beyond them. Although number and operation continue to be cornerstones of the curriculum in grades 3 through 5, each of the content standards (number, data, measurement, algebra, and geometry) is essential for building student knowledge at this level. Several "big ideas" or central mathematical themes for this grade span are woven through these areas, including multiplication, equivalence, and the notion of unit.

Likewise, knowledge and use of mathematical processes should be deepened and expanded in these grades. Students in grades 3 through 5 are capable of sophisticated reasoning and should be challenged and supported in their learning (see Photo 20-5). In grades 3 through 5, extending understanding from whole numbers to fractions and decimals is a key dimension of the mathematics curriculum. Students need many and varied experiences in order to understand what fractions and decimals represent, how they are related to each other, and how they are different from whole numbers. Suggestions for fraction and decimal activities are found at the end of this chapter.

20-9a Calculators: Grades 3–5

Appropriate use of calculators is an important part of a balanced mathematics education at all levels,

Casper Holroyd

PHOTO 20-5 Older elementary students are capable of more sophisticated reasoning and mathematical concepts.

including elementary. The National Council of Teachers of Mathematics has elaborated this position in a public statement, *Principles and Standards for School Mathematics* (NCTM, 2000). Thus, the calculator and a variety of computer software should be considered legitimate tools for learning math concepts and performing math computations and should be available to students in grades 3 through 5.

Students need access to calculators, but they also need pencil-and-paper skills. Balancing these two is an important part of an elementary teacher's work. Research has shown that students who use calculators are better at understanding mathematical concepts and solving problems (Roschelle, & Singleton, 2008). The same studies confirm that calculator use does not interfere with students' development of computational skills, and in many of these studies, students' pencil-and-paper skills increased when they also had the opportunity to use calculators.

Calculators are tools and, as such, are only as effective as the person pushing the buttons. Just as a hammer does not build a house, a calculator does not think or solve problems. This is a job for people, and a job that students can learn early on. Also, just as a hammer does not choose where to put a nail or prevent a nail from going into the wrong board, a calculator does not know what operation to use and cannot keep a person from forgetting a decimal point. These are also jobs for people, and they involve exactly the kinds of skills that teachers can help students learn. Sometimes a calculator is the right tool for a job, and sometimes it is not. Knowing when to use a calculator and when not to use one is a skill teachers can help children develop (Charlesworth, 2011).

One of the most important ways in which students can use calculators is to solve problems that they would not be able to solve otherwise. With a calculator, all children can deal with problems involving numbers that are seemingly unmanageable and that arise from their everyday experience. Whenever the teacher has a class working on developing problem-solving skills, and computational procedures are not the main point of the lesson, calculator use might be appropriate. Students can develop their decision-making and problem-solving skills far beyond what they would be able to do if they were limited to numbers that they could handle quickly using pencil and paper (Charlesworth, 2011).

Teachers need to create opportunities and make judgments about when and how math tools are used to support learning. They can arrange activities requiring students to use calculators and spreadsheets to solve problems. Students in grades 3 through 5 can use graphing and geometry software and calculators to explore, experiment, verify, and visualize mathematical ideas. For example, these children might explore geometric relationships using software to create, modify, and examine shapes. They might create graphs and consider how some presentations of data highlight or distort certain trends. They might use calculators to explore the relationship between decimals and whole numbers and between negative numbers and positive numbers. Students in this age group should also have the opportunity to learn how to search the Internet to gather information needed to solve mathematical problems.

The calculator is an important tool in teaching mathematics in grades 3 through 5. However, calculators do not circumvent the need for rapid recall of basic facts, a basic understanding of math concepts, or the ability to formulate and use strategies for computing. Rather, the calculator should support these goals by enhancing and stimulating student learning. As students solve problems involving many complex computations, the calculator should be used to perform calculations. The calculator serves as a tool for enabling the problem solver to focus on the big picture rather than become entangled in the calculating details. (See the end of this chapter for some suggested activities for grades 3 through 5.)

Did You Get It?

A fourth-grade teacher forbids the use of calculators, contending that they interfere with children's grasp of mathematical concepts. Developmentally speaking, this teacher's approach is

a. incorrect, as math instruction for fourth graders should incorporate calculators and pencil and paper.

b. incorrect, as fourth graders should be permitted calculator use to complete homework assignments, but not to assist with classroom assignments.

c. correct, as research has shown that children who use calculators have a poor understanding of math.

d. correct, as calculators distract children from the task at hand.

Take the full quiz on CourseMate.

Summary

20-1 Discuss the developmental pattern of learning mathematical concepts.

Long before a child formally uses numerals, he or she is aware of them through daily experiences. For example, a child becomes aware of sequences in events before he or she can talk about what is first, second, or third (ordinal numbers). The child recognizes, too, the difference between *one* and *many* and between *few* and *lots* before he or she acquires real number concepts. The pattern of early uses of numbers is similar to the general-to-specific pattern of physical growth. In these early stages of mathematical thinking, the child has a general understanding of numbers and will gradually move toward a more specific understanding as the developmental process continues.

20-2 Explain the purpose of the national mathematics standards.

The National Council of Teachers of Mathematics (NCTM) has developed a set of Principles and Standards for Children Pre-K–12 (2000). These standards propose mathematical content and processes students should know and be able to use as they progress through school. There are 10 standards—5 content standards and 5 process standards—that apply across the pre-K–12 grade span.

20-3 Discuss how mathematics learning occurs in learning centers in the early childhood classroom.

In the movement center, children have many chances to explore, extend, and refine their spatial discoveries. In this center, children learn to share power, space, things, and ideas as well as to use counting for access and comparing their jumping skills by measuring in a nonthreatening way.

In the language arts center, children have the opportunity to learn math through the use of children's books that encourage students to think and to reason mathematically while building their appreciation for both math and literature.

In the art center, much incidental learning related to mathematics occurs during art activities. When materials are used for a particular process, children need to remember quantity and their order of use. Children learn to consider the number of items needed and often the shapes that will be required. Many art activities are related to problem solving and measurement, which are two content standards in the national mathematics standards.

At the water table, children have many mathematical experiences measuring, pouring, and comparing. They experience the concepts of full, empty, more, and less.

In the dramatic center, children have the opportunity to translate their understanding of adult activities into their understanding of adult activities involving mathematics.

In the block center, children have the opportunity to experience real-life examples of geometric shapes and solids. They experience concepts such as classification, order, length, area, volume, number, and practice using small- and large-motor skills.

20-4 Define rote counting and rational counting.

Counting by rote (memory) is common for young children aged 3 and up. Counting with understanding (rational counting) does not occur until a child understands one-to-one correspondence.

20-5 Discuss classification and sorting.

Classification, or putting together things that are alike or that belong together, is one of the processes necessary for developing the concept of numbers. In order to classify, children must be able to sort through a group of objects and observe likenesses and differences, as well as look for other common factors.

20-6 Discuss comparing.

Comparing is another mathematical process that is appropriate in the early childhood program. Children seem to make comparisons easily and naturally, especially when the comparisons involve them personally.

20-7 Discuss ordering.

Another mathematical idea that is a vital part of a complete number concept is the idea of order. Putting things in a series or in order is a process that is appropriate for early mathematical experiences. Ordering activities can include length, height, total size, weight, and color.

20-8 Describe how to present shape and form concepts to young children.

Young children need many experiences with shapes and making comparisons between shapes before they focus on naming shapes. Usually, it is enough to introduce one new shape at a time. As the new shape is understood, other shapes may be added, thus building new learning on previous learning. As the new shape is understood, other shapes may be added, thus building new learning on previous learning.

20-9 Describe mathematics concepts appropriate for children in grades 3–5.

Sometime between grades 4 and 8, students' interest in mathematics begins to wane. It is crucial that mathematics education in the upper-elementary and early middle grades be challenging, relevant, and engaging for students.

The curriculum materials and instructional approaches a teacher uses help students connect mathematical ideas and provide a basis for making them meaningful. Because the amount of content in grades 3 through 5 expands greatly from that of the earlier grades, students need help in building connections and managing the many new concepts and procedures they are encountering. Students in grades 3 through 5 must also understand and bear responsibility for their learning. In math, this means learning how to examine, ask questions, and consider different strategies—all with the goal of making sense of mathematical ideas and fitting them to other related areas.

Key Terms

Learning Activities

A. Use one of the activities suggested at the end of this chapter with a group of young children. Evaluate your experience. Share your evaluation with your classmates.

B. Using a school supply catalog, choose three pieces of mathematical equipment appropriate for teaching seriation, geometric shapes, and size.

C. Imagine that you have $150 to spend on mathematical equipment for your classroom. Using a school supply catalog, determine how you would spend this sum. In making your selections, give the following information:
1. Developmental reason for choice
2. Purpose(s) for item

D. Choose one or two children from each of these age groups: 3-year-olds, 4-year-olds, and 5-year-olds. Assess each child's ability to count. Record and comment on the results of your assessment of each child. Discuss what math activities would be developmentally appropriate for these children.

E. Observe and talk with a preschool child, listening for comments and understanding related to numbers. If possible, ask the child such questions as "How old are you? What is your favorite number? How far can you count? Where do you see numbers?"

Observe and talk with a child between 5 and 6 years old, asking some of the same questions. Ask additional questions such as "Show me how you can add some things. Here are three pencils. How many will you have if you add two more pencils?" Challenge the child with number questions and problems. Assess the mathematical understanding of the two children you observed, keeping in mind the difference in their ages.

F. Ask children in grades 3 through 5 their opinions about math. What percent of the children liked math? Ask them why they feel the way they do about math. Report your results to the class.

G. Observe in an early childhood classroom using the Math Observation sheet in MindTap. Discuss the results of your observation with your fellow students. Did you observe any surprises? If yes, explain what they were.

H. Use one of the CCSSM-related activities at the end of this chapter for children with a group of children. Evaluate your experience. How would you change this activity?

Activities for Children

Activities such as the following help children grasp the mathematical concept of counting:

- In counting activities, have the child touch each object. Count only with number names meaningful to the child. Repeat this in various settings until touching or pointing to objects is no longer necessary. Provide for many manipulative counting experiences where children use beads, buttons, cookies, napkins, children, and chairs. For example, children might match beads to boxes or children to chairs. Determine the number of places, quantity of milk, silverware, napkins, and so on needed at the table.
- Use buttons, bottle caps, or similar objects. Have children practice counting three, putting three in a box, and taking one, two, or three out of the box. After counting, children can glue the buttons or bottle caps onto a piece of paper to make a picture.
- Have children take turns trying to toss a specified number of beanbags into a large container. Allow children to choose the number of beanbags they want to throw and count them as they throw.

Buried Treasure Count

Fill a clear plastic soda bottle two-thirds full with sand. Drop in assorted small trinkets (beads, buttons, erasers, plastic insects, charms, jewels, and so on). Cover tightly, and then secure the cover with masking tape. Let children turn and shake the bottle and try to count how many treasures are buried in it. If someone counts correctly, remove the cap, add or take out some trinkets, and then reseal the bottle.

Numbers and Snacks

Number concepts can be reinforced easily in everyday routines. Snack time is an excellent time for teaching about numbers. Once or twice a week, prepare snacks to reinforce mathematical concepts. Discuss the characteristic of each snack at service time. Then let children eat while they learn from the special snack you have prepared.

A. Choose a number and serve snack items in groups of that number (four raisins, four carrot sticks, four banana slices, four crackers, and so on).

B. Choose a geometric shape such as a circle, and serve round snack items (round crackers, cucumber slices, round cereal, carrot slices, banana slices, and so on).

Concept of Number and Counting

Cut face cards in half (make the cutting lines different on the separate cards so that only the two "matching" halves will fit together). Put the cards together as puzzles. Add these to the math center.

Place numerals from 1 to 10 around the room. Show children a card with objects on it, and ask them to find the numeral that tells how many objects are on the card.

Make a number book by pasting the correct number of colored squares or other shapes next to written numerals.

Set up at the math center a numeral recognition and numeration activity such as "Counting Marbles." Provide 10 paper cups and label them with the numerals 1 through 10. Provide a box with lots of marbles. Place these on a table for a mini math center. Have children work with a partner. One child examines the numeral printed on each cup and drops in the appropriate number of marbles. The partner counts the marbles in each cup to see if the correct amount was put in it. The marbles then go back into the box.

Recycled Math Materials

To add to your supply of math manipulatives, start saving bottle caps. You will find many uses for these recyclables. Here are a few suggestions.

Bottle Cap Sizes. Give children a number of bottle caps that vary in size. Have them organize the caps from the smallest to largest and then from the largest to smallest.

Bottle Cap Groupings. Collect a variety of bottle caps that vary in size, color, and texture. Invite children to sort the caps into like groups. Notice the different ways that children sort and classify caps. They may sort by size, shape, or color or separate the plastic caps from the metal caps. After they have completed their sorting, encourage them to describe their choice of groupings. How many more are in one group than another? Is there any other way to group them?

Bottle Cap Weights. Provide children with a pan scale and a variety of bottle caps. Have them compare the weight of plastic and metal bottle caps. Which weighs more? Have them place a large bottle cap on one side of the scale. How many small caps are equal to the weight of the large cap? Are three large caps equal to the weight of three small caps? What would happen if children put 10 more with this group? Ten less?

Bottle Cap Fill and Count. Fill a small clear plastic container with bottle caps. Ask children to estimate how many bottle caps are in the container and record each child's estimate. Have them count the number of bottle caps and compare their predictions. Then give them another container, either smaller or larger, and have them estimate how many small bottle caps will fill the container. Invite children to count the caps as they fill it up.

Bottle Cap Pairs. Collect enough bottle caps to have one pair of each. Mix them up and place them in a pile on the table. Give children time to explore the different bottle caps. Then invite one or two children to find the matching bottle caps. How many pairs of bottle caps did they find? What makes the bottle caps similar to each other? Different from the rest?

Number Roll

Position the children in a circle. Sit in the center with a ball. Pass the ball to a child while calling out a number. After the child bounces the ball the correct number of times, he or she calls out a number and passes the ball to another child. Be sure to have the child count out loud as she bounces the ball.

Variation: Practice counting with young children as their classmates run, skip, or walk laps around a short indoor course. Record results on a chart to show which child went the farthest.

Everyday Math

Try some of these simple, everyday math activities to increase your "math talk" with young children.

- **Roll Call.** Have children count how many students are present and figure out how many are absent.
- **Calendar Quiz.** Discuss the numbers on a calendar. How many days are left before the weekend? How many days are in a week? In a month?
- **Line Up.** When children are in line, have them say, "I am first," "I am second," and so on. Make a chart of the words we use to describe order.
- **Twos.** Ask children to think of things that come in ones, twos, threes, and so on. Make a chart and add to it throughout the year.
- **Learning Time.** Draw a clock on the board. Invite children to draw hands on the clock in answer to a prompt such as "When is lunch time?"

Block Activities

Birthday Candles

In which months do children celebrate birthdays? Find out and label each of 12 sheets of construction paper with a different month. Sequence and tape the pages in a line on the floor. Invite children to place a wood block in front of their birthday month. Have them stand their block on end—to represent a candle—and then attach a sticky note labeled with their name to the top of the block. After constructing the graph, compare the number of birthdays that occur in each month.

Extension: Have children graph the day of the month on which their birthdays occur.

Block Shelters

In the fall, as animals are getting ready for winter, add stuffed animals of different sizes to the block center. Encourage children to build homes for the animals. Discuss how many blocks it takes to build the animal homes. Does a bigger animal take more or fewer blocks? They can also arrange animals by size and color.

Pictographs

Make a pictograph to represent students' hand preferences. Distribute crayons and ask children to hold their crayon in the hand they draw with. Then, working in pairs, have children trace their partner's preferred hand on construction paper. Help them cut out their hand outlines. Also, trace and cut outlines of both of your hands. Draw a two-row chart on chart paper. Attach one of your hand cutouts to the left side of the top row and the other cutout to the bottom row. Then invite children to attach their cutout hand to the row that corresponds to their preferred hand: left or right. Review and discuss the results of the hand pictograph with the children.

Extension: Have boys use one color of construction paper and girls another to create a pictograph that shows hand preferences between the two groups.

Size, Seriation, and Ordinal Numbers

Ordering/Seriation

Challenge children with some of these activities.

- Have children find the shortest or longest block or tinker toy.
- Have children pick the one that is the shortest from three objects of differing heights. Have them describe the remaining two objects.
- Have students describe how the objects in a series, arranged from the shortest to the longest, differ from one another.
- Collect nesting materials, such as a set of measuring spoons or measuring cups. Have children arrange the objects in correct order so that they will properly "nest" together, one object fitting inside the other. Be sure to have children set the objects on the table in order from smallest to largest after they have finished "nesting" them.
- Supply three cans of different sizes and three beanbags in three sizes. Have students arrange the cans from smallest to largest in a row. Have children line the beanbags up next to the cans, putting the smallest by the smallest, and so on. Shuffle the cans and the beanbags. Have children order the cans from smallest to largest this time, and then match the beanbags to the cans.
- Cut out three fish. Make each fish large enough to totally conceal the next smaller fish when placed over it. Tell children that the fish go in order, with the biggest fish first leading the others. Have them find the largest fish and then the fish that will follow. Check to see if the largest fish covers the fish that follows. For self-checking, children place each fish on top of the next to see if the next fish is smaller. Variation: Have children order from the smallest fish to the largest fish.
- Have children seriate materials such as buttons, gummed stars, lids, beads, feathers, and nails in order of size. Also have children make size comparisons between two or more of the objects.
- Have children seriate boxes or cans from smallest to largest by placing them inside one another.
- Have children roll balls of various sizes from clay or play dough, and then seriate them according to size.

- Make felt or cardboard cutouts in three or more sizes of different heights (for example, trees, houses, and hats). Challenge children to arrange them in a given order beginning with shortest or tallest.
- To reinforce the use of the ordering words *first* and *last*, have children stand in line and identify the person who is first and the person who is last. See if children can figure out who is in the middle!
- Cut out triangles whose base length is the same but whose heights are different. Select a set of triangles that varies along one dimension. Lay them in front of children in mixed order but in such a way that the child does not have to turn them to discover size variations. Have children order them from smallest to largest (shortest to tallest) or largest to smallest.
- Show five blocks that have been ordered according to height. Arrange another set of blocks to match the first, third, and fifth blocks in the five-block pattern. Have children insert the two remaining blocks so that both sets match. Repeat, using different blocks, such as second or fourth, and so on.

Measurement

How Big Am I?

For this activity, you will need boxes, cartons, tables, chairs, barrels, unit blocks, and building blocks. Challenge children with questions such as the following: Can you build a building with blocks as high as you are tall? Can you build something as high as your arm is long? As high as to the top of your leg? Waist? Shoulder?

Telling Time

Use masking tape to make a large clock on the floor. Have children move around in the 12 hour spaces by stretching arms to a person in the middle of the clock as you call time. Explore different times (recess time, lunch time) and ways to move around (fast, slow, hop, slide, skip).

Number Shapes

Have students form the shapes of numbers with their bodies when you call out a signal. Encourage children to work together to form numbers if they need "extra strokes." Challenge them to make these shapes combining with time, space, and force.

Measuring with Our Bodies

Write the word *measure* on a sheet of chart paper. Ask children to share what they know about measuring. What does it mean to measure something? What type of things do we measure? What do we use to measure? Why do we measure things? Record their comments on the chart paper.

Have children use their bodies to measure different things. Have them estimate how many hands or arms long, tall, or wide something will be. Prepare another sheet of chart paper to record all the different things children measure. Include their estimations and actual measurements.

Have children use their hands to find out how many "hands long" the tables are. Invite a few children to one of the tables. Ask them to first estimate, or guess, how many hands long the table will be. Record their estimate on a chart paper. Then have them line up their hands lengthwise on the table. Count and record the actual hand length of the table. Next, ask them to compare their estimation with their answer. Then have them measure the width of the table. Estimate and then conduct the actual measurement. Are all of the classroom tables the same size?

Have children think of other ways to measure the tables with their bodies. How many hands high is the table from the floor? How many feet or bodies long are the tables? Encourage children to estimate and then compare their measurements.

Fun Measuring

Have students gather all the writing implements they can find in the room and lay them out end to end. Measure the resulting length with yardsticks and rulers. How many crayons make up a yard? How many pencils make up a foot?

Measuring Shadows

Have children pair up to trace their shadows. Show them how one child in each pair can stand in the sun on a hard surface (or on a piece of paper if you're inside) while the other child uses chalk or a pencil to trace the shadow.

When children finish, have partners trade places so everyone has a shadow tracing. Suggest that children write their names on their shadows.

Encourage children to think of ways to measure the shadows, and then invite them to test out their ideas. Have a variety of measuring tools handy, such as yarn, string, and ribbon.

Help each pair measure their shadows using the material they chose. One child can hold the yarn or other material at the head of the shadow tracing while the other stretches it to the bottom. Then, help the children cut it so that each child will have a length of material that represents the length of his or her shadow.

Encourage children to predict whether their shadow lengths are longer, shorter, or the same as their own bodies, others' shadows, and other objects they see. Show them how to compare lengths of their materials against those objects to test their predictions.

For younger children: Take large sheets of Kraft paper outdoors. Have children take turns lying on the paper. Trace and cut out the outlines of children's bodies. Later, bring paint cups and brushes outdoors, and invite children to paint their paper "shadows."

For older children: Encourage children to hunt for outdoor objects (sticks, rocks, weeds) they can use as instruments to measure their shadows.

Variation: Ask children to try to change the shape of the shadows they see outdoors by moving the objects that create them. What happens to the shadow of a tricycle, a ball, or a swing when the object is moved in one way or another?

Weather Wise Math

Shadow Stick

Put a dowel or a stake vertically in the ground away from any buildings. At the same time of day, at least once a week, measure the length of the stick's shadow using cubes or some other nonstandard unit of measure. Make a representation of your data. What is happening? Why?

Temperature

Check with your local weather station or your classroom's outside thermometer to see what the temperature is, and record the information for one week. What changes do you notice? What do you predict will happen tomorrow? Can you use towers of cubes to represent the temperatures for each day? Hint: You can find weather data in the newspaper and on the Internet.

Dress for the Weather

Imagine you have a red hat and a blue hat, as well as three sweaters—one black, one green, and one yellow—and two pairs of boots—one pair with snaps and one pair with buckles. If you wear a different combination of one hat, one sweater, and one pair of boots each day to go out and play, how many combinations can you make?

Playing Numbers

This is a fast math activity that can fill up a 5-minute period. Give each child a pair of foam dice, or regular dice, and a noise-absorbing surface, such as foam placemats or squares of fleece cloth. For children who can add, have them roll the dice and write the sum of the two numbers that come up. Keep rolling and adding until time is up. Who reached the highest number? Who had the lowest? Children who don't know how to add and subtract yet can count the dots that come up with each roll and record the numbers on paper. In 5 minutes, which number came up the most frequently? The least? Not at all?

Comparing

The following materials can be used to aid children in comparing:

- String, ribbon, pencils, rulers, clay snakes, lines, or strips of paper. Ask children which is longest, longer, shortest, and shorter.
- Buttons, dolls, cups, plastic animals, trees, boats. Have children identify the biggest one or the one bigger than another.
- Containers and coffee cans filled with various materials and sealed, or buckets or bags of items. Ask which is the heaviest or the lightest and which is heavier than another.
- Toy cars, trucks, bikes. Ask which is the fastest, the slowest, or which is faster than another.
- Paper, cardboard, books, pieces of wood, food slices, cookies. Have children make or find one that is thick, thicker, thickest, or thinnest.

Classification and Sorting

The following materials are helpful for classification and sorting activities:

- Boxes of scrap materials—velvet squares, tweeds, and net cut into uniform sizes and shapes for feeling, sorting, and classifying according to texture.
- A box or shelf of bells—cow bells, Christmas bells, decorative bells, sleigh bells—all inviting children to sort and classify on any basis they decide, perhaps size, color, shape, or sound.
- A box of various textured papers, cut into uniform shapes and sizes for the younger children and into a variety of shapes for older children. Smooth papers, watercolor paper, textured papers, and others can be obtained from a local print shop.
- Collections of nuts, nails, screws, and bolts to classify and sort according to shape, size, or function.

Sorting

Make two big loops with string on a table or on the floor. Have a set of round objects of several colors and a set of red objects of different shapes and sizes. Put a round object in one loop and a red object in the other loop. Have children sort according to this rule. Then make the loops overlap.

Tell children that only objects that are round and red can go in the middle loop. Have children re-sort the objects. Provide other sets of objects that lend themselves to this type of sorting, and let children determine the sorting rules.

Shoe Sorting

You will need 10 pairs of shoes of different sizes. To begin, put all the shoes in the middle of a circle. Have children sort them into pairs (one-to-one correspondence) and then into groups of little, middle, and big. Of course, they'll need to try them on for size!

Number Quiz

Have children make up and exchange riddles about "more" and "fewer." Examples: "I'm thinking of a number that is one more than the buttons on my shirt." "I'm thinking of a number that is one fewer than the windows in our room." Have children make up and mentally solve riddles about "same" numbers. For example, "I am the same number as legs on a dog." "I am the same number as points on a triangle."

Shapes

Blocks and Shapes

Obtain spring and/or balance scales that measure in ounces or grams, such as those for weighing letters or foods. Show children how to use them carefully. Have children weigh wooden blocks. They might also combine several blocks, balance different shapes and sizes to get the same weight, and arrange blocks from lightest to heaviest.

Make a chart to record block weights. Draw pictures of blocks and leave space to record their weights.

Have children weigh blocks together. Record block weights on the chart. Compare weights of different blocks. What combinations weigh the same?

Have children find objects that weigh the same as each block. They might build a structure with blocks and predict how much it weighs. They can find out by weighing the blocks after you take the structure apart. Have students sketch block constructions, writing the weight of each block in its picture.

Shoe Print Patterns

Collect a variety of old shoes that have interesting patterns on the soles. Tape a large sheet of brown butcher paper across a table. Help children put smocks on and give them several colors of washable tempera paint and paintbrushes. Invite them to use one or several colors to paint the soles of the shoes. Then demonstrate how to place the shoes on the paper to make a print. Have children describe the different patterns or shapes created by the soles. How are they similar, and how do they differ? Rinse the soles off with a wet cloth so the shoes can be used again. Display the shoe prints in the classroom.

Shape Matching Game

For this activity, you will need five or six colors of construction paper cut into shapes (circles, squares, triangles)—one piece per child.

Have children sit in a circle. Direct them to place their shape marker in front of them. Call out one of the shapes. All children having that shape run around the circle in the same direction and back to their places. Different kinds of movements can be used (skipping, galloping, walking, hopping).

Variation: Use colors instead of shapes. Use numbered flash cards or addition/subtraction problems.

Toothpick Shapes

For this activity, have children work in pairs. One child makes an arrangement of five toothpicks and shows it to his or her partner for 3 seconds only. The other student attempts to build a copy of the pattern. Announce "Begin!" and then "Stop!" after 3 seconds, then allow half a minute for students to build and discuss with their partners. Play four or six rounds, and discuss interesting patterns, shapes, or geometry concepts children used during this activity.

Shape Crawl

For this activity, you will need shapes cut out of cardboard. Spread the shapes around a space. Challenge children to crawl through the shapes with questions such as the following:

- Can you crawl through without touching the sides?
- Can you crawl through using one arm and both feet?
- Can you crawl through using one foot and both hands?
- Can you crawl through with one arm and one leg?
- Can you crawl through on your back using your arms and legs?

Shape Identification Game

You will need shapes of various sizes for this activity. Explain to children that each shape has a movement that goes with it. Practice the moves with each shape. Have children in a scatter formation. When you hold up a triangle, they can only move their heads. When you hold up a circle, they can move only their legs. For a square, they can move only their shoulders; for a rectangle, only their hips. For an oval, they move their entire bodies. Change shapes rapidly. This game is fun to play with some lively music, too!

Activities for Older Children (Grades 4–5)

Junk Mail

Catalogs can be used in fun lessons. Have students find two items that total $11.98; have them add up the cost of all the items on a particular page. Ask: "If you had $25 to spend for your friend's birthday, what would you select?" Have students figure shipping costs on a given item and sales tax on that item as well.

Junk Mail Collection

Have children collect all the junk mail that their families receive in a week. At the end of the week, have them count how many pieces of junk mail each family received. How much does it weigh? Have students calculate how much junk mail each family contributes to landfills each year. Have them estimate your school's contribution of junk mail.

Cafeteria Waste

For one week, have students throw their cafeteria food waste into a container that you weigh each day. Have them determine the average weight of food waste for the week. Each day, they can observe the type of food that is thrown away. Students might create a graph to display their results. Using the data they collect, they might determine the amount of food waste generated by all the classes at your school for 1 year.

Bubbling Math

Collect at least three brands of dishwashing liquid. First have students determine which brand produces the biggest bubble by blowing a straw into some solution poured onto a table. When the bubble pops, students should measure the diameter of the liquid left on the table by the burst bubble and record it. Students should conduct three trials per brand. They can then compute the average size of the bubbles. Students might also create bar graphs to compare the data they've collected.

Multiplication Activities

Memorizing the multiplication facts and understanding the concept of multiplication provide a necessary foundation for further math learning and can be particularly difficult for some students. The activities that follow help students develop this mathematical skill.

Multiplication Art

Have each student select five multiplication equations that are especially hard to remember. Then have students draw a picture of the equation and the answer. For example, a drawing for $5 \times 6 = 30$ might consist of a boy who is wearing a shirt with the number 5 on it standing in front of an apartment door with a 6 on it talking to a woman who is celebrating her thirtieth birthday with a cake that has 30 written on it.

Multiplication Building

For homework, have students choose two multiplication facts that are difficult for them. Then have them build three-dimensional creations that use those equations. For example, the equation $9 \times 6 = 54$ can be depicted by a model house with six rooms and nine objects in each room. Students should share their creations with the class without showing the equation. Students enjoy studying these models and figuring out the multiplication fact hidden within.

Multiplication Baseball

Divide the class into two teams and designate a first, second, third, and home base in the room. One group stands at the front of the room (home base) while the other group is seated. One student from Team A is "at bat," while one student from Team B "pitches" a multiplication problem. The pitcher must know the answer to their team's problem, or it's an automatic home run. After the problem is "pitched," the student at bat gives the answer and moves to first base. This continues until three students answer incorrectly, at which time, the teams trade places. To make the game more challenging, divide the multiplication problems into "singles" (easy), "doubles" (moderate), "triples" (difficult), and "home runs" (extremely difficult). Students at bat can choose which type of pitch they want. You can decide how many "innings" time will allow.

Musical Multiplication

Some students who naturally learn and store information through music will enjoy memorizing their multiplication facts through songs and jingles. Don't be surprised if you hear these students singing a multiplication fact during math time. Ask students to work in pairs to create their own multiplication jingle using one multiplication pattern ($5 \times 0, 5 \times 1, 5 \times 2$, and so on).

Multiplication Talk Show

Invite students to a multiplication talk show, where they'll participate as the guest audience and/or the featured speakers. The show is moderated by Mickey Multiplication, and the topic is "The Rough Life of a Multiplication Problem." Invite students to role-play multiplication problems after giving each number a personality. For example, Freddie Four may discuss how confused he gets when he has to play with Mr. Eight Snowman, and that the last time they played a game, he caught Mr. Snowman cheating 32 times!

Fractions and Multiple Intelligences

Some students experience a great deal of difficulty and frustration with the concept of fractions. Try some of these activities to reduce the fear of fractions and to help students understand what a fraction really is.

Fraction Order

Have students order the following fractions from largest to smallest: ¹⁄₁₀, ²⁄₈ , ³⁄₄, ¹⁄₁₅, ⁷⁄₈, and ⁵⁄₁₂. Underneath each fraction, have them draw a picture to represent it (logic, word, picture smart).

Fraction Story

Have students write a story about a fractional family. For example, the Fourth family has four members: ¹⁄₄, ²⁄₄, ³⁄₄, and ⁴⁄₄. Students should give each member of the family a unique personality relating to its fraction (word, logic smart).

Fraction Song

Invite students to make up a song to help themselves and others learn about fractions. They might want to use a familiar melody. Be sure the lyrics help students understand that fractions are used to break down a "whole" (music, word, logic smart).

Fraction P. E. Game

Have students redesign a game they already play to include fractions. For example, in softball, every time a player scores, his team could score ²⁄₃ of a point instead of one point (body smart).

The How-to Fraction Book

What problems do students have in learning fractions? They might write a how-to book to help their peers with one of these problems. Authors should include written explanations and tips from their own experience (logic, word, picture, people smart).

Fraction Skit

Have students write and perform a short skit that teaches how to reduce fractions. They may want to use props to show that certain fractions are equal even if they look different (word, person, logic smart).

Art and Math

Emphasize how artists use their knowledge of measurement and geometric shapes and forms in designing architecture, in planning beautifully proportioned vases, and in many other aspects of artistic expression.

Discuss radial balance. In radial balance, shapes and lines go out from a center. We see radial designs in many flowers and wheels. Have students collect and display examples of radial balance and radial designs in human-made and natural forms. Examples might be actual objects or photos cut from old magazines and newspapers. Examples of radial balance include starfish, wheels, snowflakes, many flowers, and the like. After students develop a display, teach them to use a compass and ruler to create precisely measured radial designs.

Shape Awareness

Discuss the difference between knowing that a shape is a circle cut from paper and the process of seeing the same shape from different angles or views. Demonstrate some of the positions from which a circle (cut from paper) can look like a wide ellipse, a narrow ellipse, and a straight line. Share art prints with students that show objects or people from different angles. Discuss how shapes are changed by angle of viewing. Encourage students to draw a familiar object from an unusual view to alter its shape and appearance.

Line Game

Every day when lining up for lunch or going to another class, have all students except the last in line stand facing forward with hands up, palms out. Give the last student a number-line problem such as "count by 3s from 6 to 30," which he or she would solve by tapping hands by 3s with the students in line. If the student does it correctly, that student is first in line the next day.

Activities Related to the Common Core State Standards for Mathematics

Grades K–2

Measurement and Data

Tell and write time using analog and digital clocks.

Bingo Time. Start by encouraging children's basic awareness of time. Set a timer for 5 minutes so children can feel how long it is. See how much they can accomplish in those 5 minutes. Then challenge them to see how much they can get done in 10, 15, and 20 minutes.

Geometry

Reason with shapes and their attributes.

Shapes in the Community. Have students make a community map using construction-paper shapes (triangle, circle, rectangle, square, and so on) to signify various landmarks. They can combine shapes to make local buildings. Then challenge them to create monsters made out of shapes and write (or dictate) stories about them.

Mathematical Practices

Make sense of problems and persevere in solving them.

Sizing Up the Glasses. Find two 16 oz. or larger clear drinking glasses, one tall and one short. Pour ½ cup of water into each glass. Ask the child: "Does the water reach the same height in each glass? Why or why not?" With a piece of masking tape or a waterproof marker, have the child make a mark on each glass to indicate his or her prediction of how high 1 cup of water will fill the glass. Have the child explain his or her thinking. Now pour the additional cup of water into the glass. How close was the prediction?

Measurement and Data

Solve problems involving measurement and estimation of liquid volume.

How Much Water? Have the child estimate how many bottle caps of water it will take to fill a cup. How many cups of water will fill a small cereal bowl? How can the child figure that out? Then have the child test his or her theory.

Measurement and Data

Solve problems involving measurement and estimation of liquid volume.

Water Waste. When you leave the water running while you brush your teeth, you waste approximately 5 gallons of water per minute. Have the children estimate how much water they use while brushing their teeth. If everyone in your class left the water on this morning while brushing their teeth, how many gallons of water did they use? Devise a campaign to encourage your students to reduce the amount of water they waste while brushing their teeth.

Measurement and Data

Tell and write time.

Race to 60. Count by ones, fives, and tens to the number 60. Then challenge your class to count to 60 in under a minute. Can they do it under 30 seconds? What about 15? Try counting to 60 in exactly a minute—give children the hint to add "one-thousand" between numbers, for example, "one one-thousand, two one-thousand, three one-thousand," and so on. Explain that time is based on the number 60: There are 60 seconds in a minute and 60 minutes in an hour.

Numbers and Operations

Understand the properties of operations to add and subtract.

Sound and Math: How Many Paper Clips? This activity is a math-and-sound experiment with a box of paper clips. Start with a small box of 50 clips and shake it. Be sure to mention to the students the number of clips in the box. Ask the children to describe the sound. Then ask them to remove 14 clips from the box. How many clips are now in the box? Have them shake the box and describe the sound again. Is it different than it was when the box had 50 clips? Continue the experiment, having children add and subtract clips from the box, giving the total number left and describing the sound.

Number and Operations in Base Ten

Understand the properties of operations to add and subtract.

Deal Me a Card! Divide students into groups of four. Each group will have a deck of playing cards. The dealer passes out seven cards to each student. (Face cards are worth 10, aces are 1, and the rest are face value.) Students make piles of cards that equal 10 (6 + 4, 9 + ace, 2 + 2 + 6, and so on). For every card they use as an addend, they get a new card. Then they repeat the process and see how many more piles they can make.

Numbers and Operations

Subtract.

Zero Game. Pass out a playing card to each student. Write "10 _ – _ =)" on the board. Ask a student with a face card or a 10 to come to the front of the room. He or she will be the beginning of the equation. Let them know that you want to get to zero using three cards. Ask another student to come to the front. Let's say that student has a 7. So far, the equation reads 10 – 7 _ = 0. Tell the students, "Raise your hand if you can finish this equation." All students with a 3 should be waving madly! Continue with other equations to zero.

Grades 3–5

Geometry

Reason with shapes and their attributes.

Using Geometric Shapes. Present the students with the following complex shapes: diamond, pentagon (five sides), trapezoid, hexagon, parallelogram, and octagon.

The student folds a sheet of paper into six equal boxes. Then, the student prints the name of a complex geometric shape at the bottom of each box. Next, distribute 12- × 18-inch black construction paper, 9- × 12-inch colored construction paper, scissors, glue, sketch paper, and pencils.

Using a pencil, students draw one complex geometric shape in each box. Ask the students how they could use these materials to make geometric shapes and fashion them into a design. Have them imagine and then sketch a design that includes these complex shapes. The children cut out the shapes from the colored construction paper and arrange them in their design on the black construction paper. They might want to use their scrap paper to design a frame or border for their design.

Numbers and Operations: Fractions

Develop an understanding of fractions as numbers.

Music and Color. Use music and color to help students understand fractions. Introduce students to whole notes, half notes, and quarter notes to reinforce the idea that a fraction is a part of a whole. Mixing colors with colored water also helps reinforce the concept of fractions. Ask the students, "How much blue and yellow do I need to make this shade of green?" Help your students figure out that a green composed of two parts blue and one part yellow is two-thirds blue and one-third yellow.

Operations and Algebraic Thinking

Represent and solve problems involving multiplication and division.

Biking to School. Present this scenario to your students: You want to bike to school, so you ask your mom for permission. She says, "If you make a strong argument with facts to convince me, I will let you ride your bike." Then tell them that you find out that your mom's car uses 1 gallon of gas a day total for the drive to and from school. If a gallon of gasoline costs $3.55, how much money is it costing your mom a week? A month? A year? Remember, she only takes you on school days. Prepare a presentation making a case for riding your bike instead of driving in a car. Be sure to include mathematical data in your argument.

Landfill Math. Present this scenario to your students: "Your town landfill is home to a large quantity of discarded plastic bottles. If each student in our class uses five water bottles per week, how many water bottles does our class use in a week? A month? A year? 10 years? 30 years? A lifetime (80 years)? If we were to recycle these water bottles instead of throwing them away, estimate how many trash cans full of water bottles you would save from going into the landfill in a week. A month, a year, 10 years, 30 years, and a lifetime. Explain how you determined your findings.

Operations and Algebraic Thinking

Represent and solve problems involving multiplication and division.

Where Does it Come from? Produce in U.S. grocery stores comes from around the world. When we buy locally grown produce, less energy is used to ship the food. Grapes may come from Chile or central California. Strawberries may come from Mexico or southern California. Corn may come from Iowa or Argentina. Apples may come from Washington State or China. Determine how many miles each product must travel from both locations to get to your hometown. Is it possible for some produce grown outside the country to be closer to your hometown than produce grown in this country? Explain.

Number and Operations: Fractions

Extend understanding of fraction equivalence and ordering.

Dominoes. Present this problem to your students: You and your friends want to play a game of dominoes. If you have a total of 24 dominoes to share among yourselves, how many tiles will each player have if everyone gets ¼ of the number of dominoes? How would your answers change if there were 16 dominoes and each player got ¼? Would the number of dominoes and players change if you started with 32 dominoes to share and each player got ¼?

Measurement and Data: Geometric Measurement

Understand concepts of area and relate area to multiplication and to addition.

Dream Home Design. Bring in real estate listings. Point out the square footage. Then show your students some home plans and blueprints. Have them design their own dream homes. Have them include the area of each room in their designs.

Numbers and Operations

Perform operations with multidigit whole numbers and with decimals to hundredths.

Shopping. Get out some sales flyers and tell your students that they're going shopping. Students tally up how much it would cost to buy a new outfit or to completely furnish their dream home. Calculating sales tax provides them with extra practice in multiplying and adding decimals.

Measurement and Data

Represent and interpret data.

Dripping Faucets. Turn on a faucet enough to drip. Place an empty gallon container under it. Have students time how long it takes the container to fill. Then, the children use this information to determine how many gallons of water are wasted each day the faucet is left dripping. How many gallons are wasted in a week? A month? A year? If a neighborhood has five leaky faucets, how many gallons are wasted in a year? The children then explain their solution.

References

Ansari, D., & Dhital, B. (2006). Age-related changes in the activation of the intraparietal sulcus during non-symbolic magnitude processing: An event-related functional magnetic resonance imaging study. *Journal of Cognitive Neuroscience, 18,* 1820–1828.

Bell, P., Lewenstein, B., Shouse, A., & Feder, M. (2009). *Learning science in informal environments: People, places and pursuits.* Washington, DC: Academies Press.

CCSSM. (2010). Key points in mathematics. Retrieved from http://www.corestandards.org/about-the-standards/key-points-in-mathematics.

Cantlon, J. F., Libertus, M. E., Dehaene, S., Brannon, E. M., & Pelphrey, K. A. (2008). The neural development of an abstract concept of number. *Journal of Cognitive Neuroscience, 21,* 2217–2229.

Charlesworth, R. (2011). *Experiences in math for young children.* (6th ed.). Boston, MA: Wadsworth.

Eisenhauer, J. J., & Feikes, D. (2009). Dolls, blocks, and puzzles: Playing with mathematical understandings. *Young Children, 64*(3), 18–25.

Geist, E. (2009). Infants and toddlers exploring mathematics. *Young Children, 64*(3), 39–41.

Geist, K., Geist, E. A., & Kuznik, K. (2012). The patterns of music: Young children learning mathematics through beat, rhythm, and melody. *Young Children, 67*(1), 74–79.

Hirsch, E. S. (Ed.). (2000). *The block book* (3rd ed.). Washington, DC: NAEYC.

Jordan, K. E., & Baker, J. (2011). Multisensory information boosts numerical matching abilities in young children. *Developmental Science, 14*(2), 205–213.

Linder, S., Powers-Costello, B., & Stegelin, D. (2011). Mathematics in early childhood: Research-based rationale and practical strategies. *Early Childhood Education Journal, 39*(1), 29–37.

National Council of Teachers of Mathematics (NCTM). (2000). *Principles and standards for school mathematics.* Reston, VA: Author. Retrieved from http://standards.nctm.org.

Roschelle, J., & Singleton, C. (2008). Graphing calculators: Enhancing math learning for all students. *International Handbook of Information Technology I Primary and Secondary Education, 20,* 951–959.

Sarama, J., & Clements, D. H. (2009). Building blocks and cognitive building blocks: Playing to know the world. *American Journal of Play, 1*(3), 313–337.

van Eimeren, L., Grabner, R. H., Koschutnig, K., Reishofer, G., Ebner, F., & Ansari, D. (2010). Structure-function relationships underlying calculation: A combined diffusion tensor imaging and fMRI study. *NeuroImage, 52,* 358–363.

Zentner, J., & Eerole, F. (2010). Rhythmic engagement with music in infancy. *Proceedings of the National Academy of Science, 107*(13), 578–73.

 Visit CourseMate for this textbook to access the eBook, Did You Get It? quizzes, Digital Downloads, TeachSource Videos, flashcards, and more. Go to CengageBrain.com to log in, register, or purchase access.

Creative Food Experiences

Children learn best when they experience the world firsthand—by touch, taste, smell, sight, and hearing. If you want to make the most of any food experience, children must be directly involved with real food and given as much responsibility as possible for growing, selecting, preparing, and eating the food.

Activities involving foods are included in most programs for young children. However, many of the food activities are under the complete direction of the teacher. Children sit and watch the teacher do the work. Sometimes children are given spoons and told to stir a mixture or are allowed to pour liquids from one container to another. Sometimes they are given the job of listening for a timer to "ding." Rarely is the child allowed to decide what foods to use, how to use them, and in what order or how long to mix ingredients.

Learning Objectives

After studying this chapter, you should be able to:

21-1 Explain why food experiences are important to the total program.

21-2 Describe the ways in which food activities develop children's skills.

21-3 Explain what curriculum areas are appropriate for creative food activities.

21-4 List the guidelines for creative food activities.

21-5 Discuss the problem of childhood obesity and ways to prevent or treat it.

naeyc
NAEYC Program Standard

5c Using their own knowledge, appropriate early learning standards, and other resources to design, implement, and evaluate meaningful, challenging curricula for each child.

DAP
DAP Criteria

2F2 To stimulate children's thinking and extend their learning, teachers pose problems, ask questions, and make comments and suggestions.

2F3 To extend the range of children's interests and the scope of their thought, teachers present novel experiences and introduce stimulating ideas, problems, experiences, or hypotheses.

21-1 Importance of Food Experiences to the Total Program

naeyc DAP The use of foods in a classroom can be one of the most creative parts of the program. Foods are a part of each child's experience. Foods and cooking are interesting to children. All of their senses are used in food activities. They see the foods. They smell them, touch them, and taste them. Children can hear many kinds of foods boiling, popping, or frying. Other learning is enhanced by food activities, too. Art, science, and aesthetics are all related to cooking. The following are some specific benefits of food activities in the early childhood curriculum.

21-1a Children Learn to Describe Things

Children experience many shapes, sizes, and colors of food. They see that some foods start out in a round shape and become long and flat during the cooking process. Many foods change in size when they are heated; some change in texture and color with mixing, heating, and cooling. In food-related activities, then, the child learns to name shapes, compare sizes, and identify and describe colors.

21-1b Children Learn About Tastes

Children find out how heating or mixing changes taste. They learn that some things, such as salt or sugar, can change the taste of foods. They discover that some foods taste good when they are mixed together and that others do not. They also learn that a change in the outward appearance of some foods does not mean that the foods taste any different. Apple juice has the same flavor as a whole apple. Frozen orange pops taste like orange juice and a frozen banana tastes just like banana ice cream.

21-1c Children Observe Changes

As they did in science activities, children observe that foods change from liquids to solids and from solids to liquids. They also see steam (a gas) rising from liquids that are heated. They smell odors as foods change from solids to liquids to gases. They see how ingredients, when mixed together, form a new substance. In baking, this same substance changes even more.

21-1d Children Learn to Express Themselves

Language skills develop as a result of food experiences. Words such as *bitter, sour, sweet,* and *salty* have real meaning. *Hot, cold, warm,* and *cool* are part of the food

vocabulary. Children may learn the words *delicious* and *tasty.* They learn a more complete meaning of terms such as *liquid* and *solid, freezing* and *boiling,* and *smelly* and *odorless.* When the words relate to direct experiences, the child's vocabulary grows.

21-1e Children Learn About Others

Food activities can be used throughout the curriculum to enhance children's learning. For example, a project on different breads from around the world can be used to teach about cultural diversity and the many types of bread individuals eat. A literature table can be set up to include children's books—both fiction and nonfiction—featuring bread themes. Children can make many types of breads from different cultures. Discussion can be held on how families and cultures use bread in celebrations and traditions. Children's literature provides many examples of how people in many different lands prepare and eat a wide variety of breads. Cooking activities can include making tortillas, wontons, waffles, fry bread, challah, hoecakes, bagels, pasta, hush puppies, latkes, and fortune cookies, to name just a few multicultural foods. Each of these foods can be used in connection with other projects to make a multicultural experience.

Did You Get It?

A group of preschool children take turns using a whisk to beat egg whites into foam. Which lesson are they likely to learn from this activity?

a. naming shapes
b. expressing oneself
c. comparing sizes
d. observing changes

Take the full quiz on CourseMate.

21-2 Food Activities and Skill Building

naeyc DAP Children can learn a number of skills from working with foods. These skills can be developed during other parts of the program also, but working with food is an excellent way to build skills in fun activities.

21-2a Small-Muscle Coordination

Mixing foods and pouring liquids from one container to another are ways in which children develop coordination (see Photo 21-1). The small muscles

PHOTO 21-1 Pouring liquid from one container to another is one way children develop coordination.

in the hands develop so that a child can hold a large spoon and help in the mixing process when using a recipe. The measuring, pouring, and mixing of foods all require the use of small muscles as well as hand–eye coordination. Thus, food activities provide excellent small-motor activities for young children.

21-2b Simple Measuring Skills

By using cups and spoons that have marks showing amounts, a child begins to understand measurements. The child is able to observe that a tablespoon is larger than a teaspoon and that a cup holds more than a tablespoon. The child can also begin to realize that if one uses too much flour, water, or salt, recipes don't turn out quite as well as when the correct amounts are used. The child begins to understand that the amount of each ingredient used makes a difference in the final product. This realization leads the child to look for ways to figure out amounts. This is when measuring tools are discovered. Older children can be challenged to make one-half of a recipe or double it. This gives them a real-life opportunity to practice multiplication, fractions, and division skills.

21-2c Social Skills

Food experiences are a natural avenue for social learning. Mixing, measuring, decorating, and eating all provide many opportunities for talking with others, exchanging ideas, sharing likes and dislikes, and learning about each other (see Photo 21-2). You will find that in preparing food, children many times will talk more freely about themselves and their lives in the homey, routine nature of this type of activity.

When cooking, a child may need help in holding a pan steady while pouring something into it. He or she may need help in carrying ingredients or finding certain foods. Children with special needs enjoy cooking activities as much as other children. By using some of the ideas presented in earlier chapters on adapting equipment and space, teachers can provide children with special needs the opportunity to enjoy cooking activities at their individual levels. One child may need an "expert" opinion on how much lemon to squeeze into a drink. These things call for working together. As children work together, social skills develop in the natural give-and-take of group experiences. Cooking activities provide children a chance to share information with each other about family recipes and food preferences. Learning about each other's cultural differences occurs naturally in cooking experiences.

21-2d Health and Safety

As children are involved in food experiences, they learn basic information about routines and cautions about food and cooking necessary to good health and safety. This information is best learned in the process of working with food and not in a lecture-type lesson.

For example, learning that cleanliness is important in all food preparation can be taught as children work with food. Both children and adults always wash their hands with soap and water before beginning and after ending any food experience (see Photo 21-3). Aprons or other cover-ups may also be necessary, especially if you are preparing foods that stain hands and fabrics easily.

PHOTO 21-2 Food experiences, such as measuring and mixing, are a natural avenue for social learning.

PHOTO 21-3 Children and adults should always wash their hands with soap and water before and after any food experiences.

© Cengage Learning 2015

Children may need encouragement to keep fingers and utensils out of their mouths while preparing food. If they do lick fingers or spoons, simply and calmly ask them to wash before proceeding. This is a good opportunity to teach children about germs and how they are transmitted. Tasting is also a good opportunity to help children learn about how foods taste at various stages of preparation and to observe changes in texture. However, no products containing raw eggs should be eaten before being fully cooked. Raw eggs are a source of salmonella bacteria and can cause digestive problems.

Any cooking adventure involving heat, sharp knives, or operating appliances should be carefully supervised. Sharp knives are rarely needed because plastic serrated knives will slice most produce items and are safe for even very young children. Children will need to be cautioned when observing food in the oven or on the range burner; utensil handles should be turned toward the center of the range at all times. Because electric burners don't always appear to be hot, children will need to learn how to identify when the burner is on by recognizing the position of the switch or by reading "on," "off," "high," and "low." Children must also be made aware that an electric burner remains hot for a while even after it has been turned off. All of these are

important health and safety lessons for young children in food experiences.

Finally, food allergies are very common among young children, and before planning any experience, you will need to know which children are allergic to specific foods. For example, in some schools, no products with peanuts are used because of children's allergies. Some children may have ethnic food restrictions that prohibit their eating certain foods. Every adult participating in food activities, whether teacher, cook, parent, or community volunteer, must have this information. If fresh produce is to be used, adults must know what parts of plants are poisonous. Children should learn that these parts and any other wild plant must never be eaten.

21-2e Activities for Toddlers and Two- and Three-Year-Old Children

Even though food preparation activities are included in the early childhood program for children 3 years and up, adults are often inclined to think that children under the age of 3 would just make a mess. For example, many cooks in early childhood centers do not want to be bothered, and of course young children underfoot in a kitchen increase the risk of accidents and injuries. An alternative is to bring the foods and the appropriate utensils for cooking activities to the children's room. The term *cooking activities* in this instance includes all the steps necessary in the preparation and serving of foods, with or without the use of heat.

The cooking-related activities that follow are listed in progressive order, from the simple to the more involved. Many toddlers and 2-year-olds are able to master many of these activities, and most 3-year-olds are capable of mastering them all.

- Exploring cooking utensils (banging, nesting, putting away)
- Exploring cooking utensils with water (cups, bowls, beaters, spoons, funnels)
- Pouring dry ingredients (corn, rice)
- Pouring wet ingredients (water)
- Tasting fresh fruit and vegetables
- Comparing tastes, textures, and colors of fresh fruits and vegetables
- Comparing tastes, textures, and colors of canned vegetables and fruits
- Dipping raw fruits and vegetables in dip or sauce
- Scrubbing vegetables with brushes
- Breaking or tearing lettuce, breaking or snapping beans, and shelling peas

- Stirring and mixing wet and dry ingredients
- Measuring wet and dry ingredients (using a rubber band to mark the desired amount on the container or measuring cup)
- Placing toppings on pizza or snacks and decorating cookies or crackers that have been spread
- Spreading on bread or crackers
- Pouring milk or juices to drink
- Shaking (making butter from cream or coloring sugar or coconut)
- Rolling with both hands (pieces of dough for cookies)
- Juicing with a hand juicer
- Peeling hard-cooked eggs and fruits
- Cutting with plastic knife (fruits, vegetables, cheese)
- Beating with a fork or egg beater
- Grinding with a hand grinder (apples or cranberries)
- Kneading bread dough
- Cleaning up

Did You Get It?

A kindergarten teacher gives her student a heavy mixing bowl full of batter, and asks him to pour the batter into a pan. What is the teacher most likely trying to develop in her student?

a. neatness skills

b. social skills

c. measuring skills

d. small-muscle coordination

Take the full quiz on CourseMate.

21-3 Creative Food Activities in Curriculum Areas

naeyc **DAP** Cooking does more than build physical, health and safety, and social skills. It is an ideal project for just about all of the curriculum areas. It involves reading, math, science, creative activities, opportunities for independent learning and following directions, and drawing and writing activities. Let's look briefly at these different areas.

21-3a Language Arts/Reading

Drawings with words and numbers can be used to help prekindergarten children understand a recipe. This is a good prereading activity in kindergarten or the primary grades. Older children can read the recipe, which itself is good practice. Many books, for both preschool- and elementary-age children, talk about food and cooking. Display some of these books in your library area for the children to look at. If you find a book that applies to a specific cooking experience, read it to the group before beginning to cook. In the language arts center, provide equipment for children to record their real and imaginary recipes, as well as paper and art materials for the recipes to be transcribed into books.

21-3b Math

For most recipes, measuring instruments—cups, tablespoons, and teaspoons—are required. Measuring cups in specific colors are helpful in cooking activities for young children. For example, the blue cup is ¼ cup, the green is ½ cup, the yellow is ⅓ cup, and the red is 1 cup. The same method can be used with different colors for each measuring spoon. It's also helpful and interesting to have a food scale for measuring. Sequencing (measuring, mixing, and then baking), estimating, counting, adding, working with fractions, and discriminating size and shape are all involved in cooking experiences. Discuss each of these objects and activities as you go along, working with small groups so everyone gets a turn. Children learn better when they do than when they merely look and listen.

Older children can handle measuring and mixing ingredients on their own. You can challenge their math skills by asking them to measure the ingredients for one-half of the recipe you're going to use. Or they can figure out how to double or triple the recipe for a larger group.

21-3c Science

Cooking develops sensory skills. It involves physical and chemical changes, the use of simple machines, and predicting the outcome of a cooking experiment. For example, when making cookies, place all the ingredients on the table and give everyone a chance to smell, touch, and taste each one. Then mix the ingredients with spoons, forks, or eggbeaters. Ask children about shape and texture as you mix. Ask them to predict the outcome of your cooking experience (see Photo 21-4). Then, after baking, have them compare their predictions with results.

Older children can suggest ways to alter the recipe to make it turn out in different ways. They enjoy experimenting with different spices to give their recipes a new and special flavor. It's fun to use spices from different cultural groups, too.

PHOTO 21-4 Ask children about shape and texture as they mix ingredients.

21-3d Science Center

Provide open-ended activities for cooking explorations. For instance, try a taste test of all the different ways apples are used in cooking and eating: juice, cider, sauce, butter, dried, and even apple cider vinegar. Or compare the appearance, taste, and texture of red, green, and yellow apples. You can also explore bananas. Brainstorm a list of how many different ways we can cook or eat them. What can you do with a frozen banana? Make ice cream! (Put chunks of frozen banana in a blender with just a hint of milk, blend until thick, and eat immediately.) How do bananas taste when they're sliced in circles? Try it and see. Try drying fruit and vegetables in the sun for tasty, healthful snacks (see recipes at chapter's end.)

21-3e Creative Activities

Almost all recipes can be extended, modified, changed, or given an unexpected twist. Use your imagination, and more important, get the children to use theirs! Use a soft pretzel recipe (recipe at end of chapter) to make animals or three-dimensional sculptures instead of the traditional pretzel shape. Add food coloring to the coating mixture (in the recipe) and paint your animals or sculptures before baking.

21-3f Drawing and Writing

Have the children dictate stories, anecdotes from home, and highlights of their experiences cooking in your classroom. Involve parents and other volunteers in this activity. Those children who want to can tell and draw about the day's cooking activity. Older children can keep personal journals of their cooking experiences. They may want to select certain favorite recipes and compile their own cookbooks.

21-3g Individual Cooking Activities in Interest Centers

Food activities can also be set up as interest centers in the early childhood program. Here is an example: It's John's turn to "cook" during free-choice activity time. First, he washes his hands; second, he puts on a white paper chef's hat; and third, he begins cutting fruit into bite-sized pieces with a plastic knife. He is following a picture recipe and will eventually put the fruit on a skewer to make a fruit kabob for his snack to be eaten later with his classmates. And, he made his snack all by himself! Independent snack preparation can easily be set up in the classroom with some basic equipment and recipes designed for individual portions. Ideas to help you set up individual cooking interest centers in your classroom and some recipe ideas follow.

Cut off one of the end flaps of a sturdy cardboard box and cut the box apart at the side seam so it will stand up using the other end flaps as supports. This will be your instruction "board." Cover the entire box with colorful contact paper. The box can be set up on a table to designate your snack and work area. Sequential picture recipes can be clipped to each section of the box/board. For example, the pictures in sequence would indicate to (1) wash hands, (2) cut fruit into pieces, (3) put fruit on skewer, and (4) place on paper plate with name on plate. Basic equipment for your snack activity center would include measuring cups, small bowls, tongue depressors, small wire whisks, five-ounce paper cups, *plastic* serrated knives, an electric skillet, blender, and paper chef's hats. ***An electric appliance should be operated by adults only***. (Figures 21-1, 21-2, and 21-3 provide sample picture recipes. Children should use only *plastic* serrated knives or have adults cut the fruit in the recipes.)

After you've designated your snack area and gathered your equipment, you're ready to begin with the recipes that follow. Before each child actually begins the snack preparation, gather the children in a group, tell them briefly about the recipe, and remind them of any specific directions. For example, a direction might be that each child may cut up only one slice of melon. While one or two children are working in the snack area, the teacher always needs to be available for assistance as children need it.

FIGURE 21-1 Picture recipe for applesauce (recipe at end of chapter).

Lettuce wrap-arounds. You'll need lettuce leaves, any combination of luncheon meats or cheese slices, and spreads such as cream cheese, peanut butter, or egg salad

What to do:

1. Lay lettuce leaf flat on cutting board.
2. Place meat and/or cheese slice on lettuce leaf.
3. Add a spread or other filler and roll up the combination, securing it with a toothpick.
4. These may be eaten rolled up or cut into bite-sized pieces with a serrated knife.

Banana shake bag. You'll need ¼ cup chopped peanuts, 1 banana

What to do:

1. After peeling a banana, cut it into 1-inch chunks.
2. Place peanuts in a plastic baggie.
3. Put a few banana chunks at a time in the bag and shake.
4. Serve bananas on paper plates.

Pineapple mix-up. You'll need ¼ cup plus 1 tablespoon instant nonfat dry milk; ½ cup pineapple juice, chilled; ½ cup cracked ice

What to do:

1. For cracked ice, wrap some ice cubes in a towel and pound with a hammer.
2. Combine all ingredients in a blender and blend on high 30 seconds until thick and foamy.

Watch the food disappear at snack time because children love these activities. Don't forget the paper chef's hats (available at a party store), or you can make your own hats! The hats make children feel like "professional" chefs.

FIGURE 21-2 Picture recipe for banana apple icy (recipe at end of chapter).

1.

2.

3.

4.

© Cengage Learning

FIGURE 21-3 Picture recipe for apple sandwiches (recipe at end of chapter).

21-4 Guidelines for Creative Food Activities

 The following are some guidelines to use to ensure that food experiences for young children are planned to enhance their creativity.

- Activities should be open ended. If all children must follow the same directions at the same time, they will not have a chance to be creative. In fact, just the opposite will happen: children will conform and do what the teacher tells them to do. Teachers who want to help children be creative must let them create their own directions and work at their own pace.

- Activities should be challenging but not too difficult for children. If food activities are too hard, children will give up. If they are too easy, children will not be challenged. It is important to start with easy things. It is also important to increase the possibilities so children will do more challenging things as they go on.

- Activities should be varied. Children get bored if they do the same thing day after day. Variety is needed. Children should work with foods they know. They should also work with new foods they have not seen or tasted before. Some activities should be very short. Others should take a longer time to finish. In some activities, children may use just one type of food. In others, they may mix in several ingredients.

- The process is more important than the product. Emphasis should not be placed on what the children create but on how they have created it. If only the final product is considered, then many children will fail. Things do not always taste good—especially when children create new recipes. But if children are rewarded for the way they create, then what they have created does not seem so important.

- Inexpensive materials and small amounts should be used. No child should feel bad if a recipe does not work. If ingredients are inexpensive, there is less chance that children will feel discouraged because something they made did not taste very good.

- Activities should be carried out in a variety of places. Food activities do not have to be limited to the indoors. They can also be done outside the classroom. They work well on the school grounds or in a nearby woods. Note: An important restriction for outdoor cooking is that the teacher should inspect all food before it is used. Poison mushrooms and berries are sometimes gathered by children. These foods must be avoided.

- Be sure to plan activities for the children who are waiting to participate in the food activity. Also, be sure that these are also high-interest activities, so that children will be just as interested in these "waiting" activities as they are for the food activity. For example, this would be a good time to break out a few new puzzles, books, or computer games for children to enjoy while they are waiting.

Caveman Cereal

Early humans survived on a diet of meat, fruits, vegetables, nuts, and the occasional tuber. Up until recently, most scientists thought cereals came later, approximately 20,000 years ago. But a study published in the *Journal of Human Evolution* hints that wild cereals were part of the human diet more than 100,000 years ago (Mercader et al., 2009).

Making cereals palatable is hard work. They have to be roasted in a fire or pounded into flour and cooked. Because the process is energy-intensive and requires specialized tools, many archeologists assumed that humans didn't begin consuming mass quantities of cereal until the advent of farming approximately 10,000 years ago.

Then, Mercader and colleagues excavated a cave in Mozambique called *Ngalue*. They uncovered an assortment of stone tools in a layer of sediment deposited on the cave floor 42,000 to 105,000 years ago. Mercader presumes that the ones buried deepest in the layer are at least 100,000 years old. Other researchers had identified tubers as an important food source during the Stone Age, so Mercader decided to check for starch residue on 70 stone tools from the cave, including scrapers, grinders, points, flakes, and drills. Approximately 80% of the tools had ample starchy residue. The vast majority of the residue came from sorghum, a grass that is still a dietary staple in many parts of Africa.

According to Mercader, the findings suggest that people living in Ngalue routinely brought starchy plants, including sorghum, to their cave. Thus, it seems like our Middle Stone Age ancestors enjoyed cereal much like we do today!

21-4a Getting Started: Planning

Careful planning is crucial to successful food experiences. All ingredients (in sufficient quantities) need to be purchased, utensils assembled, and objectives for the activity established.

Children's abilities should be matched to the food experience so that the adult does not carry out the preparation while the children watch. Depending on the complexity of the recipe, the number of children, whether children with special needs are part of the group, and the time available, it may at times be necessary for the adult to complete some tasks or to use prepared foods. Keep in mind, however, that the more the adult does, the less children learn. The extra time children take learning is well spent.

Objectives for the children's learning will help focus the activity for the adults involved. Do you want children to successfully cut celery into finger-sized strips? Is your objective to have children sample a variety of food textures and discuss the differences? Will children try less-familiar foods? Is your goal to facilitate cooperative work in a small group?

Common goals for food experiences for young children include strengthening their manipulative skills, expanding their knowledge about nutrition, and trying new foods. You will want to develop your own objectives for each recipe you choose based on your knowledge about the children in the group.

Goals for very young or inexperienced children will be different from those for more advanced food preparers. Initially, try to plan food preparation activities that involve only one or two skills and a limited number of ingredients. Squeezing orange juice involves one ingredient and two skills: squeezing and pouring. Washing vegetables or fruits (in a basin to conserve water, rather than under running water) and possibly then cutting them into convenient pieces is also a good beginning activity. For children who are just becoming competent in balancing, pouring, or cutting, these tasks are a real challenge. The following list will help you prepare for successful food experiences.

- Work out ahead of time a sequence of steps for the activity.
- Plan a series of activities that are gradually more complex.
- Encourage children to talk about what they are doing.
- Relate the activity to home experiences.
- Give the names for new foods, processes, and equipment used.
- When appropriate, involve children in getting supplies for the activities.
- Encourage discussion of what has been done. Allow a good amount of time for tasting and touching.
- Use follow-up activities to reinforce the learning. (See Figure 21-4.)

THIS ONE'S FOR YOU!

Teaching Culture Through Foods

Beginning in November in many schools, food becomes a special part of daily life. It's the main ingredient in family gatherings and holiday and cultural celebrations. Using food as the basis, children can learn a great deal about how different families prepare and enjoy a variety of food. In the process, they will be learning about each other in a natural, nonstereotypical way.

Here are some suggestions for how to use food as a way to help young children learn about each other's cultures.

● Invite children to share what they know about the way food is a part of their family celebrations. Simply asking, "How does your family prepare foods for celebrations?" will start the ball rolling. You can also ask, "Who prepares the food?" or "What foods does your family make and eat that you don't see at your friends' houses?" Note children's suggestions on a large sheet of paper, comparing similarities and differences.

● This dialogue about food can then lead to investigative questions. Write children's responses to questions like these: What do you know about cooking? What would

you like to find out about cooking? What would you like to learn how to cook?

● Based on children's answers to these questions, you can develop your next steps into learning about each other through cooking. Remember to include children in devising a plan for how to explore answers to their questions and how they want to learn about cooking.

● Invite families and friends to share their favorite cultural celebration food with the class. Be sure adults let children participate in the preparation. Encourage children to ask questions and taste new things.

● A culminating event might be a major project such as a class-created Cultural Foods Smorgasbord to share with families, or a less-demanding project such as writing and illustrating a class cookbook. You might even decide to have a multicultural bake sale and give the money earned to a charity of the children's choice. Food is a natural favorite of children. Learning about each other through preparation and enjoyment of food together is natural, fun, and delicious!

Using Food in Science Activities

- Plant an outdoor or indoor garden.
- Have a tasting party.
- Arrange unusual foods on a science table.
- Place carrot, beet, or pineapple tops in a shallow bowl of crushed stones or pebbles covered with water. Allow them to sprout.
- Cut off the top third of a sweet potato and put it part way in water; allow sprouts to vine at the top.
- Examine a coconut, then break it open.
- Examine and cut a fresh pineapple.
- Taste baby foods.
- Place seed catalogs on the reading shelf.
- Make a food dictionary.
- Draw pictures of favorite foods from each food group; make a meal; draw a picture of a plate and cup and fill them with foods to make a nutritious meal. Make sure to label each food.

Creative Art Activities with Food

- fruit-colored play dough
- broken eggshells on paintings

FIGURE 21-4 Follow-up activities to reinforce learning.   (*Continues*)

- child-made food books:
  - Foods I Like
  - Fruits I Like
  - Foods My Daddy (or Mommy, Sister, etc.) Likes
- class mural made of pictures of foods
- foods cut from flannel to arrange on a flannel or story board
- food pictures cut from newspaper or magazine advertisements to paste on colored paper
- paste pictures of foods on a chart with areas for fruits and vegetables, breads, milk, and meats
- make picture charts of favorite recipes

Table Activities—Food Experiences

- sewing cards with food pictures
- dishpans of beans with funnels, measuring cups
- food scale with beans for weighing
- balance for weighing

Field Trips—Food Experiences

- grocery store
- vegetable garden
- fruit orchard
- school kitchen
- bakery
- restaurant
- pizza restaurant
- ice cream store
- fruit and vegetable stand
- bottling company
- dairy
- canning factory
- hatchery
- cornfield, strawberry, or melon patch
- home kitchen

Games for Cooking Experiences

- Can You Remember? (Display foods on a tray; cover. Have children try to remember where each is.)
- How Many? (Arrange different foods on a tray. Have children count items.)
- Which? (Have children identify foods that can be eaten raw, foods that are yellow, etc.)
- Grouping (Have students identify those that are yellow, those that are eaten for breakfast, etc.)
- Touch and Tell (Place food in a bag; have child feel and try to identify.)
- Smell and Tell (Have child close eyes and try to identify food by smelling.)
- Guess What? (Have children describe the characteristics of food; children try to identify items.)

FIGURE 21-4 Follow-up activities to reinforce learning. (*Continued*)

Did You Get It?

A first grade teacher presents a lesson on deviled eggs. The children have to carefully remove the yolk from the hard boiled eggs that they have sliced open, mash the yolk with mayonnaise, and spoon the mixture into the indentation in the white part of the egg. Developmentally speaking, this activity

a. is appropriate, as the children will learn several new techniques simultaneously.

b. is appropriate, as the children work cooperatively together.

c. is inappropriate, because the children will probably find it too difficult and give up.

d. is inappropriate, as most first graders are likely to be allergic to eggs.

Take the full quiz on CourseMate.

21-5 Childhood Obesity

The biggest risk to young children's health is both less dramatic and more sinister than the stuff of nightly news headlines. It is one that happens incrementally as children move through early childhood into elementary school and beyond—obesity.

Overweight and obesity in children is epidemic in North America and internationally. Approximately 22 million children under 5 years of age are overweight across the world (CDC, 2012). In 2008, more than one-third of children and adolescents were overweight or obese. In the United States, the number of overweight children and adolescents has tripled in the past three decades, and similar doubling rates are being observed worldwide, including in developing countries and regions where an increase in Westernization of behavioral and dietary lifestyles is evident. The percentage of children aged 6–11 years in the United States who were obese increased from 7% in 1980 to nearly 20% in 2008. Similarly, the percentage of adolescents aged 12–19 years who were obese increased from 5% to 18% over the same period (National Center for Health Statistics, 2011).

Today, nearly one in three children in America are overweight or obese, which may lead one-third of all children born in 2000 or later to suffer from diabetes at some point in their lives (Let's Move, 2011).

With obesity the problem that it is today, this generation of American children could be the first in the history of the United States to live less healthful and shorter lives than their parents (National Center for Health Statistics, 2011).

21-5a Preventing Obesity: Empty Calories

Nutritionists and pediatricians concur that infantile and childhood obesity should be prevented. Not all overweight children are destined to become overweight adults. Conversely, not all overweight adults were overweight children. Obesity is considered the number one health risk for children in the United States.

The best plan to prevent obesity in children is to balance their caloric intake with the number of calories they expend through exercise. Children who are overweight may also have a tendency to overeat, so they may need to reduce their consumption of empty calories as well as the size of their portions.

Another way to reduce obesity is to limit empty calories—foods high in fat or sugar but low in protein, vitamins, and/or minerals. Sugar is not the only source of empty calories. High-fat and/or high-salt snacks should also be eliminated. Good choices then for snacks and meals will include vegetables, fruits, and protein-rich items.

Because young children have a limited capacity for food intake and because, for many, 22% of their caloric intake comes from snacks, it is important that empty calories be avoided. Snacks, as well as meals, must center on foods that contribute to children's need for a balanced diet.

21-5b How to Limit Children's Sugar Intake

There are four primary ways to limit children's sugar intake: (1) avoid providing obvious sources of high-sugar foods, (2) avoid giving them "hidden" sugars, (3) find alternative sources of sweetness or reduce the amount of sugar in food choices, and (4) find other ways to celebrate special events without serving foods high in sugar.

Avoid high-sugar foods. The term *sugar* is generally used to refer to sucrose, which is refined sugar from sugar cane or beets. The most common form of sucrose is white, granulated table sugar. This type of sugar is an ingredient in cakes, cookies, doughnuts, pies, candy, and soft drinks. One obvious way to reduce sugar intake is to reduce the intake of these types of foods. Another method is to use one-half or less of the sugar called for in a recipe.

Other common forms of sugar are fructose, dextrose, lactose, and maltose. Read the list of ingredients on prepared foods and watch for words ending with *-ose*, which indicates that some form of sugar

The Wonderful Banana

You may never look at a banana in the same way again after reading about the many health benefits of this common fruit. Bananas contain three natural sugars: sucrose, fructose, and glucose combined with fiber. A banana gives an instant, sustained, and substantial boost of energy. Research has proven that just two bananas provide enough energy for a strenuous 90-minute workout (Seebohar, 2011). No wonder the banana is the number one fruit with the world's leading athletes. But energy isn't the only way a banana can help us keep fit.

Bananas can also provide brain power. Two hundred students at a school in England were helped through their exams by eating bananas at breakfast, break, and lunch in a bid to boost their brain power. Research has shown that the potassium-packed fruit can assist learning by making pupils more alert (Kumar et al., 2012). Bananas can also help overcome or prevent a substantial number of illnesses and conditions, such as the following:

- **Depression.** According to a recent survey among people suffering from depression, many felt much better after eating a banana. This is because bananas contain tryptophan, a type of protein that the body converts into serotonin, known to make you relax, improve your mood, and generally make you feel happier (Kumar et al., 2012).

- **Mosquito bites.** Before reaching for the insect bite cream, try rubbing the affected area with the inside of a banana skin. Many people find it amazingly successful at reducing swelling and irritation.

- **Stress.** Potassium is a vital mineral, which helps normalize the heartbeat, sends oxygen to the brain, and regulates your body's water balance. When we are stressed, our metabolic rate rises, thereby reducing out potassium levels. These can be rebalanced with the help of a high-potassium banana snack. (Crout, 1999).

- **Body temperature.** Many other cultures see bananas as a "cooling" fruit that can lower both the physical and emotional temperature of expectant mothers. In Thailand, for example, pregnant women eat bananas to ensure their baby is born with a cool temperature. (Thakorial, et. al. 2010).

- **Overweight and pressure at work.** Studies at the Institute of Psychology in Austria found pressure at work leads to gorging on comfort food such as chocolate and chips. Looking at 5,000 hospital patients, researchers found the most obese were more likely to be in high-pressure jobs. The report concluded that to avoid panic-induced food cravings, we need to control our blood sugar levels by snacking on high carbohydrate foods (such as bananas) every two hours to keep levels steady (Hoge, 2009).

So, a banana can be a natural remedy for many ills. When you compare it to an apple, it has four times the protein, twice the carbohydrate, three times the phosphorus, and five times the vitamin A and iron. When you think about it, maybe we should be saying "A banana a day keeps the doctor away."

---

is present. These different forms of sugar have varying degrees of sweetness. For example, lactose (milk sugar) is the least sweet per unit. Fructose is nearly twice as sweet as sucrose, and invert sugar is about 30% sweeter than sucrose. All, however, provide basically empty calories.

Avoid hidden sugars. Most parents and teachers are aware that foods such as candy, cake, and soft drinks contain sugar and are low in nutritional value. Very few people are aware, however, that sugar is also present in catsup, peanut butter, luncheon meats, hot dogs, pork and beans, nondairy creamer, fruit-flavored yogurt, and canned vegetables. Although these foods do contain nutrients, the addition of sugar is usually unnecessary. Use foods that contain no sugar.

Find alternative sources of sweetness. Snacks and desserts of unsweetened foods can be emphasized at home and school. Examples include unsalted popcorn, cheese, vegetables with dip, and no-sugar-added peanut butter on apples and celery.

Fresh fruits and vegetables should be given priority. When you must use canned fruits, look for fruits canned in their own juices or in the juices of other fruits. If fresh or water-packed fruits are not available, rinse fruits canned in heavy syrup with water before serving.

21-5c Activity and Obesity

Although genetics and sugar intake play a role in obesity, they alone cannot account for the huge increase in obesity rates over the past few decades.

Eating too much and moving around too little are two other major causes of obesity. Most experts agree that watching excessive amounts of television is a significant risk factor associated with obesity; almost half of children ages 8 to 16 years watch four to five hours of television daily (CDC, 2012). Children who are the most overweight watch the most television and eat too many snacks with a high fat content (CDC, 2012). Television viewing, playing video games, and surfing the Internet often take the place of physical activity for many children. The trancelike state associated with these activities can slow children's metabolism so much that they resemble children at complete rest (Ogden et al., 2010).

21-5d Recommendations to Reduce the Risk of Obesity

The American Academy of Family Physicians offers the following tips on preventing childhood obesity:

Respect the child's appetite: Children do not need to finish every drink or clean off their plates.
Avoid prepared and sugared foods when possible.
Keep a limited amount of high-calorie foods at home.
Provide healthful meals, with 30% or fewer of the calories derived from fat.
Provide ample fiber in the child's diet.
Replace whole milk with skim milk when the child is 2 years of age.
Do not provide food for comfort or as a reward.
Do not offer sweets in exchange for a finished meal.
Limit television viewing.
Encourage active play.
Establish regular family activities such as walks, ball games, and other outdoor activities. (AAFP, 2012)

21-5e Improving Young Children's Diets

There are some very basic steps to take in order to improve a child's diet. Here are some general suggestions to accomplish this:

Serve whole organic foods that are free from artificial additives, colors, and preservatives. (See Figure 21-5 for more information on organic foods.)
Give children whole grains, eggs, seafood, and some dairy products.

● Eliminate canned fruits and vegetables, foods coated in sugar and syrup, and processed meats and cheeses.
● Encourage children to eat raw foods such as vegetables and fruits, which contain higher amounts of vitamins and minerals than cooked foods.
● Use whole-wheat or soy flour to completely or partially replace white flour in recipes.
● Use ground-up raisins, dates, or other dried fruit instead of sugar.
● Go to the USDA's ChooseMyPlate.gov website to get the latest version of the USDA's food guide based on the child's age, height, and weight.

Some more specific suggestions concerning fruit in young children's diets are listed here:

● Some fruits, especially dried fruits, berries, and solid fruits such as pears, are good sources of fiber. Offer children wedges of seedless oranges and apples. These fruits have fiber that's lost when they're made into juice.
● Generally, the more color a fruit (or vegetable) has, the more vitamins and minerals it contains.
● Avoid giving toddlers fruits with seeds. Pay special attention as toddlers eat dried or frozen fruits, and cut firm fruits to be sure they don't choke on the hard bits.
● Bananas and avocados are favorites of young children because the fruits' textures are appealing. Both are rich in potassium and other minerals.
● Products marked "juice" must contain 100% juice. "Drinks," "ades," "punches," "fruit cocktails," and other beverages may be little more than fruit-flavored sugar water.
● Giving a child juice made from concentrate is a good way to provide fluoride if your water supply is not fluoridated.

Encourage plain water for thirst. Juice is a food, and children will fill up on it and not eat other foods. The following are the American Academy of Pediatrics recommendations on offering children juice per day:

● Do not give fruit juice to infants younger than 6 months because it offers no nutritional benefit at this age.
● For children 1 to 6 years, limit juice to 4 to 6 ounces per day. For children older than 6 months, fruit juice offers no nutritional

Even if you read the labels on food and signs advertising produce, you still may be misled by the various word "plays" that apply to each of the terms *organic* and *natural*. Here is some information to help you make these distinctions.

Organic
What it *means*: Items that are **"100% organic"** are certified to have been produced using only methods thought to be good for the earth. Organic food must be grown without the use of pesticides, synthetic fertilizers, sewage sludge, genetically modified organisms, or ionizing radiation. Animals used to produce meat, poultry, eggs, and dairy products cannot be given antibiotics or growth hormones.

Items that bear the *USDA* **organic** label means that the item contains at least 95% organic ingredients. Products with at least 70% organic content can be labeled *made with organic ingredients.*

Health implications: Research has yet to show that organic foods are nutritionally superior, but they are made without potentially harmful pesticides, fertilizers, antibiotics, synthetic hormones, or genetic engineering.

Remember: Organic foods can cost up to 50% more than nonorganic products. If that cost is prohibitive to you, it's better to eat healthful choices, like fruits and vegetables that are conventionally grown, rather than skipping them.

Bottom line: Going organic never hurts, especially when it comes to avoiding pesticides, which are linked to several health issues. Produce most affected by pesticides includes peaches, apples, sweet bell peppers, nectarines, strawberries, cherries, lettuce, pears, spinach, and potatoes.

Nonorganic produce lowest in pesticides are onions, avocado, sweet corn (frozen), pineapples, mango, sweet peas, asparagus, kiwi, bananas, cabbage, broccoli, and eggplant.

100% Natural
What it means: These products typically don't contain artificial colors, flavors, or preservatives and have no synthetic ingredients. But because **natural products** are not regulated, the term has little meaning beyond its descriptive value. The ingredients on the label may look similar to those found in organic foods, but they have not necessarily been produced organically.

Health implications: As with organic foods, there is no research to prove that natural products are better for you. Most food additives, while not sounding healthy, haven't been shown to be bad for you.

Remember: Just because something is natural does not mean it's good for you. It can still have loads of sugar, fat, or calories. The soft drink 7-Up, for example, was once marketed as "100 percent natural." The label now says, "100 percent natural flavors."

Bottom line: Always check the ingredient list and nutrition-facts panel to see what's really in an item. A healthy choice will be relatively low in sugar and saturated fat, and you won't need a chemistry degree to decipher the label. For more information, visit www.foodnews.org.

FIGURE 21-5 Reading labels: Organic and natural products.

© Cengage Learning

benefits over whole fruits. Do not allow children of this age to carry a cup or box of juice throughout the day. For children 7 to 18 years of age, limit juice to 8 to 12 ounces per day (AAP, 2012).

Whole fruits also provide fiber and other nutrients. Leave that paring knife in the drawer and keep the skin of certain fruits and vegetables—such as apples, cucumbers, and baked potatoes—you could be shaving off

valuable nutrients. Temperate fruit varieties (including apples, pears, peaches, and berries) have lots of fiber, vitamins, and antioxidants. Tropical fruits (bananas, papayas, mangos) are relatively higher in calories and lower in fiber, so serve them in moderation.

21-5f Snacks and Obesity

It's hard for young children to go for long periods of time without feeling hungry. This is because their

PHOTO 21-5 Children's stomachs are small and can't hold much food at one sitting, so they need nutritious snacks during the day.

© Cengage Learning 2015

stomachs are small and can't hold much food at one sitting. Small meals or snacks can help appease the hungry child (see Photo 21-5). When snacks are chosen from a wide variety of nutritious foods, they can contribute important nutrients to the child's diet.

Today, it's easy to have a poor diet, partly because of all the foods we have to choose from. Making wise choices regarding the food we offer young children in snacks can help prevent obesity. The selection of snacks we offer young children should be based on more than taste and appearance. Nutritional value related to calories is an important indication of whether you're getting real food values in snacks and helping keep children from becoming too heavy. Consider the following guidelines when choosing snacks:

- Judge the actual nutritional contribution the snack makes to the child's diet. A nutritious snack should supply nutrients such as vitamins, calcium, and iron.
- Plan snacks around regular meal schedules. Snacks need not and should not interfere with or dull the child's appetite.
- Consider the number of calories a snack provides in the daily total. Snack foods should not be high in sugar or fat. Children enjoy sweet foods, but too much sugar can cause cavities. Too many foods high in sugar and fat can help cause children to become overweight. Try to set limits on the amount of sweet and fatty foods eaten.

- Make the snack easy to obtain. Snacks prepared ahead of time for children can provide important nutrients while being a neat treat.
- Choose foods that appeal in taste and appearance. If the snack does not look good, it is likely not going to be eaten.

See the end of this chapter for nutritious snack ideas.

▶❙❙ **TeachSource Video**

School Age: Cooking Activities

1. How would you explain to the children the reason for the eggs fluffing up? Do you consider this teacher's answer sufficient? Why or why not?

2. Using the information in your text on the steps involved in planning for cooking activities, evaluate this teacher's lesson. What specific changes would you make and why?

3. Describe a follow-up activity to this cooking activity based on the information provided in your text.

Watch on CourseMate.

Did You Get It?

In a third-grade class, one third of the students are overweight. The proportion of overweight children in this class

  a. is consistent with the average number of overweight children in the U.S.

  b. suggests that the students have an unusual propensity to be overweight.

  c. is consistent with the average seventh-grade class in the U.S.

  d. suggests that the students live in a region of the country where more children have a propensity toward obesity.

Take the full quiz on CourseMate.

Summary

21-1 Explain why food experiences are important in the total program.

Foods can be used in activities that help children become more creative in their approach to the world as they learn new information and skills. They develop knowledge about names of shapes and colors; tastes; changes in shape, size, color, and taste; and new words. They learn to describe things, learn about tastes, observe changes, and learn to express themselves.

21-2 Describe the ways in which food activities develop children's skills.

Food activities also help young children develop skills in hand–eye and small-muscle coordination, simple measuring, and socialization.

21-3 Explain what curriculum areas are appropriate for creative food activities.

Food activities are appropriate in the language arts/reading area, the science center, art activities, and in the writing center.

21-4 List the guidelines for creative food activities.

In order to ensure that food experiences for young children are planned to enhance their creativity, they must include the following basic guidelines: (1) be open ended; (2) be challenging but not too hard for 3- to 5-year-olds; (3) be varied, giving children choices; (4) emphasize the doing, not the end product; (5) involve inexpensive materials; and (6) not be dangerous to children.

21-5 Discuss the problem of childhood obesity and ways to prevent or treat it.

Adults responsible for the diets of young children must limit sugar consumption by avoiding obvious sources of sucrose and hidden sugars. Using natural sources of sweetness, reducing the focus on sweets, and finding other types of sweets for young children are all essential ways to reduce sugar in children's diets. Paying attention to the types of snacks and amount of juice given each child are others factors in planning a diet lower in sugar. Childhood obesity has become a major health problem in the United States. Some causes of childhood obesity are genetic, but sugar intake and lack of physical activity play large roles.

Key Terms

100% organic 515	Natural products 515	Organic 515

Learning Activities

A. Try testing the sense of taste of some fellow students by making "creative juice."
 1. Materials and ingredients: blender, common vegetables (cucumber, carrots, tomatoes, cabbage, celery, green pepper, parsley), salt, sugar, lemon juice.
 2. Begin with any two vegetables. Add one-half cup of cold water or crushed ice and blend. A pinch of salt and sugar and a small amount of lemon juice will improve the flavor. Taste a small amount.
 3. Add a third vegetable to the mixture. Taste. Keep track of the vegetables and amounts used. Continue to add vegetables, one at a time. Make the following.
  a. A tasty vegetable juice
  b. A juice whose vegetables no one can identify

B. Observe a group of children experiencing a type of food for the first time—perhaps eggplant, squash, or rutabaga!
 1. What kinds of expressions do they make when they taste the food?
 2. How do they react when they find out what the food was that they tasted?
 3. What can be said to make a child more willing to taste new foods?

C. Experiment with the sense of taste. Each person who tastes a food in this experiment must wear a blindfold or cover his or her eyes. Use small slices of baking apples or potatoes and a freshly sliced onion or garlic. Hold the onion under the blindfolded person's nose. Slip a small piece of apple or potato into the person's mouth. Have the person chew up the food and tell what it was.

D. With a group of children, try out at least one of the food experiences listed in this chapter. Evaluate the experience. Would you use this recipe again? Would you organize the experience in the same way next time? If not, what changes would you make?

E. Develop your own food-related activities. Develop an integrated unit on food for an elementary grade level. Share this unit with your fellow classmates for their input.

F. Keep a food diary for at least one week. Summarize your findings on your eating habits. Compare your eating habits with the recommended food at ChooseMyPlate.gov in your summary.

G. Observe a child eating lunch or dinner. What foods does the child eat? What foods are refused? Based on your observation, do you think the child is developing healthy eating habits? If there is an adult present, observe the adult's eating practices. Do you think the adult exhibits healthy eating habits? Do the adult's food likes and dislikes have any influence on what the child eats?

H. Review a menu from a child-care center. Are a variety of foods served to children? Are meals and snacks offered at times when children are likely to be hungry? Does the staff encourage children to try different foods?

I. Interview three preschool teachers. Find out what types of allergies they encounter most often and how they manage these issues in the classroom. Develop a simple 5-day snack menu for a child who is allergic to milk and milk products, chocolate, and eggs.

Activities for Children

Curriculum Ideas

Math—apple fishing game. Tie three feet of string to a wooden spoon. Attach a magnet to the end of the string. Cut and laminate many different colored and sized apples from construction paper. Attach a paper clip to each apple. Spread the apple shapes on the floor and let children try to catch the apples. Have them try to catch the red apple . . . or the biggest apple. For a twist, label the apples with letters or numbers. Have children catch a specific apple or have them identify which apple they caught.

Social studies. A trip to a local restaurant, pizzeria, or bakery can provide children with a wonderful opportunity to learn about how a favorite food is prepared. Invite children to prepare a list of questions they would like to ask during their visit. Consider taking along a portable tape recorder and camera to record the steps of the recipe the children are learning about. Children can then make the recipe at school. They can write a story about their experiences using the photos as their inspiration.

Pretend play. Wash empty yogurt containers/lids and frozen juice containers and place them in the dramatic play area. Provide children with plastic spoons, bowls, and plastic fruit or small, colored blocks to represent the fruits. Encourage children to use the snack props as they incorporate dolls and their classmates in dramatic play.

Math. Have children wash their hands. Then give them a bowl filled with crackers in a variety of shapes: goldfish, oyster, square, and oval. Place paper plates for each type of cracker on the table. Have children work together to sort the crackers onto each plate. Afterward children can pass the plates around and choose crackers to eat with their soup.

After a food activity, make a bar graph that lists all the recipes you've used in your class. Indicate the names of the children who liked each one. Which recipe did most children prefer? Which recipe was least preferred? Brainstorm with children how they might change the recipes to make them even better.

What's for Lunch?

Challenge each student to think of a favorite food that begins with the same letter as his or her first name. During morning meeting, when you ask, "What's for lunch today?" the student to your left might respond by saying, "Today for lunch we're having Megan's Meatloaf." The next student continues by saying, "Today for lunch we're having Megan's Meatloaf and Terry's Tacos," the third student says, "Today for lunch we're having Megan's Meatloaf, Terry's Tacos, and Hugh's Hamburgers," and so on. When it gets back to you, try to remember everything that's on the menu! Students will get a kick out of correcting you if you make a mistake.

Learning from Labels

Have students collect wrappers from several candy bars. Help them examine and compare the prices, nutritional components, and percentages of fat, carbohydrates, protein, and sugar in each. What conclusions can they draw?

Sun Recipes

Sun tea. The youngest of children will enjoy preparing large bottles of water with suitable herb teabags (apple cinnamon or mandarin orange spice are good choices) suspended inside and setting these out in the sunshine "to brew." From time to time have children check the color of the tea. Bring it inside when it has steeped to suit your taste. Serve your sun tea warm or ice cold and sip it together outside.

Sun-dried fruits and vegetables. Older children will be able to pare and slice apples, apricots, peaches, carrots, zucchini, and celery. Use a large, blunt-nosed needle and heavy thread to pierce and string each piece. Leave air spaces between the pieces. Lay the string on a drying rack, such as a cake rack. Place the rack outside to dry in a place that's easily observed. Be sure not to dry in direct sunlight because it may make apricots bitter. Also, be sure not to leave them out overnight. It may take several days to completely dry the fruit. Bring the rack in when the fruits are completely dried.

Fruits dried in this way will keep for months and are wonderful for snacks, either with plain yogurt or by themselves. The vegetables can also be stored until some chilly autumn day when the children toss them into chicken broth for a warming soup snack.

Apple Experiences

Count the seeds. Before you cut an apple, have children try to guess how many seeds will be inside. Cut open the apple and count them. How close were they? Write down children's guesses and the actual number of seeds that were in the apple. The next day, repeat the process. Compare your results. Were there more, less, or the same amount of seeds in the two apples?

Different apples. Next time you go to the grocery store on a field trip with children, point out all the different kinds of apples. Tell children their names. Buy a few different kinds, and when you get back to school, let children sample them. Ask them how each one tastes. Ask them how each one is different.

Apple sequencing. Gather three to five different-sized apples. Set them on a table and ask a child to arrange the apples according to size. For younger children, start with two apples and ask which is smallest.

Apple hide-and-seek. Have children stand and cover their eyes while you "hide" an apple in the room. (It should be placed in plain view.) Tell children to find the apple but not touch it. When they spot it, they should quietly go and sit back down in their place. The first one to sit down will get to hide the apple.

Apple hide-and-seek #2. Play this game the same way as the previous game, except hide the apple. Then tell children individually whether they are "hot" or "cold" in relation to the apple. Allow other children to have a chance to hide the apple and tell their classmates whether they are "hot" or "cold." It may be a good idea to discuss the meaning of "hot" and "cold" before you play this game.

Apples in the basket. You need apples and a small laundry or bushel basket. Have children place five apples in the basket. Count with children as they place the apples in the basket. How many apples will fit in the basket? Have children guess how many will fit, and then see how many it takes to fill the basket. You can also tape numbers onto the bottom of the baskets, and have the child place the appropriate number of apples into each basket.

Apple chart. Prepare sliced red and yellow apples for lunch. Ask each child which color apple she or he ate. Allow children to mark the column on a graph that corresponds to their answer.

Quinoa

Quinoa (pronounced keen-wa) is an edible seed related to leafy greens such as spinach. Cooked quinoa is fluffy and crunchy and looks somewhat like rice. Quinoa has many health benefits. It is a complete protein source, containing all nine essential amino acids, including lysine, which is important for growth. It is also gluten free, good for the heart, rich in fiber, and available in bulk. Make these quinoa dishes with children:

- Breakfast cereal. Make it like oatmeal. Add l cup quinoa to 2 cups boiling milk. Simmer with cinnamon. Add fresh berries. Sweeten to taste if needed.
- Pancakes. Add cooked quinoa to pancake batter.
- Salad. Combine equal portions of cooked quinoa, black beans, and corn with a little vinegar and fresh coriander or parsley.
- Stir fry. Sauté cooked quinoa in a wok with peas, carrots, chick peas, and tofu.
- Pudding. Cook quinoa like rice in a pudding with eggs, milk, maple syrup, dried fruits, and nuts.

See the "Recipe for Cooking Experiences" section for instructions on how to cook fluffy quinoa.

Food Riddles

Children's listening and thinking skills will improve as they identify foods by guessing the answer to riddles.

Children sit in a small group of four to five. The adult reads the entire riddle before children respond. You can write the following riddles on index cards to read to children:

1. I'm in the dairy group. I'm white. People drink me out of a glass, cup, or carton. You put me on cereal. What am I? (milk)
2. I'm in the vegetable group. I'm long, orange, and crunchy when eaten raw. What am I? (carrot)
3. I'm in the fruit group. I'm round, shiny, and smooth to touch. I'm crunchy to bite into. I grow on a tree. What am I? (apple)
4. I'm in the meat group. I'm flat and round in shape. I often come on a bun. Sometimes people put catsup on me. What am I? (hamburger)
5. I'm in the bread and cereal group. I come in a loaf. You can slice me to make sandwiches. I smell good right after I'm baked. What am I? (bread)
6. I'm a member of the meat and poultry group. I have an oval shape. I come from a chicken. You can fry me, scramble me, or boil me. Inside I am yellow and white. What am I? (egg)
7. I'm a member of the fruit group. I'm tiny, brown, and wrinkled. I used to be a grape. You can eat me in a cereal, in cookies, or just by myself. I'm sweet but not a junk food. What am I? (raisin)

Children who are familiar with the game enjoy making up their own food riddles. Riddle games could be played concentrating on only one food group, ethnic foods, and so on.

Popcorn Predictions

Materials: Paper, popped popcorn, bowl

The objective of this activity is to estimate how much popcorn will fit into various shapes. Give students a sheet of paper with different shapes on it. Then give each student one kernel of popcorn to use to estimate how many pieces it would take to fill different shapes. Give them 3 cups of popped popcorn each and have them put it on the shapes. Students can record their results and find out how close they were to their estimates. Then, everyone can eat the results!

Pop Goes the Student!

The objective of this activity is to dance using the word "pop."

Students start in a circle with the teacher in a visible location for all students to see. Start with stretching exercises that incorporate stretching the upper and lower body. Thoroughly stretch large and small muscle groups in the upper and lower body. Then have the students start low to the ground, while popcorn begins to "pop." As popcorn "pops" faster, the students begin to rise up from the lower-level position. As popcorn is "popping," the students move their arms and hands in front of them. As popcorn finishes "popping," the students then stand up and reach for the ceiling.

Variation: Do this activity while real popcorn is popping.

Your Sense of Popcorn

Materials: Air popper, popcorn, paper, pencils

The object of this activity is to have students write about popcorn using their five senses to describe it. Start by reminding the children to be careful observers. Tell them not to speak to anyone, only to listen and look. Pop up a batch of popcorn, using an electric popcorn popper. When the popcorn is finished popping, pass out paper and pencils to the children. On the paper have students write:

1. What I see.
2. What I smell.
3. What I hear.
4. What I feel.
5. What I taste.

When students are finished writing, have them share their answers with the class. Then eat the popcorn!

Fruit Feast

For this activity, you will need small plastic bowls, a large spoon, several plastic knives, a large knife (for an adult), paper or plastic plates, chart paper, and markers.

Send a note home to inform families that, as a way to learn about one another, children are requested to bring in their favorite fruit. On the day that the activity is planned, have several extra pieces of fruit handy just in case some children forget to bring their own.

Invite children to bring their piece of fruit to the meeting area. Write the question, "What is your favorite fruit?" on the top of a sheet of chart paper. Then go around the circle and invite children to show what they brought. Record children's responses, review their comments, and engage them in a discussion about the fruit that they brought in. How many children like the same fruit? Are there any fruits they have never seen before?

Ask children to place their fruit in the middle of the circle. How are the fruits similar? How are they different? Have them touch and smell the fruits. Create another chart to record their observations.

Explain that they will use their fruit to make a fruit salad bar for their snack. Divide them into two small groups, each led by an adult. Begin by washing hands and reviewing cooking safety rules. Invite children to help wash, peel, and cut the fruits with plastic knives. Ask an adult to cut the harder fruits first and give the pieces to children so that they can safely cut them and then place the different fruits into individual bowls.

Give each child a bowl and invite the group to make their own fruit salad. Before they eat, children should name the different fruits they have chosen.

Remember that many young children may not be enthusiastic about trying new foods, and some may have an aversion to specific types of food textures. Offer everyone the opportunity to participate and to touch and smell the different types of fruit. Do not require them to eat fruit if they do not want to.

Original Recipes

Ask each child to dictate a recipe to you that is made in her or his home. Write it down exactly as she or he tells you (mistakes and funny parts, too). Put the recipes together in a little booklet for parents. It will be a treasure to save and enjoy for years to come.

Sandwich Activities

Ask children about their favorite sandwich. Keep track of their answers because these can give insight into their eating habits and nutritional needs. Ask them: "Do you like mayonnaise on your sandwiches? Lettuce? Cream cheese?" "What is your favorite jelly?" (Do you know the difference between jelly and jam? Jelly is made from the juice of the fruit and it's clear. Jam has crushed fruit right in it.) "What kind of meat sandwich do you like best?" "What is your favorite bread?" (A sandwich is more bread than anything else, so it's important to have a good bread on your sandwich. A brown bread is the best because it gives your body more natural vitamins and minerals than a white bread does.)

Let their answers to these questions guide you in selecting recipes for them. Make some homemade peanut butter, homemade bread, or homemade jelly. (See recipes later in this section.)

Sandwich Collage

Materials for this activity: Small pieces of colored paper, crayons, markers, scissors, glue sticks, 12- × 18-inch white paper, brown paper or grocery bags.

Ask children, "What is your favorite sandwich?" Have them think about different kinds of sandwiches and choose a favorite. Encourage children to describe sandwiches they like and to name the colors of the foods in them. On a large piece of paper, list the sandwiches the children named. Have children close their eyes and picture themselves eating their favorite sandwich. Then say, "Let's create a sandwich collage of your favorite sandwich."

Encourage children to be aware of the colors and shapes of the food as they create their sandwich collage. Have children draw everything they want to put on their sandwiches. Then they cut them out. Different colored bits of construction paper can be used for pickles, tomatoes, lettuce, and so on.

Encourage the children to build their sandwiches from the bottom to the top. Have them use brown paper bags or brown construction paper for buns. After they are finished, have students share their collages to see if classmates can identify the ingredients.

Great Grapes

Give young children the opportunity to make choices and be creative by concocting their own snacks using only one harvest food—grapes! Set out an assortment of red, purple, and green grapes. Discuss the many grape products we eat or drink (jelly, juice, and so on). Suggest that children brainstorm new ways to prepare and eat grape snacks.

Here are a few suggestions for great grape snacks. A grape cookbook, with each recipe signed by the cook, would be a wonderful follow-up activity.

Frozen grapes. Place washed grapes on a cookie sheet with space around each one. Cut them in half to avoid the possibility of a child's choking. Freeze. When frozen, place in a plastic bag. Have children eat them frozen.

Grapes to raisins. Wash and dry a large bunch of green grapes. Place in a basket in a warm sunny spot for four to seven days. Be sure to bring them in at night! You will then have raisins!

Grape fruit cocktail. Have children slice grapes in half with plastic knives. They can add sliced grapes to a can of fruit cocktail (packed in juice, not heavy syrup) along with fresh fruit chunks as desired.

Recipes for Cooking Experiences

Fluffy Quinoa

A. Ingredients

1 cup quinoa
3 cups liquid (water, chicken stock, or vegetable stock)
½ teaspoon salt (more to taste)

B. Ingredients

1. Rinse the quinoa in a strainer until the water runs clear.
2. Bring the liquid to a boil in a saucepan. Add the salt and the quinoa. Bring back to a boil, reduce the heat to low, cover and simmer 15 minutes, or until the quinoa is tender and translucent and each grain displays a little thread.
3. Drain excess water and return to the saucepan. Cover the pan with a clean dish towel, replace the lid, and allow the quinoa to sit undisturbed for 10 minutes.
4. Fluff and serve.

Yield: About 4 cups, 6 to 8 servings.

Soft Pretzels

A. Ingredients

1½ cups warm water
3 cups flour
1 pkg. yeast
1 tablespoon sugar
1 teaspoon salt
1 tablespoon vegetable oil

B. Procedure

1. Mix together all the ingredients.
2. Add small amounts of flour until mixture does not stick to your hand.
3. Roll out 12 small balls of dough to make snakes or worms.
4. Loop ends together to make a pretzel knot.
5. Coat with a mixture of one egg yolk and two tablespoons of water.
6. Sprinkle a few pieces of salt on each pretzel.
7. Place on a slightly greased cookie sheet.
8. Bake at 425°F for 10–12 minutes.

Applesauce (refer to picture recipe in Figure 21-1)

A. Ingredients

4 to 6 medium apples
¼ cup sugar
½ stick cinnamon (or 1–2 whole cloves, if desired)

B. Procedure (if food mill is not used)

1. Peel and core the apples.
2. Cut apples into quarters, and place in pot.
3. Add a small amount of water (about 1 inch).
4. Cover the pot and cook slowly (simmer) until apples are tender. The cooked apples can then be mashed with a fork, beaten with a beater, or put through a strainer.
5. Add sugar to taste (about ½ cup to 4 apples), and continue cooking until sugar dissolves.
6. Add ½ stick of cinnamon (or 1 to 2 cloves) if desired.

Note: If a food mill is used, it is not necessary to peel and core the apples. After the apples are cooked, they are put through the food mill. Children enjoy turning the handle and watching the sauce come dripping out of the holes. Variation: For fun, add a few drops of red food coloring. What happens to the color of the applesauce? Is the flavor changed? Be sure to add them while the applesauce is still hot.

Banana Apple Icy (refer to picture recipe in Figure 21-2)

A. Ingredients

1 apple
1 banana
¼ cup milk
1 cup plain yogurt
3 ice cubes

B. Procedure

1. Peel and core 1 yellow apple.
2. Cut it into small cubes.
3. Peel and slice 1 banana.
4. Put these in a blender with the milk and yogurt.
5. Add 3 ice cubes.
6. Blend until smooth.

Makes enough for two small glasses.

Apple Sandwiches (refer to picture recipe in Figure 21-3)

A. Ingredients

1 apple
peanut butter

B. Procedure

1. Peel and core an apple.
2. Cut it crosswise into slices.
3. Spread peanut butter on one apple slice and top with another apple slice.

Fruit Soup
A. Ingredients

honeydew and/or cantaloupe melon
1 banana
1 plum
kiwifruit, grapes, and other fruits
1 cup of orange juice
1 scoop frozen yogurt

B. Procedure
1. Scoop balls from melons with a melon baller. (Kids love doing this.) Use a honeydew melon or cantaloupe or some of each.
2. Cut up banana with a butter knife.
3. Add the orange juice for the base of the soup and put in a blender.
4. Add banana pieces and whirl on high for 30 seconds.
5. Pour soup into 3 or 4 bowls or into 8–10 small cups.
6. Add cut-up fruit to each and then top off with a scoop of frozen yogurt.

Simple Nutritious Snacks

- Ants on a Log—Celery sticks filled with peanut butter and topped with raisins.
- Bunny Food—Combine grated carrots with raisins and a bit of honey and serve on crackers.
- Fancy Sandwiches—Cut bread into shapes with cookie cutters and spread with favorite toppings.
- Orange Delight—Mix in blender: ⅓ cup orange juice concentrate, ¼ cup powdered milk, ½ banana or other fruit, ¾ cup water, honey to taste, ice. (The more ice you add, the slushier the drink becomes.)
- Party Mix—Mix 2 cups dry cereal and 1 cup small pretzel sticks. Place on cookie sheet, sprinkle with parmesan cheese and ⅓ cup melted margarine. Bake at 250°F for 30 minutes, stirring occasionally.
- Roll-Up Salad—Spread a cabbage or lettuce leaf with peanut butter. Place a celery or carrot stick in the middle and roll up the leaf.

Super Snacks

Healthy strawberry shortcake. Cut the top off a low-fat bran muffin. Scoop out some muffin from the bottom half. Fill with sliced strawberries and low-fat plain yogurt. Put back the muffin top.

Fruit dip fondue. Stir together natural peanut butter and low-fat chocolate yogurt in equal proportions. Use as a dip for the fruit of your choice.

Asian veggie roll-ups. Soak rice paper (found at Asian markets) in water according to package directions until thickened. Cut veggies into julienne strips (carrots, zucchini, yellow squash, or peppers). Layer veggies on the rice paper (add some soy sauce if you like) and roll up.

Beautiful bagels. Use bagels as your "easel." Take ½ of a bagel, and have children spread it with low-fat cream cheese. Have available a variety of sliced vegetables such as carrots, cucumbers, bean sprouts, cherry tomatoes, green or red bell peppers, and black olives. Children can decorate their snack to their own "taste" both artistically and health-wise.

Banana Breakfast Split

A. Ingredients
1 banana, sliced lengthwise
½ cup low-fat cottage cheese
1 tablespoon wheat germ
1 tablespoon raisins
1 tablespoon chopped nuts

B. Procedure
1. Place banana slices in a bowl.
2. Put scoops of cottage cheese on top.
3. Sprinkle with wheat germ, raisins, and nuts. Makes one serving.

Pear Bunnies

A. Ingredients
1 ripe pear cut in half lengthwise
1 lettuce leaf
1 teaspoon cottage cheese
red cherry
raisins
almond slivers

B. Procedure: Place pear half on lettuce half, rounded side up. Decorate, using cottage cheese for "cottontail," cherry for nose, raisins for eyes, and almond slivers for ears.

Tropical smoothie. All you need is fruit and a blender to whip up a fresh fruit snack-time smoothie. Just put all of the following ingredients in a blender and whip it on high until smooth:

1 banana
2 kiwi fruit (peeled)
½ cup peeled and diced mango
½ cup peeled and diced papaya
1 cup orange juice
3 ice cubes

Makes two to three servings.

Tortilla flats. Take a small, whole grain tortilla, top with some shredded low-fat cheese, and warm in the microwave or toaster oven.

Fruit leather. This recipe reinforces the concept that fruits such as apricots, peaches, raspberries, apples, and so on, can be changed and used in new ways.

A. Ingredients
1 quart or 2 pounds of fresh fruit
sugar
cinnamon
plastic wrapping paper

B. Procedure
1. Help children break open, peel, and seed or pit fruit.
2. Puree prepared fruit in blender until smooth.
3. Add 2 tablespoons sugar and ½ teaspoon cinnamon to each 2 cups of puree.
4. Pour mixture onto sheet of plastic wrap that has been placed on a large cookie sheet. Spread mixture thinly and evenly.
5. Cover mixture with a screen or a piece of cheesecloth and place in the sun until completely dry—about one or two days. Be sure to bring it in overnight! It can then be eaten or rolled and stored.

Peanutty Pudding

A. Ingredients
1 package regular or sugar-free vanilla pudding
2 cups milk
peanut butter

B. Procedure
1. Prepare pudding as directed on package.
2. Pour cooked pudding into individual bowls.
3. While pudding is still warm, stir 1 tablespoon peanut butter into each bowl.

Fruit Kabobs

A. Ingredients
1 cup vanilla or lemon yogurt (low-fat, low-sugar variety)
2 cups fresh or canned fruit (chunk-style)
pretzel sticks

B. Procedure
1. Thread fruit chunks onto pretzel sticks. Talk about how colors and sizes look next to each other.
2. Dip each end piece into the yogurt before eating, or spoon yogurt over the entire kabob.

Strawberry Yogurt Shake

A. Ingredients
½ cup frozen unsweetened strawberries, thawed
2 tablespoons frozen orange juice concentrate, thawed
½ cup banana (optional)
1 cup vanilla or lemon yogurt

B. Procedure
1. Puree strawberries in blender.
2. Add remaining ingredients to blender and mix until frothy.
3. For holidays or special occasions, stick straws through colorful paper shapes and serve with shakes. Makes two servings, ¾ cup each.

Peanut Butter Banana Smoothie

A. Ingredients
1 cup vanilla yogurt
1 to 2 tablespoons peanut butter
1 banana

B. Procedure
1. Combine all ingredients in blender.
2. Whip for 30 to 60 seconds or until smooth.
3. Serve in a custard cup or small bowl to eat with a spoon, or pour into cups to drink.

Spider Cookies

A. Ingredients
round crackers
peanut butter
small pretzel sticks
raisins

B. Procedure
1. Cover 2 round crackers with a layer of peanut butter.
2. Break 4 small pretzel sticks in half to make 8 spider legs.
3. On one cracker, lay 4 legs on one side and 4 on the other, making sure pretzels stick out from each side.
4. Place another cracker on top.
5. Place 2 small dabs of peanut butter on the top of one end of the cracker.
6. Place 2 raisins in the peanut butter dabs for eyes.

   Make as many as you like!

Broccoli Trees and Snow

A. Ingredients
¾ cup small-curd, low-fat cottage cheese
½ cup plain yogurt
¼ cup fresh minced parsley
1 bunch broccoli

B. Procedure
1. Mix cottage cheese and yogurt in blender until smooth.
2. Add parsley and refrigerate until cool.
3. Cut broccoli into "dippers." (Cucumbers, zucchini, celery, carrots, radishes, and green peppers make good "dippers," too.)
4. Dip vegetables into yogurt mix and enjoy.

Fruit Sun

A. Ingredients
grapefruit sections
muskmelon balls
cherries
raisins

B. Procedure
1. Arrange grapefruit sections in a ring around muskmelon balls.
2. Cherries and raisins may be used to make a face.
3. Amounts depend on the number to be served; ½-cup servings are appropriate.

Carrot and Raisin Salad

A. Ingredients
3 cups shredded carrots (teacher to prepare)
¾ cup raisins
juice of one lemon

B. Procedure
1. Mix ingredients thoroughly.
2. Serve immediately.

Bird's Nest Salad

A. Ingredients
1 grated carrot
½ cup canned Chinese noodles
mayonnaise to moisten
peas or grapes

B. Procedure
1. Have the children grate the carrot.
2. Next have them mix the carrot with ½ cup canned Chinese noodles and mayonnaise to moisten.
3. Put a mound of this salad on a plate and push in the middle with a spoon to form a nest.
4. Peas or grapes can be added to the nest to represent bird's eggs. The nest could also be set on top of a lettuce leaf.

Makes two salads.

Banana Bake

A. Ingredients
1 banana, peeled
butter (melted)

B. Procedure

1. Place peeled banana in shallow baking dish and brush with melted butter.
2. Bake in moderate oven (375°F) for 10–15 minutes (until tender).
3. Serve warm.

Yield: 1 serving.

Watermelon Ice

When watermelon is in season, try this new way to use it. In a blender, puree 6 cups of seedless watermelon with 1 tbsp. lemon juice. Scoop mixture into a square baking pan and smooth the top. Cover and freeze at least 3 hours. Use an ice cream scoop to serve.

Frozen Cherries

A fun way to use cherries is to freeze them. Add them to summer drinks, giving them a subtle sweet-tartness that children will love. And when the glass is empty, let them go ahead and eat this ice—it's loaded with beta-carotene.

Carob-Nut Snack

A. Ingredients

1 cup dry-roasted unsalted peanuts
1 cup unsweetened carob chips
1 cup unsweetened dried banana chips
1 cup unsweetened cereal

B. Procedure:

Children can take turns shaking ingredients in a plastic container with lid to mix. Serve in small cups, or carry in plastic bags on field trips. Can be stored in container for several weeks.

Peanut Butter Balls

A. Ingredients

½ cup fresh peanut butter
1 tablespoon jelly
½ cup dry milk powder
1 cup bran or corn flakes
⅓ cup bran or corn flakes (crushed)

B. Procedure

1. Mix the peanut butter and jelly in bowl.
2. Stir in milk powder and 1 cup bran or corn flakes. Mix well.
3. With your hands, roll the mix into small balls. Roll the balls in the crushed flakes.

Peanut Butter Apple Rolls

A. Ingredients

1 8-ounce can refrigerated crescent rolls
2 tablespoons fresh peanut butter
1 apple, peeled and finely chopped

B. Procedure

1. Separate dough into 8 triangles.
2. Spread a thick layer of peanut butter on each triangle.
3. Top with 1 tablespoon of apple.
4. Start at the shortest side of each triangle and roll to other side. Place on cookie sheet.
5. Bake at 350°F for 10–15 minutes.

Fruit Cubes and Dip

Have the children help cut up cubes of fruit such as apples, pineapples, bananas, or fresh berries. Let them spear the fruit cubes with a toothpick and dip it into a yogurt dip, which is made from ½ cup plain yogurt and 2 tablespoons orange juice or apple juice concentrate.

Nutty Swiss Cheese Spread

A. Ingredients

2 cups Swiss cheese, shredded
½ cup fresh peanut butter
½ cup sour cream
¼ cup raisins

B. Procedure

1. Mix all ingredients well.
2. Use spread on bread or crackers.

Sandwich Roll-Ups

Have the children roll a rolling pin over a piece of whole-wheat bread to flatten it out. Next, let them spread on a sandwich spread such as: peanut butter and smashed bananas, cream cheese and pineapple bits; deviled ham, and so on. Next, have them roll their bread slices up to eat. Sandwiches can be rolled in waxed paper and saved for later.

Walking Sandwich

Core an apple, and fill it with soft cheese or peanut butter. This is a great snack for taking on a long walk.

Broiled Bananas

A. Ingredients

1 banana (unpeeled)
1 tablespoon plain low-fat yogurt

B. Procedure

1. Make a small slit in the banana peel. Place the unpeeled banana slit-side up on baking sheet.
2. Broil for 5–10 minutes, until softened.
3. Open the peel to expose banana. Serve with a dollop of yogurt.

Most children like bananas, so this recipe should be a hit. In this recipe, the banana is eaten with a spoon and the peel becomes the dish.

Frozen Banana Coins. This is an excellent use for a very ripe banana. Peel bananas. Freeze bananas on a tray. Place frozen bananas in a freezer bag or freezer container. Return to freezer until ready to use. To serve, remove bananas from freezer and slice into pieces. Serve immediately, or pieces will become soggy. Yield: ½ banana per serving.

Frozen Banana Pop. Cut banana in half horizontally. Carefully push one popsicle stick into each banana half. Freeze. Serve directly from freezer.

Popcorn Mix. For children older than 3 years of age.

A. Ingredients

2 cups plain popped popcorn
¼ cup quartered dried apricots
¼ cup raisins
¼ cup peanuts

B. Procedure

Mix all ingredients together. Store in a tightly covered container.

Yield: 2¾ cups.

Fruit Designs

In the summer when fresh fruit abounds, try these fruit designs for a fun snack time.

Boat: Cut honeydew melon into the shape of a triangle for the boat. Push one end of a small straw into the melon and the other into an orange wedge for the sail.

Toadstools: Peel hard-boiled eggs; slice a piece from the bottom so they'll stand. Top with half of a cherry tomato (remove the seeds first) and then with a bit of feta cheese.

Colored popcorn. Add several drops of food coloring to vegetable oil before staring popcorn popper. Then add popcorn kernels to the oil and food coloring. One color can be made for each batch of popcorn kernels. After popcorn cools, mix all colored popcorn together.

Have children sort the popcorn by color. They can place the different colors of popcorn in different cups. They may then want to count how many kernels are in each cup. After all this work, eat and enjoy!

Crunchy Fruit Munch

A. Ingredients

3 quarts popped popcorn
2 cups natural cereal with raisins
¾ cup dried apricots, chopped
¼ teaspoon salt
⅓ cup butter or margarine
¼ cup honey

B. Procedure

1. Preheat oven to 300°F. Combine first four ingredients in large baking pan; set aside.
2. In small saucepan, combine butter or margarine and honey. Cook over low heat until butter or margarine is melted.
3. Pour over popcorn mixture, tossing lightly until well coated.
4. Place in oven. Bake 30 minutes, stirring occasionally.

Yield: Makes 3 quarts. Store in tightly covered container up to 2 weeks.

Popcorn with Peanut Butter

A. Ingredients

2 quarts popped popcorn
1 tablespoon fresh peanut butter (creamy or chunky)
2 tablespoons butter or margarine

B. Procedure

1. In small saucepan, melt butter or margarine and peanut butter until smooth.
2. Pour over popped corn and mix well.

Popcorn Cheese Snacks

A. Ingredients

2 quarts popped popcorn
½ cup butter or margarine
½ cup grated American or parmesan cheese or both
½ teaspoon salt

B. Procedure

1. Spread freshly popped popcorn in a flat pan; keep hot and crisp in oven.
2. Melt butter and grated cheese and add salt.
3. Pour mixture over popcorn. Stir until every kernel is cheese flavored.

Vegetable People

Let the children make vegetable people one day for a snack. Give them small chunks of carrots, celery, potatoes, and so on, plus some toothpicks. Let them create creatures to devour.

Bell Pepper Snack Cups

A. Ingredients

4 green bell peppers
½ cup low fat Ranch dressing
1 red bell pepper, seeded, cut into strips, 4 inches long and ½-inch wide
12 mini peeled carrots
2 stalks celery, cut into strips, 4 inches long and ½-inch wide
8 asparagus spears, trimmed to 4 to 5 inches long

B. Procedure

1. Cut the tops off the green bell peppers and remove the seeds.
2. Place bell peppers on small plates. Pour 2 tablespoons Ranch dressing into the bottom of each snack cup.
3. Place equal amounts of red pepper strips, mini carrots, celery strips, and asparagus spears into each snack cup, then start dipping and snacking.

Homemade peanut butter. Bring to school a large bag of peanuts in the shell. Let children help you shell the peanuts. Put a cupful of peanuts into a blender. Add 1 tablespoon of peanut oil to blend the peanuts to the consistency children like.

Homemade jelly: a quick version. Defrost a 12-ounce can of frozen grape juice concentrate. Dissolve a package of unflavored gelatin into the juice. Pour this mixture into a pan and bring to a boil, stirring to dissolve the gelatin.

Remove from heat and allow to cool. Pour the mixture into a wide-mouthed jar and refrigerate.

Homemade quick whole-wheat bread. Soften 3 tablespoons of dry active yeast in 3½ to 4½ cups warm water and milk (half milk, half water) in a large bowl. Add 2 tablespoons honey, 2 teaspoons salt, ½ cup nutritional yeast (available at health food stores), and 8 cups of whole-wheat flour.

Blend well. Dough should be slippery and glutinous yet stiff enough to cling to the spoon. It shouldn't flatten out, and there should be no liquid showing in the bowl. Add more (or less) flour to achieve this texture.

Fill oiled bread pans ⅔ full. Let dough rise 15 minutes (while you are cleaning up) at 85 to 90°F, until it increases in height by 25%.

Bake at 400°F for 15 minutes. Turn down oven to 350°F and continue baking for 20 minutes more—or until it is golden brown.

Fruit smoothies. You'll need ½ cup plain yogurt, ½ cup orange juice, ¾ cup fresh fruit (strawberries, blueberries, raspberries, bananas, or a combination), 1 tablespoon honey, and ½ cup ice.

Place all ingredients in a blender. Blend for about 2 minutes or until mixture is smooth. Pour into cups and enjoy. Serves 2.

Fun Sandwiches

Break away from the usual peanut butter and jelly sandwiches with these fun and nutritious variations:

Veggie cream cheese and cucumber

Tuna salad and a sliced tomato

Almond butter with slivered almonds and dried cranberries

Hummus and chopped peppers

Apple butter and fresh apple slices

Whipped cream cheese and fresh blueberries

Laughing Cow Cheese light spreadable cheese with ham and grated carrot

Blueberry cream cheese and strawberry slices

Reduced-sugar jam and cream cheese

Sandwich Switches

In place of white bread, try crackers, bagels, corn or bran muffins, pita bread, English muffins, taco shells, raisin bread, grain bread, tortillas, or croissant rolls.

In place of lettuce, try cucumber slices, pickles, cabbage, zucchini slices, alfalfa sprouts, green pepper strips, or bean sprouts.

In place of jelly with your peanut butter sandwich, try raisins, sliced bananas, sliced apples, grated carrots, or bacon bits.

Calcium-Rich Recipes

Did you know that three out of four Americans don't get the calcium they need? Remind the children to eat three a day, that is, three servings of calcium-rich milk, cheese, or yogurt every day. To make it easier, here are some calcium-rich recipes for young children.

Polka dot milk. Fill ice trays with chocolate and strawberry-flavored milk. Drop the festive frozen milk cubes into a glass of plain milk for fun, tasty "polka dots."

Lunch in a crunch. Mix the child's favorite cereal with yogurt for a creamy and crunchy lunch.

'Nilla banana ice. Create a smooth, delicious drink by blending together 1 cup of low-fat milk, banana slices, ice, and a few drops of vanilla.

Cool cuts. Cookie cutters aren't just for cookies. Use them to cut out fun shapes from cheese slices or grilled cheese sandwiches to liven up lunches.

Festive fruity flavored milk. Mix 1 cup fat-free, skim, or 1% low-fat milk and 2 tablespoons apricot, blackberry, raspberry, or strawberry fruit syrup. For each cup of milk, stir in 2 tablespoons fruit syrup. Try experimenting with different flavors of fruit syrups until you find one that provides the perfectly pleasing color to your milk. Fruit syrups are available in natural and artificially flavored varieties and are usually found in the section with pancake mixes.

Finger lickin' good yogurt. Give kids a yogurt "palette." With a plate and two to three "colors" (flavors) of yogurt—try blueberry, strawberry, and banana—kids can paint on a graham cracker canvas and eat their great-tasting masterpiece.

Perfect cheese picks. Pair cheese with other healthy foods that will satisfy even the pickiest eaters. Wrap a slice of turkey around mild Mozzarella string cheese or slices of tangy Cheddar around apple wedges.

One-Step Cookbook

These are one-process recipes. They require some preparation, but the actual recipe uses one method that demonstrates what happens when food is prepared in that manner.

Carrot curls. For this activity, you will need carrots, a vegetable peeler, and ice water. Show children how to use a vegetable peeler safely. When peeling carrots, the peeler should be pushed down and away from the body, rather than toward the body or face.

Help children peel off the outside skin of the carrot, and then make additional carrot peels. Place peels in ice water in the refrigerator until they curl. Use the carrot curls for a snack.

Apples with cheese. Halve and core apples. Fill hollowed center with smooth cheese spread. Chill for 2 to 3 hours before serving.

Yogurt and cereal parfait. In a tall glass, layer lemon, vanilla, or fruit-flavored yogurt with a favorite breakfast cereal.

Banana breakfast bites. Peel bananas and cut into bite-sized pieces. Dip each piece in yogurt, then drop into a plastic bag filled with wheat germ. Shake to coat. Serve as finger food.

Fruit cubes. Make frozen cubes with fruit juice, placing a small piece of fruit in each cube before it freezes. Add a popsicle stick to each cube to make individual fruit treats on a stick.

Banana on ice. This is a tasty, low-calorie treat—only about 85 calories per banana. Simply peel a banana and wrap it in plastic wrap. Place it in the freezer for several hours or until hard. (Don't leave it in the freezer too long.) Eat frozen. It tastes exactly like banana ice cream.

Smiling sandwich. Spread peanut butter on a rice or corn cake. Use two raisins for eyes and a banana or apple slice for a smiling mouth.

Apple bake. Place a cored apple in a dish with a small amount of water. Cover with foil (for oven) or cover loosely with plastic wrap (for microwave) and bake at 350°F for 20 minutes (oven) or on high for 5 minutes (microwave). Add a sprinkle of cinnamon if desired.

Juice freeze. Fill a 6-ounce paper cup with sugar-free fruit juice, cover with plastic wrap, and push a plastic spoon through center of wrap. Freeze. Tear away cup to eat.

Dried banana chunks. Slice bananas into ¾-inch-thick slices. If desired, roll in chopped nuts. Place on baking sheet in 150°F oven with oven door open about 2 inches. Dry until shriveled, or about 12 hours.

Activities for Older Children (Grades 4–5)

Fruit Science

On a table, place three or four different varieties of apples. In front of each kind, place a label with the name of it. Children read the names and describe and compare the varieties. Give the children thin slices of the varieties to name, taste, and compare. Then, have them research facts about apples: uses and food value, growth, environment, and so on. Make a special dessert or salad using the apples. Children taste, describe, and enjoy.

Eggs

Read *Green Eggs and Ham* by Dr. Seuss (1976). Have the class try to state the moral of the story as succinctly as possible. The moral might be stated: "You never know if you'll like a new food until you try it" or "Try it, you'll like it." Make your own green eggs and ham.

Discuss with students purchasing environmentally sound egg cartons. Molded pulp cartons are generally made from 100 percent recycled paper. That makes these a better choice than polystyrene egg cartons. Polystyrene is not recycled, nor is it biodegradable.

Have students use their imaginations by drawing a picture of a food using eggs in the recipe. Encourage students to draw the picture so that the food looks interesting or fun to them. Students may want to write a paragraph to go with their egg-recipe pictures.

National Popcorn Month

October is National Popcorn Month and a good time to examine this popular food. Visit The Popcorn Board website for the history of popcorn, information about its nutritional value, and recipes using it. To help students practice estimation skills, pour some unpopped kernels into one glass jar and popped corn in another. How many kernels are in each? Make a Venn diagram comparing popcorn to regular kernel corn.

Food from Animals and Plants

Have students draw or cut out pictures to make a farm scene of plants and animals we eat. Have them add some plants and animals we do not eat.

Ask students to think about the grocery store. Are products from plants and animals sold together in one department, or are they in separate departments? Students should distinguish produce departments from meat/deli and dairy departments. Aisles in the middle of the stores are often combinations of plant and animal products.

Polyvinyl chloride (PVC) is a huge contributor to environmental pollution. Supermarkets package their meat, fish, and poultry in polystyrene trays and then wrap them in PVC wrap. But the deli counter will cut meat and wrap it in freezer wrap or molded pulp trays, which are better. Have students offer suggestions for alternative ways to buy and package meat.

Raising Raisins

Wash a large bunch of green grapes. Remove them from the stem and weigh the grapes carefully. Record the date and weight. Place the grapes on a cooling rack and cover them with a kitchen towel. Observe and record changes in appearance and weight over time. What is the percent of weight loss after one week? Two weeks? What factors can affect the dehydration process?

Canned Food Values

Have students bring in cans of vegetables. Sort the cans by nutritional content (vitamins, proteins, calories, sodium). Compare that data with the nutritional value of fresh vegetables. When the project is completed, donate the cans to a local food collection drive.

Fast Food Actions

This game is basically a pantomime relay race. Divide the group into three or four teams, standing along a single-file line, so that there are three or four columns of children facing the leader. The first person from each line comes up to the leader and receives a word (whispered in the ear), connected to a certain, announced topic. For example, if the topic is fast food, the person may receive the words "French fries" or "pizza" as their word/s. The person must then run back to their line and act out their word. As soon as someone in their line correctly guesses the word, the "actor" moves to the end of their line and the person at the front runs up to get a new word. The game continues until all teams have rotated through completely. Suggested topics include things found in the kitchen, things in school, jobs, occupations, movies, books, and so on.

Food and the Media

The last week of April is National Library Week. Challenge students to read a book about foods or food groups.

Provide newspapers and magazines with food advertisements. Have students cut out the ads and put them into food groups. Use food advertisements and have students "stop and think." (See the rhyme in the next paragraph.) Evaluate foods by having students respond to a series of questions related to the food groups.

Make a poster or bulletin board with the "Eating Advice" rhyme—"Eating, keep repeating, stop and think, will this help me grow?" Refer to this rhyme throughout any nutrition activities.

Food Groups

Ask students to generate a list of typical foods eaten at breakfast. Then have them write one breakfast menu. Count the number of servings from the bread, fruit, vegetable, meat, and milk groups. Knowing how many servings of each food group is recommended for a day, have the students subtract the breakfast servings to determine the food to eat the rest of the day.

After lunch, have students determine how many servings from each food group have been consumed. How many servings need to be consumed at supper in order to meet food requirements?

References

American Academy of Family Physicians (AAFP). (2012). Childhood Obesity: Assessment, prevention and treatment. Retrieved from http://www.aafp.org/online/en/home/cme/selfstudy/cmebulletin/Obesity.html.

American Academy of Pediatrics (AAP). (2012). Fruit juice and your child's diet. Retrieved from http://www.healthychildren.org/English/healthy-living/nutrition.

Center for Disease Control and Prevention (CDC). (2012). Child obesity facts. Retrieved from http://www.cdc.gov/healthyyouth/obesity/facts.htm.

Crout, J. P., & Sjoerdsma, A. (1999). The clinical and laboratory significance of serotonin and catechol amines in bananas. *New England Journal of Medicine*, 261, 23–26.

Hoge, T. (2009). When work strain transcends psychological boundaries: An inquiry into the relationship between time pressure, irritation, work-family conflict and psychosomatic complaints. *Stress and Health, 25*(1), 41–51.

Kumar, K. P., Bhowmik, D., Duraivel, S., & Umadevi, M. (2012). Traditional and medicinal uses of banana. *Journal of Pharmacognosy & Pytochemistry, 1*(3), 57–70.

Let's Move. (2011). Retrieved from http://www.letsmove.gov.

Mercader, J., Asmerom, Y., Bennett, T., Raja, M., & Skinner, A. (2009). Initial excavation and dating of Ngalu Cave: A middle stone age site along the Niassa Rift, Mozambique. *Journal of Human Evolution, 57*(1), 63–74.

National Center for Health Statistics (NCHS). (2011). *Health, United States: With special features on death and dying.* Hyattsville, MD: U.S. Department of Health and Human Services.

Ogden, C. L., Carroll, M. D., Curtin, L. R., Lamb, M. M., & Flegal, M. M. (2010). Prevalence of high body mass index in U.S. children and adolescents, 2007-2008. *JAMA, 30*(3), 242–249.

Seebohar, B. (2011). *Nutrient timing programs in sport: A case study approach.* New York, NY: Taylor & Francis Group.

Seuss, D. (1976). *Green eggs and ham.* New York, NY: Random House.

Thakorlal, J., Perera, C. O., Smith, B., Englberger, L, & Lorens, A. Resistant starch in Micronesian banana offers health benefits (2010). *Pacific Health Dialog, 16*(1), 131–140.

 Visit CourseMate for this textbook to access the eBook, Did You Get It? quizzes, Digital Downloads, TeachSource Videos, flashcards, and more. Go to CengageBrain.com to log in, register, or purchase access.

Casper Holroyd

22

Creative Social Studies

As we begin this chapter on social studies, consider these two examples of young children in social situations.

Learning Objectives

After studying this chapter, you should be able to:

22-1 Describe the appropriate approach to social studies for preschoolers.

22-2 Discuss the National Social Studies Standards.

22-3 Define the common bonds curriculum.

22-4 Describe some areas of individual development and identity appropriate in the early childhood program.

22-5 Discuss ways to include information on community workers in social studies learning experiences.

22-6 List some points to remember in planning field trips for young children.

22-7 Discuss the importance of teaching about peace in the early childhood program.

22-8 List examples of appropriate social studies activities for older children.

naeyc

NAEYC Standards

1a Knowing and understanding young children's characteristics and needs.

2c Involving families and communities in their children's development and learning.

5a Understanding content knowledge and resources in academic disciplines.

DAP

DAP Criteria

3A1 Teachers consider what children should know, understand, and be able to do across disciplines, including social studies.

5F Practitioners involve families as a source of information about the child and engage them in planning for their child.

Situation 1

Kim is waiting at home for her son Billy, who is playing next door. When he arrives 20 minutes later than scheduled, she asks what happened. "Well, Mom," he begins in a grown-up fashion, "Dao's doll broke, and I wanted to help her."

"I didn't know you knew how to fix dolls" is his mother's somewhat surprised reaction.

"Oh no, Mom. I *don't* know how. I just stayed to help her cry."

Situation 2

Greg and Marc are building together with blocks. Marc gets angry because Greg takes a block from him. They fight. The teacher intervenes and talks with Marc about using words instead of fists. She tells him to try talking to Greg. Instead of hitting him, tell Greg what was making him angry. Finally, believing she has made her point, she asks Marc, "Now, what would you like to do?"

Marc answers without hesitation, "Hit him!" And he does!

These incidents, while a bit amusing to the adults involved, both demonstrate the funny, unpredictable nature of young children in social settings. They also illustrate clearly the fact that learning to be part of a social group is not something that is natural or inborn in human beings. Young children, like those mentioned, often react in a socially unpredictable way by their very spontaneous reactions to life. Yet young children can be very sensitive to the feelings of others, even though they are direct and uninhibited in many situations. The fact is that learning about oneself, about others, and how to act with others is a long process.

Social studies is the study of human beings in their environment and of the concepts, skills, and attitudes that are needed in order to become social beings. Both the content and the processes of social studies can be integrated into activities in which even very young children can participate. As boys and girls reenact the roles of adults known to them, as they build houses, farms, airports, stores, and parks that they have seen or dramatize past experiences that have special meaning for them, they learn the content of social studies. As children become aware of community services such as fire and police protection or library and post office facilities, they incorporate them into their play.

Social studies are an important part of a child's education; they help children understand the complex world in which they live and enable them to be productive and happy within society's framework. Socially, children in the early childhood years are just coming into touch with their own feelings. Some children are so young they are just learning the names for these feelings and barely beginning to understand their meanings. Others are dealing with emotional changes as they make the transition from preschool to elementary school. Still others are moving from early childhood to middle childhood and experiencing the many emotional adjustments this entails. Guiding young children in their developing understanding of their own and others' emotions is a highly sensitive, challenging part of the teacher's job. Adults are most instrumental in helping young children deal with their feelings and those of others. To do this, adults must be able to deal with their own feelings, too.

Consider your own emotions for a moment and your own early childhood experiences. Think about all the changes you've come through to get you to the point you are now in your life. Change is inevitable in both your life and the lives of young children.

How do you feel about change? Do you look forward to the future, or do you hold on to the past? Do you accept or fight change? Does your view of the life cycle include both an appreciation for what has been and excitement about what might be?

Your personal approach to change has a direct effect on your relationship with young children (see Photo 22-1). If you are open to change yourself, you won't shy away from their concerns about growth and development or their questions about death and aging.

© Cengage Learning 2015

PHOTO 22-1 A teacher's approach to change has a direct effect on her relationship with young children.

Your attitude toward change is conveyed in a healthy acceptance of your own life and all the changes, emotions, and challenges it brings. With this approach, teaching young children social studies concepts will be a joy for you and the children.

22-1 Preschoolers and Social Studies

naeyc **DAP** Social studies have not traditionally been part of the preschool curriculum. In part, this is because the disciplines of social studies—history, geography, economics, and civics—are considered too abstract for preschoolers. But the precursors of social studies are covered in early childhood curricula in more concrete ways. Temporal awareness (history precursor; understanding the time sequence in the daily routine), spatial knowledge (geography precursor; making simple maps of familiar places), and number sense (economics precursor; playing store) are all part of the preschool curriculum. Most preschool teachers are very aware that their children are developing basic concepts about community, justice, and democracy as they learn to function as members of a social group in preschool.

Historical concepts such as "long ago" or "far in the future" have little meaning for young children, whose ideas about time do not verge far from the here and now (or the near past and immediate future). However, storytelling can introduce preschoolers to the ideas of continuity and change, similarity and difference. Young children who are beginning to sort and classify can divide time in a "binary" way ("now" and "not now") and thus comprehend that stories about history take place at a time that is "not now." Preschoolers are also interested in and capable of comparing the similarities and differences of their experiences with people in other eras. For example, 4-year-olds can try to imagine how people might communicate if they didn't have telephones (Epstein, 2009).

With regard to geography, another one of the disciplines of social studies, is a field of study that enables us to find answers to questions about the world around us—about where things are and how and why they got there. With young children, spatial awareness develops early, and children are naturally inquisitive about the places where they live and learn. Children as young as 3 spontaneously draw or build maps and can understand and use them quite proficiently in the context of their personal knowledge and experience. Learning to orient oneself in space and comparing one's own location and viewpoint to that of others is a cognitive process preschoolers are able to achieve. Social studies

can thus be relevant in preschool if it is approached through such direct experiences (Epstein, 2009).

Did You Get It?

A four-year-old tells a friend at school, "After circle time, we will have outdoor play time." Which knowledge is he developing that will prepare him to learn social studies?

a. play awareness
b. temporal awareness
c. spatial knowledge
d. number sense

Take the full quiz on CourseMate.

22-2 National Council for the Social Studies—National Standards

naeyc **DAP** The National Social Studies Standards begin at kindergarten and continue up to and including grade 12. The National Council for the Social Studies (NCSS) identified 10 thematic strands of social studies in which all children (K–12) should have learning experiences. These standards were revised in 2010 and, like the 1994 standards, continue to be structured around the 10 themes of social studies. However, the revised standards offer a sharper focus on the following:

Purposes
Questions for Exploration
Knowledge: What Learners Need to Understand
Processes: What Learners Will Be Capable of Doing
Products: How Learners Demonstrate Understanding (NCSS, 2010)

The revised standards also include the following:

- Enhancements in the descriptions of the 10 themes and the associated learning expectations
- The addition of new descriptions of standards-based class practices to time-tested descriptions that were included in the original edition of the standards
- A stronger focus on student products and their assessment
- An updated list of essential social studies skills and strategies, including literacy strategies

The themes are interrelated, and a school course in a social studies discipline is likely to touch on more than one theme. For example, the use of the

NCSS standards might support a plan to teach about a school's neighborhood drawing theme 1, Culture; theme 3, People, Places, and Environments; and theme 5, Individuals, Groups, and Institutions.

The themes point to a fundamental knowledge drawn from many subjects and most heavily from these social sciences: anthropology, archaeology, economics, geography, history, law, philosophy, political science, psychology, religion, and sociology. The first seven thematic strands are social science discipline-oriented, and the remaining three are meant to be multidisciplinary.

Each of the themes derives meaning from one or more of these subjects. The 10 strands are listed in Figure 22-1. The 10 themes are meant to serve as a framework for social studies curriculum planning. This chapter will discuss several of these themes as they relate to our discussion of the social studies curriculum. Let us now look at general social characteristics of children at various age levels in the early childhood program.

Casper Holroyd

PHOTO 22-2 Friendship patterns in preschool and early elementary grades are often characterized by best friends.

22-2a Social Characteristics

Although it is impossible to predict with any certainty the developmental pattern of any individual, general characteristics are common to age groups. It is helpful to have some general idea of what type of social characteristics to expect at various age levels. The following is a summary of age-level social characteristics.

Preschool and kindergarten. Socially at this age level, friendships are usually limited to one or two "best" friends, but these may change frequently (see Photo 22-2). Play groups are not too well organized and tend to change often. Although quarrels are frequent, they tend to be of short duration. There is great pleasure in dramatic play and beginning awareness of sex roles.

Emotional development is at a volatile stage—emotions are expressed freely, and outbursts of anger are common. A vivid imagination frequently leads to grossly exaggerated fears. Competition for adult affection breeds jealousy. Mentally, students are developing rapidly in the acquisition of language. They enjoy talking to each other and in front of groups. Imagination and fantasy are at their peak.

Primary grades (6–9 years). Although friendship patterns are still likely to be characterized by "best friends," greater selectivity is now evident in the choice of friends. Games are more organized, but there is great emphasis on "rules." Quarrels are still frequent as are physical aggression, competition, and boasting. Although the difference in interests of boys and girls becomes more pronounced at this age, there is great variation in behavior from one classroom to another because of influences exerted by teachers.

Emotionally, children become very sensitive during this period. Criticism, ridicule, and failure can be devastating. Despite their own sensitivity, they are quick to hurt others. Generally, students are eager to please the teacher and want to do well in school, for which reasons they require frequent praise.

Eagerness to learn is common to this age group. Learning occurs primarily through concrete manipulation of materials. Eagerness to talk is still evident, and there is much experimentation with language—including obscene language. Concepts of reciprocity, fairness, and right and wrong develop during this period.

Elementary grades (9–12 years). Peer groups begin to replace adults as sources of behavior standards and the recognition of achievement. Interests become more sharply different between the sexes—frequently resulting in "battles" between them for recognition and achievement, as well as the exchange of insults. Team games become more popular, along with class spirit. Crushes and hero worship are common.

1. Culture

Through the study of culture and cultural diversity, learners understand how human beings create, learn, share, and adapt to culture, and appreciate the role of culture in shaping their lives and society, as well the lives and societies of others. In schools, this theme typically appears in units and courses dealing with geography, history, sociology, and anthropology, as well as multicultural topics across the curriculum.

2. Time, Continuity, and Change

Through the study of the past and its legacy, learners examine the institutions, values, and beliefs of people in the past, acquire skills in historical inquiry and interpretation, and gain an understanding of how important historical events and developments have shaped the modern world. This theme appears in courses in history, as well as in other social studies courses for which knowledge of the past is important.

3. People, Places, and Environments

This theme helps learners develop their spatial views and perspectives of the world, to understand where people, places, and resources are located and why they are there, and to explore the relationship between human beings and the environment. In schools, this theme typically appears in courses dealing with geography and area studies, but it is also important for the study of the geographical dimension of other social studies subjects.

4. Individual Development and Identity

Personal identity is shaped by family, peers, culture, and institutional influences. Through this theme, students examine the factors that influence an individual's personal identity, development, and actions. This theme typically appears in courses and units dealing with psychology, anthropology, and sociology.

5. Individuals, Groups, and Insititutions

Institutions such as families and civic, educational, governmental, and religious organizations exert a major influence on people's lives. This theme allows students to understand how institutions are formed, maintained, and changed, and to examine their influence. In schools, this theme typically appears in units and courses dealing with sociology, anthropology, psychology, political science, and history.

6. Power, Authority, and Governance

One essential component of education for citizenship is an understanding of the historical development and contemporary forms of power, authority, and governance. Through this theme, learners become familiar with the purposes and functions of government, the scope and limits of authority, and the differences between democratic and non-democratic political systems. In schools, this theme typically appears in units and courses dealing with government, history, civics, law, politics, and other social sciences.

7. Production, Distribution, and Consumption

This theme provides for the study of how people organize for the production, distribution, and consumption of goods and services, and prepares students for the study of domestic and global economic issues. In schools, this theme typically appears in units and courses dealing with economic concepts and issues, though it is also important for the study of the economic dimension of other social studies subjects.

8. Science, Technology, and Society

By exploring the relationships among science, technology, and society, students develop an understanding of past and present advances in science and technology and their impact. This theme appears in a variety of social studies courses, including history, geography, economics, civics, and government.

9. Global Connections

The realities of global interdependence require an understanding of the increasingly important and diverse global connections among world societies. This theme prepares students to study issues arising from globalization. It typically appears in units or courses dealing with geography, culture, economics, history, political science, government, and technology.

10. Civic Ideals and Practices

An understanding of civic ideals and practices is critical to full participation in society and is an essential component of education for citizenship. This theme enables students to learn about the rights and responsibilities of citizens of a democracy, and to appreciate the importance of active citizenship. In schools, the theme typically appears in units or courses dealing with civics, history, political science, cultural anthropology, and fields such as global studies, law-related education, and the humanities.

FIGURE 22-1 National Social Studies Standards: The 10 thematic strands of social studies.

TeachSource Digital Download   Download from CourseMate.

This is the period when the conflict between adults and the group code begins to emerge. Instead of a rigid following of rules, youngsters at this age begin to understand the need for exceptions. Frequently, they set very high standards for themselves—sometimes unrealistic standards—hence, feelings of frustration are common. While the desire for independence grows, the need for adult support is still strong—therefore unpredictable behavior often results. Children at this age can behave in a very "grown-up" way one minute and revert to more "childish" behavior the next. Curiosity remains strong at this age.

With these social developmental characteristics in mind, let us now look at how the early childhood program can accommodate both developmental levels and the social studies themes/standards.

22-2b Learning About One's World

A child's universe begins with himself or herself, extends to his or her family, and then to the larger community. The development of a child's self-concept—awareness of self—is the important beginning point in social studies for young children.

To know oneself in a social sense involves learning such things as one's name, one's ethnic background, one's family grouping, and occupations in one's family. In the early childhood years, learning about oneself is at a basic level—that is, young children are learning about how their lives fit into the larger social group.

Children learn about where they live—in a house, an apartment, or a condominium—and how it is like and unlike the residences of their peers. They learn the similarities and differences among families in form, style of living, and values.

Those who work with young children from preschool through the early and later elementary years can help them discover and appreciate their own uniqueness by beginning with a positive acceptance of each child. In the early childhood years, young children need opportunities to live important experiences, to learn in an active way.

22-2c Culture (Thematic Strand #1)

The first thematic strand of the National Social Studies Standards relates to the child's awareness of culture. In today's multicultural classrooms, you, as a teacher, set the tone for the young child's developing sense of his own and other's cultures. All children have the opportunity to learn about themselves and others simply by the way you treat them and their peers. If you show respect for their worth as human beings and encourage them to respect one another, they will begin the long process of learning to celebrate human differences. Nonverbal cues, body language, and role modeling are all a part of its foundation. We may isolate ourselves from each other socially, but our classrooms become more diverse every year. Teachers confront issues of diversity in intimate ways that most adults do not, so it's crucial that teachers and administrators explore their own attitudes and beliefs regarding diversity. We cannot expect that anyone will abandon her discomfort with diversity simply because she dons the mantle of a teacher. But we can expect that all teachers develop a deeper understanding of their own diversity experiences and how they influence their interactions with children and parents. Change can be forced on you, or change can be something that you embrace and make part of yourself. In other words, you must say, "The change I believe in begins with me."

Most important of all, the development of children's appreciation of diverse cultures must be part

© Cengage Learning 2015

▶❚❚ **TeachSource** Video

Diversity: Teaching in a Multiethnic Classroom

1. What strand(s) of the National Social Studies Standards is/are represented in this video? Use specific examples in your reply.

2. Using the information in this chapter as a reference, what additional activities could Mr. Norwood add to this unit to extend the multicultural social studies experiences of the children?

Watch on CourseMate.

of the program *every day*. It must be an integral part of the early childhood curriculum of every classroom and child-care center. This does not mean that you should teach a unit on Asians or Africans or Hispanics every day . . . or any day. It does not mean you should point out differences in the way the children look or dress or speak. Teepees, tomahawks, and piñatas have little to do with developing children's appreciation of one another. What counts most of all is the following:

- A deep *belief* in the worth of every child
- An accepting *attitude* toward each child as a unique individual
- An unqualified *support* for each child's development of emotional, social, physical, cognitive, language, and creative skills on a daily basis

Casper Holroyd

PHOTO 22-3   A true mastery of language requires social interaction.

Did You Get It?

A student teacher observes that in a preschool classroom, the children seem to quarrel often. She also notices fluidity among groups of children who play together. What can she conclude?

- **a.** The children in this class have behavioral issues.
- **b.** This is a typical preschool classroom.
- **c.** This is a preschool classroom typical of special education students.
- **d.** This classroom is composed of socially gifted children.

Take the full quiz on CourseMate.

22-3 Cultural Awareness and the Common Bonds Curriculum

naeyc DAP Many preschool curricula are developed around themes such as the family, seasons, weather, holidays, animals, and community helpers. Making such programs multicultural has often meant inserting a Chinese New Year celebration or a Mexican party with a piñata. Although these activities may be fun for children, they have little to do with the immediate interpersonal concerns of children. Although such programs may seem to be teaching children to appreciate other cultures, more often than not they teach separateness instead. By focusing on a culture's differences from mainstream American culture, children from that culture may come to feel different and somehow lesser.

The creative multicultural social studies curriculum should be designed around the common bonds all of us share (see Photo 22-3). Think for a moment about what most young children have in common. Your list may include some of the following.

- They live in a family.
- They live in a neighborhood.
- They live in a natural environment.
- One or both of their parents usually work for a living.
- They eat the food their family provides.
- They speak the language their family speaks.
- They play with toys and play games.
- They like to pretend.
- They like to run, jump, and move.
- They like to draw, dance, and make music.
- They want to have friends and get along well with others
- They want to be accepted and appreciated.
- They want to feel good about themselves.
- They want to succeed.

From such a list, you can begin constructing a curriculum that speaks to the common bonds of all young children. The cultural diversity of all children can be celebrated within a **common bonds curriculum**. From the list of things children have in common in all cultures, some common bonds for a creative **multicultural curriculum** might include the following:

- Family
- Self-esteem
- Foods
- ● Arts and crafts
- Music and dance
- Physical expression
- Languages
- Earth

Once the common bonds are in place, the next step is to incorporate activities related to cultural diversity. Several examples of common bonds theme units and activities that could be used in your multicultural curriculum are provided at the end of this chapter. These ideas are only suggestions on some approaches to take to multicultural curriculum planning. Your own unique group of children will dictate what to use in your curriculum planning from the ideas provided. These ideas and all new ideas become meaningful to young children when they relate directly to the children *in your group*. Thus, if information about other cultures is to make a difference in the lives of young children, it should relate directly to the child and her or his peers. It should involve children in learning firsthand about children like themselves from different cultures.

The following sections contain suggestions for including the thematic strands of social studies in the curriculum.

Did You Get It?

A kindergarten teacher decides to spend time on jumping and movement, which many of her children like to do even though they come from different backgrounds. Which term describes her curricular approach?

a. varied background/common foreground
b. action and movement
c. shared likes
d. common bond

Take the full quiz on CourseMate.

22-4 Individual Development and Identity (Thematic Strand #4) in the Early Childhood Program

naeyc **DAP** A positive awareness and acceptance of one's own appearance is part of the social aspect of learning "Who am I?" In the room, for example, a full-length mirror in a safe but clearly visible place at child level is one way for children to see themselves and each other. Some children have few opportunities to see their reflections because mirrors in their homes are too high. Providing an unbreakable hand mirror in the room is another way to encourage children to see themselves. Magnifying makeup mirrors also produce interesting reactions from children when they see their enlarged images.

The following suggested activities are designed to develop a young child's awareness and appreciation of the uniqueness of his or her physical appearance:

- Use an unbreakable mirror to bring out the idea that we are more alike than different. Discuss color, size, and shape of eyes, hair, nose, mouth, ears, and so on. Have children draw pictures of their faces. Mount these on a low board and label them with children's names.
- Supply children with pictures of people with missing body parts. Have children describe what part is missing.
- Play the game "Policeman, Where Is My Child?" One child is the policeman, another is the parent. The parent describes the physical appearance of the missing child (dress, hair, eyes). All children become involved as they look at themselves to see if they're being described. The policeman tries to guess which child in the room belongs to the parent.
- In the art center, keep available an array of found materials for making dress-up accessories such as jewelry, hats, or masks.
- Trace the shape of children's bodies as they lie down on large sheets of paper. Children can dress these life-sized figures with fabric, felt, yarn, buttons, beads, and any other found materials that interest them.
- Offer finger paint or water-based ink for making handprints and footprints.
- Provide plaster of paris for making molds of hands.
- Encourage older children to draw self-portraits.
- Make shadow silhouettes of older children. In direct sunlight, have the child stand on a sheet of paper large enough to contain an outline of his shadow. Draw around his or her shadow on paper. Compare drawings of shadows made in the morning, at noon, and later in the day.

Additional activities are at the end of this chapter.

Casper Holroyd

PHOTO 22-4 In the early childhood program, it is important to celebrate each child's uniqueness.

22-4a Learning Names

One of the first social learnings of a young child is the recognition of his or her own name. In the early childhood program, this recognition is further developed by teachers' and peers' recognition of this name. This basic learning is directly related to a child's individual identity.

Make it a point to concentrate on individual names of children. Avoid using endearments such as "honey," "sweetie," and "sugar." Instead, use the child's first name, and alternately use the child's first and last name. This will further develop children's self-knowledge as well as help them appreciate their own uniqueness (see Photo 22-4). It also helps children learn each other's full names.

22-4b Strategies for Focusing on Each Child's Uniqueness

The following strategies are suggested in your work with young children to help focus on the uniqueness of each child:

- Write a child's name on his or her work in the upper-left corner to teach the left-to-right

sequence. While writing the child's name, say it. This provides an auditory and visual model.
- At transition times, call the child by name to go to another activity or to tell the teacher which activity he or she wants to go to. "Johnny Jones, you may ride the tricycle today. Sally Smith, you may clean off the table."
- Instruct children to go tell another child something. "Jaime, please tell Colleen it is time to come inside." Here the child is not only hearing his name, he is beginning to be able to say the other child's name and a sentence as he follows the teacher's direction.
- When children are in a group for a story, go around the group and say each child's name. Let the other children, as a group, say the child's name as you place your hand in front of the child.
- Encourage children to draw, paint, or model themselves and their families in personally meaningful ways: Me and My Best Friend; I Am Playing with My Favorite Toy; I Am Helping at My House; My Family at Dinner Time; My Family Went to . . . ; and My Wish. These renditions can be used for cooperative murals, booklets, and jigsaw puzzles.
- Provide a variety of media and found materials in the art center for children to make puppets of themselves or their families.

Additional activities are at the end of this chapter.

Concentrating on the child's voice, which is as individual as each child's name, is another good way to help develop young children's awareness of their identity. Here are some suggestions on how to actively involve young children in learning that they each have a unique voice:

- Compile a tape of all the members of the class. Discuss how each person has a different voice tone. Have children speak into the tape recorder. Afterward, play back these recordings for the group. Have children listen to the voices and guess whose they are.
- Record children telling their favorite stories (*Goldilocks and the Three Bears, Three Billy Goats Gruff, Little Red Riding Hood*), emphasizing voice inflections for the different characters.
- Play the game "Who Am I?" One child is in the center of the circle and is IT. IT tries to guess who says, "Who Am I?" The speaker disguises his or her voice after the children have mastered the game with their natural voices.

- Have children feel objects of various textures. Another day, discuss voices using familiar comparisons. "Is your voice grating? High? Low? Soft? Hard? Scratching?" Have a box or chart of textured objects for the children to feel, such as steel wool, corrugated metal, silk, velvet, cotton puffs, wool, or a small mirror.

Additional activities are at the end of this chapter.

22-4c The Block Center (Thematic Strand #3: People, Places, and Environments)

Learning about people, places, and environments is the third social studies theme in the national standards. The block center is an excellent place for learning about the community and neighborhood. Play models of various members of the family and people from various races, ethnic groups, industries, and professions, as well as small wheel toys with the blocks, all encourage true social play in the block center.

When children play together in the block center, they learn to share, communicate, and resolve conflicts. Children see that cleanup is easier when they cooperate with one another. Building with blocks builds friendships, too, as children create structures together and role-play events from daily life or their imaginations. Dramatic play using blocks also helps young children work through important emotional issues. Because there is no right or wrong way to play, building with blocks helps boost a child's self-esteem (see Photo 22-5). Knocking down block structures helps children feel powerful and in control.

Here are some ways to encourage block play for all children:

- Locate the block and housekeeping areas side by side so children can combine activities.
- Provide props and accessories that appeal to girls as well as boys. Include tools, transportation toys, and uniformed block figures as well as accessories, such as scarves, fabric pieces, and carpet samples. Be sure to include bits of colored paper, pencils, crayons, and markers. Family block and animal figures are also appealing to both boys and girls. Be sure to include family block figures of various ethnic groups and representations of children with special needs.
- Intervene when you observe gender bias. If you hear Sam and Anthony telling Roxanna she

© Cengage Learning 2015

PHOTO 22-5 Building with blocks can help build a child's self-esteem.

can't play with them because they're building a firehouse and girls can't be firemen, let children know that in your room everyone can play with everything that's available. You might teach children to use the term *firefighter* as well as other terms that do not reflect gender bias. Follow up by reading books about people in careers traditionally held by the opposite sex.

- Decorate the block center walls. Hang pictures, photos, posters, and blueprints of buildings, bridges, towers, and roadways. If children enjoy drawing their own pictures of construction sites, hang those up, too. Include pictures of men, women, and children of all races doing a variety of jobs to let children know that blocks and construction are for everyone.
- Include puppets, rocks, flashlights, pulleys, string, and other interesting extras.
- Include toy vehicles of all varieties, such as cars, trucks, airplanes, helicopters, fire engines, ambulances, buses, taxis, and boats.

22-5 Community Workers (Thematic Strand #2)

naeyc **DAP** Because a child does not exist in isolation, he or she is dependent on people in the community. Many people provide services for the child—the police officer, the bus driver, and the baker, for example. As a child meets people in the community, she learns about the many roles people play and tests some of these roles in dramatic play. The child takes a tool kit and goes to fix the telephone. He becomes involved in relationships in which adults play varied roles and people depend on each other. The child passes a firehouse in the neighborhood and sees where the firefighters are stationed. The child goes to the garage with her mother and sees the mechanic fix the family car or goes to the post office with a family member and mails a letter to Grandmother. Children learn, through everyday experiences such as these, that others help them and they help others.

A good place to begin a discussion about understanding others in the child's world, then, is to learn about people in the child's most immediate environment. This includes the people who serve the school and community. There are many people in the child's immediate environment. It is important to emphasize the importance of all of these individuals. Each member helps to make the whole community where we live and go to school what it is; all jobs are important. The following activities are designed to help develop the idea of the importance of community workers:

- Find out when the garbage is collected at the school. Be there when the truck comes. Talk to the workers about their job, the service they perform, the truck and its operation and care, and possibly how citizens can help get the garbage ready for the collector. Don't overlook the fact that these helpers are also people with personal lives. Children can learn to understand that the men and women in our labor force also have spouses, children, hobbies, pets, and so on, just like the rest of us.

- Follow the preceding procedure for postal workers, grocery store clerks, mechanics, painters, laundry workers, bus drivers, cooks in the cafeteria, and custodians.

- Follow the preceding procedure for professional and semiprofessional workers—secretary, principal, nurse, music teacher, librarian, and others. Such activity should follow careful planning with the children as well as with the people you may visit. Preparing the adults beforehand for the kind of questions they can expect will give them a chance to organize their thinking. Discussing courteous and safe behavior with children is also important. If the people you talk to can be persuaded to visit the classroom informally, the experience will be all the more effective.

- Be a worker. Learn about the world of work by visiting workplaces in the neighborhood. Then children may enjoy acting out what they observed. Costumes for this can be simple, with only a hat, a mask, or an object to carry suggesting the characterization (see Photo 22-6). Some

PHOTO 22-6 Children learn about their community by dressing up like workers in the community.

children may want to bring an article of clothing to serve as a costume. Playing the role of adults may take the form of a parade, a guessing game, pantomime, or play. Such experiences help broaden the child's understanding of life in the local community.

22-6 Field Trips into the Community

Every school is located in a community. You can safely assume that every community has members who care about the well-being of its children and who possess talents, hobbies, and resources that can enrich children's learning experiences.

An excursion into the community may help young children gain new information, clarify other information, and enhance and extend children's experiences. After one trip around the block, a group of 5-year-old children built a block barber shop and kept up their dramatic play as barbers for several days. Even the teacher sat in a chair as the children pretended to cut hair using their fingers as scissors.

Often the comment is heard, "Why take children to a fruit and vegetable store when they shop there every week with their parents?" A visit to a store with a teacher and a group of peers is a very different experience from the same trip with mother. When a teacher takes a group to a store, the purpose of the trip is to give the children a specific experience. The event focuses on them and their purposes. When children go to a store with their families, ordinarily they are hurried along, and the child's experience is not the

major consideration of the trip. Because the purposes are different on a school excursion, the experience is different.

Within the same group of children, needs will differ. For instance, a teacher taking four children to the zoo found that for three of them, the short bus trip back and forth was the exciting part of the trip because they had never been on a bus before. For the other child, the bus ride was an everyday event, and the giraffe was the highlight of the trip. When a teacher took two children to a department store to buy burlap for a bulletin board, the ride on the escalator was the event most remembered.

22-6a Planning for Trips

A teacher needs to do a good bit of planning for a trip. The purpose of a trip is to provide children with first-hand experiences. A child should not only be able to see, hear, and smell but also to touch and taste. A teacher also needs to know the children and their special interests and concerns. You should not consider any trips until you are certain you know the children well enough to anticipate any potential disruptive behavior. In many classrooms, some children may become overstimulated by the interruption of their daily routines.

You will need to familiarize yourself with the community in which the school is situated before planning excursions—become familiar with street signs and working people who come and go from the school, shops, business establishments, buildings, and service. Talk with people in the community. As you plan, try to anticipate children's reactions, remembering that you are planning for young children. This means that you will need to keep in mind these basic guidelines in planning all excursions:

- Keep it simple.
- Discuss, read about, and organize play around the places to be visited in advance.
- Encourage close observations while on the outing.
- Give small amounts of information if children are interested.
- Provide time, materials, and enthusiasm for follow-up plans and projects.

"Children are the living messages we send to a time we will not see."

—Jewish proverb

THIS ONE'S FOR YOU!

Whirled Peace: Pinwheels for Peace

The idea is simple: Take square pieces of paper and create pinwheels of all shapes and sizes. As part of the creative process, write thoughts about war and peace, tolerance, and living in harmony with others on one side. On the other side, draw, paint, collage, and so on to visually express your feelings. Assemble these pinwheels, and on International Day of Peace, September 21st, "plant" the pinwheels outside at public places as a statement and art installation. The spinning of the pinwheels in the wind will spread thoughts and feelings about peace throughout the country and maybe even the world (Ayers & McMillan, 2010).

On September 21, 2009, more than three million pinwheels were spinning in more than 37 countries around the world. The Pinwheels for Peace project has become the first big school event of the year in many schools. It has not only been a peace movement but it also has become part of anti-bullying and anti-violence campaigns (Ayers & McMillan, 2010). For details on how to make these pinwheels and for more information on this project, visit the Pinwheels for Peace website.

22-6b Celebrations (Thematic Strand #1)

In the life of any child, there are events that deserve celebrations. When a teacher observes that a child, through his or her glee or sadness, is moved by a situation, the experience is worth emphasizing with a small but **personal celebration**. For example, a boy ties his shoes by himself for the first time. For many children, this is a very special event. The teacher may take time to say, "Great! You did it," or "Show me how you did it!" or "How does it feel to do it all by yourself?" You might want to share a new accomplishment of your own at a time like this: "I just learned how to download my photos onto my computer all by myself!" Share good feelings with children, and a child begins to learn that feelings are important and worth celebrating. When a child ties his or her shoes, the teacher's knowing glance the next day reaffirms the child's positive feelings about himself or herself.

Did You Get It?

On a field trip to a grocery store, a preschool teacher is dismayed to find that her students do not pay attention to her directions and run unattended through the aisles. This teacher

- **a.** has no control over her students.
- **b.** should know that a supermarket is an inappropriate destination for a field trip.
- **c.** should have anticipated the potential for misbehavior when planning the trip.
- **d.** should have brought along one chaperone for every three children.

Take the full quiz on CourseMate.

22-7 Teaching Young Children About Peace

> "Preventing conflicts is the work of politics; establishing peace is the work of education."
>
> —Maria Montessori

naeyc **DAP** This quote very simply outlines a very complicated mission for early childhood teachers—teaching about peace. As far back as 1991, the National Association for the Education of Young Children (NAEYC) in a position statement challenged early childhood teachers to teach peace, reminding us that of all the lessons we hope to teach young children, the ability to act in peace is one of the most important. This position statement was reaffirmed in 1994 and continues to be critical in light of the increasing violence in our country, as well as in our schools. The conflicts that seem to be underway in every region of the globe demonstrate the profound need for creating paths to a peaceful and just world. Mahatma Gandhi said that if we are to have real peace in the world, we need to begin with children. Sowing the seeds for peace and justice in classrooms could nurture a new generation of world leaders and ordinary citizens who have a vision of a peaceful and just world and who have both the will and skill to bring this vision to reality (Baker, Martin, & Pence, 2008).

However, **teaching peace** is a complicated idea for many reasons. First, many adults define peace by describing what it is not. For now, examine peace in the eyes of a child. In the absence of war and fighting, peace is a time of safety, freedom, and celebration. Peace is the opportunity to play, to make friends, and to create (Lindsay, 2009). Peace is not the absence of conflict but rather the evidence of resolving differences in a positive way. Another reason peace is such a difficult topic to teach is that it's obvious that most adults have not been able to maintain peace in their own world. Finally, we certainly must ask a basic question: How can we teach young children about peace in a world so filled with strife and conflict?

Many early childhood experts have written about this challenge of teaching young children about peace. To sum up the core idea of these writings, peace begins with a basic attitude made up of trust, respect, and consideration toward everyone. When the attitudes of trust, respect, and consideration are present in the environment, it is a safe place for people to be themselves. In a safe environment, people have a sense that it is acceptable to be unique, it is acceptable to disagree, and it is expected that disputes are settled without hurting one another. Every interaction in a safe environment reflects consideration and respect for individual differences Mille, 2005; (Baker et al., 2008; Lindsay, 2009).

We can choose to create an environment that teaches children how to live peacefully with one another (see Photo 22-7). In every interaction we have with another person, we can cause hurt or not. It is our choice. It is the responsibility of a teacher to realize that this choice exists and to teach children about their choices. If we realize this, we will choose carefully. Teachers can be "conduits of peace" when they help children make positive and supportive connections with others. Maria Montessori taught us long ago to create peaceful environments where children can make choices within the context of clear limits and a sense of order. When she required children to walk around someone else's mat, she was teaching a simple lesson about respecting others.

If we respect one another, we will not choose to harm each other. In turn, we must help young children understand their choices. For example, an increase in rowdiness results in an increase of people getting hurt. Children must learn to make choices about their style of play, and they must learn that they share responsibility for the results of their actions. They also need to learn that they can choose to stop upsetting behavior in the future and to slow the pace before someone gets hurt.

22-7a Strategies for Teaching Peace

Teaching young children about peace begins with the implementation of two simple rules: (1) don't hurt anybody, and (2) use words to settle problems.

Don't hurt anybody. This is a simple rule—on the surface. Yet, just think of how many ways there are to hurt other people. Physical blows hurt. But so do unkind words, gestures, teasing, and exclusion. All of these are harmful and can interfere with a child's ability to learn in general, as well as learning how to act in peace.

Use words. Disagreements are a natural part of life, and they will occur in the lives of young children. The key to peaceful settlement is to maintain harmony in stressful situations. It is sometimes difficult for a child to take a deep breath and clearly express the feelings of the moment. At stressful times, times of conflict or disagreements, it is important for the teacher to be with the children—but to show, not to tell. Steady the children in whatever way you can. Holding them closely in your arms or on your lap often helps a child gain focus in a stressful situation. Help the child express himself or herself, but don't put words in the child's mouth. Make sure that children in a conflict listen to one another (see Photo 22-8). Asking them to repeat, or retell, what each has said to the other is one way to see if they are listening to each other.

© Cengage Learning 2015

PHOTO 22-7 Teachers can create an environment that teaches children how to live peacefully with one another.

THINK ABOUT IT

Cooperation and Social Understanding in One- and Two-Year-Olds

Development of the ability to cooperate with peers is a significant achievement. The beginnings of peer cooperation represent the child's entrance into the peer culture. The purpose of this study was two-fold: to examine developments in children's early cooperative abilities with peers and to examine associations between cooperation and social understanding in a period when both are rapidly developing (Brownell, Ramani, & Zerwas, 2012).

The researchers created a task in which 18- to 30-month-old children had to coordinate their activity with one another to achieve a single goal. The goal was provided by the task itself so that the children did not have to invent or discover it on their own, and the means to achieve the goal were demonstrated by an adult. The task also permitted children to capitalize on the imitative skills characteristics of their joint play with peers.

Two versions of the task were constructed; in both versions, each child had to perform the same single behavior (pull a handle) to activate an interesting toy. In the first version, each child pulled a separate handle, and the two handles had to be pulled at approximately the same time to activate the toy. In the second version, children again perform the same behavior with two separate handles but sequentially pulled the handles one after the other. Both versions of the task were first demonstrated to the children by an adult. In the second version, children were also individually trained to produce the sequential handle-pulling actions on a smaller version of the task before being presented with the larger, cooperative version.

Participants were 88 children (48 girls, 40 boys) divided into three age groups: 19 months, 23 months, and 27 months. Children were scheduled together with a same age (within one month), same-sex unfamiliar peer.

The cooperation task consisted of a colorful wooden box with two small plastic handles protruding horizontally from one side of the box, mounted on a small table. The handles were just below shoulder height for most children and moved freely back and forth, in and out of the box.

The researchers found age-related changes in toddlers' ability to coordinate their activities with one another on a simple task to achieve a common goal. Coordinated activity between 19-month-old peers was sporadic and primitive at best. Although they sometimes produced coordinated behavior, their efforts appeared to be more coincidental than cooperative and many dyads could not coordinate their behavior even once. Thus, 1-year-olds were relatively unskilled at taking a peer's behavior into account even when this was relevant for their own attempts to achieve a desired outcome.

In contrast, 2-year-olds appeared to be more actively cooperating toward a shared goal. By 27 months of age, children were considerably more skilled at coordinating their behavior with a peer, both monitoring and accommodating to the partner's activity and location as they attempted to achieve the goal together. These findings suggest that children begin to become true social partners with one another late in the second year or the beginning of the third year of life. The researchers concluded that this represents their developing social understanding and thereby initiating their entry into the peer culture (Brownell et al., 2012).

PHOTO 22-8 A teacher's role is to make sure children in conflict listen to one another.

22-7b A Teacher's Role

It is not necessary (or possible) for you to find solutions for every child's problems. You need only create an atmosphere in which children can work out their own solutions. It is the teacher's job to give children the tools they need to define and settle differences. Teaching children how to use words instead of actions to express emotions is one of the most important of these tools.

Classrooms are very special places, and they must be focused on the child. In these classrooms, there are many different personalities, different needs, different styles of behavior, and different ethnic and family

Respecting Other Cultures

The values, beliefs, and behaviors of the many Spanish-speaking groups in the United States may differ from group to group and from those of the larger society. When a family or child expresses a preference that does not pose an ethical dilemma, accept and support the preference.

For example, you may notice that a child from a Hispanic culture in which children are taught to be respectful and obedient to adults does not initiate or participate in interactions with the teacher beyond giving the information the teacher requests. Allow the child to find what works best for him or her within the classroom environment. Over time, the child who is supported in the classroom will gradually adjust to classroom behaviors in ways that meet his or her needs.

Another example is assuming that students with Hispanic surnames use Spanish as their dominant language. It is important to know that although 72% of first-generation Latinos are Spanish-dominant in their speech, 78% of third and older generations are English-dominant.

Here is another example. In some cultures, children are taught that particular behaviors or activities are masculine or feminine—that is, that certain things are done only by males or by females. A child so socialized may choose not to participate (or the family may discourage the child from participating) in activities that are typically associated with the other sex, such as dramatic play with aprons and dolls or climbing on the jungle gym. If a child verbalizes or shows a desire not to participate, that desire should be respected. Of course, the child should not be allowed to express this opinion in a way that negatively affects the feelings or perceptions of other children.

backgrounds. Common to all these groups is the need to feel safe. Only on this basis can we begin to build a framework of trust and respect in which each child has a chance to grow and learn. The teaching of peace must begin in the preschool class. If young children do not learn it from us, will they learn it at all?

Did You Get It?

A teacher sees two children kicking one another as they fight over a toy. She separates the children and reminds them that they cannot hurt one another, then moves on to the next activity. What else should she do to teach them about peace?

a. encourage them to speak to one another to resolve the conflict

b. give each child a five-minute turn with the toy

c. tell them that if they want to play with a toy that another child wants, they should ask the teacher for help resolving the problem

d. remind them that they may not sit near one another for the remainder of the day

Take the full quiz on CourseMate.

22-8 Social Studies for Older Children

The main focus of this chapter has been on social studies for children in the early years. Now let us briefly consider social studies for older children. As we have seen, children in the middle- and upper-elementary levels are capable of more flexible thought. Social studies activities are an excellent avenue for exploring the personal and social changes this age group is experiencing (see Photo 22-9). For example, the social studies standards theme of Individual Development and Identity can provide the basis for many learning opportunities in areas such as peer pressure, conformity, personal identity, self-concept, and social expectations, to name a few.

Casper Holroyd

PHOTO 22-9 Children in the middle- and upper-elementary grades are capable of more flexible thought, and social studies is a good avenue for exploring the personal and social changes in this age group.

22-8a Using Dance as a Means of Understanding and Expressing Culture for Older Children

All art forms are vehicles for conveying the ideas and values of their creators; they are means of coming to understand other cultures. Dance is no exception. Multicultural units are particularly appropriate contexts for using dance to help students feel sensations created by particular dance forms (for example, hip-hop, tap, jazz, ballroom, country line, jitterbug, and mazurka). Students can also view dances and then analyze them for the messages they give about what is important to the dancers and the culture represented. Through dance investigations, historical events can be understood from an entirely different point of view. For example, Native American ghost dancers in the nineteenth century created dances to celebrate the return of the lands taken by the U.S. government. The dancers tried to conjure up the powers of their ancestors and created such fervor among tribes that the government eventually forbade the dance!

Combine dance with multicultural music for another way to introduce children to other cultures. Integrate the music and dance of each culture and time period studied by analyzing how songs are historical records of how people felt, thought, and acted. Find out the significance of songs and how music even influenced history by studying France's "La Marseillaise" or the Mexican-American workers' "De Colores." Possibilities abound, including Native American music, Irish jigs, music of the Civil Rights Movement, tribal mountain music, western cowboy tunes, patriotic songs, and African tribal music. Students can come to understand how music helps create identity and explore a people's values and passions expressed in song.

22-8b Art and Social Studies

Studying the work of artists who used their work for social expression and to effect social changes is an excellent social studies activity for older children. Many artists were visual recorders of their times, just as current artists reflect their own twenty-first-century experiences. The following artists are good examples of this from different times in our history. By using the work of these artists, you can introduce students to the history of that period as well as to how these artists' work reflected that time. They can also learn that art as a social statement can be a powerful and effective tool.

Ben Shahn (Sept. 12, 1898–March 14, 1969). Ben Shahn was a Lithuanian-born American artist best known for his works of social realism. He studied art at City College in New York and at the National Academy of Design. He also studied the art of Henri Matisse, Raoul Dufy, Pablo Picasso, and Paul Klee. He was dissatisfied with the work of these artists, claiming that their work was unoriginal. He eventually outgrew his pursuit of European modern art and instead redirected his efforts toward a realistic style he used to contribute to social dialogue (Kao, 2000). His work reflected social concerns of the time. His antiwar sentiment was reflected in his paintings during World War II. He was also a commercial artist for CBS, *Time*, *Fortune*, and *Harpers*. His well-known 1965 portrait of Martin Luther King, Jr., appeared on the cover of *TIME Magazine*. Despite his growing popularity, he only accepted commissions he felt were of personal or social value. Ben Shahn's social–realist vision informed his approach to art. His examination of the status quo inspired his creative process (Kao, 2000). Although he often explored opposing themes such as modern urban life, organized labor, immigration, and injustice, he did so while maintaining a compassionate tone. He identified himself as a communicative artist. In his work, he intended to inspire social change. You might consider using one or more of the following pieces of his work to use with children:

Untitled, 1932, Houston Street Playground, New York City

The Meaning of Social Mural, 1940–1942, Federal Security Building, Washington, DC

For Full Employment after the War, Register-Vote, 1944, The Museum of Modern Art, New York

Age of Anxiety, 1953, The Joseph H. Hirschhorn Foundation, Inc.

Louise Berliawsky Nevelson (Sept. 23, 1899–April 17, 1988). Louise Berliawsky Nevelson was a Russian-born American artist known for her abstract expressionist "crates" grouped together to form a new creation. She was recognized during her lifetime as one of America's most distinguished artists, and her work continues to inspire contemporary sculptors today. In 1964, Nevelson created *Homage to 6,000,000*, a memorial to the Jews killed in the Holocaust. Once, when she was about to donate a sculpture piece to the Centre Beaubourg in Paris, the French government released a Palestinian terrorist. She compared this action to the "Hitler era." In protest, she withdrew the donation of her work to the museum.

You can access the papers of Louise Nevelson (circa 1903–1979) online in the Archives of American Art. The collection documents the life and work of the sculptor, including correspondence, personal business records, writings, scrapbooks, early art work, photographs, interviews, and an extensive amount of printed material. This collection is an excellent source for students interested in the social history of this artist.

Romare Bearden (Sept. 11, 1911–March 12, 1988). In the summer of 1963, Romare Bearden, as a member of the New York-based African American artistic collective Spiral, suggested that the group collaborate on a collage to make a statement on the Civil Rights Movement. The march on Washington was to be held that summer, and the group felt a need to speak to this issue. The group didn't take to his suggestion, but Bearden, a rising star in the American art world at the time, wasn't discouraged.

Over the next few months, he created a series of small-scale collages that would serve as his own personal statement on civil rights. He used clippings and snippets from magazines such as *Ebony* and *Life* and produced art that portrayed African American life as never before. These collages captured the sense of those times. When the collage-based paintings were discovered the following year and placed in an exhibition in New York, Romare Bearden, then in his early fifties, was suddenly a major artist.

This artist's social commentary can be seen in the following pieces of his work:

Patchwork Quilt, 1970, Museum of Modern Art, New York
Return of the Prodigal Son, 1967, Albright-Knox Gallery
Summertime (collage), 1967, St. Louis Art Museum

The quilters of Gee's Bend. This group of internationally acclaimed Black quilters creates quilts many consider modern works of art. More than 50 quilters make up the Gee's Bend Collective, owned and operated by the women of Gee's Bend, Alabama. The quilters are all descended from slaves who worked on a plantation located on the Alabama River. Most of these quilters have lived in indigence. Their quilts that once kept families warm inside drafty log cabins now hang inside some of the world's greatest museums. Quilts that were once thought worthless now

sell for thousands of dollars. In making their quilts, a new sense of self-respect has evolved in this tightly knit, family-oriented community.

The stories and graphic images of these artists are a powerful way to learn about one of the social studies—American history. Their dedication to social issues of their times is also an excellent example of civics, another part of the discipline of social studies.

22-8c Social Studies Theme of Power, Authority, and Governance

The social studies standard theme of Power, Authority, and Governance is an excellent base for developing learning experiences for students about their own individual rights and responsibilities in the increasingly complex social world of which they are a part. For example, students can be asked to develop hypothetical communities in which certain students play different power and authority roles. They can role-play enforcing rules when someone breaks one. They can also begin to study power and authority in their local community. Children often understand more about government structure than most adults give them credit for. Teachers can begin to teach the basics of government with field trips to the mayor's office and other city centers as appropriate introductions to government. Elections take place at least every other November, and they are excellent opportunities for civic education in the classroom. Rather than avoiding the voting spaces, how much more educational it would be to arrange a visit with election officials while they're in the building, and then have a space in the classroom dedicated to the election process. Photographs of people around the world voting, local political campaign materials (from two or more parties), reprinted ballots to be marked or punched, and a ballot box can make up a social studies display in November. Such a display can expand on conversations with guest speakers visiting the class from the League of Women Voters and the city clerk or municipal staff charged with running elections in the local area.

Using the NCSS theme of Culture and Cultural Diversity as a curriculum base, teachers can develop experiences to provide students an in-depth study of the specific aspects of particular cultures in similar and different places, times, conditions, and contexts (see Photo 22-10). Teachers can encourage students to consider the direct and indirect connections among the assumptions, beliefs, and values of a culture. Teachers can help students analyze ways that a people's cultural ideas and actions influence its members. Through such study, students can begin to consider the impact traditions have on a person's thoughts and actions within any particular social group.

Basing learning activities on the 10 social study themes will provide students at this age level many opportunities to explore their complex and changing social world. More activity ideas are found at the end of this chapter.

PHOTO 22-10 For older-elementary age children, teachers can develop experiences that provide an in-depth study of specific cultures.

Casper Holroyd

Did You Get It?

A fourth- grade teacher introduces the topic of bullying, encouraging her students to stand up for classmates who are being victimized. Which social-studies standards theme can pave the way for learning about standing up for oneself and others?

a. culture and common bonds
b. individual development and identity
c. people, places, and environments
d. bullies, victims, and champions

Take the full quiz on CourseMate.

Summary

22-1 Describe the appropriate approach to social studies for preschoolers.

The social studies of the preschool child must focus on the experiences of the child in his or her immediate environment. But the precursors of social studies are covered in early childhood curricula in more concrete ways. Temporal awareness (history precursor; understanding the time sequence in the daily routine), spatial knowledge (geography precursor; making simple maps of familiar places), and number sense (economics precursor; playing store) are all part of the preschool curriculum.

22-2 Discuss the National Social Studies standards.

The 10 National Social Studies Standards in which all children (K–12) should have learning experiences were revised in 2010 and like the 1994 standards, continue to be structured around the 10 themes of social studies. However, the revised standards offer a sharper focus on the following:

Purposes

Questions for Exploration

Knowledge: What Learners Need to Understand

Processes: What Learners Will Be Capable of Doing

Products: How Learners Demonstrate Understanding (NCSS, 2010)

22-3 Define the common bonds curriculum.

A common bonds curriculum is a curriculum that speaks to the common bonds of all young children. The cultural diversity of all children can be celebrated within a common bonds curriculum. From the list of things children have in common in all cultures, some common bonds for a creative multicultural curriculum might include the following:

- Family
- Self-esteem
- Foods
- Arts and crafts
- Music and dance
- Physical expression
- Languages
- Earth

22-4 Describe some areas of individual development and identity appropriate in the early childhood program.

Learning about oneself in a social sense includes learning one's name, one's ethnic background, and such things as family grouping and occupations in one's family. In the early childhood program, learning about oneself is at a basic level—that is, young children learn how their lives fit into the larger social group.

Those who work with young children from preschool through the entire period of early childhood can help them discover and appreciate their own uniqueness by beginning with a positive acceptance of each child.

22-5 Discuss ways to include information on community workers in social studies learning experiences.

A good place to begin a discussion about underst anding others in the child's world is to learn about people in the child's most immediate environment. This includes the people who serve the school and community. Some suggestions include garbage workers, postal workers, grocery store clerks, mechanics, painters, laundry workers, bus drivers, cooks, and custodians.

22-6 List some point to remember in planning field trips for young children.

Some basic guidelines in planning all excursions include the following:

- Keep it simple.
- Discuss, read about, and organize play around the places to be visited in advance.
- Encourage close observations while on the outing.
- Give small amounts of information if children are interested.
- Provide time, materials, and enthusiasm for follow-up plans and projects.

22-7 Discuss the importance of teaching about peace in the early childhood program.

This continues to be critical in light of the increasing violence in our country, as well as in our schools. The conflicts that seem to be underway in every region of the globe demonstrate the profound need for creating paths to a peaceful and just world. Mahatma Gandhi said that if we are to have real peace in the world, we need to begin with children. Sowing the seeds for peace and justice in classrooms could nurture a new generation of world leaders and ordinary citizens who have a vision of a peaceful and just world and who have both the will and skill to bring this vision to reality.

22-8 List examples of appropriate social studies activities for older children.

Social studies activities are an excellent avenue for exploring the personal and social changes this age group is experiencing. Studying the work of artists who used their work for social expression and to effect social changes is an excellent social studies activity for older children. Studying the work of socially active artists such as Ben Shahn, Louise Berliawsky, Romare Bearden, and the quilters of Gee's Bend are appropriate for these activities. The social studies theme of power, authority, and governance is also an excellent base for developing learning experiences for students about their own individual rights and responsibilities in the increasingly complex social world of which they are a part.

Key Terms

10 thematic strands of social studies   531
common bonds curriculum   535
multicultural curriculum   536
personal celebration   541
teaching peace   541

Learning Activities

A. Relate incidents similar to the opening scenes in this chapter, demonstrating young children's level of social awareness. Explain why you think the children acted the way they did. Explain how an adult (or older child) would react in the same situation.

B. What community/school "helpers" would you invite to your room to aid children's understanding of their community? What would you have these visitors talk about, bring with them to class, and do with the children?

C. What are some ways the block area can be used to teach social studies ideas?

D. Prepare a unit plan on one of the following: family, self, or a specific community worker such as a firefighter. For your unit plan, include a section titled *Children's Books,* and include stories and other appropriate language arts activities.

E. Child Study

   1. Select three children of different ages (for example, 3, 5, and 9 years), and ask each separately to describe what

fathers and mothers do, what children can or cannot do when they grow up, or what happens when they are afraid. Do not contribute your own opinions until you are sure the children have said all they would like to about the matter.

   2. What changes in ideas do you notice as you listen to children of different ages? Did any of the children have a clear misunderstanding about some aspect of the issue you discussed? If so, how did you respond? How should parents respond when this happens?

F. Observe a dispute between children in an early childhood setting. Record how it was settled. Then compare this method of settlement with the information presented in this chapter on teaching peace. How did the real-life settlement compare? Did it help the children involved learn about peace? Why or why not?

G. Interview an experienced first-, second-, or third-grade teacher. Present that teacher with each of the situations that follow. Then ask her or him to answer the questions for the situation. Write the answers down and compare them. Discuss similarities and differences in the replies.

Situation 1: Clay ignores his fellow students most of the time. When his teacher tells the class it is time for finger painting, he grabs as many paint jars as he can. When asked to share these paints, he refuses.

Question 1: In your years as a teacher, have you had children who have behaved like this? Why do you think they do it? What need or needs underlie their behavior?

Question 2: As a general rule, what would you say is the best way to respond to this kind of behavior? Why?

Question 3: What is the worst way to respond? Why?

Situation 2: Anton is a clown. If he's not making faces, he's telling jokes—and he's always disrupting the class.

The other children laugh at him, but they don't seem to like him. In the schoolyard, he's generally alone.

Ask the same questions here as in Situation 1.

H. Visit two contrasting early childhood programs. For example, visit one small suburban center and a large, federally funded urban center. Compare and contrast the social studies curriculum you observed in each setting. Review activity plans. Can you see in these activities the evidence of a multicultural curriculum? Why or why not? Do the activities and classroom materials you observed reflect the ethnic and cultural make-up of the group? Be specific in your reply. Are the activities developmentally appropriate? Explain why or why not.

Activities for Children

Sample Multicultural Lesson Plans

Skin Color

Topics: I'm Me and I'm Special, Our Five Senses, Colors, Alike and Different, Light and Dark

Goal: To help children explore shades of skin color by making and mixing different colors of play dough

Materials: Mixing bowls, measuring cups, measuring spoons, large spoon for stirring, flour, salt, alum, oil, powdered tempera paint or cake decorator's (paste) food coloring

Method: With children, prepare five batches of play dough, one in each of the following colors: black, brown, red, yellow, white. Use this recipe or another one from this book. Give each child a small ball of play dough.

Play dough recipe

Ingredients
2 cups flour
1 cup salt
2 tablespoons alum
1½ cups warm water
1 tablespoon oil
paste food coloring or powdered tempera paint

Procedure: Mix 1–3 tablespoons of powdered tempera with liquid ingredients. Stir liquids into the dry ingredients. Knead until smooth. Store in an airtight container.

Tell children there are five different colors of play dough and that they can make different colors by mixing two or three colors together. For example, combining red play dough with white play dough will make pink play dough. Have children look at the color of their skin. Encourage them to mix different colors of play dough so that their ball of play dough matches their skin color. Encourage children to experiment with combining the play dough, talk with them about the concepts of new colors, shades of color, and lighter and darker. Make a picture recipe chart that shows how to mix colors. Display it in the art center for children's use during center time.

Variations

- Make a picture recipe chart that shows how to mix colors. Display it in the art center with the five colors of play dough available for individual children's use during center time.
- Put each child's ball of skin-colored play dough in a plastic bag and let the child take it home.
- During group time, see if children can order the balls of play dough from light to dark.

Body Learning

Topics: Bodies, I'm Me and I'm Special, Alike and Different
Goal: To help children learn about their bodies and compare their height, weight, skin color, hair, and facial features with those of their classmates

Materials: Mirrors, magnifying glasses, scale, tape measure
Method: Set above materials out on a table for children to explore. Encourage them to use the materials to find out about their bodies. Children may use the tape measure to measure each other's bodies. Talk about similarities and differences.

Variations

- Make a height and weight chart of all the children in the class. Take measurements throughout the year to help children become aware of changes in their bodies.
- Write down children's words as they describe themselves and their bodies.
- Make a poster for each child that includes his or her height, weight, and a self-description. The child may want to draw a self-portrait to add to the poster.

Family Photos

Topics: Families, Changes, Alike and Different, Clothes We Wear, Bodies

Goal: To help children discover that physical characteristics stay the same throughout life (racial/ethnic constancy)

Materials: Photographs of children's parents, photographs of each child, resealable plastic bags

Method: Collect photos from parents, assuring them that they will be returned in a week or two. Put the photos in resealable plastic bags for safekeeping. Tell the children they are going to play a guessing game and that you are going to set out the photos of parents for all the children to see. Everyone must be quiet and not tell the others which photo is of their parent. Give each child the photo of himself/herself to hold. One by one ask the children to come up in front of the group with their pictures. Encourage the child to show the photo to the class. Then ask the class to look at the photos of parents. Ask, "Who can guess which photo is of _____'s parents?"

Encourage the children to notice hair color, skin color, and other physical similarities. When a correct match has been made, place the child's photo next to the one of the parents. After everyone has had a turn, encourage the children to look at all the pictures. Ask the children, "What do you think you will look like when you grow up?" Talk about how children get their skin color and physical looks from their biological parents. Adopted children can talk about the similarities and differences in their skin color and physical appearance and that of their adopted parents. Also talk about how many of our physical characteristics such as skin color and eye color stay the same as we grow older.

Peace Puppets

Create puppets that encourage children to talk about feelings and solve problems in peaceful ways.

Ask children to think about all the different ways they feel: happy, sad, angry, cranky, excited, and so on. Talk about how the same person can feel different ways at different times. Explain that they are going to make puppets and that they can decide whether their puppet will represent one feeling (and which one) or many feelings.

Provide children with a variety of materials to design their puppets: socks, paper bags, fabric, pom-poms, yarn, felt. (See Chapter 15 for puppet-making ideas.) Ask children to name their puppets. Help them label each one with the feeling or feelings they choose.

Invite children to share their finished puppets with the group. Talk about how these puppets can be used to help people talk about and sort out feelings. For instance, if someone is feeling lonely or afraid, the appropriate puppet(s) can be brought out. If there's an argument, children might enlist the help of a puppet or two to listen to the problem and help them come up with solutions. Work together to decorate a box in which the puppets can be stored. Ask children to suggest a name for the special box—Peace Place, Puppets' Place, or the like.

Playing with Peace Puppets

Seat children in a circle. One child wears one of the newly made puppets on his or her hand. Speaking quietly, ask the child sitting closest to you to create a facial expression that shows a particular emotion. You might ask the child to show sadness, anger, or happiness. The child wearing the puppet will try to "read" the child's facial expression and talk as the puppet about that feeling. "I feel sad because I wanted to go to the store last night and my mom said we couldn't go."

Continue the activity until each child in the group has had a chance to show an emotion or express an emotion as the puppet.

Suggestions for Excursions Appropriate for Young Children

Supermarket. As eager as young children are, they have a limited attention span, so do not try to do too much. Make several trips to the supermarket, each with a different focus. Watch the goods being delivered. Watch the boxes being unpacked and merchandise being stamped. Look at all the different kinds of machines in the store.

Produce department. What are some things displayed on special cardboard or wrapped in individual papers? Why are some things displayed on crushed ice or refrigerated? See if you and the children can name the fruits and vegetables.

Dairy department. What kinds of things are sold here? Why are they kept cold? Where do the various products come from?

Meat department. Watch the butcher cut and package meat. Why is the meat kept cold? Is it cold in the back, too? See how many varieties of meat you can name.

Bakery department. Compare the ovens with ovens at home and the size of the flour sacks with the sacks that you buy. Notice the quantities of baked goods and the process of baking. What kinds of clothes do the bakers wear? Why?

Shoe repair shop. Watch the person make repairs. Try to give the person something that needs fixing. What kinds of machines do they have? What kinds of materials do they use? Try to get some scraps to take back for making collages.

Dry-cleaning shop. What kinds of smells are in the air there? What kind of machine is used for ironing? How does the cleaner know which clothes are yours?

Pet store. What kinds of pets does this store have? Are there any unusual ones? What do the various pets eat? What kinds of houses do they provide for the various pets?

Florist's shop. Visiting this shop is an especially good activity on a cold winter's day when everything outside is barren and bleak. A walk through the greenhouse may bring many questions to mind: Why are the flowers growing inside the greenhouse and not outdoors? What kinds of plants are there? What kinds of smells are there? How does the florist keep cut flowers from dying? Buy a plant and learn how to take care of it. The workroom, where bouquets, baskets of flowers, and corsages are assembled, will be of interest to children.

The police officer and crossing guard. Within walking distance of your school, there is probably an intersection or a school where a police officer or crossing guard is on duty. Watch what he or she does. How does the guard tell the vehicles and pedestrians to go? To stop? The children enjoy talking to the officer and getting a good look at his or her uniform. The police station is of interest to the children, too; perhaps the desk sergeant on duty will spend a few minutes visiting with the children. (You will plan this in advance, of course.) He or she may show children the inside of a police car and the radio, and give them a short safety speech.

Mail delivery. Make arrangements to meet your own letter carrier at your mailbox and then at the nearest pick-up box on the corner to watch him or her gather the mail. Buy a stamp and mail a letter at the post office. Children are not usually allowed in the back of most post offices, but they can see a good deal if they look through the window of the parcel-post counter. Watch the packages being weighed and mailed.

Bus driver (conductor). Sit near the driver of the bus. Watch what he or she does. Look at the uniform.

Fire station. Some fire departments have open-house days. If yours does not, make an appointment for a visit ahead of time. Do not insist that children get on the equipment, even if invited to do so. Climbing on an engine can be a frightening experience for some young children. Usually the child is invited to try on a firefighter's hat, watch a firefighter slide down the pole, and inspect the engine. Find out how the fire alarm works, where the different firefighters stand on the truck, and what each of them does at a fire. Later, look at fire hydrants and fire escapes in buildings. Point out fire doors and fire extinguishers or sprinklers in various buildings.

Library. Take the children to the children's section of the library. Let them browse. Show them that all the books have letters or letters and numbers written on the bindings. Why? Perhaps your library has a storybook time that you can attend. How does the librarian know which book you take out? Check out some books so children can see the procedure.

Sanitation workers. Be aware of the sanitation workers, street sweepers, or snowplow drivers in action and how they are dressed. Why do they wear gloves?

Construction site. What kind of building is going up? What are the girders for? What kinds of machines can you see? What do they do? How do the workers dress? Why?

Repair site. Observe a surface or underground repair site. What is being fixed? What equipment is in use? How are the workers dressed? Why? What is under the street or sidewalk? Where did the rocks and soil come from?

Printing plant or newspaper plant. Call ahead of time and find out if tours are available and when the presses are operating. Remember to bring some paper remnants back for children's artwork.

Field Trip Hint

On any of the preceding field trips, try color-coding to help make the trip less stressful for chaperones. Write each student's name and number on a tab, using a specific color-coded ink. This way, chaperones only need to look for students wearing their assigned color tags. Then they can put the children in numerical order to make sure all children are accounted for—without having to call out names.

Self-Awareness Activities

Lining Up and Learning

Choose a topic, such as birth dates (with or without the year) and ask the children to line up in order of that topic.

Set two points between which the lines should be made and designate which end is, in this case, January 1 and which is December 31. To make the game more challenging (and fun), prohibit speaking. Examples of other topics to line up about could be shoe size, height, favorite color, and so on.

Name Toss

For this activity, you will need soft balls such as Koosh, Nerf, or tennis balls and enough room for the group to stand in a circle. Start by having the group stand or sit in a circle. Before starting the activity, each child says his or her name once. Using a soft ball, call out someone's name and gently toss the ball to that person, saying "What's up, (name)?" The recipient says, "Thanks, (name of tosser)," then calls out someone else's name and tosses the ball to him or her—thanking the person who tossed the ball. This repeats until the ball gets back to the person who started the activity. Each person gets the ball and tosses it once. Then challenge the group to toss the ball through the same sequence, but faster. Saying the names and thank you must still happen.

All About Us

This activity centers on the children's heads and faces. Ask them to describe everything that they all have on their heads and faces. Record their responses on chart paper.

Prepare separate sheets of chart paper for each part of the head and face (nose, eyes, ears, mouth, and hair). Tell children that each day they will focus on a different part and discuss their differences and their similarities.

Invite children to begin each investigation by discussing how they all use each body part and how they are all similar: "We all use our eyes to see." Record their responses. Ask children to examine each of their classmates' specific facial features. How are their eyes similar or different? Notice how lips have different shapes. Do ears all look the same? Record children's observations on each chart.

Have children work together to summarize what they learned about their facial features. Have them reflect on why it is special to look different. What would happen if everyone looked the same?

Provide children with a variety of art materials to create a self-portrait. Include flesh-tone markers, crayons, and paper. Encourage them to use a mirror to observe their facial features and to notice the details of their faces. Ask children to describe why they are special. Record their words on a sheet of paper and attach it beneath each self-portrait.

All About Me

- From magazines, children can cut pictures that they like or that remind them of themselves.
- Make up "Guess Who" riddles describing individual children. Suggest clues that reflect the child's positive characteristics.
- Make a set of flash cards or similar cards with pictures of community workers. Children should be encouraged

to bring pictures of their parents at their jobs or wearing clothing appropriate for that job. An additional activity could be to collect pictures of tools or items related to various jobs and have children sort them.

- Videotape interviews with community helpers. Children will be especially proud to hear their parents tell about their professions and jobs.
- Have children cut out or tear out pictures from magazines or brochures that show people or families of different ages or cultures having fun or working together. Children can use these to create a collage.
- Keep a supply of pictures of people available for very young children to paste into books. Older children might want to mount the pictures as a mural on a background they have prepared with other media.

How Do I Look?

- Discuss differences in sex. Ask: "Do girls look different from boys? How? Clothing? Hair? What else? Do men look different from ladies? How? Do they sound different?" If a child brings out the difference in sex organs, accept their comments matter-of-factly.
- Take snapshots of the children, alone or in groups, and mount them on a bulletin board or in a scrapbook with the names of the children printed beneath the pictures. These pictures are an excellent starting point for a discussion about how we all have the same body parts, even though we all look different. In this and other such activities, emphasize that we are more alike than different. Natural points in such a discussion are color, size, and shape of eyes, hair, nose, mouth, and so on.
- On a more personal level, try the following self-study activity to see how you look to the children you work with.

Self-study: How children see you. Select one or two children who are at least 4 years old. Seat them individually at a table with paper and crayons (or felt-tip pens) and ask them to draw a picture of you. Encourage them to take their time and include as much detail as they want. When they are finished, give them another sheet of paper and ask them to draw a self-portrait.

When both pictures are completed, cut them out and paste them side by side. First look at each child's drawing of you. What features appear to be most important to the children? Did they overlook any important characteristics, such as a beard, long hair, or glasses? Compare the drawing of you with the child's self-portrait. How are they similar? How are they different? Is there more detail in your picture or in the self-portrait? Is one bigger than the other? Is there a difference in emotional expression? Do these drawings reveal anything about how these children view themselves and you?

Sharing and Learning About Each Other

Send a note home requesting a baby photograph of each child. Photocopy the baby photograph if families want it returned. Then photograph each child in the class. Cover all pictures with clear Con-Tact® paper to make them more durable.

At group time, have the children share their baby photos. Ask them to describe their picture, or ask them questions to encourage discussion. Explain that they will be playing some games with their baby pictures.

Divide the children into two or three small groups, depending on the number of teachers present. Begin by placing all of their current photos face up on the table. Place their baby photos in a pile face down. Ask one child at a time to choose a baby picture and match it with the current photo on the table.

After children have become familiar with the pairs of the photos, challenge them with a game of Concentration. Mix up all of the photos and place them face down on the table. Invite one child at a time to turn over two photos to find matching sets. If the photographs do not match, turn them over and invite the next child to try. Remove the photographs after the match is found.

Follow-up activity: Make copies of the photos you took for this activity for a class book. Glue each child's picture on the upper-left corner of lined story paper. Have the child dictate information about himself or herself: age, birthday, favorite color, favorite food. Bind all the pages together. Then take a photo of the whole class for the cover of the book. Place the book in the book corner for children to enjoy.

Shoe Game

Everyone takes off one shoe, including teachers! Place all of the shoes in a bag. While sitting in a circle, ask one child at a time to close his or her eyes and pick a shoe out of the bag. The child has to find the person in the circle wearing the matching shoe. When the child comes to the person wearing the matching shoe, he or she must say, "How do you do? Is this your shoe?" and shake hands. The child or adult with the matching shoe will be the next to pick a shoe. Repeat this until everyone has had a turn, and everyone has a matching pair of shoes.

Friendly Faces

During group time, ask children if they know what a portrait is. Tell them that they are going to make a portrait of a classmate. Share some pictures of portraits done by famous artists and discuss the various styles used in each. Portraits from artists such as Van Gogh, Rembrandt, Velasquez, Picasso, and Matisse are good examples. Talk about how some portraits may look very lifelike while others may be done in very bright colors or with only a few lines.

Put the names of all children on separate slips of paper and put the slips in a hat. Draw out two slips; that will be the first pair. That pair then draws out two more names for the next pair. Continue drawing out two slips until all the children are in pairs. If you don't have an even number of children, pair a child with a teacher.

Provide children with white drawing paper; large, colored construction paper; pencils; crayons; and markers. Invite one child to sit on a chair within view of a classmate who is doing the drawing. Remind children who are drawing that they should look at their friend as they draw their portrait. The following day, have children who posed for their portraits assume the role of portrait-maker. Mount the portraits onto larger sheets of colored construction paper to create frames for the drawings. Invite children to decorate their frames. Display portraits with enough space below each portrait to add another sheet of paper.

Activities for Older Children (Grades 4–5)

Read About Artists

Encourage students to read and find out the following things about an artist of their choice:

- Life of the artist: biographical information such as birth, death, marriage, children, and friends
- Who and what most influenced the artist
- Time period in which the artist lived
- Country or countries where the artist lived
- Style in which the artist worked or school of art to which the artist belonged
- Influence the artist had on the world of art (what the artist is best known for)
- Medium(s) the artist used
- A particular work of art the artist did, for example, the most famous or controversial

Write About Art and Artists

Here is a list of possible writing and art and artist connections for language arts activities:

- Letter to the artist or someone in the picture
- Letter to the curator of a museum to request information about a work of art
- Biographical sketch of the artist
- Report on the customs of the time of the artist
- Report on the clothing styles of the time of the artist
- Story about how the work of art came to be
- Paragraph hypothesizing what the artist would do if he or she were alive today
- Play about the artist's life
- Timeline of the artist's work
- TV commercial about the artist and his or her work

African American World for Kids

Challenge your students to participate in an online Concentration-type matching game with famous African Americans as the subject matter. *African American World for Kids* is a small, focused website that will be useful as a motivational and reinforcement tool for units on African American history. Participants match drawings of famous people to descriptions of associated events. Some of the famous people included in the four levels of play are Harriet Tubman, Jesse Jackson, Jackie Robinson, Jesse Owens, Toni Morrison, Malcolm X, and Duke Ellington. The site also has an e-card section that allows students to send African American-themed postcards to their friends via email. Finally, there is a question-and-answer section with commentary from students.

National and International Treasures

National parks. Divide the class into groups. Have each group research a national park (there are 53 to choose from). Begin online. From there, each group can link to their individual selection. Have students prepare presentations that include visuals such as maps, posters, travel brochures, and the like.

Architecture and Multicultural Learning

A country's unique architecture can be a form of art to study as well as a symbol of a cultural group's pride and unity. The Taj Mahal, the Eiffel Tower, the Leaning Tower of Pisa, the Great Pyramids of Gaza, and the Great Wall of China—all are architectural symbols of a national, proudly shared identity of a people. An architectural triumph gives a nation's citizens an identity that is unique.

The Taj Mahal is an ideal architectural subject that mixes world history and art to transport a child's mind to distant horizons and cultures.

Obtain a poster of the Taj Mahal, or download an image of it from the Internet. Introduce students to the structure while playing *Scheherazade* by Rimsky-Korsakov to command their immediate attention. The building is so different, so beautiful. Ask students what it might be. Responses may range from a castle to a wealthy person's home to a palace or religious institution.

Tell students that the Taj Mahal is actually a mausoleum for a princess, Mumtaz Mahal, who died in childbirth. *Mahal* means "chosen of the palace." Her husband, the Mogul Emperor Shah Jahan of India, was heartbroken by her death and commissioned in her memory a great mausoleum like none the world had ever seen.

The Taj Mahal took 17 years to build, from 1612 to 1629 A.D. Mumtaz sarcophagus was placed directly in the center of the perfectly symmetrical structure.

While more than 75% of the people of India are Hindu, the Mogul period of rule was Muslim. There are significant differences between these two religious groups. The Taj Mahal is clearly an example of bringing a country's people together under the common symbol that is great art.

Architecture Around the World

Ask these questions to establish a broad understanding of a particular structure researched by students:

- What is a famous architectural structure of the world and where is it located?
- What is the meaning of the structure's name?
- What are the distinctive building techniques and materials used?
- What are five or more new vocabulary words associated with this structure?

Tell children that they will share something that they think is special about each person in the class. Focus on one or two children each day. Record the comments on one sheet of paper per child. Place these comments underneath each portrait.

- Is there a musical composition that can in some way be associated with this architecture and its people?

Write a paragraph about the most memorable aspects of this structure. If you have visited this place, let your five senses reflect your direct experience.

The Roman Colosseum. People have gathered at the Roman Colosseum throughout history. Search the Internet for views of the Roman Colosseum.

What was the original function of this structure? How has it been used throughout history? Does the Colosseum look different now compared to when it was created? What shapes were used in designing it? Can you think of any modern structures that might have been influenced by the Colosseum?

Art and Social Studies

Updated art. Have students create a modern-day version of an artist's work, one that reflects the current time rather than the time in which it was created. Students can change the background or subjects' dress in their portraits.

Class flags. Have students examine the flags and symbols of countries. Discuss with them how and why these countries use the colors, shapes, designs, materials, and lines that they do. Divide the class into groups to create a class flag to represent what's important about the class. Make fabric, paper, paint, and collage materials available for the design.

Famous people sculptures. Students choose a person they want to study who has made a significant contribution to history (explorer, president, artist, musician, activist). Have students brainstorm what facts about this person they would like to know. Have students use library and Internet sources to research their subject. They should try to discover details about how the person looked, moved, talked, and dressed, and what she or he ate, valued, achieved, and so on.

After researching their subject, students might construct sculptures of that person from papier mâché or make a puppet that represents that person (see Chapter 14 and Chapter 15 for papier mâché and puppet making ideas). Students can use their sculptures or puppets to role-play and do a presentation for the class. Allow time for questions.

History Makers—Social Studies Theme: Continuity and Change

On the classroom calendar, mark and label the birthdays of Betsy Ross (January 1) and Martin Luther King, Jr. (January 15). Have one-half of the class research Betsy Ross and the other half Dr. King. Have the Ross group present a research fact, and the King group presents a finding for a similar or the same category (for example, birthplace). Continue the activity until no further similarities can be found.

Freedom—Social Studies Theme: Continuity and Change

Call attention to the anniversary of the Emancipation Proclamation (January 1st). Guide children in finding and considering meanings of *emancipation* and *proclamation*. Help them research the historical actions and decisions associated with the Emancipation Proclamation. Probe for and emphasize reasons the proclamation was needed.

Regional Crafts—Social Studies Theme: Culture and Continuity

Provide reference materials showing crafts created in your area in the past 100 years. Lead a discussion about how these objects are both functional and beautiful.

Have small groups of students choose one craft that they find especially appealing. Encourage each group to choose a different craft. Have them list questions about the craft. Sample questions follow:

1. How was this (basket) made?
2. How long have people been making these (wooden boxes) by hand?
3. Do people still make these (silver buttons) today?
4. What tools were needed to create the (lace on this apron)?

Then have students do research to find the answers to their questions. Suggest that they interview craftspeople in addition to using nonfiction books, encyclopedias, and multimedia sources. Have students report their findings about the craft to the class.

Tie-Dyed Squares—Social Studies Theme: Culture and Continuity

Tell students that they will create a type of fiber art called *tie-dyeing*. Explain that this art form originated in China between A.D. 617 and 906. Tie-dyed fabrics created at that time were worn mainly by the nobility and priests.

You will need art smocks, 10-inch squares of muslin (at least one per student), acrylic or tempera paint, containers for a water-paint mixture, string, safety scissors, and rubber gloves.

Prepare several tubs of dye by mixing tempera paints or acrylic paints with water. Have students put on rubber gloves and do the following:

1. Place the muslin square on a flat surface.
2. Use their fingertips to gather a clump of material.
3. Tie the clump by tightly wrapping string around it.
4. Repeat until several clumps have been created.
5. Submerge cloth in dye for about 20 minutes.
6. Remove cloth, and untie or cut away string.
7. Dry cloth on a flat surface.

Obelisks in Egypt and Washington DC—Social Studies Theme: Culture and Continuity

Visit www.nps.gov/wamo/ for a picture of the Washington Monument. Explain that the structure was designed by an architect named Robert Mills and that he based his design on a type of ancient Egyptian structure called an *obelisk*.

Have students work with partners or in small groups to create a chart comparing the Washington Monument with an example of an Egyptian obelisk. (Students may want to research one of the obelisks called *Cleopatra's Needle*.) A sample chart is shown here. Students may want to use the categories listed or ones they create.

Washington Monument	**Egyptian Obelisk**
Height	
Weight	
Date completed	
Designer	
Today's location	
Other information	

Time Continuity and Change Strand—Activities for Multiple Intelligences

Using the theme of time, the following activities are designed for various multiple intelligences.

Time theme. Have students construct a sundial. Explain to the class how sundials were used, and give them a brief history of the sundial. (spatial/bodily–kinesthetic)

Music feelings. Play for students several pieces of music that have different rhythms and speeds. Have students write a short paper on how slow music makes them feel compared to fast music. Make sure to identify the songs and their singers or composers. (musical/intrapersonal)

Be on time! Have students prepare a 5-minute oral report on the importance of being on time. (verbal–linguistic/interpersonal)

Seasonal fashions. Have students prepare and present a report to show how the seasons influence the clothes we wear. They should include as many types of media as they can in their report. (visual/spatial/linguistic)

Family research. Have students interview their parents about what their lives were like as children. Students might look through family albums for photographs of their parents as children. Have students write a brief report about their parents' lives as children, using photos as illustrations. (verbal–linguistic/intrapersonal)

Dance. Have students learn a dance such as the waltz or the jitterbug that were popular in the past and still enjoyed today. They can demonstrate the dance for the class and relate its history. (bodily–kinesthetic/interpersonal)

Timeline. Have students construct a timeline for a period of history they've recently studied, marking the important and interesting events. Add pictures and colors to make it even more interesting. (spatial/math–logic)

Family scrapbook. Have students research their family history and create a family tree. They can see how far back they can trace their family members and where they came from. Encourage students to use their family tree to start a family scrapbook. They might add funny stories or interesting facts about family members as well as pictures, letters, and drawings. (intrapersonal/interpersonal/spatial/verbal–linguistic)

Virtual Field Trips

The Internet is a powerful tool for learning about the world. Older students will enjoy the following virtual field trips and other social studies-related Web field trips.

Visit the White House. On this Web page, you can take a tour of the First Lady's garden, read current press releases, and access information about other government agencies (www.whitehouse.gov).

Latin America. The University of New Mexico's Latin American Institute offers two resources on Latin America: the Latin America Data Base (http://ladb.unm.edu) and an outreach program, Resources for Teaching about the Americas (http://laii.unm.edu/resources/), which includes resources for art, literature, social studies, and science and math units that include Latin America.

Asia. The Asia Society has a wide range of resources for K–12 teachers and students (www.AskAsia.org). Asia for Educators (www.asiasociety.org) has materials on China, Japan, Korea, and Southeast Asia, including primary source texts and multimedia modules. The Stanford Program on International and Cross-Cultural Education (http://spice.stanford.edu/) provides teaching resources and lesson plans on many cultures.

References

Ayers, A., & McMillan, E. (2010). Whirled peace: The evolution of Pinwheels for Peace. *SchoolArts, 110*(1), 48–49.

Baker, M., Martin, D., & Pence, H. (2008). Supporting peace education in teacher education programs. *Childhood Education, 85*(1), 20–25.

Brownell, C. A., Ramani, G. B., & Zerwas, S. (2012). Becoming a social partner with peers: Cooperation and social understanding in one- and two-year-olds. *Child Development, 77*(4), 803–821.

Epstein, A. S. (2009). *Me, you, us: Social-emotional learning in preschool.* Ypsilanti, MI: High Scope Research Foundation.

Kao, D. (2000). *Ben Shahn's New York: The photography of modern times.* Cambridge, MA: Harvard University Art Museum.

Lindsay, M. H. (2009). Defining peace. *SchoolArts, 108*(7), 40–41.

Mille, S. (2005, Fall). Building a peaceful and just world—beginning with the children. *Childhood Education, 81*(3), 14–18.

National Association for the Education of Young Children (NAEYC). (1991). Guidelines for appropriate curriculum content and assessment programs serving children ages 3–8. *Young Children, 46*(3), 21–38.

National Council for the Social Studies (NCSS). (2010). *National curriculum standards for social studies: A framework for teaching, learning, and assessment.* Washington, DC: Academy Press.

 Visit CourseMate for this textbook to access the eBook, Did You Get It? quizzes, Digital Downloads, TeachSource Videos, flashcards, and more. Go to CengageBrain.com to log in, register, or purchase access.

Gross- and Fine-Motor Skills[1]

By 2 Years

Gross Motor

- Walks forward (average age 12 months)
- Walks backward (average age 15 months)
- Walks up stairs with help (average age 17 months)
- Moves self from sitting to standing (average age 18 months)
- Seats self in small chair (average age 18 months)
- Uses rocking horse or rocking chair with aid (average age 18 months)

Fine Motor

- Builds tower of two blocks (average age 15 months)
- Builds tower of three or four blocks (average age 19 months)
- Places pellet in bottle (average age 15 months)
- Places blocks in cup (average age 15 months)
- Places four rings on peg or large pegs in pegboard (average age 18 months)
- Imitates vertical line stroke (average age 20 months)
- Turns pages of book, two or three at a time (average age 21 months)

By 2½ Years

Gross Motor

- Kicks ball forward (average age 20 months)
- Jumps in place (average age 23 months)

- Runs (stiffly) (average age 2 years)
- Hurls small ball overhand, one hand, without direction (average age 22 months)
- Pedals tricycle (average age 2 years)

Fine Motor

- Builds tower of six cube blocks (average age 23 months)
- Imitates circular motion with crayon, after demonstration (average age 2¼ years)
- Turns pages of book, one at a time (average age 2 years)

By 3 Years

Gross Motor

- Walks up and down stairs without adult help, but not alternating feet (average age 22 months)
- Walks four steps on tiptoe (average age 2¼ years)
- Jumps from bottom step (average age 2 years)
- Walks backward 10 feet (average age 28 months)
- Broad jumps 24–34 inches (average age 2½ years)
- Balances on one foot, 1 second (average age 2½ years)

Fine Motor

- Imitates vertical line from demonstration (average age 22 months)
- Imitates vertical or horizontal line (average age 2½ years)

---

[1]Ninety percent of children at specific age level will have acquired skill.
Adapted from Gesell, A., Ilg, F. L., Ames, L. B., & Rodell, J. L. (1974). *Infant and child in the culture of today: The guidance of development in home and nursery school*. New York, NY: Harper and Row.

- Imitates V stroke from demonstration (average age 2½ years)
- Strings four beads in 2 minutes (average age 2½ years)
- Folds paper (average age 2½ years)
- Builds tower of seven or eight cubes (average age 2½ years)

By 3½ Years

Gross Motor

- Walks on tiptoe 10 feet (average age 3 years)
- Balances on one foot, 5 seconds (average age 3¼ years)

Fine Motor

- Imitates bridge of three blocks from demonstration (average age 3 years)
- Copies circle from picture model (average age 3 years)
- Imitates cross from demonstration (average age 3 years)
- Closes fist, wiggles thumb (average age 35 months)
- Picks longer of two lines (average age 3 years)

By 4 Years

Gross Motor

- Hops, preferred foot (average age 3½ years)
- Walks up stairs, one foot on each step, holding rail (average age 3½ years)
- Walks down stairs, one step per tread (average age 3½ years)
- Throws ball with direction (average age 3½ years)
- Balances on toes (average age 3½ years)
- Jumps over rope 8 inches high (average age 3½ years)
- Swings on swing independently (average age 3½ years)
- Jumps from height of 12 inches (average age 3½ years)
- Holds standing balance, one foot advanced, eyes closed, 15 seconds (one of two tries by 4 years)

Fine Motor

- Buttons up clothing (average age 3 years)
- Cuts with scissors (average age 3½ years)
- Touches point of nose with eyes closed (by age 4, two of three tries)
- Puts 20 coins in a box, separately (by age 4, one of two tries)

By 4½ Years

Gross Motor

- Balances standing on one foot, 5 seconds (average age 3¼ years)
- Does forward somersault with aid (average age 3½ years)
- Catches ball in arms, two of three tries (average age 4)
- Catches bounced ball (average age 4 years)
- Heel-to-toe walk (average age 3¾ years)
- Jumps from height of 2½ feet (average age 4 years)

Fine Motor

- Copies cross from picture model (average age 3¾ years)
- Draws a person, three parts (average age 4 years)
- Copies square from demonstration (average age 4 years)

By 5 Years

Gross Motor

- Balances on one foot for 10 seconds (average age 4½ years)
- Hops on nonpreferred foot (average age 4½ years)
- Bounces ball two times successively with one hand (average age 4½ years)
- Catches large bounced ball, two of three tries (average age 4 years)
- Somersaults forward without aid (average age 4¾ years)
- Balances on tiptoes for 10 seconds, one of three tries (by age 5 years)
- Jumps over cord at knee height, feet together, one of three tries (average age 4½ years)
- Walks heel to toe (average age 4¾ years)
- Walks heel to toe, backward (average age 4¾ years)
- Walks 2- by 4-inch balance beam, 3 inches off floor, without falling (average age 4½ years)

Fine Motor

- Builds pyramid of six blocks after demonstration (average age 4½ years)
- Clenches and bares teeth (by age 5 years)
- Draws diamond after demonstration (average age 4½ years)
- Copies square from picture model (average age 4¾ years)
- Ties any knot that holds with lace (average age 5 years)

Language Development Objectives and Activities for Infants and Toddlers

Level	Objective	Activity
Birth to 1 month	1. To develop intimacy and awareness of communication based on personal contact. 2. To introduce the concept of oral communication. 3. To introduce verbal communication. 4. To stimulate interest in the process of talking.	1. Whisper into the child's ear. 2. Coo at the child. 3. Talk to the child. 4. Let the child explore your mouth with his or her hands as you talk.
1 to 3 months	1. To develop oral communication. 2. To develop auditory acuity. 3. To develop the concept that different people sound different. 4. To develop the concept of oral and musical communication of feelings.	1. Imitate the sounds the child makes. 2. Talk to the child in different tones. 3. Encourage others to talk and coo to the child. 4. Sing songs of different moods, rhythms, and tempos.
3 to 6 months	1. To develop the concept of positive use of verbal communication. 2. To stimulate excitement about words. 3. To develop the concept that words and music can be linked. 4. To develop the ability to name things and events.	1. Reward the child with words. 2. Talk expressively to the child. 3. Sing or chant to the child. 4. Describe daily rituals to the child as you carry them out.
6 to 9 months	1. To develop use of words. 2. To develop the concept that things have names. 3. To develop the concept that there is joy in the written word. 4. To develop the concept that language is used to describe.	1. Talk constantly to the child and reinforce intimacy. Explain processes such as feeding, bathing, and changing clothes. 2. Name toys for the child as the child plays, foods and utensils as the child eats, and so on. 3. Read aloud to the child with expression and enthusiasm. 4. Describe sounds to the child as they are heard.
9 to 12 months	1. To develop the concept that body parts have names. 2. To reinforce the concept that things have names. 3. To stimulate rhythm and interest in words. 4. To stimulate experimentation with sounds and words.	1. Name parts of the body and encourage the child to point to them. 2. Describe and name things seen on a walk or an automobile trip. 3. Repeat simple songs, rhymes, and finger plays. 4. Respond to sounds the child makes and encourage the child to imitate sounds.

Level	Objective	Activity
12 to 18 months	1. To develop the ability to label things and follow directions. 2. To expand vocabulary and lay the foundation for later production of sentences. 3. To reinforce the concept of names and the ability to recognize names and sounds. 4. To encourage verbal communication. 5. To reinforce the concept of labels and increase vocabulary.	1. Link up various objects and, naming one, ask the child to get it. 2. Act out verbs (*sit, jump, run, smile,* and so on). 3. Use animal picture books and posters of animals. 4. Let the child talk on a real telephone. 5. Describe things at home or outside on a walk or a car trip.
18 to 24 months	1. To stimulate imitation and verbalization. 2. To improve the ability to name objects. 3. To encourage repetition, sequencing, and rhythm. 4. To develop auditory acuity, passive vocabulary, and the concept of language constancy. 5. To stimulate verbalization, selectivity, and—eventually—descriptive language. 6. To stimulate conversation.	1. Tape record the child and others familiar to the child, and play the tapes back for the child. 2. On a walk around the home or neighborhood with the child, point out and name familiar objects. 3. Play counting games, sing songs, and tell and retell familiar stories. 4. With the child, listen to the same recording of a story or song over and over. 5. Cut from magazines and mount on stiff cardboard: pictures of foods, clothing, appliances, and so on. Have the child identify them as you show them. Use memorable descriptions: " orange, buttery carrots," "the shiny blue car." 6. With the child, prepare and eat a make-believe meal.
24 to 36 months	1. To practice descriptive language and build vocabulary. 2. To encourage verbalization, repetition, comprehension, and speaking in sentences. 3. To develop the concept of written symbols. 4. To encourage specific and descriptive language. 5. To increase understanding of the relation between spoken and written language, and to stimulate the use of both.	1. Keep a box of scraps of materials and small objects. Have the child select objects, using words to describe them (*fuzzy, big, red,* and so on). 2. Ask the child: "Show me the floor, the door," and so on When the child points, say, "Here's the floor," and so on, and encourage the child to imitate you. 3. Label the child's possessions. Use the child's name repeatedly: "Mike's bed," "Mike's toy chest." 4. Ask "Which one?" when the child gives a single-word description, and expand on the child's language (for example, Child: "Cookie." You: "Yes, this is a ginger cookie."). 5. Call the child's attention to familiar brand names or identifying symbols on products, buildings, and so on.

Art Talk Summary

The following are some basic art elements to keep in mind when talking with children about their art.

Color

Hue: Primary Colors   Secondary Colors
    red   green
    blue   violet (purple)
    yellow   orange

Value

Mix black with color to make a *shade*.
Add black to a color to make it darker.
Mix white with a color to make a *tint*.
Add white to a color to make it lighter.

Line

These lines are used in artwork:
Straight
Curved
Zigzag
Horizontal
Vertical
Diagonal

Shape

These shapes are used in artwork:
Geometric
Circle
Square
Rectangle
Triangle
Oval
Diamond
Organic (natural)
Free-form

Composition

Balance in artwork can be one of the following:
Symmetrical
Radial
Asymmetrical or overall

Talk to Child About

Lines
Shapes
Colors
Content

Exhibitions and Displays

It is stimulating and educational for children to see their work displayed. Whether the purpose of the exhibit is to introduce new ideas and information, to stimulate interest in a single lesson, to show children's work, or to provide an overview of their work, the subject of the exhibition should be directly related to children's interest. Exhibits should be changed often to be of educational and decorative value.

Labels

- Make large, bold letters that can be easily read.
- Keep titles brief. Descriptive material should be in smaller letters.
- Label children's work with their names as a means of creating pride through recognition of their work.
- Vary the material in making letters. In addition to paper letters, labels can be made of paint, ink, crayon, chalk, cloth, fancy papers, string, rope, yarn, and other three-dimensional materials.

Color

- Choose a basic color scheme related to the visual material displayed. Seasonal colors can be used, such as warm colors for fall (yellow, orange, red), cool colors for winter (blue, blue-green, gray), and light and cool colors for spring (colors with yellow in the mixture, such as yellow-orange).
- Use colors for mounting that are more subdued than the materials mounted. This may be accomplished by using lighter, darker, or grayer colors.
- Select a bright color for accent, as in bands or other pleasing arrangements on the larger areas of gray or lighter or darker colors.

- Create a contrast to emphasize or attract attention. Intense color makes a visual impact, such as orange against black.
- Use both light and dark color values.
- Create color patterns that lead the eye from area to area.

Balance

Balance can be achieved formally or informally. To create formal balance, the largest piece of work may be placed in the center with similar shapes on either side. Informal balance is more interesting, subtle, and compelling. Material may be grouped in blocks of different sizes, colors, or shapes and still be balanced. Margins of the bulletin board should be wider at the bottom.

Unity

Unity in design is the quality that holds the arrangement together in harmony.

- Ideas can be unified with background paper, lettering, strips of construction paper, yarn, or ribbon.
- Repetition of similar sizes, shapes, colors, or lines can help create harmony.
- Shapes can be arranged to lead the eye from one part of the board to another.
- One large unusual background shape helps unify the design.
- Avoid cluttering the display; items placed at all angles destroy the unity.

Variety

Variety in arrangement prevents monotony. Use interesting combinations of color, form, line, and texture.

Emphasis

Emphasis is the main idea or center of interest. This can be achieved by using larger letters, a brighter color, a larger picture, an unusual shape or texture, or a three-dimensional object. Other material should be grouped into subordinate areas.

Line

Line is used to draw the eye to a specific area, to suggest direction, action, and movement, and to hold the display together. Use thick, thin, solid, dotted, or dashed lines. Diagonal lines are used to show action; zigzag lines suggest excitement; slow-moving curves are restful. Lines may be painted, cut from paper, or formed with string, yarn, ribbon, or tape.

Texture

Texture may be created with a variety of materials:
- Paper and cardboard—textured wallpaper, sandpaper, foil, egg containers, corrugated cardboard
- Fabrics—netting, flannel, burlap, fur, felt, carpet remnants, assorted felt scraps
- Miscellaneous—chicken wire, metal screen, sheet cork

Three-Dimensional Effects

- Pull letters or objects out to the head of the pin.
- Staple a shallow box to the board as a shelf to hold lightweight three-dimensional items.
- Mount a picture on a box lid and fasten it to the board.
- Use shallow boxes as buildings, animals, and people.
- Pleat a strip of paper in an accordion fold with pictures attached.
- Use paper sculpture—strips of paper can be twisted, curled, folded, rolled, fringed, perforated, or torn. Puppets, animals, birds, flowers, people, abstract forms, and masks can also be made.
- Use three-dimensional materials in displays: Styrofoam, egg cartons, paper plates, paper cups, soda straws, cupcake cups, paper lace, toweling tubes, and other discarded materials.
- Use objects from nature—branches, shells, bark, driftwood, feathers.

Background Materials

- Tissue paper, burlap, corrugated cardboard, construction paper
- Blotters, textured wallpaper, shelf paper

Display Boards for Two-Dimensional Work

- Standard cork boards or sheet of plywood to which cork tiles have been glued
- Builder's wallboard with wood strip nailed to the top with hooks for hanging
- Thick cardboard that will hold pins
- A pasteboard box open for standing on a table or the floor, depending on size
- A folding screen made from an old crate or packing box

More on Bulletin Boards—Kindergarten and Elementary Level

The most immediate evidence of an art program is the display of children's artwork. A teacher's creative approach to display is an extension of the art program in the physical environment. Bulletin boards are the most frequent form of display. Consider the following fairy tale.

> Once upon a time, there was a carpenter who was building a classroom. When he was on the very top of his ladder, a hammer fell and crashed into the wall, making a very large hole. The carpenter did not know what to do because he had no materials left to repair the wall. Suddenly he had an idea! He found a 4- × 8-foot slab of cork and hung it over the hole. Then he tacked wood strips around the edges and said, "I am well pleased." He named his creation "Bulletin Board."

The dictionary defines *bulletin board* as "a board on which bulletins and other notices are posted." Teachers often have other definitions for this term: (1) a surface that must be covered before the first day of school and before parents' night; (2) a board that is always 3 inches wider than the paper just cut for it; and (3) a rectangle that has a width never sufficient for the number of letters needed to be pinned across it.

Whatever your definition, a bulletin board is much more than a board on which notices are posted. It is a visual extension of a learning experience, a visual form of motivation, and a reflection of a curriculum area. Because bulletin boards are a visual phenomenon, teachers should be concerned about their content and appearance.

Thirty spelling papers or 15 identical paper pumpkins hanging up like someone's laundry do not constitute a good bulletin board. Mimeographed pictures, commercial cardboard turkeys, and corrugated cardboard trim are not visually appealing and certainly are not reflections of the children whose interest you are trying to catch.

A display designed for the eye is also designed for the mind. Children are very much attuned to symbols. Television commercials, billboards, posters, and cereal boxes attest to the impact of images. Bulletin boards should attract constructive attention. Stereotypical smiley faces and dog-eared paper letters with a thousand pinholes will not do it. Ideas and paper fade. Stereotyped versions of an upcoming holiday do absolutely nothing for children's art development.

For an early childhood teacher, one of the best solutions is to display the children's artwork. Art is a visual extension of the child and her or his own unique ideas and expression. It is the result of the child's own experience and serves as a motivation for others and the child herself or himself. Any subject can be the theme for an effective bulletin board, but one rule of thumb is that all boards should be student-oriented and entice student participation. Boards that ask questions, have games to play, or have objects to be handled can be fun and valuable learning experiences.

Eye-catching photographs (of the children, if possible), short stories, and poems are exercises for both the eye and mind. Whatever the mode, the key is visual impact. In order for a bulletin board to be a learning experience, it first must attract children's attention. Bright colors; bold design; legible, catchy, succinct phraseology; and relevant themes are vital to bulletin boards by, for, and about children.

Try some of these suggestions for improving your bulletin boards:

- Take advantage of interest in the World Series, Olympics, or other big sports events for a variety of projects. Find bulletin board space for newspaper clippings, pictures of heroes and heroines, and posting of scores and relative standings. Have children write reports or draw pictures of games in which they are interested. Make up graphs with scores for each team. Vary these activities according to the level of children's interest and abilities.
- If you have a bulletin board too big to cope with, cut it down to size by covering it with wallpaper samples, outlining each sample with black construction paper in a kind of giant patchwork quilt effect. Each child can use one of these squares as a personal bulletin board. Or you could use each of the squares to depict a different aspect of one main theme: kinds of animals, favorite people, and so on.
- Be sure all your bulletin boards and other kinds of displays are at children's eye level.
- When your classroom closet is awash with caps and mittens, why not bring their splashy colors and designs into the open with a self-portrait mural for a bulletin board? On a strip of butcher paper, draw a circle for each child. Have the students add features to turn these circles into self-portraits. Two lines looping down from each face become instant arms. Finally, have each child draw her or his own hat and mittens on the heads and hands. Encourage the young artists to copy the actual styles, colors, and designs of their own apparel as exactly as possible. This mural not only makes a colorful bulletin board but also helps you easily identify the owners of any stray clothing.

Display Areas for Three-Dimensional Work

- Use tops of cupboards or built-in shelves.
- Build shelves with boards supported by bricks, used permanently or temporarily.
- Attach a shelf of wood or particleboard underneath a bulletin board.
- A card table can be used for temporary exhibits, and then folded up when not in use.
- Small cardboard boxes fastened to bulletin boards make a display place for lightweight objects.
- Use driftwood as an interesting display for weaving and jewelry.
- Puppet display rods can be made with a board and some dowel sticks.
- Cover cardboard boxes and use them as bases for displaying art objects.
- Use a pegboard with hooks to hang objects on.

Recycled Materials

Creative teachers find that potential art materials abound everywhere and include old, discarded items. For example, in the following teaching suggestions, one kind of discarded item—the gallon milk container—presents a wealth of storage, display, and equipment possibilities.

Teaching Suggestions: Empty Containers Full of Promise

When that plastic gallon milk container is out of milk, it is full of potential for classroom implements you can make yourself. Scoops, funnels, sorting trays, display or storage containers, and carrying baskets are just waiting to be cut out.

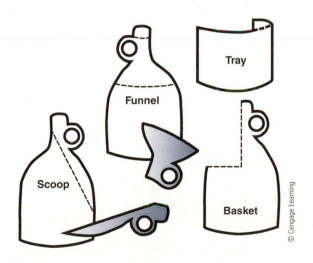

© Cengage Learning

Outline the area you want to cut with a felt-tip marker, and use a sharp knife or a small pencil-type soldering iron to do the cutting. (If you use the iron, be sure to work in a ventilated area and avoid inhaling the fumes.) Be sure that edges are not sharp and jagged. It is best to cover the cut edge with electrical tape or any other strong tape.

These containers are so readily available, you can afford to experiment with a few to find just the shapes you are after. Here are directions for some basic cuts to get you started:

- Scoop—Cut away the handle and part of the side below it. The container's handle instantly becomes the scoop's handle, while the section below becomes the scoop itself.
- Sorting trays—Cut off the bottom or the entire side opposite the handle to make trays of varying depths. These are perfect for sorting small objects, such as pebbles or shells, or for examining small amounts of sand or soil.
- Funnel—Cut the handle a few centimeters from the top. Then cut around the base of the handle to make the funnel's body from the curved section of the jug. The top of the handle becomes the spout. For a larger funnel, simply cut the bottom from the container and use the top as the spout.
- Carrying basket—Cut away the upper portion of the side opposite the handle. Children then carry the jug by the handle and use it to transport all kinds of items.

Equipment for Movement Activities from Recycled Materials

A valuable addition to the movement program in the early childhood classroom is equipment made from recycled materials. For example, empty plastic gallon milk jugs can be used as safe game goals, pins for indoor/outdoor bowling games, or cut out for scoops (see Figures E-1 and E-2) to toss yarn or other light balls in classroom movement activities.

Old pantyhose can be used to make light, child-sized rackets for great hand–eye coordination practice

FIGURE E-1 Equipment using recycled material scoops.

© Cengage Learning

Casper Holroyd

FIGURE E-2 Plastic scoop and yarn ball.

in racket games. These rackets are especially good for young children, as they are light enough to handle and yet sturdy enough to hit a yarn, Nerf, or plastic ball.

Using recycled materials has an obvious cost benefit in addition to demonstrating the importance of conservation to young children. Young children can possibly use these same materials at home for their own play experiences.

Even better, you can enlist parent participation and involvement in the program by asking parents to donate recycled materials to make movement equipment. Perhaps parents and children together could even get involved at home in making some of the equipment for the class's use, such as yarn balls or pantyhose rackets.

Other Ideas for Recycling Materials

Just as recycled materials were used for making movement equipment in Chapter 16, these same "discards" can be valuable art materials. Both conservation and creativity can be practiced in ways like the following.

- Be a scavenger. (But remember that the word is *scavenger*—not *beggar* or *receiver of junk goods*.)
- Begin your scavenger hunt by making a list of the equipment and supplies you think you might find in your community at little or no cost.
- Search for your treasures in attics, basements, garages, thrift or Goodwill Industry stores, and at garage sales.

- Ask parents to help satisfy the needs of creative children, or send a "want ad" home that is specific about what you need.
- Check with wallpaper and carpet dealers. Wallpaper dealers will sometimes give you their old sample books, and carpet dealers will often sell their sample swatches for a very small sum. These carpet swatches are useful as sit-upons, as rugs for houses the children build, as colorful mats under items on display, and as working mats for use under table toys.
- Gather paper from a variety of sources, such as the following:
  - Be a bag grabber. Collect plain paper bags. Cut them open and use them for painting, crayoning, and so on.
  - Save old newspapers for easel painting. Bright tempera (water color) paint on a newsprint background makes a very attractive and interesting work of art.
  - Check with your community or local newspaper office. They may donate or sell newsprint or old newspapers to you at a minimal cost.

Other materials listed in Figure E-3 can be valuable in the art center.

The following materials can be valuable instructional tools in the art program as well as in other curriculum areas.

1. Empty plastic containers—detergent bottles, bleach bottles, old plastic containers. These can be used for constructing scoops, storing art materials, etc.
2. Buttons—all colors and sizes. These are excellent for collages, assemblages, as well as sorting, counting, matching, etc.
3. Egg shells. These can be washed, dried, and colored with food coloring for art projects.
4. Coffee or shortening can lids and cans themselves. These can be covered with adhesive paper and used for the storage of art supplies, games, and manipulatives.
5. Magazines with colorful pictures. These are excellent for making collages, murals, and posters.
6. Scraps of fabric—felt, silk, cotton, oil cloth, etc. These can be used to make "fabric boards" with the name of each fabric written under a small swatch attached to the board, as well as for collages, puppets, etc.
7. Yarn scraps. These can be used for separating buttons into sets; also for art activities.
8. Styrofoam scraps.
9. Scraps of lace, rickrack, or decorative trim.
10. Bottles with sprinkler tops. Excellent for water play and for mixing water as children finger paint.
11. Wallpaper books of discontinued patterns.
12. Paper doilies.
13. Discarded wrapping paper.
14. Paint color cards from paint/hardware stores.
15. Old paintbrushes.
16. Old jewelry and beads.
17. Old muffin tins. These are effective for sorting small objects and mixing paint.
18. Tongue depressors or ice cream sticks. Counters for math; good for art construction projects, stick puppets, etc.
19. Wooden clothespins. For making "people," for construction projects, for hanging up paintings to dry.

FIGURE E-3 Beautiful junk list.

Sandbox Toys from the Kitchen

From the cupboard—Use plastic storage containers such as scoops, molds, or buckets. Foam cups are good scoops or molds. A plastic flowerpot with drainage holes can be a sifter.

Cut an egg carton into individual egg cups for molds.

Make an egg-carton sifter by cutting the lid off an egg carton and cutting the egg cup section in half the short way. In the bottom of each cup, poke a hole. The holes may be the same size or of varying sizes.

Musical Instruments from Recycled Materials

Recycling egg cartons for tambourines. Young children can make a simple tambourine from egg cartons and bottle caps. Simply put a few bottle caps in each egg carton, tape the carton closed, and you have an instrument that players can shake or hit. Children will love playing it both in rhythm and creative movement activities.

Recycling nuts and bolts for rattles. For an unusual set of musical instruments, assemble an assortment of large nuts, bolts, and washers. Young children will get excellent practice in fine finger movements when they create musical rattles out of these. All you have to do is place several washers on each bolt and loosely turn the nut onto the bolt. Place these inside empty, metal boxes, tape shut, and use as interesting sound instruments (rattles).

Making music with bottles. Gather a collection of bottles with both small and large mouths, such as soft drink bottles, ketchup bottles, quart canning jars, mayonnaise jars, and so on.

Show children how different sounds can be made with different-sized bottles by blowing across the various openings. Have them listen for high and low sounds. Stand the bottles on a table and gently tap them with a spoon. Children can explore different sounds the bottles make by blowing across them and by tapping them with a spoon.

Rhythm instruments from recycled materials. The following are suggestions for simple rhythm instruments children can make to use in their musical experiences. Creating rhythm instruments from found objects gives young children another opportunity for self-expression. They receive satisfaction and pleasure from beating rhythmic sounds and keeping time to music with instruments they have created.

Materials

paper plates	plastic egg-shaped containers
empty spools	small plastic bottles
pebbles	sticks
nails	old Christmas bells
toweling rolls	bottle caps
embroidery hoops	dried peas, beans, or corn wire
small boxes or cartons	

Bottle cap shaker. Remove plastic from inside bottle caps. Punch a hole in the center of the bottle cap. String bottle caps on a string and attach to a package handle. Paint if desired.

Spool shaker. Paint designs on a large spool. Force four pipe cleaners through the center of the spool. Attach a Christmas bell to the end of each pipe cleaner by bending the pipe cleaner to hold the bell.

Plate shaker. Decorate two paper plates with crayons or paint. Put pebbles or dried corn, peas, or beans between them and staple or sew the plates together with bright yarn or string. Bend wire to form a handle, and fit the ends inside.

Box shaker. Place small pebbles, beans, or seeds in a small box or empty, clean milk carton to make a shaker. It can be used with or without a handle. Decorate as desired.

Flute. Use a paper towel or tissue paper roll. With a pencil, punch three or four holes (about 1 inch apart) in the cardboard tube. Cover one end of the roll with a piece of waxed paper, as described later in the instructions for the Hummer. Children hum a tune in the open end, moving their fingers over the holes.

Sandpaper blocks. Paint two small wooden blocks. Place a strip of sandpaper on the surface, allowing an overlap on each end for fastening with thumbtacks. Children rub the blocks together to make a sound.

Clappers. Thumbtack bottle caps to a painted wooden block.

Cymbals. Cover the edges of two tin can lids with electric tape to be sure they are not sharp. Then decorate the lids. Fasten a small spool or block of wood on for a handle.

Tambourine. Punch holes in bottle caps and tie them together with thin wire, pipe cleaners, or string. Punch a hole in a paper or tinfoil plate and tie on the bottle caps.

Hummer. Decorate a tube from a waxed paper or paper towel roll. Fasten a piece of wax paper over one end of the tube. Humming through the wax paper is fun for children. Be sure to change the paper after each use.

Circle shakers. Stretch two layers of plastic cloth with uncooked rice or tapioca between them over one-half of an embroidery hoop. Fasten with the other half of the hoop to make a circle shaker. (When making any shaker-type toys, be sure that the small objects used are sealed securely inside. Small objects such as beans, peas, and rice can pose a serious choking risk to young children.)

Egg shakers. Fill plastic egg-shaped containers (plastic Easter eggs) with dried beans. Tape the halves together. Children use them as maracas.

Bottle shakers. Collect empty, small plastic bottles. Fill with rice, beans, or nuts until half full. Seal bottles that don't have childproof lids with tape. These are excellent shakers for tiny hands.

Drums. Glue lids on round-shaped boxes such as those containing salt, cereal, or ice cream, and decorate with paint to use as drums. Older children may make drums from restaurant-size tin cans with canvas or heavy paper stretched and laced to cover the ends.

Kazoo. Use a piece of wax paper over a clean comb. Children play by pressing their lips against the paper and humming. Change the paper after each use.

Gong. Use an old license plate (the older the better). Children strike with a mallet to play. They might describe the sounds.

Jingle instrument. Use a set of metal measuring spoons. Children play by shaking or slapping them in their hand.

Wrist or ankle bells. Lace a shoestring through two or three bells. Tie to children's wrists or ankles. Children move to shake their bells.

Rubber band box. Another addition to rhythm instruments is a rubber band box. Gather together 1 cigar box (or similar size and weight box), 5 rubber bands of several lengths and thicknesses, and 10 brass fasteners.

Punch five holes 1½ inches apart in each end of the box. Attach a rubber band to a brass fastener, push through one of the holes, and open the fastener on the inside of the box to hold it down. Stretch the rubber band tight to the other end of the box and attach it in the same way. Attach the rest of the rubber bands.

The rubber band box can be held, placed on a table, or placed on the floor. Encourage children to pluck the rubber bands with their fingers or strum the bands with their thumbs. They can experiment with sounds and beats: high–low, fast–slow, and loud–soft.

Sound box. Another rhythm instrument is the sandpaper sound box. Gather together a box, four pieces of sandpaper (of various grades from fine to coarse), glue, scissors, and a dowel (½" × 6" long). Glue the top and bottom of the box closed. Allow enough time for it to dry completely. Cut the sandpaper to fit all sides of the box. Glue the sandpaper strips to the box.

Rub the dowel on the sandpaper. While children are using the sound boxes, you can introduce such musical concepts as loud–soft and fast–slow. The dowels can also be used alone in a rhythm band or in a parade. Extend this activity by having children make their own sound boxes if they are interested.

Clickers. Glue two baby food jar lids together (you can use a glue gun) with the tops opposite each other. Children can paint or decorate with paper or markers. When completed, children squeeze the two lids together with their fingers to make a clicking sound.

Homemade bell. You will need the following:
- Soup can with one end removed and smoothed
- Empty thread spool (wooden is best)
- 2 large buttons
- Masking tape
- Glue and yarn or string
- Hammer and large nail
- Material to decorate the outside of the bell

Punch a hole in the end of the soup can with the large nail. Cover the cut edges of the can with masking (or electric) tape. Tie two buttons to the end of a piece of yarn or string. Put masking tape on the other end of the string to make it easier to thread through the can and empty thread spool. Thread the string from inside the can to the outside. Spread glue on the bottom of the thread spool before threading the yarn or string through it. Press the thread spool tightly against the can to secure the handle. Lower the string so that the buttons hand about 1/3 of the way down the can. Tie a large knot in the string close to the top of the thread spool.

Children can decorate the can, if they so desire.

Drumsticks. Use wooden dowels with the ends wrapped in soft cloth, secured with a rubber band.

Rain sticks. Put beans, rice, or the like into a tube that can be closed tightly on both ends. Decorate with feathers, ribbon, designs, and so on.

Rhythm sticks. Use wooden dowels with the ends smoothed. Paint stirrers from the local hardware store work well, too.

Shakers. Fill empty film canisters and small plastic soda bottles with rice, beans, or popping corn. Make sure to either glue the tops closed or secure them with tape.

Criteria for Selecting Play Equipment for Young Children

1. *A young child's playthings should be as free of detail as possible.* A child needs freedom to express himself or herself by creating his or her own world; too much detail hampers rather than assists. Blocks are the best example of unstructured toys. Blocks, construction sets, and other unstructured toys and equipment such as clay, sand, and paints allow the imagination free rein and are basic playthings.

2. *A good plaything should stimulate children to do things for themselves.* Equipment that makes the child a spectator, such as a mechanical toy, may entertain for the moment but has little or no play value. The equipment provided for play should encourage children to explore and create or offer the opportunity for dramatic play.

3. *Young children need large, easily manipulated playthings.* Toys that are too small can be a source of frustration because the child's muscular coordination is not yet developed enough to handle smaller forms and shapes. A child's muscles develop through play. A child needs equipment for climbing and balancing.

4. *The material from which a plaything is made has an important role in the play of the young child.* Warmth and pleasurable touch are significant to a child. The most satisfactory materials have been established as wood and cloth.

5. *The durability of the plaything is of utmost importance.* Play materials must be sturdy. Children hate to see their toys break. Axles and wheels must be strong to support a child's weight. Some materials break so readily that they prove to be very expensive.

6. *The toy must work.* What frustration when a door or drawer won't shut, wheels get stuck, or figures won't stand up! Be sure parts move correctly and that maintenance will be easy.

7. *The construction of a plaything should be simple enough for a child to comprehend.* This strengthens his or her understanding and experience of the world. The mechanics, too, should be visible and easily grasped. Small children will take them apart to see how they work.

8. *A plaything should encourage cooperative play.* As we seek to teach children to work and play together, we should provide the environment that stimulates such play.

9. *The total usefulness of the plaything must be considered in comparing price.* Will it last several children through several stages of their playing lives?

What are some good toys and play materials for young children?
All ages are approximate. Most suggestions for younger children are also appropriate for older children.

Sensory Materials	Active Play Equipment	Construction Materials	Manipulative Toys	Dolls and Dramatic Play	Books and Music	Art Materials
2-Year-Olds and Young 3-Year-Olds						
Water and sand toys: cups, shovels Modeling dough Sound-matching games Bells, wood block, triangle, drum Texture-matching games, feel box	Low climber Canvas swing Low slide, wagon, cart, or wheelbarrow Large rubber balls Low three-wheeled, steerable vehicle with pedals	Unit blocks and accessories: animals, people, simple wood cars and trucks Interlocking construction set with large pieces Wood train and track set Hammer (13 oz. steel shanked), soft wood, roofing nails, nailing block	Wooden puzzles with 4–20 large pieces Pegboards Big beads or spools to string Sewing cards Stacking toys Picture lotto, picture dominoes	Washable dolls with a few clothes Doll bed Child-sized table and chairs Dishes, pots, and pans Dress-up clothes: hats, shoes, shirts Hand puppets Shopping cart	Clear picture books, stories, and poems about things children know CDs or tapes of classical music, folk music, or children's songs	Wide-tip water color markers Large sheets of paper, easel Finger or tempera paint, brushes Blunt-nose scissors White glue
Older 3- and 4-Year-Olds						
Water toys: measuring cups, egg beaters Sand toys: muffin tins, vehicles Xylophone, maracas, tambourine	Bicycle Roller skates Climbing structure Rope or tire swing Plastic bats and various sizes rubber balls Balance board Planks, boxes, old tires Bowling pins, rings to toss, bean bags, and target	More unit blocks, shapes, and accessories Table blocks Realistic model vehicles Construction set with smaller pieces Woodworking bench, saw, sandpaper, nails	Puzzles, pegboard, small beads to string Parquetry blocks Small objects to sort Marbles Magnifying glass Simple card or board games Flannel board with pictures, letters	Dolls and accessories Doll carriage Child-sized stove or sink More dress-up clothes Play food, cardboard cartons Airport, doll house, or other settings with accessories Finger or stick puppets	Simple science books More detailed picture and story books Sturdy CD player Wider variety of music Book and CD Sets	Easel, narrower brushes Thick crayons, chalk Paste, tape with dispenser Collage materials Potter's clay

	Sensory Materials	Active Play Equipment	Construction Materials	Manipulative Toys	Dolls and Dramatic Play	Books and Music	Art Materials
5- and 6-Year-Olds	Water toys: food coloring, pumps, funnels Sand toys: containers, utensils Harmonica, kazoo, guitar, recorder	Outdoor games: bocce, tetherball, shuffleboard, jump rope, Frisbee, bicycle	More unit blocks, shapes, and accessories Props for roads, towns Hollow blocks Brace and bits, screwdrivers, screws, metric measure, accessories	More complex puzzles Dominoes More difficult board and card games Yarn, big needles, mesh fabric, weaving materials Magnets, balances Attribute blocks	Cash register, play money, accessories, or props for other dramatic play settings: gas station, construction, office Typewriter	Books on cultures Stories with chapters Favorite stories children can read Children's recipe books	Watercolors, smaller paper, stapler, hole punch Chalkboard Oil crayons, paint, crayons, charcoal Simple camera, film Tools for working with clay
7- to 10-Year-Olds	Modeling materials, papier-mâché, wire for sculpture	Jump ropes, roller skates, skateboards, equipment for team sports and ball tossing and catching	Woodworking bench; full range of tools and equipment	Computer games, puzzles, crochet and knitting supplies	Materials for skits and short dramatic activities	CDs of classical, folk, jazz, and popular music Fiction and nonfiction books	Materials for easel painting, printing, sculpting, collage, rubbings Computer programs for graphic design experiences Potter's clay

Glossary

10 thematic strands of social studies—Developed by the National Council for the Social Studies, these 10 themes point to a fundamental knowledge of social studies for children (K–12).

100% organic—Refers to items that are certified to have been produced using only methods thought to be good for the earth.

accent (music) (or beat)—The rhythmic pulse of the music.

acceptance in teaching music—Teachers should accept more than one kind of response to music activities.

activity centers—A part of the early childhood environment identified by specific activities and materials. In activity centers, young children can manipulate objects, engage in conversation and role-playing, and learn at their own levels and at their own pace.

activity pattern—Varying activities so that the new and old are in an interesting as well as developmentally appropriate pattern for young children.

actualizing tendency—In the theory of Carl Rogers, the drive of every human being to do his best in life.

aesthetic development—The process of continuously finding beauty and wonder in the world.

aesthetic experience—Doing things for the pure joy of it. The goal of aesthetic experiences is a full, rich life for the child.

aesthetic learning—Joining what one thinks with what one feels.

Aesthetic Movement, the—An artistic movement in the 1880s in the United States. The chief characteristic was its concentration on the "science of the beautiful" or the "philosophy of taste."

aesthetic sense—The sense that the child is using taste or preference: "I enjoy what I see" or "I like what I hear."

aesthetic sensitivity—Involves three types of sensing and feeling. First is contact with the world outside of the person, seeing, hearing, smelling, tasting, and touching. The second is what people feel within themselves. The third type goes beyond the present and reality.

aesthetics—An appreciation for beauty and a feeling of wonder; a sensibility that uses the imagination as well as the five senses.

affective readiness (for reading)—A prerequisite to reading involving the child's positive self-concept.

afterimage—After staring at a page of solid color for about 30 seconds, and then looking at a dot on a page of white or gray, our eyes will see color on the blank page. The color is usually the complement or near complement of the color first looked upon.

aggregates—In Rhoda Kellogg's art theory, the early pictorial stage when children begin putting diagrams together. This is also referred to as *combines*.

analytic—Referring to the left-brain approach, which approaches learning in a step-by-step sequential format.

antibias curriculum (ABC)—A curriculum developed by the NAEYC to be a starting point for planning an inclusive, antibias curriculum.

appropriate music activities—These music activities can only be planned if the teacher understands the developmental levels of the children involved.

art appreciation—Seeing and appreciating good artwork.

art area—An activity center for painting, collage-making, cutting, pasting, and so on. It needs to be located near water and light.

art elements—The language of art, including color, line, shape, contrast, texture, and size.

arts and crafts—A term that has its origin in folk arts. Examples of arts and crafts are hand-shaped clay pots, original carving, and weaving. Also refers to a creative activity producing a utilitarian (or craft) item.

Asperger's Syndrome—One of the autistic spectrum disorders. The list of ASD symptoms includes notable difficulty with social interaction, sensitivity to stimulation, and intense fixation on particular objects or tasks.

assemblage—A three-dimensional art form involving placement of a number of three-dimensional objects, natural or manmade, in juxtaposition to create a unified composition.

assistive technology—Computer technology that aids children with special learning needs.

associative play—A type of play characterized simply by being present in a group. An example is the child who participates in finger plays during circle time but does not interact with others in the circle.

attention span—The length of time a child's interest lasts. Generally, the younger the child, the shorter the attention span.

bag puppet—A common paper bag stuffed with newspapers and fastened shut. A body is made with a second bag attached to the first, leaving room for the child's hand to slip in and work the puppet.

balance—A principle of design that deals with visual weight in a work of art.

basic forms stage—The stage in the development of art when a child finds, recognizes, and repeats at will basic shapes such as rectangles, squares, and circles.

beat (music)—See *accent*.

block-building area—In the early childhood classroom, an activity or interest center where young children can create with both large and small blocks, Legos®, and the like.

blog—An online journal that can substitute for a traditional website.

Bloom's taxonomy—A six-level classification system for categorizing questions and designing instruction from lower- to higher-order levels of thinking.

bodily/kinesthetic learner—In Gardner's theory, this learner is physically active, prefers hands-on learning, and is talkative. He or she is often called the "mover."

books and quiet area—In the early childhood classroom, the place where children can be alone with their thoughts or explore the world of books.

brain stem—Located at the base of the skull, it controls most basic life activities, including blood pressure and body temperature.

brayer—An ink roller used with a printing plate. The brayer is rolled in a shallow pan filled with water-soluble ink or tempera paint.

brush painting—Creating art using a brush.

capital C creativity—Creativity that involves bringing into existence something genuinely new that receives social validation enough to be added to the culture. An example of capital C creativity is the invention of the lightbulb.

cardboard cylinder puppet—A puppet made by placing the cardboard cylinder from a roll of paper towels or toilet tissue over the fingers.

cardinal numbers—Number names (examples—*one, two, three*).

celebration—A term that is used synonymously with the term *holiday* to reflect a broader approach to special days in a child's life.

cephalocaudal development—The pattern of physical development in the human body from head to toe (or top to bottom).

cerebellum—Located behind the brain stem in the human brain; it coordinates movement and balance.

chalking materials and use—Materials including a blackboard and eraser, and/or a stack of wet or dry (or both) paper and a container full of colored and white chalk. Most children will select and use chalks easily on these materials.

childhood chants—The teasing chants sung by children that are most often heard on the playground.

classification and sorting—Putting together things that are alike or belong together. This is one of the processes necessary for developing the concept of numbers.

classroom blog—A blog used to share news and information with parents and students.

classroom museum—A collection of items and artifacts on a specific theme. These items and artifacts are brought in by children for display.

cognitive development theory (of children's art)—Developed by Piaget, this theory holds that children's art is related to their ability to understand the permanent existence of objects.

cognitive readiness (for reading)—The abilities of comprehension, problem solving, and reasoning required in order to learn to read.

collage—A French word meaning "to paste." This two-dimensional art activity involves selecting, organizing, and arranging materials, and then attaching them to a flat surface.

color—The property of reflecting light of a particular visible light wavelength; the colors of the spectrum are red, orange, yellow, green, blue, indigo, and violet.

color relativity—The color gray appears much lighter when placed on a black background than it does against a white one. This dark/light effect holds true for many other colors as well.

combination of phrase-wise and whole-song method—A method of introducing a song to children where the entire song is presented, but the teacher only asks the children to respond to the easiest parts of it with voices, hands, or an instrument.

combines—In Rhoda Kellogg's art theory, the stage when children put diagrams together and enter the pictorial stage. Combines are also referred to as *aggregates*.

common bonds curriculum—A curriculum that celebrates the cultural diversity of all children by focusing on common bonds all people share, such as family, home, and food.

Common Core State Standards—Standards in English language arts and mathematics begun in 2009 as an initiative of the National Governor's Association and the Council of Chief State School Offices. These standards establish a clear and consistent map for what students should learn from kindergarten through high school to better prepare them for college and career.

Common Core State Standards for Mathematics (CCSSM)—The CCSSM are built on the National Math standards, but they also introduce significant changes to how mathematics is to be taught. The 8 Standards for Mathematics Practice describe varieties of expertise that mathematics educators at all levels should seek to develop in their students.

communication sites—On the Internet, communication sites allow children to interact with friends, relatives, or classrooms across the street, in another city, or even across the globe.

comparing—A mathematical skill involving the perception of differences in items (example: "My shoes are bigger than yours.").

composition—An art term referring to the arrangement of the objects and spaces in a piece of art.

concrete operations stage (Piaget)—Ages 7–11 when a child develops basic concepts of objects, numbers, time, space, and causality, and develops reversibility (two-way thinking).

contrast—In art, the degree of difference in form, color, size, and texture in objects (example: The rough bark of a tree contrasts with its smooth leaves.).

controlled scribbling—A later point in the scribble stage when the child connects his or her motions with the marks on the page. The child has found it possible to control the marks.

convergent thinking—Encouraging one correct answer or one way to do things; single-focused.

cooperative play—A type of play marked by mutual involvement in a play activity.

cortex—Part of the brain containing 80% of the neurons, located at the top layer of the brain. Called the "executive branch" of the brain, it regulates decision making and controls thinking, reasoning, and language.

crayons—The most basic, most familiar, and easiest tool for young preschoolers to use. Crayons can be used to make attractive colored marks on paper.

creative dramatics—A form of imaginative play that helps students learn and uses no written dialogue. It is different from a play performed on stage. In creative dramatics, actors create their own words to convey meaning.

creative movement—Movement that reflects the mood or inner state of a child.

creative movement activities—Natural activities for children to express their creative selves by physical movement.

creativity—The process of bringing something new into being.

Csikszentmihalyi's 5 steps—Researcher on the creative process who described creativity as a process involving the five steps: preparation, incubation, insight, evaluation, and elaboration.

deficit perspective—This approach to working with non-English-speaking children perceives the child as lacking skills, a deficit caused by not speaking English.

design—The organization of an artwork, including symmetry/asymmetry, repetition, alternation, and variation.

developmental level—Referring to a framework upon which we organize our knowledge and observations of children. Includes four major areas of growth: physical, social, emotional, and intellectual.

developmental levels (of art)—A guide to what a child can do in art at different ages; not a strict guideline.

developmentally appropriate early childhood classrooms—Classrooms that evidence maximum interaction among children; an environment filled with challenging and interesting materials and a variety of independent and small-group tasks.

developmentally appropriate music activities—Musical activities that are planned around the developmental levels of the children involved.

Developmentally Appropriate Practice (DAP)—A position of the National Association for the Education of Young Children defining and describing appropriate practice in early childhood programs.

diagram stage—In Rhoda Kellogg's art development theory, the point at which the child begins to draw six different diagrams: the rectangle, the oval, the triangle, the Greek cross, the diagonal cross, and the odd shape.

differentiated instruction—A way of thinking about teaching and learning. Its aim is to maximize each child's growth by meeting each child where he or she is and helping the child progress from that point.

digital cameras—Cameras that make it possible to instantly see the picture you've just taken and erase it if you don't like it. The power of a digital camera is measured in megapixels—the more a camera has, the sharper the picture.

dimensionality—Experiencing the world through three dimensions: height, width, and depth.

disordered or random scribbling—An early part of the scribble stage, characterized by the child's lack of control over hand movements or the marks on a page. The marks are random and go in many directions.

divergent thinking—Encouraging many different answers or ways to do things; open-ended.

DLL—Dual-language learner.

dramatic play—A free, unstructured form of play in which young children are able to express their inner feelings.

drawing materials and uses—Drawing materials include sturdy sheets of paper, a basket of jumbo crayons, and watercolor markers in many colors and tip widths. These materials are ideal for children to use in the early childhood program.

dynamics (music)—Volume or relative loudness or softness of the sound, giving emotional intensity.

early basic forms stage—The circle and oval are generally the first basic forms. This stage in art development occurs when children recognize the simple circle in their scribbles and are able to repeat it.

early pictorial (first drawings) stage—The stage in art development when a child works on making and perfecting one or many symbols.

ecology—The study of all elements of an environment, both the living and nonliving, and the interrelation of these elements.

emergent curriculum—A curriculum that is built on the strengths of the child and arises from the play of children and the play of teachers.

emergent diagram shapes—The term for basic forms in Kellogg's theory of art development.

emerging literacy—The developmental process involving the time immediately before a child learns to read printed symbols, but also the continuous development of prereading skills that begin at birth. The term *emergent literacy* is preferred over the term *reading readiness*, which describes a narrower range of skills.

emotional brain—The first part of the brain to receive input and the first to react.

environment—The manmade and natural things that children meet in their surroundings.

environmental motivation (for picture making)—Children must have the opportunity to reflect on experiences they have in their environment before expressing them visually.

Erik Erickson's stages of psychosocial development—Stages of social development that include: Stage 1 – trust vs. mistrust; stage 2 – autonomy vs. shame and doubt; stage 3 – initiative vs. guilt; and stage 4 – industry vs. inferiority.

ESL learner—English as a second language learner.

executive function skills—The ability to focus, hold, and work with information in mind, filter distractions, and switch gears.

facilitate—To help along, to guide, to provide opportunities, and to be sensitive and caring without interfering.

fine-motor development—The development of the small muscles of the body, such as those in the fingers, hands, wrists, and eyes.

finger painting materials and use—These materials include paper with a shiny surface, water supply to make the paper damp, finger paint, racks to dry the finished work, a smock for each child, and a nearby sink with running water for washing hands and cleaning up. Finger painting materials allow children to experiment with the paint using fingers, palms of their hands, their wrists, and their arms.

finger puppets—Puppets made by using the child's fingers. They include three general types: finger-leg, finger-cap, and finger-face.

flexibility in teaching music—Teachers should adapt music activities based on the various responses children communicate.

flexible thinking—The ability to think of things in many ways; to think of things in the context of change, that not all things are permanent.

folk and traditional songs—Songs that are part of our heritage and that have been sung by children for centuries (examples: "Bingo" and "I'm a Little Teapot.").

foreground, middle ground, and background—The areas in a piece of art that appear closer to the viewer (foreground), next closest (middle ground), and farthest away (background).

form or shape—Essential elements of all artwork that are combined, that occur in various sizes, and that can be filled, empty, separate, connecting, or overlapping.

formal operations stage (Piaget)—Ages 11–15 when a child can think abstractly and hypothetically generate diverse solutions for problems and evaluate alternatives based on many criteria.

formal science—A science experience planned by the teacher to develop particular skills.

Framework for K-12 Science Education—Science standards that identify the key scientific ideas and practices all students should learn by the end of high school.

free play—See *spontaneous play*.

functional/physical movement—Movement that serves a practical purpose.

gang stage—In Lowenfeld's theory, stage in art development occurring in children ages 9 to 12, when they become more aware of how things look in their drawings. This awareness is often expressed with more detail in the child's schema. The use of the word *gang* refers to the fact that the peer group assumes more importance to the child at this point.

Gardner's multiple intelligence theory—According to this theory, each of us possesses eight "intelligences," or ways to be smart: word smart, logic smart, picture smart, music smart, body smart, person smart, self smart, and nature smart.

global thinking—Referring to the right brain, which prefers to begin with a general concept and then to specifics.

gross-motor development—The development of large (gross) muscles in the body, such as those in the neck, trunk, arms, and legs.

hand–eye coordination—The use of hand(s) and eyes at the same time.

hard thinking—Referring to the left brain, which processes information in an analytical and sequential way.

harmony (music)—The blending of sounds, for example, chords; two or more pitches simultaneously.

Haugland Software Development Scale—An evaluation tool for teachers to understand the key components of quality software.

holistically—In an overall way; as a whole. A holistic approach to early childhood education takes into consideration the intellectual, social, emotional, and behavioral needs of children.

housekeeping/dramatic play center—A place for acting out familiar home scenes with various real-life props.

hue—The color name for a color, such as "blue-green."

humanettes—See *people puppet*.

imaginative play—In Piaget's theory of play, one of the purest forms of symbolic thought available to the young child.

incidental science—The open, unstructured, free exploration by young children of their world.

inclusive environment—An environment that addresses both the daily life realities of cultural diversity as well as the potentially biased attitudes and behaviors that are part of this reality.

individual differences—The unique, different levels of development present in each child.

informal science—A term referring to children's independent exploration of science; there is little or no teacher involvement in this exploration.

information sites—On the Internet, information sites are rich reference resources that teachers and parents can use to assist children in answering questions, making new discoveries, and building knowledge.

inquiry-based learning—Term in science education referring to investigating to gather information, which is part of human behavior from birth.

integrated curriculum—A curriculum in which the artificial divisions among content areas are reduced. Most often an integrated curriculum is designed around a unit of study, that is, centered around a specific theme or project.

intensity—Depth of a color that is varied by adding a hue's complementary color; the color opposite it on the color wheel.

interaction sites—On the Internet, interaction sites are similar to software programs, using sound, animation, sound effects, and high-quality, realistic graphics.

interactive (refers to computers)—The computer, when used with young children, provides a vehicle for two types of interaction: child-to-computer and child-to-child. Placing two child-sized seats in front of the computer and one at the side for adults encourages an interactive experience for both the children and the teacher with the computer.

interactive/shared reading—Reading and talking about books with children.

interest centers—See *activity centers*.

interpersonal learner—In Gardner's theory, this learner is group-oriented, extroverted, communicative, and enjoys interacting with others. He or she is often called the "socializer."

intrapersonal learner—In Gardner's theory, this learner is reflective, introverted, solitary, and prefers learning alone. He or she is often called the "individual."

juxtaposition—An artistic technique whereby pigments placed side by side in small repeated strokes are altered by our vision to appear to combine, thus forming a different hue.

key indicators—In the Interstate New Teacher Assessment and Support Consortium (INTASC), these describe what teachers should know and be able to do, rather than listing courses that teachers should take in order to be awarded a license.

kid culture—A broad range of media for children, including TV, computer games, movies, books, comic books, advertising, entertainment, toys, games, and trading cards.

language enhancement—Providing children many experiences to enrich their language development.

language of art—Just as there are basic visual symbols in a spoken language, there are basic elements that make up the language of art.

later basic forms stage—In this stage of art development, the child can purposely draw separate lines of any length desired, and thus can form rectangle and square shapes.

later pictorial (first drawings) stage—A later point in the pictorial stage when the child draws symbols more easily and exactly.

left-brained—Having a preference for learning that involves the left hemisphere of the brain.

limbic system—Located in the central part of the brain, it controls emotions, attachment, and memory.

line—An element present in all art. Every line in a piece of art has length, a beginning, an end, and direction.

linguistic readiness (for reading)—A prerequisite to reading that involves skill in using oral language.

listening—The part of language development that involves receiving and processing incoming information. Listening is more than simply hearing because good listeners filter out much of what they hear in order to concentrate on a message.

literacy—The mastery of language: speaking, listening, writing, and reading.

literature response blog—A blog on which a teacher posts a prompt and invites students to respond to a text.

logical/mathematical learner—In Gardner's theory, this learner is inquisitive, experimental, and oriented toward numbers, patterns, and relationships. He or she is often called the "questioner."

mandala—A universal form found most often in the later scribble stage.

manipulative area—In the early childhood classroom, a place to enhance motor skills, hand–eye coordination, and mental, language, and social skills through the use of play materials such as pegboards, puzzles, and games.

media—Any material used to create or enhance learning experiences for young children.

melody (music)—A series (more than one) of musical tones falling into a recognizable pattern.

midbrain—Located at the top of the brain stem, it controls motor activity, appetite, and sleep.

mirror blogs—A blog that allows bloggers to reflect on their thinking.

mirror neurons—Nerve cells in the human brain that allow us, without thinking, to mimic the feelings and movements of people around us.

mixing paint—The process of preparing paint for use in artwork. Children enjoy mixing paint, and it is a good learning experience for them.

mobile—A three-dimensional art form that involves balance, design, sculpture, form, space, and color.

modeling—The process of manipulating and shaping flexible material.

modeling behavior—A characteristic of dramatic play in which children imitate what they have observed.

modeling (three-dimensional)—Using flexible materials to create objects in the round.

monoprint—A single-colored print.

montage—An art form consisting of a number of smaller items joined together.

mosaics—An art form made with small pieces of torn or cut colored paper and glued into a design or shape.

motivate children—Helping children recall their experiences and record these in art media.

motor development—Physical growth; the ability to use one's body.

multicultural activities—Routine curriculum activities as well as special events in the child's week that expose the child to his or her own and many other cultures.

multicultural aesthetics—Experiences that honor heritage, community, and tradition as a way of conveying multiculturalism.

multicultural centers—Learning centers that have incorporated materials from other cultures.

multicultural curriculum—A curriculum that reflects the culture of the children in the group and the local community.

multimedia artwork—An art form and contemporary art movement that emphasizes the integration of all art forms.

mural—A storytelling picture or panel intended for a large wall space.

music center—In the early childhood classroom, a place for listening to CDs and tapes, singing, creating dance, and playing musical instruments.

music elements—The language of music, including rhythm, beat, accent, tempo, syncopation, melody, pitch, timbre, dynamics, texture, harmony, form, and ostinato.

musical/rhythmic learner—In Gardner's theory, this learner is oriented toward music, rhythmic sounds, and environmental sounds. He or she is often called the "music lover."

National Council for the Social Studies National Standards—A set of national standards developed for children (K–12) identifying learning experiences that make up a fundamental knowledge of social studies.

National Science Education Standards—A set of national standards on science education, presenting an outline of what students (K–12) need to know, understand, and be able to do to be "scientifically literate" at each grade level.

national standards—Standards that are written for grades K–12 in broad language to cover the basic areas of the curriculum, such as language arts, math, and science.

natural products—These foods typically don't contain artificial colors, flavors, or preservatives and have no synthetic ingredients.

neurons—Nerve cells in the brain.

Next Generation Science Standards—Developed by a joint effort between the National Research Council, the National Science Teachers Association, and the American Association for the Advancement of Science, these standards will be K–12 science standards created through a collaborative, state-led process.

No Child Left Behind (NCLB) Act—Authorized by Congress in 2001, the NCLB act was designed to improve U.S. schools to create more equitable educational opportunities for all children.

one-to-one correspondence—A concept basic to rational counting, giving one number per item in a series.

onlooker behavior—The earliest stage of play in which the child plays passively by watching or conversing with other children engaged in play activities.

onlooker play—The earliest stage of play in which the child is playing passively by watching or conversing with other children engaged in play activities.

oral language—Children's ability to receive and express thoughts, wants, needs, and feelings.

ordering (seriation)—A mathematical skill involving the ability to perceive opposite ends of a series (example: big to little).

ordinal number—Number that refers to the place of an object in a series of numbers (example: *second* book, *third* window).

organic—Food that is grown without the use of pesticides, synthetic fertilizers, sewage sludge, genetically modified organisms, or ionizing radiation.

organized play—An open, flexible type of play, with some structure provided in terms of materials.

ostinato—Simple, rhythmic, or melodic content repeated over and over to accompany a song.

painting with a brush—Creating artwork by means of brush and paint.

paper pulp (papier-mâché)—An easy-to-work-with clay substitute made from newspaper and powder paste.

parallel play—A form of play in which a child plays side by side with other children with some interaction but without direct involvement.

passive listening—A stage in the development of listening skills when the child simply sits, with little or no reaction.

pasting materials and use—The basic pasting materials are small jars of paste, sheets of plain or colored paper, and blunt scissors for both left- and right-handed children. Pasting should be done away from climbing toys, building blocks, and similar large-motor activities.

pattern (repetition and rhythm)—An art term referring to the harmonious or decorative effects created when a particular shape, color, or motif are designed and repeated in a rhythmic way.

people puppet—Also called *humanettes*, puppets that are half-person, half-puppet. They are made by placing a large paper grocery bag over the head. Holes are cut for eyes and other facial features.

perceptual readiness (for reading)—The prerequisite skill to reading involving the ability to associate printed language with spoken language and to discriminate among letters and sounds.

personal celebration—A celebration emphasizing an experience of individual, special significance to a child (example: losing the first tooth).

personal creative movement—Movement that reflects the mood or inner state of an individual.

personal learning network—A collection of people and resources you can consult to learn something or to get answers to your questions.

personal space—A place for each child for his or her own personal use.

phrase-wise method—A method of introducing a song to children through the use of a brief story, discussion, or question.

pictorial stage—The stage in art development when children have the ability to draw the variety of marks that make up their first representational pictures.

picture making/drawing—Any and all forms of purposeful expressions, beginning with controlled scribbling.

pitch (music)—The high or low tones in the sound pattern.

portfolio—A representative collection of an artist's work, including samples from various periods, showing how the artist's talent has developed over time.

positive self-concept—A good feeling about one's self, or self-esteem.

potter's clay/play dough materials and use—Basic materials for three-dimensional art work best used at a table that is easy to clean with tools for clay/dough work such as cookie cutters, spoons, and blunt plastic knives.

pre-operational stage (Piaget)—Ages 2–7 years when a child begins to carry out mental actions (operations) that require forming and using images and symbols.

preschematic stage—A term that refers to the basic forms stage. Generally refers to the fact that basic forms are drawn in and of themselves and not to represent a particular object.

pretend reading—Also called "reenactment" or "emergent reading." Children practice reading-like behaviors that build confidence in themselves as readers.

primary colors—Red, yellow, and blue.

Principles and Standards for Mathematics Children Pre-K–12—A set of standards developed by the National Council of Teachers of Mathematics proposing mathematical content and processes students should know and be able to use as they progress through school.

print concepts—A child's understanding that we can communicate through spoken or sign language words and sentences and that words can be written down for others to see and understand.

printing—In a basic printing activity, the child learns that an object dipped in or brushed with paint makes its own mark, or print, on paper.

printmaking activity—Activities that involve the creation of prints, either alone or in patterns by dipping an object in paint and pressing it down to make its mark on the paper.

process learning—A concept that conceives of learning in terms of its processes rather than its products. In process learning, the focus is on providing children experiences that promote thinking and problem solving without specifically identified outcomes.

process over product—Phrase referring to the belief that the process that leads to originality (exploration and experimentation with materials) is more important than the end product.

proximodistal development—The pattern of human growth from inside to outside (or from center to outside).

publication sites—On the Internet, sites that publish children's work.

psychologically safe environment—An environment in which the child is accepted for himself or herself with unconditional acceptance.

quality (in music experiences) vs. quantity—Children develop musical preferences at an early age so listening experiences should include a variety of styles and cultures, not just children's music.

random manipulation—Squeezing clay in an uncontrolled way; comparable to the early scribble stage in drawing.

random scribbling—See *disordered scribbling*.

rapport—A warm and friendly feeling and relationship between people.

rational counting—Comprehension of the concept that the last number counted in a sequence of objects represents all the objects in the sequence.

reading readiness—See *emerging literacy*. Often used to describe the skills involved in getting ready to read.

Reggio Emilia approach—An approach to early childhood education started in the Italian town, Reggio Emilia, in which children spend time each day expressing their ideas through art media.

representational art—Art in which symbols are used to make a visual representation of something important to the child.

reticular activating system (RAS)—A screening device located at the base of our brain that helps decide what we are to be conscious of as it filters out other information.

rhythm—The element of art found in repeated shapes, colors, textures, and other patterns.

rhythm instruments—Musical instruments used by children to copy the rhythmic patterns heard in songs.

right-brained—Preference for learning that involves the right hemisphere of the brain.

rote counting—Memorization of a number sequence with no comprehension of what the numbers mean.

schema—An individual way or pattern of drawing. Schema develops from repeated practice with drawing symbols.

schematic stage—Another term for the pictorial stage; refers to the child's ability to use his or her own special variety of marks or schema.

science—A study consisting of investigation and knowledge: two phases that cannot be separated.

science/discovery center—In the early childhood classroom, a place where children learn about nature and science.

scrap art materials and use—Basic scrap materials include paste, glue, tape or stapler; colored tissue paper; colored tape; gummed circles, stars, and designs; tempera paint; chalk crayons and colored markers; and odds and ends of scrap materials. Children choose materials to organize and use in artwork.

scribble stage—The first stage in the development of art beginning with a child's first scribbles, usually at about 1 ½ to 2 years of age.

secondary colors—Orange, violet (purple), and green.

self-actualization (Carl Rogers)—Growing and developing into one's full potential.

sensorimotor—Derived from the two words *sensory* (referring to the five bodily senses) and *motor* (referring to the physical act of doing). Sensorimotor learning involves the body and its senses as they are used in doing.

sensory awareness—Using the senses to experience the world more fully with more than one sense.

seriation—See *ordering*.

shape/form—An art element that refers to geometric shapes, organic (natural), or free-form shapes.

showcase blogs—A blog used to post student art projects, podcasts, and writing.

simultaneous processor—Term associated with the right brain, as a person who prefers to learn beginning with the general concept and then go on to specifics.

small c creativity—Creativity that involves ideas or products that are new to the person but only to the person. An example of small c creativity is a child's new use of blending finger paint colors.

smart toys—Toys with microprocessors that offer high-quality interactive learning opportunities.

social competence—The ability to get along with others, which is an important factor in child-to-child relationships.

social–emotional growth—Term referring to the development of a child's feelings in conjunction with his or her growth as a member of a group.

soft thinking—Referring to the right side of the brain, looking first at the whole picture and then at the details, processing information in an intuitive way.

software—Collective term for films, tapes, computer disks, and all other materials used on hardware (or machines) as media (example—a DVD).

solitary play—The form of play in early toddlerhood when the child plays primarily alone.

space—An art element referring to the distance within or between aspects in an artwork.

spatter/spray painting—Creating designs by placing small, flat objects on paper; dipping small brushes (toothbrushes) into paint; and gently pulling a straight-edged object (ruler, emery board, or tongue depressor) across the ends of the bristles. This causes the bristles to snap forward, throwing small particles of paint onto the paper, creating interesting designs around the edges of the flat objects.

spiral teaching—Teaching methodology in which the teacher presents the basic facts without worrying about the details. As learning progresses, more and more details are introduced.

spontaneous play (free play)—Free, unplanned, flexible play.

stabile—A three-dimensional art form that is stationary and made on a freestanding and immobile base.

STEAM—Acronym for Science, Technology, Engineering, Arts, and Math.

STEM—Acronym for Science, Technology, Engineering, and Math.

stencils—Cutting out different shapes from several pieces of drawing paper to make a stencil. The drawing paper stencil is placed on top of another piece of paper. Then the child rubs a chalk filled tissue across the stencil, making the shape appear on the paper underneath.

successive processor—Referring to the left-side of the brain, a person who prefers to learn in a step-by-step sequential format, beginning with details leading up to understanding a concept or acquiring a skill.

sugar—A nutritional term generally used to refer to sucrose, which is refined sugar from sugar cane or beets. Other sources of sugar are fructose, dextrose, lactose, and maltose.

symbol (in children's art)—A visual representation of something of importance to the child.

syncopation (music)—Uneven rhythms as in jazz.

tableaus—"Frozen pictures" in which groups of students "freeze" or pose to act out a scene, a saying, a book title, and so on.

teacher talk—A key form of adult support that early childhood teachers can use to enhance the play of children with disabilities and promote peer interaction. Refers to specific help that teachers provide to children to encourage richer play experiences.

teaching peace—Teaching children a basic attitude of trust in, acceptance of, and consideration toward everyone.

teaching songs from recordings—A method of introducing a song where children respond to the whole song rhythmically, dramatically, and with instruments.

tempera—Powdered paint that is mixed with water for use in painting activities.

tempo—The speed, how fast or slow the music is.

tertiary colors—Red-violet, red-orange, blue-violet, blue-green, yellow-orange, and yellow-green.

texture (music)—Layering of instruments and/or voices to create a thin or full feeling.

thinking brain—The part of the brain that thinks logically. It reacts after the emotional brain.

three-dimensional art—Refers to any art form that has at least three sides. Art that is "in the round," which means that one can look at it from many sides.

timbre (music)—Tone color or unique qualities of sound.

toddler-appropriate art activities—Art activities that involve sturdy materials with no tiny pieces that might be swallowed.

tourist curriculum—Teaching about cultures only through artifacts such as food, traditional clothing, and household implements.

traffic flow—Movement in a room.

transformational perspective—In working with non-English speaking children, an approach based on the assumption that communities possess "funds of knowledge," reservoirs of knowledge and skills shared by community members.

two-dimensional media—A term used to refer to any art form that has only two sides: front and back.

unconditional positive acceptance—In the theory of Carl Rogers, accepting the child as he or she is.

unity—Feeling of wholeness or oneness in an art work.

value—The lightness or darkness of a color or hue.

varying the rhythm of the music program—A process of adding variety to the music program through choice of music, method of presentation, and lesson planning that helps hold children's interests and makes the experience enjoyable.

verbal/linguistic learner—In Gardner's theory, this learner is oriented toward language, words, reading, and writing. He or she is often called the "word player."

visual acuity—The ability to see and recognize shape and form.

visual spatial learner—In Gardner's theory, this learner is imaginative, creative, and oriented toward colors and pictures. He or she is often called the "visualizer."

whole-song method—A method of introducing a song to children by presenting the whole song in a variety of ways.

wiki—A website that allows readers to add and edit content.

woodworking materials and use—Basic woodworking materials include soft lumber pieces, nails with large heads, wooden spools, corks, twigs, bottle caps, small hand tools, workbench, sandpaper, C-clamp vise, and safety goggles. Carpentry needs to be done in a special area away from other activities.

Index